Fire, Death And Philosophy

A History of Ancient Indian Thinking

FIRE, DEATH AND PHILOSOPHY

A History of Ancient Indian Thinking

JOANNA JUREWICZ

MOTILAL BANARSIDASS PUBLISHERS
PRIVATE LIMITED • DELHI

First Edition : Delhi, 2018

Earlier printed by Dom Wydawniczy, ELIPSA, Warszawa in 2016

ISBN : 978-81-208-4189-5

Also available at

MOTILAL BANARSIDASS

41 U.A. Bungalow Road, Jawahar Nagar, Delhi 110 007
1 B, J.S. Compound, Kennedy Bridge, Nana Chowk, Mumbai 400 007
203 Royapettah High Road, Mylapore, Chennai 600 004
236, 9th Main III Block, Jayanagar, Bengaluru 560 011
8 Camac Street, Kolkata 700 017
Ashok Rajpath, Patna 800 004
Chowk, Varanasi 221001

MLBD Cataloging-in-Publication Data

Fire, Death and Philosophy: A History of Ancient Indian thinking
by JOANNA JUREWICZ
Includes Bibliography and Index
ISBN : 978-81-208-4189-5
I. Philosophy II. Rituals of Fire and Death
III. References in Rigveda, Atharvaveda Satapath
Brahmana and Upanisads. IV. Jurewicz, Joanna

Published by

Motilal Banarsidass Publishers Private Limited
www.mlbd.com • mlbd@mlbd.com
Printed by Replika Press Pvt. Ltd.

To Zosia
my beloved daughter

Table of contents

Introduction

1. The aim of the book

This book is an attempt to reconstruct the foundations of Indian philosophy which are reflected in early Indian texts dated between 13th and 6th B.C.E. They are religious texts composed in Sanskrit which were transmitted orally in the families of priests called Brahmins[1]. They constitute the intellectual foundation of Indian culture called Śruti (*śruti*), literally, 'what has been heard'. They are generally called Veda (*veda*) which means 'knowledge'. These two names reveal a specific feature of early Indian culture that it is founded on knowledge preserved in texts remembered by priests who heard them from their teachers. For this period, we do not have other archaeological evidence of religious cults such as temples or images of gods[2]. Even if they were created, the fact that they disappeared shows that they were less important for the culture and its survival than the corpus of the Veda which has come down to us in a magnificent and well maintained condition as a literary text.

The sources forming the basis for the analysis presented in this book come from three layers of the Vedic tradition. The earliest layer is the four Vedas: the Veda of Ṛk-stanzas (*Ṛgveda*, ṚV), the Veda of Sāman-chants (*Sāmaveda*, SV), the Veda of Yajus-formulas (*Yajurveda*, YV) and the Veda of Atharvans (*Atharvaveda*, AV). The ṚV is the oldest from around 15th–13th B.C.E. It preserves many traces of the earlier Indo-European tradition and defines the conceptual frames for later Indian thinking and practice. Its role can be compared to the role of Presocratics in ancient Greece in that we witness here the beginnings of philosophical investigation which chart the pathway, both conceptually and linguistically, for the later tradition. Due to

1 For education in ancient India, see Scharfe (2002).

2 Staal (1983, I: 94). As Kulke, Rothermund (2008[1986]: 35) write: 'The Vedic texts, and in particular, the Rigveda, still remain our major source concerning the early phases of Vedic culture in northwest India. But we always have to keep in mind that these texts express the priestly world-view of the Brahmins.'

the power of human memory, we are fortunate to have 1028 hymns, composed in a highly sophisticated way, which give us an insight into these beginnings.

While most of the Ṛgvedic hymns or stanzas were recited, some of the stanzas were intended for singing. They are gathered in the SV which comprises 1549 stanzas (Michaels 2004), primarily from the ṚV, some of which are changed due to the specific way in which they were to be sung. It also contains manuals for the correct singing of the stanzas. Composition of the SV was a consequence of the growing role of priests and ritual in Vedic ritual. It is also reflected in the YV which is divided into two schools called the White YV (*śuklayajurveda*) and the Black YV (*kṛṣṇayajurveda*). The former contains stanzas, partly from the ṚV, used in sacrifices, while the latter also explains their meaning, the meaning of the ritual implements and the actions to be taken. As they are composed, ritual becomes as important as sacred texts. Similarly to memorisation and recitation, ritual is an activity which does not leave archaeological evidence. So again we owe our knowledge of this further cultural treasure of ancient India to the power of human memory.

The AV was not included among the sacred Vedas from the beginnings of Indian tradition[3]. It is commonly known as the 'Veda of charms', though, as Brockington comments, there is not much difference between charm and sacrifice because their aims are similar (1990: 29). Moreover, the Sanskrit term, which is usually translated as 'charm', in the context of the AV is *bráhman*. The same term is used in the early Vedic text to denote the sacred word and its power. The difference lies in their use: while the Ṛgvedic hymns and stanzas were mostly used in solemn rituals destined for establishing and maintaining the social order, those in the Atharvavedic were more connected with the everyday needs of people[4].

Four Vedas, called *saṃhitā* ('what is put together'), constitute the first layer of the early Indian tradition. The next layer is constituted by the Brāhmaṇas the name of which is derived from the word *bráhman*. They are an exegesis of the sacred word and its power and, since in the Brāhmaṇas the word *bráhman* also includes three Vedas (ṚV, YV, SV), they are their exegesis as

3 Witzel (1987a, 1997).

4 But there are parts of the AV which are also connected with solemn ritual (Rājasūya), Lelli (2015). Indian tradition discerns one more layer of the Śruti which are the Āryaṇyakas, composed between the Brāhmaṇas and the Upaniṣads. The distinction between the Āryaṇyakas on the one hand, and the Brāhmaṇas, on the other, is not very distinct, sometimes the Āryaṇyakas form the last part of the Brāhmaṇas, e.g. *Bṛhadāryaṇyaka Upaniṣad* is included into Śatapatha Brāhmaṇa in its Mādhyandina recension (see Keith 1989 [1925], Keith 1969, Gonda 1975c, Malamoud 1997, Houben 1991, Pataskar 2009).

well. Thus the Brāhmaṇas continue the exegetical tradition of the YV with each Saṃhitā commented on by at least two Brāhmaṇas[5].

The life of Indian priests focused on ritual and, therefore, an explanation of ritual is an explanation of their life. Thus seen, the Brāhmaṇas are proof of the basic human need to make life meaningful[6]. The composers of the Vedas were looking for the meaning of reality and that meaning is then realised in ritual. Ritual is therefore a meticulous and perceptible manifestation of the thought and speech of ancient Indians constructed in the sacred sphere.

The third and final layer of early Indian tradition that is examined in this study is the Upaniṣads which were composed before the Buddha, i.e. before the 5th century BC (Gombrich 1992)[7]. These texts can also be seen as resulting from the exegesis on the concept of *bráhman*. Now the concept becomes ontological and refers to absolute reality which transforms its aspect in cosmos and man. Reality also manifests itself as their innermost essence. Ritual activity becomes internalised as a pattern of human activity which leads towards the cognition of reality.

The first part of this book's title refers to these three layers of ancient Indian tradition. The concept of fire is the central metaphysical concept of Ṛgvedic thought (Jurewicz 2010a) and remains such until the Brāhmaṇas. However, the primary focus of the composers of the Brāhmaṇas was on the concept of death seen as a manifestation of fiery reality. It will be argued that Upaniṣadic thought could not develop without this rich earlier background, therefore the word 'philosophy' refers not only to Upaniṣads, but also covers the whole of early Indian tradition. I come back to this problem later.

The second part of the title refers to a further aim of the book, which is to present a history of ancient Indian thought. I will focus on its development and show how tradition is transformed and redefined. This approach is in line

---

5 The Brāhmaṇas of the RV: *Aitareya Brāhmaṇa* and *Kauṣītaki Brāhmaṇa*. The main Brāhmaṇas of the SV: *Tāṇḍya Mahābrāhmaṇa* or *Pañcaviṃśa Brāhmaṇa*, *Ṣaḍviṃśa Brāhmaṇa* (Kauthuma and Rānāyanīya schools), *Jaiminīya Brāhmaṇa*, *Jaiminīya Upaniṣad Brāhmaṇa* (Jaimīniya school). In the Black YV, exegetical texts are already included in the Saṃhitās (*Maitrāyaṇī*, *Kaṭha*, *Kapiṣṭhalakaṭha*, *Taittirīya*), the separate Brāhmaṇas are *Kaṭha Brāhmaṇa*, *Kapiṣṭhala Brāhmaṇa* (both in fragments), *Taittirīya Brāhmaṇa*. White YV: *Śatapatha Brāhmaṇa* in two recensions (*Mādhyandina*, *Kāṇva*). The Brāhmaṇa of the AV: *Gopatha Brāhmaṇa*. For details, see Jamison, Witzel (2003). For the commentarial character of Brāhmaṇas, see Lubin (20100).

6 For the role of religion in making human life meaningful, see Geertz (1973b).

7 The Upaniṣads of the RV: *Aitareya Upaniṣad* and *Kauṣītaki Upaniṣad*. The Upaniṣad of the SV: *Chāndogya Upaniṣad* (Kauthuma school), *Kena Upaniṣad* (Jaiminīya school). The Upaniṣads of the Black YV: *Taittirīya Upaniṣad*, *Katha Upaniṣad*, *Śvetāśvatara Upaniṣad*. The Upaniṣads of the White YV: *Chāndogya Upaniṣad*, *Īśā Upaniṣad*. The Upaniṣads of the AV: *Muṇḍaka Upaniṣad*, *Māṇḍukya Upaniṣad* (Śaunakīya school), *Praśna Upaniṣad* (Paippalāda school).

with the attitude of the Vedic priests towards their own tradition, who saw each layer as a commentary on that which came earlier[8]. We could say that they realised in practice Gadamer's concept of the fusing of horizons within the frame of which man can then meet his tradition and enter into dialogue with it (1993 [1975]). This dialogue allows man to understand himself and the world in which he lives. The Indian priests were fully immersed in their cultural heritage which, during everyday loud recitation, would have been experienced more vividly and intensely than *via* other means of transmission. I will try to reconstruct the main lines of this dialogue.

Most histories of Indian philosophy begin with the Upaniṣads and the earlier texts are only briefly mentioned[9]. The reference to the earlier tradition is limited to most explicit and late hymns of the ṚV (mainly the *Nāsadīyasūkta*, 10.129) and the *Puruṣasūkta* (10.90). The philosophical hymns of the AV are mentioned more rarely while the Brāhmaṇas are either mentioned generally or not mentioned at all. Moreover, early Vedic thought, even if it is mentioned, is treated as an example of mythological thinking and ritualistic speculations with the implication that it cannot be treated as a subject for serious philosophical investigation. In my view, this is the result of the specific bias in Western thinking which narrows the meaning of philosophy to one kind of mental activity.

True, if we define philosophy as a discipline performed with aid of reason and logic, there is no philosophy in ancient Indian thought even in the Upaniṣads. Such kind of investigation appears only with the beginning of the six classical philosophical schools called Darśanas in the first half of the first millennium B.C.E (Potter et al. 1981–2015). However, the problem in which I am interested is how philosophy began. As mentioned above, Indian tradition preserves multiple texts which provide us with the possibility of tracing back through time human endeavours for understanding the world and themselves. They are therefore of great value not only for Indological studies but also for general studies on the human mind and its ability to create philosophy. Within the scope of Indology, which is the main field of research here, my argument is that Upaniṣadic philosophy could not evolve without the efforts of earlier philosophers and that it is deeply grounded in a tradition which begins already in the ṚV.

Ancient Indian texts attest mental activity which can be called philosophical if we enlarge the definition of philosophy and understand that it is a mental activity the aim of which is to answer some of the most basic questions of

---

8 See the study of exegetical strategies attested in the *Bṛhaddevatā* and its role for the later Indian canonical texts by Patton (1996).

9 Just to mention Dasgupta (1951–1955), Frauwallner (1990[1953]), Kumar (1991), Gupta (2012).

thinking man. These include the beginnings of the world and its functioning, the role of man, the problem of evil and the problem of death. Philosophy in these terms is a conscious activity by which people try to construe a coherent conceptual structure whose elements explain other elements and which can be treated as an overall explanation of such basic questions.

It is generally agreed that abstract terms are necessary for philosophical investigation. Abstract terms refer to abstract concepts which at their broadest do not refer to immediate experience. So it could be argued that if there are no abstract terms, then thinking is not abstract. In his study of Presocratic thought, Havelock (1983) mentions such terms as being, change, time, dimension and space, body and matter and so on, which were coined by the early Greek philosophers. And it is true that early Indian texts, especially those composed before the Upaniṣads, do not contain many such terms. The question is if this means that their composers were not thinking in an abstract way that could be considered philosophical.

The problem of the relationship between concepts and language is very much discussed in the philosophy of mind and in cognitive science[10]. Experiments done by Mandler and others on infants younger than one year show that it is possible to have simple concepts without an accompanying language[11]. Moreover, the concepts created by infants are abstract and general, though, of course, more detailed conceptualisation comes with acquisition of language. As far as adult human who have language are concerned, it seems that there is a group of abstract concept which may exist without linguistical expression. Such mental abstract concepts are unconsciously used in a coherent way and motivates linguistic and the bodily behaviour.

For example, the concept of category is such a concept. We can infer its existence on the basis of the fact that people are able to organise their knowledge and experience in conceptual wholes and include various elements within specific slots and create new ones. Even if a culture does not have a word for category, and many cultures do not, its participants do categorise[12]. Another example is number. Again, even if a given culture does not have the word for this concept, its participants calculate objects and they treat some objects as being impossible to count. The image schemas (VERTICALITY, SOURCE-PATH-GOAL, CENTRE-PERIPHERY etc., see below) which are developed in early childhood are further examples of abstract concepts which do not

---

[10] See e.g.: Givón (1988), Paivio (2007), Logan (2008).

[11] Mandler (1992, 2000, 2004, 2008, 2012b, b, 2014), Mandler, McDonough (1996).

[12] See categorisation in Dyirbal language in Lakoff (1987).

have verbal expression[13]. The existence of image schemas can be inferred on basis of the way people conceive and evaluate various aspects of their experience (Johnson 1987). Yet another example is the syntax of a given language. It is a whole conceptual system of rules that govern the structure of sentences which the speakers of a given language use often without being aware of it.

In Jurewicz (2010a), I have argued that the Ṛgvedic poets had general concepts which I called general domains and this allowed them to gather various kinds of experiences into conceptual units (see also below, section 7). I have also argued for the existence of an overall metaphysical system the core of which is the concept of an internally contradictory reality called Agni the existence of which can be inferred from textual evidence[14]. The main difference between the examples given above and the abstract concepts in the ṚV is that the analysis of the latter allows me to postulate that their composers consciously created and transformed them in order to create a coherent system of thought[15].

In case of ancient Vedic texts, at least in the ṚV, AV and in the Brāhmaṇas, the situation looks as follows. At the level of linguistic exposition, these texts evoke many concrete situations which refer to abstract cosmogonical and cosmological systems. There is no doubt that the composers of the ṚV did not want to describe what happened to them in everyday life. Although they mention its elements (elements of social life and individual experience), reconstruction of what really happened to them is very difficult, if not impossible, as the ṚV is not an historical text. The composers of the AV present mantras which refer everyday life situations, but again, these situations are difficult to reconstruct. And the so called philosophical hymns of the AV are clearly far from everyday life experience, although they abound in everyday

13 Image schemas were described only in second half of the previous century (Johnson 1987). As far as I know, they only have technical terms created by scholars.

14 In her monumental study about multiplicity in Indian art, Srinivasan (1997) also looks for the abstract concepts which are not expressed in language. She discerns three definitions of the multiplicity convention in the RV. They can be reconstructed because they are applied remarkably consistently throughout the whole text and are 'unexpectedly stable' (1997: 24). The basic symbolism of the convention is preserved, notwithstanding the type of deity to which it applies. Moreover, she shows that the multiplicity convention expressed by these definitions motivates in a significant way later Vedic and Hindu thought as its conceptual basis. Her study is the proof that general and abstract concepts are possible to be created and understood even if they are not expressed in language.

15 In her research on the Ṛgvedic mantra, Findly (1989) argues that although the term *mantra* is a late Ṛgvedic concept it is possible to look for its concept in the earlier strands of the RV. As she writes: 'inattention to a term in the ṚV does not always mean inattention to the corresponding concept' (Findly 1989: 15).

life terms. Finally, the ŚB allows us to reconstruct ritual whose exegesis was one of the reasons for its composition. However, a further reason is to explain the metaphysical rationale which makes the ritual meaningful and this explanation is based on earlier metaphysical thought. Yet, the composers of the ŚB present reality in very concrete terms. Although one can see on the level of words some mutual dependence between elements of ritual and the elements of a cosmogony the ritual is supposed to explain, it is usually difficult at first glance to see such dependence on the level of concepts. It is only in the Upaniṣads that concrete descriptions appear in contexts which leave no doubts that they are being used by the composers to illustrate abstract concepts.

This peculiar feature of Vedic thinking is closely connected with the fact that the texts in which it is expressed were created and transmitted orally. One of the peculiarities of oral transmission is wording which is relatively concise by comparison with the thought expressed by it[16]. The composer of an oral text must know the ways how, using such concise wording, to make his recipient understand its richer content. The concept of script used in the investigation of oral poetry[17] is a further example of an abstract concept which is not expressed verbally but governs its creation in a structured way.

The dual-coding theory (DTC) proposed by Paivio (2007) can be useful to explain the relationship between the level of words and of thoughts in oral poetry. According to this theory, knowledge is coded in verbal and nonverbal subsystems. They are composed of representational units called logogens and imagens. These units 'are activated when one recognises, manipulates or just thinks about words or things' (Paivio 2006). The relationship between them in this respect is seen by Paivio as follows:

> The verbal system is a necessary player in all 'language games' but it is sufficient in only a few. In the most interesting and meaningful ones, the verbal system draws on the rich knowledge base and gamesmanship of the nonverbal system. Conversely, the nonverbal system cannot play language games on its own, but it can play complex nonverbal 'solitaire'. (2006: 3)

Pavio and his collaborators have been doing research on memorisation by application of the DTC. Inter alia, this has resulted in the formulation of the conceptual peg hypothesis. This has been supported by experiments

16 See Jamison (2002, 2007, and 2015). For peculiarities of Indian oral tradition, see Staal (1986), Scharfe (2002).

17 Schank, Abelson (1977, 1995), Minchin (2001, 2008, 2011).

that demonstrate that a logogen creates imagen which further activates other logogens and imagens which thereby facilitates memorisation (2007: 23, 60 ff.)[18]. Experiments have shown that concrete words and images are more effective in activating abstract content in memory than an abstract phrase. To quote one simple example (Begg 1972, quoted in Paivio 2007: 74):

> [A] concrete phrase such a *white horse* can be remembered as a single integrated image (a white horse), whereas an abstract phrases such as *basic truth* does not activate an image and therefore must be remembered as two words.

A further example of the conceptual peg is the famous madeleine sponge dipped in tea which activated Proust's memory of times past which he then proceeded to set out in his *À la Recherche du Temps Perdu* (2007: 60). Oral texts usually preserve such conceptual pegs which are meant to do the same. Proust could compose his book only because he could write those memories down. If, on the other hand, he were an oral composer, he would probably describe the madeleine sponge in more detail and only briefly mention some important moments of his life. But Proust would have to have profile the description in such a way that he could be sure that the recipient would think about 'home, garden, street, village, the pleasures experienced' and feel the feelings expected of him (Paivio 2007: 60). In other words, he would have to be a specialist in the relationship between words and thoughts as are oral composers.

Taking this into account, it is not surprising that early Indian texts are much more concrete in their verbal exposition even when their intention is to convey abstract content. This content is reintegrated and understood on the unconscious level. As Paivio argues:

> It has become increasingly clear over more than a century that much cognitive work goes on at an unconscious level, psychologically inaccessible to introspection and verbal description. (2007: 55)

Oral composition and transmission of texts would not be possible if their composers were unable to reach this unconscious level and manipulate words that make their art meaningful to recipients. As I have argued in Jurewicz (2010a), the Ṛgvedic composers went a step further as they elaborated material stored in the collective memory to build a coherent system which made life meaningful.

---

[18] See also Paivio, Walsh (1993[1979]).

2. Cognitive linguistics and semantics

In order to reconstruct the abstract concepts, the way they were created and how they changed, I will use the methodology of cognitive linguistics. It is a young discipline of linguistics which began with George Lakoff and Mark Johnson's book *Metaphors we live by* (1980). Since then it has developed into an independent branch of humanities to become an important part of cognitive science. Its main focus is relationship between signs, both verbal and nonverbal, and their meanings. In other words, how such signs are construed and how they are understood. It also proposes models which reconstruct links between thought and signs.

The basic assumption accepted by cognitive linguists is that meaning is embodied. This assumption is experimentally investigated in cognitive science and psychology[19]. The outcomes of this assumption are that meaning is motivated by biological, physical and cultural experience and that this fact should be taken into account in its analysis. This assumption is especially important for the investigation of oral literature. It is everyday experience, shared by a linguistic community, which is the source of the conceptual pegs which anchors people's thinking and triggers associations. The research of Paivio and his collaborators confirms the crucial role of experience in the creation of abstract concepts such as syntax. The concept of syntax develops in early childhood by observation of motions and relations between the objects together with learning their names. As Paivio (2007: 110) puts it:

> [T]he theory suggests that the grammars first learned by children will be "tied to" the syntax of concrete objects and events… *via* the medium of imagery… and only later will more abstract grammar emerge.

This is a further argument for my claim that a text which on the verbal level seems to refer to concrete concepts does not have necessarily only refer to those concrete concepts. The problem is how to reconstruct hidden abstract ideas on the basis of their concrete verbalisation.

According to cognitive linguists, the meaning of words is also embodied. This is the first guiding principle which 'characterises a cognitive approach to semantics' (Evans, Bergen, Zinken 2007). According to the second principle, the meanings of words refer to concepts of mind more than to the external world. Evans, Bergen, Zinken (2007: 7) write that 'semantic structure… can be equated with conceptual structure'. This does not mean that they are the

[19] Johnson (1987), Gibbs (2005a, b, 2008), Tyler, Evans (2003), Hampe, Grady (2005), Evans, Green (2006), Rohrer (2007), Maaley, Yu (2011).

same. On the contrary, the conceptual structure evoked by a word is usually richer. This fact is connected with the third principle according to which words serve as 'points of access' to the repository of knowledge related with their conventional meaning (Evans, Bergen, Zinken 2007: 8). Meaning is conceptually construed in context and we could say that it does not exist out of that context. This dynamic understanding of meaning constitutes the fourth principle in the light of which 'meaning' is a process rather than a discrete 'thing' that can be 'packaged' by language' (Evans, Bergen, Zinken 2007: 9)[20].

Such an approach to meaning seems to be very appropriate as far as oral literature is concerned. Using Paivio's terminology, words are conceptual pegs which prompt the recipients to unfold the conceptual structure stored in verbal and imagery subsystems. Depending on context, various associations may lead a recipient along the concrete imaginarium, but may also lead them into more abstract and general thinking. Proper context is one of the crucial devices to realise the composer's aim. The words and phrases can be put in a context that forces the recipient to violate their everyday meaning and to look for a new one which could endow the whole utterance with sense[21]. This, in my view, is one of the reasons why the ṚV is so difficult. The words which refer to everyday experience are placed in particular contexts in order to prompt the recipient to create their new meaning which refers to metaphysical issues and thereby convey abstract content. As I will show, this was also done by the composers of the AV and ŚB. The Upaniṣadic philosophers could therefore draw on a vast repository of such concepts that had become abstract and had been coined by their predecessors.

Cognitive linguists propose three main models which allow them to reach the thought hidden in language and non-verbal signs. These are conceptual metonymy, conceptual metaphor and conceptual blending. All the models are based on the principles presented above. In order to accept the principles, and to understand the relationship between a sign and thinking, we need a theory as to how our knowledge is structured in mind and how this knowledge is activated when a sign is perceived.

We must first consider the problem of categorisation, which is now much discussed in cognitive science and its presentation would go far beyond the topic of my book[22]. Generally speaking, there are two main theories of

20 See also Tyler, Evans (2001, 2003), Evans (2005, 2006), Coulson (2000), Porto Requejo (2007).

21 It has been argued that 'novel metaphors may be used deliberately by the speaker in order to force the listener to see a concept in a new perspective, whereas conventional metaphors do not have this communicative goal' (Pecher, Boot, Van Dantzig 2011: 239).

22 Lakoff (1987), Kövecses (2011[2006]).

categorisation; classical theory and prototype theory[23]. Both agree that humans store their knowledge in conceptual wholes, but the nature of those wholes, the way they are created and the way the elements are included within them are interpreted differently. Cognitive semantics is based on the prototype theory.

Lakoff (1987) proposes that we understand categorisation as a process of creating idealised cognitive models (ICM) which are relatively stable conceptual structures stored in long-term memory. These structures constitute a mental basis which is activated when a sign is perceived and which guides further categorisation and reasoning. We do not activate our whole knowledge about Christianity (i.e. our idealised cognitive model) when we hear the word *Jesus*, but only the parts which are relevant in a particular context. When we hear this word during Christmas, we will think about his birth, on Good Friday we will think about his death. In everyday prayer, we will think about his mercifulness, in the museum, we will think about the ways he is presented in painting, etc.[24]

The parts of ICM's that are activated during the perception of a sign have various names in cognitive semantics (Cienki 2007). In order to present them, I will limit myself in two respects. First, I will limit myself to linguistic signs. Second, I will discuss the topic only as far as it is relevant for understanding the models which enable us to understand the relationship between language and thought.

Within the approach which investigates the models of conceptual metonymy and metaphor, the term 'conceptual domain' is most often used. Conceptual domain is understood as 'any knowledge configuration which provides a context for conceptualisation' (Taylor 2002: 589). In order to understand the word *tail*, we have to activate the concept of an animal and context decides if it is to be that of a dog or a dragon. This concept is called the conceptual domain. The term 'mental space' is used especially when using the model of conceptual blending and this term is explained below.

Conceptual metonymy is a model of a mental process which occurs within one conceptual domain or, more broadly, within one ICM[25]. A linguistic item is a prompt which gives us access to other aspects of a given conceptual domain or to the whole domain. It often happens that the linguistic item refers

---

23 Lakoff (1987), Croft, Cruse (2004), Kövecses (2011[2006]). Evans, Berger, Zinken (2007). For a concise survey see: http://plato.stanford.edu/entries/concepts/.

24 For an interpretation of categorisation on the neural level, see Barsalou (2005a), Feldman (2006).

25 For list of metonymies in English, see Radden, Kövecses (1999). See also Lakoff (1987), Croft-Cruse (2004).

to whole domain and is used in such a way that the recipient is triggered to activate its aspect.

Metonymy, which operates between particular aspects of a conceptual domain, is usually connected with the conceptualisation of events[26]. For example, when we hear the sentence *I like Bach*, we understand that the speaker means Bach's music and the domain is the creation of music. Metonymy, which operates between the whole domain and its aspects, is usually connected with the conceptualisation of things. When we hear the sentence during dinner *Pass me the salt, please*, we expect to get the salt cellar. This metonymy operates within the conceptual domain of salt cellar filled with salt. Similarly, the word *Christmas tree* in the sentence *Let's light the Christmas tree now* makes us to think about candles which should be lit. This metonymy operates within the conceptual domain of Christmas tree.

The concept which triggers our thinking is called 'the vehicle' while the concept which is mentally reached is called 'the target domain'[27]. The recipient of the linguistic expressions discussed above activates in his mind the target domains (music, salt cellar, candles) *via* its vehicle (*Bach*, *salt*, *Christmas tree*), but he mentally operates within one conceptual domain (creation of music, salt cellar filled with salt, Christmas tree).

Radden and Kövesces (1999) have classified the most important metonymies on the basis of data coming from English. In my book, I will use their classification and we will see that on the general level many of these metonymies also motivate Vedic thinking. Their particular realisations, however, will be different because of the different cultural and textual context.

Conceptual metaphor is the next model proposed by cognitive linguists[28]. It is a model of conceptual mapping which takes place between two conceptual domains. It enables us to think about a concept in terms of another one. For example, a cause of something can be conceived in terms of physical forces. When we hear a sentence *He pushed me to do that*, we understand that the speaker was forced to do something against his or her will. Such thinking about causality is so deeply rooted in our culture that we do not easily recognise its metaphoric character and the empirical character of the source domain.

The concept that lends its categories is called 'the source domain' while the concept that is conceived in terms of these categories is called 'the target

26 Radden, Kövecses (1999: 30–44).

27 Radden, Kövecses (1999: 21). See also Lakoff, Turner (1989), Panther, Radden (1999), Panther, Thornburg (2004), Kövecses (2011 [2006]).

28 Theory of conceptual metaphor belongs to the vast field of research which also includes Pavio's Dual Coding Theory, the theory of linguistic co-occurrence and hybrid models (Pecher, Boot, Van Dantzig 2011, Jelec 2014).

domain'. In the example given above, the concept of physical force is the source domain, while the concept of cause is the target domain. The concepts which serve as the source domain are often more concrete than their target domains. The lists of main metaphors for English can be found in Lakoff, Johnson (1999: 49–54)[29]. The source for their classification is English. Many of them are also attested in the Vedic thinking but of course there are a lot of metaphors which are culturally specific on the general level and in their specific realisation.

There is a class of conceptual metaphors the source domain of which are image schemas[30]. The term 'image schema' has been introduced by Johnson (1987) to name the basic patterns that are acquired during early perceptual and sensorimotor experience and which significantly motivate our thinking. As he writes:

> [I]n order for us to have meaningful, connected experiences that we can comprehend and reason about, there must be pattern and order for our actions, perceptions, and conceptions. A schema is a continuous structure of an organising activity (1987: 29)

Image schemas are dynamic patterns because 'they are structures of an activity by which we organise our experience in ways that we can comprehend' (1987: 29–30). They are also flexible 'in that they can take on any number of specific instantiations in varying contexts' (1987: 30). As such they are proof of the human ability for abstraction we have from birth. Johnson gives as example image schema of BALANCE. As he says we learn this schema 'with our bodies and not by grasping a set of rules' (Johnson, 1987: 74). It is impossible to teach balance through rules. Yet, the image schema of balance becomes the source domain for various abstract concepts such as justice, harmony, beauty, health, system etc. We use it unconsciously when we set the table for a formal dinner or think that a punishment should be in accordance with the crime.

In their research in developmental psychology, Mandler, Cánovas (2014) use the term 'image schema' slightly differently to its use in cognitive linguistics. Their experiments show that the first human conceptualisation, which occurs at the age of three months, is spatial conceptualisation which involves moving objects. Mandler (2008) calls such concepts spatial primitives and shows that they are general and belong to the superordinate level of categories. Mandler, Cánovas (2014) argue that the next stage of development in early cognition is

29 See also Lakoff, Johnson (1980: 46–51).
30 Lakoff (1987), Clausner, Croft (1999).

representations of simple spatial events. They call these representations image schemas. The next step of development is schematic integrations which include non-spatial elements. In their view image schemas are 'the first conceptual structures' (2014: 17).

However, in cognitive linguistics this term is used in the broader sense of 'a condensed redescription of perceptual experience for the purpose of mapping spatial structure onto conceptual structure' (Oakley 2007: 215). The embodied character of image schemas is due to the fact that they arise from and are created in the very early, preconceptual and prelinguistic stage of human development. At the same time, they are abstract conceptual organisation of experience. A tentative list of image schemas has been created (Johnson 1987: 126, Lakoff, Turner 1989, Clausner, Croft 1999: 15, Hampe 2005: 2–3)[31]. We will see that many of them are attested in Vedic thinking which is not surprising when we take into account that our early development is biologically similar.

The third model is conceptual blending. This model was created by Fauconnier and Turner (1993)[32]. It is based on the assumption that construction of meaning involves more than two concepts (as in the model of conceptual metaphor) and that it consists not only in the mapping of some elements of one concept onto another, but in the integration of some elements of the concepts involved in the process. The concepts involved in integration are called 'mental spaces'. As Turner (2007: 351) defines them they are 'very partial assemblies constructed as we think and talk for purposes of local understanding and action'. The mental spaces are structured by knowledge organised by ICMs preserved in long term memory and mostly operate in working memory activating elements of our knowledge.

The basic conceptual network model consists of four mental spaces each of which has a different function. Two are the mental spaces which provide information necessary to create a meaningful conceptual unit. They are called 'input spaces' while the conceptual unit which is the result of integration is called 'blend'. It is a concept which recruits elements from both input spaces and conveys new information in comparison to the input spaces[33].

---

[31] *SPACE*: UP-DOWN, FRONT-BACK, LEFT-RIGHT, NEAR-FAR, CENTER-PERIPHERY, CONTACT; *SCALE*: PATH, *CONTAINER*: CONTAINMENT, IN-OUT, SURFACE, FULL-EMPTY, CONTENT; *FORCE*: BALANCE, COUNTERFORCE, COMPULSION, RESTRAINT, ENABLEMENT, BLOCKAGE, DIVERSION, ATTRACTION; *UNITY/MULTIPLICITY*: MERGING, COLLECTION, SPLITTING, ITERATION, PART-WHOLE, MASS-COUNT, LINK; *IDENTITY*: MATCHING, SUPERIMPOSITION, *EXISTENCE*: REMOVAL, BOUNDED SPACE, CYCLE, OBJECT, PROCESS (Croft, Cruse 2004: 45).

[32] See also Coulson, Oakley (2000), Grady, Oakley, Coulson (2007), Turner (2007).

[33] For primary metaphors as the inputs in blending, see Grady (2005).

Generation of the blend is governed by three processes. The first process is the composition of elements from the input spaces. The second is the process of completion which needs activation of elements of knowledge stored in the long term memory. The third is the process of elaboration during which the content of the blend is developed according to the principles and logic provided by the input spaces and the blend itself[34]. It is important to add that conceptual networks may have more than two input spaces and, as we will see, this happens very often in the Vedic texts.

The fourth mental space in the model is called the 'generic space'. It contains the elements of input spaces which are recognised as common. Generic space is often very schematic and devoid of the details which differentiate the input spaces and are usually much more numerous than elements which are common.

The concept of angel is a good example of conceptual blend. It integrates elements of two concepts (two input spaces): that of human beings and that of bird. From the input space of bird, the concept of wings is transferred to the blend and from the input space of a human being, the overall shape. Thus we compose the blend. However, the concept of angel has more meaning than that of a flying man. It is conceived as living being endowed with cognitive abilities. The feature of life comes from both input spaces because we know that men and birds are living beings. Cognitive abilities are transferred into the blend only from the input space of man because we know that men are (or we hope they are) endowed with these abilities. In this way, the blend is completed with elements of our general knowledge about men and birds. The generic space of the conceptual network is the concept of a being.

The concept of angel is so well entrenched in our thinking we do not realise that it is a fictive concept. But this concept is not only stored in our long term memory. Or rather, it is stored in order to be elaborated. For example, Aquinas conceived angels as possessing intelligence and power and saw them as worshippers of God who implement his will and are his messengers. A whole branch of theology called angelology was created in the Middle Ages to explain their nature. On the other hand, Wim Wenders in his movie *Wings of Desire* created an angel with the ability to experience love which finally transformed him into a human being. This is how a blended concept is elaborated.

---

[34] 'Elaboration develops the blend through imaginative mental simulation according to principles and logic in the blend. Some of these principles will have been brought to the blend by completion. Continued dynamic completion can recruit new principles and logic during elaboration. But new principles and logic may also arise through elaboration itself. We can "run the blend" indefinitely' (Fauconnier, Turner 1998: 144).

Conceptual blending involves compression of relations that occur between input spaces. Fauconnier and Turner (2000) present a set of such relations among which are cause-effect, analogy-disanalogy, time, space, identity, part-whole and representation[35]. The main aim of compression is to facilitate global insight into diffuse conceptual structures and to bring complex situations to a human scale which thereby become intelligible and mentally manipulable.

Let us take as a further example the blended concept of Holy Communion in the Catholic tradition. This concept integrates input spaces which are linked by various relations such as relations of Time, Space, Analogy and Disanalogy. The Last Supper (the first input space of the network) is an event very remote from the Sunday Mass (the second input space of the network) in all these respects. Yet, in the blend, the bread and wine *are* the flesh and blood of Christ. For the believer there is no place for any quotation marks and the blend is treated as the ontological truth. All relations are fully compressed[36].

The theory of conceptual blending encompasses the analysis of conceptual metaphors and sees them as the result of integration[37]. Turner also argues that when a mapping and its expression is conventionalised and well entrenched, the generic and blended spaces are invisible, but that proper analysis will show their existence (1996: 88).

In my book, I will combine both approaches. I will use the model of conceptual metaphor in reference to conventionalised mappings between two conceptual domains. For more complex thinking, the model of conceptual blending will be necessary. Conceptual blends that are created by the Vedic authors usually consist of many input spaces some of which give structure and scenario to others. In my analysis, I will sometimes call the former 'source domains' and the latter 'target domains' in order to precisely express the mapping but it should be remembered that the mapping occurs within the blend.

All three conceptual processes are processes of which we are not usually aware. They are neuronal patters activated automatically and instantly when we perceive a sign. These patterns are created during the process of enculturation, but also on the basis of our sensorimotor activity. They can be consciously activated when we want to explain the meaning of an image or a sentence to someone who does not understand them. But even then we do not use this model, but simply explain in everyday language that when I ask for salt at the table I mean the salt cellar. Similarly, when I say that I am pushed by someone to do something, although he is thousands kilometres far away,

35 See also Fauconnier (2005).

36 For ritual blends: Sweetser (2000), Sørensen (2007).

37 Turner, Fauconnier (2003), Grady, Oakley, Coulson (2007).

I mean that he insists on me doing something. In the same way, we can explain blends. Angels can think and feel because in this respect they are like us and transformation of bread and wine into flesh and blood of Christ is a mystery that has just to be accepted.

Usually, all we know about the conceptual processes just discussed is the meaning that has emerged thanks to them. Since people are different the meaning can also be different. The fruitfulness of communication is anchored in the way we use these unconscious processes to understand each other and everything we create from day to day talks to the complex social institutions. Creation of metaphysical texts is part of this endeavour to communicate meaning.

3. The creation of abstract concepts in cognitive semantics

Research undertaken in cognitive science shows that abstract concepts are also embodied in that they are grounded in experience. As Barsalou shows 'abstract concepts are perceptual being grounded in temporally extended simulations of external and internal events' (1999: 603[38]). His experiments confirm the dynamic nature of abstraction (2005a) and the role of situation for understanding and representing abstract concepts which focus on relations, events and introspections (2005b). Moreover, 'the representation of abstract concepts is more complex, being less localised in situational content than the content of concrete concepts' (Barsalou 2005b: 134). Experiments by Prinz (2005) confirm that moral concepts have their grounding in emotions[39]. Barsalou, referring to Prinz, claims that this shows that abstract concepts are experienced directly (2005b: 133). It has also been shown that some abstract concepts can be seen in patterns of forces (Talmy 1988, 2000: 409ff).

The ability to perform conceptual operations modelled as conceptual metonymy, metaphor and blending is already proof of our ability for abstraction. At the same time, they play an important role in the creation of abstract concepts. I will now briefly discuss this topic. It should be noted that very often they co-occur in this process, but I will present them separately for the sake of clarity.

Let me begin with the role of metonymy in creation of abstract concepts. Radden (2004) shows that, in many languages, the concept of language is denoted by words which refer to the organ of speech ('tongue'), articulation

[38] See also Barsalou (2003), Ramscar, Matlock, Boroditsky (2010), Zwaan (2014).

[39] See also Kövecses (2008), Kousta et al. (2011), Cánovas (2011).

('voice'), linguistic action ('speak'), or a linguistic unit ('word'). He comments that 'these metonymic shifts allow us to access the notion of language as a fairly abstract target *via* a more tangible reference point' (2004: 1). He then reconstructs the folk model of language which comprises four levels (2004:2):

> The following four levels may be distinguished, which display increasing degrees of complexity or abstractness: (i) articulation, focusing on voice and speech organs such as the tongue, (ii) speaking, including various aspects related to speaking such as gossiping, (iii) speech, i.e. parole, focusing on spoken language, and (iv) language as a system, i.e. langue.

He concludes his analysis with the comment that 'conceptual metonymy allows us to understand abstract notions in terms of experientially basic notions' (2004: 14). Paivio gives a very simple example of metonymic abstraction, namely, the onomatopoeic *bow wow* which is the metonymic[40] extension of the vocal property of dogs (2007: 292). The child will abstract the features of all dogs into one which is the most salient. Putting this within the frame of the model of conceptual metonymy, we could say that the abstract phrase *bow wow* is the vehicle which gives the child access to the abstract concept of dog or a concrete example of it.

However, in many cases, the metonymic thinking would not be effective if it were not accompanied by metaphoric thinking. Yu (2008: 249) writes:

> 'metonymy very often is the link between bodily experience and metaphor in the mapping process from concrete experience to abstract concepts: bodily experience → metonymy → metaphor → abstract concepts.'

In her study of conceptual interaction patterns, Diez Velasco (2001/2002: 52–53) shows how metonymy gives access to abstract concepts taking as the example the expression *to have the stomach for something*, i.e. to have courage. The abstract concept of courage is activated *via* the concept of its locus *stomach*. But the meaning of this expression is also built on metaphoric thinking about qualities as physical entities which may be possessed. Moreover, *stomach* is conceived in terms of the image schema of a CONTAINER[41]. Diez Velasco claims that, 'unless we metaphorically understand *stomach* as a *container* and courage as its content, the relationship between them is impossible and the

[40] Paivio calls it metaphoric extension, but also 'kind of synecdoche'. In cognitive linguistics, these two mappings are seen as different operations and *bow wow* is an example of metonymic extension.

[41] Example provided by Diez Velasco for this mapping is *I have butterflies in my stomach* (2001/2002: 53).

sentence (1)[42] would be meaningless' (2001: 53). Thus the abstract concept of courage is understood in terms of the contents of an actual container which is part of our body.

The role of metaphoric thinking in the creation of abstract concepts can already be seen in that its source domain is usually more concrete than its target domain. Thus a metaphor gives us conceptual access to what is abstract so that we can think and speak about it. In his study, Paivio uses the example of the term *metaphor* to show that (2007: 292)

> 'metaphoric expressions pervade even the most literal language, to the point where it is often claimed that existing languages consist mainly of words and expressions that had metaphoric origin.'

The Greek term *metaphora* originally meant 'transfer'. It is a compound which consists of *meta* ('over') and *phoreo* ('to carry'). Paivio writes: 'the literal meaning survives in that "metaphora" is the identifying label for removal vans in Greece' (2007: 292). Within the frames of this conceptualisation, the concept of a removal van is the source domain while a change in the meaning of words is the target domain. Meaning is conceived in terms of a load which is carried by a van from one place into another and words are conceived in terms of places. In the course of usage of this term in a linguistic and philosophical context, it became lexicalised as an abstract term (Jurewicz 2014).

The pervasiveness of metaphoric thinking which enables conceptualisation of abstract concepts is an important part of cognitive semantics research. It has been shown, for example, that our thinking about abstract concepts such as time is based on metaphorical relationships (Evans 2004). Özçalişkan and Stites (2013) show that the concept of motion metaphorically structures a wide range of abstract concepts, from time to mental states and that this ability is learned by children by the age of five. People will also mentally simulate actions provided by source domains even if the target domains are abstract (such as 'grasping' in *to grasp a concept* or 'stomping' in *to stomp out racism*, Gibbs, Matlock 2008). They will do it even when the motion is fictive, that is, when a sentence or expression refers to a concrete situation conceived in a metaphoric way, for example *the road goes through the park*. This means that people mentally simulate situations which are impossible in the real world where a concept cannot be grasped, racism cannot be stomped out and a road does not go. Moreover, simulation of action does not inhibit abstract understanding but rather enhances it.

---

42 *The conscripts have no stomach for a fight* (Diez Velasco 2001/2002: 52).

As mentioned above, image schema, as the basic conceptual redescription of human early experience, are proof of our ability for abstraction. Moreover, they play an important role in the creation of abstract concepts such as categories understood in term of containers or event structures conceived in terms of source-path-goal schema[43]. Moral evaluation and moral concepts are based on image schemas of VERTICALITY and CENTRE-PERIPHERY (Krzeszowski 1997). One of the most abstract human creations is music and it is structured and understood in terms of image schemas, as is shown by Snyder (2000).

Metonymic and metaphoric conceptualisation of abstract concepts is also one of the main reasons why it is possible to use signs in communication (Gibbs, Matlock 2008: 162–163):

> Imagine, for instance, that you are sitting in a restaurant in a foreign country. You have long finished your meal and want to pay the bill. Eventually, you manage to catch your waiter's attention and pretend to scribble something in the air. In doing so, you are replacing the word *bill*, or its appropriate equivalent, with an iconic gesture that you assume will be familiar to him. The waiter understands and brings you the bill. Imagine next that you have just gotten on a crowded bus and see an old friend outside on the street. She waves and you then hold your hand up to your ear as if you are holding a cell phone. As the bus is pulling away, your friend nods and does the same in return. In both the restaurant and on the bus, you do a physical action that communicates something clear and unambiguous to your interlocutor. You simulate physical actions (signing a bill, making a phone call) that are familiar and grounded in shared knowledge.

Activation of the concepts of signing a bill and making a phone call is metonymic. In the first case, the concept of writing is activated by the specific movement of one's hand, which in turn activates the complex concept of the waiter preparing the bill and customer paying for the meal. Moreover, we must have an appropriate idealised cognitive model of *restaurant* which provides us with the knowledge that it is a place where one pays for a meal. It is metonymy which operates between the elements of action in which the last phase (paying) is activated by concept of the first phase (writing a bill)[44]. The concept of writing is the vehicle while the concept of paying is target domain. In the second case, the vehicle is the concept of a telephone and the target is the making a phone call. It is also the metonymy which operates between elements of action. Again one has to have an appropriate idealised

[43] Lakoff (1990, 1999), Gibbs (2005a, b), Richardson et al. (2001), Boot, Pecher (2011).

[44] 'In our conception of events, an initial or final phase may be seen as being more important than the central phase. *to pull the trigger* for 'to shoot' focuses on an event's initial phase, *to sign a contract* for 'to make a contract' focuses on an event's final phase.' (Radden, Kövecses 1999: 49).

model about communication with the use of telephones and one has to have had experience of their usage. From my point of view the most interesting is the third gesture which is nodding. In the first two actions of writing and telephoning, a body sign replaces action. In the case of nodding, there is a movement of the body which accompanies an understanding of someone else's intention and an agreement to that which is suggested. Although the concept of paying a bill and making a phone call are already abstract concepts, the concepts of understanding and agreement are even more abstract. Yet they are being activated in everyday life *via* a very simple bodily gesture.

The cognitive research on gestures confirms the experiential ground for thinking about abstract concepts. A metaphoric gesture is a movement of hands which represents the source domain for a metaphor the target domain of which can (and often is) an abstract concept[45]. According to McNeill (1992: 14), the pictorial content of metaphoric gestures 'presents an abstract idea rather than a concrete object or event. The gesture presents an image of the invisible – an image of an abstraction.' The ability for metonymic and metaphoric thinking is the basis for the creation of conventionalised sing languages such as ASL (Wilcox 2004) or LIS (Borghi 2014[46]) or sign language in classical Indian theatre[47]. In his study of metonymic and metaphoric mappings in ALS, Wilcox (2004) shows how abstract concepts connected with thinking are activated *via* the signs which are icons for the parts of a computer. Within the frames of this conceptualisation, the mind is conceived in terms of a computer and, more generally, in terms of container (Wilcox 2004: 203–204):

> The forehead is an icon for the keyboard, which is in turn a metonym for the entire computer. The index finger metonymically represents all of the fingers of a hand that types on a keyboard. Metonymy expands from fingers on the keyboard to the working components of an electronic computer. In turn, a finger punching along the crease at the forehead metonymically and metaphorically represents specific thoughts being created by Jose's intellect. Although we cannot actually punch at our foreheads and produce ideas, we know that the physical motion of typing on a keyboard creates printed letters. This source domain of typing movements – printing words – at the forehead maps to the domain of creating ideas.

The meaningfulness of sign languages and of everyday languages lies in the way abstract concepts are structured by our experience and conventionalised in metonymic and metaphoric mappings stored in our long term memory.

[45] Cienki, Müller (2008a, b).
[46] Lingua dei Segni Italiana.
[47] This is a fascinating field of future research for Indologists and cognitive linguists.

Our ability to conceive abstract concepts metaphorically extends to such abstract concepts like those to be found in grammar and mathematics. Our general conceptualisation of theories in terms of building[48] allowed grammarians from the 16th and 17th century to visualise grammar. Mittelberg (2002) analyses the famous *Tower of Grammar* (Zurich 1548) and shows that coherence of this visualisation is grounded in metonymic and metaphoric thinking including those of image schemas. She draws our attention to the fact that generative linguists also conceive of grammar in concrete terms, namely, that of a tree which is an instantiation of another metaphor IDEAS ARE PLANTS[49]. As she writes,

> the *Tower of Grammar* constitutes an image of grammar using spatial and social structures, in addition to human qualities to make the meaning of abstract notions accessible' (2002: 84).

Moreover, she points out that the *Tower of Grammar* belongs to a tradition of the *ars memorativa* which created models that facilitated learning and memorisation. Its efficiency was enhanced as it combined words and images. Thus we are led back to Paivio's theory of memory based on dual-coding according to which our memory is most efficient when there is cooperation of logogen and imagen subsystems (2007). In case of oral poetry, the imagen system operates mentally, while in case of *ars memorativa* it is visualised.

Even mathematical concepts, the most abstract concepts of humanity, have their grounding in experience and are motivated metaphorically (Núñez 2007: 356)[50]:

> even the most abstract conceptual system we can think of, mathematics(!), is ultimately embodied in the nature of our bodies, language, and cognition. Conceptual metaphor and fictive motion, being extremely fast, highly efficient, and effortless cognitive mechanisms that preserve inferences, play a fundamental role in bringing many mathematical concepts into being.

Núñez argues that formal mathematical systems are not rich enough to fully grasp the inferential structure of mathematical ideas which arise from the cognitive science of mathematics (Núñez 2008: 356). In his paper, he demonstrates how abstract thinking is embodied by studying gestures used by the teachers of mathematics. Similar research was undertaken by Mittelberg

48 See e.g. Lakoff, Johnson (1980: 46).
49 See e.g. Lakoff, Johnson (1980: 47).
50 Lakoff, Núñez (2000), Winter, Matlock (2013).

(2003) in the teaching of grammatical phenomena. In both cases, teachers conceived abstract concepts in terms of source domains. The explanative role of such gestures would not be possible if we did not possess a common conceptual system structured by metonymies and metaphors which enabled us think about abstract concepts and to elaborate them[51]. Artistic creation is also structured by the metaphoric conceptualisations of abstract concepts. For example, Forceville shows how films and comics visualise abstract concepts such as life, knowledge, development and anger.

Our ability to create conceptual blends is also based on our ability for abstraction. The generic space which shares common features of input spaces is abstracted from their specific elements. As Turner (1996) shows, the generic space is often difficult to recognise, especially in the expression of conventional projections, but he argues it motivates thinking and can be elaborated, especially in artistic creativity to create a coherent story (1996: 91–92). The fact that it is often dofficult to find a linguistic expression for generic space can be viewed as a further example of mental concepts which motivate and structure thinking as concepts of category, number, syntax and image schemas[52]. Turner argues that generic spaces have an actual conceptual existence of their own and this feature enables us to project it onto various targets (1996: 86–87).

At the same time, conceptual blending is an important process which facilitates abstraction. As mentioned, blending involves the compression of relationships. One of the aims of this process is to achieve a human scale for complex situations. This enhances our comprehension of abstract concepts (Coulson, Oakley 2005: 1532–1533). In their research on early human cognition, Mandler, Cánovas (2014) show the role of blending in schematic integration, i.e. the process which involves integration of non-spatial elements into spatial events. As they argue, this process is crucial for creating abstract concepts of emotions both for infants (Mandler, Cánovas 2014) and adults (Cánovas 2010). The role of blending in the conceptualisation of abstract concepts in science and the use of gestures in teaching has been analysed by Dreyfus, Gupta, Reddish (2014), in mathematical thinking by Turner (2012) and in physics (the concept of energy) by Dreyfus, Gupta, Reddish 2014). In literary art, abstraction has been shown to be reached by blending source and target domains (Szelid 2010). Conceptual blending is also one of the mechanisms of iconicity which is another example of human ability for abstraction (Freeman 2002, 2006, 2007, 2012) Another example is painting which allows the artist to present abstract concepts like movement (Turner 2006). A lot of research

[51] For the role of image schema in scientific models, see Amin, Smith, Wiser (2014). See also Semino (2008: 125–167).

[52] Actually, the generic space is often an image schema.

on the role of conceptual blending in creation of abstract concepts in design has been done by Taura et. al. (Taura, Yukari, Tanaka 2005, Harakawa, Nagai, Taura 2005, Nagai, Taura, Mukai 2009, Taura, Nagai 2013).

4. The creation of abstract concepts of philosophy using cognitive semantics

There is ongoing research which shows that philosophical abstract concepts are also embodied. Lakoff and Johnson (1999) have shown that abstract philosophical concepts in Western philosophy such as time, events and causes, the mind, the self, morality are built on simple, often image schematic concepts, and are then elaborated in metaphoric thinking. The later philosophers tacitly assume this metaphoric system and use it in the creation of theories and arguments. For example, the Decartes' concept of intuition as a mental faculty 'to *see clearly*' in 'the *light* of reason' is based on a set of metaphors: COGNITION IS SEEING, REASON IS A SOURCE OF LIGHT, LACK OF KNOWLEDGE IS LACK OF THE POSSIBILITY TO SEE, OBSTACLES IN COGNITION ARE OBSTACLES IN SEEING (e.g. a veil which obscures an object), THE MIND IS CONTAINER, THE IDEAS ARE OBJECTS (Lakoff, Johnson 1999). It is worth noting that it would be very difficult, if not impossible, to express Decartes' concept of intuition without these metaphors. This state of affair is caused by the embodied nature of our thinking in any specific instance. We would like philosophy and, more generally, science to be the exception to this fact, but as the research shows, it is not true. This does not mean that we are helpless in our search for rationality which Western thought generally considers can only be fully realised when expressed in literal statements. As Johnson (2008: 51),

> once you understand how conceptual metaphors lie at the heart of our abstract conceptualisation and reasoning, you acquire a new set of tools for analysing, explaining, and criticising philosophical theories. (…) [w]e *can* become aware of those metaphors, we can subject them to critical evaluation, and we can creatively elaborate them in developing new philosophies to help us deal with the problems that confront us in our daily lives.

In other words, we can use our rational thinking to deconstruct metonymies, metaphors and blends once we know their structure. We cannot be totally free from such operations, but if we are aware of them, we are freer. I would argue that early Indian philosophers were aware of the experiential entailment of our cognition and its influence on thinking. It also seems that they were aware that thinking is not literal and that they could use this feature in their metaphysical endeavours. Since their metaphysics was created in supra-natural states of mind, such as when exulted with the juice of Soma or from various deprivational experiences, it was characterised by specific features the most important of which is the internal contradictions of reality. It is impossible to conceive and express such a world view through rational thinking that is governed by rules that exclude contradiction. Conceptual metaphor and blending, adequately elaborated, were the only choice for the Vedic composers. On the other hand, such conscious work on their cultural heritage makes the early Vedic texts different from myths understood as stories repeated by generations without changes motivated by a desire to compose a coherent system. I am not saying that such efforts similar to those of the Vedic composers did not exist elsewhere in the world, but rather that they did exist in early India.

The conceptual awareness of the Vedic philosophers postulated by me could have many sources and I will discuss two of them. The first is that philosophical endeavour (or an important part of that endeavour) is in practice not only based on mind but also on body.

It has been stated that thinking is embodied and that cognitive thought is also embodied. The mental practices of the Vedic composers made it even more embodied because it was part of a process which took over the whole organism. It can be seen for example in the conceptualisation of thinking in the Veda. Among many metaphors, such as COGNITION IS SEEING, an important one in the Vedas is COGNITION IS HEATING OF THE AGENT. When I keyed in the phrase *cognition is seeing* in the Google (June 26, 2015), I found many references to cognition in various contexts. On the first page of the website, there was a paper 'Is Seeing All It Seems? Action, Reason and the Grand Illusion' by Andy Clark, a paper by Pierre Jacob, Marc Jeannerod 'Précis of Ways of Seeing, the Scope and Limits of Visual Cognition', a collection of papers on perception published on the website of Department of Psychology at the Stanford University, a review of a book *Ways of seeing. The scope and limits of visual cognition* by Pierre Jacob and Marc Jeannerod, a PhD thesis in the Graduate College of the University of *Iowa Seeing God: Theology, Beatitude and Cognition in the Thirteenth Century* by William Owen Duba (2006), a paper about perceptual cognition in Nyaya-Kantian approach by Monima Chadha. There was also information about a book on cognitive analysis of perceptual metaphors for knowledge (*Sensuous Cognition: Exploration into Human Sentience: Imagination,(E)motion and Perception* edited by Rosario Caballero and Javier E. Díaz Vera). I also found information about a conference on neuroesthetic *Seeing Knowing: Vision, Knowledge, Cognition, and Aesthetics*. When I keyed the phrase *cognition is heating,*

I found several papers about bad influence of excessive heat on humans and their cognition. Even this very short survey shows that in our culture metaphor COGNITION IS HEATING OF THE AGENT does not prevail, although some verbal expression, such as *my mind is warming up*, betray this conceptualisation too. They are, however, rare. On the other hand, the concept of heating is a conventionalised source domain for Vedic thinkers and is attested already in the ṚV (Jurewicz 2010a).

Such a conceptualisation can be explained experientially. From the Ṛgvedic testimony, we can infer that Somic exultation produced a sensation of heat which led to sweating (Jurewicz 2010a: 267). My argument is that this sensation was so strong that it could become a sign for the beginning of supra-natural cognition. Such a conceptualisation is motivated by the metonymy THE INITIAL PHASE OF THE PROCESS FOR THE WHOLE PROCESS, which also motivates English speakers[53]. When the Vedic community left the regions where Soma, the plant which gave the supra-natural experience, grew[54] (see below, section 6), they began to look for ways of achieving a post-Somic state without Soma. The activity they undertook to achieve this objective was connected with bodily heating. During the time of the early Upaniṣads the practice was mastered to such an extent that it became possible to analyse it theoretically. It seems that the sensation of heating as a necessary factor to begin the practice gradually lost its value. However, its importance is preserved in the word *tapas*, which literally means 'heat' (still in the ŚB), and it then acquires an extended general meaning relating to ascetic practice[55].

The next possible reason for the specific conceptual awareness of early Indian thinkers is the nature of oral composition and the transmission of texts. It is an art present in every oral tradition and the early Indian philosophers took it a step further. They were not only aware of their conceptual heritage, but knew how to elaborate it in a way they wanted. The final redaction of the ṚV took place circa 7th B.C.E. We do not know much about the social and psychological environment of the time (see below), but it was done orally. If the composers of the ṚV had any coherent concept of reality (as I argue here and in Jurewicz 2010a), they had to use techniques they had mastered for centuries. We could say that Vedic philosophers did what Johnson proposed: they were aware of metaphors and because of that they knew how to use metaphors and transform them to create abstract theory. They were

53 Radden, Kövecses (1999: 49), see note 46.

54 For Soma see Oldenberg (1993[1894]), Keith (1989 [1925]), Hillebrandt (1990[1927–29]). Wasson (1968), Falk (1989), Nyberg (1995), Parpola (1995), Oberlies (1998), Staal (2001), Houben 2003, Stuhrmann 2006.

55 For the concept of *tapas*, see Knipe (1975), Kaelberg (1990), Malamoud (1996b).

not 'slaves operating blindly under the harsh influence' (Johnson 2008: 51) of their metaphors. Just the opposite, they created philosophical structures from them.

My claim enriches research done in the field of oral tradition especially that of philosophical thinking. Havelock connects the beginnings of abstract thinking in ancient Greece with the appearance of writing (1983, 2006[1986]), and Seaford (2004) with the appearance of money. My research shows that none of these are essential factors in ancient India. The earliest accounts of writing date from circa 4th B.C.E (Salomon 1995, 1998)[56], the earliest coins of India dated to the end of the 6th or late 5th century B.C.E (Dhavalikar 1975)[57]. However, the cognitive approach shows that we do not necessarily need to look for the beginnings of abstract thinking in the external environment. It can be an internal work with the contents of one's mind modelled by shared experience, both human and social, that facilitated by mental practices. Such a way towards abstract thinking is expressed in the *Nāsadīyasūkta* (ṚV 10.129) the composer of which says that the relation between being and truth (*sát*), and non-being-untruth (*ásat*) is found by poets in their heart which is also the locus for thinking in the ṚV (Reat 1990).

The different paths to abstract thought lead to different models of reality. As Havelock (1983: 14) writes:

> His (Heziod's – JJ) poem is the earliest attempt we have in a style in which the resources of documentation have begun to intrude upon the manner of an acoustic composition. But his account is still a narrative of events, of "beginnings", that is, "birth", as his critics the Presocratic were to put it. From the standpoint of sophisticated philosophical language, such as was available to Aristotle, what was lacking was a set of commonplace but abstract terms which by their interrelations could describe the physical world conceptually; terms such as space, void, matter, body, element, motion, immobility, change, permanence, substratum, quantity, quality, dimension, unit, and the like. Aside altogether from the coinage of abstract nouns, the conceptual task also required elimination of verbs of doing and acting and happening, one may even say, of living and dying, in favour of a syntax which states permanent relationships between conceptual terms systematically. For this purpose the required linguistic mechanism was furnished by the timeless

[56] For the beginnings of writing in India, see Thapar (1966), Salomon (1995, 1998), Scharfe (2002: 12).

[57] But see also: 'The first documented coinage is deemed to start with '*Punch Marked*' coins issued between the 7th–6th century BC and 1st century AD. These coins are called 'punch-marked' coins because of their manufacturing technique. Mostly made of silver, these bear symbols, each of which was punched on the coin with a separate punch.' (https://www.rbi.org.in/currency/museum/c-ancient.html).

> present of the verb to be – the copula of analytic statement. The angles *are* equal to two right angles. They are not born that way or become or are made so.

So philosophy was concerned with what is eternal and unchanging. Ancient Greeks aimed at creation of a perfectly static model of reality. This could be the effect of literacy because written text freezes the dynamic flux of speech. Yet the reality experienced by ancient Indians was internally contradictory and constantly dynamic. It could not be expressed by a model which grasps what is eternal and unchanging because such a model would be false for them. Moreover, it seems that even within the model postulated by the ancient Greeks only assertive and negative sentences about existence of something are possible. Whenever one want to express anything more, e.g. not only that time is, but also the implications of this fact, one cannot do so without reference to metaphor.

As Havelock (1983: 21) shows, in their creation of abstract concept the Precocratics had to begin with what was available to them:

> namely, the vocabulary and syntax of orally memorised speech, in particular the language of Homer and Heziod. What they proceeded to do was to take language of the mythos and manipulate it, forcing its terms into fresh syntactical relationships which had the constant effect of stretching and extending their application, giving them a cosmic rather than a particular reference

There is no place here to analyse the cognitive processes through which the Presocratics constructed their philosophical apparatus. I will limit therefore myself to a few examples of how Havelock describes shifts in the meaning of concrete words to create abstract meaning. For example, the word *cosmos*

> is borrowed from the epic vocabulary, in particular from previous application to the orderly array of an army controlled by its 'orderer' (cosmetor); but it is now "stretched", so to speak, just as the neither of the numeral one is being stretched, to cover a whole world or universe or physical system. (1983: 21).

In order to express the semantic changes conveyed by the Presocratics, Havelock uses the verb *to stretch*. He is aware of its metaphoric usage in this context, but he does this in the hope that the recipient will do the same and understand the abstract content of what is being said. The ground for his hope is the conceptual mapping which has occurred in his mind and should occur in the mind of his recipient within the frame of which a change of meaning is conceived in terms of the physical manipulation of objects. We are very close here to the ancient Greek concept of metaphor in terms of transferring a burden from one van onto another (Paivio 2007, see above). However, Havelock's metaphor implies that this is a forceful activity as if the words kept their meaning tightly which they did not want to lose. Cognitive semantics provides the tools to explain this mysterious process of 'stretching the meaning' which enable us to analyse the process in more precise terms and understand its nature. In case of word *cosmos*, the following conceptual changes occurred.

In Jurewicz (2014), I argued that the conceptual mechanisms by which abstract concepts are created are similar to those that underlie grammaticalisation in that both processes involve metonymic and metaphoric thinking and the manipulation of context. The research done by Heine (2002) provides a useful model of the process of grammaticalisation which can also be used to analyse the creation of abstract concepts. In the first stage, the context is unconstrained and the meaning of a linguistic expression is its source meaning. When the word begins to be used in a different context (which is called by Heine 'the bridging context'), the recipient looks for another meaning of the expression which is more plausible in this context and which is the target meaning. In this stage, however, the source meaning is still easily activated. The next stage is the use of an expression in a context (called 'the switch context') which rules out the interpretation of the target meanings in terms of the source meaning. In the final stage, called conventionalisation, the target meaning does not need to be supported by the context and becomes the only meaning of a particular linguistic expression which may contradict or violate the source meaning.

If we apply this model to Havelock's stretching metaphor, we could say that he himself creates the switch context for the verb *to stretch*. He uses this verb in his paper so consistently that it becomes conventionalised and he does not have to add 'so to speak' as he does in the passage quoted above. The Precocratics did the same with nouns like *cosmos* and many others. It is worth adding that usually the bridging and the switch contexts activate metonymic and metaphoric mappings. According to some scholars, the process of metaphorisation can be seen as the process of objectivisation, that is, the process which facilitates conceptualisation of all abstract concepts (even relations) in terms of physical concepts (Szwedek 2008: 312[58]). Since conceptualisation in terms of objects causes reification this confirms, a bit

[58] 'The metaphorisation of all abstract concepts (including relations) in terms of physical objects I call *objectification*. In that theory the OBJECT refers to any material entity, including animate beings, plants and (inorganic) things'. For analysis of metaphorical models of abstract domains, see Zelinsky-Wibbelt (2000: 240 ff.).

paradoxically, that the static models in Greek philosophy is also the results of metaphorisation.

The advantages of using cognitive linguistics in any investigation of the early Veda are as follows. Firstly, it allows one to create a meta-language, so one can speak about the Vedic contents without using its concrete and figurative expressions. Secondly, it is a precise analytical tool for the deconstruction of the condensed exposition that is its content. Thirdly, its usage shows the universal character of human thought and demonstrates that the Vedic composers thought in the same way as we do in everyday life, in science, in art, and in philosophy. The search for universal aspects of the ancient Indian thinking has already been postulated by (Witzel 1979). He based his investigation on the concept of 'noematic aggregates', accepted by Hoffmann (1975/76) to analyse the rich semantics of Sanskrit words and their cultural entrenchment. The models of cognitive linguistics, developed since then, allow us to analyse the problem in more precise way.

In my reconstruction of the creation of abstract concepts in the Vedic thoughts, I use all three conceptual models proposed by cognitive semantics, namely, conceptual metonymy, conceptual metaphor and conceptual blending. The role of metonymy in creation of abstract concepts can be seen as follows. The vehicle loses its connection with the target concept and it becomes independent in that it does not activate its target domain. However, the recipient is also expected to activate the target domain and thus create a blend which consists of two input spaces. The first input space is the vehicle while the second input space is the target concept. The metonymic abstract concepts preserve elements from both input spaces, but combine them in such a way that the elements from the vehicle input space are not expected to activate any concrete reference, only its general topology and scenario.

A similar process occurs in case of metaphoric thinking. The conceptual network consists of two input spaces: the source and target domains the elements of which are transferred into the abstract blend. In both cases, the role of the generic space is very important because it links two concepts that cannot be linked on the basis of everyday experience. Thus its content comprises the most abstract common feature of both concepts. As Pecher, Zwaan (2005: 238–239) write: 'Indeed, being able to see structural similarities might be at the very core of representing and understanding abstract concepts.'

However, since the main topic of my book is history of ancient Indian thinking and not the role of conceptual operations in creation of abstract concepts, my analysis does not exhaust the latter topic. I am sure, however, that such research is indispensable preferably in a comparative perspective that at the very least involves early Greek and Indian philosophy.

5. The content of the book and basic interpretative assumptions

The repository of texts memorised by ancient Indian priests is surprisingly large. While the ṚV has come to our times only in one recension, other Vedic texts are preserved in more than one version. The full analysis of all of them would need a not inconsiderable cooperative effort. For this present work, I had to choose sources which were the most representative for the topic of my analysis.

The first chapter will discuss selected hymns of the late books of ṚV, namely, those hymns which come from the tenth book and one hymn from the first book (ṚV 1.164)[59]. The second chapter is devoted to an analysis of nearly all of the so called philosophical hymns of the AV (Śaunaka recension). The source for the third chapter are the cosmogonies presented in the *Śatapatha Brāhmaṇa* (ŚB) of the Mādhyandina recension. This is a commentary to the White Yajurveda. I decided to choose this Brāhmaṇa because cosmogonies presented in it are very elaborated, in many cases much more than in other Brāhmaṇas. As far as the Upaniṣads are concerned, which will be discussed in chapter four, I will analyse selected chapters of the main ones composed before the Buddha. These are the *Bṛhadāraṇyaka Upaniṣad* (BU) belonging to the White Yajurveda commentary tradition, *Chāndogya Upaniṣad* (CU) belonging to the *Sāmaveda* tradition, the *Aitareya Upaniṣad* (AU) belonging to the *Ṛgveda* tradition, and the *Taittirīya Upaniṣad* (TU) belonging to the Black Yajurveda tradition. The fifth chapter is devoted to the problem of belief in rebirth and here the sources are selected chapters of the *Jaiminīya Brāhmaṇa* (JB), the *Jaiminīyopaniṣad Brāhmaṇa* (JUB) belonging to the *Sāmaveda* tradition, and the *Kauṣītaki Upaniṣad* (KU) which belongs to the *Ṛgveda* tradition.

Such an approach allows me to see the development of concepts and language in their broader context. In researches of Indian philosophy up until today, the point of reference has been the later thought formulated in the classical Darśanas. This perspective makes scholars look at the earlier thought from one specific perspective which gives them insight to the conceptual roots of a given philosophical theory. This is clearly seen in the research done on the history of the Sāṃkhya (Larson 1969, Hulin 1978[60]). However, this approach takes the earlier concepts out of context which obscures their original meaning. The same approach is visible in the interpretation of the Vedic thought (especially Upaniṣadic) using the later Indian commentaries. Such an investigation gives us knowledge about the way the earlier texts

[59] These books are considered to be the youngest, see Oldenberg (2005[1888]), Witzel (1995a, b).

[60] See also Crangle's (1994) research on the early Indian origins of contemplative practices.

were understood by the later tradition, but not as to how they were originally understood by their composers.

I understand the original meaning as that which can be reconstructed on the basis of the wider context, contemporaneous and earlier, available to the composer. Of course, we can never be sure of the real intention of the author and how the text was understood by its recipients. It will be shown, however, that the full context considerably enlarges our understanding (Witzel 1996). It is also enlarged by the use of conceptual models proposed by cognitive linguistics which show just how many aspects of human thinking are common.

In their interpretation of the Vedic texts, some scholars seem to assume that the Indian authors were not always fully aware of the sense of their own creation. The difficult passages are sometimes explained as insertions of fragments composed at various times. The aim of these manipulations is to prove consistency of tradition, but it is done without taking care as to how such passages fit into the whole (e.g. Gotō 1986, Bronkhorst 2007: 125–126, Bodewitz 1997b: 593). However, the work of Witzel (1987a,b, 1995c, 1997) shows that the composition of the texts was a conscious elaboration of earlier tradition to make it meaningful in new, social, religious and intellectual contexts. In my view, therefore, the Sanskrit texts are worth investigation only if it is assumed they were composed by rational people who wanted to express their thoughts as clearly as possible, even if the range of their recipients was a narrow group of specialised Brahmins (Witzel 1997). When a meaning could be considered obscure, they gave keys to aid understanding which can usually be reconstructed if the broader context, both contemporaneous and earlier, is taken into account. In Jurewicz (2010a), I have shown how the key for understanding the metaphysical assumption of Agni as reality can be found if one analyses the whole hymns or the groups of hymns.

The broad context and an analysis undertaken with use of cognitive models allow us to see the philosophical character of the passages which are devoid of purely abstract terms. As mentioned, the Upaniṣads are more abstract in their exposition than the earlier texts and they have fragments which seem to be explicit in their meaning. These fragments are quoted in the studies on the history of Indian philosophy. Their context, however, is very often omitted as it is not so overt. In the present analysis, I will look at these fragments within the context of the whole chapters and books and will show how deeply they are interrelated. This approach enriches the meaning of the abstract passages and proves the rational efforts of their composers who wanted to create a coherent exposition. The earlier context will be seen to provide meaning for passages which are otherwise obscure. The same approach will be realised in case of the hymns of the ṚV and AV and the cosmogonies of the ŚB.

Classical Indological research has been grounded on a philological methodology based on the investigation of lexemes. The tools of the cognitive linguistics enrich this approach with the investigation of concepts that can be reconstructed on the basis of linguistic expressions. Research based only on lexemes has its limits, as one concept or conviction can be expressed in various ways. People store shared cultural knowledge in their memory, which is evoked by the use of various signs and different words and expressions. It will be shown that it is possible to find how some ideas, characteristic for the later stage of the development of thought and culture, are already present in the earlier strands of texts even though the specific word does not yet appear. For example, the concept of time is already elaborated in the ṚV, although the term *kālá* is what actually appears in the AV. This is also the case of *yoga*. This term in its specific meaning is not used in the early Upaniṣads, but the stages of the process are already there in general outline. The diachronic investigation of thought, therefore, requires these two explorative perspectives, namely, the research on lexemes and on concepts, and their constant and mutual crosschecking.

The fact that thought develops on two levels, conceptual and linguistic, allows one to propose a slightly different understanding of the intertextuality of early Indian thinking. It is well known that the Vedic composers repeated and rephrased passages of other texts. This is not unusual in human culture and is done not only with verbal creations but also in other forms of communication (painting and others kinds of visual art, music and, nowadays, film). Such repetitions are based on the common cultural knowledge that is shared by the members of a community. The aim is not to repeat the linguistic (or other) form, but to activate thinking about its meaning in a new context. In case of the Vedic tradition, it is usually done to highlight continuity. However, we should remember that, although the amount of preserved texts is great, there were also texts which are lost to us. Moreover, shared knowledge is often preserved not in a particular text, but in the sayings and phrases which are circulating among people of a particular community. For the convenience of exposition, we may say that a composer of a particular text quotes or refers to another particular text, but one can never sure if this is the case or if the composer is referring to something that was embedded in 'common' knowledge. For example, the definition of the name of the god Indra as *índha* is attested in ŚB 6.1.1.2 and is repeated in BU 4.2.2-3, but it is difficult to state if its composer wanted his recipient to activate exactly that passage of the ŚB or just activated knowledge that everyone knew and accepted.

Human cultures are usually based on some implicit assumptions and models which are not questioned in their most basic frame. They are treated as ontological truths rather than just one of a number of possible ways to interpret the world. It is only now in our post-modern Western culture that people have come to realise the fragility of these frames which for some is fascinating and for others frightening. The conceptual frame of the Vedic tradition was established in the RV. It was the most important model of reality for explaining the creation of the world and the role of man. It resulted in cognition and ritual being formulated in a more or less explicit way. I have reconstructed these frames in Jurewicz (2010a) and will now show their stability while, at the same time, demonstrate the flexibility they offer which allowed later thinkers to develop, transform, redefine and often explicitly express concepts accordingly to the needs of their times. The problem which philosophers contributed to this proces, I leave for another type of research. Here I am interested in their common effort to create a coherent theory of the world and how this theory might look. It is important to note that oral preservation of texts needs cooperation and constant mutual contact of people who recite the texts together. We do not know how composition and compilation of new versions of the texts were created, but we can be sure that they were done by groups of Brahmins who manipulated texts during loud recitation. Their mind was extended in that it was kept in texts which did not exist if they were not recited[61]. The next level for extending the Vedic mind was that of ritual which embodied philosophical thinking[62]. In Vedic India, one cannot envisage someone like Kant who created his *opus magnum* in solitude in Königsberg. It was just not possible.

This most basic model of the Vedic thinkers looks as follows. Reality is one. It is internally contradictory. It manifests its aspect which becomes cosmos and man and yet, in other aspects, reality is still unmanifest. The motive of creation is self-cognition and reality cognises itself through cosmos and man. Man as such is a manifestation of reality which is able to perform self-cognition on the micro-scale. In the early strands of Vedic thought (from the ṚV to the Brāhmaṇas), man can do so thanks to cognition and ritual. The Upaniṣadic philosophers emphasise the role of cognition in this process, although they also try to present it as ritual which takes place within the

61 For the concept of extended mind in philosophy of mind, see Clark, Chalmers (1998), Clark (2008), Logan 2008. See also Geertz (1973a: 45): 'Human thought is basically both social and public – (…) its natural habitat is the house yard, the market place, and the town square. Thinking consists not of "happenings in the head" (though happenings there and elsewhere are necessary for it to occur) but of a traffic in (…) significant symbols – words for the most part but also gestures, drawings, musical devices like clocks, or natural objects like jewels, anything, in fact, that is disengaged from its mere actuality and used to impose meaning upon experience.'

62 Because of this each explanation of particular sacrifice begins with cosmogony.

human mind. Cognition is prior to being and results in ontic transformation of the cognising subject and the objects of his cognition. The final aim of cognition is realisation of the unity of reality.

The term 'reality' is the most abstract term which includes all conceptualisations of the Vedic composers about 'that what is'. In the ṚV, reality is conceived in terms of fire, Agni. Such a conceptualisation is valid until the Brāhmaṇas the composers of which express reality in a visible form through ritual. In the late ŚB, the term *bráhman* begins to be used to denote reality. This term becomes prevalent in the Upaniṣads. The term *ātman*, which in the Upaniṣads denotes the manifestation of reality in man and cosmos, is already used in the ṚV to denote the essence of a whole together with its outward appearance (Jurewicz 1997). In the AV, the term begins to be used in the meaning of the essence of cosmos, while in the Brāhmaṇas it is used to denote the manifest aspect of reality and the immortal essence of man built in ritual.

However, as cognitive research shows, although human beings can create purely abstract concepts, when they want to say anything more about their designates than merely to state or negate their existence, they have to conceive a concept in some way and this always includes reference to something concrete. The model of conceptual blend seems to be a very good tool to search for such conceptualisations that are in themselves abstract but which are then open to more analytic discourse. As mentioned, the model assumes the fusion of at least two concepts (input spaces). These concepts must have something in common (at least conceptually) and this common feature is called the generic space. Its isolation allows one to find the possible and most basic conceptualisation of reality.

The composers of the hymns of the ṚV analysed in this book continue the earlier conceptualisation in that they create blends the generic space of which is the appearance of the symbol of light from the symbol of darkness (Jurewicz 2010a, see below, section 7). In the late ṚV, however, a new generic space of blends appears which includes the concept of reality. This is the image schema of SELF-MOTION (Mandler 1992, 2000). The composers of the AV continue this conceptualisation. They also create new kind of blends with the concept of transformation under the influence of heat as the generic space. This concept is the basic generic space in the ŚB which in later chapters becomes a more general concept of transformation. The Upaniṣadic philosophers then create further blends, with this concept as the generic space, of which the most common blend is that of self-cognition. In each layer of the text, other generic spaces appear but they are less commonly used. The use of the cognitive tools, therefore, allows us to reconstruct the main line of development of the concept of reality. It also confirms that even the most abstract concept is somehow framed in more concrete terms which render their analysis possible.

6. An outline of the historical and cultural background

The period between the composition of the ṚV and the earliest Upaniṣads comprises almost one thousand years. We do not have much archaeological evidence for this period, especially for that commensurate with the earliest text, i.e. the ṚV[63]. However, the texts themselves, although they were not composed as an historical testimony, can be used as sources of evidence for historical change provided they are treated with utmost circumspection. The work of Witzel (1995a, b, c, 1997) is the most recent and the most exhaustive example of such cautious investigation and in the present section, I will summarise its outcomes. In his papers, Witzel shows the complex development of the Vedic Canon, but here I will limit myself to the texts analysed in this book.

The most ancient text of the Veda, the ṚV, was composed by Indo-European tribes belonging to the eastern Indo-Iranian branch of tribes who gradually settled on the Panjab plateau during the second millennium B.C. At its peak, this Ṛgvedic civilisation extended from the Kabul River to the Gangā (Witzel 1995a: 93). The earliest hymns were probably composed around 1500 BC[64]. Witzel (1995c, 1997) discerns two stages in the early compilation of the Ṛgvedic materials. The first stage is attested in the collection of the family books (2–7) and the second is attested in the collections composed by the Kāṇva and Āṅgirasa in books 8 and 1, and the late book 10 (Witzel 1997: 264–265). The final codification of the ṚV took place possibly around the 7th century B.C.E., in eastern North India during the late Brāhmaṇa period (Witzel 1997: 265), and is a testament of the further rearrangement of the Vedic Canon (Witzel 1997, 322 ff.). It is then that the analytic version of the ṚV, in which words are reconstructed without euphonic changes (*padapāṭha*), was created and it is ascribed to Śākalya[65].

---

63 Thapar (1996), Kulke, Rothermund (2008[1986]).

64 Witzel (1995a: 98), see also Oberlies (1998: 155–156).

65 The version for continuous recitation (*saṃhitāpāṭha*). For hypothesis of an early written version of *padapātha* see Bronkhorst (1982). For contestation of his approach, see Scharfe (2002: 12) who writes: 'The best evidence today is that no script was used or even known in India before 300 B.C., except in the extreme Northwest that was under Persian domination'. For the issues connected with oral and written tradition in India, see Rocher (1994). came to us in one recension ascribed to, although we know that there were others. The names of the other schools of the ṚV are *Bāṣkala*, *Āśvalāyana*, *Śāṃkhāyana* and *Māṇḍūkāyana*;

The centre of Kuru rule was located at Kurukṣetra and it comprised eastern Panjab and Haryana in the west, to upper Doab of the Yamunā and Gaṅgā in the east (Witzel 1997: 266). Information about the political and social changes which took place in this time can be found in the mantras of the additional collection of the ṚV (ṚV Khila) and the early mantras of other Saṃhitās (SV, YV, AV, Witzel 1995c: 6, 1997: 268). In the AV (*Śaunakīya* and *Paippalāda*), the first mention of iron appears which allows us to date this text circa 1200 B.C.E (Witzel 1997: 280).

The early YV Saṃhitās attest the development of the Kuru culture towards the east and the south (Witzel 1997: 299) and the growing importance of the Pañcāla tribe, "the other half of the 'classical' Vedic tribal moiety" (Witzel 1997: 301). In the beginning of the first millennium B.C.E., the centre of Vedic culture was located in Uttar Pradesh (Witzel 1997: 302–303). It is there where the texts of the Jaiminīya schools (JB, JUB) were composed.

The late Brāhmaṇa texts mention another political and cultural centre located to the east of the Kuru- Pañcāla realm which is occupied by the Kosala and Videha tribes (Witzel 1997: 307). It was located in eastern Uttar Pradesh and in Bihar north of the Ganges. On the basis of linguistic and archaeological evidence, it can be inferred that the people living in the east of northern India did not participate in the Vedic Kuru-Pañcāla culture which was imported by the Brahmins from the West and invited to the eastern territory in order to elevate the cultural heritage of the population that lived there (Witzel 1997: 307–308). One of the results of these efforts is the ŚB in its Kāṇva and Mādhyandina recensions and the earliest ritual manual the *Baudhāyana Śrautasūtra* (Witzel 1997: 315 ff.). Here the Śākalya ṚV was composed and also the *Vājasaneyi Saṃhitā* (belonging to the White YV school) (Witzel 1997: 322–326).

The general geographical localisation of the early Upaniṣads (BU, CU, AU, KU and TU) was probably the regions of Kuru-Pañcāla and Kosala-Videha together with the areas directly to the south and west of these[66]. They were composed around 6–5th B.C.E., most probably before the Buddha.

As Witzel summarises (1995c: 4–5), the ṚV attests the free organisation of a society which was composed of many tribes which contended among themselves and with the aboriginal people over land and access to water. The second stage of development of the ṚV reflects the unification of various Ṛgvedic tribes under the rule of the dynasty of Parikṣit from the Kuru tribe (Witzel 1995c, 1997: 265). In the Mantra period, the way of living was still

see Scheftelowitz (1906), Renou (1947). For use of cognitive linguistics in research on oral literature, see Cánovas, Antović (forthcoming a, b).

66 See also Olivelle (1998: 13).

semi-nomadic with periods of treks (*yóga*) and peaceful settlement (*kṣéma*) along the rivers and later in the interior (Witzel 1997: 266). By the late Vedic period (late Brāhmaṇas and early Upaniṣads), the northern Indian territory is divided into several kingdoms the main ones of which of which are the Kuru-Pañcāla, the Kāśi, the Kosala and the Videha.

The main social classes were the Brahmins (*brāhmaṇa*), the priests and the Kṣatriyas (*kṣatriya*), the warriors. While the Kṣatriyas kept political power, the Brahmins preserved cultural values through the texts they memorised and realised in ritual which, by the time of the Brāhmaṇas, had become very complex. The next social class was the people (*vaiśya*), peasants and artisans, while the lowest state was that of the Śūdras (*śūdra*) who were supposed to serve the three upper classes. Three upper classes could learn the Veda and participate in ritual and the Brahmins could teach the Veda and perform rituals. The Śūdras were excluded from both forms of culture. The ritual was divided into the public (*śrauta*) and the private (*gṛhya*). The former constituted the basic frames for the social structure while the latter, the description of which begins already in the AV, was connected with the everyday life of the Vedic people.

According to Witzel (1995c, 1997), the formation of the Śrauta ritual had already began during the Mantra period under the kings of Kuru who wanted to control members of the royal and priestly classes. This was the first reason for codification of the early Vedic Canon. Ritual framed the structure of society and relieved tensions, especially between the Brahmins and the Kṣatriyas, who became mutually interdependent. Although in real life the Brahmins were dependent on the Kṣatriyas and their donations, they were indispensable for legitimisation of the political power of the Kṣatriyas and for their spiritual progress during life and after death[67]. The great solemn royal rituals such as Aśvamedha and Rājasūya can be seen as the results of these efforts. The ritual of Agnicayana, which is a sophisticated development of the Soma sacrifice performed already in the RV, is a further result of these efforts.

The development of Vedic Canon was also motivated by the need for brahmanisation and sanskritisation of the territories which were gradually occupied by Vedic civilisation and 'was carried out by the well-tested alliance of the Ksatriyas and Brahmins (*brahmakṣatra*)' (Witzel 1997: 336). This affected not only the Āryan population, but also the aboriginal tribes (Witzel 1997: 297, 313–314, 323).

The next factor motivating the composition of the Canon was rivalry between various groups of priests within the Śrauta ritual. At the end of its

---

67 See also Olivelle (1998).

formation, the priests were divided into four groups: the priests of the ṚV (Hotar) were responsible for the recitation of Ṛgvedic mantras, the priests of the YV (Adhvaryu) were responsible for reciting Yajus during the performance of ritual, the priests of the SV (Udgātar) performed Sāman-chants and the priests of the AV (Brahmán) prevented any mistakes occurring during ritual which could be fatal. The members of each group were also responsible for preservation and transmission of texts within their school. The growing role of the Adhvaryu priests in the post-Ṛgvedic ritual marks the first important step in the early formation of the Canon (Witzel 1997: 270 ff.). The Ṛgvedic priests aimed to preserve their role which is reflected in the composition of the speculative hymns of the AV (Witzel 1997: 293). As Witzel writes:

> To the *trayī* collections the Āṅgirasa of the AV had added their own new speculative hymns. They represent just one aspect of the ongoing deliberations on the meaning and the secret import of the new *Śrauta* ritual. (1997: 295)

As to the origination of the present version of the ŚB, Witzel presupposes (after Weber 1914[1852] and Mylius 1965) that the original 'centre of attention' of the earliest parts of ŚB in the Mādhyandina recension 1–5 is Kuru-Pañcāla territory (1987b: 196), while books 6–10 originated more to the west (1987b: 197). At the same time, it portrays some knowledge of the eastern territory of Videha. The ŚB in the Kāṇva recension (1–7) corresponds to ŚBM 1–5, but its final redaction probably took place in Kosala lands (1987b: 199). The late books of both versions (ŚBM 11–13, ŚBK: 13–15) betray knowledge of the western homeland (Kurukṣetra), but the final compilation was made in the east (Witzel 1987b: 199–200). The debates at court as to role of Janaka, the king of Videha, are a good example of possible intellectual efforts aiming at crystallisation of the Canon[68]. Let me quote Witzel again:

> when the western texts were introduced into the east (AB[69], the Śākala RV, the eastern Kaṭha texts, and PB/BhallaviB[70]), the ŚB collection was looked into by one of the many imported Kuru-Pañcāla

[68] 'We might regard the present ŚB consisting of the two parts represented by the eastern "Yājñavalkya" section (ŚBM 1–5 = ŚBK 1–7) vs. the western 'Śāṇḍilya' section (ŚBM 6–10 = ŚBK 8–12) as a close descendant of the *original* version. However, this combined version (which includes, as an addition ŚBM 11–14 = ŚBK 13–17) has again come down in the western (Kosala) Kāṇva and the eastern (Videha) Mādhyandina versions. Both schools have revised the lost older text independently, and have then influenced each other subsequently.' (Witzel 1997: 317).

[69] *Aitareya Brāhmaṇa.*

[70] *Pañcaviṃśa Brāhmaṇa/Bhallavi Brāhmaṇa.*

> Brahmins, a sort of *Veda-Vyāsa*, – perhaps Yājñavalkya himself, who quite uncharacteristically is said to directly "have received the Mantras from the Sun" and not from his teacher(s)' (1997: 328)

The early Upaniṣads were created on the eve of the second Indian urbanisation[71], when 'the large mass of texts' (Witzel 1997: 327) had already been imported to the east, collected and compiled. The rulers of the emerging kingdoms and their priests aimed at the creation of the basic concept of the Śrauta ritual which could put various strands of Vedic thought and ritual practice into a coherent system.

My analysis supports Witzel's reconstruction in that the texts that are taken into account here reflect efforts to develop a coherent version of the Canon at the conceptual level. As already mentioned, the reflection over ritual goes beyond its correct performance and basic meaning. The priests wanted to create metaphysical foundations for their activity, which would not only explain the importance of ritual, but which could also justify their high status in society. Although they did not succeed in the creation of a totally unified metaphysical system, there is no doubt that was their aim. On the one hand, they wanted to preserve the basic assumptions derived from the ṚV while, on the other, they wanted to adapt such assumptions to new social, political and religious circumstances. The Vedic testimony gives us the possibility to reconstruct the human search for making life meaningful and how this search motivates the development of tradition.

7. Fire and cognition in the *Ṛgveda*

The present book continues the research set out in the *book Fire and Cognition in the Ṛgveda* (Jurewicz 2010a). Its main claim is that the ṚV, in the final form that has survived till modern times, can be seen as attempt to build abstract concepts and models. I have shown the metaphysical assumptions which constituted the basis for the models concerning creation of the world, its functioning and the role of man. In order to do that, I had to go beyond classical philology and use the methodology of cognitive linguistics.

The main metaphysical assumption is that reality is conceived in terms of fire which is internally contradictory in that it has fiery and liquid (Somic) aspects. Reality thus conceived creates the world through a process of alternate manifestation of its aspects beginning with the Somic aspect. The functioning

---

71 The first took place c.a. 2500–1900 B.C.E., the archaeological remnants of which are preserved in Mohenjo Daro and Harappa (Thapar 1966, Kulke, Rothermund 2008[1986], Witzel 2010).

of the world repeats the creation and the role of man is crucial in this process. In the morning, he pours Soma, ritually pressed and purified, into fire. Mixed with Soma, fire becomes the rising sun. When the sun reaches its zenith, the Soma of which it is comprised becomes finally purified and falls on the earth in the form of rain. At the same time man, having poured Soma into fire, drinks what remains and, exulted with it, enters a supra-natural state of omniscience, freedom and immortality. The exultation is presented as alternate manifestations of the fiery and the liquid stages. The realisation of the supra-natural state is mentally realised when the sun is at its zenith. When man dies, he repeats his ritual journey. The heat of the cremation fire replaces the heat of Soma and the deceased reaches the sun where he again experiences the same supra-natural state which he experienced during his life. Then he comes back to the earth in the form of rain to be reborn among his relatives. This cosmic and human cycle is therefore conceived, at the deepest level, as alternative transformations of the fiery and Somic aspects of reality. I have called this the general model of reality transformation.

This model was never expressed explicitly in the ṚV even in the so called philosophical hymns of the tenth maṇḍala. But the Ṛgvedic hymns are composed in such a way that it is possible for it to be reconstructed. Further, it is not only possible to reconstruct it for the contemporary recipients of the ṚV, but also by those for whom the ṚV was a basis for further interpretations, i.e. the composers of the later Vedic texts.

In Jurewicz (2010a), I have shown that most of the abstract and general concepts were rooted in concrete experience which was transformed to convey the metaphysical meaning. I divided my analysis into two parts. In the first, I reconstructed the main elements of the experience of the Ṛgvedic poets attested in the ṚV. I have called them the defining events. These are cosmic events (the appearance of the morning light), social events (war and ritual, i.e. producing fire and preparing Somic juice) and cognition undertaken under the influence of Soma. I have shown that all these events are presented in the ṚV and have the same scenario which I generally labelled as the appearance of the symbol of light from the symbol of darkness, through the destruction/disappearance of darkness. The symbols of light are not only the ultimate aim of the defining events, but are also the agents which cause the destruction/disappearance of the symbols of darkness. Conceived in this way, the defining events can be viewed as reflexive processes in which subject and object is the same. I have also shown that Agni, fire, is conceived as being the most important agent of the process and also its aim.

In the second part of the book, I analysed philosophical models which aim at a more abstract and general theory of reality. Those models are the model of Child Of The Waters, of The Boiled In The Raw, of The Wave Of Honey, of Streams Of Clarified Butter, of The Aṅgirases Freeing Cows, of Indra's Fight With Vṛtra, of Footprints Of Viṣṇu and of The Copper Pillar. They are complex conceptual wholes which fuse several concepts and they are to some extent conventionalised and often evoked by conventionalised verbal expression. Their aim is to evoke the holistic insight into reality in all its aspects: cosmic, social and cognitive. All of them are structured by the common scenario of the defining events and, on the most general level, express the transformations of Agni. At the same time, each of them highlights different aspects of this process. Each include an image of a simple everyday situation which facilitates an understanding of the whole model and activates the understanding intended by the composer.

In my analysis, I also reconstructed the superordinate categories which I have called the general domains. These are Water and A Rocky Hill, A Vessel Filled With Liquid, Procreation, Creation Of Space, Finding The Hidden, Freeing Cows and Cleansing By Heat. They are evoked by verbal phrases or words denoting everyday experience (natural phenomena, objects and activities). Their aim is to endow complex concepts with a simple frame and scenario which will facilitates mental associations between different concepts.

I have argued that the defining events, philosophical models, general domains and the general model of reality transformation are important proofs for a tendency to abstraction and generalisation. The problem is that they have never been expressed verbally and can only be reconstructed taking into account context. Sometimes, the close context of a stanza or a hymn is enough to activate them but more often the recipient has to take the whole of the ṚV into account. Such a mental journey within the ṚV was guaranteed as text was preserved not only in the long term memory, but first of all in the short term memory as a result of constant repetition.

The ṚV is unique in Indian tradition (and the whole of human tradition) for many reasons. Its careful composition is important not only from the point of view of mnemonic values. In Jurewicz (2010a), I argue that its final composers wanted to arrange it in such a way that they could reasonably expect that the recipient would follow their line of reasoning in spite of its concise verbal expression. The composition of the later Vedic texts is less restricted and it is not possible for some of the conceptual models proposed in them to be reconstructed in as clear a form as in the RV, beginning with the AV. Some of them disappeared and some of them remained as a basic conceptual frame for thinking about reality. The latter can be divided into two kinds. The first are the models which became the cultural axioms accepted by the members of community of the Vedic composers and formed the basis on which their conceptual edifice was built. Models of this kind were taken for granted and were not questioned as they were considered part of reality itself and not its description. The second kind are those models the aspects of which were still productive and used to conceive various processes and states. In both cases, it often happened that the concepts used in the model which evoked the experience were transformed into those which were more familiar from the point of view of the geographical and cultural environment of the composers.

The models which disappeared are the model of The Boiled In The Raw and that of The Aṅgirases Freeing Cows. The model which formed a part of the conceptual foundation is the model of Child Of The Waters. It is evoked in various ways, the most abstract being the concept of the golden egg floating on waters.

The models the aspects of which are productive can be further divided into two kinds. The first are models which are built on the basis of cultural knowledge. These are the models of Indra's Fight With Vṛtra, of Footprints Of Viṣṇu and of The Copper Pillar. They are evoked *via* the concepts of the gods, i.e. Indra, Viṣṇu and Varuṇa. The recipient is not, however, expected to activate the whole meaning of these models as presented in the ṚV, but only their main general meaning. In the case of the model of Indra's Fight With Vṛtra, the concept of his creative fight is evoked in order to conceive the situation of the sacrificer in those terms. The later Vedic composers also prompt their recipient to activate the concept of Indra, who becomes heated having drunk Soma, to conceive of creation and of supernatural cognition. In the case of Footprints Of Viṣṇu, the concept of the creation of space, both in cosmic terms and in the sacrificial place, is to be activated. In the case of the model of The Copper Pillar, the concept of Varuṇa and the meaning of cognition realised in ritual is supposed to be activated. In Jurewicz (2010a), I have interpreted the concept of Varuṇa's nooses as the source domain for the results of unsuccessful cognition. In the Brāhmaṇas, it is transformed into a concept in terms of which the situation of living beings, when creation fails, may be understood. However, transformation of the concepts of these three gods in the later Vedic thought and ritual needs a separate study which goes beyond the present one.

The model of The Wave Of Honey is not often evoked in later Vedic thought, but its use is well-thought-out. It is activated in explanation of the general structure of the world and society. In some places, the recipient is prompted to activate one of its input spaces which is the concept of a baby united with its mother *via* the umbilical cord. The concept of clarified butter used in the model of Streams Of Clarified Butter is replaced by the concept of milk, sweat and gold while its meaning of cognition is highlighted.

The general domains are less numerous in the Ṛgvedic hymns analysed in this book in comparison to those in the earlier RV. Some of them became a part of the general conceptual frame of thinking about creation and cognition (Creation Of Space, Finding The Hidden), other disappear (A Rocky Hill, A Vessel Filled With Liquid and Freeing Cows).

The most common general domain used in later thought is the general domain of Procreation which is elaborated in that the concept of growth and development of a calf/child is included as its specific realisation. Contrary to the earlier Ṛgvedic general domains, it has one main target domain which is creation. In the Upaniṣads, aspects of liberating cognition are also conceived in its terms while their composers mainly activate its specific realisation of the sexual act. The use of this domain is not only explained by the universal conceptualisation of the appearance of something new in terms of delivery. It is also motivated by the cultural conviction shared by the Vedic people that the father is reborn in the son[72]. Thus the general domain of Procreation endows the target concepts and blends with the reflexive meaning thanks to which transformation of one reality can be conceived.

The next general domain which is preserved and elaborated in later thought is Cleansing By Heat. The composers of the ŚB enlarge it so that new experiences are evoked as its specific realisation. These are the boiling of water and production of cream, butter and iron. They also elaborate the concept of purification of gold. The Upaniṣadic philosophers elaborate this general domain in its specific realisation of the transformation of milk to produce cream or butter. The salt-metaphor, analysed by Slaje (2001a,b, 2002), can also be seen as a further example of the specific realisation of this general domain[73]. Cleansing By Heat has two target domains: creation and cognition.

The composers of the ŚB also created a new general domain, namely, the general domain of Cooking which includes all scenarios of preparation of food, its cooking and eating. It can be seen as the elaboration of the general domain of Cleansing By Heat but, taking into account its reach, I will treat is as a separate domain. Its target domain, is very broad and it is used to conceive creation, the functioning of world, ritual and cognition. In the Upaniṣads, its range is narrowed as it is mostly evoked in its specific realisation of eating to conceive subjective-objective cognition.

---

72 Olivelle (1993: 41–46).

73 Another source domain which implies transformation under the influence of heating is metaphor of producing honey elaborated in CU 3.1-10 (see chapter 4.4.2.1).

The general model of reality transformation becomes the main metaphysical assumption as far as the internally contradictory nature of reality is concerned and it is expressed in more and more abstract ways. In the ŚB, it is conceived of in terms of the opposition of the fiery and liquid aspects of reality while in the Upaniṣads it is conceived of in terms of opposition between the subject and the object of cognition.

There is one more model accepted by later Vedic thought which is the model of creation established in the *Nāsadīyasūkta*. It is possible to discern seven stages of creation presented in the hymn.

1. The pre-creative inexpressible state (*nā́sad āsīn nó sád āsīt tadā́nīṃ*, 'There was neither being/truth nor non-being/untruth then').
2. The first act is the passage from the pre-creative inexpressible state to the state which can be expressed (*ā́nīd avātáṃ svadháyā tád ékaṃ*, 'That One was breathing breathlessly with its own will').
3. Reality inchoately divides into aspects unmanifest and manifested (*táma āsīt támasā gūḷhám ágre*, 'darkness was hidden by darkness in the beginning').
4. The appearance of the first expressible form of the manifested aspect (*apraketáṃ salilám sárvam ā idám*, 'everything was flood without any sign').
5. The final constitution of the manifested aspect (*tuchyénābhú ápihitaṃ yád ā́sīt tápasas tán mahinā́jāyataíkam*, 'That which was about to be/that which was empty was surrounded by the void. That was born thanks to the power of heat – One.').
6. The appearance of desire for the manifested aspect (*kā́mas tád ágre sám avartatā́dhi mánaso rétaḥ prathamáṃ yád ā́sīt*, 'Desire firstly came upon that which was the first semen of thought/mind').
7. The creative activity of the poets (*sató bándhum ásati nír avindan hṛdí pratī́ṣyā kaváyo manīṣā́*, 'The poets, having searched in the heart with their thinking, found the kinship of being/truth in non-being/untruth. Their ray/reins streamed sideways').
8. Realisation of the creative activity by concrete human beings (stanzas 6–7)[74].

As it will be shown, later composers generally accepted this model, although they usually began their creative accounts with the description of the first stage.

The Brāhmaṇas attest the validity of the metaphysics composed in the ṚV not only on the conceptual level. Ritual can be seen as its visible manifestation. This issue needs separate research, but correspondence between thought and

---

74 Jurewicz (2010a: 58–59).

ritual is the main reason why cosmogonies have explanative value. Their composers interpret earlier thinking and elaborate it according to the conceptual and social needs of their recipients in order to express in ritual that which makes human life meaningful. Because of this the Vedic sacrifice can be treated as a model of reality. Thus the tendency for abstraction finds its ultimate realisation in activity in ritual space.

*

Before I go on, I would like to warmly thank my dear friends who for years have accompanied me on the crossroads of Indology, cognitive linguistics and philosophy: Richard Gombrich, Sven Sellmer, Elżbieta Górska, Richard Seaford and George Thompson.

During the realisation of my project I was fortunate to meet colleagues who gave me inspiration and support when it was needed: Michael Witzel, Alexander Lubotsky, Clara Robbiano, Jarrod Whitaker, Caley Smith, Paolo Magnone, Frank Köhler, Hanna Urbańska and Marcin Lisiecki. I thank you all very much.

I wish to thank Tim Clapham who reviewed the English text and helped make the book more accessible for English speaking readers.

Many thanks to my colleagues in the Chair of South Asia, Faculty of Oriental Studies, especially to Anna Trynkowska, Monika Nowakowska, Justyna Wiśniewska and Wiesława Marczuk.

I would also like to thank my father who has always believed in me and to my close friends who make my life more colourful.

I could not write this book without two more persons. And it is also dedicated to them: to Wirginia who teaches me how to sing and to you who teaches me how to fly.

Chapter One

The *Ṛgveda*

In the first part of this chapter, I will discuss the tendency for abstraction which consists on the redefinition of the concept of Agni attested in ṚV 10.81-82 and 10.121. The redefinition consists of the creation of conceptual blends. Two input spaces are the source and the target domains of metaphors which in the earlier Veda are used to conceive fire, namely, FIRE IS A TREE/WOOD, FIRE IS AN EMBRYO. The third input space is reality or its manifest aspect. In the blend, reality is conceived in terms of tree/wood, or its manifest aspect is conceived in terms of the embryo. The features of reality are imparted from both input spaces which come from metaphor. Thus the concept of fire motivates thinking about reality.

The next kind of blend, created in ṚV 10.125, is similar in its construction. The difference is that the metaphor the domains of which become the input space is a metaphor in which fire is the source domain used to conceptualise speech (SPEECH IS FIRE).

Recognition of the generic space which unites concrete concepts and the concept of reality is difficult. As I have argued in the *Introduction*, it is possible to create a static abstract concept without any reference to experience and this is attested in the early Greek philosophy. However, it is impossible to think and talk about such concepts other than to assert their existence or non-existence. So reality, in order to be explained, must be already conceived in some terms. These terms must be general enough to make them the input spaces of the blends which also recruit from experience. Mandler shows in her research that the first conceptualisation of children is spatial (1992, 2008, 2010, and 2012).

She enumerates the most basic image schematic concepts created by infants which are the earliest redescription of the spatial experience. These concepts constitute the basic network of human thinking which evolves into complex structures when language appears. I think that these most basic concepts can be seen as source domains for the abstract concept of reality in the early Veda and constitute the generic space of blends. For my research, the following image schemas are most relevant: SELF-MOTION (Mandler 1992: 593), SOURCE-PATH-GOAL, CONTAINER, and CONTAINMENT. Moreover, the generic input space which unites source and target domains (as described above) also motivates thinking about reality in a considerable depth. In some blends, created in the later ṚV, the generic space is still the appearance of symbol of light from the symbol of darkness.

Then I will analyse the *Puruṣasūkta* (ṚV 10.90) the composer of which conceives reality in terms of man (*púruṣa*) and consequently uses it to present manifestation of reality in cosmos and society. Next, I will analyse the concept 'the Maker of Everything' (*víśvákarman*, ṚV 10.81-82) which is a blend the main input spaces of which are concepts of man and fire.

In the next section, I will analyse ṚV 10.72 which is similar to the *Nāsadīyasūkta*'s attempt to create an abstract model of creation with the use of abstract and general concepts. Then I will analyse ṚV 1.164 which is an attempt to describe the cognitive experience of a poet and present it within the frames of metaphysical and ritual knowledge. Finally, I will analyse the complex concept of fame, expressed by words *śrī́*, *śrávas*, *yáśas* and *kṣatrá* in the ṚV. This concept is important from the point of view of the later thought which activates it in contexts describing *summum bonum* of human beings.

I will refer to the translation of Jamison, Brereton (2014). However, since in many cases I propose a different interpretation, I am giving their interpretation in the footnotes. The quotations are from Holland, van Nooten (1994).

1.1. The blended abstract concepts. Wood, tree and embryo of the waters

In this section, I will analyse concepts which are motivated by the concept of Agni which is the result of looking for a more abstract way of expression of philosophical issues. The first are the concepts of tree and wood which is a metonymic extension of the concept of tree. It is evoked in one stanza of the ṚV (10.81.4) where the poet asks about wood (*vána*) and tree (*vr̥kṣá*) from which the world was carved (*nís takṣ-*)[1]. In this short question, the poet creates a rich conceptual network. Its first input space is the creation of the world which is evoked on the basis of the general context of the stanza. The second is carving or chopping. Since in the ṚV, the creation of poems is conceived in terms of carving or chopping (see section 1.6), the third input space is creation of speech. The generic space is the appearance of the symbol of light from the symbol of darkness. In the blend, the creation of world is the creation of speech and it is conceived in terms of carving or chopping. At first glance, the concept of fire is invisible. However, the concept of wood (*vána*) evokes one of the hiding places of fire (Jurewicz 2010a: 124–125), so operations on wood are operations on the fire hidden in it. The concept of fire is also evoked by the concept of tree (*vṛkṣá*) in terms of which fire is conceived as the world and its *axis mundi* (ṚV 2.35.8, see ṚV 1.164.20-22, section 1.6). Thus the recipient can add the next input space which is the transformation of fire and incorporate it in the blend. However, it seems that the intention of the poet is rather to put the concept of creation in abstract terms of transformation of a material without evoking any concrete image. This is contrary to ṚV 2.35.8 that create a concrete image of a tree with branches that grow in waters. But the conceptual link between the abstract concepts of *vána* and *vṛkṣá* and the concept of fire can easily be reconstructed.

The tenth mandala of the ṚV also attests the transformation of the philosophical model of Child Of The Waters which is the next example of the creation of abstract concepts. ṚV 2.35 presents a rich image of fire burning in waters in terms of which reality is conceived. In order to facilitate understanding of this image, the composer evokes everyday experience: fire is conceived in terms of a calf born from cows, it is licked by them and has sexual intercourse with them (Jurewicz 2010a: 207–208). ṚV 10.82.5-6 can be seen as the next step of this conceptualisation of reality towards a more abstract level (for analysis of these stanzas see also Jurewicz 2010a: 331–332):

---

1 ṚV 10.81.4ab: *kíṃ svid vánaṃ ká u sá vṛkṣá āsa yáto dyā́vāpṛthivī́ niṣṭatakṣúḥ*. See Havelock (1983: 32): 'The term adopted by Aristotle to signify undifferentiated matter which constitutes the raw material of touchable body was *hulë*, the Homeric word for a forest or its firewood, or timber, the Latin '*materies*' our 'matter'. However, abstract may be the intention of this usage, its connotation is still that of solidity and touchability'.

ṚV 10.82.5-6

paró divā́ pará enā́ pṛthivyā́ paró devébhir ásurair yád ásti |
kám svid gárbham prathamáṃ dadhra ā́po yátra devā́ḥ samápaśyanta víśve || (5)
tám íd gárbham prathamáṃ dadhra ā́po yátra devā́ḥ samágachanta víśve |
ajásya nā́bhāv ádhi ékam árpitaṃ yásmin víśvāni bhúvanāni tasthúḥ || (6)

Was it beyond heaven, beyond this earth, beyond lords and gods?
What first embryo did the waters receive, where all the gods appeared together? (5)
Just this first embryo did the waters receive, where all the gods gathered together;
the one fitted upon the navel of the unborn, where all living beings have been taken their place. (6)

As in in case of the model of Child of the Waters, the unmanifest aspect of reality is conceived in terms of water but here the world is conceived in terms of the embryo. In the ṚV, fire is conceived in these terms. This conceptualisation is also activated by ṚV 2.35 the composer of which presents fire as a calf born from cows. As the logic of the general domain of Procreation presupposes, the concept of pregnancy and presence of the embryo within the mother's womb.

Jamison, Brereton (2014) translate *samápaśyanta* as 'appeared'[2]. It is also possible to understand this word as 'to see'[3]. This interpretation allows the recipient to understand that the gods see themselves in the embryo in terms of which the world is conceived because creation of the world is creation of the possibility to cognise. The priority of cognition is preserved in the stanzas. The gods first see themselves in the embryo and can then exist within its range. If the recipient understands the embryo as fire and the sun, he will understand that the gods can see themselves and can exist thanks to the sacrifices that are performed in cosmic and human dimensions.

At the same time, the monistic character of creation is preserved. The concept of the navel (*nā́bhi*, ṚV 10.82.6c) evokes the concept of birth-giving in terms of which creation is conceived. The aspect that is born is called *ékam*. As the *Nāsadīyasūkta* tells us, *ékam* is also the name of the pre-creative reality which manifests itself in the first stage of creation (see Jurewicz 2010a: 47–48). That the pre-creative reality manifests itself in creation is confirmed in that, according to ṚV 10.82.6d, on the one all the worlds have rested. The concept of navel may trigger the recipient to evoke the model of The Wave Of Honey with its whole imagery of the wave rising from the ocean, the Somic plant growing from the soil and a child linked with its mother by

2 In the same way understands it Elizarenkova (1999), Geldner (1957, I).
3 Edgerton (1965).

umbilical cord. It has been shown (Jurewicz 2010a: 240 ff.) that the deepest meaning of the blend created in this hymn are the transformations of Agni. But this activation is not necessary in order to understand the content of ṚV 10.82.6 thanks to the abstract character of the description. Even the concept of a navel can be understood more generally as the source of existence linking cause and effect[4].

The input spaces of the blend created in the stanzas are already abstract. These are the philosophical model of Child Of The Waters and the general domain of Procreation. The next two input spaces are the concepts of cognition and reality. The generic space is the appearance of the symbol of light from the symbol of darkness. In the blend, the concept of water comes from the model of Child Of The Waters while the concepts of embryo and navel come from the general domain of Procreation. They are used to conceive the cognitive and the creative activity of reality.

The most abstract form of the model of Child Of The Waters in the ṚV is attested in the following stanza:

ṚV 10.121.1

hiraṇyagarbháḥ sám avartatā́gre bhūtásya jātáḥ pátir éka āsīt |
sá dādhāra pṛthivī́ṃ dyā́m utémā́ṃ kásmai devā́ya havíṣā vidhema ||

The golden embryo evolved in the beginning. Born the lord of what came to be. he alone existed.
He supports the earth and the heaven there – Who is the god to whom we should do homage with our oblation?

In Jurewicz (2010a: 96–97), I have shown that the conceptual operations which motivated the concept of the Golden Embryo and the Golden Egg derive from the source domain of an egg with its nestling. However, the model of Child Of The Waters is also the motivating factor for the composer of ṚV 10.121 in that it endows the concepts of the Golden Embryo and the Golden Egg with metaphysical meaning. In the stanza just quoted, the context is so general that the recipient is not expected to evoke any concrete image to understand its general reference which is the creative power transforming itself into the world. Only the golden colour of the embryo betrays its fiery origin because, as we remember, the fire in the model of Child Of The Waters is also conceived as golden (ṚV 2.35.10).

The concept of the Golden Embryo, later transformed into the Golden Egg, became the main concept in terms of which the cosmos was conceived

---

4 As *bándhu* in the *Nāsadīyasūkta*.

in later Indian thought. It became a purely abstract concept with no reference to experience. On the other hand, the concept of wood/tree as the source domain for the material of the cosmos has disappeared.

1.2. Reality as speech (*vā́c*)

Conceptualisation of reality in terms of speech is elaborated in ṚV 10.125[5]. It can be argued that this conceptualisation is based on the specific experience of recitation. This experience is more and more important in the Vedic tradition, and, as it will be shown, it became an important factor motivating philosophical thought in the later Veda.

Speech is conceived in terms of a woman, more specifically in terms of a queen (10.125.3a) who is able to make those whom she loves full of strength, power and poetic ability (ṚV 10.125.5cd)[6]. In order to express the relationship between living beings and speech, the composer activates the image schema of CONTAINER: speech is conceived in terms of a container in which sentient beings exist without being aware of it (10.125.04c *amantávo mā́ṃ tá úpa kṣiyanti*)[7]. We may presume that this lack of this knowledge is characteristic for everyday cognition which can be overcome in Somic exultation. The dynamic nature of speech is conceived in terms of its roaming or walking (ṚV 10.125.1a: *ahám...carāmi*). As will be shown, the concept of moving is used to conceive the first manifestation of reality as free (AVŚ 11.5 and the *Vrātyakāṇḍa* (AVŚ 15) see chapters 2.2.1-2) and it is possible that reality conceived in terms of speech is also seen in this way.

The relationship between speech and gods is expressed in ṚV 10.125.1-2ab, where speech is presented as moving together with the gods and carrying them[8]. The concept of carrying activates the concept of a pregnant mother of a mother carrying a baby which is the specific realisation of the general domain of Procreation. In these terms, the dependence of the gods on speech is conceived.

---

5 For similarity of the concept of speech in ṚV 10.125, 10.71 and 1.164, see Brown (1968b).

6 ṚV 10.125.5cd: *yáṃ kāmáye táṃ-tam ugráṃ kr̥ṇomi tám brahmā́ṇaṃ tám ŕ̥ṣiṃ táṃ sumedhā́m.*

7 This foreshadows much later concepts according to which the Absolute in this unmanifest aspect knows all its manifestations contrary to them (Jurewicz 1994).

8 ṚV 10.125.1: *aháṃ rudrébhir vásubhiś carāmi ahám ādityaír utá viśvádevaiḥ* | *ahám mitrā́váruṇobhā́ bibharmi ahám indrāgnī́ ahám aśvínobhā́* ||
10.125.2: *aháṃ sómam āhanásam bibharmi aháṃ tváṣṭāram utá pūṣáṇam bhágam* | *aháṃ dadhāmi dráviṇaṃ havíṣmate suprāvíye yájamānāya sunvaté* ||

According to verses *c–d* of the second stanza, it is speech which gives wealth to the sacrificer. The typical addressees of sacrifices are gods who reward human ritual efforts. So the recipient understands that speech is the main power that makes a sacrifice successful. Its superiority over the gods is also implied in that in the third stanza it is called 'foremost among those deserving the sacrifice' (*prathamā́ yajñíyānām*, ṚV 10.125.3b).

Features of speech are also motivated by the concept of Agni. In the earlier ṚV, conceptualisation of speech in terms of fire is clearly seen in the descriptions of the Aṅgirases and Bṛhaspati (Jurewicz 2010a: 264 ff., 379 ff.). Such a conceptualisation of speech is grounded in experiential correlation as, when one speaks, one exhales warm breath. The mechanism which creates abstraction is as follows: the target domain (speech) loses its source domain (fire) and becomes the independent concept used to think about reality, the features of fire are therefore blended within the concept of speech. The conceptual network looks as follows: the first input space is the concept of fire and the second input space is the concept of speech. The features of fire and speech are transferred to the emergent space and thus the new concept of speech is created. The generic space of this blend are concepts of heat, sound and cognition. The next input space is the concept of reality which in the blend is identified with speech. Speech, although is one of most intimate human experience, seems to be more abstract than fire because it conveys human thought and allows for communication. The generic space of this new conceptual network is the image schema of SELF-MOTION.

The construction of first two stanzas is similar to the construction of ṚV 2.1 which is devoted to Agni there identified with all gods. Each verse ṚV 10.125.1-2ac begins with the pronoun *ahám*, while verses of ṚV 2.1.1-14a begin with the pronoun *tvám*. The similarity of construction triggers the recipient to think about Agni and to identify speech with it. In ṚV 10.125.3a speech is called 'gatherer of riches' (*saṃgámanī vásūnāṃ*) and Agni is described in ṚV 1.96.6a[9] in the same way. Speech is also presented as being placed everywhere by the gods (*tā́m mā devā́ ví adadhuḥ purutrā́*, ṚV 10.15.3c) and again Agni is presented in 10.45.2b, 10.80.4d, 3.55.4.a and 7.1.9[10] in the same way. According to the fourth stanza, every sentient being eats food thanks

[9] This is repeated in ṚV 10.139.3a; here the addressee is the sun.

[10] The root *dhā-* is not used in these contexts, but the idea is the same; ṚV 10.45.2b: *vidmā́ te dhā́ma víbhṛtā purutrā́-*; 10.80.4d: *agnér dhā́māni víbhṛtā purutrā́*; 3.55.4a: *samānó rā́jā víbhṛtaḥ purutrā́*; 7.1.9ab: *ví yé te agne bhejiré ánīkam mártā náraḥ pítriyāsaḥ purutrā́*; 7.1.9c: *utó na ebhíḥ sumánā ihá syāḥ.*

to speech[11]. The reason for such a conceptualisation of speech is not only the fact that speech is produced in the mouth through which food is eaten[12], but also by the concept of speech deriving from the concept of fire which is conceived in the ṚV as the eater of food (ṚV 4.7.10, 7.7.2, 843.3, 10.15.2).

In stanzas 5–6, speech is conceived as ambivalent as it is benevolent to some and dangerous to others. Its nature then is the same as that of Agni and Soma (Jurewicz 2010a: 294 ff.). It has power to transform people, to make them powerful and strong (*ugrá*) and full of poetic ability (*brahmā́*; *ṛ́ṣi*, *sumedhā́*)[13]. In the ṚV, Agni is conceived as having transformative power as it transforms ordinary men into those who can drink Soma and it transforms the deceased into the father (Jurewicz 2010a: 294ff). Soma is conceived as having the power to transform its drinker into a seer, it is called *ṛṣikṛ́t* in ṚV 9.96.18. This power of Soma manifests especially in Indra who is transformed in a similar way (Jurewicz 2010a: 301–302, 342) . Speech is also presented as the power that stretches the bow of Rudra to kill enemies of the sacred word (*bráhman*)[14]. This evokes the destructive aspect of Agni who destroys enemies in battle and eats their corpses[15]. Also the fact that speech is presented as entering the earth and the sky (10.125.6d: *ahám dyā́vāpṛthivī́ ā́ viveśa*) shows that this concept draws on the concepts of Agni and Soma in their cosmic, solar form.

The next stanza can be seen as an attempt to settle the relationship between concepts of speech and Agni:

ṚV 10.125.7

aháṃ suve pitáram asya mūrdhán máma yónir apsú antáḥ samudré |
táto ví tiṣṭhe bhúvanā́nu víśvā utā́mū́ṃ dyā́ṃ varṣmáṇópa spṛśāmi ||

I give birth to Father[16] on his[17] head[18]; my womb is in the waters, in the sea. Thence I spread forth across all the worlds, and yonder heaven with its height I touch.

---

11 ṚV 10.125.4 *máyā só ánnam atti yó vipáśyati yáḥ prā́ṇiti yá īṃ śṛṇóti uktám | amantávo mā́ṃ tá úpa kṣiyanti śrudhí śruta śraddhiváṃ te vadāmi ||*

12 Metonymy MEANS FOR ACTION is elaborated in ŚB 2.2.4.1 in the definition of Agni, see chapter 3.1.1.

13 ṚV 10.125.5: *ahám evá svayám idáṃ vadāmi júṣṭaṃ devébhir utá mā́nuṣebhiḥ | yáṃ kāmáye táṃ-tam ugráṃ kṛṇomi tám brahmā́ṇaṃ tám ṛ́ṣiṃ táṃ sumedhā́m ||*

14 ṚV 10.125.6a-c: *aháṃ rudrā́ya dhánur ā́ tanomi brahmadvíṣe śárave hántavā́ u | aháṃ jánāya samádaṃ kṛṇomi ||*

15 Such a conceptualisation of speech can also be motivated by the concept of Bṛhaspati who is often presented as destroying enemies of the sacred word (*bráhman*).

16 Jamison, Brereton 2014: '(Heaven?)'.

17 Jamison, Brereton 2014: '(own?)'.

18 Jamison, Brereton 2014: '[Agni?]'.

In verse *a*, speech is presented as giving birth to father on his head. The concept of father is used in the earlier ṚV in reference to the unmanifest aspect of reality, conceived in terms of Agni (Jurewicz 2010a: 249–250, see below, section 1.6). If speech is presented as the mother of the father[19], it implies that it is seen as the primordial reality and is prior even to Agni. At the same time, it is presented as giving birth on the head of the father. This implies that the father is born from his own head that in the later Veda is identified with womb (BU 1.4.6, see chapter 4.1.2). Speech is the intermediate element which makes the birth possible and which, conceived as female, opposes both father and son. The relationship between aspects of reality is conceived in the model of Child Of The Waters in the same ambiguous way. The relationship between speech and gods is similarly ambiguous: on the one hand, it carries them (ṚV 1.125.1cd-2ab), though, on the other, it is distributed by them within the cosmos (ṚV 10.125.3c).

In ṚV 10.125.7b, the composer resolves the ambiguity. The womb of speech is in the water, in the sea. In my analysis of ṚV 4.58.1, I reconstructed the basic ontology of the model of the Wave Of Honey (Jurewicz 2010a). In that model, Agni is identified with the ocean from which Soma arises. If the recipient activates the model, he will understand that speech is the next manifestation of the father. He will then understand the creative stages in the following sequence: Father – Speech – Father (= Agni = Ocean) – Speech. This sequence is elaborated in the models Puruṣa – Virāj – Puruṣa and Aditi – Dakṣa – Aditi (see sections 1.3, 1.5).

The presence of speech within the cosmos is described in ṚV 10.125.7cd. It extends 'across all the worlds' (*táto ví tiṣṭhe bhúvanā́nu víśvā*) and reaches zenith in the form of the rising sun (*utā́mū́ṃ dyā́ṃ varṣmáṇópa spṛśāmi*). Agni is presented in its solar form in the same way (ṚV 5.8.7, 3.5.9, Jurewicz 2010a: 134 ff.). Within the frames of thinking just reconstructed, speech is the form through which Agni pervades the universe as the sun.

In verse *a* of ṚV 10.125.8, speech is compared to the wind (*ahám evá vā́ta iva prá vāmi*). Comparison of speech with wind is based on experiential correlation: when one speaks one breaths. Since in the earlier ṚV fire is identified with wind, the recipient again sees the identity of speech and fire.[20] In verse *b*, speech is presented as taking the world to itself (*ārábhamāṇā bhúvanāni víśvā*). Thus the burning activity of fire, conceived in terms of eating, is evoked. The blend, profiled in this way, is an important source for

---

[19] This conceptualisation will be elaborated in ṚV 1.164.8, see section 1.6.

[20] ṚV 7.3.2, see also ṚV 1.148.4, 4.7.10, 10.142.4. Agni is called 'wind' in ṚV 6.4.7. Agni is compared to wind in ṚV 7.5.7, 10.46.7. Agni breathes (*śvas-*) in ṚV 1.65.9, 1.140.5. Agni is called 'breath' (*prāṇá*) in ṚV 1.66. (Jurewicz 2010a: 266, note 30).

the conceptualisation of the creative activity of reality in AU 1.3.10 within its manifest aspect (see chapter 4.1.3). The second hemistich of the last stanza presents speech as identical with the unmanifest aspect: it extends beyond the sky and the earth[21].

From the diachronic view, identification of reality with speech and the way of thinking about it is motivated by the concept of Agni. In the earlier parts of the ṚV, reality is conceived in terms of fire that burns, speaks, is omnipresent and is ambivalent. Speech has the same features. At the same time, to conceive reality in terms of speech is proof of abstraction. Reality, conceived in terms of speech, is dynamic and cognitive.

From the synchronic view, the concept of speech in the ṚV 10.125 is a blend of features of Agni and of speech. The features of Agni are based on the way it is conceived in the ṚV, on the metaphors of its activity, on its role it plays in society and cosmos and on its metaphysic conceptualisation. The features of speech are also based on its metaphoric conceptualisation, especially in terms of woman/queen/mother. Those features are transferred into the blend to create a metaphysical concept of reality. The input spaces of Agni and speech endow the concept of reality with meanings of cognition while the conceptualisation of speech in terms of a woman imparts to the blend the concept of agency. The generic space which unites those input spaces with the input space of reality is the image schema of SELF-MOTION.

1.3. Man is the measure of all things (RV 10.90)

The *Puruṣasūkta* begins a long and well established tradition in Indian philosophy to conceive of reality in terms of man (*púruṣa*). This hymn can be seen as the explicit verbalisation of Ṛgvedic thinking about reality in such terms. It is possible that conceptualisation of reality in terms of a man is motivated by the concept of Agni which is conceived as a man, principally as a poet, a priest and a messenger[22]. The concept of man is also implicitly evoked by the *Nāsadīyasūkta via* the concepts of cognition and procreation in terms of which the creative process is conceived (metonymy ACTION FOR AGENT, Jurewicz 2010a: 45 ff.[23]). Mus (1968) looks for reasons for this conceptualisation in the historical context and in contemporary political and

21 ṚV 10.125.8: *ahám evá vā́ta iva prá vāmi ārábhamāṇā bhúvanāni víśvā | paró divā́ pará enā́ pṛthivyā́ etā́vatī mahinā́ sám babhūva ||*

22 Already Brown (1931: 109–110) has shown that the concept of *púruṣa* shares features with the earlier concept of Agni and Sūrya.

23 Radden, Kövecses (1990). See Jurewicz (2010a: 45 ff.).

social changes. The Brahmins and the Kṣatriyas needed an established alliance between spiritual power (*bráhman*) and secular power (*kṣatrá*) and a clearer concept of a society which was becoming more and more complex.

The composer of the *Puruṣasūkta*, on the one hand, evokes the domains used by the *Nāsadīyasūkta* and, on the other, he elaborates the concept of the sacrifice. As it will be shown, while the first five stanzas present creation the main schema of which agrees with that of the *Nāsadīyasūkta*, the remaining stanzas of the hymn introduce a new perspective which allows the composer to define ontology and anthropology in a different way. This reflects the social changes that took place in the Āryan society as far as ritual is concerned. It had become more complex and had begun to play the role of a common activity that organised all of society. The main input spaces of the conceptual network created by the composer are concepts of man and of reality. The third input space is the cosmos understood in the blend as the manifest aspect of reality. The generic space is the concept of transformation.

ṚV 10.90.1

sahásraśīrṣā púruṣaḥ sahasrākṣáḥ sahásrapāt |
sá *bhū́mim viśváto vṛtvā́* áty *atiṣṭhad daśāṅgulám* ||

The Man has a thousand heads, a thousand eyes, and a thousand feet.
Having covered the earth on all sides, he extended ten fingers' breadth beyond.

Contrary to the *Nāsadīyasūkta*, here the composer begins his description with a positive statement, although the content of the statement is paradoxical: it is the image of a man with a thousand heads, eyes and feet. The first act of creation is conceived in the *Nāsadīyasūkta* in a similarly paradoxical way (Jurewicz 2010a). Since, in everyday life, there is no living being which could have a thousand heads and feet, the recipient understands that this impossible concept expresses the paradoxical nature of reality. The number 'thousand' is probably meant to metonymically evoke the concept of infinity[24]. If this is the case, the recipient understands that reality manifests itself as infinite. The concept of the head metonymically evokes the concept of thinking, the concept of eye evokes it metonymically (PART OF THE BODY FOR ACTION[25]) and metaphorically (COGNITION IS SEEING[26]). So from the man having a thousand heads and eyes, the recipient can understand that reality

[24] Srinivasan (1997: 75): '1,000 = totality of numbers of things; completeness prior to the introduction of distinction'.

[25] This metonymy can be seen as an instantiation of the metonymy MEANS FOR ACTION (as in the sentence *He sneezed the tissue off the* table, Radden, Kövecses 1999: 37).

[26] For the importance of this metaphor in the ṚV, see Gonda (1963: 28 ff. *passim*).

is omniscient. From the man also having a thousand feet, the recipient can understand that reality is omnipresent: omnipresence is conceived in terms of the ability to go everywhere at the same time[27] and he may infer from it that, in the first act of creation, reality begins to move. In the same way, speech is conceived in ṚV 10.125.1a with use of the source domain of walking (see section 1.2). Moreover, the ability to go everywhere implies a lack of restriction. On this basis, the recipient can understand that reality manifests itself as free (FREEDOM IS LACK OF BONDAGE)[28]. The first manifestation of reality in the *Nāsadīyasūkta* is conceived in the same way, although with the use of a different concept of breathing without breath (Jurewicz 2010a: 46–48). Such a conceptualisation of the first manifestation of reality is continued in AVŚ 11.5 and 15.1 (see chapters 2.2.1-2).

The earth in verses *c–d* is the source domain for the conceptualisation of the world in its pre-creative state[29]. It is presented as being encompassed by reality. In the same way, the composer describes the next stage of creation. This is conceived similarly to the *Nāsadīyasūkta* which presents it as darkness hiding darkness (*táma āsīt támasā gūḷhám ágre*, Jurewicz 2010a: 48–49). The verb *vr̥-* (*vr̥tvā́*) evokes the concept of Vr̥tra who is the embodiment of the power that hides the future world. In Jurewicz (2010a: 343 ff.), it is shown that, in the descriptions of the fight of Indra with Vr̥tra, the appearance of Vr̥tra corresponds to the second stage of creation in the model of the *Nāsadīyasūkta.* Moreover, if the recipient activates the concept of Vr̥tra here, he may interpret the thousand-headed and thousand-feet being as a monster which in the second stage of creation manifests its destroying power[30].

In the interpretation of *daśāṅgulám*, I follow the interpretation of Coomaraswamy (1941) and Mus (1968)[31] who argue that this expression refers to the measure of face. According to Mus (1968: 548–549), its upper part measures ten fingers while the lower jaw measures two fingers. This interpretation implies that, in order to understand the state described in the stanza, the recipient must think about the head of man and conceive reality in these terms; the concepts of head and of reality are the input space of this conceptual network. The conceptualisation can be run in the blend in two ways. According to the first interpretation, the upper immovable part of the head is

---

27 Expressed by later *sarvagata*.

28 Lakoff (1987: 274): 'Slavery is understood as bondage, and freedom as the absence of anything tying us down'.

29 In ŚB 2.2.4.3 the pre-creative state of the world is conceived in terms of the bald earth, see chapter 3.1.1.

30 See Coomaraswamy (1935). This is the case in some cosmogonies of the ŚB, see chapter 3.1.

31 See also Jamison, Brereton (2014: 1538). Brown (1931) and Coomaraswamy (1946) interpret *áty atiṣṭhad* as 'ruled over'. According to Brown (1931), *daśangulám* refers to 'heart'.

the unmanifest aspect of reality while its lower movable part and the space which is created when mouth is open, is the manifest one. According to the second interpretation, the upper immovable part is the borderline sphere of the cosmos reached in sacrifice while the whole body is the unmanifest aspect[32]. The generic input space is the concept of the image schema of CONTAINER. In the blend, the creation is conceived in terms of man who opens his mouth in order to speak or to eat; the existence of the world is conceived in terms of speaking and eating[33]. This again brings us back to the concept of Agni whose burning is conceived in these terms. Moreover, this foreshadows later metaphysical concepts of the ŚB.

ṚV 10.90.2

púruṣa evédáṃ sárvaṃ yád bhūtáṃ yác ca bháviyam |
utā́mṛtatvásyéśāno yád ánnenātiróhati ||

The Man is this whole[34]: what has come into being been and what is to be. Moreover, he is master of immortality when he climbs beyond[35] through food.

Already in the ṚV, the expression *idáṃ sárvam* (verse *a*) refers to the manifest world[36] so, in verse *a*, the composer identifies reality with its creation. In this way, the monistic assumption is expressed. According to verse *b*, reality is what has come to being and what is to be (*yád bhūtáṃ yác ca bháviyam*), i.e. it is subject to the influence of time. The concept of time is not yet expressed verbally (it will be in AVŚ 19.53, see chapter 2.1.3), but clearly it exists in the mind of composer. The concept of time is the consequence of the conceptualisation of the manifest aspect in terms of a moving jaw which metonymically activates concepts of speaking and eating. From everyday experience, the recipient knows that any activity occurs in time.

In verse *c*, reality is called 'the master of immortality' (*amṛtatvásyéśāno*) which implies that reality is beyond the influence of time. There two possible interpretations of this expression. The first is that it refers to the unmanifest aspect of reality. However, the composer states in verse *d*, that the stage of immortality can be gained thanks to food (*yád ánnenātiróhati*).

---

32 In this way, it is interpreted in ŚB 6.1.1, see chapter 3.2.2.

33 Here I would see the roots of the AU conceptualisation of the beginnings of the creative process in terms of an egg which appears from an open mouth (see chapter 4.1.3). The earth covered by man from all sides may evoke the image of an egg kept in a mouth.

34 Jamison, Brereton 2014: '(world)'.

35 Jamison, Brereton 2014: '(this world)'.

36 ṚV 8.58.2: *éka evā́gnír bahudhā́ sámiddha ékaḥ sū́ryo víśvam ánu prábhūtaḥ | ékaivóṣā́ḥ sárvam idáṃ ví bhāti ékaṃ vā́ idáṃ ví babhūva sárvam ||*

As I have already mentioned (see *Introduction*), in the early Veda the range of philosophical interest was limited to what is manifest (*sát*), the sphere that can be defined and experienced. Although the composers assumed the existence of the unmanifest aspect of reality, which is the source of the world, they did not explore it mentally. However, they accepted the existence of the sphere within the manifest aspect, which is beyond everyday life experience, but which can be acquired in Somic exultation. It is conceptualised in the ṚV as being realised on the sun. The sun is the visible form of the highest heaven, *paramá vyòman*, which is the borderline sphere of the cosmos seen as the spatio-temporal beginnings of the world (Jurewicz 2010a: 296 ff.)[37]. However, as I have also mentioned in the *Introduction*, in the late Veda the composers begin to recognise more clearly this sphere and see it as the borderline sphere of the cosmos which is manifest but not subjected to limitation of everyday life experience. The expression 'the master of immortality' (*amṛtatvásyéśāno*) may refer to this very sphere. In the ṚV, the concept of immortality (*amrtatvá*) metonymically activates the concept of the sun in zenith filled with Somic juice which is gained by men during sacrifice (STATE FOR THE PLACE THE STATE IS REALISED[38]). According to this interpretation, death and immortality belong to the manifest aspect of reality which is divided into two parts: the part subjected to time (the earth), and the part where immortality is gained (the sun filled with heavenly Soma). Thus the recipient understands that reality, in the creative act, manifests as mortal and immortal.

To the best of my knowledge, this account of the *Puruṣasūkta* is the first testimony in the ṚV of an attempt to create a clear division between both aspects of reality and between the spheres of the cosmos. Such a division is implied in the earlier parts of the ṚV with use of conceptual metaphors the target domain of which is a tripartite whole, the middle sphere of which can be interpreted both as a symbol of darkness and as a symbol of light[39]. In the earlier hymns, however, the source domains are concepts connected with experience. Here this tripartite reality is conceived in abstract terms: of past and future (i.e. subjected to the power of time), of immortality and of what is beyond both states (see ṚV 10.129.2a: *ná mṛtyúr āsīd amṛ́taṃ ná tárhi*). The first two states constitute the manifest aspect, the third is the unmanifest one.

---

37 As we will see, this sphere will be thoroughly penetrated by the Upaniṣadic thinkers in their liberating practice, see chapter 4.4.

38 This could be treated as specific instantiation of metonymy PLACE FOR EVENT (Radden, Kövecses 1999: 42). The word *amrtatvá* is used in ṚV 4.58.1 in this meaning (Jurewicz 2010a: 227–228).

39 Treasure – treasury – mountain; bird – nestling – egg; milk – cow – its enclosure; milk – udder – cow (Jurewicz 2010a: 2010: 94–95).

In verse *d*, the composer explains the way reality becomes 'the master of immortality' (*amṛtatvásyéśāno*). He conceives this process in terms of a living being which grows when it is well fed. This may occur in everyday feeding, but also during ritual when gods and men are fed with oblation. The name *púruṣa* used in reference to reality allows the composer to express the simultaneity of reality and of human transformations. Thus the essence of sacrifice is conceived in terms of eating. This interpretation conforms with the conceptualisation of the world in terms of a moving jaw (ṚV 10.90.1).

ṚV 10.90.3

etā́vān asya mahimā́ áto jyā́yāṃś ca pū́ruṣaḥ |
pā́do 'sya víśvā bhūtā́ni tripā́d asyāmṛ́taṃ diví ||

So much is his greatness, but the Man is more than this;
a quarter of him is all living beings; three quarters are the immortal in heaven.

In verse *a*, the composer activates a spatial conceptualisation of the manifest aspect of reality which he presents as great. In this way, he implies that it can be measured, contrary to the unmanifest aspect which is immeasurable. Such a conceptualisation of the manifest aspect in the early stages of creation will be continued in later Indian philosophical thought[40]. In verse *b*, the poet states that reality as a whole is 'greater' (*jyā́yān*) than its manifest aspect. Thus, he proposes a panentheistic theory according to which the manifest aspect is only a part of the unmanifest whole.

In verses *c–d*, the composer evokes the concept of an animal (most probably a cow) of which only one leg can be seen and three are invisible. This conceptualisation can be activated if the recipient understands *padá* as 'leg' (not as 'quarter' as Jamison, Brereton propose). Activation of the experiential meaning allows the recipient to understand much more of the abstract content than the seemingly abstract meaning of part.

Again, two interpretations are possible here which are not mutually exclusive. In the first, all reality is conceived according to a zoomorphic model: the world is conceptualised in terms of legs of the cow while the unmanifest aspect of reality is conceptualised in terms of the body of the cow. According to the second, only the manifest aspect is conceived in terms of the zoomorphic model. The first interpretation logically follows from the first hemistich of the stanza which describes reality as greater than its manifest aspect. The second interpretation is activated *via* the expression *amṛ́taṃ diví* ('the immortal in heaven', verse *d*). Most probably this expression refers to

[40] For the use of the concept of greatness in the AV see chapter 2.2.2.

the borderline sphere of the cosmos where immortality can be gained during life and after death thanks to ritual; this sphere is called *amrtatvá* in the previous stanza. The possibility to interpret the stanza equivocally may be caused by the composer wanting to express the idea that the state realised in the highest place of the sky opens the way to what is unmanifest and beyond any human condition, although this condition cannot be cognised and described by discursive categories.

The concept of a visible leg is the source domain for the *axis mundi* and three legs are hidden in the sun where the state of immortality can be realised. It should be noted that the Ṛgvedic composers believed that the *axis mundi* marked the sacrificial route between the earth and the sky: the oblations and the sacrificer go up it and the gods come to sit on the sacrificial grass, *barhís* (Jurewicz 2010a: 276 ff., 284). Thus understood the *axis mundi* is sometimes conceptualised in terms of a tree. This can be seen in the Āprī hymns of the ṚV where the sacrificial post (*yū́pa*), the ritual embodiment of the *axis mundi*, is called tree[41]. The concept of climbing a tree is also the source domain to conceive of cognition gained during sacrifice (ṚV 1.164.40-43, see section 1.6). It is also worth noting that the image of an animal standing on one leg with three legs up (a situation impossible from the point of view of everyday experience of course) is schematically similar to the image of a tree: one leg corresponds to the trunk, the three legs its branches.

Moreover, if the recipient elaborates the scenario of a jaw moving in speaking and eating, he will understand that the *axis mundi* stops this movement. According to Ṛgvedic beliefs, the *axis mundi* appeared in the morning and on its top the sun is raised (Jurewicz 2010a). According to the conceptualisation of the *Puruṣasūkta*, the midday is conceived as the moment when mouth is opened and cannot move. At the same time, as stated above, dynamism characterising the manifest aspect of reality is conceived in terms of constant eating and speaking. Thus the experience is again violated in order to express movement of what is immovable.

The concept of a cow is elaborated in ṚV 1.164.45 where speech is presented as divided into four footprints (*padá*) of which one is spoken by living beings and three are hidden (see section 1.6); the phonetic association between *padá* and *pā́da* reinforces the similarity of expositions of the two hymns. If the recipient evokes this conceptualisation of speech and blends it with the concept of manifestation of reality as the cosmos, he will understand that creation is conceived as manifestation of speech. The blending is justified in that speech is conceived in terms of a cow in the ṚV (ṚV 8.100.100-11,

[41] Potdar (1944–46, 1946–47), Bosch (1985).

10.101.9, it is elaborated in ṚV 1.164, see section 1.6). It is also justified on the ground of the *Puruṣasūkta* itself the composer of which evokes the concept of a moving jaw in the first stanza. We can see that all these meanings could not be grasped without activation of the experiential meaning of *pā́da* which is 'leg'. The input space of cow imparts to the blend topology, while the input space of speech imparts the cognitive nature of creative transformations of reality. The generic space of this blend is the image schema of SELF-MOTION.

ṚV 10.90.4

tripā́d ūrdhvá úd ait púruṣaḥ pā́do 'syehā́bhavat púnaḥ |
táto víṣvaṅ ví akrāmat sāśanānaśané abhí ||

With three quarters the Man went upwards, but a quarter of him came to be here again.
From there he strode out in different directions towards what eats and what does not eat.

In verses *a–b*, the composer elaborates the ontology presented in the previous stanza and highlights its dynamism with use of the image schema of VERTICALITY. It is implied that three parts of reality, which constitute the heavenly sphere of immortality and lead to what is unmanifest, are created in the upward movement and then the downward movement of one part of reality created the *axis mundi.*

The use of the verb *ví kram-* in verse *c* evokes the model of Footprints Of Viṣṇu whose activity is expressed with the same verb (ṚV 1.154.1,2). The recipient can also evoke this model on the basis of the phonetic resemblance between *pā́da* and *padá*. Since the main meaning of the model Footprints Of Viṣṇu is the sunrise, the activity of reality presented in verse *a* can be interpreted as sunrise. In such a case, there would be a difference in conceptualisation between the *Puruṣasūkta* and the model of Footprints Of Viṣṇu: according to the former, three parts (conceived in terms of legs) constitute the sky, while, according to the latter, three parts (conceived in terms of footprints) constitute the earth, the space and the sky (Jurewicz 2010a: 387 ff.).

However, in the *Puruṣasūkta*, the word *ví kram-* has a wider meaning than in the model of Footprints Of Viṣṇu. It is used to express the monism of two spheres of the manifest aspect: reality encompasses everything 'what eats and what does not eat' (*sāśanānaśané abhí*, verse *d*). Since immortality is gained thanks to eating, the recipient understands that the phrase 'what eats' refers to the borderline of the cosmos reached in sacrifices while 'what does not eat' is everything which is the food. Thus the opposition between immortality and mortality realised within the manifest aspect is again expressed. Verses *c–d*, therefore, express that reality confirms the identity of its two opposing spheres of the world.

The description of ṚV 10.90.3-4 is a good example how abstract thought is created. The main source domain is a moving cow: the functioning of the world is conceived in terms of its moving legs while the borderline of the cosmos and the unmanifest aspect of reality is conceived in terms of the body of the cow. The recipient need not activate all his knowledge about a cow, but only focus on the movement of its legs. What is more, such a movement is impossible from the point of view of everyday experience. In this way, association between the legs and the whole animal is blocked and the concept of the legs becomes an independent concept for conceptualisation of creation of the world and its functioning.

It should be added that this is not a new metaphor of creation in the ṚV. As I have shown elsewhere (Jurewicz 2010a: 88–89, 121), creation of the world is conceived in terms of creation of legs. The earliest stages of creation are conceived in terms of a living being without legs (e.g. ṚV 1.24.8) while the next stages of creation are conceived in terms of acquiring legs and their movement (ṚV 1.164.41, see section 1.6). The ability for movement, gained thanks to legs, is the ground for the abstract concept of *ṛtá*, literally 'something that has gone', which generally refers to the manifest aspect of reality[42]. The composer of *Puruṣasūkta* elaborates this metaphor to explain the structure and dynamism of the manifest aspect of reality and the role of the *axis mundi*. Moreover, by activating the concept of a cow, he triggers activation of speech in these terms (SPEECH IS COW, ṚV 8.100.10-11). Thus he can enrich the meaning of creation with this concept. The abstraction is built on the basis of a very concrete word 'leg' (*pā́da*) and knowledge about everyday processes. In the blend, the logic of everyday processes is violated which allows the composer to precisely express the impossible activity of reality.

It can be concluded that in the stanzas 3–4 the composer settles the general rules for functioning of the future world. The manifest aspect is divided into the mortal and the immortal sphere, the link between them is settled and the upwards activity that allows the future men to gain immortality is performed.

The next stanza presents the further arrangement of the manifest aspect.

ṚV 10.90.5

tásmād virā́ḷ ajāyata virā́jo ádhi pū́ruṣaḥ |
sá jātó áty aricyata paścā́d bhū́mim átho puráḥ ||

From him the Virā́j was born; from the Virā́j the Man.
Upon his birth, he reached beyond the earth from behind and also from the front.

42 Jurewicz (2016a).

Verses *a–b* activate complex creative process. The verb *jan-*, 'to generate, to beget, to give birth to' activates the general domain of Procreation. On the basis of metonymy THE LAST PHASE OF THE PROCESS (DELIVERY) FOR THE WHOLE PROCESS (PREGNANCY)[43], the recipient is able to reconstruct the phases of creation on this basis. The internal contradictoriness of reality is conceived in terms of androgyny[44]. The primeval creative impulse, which takes place in this stage, is conceived in terms of the sexual act between its two opposing aspects[45]. Thanks to it, reality manifests itself as a female called *virā́j*; such an interpretation of *virā́j* is based on its grammatical gender which is feminine. The next creative impulse is conceived in terms of a sexual act between the male aspect of reality and the female aspect *virā́j*. This stage of creation is conceived in terms of a pregnant woman. If the recipient metonymically activates the concept of water *via* the concept of womb full of fetal waters, he will see that this stage of creation is conceived in the same way as in the third act of creation in the *Nāsadīyasūkta* model. It is important to note that the scenario of the general domain of Procreation is prompted in the recipient's mind *via* very concise wording which enumerates the nouns in masculine and feminine gender. Thus *púruṣa* and *virā́j* can be seen as abstract words which name the stages of creation[46].

However, the recipient may activate even more concepts *via* the word *virā́j*. Its meaning is 'the shining one' and it metonymically evokes the concept of luminary bodies. If the recipient activates the concept of dawn and the metaphor DAWNS ARE WATERS, he may understand this stage of creation in terms of the appearance of water as in the third stage of the *Nāsadīyasūkta*. If he thinks about the sun, he will understand this stage of creation as the sunrise. Activation of the concept of the sun is based not only of the meaning of *virā́j* which is 'shining'. As Gonda (1969: 115ff.) has shown, *virā́j* also conveys the meaning of an extended rule of a king and the sun is conceived in terms of a king in the ṚV. Thus interpreted, verse *a* also evokes the fourth stage of creation according to the model of the *Nāsadīyasūkta* which is conceived as the manifestation thanks to the power of heat.

The word *virā́j* is also the name of a metre composed of ten syllables. In the first stanza of the hymn, reality is presented as extending ten fingers

43 The same metonymy motivates English expression 'to sign a contract' for 'to make a contract', Radden, Kövecses (1999: 49).

44 This conceptualisation of reality is elaborated in the ŚB, see chapter 3.2.

45 The composer of the *Nāsadīyasūkta* activates the concept That One which drinks Soma within itself (Jurewicz 2010a: 325–327).

46 In CU 6.2.3-4 (see chapter 4.1.4), the words *tapas*, *āpas* and *anna* can be similarly interpreted: as evoking the earlier general model of reality transformation and as abstract concepts which only refer to the stages of creation.

beyond the manifest aspect. Activation of the meaning of *virāj* as a ten-syllable-metre may allow the recipient to understand that the unmanifest aspect is born within the manifest one[47]. Thus the meaning of the monistic nature of reality will be highlighted.

The recipient may also metonymically understand that in this stage of creation, speech organised in metres appears. Taking into account the possibility of the activation of the concept of speech on the basis of the previous stanzas (ṚV 10.90.3-4), the speech organised in metres is its quarter conceived in terms of one leg. In ṚV 1.164.45, speech spoken by men is conceived in the same way, as a quarter of the whole speech (see section 1.6).

If the recipient activates all the associations mentioned, he will create a conceptual network with the following input spaces. The first is the general domain of Procreation, more specifically, a male and a female engaged in sexual activity. Since there is one actor in the activity described by the hymn, the recipient will understands that an incestuous act is implied here: the male element gives birth to the female element with which he sexually unites in order to be reborn in her as his own son. Such a conceptualisation of creation is expressed by the model of the Child Of The Waters (Jurewicz 2010a: 213), in the conceptualisation of relationship between speech and the manifest aspect of reality in ṚV 10.125 (see above, section 1.5) and is formalised in another way as the sequence Aditi – Dakṣa – Aditi in ṚV 10.72 (see below, section 1.5). The main difference is that in the *Puruṣasūkta*, the male aspect of reality is conceived as that which gives birth to the female to be reborn from it. It is in this form that it is accepted in the later thought.

The second input space is the appearance of the morning light, the third is the appearance of waters and the fourth is the concept of a king. As will be shown, the conceptualisation of creation in terms of enthronement is elaborated in the *Vrātyakāṇḍa* (see chapter 2.2.2) and it is possible that the recipient is triggered to activate this concept in this context. The fifth input space is the recitation of metrical speech which the recipient may imagine in more concrete terms of a priest or a poet singing hymns in the morning. The sixth input space is the concept of reality. The general domain of Procreation gives scenario to the blend and the concept of an incestuous act allows for conceptualisation of the reflexive nature of transformation of one reality. This transformation causes the appearance of life-giving elements in the cosmos and establishes the sacral and political power of the future society. The concepts of a king and a priest endow the blend with the concept of agency. The generic space is the appearance of the symbol of light from the symbol of darkness.

47 This is expressed in AU in the description of *ātman* which is born within man (see chapter 4.1.3).

According to verses *c–d*, reality reaches beyond the earth. The words *paścā́d* and *purás* mean not only 'behind' and 'in front', but also 'eastward' and 'westward', 'earlier' and 'later'. Since, as I have argued, the first form of the world is conceived in terms of earth, the composer now seems to express the idea that reality confirms the identity of the world and its unmanifest aspect which has been conceived in the first stanza in terms of ten fingers extending beyond the earth.

The scenario of creation presented in the *Puruṣasūkta* is, in its basic scheme, similar to the scenario presented in the *Nāsadīyasūkta*, although the pre-creative state of reality is not described here. The concept of reality is a blend of two input spaces: the concepts of a human and of a monstrous being (ṚV 10.90.1ab). This state corresponds to the first stage of the model of the *Nāsadīyasūkta* where reality manifests as the One breathing without breath. The description of reality which covers the earth and extends beyond it for ten fingers length refers to the second stage of creation described by the *Nāsadīyasūkta* in terms of a darkness that covers the darkness: two aspects of the one reality are outlined here. One is the earth which is the manifest, the second one is the ummanifest conceived as surrounding the manifest. The word *virā́j*, used in stanza 5, evokes the concepts of water and light and in this concise way activates the third and fourth creative stages.

Now the implications of conceptualisation of reality in terms of man are elaborated and further creation is conceived in terms of sacrifice that was performed *in illo tempore*. This part of the hymn is the detailed description of the final arrangement of the world which is described in the *Nāsadīyasūkta* in the concise image of the seers who extend their ray/reins (see Jurewicz 2010a: 53–54).

ṚV 10.90.6

yát púruṣeṇa havíṣā devā́ yajñám átanvata |
vasantó asyāsīd ā́jyaṃ grīṣmá idhmáḥ śarád dhavíḥ ||

When, with Man as the offering, the gods extended the sacrifice,
spring was the melted butter, summer its firewood, autumn its offering.

Similarly to the *Nāsadīyasūkta*, the source domain which facilitates conceptualisation of this stage of creation is the sacrifice; here it is the animal sacrifice. The composer of the *Puruṣasūkta* elaborates this source domain in a detailed way. We are told that in this sacrifice man is the oblation, the gods are the priests. The appearance of gods is not mentioned in the hymn (it is not mentioned in the *Nāsadīyasūkta* either). However, it is implied by the general domain of Procreation elaborated in the previous stanza. The recipient may assume that the gods are born together with manifest aspecrt. I would see them (and the Sādhyas and the seers mentioned in ṚV 10.90.7d) as the manifestation of the subjective power of reality which is able to perform its creative activity within the manifest aspect. I have interpreted poets in the *Nāsadīyasūkta* in the same way (Jurewicz 2010a: 51). Thus, within this aspect, reality manifests itself as the subject and object of its activity.

In ṚV 10.90.6cd, the seasons are conceived in terms of the various kinds of elements that kindle and sustain fire: spring is conceived in terms of the melted butter, summer in terms of firewood and autumn in terms of oblation which is the flesh of the animal. The target domain is time in its most basic form that is the year divided into seasons. It begins when the subjective manifestations of reality begin to act. Conceptualisation of the seasons in terms of the elements kindling fire foreshadows the Brāhmaṇic conceptualisation of time in terms of cooking.

ṚV 10.90.7

táṃ yajñám barhíṣi praúkṣan púruṣaṃ jātám agratáḥ |
téna devā́ ayajanta sādhiyā́ ṛ́ṣayaś ca yé ||

On the ritual grass they consecrated that sacrifice, the Man, born at the beginning. With him the gods sacrificed,[48] the Sādhyas and those who were seers.

The verb *praukṣ-* (verse *a*) can be understood in three ways. If we take into account the later descriptions of the animal sacrifice, we can understand this verb as activating the moment when the victim is sprinkled with water before killing (ŚB 3.7.7.4) and after its killing (ŚB 3.8.2.7 ff.[49]). In the light of this interpretation, reality manifests itself as the oblation. Secondly, in the ṚV, the verb *praukṣ-* is used to denote the pouring of fire with clarified butter on the ritual grass (*barhís*)[50]. In the light of this interpretation, reality manifests itself as fire. And thirdly, the verb *praukṣ-* can refer to the worship of the guest who is given water when he comes to someone's home. Since in the ṚV gods coming for the sacrifice were conceived in terms of guests, the recipient can understand that reality is also a god who comes for the sacrifice to eat the oblation. In this way, the reflexive character of the temporal transformations of the manifest aspect is expressed. On the one hand, reality manifest in oblation is its object. On the other hand, it is its subject which

48 Jamison, Brereton (2014): '(also)'.

49 Thite (1975).

50 ṚV 3.9.9: *trī́ṇi śatā́ trī́ sahásrāṇi agníṃ triṃśác ca devā́ náva cāsaparyan | aúkṣan ghṛtaír ástṛṇan barhír asmā ā́d íd dhótāraṃ ní asādayanta ||*

manifests in two ways: as the gods and men performing sacrifice and as the gods who eat the oblation.

ṚV 10.90.8

tásmād yajñā́t sarvahútaḥ sámbhr̥tam pr̥ṣadājiyám |
paśū́n tā́ṃś cakre vāyavyā̀n āraṇyā́n grāmiyā́ś ca yé ||

From that sacrifice, when it was offered in full, the clotted mixture was collected. It[51] was made into the animals: those of the air[52] those that belong to the wilderness and those that belong to the village.

In the animal sacrifice attested in texts later than those of the ṚV, the first part of animal which is offered is the omentum cooked on the Āhavanīya fire. Its drops fall into the fire (Minkowski 1992: 51–53). Then the Maitrāvaruṇa priest recites ṚV 1.75.1 and 3.21.1-5 which is devoted to the drops (*stóka*). The 'clotted mixture' (*pr̥ṣadājyá*), mentioned in the ŚB in reference to clarified butter used in animal sacrifice (2.5, 2.6, 2.8, 3.6, and 3.8) and the formulation of ṚV 10.90.8, implies that the clotted mixture is the fat which drips from the baking meat.

The sacrifice, in terms of which creation is conceived, is a special activity during which nothing is wasted. The fat which flows from the baking meat becomes the material from which animals are created. This source domain can be seen as the specific instantiation of the general domain of Cleansing By Heat (see Jurewicz 2010a) which is here used to conceive creation[53]. The use of this domain in conceptualisation of the ontological transformations foreshadows its use in the later Veda. The fact that omentum was burn on the Āhavanīya fire strengthens the concept of its immediate transformation under the influence of the offetorial fire which brings about life-giving transformation (see chapter 3.2.3). It is worth mentioning that *pr̥ṣadājyá* is identified with breath (*prāṇá*) and food (*ánna*) in later thought (ŚB 3.8.4.8). If this identification was already accepted when the *Puruṣasūkta* was created, this would reinforce the description of the creation of animals from clotted butter.

The animals correspond to three spheres of the world that are metonymically evoked (INHABITANTS FOR PLACE, Radden, Kövecses 1999: 41). The animals called *vāyavyà* live in the air, those called *grāmyá* are animals that live close to men, i.e. on earth, those called āranyà are those that live in regions completely strange to men probably not only those in woods but also far up in the sky.

---

51 Jamison, Brereton (2014): '[= the sacrifice]'.

52 Jamison, Brereton (2014): '(and both)'.

53 In the same way creation is conceived in ŚB 10.5.3 (see chapter 2.5.2) and AU (see chapters 4.1.3).

Thus understood, the stanza presents the creation of space. At the same time, the three kinds of animal evoke three kinds of relationship between men and other living beings: the relationship that one feels towards someone close to him (*grāmyá*), the relationship that one feels towards a stranger (*āranyà*) and those to whom one feels indifferent (*vāyavyà*). Moreover, the distinction between animals which can be sacrificed (*grāmyá*) and those which cannot (*āranyà*) is settled.

It is also possible that the intention of the poet was to evoke the expression *pŕ̥ṣadaśva*, 'a dappled horse', which is phonetically similar to *pṛṣadājyá*. Since in the ṚV the sun is conceived in terms of a dappled horse (Jurewicz 2010a), the recipient could understand that the sunrise is described here conceived in terms of collecting the fat. In this way, the general domain of Cleansing By Heat is again used in conceptualisation of ontological transformation. In the light of this interpretation, the temporal manifestation is further developed in that the measure of the day appears.

The following stanzas describe the creation of the elements of the sacrifice. ṚV 10.90.9 presents the division of reality's speech into metrical units (Ṛk-stanzas and Sāman-chants) and Yajus-formulas which, being composed as prose, are created after the creation of metres (*chándas*)[54]. Then (ṚV 10.90.10) the creation of five kinds of animals is described[55]. Four of them, horses, cattle, goats and sheep, are the animals the heads of which are buried under the altar in the Agnicayana ritual. So one can presume that the specific group of the sacrificial animals is created within the general category of the *grāmyá* animals. The fifth kind of animal is called *ubhayā́dant*. It could be argued that this compound means not only the creatures which have teeth in both jaws, but also creatures that have both kinds of teeth, i.e. milk and permanent teeth. Thus the fifth victim of the Agnicayana would be created, i.e. man. Since the creation of the *várṇa* system takes place later, we could presume that in ṚV 10.90.10, the composer describes the creation of men who do not belong to this system. If the human sacrifice was really performed in times of the Veda, probably the humans chosen were among communities that were outside the Āryan one[56].

Creation of man is presented in ṚV 10.90.11-12. Man will be the one who will continue the creative activity of reality and perform the sacrifice. The four social states (*várṇa*) are presented as being created from man's

---

54 ṚV 10.90.9 *tásmād yajñā́t sarvahúta ŕ̥caḥ sā́māni jajñire | chándāṃsi jajñire tásmād yájus tásmād ajāyata ||*

55 ṚV 10.90.10 *tásmād áśvā ajāyanta yé ké ca ubhayā́dataḥ | gā́vo ha jajñire tásmāt tásmāj jātā́ ajāváyaḥ ||*

56 For the problem of human sacrifice in the early India, see Parpola (1992, 2007), Bakker (2007).

body. This manifestation also has the form of man and the social states come from its parts: the Brāhmaṇa from the mouth, the Kṣatriya from the arms, the Vaiśya from the thighs and the Śūdras from the feet[57]. However, as Mus (1968) has shown, there is a difference as far as the way each *várṇa* is created. The Brāhmaṇa is the mouth of reality (*brāhmaṇò 'sya múkham āsīd*) which implies a relation of identity between this *várṇa* and reality. Mus also argues that verses *b–c* (*bāhū́ rājaníyaḥ kṛtáḥ ūrū́ tád asya yád vaíśyaḥ*) should be translated more literally:

> 'Into his arms was made the Rājanya.
> (And as for) his thighs, that was what the Vaiśya became.'[58]

This implies a transformation of the parts of the man's body, but identity is still implied. Creation of the Śūdra is conceived in terms of birth (*padbhyā́ṃ śūdró ajāyata*). Although in Vedic thought the son is conceived as identical with his father, in this case a transformation occurs. On the basis of this difference, it can be inferred that two opposed parts of reality manifest in the cosmos are realised in society: those who are the direct part of the manifestation of reality (three upper *várṇas*) and those whose link with reality is indirect (the Śūdras). The three upper *várṇas* are those who can participate in the sacrifice, the Śūdras cannot. Since creative activity is conceived in terms of the sacrifice, we can interpret the three upper *várṇas* as the manifestation of the subjective power of this activity: the Brahmins are embodiments of the cognising abilities of reality, the Kṣatriyas are the embodiment of its destructive power while the Vaiśyas are embodiment of his creative power. The Śūdras are manifestation of the objective power of reality[59].

It is worth mentioning that the general domain of Procreation can be evoked by the sequence of creation of the four *várṇas* which is the same

---

[57] ṚV 10.90.11: *yát púruṣaṃ ví ádadhuḥ katidhā́ ví akalpayan | múkhaṃ kím asya kaú bāhū́ kā́ ūrū́ pā́dā ucyete* || ṚV 10.90.12: *brāhmaṇò 'sya múkham āsīd bāhū́ rājaníyaḥ kṛtáḥ | ūrū́ tád asya yád vaíśyaḥ padbhyā́ṃ śūdró ajāyata* ||

[58] Jamison, Brereton (2014): 'The ruler was made his two arms. As to his thighs – that is what the freeman was.'

[59] It is also worth noting that the social functions are determined by the function of the parts of the body. The activity of the Brāhmaṇas is the activity of mouth conceived in the ṚV in terms of fire. So the Brāhmana recites Veda and cooks the oblation. The activity of the Kṣatriya is the activity of the arms: he embraces his kingdom with his arms and thus he protects it as arms protect the body (Gonda 1969). The activity of the Vaiśya is the activity of the thighs or loins: he cultivates the plants and cattle and thus prepares the oblations for the sacrifice. Mus (1968: 181) interprets this stanza as reflecting the social situation: 'c'est la démarcation entre les éléments āryennes de plein droit, qui manifestent et consacrant ce droit par leur accès au sacrifice, et la "classe serivile indigène", exclue de cette communication qui mène rituellement à l'immortalité.'

as the sequence of appearance of baby during delivery: the head comes first followed by the rest of the body. So the recipient can understand the manifestation of reality as society in terms of delivery. Within the frames of this conceptualisation, the creation of three upper *várṇas* is the result of the creative impulse conceived in terms of an incestuous act (see above, analysis of ṚV 10.90.5ab), the creation of the Śūdras, who are presented as being born from feet, is the result of the next creative impulse.

In the next two stanzas, the composer presents the final spatial arrangement of the manifest aspect (ṚV 10.90.13-14). The parts of the cosmos are created from the parts of the manifest aspect of reality conceived in terms of man: the moon is created from the mind, the sun from the eye, Indra and Agni from the mouth, the wind from breath, the space between the earth and the sky from the navel, the sky from the head, the earth from the feet and directions from the ear[60]. The sequence of their creation is not random. It is again arranged according to the stages of development of a child and the recipient is again expected to evoke the general domain of Procreation and to follow the logic implied by it. In stanza 13, mind is created first followed by the eye, the mouth and then breath. This sequence reflects the order of cognition. Reality in its cosmic manifestation first thinks with its mind (the concept of thinking is evoked metonymically by the concept of the mind). If the recipient activates the metaphor COGNITION IS SEEING, he will understand that reality continues its cognitive activity. The next stage is when reality begins to verbalise its cognition and to breath which is not only the inseparable element of speaking, but also evokes the concept of living. Then the space between the earth and sky is created from the navel (ṚV 10.90.14a).

This elliptic description evokes the general domain of Procreation with its specific realisation of pregnancy and birth giving during which a baby is linked with its mother by the umbilical cord. This is one of the input spaces in the philosophical model of The Wave Of Honey created in ṚV 4.58.1 (Jurewicz 2010a: 227 ff.). The composer of this hymn creates a conceptual network which evokes the following input spaces. The first is the concept of a child linked with its mother by the umbilical cord. The next input spaces are the concepts of growth of a plant, the rise of the wave and the sunrise. In the blend, the mother corresponds to the soil from which the plant grows, to the ocean and to the nocturnal sky, the baby corresponds to the top of the plant, to the wave and to the rising sun and the umbilical cord corresponds to the stalk of the plant in terms of which the cosmic pillar is conceived.

---

60 ṚV 10.90.13: *candrámā mánaso jātáś cákṣoḥ sū́ryo ajāyata | múkhād índraś ca agníś ca prāṇā́d vāyúr ajāyata* || ṚV 10.90.14ab: *nā́bhyā āsīd antárikṣaṃ śīrṣṇó dyaúḥ sám avartata.*

The generic space is the appearance of the symbol of light from the symbol of darkness.

If the recipient of ṚV 10.90.12 activates the metonymy NAVEL FOR THE UMBILICAL CORD[61] and evokes the blend created in the model of The Wave Of Honey, he will understand why the space is created from the navel. The concept of the navel metonymically evokes the concept of the umbilical cord and, in the blend, it becomes the *axis mundi*. Creation of the sky and the earth from the head and the feet (verses *b–c*) follows the logic created by the blend: the child, being born, stands up. It can be seen then that the final spatial arrangement of the world is conceptualised in terms of the cognitive and physical development of man. Such a conceptualisation of creation will be elaborated in later thought (ŚB 11.1.6, see chapter 3.5.2).

It is also worth noting that the gods are mentioned earlier as those who perform the sacrifice together with the seers; in the same role they are mentioned in the next stanza (10.90.15, see below). We can presume that their sacrifice was fulfilled and thanks to that they were transformed into divine forms of the cosmos. This concept will evolve later, in the AU, where the divine parts of the cosmos are called its guardians (see chapter 4.1.3). In this way, the division of the world into subjective and objective parts is continued: the gods as the recipients of the sacrifice are the subjects, while as the elements of the world are the objects.

Thus the cosmogonic activity of reality is rewritten into spatiotemporal frames and can be repeated in everyday ritual activity. There are the multiple agents of the sacrifice who are the members of the four *várṇas*, there is speech recited during it, there are the sacrificial animals and there are the gods.

The last two stanzas (ṚV 10.90.15-16) are the conclusion of the hymn. However, some expressions are difficult to interpret[62]. In ṚV 10.90.15ab, the composer mentions seven surrounding sticks (*saptā́syāsan paridháyas*) and thrice seven pieces of kindling wood (*tríḥ saptá samídhaḥ*). Their full interpretation would need a separate analysis. The expression *saptā́syāsa* phonetically evokes the *saptā́sya* that is used to qualify, among others, Bṛhaspati and priests[63]. Thus we can presume that, notwithstanding other meanings, the intention of the poet is to evoke the concept of seven seers and, more specifically, the Aṅgirases. This is supported in that *tríh saptá*,

61 A more general interpretation of this metonymy depends on the way the relationship between the navel and the umbilical cord is conceived. It can be conceived in terms of a part and the whole (metonymy PART OF A THING FOR THE WHOLE THING). However, the Vedic texts do not provide sufficient sources for the reconstruction of this conceptualisation.

62 ṚV 10.90.15: *saptā́syāsan paridháyas tríḥ saptá samídhaḥ kṛtā́ḥ | devā́ yád yajñáṃ tanvānā́ ábadhnan púruṣam paśúm ||*

63 ṚV 4.54.4c, ṚV 4.51.4, ṚV 9.11.1g. In ṚV 10.40.8.d *vrajá* is qualified in this way.

which here refers to the kindling sticks (verse *b*), in ṚV 4.1.16 is used to denote the names of a cow found by the Aṅgirases (Jurewicz 2010a: 259 ff.). As Thieme has shown (1985), this expression metonymically evokes the concept of sacred speech. The fact that here the number refers to the kindling sticks agrees with the conceptualisation of speech in terms of fire. Thus understood, ṚV 10.90.15ab describe the activity of the seers who name the created world.

According to ṚV 10.90.15cd, reality is the sacrificial animal which is tied up during sacrifice (*devā́ yád yajñáṃ tanvānā́ ábadhnan púruṣam paśúm*). In this way, the reflexive character of its activity is expressed (which will be continued in the next stanza). At the same time, the recipient may understand that during creation reality limits itself which is conceived in terms of tethering a victim.

ṚV 10.90.16a explicitly expresses the self-reflexive character of the cosmogony: the activity, the instrument and the object is the same called with the general name *yajñá*, the agents are the gods who are manifestation of the subjective power of reality (*yajñéna yajñám ayajanta devā́s*)[64]. According to verse *b*, during the first cosmogonic sacrifice, the rules are settled that will constrain those who will perform it in the future especially the men who are the members of the social body of reality (*tā́ni dhármāṇi prathamā́ni āsan*).

Verse *c* mentions greatnesses (*mahimā́naḥ*) that reach the sky where there are those who performed the primeval cosmogonic sacrifice (*yátra pū́rve sādhiyā́ḥ sánti devā́ḥ*). As I argue (see analysis of ṚV 10.90.3), the concept of greatness is used in the Veda to conceive the early stages of creation when it becomes possible to measure reality. The context implied by the composer is ritual thanks to which the sacrificer can reach the sun and drink Soma from its source. The concept of greatness is used in the description of Indra who drinks Soma before his fight with Vṛtra and becomes great (Jurewicz 2010a: 341–343). The same state of greatness is realised by the sacrificer. In this stanza, the word *mahimán* can be seen as the proof for abstraction: the sacrificer reaches the sun only mentally *via* its most powerful part.

*

The main input spaces of the conceptual network created in the *Puruṣasūkta* are the concepts of man, of cosmos and of reality. Conceptualisation of the activity of reality is elaborated according to the logic of human activity. In the first stanza, the concept of a moving mouth is elaborated which evokes

64 This stanza also appears in ṚV 1.164.50, see section 1.6.

the concepts of eating and speaking. The second stanza introduces the concept of a child who grows thanks to food. In the blend, the first creative act of reality and its manifestation as mortal and immortal is conceived. The next two stanzas introduce the concept of a cow as the next input space and the manifestation of reality is conceived in terms of its legs which move. In both input experiential input spaces (namely, the input spaces of man and of cow), features are transformed in a way that violates experience: man has a thousand heads, eyes and feet, a cow stands on one leg, a mouth moves and does not move at the same time. This transformation comes from the input space of reality which is omnipotent and omniscient. It is worth mentioning that the concepts implied by the concept of moving jaw, i.e. eating and speaking, can be seen as the grounding concepts in conceptualisation of the early stages of creation. The concept of eating is elaborated in the first two stanzas while the concept of speaking is activated *via* the metaphoric conceptualisation of speech in terms of a cow in the next two stanzas. In the fifth stanza, the general domain of Procreation is activated. The final division of reality into unmanifest and manifest aspects is conceived in these terms. This stanza emphasises the identity of both aspects.

In the remaining stanzas of the hymn, the composer elaborate the input space of man who performs animal sacrifice. Since in ṚV 1.164.35b, the sacrifice is conceived as the navel of the world (*ayáṃ yajñó bhúvanasya nā́bhiḥ*, see section 1.6), we can see the coherence between this concept and the general domain of Procreation elaborated earlier by the composer of the *Puruṣasūkta*. In the blend, reality is agent, object and recipient of this sacrifice. The sequence of the stages of arrangement of the manifest aspect conforms to the stages of ritual: first, time is created, then space with animals generally conceived, then speech composed in the three Vedas and then the five main animals used in ritual. The recipient may presume that all of them are created from the clotted butter which drained from the heated body of man. The next two manifestations, human society and cosmos, are the result of transformation of man's body, although they appear from its different parts and in various ways. In the blend, various levels of reality's manifestation are conceived in these terms, but everything within the world is also a part of unmanifest reality.

The composer of the *Puruṣasūkta*, thanks to use the concept of man as the main source domain for conceptualisation of reality, can present creation as its successive manifestations in the cosmic and social forms which are identical with it in it. In its most schematic form, the structure of reality can be seen as concentric human form conceived in terms of the image schema of CONTAINER. This concept is the generic space of the blend.

In the beginning of creation, the manifest aspect is called the earth and it is surrounded by the unmanifest aspect (ṚV 10.90.1cd, 3c, 5cd). Stanza 5 evokes the general domain of Procreation in its specific realisation of pregnancy and birth giving. This input space enlarges the generic space with the meaning of process. Thus the schema of concentric human forms, one of which (child) is present inside another (mother) is enriched with the concept of an agent which goes out from the container. Man is born from *virā́j* to become the cosmos and society and one can conceive of society as a human form within another human form which is the cosmos. This way of thinking about the structure of reality, established in the *Puruṣasūkta*, will be elaborated in later Vedic thought[65].

1.4. The Maker of Everything (*víśvákarman*)

The next example of the tendency to present reality and its activity in more abstract terms is the concept of *víśvákarman*, 'the Maker of Everything', which is elaborated in two hymns of the tenth mandala (ṚV 10.81-82). This concept is more abstract than the concept of man because it does not refer to any concrete human form and only highlights the creative, efficient power of reality. However, ṚV 10.81.3 betrays that it is motivated by the concept of man and that this source domain is similarly transformed as in ṚV 10.90.1. Reality called *víśvákarman* is conceived as having eyes, faces, arms and feet in all directions (10.81.3ab[66]). Its omniscience, omnipresence and omnipotence is expressed in this way. Another similarity with the *Puruṣasūkta* is that creation is conceived in terms of the self-sacrifice of reality within its manifest aspect (ṚV 10.81.5d, 10.81.6ab)[67].

On the other hand, there is clear evidence that the concept of *víśvákarman* is motivated by the concept of Agni. It can be seen in the metaphors used to conceptualise *víśvákarman*, in epithets that are given to him and the features that are ascribed to him. In two cases, the recipient is expected to activate the general domain of Cleansing By Heat. In ṚV 10.81.3c, Viśvakarman is conceived in terms of a smith who forges together the earth and the sky (ṚV 10.81.3cd)[68]. The concept of a smith metonymically evokes the concept

---

65 Especially in the AU (see chapter 4.1.3).

66 *viśvátaścakṣur utá viśvátomukho viśvátobāhur utá viśvátaspāt.*

67 ṚV 10.81.6ab: *víśvakarman havíṣā vāvṛdhānáḥ svayáṃ yajasva pṛthivī́m utá dyā́m* | ṚV 10.81.5cd: *śíkṣā sákhibhyo havíṣi svadhāvaḥ svayáṃ yajasva tanúvaṃ vṛdhānáḥ* ||

68 ṚV 10.81.3cd: *sám bāhúbhyāṃ dhámati sám pátatrair dyā́vābhū́mī janáyan devá ékaḥ* ||

of fire (metonymy AGENT FOR THE OBJECT OF ACTION[69]). Creation, conceived in terms of forging, allows the recipient to understand it in terms of sharpening which is the source domain for cognition and speaking in the ṚV (Jurewicz 2010a: 266–267). At the same time, within the frames of this conceptualisation, the creation of the earth and the sky is making them shining and warm just as an object that is sharpened becomes shining and warm. Thus we are close to the imagery of the *Nāsadīyasūkta* where the crucial creative moment is conceived in terms of appearance of light in darkness (*tápasas tán mahinā́jāyataíkam*, Jurewicz 2010a: 49–50)

The general domain of Cleansing By Heat is also activated in ṚV 10.82.1c where the earth and the sky are conceived in terms of clarified butter, so the recipient may create the conceptualisation of their creation in terms of preparation of clarified butter[70]. This source domain evokes the concept of fire on the basis of metonymy EFFECT FOR CAUSE: fire is the cause of clarified butter which, in order to be prepared, must be heated.

The motivating influence of the concept of Agni on the concept of *viśvákarman* can also be seen in the epithets of The Maker of Everything: he is called *ṛ́ṣir*, *hótā* and *pitā́* which are also the epithets of Agni in the ṚV[71]. Viśvakarman is also presented as having highest and lowest abodes (ṚV 10.82.3)[72] and as a knower of the worlds who is asked by the living beings[73]. Agni is presented in the same way in the ṚV as the one has various abodes and as the wise to whom creatures ask questions[74].

So the concept of the Maker of Everything is a blend which consists of the following input spaces. The first is the concept of man, the second is the concept of Agni and the third is the concept of reality. In the blend, the concept of agency comes from the input space of man. The overall concept of *viśvákarman* also comes from this input space, but it is transformed in an impossible way under the influence of the concepts of omniscience and omnipotence coming from the input space of reality. Creative power also comes from this input space. Its ability to heat comes from the input space of

---

69 Radden, Kövecses (1999) do not recognise this metonymy.

70 ṚV 10.82.1: *cákṣuṣaḥ pitā́ mánasā hí dhī́ro ghṛtám ene ajanan nánnamāne | yadéd ántā ádadṛhanta pū́rva ā́d íd dyā́vāpṛthivī́ aprathetām ||* This source domain foreshadows later usages of the metaphor which highlight the solid results of milk transformation that is cream (AU 1.1.2, see chapter 4.1.3, BU 1.2.2, see chapter 4.1.1).

71 ṚV 10.81.1ab: *yá imā́ víśvā bhúvanāni júhvad ṛ́ṣir hótā ní ásīdat pitā́ naḥ*. ṚV 10.81.1cd: *sá āśíṣā dráviṇam ichámānaḥ prathamachád ávarām̐ ā́ viveśa*. See also ṚV 10.82.3: *yó naḥ pitā́ janitā́ yó vidhātā́*

72 ṚV 10.81.5: *yā́ te dhā́māni paramā́ṇi yā́vamā́ yā́ madhyamā́ viśvakarmann utémā́ | śíkṣā sákhibhyo havíṣi svadhāvaḥ svayáṃ yajasva tanúvaṃ vṛdhānáḥ ||*

73 ṚV 10.82.3cd: *yó devā́nāṃ nāmadhā́ éka evá táṃ sampraśnám bhúvanā yanti anyā́.*

74 ṚV 1.105.4, 1.145.2, 10.79.6.

Agni, but in the blend it is conceived in terms of a smith which is a specific instance of human activity. Its other features are also motivated by the input space of Agni. The generic space of this conceptual network is the image schema of SELF-MOTION.

1.5. The search for abstraction (ṚV 10.72).

ṚV 10.72 is important evidence for the attempt to conceive creation in abstract and general terms. The first stanza explicitly says that the topic of the hymn will be creation (10.72.1ab: *devā́nāṃ nú vayáṃ jā́nā prá vocāma vipanyáyā*)[75]. The next stanzas present reality in its first creative manifestation and explain the nature of creation:

ṚV 10.72.2-3ab

bráhmaṇas pátir etā́ sáṃ karmā́ra ivādhamat |
devā́nām pūrviyé yugé ásataḥ sád ajāyata || (2)
devā́nāṃ yugé prathamé ásataḥ sád ajāyata | (3ab)

The Lord of the Sacred Formulation[76] smelted these[77] like a smith.
In the ancient generation of the gods, what exists was born from what does not exist.
In the first generation of the gods, what exists was born from what does not exist.

Reality in its creative manifestation is called *bráhmaṇas páti* 'the Lord of the Sacred Formulation'. There are similarities between this conceptualisation of reality and its conceptualisation in terms of Viśvakarman (see section 1.4). Firstly, Viśvakarman is called *vācáspáti*, 'the lord of the speech' in ṚV 10.81.7a[78]. So the authors of both hymns want to highlight the cognitive ability of reality which can be expressed in speech; the first stage of creation is conceived as the manifestation of this ability. Such a conceptualisation of reality brings us back to the concept of Agni. As I have shown elsewhere (Jurewicz 2010a: 380 ff.), the concept of Bṛhaspati/Brahmaṇaspati is a metaphysical elaboration of the concept of Agni who manifests himself as Indra and thus realises the internally contradictory nature of his killing and creating aspects. Within the frames of this conceptualisation, the main instrument of Agni is speech

75 ṚV 10.72.1: *devā́nāṃ nú vayáṃ jā́nā prá vocāma vipanyáyā* | *ukthéṣu śasyámāneṣu yáḥ páśyād úttare yugé* ||
76 Jamison, Brereton 2014: '[= Bṛhaspati]'.
77 Jamison, Brereton 2014: '(births)'.
78 ṚV 10.81.7ab: *vācás pátiṃ viśvákarmāṇam ūtáye manojúvaṃ vā́je adyā́ huvema.*

conceived in terms of Indra's thunderbolt (*vájra*)[79]. The appellation of reality as *bráhmaṇas páti* in ṚV 10.72.2a is further proof of the motivating influence of the concept of Agni on the metaphysical thinking of the Ṛgvedic poets. At the same time, it allows the poet to conceive creation as the appearance of speech.

The next similarity between the two concepts of reality presented in ṚV 10.72 and 10.81-82 is that reality in both is conceived in terms of a smith (ṚV 10. 81.3c). Thus the authors of both hymns activate the general domain of Cleansing By Heat in its specific realisations of sharpening a metal object (see Jurewicz 2010a: 266–267). In these terms, cognition is conceived in the ṚV and the composers of both hymns in this way imply the cognitive nature of transformations of reality. At the same time, if the recipient elaborates the source domain which is activity of fire, he will understand that the intention of the composer is to imply the fiery nature of reality.

In ṚV 10.72.3b, the composer presents creation in abstract terms as the appearance of existence (*sát*) from the non-existent (*ásat*)[80]. In the same way, the *Nāsadīyasūkta* conceives creation of the seers who take the existent (*sát*) from the non-existent (*ásat*). The recipient can assume that *ásat* refers to the unmanifest aspect of reality and *sát* to its manifest aspect. The verb *jan-* 'to generate, to beget, to give birth to', used to express the appearance of *sát*, loses its concrete meaning in this context. However, in the next hemistiches, the composer elaborates the concept of the general domain of Procreation in order to present the next stage of creation:

ṚV 10.72.2cd-10.72.3ab

tád ā́śā ánv ajāyanta tád uttānápadas pári || 2cd
bhū́r jajña uttānápado bhuvá ā́śā ajāyanta | 3ad

The regions of space were born following that[81] – that[82] was born from the one whose feet were open up.
The earth was born from the one whose feet were open up; from the earth the regions of space were born.

The appearance of the regions of space (*ā́śā*) is conceived in terms of delivery. This concept is activated *via* the expression *uttānápad*, literally 'with legs directed upwards'[83]. The concept of delivery is also elaborated

[79] For the connection between speech and thunderbolt (*vájra*) see JUB 3.19.1, see chapter 5.2.3.
[80] *ásataḥ sád ajāyata.*
[81] Jamison, Brereton (2014): '(which exists)'.
[82] Jamison, Brereton (2014): '(which exists)'.
[83] Falk, Jamison, Brereton (2014: 1499).

in the cosmogony of the *Nāsadīyasūkta* where the poets are conceived in terms of midwives who take the existent (*sát*) as if from the mother's womb (see Jurewicz 2010a: 53). In ṚV 10.72.2cd, the agent who acts as a midwife is not mentioned, so the recipient may presume that it is reality in its reflexive activity, who is both the agent and the object. In this case, the object is the space conceived in terms of the space between the two legs of a woman giving birth. According to ṚV 10.72.3ab, the earth is created in the same way and from the earth space is created again.

The sequence of creation can be reconstructed as alternative manifestations of a lack of being and of being: from what does not exist (*ásat*) the existent (*sát*) appears, then regions (*ā́śā*) appear. The concept of *ā́śa* implies the concept of an emptiness, similarly to the concept of *ásat*, then the earth seen as the manifestation of what exists and then regions (*ā́śā*) again. A comparison with the *Nāsadīyasūkta* will shed more light on the concept of creation presented in the hymn. As already stated, the concept of Brahmaṇaspati, who smelts the earth and the sky, refers to the first stage of creation when reality manifests its cognitive power. Then the composer introduces the concept of what does not exist (*ásat*, ṚV 10.72.2c). In this way, he activates the concept of the creative state which anticipates the later theories that are elaborated in the ŚB (see chapter 3), according to which reality creates a place for the future world which then is filled with the world which is identical with reality. From *ásat*, *sat*, i.e. what exists, appears. Then within the world the pattern of creation is repeated: firstly space appears (*ā́śa*), it is filled with earth and again space (*ā́śa*) appears.

The tendency to create abstract concepts is clear. The description is very concise and the general domain of Procreation is not elaborated in much detail. It endows the content presented by the poet with a general scenario which can be seen in terms of a cause-effect relationship. The nature of this relationship is concisely described in the next two hemistiches:

ṚV 10.72.4cd-10.72.5ab

áditer dákṣo 'jāyata° dákṣād u áditiḥ pári || (4cd)
áditir hí ájaniṣṭa dákṣa yā́ duhitā́ táva | (5ab)

From Aditi, Dakṣa was born, and from Dakṣa, Aditi.
Because Aditi was born – she who is thy daughter, o Dakṣa.

In my view, in these verses the composer replaces the schema: space (*ā́śa*) – earth (*bhū́*) – space (*ā́śa*) with the schema: Aditi – Dakṣa – Aditi. Similarly to the schema Puruṣa – Virāj – Puruṣa (see above, section 1.3), this schema is meant to express the monistic nature of creation which is the transformation of one reality. It also expresses the internal contradictory character of creation which is the alternate manifestation of opposing aspects conceived here as opposition of female and male. This contradictory character of reality allows it to reproduce conceived in terms of the sexual act occurring between its male and female aspects.

However, when the recipient takes into account the meaning of words used in the schemas, he will see the difference with the schema proposed in the *Puruṣasūkta*. The word *áditi* means 'infinity' and *dákṣa* the power of thought that facilitates the realisation of intention (*krátu*, Reat 1990). So the schema highlights the internal contradictory character of creation in that creation is the process during which infinity (*áditi*) manifests itself in what is finite[84]. Moreover, the next stage is manifestation of infinity within the manifest, i.e. finite, aspect. The schema also highlights the cognitive dimension of creation: the intermediate stage between two forms of infinity is conceived in terms of mental activity. Taking into account that reality is also conceived in terms of speech (ṚV 10.125, see section 1.2), Aditi can also be interpreted as speech which gives rise to thinking which again produces speech (see ṚV 1.164.8, section 1.6)

If the recipient applies the schema Aditi – Dakṣa – Aditi to the earlier stages of creation presented in ṚV 10.72, he will understand that appearance of what is existent (*sát*) is the stage of Dakṣa, when reality manifests its cognitive power. The appearance of the space (*ā́śa*) is the stage of manifestation of what is infinite (Aditi). Creation of the earth is the stage of Dakṣa, then again infinity manifests itself in space. Thus the schema Aditi – Dakṣa – Aditi is an abstract general way to express the internally contradictory nature of creation conceived as the manifestation of opposing aspects of reality: the infinite and the finite.

The schema Aditi – Dakṣa – Aditi also allows for interpretation of creation as manifestation of Agni because Agni in the ṚV is called by both terms[85]. Moreover, it is possible to reconstruct the concept of producing fire in the description of creation of the space and the earth 'from the one whose feet were opened up' (*uttānápadas pári*). Production of fire is presented in the same way: fire is born in the 'raised up' (*uttānā́yām*) which can refer to the kindling sticks. In the Veda, fire is a counterpart of the earth (Smith 1994). Thus the recipient can interpret creation of the earth as the creation of fire as well.

---

[84] Such conceptualisation of creation is also expressed in the formula *tátaḥ kṣarati akṣáraṃ* which, as I have shown elsewhere (Jurewicz 2012a), is another example of the attempts of the Ṛgvedic poets to create abstract concepts.

[85] Agni is called *áditi* in ṚV 7.9.3 Agni, *dákṣa* refers to Agni in ṚV 10.5.7, Jurewicz (2010a: 297).

The next hemistich presents the appearance of gods who will continue creation within the manifest aspect:

ṚV 10.72.5cd

tā́ṃ devā́ ánv ajāyanta bhadrā́ amṛ́tabandhavaḥ ||

Following her, the gods were born, the auspicious kin of the immortal one.

Qualification of the gods as *amṛ́tabandhu* (verse *d*) activates two main associations. Firstly, *bándhu* means kinship with mother (ṚV 1.164.33, see section 1.6), so the recipient may understand that they are manifestation of what is immortal. Following the logic of the hymn, the recipient understands that immortal is Aditi born from Dakṣa, i.e. infinity is manifested within the finite aspect. Within the frames of the general cosmogonic schema Aditi – Dakṣa – Aditi, the recipient may understand that the gods can be seen as Dakṣa again.

Qualification of gods as the 'kin of the immortal one' (*amṛ́tabandhavas*) also allows the recipient to unfold the scenario of the sacrifice. In order to explain this, I refer to other hymns of the ṚV. The word *amṛ́ta* metonymically refers to Soma in the ṚV (EFFECT FOR CAUSE). The abstract noun *amrtatvá* is used in ṚV 4.58.1 to denote the top of the Somic plant which is identified with the sun in zenith where Soma is finally purified (Jurewicz 2010a: 227 ff.). The next conceptualisation of the sun in zenith filled with Soma is attested in ṚV 1.154.5 where it is conceived in terms of the third footprint of Viṣṇu (Jurewicz 2010a: 387 ff.). According to this stanza, in the third footprint, there is a spring of honey which is called the kin (*bándhu*) of Viṣṇu and from which the pious people drink Soma and get exulted. In the *Nāsadīyasūkta*, the word *bándhu* is used to denote the link between the two aspects of reality (Jurewicz 2010a: 50 ff.). Taking all this into account, I would argue that the expression *amṛ́tabandhu* used in reference to the gods in ṚV 10.72.5d is meant to metonymically activate the concept of the sacrifice with its initial phase of drinking Soma on earth and its final realisation in the state of immortality.

Now the creative activity of the gods is presented:

ṚV 10.72.6-7

yád devā adáḥ salilé súsaṃrabdhā átiṣṭhata |
átrā vo nṛ́tyatām iva tīvró reṇúr ápāyata (6)
yád devā yátayo yathā bhúvanāni ápinvata ||
átrā samudrá ā́ gūḷhám ā́ sū́ryam ajabhartana (7)

When, o gods, well clasped to one another, you stood there in the ocean,
then the bitter dust[86] dispersed from you, like[87] of those dancing. (6)
When o gods, just as the Yatis did, you swelled the living worlds,
then you brought here the sun, which was hidden in the sea. (7)

In stanza 6 the composer creates the image of dancers who dance holding hands. They dance so quickly that the dust rises from earth. The final creation of the world is conceived in these terms. The rotating movement of the dance allows the recipient's activation of other activities that need rotation: producing fire and the preparation of butter[88]. Since the adjective *tīvrá* most often qualifies the Somic juice in the ṚV[89], the recipient may also activate the concept of the preparation of Soma with mortar and pestle. Jamison, Brereton suggest that the dust can be identifiedwith the sweat of the dancers (2014: 1500). Activation of this concept triggers the recipient to activate the conceptualisation of cognition in terms of heating the external manifestation of which is sweating (see ṚV 1.164, section 1.6, Jurewicz 2010a: 267–269[90]). The concepts of all these activities are the input spaces of the conceptual network created by the poet. In the blend, the gods perform the first sacrifice, i.e. kindle fire, prepare Soma, cognise and dance; the main result of this activity is the appearance of light and movement which are the next input spaces of the blend. The next input space is the concept of reality which manifests itself. The generic space is the appearance of the symbol of light from the symbol of darkness.

In stanza 7, the gods are presented as swelling the worlds and bringing the sun which was hidden in the sea. The concept of swelling metonymically evokes the concept of a cow's udder before its milking; creation of rain was conceived in terms of milking in the ṚV (e.g. ṚV 9.85.9, Jurewicz 2010a). It is also possible that the recipient is expected to evoke the concept of concealing in the same way as it is evoked in the description of creation of rain by Mitra and Varuṇa who conceal the sun with clouds (Jurewicz 2010a: 400 ff.). The concept of raining can also be evoked *via* the concept of the Yatis to which the gods are compared. Jamison (1991: 111) argues that the ritual death of

86 Jamison, Brereton 2014: '[= spray]'.
87 Jamison, Brereton 2014: '(the dust [= sweat?])'
88 This is the earliest instance of usage of the image of preparation of butter to express creation, so often used in the later thought (see chapters 4.1.1, 4.1.3) and the earliest source of later concept of the *amṛtamanthana* myth described in the ŚB and, first of all, in the *Mahābhārata* (Lidova 1994).
89 E.g. ṚV 2.41.14, 4.35.6, 5.5.1, 5.37.4, 6.47.1, 9.17.8, 9.65.15.
90 The concept of sweating is elaborated in ŚB 6.1.1.13 (see chapter 3.2.2), ŚB 6.1.3.1-2 (see chapter 3.5.1, see also chapter 3.4).

the Yatis brings rain and that the Yatis themselves become that rain. If the recipient enriches the conceptual network created on the basis of the stanza 6, he will understand that the next stage of the gods' activity is rain. This agrees with the general model of reality transformation: firstly, the fiery aspect of reality manifests itself, then the fluid aspects[91].

The second hemistich of stanza 7 presents the appearance of the sun from the sea where it was hidden. The composer activates metaphorical thinking which is well entrenched in the ṚV. The nocturnal sky is conceived in the ṚV in terms of the sea and creation of the sun is conceived in terms of the general domain Finding The Hidden (Jurewicz 2010a). In my view, the composer presents here the first cosmogonical sunrise and implies the final arrangement of the manifest aspect of reality. It exists thanks to the circular movement of the sun the result of which is rain.

The general cosmogonic scheme Aditi – Dakṣa – Aditi implies that now the manifestation of Aditi should take place. As I have argued above, we can understand the manifestation of Aditi within the manifest aspect of reality in terms of the creation of the regions of space. The composers of the ṚV clearly imply that creation of sunrise and rain is the creation of space (see Jurewicz 2010a: 112 ff.), so the recipient can understand the activity of the gods as the repeated manifestation of infinity within the frames of the space of the cosmos. In other words, the gods, who are manifestation of Dakṣa aspect of reality, bring about the manifestation of the Aditi aspect.

In the last two stanzas, the composer presents the creation of men:

ṚV 10.72.8-9

aṣṭaú putrā́so áditer yé jātā́s tanúvas pári |
devā́m̐ úpa praít saptábhiḥ párā mārtāṇḍám āsiyat || (8)
saptábhiḥ putraír áditir úpa praít pūrviyám̐ yugám |
prajā́yai mṛtyáve tuvat púnar mārtāṇḍám ā́bharat || (9)

Eight are the sons of Aditi, which were born from her body.
With seven she went forth to the gods. She cast away the one stemming from a dead egg.
With seven sons Aditi went forth to the ancient generation.
For procreation but also for death, she brought here again the one stemming from a dead egg.

Taking into account the alternate character of the creative process expressed in the scheme Aditi – Dakṣa – Aditi, the creation of man should be seen as the next manifestation of Dakṣa's aspect. During this stage, reality within its

[91] As it will be shown this model will also be elaborated in cosmogonies of the ŚB and Upaniṣads.

manifest aspect multiplicates itself into eight forms thanks to its cognitive power. The reflexive nature of the process is expressed in that the sons are born from the body (*tanúvas pári*, ṚV 10.72.b) of Aditi which implies their identity with it. Since, as I have mentioned above, the word *dákṣa* refers to fire, we can interpret this form of reality as the Aṅgirases. The Aṅgirases perform the first sacrifice which involves their journey up to zenith where they drink Soma from the heavenly source and gained immortality. Using the words of the hymn, we could say that they become *amṛ́tabandhavas* as are the gods.

Seven Aṅgirases remain there, but one of them comes back as mortal man (ṚV 10.72.9ab). The term *mārtāṇḍá*, 'the dead egg' (ṚV 10.72.9c), evokes the scenario of the hatching of a nestling. The recipient can elaborate this scenario and imagine the sacrificial journey of the Aṅgirases to the sky in terms of a bird that flies to the top of a tree. Such a conceptualisation is also evoked in ṚV 1.164.40-42 (see section 1.6). Within the frames of this conceptualisation, the return of the mortal sacrificer to earth is conceived in terms of an egg that falls down from the nest. This conceptualisation will be elaborated in the description of rebirth in JUB 3.7-28 (see chapter 5.2).

*

ṚV 10.72 is a bold attempt towards abstraction. Its composer puts creation in a simple scheme of alternating aspects of reality opposed to each other. Their names convey philosophical meaning which allows the poet to express the metaphysical assumption according to which creation is an impossible manifestation of infinity thanks to the power of thought. Creation is also seen as alternating manifestation of lack of being and being which will later will be expressed with the metaphor of fullness (AVŚ 10.8.29, BU 5.1.1, see chapters 2.6.1, 4.2.2). At the same time, however, the description evokes rich images, deeply immersed in experience, which are used as source domains for the abstract content. These are the images of a smith who forges metal, of a woman giving birth, of dancers, of a nestling in the egg and its hatching. They are evoked in a very concise way and in order to reconstruct them, the recipient needs to refer to the whole ṚV. This means that the concepts used by the composer of the hymn are not abstract enough to produce meaning on their own. In other words, the blending, which fuses concrete experience and abstract meaning, has not occurred in this case. This is not the case of the *Nāsadīyasūkta* which is construed in such a way that the main idea can be understood without reference to the larger background (see Jurewicz 2010a). It is needed only if the recipient desires to enrich his knowledge.

The general conceptualisation of creation presented by the composer of the hymn did not influence much of later tradition, contrary to the *Nāsadīyasūkta* the model of which became the main cosmogonical frame for Indian philosophers. However, two concepts elaborated here will become important for later philosophy. The concept of a smith's activity in its realisation as the purification of gold becomes an important concept for thinking, especially in Buddhism (Covill 2009), while the concept of dance as a source domain for creation is used in later Hinduism.

1.6. The first philosophical treatise (ṚV 1.164)

In this section, I will analyse ṚV 1.164. This hymn is considered one of the most difficult hymns in the ṚV[92] and it is difficult to reconstruct its full meaning but I will try to look it in a slightly different way than is usually done. Recent research shows that it is strongly motivated by the ritual context (see Houben 2000a) which allows us to understand more of it. My perspective will be different in that I will look at the hymn as a description of a way to acquire supernatural cognition and only then describe its content which is often put in abstract terms. The author of the hymn elaborates the problem of the theoretical knowledge which has to be not only understood, but also experienced by the poet the protagonist of the hymn[93]. This problem is expressed implicitly in the structure of some hymns in the ṚV (e.g. 4.1, 4.58, 6.9, Jurewicz 2010a) which firstly present the state of affairs and then the way it is confirmed and experienced by those who are described in the hymn. The state of affairs is cognised by the first seers who repeat the creative activity of reality and thus create a pattern for their followers. The structure of the *Nāsadīyasūkta* is different in that its author describes the state of affairs in the majority of the stanzas and only in two last stanzas does he triggers the recipient to confirm the content presented earlier (Jurewicz 2010a).

ṚV 1.164 is unique in early Vedic thought in that it presents the process through which the poet confronts his own experience with the knowledge he possesses, fails, tries again and finally overcomes all difficulties (Brown 1968a: 206). This may be connected with changes in practice which lead to supernatural cognition. The main means which lead to this state are, in this hymn, sacred speech and ritual. The ultimate content of the poet's knowledge is that Agni is reality which manifests itself in the world and in men; as I will

92 See Brown (1968a), Houben (2000a).

93 In the analysis of this hymn, the term 'poet' refers to the protagonist of the hymn, the term 'composer' to its author.

show, the hymn can be interpreted as the dialogue between Agni and the poet who aims at its cognition[94].

I would like to emphasise that my interpretation should not be treated as opposing those who see ṚV 1.164 as referring to ritual. Just the opposite, I am fully convinced by the results done by Houben (2000a). My interpretation of this hymn as describing cognition should rather be treated as complementary. It allows me to see the main line of thinking which motivated its arrangement and its importance for the development of philosophical concepts.

Jamison, Brereton write in their commentary to the hymn that '[t]he linkage of fire and water or sun and rain is a constant throughout the hymn' (2014: 351). This linkage is the core of the Ṛgvedic general model of reality transformation according to which creation and the functioning of the world is a manifestation of the internally contradictory nature of reality conceived in terms of Agni transforming into Soma (see Jurewicz 2010a). The composer of ṚV 1.164 presents consecutive stages of the poet's cognition and the specific circular composition of the hymn, in which images recur in new contexts, allows the composer to show the deeper layers of cognition described in the hymn.

The main input spaces of the conceptual network created by the composers are: the concept of reality conceived in terms of fire, cosmos in its solar-rain cycle, and man who cognises and performs ritual. The next two input spaces, which give scenario and structure to the processes described in the blend, are the concept of riding on a chariot, the concept of a cow and its calf, the general domain of Procreation and the model of Child Of The Waters. The network is enriched with additional input spaces created online in the stanzas. These are the philosophical model of The Wave Of Honey, of Indra's Fight With Vṛtra, and the concepts of flow of waters, tree with birds, weaving and carving/chopping. The generic space of blends depends on the context in which they are created.

ṚV 1.164.1

asyá vāmásya palitásya hótus tásya bhrā́tā madhyamó asti áśnaḥ |
tṛtī́yo bhrā́tā ghṛtápṛṣṭho asya átrāpaśyaṃ viśpátiṃ saptáputram ||

This treasured one, the grey Hotar – his middle brother is the ravenous one; his third brother is the one with ghee-smeared back. In him I saw the clanlord with seven sons.

Jamison, Brereton (2014) and Houben (2000a) interpret three fires as referring to elements of the cosmos or to three sacrificial fire. Geldner (1951, I)

[94] Thus, contrary to Brown (1968a), I will treat the hymn as a unity.

interprets fires as three domestic fires. I would like to enrich their interpretation with one more dimension, that of a poet (the protagonist of the hymn) who kindles fire and looks how it grows. It is evoked by the imperfect form *apaśyam*, which also expresses 'actions that are not remote in time, or which directly concern the speaker or the present' (Houben 2000a: 519). Fire in its first form is called *hótr̥* and its kindling is conceived in terms of its sitting down (see Jurewicz 2010a: 269 ff.). It is also qualified as 'dear', *vāmá*; in the same way Agni in qualified in R̥V 10.122.1. This positive evaluation of fire is not surprising taking into account its role for human existence and its metaphysical role in the R̥V. As kindling begins, smoke appears and the fire cannot be clearly seen. The concept of smoke is metonymically evoked *via* the concept of grey, *palitá* (DEFINING PROPERTY FOR CATEGORY[95]). The word *palitá* is used four more times more in the R̥V either in reference to fire (R̥V 1.144.4, 10.4.5), or to its smoke (R̥V 3.55.9, 10.55.5, Jamison, Brereton 2014: 1465)[96].

The stages of kindled fire are conceived in terms of brothers which triggers the recipient to activate the general domain of Procreation and the concept of delivery. The second form is conceived in terms of a middle brother called 'the ravenous' (*áśna*). This word is used in R̥V 1.173.2 as a qualification of the wild beast to which Indra is compared. If the recipient activates the concept of Indra, he would understand that it is in these terms that Agni's manifestation in the world is conceived which agrees with other R̥gvedic testimony (Jurewicz 2010a: 360 ff.). In the last three contexts, *áśna* is used in reference to a demon killed either by Indra (R̥V 2.14.5, 2.20.5) or by Agni (R̥V 6.4.3). Such a conceptualisation of this stage of a fire is based on experience as there is a moment during its kindling when it suddenly bursts into flame. If we take into account that fire was kindled with the use of a fire-drill which required blowing on it from the close distance, it could happen that it burns its kindler. Moreover, as it will be shown, fire is presented in a voracious form in some cosmogonies of the ŚB, especially in ŚB 2.2.4 where it wants to eat Prajāpati (see chapter 3.1.1). If the recipient interprets the form *áśnaḥ* as a genitive of *áśman* (Houben 2000a: 618), then he would evoke the general domain of A Rocky Hill in its specific realisation of stone in terms of which the hiding places of Agni and Soma are conceived (Jurewicz 2010a). This would imply that in this moment of kindling the use of flint was necessary. The recipient could also understand that the second form of fire is Soma, which agrees with the general model of reality transformation. As has

[95] More specifically, COLOUR FOR SUBSTANCE (Radden, Kövecses 1999: 35).

[96] In R̥V 5.2.4 the female form *páliknī* appears also in the context of kindling fire.

been shown (Jurewicz 2010a: 145 ff.), Soma is also conceived as appearing from the stones which press it.

The last form of fire, conceived in terms of the third brother, is qualified as 'the one with ghee-smeared back' (*ghṛtápṛṣṭha*). This compound is often used in the ṚV in reference to fire. Within the frames of this conceptualisation, fire is conceived in terms of a horse and the clarified butter which pours from it in terms of a horse's sweat (e.g. ṚV 5.4.3, 7.2.4). In this way, the composer can imply that when fire ignites, it should be immediately fuelled with clarified butter lest it fade away. Since the rising sun is conceived in the ṚV in terms of the horse (Jurewicz 2010a), the recipient may identify the third form of fire as the sun.

The word *viśpati* (verse *d*) is used in the ṚV 33 times (Lubotsky 1997, II, 1311) and in only six stanzas does it not refer to fire. So we may safely presume that the object seen by the poet is fire. In ṚV 8.25.16b, the sun is called *viśpáti*[97] which confirms the identification of the kindled fire with the sun and agrees with the Ṛgvedic general model of reality transformation. In ṚV 10.135.1, the word *viśpáti* denotes the dead father of the protagonist of the hymn; the place of his staying is conceived in terms of the top of a tree and the father is accompanied by Yama (Jurewicz 2010a: 303–304). If the recipient evokes this stanza, he will understand that the poet sees the sun in zenith which is the location of the deceased.

Qualification of fire as *saptáputra* agrees with conceptualisation of its flames in terms of men. In ṚV 3.29.14, fire is qualified as *saptáhotṛ*, in ṚV 8.39.8, as *saptámānuṣa*. The number seven in this context may evoke the concept of the seven seers in terms of which the flames of fire are conceived: in ṚV 4.1.12, seven Aṅgirases are conceived in terms of his seven beloved or own (*priyá*) sons (see Jurewicz 2010a: 258–259)[98]. Thus the creation of the seven seers is presented, who undertake the further creation of the world and whose activity supports its existence.

Thus the first stanza in a concise way presents the experience of kindling of fire and the knowledge of the poet about the general model of reality transformations, according to which creation and the existence of the world is a manifestation of fire and its opposing aspect conceived in terms of Soma.

The next two stanzas present the knowledge of the poet as to the temporal structure of the cosmos and the role of the primeval seers:

---

[97] ṚV 8.25.16: *ayám éka itthā́ purú urú caṣṭe ví viśpátiḥ | tásya vratā́ni ánu vaś carāmasi ||* See also Houben 2000a: 520).

[98] In ṚV 6.7.6d flames of fire are conceived in terms of its seven outgrowths (*vayā́ iva ruruhuḥ saptá visrúhaḥ*).

ṚV 1.164.2

saptá yuñjanti rátham ékacakram éko áśvo vahati saptánāmā |
trinā́bhi cakrám ajáram anarvám̐ yátremā́ víśvā bhúvanā́dhi tasthúḥ ||

The seven harness the chariot with a single wheel[99]. A single horse with seven names draws it.
Triple-naved[100] is the unaging, unassaible wheel, on which all these living beings rest.

In verse *a*, the image of a chariot harnessed by seven charioteers, evoked metonymically by the adjective *saptá*, 'seven', is presented. This is the first input space of the conceptual network. The next is the concept of the sunrise. In the blend, sunrise is conceived in terms of men harnessing horses to the chariot (Jurewicz 2010a: 150–151). The recipient understands that these are the seven sons of fire mentioned in the previous stanza who are supposed to continue his activity. Qualification of the horse as having seven names (*saptánāmā*, verse *b*) may imply its identification with the seven seers: in the blend, the seers are both those who harness and what is harnessed. The reflexive activity is implied in this way. This interpretation agrees with the general model of reality transformations according to which man causes the sunrise and rises up together with the sun to zenith; the recipient may activate this model as the next input space of the network. This conceptualisation of the sun is elaborated in the AVŚ in a more general context with use of the abstract noun *kālá*, 'time' (see chapter 2.1.3).

The chariot has one wheel with three naves which is assumed by scholars to mean to refer to the divisions of time (Jamison, Brereton 2014: 354). In the later stanzas of the hymn, other numbers will be mentioned. The translators of this hymn try to identify them. It seems, however, that their exact meaning is lost in this context. The composer probably referred to shared knowledge which is not now accessible to us, except for some of its parts (e.g. twelve and seven hundred and twenty in ṚV 1.164.11 which probably refer to months, and days and nights).

From the point of view of my argument, it is important that the composer transforms the concepts which come from experience to convey abstract content: real chariots had two wheels (Sparreboom 1985). The conceptual network created by the composer consists of the following input spaces. The first is a chariot pulled by a horse, the second is the rising sun and the third is the world. In the blend, the world is placed in the revolving wheel of the chariot. The generic space is the concept of motion.

---

[99] Jamison, Brereton (2014): '[= the sun]'.
[100] Jamison, Brereton (2014): '[= with three seasons?]'.

At the same time, the wheel is qualified as unaging (*ajára*) and unassaible (*anarvá*) which allows the recipient to activate the next input space, i.e. is reality beyond the influence of time (on the basis of metonymy DEFINING PROPERTY FOR CATEGORY[101]). Thus the recipient is triggered to run the blend. The first hemistich prompts him to understand the sunrise in terms of harnessing a chariot and its ascending. The second hemistich makes him see all reality in terms of a chariot with a horse. The concept of reality is the next input space of the network. The wheel of the chariot corresponds to the borderline sphere of the cosmos where reality is already manifest, but is not yet subject to the power of time; within the wheel the world is influenced by time divided into three. Such a concentric conceptualisation of reality is attested in other places of the ṚV[102] and it will be elaborated by the composers of the AV (see chapter 2.5). Conceptualisation of the cosmos (the concept of which is the next input space) as being within the wheel allows the composer to identify it with time. The topology of the blend comes from the input space of the chariot and the temporal nature of reality which manifests in the cosmos comes from the input space of the sunrise. The recipient understands that the poet now cognises the temporal dimension of the cosmos and the role of the seven seers in its creation.

ṚV 1.164.3

imáṃ rátham ádhi yé saptá tasthúḥ saptácakraṃ saptá vahanti áśvāḥ |
saptá svásāro abhí sáṃ navante yátra gávāṃ níhitā saptá nā́ma ||

As its seven horses, the seven[103] who stand upon this chariot[104] draw the seven-wheeled[105].
Seven sisters[106] together cry out[107]in which the seven names of the cows[108] are imprinted.

The concept of the seven seers who ride on the chariot, again evoked metonymically by the adjective *saptá* 'seven' in verses *a–b*, agrees with the logic of the source domain: in the previous stanza the horses are harnessed to the chariot, now the seers ride on it. The recipient may understand that in these terms the mental trip of the seers is conceived that is realised during

[101] Radden, Kövecses (1999: 35).
[102] ṚV 10.125 (see section 1.2), ṚV 10.90 (see section 1.3), see also Jurewicz (2010a: 94).
[103] Jamison, Brereton (2014): '[= the priests]'.
[104] Jamison, Brereton (2014): '[= the sacrifice].
[105] Jamison, Brereton (2014): '(chariot)'.
[106] Jamison, Brereton (2014): '[= voices of the priests]'.
[107] Jamison, Brereton (2014): '(the words)'.
[108] Jamison, Brereton (2014): '[= poetic speech]'.

ritual (Jurewicz 2010a). The composer again implies the identity of the seers and the horses: the seers, the wheel and the horses are seven. Such a use of the word *saptá* betrays the tendency to create an abstract and general noun which can refer both to the agent which causes action (the seers who harness the horses) and renders it possible (the horses which pulls the chariot and the seers who drive it).

In verse *c*, the seven sisters, who cry out, are presented. The composer evokes the philosophical model of Child Of The Waters in this way. Generally speaking, this model facilitates conceptualisation of creation and existence of the world in terms of origination of a male principle (most often Agni, sometimes Soma and the sun) thanks to female agents (Jurewicz 2010a: 203 ff.). The female agents are often seven. In the case of fire, the seven females are the spoons or tongues (ṚV 1.58.7), however, in most places, the females are evoked by the adjective 'young', *yahvī́*, which is supposed to metonymically evoke the corresponding noun (ṚV 1.71.7, 1.72.8, 3.1.4). Often in the ṚV, the use of adjectives instead of nouns is proof of abstraction because, as we can see, the female principle is variously conceived in the model. The use of adjectives makes the recipient think about all of them. The adjective *yahvī́* in reference to females which give birth to fire, within the frames of the model of Child Of The Waters, is used in ṚV 2.35 where it qualifies waters in two stanzas (this is the only use of this adjective in the second maṇḍala, ṚV 2.35.9, 14). In case of Soma, various females are mentioned: young rivers (ṚV 9.92.4), cows (in terms of which milk is metonymically conceived, ṚV 9.86.25), but most often thoughts (*dhītí*, ṚV 9.8.04, 9.9.4, 9.15.8, 9.62.17). In case of the sun, the female agents are young mares (ṚV 1.50.8,9, 4.13.3, 7.60.3). These females are conceived in terms of sisters (*svásṛ*, *jāmí*, ṚV 7.066.15, 8.59.4, 9.66.8) and mothers (*mātṛ́*, ṚV 9.102.4); once sisters are identified with mothers (ṚV 9.86.36). This also agrees with the self-reflective nature of the process presented in the model of Child Of The Waters according to which the child of the waters becomes their husband. The females are also conceived in terms of voices (*vā́ṇī*, ṚV 3.7.1, 9.103.3, 8.59.3). So the recipient can evoke this model and understand that the composer in verse *c* presents creation of fire, Soma and the sun. On the basis of the general model of reality transformation, the recipient can reconstruct the sequence of their appearance thanks to morning sacrifice: the fire is kindled, Soma is poured into it and the sun rises as the solar manifestation of fire.

The sisters are presented as crying out (*abhí sáṃ navante*). The image of beings which cry when the sun rises probably refers to pastoral experience when the cows bellow in the morning. This experience is evoked in ṚV 1.66.10b (*návanta gā́vaḥ súvar dṛ́śīke*). ṚV 1.69.10b repeats the same verse, but replaces *gā́vaḥ* with *víśve* (*návanta víśve súvar dṛ́śīke*). Together with cows, the Aṅgirases shout in the morning (ṚV 4.3.11, 5.5.08) while in ṚV 4.1.16, 10.123.2 the female troop (*vrā́*) is presented as shouting. Another experience, which motivates the image of female agents crying out at something, is the loud expression of wonder when a child is born. It is activated in ṚV 6.7.4 where the gods are presented as crying out at fire as at a child being born. The next experience is evoked in ṚV 9.56.3 where the ten fingers which clarify Soma is expressed with the verb *abhí nu-* and the fingers are compared to a young girl who calls her lover. Jamison, Brereton propose yet another experience which is announcing the bridegroom choice by the maidens (2014: 558, ad ṚV 4.1.16).

The verb *abhí/sám nu-/nū* is most often used with a direct object in accusative which expresses in the source domain the direction of action (cows bellow towards the sun) and, in the target domain, the object extolled in songs (e.g. ṚV 1.7.1, 8.12.22, 8.21.5, 10.68.1) or the object which is transformed (most often Soma, e.g. 8.69.11, 9.26.2, 9,86.25). I would, therefore, argue that the same metaphor is evoked here. In the source domain, cows bellow looking at the sun, in the target domain, people extoll the sun which is the place where 'seven names of cows is hidden' (*yátra gávāṃ níhitā saptá nā́ma*, verse *d*).

According to the general model of reality transformation, during sacrifice man mentally reaches the sun where he achieves the state of immortality and omniscience which is conceived in terms of drinking Soma from the solar source (Jurewicz 2010a). In ṚV 9.87.3cd, it is said that Soma finds 'the hidden name of cows' (*sá cid viveda níhitaṃ yád āsām apīcíyaṃ gúhiyaṃ nā́ma gónām*). In ṚV 10.68.7, Bṛhaspati is described as creating the morning when he thinks about the hidden name of 'these who were resounding' (*nā́ma svarī́ṇāṃ sádane gúhā yát*). These are the cows in terms of which sacred speech is conceived. In ṚV 4.1, the Aṅgirases cognise twenty one highest names of mother which is a red cow appearing with its shine when the female group cries out[109]. In these terms, the appearance of speech in the morning sacrifice is conceived.

It can be assumed then that in this stanza the composer presents the morning ritual activity of the primeval seers during which they mentally reach the sun in zenith and realise the state of omniscience which can be verbalised in speech. Their activity is repeated by the poets (*kaví*, ṚV 1.164.5) and will become the pattern for the poet (protagonist of the hymn, ṚV 164.6,16,18). As I have already mentioned, in other hymns of the ṚV, the description of

[109] ṚV 4.1.16: *té manvata prathamáṃ nā́ma dhenós tríḥ saptá mātúḥ paramā́ṇi vindan | táj jānatī́r abhí anūṣata vrā́ āvír bhuvad aruṇī́r yaśásā góḥ ||*

the successful ritual and cognitive activity is presented in this moment. But in this hymn, the realisation of the supernatural cognition by the poet will be described later (beginning from stanza 26). Now, the poet asks questions about the beginning of the world on the basis of which the recipient understands that he is not satisfied with the knowledge he possesses:

ṚV 1.164.4

kó dadarśa prathamáṃ jā́yamānam asthanvántaṃ yád anasthā́ bíbharti |
bhū́myā ásur ásṛg ātmā́ kúva svit kó vidvā́ṃsam úpa gāt práṣṭum etát ||

Who has seen the first one[110] as he is being born, when the[111] boneless[112] carries the one having bones[113]?
Where is life, blood, and breath of the earth? Who will approach the knowing one to ask?

In verse *a*, the poet asks about the first manifestation of reality conceived in terms of being born. The answer to the question in verse *a* seems to be given in ṚV 4.17.7a which presents Agni as the first being born (ṚV 4.17.7a: *tuvám ádha prathamáṃ jā́yamāno*). Agni as the first born is also mentioned in ṚV 10.45.1 a (*divás pári prathamáṃ jajñe agnír*). In ṚV 4.50.4c, Bṛhaspati, which in the ṚV is a blended concept of Agni who acts as Indra (Jurewicz 2010a: 360 ff.[114]), is presented as being the first born (*bṛ́haspátiḥ prathamáṃ jā́yamāno*). In ṚV 1.163.1a, a sacrificial horse is described in the same way (*yád ákrandaḥ prathamáṃ jā́yamāna*). Taking into account that, in the ṚV, Agni is conceived in terms of a horse, it is possible that the intention of the composer of ṚV 1.163.1 is to also evoke the concept of Agni[115].

Verse *b* presents a conceptualisation of the pre-creative state of the world in terms of pregnancy: the pregnant female is conceived as boneless, the embryo as having bones. Such a conceptualisation is unique in the ṚV, but it may bring the recipient's mind to the model of the Boiled In The Raw (Jurewicz 2010a: 215 ff.). Within the frames of this conceptualisation, reality is conceived in terms of a cow qualified as raw, the world in its pre-creative state in terms of boiled milk. Thus the recipient activates the zoomorphic model of reality. The earth in verse *c* is also conceived in terms of a living being endowed

[110] Jamison, Brereton (2014): '[= the Sun/Agni].
[111] Jamison, Brereton (2014): add 'his'.
[112] Jamison, Brereton (2014): '(mother) [= the Waters?].
[113] Jamison, Brereton (2014): '[= the one who is a living being].
[114] For interpretation of Bṛhaspati see also Schmidt (1868).
[115] This assumption needs more research which would go beyond the scope of the present work.

with breath and blood[116] and constituting a whole called *ātmán* (Jurewicz 1997). The earth metonymically stands for the whole creation, as it is in the *Puruṣasūkta* (ṚV 10.90.1cd, see section 1.3) and in the ŚB (see chapter 3).

In verse *d*, the composer asks who can approach the knowing one in order to obtain knowledge about the origins of the world. In the ṚV, it is Agni who is conceived in terms of all-knowing and who should be asked by the poets[117]. So the recipient understands that the knowing one is Agni. If we accept that in verse *a* of the stanza Agni is mentioned, we would see the coherence of the thought of the composer: the one who knows about the first manifestation of reality is the one who manifests itself as the first.

However, the poet cannot ask these questions directly to Agni. He needs the help of those who have successfully realised the state of supernatural cognition:

ṚV 1.164.5

pā́kaḥ pṛchāmi mánasā́vijānan devā́nām enā́ níhitā padā́ni |
vatsé baṣkáye ádhi saptá tántūn ví tatnire kaváya ótavā́ u ||

Naïve, not understanding, in my mind I ask about these imprinted tracks of the gods.
Upon the full-grown calf[118] the poets have stretched the seven warp-threads in order to weave.

The poets whom the protagonist of the hymn wants to ask (verse *a*) are most probably those who, thanks to their knowledge, were or are able to repeat the activity of the seven seers described in ṚV 1.164.2-3. In verse *b*, the poet asks about the tracks of the gods. The composers of the ṚV elaborate the scenario of following the tracks or footprints of the cattle (or its thief) and their finding to conceive the kindling of fire and cognition which can be verbalised in sacred speech (Jurewicz 2010a: 128 ff.). This is a specific realisation of the general domain of Finding The Hidden. Within the frames of this conceptualisation, words are conceived in terms of footprints, Agni is conceived in terms of a calf and sacred speech in terms of a cow[119]. The scenario implies that if one knows the footprints, one will find the object.

---

116 This is also a unique conceptualisation in the ṚV. It is possible that bones and blood as the elements of the source domain come from the experience of animal sacrifice. It cannot be excluded that this sacrifice is a horse sacrifice described in two preceding hymns, but this hypothesis needs more investigation to be confirmed.

117 ṚV 1.105.4, 1.145.2, 10.79.6.

118 Jamison, Brereton (2014); '[= the fire]'.

119 The coherence of this conceptualisation can be seen in that cognition is conceived in terms of kindling fire in the ṚV (Jurewicz 2010a).

The concept of a path made of footprints (probably this was the way paths were created during the times of the ṚV) is also evoked in the model of Footprints Of Viṣṇu who leaves three footprints: the earth is conceived in terms of the first footprint, space in terms of the second footprint and the sun filled with Soma in terms of the third footprint (Jurewicz 2010a: 387 ff.). Along this path men walk to the solar source of Soma in sacrifices.

This complex conceptualisation is evoked by ṚV 1.164.5. The expression 'tracks of the gods' (*devā́nām padā́ni*, verse *b*) evokes conceptualisation of sacred words in terms of footprints which are left by Viṣṇu and other gods and which are followed by men. The poet states his lack of knowledge about sacred speech thanks to which he could cognise the first manifestation of reality which is Agni.

In the second hemistich, the composer creates the image of a calf upon which the threads are stretched. If the recipient activates the scenario of a lost calf, he will understand that, when it is finally found by the poets, it has grown so much it has to be bound with a rope so that it not escape again. However, in verse *d*, the composer activates the next input spaces of the network which are the source and the target domain of the metaphor COGNITION IS WEAVING (Jurewicz 2010a: 117–118). In the blend, Agni is conceived in terms of a calf. It can be cognised thanks to sacred speech. This cognition can be realised when one follows the footprints left by Viṣṇu; using the Ṛgvedic metaphor, the calf can only be caught on the sun. It is also implied that the act conceived in terms of catching a calf is only the beginning of cognition: the poets have seven threads with which they have bounded the calf, i.e. kindled fire and now can begin to weave, i.e. to cognise. The image of the poets manipulating threads is coherent with earlier descriptions of the seers who drive the chariot because the concept of thread (*tántu*) is synonymous with the concept of reins (*raśmí*).

So the network created in this stanza consists of the following input spaces: the poets who cognise, people who look for a lost calf, people who weave and the model of Footprints Of Viṣṇu. The latter three input spaces impart to the blend a topology of the world and a scenario of supernatural cognition which easier to be understood thanks to this. The generic space are the image schema of SELF-MOTION and SOURCE-PATH-GOAL. As we will see, while the activity of the seven seers is conceived in terms of riding on chariot, the activity of the poets which are the closest example for the poet (protagonist of the hymn) is conceived in terms of cowherding.

In the next two stanzas, the poet asks those, who have realised the supernatural state of consciousness as to the origin of the world and the nature of its functioning, about the way to find answers to these questions.

ṚV 1.164.6

ácikitvā̃n cikitúṣaś cid átra kavī́n pṛchāmi vidmáne ná vidvā́n |
ví yás tastámbha ṣáḷ imā́ rájāṃsi ajásya rūpé kím ápi svid ékam ||

Unperceptive, I ask also the perceptive poets about this in order to know, since I am unknowing.
What also is the one in the form of the Unborn[120] that has propped apart these six realms[121]?

In the first hemistich, the composer presents the poet who wants to realise the same cognition as the poets described in ṚV 1.164.5. In the second hemistich, the object of knowledge is presented. The concept of an unborn or a goat (*ajá*, verse *d*) which props apart the spheres of the world is evoked in ṚV 1.67.5 (*ajó ná kṣā́ṃ dādhā́ra pṛthivī́ṃ tastámbha diyā́m mántrebhiḥ satyaíḥ*)[122]. Since this hymn is devoted to Agni, the recipient of ṚV 1.164.6 can understand that the poet again asks about it. If the recipient understands the word *ajá* as 'unborn', which assumes a form, *rūpá*, he will understand the internally contradictory nature of reality when it manifests itself. In order to remove this contradiction, the recipient may understand the meaning of *ajá* which is 'a goat'. Then he will activate the concept of *ajá ékapād* which is elaborated in the next stanza in the description of the world's functioning. In the ritual, the goat is an oblation devoted to Agni (ṚV 10.16.4) which confirms the conceptual links between them. It seems that the triple concentric structure of the world is again implied: within the unmanifest, unborn reality, there is its borderline form which can be called its *rūpá*, probably conceived in terms of a goat's body. Its leg becomes the *axis mundi* which props apart the realms of the world. This reality is conceived as Agni.

ṚV 1.164.7

ihá bravītu yá īm aṅgá véda asyá vāmásya níhitam padáṃ véḥ |
śīrṣṇáḥ kṣīráṃ duhrate gā́vo asya vavríṃ vásānā udakám padā́puḥ ||

Let him speak here, who knows the imprinted tracks of this treasured bird[123].
The cows [124] yield milk[125] from his head[126]. Clothing themselves in a cloak, they have drunk water with the foot[127].

---

[120] Jamison, Brereton (2014): '[= the Sun]'.
[121] Jamison, Brereton (2014): '(of heaven and earth)'.
[122] Agni measures six broad spaces: ṚV 6.47.3. Indra sets apart six: ṚV 2.13.10, The one carries six: ṚV 3.56.2.
[123] Jamison, Brereton (2014): '[= the Sun]'.
[124] Jamison, Brereton (2014): '[= rain-clouds]'.
[125] Jamison, Brereton (2014): '[= rain]'.
[126] Jamison, Brereton (2014): '[= the Sun]'.
[127] Jamison, Brereton (2014): '[= the Sun's rays]'.

Verse *a* is similar to ṚV 10.129.7 where the composer asks about the beginnings of the world, the nature of creation and about the eye-witness in the highest heaven who either knows or does not (*só aṅgá veda yádi vā ná véda*, verse *d*). Since in the ṚV the word *ádhyakṣa* is always used in reference to Agni, the composer of the *Nāsadīyasūkta* implies that the eye-witness is also Agni (Jurewicz 2010a: 332–333). So the recipient of ṚV 1.164.7a may assume that it is Agni who is expected to answer the poet's question which agrees with Agni's conceptualisation as an omniscient person who should be asked (ṚV 1.164.4)[128].

Verse *b* begins with phrase *asyá vāmásya* in the same way as the whole hymn. So the recipient may interpret the further verses of the stanza as the opening answer to the poet's doubts. Since in terms of a bird the sun is conceived, the recipient may understand that the expression *padáṃ véḥ* refers to it: the sunrise is conceived in terms of a bird which flies up. According to the Ṛgvedic poets, birds leave tracks; they are invisible for men, but Varuṇa knows them (ṚV 1.25.7). In ṚV 10.5.1d, the track of bird is presented as being in the middle of the spring (*útsasya mádhye níhitam padáṃ véḥ*). This image agrees with the general conceptualisation of the sun in the ṚV: it is conceived in terms of a vessel or a spring filled with Soma (see Jurewicz 2010a: 164 ff.). According to ṚV 10.5.1, the track of bird is on the sun. If the recipient of ṚV 1.164.7 evokes this conceptualisation, he will understand the track of 'this treasured bird' in the same way. This track belongs to Agni evoked by its qualification *asyá vāmásya*. The composer implies the following conceptualisation of the sunrise: fire becomes the rising sun which is conceived in terms of a bird flying up. When the sun reaches zenith, fire disappears in it, leaving its track which is the sun filled with Soma. According to ṚV (3.5.5, 3.5.6, 4.5.8), it is Agni who guards the track of the bird, so we can presume that he knows it. Thus the composer implies that the poet again wants to ask Agni about its nature.

Verse *c* presents the cows which, as Jamison, Brereton (2014) interpret, 'yield milk from his head' and interprets it as the beginning of rain. According to Houben (2000a: 534), cows milk rain 'from the head of him (the sun)'. The fact that rain appears conforms to the general model of reality transformation. The everyday experience of milking is transformed in order to express the beginning of rain: cows are not milked, but they are the agents of milking. The composer creates the conceptual network consisting of two input spaces, milking a cow and raining. In the blend, the udder is identified with the head.

[128] For Agni as the giver of insight, see ṚV 4.5.3cd: *padáṃ ná gór ápagūḷhaṃ vividvā́n agnír máhyam préd u vocan manīṣā́m*. See Findly (1989: 37–40).

The generic space of this blend is the appearance of the symbol of light from the symbol of darkness.

In the blend, the logic of scenario of milking allows the recipient to identify the head with the udder. In ṚV 9.71.4 the image of cows is built, which heat[129] Somic juice in the head identified with the udder. Activation of this stanza allows the composer of ṚV 1.164.7 to express the reflexive action: cows are the agents of milking and, at the same time, they are milk which flows from the udder. In terms of milk, rain is conceived. Such a conceptualisation agrees with the general model of reality transformation which in its deepest meaning presents the appearance of rain as the result of self-transformations of fire into Soma and Soma into rain under the influence of fire. Within the frames of my interpretation, the streams of rain are conceived in terms of cows and the rain-cloud is conceived in terms of a cloak (*vavrí*)[130]. This is confirmed by the word *vavrí* being used in ṚV 1.164.29 in the description of speech conceived in terms of the lightning emerging from its hiding-place (*vavrí*, ṚV 1.164.29); in this context *vavrí* surely refers to the rain-cloud.

In verse *d*, the cows are presented as drinking water with the foot. My interpretation of this verse is as follows. The cows now refer to real cows which live on earth and drink rainy water. The foot is the leg of the Aja Ekapād which is the *axis mundi* along which the rain flows down. Conceptualisation of the *axis mundi* in terms of the leg of an animal is elaborated in the *Puruṣasūkta* (see section 1.3[131]). The polysemy of the word *gó* allows the composer to activate the concept of real cows, the concept of their milk (on the basis of metonymy COW FOR MILK[132]), and the concept of rain (on the basis of metaphor RAIN IS MILK). Thank to that he can present the cosmic cycle which ends with rain and its life-giving role. If the recipient activates the concept of *ajá ékapād*, he will understand that the head belongs to Agni and that Agni is the creator of rain.

Thus the poet obtains knowledge of the functioning of cosmos, but in a different terms than described in ṚV 1.164.2-3. The main source domain activated in those stanzas is the concept of a chariot and its wheel. The source

129 As I have argued (Jurewicz 2010a), the verb *śrī-* can be interpreted as conveying the meaning of heating.

130 Jamison, Brereton (2014) and Houben (2000) interpret the concept of cows as referring to rain-clouds. Brown (1968a: 205) interprets this image as appearance of light and rain: 'In the sky the cows (rays) draw milk from the Sun's head (7) and then descend from the sky to the earth. The water which thy take to earth with them is now metaphorically called milk, since it is the nourishing rain'.

131 And in the AVŚ where *axis mundi* is conceived in terms of leg of a wild goose, see chapter 2.5.3.

132 More general interpretation of this metonymy can be either WHOLE THING FOR A PART OF THE THING or CAUSE FOR EFFECT. The cows are presented as flowing from the udder in ṚV 4.22.6.

domains activated in ṚV 1.164.5-7 are the concept of animals, such as a bird, a goat and a cow which will be the main source domain for conceptualisation of the sacred speech elaborated in the next stanzas. The concepts of a path made of footprints and of an head identified with udder, in terms of which the sun is conceived, presuppose the possibility to repeat the poets' activity (described in ṚV 1.164.5) conceived in terms of following footprints and drinking from the udder. The concept of weaving activated in this stanza strengthens the meaning of successful cognition which can be verbalised and which is realised on the sun.

In the next three stanzas, knowledge about the origins of the world is presented which can be treated as the answer given to the poet. One gets impression as if the composer of the hymn now wanted to explain the cosmological proces described in the previous stanza.

ṚV 1.164.8

mātā́ pitáram ṛtá ā́ babhāja dhītī ágre mánasā sáṃ hí jagmé |
sā́ bībhatsúr gárbharasā níviddhā námasvanta íd upavākám īyuḥ ||

The mother[133] gave[134] father[135] a share in the truth, for in the beginning, through[136] insight, she united[137] by her mind.
Recoiling, she whose essence was her child[138] was pierced[139]. Just those offering their reverence went to the[140] invocation.

Verse *a* is composed ambiguously. In their translation, Jamison, Brereton (2014) interpret that the father is the father of the mother. However, it is also possible that 'mother' is the one who is boneless, mentioned in ṚV 1.164.4. I will present this interpretation now, while the second possibility will be presented at the end of the hymn. If mother is 'the boneless one', the recipient may understand mother as reality in its unmanifest aspect[141]. The verb *sám gam-* implies sexual union of mother and father, from which the father is born again[142]. If we use the schema presented in ṚV 10.72, we could say that mother is Aditi and father is Dakṣa. The same internally contradictory

---

133 Jamison, Brereton (2014): '[= the Dawn]'.
134 Jamison, Brereton (2014): add 'her'.
135 Jamison, Brereton (2014): '[= the Sun/Heaven]'.
136 Jamison, Brereton (2014): add 'her'.
137 Jamison, Brereton (2014): '(with him)'.
138 Jamison, Brereton (2014): '[= Agni/the Sun]'.
139 Jamison, Brereton (2014): '(by her father)'.
140 Jamison, Brereton (2014): '(morning)'.
141 Aditi is called 'mother' (*mātṛ́*) in ṚV 1.72.9, 1.89.10.
142 For rebirth of father in his son in the early Veda, see Kaelber (1975: 351–355).

process is elaborated in the model of Child Of The Waters and in the general model of reality transformation which sees transformations of reality in terms of alternative and contradictory transformations of Agni and Soma.

In ṚV 1.164.8, the cognitive nature of this first creative act is expressed in that the union occurs with aid of insight (*dhītí*) and of mind or thought (*mánas*). This cognitive nature allows the recipient to understand mother as speech which renders true cognition possible[143]. This interpretation agrees with conceptualisation of reality in terms of speech which is presented in ṚV 10.125.7. As has been shown, speech is conceived in terms of the mother of the father (see section 1.2). On the other hand, the fact that the father is born from this union is more clearly seen when the meaning of *ṛtá* which is also 'the order of the world, the world' is highlighted. The input spaces of the conceptual network are the concepts of reality and of cognition which can be verbalised. In the blend, reality can manifest itself as existing which in the *Nāsadīyasūkta* is expressed with the word *sát*. The next input spaces are the general domain of Procreation and the model of Child of the Waters. These input spaces impart to the blend the concept of the appearance of something new, of agency and of self-transformations. In terms of a father, the manifest aspect of reality is conceived[144]. The generic space is the image schema of SELF-MOTION.

The recipient may presume now that the next hemistich presents transformations within the manifest aspect. Verse *c* presents a female which recoils, is pregnant and is pierced (*sā́ bībhatsúr gárbharasā níviddhā*). The form *bibhatsú* is used twice more in ṚV 10.124.8-9 in reference to waters. The context of ṚV 10.124.8 implies that they recoil from Vṛtra which encloses them. ṚV 10.124.9 creates the image of Indra, conceived in terms of a golden goose, who is the friend of the recoiling waters[145]. Within the frames of ṚV 10.124,

143 Malamoud (2004 (1): 144): 'Aditi, en effet, qui est la Terre, le tout primordial (et féminin), la mère innombrable, la nourriture inépuisable (à l'instar de Virāj à laquelle elle est souvant identifiée), est aussi une figure de la Parole'.

144 This conceptualisation differs from the conceptualisation of ṚV 6.9 where the unmanifest aspect is conceived in terms of a father (Jurewicz 2010a: 249–250). This difference can be interpreted in two ways. Firstly, the composer may refer to the model of Wave Of Honey according to which the unmanifest aspect is conceived in terms of a mother (Jurewicz 2010a: 230–231). Secondly, this conceptualisation may attest the change in the content of supra-natural cognition which leads the agent to understand that the range of cognition of the unmanifest aspect of reality can be expanded. Thus the sphere of reality conceptualised in terms of a father is not the final one. It has its unmanifest source, conceived in terms of a mother.

145 Jamison, Brereton (2014) interpret this stanza as referring to the incest between the father and his daughter in terms of whom the appearance of Agni or the sun, as a child of the Dawn and the sun or the sky, is conceived (2014: 352). The concept of incest is activated in verse *c* where female is qualified as *bibhatsú* and presented as pregnant (*gárbharasā níviddhā*).

waters are conceived as lovers of Vṛtra from whom they recoil, then Indra saves them and thus becomes their friend. At the same time, conceptualisation of Indra as a golden goose amidst waters evokes the model of Child Of The Waters which implies an incestual sexual act between mothers and their son (Jurewicz 2010a: 432–333).

In ṚV 1.164.8 a female that recoils from the sexual act is either a mother who does not want to unite with her son or daughter who does not want to unite with her father. Taking into account the unity of reality, these two possibilities are not mutually exclusive. As the model of the Child Of The Waters shows, waters are mothers, sisters and daughters of fire. The schema Aditi – Dakṣa – Aditi puts this impossible situation in a linear sequence which is easier to be understood, but simplifies the contradictoriness caused by the monistic assumption.

The concise verse *d* presents agents who pay homage and sing invocations which Jamison, Brereton (2014) interpret as taking place in the morning. In its general meaning, it is similar to ṚV 1.163.3cd which presents seven sisters who cry out, although here the group consists of males. So the recipient may assume that a child is again born. If we accept the interpretation that the father unites with his daughter, the child would be Dakṣa. If we accept the interpretation that the father unites with his mother, the child will be Aditi. The same ambiguity in the relationship between speech and the male element conceived in terms of a father can be seen in ṚV 10.125.7 (see section 1.2). Its aim is to express the reflexive nature of the creative process which is the transformation of one reality. In the blend, reality manifests itself in speech.

ṚV 1.164.9

yuktā́ mātā́sīd dhurí dákṣiṇāyā átiṣṭhad gárbho vṛjanī́ṣu antáḥ |
ámīmed vatsó ánu gā́m apaśyad viśvarūpíyaṃ triṣú yójaneṣu ||

The mother was harnessed to the yoke-pole of the sacrificial rewards; her child stood up amid the penned cows.
The calf[146] bellowed and looked toward the cow of every colour[147], three wagon-treks[148].

This stanza can be interpreted in two ways. The first possibility is that it describes the same process as described in the previous stanza, but in more clear way, with use of the simple scenario of the birth of a calf and not an abstract model such as Child Of The Waters. The second is that it describes

146 Jamison, Brereton (2014): '[= Agni]'.
147 Jamison, Brereton (2014): '[= the Dawn]'.
148 Jamison, Brereton (2014): '(in the distance)'.

the next stages of the process described in the previous stanza. I would see this ambiguity as the attempt to create an abstract and general model enabling the composer to express the conviction that manifestation of reality within the cosmos is the same as its first creative act.

In verse *a*, the concept of mother is again activated. In this context, it may be either reality in its unmanifest aspect or in its manifest form conceived as the offspring of the father. The concepts of mother and father metonymically evoke the general domain of Procreation.

Mother is presented as yoked to the yoke-pole of *dákṣiṇā*. This implies its conceptualisation as a cow (ṚV 1.84.16a *kó adyá yuṅkte dhurí gā́ ṛtásya*) which strengthens the possibility of its interpretation as speech. In the ṚV, the word *dákṣiṇā* still activates its meaning of cow which in later thought becomes a conventional metonymic concept used in reference to the sacrificial fee consisting mainly of cows[149]. On more general level, cow harnesses a cow which implies reflexive activity of reality in the same way as it is implied by use of numeral *saptá* in ṚV 1.164.2-3.

The concept of yoke-pole metonymically evokes the concept of the chariot used to conceive the passage of time (see above, ṚV 1.164.9). Since in the ṚV the passage of time is observed on the basis of the appearance of dawns and since dawn is conceived in terms of a cow or a female who rides on chariot yoked with cows (Srinivasan 1979, Jurewicz 2010a)[150], the recipient can also activate this concept. So the general concept of yoking a cow by a cow is the source domain for conceptualising the appearance of speech and dawn. Since in the ṚV the appearance of the morning light brings the possibility to cognise and to live (Jurewicz 2010a), the recipient may understand verse *a* as expressing in cosmic terms the abstract content of the previous stanza which presents a mother as giving to a father 'a share in the truth' (ṚV 1.164.8a: *mātā́ pitáram ṛtá ā́ babhāja*), but he may also understand it as the next stage of the process described in the previous stanza. Within the frames of this interpretation, Aditi is born from Dakṣa in the more concrete forms of the appearance of morning light and speech.

Verse *b* presents the embryo which stands 'amid the penned cows' (*vṛjanī́ṣu antáḥ*). The concept of embryo metonymically evokes the sexual union[151] and it corresponds to the father or to Dakṣa. The embryo has many mothers conceived in terms of cows which again evokes the model of Child Of The Waters and the concept of incest. Since the child is most often Agni, the

[149] ṚV 1.125.5, 2.11.21, 2.18.9, 6.64.1, 7.27.4, 3.58.1.

[150] *Dákṣiṇā* in reference to dawn: ṚV 6.64.1, 10.107.1

[151] Metonymy THE FINAL PHASE OF THE PROCESS FOR THE WHOLE PROCESS (Radden, Kövecses 1999).

recipient may elaborate this concept in the blend and understand that fire kindled in the morning, which becomes the rising sun, is conceived in terms of the embryo. This interpretation is consistent in that the nocturnal sky is conceived in terms of a cow-pen in the ṚV while the appearance of the dawns is conceived in terms of cows which go out to pasture (ṚV 1.92.4, 4.51.2). Fire and its cosmic solar form is born among the light of dawns.

The logic of the general domain of Procreation implies that the embryo is born. The logic of verse *a*, which presents the mother of a calf which is yoked to a pole, implies that mother goes away. In verse *c*, the calf is presented as bellowing at its mother[152]. In the source domain, the cow leaves its calf which bellows at it. The fact that the cow leaves its calf is confirmed as the cow is presented as being three wagon-treks afar (*triṣú yójaneṣu*, verse *d*). The concept of the three-wagon treks introduces the concept of a journey. In the blend, the dawn disappears having covered the sky with its light; the three wagon-treks may be understood as the earth, the space and the sky. The cow, in terms of which the dawn is conceived, is qualified as all-formed or all-coloured (*viśvarūpíya*). In ṚV 3.55.19 and 10.10.5, the word *viśvárūpa* is used in reference to Savitar[153] and in ṚV 3.38.4, it is used in reference to the sun conceived in terms of a bull. At the same time, the flames of fire are called *viśvárūpa* in ṚV 3.1.7. So it is possible that adjective *viśvarūpíya* is meant to imply that the cow is connected with fire and its solar form[154].

The input spaces of the conceptual network elaborated in this stanza are as follows. The concepts of the manifestation of reality in speech and the appearance of the morning light (kindling of fire and appearance of dawn) are the input spaces which transfer to the blend the content of the cognition of the poet who wants to understand their nature. The concepts of yoking a cow to the chariot and of cow and its calf are the input spaces which trigger the recipient to conceive these complex processes in simple terms of everyday experience. The concept of yoking imparts to the blend the concept of agency. The next input space is the image schemas of SOURCE-PATH-GOAL and of VERTICALITY which allow the recipient to see the movement of processes described in the blend in simple terms of an upward, intentional movement. The next two input spaces, namely, the model of Child Of The Waters and the general domain of Procreation, endow the blend with the meaning of reflexive process and the appearance of something new. The generic space is the image schema of SELF-MOTION.

152 ṚV 2.2.2, 2.16.8, 3.33.3, 3.41.5, 6.45.25, 28, 8.88.1.

153 ṚV 3.55.19 = 10.10.5.

154 The adjective *viśvárūpa* is also used in ṚV 4.33.8.b, in reference to a cow created by Ṛbhus, in the same context it is used in ṚV 1.161.6a.

ṚV 1.164.10

tisró mātṝ́s trī́n pitṝ́n bíbhrad éka ūrdhvás tasthau ném áva glāpayanti |
mantráyante divó amúṣya pṛṣṭhé viśvavídaṃ vā́cam áviśvaminvām ||

Carrying three mothers[155] and three fathers[156] alone, he[157] stands uprights; they do not cause him to weary.
On the back of the yonder heaven they[158] recite the speech that knows everything but does not inspire everyone.

In verse *a*, the composer presents the image of the one (*éka*) which carries the six. I would interpret the one as Agni described in ṚV 1.164.6 who props apart the six realms of the world[159]. In verse *b*, the one is presented as standing up. Thus the composer uses the logic of the input space of a calf which bellows at the cow. In the blend, fire, conceived in terms of a calf, stands up and runs after a cow. Thus it becomes the rising sun. The sunrise is also conceived in the ṚV in terms of a man standing erect (Jurewicz 2010a: 139–141)[160]. So the concept of the birth of a man is the next input space of the conceptual network. In the blend, fire, conceived in terms of a man, stands firmly erect; its flames, conceived in terms of the body, are the *axis mundi*. The *axis mundi* is also conceived in terms of footprints left by the calf.

In verse *c*, the composer evokes the zoomorphic model of the world, according to which the sky is conceived in terms of a cow/bull (Jurewicz 2014a). The borderline sphere of the cosmos is conceived in terms of its back. If the recipient elaborates the input space of the cow and a calf and understands the sunrise in terms of a calf following his mother, he would understand that now the calf sucks her udder; in terms of the udder the sun filled with Soma is conceived in the ṚV (Jurewicz 2010a: 261 ff., 2014). In this way, the composer can express various aspects of the sunrise: if the recipient conceives it in terms of a standing man, he will highlight the possibility of reaching the sun, if he conceives it in terms of a calf sucking his mother's udder, he will highlight the possibility of obtaining omniscient cognition and speech thanks to solar Soma present in the sun.

This supernatural state is realised by those who are present in the borderline sphere of the cosmos and 'recite the speech that knows everything' (*mantráyante*

155 Jamison, Brereton (2014): '[= earths]'.
156 Jamison, Brereton (2014): '[= heavens]'.
157 Jamison, Brereton (2014): '[= the Sun]'.
158 Jamison, Brereton (2014): '[= the gods]'.
159 The same image is created in ṚV 3.56.2.
160 This conceptualisation will be elaborated in ŚB 11.1.6 (see chapter 3.5.2).

divó amúṣya pṛṣṭhé viśvavídaṃ vā́cam). The recipient may presume that they are the seven seers who are evoked in ṚV 1.164.2-3 and the poets described in ṚV 1.164.5.

In verse *d*, it is stated that not everyone can realise this state. According to ṚV 9.83.1, there are people who are unprepared for Somic exultation; they are conceived as 'raw' and their body is not heated. According to ṚV 9.73.8-9, such people fall into a pit and are lost; the recipient may understand that they fall from the *axis mundi*.

So we can conclude that now the poet understands the world and its source. The world is the manifestation of one reality in speech and time and is conceived as fiery. He also understands the way to finally cognise this impossible state of affairs. Man can use the manifestation of reality in order to cognise it because he possesses sacred speech which is acquired in a supernatural state realised in the sun.

The next group of stanzas (ṚV 1.164.11-15) presents the poet as one who elaborates in more detail knowledge about the temporal structure of the world presented in ṚV 1.164.2-3 and who uses the chariot metaphor to understand its paradoxical nature.

ṚV 1.164.11

duvā́daśāraṃ nahí táj járāya várvarti cakrám pári dyā́m ṛtásya |
ā́ putrā́ agne mithunā́so átra saptá śatā́ni viṃśatíś ca tasthuḥ ||

Twelve-spoked, the wheel of truth[161] ever rolls around of heaven – yet not to old age.
Upon it, o Agni, stand seven hundred twenty sons in pairs[162].

The composer again elaborates the concept of the world conceived in terms of a wheel. In terms of the seven hundred and twenty sons, nights and days are conceived (Geldner 1951, I, Jamison, Brereton 2014, Witzel, Gotō 2007). Thus the temporal dimension of the world is expressed. The wheel is called 'the wheel of truth' (*cakrám pári dyā́m ṛtásya*) because speech manifests in time. Creation is conceived in terms of giving the father a share in truth (ṚV 1.164.8). Reality manifests itself as truth and then time begins which is realised in the transformations of fire. These transformations of fire are conceived in the general model of reality transformation. The paradoxical nature of the temporal existence of the world is expressed by verse *a* where the composer states that the wheel rolls 'not to old age' (*nahí táj járāya*), which means that

[161] Jamison, Brereton (2014): '[= the Sun]'.
[162] Jamison, Brereton (2014): '[= the nights and days of the year]'.

although a living being get old, the world as such does not. This is because the world is a manifestation of unaging reality.

It seems that the intention of the composer is to imply that now the poet has access to the omniscience of those who are in the sun at zenith, described in the previous stanza (similarly to the poets described in ṚV 1.164.5). He knows what he should know and do. But he has still not realised this state as his experience. The vocative form *agne* (verse *c*) confirms that it is Agni who gives the answer to those who seek knowledge (ṚV 1.164.4).

ṚV 1.164.12

páñcapādam pitáraṃ dvā́daśākr̥tiṃ diváḥ āhuḥ páre árdhe purīṣíṇam |
átheme anyá úpare vicakṣaṇáṃ saptácakre ṣáḷara āhur árpitam ||

They speak of the father[163] with five feet[164] and twelve forms[165], the overflowing one in the upper half of heaven.
But these others speak of the far-gazing one[166] in the nearer[167] fixed on[168] with seven wheels[169] and six spokes[170].

Jamison, Brereton (2014) interpret the first hemistich as referring to the moon[171]. However, the concept of the moon is not elaborated much in the ṚV. Moreover, the word *púrīṣa*, 'overflowing', is used in the ṚV 10.27.21 in reference to the sun (*sū́ryasya br̥hatáḥ púrīṣāt*)[172]. In ṚV 6.49.6, it denotes Parjanya and Vāta who, conceived in terms of the bulls, quicken 'the watery outpourings', in ṚV 5.55.5, the Maruts, who create rain, are called *purīṣíṇaḥ* 'the overflowing ones' and in ṚV 10.65.9, Parjanya and Vāta are called similarly. Taking into account the Ṛgvedic cosmological model, I would argue that the composer, using the word *purīṣín* in reference to the father with five feet, wants to activate the concept of the sun filled with Soma as the source of rain. This would also agree with the interpretation of ṚV 1.164.9 where Agni is conceived in terms of the father who becomes the rising sun.

The father is presented as having five feet. In this way, everyday experience is again violated. The recipient is probably prompted to create the image of

163 Jamison, Brereton (2014): '[= the Moon]'.
164 Jamison, Brereton (2014): '[= the Seasons]'.
165 Jamison, Brereton (2014): '[= the months]'.
166 Jamison, Brereton (2014): '[= the Sun]'.
167 Jamison, Brereton (2014): '(half)'.
168 Jamison, Brereton (2014): '[= the chariot]'.
169 Jamison, Brereton (2014): '[= the Sun, Moon and visible planets]'.
170 Jamison, Brereton (2014): 'the seasons, in a different reckoning'.
171 Bergaigne (1963 [1878–83], II: 126) interprets the father as Aja Ekapād. He argues that one foot corresponds to the invisible world and four foots to cardinal directions.
172 For the meaning of the word *púrīṣa* see Renou (1960).

a bull or horse whose five feet may correspond to the sun's rays. It is also possible that the bull or horse's penis is conceived in terms of the fifth foot from which, in the blend, rain appears conceived in terms of semen and urine (Jurewicz 2010a[173]). If this interpretation is correct, this would mean that the composer blends the concept of a cow (ṚV 1.164.9-10) and a bull to express the extraordinary nature of the appearance of rain from the heated sun: it is conceived in terms of the appearance of milk from the udder and of semen or urine from the penis. The generic space of the conceptual network is the appearance of the symbol of light from the symbol of darkness.

Moreover, in later thought, the moon is seen as a gate to the sun (see chapter 5), so it seems that it is conceived as placed in the nearer half of the sky than the sun. This is contrary to the topology presented in this stanza according to which the father is in the upper half of the sky and 'the far-gazing one' (*vicakṣaṇá*)[174] is in the nearer half of the sky. So it rather seems that in this stanza, the composer wants to present two ways of understanding the cosmic function of the sun and the divisions of time and not the difference between the moon and the sun. It is possible to think that, in the first hemistich, the composer presents the sun as the source of Soma cognised in the supernatural cognition realised at the borderline sphere of the cosmos while, in the second hemistich, the sun is the seen seen in everyday cognition. My interpretation is confirmed in that the composer, in the first hemistich, elaborates the concept of an animal while, in the second, he has the concept of wheels which belong to the chariot being drawn by the animal. The logic of everyday experience implies that when a chariot moves away, we cannot see the animal which pulls it. In the blend, the sunrise is conceived in terms of a chariot ascending of which people can see only the back. The generic space is the image schema of SOURCE-PATH-GOAL.

ṚV 1.164.13

páñcāre cakré parivártamāne tásminn ā́ tasthur bhúvanāni víśvā |
tásya nā́kṣas tapyate bhū́ribhāraḥ sanā́d evá ná śīryate sánābhiḥ ||

In the five-spoked wheel[175] that rolls round – on that do all living beings take their stand.
Its axle does not become hot, though its load is heavy. From of old it, along with its nave, does not break apart.

---

[173] The metaphor RAIN IS SEMEN is also elaborated in the AV, see chapter 2.1.2.

[174] Jamison, Brereton (2014) interpret it as the sun, Witzel, Gotō (1997) accept following possibilities: the moon, the sun or constellation.

[175] Jamison, Brereton (2014): '[= the year]'.

The use of the compound *páñcāra* (verse *a*) evokes the compound *páñcapādam* which may imply that the composer now metonymically compresses the concepts of a chariot, its wheels and the animal that pulls it[176]. He uses the most abstract concept of a wheel to describe the borderline sphere of the cosmos. Verse *b* of this stanza (*yátremā́ víśvā bhúvanā́dhi tasthúḥ*) is almost the same as verse *d* of ṚV 1.164.2 (*tásminn ā́ tasthur bhúvanāni víśvā*) and the general meaning is the same: the world is conceived in terms of a revolving wheel within which are all living beings. The main difference lies in that now the poet knows the nature of the world conceived in the previous stanza in simple terms of a cow with its calf and an animal yoked to a chariot.

In the second hemistich, the composer transforms everyday experience. He states that although the chariot (the concept of which is metonymically evoked by the concept of a wheel) has a very heavy burden and its way is very long, its axle does not become heated and it does not break. In this way, he can express the internally contradictory nature of reality within the frames of world and time.

ṚV 1.164.14

sánemi cakrám ajáraṃ ví vāvr̥ta uttānā́yāṃ dáśa yuktā́ vahanti |
sū́ryasya cákṣū rájasaiti ā́vr̥taṃ tásminn ā́rpitā bhúvanāni víśvā ||

Along with its felly, the unaging wheel[177] has turned away. Harnessed to the outstretched[178], ten[179] draw it.
Covered over, the eye of the Sun moves through the airy realm. All living beings are fixed upon it.

Jamison, Brereton (2014) interpret the word *ví vr̥t-* (verse *a*) as 'turned away'[180], but in its other usages in the ṚV they interpret this verb as conveying the meaning of unrolling (ad ṚV 5.48.3d, 8.14.5b, 8.103.2c) or rolling out (ad ṚV 6.8.3c) or separately (ad ṚV 1.166.9). The intention of the composer is to present the beginnings of time in terms of the wheel which begins to revolve. The word *uttānā́yām* (verse *b*) evokes the concept of the kindling of

176 Metonymies CHARIOT FOR THE ANIMAL WHICH DRAGS IT (OBJECT OF ACTION FOR AGENT) and WHEEL FOR A CHARIOT (PART FOR WHOLE). The first metonymy is not recognised by Radden, Kövecses (1999).

177 Jamison, Brereton (2014): '[= the night Sun]'.

178 Jamison, Brereton (2014): '(yoke-pole) [= the airy realm?]'.

179 Jamison, Brereton (2014): '(horses)'.

180 Witzel, Gotō (2007): 'Mitsamt der Felge hat sich das Rad, ohne sich abzunutzen, (immer) gedreht'. In ṚV 1.164.11 the verb *vr̥t-* (without *ví*) is used in the same context of revolving wheel.

fire (ṚV 2.10.3, 3.29.2); within the frames of this conceptualisation, kindling sticks are conceived in terms of the legs of a women during delivery[181]. The word *dáśa*, 'ten', used without the noun, can activate the concept of the ten fingers of men who kindle fire (ṚV 3.23.3) or prepare Soma (ṚV 5.43.4, 9.15.8, 9.46.6, 9.61.7). At the same time, the participle *yuktá* evokes the concept of the horses which draw the chariot. The input spaces of the blend are the concepts of reality, the concept of a temporal cosmos, the concepts of a chariot, of kindling fire, of pressing of Soma and the general domain of Procreation. In the blend, the morning sacrifice, during which fire is kindled and Soma is prepared, creates or supports manifestation of reality in time which is conceived in terms of a revolving wheel. The generic space is the image schema of SELF-MOTION.

Verse *c* presents the eye of the sun which goes along the space and is 'covered over' (*ā́vṛta*). This participle is used five times more in the ṚV, two times in reference to Indra and one to Agni enveloped with power (*táviṣībhir ā́vṛtam*, ṚV 1.51.2b, 8.88.2a, 3.3.5c), one time to Indra's thunderbolt (*vájra*) identified with Soma covered with milk (*pári góbhir ā́vṛtam*, ṚV 6.47.27c) and one time to Soma (*pári góbhir ā́vṛtam*, 9.86.27c). Interestingly enough, the concept of space is evoked in three cases: in ṚV 1.51.2b, Indra is qualified as *antarikṣaprā́*, in 8.88.2a, as *dyukṣá* while in ṚV 9.86.27d, Soma that is covered with milk is presented as being 'on the third back in the luminous realm of heaven' (*tṛtī́ye pṛṣṭhé ádhi rocané diváḥ*). If the recipient of ṚV 1.164.14 activates those usages, he would understand that the eye of the sun is full of power, that its essence is Agni and Soma and that it can be conceived as Indra with his thunderbolt (*vájra*) when he, having drunk Soma, stands up to fight with Vṛtra (see Jurewicz 2010a: 341–343). Moreover, the concept of covering implies that either the sun cannot see clearly[182] or men cannot see it as the power of the sun and the space through which it goes hide its essence. This would confirm my interpretation of ṚV 1.164.12. The solar-rainy transformations of fire, described in the first hemistich of this stanza, are hidden and in everyday cognition people can only see the eye of the sun, i.e. its shining form in the sky presented in the second hemistich as the 'far-gazing one' (*vicakṣaṇá*)[183].

In verse *d*, the composer again presents all beings which live in the world and time; now they are presented as fixed in the eye of the sun (*tásminn ā́rpitā bhúvanāni víśvā*). The participle *árpita* is used in ṚV 1.164.12d in

---

[181] This image is used in ṚV 10.72, see section 1.5.

[182] Seeing is the prototypical feature of the sun in the ṚV.

[183] It is possible that the word *vicakṣaṇá* in the verse *vicaksanā́d*... which should be recited by the deceased (see chapter 5.1) refers to this form of the sun.

reference to the far-gazing one in the nearer half of the sky which is fixed on the chariot with seven wheels and six spokes. It is possible that in this way the composer wants to imply that all beings are fixed upon the everyday movement of the sun because they cannot get through space to the sun as the source of Soma.

We can now conclude that the poet has understood the temporal manifestation of reality conceived in terms of the chariot-metaphor presented in ṚV 1.164.2-3. In these stanzas, the concept of seven seers is metonymically activated and now the composer explains their role within the structure of the world:

ṚV 1.164.15

sākaṃjā́nāṃ saptátham āhur ekajáṃ ṣáḷ íd yamā́ ṛ́ṣayo devajā́ íti |
téṣām iṣṭā́ni víhitāni dhāmaśá sthātré rejante víkṛtāni rūpaśáḥ ||

They speak of the seventh of the same who are born at the same time as the one born alone, saying 'the twins, the seers of the gods, are only six'.
What[184] are desired by these[185] are distributed according to their spheres. While (the one)[186] stands still, the ones varies in appearance[187] quiver.

In the first hemistich, the composer of the hymn evokes the same concept as in ṚV 10.72.8-9 (see section 1.5). Its composer mentions eight sons of Aditi, with seven she went to the gods while one was born from a dead egg and is destined to be born and die repeatedly. In ṚV 1.164.15, reality is conceived in a reverse topology: seven sons of Aditi are born. Of them six are distributed according to their wish and acquire forms in movement while the seventh does not move and is a stable principle of everything which moves (verses *c–d*)[188]. Jamison, Brereton (2014), and Witzel, Gotō (1997) interpret them as the seven stars of Ursa Maior, called the Seven Seers, of which the polar star does not move. It is possible to interpret this concept more generally as referring to the whole construction of the world which is visible in the structure of Ursa Maior identified with seven seers. Therefore, it may also be assumed that the one which does not move is the one which supports the six realms of the world (ṚV 1.164.6, 10).

[184] Jamison, Brereton (2014): '(places)'.
[185] Jamison, Brereton (2014): '[= the seven seers]'.
[186] Jamison, Brereton (2014): '[= the pole star]'.
[187] Jamison, Brereton (2014): '[= the stars of the Seven Seers]'.
[188] In the same way, the poets of the ṚV play with the division into four of which either one fourth part is hidden (see ṚV 10.90, see section 1.3), or three parts are hidden (see ṚV 1.164.45, section 1.6, see also Bhattacharya 1978)

The next group of stanzas (ṚV 1.164.16-22) presents the nature of cognition which confirms the theoretical knowledge of the poet:

ṚV 1.164.16

stríyaḥ satī́s tā́m̐ u me puṃsá āhuḥ páśyad akṣaṇvā́n ná ví cetad andháḥ |
kavír yáḥ putráḥ sá īm ā́ ciketa yás tā́ vijānā́t sá pitúṣ pitā́sat ||

Though they[189] are women, yet they speak as men to me. He who has eyes sees; the blind man does not differentiate.
One who is a poet, a son[190], perceives him. One who recognises these[191], he will be the father of his father.

Some scholars[192] interpret the multiple female subjects (verse *a*) as Pleiades. According to the interpretation proposed by Elizarenkova (1989) and O'Flaherty (1981), the androgynic character of the creative principle is expressed here: the females as mothers of the males become the males. Notwithstanding the possibility of their final identity, the general meaning of the verse seems to be that true knowledge requires the suspension of everyday knowledge: what seems to be female should be understood as male. The cognising agent, who uses everyday knowledge to understand what is beyond, is conceived in terms of a blind man (verse *b*).

In the second hemistich, the composer states that the poet who is the son can realise true knowledge and will then become a father of his father. The concept of poet activates the concept of poets described in ṚV 1.164.5 who are an example for the activity of the protagonist of the hymn. Since many times in the ṚV Agni is called poet, the recipient may presume that the protagonist of the hymn is expected to realise his identity with it in his supernatural cognition. The analysis of the other metaphors used in this stanza confirm this presumption.

The concept of father has already been used in the hymn. In ṚV 1.164.8, the father is presented as having a share in truth thanks to the mother (in terms of which speech is conceived) and, thanks to this, reality can manifest itself in the world. In ṚV 1.164.12, the concept of a father with five legs is introduced, in terms of which, as I have argued, the sun cognised in supernatural vision is conceived. Now this concept refers to a particular man who can undertake cognition of the world and, if he realises it, he will be called 'the father of the father'. It is worth adding that in the same way Agni is qualified

[189] Jamison, Brereton (2014): '[= the Kṛttikas, the Pleiades]'.
[190] Jamison, Brereton (2014): '(poet's)'.
[191] Jamison, Brereton (2014): '(women)'.
[192] Thieme (1987), Witzel, Gotō (2007), Jamison, Brereton (2014).

in ṚV 6.16.35[193], so the recipient may assume that man in his cognition becomes Agni.

As has been already mentioned, the relationship between the teacher and the pupil is conceived in terms of the relationship between the father and the son in the ṚV (Jurewicz 2010a: 249 ff.[194]). In ṚV 1.164.16, the pupil is conceived in terms of the son who, when knows the right answer, becomes the father of his father. In this way, the composer implies that in order to gain knowledge about the origins of the world, one should frame oneself within the traditional frames of teaching which is the only way to learn the sacred speech. The possibility to surpass one's teacher, implied by verse *d*, is granted by knowledge which goes beyond the scope of the knowledge taught by the teacher.

However, as also mentioned, the concepts of father and son are used to conceive the ontological relationship between aspects of reality. Within the frames of this conceptualisation, Agni is the father. Its cosmic manifestations within which it is born are conceived in terms of the son. In microscale, Agni manifests itself in men to cognise its identity with its unmanifest aspect thanks to ritual action during which men reach the sun and get omniscience there.

Taking this into account, the second hemistich of the stanza can be interpreted as activating this conceptualisation: the poet, who realises his identity with Agni, will become Agni's father. Then he will be able to create the manifest aspect of his own father in microscale. He will also know the answer to the question asked in ṚV 1.164.4 about the origins of the world. It is worth mentioning that according to ṚV 1.164.8-9, the father is born from the mother. As has been argued, Aditi is conceived in terms of the mother who is identified with speech. Thus the recipient may understand that the poet gains his supernatural cognition thanks to speech. Thus he will have 'share in truth'. The gaining of cognition is conceived in terms of being born.

ṚV 1.164.17

aváḥ páreṇa pará enā̆vareṇa padā̆ vatsám bíbhratī gaúr úd asthāt |
sā̆ kadrī́cī káṃ svid árdham párāgāt kúva svit sūte nahí yūthé antáḥ ||

Below the upper[195], above the lower here[196], the cow[197] carrying her calf[198] has stood up by her foot.
In which direction is she? Towards which side did she go away? Where does she give birth, for it is not within the fold?

[193] ṚV 6.16.35: *gárbhe mātúḥ pitúṣ pitā̆ vididyutānó akṣáre* | *sī́dann ṛtásya yónim ā̆* ||
[194] It is elaborated in AVŚ 10.5, see chapter 2.2.1.
[195] Jamison, Brereton (2014): '(realm)'.
[196] Jamison, Brereton (2014): '[= at the horizon]'.
[197] Jamison, Brereton (2014): '[=Dawn]'.
[198] Jamison, Brereton (2014): '[=the Sun]'.

In verse *a*, the composer creates the image of two halves of the world: 'the upper' (*pará*) is the sky and 'the lower' (*ávara*) is the earth. In verse *b*, the composer presents a cow which stands up. Jamison, Brereton (2014) interpret that it stands up by her foot, but it is also possible to understand that she carries her calf with her foot (Geldner 1951, Elizarenkova 1989, Witzel, Gotō 2007). The image of a cow which carries a calf with her foot breaks the logic of everyday experience, but allows the composer in the blend to create the image of the *axis mundi* (conceived in terms of cow's leg) with the sun on its top (conceived in terms of a calf). In the same way, the structure of reality is conceived in the model of The Wave Of Honey (ṚV 4.58.1). Its composer evokes the image of a baby to conceive of the sun as linked by the umbilical cord to its mother evoked *via* the concept of the sea (*samudrá*). In terms of the umbilical cord, the *axis mundi* is conceived (Jurewicz 2010a: 230–231)[199].

In the second hemistich, the composer asks questions about the place the cow went to give birth to its child. In this way, the composer presents the lack of knowledge of the poet about sacred speech. In terms of a calf which is not born in the fold, presumably that of the poet, manifestation of speech which cannot be acquired by men is conceived. The scenario of the general domain of Finding The Hidden implies that the cow has left its footprints. The poet is in the same situation as the poets described in ṚV 1.164.5: he knows that the cow with its calf is somewhere and he has to follow its tracks in order to find it.

The blend consists of four input spaces. The first two of them, the concepts of cow with its calf and of a pregnant mother with her child linked to her by the umbilical cord, endow the third input space, which is the cosmos with the *axis mundi*, with topology. The input space of cow activates the next input space which is cognition verbalised in speech (SPEECH IS A COW). The next input space, the general domain of Finding The Hidden, enriches the blend with the concept of a path made of cow's tracks. The generic space is the image schema of SOURCE-PATH-GOAL.

ṚV 1.164.18

aváḥ páreṇa pitáraṃ yó asya anuvéda pará enā̆vareṇa |
kavīyámānaḥ ká ihá prá vocad devám mánaḥ kúto ádhi prájātam ||

[199] We can see that the Ṛgvedic composers had a great ability not only to create images, but also to treat them dynamically. Thus they could convey rich meaning with relatively small number of crucial concepts. The concept of a cow can be used as the source domain for the sky in the zoomorphic model and for the earth in the Wave Of Honey model depending on the needs of the meaning the composers wanted to express.

> Below the upper[200], above the lower here is he[201] who knows his father.
> Showing himself to be a poet, who will proclaim this here: from when has divine thought has been born?

The topology of the image created by the first hemistich reflects the topology of the world presented in the previous stanza as the two halves of the world are mentioned. The son is presented as being between them, below the upper half of the world (i.e. below the sky) and above the lower half (i.e. the earth). As I have argued (see above, ṚV 1.164.16), the concept of the son is the source domain to conceive of the cosmic manifestations of Agni and a pupil who looks for supernatural cognition. We could say that the poet now realises its situation in the cosmos and its cognitive possibilities.

In verses *c–d*, a person called *kavīyámāna*, one who behaves like a poet[202], is presented as being able to answer the questions about the origins of divine thought (*devám mánaḥ*). This qualification can refer to the poets described in ṚV 1.164.5, but also to Agni who is called poet in the ṚV many times. Moreover, since other gods are called *kaví* in the ṚV, the recipient may understand that a man called *kavīyámāna* realises his identity with all the godly manifestations of Agni.

The recipient may presume that a person called *kavīyámāna* is an example for the poet whose activity he is able to follow.

ṚV 1.164.19

> *yé arvā́ñcas tā́m̐ u párāca āhur yé párāñcas tā́m̐ u arvā́ca āhuḥ |*
> *índraś ca yā́ cakráthuḥ soma tā́ni dhurā́ ná yuktā́ rájaso vahanti ||*

> What[203] this way – as they say that those[204] away; what[205] away – they say those[206] this way.
> O Soma and Indra,[207] that you two have done, these draw[208] like[209] harnessed to the yoke-pole of the airy realm.

[200] Jamison, Brereton (2014): '(realm)'.
[201] Jamison, Brereton (2014): '[= the Sun]'.
[202] O'Flaherty (1981): 'with such mystical insight', Witzel, Gotō (2007): 'wer verkünder [das] hier, sich als Seher erweisend', Elizarenkova (1989): 'projavljaja sebja prozorlivcem'.
[203] Jamison, Brereton (2014): '(chariots [sacrifices?] come]'.
[204] Jamison, Brereton (2014): '(will go)'.
[205] Jamison, Brereton (2014): '(chariots go)'.
[206] Jamison, Brereton (2014): '(will come)'.
[207] Jamison, Brereton (2014): '(the deeds)'.
[208] Jamison, Brereton (2014): '(those chariots)'.
[209] Jamison, Brereton (2014): '(horses)'.

In the first hemistich, the composer again implies that knowledge of the divine mind implies the reversal of the everyday logic: what seems to be near is far away while what seems to be far away is near.

In verse *c*, the composer presents the deeds done by Indra and Soma in terms of horses which are harnessed to the pole of a chariot and draw the chariot. In ṚV 6.72.01, the great deeds of Indra and Soma are a creation of the morning. In ṚV 8.59.6, Indra together with Varuṇa are presented as creating places which are seen by the poet thanks to his heat (*tápas*) created during sacrifice. If the recipient evokes these concepts, he may understand the deeds of Indra and Soma as a creation of the sunrise that provide a possibility for supernatural cognition. These deeds drag men as horses drag men sitting on a chariot. The fact that the pole of the horse can be interpreted as the *axis mundi* strengthens the concept of the mental journey up to zenith. The recipient may presume that now the poet is mentally dragged by the deeds performed *in illo tempore* by Indra and Soma. And this journey is described in the following stanzas with use of the source domain of climbing a tree:

ṚV 1.164.20-22

duvā́ suparṇā́ sayújā sákhāyā samānáṃ vṛkṣám pári ṣasvajāte
táyor anyáḥ píppalaṃ svādú átti ánaśnann anyó abhí cākaśīti (20)
yátrā suparṇā́ amṛ́tasya bhāgám ánimeṣaṃ vidáthābhisváranti
inó víśvasya bhúvanasya gopā́ḥ sá mā dhī́raḥ pā́kam átrā́ viveśa (21)
yásmin vṛkṣé madhuádaḥ suparṇā́ niviśánte súvate cā́dhi víśve
tásyéd āhuḥ píppalaṃ svādú ágre tán nón naśad yáḥ pitáraṃ ná véda (22)

Two well-feathered[210], yokemates and companions, embrace the same tree.
Of those two the one eats the sweet fig; the other, not eating, keeps watch. (20)
Where the well-feathered[211], never blinking, cry out for a share of immortality and ritual distributions,
here the forceful herdsman of the whole living world, the insightful one, has entered me, the naïve one. (21)
Just that tree on which all the honey-eating, well-feathered ones settle and give birth,
they say, has the sweet fig as its top. He who does not know the father will not reach up to that. (22)

I have already analysed these stanzas (Jurewicz 2010a: 304–305), so here I will only repeat my main conclusions and show how they form a part of the whole hymn[212]. In terms of the sweet fig (ṚV 1.164.20c), the sun filled

[210] Jamison, Brereton (2014): '(birds)'.
[211] Jamison, Brereton (2014): '(birds)'.
[212] For interpretation of these stanzas as the poetic competition, see Johnson (1976).

with Soma is conceived, in terms of tree, the *axis mundi*. The bird which eats the fig is a man who realises the omniscient state thanks to the solar Soma, the bird which does not eat, is a man who does not cognise and only watches (ṚV 1.164.20cd)[213]. Cognition is conceived in terms of climbing a tree which agrees with the earlier images of the men rising up on a chariot. The concept of birds which, without blinking, cry for the share in immortality and ritual distributions (ṚV 1.164.21ab) are the source domain for the gods who eat the sacrificial oblations. Among them is Agni conceived in terms of a herdsman (ṚV 1.164.21c[214]). The birds, which are settled on the tree, eat the sweat fig and give birth (ṚV 1.164.22ab), are men who realise supernatural cognition in ritual.

Cognition of Agni is conceived in terms of its entering into the poet (ṚV 1.164.21d). Since other Ṛgvedic gods are conceived in terms of herdsmen, the recipient can understand that, together with the knowledge of Agni, the poet gains knowledge of all gods. In ṚV 1.164.22cd, the composer states that a man who does not know the father will not reach the sun. The context clearly implies that Agni is conceived in terms of a father. If the recipient evokes the conceptualisation of Agni in terms of a tree, he may construe the image of a fiery tree. Then cognition of Agni is seen as a reflexive activity: Agni leads men so that they may know it[215]. This agrees with the implication of ṚV 1.164 according to which the poet looks for Agni.

The next two stanzas (ṚV 1.164.23-24) describe creation of the sacred speech:

ṚV 1.164.23

yád gāyatré ádhi gāyatrám ā́hitaṃ traíṣṭubhād vā traíṣṭubhaṃ nirátakṣata |
yád vā jágaj jágati ā́hitam padáṃ yá ít tád vidús té amṛtatvám ānaśuḥ ||

How *gāyatrī* (track)[216] is based upon a *gāyatrī* (hymn) or how a *triṣṭubh* track[217] was fashioned out of a *triṣṭubh* (hymn),
or how the *jagat* track[218] is based on the *jagat*[219] (hymn) – only those who know this have reached immortality.

---

[213] Later tradition conceives in terms of this bird someone who is beyond subjective-objective cognition and does not need Soma to remain in eternal happiness.

[214] Agni as the herdsman, see e.g. ṚV 1.1.8.

[215] Such a conceptualisation of the sacred knowledge is the reason why Vedic schools are called 'branches of a tree' (*śākhā*).

[216] Jamison, Brereton (2014): '[= *gāyatrī* line]'.

[217] Jamison, Brereton (2014): '[= *triṣṭubh* line]'.

[218] Jamison, Brereton (2014): '[= line]'.

[219] Jamison, Brereton (2014): '[= *jagatī*]'.

The subject of the activities described in the stanza is not specified, but the recipient may infer on the basis of the context that the composer describes the seers who create sacred speech (as in ṚV 10.130). It is worth noting that the composer of the hymn does not use the technical words for the three kinds of stanzas, i.e. *gāyatrī́*, *triṣṭúbh* and *jágatī*, but is more general[220]. The word *gāyatrá* generally means a song in the ṚV, the word *traíṣṭubha* is used twice (ṚV 2.43.1 and 5.29.6), in both cases together with the *arká*-speech[221]. The word *jágat* is mostly used in a general sense of 'a moving one'. In the ṚV 1.57.7 and in 6.72.4, *jágatī* is used in its literal meaning of 'a moving female'[222]. It is also worth mentioning that the meaning of *padá*, which is 'verse or line', is not attested in the ṚV; this word is mainly used in the sense of a track or footprint, of a step and, metaphorically, of a place. As the last member of the compounds, it means 'foot' (see above, ṚV 1.164.12 and below, ṚV 1.164.24, 41).

The composer elaborates two main input spaces of his blend: that of a cow that went away and left its footprints and that of various kinds of sacred speech. In the blend, the seers find the footprints of cow: having found one footprint, they can find another. The footprints already exist because they were made *in illo tempore* when reality manifested itself for the first time. It seems that they are conceived as having different shapes. The seers find the footprints in the shape of *gāyatrá*, *triṣṭúbh* and *jágat* and thus it is as if they create the footprints for themselves. The logic of the input space of a lost cow implies that, in this way, the seers finally learn the whole of sacred speech. In verse *b*, the blend is enriched with the input space of carving in terms of which creation of hymns is conceived in the ṚV. The generic space is the concept of the appearance of the symbol of light from the symbol of darkness.

Verse *d* presents those who know the origins of sacred speech and thanks to that they became immortal. These are probably the poets described in ṚV 1.164.5.

---

220 *Gāyatrī́* appears in ṚV 10.14.16, 10.130.4, *triṣṭúbh* appears in ṚV 8.7.1, 8.69.1, 9.97.35, 10.14.16, 10.130.5, *jágatī* in ṚV 10.130.5. Witzel, Gotō (2007): '*gāyatrī*sche (Fuss)', '*triṣṭubh*ische (Fuss)', '*Jagat*-Fuss'.

221 *traíṣṭubha* is used in ṚV 2.43.1 and 5.29.6.

222 In the later thought, the three metres mentioned in the stanza are connected with the gods and spheres of the world: *gāyatrī* is connected with the earth and Agni, *triṣṭubh* is connected with the space (ŚB 8.3.4.11), with Vayu and Indra (Eggeling 1894: 40, note 2), *jagatī* is connected with the sky and the sun (see Smith 1994). So the sequence in which the metres are mentioned iconically reflects the way of the rising sun.

ṚV 1.164.24

> *gāyatréṇa práti mimīte arkám arkéṇa sā́ma traíṣṭubhena vākám |*
> *vākéna vākám̐ dvipádā cátuṣpadā akṣáreṇa mimate saptá vā́ṇīḥ ||*
>
> By a song[223] one measures the chant; by the chant the melody; by the speech composed in *triṣṭubh*[224] the recitation;
> by two-footed and four-footed recitation the[225] recitation. By the syllable the seven voices assume their measure.

The subject of the stanza is again not specified, but the recipient may understand that the poet now understands the general rule for the creation of various kinds of sacred speech. This is the rule which he will have to obey to obtain supernatural knowledge.

As far as the composition of types of speech is concerned, a song (*gāyatrá*) creates a chant (*arká*), the chants (*arká*) compose the Sāman-chants and recitation (*vāká*) is composed by the speech called *traiṣṭubha* (verses *a–b*). It seems that the creation of these kinds of speech is again conceived in terms of following footprints: if the subject follows the footprint in the shape of the song, he creates the chant, if the subject follows the footprint in the shape of *triṣṭúbh*, he creates recitation. According to verse *c* recitation, conceived in terms of a two-footed being (*dvipád*) and a four-footed being (*cátuspad*), creates recitation; the recipient again may activate the image of following footprints in these shapes.

In the ṚV, the chant named by the word *arká* is specifically conceived. It is conceived as shining (*citrá*, ṚV 10.112.9) and, in ṚV 10.68.6, it is heated by fire. In ṚV 6.4.7, the word *arká* denotes flames of fire[226]. The power of the chant thus conceived destroys darkness (ṚV 3.31.11, 6.65.5, 10.68.6,9) and, in some stanzas, the composer create a blend which identifies the chant with the rays of the sun or the sun itself (ṚV 4.16.4, 4.56.2, 6.4.6, 9.97.31). So the intention of the composer of the present hymn is to create the image of a man who recites words which burn and thus causes the sunrise[227]. This powerful chant creates the Sāman-chant. In ṚV 10.99.2, the Sāman-chant is connected with lightning and the recipient may understand that thanks to its creation rain comes. The meaning of rain is confirmed in that the chant

---

223 Jamison, Brereton (2014): 'by the *gāyatrī* (track) [= line]'.
224 Jamison, Brereton (2014): 'by the *triṣṭubh* (track) [line] (one measures)'.
225 Jamison, Brereton (2014): '(full)'.
226 ṚV 6.4.7: *tuvā́m̐ hí mandrátamam arkaśokaír vavṛmáhe máhi naḥ śróṣi agne | índram̐ ná tvā śávasā devátā vāyúm pṛṇanti rā́dhasā nṛ́tamāḥ ||*
227 In this way, the creative activity of the Aṅgirases is conceived in ṚV 4.1, see Jurewicz (2010a).

(*arká*) is conceived in terms of water which is poured (ṚV 8.63.4) and, in ṚV 10.67.5, it is connected with the appearance of rain. In its *traíṣṭubha* form, sacred speech is qualified as two-footed and four-footed. Taking into account that living beings are usually conceived in the ṚV in this metonymic way, the recipient may evoke this concept and understand that they are created in recitation: when two-footed recitation is performed men are created and with four-footed recitation animals[228]. It is worth adding that ṚV 1.164.23 uses the word *jágat*, 'a moving one', in the same verse (*c*) which may confirm that now, in ṚV 1.164.24c, the composer wants the recipient to think about moving living beings (for the next interpretation of verses *c–d* see below, ṚV 1.164.41).

The expression *saptá vā́ṇīḥ* evokes the situation in the morning described in ṚV 10.164.3 when men and cattle cry out seeing the sun. As we can see, the composer again presents the same content as in the beginning of the hymn, but places it in a context which allows the recipient to understand that creative and cosmic changes performed by the seers and the poets are transformations of sacred speech. Since, as I have already mentioned, kindling of fire and clarification of Soma are conceived in the ṚV as being created by seven voices (kindling of fire: ṚV 3.7.1; clarification of Soma: ṚV 8.59.3, 9.103.3, 9.104.4), the recipient can also evoke these concepts and understand that the cosmic cycle implied by the stanza begins with the morning ritual. It is possible that phonetic similarity between the verbs *mā-*, 'to measure' and *mā-/mī-*, 'to bellow' is played here too and that man is conceived in terms of a bellowing bull.

The next stanza simultaneously presents the creation of the world with the aid of sacred speech and the magnificent outcome of its knowledge:

ṚV 1.164.25

jágatā síndhuṃ diví astabhāyad rathaṃtaré sū́riyam páry apaśyat |
gāyatrásya samídhas tisrá āhus táto mahnā́ prá ririce mahitvā́ ||
By the *jagat*[229] he buttressed the river in heaven; in the rathantara (chant), he watched over the Sun.
They say that there are three kindling sticks[230] belonging to the song[231]. By this greatness it[232] has passed beyond those in greatness.

---

[228] For interpretation of this hemistich, see also below, analysis of ṚV 1.164.45.
[229] Jamison, Brereton (2014): '[= *jagatī*] (stanza)'.
[230] Jamison, Brereton (2014): '[= three lines in a *gāyatrī* stanza]'.
[231] Jamison, Brereton (2014): 'to the *gāyatrī* (stanza)'.
[232] Jamison, Brereton (2014): '[= the *gāyatrī* stanza]'.

In verse *a*, the composer presents a subject which buttresses the river in the sky with aid of *jágat*. Activation of the literal meaning of the word *jágat* implies movement of the subject and the recipient may understand that the subject in his recitation reaches the sky. O'Flaherty (1981) reminds us that it is in this way that Indra's activity is evoked in the ṚV when he is presented as freeing waters by killing Vṛtra. Thus the composer would include the model of Indra's Fight With Vṛtra with its image schematic meaning of growing in terms of which the sunrise, which results in rain, is conceived (see Jurewicz 2010a).

The creation of a river is fully justified in the context of the model of Indra's Fight With Vṛtra. Moreover, the word *síndhu* is used many times in the ṚV in the context of the clarification of Soma by reference to water with which it is mixed[233]. In ṚV 4.22.8a, the sweet stalk of Soma is presented as being squeezed like a river (*pipīḷé aṃśúr mádiyo ná síndhur*). If the recipient activates these usages of the word *síndhu*, he will understand that, in his ride up to the sky, the subject creates the solar Somic source[234]. The recipient may create an image of a river the sources of which are in the sky and which flows downwards to the earth and thus becomes the *axis mundi*.

The word *rathaṃtará* in reference to the chant is used once more in ṚV 1.181.1 where it is brought by Vasiṣṭha 'from the flashing Founder and from Savitar and Viṣṇu' (*dhātúr dyútānāt savitúś ca víṣṇo*)[235]. But if the recipient activates the literal meaning of this compound, which is 'a chariot which goes fast' (Grassmann 1999[1873–1875]: 1139), he would see the conceptual consistency of verse *b*: the subject who recites sacred speech in the shape of *rathaṃtará* is conceived in terms of someone who rides a chariot in the sky and thus can watch the sun and the whole world. In both cases, the recipient may activate the input space of following footprints and understand recitation in these terms. When the subject follows the footprints in the shape of *jágat*, he goes to the sky and when he follows the footprints in the shape of *rathaṃtará*, he circulates the sky.

The word *gāyatrá* in verse *c* should also be interpreted more generally as a song than as the *Gāyatrī*-stanza[236]. The concept of *samídh* evokes the image of fire and the intention of the composer is to create a blend within

---

[233] In genitive form: ṚV 9.12.3, 9.14.1, 9.21.3, 9.39.4, 9.50.4, 9.69.7, 9.73.2, 9.80.5, 9.85.10, 43.

[234] The phrase *síndhur ná kṣódah* is used in order to express the vehemence of the light of fire (ṚV 1.65.6b, 1.66.10a) or of the dawn (ṚV 1.92.12b)

[235] In the same way, the Bṛhat – chant and the hot milk are brought for the Pravargya in ṚV 10.181.2-3.

[236] Jamison, Brereton (2014): interpret kindling-sticks as 'three lines in a *gāyatrī* stanza'. Witzel, Gotō (2007) generally: 'Das Gāyatrische habe drei Stück Brennholz', Elizarenkova (1989): 'w (razmere) gayatrī', Geldner (1951, I): 'das Gāyatri(versmass)'.

the frames of which singing of a song and the kindling of fire are identified. This blend opens the way to the later explanations of links between the *Gāyatrī*-stanza and fire in ŚB 6.1.15 where Agni, called *gāyatrá*, is presented as sitting at the back of the earth (see chapter 3.2.2). This link is already attested in ṚV 10.130.4.

Verse *d* presents a subject who surpasses (presumably everything) with his greatness and might (*táto mahnā́ prá ririce mahitvā́*). In the ṚV, it is Indra who is most often presented as going beyond the elements of the manifest aspect with his might (ṚV 1.61.9, 1.102.7, 3.46.3, 6.21.2, 6.24.3, 6.30.1, 8.88.5, 10.89.11). Moreover, the model of Indra's Fight With Vṛtra is used to conceive the sacrificial situation of man who identified himself with Indra (Jurewicz 2010a: 353a, Whitaker 2011). So it can be assumed that in the second hemistich of ṚV 1.164.25, the composer, in a concise way, evokes the ritual situation. In verse *c*, he evokes the kindling of fire which should be accompanied with singing and, in verse *d*, he evokes the results of sacrifice thanks to which the sacrificer mentally realises the state of Indra.

In this way, the composer introduces the ritual context which is necessary not only to understand the mystery of the world, but to experience it as an agent of cosmic and cognitive processes. There are two accounts which imply that the ultimate subject of this stanza (and, possibly, the previous one) is Agni. Indra is the form under which Agni acts in the world (Jurewicz 2010a: 360 ff.). Agni is also presented as surpassing the might of the sky and becoming the king of living beings (ṚV 1.59.5). So the recipient may understand that the final aim of ritual is realisation of the poet's identity with Agni.

As Houben (2000a) has convincingly shown, the next stanzas of the hymn can be interpreted as relating to the Pravargya ritual. Jamison, Brereton (2014: 349) also refer to Mahāvrata ritual as the another possible context of the hymn. My interpretation will supplement their interpretation in that I will try to show how ritual activity is supposed to be accompanied with mental transformations without which the ritual is meaningless. In other words, the ritual is the external manifestation of what happens inside the sacrificer. Mentally he is in the sun at the borderline sphere of the cosmos where he participates in reality manifest in speech and time. Using the metaphors of the hymn, he rides on a chariot and finds a cow with its calf.

The next group of stanzas (ṚV 1.164.26-36) presents the moment when the poet begins to perform his own cognition and to realise a supernatural state. As I have already stated, the structure of the hymn agrees with the structure of other Ṛgvedic hymns which in the beginning present the state of affairs cognised by the primeval poets and which should be known by the protagonist of the hymn (e.g. 4.58, 6.1, see also AVŚ 2.1, chapter 2.4).

ṚV 1.164.26

úpa hvaye sudúghāṃ dhenúm etā́ṃ suhásto godhúg utá dohad enām |
śréṣṭhaṃ savā́ṃ savitā́ sāviṣan no abhī́ddho gharmás tád u ṣú prá vocam ||

I summon this milk-cow giving good milk, and deft-handed milker will milk her. Savitar will impel the most excellent impetus in us. The *gharma* pot has been heated: this I shall proclaim.

Since the composer of the hymn elaborates the concept of cow as the source domain of speech, the recipient can understand that the poet has reached the state when he is able to cognise it. This is expressed in terms of calling a cow (verse *a*).

In verse *b*, a dexterous milker is presented who is supposed to milk a cow. As Houben (2000a) points out the word *suhásta* refers to the Adhvaryu. I would like to draw attention to the fact that in several places the word *suhásta* (or *suhástya*) is used in the context of the pressing of Soma: ten fingers are conceived in terms of the dexterous slaughterers (in the sense of butcher, but Indologists use the word 'slaughterer' in this case) of Soma (ṚV 5.43.4, 5.43.4, 9.46.4, 9.97.37, 9.107.21, 10.30.2). Cognition is conceived in terms of milking a cow and of clarification of Soma, so the recipient may evoke this concept too and understand that the poet begins to cognise sacred speech.

The concept of the beginning of cognition is also evoked in verse *c* where Savitar is asked to drive the process. Savitar is the embodiment of the impelling force of the morning light and the rising sun and, in ṚV 3.62.10, is asked to impel the inspired thoughts of the poets. Moreover, the concept of the appearance of the morning light is conceived in the ṚV as the moment when people are able to cognise (see Jurewicz 2010a: 109 ff.)

The word *gharmá* (verse *d*) may not merely refer to a real pot heated on fire and filled with milk (metonymy CONTENT FOR CONTAINER/CONTAINER FOR CONTENT[237]). As I have shown, cognition is conceived in terms of the general domain of Cleansing By Heat in the ṚV; the experiential ground for this conceptualisation is the heating influence of Soma (see Jurewicz 2010a: 193–194). The word *gharmá* is used in ṚV 10.67.7, in the compound *gharmásveda*, in reference to the Aṅgirases conceived in terms of sweating boars. Their cognition is conceived in terms of the boiling of milk which overflows the pot, so sweat, conceived in terms of milk, is the external sign of their cognition (see Jurewicz 2010a: 268, 382–383).

In this way, the composer of the hymn enriches the conceptual network with the input space of ritual which actually takes place. In the blend, the

[237] Radden, Kövecses (1999: 41).

ritual activity has two dimensions, an external one and an internal cognitive one. As Sweetser (2000) and Sorensen (2007) have shown, such ritual blends make ritual meaningful. Within the blend created by the composer of ṚV 1.164, a cow which is milked corresponds to speech appearing in the mind of the poet, while the heating of the pot corresponds to his cognitive activity which externally manifests itself in his sweating. The generic space is the concept of the appearance of the symbol of light from the symbol of darkness.

ṚV 1.164.27

hiṅkṛṇvatī́ vasupátnī vásūnāṃ vatsám ichántī mánasābhi ā́gāt |
duhā́m aśvíbhyām páyo aghniyéyáṃ sā́ vardhatām mahaté saúbhagāya ||

Making the sound him, the good-mistress of gods, seeking her calf, has come near through[238] thinking.
Let this inviolable cow give milk to the Aśvins. Let her increase for our great good fortune.

That the description also refers to cognition is confirmed in that the cow comes thanks to the thought of the poet. It is worth noting that the scenario of the relationship between the cow and its calf is reversed in comparison with ṚV 1.164.9c as it is now the cow which bellows at its calf and looks for it. I will now reconstruct the full scenario of this source domain as follows: 1. a cow leaves a calf, 2. a calf runs after it, 3. both are lost, 4. men look for them following their footprints, 5. they find a calf, 6. a cow will come hearing its bellowing. The next input spaces of the conceptual network are the appearance of the morning light, kindling fire and cognition which can be verbalised in the sacred speech. In the blend, all the processes are identified and conceived in terms of relationship between a cow and its calf. The generic space of the blend is the appearance of the symbol of light from the symbol of darkness.

Within the frames of this conceptualisation, the appearance of the dawn (DAWN IS A COW) and the kindling of fire is conceived in terms of the separation of a cow from its calf. The appearance of the dawn allows man to discern the sky from the earth. The sunrise, caused by kindling of fire, is conceived in terms of a calf running after the cow; it is implied that both a cow and a calf leave their footprints and that a calf grows. In the third stage, the situation of men wanting to cognise is conceived in terms of a cow and a calf that cannot be seen and men beginning to look for them *via* their footprints. The object they look for is both fire in its solar manifestation and speech. Their mental

---

238 Jamison, Brereton (2014): '(my)'.

trip along the *axis mundi* is conceived in terms of following footprints. In the fifth stage, men reach the sun at zenith which is conceived in terms of catching a calf. In the sixth stage, they drink Soma from its solar source and get omniscience which can be verbalised in sacred speech. This is conceived in terms of drinking cow's milk. Thus we can see that very complex cognitive and ontic processes are conceived in simple terms of the relationship between a cow and its calf. This is the proof of the creation of an abstract and general apparatus which in the ṚV was successful, but later disappeared, probably because of a change in experience.

If we apply the scenario of ṚV 1.164.2, we can understand the poet has now reached the sun, which is conceived in terms of catching a calf, similarly to the poets described in ṚV 1.164.5. A real fire burning during ritual and the *gharma* pot are conceived in terms of a calf and so is the beginnings of supernatural cognition.

The presence of Aśvins is justified by the Pravargya framework, but I would like to try to interpret it within the cognitive frames. Aśvins in the ṚV are often presented as saving men from various difficult situations (e.g. ṚV 1.112, 116, 117, 118); one of them is Atri who is lost in a dark chasm (Macdonell 1897: 51–53, 145) and who, in ṚV 4.50.6-8, is presented as finding the hidden sun (Jamison 1991). If the recipient evokes this concept in the context of ṚV 1.164.27, he may understand that oblation to Aśvins is meant to evoke them to help the poet in his mental transformations conceived as taking place on the sun.

ṚV 1.164.28

gaúr amīmed ánu vatsám miṣántam mūrdhā́nam híṅṅ akr̥ṇon mātavā́ u |
sŕ̥kvāṇam gharmám abhí vāvaśānā́ mímāti māyúm páyate páyobhiḥ ||

The cow bellowed after her blinking calf. She made the sound *híṅ*[239] against[240] head[241] to bellow.
Lowing toward[242] hot jaw, she bellows her bellow and swells her swell of milk.

In verse *a*, the composer again presents the cow as bellowing at its calf, so the recipient may presume that the poet hears sacred speech. The calf is qualified as blinking (*miṣánt*). In the ṚV, the gods are presented as not blinking (3.29.14, 9.73.4, 10.10.8) and the living beings as blinking (10.121.3, 10.190.2), so the recipient may understand that in terms of a blinking calf

[239] Jamison, Brereton (2014): add: 'him'.
[240] Jamison, Brereton (2014): add: 'his'.
[241] Jamison, Brereton (2014): '(for him)'.
[242] Jamison, Brereton (2014): add: 'his'.

a living being is conceived. However, the concept of blinking evokes the concept of seeing in terms of which cognition is conceived[243]. A blinking calf is the source domain for the beginnings of cognition.

The concept of cognition is also evoked *via* the concept of head, *mūrdhán*; it is not explicitly stated whose head is meant (verse *b*). In the ṚV, Agni is often called the head (*mūrdhán*) of the sky or of the world (ṚV 1.59.2, 3.2.14, 6.7.18.44.16, 8.75.4, 10.88.5,6). The word *mūrdhán* is used twice to denote the head of a cow: in ṚV 10.46.3, Agni is found in the head of the inviolable cow (*mūrdháni ághniyāyāḥ*) and, in ṚV 1.30.19, one wheel of the chariot of the Aśvins is placed in the head of the inviolable cow (*mūrdháni ághniyāyāḥ*) while the other one drives round the sky. If the recipient activates the concept of Agni as the head of the sky/world, he will confirm the meaning of zenith where the events described by the composer take place. Taking into account ṚV 1.30.19, this place is conceived in terms of a wheel fixed in one place while the sun encircling the sky is conceived in terms of the second wheel. Activation of the concept of Aśvins is justified as the recipient may presume that they, having eaten the oblation (ṚV 1.164.27, see below), manifest themselves to the poet.

If the head belongs to the cow, this would mean that the cow makes her head resound with the sound *híṅ*. Most of scholars understand *mā́tavaí* as 'to bellow' (Geldner 1951, Houben 2001a, Witzel, Gotō 2007, Jamison, Brereton 2014), but Elizarenkova (1989) interprets it as 'to measure'. Taking into account ṚV 1.164.5 which presents poets binding a calf in order to weave, we could think that the concept of weaving is evoked here as well. Moreover, cognition is conceived in terms of measuring in the ṚV.

In verse *c*, the composer presents the cow which bellows 'toward hot jaw' (*sṛ́kvāṇaṃ gharmám*). As Houben argues, the heated *gharma* pot is described in this way (2000a: 535). The word *sṛ́kvan* is a hapax. In ṚV 9.73.1, the word *srákva* is used in the description of the pressing of Soma, probably in reference to the pressing stones which are conceived in terms of eating mouths and, in ṚV 7.55.2, the word *srákva* is used in reference to the mouth of a dog which is urged to go to sleep (Jamison, Brereton 2014: 947). The hot mouth may belong to a calf at which the cow bellows, but also to a poet whose head is heated by cognition (see ṚV 4.2.6); the beginning of cognition is conceived in terms of a calf and, within the ritual space, in terms of a *gharma* pot filled with hot milk (ṚV 1.164.26, see above). It may be assumed that, in this way, sacred speech is conceived as entering the poet through his mouth; in the same way the entering of cognition of Agni is conceived in ṚV 1.164.21.

[243] This conceptualisation is elaborated in AU 1.1 (see chapter 4.1.3)

It may also be assumed that the image of a swelling cow (verse *d*) is meant to conceive the experience of the poet who, under the influence of Soma, feels bigger (see 9.119.7,11, 12, Jurewicz 2010a: 177 ff.). According to ṚV 10.164.25, the achievement of greatness is the promised result of the ritual.

ṚV 1.164.29

ayáṃ sá śiṅkte yéna gaúr abhī́vṛtā mímāti māyúṃ dhvasánāv ádhi śritā́ |
sā́ cittíbhir ní hí cakā́ra mártiyaṃ vidyúd bhávantī práti vavrím auhata ||

This hums – that by which the cow is enclosed. She bellows her bellow, resting upon the smoky[244].
Because she has put down[245] mortal with the sound 'chit-chit', becoming lightning, she pushed away her covering.

As Houben (2000a) shows, within the ritual context, the stanza describes the heated *gharma* pot into which milk is poured: the pot is on fire and makes crackling sounds. I will again focus on the interpretation of the mental state of the poet. In verse *a*, the cow is presented as being enveloped by something which hums. The verb *śiñj-* is used once again in ṚV 6.75.3, in reference to the sound of the bow string compared to a ringing sound of a women (or her anklets as Jamison, Brereton 2014 presume). If the recipient understands that in the previous stanza sacred speech is presented as entering the poet, he could understand that it is the poet himself who begins to speak. Taking into account that the sound of a cow is *hiṅ* (ṚV 1.164.27-28, see above), it is possible that the sounds spoken by the poet can be described as a kind of whizzing similar to the sound of the bow string.

In verse *b*, the cow is presented as resting upon a smoky fire (*dhvasána*) which Houben translates as sparkling (in the same way Geldner 1951, Elizarenkova 1989, Witzel, Gotō 2007). In this way, the recipient may evoke the concept of boiling milk and not only elaborate the Pravargya ritual, but also cognition conceived in these terms.

The concept of cognition is evoked by the word *cittí* (verse *c*). Notwithstanding its phonetic resemblance to the word *cítti* which refers to thinking, the word *cittí* is used in ṚV 8.79.4 in reference to Soma; its meaning is cognitive ability:

---

244 Jamison, Brereton (2014): '(fire)'.
245 Jamison, Brereton (2014): '(what is)'.

ṚV 8.79.4

tuváṃ cittī́ táva dákṣair divá ā́ pṛthivyā́ ṛjīṣin |
yā́vīr aghásya cid dvéṣaḥ ||

You possessor of the silvery drink – through your perception, through your skills
you keep away from heaven and earth
the hatred of any evil man.

In ṚV 1.164.24c, the cow is presented as putting down the mortal with its *cittí*. In the same way, Soma is presented as conquering with the aid of its *dákṣa* and *cittí* in ṚV 8.79.4 just quoted. The recipient can understand that, on the external level *cittí*, means the sound of boiling milk and, on the internal level, *cittí* means thought which disperses a lack of knowledge.

In verse *d*, the composer creates the image of lightning which emerges from its hiding place (*vavrí*). On the most literal level, *vavrí* in this context refers to the rain-clouds. Houben interprets this verse as referring to the fire blazing up, when milk is added to the clarified butter in the pot (2000a: 506–507). The realisation of cognition is conceived in terms of lightning and such a conceptualisation of cognition is elaborated in later thought (see chapter 4.4.2.4).

ṚV 1.164.30

anác chaye turágātu jīvám éjad dhruvám mádhya ā́ pastíyānām |
jīvó mṛtásya carati svadhā́bhir ámartiyo mártiyenā sáyoniḥ ||

Breathing, life rests[246] on its headlong course, stirring[247] steadfast in the midst of dwelling places.
The living one keeps moving by the will of the dead one; the immortal one shares the same womb with the mortal one.

Within the frames of the ritual input space, the relationship between the pot and fire is described (see Houben 2000a: 510–511). Within the frames of the input space of the internal transformations of the poet, the content of the knowledge now gained by the poet is described. The word *mártya* used in the previous stanza metonymically evokes the concept of death strengthened by the concept of the expansive conquest which conveys the meaning of killing. In Jurewicz (2010a: 298 ff.), I have analysed this stanza as describing the internally contradictory nature of the deceased. I have interpreted *mṛtásya* in verse *c* as a qualifier of *jīvá* which strengthens the contradictoriness of the state of the deceased. However, within the context of the whole hymn the

[246] Jamison, Brereton (2014): '(though remaining)'.
[247] Jamison, Brereton (2014): '(though)'.

stanza has more meaning. Verses *a–b* present, in a general way, life (*jīvá*, n) the movement of which is contradictory; the masculine *jīvá* in verses *c–d* is the realisation of life in a particular man. The power which enables union of what is alive and what is dead is called *svadhā́* which in the ṚV is used to denote the contradictory situation or movement (Jurewicz 2010a: 298–299).

Qualification of life as being 'in the midst of dwelling places' (*mádhya ā́ pastíyānām*, verse *b*) is meant to evoke the concept of fire which is presented as being born in the dwelling places of people who kindle it; these places are called *pastyā́* (6.49.9). Moreover, the word *pastyā́* may highlight the meaning of a watery dwelling. According to Brereton (1981: 94–96), there is no place in the ṚV where the meaning of water can be unambiguously ascribed to the word *pastyā́* and he proposes to consistently translate it as 'home, dwelling place' like *pastyà*. Houben (2000a, 2000b) does not agree with that. In some contexts, the meaning of water can be activated as specific kind of a dwelling, namely, a watery dwelling. Such is the case in the descriptions of Agni which activate the philosophical model of Child Of The Waters. One of the examples is ṚV 10.46.6 where Agni is presented as being covered in *pastyā̀su* and as sitting in the womb (*ní pastíyāsu tritá stabhūyán párivīto yónau sīdad antáḥ*). In this stanza, *yóni* not only means the place where Agni is settled, but also evokes the scenario of pregnancy and the concept of a womb from which Agni will be born. The womb is conceived as a dwelling full of fetal waters. The description of ṚV 4.1.11 also activates the meaning of the watery dwelling of *pastyā̀su*. Here Agni is presented as being born 'in the bottom of the great space' (*mahó budhné rájaso*) and in the womb (*yónau*; Jurewicz 2010a: 257–258). The space between the earth and the sky is conceived in terms of the general domain of A Vessel Filled With Liquid and the concept of a womb evokes the dwelling filled with concept of fetal waters within which Agni is born.

Taking this into account, it can be argued that the recipient of ṚV 1.164.30b is expected to activate the model of Child Of The Waters; within its frame the activity of fire is also conceived as contradictory. In other places in the ṚV, fire is presented as being born alive (*jīvá*) from dry wood, as breathing in waters (ṚV 1.65.9) and as giving breath (*ásu*) and life (*jīvá*, Jurewicz 2010a: 208–209[248]).

So the content of the knowledge presented by the poet is that the principle of life and death is Agni present in what is mortal: in the cosmos and in men. It has a common womb with what is mortal because it is born within men

[248] Life is conceived as coming together with the appearance of the dawns when fire is kindled (ṚV 1.92.9, 1.113.16, 4.51.5, 7.77.1, 10.107.1).

when they are born and it resides in their hearts (see e.g. ṚV 10.5.1[249]). My interpretation agrees with Houben's interpretation who identifies this principle with breath *prāṇá* (2000a: 508ff) with which Agni is identified in the ṚV (1.66.1b). Here again we see the roots of the later elaboration of *prāṇá* as the fiery cosmic principle (AVŚ 11.4, see chapter 2.1.2) and as the principle of man identified with *ātmán* (Jurewicz 1997).

That Agni is the principle of the manifest aspect is expressed almost explicitly in the next stanza:

ṚV 1.164.31

ápaśyaṃ gopā́m ánipadyamānam ā́ ca párā ca pathíbhiś cárantam |
sá sadhrī́cīḥ sá víṣūcīr vásāna ā́ varīvarti bhúvaneṣu antáḥ ||

I saw the herdsman who never settles down, roaming here and afar along his paths. Clothing himself in those that converge and diverge, he moves back and forth among living beings[250].

The word *gopā́* (verse *a*) appears in ṚV 10.164.21 where, as I have argued, it denotes Agni the cognition of which is conceived in terms of it entering into the poet. If the recipient evokes the image of climbing a tree in order to get a sweet fig, he will understand that the poet now realises his omniscience having mentally reached the sun in zenith. In its solar form, fire comes and goes away (verse *b*); the recipient may also understand that the movement of fire is contradictory: at the same time it goes hither and thither (Houben: 2000a).

It is worth mentioning that Pūṣan is described in the same way in ṚV 10.17.6d, as 'going back and forth' (Jamison, Brereton 2014); again the ambiguity of this movement can be highlighted by the recipient. In ṚV 10.17.3b, Pusan is conceived in the same terms as Agni and, in ṚV 1.164.31a, as a herdsman (*gopā́*). In ṚV 10.17.3c, Pūṣan is presented as leading the deceased men to their fathers and in ṚV 10.17.3d Agni is mentioned as leading them to gods. Taking into account that, in the ṚV, the place reached in rituals and after death is the same, i.e. the sun (Jurewicz 2008b, 2010a: 294–296), I would argue that Pūṣan is identified with Agni. Their identity is also implied in that, in ṚV 10.17.4a, Pūṣan is called the lifetime (*ā́yus*), to which Agni, conceived as breath *prāṇá*, is compared in ṚV 1.66.1b. These similarities

[249] ṚV 10.5.1ab: *ékaḥ samudró dharúṇo rayīṇā́m asmád dhṛdó bhū́rijanmā ví caṣṭe*; for identification of the ocean and fire see Jurewicz (2010a: 188 ff.).

[250] This stanza also appears in ṚV 10.177. For its interpretation in its ritual use (the Pravargya rite), see Patton (2005: 132–137).

between Pusan and Agni strengthen the interpretation that ṚV 1.164.31ab presents Agni which, in its solar form, is now visible to the poet[251].

Verse *c* presents fire as clothed with females. They surround it and gradually disperse. It evokes the model of Child Of The Waters and the recipient may elaborate its general meaning of the creation of the world. He may also evoke a specific image of streams of waters from which lightning appears; thus he will understand that raining is the result of the sunrise.

Verse *d* expresses the presence of fire within the manifest aspect: in the macrocosmic dimension, it circulates among the worldly spheres in its solar form, in the microcosmic dimension, it circulates within living beings as their innermost principle.

ṚV 1.164.32

yá īṃ cakā́ra ná só asyá veda yá īṃ dadárśa hírug ín nú tásmāt |
sá mātúr yónā párivīto antár bahuprajā́ nírṛtim ā́ viveśa ||

He who created him does not know him. He is far away from him who has seen him.
He is surrounded within the womb of his mother. Having many offspring, he has entered into destruction.

I would interpret verses *a–b* as referring to the lack of knowledge of people who create fire in their everyday life; although it is close to them, they do not know its essence and nature. The same kind of superficial knowledge is expressed in AVŚ 10.8.14 where it is said that everyone sees the movement of the sun, but not everyone understands its cause (see chapter 2.6.1). If someone knows of fire's transformations and kindles fire, he knows that it will become far from him because it will assume its form of the rising sun.

In verses *c–d*, the composer explains why it is difficult to cognise Agni. In verse *c*, it is presented as hidden within the womb of his mother. This general statement refers to fire's hidden presence in the wood, in the sun and in rain. If the recipient activates ṚV 1.164.8, he will conceive Agni as father which will be born from the mother and thus share in truth (*ṛtá*).

In verse *d*, Agni is presented as having many offspring (*bahuprajā́*). In this way, various manifestations of fire are conceived. The phrase *nírṛtim ā́ viveśa* implies that in its manifestations fire somehow disappears. The literal meaning of *nírṛti* is the state opposite to *ṛtá*, which also means 'truth'. Taking this into account, I would argue that fire becomes uncognisable in its manifold manifestations. Such a meaning seems to be activated in ṚV 7.104.14 where

[251] For Pūṣan and his relationship with Agni, see Kramrisch (1961). For Pūṣan and his relationship with Sarasvatī, see Gonda (1985).

those whose speech is deceitful (*droghavā́cas*) are supposed to unite with *nirṛthá*, the word cognate with *nírṛti* (Mayrhofer 1996: 45).

However, the use of the word *nírṛti* in the ṚV implies a further ontological situation for Agni manifest in the world. If the recipient again activates ṚV 1.164.8, he can understand that in its manifestations, Agni loses its share in truth and comes back to its unmanifest aspect. Moreover, the word *nírṛti* is often used to name the state from which the poets want to be saved (ṚV 1.24.9, 1.38.6, 6.74.2, 8.24.24, 10.36.2,4, 10.59.1-4). Renou (EVP 16: 21) shows that it is possible to understand *nírṛti* as opposing *sám ṛṇvati* which highlights the meaning of lack of movement. In ṚV 1.117.5, *nírṛti* denotes the place of sleeping people. In ṚV 7.58.1, it denotes the place from which the Maruts reach the sky and is used in apposition with *avaṃśá*, 'the propless'. The lack of movement and support and the state of sleep are features of the pre-creative state which is where the enemies of the Āryans are supposed to be (ṚV 7.104.3, Jurewicz 2010a: 72). Thus understood, the word *nírṛti* evokes the concept of death[252]. Conceptualisation of fire as dying in its manifestation would anticipate thought presented in the ŚB which conceives of creation in these terms (see chapter 3.2). Conceptualisation of fire as sleeping in its manifestation anticipates Upaniṣadic thinking where the concept of sleep is used to conceive manifestations of *ātmán* (see chapter 4.4.2.3).

ṚV 1.164.33

dyaúr me pitā́ janitā́ nā́bhir átra bándhur me mātā́ pṛthivī́ mahī́yám |
uttānáyoś camúvor yónir antár átrā pitā́ duhitúr gárbham ā́dhāt[253] ||

My father, my progenitor, is Heaven; here is my navel. My mother, this great Earth, is my relation.
My womb is within the two open cups[254]. Here my father placed the child[255] of his daughter[256].

Jamison, Brereton (2014) interpret this stanza as being spoken by the sun while Geldner (1951) supposes that the speaker is the wind and breath. However, I would argue that the speaker is the poet who now understands his identity with fire. In many places in the ṚV, Agni is described as the son of the earth and the sky. The word *uttānáyoḥ* (verse *c*) evokes the form *uttānā́yām* (ṚV 1.164.14) which, as I have shown, is used in the description of

252 See Bodewitz (1999a,b).
253 Jamison, Brereton (2014): interpret this stanza as presenting the words of the sun.
254 Jamison, Brereton (2014): '[= Heaven and Earth]'.
255 Jamison, Brereton (2014): '[= the Sun]'.
256 Jamison, Brereton (2014): '[= Dawn]'.

kindling of fire. The word *camú* is used in the description of the clarification of Soma and its drinking, so the poet realises his identity with Soma which is the first manifestation of Agni and is poured in the morning sacrifice to create sunrise and is then finally purified in zenith. Verse *d* evokes the concept of incestual sexual union. Since raining is conceived in terms of impregnating earth, the recipient may activate this concept in this context and reconstruct the solar-rainy cycle of Agni with which the poet understands his identity[257].

Taking into account the previous stanza which implies the disappearance of fire during its manifestation, it may be assumed that it now reappears during the cognitive activity of a cognising man.

ṚV 1.164.34-35

pr̥chā́mi tvā páram ántam pr̥thivyā́ḥ pr̥chā́mi yátra bhúvanasya nā́bhiḥ |
pr̥chā́mi tvā vŕ̥ṣṇo áśvasya rétaḥ pr̥chā́mi vācáḥ paramám víoma || (34)
iyám védiḥ páro ántaḥ pr̥thivyā́ ayám yajñó bhúvanasya nā́bhiḥ |
ayám sómo vŕ̥ṣṇo áśvasya réto brahmā́yám vācáḥ paramám víoma || (35)

I ask you about the farthest end of the earth. I ask where is the navel of the living world.
I ask you about the seed of the bull(-like) horse. I ask about the highest heaven of the speech. (34)
The altar here is the farthest end of the earth. This sacrifice here is the navel of the living world.
This soma is the seed of the bull(-like) horse. This formulator here is the highest heaven of the speech. (35)

This *brahmodya* may take place during the sacrifice actually performed (Thompson 1997). However, it can also be seen as a *brahmodya* which takes place between 'the father', i.e. Agni recognised by the poet and 'the son', i.e. the poet himself. In the beginning of this section, I proposed interpretation of the hymn as a dialogue between Agni hidden within the poet and the poet who wants to cognise it. In ṚV 1.164.4, the poet looks for someone who should be asked in order to get knowledge and, in ṚV 1.164.11, the vocative *agne* is used. Agni is conceived in terms of a person who poses questions, as the poet's father and teacher, and the poet as a person who answers them. The topic of their dialogue is knowledge about the meaning of ritual.

The altar is called the farthest end of the earth (ṚV 1.164.35a). The concept of earth metonymically evokes the concept of the world. Thus the recipient understands that the range of the world is marked by a sacrificial place. Sacrifice is called the navel of the living world (*bhúvanasya nā́bhiḥ*,

[257] Raining is conceived in terms of incestuous sexual union in ṚV 1.71.5.

ṚV 1.164.35b). The concept of navel metonymically evokes the concepts of the umbilical cord and of a mother giving birth which allows the recipient to understand that during sacrifice the world is created. The same is expressed by the general model of reality transformation as fire, and the Soma which is poured into it in the morning sacrifice, become the sun; thus ritual creates the world. Soma is called the seed of a potent stallion (Houben 2000a: 535, ṚV 1.164.35c). In the ṚV, Soma is conceived in terms of semen and the sun is conceived in terms of a bull or a stallion; its semen becomes rain (Jurewicz 2010a). According to the general model of reality transformation, rain is Soma purified in the sun. Finally, the Brahman-priest is called 'the highest heaven of the speech' (ṚV 1.164.35d, see Thompson 1997). The expression *paramá vyòman* denotes the sun in zenith which is the visible form of the spatio-temporal beginnings of the world (Jurewicz 2010a: 296–298[258]). The expression 'the highest heaven of the speech' (*vācáḥ paramáṃ víoma*) implies that the world is conceived in terms of sacred speech which agrees with the earlier content of the hymn (ṚV 1.164.11). The Brahman-priest is the ritual embodiment of the highest heaven in the sacrificial place.

The conceptual network elaborated by the composer of the hymn in this stanza is not only addressed to the recipient of the hymn, but also to the performers of the ritual. Its input spaces are the concepts of ritual and of the world. In the blend, the former input space gives topology and scenario to the latter. The generic space is the image schema of CONTAINER. In the blend, the sacrificial place is the whole world and ritual is the activity which creates it, Soma poured into fire will become rain when it will be finally clarified in the sun in zenith called 'the highest heaven' (*paramá vyòman*). The visual representation of the highest heaven, identical with it, is the Brahman-priest whose presence assures the mental transformation of the participants conceived in terms of drinking Soma from its solar source in the highest heaven. Such an understanding of the priests in ritual is elaborated by the JUB the composer of which shows his crucial influence on the afterlife state of man (see chapter 5.2). This blend allows for conceptualisation of sacrifice as the model of the world which is identical with it. Whatever happens in the sacrifice, happens in the world. Such a conceptualisation of sacrifice will be elaborated in the ŚB (see chapter 3). So the poet now understands that supernatural cognition can be realised within the frames of ritual.

[258] The problem of the highest heaven will be discussed more by the composer in the next stanzas (ṚV 1.164.39, 41).

ṚV 1.164.36

saptā́rdhagarbhā́ bhúvanasya réto víṣṇos tiṣṭhanti pradíśā vídharmaṇi |
té dhītíbhir mánasā té vipaścítaḥ paribhúvaḥ pári bhavanti viśvátaḥ ||

The seven children of the[259] halves[260], the seed of the living world, take their place by the direction of Viṣṇu in the spreading expanse.
By their insights and their thought these encompassing perceivers of inspired words encompass[261] here.

In the first hemistich, the composer presents seven children of the halves of the world, i.e. the earth and the sky who, it may be assumed, are the seven sons of Aditi present in the world (ṚV 1.164.15). Thus the composer again repeats the same content in a new context.

The structure of the world is conceived as being six spheres or elements that move and a seventh that does not. These elements are qualified as 'the seed of the living world' (*bhúvanasya réto*, verse *a*) which is an equivocal expression. The word *rétas* can refer to the offspring and to the father. In the first case, the expression confirms that the elements originate from the earth and the sky. In the second case, they are the source of the world. The same equivocality characterises the expression *mánaso rétas* in the *Nāsadīyasūkta* (Jurewicz 2010a: 51) and it may be assumed that this equivocality is intentional.

Since the word *rétas* is followed by the word *víṣṇu*, the listener can also understand that the seven elements are the seed of Viṣṇu. On the one hand, they create Viṣṇu in the morning and, on the other, they appear when Viṣṇu makes his three steps corresponding to the earth, space and sky created in the morning and they then take their places in the cosmos. Such a conceptualisation anticipates the later concept of the elements of the world in terms of gods (*devatā*, see chapter 4.1.3). The elements are endowed with cognitive abilities (verse *c*) and are presented as circulating (*paribhúvaḥ pári bhavanti*, verse *d*) which allows the recipient to understand them as identified with the sun conceived in terms of a wheel the spokes of which move and the axle of which does not. Since the concept of a wheel is the source domain for conceptualisation of the world (see ṚV 1.164.2 and 11,13-14), the recipient may understand that the poet understands the structure of the whole world.

If we interpret the seven sons of Aditi as seven seers, we get a coherent image of the seers present in the sun. Moreover, the fact that they are sons of the halves of the world implies their affinity with the poet who has recognised

---

259 Jamison, Brereton (2014): '(two world-)'.
260 Jamison, Brereton (2014): '[= the Seven Seers]'.
261 Jamison, Brereton (2014): '(everything)'.

himself as the child of the earth and the sky (ṚV 1.164.33, see above). Thus it is implied that he has the same cognitive abilities as they have. And since the seers are elements of the world, we may also presume that the poet realises his identity with the world.

The next stanza presents the moment when the poet loses his knowledge and recovers it thanks to his recognition of Agni.

ṚV 1.164.37

ná ví jānāmi yád ivedám ásmi niṇyáḥ sáṃnaddho mánasā carāmi |
yadā́ mā́gan prathamajā́ ṛtásya ā́d íd vācó aśnuve bhāgám asyā́ḥ ||

I do not understand what sort of thing I am here: though bound, I roam about in secret by my thinking.
When the first-born of truth[262] has come to me, only then I attain a share of this speech here.

Taking into account the context of the hymn, it can be assumed that the poet is lost in his omniscience gained during sacrifice conceived in terms of reaching the zenith. Using the words of the ṚV, the poet seems to be lost in the highest heaven (*paramá vyòman*) which he has reached thanks to the ritual and the activity of the Brahman-priest. This topic will be elaborated in the description of the afterlife state of man in the JUB (see chapter 5.2).

The poet is qualified as 'hidden' or 'concealed', *niṇyá* (verse *b*). Houben (2000a) interprets this qualification as referring to the Avānataradīkṣā of the Pravargya (512–513). Within the frames of my interpretation, this qualification also implies that the poet is mentally somewhere else. As the composer says he roams about by his thinking (*mánasā carāmi*). In this way, his mental presence in the highest heaven is expressed; the poet is somehow invisible to the other participants of the ritual. Although he has recognised his affinity with the seers and with the world, he does not understand himself. It is possible that this is meant to imply his radical mental transformation goes beyond human understanding.

The concept of being bound (*sáṃnaddho*, verse *b*) is used in the ṚV to conceive of the state of a lack of knowledge connected with sin: in ṚV 2.28.6 and 7.86.5, the poet asks Varuṇa to release him from this state as a calf is released from a rope; ṚV 2.28.6 calls this state by the general noun *áṃhas* (Jurewicz 2013a)[263]. If the recipient activates this conceptualisation, he could understand the state of the poet as a loss of all features which make a living being a human being. In the ṚV, *áṃhas* is connected with enemies of the

[262] Jamison, Brereton (2014): '[= Agni]'.
[263] See also ṚV 2.28.5.

Aryans who are treated as non-human (Jurewicz 2010a: 68, 2013a). In ṚV 1.164.32cd (see above), Agni is described as disappearing in his manifestations. It is possible that the poet, having realised his seer-ness which implies his identity with the world (see previous stanza), is now lost in it.

In verse *c*, the composer states that 'the first-born of truth' (*prathamajā́ ṛtásya*) has entered the poet. This qualification is used in ṚV 10.61.19 in reference to Agni in a very significant context:

> *iyám me nā́bhir ihá me sadhástham imé me devā́ ayám asmi sárvaḥ |*
> *dvijā́ áha prathamajā́ ṛtásya idáṃ dhenúr aduhaj jā́yamānā ||*
>
> [Agni:]: "This, here, is my navel, and here is my seat. These gods here are mine, and here am I – the whole –
> having two births, first born of truth. This[264] here did the cow give as her milk as she was being born.

I would interpret the pronoun *iyám* in verse *a* differently to Jamison, Brereton (2014). Taking into account ṚV 1.164.35, it can be interpreted as evoking the altar (*védi*) and, metonymically, the sacrifice (*yajñá*). The altar is the navel of Agni which manifests itself in the ritual fire as it is only because of that can the sacrifice be called 'the navel of the living world' (*bhúvanasya nā́bhiḥ*). Verse *b* of ṚV 10.61.19 explicitly states the superiority of Agni over other gods. On the other hand, the pronoun *idám* (verse *d*) metonymically evokes the phrase *idám sárvam* (this activation is strengthened by the word *sárva* in verse *b*) which refers to the world (ṚV 8.58.2). The cow is the source domain for sacred speech thanks to which the world exists. Its existence is ensured by rain conceived in terms of a cow's milk. It is also possible to understand the stanza as expressing the words of the seer Nābhānediṣṭha who has experienced his identity with Agni realised in supernatural cognition. Agni is also called *prathamajā́ ṛtásya* ṚV 10.5.7. Since cognition is conceived in terms of the object of knowledge entering into its subject (ṚV 1.164.21), the recipient of ṚV 1.164.37 understands that the poet has cognised Agni (Brown 1968a: 206).

This knowledge is the basis for further cognition which requires knowledge of sacred speech (verse *d*). Knowledge of speech is conceived in terms of having a share in it (*ā́d íd vācó aśnuve bhāgám asyā́ḥ*). This conceptualisation is evoked in ṚV 1.164.8 (see above) where speech is conceived in terms of a mother who gives a share in truth to a father (*mātā́ pitáram ṛtá ā́ babhāja*). The poet is to be seen in the same terms: having cognised Agni (the father), he becomes able to cognise and thus becomes the

[264] Jamison, Brereton (2014): '(earth?)'.

father. This is the situation which ṚV 1.164.16 conceives as being 'the father of his father' (*sá pitúṣ pitā́sat*).

The next three stanzas describe the further cognition of the poet who again focuses on the role of sacred speech.

ṚV 1.164.38

ápāṅ prā́ṅ eti svadháyā gṛbhītó ámartiyo mártiyenā sáyoniḥ |
tā́ śáśvantā viṣūcī́nā viyántā ní anyáṃ cikyúr ná ní cikyur anyám ||

He goes inward and outward, controlled by his own will – he, the immortal one of the same womb as the mortal one.
Those two are ever going apart in different directions. They observe the one; they do not observe the other.

In the first hemistich, the composer again repeats the earlier content now the content of ṚV 1.164.30-31. In verse *a*, he evokes the concept of Agni in its solar form conceived in terms of a herdsman who goes forwards and backwards (ṚV 1.164.31c: *ā́ ca párā ca pathíbhiś cárantam*). In verse *b*, he evokes the concept of the life of an individual man conceived as immortal who has a common womb with the mortal (ṚV 1.164.30d: *ámartiyo mártiyenā sáyoniḥ*). The power, which enables the movement of Agni and life, is called *svadhā́*, as in ṚV 1.164.30 where this word is used to qualify the coexistence of what is immortal and what is mortal. In this way, the composer states the unity of Agni manifest in the cosmos and life manifest in man. Thus the poet recognises his identity with Agni and overcomes the state of an inability to cognise expressed in the previous stanza.

In verse *c*, two elements are mentioned which are qualified as going apart (*viṣūcī́nā*); they are also qualified as *śáśvantā* which Jamison, Brereton (2014) translate as 'ever' (Houben 2000a: 'always', Geldner 1951, I: 'bestanendig', Elizarenkova 1989: 'postojanno'). The word *śáśvat* also means 'perpetual, frequent, ever-recurring'. In this meaning, it is used in the descriptions of the dawns which come back every day (ṚV 1.113.8, 15, 1.171.5) and it can also be highlighted here (Witzel, Gotō 2007: 'aufeinanderfolgend'). So verses *c–d* can be interpreted as expressing the conviction that the immortal and mortal spheres repeatedly separate: when the body dies, it is seen while the immortal principle is not. Such an interpretation would be further proof of the early belief in rebirth with the immortal life principle. At the same time, the wording of verse c phonetically evokes ṚV 1.164.31cd (*sá sadhrī́cīḥ sá víṣūcīr vásāna ā́ varīvarti bhúvaneṣu antáḥ*) and the recipient may understand that it is Agni which is seen by some people and cannot be seen by others.

ṚV 1.164.39

ṛcó akṣáre paramé víoman yásmin devā́ ádhi víśve niṣedúḥ |
yás tán ná véda kím ṛcā́ kariṣyati yá ít tád vidús tá imé sám āsate ||

The syllable of the verse, upon which all the gods have settled, is in the highest heaven –
he who does not know that[265], what will he accomplish by his verse? Only those who know it sit together here.

In verse *a*, the composer equates the highest heaven, *paramá vyòman*, with the syllable of the Ṛk-stanza (*ṛcó akṣáre*). Taking into account that *paramá vyòman* denotes the spatio-temporal beginnings of the world and that the world is the manifestation of speech, the recipient understands that the first act of manifestation of reality is conceived in terms of pronouncing the syllable (*akṣára*) of the Ṛk-stanza. The word *akṣára* means also 'imperishable'. Thus the most mysterious moment of creation is expressed as paradoxical. On the one hand, speech manifests itself in time and such a manifestation involves change. On the other hand, it is imperishable so it does not change. This paradoxical nature of the first creative act will be elaborated in ṚV 1.164.42 (see below). Within the frames of the cosmos, *paramá vyòman*, the visible form of which is the sun in zenith, is the borderline sphere of the cosmos. It is the most mysterious sphere of what is manifest because at the same time it is not manifest at all. Recognition of the paradoxical nature of this sphere shows that the composers of the ṚV were aware of problems connected with monistic assumptions. Although it is possible to call aspects of reality as existing and true (*sát*, *ṛtá*) and non-existing and untrue (*ásat*, *ánṛta*), it is impossible to name the sphere between these two aspects in those terms. The only solution is paradox or metaphor. The presence of the gods in the highest heaven (verse *b*) agrees with the Ṛgvedic cosmological thinking according to which the gods are on the sun and the recipient infers that they possess the knowledge about *akṣára* because they drink solar Soma.

In verses *c–d*, the composer states that without knowledge of the syllable (*akṣára*), the knowledge of the Ṛk-stanza is useless. Only those who know it, can realise the state which is now conceived in terms of sitting together. In ṚV 3.9.7, men are presented as sitting around fire[266]. In ṚV 10.65.7, the gods who live in the sky with tongues of fire are presented as sitting at the womb of the truth and stroking it (*ví mṛś-*)[267]. In these terms, kindling

---

[265] Jamison, Brereton (2014): '(syllable)'.
[266] In the ṚV, kindling of fire is conceived in terms of its seating (Jurewicz 2010a: 269–70).
[267] The concept of stroking (*mṛś-*) can be seen as an instantiation of metaphors the source domain of which is general domain of Cleansing By Heat.

fire and cognition is conceived in the ṚV (Jurewicz 2010a). It can be argued then that the intention of the composer is to activate this conceptualisation to express that those who know the syllable of the Ṛk-stanza, having kindled ritual fire on earth, realise supernatural knowledge sitting around the solar source of fiery Soma. And the recipient may presume that the poet wants to cognise the imperishable element of sacred speech expressed in a syllable.

ṚV 1.164.40

sūyavasā́d bhágavatī hí bhūyā́ átho vayám bhágavantaḥ siyāma |
addhí tṛ́ṇam aghniye viśvadā́nīm píba śuddhám udakám ācárantī ||

Because you would become blessed, feeding upon good pasturage, so then we would also be blessed.
Feed on grass always, o inviolable cow[268]! Come here, drink pure water!

Notwithstanding the possibility of interpreting the concept of a cow literally (Houben 2000a), it can also be interpreted as the source domain of sacred speech. Its excellence is conceived in terms of a cow which is well-fed. I am tempted to argue that the verbal form *bhūyā́ḥ* (verse *a*) phonetically evokes the adverb *bhū́yas* which means 'more'. This would be suitable in the context of the hymn according to which speech has already been cognised by the poet and now he wants to know more, i.e. its imperishable element. Thanks to his knowledge of speech, the poet will be called *bhágavant*, i.e. someone who has a share in it. Using the words of the ṚV 1.164.8, he will be in the same situation as reality *in illo tempore* which gives its manifest part, conceived in terms of a father, a share in truth. Thus his wish, expressed in the same way in ṚV 1.164.37d (*ā́d íd vācó aśnuve bhāgám asyā́ḥ*), will be fulfilled.

And sacred speech manifests itself in a really magnificent way:

ṚV 1.164.41-42

gaurī́r mimāya salilā́ni tákṣatī ékapadī dvipádī sā́ cátuṣpadī |
aṣṭā́padī návapadī babhūvúṣī sahásrākṣarā paramé víoman || (41)
tásyāḥ samudrā́ ádhi ví kṣaranti téna jīvanti pradíśaś cátasraḥ |
tátaḥ kṣarati akṣáram tád víśvam úpa jīvati || (42)

The buffalo-cow[269] has bellowed, fashioning oceans. One-footed and two-footed, she is four-footed,
having become eight-footed and nine-footed: she has a thousand syllables in the highest heaven.
Seas flow everywhere from her: by that four directions live,
from that the syllable flows, upon that does everything lives.

[268] Jamison, Brereton (2014): '[= Speech]'.
[269] Jamison, Brereton (2014): '[= Speech]'.

As I have argued elsewhere (Jurewicz 2010a: 85 ff., 2012a), these stanzas are proof of the creation of an abstract concept of *akṣára* which expresses the contradictionary nature of the manifest aspect of reality conceived in terms of something that does not flow and flows at the same time. I have also shown that this concept is widely used in later thought (Jurewicz 2012a, see also chapters 2.6.1, 3.5.1). If the recipient understands the word *salilá* (ṚV 1.164.41a) literally, he will create an image of a buffalo-cow which stamps in muddy water and creates lumps of mud. Thus the concept of solidification of something fluid can be evoked and, as it will be shown, this concept is used to conceive creation in later thought (see ŚB 6.1.3, ŚB 10.5.3, chapter 3.5.1, AU, chapter 4.1.3). It is possible that the intention of the composer is also to evoke the concept of heating which, in later thought, is expressed with the use of the verb *mūrch-*, 'to solidify' (ŚB 10.5.3, see chapter 3.5.1, AU 1.1.2, chapter 4.1.3). In terms of solidification under the influence of heat, cognition is conceived. The concept of cognition is also evoked *via* the verb *takṣ-*, 'to carve'; this conceptualisation is evoked in ṚV 1.164.23 referring to the creation of *traíṣṭubha* speech (see above). The cognition of sacred speech by the poet is conceived in terms of the buffalo-cow the legs of which multiply sacred speech; the recipient is prompted to imagine it as unfolding in its infinite[270] forms before the eyes of the poet. The activity of the buffalo-cow is presented as taking place in the highest heaven which is where the poet is. Thus the recipient understands that he has access to the whole of speech. If the recipient elaborates the metaphoric meaning of the *salilá* which is the pre-creative state of the world, he will understand that when speech is created, the world begins to be created in all its potential forms (see Jurewicz 2010a: 85 ff.). In my view, the poet now cognises the aspect of reality conceived in terms of mother in ṚV 1.164.8-9 and which I interpret as Aditi and speech.

Creation of the world is presented in ṚV 1.164.42 and conceived in terms of flowing (Jurewicz 2012a). The internally contradictory nature of creation is expressed in ṚV 10.164.42c: *tátaḥ kṣarati akṣáram*, 'from it flows what does not flow'. Conceived in these terms, the world is a syllable which is pronounced and not pronounced at the same time. Its conceptualisation in terms of water also agrees with conceptualisation of speech in terms of flowing water (see Jurewicz 2012a). If the recipient takes into account that reality is Agni, he will understand the internal contradiction of its manifestation in terms of the appearance of water from fire. This internal contradiction is

[270] Like in ṚV 10.90.1, see section 1.3.

expressed in the Ṛgvedic cosmological model which assumes the appearance of rain from the sun.

I would also like to refer to ṚV 4.12.6 and 10.126.8 the composer of which asks the good gods (Vasu) to release the poets from constraint (*áṃhas*) in the same way as they release a buffalo-cow tied by its foot. Taking these stanzas into account, it is possible that the buffalo-cow in ṚV 1.164.41-42 is also released from bondage; her fury with which it stamps in the water, implied by its roar and the multiplication of its legs, may be caused by it trying to escape from this state for a long time. Conceived in these terms, the creation of the world is the liberation of reality from the state in which it is bound. The state of being bound should not be understood as the pre-creative state, but rather as a very early creative state. It will be shown that the concept of confinement as the first manifestation of reality is elaborated in AVŚ 11.5 and the *Vrātyakāṇḍa* using the concepts of Brahmacārin (*brahmacārín*) and Vrātya (*vrā́tya*), i.e. someone who subjects himself to the rules (*brahmacárya*, *vratá*, see chapter 2.2.1-2).

Thus the recipient understands that the poet has recognised *akṣára* of the Ṛk-stanza. It is this imperishable element of sacred speech which is unmanifest and, at the same time, manifest in the Ṛk-stanzas as the world.

ṚV 1.164.43

śakamáyaṃ dhūmám ārā́d apaśyaṃ viṣūvátā pará enā́vareṇa |
ukṣā́ṇam pṛ́śnim apacanta vīrā́s tā́ni dhármāṇi prathamā́ni āsan ||

At the midpoint, beyond this nearer[271], I saw dung-smoke from afar.
Heroes cooked the dappled bullock. These were the first foundations[272].

I will supply the interpretation of this stanza, apart from its ritual meaning connected with Pravargya (Houben 2000a), with a meaning which derives from my analysis of the hymn as presenting the supernatural cognition of the poet.

The poet is presented as observing smoke from the sacrificial fire. The expression *pará enā́vareṇa* (verse *b*) is used in ṚV 1.164.17-18 in reference to the earth, so I think that the intention of the composer of the hymn is to evoke this meaning. According to Jamison and Brereton (2014: 354), the word *viṣūvánt* 'can refer to the Viṣūvant day (as in 1.84.10), the summer solstice, which is the ritual midpoint of a year-long Sattra ceremony'. This word is used in the ṚV only in these two stanzas. In ṚV 1.84.10, it denotes the midpoint

---

271 Jamison, Brereton (2014): '(fire)'.
272 Jamison, Brereton (2014): '(of the rite)'.

of a vessel from which the buffalo-cows drink sweet Somic juice. Jamison, Brereton (2014: 212) and Elizarenkova (1989: 592) understand the concept of *gaurī́*, used in verse *b* of this stanza, as metonymically activating the milk with which Soma is mixed. Witzel, Gotō (2007) refer to ṚV 9.12.3 where the word *gaurī́* is clearly meant to evoke this meaning; in this stanza Soma is qualified as *madacyút*. It is possible then that the composer of ṚV 1.164.42 wants the recipient to think about Soma which is prepared in ritual and becomes the sun rising over the earth; the concept of smoke metonymically evokes the concept of fire into which Soma is poured[273]. But taking into account the hemistich more generally, the recipient is prompted to create the image of smoke which rises in the middle of space in terms of which the *axis mundi* is conceived (Jurewicz 2010a: 135–136). Since the sacrifice is conceived in terms of the navel of the world (ṚV 1.164.35), the recipient can activate this concept and identify the smoke with the umbilical cord in the blend. The logic of this image evokes the concept of the sun which is on the top of the *axis mundi*. Jamison, Brereton (2014: 354), on the basis of their interpretation of *viṣūvánt*, write that it 'suggests that the fire beyond the earthly fire is the sun, perhaps wrapped in cloud, the "dung-smoke", since the solstice should occur around the beginning of the rainy season'. Within the frames of the interpretation I present in Jurewicz (2010a), the general model of reality transformation is an abstraction from everyday experience and does not refer to any concrete ritual, but rather presents the general functioning of the cosmos in terms of the transformation of fire and Soma into sun and rain.

The concept of the sun is also evoked by the expression 'the dappled bull' (*ukṣáṇam pṛ́śnim*). The sun is conceived in terms of a bull in the ṚV and the adjective *pṛ́śni* is used in contexts evoking the sun. In ṚV 9.83.3, Soma in its solar form is called *pṛ́śni* and, in ṚV 4.57.3, the sun is called *pṛ́śnir* áśman. In this concise way, the composer evokes the concept of the sacrifice during which Soma is prepared and the result of which is sunrise. The fact that the poet sees the smoke from afar may also imply that he is still conceived as being in the highest heaven from where he observes the earth thanks to his omniscience. This omniscience comes thanks to gaining the imperishable syllable of sacred speech.

[273] Fire is called *dhūmáketu* (e.g. RV 1.27.11, 1.94.10, 8.43.4, 10.4.5).

ṚV 1.164.44

tráyaḥ keśína ṛtuthā́ ví cakṣate saṃvatsaré vapata éka eṣām |
víśvam éko abhí caṣṭe śácībhir dhrā́jir ékasya dadṛśe ná rūpám ||

Three long-haired ones gaze out in succession: in a year one[274] of them shears away[275] for himself;
another[276] gazes upon everything with his powers; the rush of another[277] is visible but not his form.

In this stanza, the composer presents the three main elements of the world which are fire, the sun and the wind[278]. They are metonymically evoked *via* their most salient features.

The verb *vap-*, 'to scatter, to sow' and the verb *vap-* 'to shear' can be seen as the one verb (see 1992, see also Gotō 1987: 287); their meanings can be subsumed into one as they are extension of the main concept of scattering. On a more general level, sowing and shearing are the activities during which small objects fall down: in the case of sowing, it is seed and, in the case of shearing, it is hair. In terms of shearing, burning is conceived while in terms of sowing, raining is conceived (Jurewicz 2010a: 315–316). In this way, *via* the double meaning of the verb *vap-*, the composer can evoke the activity of fire in the cosmos which is the creation of sunrise and rain. The medial form of the verb implies the reflexive activity of reality conceived in terms of fire which manifests itself in solar-rainy transformations.

The concept of the sun is evoked *via* its salient feature which is that of seeing everything in the world. The concept of the wind is evoked *via* its rushing and invisibility which are its salient features. Since in the ṚV the word *keśín* (verse *a*) qualifies the horses of Indra in most cases, the recipient can conceive these elements of the world in terms of horses the hair of which are, as Houben proposes (2000a: 536), flames of fire, rays of the sun and lightning; in the last case I would rather propose streams of rain. Moreover, the concept of these elements metonymically evokes the concept of the spheres of the world which are the earth, the sky and the space between them. The recipient may infer that the sequence in which they are mentioned iconically reflect the sentence of their appearance during sacrifice: firstly, fire with air

[274] Jamison, Brereton (2014): '[= Agni]'.
[275] Jamison, Brereton (2014): '(the land)'.
[276] Jamison, Brereton (2014): '[= the Sun]'.
[277] Jamison, Brereton (2014): '[= Wind]'.
[278] Thus they are interpreted by Sāyaṇa and Geldner (1951, I) and Witzel, Gotō (2007) who refer to him. Elizarenkova (1989) interprets as the moon, the sun and the wind. O'Flaherty (181): 'Three forms of Agni with flames for hair, or three ecstatic sages (cf. 10.136.1)'.

appears, then the sky appears created during sunrise, space is visible when rain comes from the sun with wind[279].

Thus the cosmic processes are conceived in terms of horses. We may presume they are released in the morning to run freely in the pasture. In the blend, they become one horse transforming itself. Such a conceptualisation allows the composer to present complex cosmic processes in simple terms that are well known to his recipients. The adverb *ṛtuthā́* activates the concept of the passage of time and its order. The world is identified with time and it is understood in the same way with the use of the concept of a wheel (ṚV 1.164.2, 3, 11, 14).

The verb *ví cakṣ-* (verse *a*) can be interpreted as 'to see, to gaze' (Jamison, Brereton 2014, Witzel, Gotō 2007) or 'to become visible' (Houben 2000a, Elizarenkova 1989, O'Flaherty 1981). Both interpretations suit the context: the world exists thanks to the movement incited in ritual and its essence is constituted by the cognitive activity of reality which manifests itself when it begins to cognise and thus sets itself in motion. At the same time, the reduction of the complexity of the world into three elements is proof of the search for abstraction. Moreover, this process of abstraction is continued in the next stanzas. In the previous stanza (ṚV 1.164.43), the poet observes the sacrificial cycle. In the present stanza, he understands its ontological basis which is expressed in the general model of reality transformations. Now, he will understand the deepest nature of reality which is speech.

ṚV 1.164.45

catvā́ri vā́k párimitā padā́ni tā́ni vidur brāhmaṇā́ yé manīṣíṇaḥ |
gúhā trī́ṇi níhitā néṅgayanti turī́yaṃ vācó manuṣyà vadanti ||

Speech is measured in four feet[280]. Brahmins of inspired thinking know these. They do not set in motion the three that are inspired in secret; the sons of Manu speak the fourth[281] of speech.

The composer presents speech which is conceived as divided into four feet or footprints. In this way, he elaborates the concept of a cow in terms of which speech is conceived in the hymn. The logic of the concept of cow triggers the recipient to activate the triple structure of reality. Its interpretation depends on an interpretation of the word *padá*. If the recipient interprets it as 'foot', then the manifest aspect is conceived in terms of one foot, the borderline sphere of

279 This is the sequence of creative stages in CU 6.1-7 (see chapter 4.1.4).
280 Jamison, Brereton (2014): '[/quarters]'.
281 Jamison, Brereton (2014): '(foot/quarter)'.

the cosmos as three feet and the unmanifest aspect as the body of a cow[282]. If he interprets *padá* as 'footprint', he will understand the word in terms of one footprint, the way to the borderline sphere of the cosmos in terms of three footprints and reality in terms of the whole cow. Probably, the dual meaning of the word *padá* prompts the recipient to refer to everyday knowledge in order to facilitate supernatural cognition in precise terms. As mentioned above, it is based on the experience of following the footprints of lost or stolen cattle although, as we shall see, experience is again violated. One visible footprint leads one to the leg in terms of which the *axis mundi* is conceived. Since the *axis mundi* is also conceived in terms of a path made of three footprints, when one climbs mentally *via* these three footprints, one gets access to three legs in terms of which the borderline of the cosmos is conceived[283]. Then the way to the unmanifest aspect of reality is open, but, as already mentioned many times, the composers of the Veda do not enter it before the Upaniṣads. Moreover, the composer of ṚV 1.164 seems to think that the whole of reality can be conceived in terms of speech.

We can see yet again how the concepts of simple experience motivate abstract thinking. Their use allows the composer to present precisely a complex and difficult concept of supernatural cognition and its different stages. Moreover, he can express the situation of profane life. Within the frames of this interpretation, men in everyday life cognise only one footprint of the cow which leads nowhere. We could say that they follow an empty footprint (*réku padá*). This phrase is used twice in the ṚV. Once in ṚV 4.5.12, in the dialogue between Agni and the poet who cannot recognise the hidden end of the road leading to riches that is announced by Agni. The second is ṚV 10.108.7, in the dialogue of the Paṇis with Saramā: the Paṇis claim that Saramā will not get their riches and have come in vain. Since in terms of the conquest of riches cognition is conceived in the ṚV (Jurewicz 2010a: 91 ff.), the recipient may interpret these stanzas as expressing futile cognition. Such is the situation of men who do not know sacred speech, or, more precisely, the *akṣára* of the Ṛk-stanza. Those who know it get access to other footprints which form a path leading to supernatural cognition conceived in terms of drinking Soma from the solar source in the highest heaven, at the borderline sphere of the cosmos.

Within the context of the whole hymn, the recipient may presume that, in his presentation of speech divided into four, the composer refers to the

---

282 This is conceptualisation of reality proposed in *Puruṣasūkta* with use of the word *pắda*. For the problem of division into four in the Veda, see Bhattacharya (1978).

283 In the same way a simple experience of drinking a juice to get its essence (*rása*) is used in BU 2.3, see chapter 4.4.2.2.

akṣára of the Ṛk-stanza which should be known if one wants his recitation to be successful (ṚV 1.164.39, see above) and which is conceived in terms of the buffalo-cow (ṚV 1.164.41-42, see above). My argument is as follows. The word *akṣára* is used for the first time in the hymn in stanza 24c; I would like to quote once again its second hemistich:

> *vākéna vākáṃ dvipádā cátuṣpadā akṣáreṇa mimate saptá vā́ṇīḥ*
>
> by two-footed and four-footed recitation the[284] recitation. By the syllable the seven voices assume their measure.

When the listener hears the whole hemistich, he may understand that *cátuṣpad* also refers to *akṣára* which is divided in four footprints. And this is also the intention of the poet: he wants not only to present the structure of speech and the creation of living beings, but also to imply that *akṣára*, the essence of the world and speech, is divided into four. In this way, he implies that the seven voices, which metonymically evoke the seven seers, have access to the whole syllable. And this is confirmed by ṚV 1.164.45b where the composer says that Brahmins endowed with insight, *manīṣā́*, know it. The word *manīṣā́* is used in ṚV 10.129.4 to denote the power of thinking of poets who are able to discern the unmanifest aspect of reality, called *ásat*, from the manifest, called *sát* (Jurewicz 2010a: 52–53).

In the light of this interpretation, the recipient can enrich the meaning of ṚV 1.164.24c. As I have argued, it is possible to understand *dvipád* and *cátuṣpad* as 'two-footed', i.e. men and 'four-footed', i.e. animals. It follows then that, if we take *cátuṣpadā* as a qualifier of *akṣára*, it would be connected with animals. In order to resolve this contradiction, I will refer to the Brāhmaṇas. Firstly, speech as a whole is not-uttered (*ánirukta*); in the same way speech of animals is conceived (ŚB 4.1.316). Secondly, in ŚB 11.1.6.3-5 (see chapter 3.5.2), the creation of the world is conceived in terms of the development of man who firstly utters words consisting of one and two syllables and then utters words consisting of more syllables. Taking this into account, we can assume that *dvipád* can also refer to animals the speech of which consists only of two syllables while *cátuṣpad* refers to men whose speech is more complex. The recipient may play with the ambiguity of the meaning of *dvipád* and *cátuṣpad* and see the process of creation in a holistic way.

Coming back to ṚV 1.164.45, the three feet/footprints of the buffalo-cow, in terms of which hidden parts of speech are conceived, are beyond the scope

[284] Jamison, Brereton (2014): '(full)'.

of everyday cognition[285]. Their state is expressed with the negative use of the verb *iṅg-*. This verb is used three times in the ṚV. Its two other usages evoke experience. In ṚV 4.57.4, it is used with the concept of a goad for driving cattle as its direct object. In ṚV 5.78.7, it is used to denote action of the wind which moves waves of ponds covered with lotuses, in the same way as a child during delivery expected to be born is easily incited by the internal power of mother. Both concepts are suitable source domains for the concept of speech. Within the frames of the first conceptualisation, speech is conceived in terms of a man who drives his cattle while within the frames of the second, speech is conceived in terms of wind which moves various objects. In the blend, the hidden part of speech is conceived as a factor which may inspire men, but which does not do so for those who do not know it (as it is stated in ṚV 1.164.39, see above) and who only have access to its manifest part. If the recipient activates conceptualisation of speech in terms of fire, he will understand that fire is present within men as their ultimate cognitive principle in its potential form. When it is kindled thanks to Soma drunk during ritual, it inspires men which is conceived in terms of their burning (see Jurewicz 2010a: 264 ff., 270–272).

ṚV 1.164.46

índram mitrám̐ váruṇam agním āhur átho divyáḥ sá suparṇó garútmān |
ékaṃ sád víprā bahudhā́ vadanti agníṃ yamám mātaríśvānam āhuḥ ||

They say it is Indra, Mitra, Varuṇa and Agni, and also it is the winged, well-feathered[286] of heaven[287].
Though it is One, inspired poets speak of it in many ways. They say it is Agni, Yama and Mātariśvan.

Now the cognition of the poet reaches the final state. He understands the unity of reality which seems to be many because of many names given to it. Verse *a* draws the recipient's attention to ṚV 1.106.1 the composer of which asks various gods for help; the names of Indra, Mitra, Varuṇa and Agni are

[285] The idea that only part of our thinking is conscious, which is implied by its Ṛgvedic conceptualisation, anticipates the findings of modern cognitive science which find this is the case. As Lakoff, Johnson (1999: 391 ff.) point out the philosophy of mind conviction that all thought is conscious that is widespread in European was inherited from Descartes and his metaphoric conceptualisation of knowing in terms of seeing. As they write 'Remarkably enough Descartes' view is not a quaint seventeenth oddity of mere historical interest. It is very much with us today, and the only justification for it today is Descartes' argument, which is constituted by his metaphors and which could not be made without them' (Lakoff, Johnson 1999: 397).

[286] Jamison, Brereton (2014): '(bird)'.

[287] Jamison, Brereton (2014): '[= the Sun]'.

mentioned in the same sequence[288]. At the same time, Agni is called Mitra and Varuṇa is called Agni in the ṚV (Jurewicz 2010a: 419–421). But there are stanzas which have the tendency to identify Indra with Agni (Jurewicz 2010a: 360 ff.), so I would argue that the composer implies that all gods called on during sacrifices are manifestations of Agni.

The word *garútmant* (verse *b*) is used in once more in the ṚV (10.149), in the hymn describing creation performed by Savitar. ṚV 10.149.1ab presents creation in terms of fastening the earth and stabilising the sky in a place which has no prop; the concept of Savitar metonymically evokes the concept of the sunrise *via* the concept of Savitar's impelling power. ṚV 10.149.1cd presents the creation of space in terms of milking a horse. Thus the recipient understands that creation of space takes place when it rains: in terms of a horse, the sun is conceived and, in terms of milking, raining. Space is conceived in terms of a sea bound in an unlimited sphere. It is worth adding that the sequence of creation, which is the earth, the sky and the space between them, agrees with the sequence of creation presented in ṚV 1.164.44 (see above).

In the second stanza of ṚV 10.149, the composer seems to put creation in more abstract terms. In the first hemistich, he states that only Savitar knows the place where this sea flows forth. The sequence of creation presented in the second hemistich is similar to that in ṚV 10.72 (see section 1.5): the earth called *bhū́r*, appears, then the space called *bhúvas* and, then, the earth and the sky are created. Creation is conceived in terms of flowing (*ví aúnad*) or rising or standing up (*útthitaṃ*) and in terms of spreading out (*aprathetām*) which are more image schematic than the source domains evoked in the description of the first stanza.

In ṚV 10.149.3[289] the composer states that a being, conceived in terms of 'the fine feathered Garutmant(-bird) of Savitar' (*suparṇó savitúr garútmān*), was created earlier. So the recipient may infer that *garútmant* appears before the world is created. Conceptualisation of the sun in terms of a bird allows us to interpret *garútmant* as the sun. This stage of creation corresponds to the fourth stage of creation in the *Nāsadīyasūkta* conceived in terms of the heating of part of reality (see Jurewicz 2010a: 50). Within the frames of this

---

[288] ṚV 1.106.1: *índram mitrám váruṇam agním ūtáye mā́rutaṃ śárdho áditiṃ havāmahe |ráthaṃ ná durgā́d vasavaḥ sudānavo víśvasmān no áṃhaso níṣ pipartana* || See also ṚV 10.35.10: *ā́ no barhíḥ sadhamā́de bṛhád diví devā́m̐ īḷe sādáyā saptá hótṝn* | *índram mitrám váruṇaṃ sātáye bhágaṃ suastí agníṃ samidhānám īmahe* |

[289] It is worth adding that the last stanza of the hymn (ṚV 10.149.5cd: *evā́ tvā́rcann ávase vándamānaḥ sómasyevāṃśúm práti jāgarāhám*) attests meditation on the sun: the poet stays wakeful facing the sun as if he stayed facing the stalk of Soma. In this way, the composer evokes ṚV 4.58.1 with its image of the Somic wave which rises in the form of the stalk of Soma (see Jurewicz 2010a: 227 ff.).

conceptualisation, the whole of reality would be conceived in terms of Savitar. *Garútmant* is presented as appearing with the abundance of the immortal world (*ámartiyasya bhúvanasya bhūnā́*) which implies that it is an excellent manifestation of reality. It is also possible to understand the instrumental form *bhūnā́* as expressing the way reality manifests itself in the world: it manifests thanks to its greatness. In other words, reality becomes shining and great and this form of reality, which will become the world, is called *garútmant*. This form of reality can be conceived in terms of the sun, but it is not yet the sun. I would see this form as the borderline sphere of the cosmos reached in Somic exultation.

Taking the concept of *garútmant* thus understood in the frames of ṚV 1.164.46, we can assume that the composer, having described everyday ritual activity which needs the concepts of various gods that can be called on by the poets for help, now refers to the first manifestation of reality in the world. In verse *c*, he states that reality thus conceived is one, although men give various names to it.

In verse *d*, the composer enumerates the names Agni, Yama and Mātariśvan. The possibility to identify Agni with Mātariśvan is attested in that the word *mātariśvan* either refers to a power which kindles fire or to fire itself. The identity of Yama and Agni has been already argued by Bergaigne (1963[1878–83], I: 89 ff.). I would like to add few arguments which confirm this thesis within the frames of the present work.

Yama is presented as being in the highest heaven together with the ancestors (ṚV 10.14.8). The highest heaven is at the top of the cosmic tree (ṚV 10.135) and is the same place as reached by men during sacrifices (Jurewicz 2010a: 303–305). In ṚV 1.66.8, Agni is called a being born as Yama and Yama is what is to be born (*yamó ha jātó yamó jánitvam̐*). Either the poet wants to express the identity of Agni with Yama or he conceives Yama and Agni in terms of twins; the second conceptualisation also implies their close similarity, if not identity. In ṚV 10.52.3, the poet asks who is Agni for Yama (*ayám̐ yó hótā kír u sá yamásya*) and about their relationship conceived, as we may presume in the light of ṚV 1.66.8, in terms of their twinship. The concept of Yama also appears in the description of the creation of fire in ṚV 10.51.3 the composer of which creates an image of Agni who hides from the gods who want him to become the Hotar. In the third, stanza Yama finds Agni. If the recipient takes into account that Yama is the first who died and thus created the path of men (ṚV 10.14.1 see Jurewicz 2010a: 289 ff.), he can interpret that Agni dies when Yama finds him. This would explain why Agni is so afraid of the gods: because he is afraid of death. The death of Agni is also implied in ṚV 1.164.32 where Agni is presented as entering *nírṛti* (see above). It is elaborated in ŚB 6.1.2 where Agni is afraid that Prajāpati will kill him and hides itself in five animals. Because of that the gods promise Agni that he will not age and he will not be hurt in his function as the Hotar (ṚV 10.53.7).

In ṚV 10.21.5, Agni is presented as being born thanks to Atharvan and, having found all the poetic arts, becomes the messenger of Vivasvant, i.e. the sun that is the father of Yama. The composer of this stanza calls Agni dear and beloved of Yama (*priyó yamásya kā́miyo*, ṚV 10.21.5e). Such a qualification may prompt the recipient to infer that Yama does not really kill Agni.

ṚV 1.83.5 seems to refer to the same (as in ṚV 10.21.5) conceptualisation of the creation of Agni in terms of which the creation of the world is conceived[290]. In verse *a*, Atharvan creates paths in ritual action. In the ṚV, the dawn is conceived in the same way paths are created (Jurewicz 2010a: 114–115). Verse *b* presents the appearance of the sun which agrees with the scenario of the appearance of the morning light: first we see dawn, then the sun. Verse *c* presents the morning ritual activity of men conceived in terms of freeing cows; men are metonymically evoked *via* the concept of the priest (Uśanā Kāvya). In verse *d*, the composer states that men sacrifice to *yamásya jātám amṛ́taṃ*. Jamison, Brereton (2014) interpret this phrase as 'immortal birth of Yama'[291], but it is also possible to interpret it as '[something which is] immortal [and] born [and belongs] to Yama'. The immortal being is Agni which is born in its form of fire and of the rising sun.

So verse ṚV 1.164.46d, enumerating the names *agní, yamá, mātaríśvan* could metonymically evoke the phases of manifestation of Agni which first dies and is then kindled within the world. Yama, conceived in terms of Agni's twin, is a manifestation of Agni's ability to hide itself and die. Men in their ritual activity mentally reach the state in which they able to realise their identity with the internally contradictory nature of reality.

ṚV 1.164.47

kṛṣṇáṃ niyā́naṃ hárayaḥ suparṇā́ apó vásānā dívam út patanti |
tá ā́vavṛtran sádanād ṛtásya ā́d íd ghṛténa pṛthivī́ ví udyate ||

Along the dark course, tawny well-feathered[292], clothing themselves in the water, fly up towards heaven.
These have returned here[293] from the seat of truth[294]. Only then is the earth moistened with ghee.

---

[290] ṚV 1.83.5: *yajñaír átharvā prathamáḥ pathás tate tátaḥ sū́ryo vratapā́ vená ā́jani | ā́ gā́ ājad uśánā kāviyáḥ sácā yamásya jātám amṛ́taṃ yajāmahe ||*
[291] In the same way Elizarenkova (1989), Geldner (1951), Witzel Gotō (2007).
[292] Jamison, Brereton (2014): '(birds) [= flames]'.
[293] Jamison, Brereton (2014): '(as rain)'.
[294] Jamison, Brereton (2014): '[= heaven]'.

In this stanza, the composer presents the general model of reality transformation[295]. Flames of fire, conceived in terms of birds (verse *a*), fly up to the sky along the black way marked by its smoke in terms of which the *axis mundi* is conceived (ṚV 1.164.43, see above). It is possible that the composer wants to evoke the concept of *suparṇá* from the previous stanza in order to imply that the flames of fire are the same reality which manifests itself in the world in the creative act. In this way, transformation of one into many is conceived.

Qualification of the flames of fire as 'clothing themselves in water' (*apó vásānā*, verse *b*) activates the concept of Soma which is most often qualified in this way when it is mixed with water (SOMA IS A KING, MIXING SOMA WITH A FLUID IS CLOTHING A KING)[296]. The concept of Soma is also activated *via* the concept of birds in terms which its streams are conceived (see Jurewicz 2010a: 165–166).

The concept of the seat of truth (*sádanād ṛtásya*, verse *c*) is used in ṚV 4.21.3 in reference to a place from which Indra is expected to come. In this stanza, this place is qualified as being far away (*parāvátas*). According to ṚV 7.36.1, the sacred word is supposed to come from the seat of truth (*prá bráhma etu sádanād ṛtásya*) when the sun rises, the earth appears in the morning light and fire is kindled. In ṚV 4.42.4, the protagonist of the hymn (king Trasadasyu who identifies himself with Varuṇa and Indra, see Smith 1992) states that he has supported the sky on the seat of truth (*dhāráyaṃ dívaṃ sádana ṛtásya*). These contexts allow me to assume that the expression *sádana ṛtásya* refers to zenith, i.e. to the place which is conceived in terms of the highest heaven at the borderline sphere of the cosmos. This expression is also used in a context which implies that it also denotes the sacrificial place (ṚV 7.53.2, 8.59.4) but, taking into account that *paramá vyòman* is already present embodied in the Brahman-priest, we can presume that the Ṛgvedic poets wanted to create a conceptual blend within which the sacrifice is a mysterious sphere beyond space and time where the earth and the sky are united as they were in the pre-creative state (Jurewicz 2010a: 284–285). This is confirmed in ṚV 9.72.6 where the poets are described as milking the undecaying stalk which thunders; in this way, the creation of rain during the Soma ritual, conceived in terms of milking, is presented (see Jurewicz 2010a). According to verses *c–d* of this stanza, cows and thoughts go together and they are presented as being in the womb, in the seat of truth (*ṛtásya yónā sádane punarbhúvaḥ*). The activity of the poets takes place on earth, but they manipulate processes which take place in the sky. Thus the unity of those spheres is implied. If the

[295] Oberlies (1998: 478–479).

[296] ṚV 9.16.2, 9.42.1, 9.78.1, 9.86.40, 9.96.13, 9.109.21, 9.107.4,18,26.

recipient highlights the meaning of *punarbhū́*, which can also be 'appearing once again'[297], he would add the meaning of rain which comes back to the earth conceived in terms of a sacrificial place.

So in the context of ṚV 1.164.47, the recipient understands that the flames of fire mixed with Soma, in the form of the sun, reach the highest point in the sky and come back to the earth. It is worth adding that the form *ā́vavṛtran* (verse *c*) is used in ṚV 3.32.15 to express the streams of Soma which come back to exult Indra; the recipient is triggered to understand that they come back from the sky to feed Indra at the sacrificial place. That the rain forms flames of fire is confirmed by verse *d* where it is stated that only then when they come back from the sky, the earth is moistened with clarified butter. In terms of clarified butter, rain is conceived in the ṚV (Jurewicz 2010a).

ṚV 1.164.48

duvā́daśa pradháyaś cakrám ékaṃ trī́ṇi nábhyāni ká u tác ciketa |
tásmin sākáṃ triśatā́ ná śaṅkávo arpitā́ḥ ṣaṣṭír ná calācalā́saḥ ||

The chariot-wheel[298] is one, its wheel-segments are twelve, its wheel-naves are three: who understands this?
They[299] that wander on and on are fitted together on that, like three hundred pegs, like sixty[300].

The composer of the hymn comes back to the chariot-metaphor elaborated in ṚV 1.164.2-3 and then in ṚV 1.164.11-14. The processes described in the previous stanza with use of the general model of reality transformation are now conceived in terms of a wheel. These processes constitute the temporal and spatial dimension of the world. The wheel with twelve spokes is mentioned in ṚV 1.164.11 to conceive the temporal dimension of the manifest aspect. It is possible that the composer now wants to activate this image of a wheel, although here the word *pradhí* is used instead of *ará*. According to Sparreboom (1985: 123), the word *pradhí* can refer to 'an element of the solid disc wheel', but it is not possible to reconstruct its exact meaning. The concept of a wheel with three navels (*trinā́bhi cakrám*) is evoked in ṚV 1.164.2 and, again, it is possible that the recipient is expected to evoke it here *via* the word *nábhya* which can be the synonym of *nā́bhi* (see Sparreboom 1985: 123). The phrase 'like three hundred pegs, like sixty' (*triśatā́ ná... ṣaṣṭír ná...*) which qualifies pegs makes the recipient think about the number three hundred and sixty and

[297] As Elizarenkova (1989) does.
[298] Jamison, Brereton (2014): '(of the Sun)'.
[299] Jamison, Brereton (2014): '[= the days]'.
[300] Jamison, Brereton (2014): '(more)'.

to conceive days in terms of pegs. As has been argued, the days and nights are conceived in terms of seven hundred and twenty sons in ṚV 1.164.11 (which is two times three hundred and sixty). If this interpretation is accepted, the days are presented in this stanza as moving and not moving at the same time. Taking into account the construction of the chariot, pegs do not move in reference to the wheel, but move, when the wheel moves. Since according to ṚV 1.164.2, all the worlds or living beings are on the wheel, the recipient may presume that they are in the same situation: they do not move and move. Thus the internally contradictory condition of the manifest aspect of reality is expressed. Moreover, it seems that days and nights are conceived in the same way in ṚV 1.164.11 where they are presented as seven hundred and twenty sons who, it is implied, sit on the wheel.

It is worth noting that numbers are quite consistent as far as stanzas evoking the concept of a wheel are concerned: most often it is one wheel with twelve or six spokes (which is half of twelve) that is mentioned and seven hundred and twenty or three hundred and sixty elements on the wheels; only once is a wheel with five spokes mentioned. The descriptions differ as far as the number of horses is concerned (in 1.164.2 seven horses are harnessed by seven drivers and in ṚV 1.164.1 ten horses are harnessed) and as far as the number of wheels (in ṚV 1.164.3.12 a chariot a chariot with seven wheels is mentioned). It is difficult in the present state of research to reconstruct the exact meanings of these conceptualisation, but its general consistency allows one to assume the general division of time into twelve months, six seasons and seven-hundred days and nights. This conceptualisation of time appears in the beginning of the hymn (ṚV 1.164.2-3), in the description of the beginning of supernatural cognition (ṚV 1.164.11-14), and now, when the cognition of the poet is finally fulfilled. So the problem of manifestation of reality in time and its cognition seems to be the crucial problem of this hymn. Reality, conceived as infinite (*áditi*) and imperishable (*akṣára*), manifests itself as finite and perishable fiery speech expressed in time.

It is worth mentioning that concept of a chariot, speech and fire are an effective experiential basis for the conceptualisation of time. The concept of a chariot activates the concept of a journey during which the passage of time is experienced. Long recitation is also an activity which is connected with the experiencing of the passage of time. Sitting in front of a fire and waiting for milk to boil is also an activity closely connected with the experience of time. Thus the ritual setting allows its participants to experience the flow of time. The source domains of fire and a chariot allow for its understanding.

Conceptualisation of time in terms of a chariot's wheel, identified with the world, is important proof of the tendency for abstraction. The fact that the composer repeatedly evokes it in the hymn implies that he wants to focus the recipient's attention on an abstract way of thinking about the manifest aspect of reality. This tendency will be developed in later thought: the composers of the AVŚ will elaborate the concept of the wheel and time (see chapter 2.1.3, 2.5.1.2) while the composers of the ŚB will conceive the temporal character of the manifest aspect of reality using different source domains, but will see it as the most important reason for the human condition (see chapter 3.2.3).

ṚV 1.164.49

yás te stánaḥ śaśayó yó mayobhū́r yéna víśvā púṣyasi vā́riyāṇi |
yó ratnadhā́ vasuvíd yáḥ sudátraḥ sárasvati tám ihá dhā́tave kaḥ ||

Your breast, which is ever full, which is joy itself, by which you make all desirable things prosper,
which confers treasure and finds wealth, which brings good gifts – o Sarasvatī, you prepare to suckle us here.

This stanza is an invocation of Sarasvatī [301]. Before I place this concept within the context of the whole hymn, I will briefly analyse the Ṛgvedic use of the words *sáras* and of *sárasvant*.

The word *sáras* denotes a pond or lake. It is evoked in comparisons: frogs lie in it like a dried leather gag (ṚV 7.103.2), the bulls given to the poet are compared to reeds from a pond (ṚV 8.1.33). Frogs are compared to Brahmins who surround a vessel full of Soma like frogs round a pond (ṚV 7.103.7). However, it appears most often in connection with the amount of Soma drunk by Indra: he drinks Soma like a buffalo from a pond (ṚV 8.45.24), streams of Soma fill him like water fills a pond (ṚV 8.49.3) or he is filled with them like a pond (8.1.23). In several stanzas, *sáras* is used in reference to Soma: Indra drinks three or three hundred lakes of Soma (ṚV 5.29.7,8, 8.77.4, 6.17.11, 8.7.10). In ṚV 9.54.2, Soma is presented as looking like the sun and flowing along the seven slopes to the lakes (*sárāṃsi*) and the sky. The concept of *sáras* can be understood as metonymically referring to the vessels into which Soma is poured[302], but the context also implies that it refers to the vessels which are in the sky, i.e. to the sun where Soma is finally purified. Such blends conflating the concepts of clarification of Soma both on earth and in the sky are created by the composers of the ṚV (Jurewicz 2010a:

[301] For a recent concise survey of the concept of Sarasvatī in the ṚV, see Ludvik (2007: 11–36). For identification of Sarasvatī with Milky Way, see Witzel (1984). For Sarasvatī as river, cows and speech (also in the later thought, see Gonda (1985).

[302] In this metonymic way, Jamison, Brereton (2014) understand *sáras* in ṚV 7.103.7.

165–166)[303]. So the contexts of the usages of the word *sáras* highlight its meaning of a lake of Soma.

Taking this into account, the word *sárasvant* can be interpreted as someone or something filled with Soma. Such a conceptualisation of Sarasvatī is most clear in ṚV 7.95.1 where it is conceived in terms of a copper stronghold (*ā́yasī pū́ḥ*). As I have shown elsewhere (Jurewicz 2010b), the concept of a copper stronghold is the result of the transformation of the concept of a stronghold hiding desired riches which metonymically identifies the contents with the container (DESIRED RICHES FOR A STRONGHOLD). The copper stronghold becomes a desired good; it belongs to the poets and protects them (Jurewicz 2010b). In some contexts, the concept of copper stronghold is the source domain for conceptualisation of the sun and, in ṚV 8.100.8, Soma is presented as hidden in it. Conceptualisation of Sarasvatī as filled with Soma is also confirmed in that the rivers' water is identified with it (e.g. ṚV 7.47.1).

This conceptualisation is evoked in ṚV 1.164.49. The composer of which presents Sarasvatī as a female with breasts which are ever full and thanks to which she makes 'all the desirable things prosper' (*yéna víśvā púṣyasi vā́riyāṇi*, verses *a–b*). She gives her breast to suckle as someone who gives treasure and good gifts (verses *c–d*).

The word *stána* (verse *a*) is used in the ṚV three more times. In ṚV 1.69.4, it is used in reference to a cow', so the recipient can conceive Sarasvatī in these terms which agrees with its Ṛgvedic conceptualisation that is attested in many places: it is presented as a cow swelling with milk, honey and clarified butter which can be milked (ṚV 5.43.11, 6.61.14, 7.36.6, 7.95.2, 9.67.32, 10.17.10, 10.64.9). On the other hand, the word *stána* is used in ṚV 2.39.6 the composer of which extolls the Aśvins and compares them to various phenomena appearing in pairs like two breasts of a woman[304].

If the recipient highlights the meaning of cow, he will understand Sarasvatī as speech[305]. If he highlights the meaning of a woman, he may understand that Sarasvatī is the mother of the cognising poet; Sarasvatī is called 'the best mother' (*ámbitama*) in ṚV 2.41.16a. The concept of mother appears in ṚV 1.164.8 where she is presented as giving a share in truth to the father. I interpret mother as Aditi and speech. Now, at the end of his cognition, the poet understands her as Sarasvatī.

---

303 In ṚV 9.97.5, Soma, clarified in the morning, is asked to flow into the lake which can also be understood in both ways: as the earthly vessel and as the sun.

304 The fourth use of the word *stána* is ṚV 7.96.6 which will be discussed below.

305 Toporov (2008) shows a possible experiential basis of conceptual connection between river and speech which is their common feature of making noise. It can also be the basis for metaphorical conceptualisation of speech in terms of a liquid, attested already in the ṚV (Jurewicz 2010a: 379) and elaborated in ŚB 6.1.1 (see chapter 3.2.2).

The concept of suckling an udder or a breast (verse *d*) is the source domain for the conceptualisation of cognition realised during sacrifices which leads to omniscience and immortality (Jurewicz 2014a). In the ṚV, Sarasvatī is presented as closely connected with the inspired thought *dhī́*: it rules over it (ṚV 1.3.12), it realises it (ṚV 2.3.8), it gives it (ṚV 6.49.7), it helps it (ṚV 6.61.4) and it comes with it (ṚV 7.35.11, 10.65.13). The possibility to understand Sarasvatī as a symbol of light agrees with the conceptualisation as speech, presented in ṚV 1.164, as the powerful factor which leads the sacrificer in his journey to the sky. In ṚV 1.188.8, Sarasvatī is presented as impelling to glory (*śrī́*), which metonymically activates the state of fame which is conceived as the state of immortality and omniscience realised on the sun[306] (see section 1.7). Since the state realised under the influence of Soma is also conceived in the ṚV in terms of coming back home (Jurewicz 2010a: 416–417), the description of the composer of ṚV 1.164.49 is even more coherent: it can be understood as coming back to the mother's home. It further confirms my interpretation that Sarasvatī is the mother who gives share in truth to the father with her insight and mind that is described in ṚV 1.164.8.

The person who is allowed to suck is called *ratnadhā́* (verse *c*). This word is most often used in the ṚV in reference to Agni (ṚV 1.1.1, 2.1.7, 5.8.3, 7.16.6), then to Soma (ṚV 9.67.13, 9.90.2, 9.107.4). In ṚV 10.35.7, it is also used in reference to Savitar, to Ṛbhus (ṚV 4.34.6) and to the wives of gods (ṚV 4.36.7). Such a qualification of the man who will suck the breasts of Sarasvatī suggests he is a person who is able to realise his identity with Agni and its Somic and solar manifestations. The compound *vasuvíd* evokes the conceptualisation of cognition in terms of gaining riches (Jurewicz 2010a: 91 ff.). It is confirmed in that inspired thought (*dhī́*) is twice qualified in this way (ṚV 1.46.2, 8.60.12).

ṚV 1.164.50

yajñéna yajñám ayajanta devā́s tā́ni dhármāṇi prathamā́ni āsan |
té ha nā́kam mahimā́naḥ sacanta yátra pū́rve sādhiyā́ḥ sánti devā́ḥ ||

With the sacrifice the gods performer the sacrifice: these were the first foundations. These, its greatnesses, followed to heaven's vault, where the ancient Sādhyas and the gods are.

[306] The same state is evoked in ṚV 2.41.17 where Sarasvatī is conceived as containing 'all lifetimes' (*víśvā ā́yūṃṣi*).

This stanza is the same as the last stanza of the *Puruṣasūkta* (see section 1.3). Verse *b* is already evoked in ṚV 1.164.43d. I have interpreted this stanza as presenting a poet who understands the cosmic and cognitive dimension of ritual which causes the sunrise and leads the sacrificer to the supernatural state. The concept of greatness (*mahimán*, verse *c*) has also been evoked by the composer of ṚV 1.164.25d (*táto mahnā́ prá ririce mahitvā́*) who in this way wants his recipient to think about Indra who drinks Soma before his fight with Vṛtra and thus becomes great. At the sacrificial place, the sacrificer identifies himself with Indra and realises the same supernatural state conceived in terms of greatness. Taking into account the larger context of ṚV 1.164.50, the recipient may understand that the sacrifice described in the hymn is a reflexive activity expressed by the verbal and nominal forms of the root *yaj-*. It is the same sacrifice which was performed *in illo tempore* by reality. Thus the poet finally gets the answer to his doubt as to the nature of reality and the beginnings of the world expressed in the initial stanzas of the hymn.

ṚV 1.164.51

samānám etád udakám úc caíti áva cā́habhiḥ |
bhū́mim parjányā jínvanti dívaṃ jinvanti agnáyaḥ ||

This water remains the same: it goes up and down throughout the days.
Thunderstorms vivify the earth, and fires vivify heaven.

In this stanza, the general model of reality transformation is expressed without the use of metaphors, contrary to ṚV 1.164.47. It is presented as the circulation of water between the earth and the sky. The elimination of metaphors has its price: the fiery-solar nature of transformations of reality is hidden, it can only be evoked *via* the concept of fires which vivify the sky (verse *d*). On the basis of this concept, the recipient can evoke the concept of morning sacrifice which creates the sun. The composer is concentrated on what men see and not on its hidden nature. This conceptualisation will be elaborated in AVŚ 10.8.29 within the context of the abstract concept of the full (see chapter 2.6.1).

ṚV 1.164.52

divyáṃ suparṇáṃ vāyasám bṛhántam apā́ṃ gárbhaṃ darśatám óṣadhīnām |
abhīpató vṛṣṭíbhis tarpáyantaṃ sárasvantam ávase johavīmi ||

The heavenly well-feathered, lofty birth, child of the waters, and beautiful (child) of the plants,
the one bringing satisfaction by the rains from what is bounded by waters: Sarasvant! – him do I call upon again and again for help.

The word *suparṇá* in verse *a* is used several times in the hymn. In ṚV 1.164.20-22, it is used as the source domain to conceive of two men one of whom gets supernatural cognition, while the other does not. In ṚV 1.164.46, the word *suparṇá*, in apposition with *garútmant*, is used as the source domain for the first manifestation of reality as the world. In ṚV 1.164.47, the word *suparṇá* in plural is used in reference to flames of fire mixed with streams of Soma which become the rising sun. As I have argued, it is possible that the composer intentionally uses the same word in reference to the first form of reality in the world, and its specific manifestation in fire and Soma, in order to activate the concept of multiplication conceived in terms of the multiplication of birds. In ṚV 1.164.52a, the word *suparṇá* is used to activate the concept of the sun conceived in terms of a bird; it is activated *via* the words *divyáṃ* and *bṛhánt*. In this way, the composer implies that the cognition of reality should begin with cognition of the nature of the sun. Its ambivalent fiery-Somic nature may lead men to unfold the whole cosmic and cosmogonic cycle of the manifestations of reality. This will be elaborated in the AVŚ where an understanding of the sun leads to an understanding of the whole of reality (see chapter 2).

In verse *b*, the composer evokes the model of Child Of The Waters. The child is called the child of the plants, *gárbhaṃ óṣadhīnām*. In this way, the concept of fire is evoked which, as it was believed, exists in hidden forms in plants. The expression *apā́ṃ gárbhaṃ darśatám óṣadhīnām* also appears in ṚV 3.1.13b in a clear reference to Agni. Thus the composer of ṚV 1.164.53 creates a blend identifying the sun, presented in verse *a*, with fire.

If the recipient evokes the use of the phrase *gárbhaṃ óṣadhīnām* in ṚV 7.101.1, he will get more knowledge about the sun. This hymn is devoted to Parjanya. In the first hemistich of the first stanza, the composer creates the conceptual network which consists of the input spaces of a storm with thunder and lightning, human speech and a cow which bellows and gives milk. The generic space of this blend is the concept of sound. In the blend, thunder and lightning are conceived in terms of speech which in turn is conceived in terms of a cow which gives milk from its udder. In verse *c*, the image of a calf created by the bull is evoked and the calf is called 'the embryo of plants' (*gárbhaṃ óṣadhīnām*). In this way, the blend is enriched with the input space of kindling fire; according to verse *d* fire becomes a bull which bellows as soon as it is born. Since burning fire also makes sounds, this input space is coherent with the generic space. On the basis of everyday experience, the recipient knows that fire can be kindled by men in ritual, but also by thunderbolts.

Moreover, both blazing fire and the sun, which is the solar form of fire from which rain comes, are conceived in terms of a bull; this solar-rainy form of fire is personified as Parjanya. Thus the recipient of ṚV 7.101.1 can unfold the whole cycle of fire-rainy transformations which ends with the growth of plants in which fire is hidden. In ṚV 7.101.3, the bull is conceived as androgynic: it is also a cow. Moreover, it is stated that it is sometimes a barren cow and sometimes a cow which gives birth. In this way, the composer expresses the contradictory activity of reality manifesting itself in cosmic phenomena. The recipient can also understand the lightning as the moment when a bull is manifest born to a cow. In ṚV 7.101.3b, the bull is presented as transforming its body according to its will; the recipient understands that because of this power it can become a cow. Indra is described in the same way (ṚV 3.53.8, 6.47.18[307]), so the recipient may also enrich the blend with this input space. In ṚV 7.101.3c, the composer conceptualises raining in terms of a mother who accepts the milk of a father; in terms of the father, Parjanya is conceived, in terms of the mother, the earth and, in terms of milk, semen and rain. In verse *d*, the composer states that by this act the father and son are born. In this way, the belief that father is reborn in his son is evoked and the rebirth of fire within plants is conceived: firstly, fire becomes the sun, then it becomes the rain (father) to be finally reborn in plants (son).

Activation of this scenario and conceptualisation of rain in ṚV 1.164.52b *via* the phrase *gárbhaṃ óṣadhīnām* agrees with the previous stanza which presents the functioning of the world as the circulation of water generated by fire. ṚV 7.101 presents it in the same way, but in more detail. At the same time, the composer of ṚV 1.164.52 triggers its recipient to unfold the meaning of the model of Child Of The Waters which is raining too (see Jurewicz 2010a: 203 ff.). This meaning is explicitly evoked in verse *c*.[308]

In verse *d*, the composer of ṚV 1.164.52 calls reality, manifest in the world, as *sárasvant*. Taking into account the literal meaning of *sárasvant* which is, as I have argued above, someone or something filled with Soma, this qualification expresses the nature of Agni which is conceived full of Soma and only because of that can it produce rain in its solar form. However, I would like to devote a bit more attention to the concept of *sárasvant* in the ṚV and its relationship with *sárasvatī*.

As far as the relationship between *sárasvant* and *sárasvatī* is concerned, the most instructive is ṚV 7.96. Its first three stanzas refer to *sárasvatī* and the next three to *sárasvant* which Jamison, Brereton (1024: 1003) call 'her shadowy male counterpart'. In stanza 5, *sárasvant* is presented as having

[307] He transforms himself according to his wondrous power (*māyā́*).

[308] Mayrhofer (1992): 'von beiden Seites (des Wassers), allseitig'.

waves which are full of honey and drip with clarified butter, so he is clearly identified with *sárasvatī* described in the previous stanzas. This identification allows the composer to create a blended concept of an androgynous being conceived in terms of a river with its waves. I am tempted to think that the intention of the composer is to evoke the concept of the flood (usually called *salilá*) which is used to conceive the pre-creative state of the world (see above, ṚV 1.164.41, see also Jurewicz 2012a). Within the frames of this conceptualisation, shining waves are the manifestation of reality as the world is conceived (as in the model of the Wave Of Honey, Jurewicz 2010a). Sarasvant helps the poets with these shining waves (ṚV 7.69.5c) because man can access reality only through its manifest aspect. The concept of an androgynic being is elaborated in the next stanza of ṚV 7.96. Sarasvant is presented as having a breast (*stána*) which swells and which is lovely to see (*darśatá*). Taking into account the description of the previous stanza which evokes the image of a shining fluid, similar to clarified butter and honey, the qualification of the breast of Sarasvant in this way is not surprising. If we assume that the sequence of stanzas in ṚV 7.96 iconically reflects the sequence of cognition, we could interpret the hymn in the following way. Firstly, Sarasvatī is cognised in her manifestation as a river, but also in her manifestation as speech and the factor which induces inspired thoughts (*dhī́*, see above, ṚV 1.164.49). The poets then look for the deeper meaning of the world. In their search, they are presented as unmarried men who look for wives and sons and call upon *sárasvant* (ṚV 7.96.4). Taking into account the belief that the father is reborn in his son, the search for wives and sons can be interpreted as the search for oneself. Then the poets realise the structure of reality which in its unmanifest aspect is conceived as an androgynous being and in its manifest aspect is conceived in terms of shining waves conceptually blended with a breast from which bright milk flows. The relationship between aspects of reality is similar to that of ṚV 4.58.1 which is evoked by the image of a honey wave rising from the ocean (the philosophical model of Wave Of Honey, Jurewicz 2010a: 227 ff.). In the context of ṚV 7.96, the waves seem to be conceived in terms of *sárasvatī* and the place of their origin in terms of *sárasvant* conceived as androgynous.

As I have also argued in Jurewicz (2010a), the ocean in ṚV 4.58.1 can be interpreted as Agni. The ṚV attests to a relationship between *agní* and *sárasvatī*. The composer of ṚV 7.95, which is devoted to Sarasvatī, in the third stanza presents a calf which is born in her streams; the recipient can understand that *sárasvant* is *agní*. In verse *d*, it is expected to 'groom his body for winning' (*ví sātáye tanúvam māmṛjīta*) which allows the recipient to activate the general domain of Cleansing By Heat in its specific realisation of grooming a horse. This domain is evoked in ṚV 2.35 which elaborates the model of Child Of The Water, and in many other places in the ṚV to conceive the activity of fire (Jurewicz 2010a).

This model is also evoked in ṚV 3.23.4d where, according to Jamison, Brereton (2014) and Witzel, Gotō (2007), Agni is expected to shine richly on the *sárasvatī* (*sárasvatyāṃ revád agne didīhi*). However, the word *revát* can also be understood as noun and then *agní* is presented as illuminating the riches on *sárasvatī*[309]; the recipient may then also identify *agní* with riches. It is also possible to understand the verse as a request to Agni to illuminate riches in *sárasvatī* which agrees with her conceptualisation in terms of a copper stronghold (ṚV 1.164.49, see above). So Agni is presented as the child of Sarasvatī (ṚV 7.95.3) and, according to the model of Child Of The Waters, it is also her father; searching for riches in Sarasvatī (ṚV 3.23.4) can be understood as the source domain of their sexual act.

Agni is also presented in ṚV 7.40.3 as an impelling factor, together with Sarasvatī (and other gods who are evoked *via* the plural form of the predicate *junanti*), of a man who is helped by the Maruts. Coming back to ṚV 7.96 which is devoted to Sarasvatī and Sarasvant, if the recipient understands that Sarasvant is Agni, then he would construe the same cosmological structure as in ṚV 4.58: the unmanifest aspect of reality is internally contradictory Agni conceived in terms of an androgynous being while the manifest aspect of reality is Sarasvatī conceived in terms of a shining river erupting and turbulent with glistening waters.

So it may be argued that the composer of ṚV 1.164, wants his recipient to interpret *sárasvant* as Agni. Thus the poet would end his supernatural cognition with a vision of the fiery reality as in ṚV 6.9.7 (Jurewicz 2010a: 253–254). In the analysis of ṚV 1.164.8, I have argued that reality in its unmanifest aspect is Aditi; its manifest aspect is conceived in terms of a father. At the end of his cognitive process the poet understands reality as androgynous Agni and its conceptualisation as a mother gives access to it. As I have mentioned, it is possible for the concept of a father to be that of father of a mother. Thus the mother, identified by me as Aditi, is born from her own father called in the last stanzas of the hymn Sarasvant. She becomes the manifestation of sacred speech which allows the unmanifest aspect to manifest within its frames. In ṚV 10.66.5, Sarasvant is summoned together with inspired thoughts (*dhībhís*) which, as I have mentioned above, are given by Sarasvatī[310].

[309] Thus Elizarenkova (1989) and Renou (EVP 12).

[310] In ṚV 10.66.5, the word *sárasvant* is used together with other gods who are summoned to give shelter to the poets; he is expected to come with or thanks to inspired thoughts.

In fact, ṚV 1.164.8a creates a vicious circle. It is impossible to settle finally how the ultimate form of reality is conceived. In this masterly way, the composer can express the internally contradictoriness of reality which can be conceived as a mother or a father because it contains both aspects. However, men need linear thinking especially if they want to find a way to realise their identity with reality thus conceived. In the light of the last stanzas of ṚV 1.164, one has to reach the state of manifestation through power of sacred speech called Sarasvatī. The word *sáras* implies that it is power of Soma but, taking into account that the composer of the hymn is more focused on speech than on Soma as a necessary condition for supernatural knowledge, I would argue that Sarasvatī is conceived in terms of a more general power. This is Aditi, infinity, a general term for the fiery reality which is able to bound itself in speech and manifest itself in the cosmos as time. In an individual dimension, during ritual, it manifests as Sarasvatī.

*

From the analysis undertaken above it can be seen that the hymn is a very coherent composition. The hymn can be seen on several levels.

One level is the experience of the poet who looks at fire which is kindled. Then ritual is performed the crucial moment of which is, according to the hymn, the cooking of milk in a pot, offering Soma and bull sacrifice. This experience leads the poet to see the transformations of fire in the world. He wants to confirm his own identity with it and to know the source of its manifestation and of himself. This process is conceived in terms of a dialogue with Agni. It is also conceived in terms of climbing a tree.

The poet realises supernatural mental state during which he confirms his theoretical knowledge in practice. Contrary to the earlier ṚV, here, Soma, as the indispensable factor of this process, is not elaborated, but the knowledge of sacred speech and its most mysterious meaning is conceived in terms of the imperishable syllable (*akṣára*). The moment of gaining knowledge of this syllable is conceived in terms of a buffalo-cow which makes waters flow. Thus the composer can express the paradoxical content of that knowledge in terms of the flowing of something which does not flow. The twofold conceptualisation of speech, in terms of Aditi and in terms of Sarasvatī allows me to propose that the composer discerns two kinds of thinking: the philosophical and the religious. The philosophical thinking uses the abstract concept of Aditi which has already in the ṚV lost its connections with experience, although it is still called 'mother' (*mātṛ́*). Sarasvatī is conceptualised in more concrete terms, as a feeding mother. In ṚV 6.49.7, she is presented as the daughter of Pavīru (*pā́vīravī*)[311] and her husbands are heroes (*vīrápatnī*[312]), her life is brilliant (*citrā́āyuḥ*). According to ṚV 10.17.8, she rides on chariot. So the recipient can conceive her in similar terms to other Ṛgvedic goddesses, especially to the Dawn. Within the frames of individual ritual, she could be imagined to appear in this form.

The next level is ontology presented by the composer. The main metaphysical assumption about reality is conceived in terms of Agni which manifests itself and its manifest aspect is time and speech. Manifestation in time is constitutes the cosmic dimension, manifestation in speech constitutes the human dimension. The latter enables man to understand the former. At the same time, speech is also seen as cosmic manifestation similarly as time is human experience.

Another level is that of metaphor used to conceptualise manifestations of Agni. Its manifestation in time is conceived in terms of a chariot and its wheel. Its manifestation in speech is conceived in terms of a cow and its calf. These two metaphors are used in a coherent way. Cognitive activity of the seven seers, who take part in creation, is conceived in terms of the former metaphor while the cognitive activity of poets, who repeat their activity, is conceived in terms of the latter. The use of these two metaphors allows the composer to express the possibility of realising a supernatural state which is conceived in terms of yoking a cow to the chariot.

Manifestation of Agni is also conceived in terms of a relationship between a mother and a father. This metaphor is ambiguous. On the one hand, Agni in its unmanifest aspect is conceived in terms of a mother who gives birth to a father. In terms of father, manifest aspect of Agni is conceived within which mother, speech, is again born. On the other hand, Agni in its unmanifest aspect is conceived in terms of a father and its manifestation in speech in terms of a mother while its manifestations in the cosmos is conceived again in terms of a father. In this way, the poet expresses internally contradictory nature of reality. At the same time, the composer also activates the philosophical models created in the ṚV to conceive manifestations of Agni. These are the general model of reality transformations, the models of Child Of The Waters and of The Wave of Honey and the general domain of Procreation.

It is worth noting that the sources domains, used for the conceptualisation of the abstract concepts of time, speech and cognition, imply the same conceptualisation of the world and of the possibility to reach a supernatural state. Their most simple topology is based on the image schema of SOURCE-

[311] This epithet also appears in ṚV 10.65.13a as the first epithet of the gods summoned in this stanza. Sarasvatī is summoned in verse *c* of this hymn, as the last goddess.

[312] According to Jamison, Brereton (2014), this epithet also refers to Sarasvatī in ṚV 1.104.4c.

PATH-GOAL where the path is the *axis mundi*. The *axis mundi* is conceived in terms of a tree, a yoke-pole, a path left by a chariot, a path left by a cow and its calf, and an umbilical cord. In case of an outflow of water, it is the stream of rain flowing from the sun. There is no doubt that the composer consciously choses concepts in his exposition of metaphysical issues. In the context of the hymn, the everyday concepts of chariot, cow, mother and father become abstract concepts created in the way I have described in the previous sections. Their input spaces are concrete concepts and concepts of time, speech and manifestations of reality. In the blends, the basic logic is imparted by the concrete input spaces in order to conceive the content coming from the abstract ones. In comparison with the earlier content of the ṚV, where the concept of passage of time is conceived in terms of dawns coming every day in the morning (Jurewicz 2010a: 119–121), the concept of time presented in ṚV 1.164 is more abstract and general. As I have also argued, conceptualisation of the manifest aspect in terms of speech is more abstract than its conceptualisation in terms of fire (see section 1.6). There is no mention of *vā́c* (speech), *kālá* (time) or *sṛ́ṣṭi* (creation) which will be used in later thought, but there is no doubts that these concepts are intended by the composer. They are sufficiently clear in his mind for him to analyse and express them.

The hymn is the first in early Indian thinking to devote so much space to supernatural cognition and the lack of knowledge which precedes it. Sacred speech plays the main role in this process which foreshadows the later attempts to gain the supernatural state, characteristic for those which are under influence of Soma, without Soma.

Conceptualisation of the first manifestation of reality in terms of speech shows a changes in the means of obtaining supernatural cognition as if Soma was less accessible or recitation had begun to give supernatural results additional to those from Somic exultation. It seems that when the late layers of the ṚV were composed, the role of recitation of sacred texts had become a part of practice leading to supernatural cognition. At the same time, it is possible that the composer wanted to create a meta-language on the basis of the Ṛgvedic heritage which could be used in theoretical thought about reality and supernatural experience. In this sense, ṚV 1.164 is close to the attempts of the composers of the AV.

In my view, the interpretations which refer to specific rituals, such as Mahāvrata and Pravargya (Jamison, Brereton 2014, Houben 2000a), endow us with much information about the meaning of the hymn, but it cannot be denied they are based on later tradition. My interpretation, based on the Ṛgvedic context, shows that it is possible to reconstruct the main line of the composer's reasoning within its frames. I am aware that I have not solved all the problems connected with the interpretation of this hymn, but my conclusion is that its composer presented his thought in a coherent way. This allowed his recipients to understand it and there is no doubt that they understood much more than we can now.

1.7. The Ṛgvedic concept of fame (*śrī́*, *śrávas*, *yáśas* and *kṣatrá*)[313]

The aim of this section is to analyse the conceptual cluster elaborated by the Ṛgvedic poets which is important from the point of view of later thought. This conceptual cluster in the ṚV is activated by four words: *śrī́*, *śrávas*, *yáśas* and *kṣatrá*. The concept is metaphoric. The target domain is the supernatural state gained thanks to Soma which is conceived as realised on the sun. The source domains impart various semantic aspects of light, beauty, power, and excellence. This is one of the proofs for the ability of the Ṛgvedic poets to construe general and abstract concepts which are not expressed verbally. Later Vedic thought evokes this state most often *via* the word *śrī́*, more rarely *via* the word *yáśas*. This fact betrays the strong conceptual continuity in the Vedic tradition. Even when Soma was not in use and the supernatural state was gained with aid of various techniques, mainly breathing practices, the words *śrī́* and *yáśas* are used in a context which is supposed to trigger the recipient to activate the concept coined in the ṚV.

I will analyse the semantic range of the words *śrī́*, *śrávas*, *yáśas* and *kṣatrá* in order to reconstruct the concepts denoted by them. I will also show the internal motivation of the meaning of each word and the coherence of the whole conceptual cluster.

1.7.1. *Śrī́*

Grassmann (1999[1873–1875]) translates *śrī́* as 'Licht, Glanz, Herrlichkeit, Pracht, Schmuck', Mayrhofer (1996) as 'Schönheit, Glanz, Pracht, Herrlichkeit'[314]. The word *śrī́* is very often used in reference to the light of dawn, the sun and fire[315]. In ṚV 10.91.5, the flames of fire are called *śrī́* and

---

[313] I have analysed this problem in Jurewicz (2008c).

[314] For the survey of meanings of *śrī́* in the Veda, see Gonda (1954: 176 ff.), in the ṚV, see Renou (1958).

[315] Light of dawn: ṚV 1.46.14, 1.92.6, 1.117.13, 1.188.6, 5.45.2, 6.63.5, 6.64.1, 10.95.6. Light of the sun: ṚV 1.122.2, 5.45.2, 6.48.19. Light of fire: ṚV 2.1.12, 2.8.3, 3.1.5, 5.3.4, 5.28.4, 7.15.5, 10.91.5.

compared to flashes of lightning. In some contexts, *śrī́* highlights the meaning of the desired state which the agent wants to gain. This is especially clear in the descriptions of the Maruts who balm their bodies and put on ornaments in order to achieve the state called *śrī́* (ṚV 1.88.3, 5.55.3, 5.60.4, 8.7.25, 10.77.2). In this context, the meaning of *śrī́* is not only light, but also beauty. The dative use of the word *śrī́* in the descriptions of the preparation of the juice of Soma (ṚV 9.94.4b, 9.102.1c, 9.104.1c) and of kindling of fire (ṚV 4.5.15, 4.10.5, 5.3.3, 5.44.2. 4.5.15) highlights the meaning of excellence in that the final form of the juice and blazing form of fire are their best forms. The meaning of beauty and excellence can also be activated in the descriptions of the appearance of dawn which is described as a beautiful woman and which aims at its best form (ṚV 1.92.6, 6.63.5, 6.64.1, 7.67.2). In ṚV 2.33.3, *śrī́* is the feature which makes Rudra better than other beings which clearly activates the meaning of excellence. The word *śrī́* means also 'ornament'. This use is metonymically motivated because the ornament is something which makes the agent beautiful (ṚV 1.85.2, 1.166.10, 8.28.5, 10.21.3, 10.110.6, 10.127.1). In ṚV 5.61.12, the Maruts are presented as shining with *śrī́* and are compared to the sun conceived in terms of a golden ornament. In reference to men, the word *śrī́* is used in contexts which highlight the beauty of the body (ṚV 1.179.1) and excellence of mind (ṚV 6.44.8, 4.41.8). In ṚV 9.94.4, people, who are endowed with *śrī́* thanks to Soma, become immortal. As such this state is desired by men.

So the semantic structure of *śrī́* looks as follows[316]. The meaning of light and beauty are in the centre. The meaning of beauty metonymically motivates the meaning of ornament. The meaning of excellence is motivated by the meaning of light and beauty and is especially highlighted in the dative use of the word *śrī́*. The meaning of excellence is the basis for the meaning of a factor which makes the agent better than others.

1.7.2. *Śrávas*

According to Mayrhofer (1996), the main meaning of *śrávas* is 'fame' ('Ruhm, Preis, Lobpreisung, Ansehen'). Grassmann (1999[1873–1875]) sees more semantic aspects of this word: 'lauter Ruf, Lob, Preis, Preislied, Ruhm'. However, as we shall see, the semantic range of this word is even wider. It used in reference to the light of the dawn, the sun and fire and it is implied

[316] According to the prototype theory of categorisation, the structure of word meaning reflects the structure of categories. As Taylor (2011: 643) 'To the extent that words can be said to be names of categories, prototype theory becomes a theory of word meaning'. Thus the semantic structure is the radial structure with the most common and literal meanings in its centre.

that the light is strong[317]. It seems that *śrávas* does not refer to light when the dawn, the sun and fire begin to shine, but when they shine brightest. In these contexts, the word *śrávas* highlights the meaning of the final form of shining elements, the form which is excellent and beautiful[318]. The meaning of excellence is highlighted in the stanzas which describe the purification of Soma when the word *śrávas* denotes its final form (ṚV 9.1.4, 9.4.1, 9.6.3, 9.51.5, 9.62.22, 9.63.12). The same meaning is highlighted when *śrávas* is used in reference to the state for which Indra aims.

The state denoted by the word *śrávas* is qualified as shining (*dyumát*, ṚV 5.18.5, 6.17.14, 9.32.6). It is used in apposition to *dyumná* (shine, radiance, ṚV 3.37.7,10, 5.7.9, 6.5.5, 8.5.32, 8.74.9). It is also qualified as lofty (*bṛhát*)[319] which activates its conceptualisation in terms of the image schema VERTICALITY. It is 'not ageing' (*ajára*, *ajūryá*, ṚV 1.126.2, *ajūryá*, ṚV 3.53.15), is 'immortal' (*amṛ́ta*, ṚV 7.81.6, *ámṛtyu* 6.48.12), is realised in heaven (*diví*, ṚV 1.73.7, 4.31.15, 5.35.8, 10.28.12) and among the gods (*devéṣu*, ṚV 1.73.5, 8.65.12, 10.62.7. 4.31.15)[320]. It is also 'broad' (*pṛthú*, ṚV 7.5.8) and 'far-reaching' (*urugāyá*, ṚV 6.65.). Such a qualification can be motivated not only because this state is visible from far away because it is shining brightly, but because it can be heard (see below, section 1.5.7). This state is desired by men who ask the gods for it (ṚV 7.16.10, 1.126.5, 8.9.17). As Whitaker (2011: 102ff.), has shown it is also the state realised by Indra.

In many respects, the semantic range of the word *śrávas* is close to that of *śrī́*. Although its central meaning is fame, the meanings of light of the dawn, the sun and fire are also present. The meaning of excellence is also clear. On the other hand, the meaning of beauty, which is one of the central meanings of *śrī́*, is not so distinct; it can rather be inferred on the basis of the meanings of excellence. The semantic proximity between *śrávas* and *śrī́* is highlighted in the following stanza where they refer to the state of the same feature, i.e. manliness:

ṚV 1.43.7

asmé soma śríyam ádhi ní dhehi śatásya nṝṇā́m+ |
máhi śrávas tuvinṛmṇám ||

Upon us, Soma, set down the glory of a hundred men,
great, powerfully manly fame.

317 Light of the dawn: ṚV 1.92.8. Light of the sun: ṚV 8.101.12. Light of fire: ṚV 6.1.11, 10.140.1.

318 In ṚV 1.95.11 the word *śrávas* is used to denote the state to which Agni aims.

319 ṚV 1.9.7-8, 1.44.2, 3.37.10, 5.18.5, 5.86.6, 8.9.17, 8.89.4, 8.31.7, 8.65.9, 9.83.5, 9.86.40, 9.98.8

320 Among immortals (*ámartyeṣu*): ṚV 1.110.05.

1.7.3. *Yáśas*

According to Grassmann (1999[1873–1875]), the meanings of *yáśas* are: 'Herrlichkeit, Glanz, Segen, Heil, Segen, Heil, Wohlstand' and according to Mayrhofer (1996): 'Ansehen, Ruhm'. The meaning of light can be easily activated in the usages of its adjectival derivates such as *yaśás*, *yáśasvant* and *yaśástama* which are used to denote the light of the dawn and fire[321]. The state denoted by *yáśa*s is qualified as shining (*dyumát*, ṚV 9.32.6, *dyumnítama*, ṚV 8.19.6) and is used in apposition to *dyumná* (ṚV 5.79.7, 9.108.9). It is qualified as 'lofty' (*brhát*, ṚV 9.20.4, 9.108.9) and is realised among the gods (*devéṣu*, ṚV 9.94.3). It is the state desired by men (ṚV 5.4.10, 9.32.6).

The semantic proximity between the word *yáśas*, the word *śrī́* and the word *śrávas* is clear: its central meaning is glory and light. The state denoted by it is also conceptualised in the same way as the state denoted by *śrávas*. The words *yáśas* and *śrávas* are used in the following stanza:

ṚV 6.2.1

tuváṃ hí kṣaítavad yáśo ágne mitró ná pátyase |
tuváṃ vicarṣaṇe śrávo váso puṣṭíṃ ná puṣyasi ||

You, o Agni, like Mitra are indeed master of the glory belonging to the settlements.
You prosper fame like prosperity, o good one without boundaries.

1.7.4 *Ksatrá*

According to Mayrhofer (1992), the meanings of the word *kṣatrá* are 'Herrschaft, Macht, Gewalt, Regierung' and Grassmann (1999[1873–1875]) mentions 'Herrschaft' and 'Gesammtheit der Herrscher'. The state denoted by this word is similarly conceived to the state denoted by other words analysed in this section. In the following stanza, it is used together with the word *śrávas* and is qualified as 'lofty' (*bṛhát*); the stanza also betrays the conceptualisation of the state called *śrávas* and *kṣatrá* in terms of the image schema of VERTICALITY:

---

[321] Light of the dawn: ṚV 4.1.16 (*yaśás*), ṚV 1.79.1, 10.11.3 (*yáśasvatī*). Light of fire: ṚV 1.60.1, 5.8.4 (*yaśás*), ṚV 7.16.4, 8.102.10, 2.8.1 (*yaśástama*), ṚV 1.9.6, 3.16.6, 10.20.9 (*yáśasvant*).

ṚV 1.160.5

té no gr̥ṇāné mahinī́ máhi śrávaḥ kṣatrám̐ dyāvāpr̥thivī dhāsatho br̥hát |
yénābhí kr̥ṣṭī́s tatánāma viśváhā panā́yiyam ójo asmé sám invatam ||

While being sung, o great one, you will establish great fame for us and lofty dominion, o Heaven and Earth,
by which we will extend (our control) over the communities all the days. Jointly impel to us power worthy of wonder.[322]

In ṚV 8.19.33, the word *ksatrá* in plural refers to flames of fire. The state denoted by this word is also qualified as shining (*jyótismat*, ṚV 1.136.3) and used in apposition to *dyumná* (ṚV 1.54.11, 8.19.33). It is also qualified as lofty (*br̥hát*, ṚV 5.27.6, 5.64.6) and unageing (*ajára*, ṚV 6.8.6, 7.18.25). It is compared to the sun in the sky (ṚV 5.27.6, 10.60.5) and to the sky (ṚV 4.21.1). So, the use of the word *kṣatrá* is similar to the use of the words *śrávas* and *yáśas* and, besides its main meaning of dominion, it conveys the meaning of a state conceived as shining, lofty and beyond death.

1.7.5. One concept, four words

The above analysis confirms the Ṛgvedic poets created a general concept of a state expressed by the words *śrī́*, *śrávas*, *yáśas* and *kṣatrá*. This concept unites the ideas of light, beauty, excellence, fame, and dominion. It is qualified as immortal and divine. This complex is also activated in the synonymous use of derivative forms of these words, e.g.:

ṚV 7.75.2

mahé no adyá suvitā́ya bodhi úṣo mahé saúbhagāya prá yandhi |
citrám̐ rayím̐ yaśásam̐ dhehi asmé dévi márteṣu mānuṣi śravasyúm ||

For our great faring take note of us today; o Dawn, for our great good fortune provide (for us).
Establish for us bright, glorious wealth that seeks fame – o goddess among mortals, belonging to the sons of Manu.

There is one more feature shared by the state denoted by the words analysed in this section. It is fluidity. Let us begin with the use of the word *śrī́* in the meaning of milk:

---

[322] See also ṚV 1.113.6.

ṚV 8.72.13ab

ā́ suté siñcata śríyaṃ ródasīyor abhiśríyam |

Into the pressed Soma pour glory [= milk], the full glory of the two world-halves. ||

If the word *śrī́* can be used in reference to milk, the conceptualisation of its designate must be such that it justifies such a usage. The liquidity of the concept denoted by *śrī́* can also be seen in that it is used as the direct object of the participle *vásānā*, literally 'clothed in' (ṚV 2.10.1: *śríyaṃ vásāno*, ṚV 3.38.4: *chríyo vásānaś*, ṚV 9.94.4: *śríyaṃ vásānā*). The concept of clothing is used in the ṚV as the source domain for mixing with fluid (water, milk and clarified butter[323]). These usages of the word *śrī́* imply that its designate is also conceived as liquid and that its liquidity is conceived in terms of milk.

The word *śrávas* is used twice in contexts which imply the fluid nature of its designate. In ṚV 6.10.3ab, the worshipper of Agni is presented as swelling with *śrávas* (*pīpā́ya sá śrávasā mártiyeṣu yó agnáye dadā́śa vípra ukthaíḥ*); the verb *pī-* is used in the ṚV to denote the swelling of a cow's udder with milk and the swelling of Soma (e.g. ṚV 1.153.3, 7.23.4, 7.24.4, 7.36.6, 9.93.3, 9.107.12). In ṚV 6.48.12, a cow milks *śrávas* for the Maruts (*yā́ śárdhāya mā́rutāya svábhānave śrávo ámṛtyu dhúkṣata*). In both cases, the concept of milk can easily be evoked. The qualification of the word *śrávas* as unexhausting (*akṣiti*, ṚV 1.40.4, 8.103.5, 9.66.7, *ákṣita*, ṚV 1.9.7, *ákṣita*) also implies the conceptualisation of the state denoted by it as liquid.

The examples of the use of the conceptualisation of the designate of *yáśas* for milk are as follows. In ṚV 10.106.11, the milk in a cows' udder is compared to *yáśas*. In ṚV 9.81.1, the adjective *yaśás* qualifies cow's milk mixed with Soma. In ṚV 7.104.11cd, the poet wishes that the *yáśas* of his enemy dries up. If the recipient activates the concept of milk, he could understand the hemistich more literally as a wish that cows belonging to the enemy do not give milk; he may also understand that women would have no milk for children. However, it is worth noting that *yáśas* is often qualified as *vīravánt* (ṚV 4.32.12, 7.15.12, 8.23.21, 8.103.9, 9.61.26, 9.103.13, 10.36.10) and that semen is identified with milk in the ṚV. So the recipient of the hemistich may also think about semen which dries up; thus he will understand that the composer's wish for his enemy to be sterile.

As far as the word *kṣatrá* is concerned, the idea of fluidity of its designate is much less discernible. There is one context which might imply it:

---

[323] E.g. ṚV 9.47.1, 9.86.40, 9.78.1, 9.82.2

ṚV 1.157.2ab

yád yuñjā́the vŕ̥ṣaṇam aśvinā rátham̐ ghr̥téna no mádhunā kṣatrám ukṣatam |

When you harness the bull that is your chariot, Aśvins, then increase [/sprinkle] our dominion with ghee and honey!

If we interpret *naḥ* as dative (and not genitive), we could understand verse *b* as: 'sprinkle dominion for us with ghee and honey'; the possibility of use the verb *ukṣ-* in such collocation is attested in the following stanza:

ṚV 1.87.2cd

ścótanti kóśā úpa vo rátheṣu ā́ ghr̥tám ukṣatā mádhuvarṇam árcate ||

The casks on your chariot drip. Sprinkle ghee the colour of honey for the one who chants.

Notwithstanding if we agree with my last interpretation, there is no doubt that the words *śrī́*, *śrávas* and *yáśas* are used in a way which implies correlation of its designate with fluidity conceived specifically as milk. This confirms the existence of a common general concept named by these words.

This concept is very abstract. It unites features of light, immortality, excellence, fame, glory and rule, fluidity and being in the sky where the gods are. One could ask if there is any more concrete concept in the ṚV which could be used as its source domain. And indeed, there is such a concept. It is the sun.

The sun is shining and is in the sky. According to the Ṛgvedic beliefs, the gods are in the sun (Jurewicz 2010a). The immortal state gained under the influence of Soma is conceived as being realised in the sun[324]. Moreover, the sun is conceived as a fiery container filled with Soma which becomes rain (Jurewicz 2010a: 164 ff.). In the frames of this conceptualisation, the container in terms of which the sun is conceived is called 'unfailing' (Jurewicz 2006). The concept of milk evoked in the usages of *śrī́*, *śrávas* and *kṣatrá* confirms that the sun, as the container for Soma, is also conceived in terms of a cow's udder (Jurewicz 2014a).

Some usages of *śrávas* activate the concept of the sun in zenith. I will begin with the following stanza:

324 ṚV 9.113.7-10, see Jurewicz (2010a: 294–296). In ṚV 7.76.1, the light of the sun is called *amŕ̥ta*.

ṚV 8.101.12

báṭ sūriya śrávasā mahā́m̐ asi satrā́ deva mahā́m̐ asi |
mahnā́ devā́nām asuryàḥ puróhito vibhú jyótir ádābhiyam ||

Yes, indeed! Surya, you are great in fame; in every way, god, you are great.
Because of his greatness the lordly one was set in front for the gods, as the extensive undeceivable light.

The composer creates a blend consisting of two input spaces (verses *a–b*). The first one is of a warrior, most probably a victorious king, famous thanks to his deeds. The second one is the shining sun. The generic space is the image schema of SOURCE-PATH-GOAL. In the blend, sunshine is conceived in terms of a king's fame. Its activity makes possible the existence of the world. The term *puróhita* (verse *c*) refers to Agni in its role as the initial factor of everything: he leads the people in war, is kindled in the morning and is thus the cause of the appearance of the morning light and rain. The word *śrávas* is used in reference to the sun's light which is qualified as strong.

In the following two stanzas, *śrávas* denotes the solar form of Soma realised in zenith:

ṚV 9.83.5

havír haviṣmo máhi sádma daíviyaṃ nábho vásānaḥ pári yāsi adhvarám |
rā́jā pavítraratho vā́jam ā́ruhaḥ sahásrabhṛṣṭir jayasi śrávo bṛhát ||

You possessor of the oblation, as an oblation yourself you drive around the great heavenly seat, around the ceremonial course, clothing yourself in cloud.
As king, having the filter as your chariot, you have mounted the prize. Having thousand spikes, you win lofty fame.

ṚV 9.86.40

ún mádhva ūrmír vanánā atiṣṭhipad apó vásāno mahiṣó ví gāhate |
rā́jā pavítraratho vā́jam ā́ruhat sahásrabhṛṣṭir jayati śrávo bṛhát ||

The wave of honey has raised (our?) desires; clothing himself in waters, the buffalo plunges through them.
The king whose chariot is filter has mounted the prize. He of a thousand spikes wins lofty fame.

In ṚV 9.83.5*a*, Soma is presented as the oblation and as the person who possesses oblation. This person can be both sacrificer and the god who receives oblation. In this way, the identity of the agent and the object of ritual activity is expressed. It is realised on earth. In ṚV 9.86.40a, the situation of the agent is presented as one whose desires are inspired by a Somic wave (Jurewicz 2010a: 228–229).

In ṚV 9.83.5*b*, Soma is qualified as 'clothed in cloud' which implies that Soma reaches the sky. At the same time, since the Ṛgvedic poets create a blend in which cosmic and ritual processes are the same, *nábhas* can also refer to the woollen strainers in which Soma is purified. This meaning is activated in ṚV 9.97.21b (*pári srava nábho árṇaś camū́ṣu*). Because of that, Soma can be presented as circulating around the sacrifice. In ṚV 9.86.40b, the mixing of Soma with water is conceived in terms of clothing. Here, Soma is conceived in terms of a bull which bathes in water. This description creates a blend which unites earthly and cosmic processes: Soma, having been purified in a strainer, is mixed with water. At the same time, since the concept of bull is the source domain for the sun in the ṚV (Jurewicz 2010a), Soma becomes the rising sun.

In verses *c* of both stanzas, Soma is called the king whose chariot is made of a strainer. If the recipient highlights the meaning of *nábhas* as a strainer and activates the metaphor THE SUN IS A KING[325], he will understand that Soma becomes the sun having been purified. The source domain of king is elaborated in that Soma is presented as achieving the prize. The epithet *sahásrabhr̥ṣṭi* is most often used as a qualification of Indra's thunderbolt (*vájra*, ṚV 1.80.12, 1.85.9, 5.34.2, 6.17.10), so the recipient may further elaborate the source domain of the king and understand that he pierces the hiding place of the prize and thus wins it. This source domain is further elaborated in verse *d* of both stanzas where the king achieves lofty fame. However, there is more meaning in this expression. The concept of Indra's thunderbolt (*vájra*) is used as the source domain, so the recipient understands that rain appears as the result of earthly ritual. Qualification of *śrávas* as lofty activates the image schema of VERTICALITY and, if the recipient activates qualifications of *śrávas* as immortal and divine, he will evoke the concept of the sun in zenith from which rain appears. Since ṚV 9.83.5a identifies the person who possesses oblation with Soma, the recipient may understand that the sacrificer reaches the same state of immortality and divinity which is called *śrávas* here and is conceptualised as being realised in the sun in zenith.

The word *śrávas* is used to denote the place which is gained by Soma in the following stanza:

ṚV 9.100.8

pávamāna máhi śrávaś citrébhir yāsi raśmíbhiḥ |
śárdhan támāṃsi jighnase víśvāni dāśúṣo gr̥hé ||

O self-purifying one, you drive to great fame with your brilliant rays.
Vaunting yourself, you keep smashing away all dark shades in the house of the pious man.

[325] See Auboyer (1968: 79 ff.), Heesterman (1957: 52,102, 111).

Soma is presented as having rays, so the recipient can understand that it is his solar form that is meant in the first hemistich. The aim of journey of Soma is called *máhi śrávas* and the recipient may presume that in his solar form Soma will reach zenith and will destroy darkness with his strong light[326].

The word *śrávas* is also used in reference to the power of the solar form of Soma realised in zenith:

ṚV 9.110.5

abhí-abhi hí śrávasā tatárditha útsaṃ ná káṃ cij janapā́nam ákṣitam |
śáryābhir ná bháramāṇo gábhastiyoḥ ||

Because with your fame you drilled ever closer to the inexhaustible drink for men, as if to some kind of wellspring,
while being carried in the (priest's) hands, like (booty by someone) with arrows in his hands.

As I have shown elsewhere, the concept of *útsa* is used as the source domain for the sun from which rain appears (Jurewicz 2006). The composer of the stanza again elaborates the concept of a victorious warrior to express the appearance of rain which is Somic juice purified in the sun. The word *śrávas* denotes the power of Soma which creates rain. Rain appears when Soma is finally clarified in the sun in zenith under the influence of its heat.

The word *śrávas* derives from the verb *śru-* which means 'to hear'. It is possible that the concept of being heard is present within the concept denoted by the words analysed in this section. In one stanza, the adjective *yaśás* is used in such a way that the recipient is prompted to activate the meaning of hearing:

ṚV 5.32.11ab

ékaṃ nú tvā sátpatim pā́ñcajanyaṃ jātáṃ śṛṇomi yaśásaṃ jáneṣu |

I hear of you as born the sole master of settlements, belonging to the five peoples, glorious among the peoples.

The hemistich can be interpreted as expressing that the composer hears about Indra from other people, but it is also possible to understand that he hears Indra himself. It is worth mentioning that the impelling power of the sun (*savitṛ́*) is also conceived as making sounds. These sounds are called *ślóka* which derives, similarly to *śrávas*, from the verb *śru-*, 'to hear':

---

326 The next input space is cognition.

ṚV 5.82.9

yá imā́ víśvā jātā́ni āśrāváyati ślókena |
prá ca suvā́ti savitā́ ||

Wo makes all these creatures hearken with his signal-call
and will impel[327] forth: Savitar[328].

This fact confirms that the state denoted by *śrávas* and other words is conceived as being realised on the sun. The state called *śrávas* can be heard in the same way as the rising sun is heard. At the same time, the qualification of the state of *śrávas* as 'broad' (*pṛthú*) can be based on the fact that it is conceptualised as the state which is not only visible from far away, but can also be heard from a distance.

Since *śrávas* is the most commonly used word in the ṚV among those analysed in this section, and since it is used with all of them, I would assume that in the ṚV it is the main name for the conceptual cluster reconstructed in this section. As I have already mentioned, this word is not in use in later thought although, as it will be shown, the concept survived and is evoked mainly by the word *śrī́*, more rarely by *yáśas*. It will be shown that it is impossible to find the full justification of the use of these words in the later texts without reference to the Ṛgvedic background.

The full reconstruction of the conceptual cluster referred to by words *śrī́*, *śrávas*, *yáśas* and *kṣatrá* would look as follows. Its central meaning is fame (conveyed by words *śrávas* and *yáśas*). This state is conceived as shining (conveyed by *śrī́*, *śrávas* and *yáśas*), beautiful (conveyed by *śrī́*), excellent (conveyed by *śrī́* and *śrávas*), immortal, realised high up in the sky and among the gods (conveyed by all four words). It is also the state of dominion (conveyed by *kṣatrá*). It is conceptualised as being realised in the sun and desired by men. Such a conceptualisation of this state implies that it can be achieved under the influence of Soma which, as I have shown, is conceived in the same way (Jurewicz 2010a).

The concept reconstructed in this section betrays formal and conceptual connections with the ancient Greek concept of fame. As Nagy (1974) has shown, the expression 'inexhaustible fame' *śrávas ákṣitam*, is a poetic formula which has its correspondent in the Greek *kleos aphthiton*. In his book, Nagy analyses the usages of both words[329]. He concludes that in both cases the

---

327 Jamison, Brereton 2014: '(them)'
328 See also ṚV 4.53.3, 7.82.10.
329 As far as *ákṣita*, it is used as qualification of 'spring' (*útsa*), 'well' (*avatá*), 'Somic juice' (*índu*), 'Somic stalk' (*aṃśú*), and, by metonymic and metaphoric extension to seed (*bī́ja*), 'stream of light' (*pā́jas*), space (*rájas*), 'aim' (*ártha*), 'Asura-power' (*asuryà*), 'municence'

adjectives qualify 'an unfailing stream' of fire, water, semen or vegetal extract (juice of Soma or wine, 1974: 240, 244), *ákṣita* also qualifies milk and urine and *aphthiton* qualifies royal attributes.

The word *kleos* refers to the song of the singer thanks to which gods and heroes gain fame (Nagy 1974: 250). Similarly, the word *śrávas* connotes the meaning of song of praise. Nagy interprets *śrávas* in ṚV 9.110.5 (see above) as "craft of song' *in the specialised language of the Singer himself*' (Nagy 1974: 253) which in the human sphere 'glorifies valour or generosity; in the divine sphere it praises gods for their cosmic function because divine performance depends on praise' (Nagy 1974: 253–254). He interprets the use of *śrávas* in ṚV 1.92.8 in the same way (Nagy 1974: 254). He concludes that the Indo-European lexeme **klewos* which is the common source of *kleos* and *śrávas* 'was the word once used to designate the hieratic art of song which ensured unfailing streams of water, light, vegetal sap, and so on. Since these streams were unfailing, the art of song itself could be idealised and self-servingly glorified by the Singer as 'unfailing'" (Nagy 1974: 254). This meaning is preserved in the formulaic expressions *kleos aphthiton* and *śrávas ákṣitam* which implies that '*śrávas* /*kleos*' flows 'like a stream' (Nagy 1974: 254).

As I have shown, such a conceptualisation of fame is still preserved in the ṚV and is activated when the fame is called with use of the words *śrī́* and *yáśas*. It is probable that it was preserved because of the cosmological assumption of the Ṛgvedic poets who conceived the sun as the fiery container of Soma. It seems that in case of the ṚV, the expression *śrávas ákṣitam* is not the 'fanciful metaphor' (1974: 254) that Nagy sees, but is justified on cosmological Ṛgvedic grounds. At the same time, the fact that **klewos* could denote the art of song of the poet strengthens my claim that the state called by use of the words analysed in this section is realised under the influence of Soma which in the ṚV was the necessary condition for poetic creation. In the light of Nagy's research, it may be argued that the concept of fame in the ṚV was inherited from earlier Indo-European tradition; it was then elaborated by the poets with the use of other words in order to appropriate it in their cultural situation.

(*sumná*) and 'land' (*dhánvan*). As far as for *aphthiton*, it qualifies 'throne' (*thronos*), 'palace (*domon*/*domata*), 'scepter' (*skepthron*), water (*hydor*), river Stiks, 'wheel-rim' (*itus*), grape-wines (*ampeloi*).

1.8. Conclusion

My general conclusion is that the differences in the models of creation presented in the late hymns of the ṚV are due to the fact that the hymns reveal attempts to construct an abstract description of cosmogony. Moreover, the range of philosophical interest of their composers was not limited to the problem of the origin of the world. They are concerned with other problems such as the nature of reality, the relationship between its aspects, the essence of the cosmos and the role of man. They transform concepts which come from experience in such a way that they become an apparatus that is good enough to express their views. They elaborate the concepts of tree/wood, of egg, of chariot and its wheels, of a cow and its calf, of woman and man, of father and son, of human activities in order transform them into abstract and general concepts enabling conceptualisation of the whole of reality and its manifestations.

In ṚV 10.125, reality is conceived in terms of speech. This conceptualisation allows the composer to present its transformation as a cognitive process of the appearance of sound and heat. Conceptualisation of speech in terms queen allows the composer to present his conviction about its supremacy over gods and the world.

In the *Puruṣasūkta*, reality conceived in terms of man. This concept is consequently used to conceive the first manifestation of reality and its manifestations as society and the cosmos. Creation seen in these terms is a conscious and intentional action and ritual activity allows men to participate in it. This is again proof of the search for one general and abstract concept which could encompass all aspects of reality within its range. This source domain is further abstracted as the concept of the Maker of Everything (*viśvákarman*, ṚV 10.81-82).

ṚV 10.72 is an attempt to construe an abstract model of creation. The terms *sát* and *ásat* are used. Moreover, its composer uses other terms such as *áditi*, *dákṣa*, *ā́śā* in their general meaning of 'infinity', 'intention' and 'space'. Even the compound *uttānápad* conveys a more general meaning of the source of the world. The general domain of Procreation in its specific realisation of delivery also conveys the general meaning of origin. It is also evoked *via* the opposing genders of the words *áditi* and *dákṣa*, but only to express the internally contradictory nature of reality which allows it to manifest. The first five stanzas of this hymn can be seen as similarly abstract and general as the *Nāsadīyasūkta*.

Finally, ṚV 1.164 can be considered the first philosophical treatise in Indian culture. The most important topic of the hymn is supernatural cognition and possibility of its realisation through sacred speech and ritual. The content of this cognition is manifestation of reality in time and speech. The lynchpin of the content of ṚV 1.164 is the general model of reality transformation elaborated especially in its ritual dimension.

As it has been shown, thinking of the poets is motivated by the earlier Ṛgvedic philosophical assumptions about Agni. The metonymic and metaphoric operations leading to new conceptual blends are the important factor in creation of new concepts which seem to be more abstract that the concept of fire. The concepts of speech, man, tree and wood, of the Maker of Everything and embryo of the waters are blends which share some features of the input space of Agni and, at the same time, are elaborated according to the logic of the input spaces which come from experience. In many cases, the concept of fire is not necessary to be activated in order to understand the blended concept, but if one wants to explain its specific features, one has to do that. Thinking of the poets is also motivated by the earlier cultural knowledge which still, in many cases, has to be activated in order to understand the meaning conveyed by them. A good example is ṚV 10.72.6-9 where a myth about Aditi and her eight sons is activated in order to express the role of man in the world. ṚV 10.90 and 1.164 activate aspects of the earlier background and also refer to ritual practice in the conceptualisation of philosophical target domains.

In the last section of this chapter, I have reconstructed the Ṛgvedic concept of fame evoked by the words *śrī́*, *śrávas*, *yáśas* and *kṣatrá*. It refers to the supernatural state conceived as realised in the sun under the influence of Soma. I have shown that the concept of this state is motivated by the Ṛgvedic cosmological assumptions according to which rain is created in the sun. Comparison with Nagy's research shows the antiquity of this concept which may reflect Indo-European thinking.

The general line of thought of the composers of the late Ṛgvedic hymns preserves earlier assumptions (Jurewicz 2010a). Reality is one and internally contradictory, the world is its manifest aspect. Cognition is the motive of creation, being is the result of it. The fundamental role of speech and ritual in human condition, present in the earlier books of the ṚV, is now highlighted and elaborated which will be continued in the later thought.

Chapter Two

The *Atharvaveda*

The AV does not contain many hymns that are strictly philosophical[1]. I will show, however, that its accounts are very important from the point of view of the history of ancient Indian thought. On the one hand, they develop Ṛgvedic metaphysics while, on the other, they provide the basis for the later theories that presented particularly in the Upaniṣads.

The process of looking for the abstract conceptualisation of reality, already begun in the ṚV, is continued. This is done in two ways. Firstly, reality is conceived in terms of blended concepts with one of the input space constituted by some aspects of Agni. Secondly, the concepts of man and of pillar are elaborated. I will discuss those problems in sections 2.1-3. Then I will present the stanzas of the hymns in which the fiery nature of reality is expressed directly (section 2.3). In the next section, I will analyse how the tendency to continue the abstract and general concepts created in the ṚV can be seen in a wider exposition of the first two stanzas of AVŚ 2.1 (2.1, section 2.4).

The AV also attests efforts to create abstract language on the basis of concepts which refer to experience, but which are consciously transformed in order to express philosophical matters[2]. I will analyse such concepts in

1 For the general survey of the AVŚ see Bloomfield (1899). For its Paippalāda recension see Griffith, Schmiedchen (2007).

2 Srinivasan notices the abstract tendency in the AVŚ (1997: 35 ff.). The tendency to put the content of the Ṛgvedic hymns in more simple terms by the composers of the AVŚ does not allow us to interpret that they did not understand the content of the ṚV (as Edgerton 1920 supposes). Just the opposite, these more literal versions should be treated as commentaries explaining the meaning which had been gradually lost by the times of the AVŚ.

section 2.5. The last part of the chapter will be devoted to more general descriptions of reality which are important for the later thought (section 2.6).

The quotations are from the Titus Text Database (*Śaunaka Recension*[3]). The translations not marked on are by Whitney (1905).

2.1. Blended concepts with Agni as the input space

In this section, I will discuss the conceptualisation of reality in terms of breath (*prāṇá*), the ruddy one (*róhita*) and time (*kālá*). These concepts are the main input spaces of the blends. The next input space is Agni. The relationship between concepts, which constitute the main input spaces of the blends and the concept of Agni, is more diversified that it is in case of the ṚV. The relationship between breath and Agni is metaphoric (BREATH IS FIRE) while the relationship between the ruddy one and Agni is metonymic (DEFINING PROPERTY FOR CATEGORY, COLOUR FOR SUBSTANCE, RUDDY FOR FIRE). In the case of time, the relationship can be seen as identity.

The blends express and the whole of reality and its essence. The identity of reality with its essence is already attested in the Ṛgvedic concept of *ātmán* which, as I have shown elsewhere (Jurewicz 1997), denotes the whole entity and its defining essence. Although, in the Atharvavedic philosophical hymns, this word is not very often used, the conviction about identity of reality with its essence is commonly accepted and expressed.

2.1.1. Reality as the ruddy one (*róhita*)

Proferes (2007) shows the connections between the ruddy sun (*róhita*) in AVŚ 13.1 and the king. He refers to Bloomfield (1891) 'who argued that the name or epithet *róhita* permits a connection both with the ruddy (*róhita*) sun that mounts (*ruh-*) the sky, and with the king who, in course of his consecration, mounts (*ā́ ruh-*) the throne.' (2007: 85)[4]. Witzel (1997: 277–278 and note 81) includes AVŚ 13 that is devoted to *róhita* among the books concerning the Gṛhya ritual: 'The Rohita book is "gṛhya" in so far as it does not deal with official ceremonies such as the royal consecration (*abhiṣeka*), but with the more general, "domestic" concerns of the king'. He also refers to the hymns of the AV that deal with Rohita, the '"red (sun)" as a symbol of royal power' (1997: 267).

3 http://titus.uni-frankfurt.de/texte/etcs/ind/aind/ved/av/avs/avs.htm.

4 See also Gonda 1969: (133–134).

Conceptualisation of the sun in terms of king is attested already in the ṚV (Jurewicz 2010a), but the cognitive analysis of this specific topic would go beyond the scope of the present study[5]. Instead, I will look at the concept of *róhita* from a different perspective and see it as an abstraction of one of the most salient feature of fire which is its redness. The whole of book XIII of the AVŚ is devoted to the description of reality understood in this way[6]. I will discuss here only those passages which, firstly, betray the motivation of the concept of Agni on the concept of *róhita* that, secondly, show the convergence of thought with Ṛgvedic metaphysics concepts and that, thirdly, show reality as conceived in terms of *róhita*. The fact that AVŚ 13.2 is full of quotations from the ṚV, that are more or less literal, is proof that the composers of this text were aware of their Ṛgvedic conceptual heritage in their attempts to create a more abstract and general language for philosophy.

There are stanzas in the AVŚ which imply identity of *róhita* and Agni. The term *róhita* explicitly is used in reference to the sun conceived as the cosmic form of fire in AVŚ 13.1.11[7]. Verse *c* of this stanza calls *róhita* Agni that shines with its sharp light (*tigména jyótiṣā*). At the same time, it shines in the third space (*tṛtī́ye rájasi*) and is present in the sky (*ádhi nā́ke asthād*) which implies that it is the sun. The next hemistich of the hymn[8] calls *róhita* by the name *jātávedas* which is the conventionalised epithet for Agni in the ṚV. The identity of *róhita* with Agni can also be seen in that it is conceived here in terms of a bull with a thousand horns (*sahásraśṛṅgo vṛṣabhó*) which is the way Agni and Soma are conceived in the ṚV (e.g. ṚV 5.2.9d, 9.70.7b). Its appellation as 'poured with the clarified butter' (*ghṛtā́hutaḥ*) evokes the image of fire which is kindled by pouring on clarified butter (ṚV 8.19.22-23, ṚV 10.61.1-2)[9]. Finally, the epithet *sómapṛṣṭhaḥ* also evokes the image of fire into which Soma is poured. This epithet is used twice in reference to fire in the ṚV (ṚV 8.43.11, 10.91.14). If the recipient elaborates the image of a bull in terms of which fire is conceived in the ṚV, he can understand fire

5 This analysis should include the fact that the main scenario of the royal consecration realises the cosmic cycle in accordance with the general model of reality transformation. According to Proferes (2007: 82), the unction waters make the king arise as the sun. In my view, however, the meaning of this is more complex: the king not only arises thanks to waters, but also creates them in its solar form which is ritually reflected by sprinkling him with water from four cups (Heesterman 1957: 120 ff.). In the blend, the cosmic and social processes are one two-dimensional process which guarantees life on earth and among people.

6 For the discussion about the interpretations of AVŚ 13 in the Western scholarship, see Dore (2015: 39 ff.).

7 AVŚ 13.1.11: *ūrdhvó róhito ádhi nā́ke asthād víśvā rūpā́ṇi janáyan yúvā kavíḥ | tigménāgnír jyótiṣā ví bhāti tṛtī́ye cakre rájasi priyā́ṇi ||*

8 AVŚ 13.1.11ab: *sahásraśṛṅgo vṛṣabhó jātávedā ghṛtā́hutaḥ sómapṛṣṭhaḥ suvī́raḥ.*

9 Whitney (1905): 'offered to with ghee', Edgerton 1965: 'receiver of sacrifices with ghee'.

as a bull which drinks Soma to such an extent that it overflows and trickles down on its back. Thus understood, the epithet expresses the same metaphysic situation as the composers of the ṚV according to whom Soma is the first manifestation of Agni (see Jurewicz 2010a).

Róhita is also called Agni in AVŚ 13.3.13 where it is presented as assuming the forms of various gods depending of its activity: it is Varuṇa in the evening and it is Mitra in the morning while he is also Savitar and Indra[10]. Agni is conceived in the same way in the ṚV, although his identification with gods varies (ṚV 3.5.4, 5.3.1, 10.8.5).

The motivation of the Ṛgvedic concept of Agni in creation of the concept of *róhita* can also be seen in that both are conceived in the same way. The fiery and solar character of *róhita* has been just described. Similarly to Agni in his solar form, *róhita* is presented as having a rainy aspect: it releases waters (AVŚ 13.1.21), thunders, and flashes, throws thunderbolts (AVŚ 13.4.41) and rains (AVŚ 13.4.43).

Moreover, in its solar form *róhita,* similarly to Agni and Soma in the ṚV, creates a world which creation is conceived in images well known from the RV:

AVŚ 13.1.6-7

róhito dyā́vāpṛthivī́ jajāna tátra tántuṃ parameṣṭhī́ tatāna |
tátra śiśriye ,já ékapādó ,dṛṃhad dyā́vāpṛthivī́ bálena || (6)
róhito dyā́vāpṛthivī́ adṛṃhat téna svà stabhitáṃ téna nā́kaḥ |
ténāntárikṣaṃ vímitā rájāṃsi téna devā́ amṛ́tam ánv avindan || (7)

The Ruddy One begot heaven and Earth; there He that is in the Highest (Parameṣṭhín) extended the thread (of the sacrifice); there supported himself the one-footed Unborn; he made firm heaven and earth by might. (6)
The Ruddy One made firm heaven and earth; by him was established the (heavenly) light, by him the firmament. By him the atmosphere and (its) spaces were measured out; by him the gods found immortality. (7) (Edgerton 1965)

In the ṚV, the ray of the sun is conceived in terms of thread, and the concept of its extending is the source domain for conceptualisation of the morning light created by the dawn (Jurewicz 2010a: 116 ff.). The ray of the sun becomes the *axis mundi* (Jurewicz 2010a: 112–113) which in AVŚ 13.1.6c is evoked *via* the concept of a one-footed entity. The *axis mundi* is conceived in the same way in the *Puruṣasūkta* where one leg of man is present in the world while three legs are invisible in the sky (see chapter 1.3, see also ṚV 1.164.6-7,

[10] AVŚ 13.3.13: *sá váruṇaḥ sāyám agnír bhavati sá mitró bhavati prātár udyán | sá savitā́ bhūtvā́ntárikṣeṇa yāti sá índro bhūtvā́ tapati madhyató dívam ||*

chapter 1.6). The creation of the world in the morning is conceived here in the way well entrenched in the Veda: as supporting, making firm and measuring (*dr̥m̐h-*, AVŚ 13.1.6.d, 13.1.7.a, *stambh-*, AVŚ 13.1.7b, *mā-*, AVŚ 13.1.7.c[11]). The gods find immortality thanks to *róhita* because it is the sun filled with Soma. In the following stanza, *róhita* is not identified with Agni and the sun, but is presented as the entity which encompasses them:

AVŚ 13.1.25

yó róhito vr̥ṣabhás tigmáśr̥ṅgaḥ páry agníṃ pári sū́ryaṃ babhū́va
yó viṣṭabhnā́ti pr̥thivī́ṃ dívaṃ ca tásmād devā́ ádhi sŕ̥ṣṭīḥ sr̥jante ||

The ruddy one, the sharp-horned bull, who encompassed Agni, the sun, who props asunder the earth and the heaven – out of him do the gods create creations.

In verse *a*, *róhita* is conceived in terms of a bull with sharp horns. This is a conventionalised conceptualisation of Agni and Soma in the R̥V. According to verse *c*, *róhita* is the creator of the space between the earth and the sky and, according to verse *d*, it is the material out of which the world is created. This implies that *róhita* is both reality in its unmanifest aspect that creates the world and reality which manifests itself in the world. In such a metaphysic, creation is seen as the self-transformation of reality which the R̥V puts in the schemas: Aditi – Dakṣa – Aditi, Puruṣa – Virāj – Puruṣa (see chapters 1.3, 1.5). AVŚ elaborates this schema: in 13.4.29-38 *róhita* is presented as being born from various elements of the world (day, night, space, wind, sky, cardinal points, earth, fire, the sun, waters, hymns and sacrifice) and as giving birth to them. As the reality which creates the world, *róhita* is seen as the source of all activities of the world: it is the source of winds and the oceans, it kills and gives life (AVŚ 13.3.2ab, 13.3.3ab). This stanza shows a similar tendency to that in the late R̥V. The composers become more aware of the unmanifest aspect of reality and they want to analyse it. Finally, the fact that the concept of *róhita* was motivated by the R̥gvedic concept of fire is also confirmed by the way its activity is cognitive:

AVŚ 13.1.39

amútra sánn ihá vetthetáḥ sáṃs tā́ni paśyasi |
itáḥ paśyanti rocanáṃ diví sū́ryaṃ vipaścítam ||

When you are yonder, you know (what is here); when here, you see those things yonder. From here (men) see the shining space, the inspired Sun in the sky. (Edgerton 1965)

---

11 *dr̥m̐h-*: e.g., R̥V 10.149.1b, *stambh-*: e.g. R̥V 4.5.1.d, *mā-*: e.g. R̥V 1.154.1b

The stanza presents reality which, in its form of the sun, knows what happens in the earth and, in its form of fire, knows what happens in the sky. The role of cognition in creation is expressed in AVŚ 13.2.10 where *róhita*, in its solar form, is presented as illuminating with his intention (*krátu*) two oceans and embracing all the worlds:

AVŚ 13.2.10

udyán raśmī́n ā́ tanuṣe víśvā rupā́ṇi puṣyasi |
ubhā́ samudraú krátunā ví bhāsi sárvāṃl lokā́n paribhū́r bhrā́jamānaḥ ||

Rising, thou extendest thy rays; thou adornest thyself with all forms; thou illuminest with might (? kratu) both oceans, encompassing all worlds, shining.

From what has been said above it can be seen that the concept of *róhita* is motivated by the Ṛgvedic concept of fire. They are qualified and conceived in the same way. At the same time, the concept of *róhita* is more general because both earthly fire and fire in its solar form are present within its semantic range.

2.1.2. Reality as breath (*prāṇá*)

The composer of AVŚ 11.4 conceives reality in terms of breath (*prāṇá*). Such a conceptualisation of reality already has roots in the ṚV. In one stanza of the ṚV, fire is identified with breath (ṚV 1.66.1.b, Jurewicz 2010a: 266–267). As far as experience is concerned, fire is closely connected with blowing which is necessary for its kindling. Fire is also connected with wind which makes it greater and wind is identified with fire in the ṚV (Jurewicz 2010a: 266). Finally, a living entity is warm but cold when dead which could also be the experiential reason for the identification of fire and breath. However, breath is a more abstract notion than fire because it cannot be perceived and yet it maintains the life of living beings. As such, it is more adequate for philosophical use.

At the same time, speech is conceived in the early Veda in terms of fire (Jurewicz 2010a: 380ff, see also chapter 1.2). We have already seen that the Ṛgvedic poets conceived reality in terms of speech (see chapter 1.6). Since there is the experiential connection between speaking and breathing, we can say that the Atharvavedic philosophers who saw reality in terms of breath are also referring to the Ṛgvedic identification of reality as speech. At the same time, the identification of reality with speech can be proof of a breathing practice which was connected with recitation (Zysk 1993) and which led to the supernatural cognition or facilitated cognition gained under the influence of Soma.

According to AVŚ 11.4, breath is the essence of everything what exists: it rules everything and supports everything; past and future is in breath (AVŚ 11.4.1, 10, 15cd, 20c). The hymn focusses on the rainy aspect of breath: it is seen as the source of rain and is identified with rain, lighting and thunder (AVŚ 11.4.2, 5c). Identified with rain, it is seen as the giver of life to human beings, cattle and plants (AVŚ 11.4.3-6, 17). The identification of breath with rain is motivated by the Ṛgvedic concept of Agni which has a rainy aspect (Jurewicz 2010a: 184–186). It is also possible that during the times of the AVŚ which was composed in a warmer climate than the ṚV rain, as the cosmic life-giving phenomenon, was more important than sunrise.

There are other features of breath which suggest that this concept is motivated by the concept of fire. It is called *mātariśvan* which in the ṚV is the name of fire and of someone who kindles it (*prāṇáṃ āhur mātariśvānaṃ vā́to ha prāṇá ucyate*, AVŚ 11.4.15.a-b). It has favourable aspects which can cure sickness (*yā́ te prāṇa priyā́ tanū́r yó te prāṇa préyasī | átho yád bheṣajáṃ táva tásya no dhehi jīváse*, AVŚ 11.4.9) The cremation fire is also presented as having favourable aspects with which he carries the dead to the world of those who did good deeds (*yā́s te śivā́s tanúvo jātavedas tā́bhir vahainaṃ sukŕ̥tām ulokám*, ṚV 10.16.4cd).

The next common feature of breath in the AVŚ and fire in the ṚV is that both are conceived as receiving tribute (*balí*)[12]; in the frames of this conceptualisation, both fire and breath are conceived in terms of a king. In the ṚV, the word *balí* is used four times. Once *balí* denotes tribute gained by Indra and it is here that the source domain of a conquering king who receives *balí,* is the most clear[13]. Twice it is used to denote tribute paid to Agni (ṚV 1.70.9, ṚV 5.1.10). In ṚV 8.100.9, it is used to denote the tribute paid to the thunderbolt (*vájra*)[14]. In this stanza, tribute is offered to the thunderbolt by waters that surround it. This clearly evokes the model of Child Of The Waters and *vájra* is seen as the cosmic form of fire in the ṚV (e.g. 10.45.4a-b). So in this case, *balí* can also be seen as the tribute paid to Agni in his cosmic form. Conceptualisation of breath in terms of a king

12 AVŚ 11.4.18: *yás te prāṇedáṃ veda yásmiṃś cāsi prátiṣṭʰitaḥ |sárve tásmai balíṃ harān amúṣmiṃl loká uttamé* ||;
AVŚ 11.4.19: *yátʰā prāṇa balihŕ̥tas túbʰyaṃ sárvāḥ prajā́ imā́ḥ |evā́ tásmai balíṃ harān yás tvā śr̥ṇávat suśravaḥ* ||

13 ṚV 7.18.19: *ā́vad índraṃ yamúnā tŕ̥tsavaś ca prā́tra bhedáṃ sarvátātā muṣāyat | ajā́saś ca śigravo yákṣavaś ca balíṃ śīrṣā́ṇi jabhrur áśviyāni* ||

14 ṚV 8.100.9: *samudré antáḥ śayata udnā́ vájro abhī́vr̥taḥ | bháranti asmai saṃyátaḥ puráḥprasravaṇā balím* ||

receiving tribute betrays the motivating influence of the Ṛgvedic concept of fire. This conceptualisation of breath will be elaborated in the Upaniṣads.

Similarly to fire in the ṚV, breath in AVŚ 11.4 is ambivalent. On the one hand, it gives life in the human and cosmic (as the source of rain) dimensions. But it also is dangerous. It is called death and fever (AVŚ 11.4.11ab). Identification of breath with fever again betrays its conceptual connection with fire: the ill person becomes hot as if fire was being kindled inside. Fire in the ṚV is also seen as bringing death, especially towards enemies of the poets (Jurewicz 2010a: 127–128).

Ambivalence of breath is explicitly expressed in the following stanzas as the ability to perform contradictory activities:

AVŚ 11.4.7-8

námas te astv āyaté námo astu parāyaté |
námas te prāṇa tíṣṭhata ā́sīnāyotá te námaḥ || (7)
námas te prāṇa prāṇaté námo astv apānaté |
parācī́nāya te námaḥ pratīcī́nāya te námaḥ sárvasmai ta idáṃ námaḥ || (8)

Homage be to you coming, homage to you departing; homage, breath, to you standing, and homage to you sitting. (7)
Homage, breath, to you breathing up, homage to you breathing down, homage to you turning away, homage to you turning thither, here is homage to all of you. (8) (Edgerton 1965)

On one level, this stanza refers to the movement of breath. It may describe not only everyday breathing, but also breath during a breath practice[15]. Moreover, as I have shown elsewhere, transformations of the deceased, i.e. of the part which survives death, can be seen as transformations of fire and the deceased can be seen as having a fiery form (Jurewicz 2010a: 307 ff.). The movement of the living part of the deceased is described in a similarly contradictory way (ṚV 1.164.30cd, 38ab, see chapter 1.6) as the movement of breath in the stanzas quoted above: it moves forwards and backwards at the same time[16]. In fact, the ability of the deceased for movement, despite having lost his body which is the vehicle that allows human beings to move,

---

[15] In his book on the origins of early Indian contemplative practice, Crangle (1994) looks for terms which are characteristic for the classical Buddhist and Hindu yoga and shows their development. As has been said, the research of lexemes allows us to understand well their history, but often it does not give access to the concepts which are not expressed explicitly. A breath practice postulated by me is such a concept and is an important source of classical yoga too.

[16] ṚV 1.164.30cd: *jīvó mṛtásya carati svadhā́bhir ámartiyo mártiyenā sáyoniḥ*;
ṚV 1.164.38ab: *ápāṅ prā́ṅ eti svadháyā gṛbhītó ámartiyo mártiyenā sáyoniḥ.*

is extraordinary. The Upaniṣadic conceptualisation of the part which survives death as being the self made of breath finds its roots already in the AVŚ.

The motivating influence of the concept of fire on the concept of breath can also be seen in that in AVŚ 11.4 breath is presented in such a way that it evokes the model of Child Of The Waters. This model is evoked indirectly in the following stanza:

AVŚ 11.4.20

antár gárbhaś carati devátāsv ā́bhūto bhūtáḥ sá u jāyate púnaḥ |
sá bhūtó bhávyaṃ bhaviṣyát pitā́ putrám prá viveśā śácībhiḥ || 11.4.20

He moves within the deities as a germ; having come into being, being in existence, he is born again; he has entered with his powers into the world that has been, that is, and that will be, as a father (approaches) his son. (Edgerton 1965)

The composer in a concise way presents the process of creation according to the model formulated in the *Nāsadīyasūkta*. Verse *a* presents breath as the embryo within the womb of the deities. The plural form of the feminine noun *devátā* activates the feminine plural concept of waters. This corresponds to the second stage of creation when the future world is already delineated, but still not manifest. The composer of the *Nāsadīyasūkta* conceives this stage in terms of darkness hidden within darkness. Here the embryo is conceived as moving. The recipient may interpret this as the response to the question *kím ā́varīvaḥ* in the first stanza of the *Nāsadīyasūkta*. As will be shown, the first manifest form of reality is conceived in terms of moving in the AVŚ (see sections 2.2.1-2).

In verse *b*, breath is presented as coming into being, as being and as being born. In the same way, the state of reality, just before its final manifestation in the world, is presented in the *Nāsadīyasūkta* as the future world about to be (*abhū*, Jurewicz 2010a).

According to verse *c*, breath is called the past and the future[17]. Thus its temporal character as manifest in the world is expressed. The manifest aspect of reality is conceived in the same way in the *Puruṣasūkta* (10.90.2ab, see chapter 1.3). Verse *d* presents the monistic nature of creative transformations in terms of the self-birth of the father from his son. Both translators interpret *pitā́ putrám* as comparison, though I would see it as an ontological statement. In the ṚV, this reflexive relationship between a father and a son is used in the context of the model of Child Of The Waters. ṚV 3.1.10 presents Agni

[17] In a similar way the temporal character of the world which is an aspect of reality is presented in ṚV 10.90.2, see chapter 1.3.

as pregnant with his own father, so he is identified with waters. At the same time, as Agni is the one who sucks waters, he is also the child. In ṚV 6.16.35, Agni is depicted as his own grand-father ('father of his father', pitús *pitā́*) who remains in the womb of his mother and – we can presume – is born from it. Here, breath is conceived in terms of a father who is born in his own son. Such a description of breath evokes the Ṛgvedic descriptions of fire which is its own father and son which again confirms that this concept is motivated by earlier thought.

The last stanza of AVŚ 11.4 explicitly evokes the model of Child Of The Waters:

AVŚ 11.4.26

prā́ṇa mā́ mát paryā́vṛto ná mád anyó bhaviṣyasi |
apā́ṃ gárbham iva jīváse prā́ṇa badhnā́mi tvā máyi ||

O breath, turn not away from me; you shall be no other than myself. I bind you to myself, breath like the child of the waters that I may live.

Since breath is necessary for life, the composer wants to have it within himself. In order to express the relationship between breath and a particular man, he evokes the model of Child Of The Waters. In this way, he identifies breath with fire which is both a condition of life and its sign. One could say that breath is the father who is born as a child in man.

It is worth adding that reality, conceived in terms of *róhita* (see above, section 2.1.1), is seen as the source of breathing of the world (13.3.4ab). This identification is justified in that both concepts, *róhita* and breath, are motivated by the concept of Agni. The same reasoning lies behind the conviction that the wind purifies and its later appellation as *mātaríśvan*. The following stanza can be seen as testifying a transitional period between the Ṛgvedic concept of fire which purifies and the later concept of purifying wind:

AVŚ 13.3.19cd

ṛtásya tántuṃ mánasā mimā́naḥ sárvā díśaḥ pavate mātaríśvā |

Measuring out with his thought the cord of Right, he purifies as Mātariśvan (the wind) all quarters. (Edgerton 1965)

The subject presented in this hemistich is the sun treated as the solar form of fire. The shining of the sun is conceived in terms of extending a thread (Jurewicz 2010a: 113, 116 ff.). The composer creates a blend here. The sun is the first input space, the second input space is a cognising agent evoked by the concept of mind (*mánas*) and the third input space is a measuring agent. The generic space is the concept of a conscious agent. The general noun *ṛtá*, ('truth, law, cosmos') strengthens the meaning of thinking and also activates the fourth input space which is the creation of the cosmos. In my view, within the frames of this conceptual network, the shining of the sun and creation is already conceived in terms of the activity of a conscious agent. In the blend, sunshine is identified with thinking and the creation of the world and these processes are conceived in terms of measuring. As already stated, in the ṚV, the word *mātariśvan* was used either for the kindling power of fire (e.g. ṚV 1.71.4. 1.148.1) or for the fire itself (ṚV 3.29.11). Purification is one of the most salient features of fire and as a purifier it is called *pāvaká* (e.g. ṚV 5.4.7, 6.2.6). In AVŚ 13.3.19, *róhita* is called *mātariśvan* and its activity is purification which clearly evokes the concept of fire. At the same time, its action takes place in space like the action of the wind. The Vedic identification of wind with breath together with identification of breath with Agni gives additional justification for such a description of *róhita*.

*

The concept of breath can be seen as a blend of features of Agni, wind, speech and breath. Breath shares its features with Agni and both concepts are presented in the same way with the use of the model of Child Of The Waters. Its role of the originator of rain comes from the input space of Agni which is wind and speech (THUNDERING IS SPEAKING). Its conceptual connection with speech is based on the experience of recitation which will be more and more important as the motivating factor for philosophical thinking. The next input space of the conceptual network is the concept of reality. The generic space is the image schema of SELF-MOTION.

2.1.3. Reality as time (*kālá*)

Time, called with the abstract term *kālá*, is described in two hymns of the AVŚ (19.53-54). I will analyse AVŚ 19.53 in order to show the way time is conceived and the motivating influence of the concept of fire. The main input spaces of the blend created in this hymn are the concept of time, the concept of fire, the concept of chariot and the concept of reality. Other input spaces are activated on-line which allow the composer to express precisely various aspects of time. The generic space is the image schema of SELF-MOTION.

AVŚ 19.53.1

kāló áśvo vahati saptáraśmiḥ sahasrākṣó ajáro bhū́riretāḥ |
tám ā́ rohanti kaváyo vipaścítas tásya cakrā́ bhúvanāni víśvā ||

Time drives (as) a steed with seven reins (rays), thousand-eyed, unageing, of abundant seed. Him mount the poets that know holy hymns; his wheels are all worlds (or beings). (Edgerton 1965)

In verse *a*, time is conceived in terms of a horse which pulls a chariot. Such a conceptualisation evokes the Ṛgvedic conceptualisation of the sun in these terms (THE SUN IN A CHARIOT). In ṚV 2.18.1, the epithet *saptáraśmi* is used for a chariot in terms of which the sun is conceived the rise of which is incited by human wishes and thoughts. In ṚV 1.146.1, it qualifies Agni which is being kindled and which will become the sun which fills space with light. In ṚV 6.44.24, the chariot yoked by Indra, qualified as *saptáraśmi,* is the source domain for the sun from which rain appears (Jurewicz 2010a: 217–218). In ṚV 4.50.4, Bṛhaspati creating the morning light is qualified in this way. In ṚV 2.12.12, Indra, who frees cows, is called *saptáraśmi* and the result of this act is the creation of the morning light (Jurewicz 2010a: 349–350)[18]. So the epithet *saptáraśmi* evokes the general model of reality transformation according to which fire becomes the sun. The input spaces of the blend are the concepts of time, of fire, of sunrise and of a horse pulling a chariot. The generic space is the image schema of SELF-MOTION. In the blend, the sunrise is conceived in terms of chariot being driven. As we have seen, such a conceptualisation of the sunrise is elaborated in ṚV 1.164 (see chapter 1.6). However, the composer of the AVŚ creates an abstract concept of time to express the power that makes sunrise.

In verse *b*, the composer presents the horse as having a thousand eyes (*sahasrākṣá*)[19]. Such a qualification evokes the metaphor COGNITION IS SEEING and the feature of the sun which is omniscience. It also evokes conceptualisation of reality in its first stage of manifestation as a thousand-eyed man (ṚV 10.90.1, see chapter 1.3). Thus the recipient can enrich the blend with the concept of reality. The horse is also abundant with semen (*bhū́riretās*) which evokes the rainy aspect of the sun together with the conceptualisation of rain in terms of semen[20]. Finally, the horse is qualified as unageing (*ajára*). In the same way, the wheel is qualified in ṚV 1.164.2 (*ajára*) and in ṚV 1.164.11 (*nahí*

[18] The epithet *saptáraśmi* is once used in reference to a being killed by Āptya incited by Indra (ṚV 10.8.8).

[19] It is used in ṚV 1.79.12 (Agni), 10.90.1 (Puruṣa), 1.23.3 (Indra and Vāyu), and 10.161.3 (*havís*).

[20] *Bhū́riretas* in RV: 3.3.11 (Agni), 6.70.1, 10.92.11 (Heaven and Earth).

táj járāya). This implies the paradoxical nature of time which, although it moves, is not subject to change leading to old age.

Verse *c* creates the image of people who mount a chariot pulled by the horse, metonymically evoked by the verb *vah-*; the people are the poets. The recipient may presume that they sit on the seat of the chariot. In these terms, the Somic exultation of men and their mental journey to the sun is conceived. This concept will be elaborated in AVŚ 19.53.3 (see below); it is also activated in ṚV 1.164.3 (see chapter 1.6). In verse *d*, all the worlds or living beings (*bhúvana*) are conceived in terms of wheels of the chariot (see ṚV 1.164.2, 13, 14, see chapter 1.6). The input space of a horse which pulls a chariot endows the blend with topology which allows the recipient to understand the structure of reality. It seems to be identified with time and is conceived in terms of a horse. The borderline between the two aspects of reality is conceived in terms of seat of the chariot and the manifest aspect in terms of its wheels.

AVŚ 19.53.2

saptá cakrā́n vahati kālá eṣá saptā́sya nā́bhīr amŕ̥taṃ nv ákṣaḥ |
sá imā́ víśvā bhúvanāny añjat kāláḥ sá īyate prathamó nú deváḥ ||

The Time drives seven wheels; seven are his naves, his axle is immortality. He, adorning (anointing) all these worlds, he, Time, moves on as foremost god. (Edgerton 1965)

In verses *a–b*, the composer elaborates the concept of the chariot. Similarly to ṚV 1.164.12 the wheels are seven. The axle, however, is one and is qualified as immortal (*amŕ̥ta*). The topology of the concept of the chariot is transformed in order to express the target domain. The manifest aspect is conceived in terms of seven wheels. Qualification of the axle as immortal allows the recipient to interpret it as either the unmanifest aspect or as the borderline sphere of the cosmos. We can again see how a concept which comes from experience is elaborated in order to make it a suitable source domain for abstract concepts. Since an axle is the centre of the chariot, the recipient understands that in the same way what is immortal is present within the world. Such a conceptualisation of reality is new in the Veda and is attested in other Atharvavedic metaphors (see section 2.5.1.2). It foreshadows the Upaniṣadic concept of the immortal self (*ātmán*) present within cosmos and man.

In verse *c*, the activity of time is conceived in terms of anointing. For the present argumentation it is important that, in the ṚV, the activity of fire in its cosmic form is conceived in these terms (ṚV 10.45.4, Jurewicz 2010a: 185). On the one hand, anointing makes an object warm, so in this way heating and the burning activity of the sun is expressed. On the other hand, the concept of anointing includes the idea of moistening which evokes the Ṛgvedic conceptualisation of the sun as the source of rain. The rainy aspect of time is also expressed in AVŚ 19.53.7 according to which 'all creatures rejoice in Time when it arrives'[21] (*kāléna sárvā nandanty ā́gatena prajā́ imā́ḥ*). The ṚV conceives the coming of rain which is happily greeted by plants and other inhabitants of the earth in the same way[22]. So the conceptualisation of the activity of time in terms of anointing betrays its roots in Ṛgvedic thinking about fire.

Verse *d* presents time as being the first among the gods and this also brings us back to the Ṛgvedic concept of fire because, as I have shown elsewhere (Jurewicz 2016c), precedence is the main feature of fire in the ṚV.

AVŚ 19.53.3

pūrṇáḥ kumbhó 'dhi kālá ā́hitas táṃ vaí páśyāmo bahudhā́ nú sántam |
sá imā́ víśvā bhúvanāni pratyáṅ kāláṃ tám āhúḥ paramé vyòman ||

A full vessel is set upon Time; we see him, verily, through his many forms; he faces all these worlds; they say that he, Time, is in the highest heaven. (Edgerton 1965)

In verse *a*, the composer creates the image of a full vessel which is set upon time. In the ṚV, the sun filled with Soma is conceived in terms of a vessel filled with liquid (Jurewicz 2010a: 264 ff.). This vessel is most often expressed with use of the word *kóśa* which also means 'the body of the chariot'. If the recipient activates this conceptualisation of the sun and the double meaning of *kóśa*, he will see coherence in the verse which blends the concepts of the sun filled with Soma, the vessel filled with liquid and the chariot. In the blend, the vessel is upon the chariot as its seat and in these terms the sun in zenith is conceived. The vessel is full. Such a qualification strengthens the liquid aspect of the sun. Moreover, the concept of the full is already an abstract concept in the AVŚ which is attested in AVŚ 14-15, 29 and the present stanza is the example of its formation. The concept of vessel is elaborated with the same meaning in AVŚ 10.8.9 (see section 2.5.1.3).

According to verse *b*, the vessel is seen by the poets. This sentence can be understood in two ways. It may refer to the everyday possibility of seeing the

[21] Edgerton's translation (1965).

[22] ṚV 5.83.9: *yát parjanya kánikradat stanáyan háṃsi duṣkṛ́taḥ | prátīdáṃ víśvam modate yát kíṃ ca pṛthivyā́m ádhi ||* As it has been shown, in a similar way the rainy aspect of breath is conceived.

sun. It may also refer to supernatural cognition realised under the influence of Soma which allows the poets to see the fiery-rainy nature of the sun (Jurewicz 2010a). The composer emphasises that the sun can be seen because it manifests in many forms (*bahudhā̆ nú sántam*). This may trigger the recipient to think about ṚV 1.164.9 where a cow, in terms of which the dawn is conceived, is qualified as *viśvarūpíya*, 'all-formed' or 'all-coloured' (see chapter 1.6). As I have shown, this adjective activates the concept of both fire and the sun. Moreover, it is possible that the composer of AVŚ 19.53.3b understands the sun as identical with the whole manifest aspect and because of this he calls it as having many forms. As it will be shown, the identification of the sun with the cosmos is attested in the AVŚ and it is implied that knowledge about the sun leads to the knowledge about the world. The structure of the hymn agrees with the structure of many Ṛgvedic hymns the composers of which firstly present the state of affairs which should be known and then the cognition of those who are described in the hymn. The first two stanzas elaborate the concept of reality identified with time and the way it manifests itself. The poets who mount the chariot (AVŚ 19.53.1c) are those who first cognised reality and set an example for other generations. Now, man repeats their activity and can see the same as those first poets.

In verse *c*, the composer identifies time with Agni in its earthly and solar form. It is presented as facing all the worlds. In such a way, fire and the sun are presented in the ṚV (ṚV 1.50.5, 1.144.7, 2.3.1, 5.28.1, 9.80.3, 10.12.1, 10.79.5, 10.88.16, 10.123.7, 10.141.1).

In verse *d*, time is presented as being in the highest heaven (*paramá vyòman*). This concept is used in the ṚV to denote the initial spatial and temporal beginnings of creation manifest in the sun in zenith (see chapter 1.6). I have also shown that *ádhyakṣa* which is in the highest heaven (ṚV 10.129.7) can be interpreted as Agni (Jurewicz 2010a: 332). Location of time in the same place again betrays the Ṛgvedic motivating influence of the concept of fire. In the blend, time manifests itself in the sun in zenith which can be mentally reached in the supernatural cognition under the influence of Soma. The scenario of riding a chariot allows the composer to present the stages of cognition and the structure of reality in a precise way. The early stages of cognition are conceived in terms of riding upwards on a chariot, but it seems that men finally reach its seat only in zenith. Then they can see the contradictory nature of the sun which is the visible manifestation of time. The next stages of cognition are presupposed by the logic of this scenario. Since time is conceived in terms of a horse, the recipient may presume that it can be cognised only when men sit comfortably on the chariot's seat. The composer of AVŚ 19.53 does not present the content of cognition realised in these stage because, as I have mentioned many times, the range of interest of the early Vedic thinker is limited to the manifest aspect. We can, however, see the shift in accent in comparison with the ṚV. In the ṚV, the unmanifest aspect, conceived only apophatically as non-existent and untrue, is totally beyond human cognitive abilities. Conceptualisation of the unmanifest aspect in terms of an invisible horse towards which one can get closer when one reaches the seat of the chariot implies the possibility of its cognition.

AVŚ 19.53.4

> *sá evá sáṃ bhúvanāny ā́bharat sá evá sáṃ bhúvanāni páry ait |*
> *pitā́ sánn abhavat putrá eṣāṃ tásmād vaí nā́nyát páram asti téjaḥ ||*
>
> He alone assembled the worlds (or beings); he alone encompassed the worlds (beings). Though their father, he became their son, than him there is no other majesty higher. (Edgerton 1965)

I see the image of bringing worlds by time (verse *a*) as a specific instance of a more general metaphor LIFE IS BEING HERE. Within the frames of the conceptualisation elaborated in the hymn, the creation of the world is conceived in terms of riches which are brought on a chariot by a victorious warrior. In this way, the full cosmological cycle, expressed by the general model of reality transformation, is presented. As the chariot goes away to bring back booty, in the same way the sun rises up to bring back rain. And since the sunrise is incited in ritual, the fulfilment of sacrificers' wishes are conceived in terms of the riches brought back to earth. The composer presents the first cosmogonic act of reality as time which is repeated by the sacrifices of men.

In verse *b*, time is presented as encircling the worlds. In this way, Agni in its solar form and the sun are conceived in the ṚV (ṚV 1.11.5, 1.128.3). The concept of Agni is also evoked by verse *c* where time is presented as the father of the worlds and their son. The relationship between father and son is used in the ṚV to conceive the relationship between aspects of reality and Agni is conceived in terms of a father (see chapter 1.6). This relationship is elaborated in the philosophical model of Child Of The Waters where Agni is both father and the son of waters. The formulation of verse *c* evokes the Ṛgvedic formulation which describes Agni: *bhúvo devā́nām pitā́ putráḥ sán* (ṚV 1.69.2b). In the blend, time is fire. This identification is strengthened by the qualification of time as *téjas* (verse *d*).

The following stanzas describe time as the creator of the sky and the earth (AVŚ 19.53.5) and present a panentheistic vision: in time are all elements of the world, both cosmic and psychic, and its powers (AVŚ 19.53.6-8). The composer also mentions abstract concepts such as *bráhman* and *parameṣṭhín* as being created by time[23]. Time also creates Prajāpati and the seer Kaśyapa.

*

From what has been said above it can be seen that the concept of time proposed in AVŚ 19.53 is an elaboration of earlier metaphysical concepts. The cosmology and the role of man are conceived in terms of the general model of reality transformation. The abstract concept of time emerges from its earlier conceptualisations presented, first of all, in ṚV 1.164. And this concept is an important proof for a tendency to abstraction. However, it could not be created without earlier efforts. Conformity of thinking in ṚV 1.164 and AVŚ 19.53 strengthens my thesis that the Ṛgvedic poets had created conceptual abstracts which in the exegetical tradition were not only understood but also named. Another new feature in this hymn is the potential possibility of cognising the unmanifest aspect of reality. One could argue that if reality is identified with time, it is already cognised. This possibility is attested in other philosophical hymns of the AVŚ and will be realised by the Upaniṣadic thinkers.

2.2. Conceptualisation of reality in terms of man

The composers of the AVŚ also elaborate the conceptualisation of reality in terms of man formulated in the *Puruṣasūkta*.

I will analyse two examples of this conceptualisation. The first one is the conceptualisation in terms of the Brahminic student (*brahmacārín*, AVŚ 11.5) and in terms of Vrātya (*vrā́tya*, AVŚ 15). Then I will analyse the conceptualisation of reality in general terms of man (10.2, 11.8) which allows the composers to create a description which also refers to a particular human being. Finally, AVŚ 10.7-8 elaborates the conceptualisation of reality in terms of a pillar (*skambhá*), but I will include this conceptualisation in this section because the concept of pillar is blended with the concept of man.

[23] For discussion of these terms, see section 2.2.2.

2.2.1. The concept of the Vedic pupil (*brahmacārín*)

The concept of a fiery man, used in order to conceive reality, is elaborated in AVŚ 11.5. The hymn has some stanzas that are difficult to understand in the present stage of the research. However, it is possible to reconstruct the general way of thinking presented by its composer. The main input spaces of the blend run in the whole hymn are the concept of the Upanayana rite and the concept of reality. In the blend, the teacher is reality while the student is the manifestation of its power in the cosmos. The input space of Upanayana imparts to the blend the concepts of confinement and cognition. It also allows the composer to present the stages of the processes described in the hymn in a clear scenario. The next input space is the general domain of Procreation which endows the processes described in the blend with a more general scenario. Finally, the model of the Child Of The Waters is also evoked in some stanzas to become the next input space of the blend. The generic space is the concepts of transformation under the influence of heat.

The hymn has a round composition in that its composer repeats the description of creation several times. The first two stanzas are a general presentation of creation, the next are the following groups of stanzas: 3–7, 8–13, 14–17, 18–22, 23–25 and 26. In this way, the composer can present various aspects of the manifestation of reality. He also puts the metaphysic content in general terms and in schemas. The conceptualisations of reality in terms of Brahmacārin is an attempt to highlight the fiery nature of reality conceived in terms of man in the *Puruṣasūkta*.

Stanzas 1–2

AVŚ 11.5.1

brahmacārī́ṣṇáṃś carati ródasī ubhé tásmin devā́ḥ sáṃmanaso bhavanti |
sá dādhāra pṛthivī́ṃ dívaṃ ca sá ācāryàṃ tápasā piparti ||

The Vedic student goes on setting in motion both firmaments; in him the gods become like minded; he maintains earth and heaven; he fills his teacher with fervour.

In verse *a*, Brahmacārin is presented as moving and as impelling the world[24]. In the same way, speech is conceived in ṚV 10.125.01a (*aháṃ rudrébhir vásubhiś carāmi*, see chapter 1.2). In these terms, the first stage of creation is conceived in which reality manifests itself. The concept of

[24] In a similar way, the Vrātya is presented in AVŚ 15.1.1 (see section 2.2.2). For the similarities between AVŚ 11.5, AVŚ 15.1 and AVŚ 13.4, see Dore 2015.

movement can be seen as the source domain for conceptualisation of freedom. One may also presume that this concept also reflect a practice which led to supernatural cognition connected with breathing and recitation. This practice would consist on the extensive effort, as it is attested in the cosmogonies of the ŚB in their initial sentence *sò 'śrāmyat sá tápo 'tapyata* (see chapter 3).

However, since the action of the Vedic student consists mainly of restrictive actions, the recipient may understand that, in the first act of creation, reality manifests not only its freedom, but also its ability to constrain itself and to make itself subject to its own rules. Such a conceptualisation of creation is also attested in the *Vrātyakāṇḍa* (AVŚ 15, see section 2.2.2) and in ŚB 11.1.6 where it is implied that reality subjects itself to the rules of time it creates (see chapter 3.5.2)[25]. Moreover, the idea of limitation during creation is implied by ontological theory according to which unique reality manifests itself within its aspect and its creative transformations do not influence its unmanifest existence.

Verse *b* presents the gods whose minds are united (*sáṃmanaso*) in Brahmacārin. I would interpret this description as expressing the moment when reality unites its cognitive powers in one subject. The meaning of this statement will be explained in AVŚ 11.5.7d.

According to verse *c*, Brahmacārin supports the earth and the sky; the recipient may presume that he functions as the *axis mundi* which will also be confirmed in later stanzas of the hymn (AVŚ 11.5.12, 11.5.26, see below). In the ṚV, the act of creation is also conceived in terms of supporting what is unstable (e.g. ṚV 2.12.2. 2.175, 10.149.1). At the same time, in the Ṛgvedic conceptualisation of the morning, the space between the earth and the sky is created thanks to the appearance of the *axis mundi* (Jurewicz 2010a: 112–113). If the recipient activates this conceptualisation, he can understand that in this initial stage of creation the space for the future world is created; this concept will be elaborated in the ŚB. While the future world is outlined, reality becomes limited within these very frames.

I would interpret that in the first three verses of the first stanza the composer presents the general content of the hymn which then will be elaborated. He presents Brahmacārin as the efficient power of reality which becomes able to cognise and will support the manifest aspect.

In the last verse, the composer presents Brahmacārin as filling his teacher with heat which is conceived in terms of the teacher's pregnancy (see below, AVŚ 11.5.3). Thus the composer generally presents the relationship between reality and its efficient power in terms of heating. The structure of reality is

[25] It is mostly elaborated in the *Smṛti* philosophy (Jurewicz 1994).

conceived in terms of the image schema of CONTAINER. It is worth adding that in the cosmogonies of the ŚB space, created in the beginning of creation, is filled with fire; the composers often use the image of the hungry belly of Prajāpati to conceive this creative stage (see chapter 3.1.1). The description of AVŚ 11.5 foreshadows this later concept.

In the second stanza of the hymn, the composer introduces the concept of a train formed by the fathers, the god-folk, Gandharvas and the gods who follow Brahmacārin [26]. The concepts of gods, seers and other divine beings are the source domains for the conceptualisation of the creative powers of reality which facilitate its organisation within the cosmos. This is especially clear in the *Puruṣasūkta* (see chapter 1.3) and will be continued in later thought. According to AVŚ 11.5, they are conceived as subservient to the main efficient power conceived in terms of Brahmacārin. The concept of train is elaborated in the description of the creative activity of reality conceived in terms of Vrātya (AVŚ 15, see section 2.2.2) which is imparted to the blend from the input space of a king and his consecration. This input space is not much elaborated in AVŚ 11.5, contrary to AVŚ 15. However, it allows the composer to express the relationship between the efficient power of reality and its other powers: it is conceived in terms of the servants of a king.

Verse *d* describes Brahmacārin who fills the gods with heat (*sárvānt sá devā́ṃs tápasā piparti*). The concept of heating activates the concept of smelting (as in ṚV 10.72.2, 10.83.3c, see sections 1.4-5) in terms of which the final unification of the gods' mind is conceived. At the same time, it evokes the concept of their enlivening (A LIVING BEING IS A HEATING BEING). Since the concept of *tápas* also includes the concept of light, heating of the gods means endowing them with cognitive powers which can be realised in seeing (COGNITION IS SEEING). Thus the composer can express the nature of the subjection of other powers of reality to the main efficient power of reality.

Stanzas 3–7

AVŚ 11.5.3

ācāryà upanáyamāno brahmacāríṇaṃ kṛṇute gárbham antáḥ |
tám rā́trīs tisrá udáre bibharti táṃ jātáṃ drá̇ṣṭum abhisáṃyanti devā́ḥ ||

The teacher, taking (him) in charge, makes the Vedic student an embryo within; he bears him in his belly three nights; the gods gather unto him to see him when born.

---

[26] AVŚ 11.5.2: *brahmacāríṇaṃ pitáro devajanā́ḥ pṛ́thag devā́ anusáṃyanti sárve | gandharvā́ enam ánv āyan tráyastriṃśat triśatā́ḥ ṣaṭsahasrā́ḥ sárvānt sá devā́ṃs tápasā piparti ||*

The relationship between the teacher and the student is seen in terms of the general domain of Procreation in its specific realisation of pregnancy and giving birth. The Upanayana and the general model of Procreation are two input spaces of the blend while the next input space is reality which manifests itself. In the blend, the manifest aspect of reality is conceived in terms of the pregnant belly of the teacher filled with heat while the unmanifest aspect of reality is conceived in terms of his whole body.

The concept of embryo is used in AVŚ 11.4.20 in the description of the manifestation of reality identified with breath (see section 2.1.2). The embryo is conceived as moving (*antár gárbhaś carati devátāsu*, AVŚ 11.4.20a). I have argued that this stage corresponds to the second stage of creation in the *Nāsadīyasūkta*. Thus, while AVŚ 11.5.1a describes the first stage of creation, AVŚ 11.5.3ab can be interpreted as describing the stage corresponding to its second stage.

The concept of a male who can be pregnant is a concept of an androgynous being which agrees with Vedic thinking about reality. The input space of the Upanayana rite, which begins the period of learning, imparts to the blend the concept of confinement to strict rules which imply that creation is conceived in terms of giving a boundary to what is unmanifest and unbounded[27]. It is worth adding that the image of the gods gathering around Brahmacārin probably evokes the experience of gathering around a new-born baby. Thus the gods are presented as realising their cognitive power. Moreover, as shown, this experience is elaborated in the descriptions of the morning which present living beings (cows and men) shouting at the rising sun (see chapter 1.6). So the recipient may enrich the blend with the input space of the appearance of the morning light. He will then understand that the gods can see not only because they are able to cognise, but because the conditions which enable cognition are also created[28]. We could say that in this moment, the first subjective-objective act is performed: reality divides itself into those who cognise (the gods) and into the cognised object (Brahmacārin).

The logic of the Upanayana rite implies that further creation is generally conceived in terms of the period of learning which ends with the final bath of the student (see below, AVŚ 11.5.26). The concept of Brahmacārin is used as the source domain for conceptualisation of the efficient creative power of reality within its manifest aspect. Conceived as a new-born baby, this power is viewed as the object of the gods' cognition. However, it becomes endowed

27 The same concept is expressed in the *Vrātyakāṇḍa*, see section 2.2.2.

28 In the ṚV, the appearance of the morning light is seen as the creation of possibility to cognise (Jurewicz 2010a: 109–110).

with cognitive powers enabling further creation which is conceived in terms of the activity of the Vedic student.

AVŚ 11.5.4

> *iyáṃ samít pṛthivī́ dyaúr dvitī́yotā́ntárikṣaṃ samídhā pṛṇāti |*
> *brahmacārī́ samídhā mékhalayā śrámeṇa lokā́ṃs tápasā piparti ||*
>
> This piece of fuel (is) earth, sky is the second; also the atmosphere he fills with fuel; the Vedic student fills the worlds with fuel, girdle, toil, fervour.

Verses *a–b* present a world filled with fuel. The concept of fuel comes from the input space of the Upanayana rite: its bringing is one of the main duties of the pupil. This image may activate the concept of the material of the world conceived as wood as in ṚV 10.81.4 and ṚV 1.164.41-42 (see chapter 1.6).

Verses *c – d* present the worlds as filled by Brahmacārin not only with fuel, but also by his girdle, by toil and by fervour (AVŚ 11.5.4cd). The sequence of the nouns iconically reflects the sequence of kindling fire: first, the fuel is gathered, then an effort is made which leads to heating the fuel and finally fire is created. If the recipient evokes the conceptualisation of the creation of sacred speech in terms of carving chopping, he will understand that creation of the world is the creation of speech conceived in terms of fire. The coherence of this conceptualisation is strengthened in that learning the Veda was the main duty of the Vedic student. The recipient may also take into account the Ṛgvedic identification of wood with water (and ṚV 1.164.41-42, see chapter 1.6). Thus he will activate the next input space of the blend which is the model of Child of The Waters and he will understand the process described in the stanza in terms of general image of fire which appears from waters.

Verse *d* ends with a description of the worlds which are filled with Brahmacārin's heat. Since cognition is conceived in terms of heating in the Veda, the recipient understands that the activity of the efficient power of reality is cognitive. At the same time, on the basis of metaphors LIFE IS FIRE and BREATH IS FIRE, the recipient understands that the space for the future world is now enlivened and filled with breath.

Generally speaking, the main creative pattern presented in AVŚ 11.5 agrees with the pattern presented in the *Nāsadīyasūkta*. The first stage of creation is the manifestation of the freedom of reality conceived in terms of free movement. The composer of the AVŚ adds the new meaning of bounding which outlines the future world. The second stage is conceived in terms of a teacher pregnant with a fiery embryo; the image of the pregnant being conveys the same general meaning of the future world hidden within the unmanifest sphere. As I have argued, the description of the second stage presented in the *Nāsadīyasūkta* triggers the recipient to activate the concept of dark fire (Jurewicz 2010a: 327-329) which is also implied in the description of AVŚ 11.5. I have also argued that the concept of pregnancy can be activated in the description of the second stage of creation in the *Nāsadīyasūkta*. The third stage of creation, conceived in terms of an unmarked flood in the *Nāsadīyasūkta*, can be metonymically activated *via* the concept of pregnancy (PREGNANCY FOR AMNIOTIC FLUID[29]). The fourth stage, which is presented in the *Nāsadīyasūkta* as the appearance of heat, is presented in AVŚ 11.5 with more detail as far as the source domain is concerned. As I have shown, the composer evokes the whole scenario of kindling fire.

Taking into account the general cosmogonic scenario, the recipient may presume that the further description refers to what happens within the manifest aspect of reality.

AVŚ 11.5.5

pū́rvo jātó bráhmaṇo brahmacārī́ gharmáṃ vásānas tápasód atiṣṭhat |
tásmāj jātáṃ brā́hmaṇaṃ bráhma jyeṣṭháṃ devā́ś ca sárve amṛ́tena sākám ||

Prior born of the *bráhman*, the Vedic student, clothing himself with heat, stood up with fervour; from him (was) born the *brā́hmaṇa*, the chief *bráhman*, and all the gods, together with immortality.

In verse *a*, the composer states that Brahmacārin is born first from *bráhman*. If the recipient activates the meaning of *bráhman* as sacred speech, he will understand that creation is conceived in terms of recitation. This agrees with the conceptualisation of the unmanifest aspect in terms of the teacher who teaches the Veda to his pupil; the pupil is born as he learns the Veda by heart. As we have seen, conceptualisation of creation in terms of the creation of speech is attested already in ṚV 1.164 (see chapter 1.6). Such a conceptualisation of creation presupposes its cognitive nature. At the same time, the use of the word *bráhman* as the source of what is manifest foreshadows its later usage in reference to the unmanifest aspect of reality.

In verse *b*, Brahmacārin is presented as clothing himself in heat and standing erect with heat. Since in the ṚV the mixing of fluids, first of all Soma with milk and clarified butter, is conceived in terms of clothing (e.g. ṚV 9.42.1, 9.78.1, 9.82.2), we can also presume that the image of fire, into which hot milk is poured, is created here. In the blend, the recipient may conceive Brahmacārin in terms of a high flame of fire which reaches the sky and is the *axis mundi*.

[29] This metonymy can be seen as an instantiation of the metonymy EFFECT FOR CAUSE (pregnancy is the cause of the appearance of the amniotic fluid).

According to verse *c*, Brahmacārin creates the form of reality called *brāhmaṇa* and creation is conceived in terms of giving birth. In this way, the reflexive nature of creation can be expressed in the model: Brahman – Brahmacārin – Brāhmaṇa, similar to that of *Puruṣasūkta* (Puruṣa – Virāj – Puruṣa). Since the word *brāhmaṇa* is used in the neuter gender, it may be presumed that a more general meaning is conveyed here: it refers to the manifest aspect conceived in terms of a grand-son of the unmanifest aspect.

The next form, which is created by Brahmacārin in AVŚ 11.5.5c, is 'the highest[30] *bráhman* (*bráhman jyeṣṭhám*). The analysis of this concept in the AVŚ needs separate research. For the moment, I will limit myself to saying that the phrase *bráhman jyeṣṭhám* seems to have ontological meaning. In other places in the AVŚ, it is presented as being known by the knowers of *bráhman* (AVŚ 10.7.17, 24), homage should be paid to it (AVŚ 10.7.17, 32-34, 36 10.8.1) and it appears in the beginning of creation (AVŚ 19.23.30). It is important to note that the word *jyeṣṭhá* can also be interpreted as 'the eldest'. Since in AVŚ 11.5 creation is conceived in terms of pregnancy and giving birth, the forms of the manifest aspect created by Brahmacārin can be conceived in terms of the eldest brother. This conceptualisation is evoked in ṚV 1.164.1 in reference to manifest forms of Agni (see chapter 1.6). While I would interpret the term *brāhmaṇa* as a general term for everything which is created by Brahmacārin within the manifest aspect of reality, the term *bráhman jyeṣṭhám* seems to refer to the sun which gives access to the borderline sphere of the cosmos (see also below, AVŚ 15.1.3). My interpretation is supported in that, in verse *d*, the gods with immortality are created. In the ṚV, the immortal state gained thanks to Soma is conceptualised as being realised on the sun where the gods are (Jurewicz 2010a: 276 ff.). It also agrees with the general pattern of Vedic cosmogonies which use the image schema of VERTICALITY in order to conceive creation of the sun as taking place when the moving object reaches the highest point of its upward path (e.g. ṚV 4.58.1, see Jurewicz 2010a: 227 ff., ŚB 11.1.6, see chapter 3.5.2).

AVŚ 11.5.6

brahmacāry èti samídhā sámiddhaḥ kā́rṣṇaṃ vásāno dīkṣitó dīrghásmaśruḥ |
sá sadyá eti pū́rvasmād úttaraṃ samudráṃ lokā́nt saṃgŕ̥bhya múhur ācárikrat ||

The Vedic student goes kindled with fuel, clothing himself in the black-antelope-skin, consecrated, long-bearded; he goes at once from the eastern to the northern ocean, having grasped the worlds, again and again violently shaping (?) (them).

[30] As Bloomfield (1897) translates it: 'From him sprung the *brā́hmaṇam* (Brāhmaṇic life) and the highest *brahma*, and all the gods together with immortality (*amrita*)'.

In verses *a–b*, the composer elaborates the input space of the Upanayana rite and presents Brahmacārin who has performed his initiation (*dīkṣā*); he is covered by the skin of the black antelope and has a long beard. It is possible that the composer wants the recipient to activate the general concept of *keśín* (ṚV 10.136) which literary means 'hairy'. This qualification refers to men who are not shaved and who have long hair and beards. In these terms, the activity of the efficient power of reality is conceived.

Brahmacārin is presented as kindled with fuel. Such a qualification metonymically refers to the everyday duties of the Vedic student. However, in the blend, a more general image is created: the creative power of reality within its manifest aspect becomes heated. One is reminded of the cosmogony of ŚB 6.1.12 the composer of which presents the main breath which is kindled, *índha*, which is the reason for its name *índra* (see chapter 3.2.2). As will be shown, the intention of the composer of AVŚ 11.5 is to trigger identification of Brahmacārin with Indra conceived as the efficient power of Agni which acts in the world.

In verse *c*, Brahmacārin is presented as going from the eastern to the northern ocean. If the recipient activates the meaning of *úttara* as 'upper', he may activate the image schema of VERTICALITY and understand the sunrise in these terms: the sun appears in the east and then goes upwards. If the recipient interprets *bráhman jyeṣṭhám* as the sun, the present stanza, which implies identity of Brahmacārin and the sun, would describe the act of realisation of the immortal state by the efficient power of reality within its manifest aspect. It is worth mentioning that the sun's rays are conceived in terms of hair in the Veda (ṚV 1.164.44, see section 1.6) and that the hairy face of Brahmacārin is the source domain for conceptualising the sunshine.

The word *sadyás* evokes the Ṛgvedic thinking about the birth of Agni and Indra who, as soon as they are born, become great (e.g. Agni 3.5.8, Indra ṚV 6.19.2) and are able to perform their specific activity such as being a messenger (ṚV 4.7.9) or drinking Soma (e.g. ṚV 3.32.9-10). In verse *d*, Brahmacārin is presented as repeatedly giving form to the worlds. This agrees with the conceptualisation of the appearance of the morning light during which the elements of the world acquire shape; the fact that Brahmacārin does this repeatedly (*múhur*) strengthens the identification of Brahmacārin with the sun in the blend. In ṚV 1.6.3, Indra is presented as giving signs and forms to what is without sign and form in the morning. Moreover, in ṚV 6.45.5ab, Indra's activity is presented with use of the same phrase *múhur ā́ kr̥-* (*anyád adyá kárvaram anyád u śvó ásac ca sán múhur ācakrír índraḥ*). As I have argued, in the ṚV, Indra is conceived as the form of Agni through which it acts in the world (Jurewicz 2010a: 360 ff., 425 ff.). And the recipient may also evoke this conceptualisation here. It will be confirmed by the next stanza. It seems to explain the activity of Brahmacārin which is described in AVŚ 11.5.5-6:

AVŚ 11.5.7

brahmacārī́ janáyan bráhmāpó lokám̐ prajā́patim̐ parameṣṭhínam virā́jam |
gárbho bhūtvā́mṛ́tasya yónāv índro ha bhūtvā́surām̐s tatarha ||

The Vedic student, generating the *bráhman*, the waters, the world, Prajāpati, the most exalted one, the *virāj*, having become an embryo in the womb of immortality, having become Indra, he has shattered the Asuras.

The first hemistich of the stanza again enumerates forms of reality created by its efficient power. In verse *a*, the composer presents Brahmacārin as creating *bráhman*, waters and the world. If the recipient elaborates the input space of the Upanayana rite, he can create the image of the Vedic student who recites the Veda. The result of recitation is the creation of waters which, on the one hand, is consistent with conceptualisation of speech in terms of water. It is also possible that recitation gives the reciting man such a sensation of heat that he begins to sweat[31]. On the other hand, in the ṚV, the concept of waters is the source domain for the unmanifest aspect of reality from which the world appears. This is elaborated in the abstract way in the model of Child Of The Waters and in the cosmogony of the *Nāsadīyasūkta*. The composer of AVŚ 11.5 activates this conceptualisation and presents the world as the next creation of Brahmacārin after the creation of water. The recipient may presume that the efficient power of reality, having reached the sun, realises the supernatural state which is not only the state of omniscience, but also of the ability to create.

The exact meaning of the concepts used in verse *b* (*prajā́pati*, *parameṣṭhín* and *virā́j*, AVŚ 11.5.7.b) is difficult to be reconstructed in the present state of research. In the AVŚ, all of them refer to the manifestations of reality conceived in abstract and general terms. In AVŚ 10.7.17, knowledge of *bráhman*, which may again be interpreted in this context as sacred speech, guarantees the knowledge of *parameṣṭhín* and *prajā́pati*. The term *virā́j* will be used in AVŚ 11.5.16 (see below) in a context which also implies its identity with Brahmacārin. In some stanzas, *prajā́pati*, *parameṣṭhín* and *virā́j* are evoked together (AVŚ 4.11.7b, 8.5.10c, 13.3.5a), in other stanzas, *prajā́pati* and *parameṣṭhín* are conceived separately (AVŚ 9.7.1a, 15.6.9bc, 15.7.2a). However, the later stanzas of AVŚ 11.5 (AVŚ 11.5.15-16) imply

31 This is attested in BU 1.2.1, see chapter 4.1.1.

that *parameṣṭhín* qualifies *prajā́pati* and that it should not treated as denoting a separate being in the context of this hymn. Notwithstanding the exact meaning of these words, I would presume that they denote the first manifest forms of reality similarly to the words *brā́hmaṇaṃ* and *bráhma jyeṣṭhám* in AVŚ 11.5.5.c.

Then the form called *virā́j* is created. In the *Puruṣasūkta*, the intermediate form between aspects of reality is called in this way (see chapter 1.3) and it has the same meaning here to denote the intermediate form between *prajā́pati parameṣṭhín* and the form described in verses *c–d* of the stanza.

In the second hemistich, the composer presents Brahmacārin as becoming the embryo in the womb of what is immortal. Thus the recipient can conceptualise the form called *virā́j* as a pregnant woman (as in the *Puruṣasūkta*, see chapter 1.3). This conceptualisation is elaborated by the composer who states that Brahmacārin is the embryo in the womb of immortality (*amṛ́tasya yónāv*). This expression is equivocal. If the recipient understands that the womb belongs to what is immortal, he will interpret Brahmacārin as the son of immortality. If he understands that from the womb what is immortal is born, he will understand that Brahmacārin is immortal. In this way, the reflexive nature of transformations of the one reality is conceived.

According to verse *d*, Brahmacārin becomes Indra and kills Asuras. This description evokes the description of Agni in ṚV 10.124 which presents Agni who remains inside his father and then leaves him to choose Indra (*bahvī́ḥ sámā akaram antár asminn índraṃ vṛṇānáḥ pitáraṃ jahāmi*). As I have shown, this hymn can be interpreted as presenting a cosmogony in which Agni manifests itself and assumes forms of various gods (Jurewicz 2010a: 435 ff.). In the present context, it is important that, according to ṚV 10.124, Agni destroys Asuras in the form of Indra (10.124.5a *nírmāyā u tyé ásurā abhūvan*). The recipient is of AVŚ 11.5.7d is prompted to activate this conceptualisation of Agni's activity.

Thus the composer explains the manifestation of the efficient power of reality, described earlier in AVŚ 11.5.6. Manifestation is conceived in terms of the general domain of Procreation in its specific realisation of pregnancy and birth giving and the activity of reality within the cosmos is conceived in terms of Indra killing the Asuras. Since cognition is conceived in terms of fighting with enemies (Jurewicz 2010a), the recipient may understand that the efficient power of reality cognises its manifest aspect.

Stanzas 8–13

AVŚ 11.5.8

ācāryàs tatakṣa nábhasī ubhé imé urvī́ gambhīré pṛthivī́ṃ dívaṃ ca |
té rakṣati tápasā brahmacārī́ tásmin devā́ḥ sáṃmanaso bhavanti ||

The teacher fabricated both these envelops (nábhas), the wide, profound (namely) earth and sky; them the Vedic student defends by fervour; in him gods become like-minded.

In verses *a–b*, the creation of the earth and the sky is conceived in terms of their chopping (*takṣ-*) by the teacher in the same way as wood is chopped to become fuel. If the recipient takes into account AVŚ 11.5.4, he will now understand that the unmanifest aspect is the ultimate cause of creation of the world conceived in terms of kindling fire. At the same time, the earth and the sky are called *nábhasī* which in the ṚV is used to denote 'mist, vapour' and 'cloud, rain-cloud' (Mayrhofer 1996). Thus the recipient may understand that the unmanifest aspect of reality is the deepest source of rain as it is also the deepest source of fire.

According to verse *c*, Brahmacārin guards the earth and the sky. The verb *rakṣ-* is used in the ṚV in reference to gods who guard the rules of the world (often called *vratá*) which are not broken by any living being (e.g. ṚV 1.62.10, 1.90.2, 1.93.8, 4.53.4, 5, 5.69.1, 6.8.2, 7.83.9, 8.63.13, 9.73.3, 10.37.5). The intention of the composer is to imply that reality is subjected to its own rules within its manifest aspect. This idea is elaborated in the *Vrātyakāṇḍa* the composer of which conceives the manifest aspects of reality in terms of Vrātya, i.e., the one who is subjected to the rule (see section 2.2.2). If the recipient takes into account the monistic assumption of the hymn, expressed explicitly in AVŚ 11.5.16, he could understand in these terms the ability of reality for self-confinement. Its freedom is restricted by its own rules as a young boy restricts his freedom after Upanayana.

Verse *d* repeats AVŚ 11.5.1b: the gods are presented as having united their minds (*sáṃmanaso*) in Brahmacārin. A new context allows the composer to explain the meaning of this statement. In AVŚ 11.5.3d, the gods are presented as gathering around Brahmacārin which I have interpreted as expressing the division of the manifest aspect of reality into subjective (the gods) and objective (Brahmacārin) spheres. Now, they become unanimous in Brahmacārin which implies their participation in his cognitive activity. It is possible that this participation is conceived in terms of their entering into the mind of Brahmacārin. This interpretation is confirmed by AVŚ 11.8.19, 24 where cognitive and emotional states, conceived in terms of gods, enter the manifest aspect conceived in terms of man (see section 2.2.3). As it will be shown, the concept of unification of cognitive powers in one subject is elaborated in ŚB 6.1.1.3 (see chapter 3.2.2). So the state conceived in terms of gods, who become unanimous in Brahmacārin, can be understood as the state when the cognitive unity of the manifest aspect of reality is realised. The composer implies that cognitive activity of reality, performed by the gods, can occur only when reality manifests in the cosmos.

AVŚ 11.5.9

imā́ṃ bhū́miṃ pṛthivī́ṃ brahmacārī́ bhikṣā́m ā́ jabhāra prathamó dívaṃ ca |
té kṛtvā́ samídhāv úpāste táyor ā́rpitā bhúvanāni víśvā ||

This broad earth, and the sky, the Vedic student first brought (as) alms; having made them (both) fuel, he worships; in them are set all beings.

In verses *a–b*, the composer elaborates the input space of the Upanayana in order to conceive the functioning of the cosmos and its relationship with the unmanifest aspect of reality. The earth and the sky are conceived in terms of alms which are brought by the pupil to his teacher. Bringing food was the next duty of the Vedic student. The concept of eating becomes the next input space of the conceptual network and, in the blend, the world becomes the food of reality. Such a conceptualisation will be elaborated by the composers of the ŚB who will see cognition in terms of eating.

In verse *c*, the composer further elaborates the input space of the Upanayana rite and presents the earth and the sky as fuel which is kindled by Brahmacārin. In the blend, the food eaten by the teacher becomes digested (on the basis of metaphor DIGESTING IS BURNING, see chapter 3.2.3); the functioning of the cosmos is conceived in these terms. Since cognition is conceived in terms of eating, the recipient understands that now the unity of both aspects of reality is realised in the same way as food becomes one with the eater. At the same time, if the recipient highlights the literal meaning of kindling, he will conceive the functioning of the cosmos in terms of the constant kindling of fire and its keeping. I would understand the verb *upās-* in its more literal sense of sitting next to a fire in order to kindle it (Jurewicz 2010a: 269–270). The rotating movement of fire-sticks evokes the image of the circular dance of gods in terms of which creation is conceived in ṚV 10.72.6 (see chapter 1.5), here its meaning is enlarged to become the source domain for the dynamic existence of the world. The recipient is expected to activate both possible interpretations of verse *c* in order to get a more comprehensive understanding of the world's functioning.

In AVŚ 11.5.6, the composer presented the movement of the sun as resulting from the activity of the efficient power of reality. In the next three stanzas, he explains the functioning of the cosmos in detail.

AVŚ 11.5.10

arvā́g anyáḥ paró anyó divás pṛṣṭhā́d gúhā nidhī́ níhitau brā́hmaṇasya |
táu rakṣati tápasā brahmacārī́ tát kévalaṃ kṛṇute bráhma vidvā́n ||

The one this side, the other beyond the back of the sky, in secret (are) deposited the two treasures of the *brā́hmaṇa*; them the Vedic student defends by fervour; the whole of that he, knowing, makes *bráhman* himself.

In verse *a*, the composer mentions two fires. One of them is directed downwards and the second is beyond the back of the sky. I would interpret the former as the sun perceived in everyday life cognition and the latter as referring to the place at the borderline of the cosmos which is reached in supernatural cognition. The same conceptualisation in implied by ṚV 1.164.12 (see chapter 1.6).

Fires are called two treasures (or treasuries, *nidhí*, verse *b*) of *brā́hmaṇa*. If the recipient activates the Ṛgvedic general domain of Finding The Hidden in terms of which cognition is conceived, he will understand that both fires should be known. As it will be shown, the way to supernatural cognition leads through the cognition of the cosmic sun. The fires are presented as belonging to *brā́hmaṇa* which I have interpreted as a general concept denoting the first creation of Brahmacārin. This confirms my interpretation of the fires because the borderline sphere of the cosmos is the sphere which appears first in creation.

In verse *c*, two fires are presented as being guarded by Brahmacārin. I would interpret this in a way that is similar to the way I interpret the concept of guarding the earth and the sky expressed in AVŚ 11.5.8.c. Reality subjects to its own rules not only the cosmos, but also its borderline sphere. If this sphere is not guarded, the world would collapse into its unmanifest source[32]. The power of guarding is conceived in the same way as in AVŚ 11.5.8.c, namely, in terms of heating (*tápas*).

According to verse *d*, Brahmacārin knowing *brahman*, i.e. sacred speech, makes all what exists his own. In this way, the cognitive nature of the existence of the world is expressed and, at the same time, its ontic results: knowledge of sacred speech allows the speaker to identify with his object. In this way, in the blend, reality cognises itself and confirms its unity through the activity of Brahmacārin.

---

[32] The same conviction is implied in AV 11.4.21, see section 2.1.2.

AVŚ 11.5.11

arvā́g anyá itó anyáḥ pṛthivyā́ agnī́ saméto nábhasī antarémé |
táyoḥ śrayante raśmáyó 'dhi dṛḍhā́s tā́n ā́ tiṣṭhati tápasā brahmacārī́ ||

The one this side; the other hence, from earth, the two fires come together between these two envelops; upon them are set the firm rays; these the Vedic students stands upon by fervour.

Verse *a* repeats the content of AVŚ 11.5.10a with a small difference: the second fire now goes from the earth i.e. upwards. This is the terrestrial fire which in the morning becomes the rising sun thanks to sacrificial activity. When it reaches zenith, it becomes the fire directed downwards. Verse *c* mentions rays which are set upon these two fires; the genitive *táyoḥ* can also be interpreted as the rays being those of the two fires. In the ṚV, the *axis mundi* is conceived in terms of a ray which appears in the morning (Jurewicz 2010a: 112–113) and this conceptualisation can be evoked here. In verse *d*, Brahmacārin is presented as ascending the rays. Such a description allows the recipient to understand him as Agni who becomes the rising sun and ascends. The composer now shows the way which leads to the sun and this opens the possibility for realising supernatural cognition to those men who will pattern the cognitive activity of Brahmacārin presented in the previous stanza.

In the next stanza, the solar-rain cycle of cosmos is presented which in the ṚV is conceived in the general model of reality transformation:

AVŚ 11.5.12

abhikrándan stanáyann aruṇáḥ śitiṅgó bṛhác chépó 'nu bhū́mau jabhāra |
brahmacārī́ siñcati sā́nau rétaḥ pṛthivyā́ṃ téna jīvanti pradíśaś cátasraḥ ||

Roaring on, thundering, the ruddy white-goer has introduced in the earth a great virile member; the Vedic student pours seed upon the surface, on the earth, by that live the four directions.

Verse *a* expresses the solar aspect of Brahmacārin on the basis of his qualification as ruddy (*aruṇá*, DEFINING PROPERTY FOR CATEGORY[33]). The concepts of roaring and thundering metonymically evoke the concept of rain. In verses *b–d*, the composer elaborates the metaphor RAINING IS INSEMINATING THE EARTH: Brahmacārin is presented as pouring semen from his penis in terms of which, as we may presume, the *axis mundi* is now conceived. Taking into account the context of the previous stanza, the recipient understands that the solar-rain cycle of the cosmos is the result of the sacrificial activity of men.

[33] Radden, Kövecses (1999: 35).

The life-giving character of the rain is expressed in verse *d*. It is worth mentioning that this verse quotes ṚV 1.164.42.b which presents the creative and life-giving nature of the manifestation of sacred speech (see chapter 1.6). Activation of this meaning allows the composer to conceive raining as the cosmic manifestation of sacred speech. The coherence of this activation is strengthened in that speech is conceived in terms of flowing water (Jurewicz 2010a: 85 ff.).

AVŚ 11.5.13

> *agnaú sū́rye candrámasi mātaríśvan brahmacāry àpsú samídham ā́ dadhāti* |
> *tā́sām arcī́ṣi pṛ́thag abhré caranti tā́sām ā́jyaṃ púruṣo varṣám ā́paḥ* ||
>
> In the fire, in the sun, in the moon, in Mātariśvan, in the waters, the Vedic student puts fuel; their gleams go about separately in the cloud; their sacrificial butter is man, rain, waters.

In verses *a–b*, Brahmacārin is presented as placing fuel in the fire, in the sun, in the moon, in Mātariśvan and in waters in order, as the recipient may suppose, to kindle them. Conceptualisation of the fire as being kindled is obvious. Conceptualisation of the sun as being kindled is based on the Ṛgvedic general model of reality transformation: the sun is the form of fire kindled in ritual. Conceptualisation of the moon as being kindled is patterned according to the conceptualisation of the sun and it is a new element in comparison to the ṚV where the concept of the moon is not much elaborated. As has been already mentioned, in the ṚV, Mātariśvan denotes the power which kindles fire and fire itself. In the AVŚ, it also begins to denote wind which is still closely connected with fire (see section 2.1.2, ad AVŚ 11.4.15). So its conceptualisation as being kindled is coherent.

In verse *b*, Brahmacārin is presented as kindling water. Thus the composer creates a blend which consists of two input spaces. The first consists of concepts of luminous bodies, the second of heating water by fire while the generic space is heating. In the blend, shining is conceived in terms of boiling. The recipient can also activate the input space of Child Of The Waters and impart to the blend the general image of fire in waters. I would argue that the composer of AVŚ 11.5.13b also wants to subsume all the sources of light and heat under one general concept of waters on the basis of this model.

In verse *c*, the composer states that lights of the luminous bodies are dispersed in the cloud. If the recipient elaborates the heating of water, he will understand that now it boils and vapor arises. But the concept of cloud makes him to think about rain which, according to the general model of reality functioning, appears from what is heated, i.e. fire becoming the sun.

The concept of rain is metonymically evoked by the concept of Mātariśvan which, as I have just stated, begins to mean 'wind' in the AVŚ. The image of lights going separately in the cloud evokes the concept of lightning.

Verse *d* is very concise: the sacrificial butter (*ā́jya*) of the luminous body is identified with man, rain and waters. I would again see the sequence of these words as iconically reflecting the sequence of transformation. The concept of sacrificial butter (*ā́jya*) evokes the concept of animal sacrifice. The word *ā́jya* is used in ṚV 10.90.8b to denote the fat which flows from the heated sacrificial victim (i.e. man in terms of which the manifest aspect of reality is conceived, see chapter 1.3). If the recipient evokes this concept here, he would metonymically activate the concept of sacrifice and conceive the appearance of rain in these terms.

However, the sacrifice implied by the stanza, the result of which is fat, can be interpreted not only as animal sacrifice, but also as cremation. In this way, the composer having described in the previous stanza the solar-rain cycle of the cosmos that is realised thanks to the sacrificial activity of men, now presents the afterlife[34]. It would be interesting to see verse *d* against the later context attested in JB, BU and CU (see chapters 4.3.1, 5.1). They present the functioning of the world in terms of sacrifice during which various elements of the cosmos are fire and oblation. In the first cosmic sacrifice, oblation is constituted by man, burnt on the cremation pyre, who then becomes rain. The same concept of an afterlife can be reconstructed here. The deceased is burnt on cremation pyre. Part of him, conceived in terms of butter, survives death and is called *púruṣa*. This part becomes rain. In the light of this interpretation, it is interesting to note that the sequence of luminous entities in verse *a* (fire, sun, moon, fire/wind) also may reflect the afterlife path of the deceased: he is burnt in fire, reaches the sun then, the moon to finally become the wind and come back to the earth in the form of rain. If my interpretation of is correct, this would mean that the concept of rebirth was enough well entrenched in the times of the AVŚ to be metonymically evoked.

The concept of waters (*ā́pas*) mentioned at the end of the stanza can be interpreted on several levels. It metonymically evokes the concept of a pregnant woman from which man will be born. It also activates the general concept of any source of light and heat as it is implied by verse *b*. Having been born, man also becomes the source of light and heat thanks to his sacrificial activity. Finally, the concept of waters also activates the fluid aspect of reality which manifests from its fiery aspect activated by the first word of the stanza

[34] It will also be presented in the next stanza.

which is *agní*. The most general message of the stanza is that fire and water are the same and their transformation is self-transformation.

This stanza is the example of a tendency to present the functioning of the world in abstract terms. As I have shown, its interpretation requires reference to general assumptions of Vedic metaphysical thinking expressed in the general model of reality transformation and in the philosophical model of Child Of The Waters. The only concrete experience evoked by the composer is the heating of water by fire. It seems, however, that its activation is not necessary to understand the meaning of the stanza.

Stanzas 14–17

AVŚ 11.5.14

ācāryò mṛtyúr váruṇaḥ sómo óṣadhayaḥ páyaḥ |
jībhū́tā āsant sátvānas taír idáṃ svàr ā́bhṛtam ||

The teacher (was) death, Varuṇa, Soma, the herbs, milk; the thunder were warriors; by them (was) this heaven brought.

This group of stanzas is an attempt to present the relationship between aspects of reality and put it in abstract terms that are recruited from the Ṛgvedic concepts, especially ṚV 10.124 and the *Puruṣasūkta*. At the same time, the composer defines the concept of Prajāpati as the generating power of Brahmacārin.

In verse *a*, the teacher is first called death. The concept of teacher is used as the source domain to conceive reality in its unmanifest aspect. The concept of death can be interpreted as the ability to kill and also a state that is subject to death and metonymically it evokes a being which kills and dies. The first act of creation is conceived in these terms: reality manifests itself as killing and dying at the same time[35]. Such a conceptualisation of the initial state of creation is attested in ṚV 10.124 the composer of which describes it as a sphere where there is no gods and sacrifice is impossible[36]. As I have shown, these are the features of symbols of darkness which are characterised by killing and death at the same time. The ability to kill is also a feature of Agni in the ṚV (Jurewicz 2010a, Blair 1961). On the other hand, the authors of the ŚB elaborate a fire's ability to die if there is no proper fuel for it (see chapter 3.1.1). The recipient may also conceive the first manifest form of reality in more concrete terms of a Vedic students who kills and dies.

35 Elaborated in the ŚB, see chapter 3.2.3.

36 ṚV 10.124.2a: *ádevād deváḥ pracátā gúhā yán*; ṚV 10.124.3d *ayajñiyā́d yajñíyam bhāgám emi.*

The teacher is called Varuṇa. This identification again evokes ṚV 10.124. As I have shown, it is possible to interpret the father in whom Agni remains as Varuṇa (Jurewicz 2010a: 425). The recipient can understand that Brahmacārin, within the womb of the teacher, now identifies himself as Varuṇa. This is confirmed in that the next concept mentioned in verse *a* is Soma which metonymically evokes the concept of exultation. Moreover, in ṚV 7.86-88 exultation is conceived in terms of a close relationship with Varuṇa (Jurewicz 2010a: 413 ff.). Since this state of exultation is seen in the ṚV as the state of immortality (Jurewicz 2010a: 177 ff.), the recipient understands that now reality manifests its immortal nature. It is worth mentioning that immortality is also the next stage of transformation of Agni in ṚV 10.124 which is presented as going towards immortality[37].

At the same time, the concept of Soma activates the concept of rain (RAIN IS SOMA). So the next stage of creation is the manifestation of the fluid aspect of reality which agrees with the general model of reality transformation. The concepts of plants and milk also metonymically activate the life-giving aspect of reality: the result of rain is the growth of plants which are food for living beings. The concept of milk metonymically evokes the concept of cows which eat grass and, more generally, the concept of food.

So the general schema of creation presented in this hemistich can be reconstructed in the following way. Reality (metaphorically conceived in terms of the teacher) manifests its dangerous power (metonymically evoked by the concept of death). Then it manifest its immortality (metonymically evoked by the concept of Soma) and its benevolent aspect (metonymically evoked by the concepts of rain and milk).

However, I would argue that the first hemistich is also meant to evoke the concept of rebirth. The concept of death is explicitly evoked in verse *a*. In the ṚV, the deceased is conceived as exulting with Soma on the sun (Jurewicz 2010a: 294 ff.). In ṚV 7.87.5, the exultation of the poet is conceived in terms of swinging on a golden swing together with Varuṇa; the swing is a source domain for the sun (Jurewicz 2010a: 415–417). So the concepts of Varuṇa and Soma may trigger the recipient to reconstruct the afterlife state of the deceased conceived as being realised on the sun. The form in which the deceased comes back to the earth is rain which is evoked by the concept of Soma. The next stage of the deceased's return to earth is evoked by the concepts of plants and milk. It is worth noting that these stages are conceived by the composers of the JB, BU and CU (see chapter 4.3.1, 5.1) in the same way. The penultimate form realised by the deceased is in the form of semen

37 ṚV 10.124.2b: *prapáśyamāno amṛtatvám emi.*

the concept of which can be evoked in AVŚ 11.5.14 on the basis of the metaphor SEMEN IS MILK (Jurewicz 2010a).

The concept of rain is also metonymically evoked in verse *c* where it is stated that clouds were the warriors. The concept of warriors activates the concept of Indra who accompanies the troop of the Maruts. The result of their activity is presented in verse *d*: they bring the sun (*idáṃ svàr ā́bhṛtam*). In the ṚV, the creation of the sun is one of the results of killing Vṛtra (Jurewicz 2010a: 347 ff.). This wording also brings the recipient's mind to ṚV 10.124: in the sixth stanza of this hymn Agni is presented as Indra who brings the sun (ṚV 10.124.6a: *idáṃ súvar idám íd āsa vāmám*).

AVŚ 11.5.15

> *amā́ ghṛtáṃ kṛṇute kévalam ācāryò bhūtvā́ váruṇo yád yad aíchat prajā́patau|*
> *tád brahmacārī́ prā́yachat svā́n mitró ádhy ātmánaḥ ||*
>
> Varuṇa, having become teacher, makes his own the entire ghee; whatever he sought of Prajāpati, that the Vedic student furnished, a friend from his own self.

In the first hemistich, the composer presents the teacher who prepares clarified butter at home, having become Varuṇa. The concept of the preparation of clarified butter evokes the concept of cognition performed under the influence of Soma; this conceptualisation is elaborated in ṚV 4.58 (Jurewicz 2010a). Somic exultation is also metonymically activated *via* the concept of home. So the recipient may understand the first creative transformations of reality which are elliptically presented in the previous stanza by the chain of identifications (teacher, death, Varuṇa) in more detail. The composer first highlights the source domain of creative transformation which is the concept of exultation. He then says that the teacher becomes Varuṇa and he implies that during creative transformations it becomes possible to call reality with this name. Reality can be called Varuṇa when it is cognised by its efficient power called Brahmacārin.

Then the composer states that whatever Prajāpati wanted was done by Brahmacārin (verses *b–c*). As discussed above in AVŚ 11.5.7c Prajāpati, qualified as *parameṣṭhín,* is created by Brahmacārin. In the context of the present hymn, it is relevant that one of the important semantic aspects of the concept of Prajāpati in the AVŚ is the connection with generation. In AVŚ 19.17, various gods, defined by their essential features, are evoked among them is Prajāpati who is called *prajánanavānt* (see also AVŚ 19.8.9). Its generating function is explicitly expressed in AVŚ 7.19.1a *prajā́patir janayati prajā́ imā́* (see also AVŚ 2.34.4, 3.23.5, 5.25.5, 9.1.24). Taking this meaning into account, I would argue that the source domain of Somic exultation is elaborated here and that the term *prajā́pati* is used to denote the generating power which arises in this state. Within the frames of this interpretation, Brahmacārin is the efficient power which makes thoughts of reality true and makes them existent. The same idea is expressed in ṚV 1.164.8 where the mother is presented as giving a share in truth to the father (see chapter 1.6).

In verse *d*, Brahmacārin is presented as creating everything from himself. In this way, the monistic assumption is expressed: since Brahmacārin is explicitly identified with the teacher (see the next stanza, AVŚ 11.5.16), the recipient understands that everything is created from unmanifest reality. Brahmacārin is also called 'a friend' (*mitrá*). The form *ātmánas* plays a double role here. On the one hand, as ablative, it expresses the source of creation which is Brahmacārin's self. On the other hand, as genitive, it qualifies *mitrá*; thus Brahmacārin is presented as his own friend. In the ṚV, Agni is presented as becoming *mitrá* (1.94.13, 2.1.4, 3.5.9, 10.20.2), so we can see again the tendency to identify Brahmacārin with fire. In AU 2.2-3 *ātmán,* which manifests in a woman's womb, does hurt her (see chapter 4.1.3)[38]. It is possible that the composer of AVŚ 11.5.16 wants to express the same conviction. According to BU 1.4.8, the possibility to feel love to various forms of manifest reality is grounded in recognition of its unity (see chapter 4.1.2). Taking into account that the monistic assumption is explicitly expressed in the next stanza of the AVŚ, it can be argued that the composer of the AVŚ sees the same reason for the benevolent nature of reality.

AVŚ 11.5.16

ācāryò brahmacārī́ brahmacārī́ prajā́patiḥ |
prajā́patir ví rājati virā́ḍ índro 'bhavad vaśī́ ||

The teacher (is) the Vedic student; the Vedic student (is) Prajāpati; Prajāpati bears rule, the *virāj* became the controlling Indra.

In the first hemistich, the teacher is identified with Brahmacārin and Brahmacārin with Prajāpati. Thus the identity of reality and its efficient creative powers is expressed.

In the second hemistich, the composer evokes the model proposed in *Puruṣasūkta* the composer of which presents the creative sequences in terms of the pattern: Puruṣa – Virāj – Puruṣa (see chapter 1.3). He focuses on the middle stage called *virā́j*. In verse *c*, Prajāpati is presented as ruling or shining (*ví rājati*). In this way, the composer explains the nature of the activity of

38 This also reminds us a much later presentation of the *Bhagavadgītā* 6.5-6 where the ultimate liberating experience is conceived in terms of being one's own friend.

the generating power of Brahmacārin: it is conceived in terms of shining and ruling. The first source domain is coherent with the general metaphor COGNITION IS SEEING, the second implies that cognition gives power. This second source domain is elaborated in verse *d* where Virāj is presented as becoming Indra the ruler. The concept of Indra has already been used by the composer of the hymn to express the creative activity of Brahmacārin in the world. The chain of identifications: teacher – Brahmacārin – Prajāpati – Virāj – Indra implies that creation is self-transformation of one reality.

Stanzas 18–22

In AVŚ 11.6.17-19, the author identifies Brahmacārin's activity (*brahmacárya*) with heat (*tapas*) and sees it as the source of various social (AVŚ 11.5.17, 11.5.18ab) and natural (AVŚ 11.5.18cd) processes: a king defeats a kingdom, a teacher finds a student, a woman finds a husband and cattle find food[39]. In AVŚ 11.5.19ab, the composer presents the gods who smote away death thanks to Brahmacārin, the second hemistich mentions Indra who, thanks to *brahmacárya*, has brought the sun to the gods. Thus the Ṛgvedic conceptual heritage is reinterpreted in more abstract terms which subsume all the processes of the world under one concept of activity of reality conceived in its manifest aspect as Brahmacārin. In the next two stanzas, the composer enumerates various elements of the world which are created by Brahmacārin: plants and elements of time (AVŚ 11.5.20) and animals (AVŚ 11.5.21[40]).

AVŚ 11.5.22

pṛ́thak sárve prājāpatyā̃ḥ prāṇā̃n ātmásu bibhrati |
tā̃nt sárvān bráhma rakṣati brahmacāríṇy ā̃bhṛtam ||

Individually do all that are of Prajāpati bear breaths in their bodies; all these the *bráhman* defends, brought in the Vedic student.

In verses *a–b*, all beings are called 'the descendants of Prajāpati' (*prājāpatyā̃ḥ*) who carry their breaths in themselves (*ātmásu*). Qualification of beings as *prājāpatyā̃s* agrees with the interpretation of the concept of Prajāpati as the manifestation of the generating power of reality in its form

[39] AVŚ 11.5.17-19:
brahmacáryeṇa tápasā rā̃jā rāṣṭrám ví rakṣati | ācāryò brahmacáryeṇa brahmacāríṇam ichate||
brahmacáryeṇa kanyā̃ yúvānam vindate pátim | anaḍvā̃n brahmacáryeṇā̃śvo ghāsám jigīrṣati ||

[40] Verse *c* (*āraṇyā̃ grāmyā̃ś ca yé*) repeats ṚV 10.90.8d.

of Brahmacārin [41]. The realisation of this power is conceived in terms of the ability to conceive and give birth to offspring.

In verses *c–d* , the relationship between the manifestations of reality called *bráhman* and *brahmacārín* is conceived in terms of the image schema of CONTAINER: *bráhman* is within Brahmacārin. Such a conceptualisation is coherent with the input space of Upanayana the main aim of which was the acquisition of the sacred speech expressed in the Veda. The learned pupil became the container for this knowledge. So we may presume that in this stanza *bráhman* means sacred speech present not only in the world, but also in separate men and other beings. Breaths or living beings are guarded by sacred speech. The coherence of this sentence is based on the fact that recitation is closely connected with breath and sacred speech can exist only when is recited.

Stanzas 23–25

In this group of stanzas, the composer presents the way to gain supernatural cognition.

AVŚ 11.5.23

devā́nām etát pariṣūtám ánabhyārūḍhaṃ carati rócamānam |
tásmāj jātáṃ brā́hmaṇaṃ bráhma jyeṣṭháṃ devā́ś ca sárve amŕ̥tena sākám ||

That, sent forth (? pariṣūta) of the gods, not mounted onto, goes about shining; from that (was) born the *brā́hmaṇa*, the chief *bráhman*, and all the gods together with immortality.

In the first hemistich, the composer presents the sun in its daily movement; the concept of the sun is metonymically evoked by verse *b via* the concept of shining and movement. Since the cognitive powers of Brahmacārin are conceived in terms of gods, the sun is presented as being set into motion by them. The sun cannot be mounted (*ánabhyārūḍha*) in everyday experience. The recipient may, however, presume that, since Brahmacārin is able to do that (see above, AVŚ 11.5.6), there are people who can possess the same supernatural knowledge and are able to do that.

The second hemistich is the same as that of AVŚ 11.5.5cd and can be seen as its explanation. Within the context of the present stanza, the *brā́hmaṇa*, the highest *bráhman* and the gods with immortality are born from the sun seen in everyday life experience. Now the recipient understands that the way to immortality, along the *axis mundi* conceived in terms of Brahmacārin,

[41] In AVŚ 3.23.5, this word is used in reference to a woman who is expected to be pregnant.

begins with the cosmic sun. One could presume that it is also implied that man, mounting mentally the *axis mundi* thus conceived, becomes himself Brahmacārin. The same is implied in ṚV 1.164.20-22 where the *axis mundi* is conceived in terms of a fiery tree and the man who mounts it realises his identity with Agni (see chapter 1.6).

AVŚ 11.5.24-25

brahmacārī́ bráhma bhrā́jad bibharti tásmin devā́ ádhi víśve samótāḥ |
prāṇāpānaú janáyann ā́d vyānáṃ vā́caṃ máno hṛ́dayaṃ bráhma medhā́m || (24)
cákṣuḥ śrótraṃ yáśo asmā́su dhehy ánnaṃ réto lóhitam udáram || (25)

The Vedic student bears a shining *bráhman*; in that (are) woven together all the gods; (he) generating breath-and-expiration, then out-breathing, speech, mind, heart, bráhman, wisdom. (24)
Sight, hearing, glory put in us; food, seed, blood, belly. (25)

In verse *a*, the composer presents Brahmacārin as bearing shining *bráhman*. The recipient may again understand the term *bráhman* as sacred speech, its shining nature is due to the metaphoric conceptualisation of speech in terms of fire. At the same time, qualification of *bráhman* as shining (*bhrā́jat*) may imply that this expression refers to the sun. Interpretation of *bráhman* as sacred speech is confirmed in that the gods are present in *bráhman* in verse *b*. The gods are cognitively present in sacred speech as its object and they are ontologically present at the sun.

The gods are conceived in terms of threads that are woven in the loom. In the ṚV, the concept of weaving is the source domain for the creation of light and cognition (see ṚV 1.164.5, chapter 1.6). The conceptual network is enriched with this concept. In the blend, the image of shining threads stretched in Brahmacārin is created. In these terms, sacred speech, with gods as its epistemological and ontological content, is conceived. At the same time, this image evokes the concept of a Somic strainer stretched in the sun and in the heart of the poet that is elaborated in the ṚV (Jurewicz 2010a: 161–162). In this way, the composer expresses that knowledge of sacred speech leads to the same results as Somic exultation.

As we have seen, the concept of the gods is elaborated earlier by the composer of the hymn. In AVŚ 11.5.3d, they are the first to see Brahmacārin. In AVŚ 11.5.1b. 11.5.8d, their minds become one in Brahmacārin. Now, the unity of subjective and objective aspects of reality is finally realised: the gods are within Brahmacārin thanks to sacred speech. The same interiorisation of cognitive powers conceived in terms of gods is expressed in ṚV 10.82.5-6 where the gods are presented as seeing the womb of waters and gathering within it (Jurewicz 2010a: 331–332)[42]. Moreover, the composer of the hymn also expresses the reflexive nature of creation: according to AVŚ 11.5.3, the gods are prior to Brahmacārin and now they are present within him. In the same way, the relationship between gods and speech is conceived in ṚV 1.125 (see chapter 1.2).

According to the second hemistich of AVŚ 11.5.24, Brahmacārin creates three breaths (*prāṇá*, *apānā*, *vyānā*), speech, mind, heart, *bráhman* and wisdom. (*prāṇāpānaú janáyann ā́d vyānám vā́cam máno hŕ̥dayam bráhma medhā́m*). The recipient may presume that these powers will enable men to reach this state in supernatural cognition. In the next stanza (AVŚ 11.5.25), Brahmacārin is requested to grant seeing, hearing, glory, food, semen, blood and belly to the people. The concept of glory (*yáśas*) evokes the concept of fame which is the state realised in the sun under the influence of Soma (see chapter 1.7), so the recipient may understand that the concepts of seeing and hearing refer not only to everyday cognition, but also to supernatural cognition. The concepts of food, semen, blood and belly refer to the everyday functioning of the world. The concept of food metonymically evokes the concept of eating, the concept of semen evokes the concept of procreation, the concept of blood evokes the concept of life. The belly seems to be the general concept here as it denotes the part of the human organism where the life-giving processes take place.

AVŚ 11.5.26

tā́ni kálpan brahmacārī́ salilásya pr̥ṣṭhé tápo 'tiṣṭhat tapyámānaḥ samudré |
sá snātó babhrúḥ piṅgaláḥ pr̥thivyā́m bahú rocate ||

Shaping (?) these things, the Vedic student stood performing penance on the back of the sea, in the ocean; he, bathed, brown ruddy, shines much on the earth.

In verse *a*, the composer uses the verb *kl̥p-* to denote the creative activity of Brahmacārin; this verb is used in ṚV 10.90.14d to express the creative activity of gods and seers conceived in terms of sacrifice.

Brahmacārin is called 'bathed', *snātá* (AVŚ 11.5.26c). The concept of bath comes from the input space of the Upanayana rite; the final bath marks the end of learning. In the blend, Brahmacārin, having finished creation, stands on the surface of water. The logic of the image implies that he has emerged from it and because of this he is called 'bathed'. He is brown (*babhrú*, AVŚ 11.5.26c), which is the colour of Agni and Soma in the ṚV, and burns and illuminates the earth. It is also called 'yellow' (*piṅgalá*). Such a description triggers the

42 The same is presented in AU, see chapter 4.1.3.

recipient to evoke the image of fire emerging from waters which is the *axis mundi* sustaining the earth and the sky, as presented in the first stanza.

The structure of reality presented in this stanza is the same as the model of Wave Of Honey (ṚV 4.58.1) where the wave identified with its plant rises from the ocean: in terms of the wave, the *axis mundi* is conceived, in terms of the ocean, its unmanifest source identified with Agni (Jurewicz 2010a: 242–244). If the recipient activates this concept, he will identify the teacher with Agni in its unmanifest aspect and Brahmacārin in terms of Soma which metonymically evokes the concept of Indra elaborated by the composer of the hymn.

*

AVŚ 11.5 is a coherent exposition of the metaphysical assumptions of its composer. In order to explain them, the composer elaborates the concept of the Upanayana rite which allows him to express the relationship between two aspects of reality, the nature of creation and its final result. The first thirteen stanzas elaborate in detail the elements of the source domain, the next three (AVŚ 11.5.14-16) can be seen as the attempt to create and define general metaphysical concepts. The composer repeats his exposition, beginning with the general description, which is then explained in contexts that enable the recipient to understand aspects of creative activity and the role of man within its frame.

The composer draws upon the earlier conceptual background. He conceives reality as manifesting in creation with its opposing aspects conceived in terms of fiery and fluid ones and conceives the functioning of the world in the same terms. The concept of Brahmacārin, in terms of which reality's creative power is conceived, clearly betrays the motivating influence of the Ṛgvedic concept of Agni. The concept of Indra is used to conceive the creative activity of reality in its manifest aspect. The composer also refers to concrete Ṛgvedic hymns, mainly to ṚV 10.124, but also to ṚV 10.90, 1.164, 4.58. Conceptualisation of reality in terms of the teacher and his pupil also comes from the ṚV (see chapter 1.6). The creative pattern is also the pattern of the afterlife.

At the same time, in many stanzas, the composer uses abstract and general terms to express the stages of the creation and supernatural cognition. From the point of view of later thought, the use of the words *prajā́pati*, *bráhman*, *brā́hmaṇa* is important. Although their exact meaning in the hymn can be proposed only tentatively, the efforts of the author to define them are clear. The word *prajā́pati* refers to the generative power of reality while the word *bráhman* refers to sacred speech and its power, though in one place it can also be interpreted as referring to the unmanifest aspect of reality (AVŚ 11.5.3a). Qualified as *jyeṣṭhá*, it refers to the borderline sphere of the cosmos and the sun. The word *brā́hmaṇa* is a general word denoting the first manifestation of reality created by its power called Brahmacārin. Seen in these general terms, this creative power is that 'which follows *bráhman*' in the ontic sense, i.e. it makes true the creative wishes of reality. Using the concepts of the ṚV, we could say that Brahmacārin is 'a body of the other' (ṚV 2.35.13d[43]) of reality thanks to which it can be active in its manifest forms as the world.

It can be said that the metaphysical Ṛgvedic assumptions, expressed in the general model of reality transformation, constitute the uncontested background which is now expressed in new metaphors and concepts.

2.2.2. The concept of Vrātya

The conceptualisation of reality in terms of man is also elaborated in the *Vrātyakāṇḍa* (AVŚ 15) where reality is identified with Vrātya[44]. It is not the aim of the present section to deal with the problem of the Vrātyas and their historical significance[45]. I rather identify the issues which are important for understanding the development of early Indian philosophy. It will be shown that the basic cosmogonic pattern of the *Vrātyakāṇḍa* agrees with the general Vedic cosmogonic pattern and elaborates the cosmic transformation of reality in terms of man. We will see that the cosmogony of the *Vrātyakāṇḍa* evokes many cosmological concepts characteristic for the ŚB[46] and they can be used in its explanation. It can be assumed that it belongs to a later period than AVŚ 11.5. This assumption is also supported by the way of thinking about creation presented in the *Vrātyakāṇḍa* displays convergence with the ritual of royal consecration (Rājasūya).

Etymology of the word *vrā́tya* is discussed in the field with two words seen as possibilities for the root of the word, either *vratá*, 'rule, law' or *vrā́ta*, 'multitude, troupe, group' (Mucciarelli 2015: 66). I am not going to solve the problem in this study. However, if we accept the former possibility, then

---

43 *anyásyevehá tanúvā viveṣa*. See Jurewicz (2010a: 361).

44 According to Witzel (1997: 277–278 and note 81), while AVŚ 13 devoted to *róhita*, should be included among books concerning with the Gṛhya ritual, 'the Vrātya book deals with an "anti-gṛhya" topic'.

45 For the present state of discussion, see: Pontillo, Bignami, Dore, Mucciarelli (2015). See also Parpola (2015: 130–144). For earlier studies, see: Hauer (1927), Choudhary (1964), Parpola (1983), Falk (1986). For interpretation of Vrātya in terms of Girard's theory of culture, see Collins (2014: 112 ff.).

46 According to Witzel (1987b), the *Vrātyakāṇḍa* which is composed in prose agrees with the Brāhmaṇas in language and style.

the word *vrātya* could be interpreted in the same way as the word *brāhmaṇa* used in reference to the priests generally. As *brāhmaṇa* is someone whose essence is the sacred word and its power (*bráhman*), in the same way *vrātya* is someone whose essence is rule (*vratá*).

In ṚV 7.103.1, the compound *vratacārín* is a qualification of Brahmins to whom frogs at the beginning of rainy season are compared (Scharfe 2002: 91). As Jamison, Brereton (2014: 1012) argue, one of the meanings of this hymn is to describe 'a pedagogical situation (see esp. vss. 3, 5), in which father/teacher speaks and the pupils exactly repeat his utterance'. According to Scharfe (2002: 217), '[t]he student's life was made more strenuous on purpose by a string of vows (*vratá*) that he was to undertake'. On the other hand, it is possible, as Scharfe argues, that some students could temporarily return home to see their parents (Scharfe 2002: 216). Thus the term *vrātya* could refer to 'the older Veda students during their study break' (Scharfe 2002: 217). This fact could also explain similarities between AVŚ 11.5 and AVŚ 15.1[47]. At the same time, the king's observations are called *devavrata* (Gonda 1969: 21) which links the concept of *vrātya* with the concept of king. As it will be shown, the concept of king is one of the main source domains to conceive Vrātya used in *Vrātyakāṇḍa*.

The main input spaces of the conceptual network created by the composer are the concepts of Vrātya, of king and reality. The input space of Vrātya imparts to the blend the concepts of supernatural cognition and self-restriction. The concept of king and his enthronement imparts the concept of power, and provides the scenario for the processes described in the blend. The next are the general domain of Procreation and the model of Child Of The Waters. Other input spaces are created on-line in order to specify the nature of creative activity of reality. The generic space is transformation under the influence of heat.

In the beginning of the cosmogony, the composer creates the image of a wandering man called Vrātya:

AVŚ 15.1.1

vrā́tya āsīd ī́yamāna evá sá prajā́patiṃ sám airayat |

A Vrātya there was, just going about; he stirred up Prajāpati.

The concept of a wandering man is also used in AVŚ 11.5.1 in the description of the first manifestation of reality (see section 2.2.1). I have interpreted this concept as the source domain for the conceptualisation of

47 See Dore (2015) who interprets AVŚ 15.1 and 11.5 in connection with AVŚ 13.4.

the freedom of reality (conceived in terms of movement) and its ability to constrain its freedom (conceived in terms of the rules to which *brahmacárya* subjects himself). The concept of rule is even more explicit in AVŚ 15.1 *via* the word *vrā́tya* which can be interpreted as 'someone whose essence is rule'. Thus it is implied that in the first creative stage reality manifests its freedom and its ability to control and limit itself.

In the next sentence, the composer introduces the concept of Prajāpati. In AVŚ 11.5, the concept of Prajāpati is used in reference to the generative power of Brahmacārin and here it can be interpreted in the same way. The recipient will then activate the next input space of the conceptual network which is the general domain of Procreation and will conceive the first creative stage in terms of the sexual act and insemination. It is also possible that the composer evokes the experience of goading cattle in order to conceive the appearance of the power of creation. Another experience, which incited men to activity, was Somic exultation. These concepts, if activated, become the input spaces of the blend created in this passage.

AVŚ 15.1.2

sá prajā́patiḥ suvárṇam ātmánn apaśyat tát prā́janayat |

He, Prajāpati, saw in himself gold; he generated that.

The composer enriches the conceptual network with his next input space. It is the purification of gold, metonymically activated *via* the concept of gold[48]. The verb *prá jan-* strengthens the input space of Procreation[49]. In the blend, the first form of the future world is conceived in terms of gold and an inseminated woman. As we have seen, conceptualisation in terms of sexual act is common in Vedic thinking[50]. The concept of purification of gold as the source domain for other activities is already used in the ṚV 9.86.43 (see Jurewicz 2010a: 181) and is then elaborated in the ŚB (6.1.3, see chapter 3.2.2). The word *suvárṇa* not only conveys the meaning of 'gold', but also evokes the beauty of the offspring in terms of which the future world is conceived[51]. There is a correspondence between the concept of purification of gold and the growth of an embryo because both consist of

---

48 Metonymy RESULT FOR ACTION; GOLD FOR ITS PURIFICATION (Radden, Kövecses 1999: 37).

49 Metonymy THE LAST PHASE OF THE PROCESS FOR THE WHOLE PROCESS (Radden, Kövecses 1999: 49). INSEMINATION FOR THE SEXUAL ACT.

50 Already in the ṚV, see Jurewicz (2010a) and elaborated in the Upaniṣads, e.g. BU 1.4 (see chapter 4.1.2).

51 Metaphor THE EARTH IS A BEAUTIFUL WOMAN (ŚB 6.1.1.15, see chapter 3.2.2),

heating[52]. So the sentence *sá suvárṇam apaśyat* activates the concept of the growth of an embryo conceived in terms of purification of gold. In these terms, this stage of creation is conceived. Since the concept of gold metonymically activates the concept of shine[53], the recipient can activate the next input space of the conceptual network, which is the appearance of light from darkness, and understand this stage of creation in those terms. The fact that Prajāpati sees the gold in himself (*ātmán*) implies the reflexive character of the creative process.

In the next passage, the composer elaborates the general domain of Procreation in its specific realisations of pregnancy and of the development of an embryo. On the basis of the belief that the father in reborn in his own son, the recipient may identify the embryo with Prajāpati:

AVŚ 15.1.3

tád ékam abhavat tál lalā́mam abhavat tán mahád abhavat táj jyeṣṭhám abhavat tád |
bráhmābhavat tát tápo 'bhavat tát satyám abhavat téna prā́jāyata |

That became one; that became star-marked; that became great; that became chief; that became *bráhman*; that became heat[54] that became truth; therewith he had progeny.

On the basis of the expression *tád ékam*, a recipient well versed in the Veda may evoke the concept of That One used in the *Nāsadīyasūkta* in reference to reality in the first stage of creation. The next phases of the development of an embryo are metonymically evoked by the words *lalā́ma*, *mahát*, *jyeṣṭhá*, *bráhman*, *tápas* and *satyá*. To the best of my knowledge it is only here that the word *lalā́ma* appears the AVŚ, though in two places its feminine form is used in reference to a female demon (AVŚ 1.18.1,4). This word, interpreted by Whitney as 'star-marked', is interpreted by Monier Williams as 'having a mark or spot on the forehead marked with paint &c (as cattle)'. If this is the case, the domain of cow pregnant with a calf can be activated. If, on the other

---

52 *Taittirīya Brāhmaṇa* 3.11.7-8 presents creation in terms of heating of gold in the internal fire of Prajāpati:
prajā́patir vái prajā́kāmas tápo 'tapyata | sá híraṇyam údāsyat| tád agnaú prā́syat | tád asmai nā́cchadayat | tád dvitī́yaṃ prā́syat | tád asmaí ná_evā́cchadayat | tát tṛtī́yaṃ prā́syat | tád asmaí ná_evā́cchadayat | tád ātmánn evá hṛdayyè 'gnaú vaiśvānaré prā́syat | tád asmā acchadayat | tásmād dhíraṇyaṃ kániṣṭhaṃ dhánānām | bhuñját priyátamam | hṛdayajám̐ hí | sá vái tám evá nā́vindat | yásmai tā́ṃ dákṣiṇām áneṣyat | tā́m̐ svā́ya_evá hástāya dákṣiṇāyānayat | tā́ṃ prátyagṛhṇāt |

53 SHINE FOR GOLD, an instantiation of metonymy DEFINING PROPERTY FOR A CATEGORY (Radden, Kövecses 1999.

54 Whitney (1905) omits the phrase *tát tápo 'bhavat* in his translation.

hand, the recipient evokes the concept of a female demon, he would understand this stage of creation in terms of the appearance of a terrifying form. I have shown that the concept of darkness used in the *Nāsadīyasūkta* activates the concept of Vr̥tra (see Jurewicz 2010a: 345). Such a conceptualisation of the second stage of creation is also elaborated in ŚB 2.2.4 where Prajāpati creates a terrifying fiery form which threatens him with death (see chapter 3.1.1).

The words *mahát* ('great') and *jyeṣṭhá* ('excellent') imply a further development of the embryo which grows to assume a fully mature form. However, in the AVŚ they are also used in more philosophical contexts[55].

The word *mahát* is used in AVŚ 10.8.6 to qualify the sphere of reality conceived in terms of a track (*mahát padám*)[56]. Within the monistic frame, it is the most mysterious sphere on the borderline between what is manifest and unmanifest (*āvíḥ sán níhitaṃ gúhā*) that is already subjected to the power of time (it is aging, *járat*). It is the basis for the world (*tátredáṃ sárvam ā́rpitam éjat prāṇát prátiṣṭhitam*). On the other hand, in AVŚ 8.8.8, the word *mahát* is used to qualify the world[57]. In AVŚ 10.8.16, the world, qualified as *mahát*, is conceived in terms of the human body[58]. In AVŚ 10.7.38 and 10.8.15, the word *mahát* qualifies *yaksá* who is a mysterious being in terms of which the essence of the world is conceived (see section 2.5.2.2, 2.6.1). In AVŚ 1.32.1, *mahát* qualifies *bráhman* understood as speech pronounced during sacrificial gatherings[59].

The word *mahát* is also used without a noun. In AVŚ 10.8.9d, the seers, who are in the sun (conceived in terms of a vessel turned upside down see section 2.5.1.2), are called the guardians of the great (*gopā́ maható*). In AVŚ 10.8.33, 37-38, the phrase *brā́hmaṇam mahát* is used to denote the object of knowledge reached by the words spoken 'by the One who had no predecessor' (as Edgerton 1965 translates *apūrvéṇeṣitā́ vā́cas*) and it is called 'the thread of the thread' (*sū́traṃ sū́trasya*)[60].

Such uses of the word *mahát* are further proof of the search for abstract concepts. It metonymically evokes the concepts it qualifies: the world, its beginning, its supreme essence and the speech which enables its cognition. At

---

55 For *jyeṣṭhá* in context of Vrātyastoma, see Candotti, Pontillo (2015).

56 AVŚ 10.8.6: *āvíḥ sán níhitaṃ gúhā járan nā́ma mahát padám | tátredáṃ sárvam ā́rpitam éjat prāṇát prátiṣṭhitam ||*

57 AVŚ 8.8.8: *ayáṃ lokó jā́lam āsīc chakrásya maható mahā́n | ténāhám indrajālénāmū́ṃs támasābhí dadhāmi sárvān ||*

58 AVŚ 11.8.16: *yát tác chárīram áśayat saṃdháyā sáṃhitaṃ mahát | yénedám adyá rócate kó asmin várṇam ā́bharat ||*

59 AVŚ 1.32.1: *idáṃ janā́so vidátha mahád bráhma vadiṣyati | ná tát pr̥thivyā́ṃ no diví yéna prāṇánti vīrúdhaḥ ||*

60 For the meaning of the related noun *mahás*, see Gonda (1975a). See also Buitenen (1988a).

the same time, the fact that the world in this stage of creation can be qualified as great implies that reality manifests itself in a form that can be measured with the use of the concept of size[61]. Such a conceptualisation implies that it is already limited and bounded because in its unmanifest aspect it is unlimited, unbounded and cannot be measured.

The uses of the word *jyeṣṭhá* also betray the search for abstraction. This word is used in apposition to *bráhman* in AVŚ 11.5.5, 23: *bráhma jyeṣṭhá* is born from the Brahmacārin (see above, section 2.2.1). As already argued, it can be interpreted as referring to the borderline sphere of the cosmos or to the sun. The word *jyeṣṭhá* is used in AVŚ 10.7.17 in apposition to the adjective *brā́hmaṇa*; its composer states that they who know the *jyeṣṭhám brā́hmaṇam* know the pillar. In AVŚ 10.8.16, the word *jyeṣṭhá* is used to denote the sphere of the world from which the sun rises and where it sets. In AVŚ 10.8.19, it is used to denote a principle which shines upwards by truth, looks downwards by *bráhman* and breathes transversely by breath. In AVŚ 11.53.8ab, *jyeṣṭhá* is presented as located in time, similarly to heat (*tápas*) and *bráhman*. Such usages of the word *jyeṣṭhá* may allow us to understand it as referring to the borderline sphere which enables its spatial and temporal functioning.

Let us consider one more stanza which uses both of the words *mahát* and *jyeṣṭhá* together with the adjective *brā́hmaṇa*:

AVŚ 10.8.20

yó vaí té vidyā́d aráṇī yā́bhyāṃ nirmathyáte vásu |
sá vidvā́n jyeṣṭháṃ manyeta sá vidyā́d brā́hmaṇaṃ mahát ||

Verily who knows these two kindling-sticks (rubbed together in lightning the sacred Fire), by which is rubbed out wealth (through sacrifice), he may be considered a knower of the Supreme; he would know the bráhman power.

The composer of the stanza implies that knowledge of the origination of fire leads to knowledge of the manifest aspect of reality which is evoked metonymically *via* the adjectives *jyeṣṭhá*, *mahát* and *brā́hmaṇam*. The conceptual network consists of two input spaces, the kindling of fire and cognition. In the blend, when a man kindles fire, he is mentally able to reach to the beginnings of the world (*mahát padám*[62]) and to understand the structure of the world. We again see the motivating influence of the Ṛgvedic thought as knowledge about fire is knowledge about reality.

---

61 Here I would look for the earliest roots of the late use of *mahā́nt* in the Smṛti and Sāṃkhya cosmogonies.

62 See above, analysis of AVŚ 10.8.6, section 2.2.2.

Taking into account these usages of the words *mahát* and *jyeṣṭhá*, we may assume that the recipient of AVŚ 15.1.3 is expected to activate their abstract meaning. In the blend, Prajāpati, conceived in the form of the embryo, manifests himself in a form which is great and outlines the borderline sphere of the future cosmos the visual form of which is the sun.

The next form of Prajāpati is called *bráhman* which I would again interpret as sacred speech. Prajāpati is conceived in terms of man who recites the sacred speech. Recitation results in heating (*tát tápo 'bhavat*). The word *satyá*, used in the next sentence (*tát satyám abhavat*), has two meanings here: epistemological (sacred speech is true) and ontological (sacred speech is what exists, i.e. the world). The use of the word *satyá* in reference to the manifest aspect of reality is in accordance with its use in the early Veda which calls it by the cognate word *sát* (see Jurewicz 2010a: 52).

The last sentence (*téna prā́jāyata*) is translated by Whitney as 'therewith he had progeny', but I would argue that its meaning is 'by this he was born'. This interpretation agrees with the self-reflexive nature of the creative process which is conceived in terms of the rebirth of a father in his own son. In these terms, the final manifestation of Prajāpati, as the generative power of reality within its manifest aspect, is conceived.

AVŚ 15.1.4-5

só 'vardhata sá mahā́n abhavat sá mahādevó 'bhavat | (4)
sá devā́nām ī́śā́ṃ páry ait sá ī́śāno 'bhavat | (5)

He increased; he became great; he became the great god.
He compassed the lordship of the gods; he became the Lord.

The composer describes transformations of Prajāpati in terms of the growth of a child: he grows and becomes great. The same scenario is elaborated in ŚB 11.1.6 where Prajāpati, having been born from an egg, grows, stands on his legs, speaks and creates the cosmos (see chapter 3.2.2). Because he is great, he is called the great god. The compound *mahādevá*, taken against the context of the Vedic cosmogonies, does not need to be interpreted as referring to Śiva. It can be just a statement referring to Prajāpati who becomes the manifest aspect of reality understood as great (see above, analysis of AVŚ 15.1.3 and below, analysis of AVŚ 15.4-6).

The next sentence introduces the input space of a king: Prajāpati, having fully grown, encompasses rulership of all the gods, so he is their ruler. It is worth noting that the concept of a king is used as the source domain for conceptualisation of transformation of reality in the *Puruṣasūkta*: its intermediate form is called *virā́j* which, as I have shown, activates the concept of a king (see chapter 1.3, see also AVŚ 11.5, section 2.2.1). The concept of a ruler (*vaśín*) is also evoked in AVŚ 11.5.16 to conceive reality acting in its manifest aspect with the ruler identified as Indra (see above, section 2.2.1).

AVŚ 15.1.6

sá ekavrātyó bhavat sá dhánur ā́datta tád evéndradhanúḥ |

He became the sole Vrātya; he took to himself a bow; that was Indra's bow.

In this stage of creation, the creative power of reality conceived in terms of Prajāpati is called *ekavrātyá*. Thus the composer elaborates the pattern of cosmogony which agrees with the general Vedic pattern. It is explicitly expressed by the Ṛgvedic poets who use the concept of self-birth to conceive the monistic character of the cosmogonic transformations (Father – Speech – Father, Aditi – Dakṣa – Aditi, Puruṣa – Virāj – Puruṣa, *tád ékam – tápas – tád ékam*, see chapters 1.2, 1.5, 1.3). Here, the initial cosmogonic principle called Vrātya is reborn as Vrātya and manifests itself as one. This process can be patterned as: Vrātya – Prajāpati – Ekavrātya. The name of this form of reality 'one Vrātya' (*ekavrātyá*) evokes the name of reality in the *Nāsadīyasūkta, tád ékam*. In this way, the unity of reality is expressed.

This form of reality is conceived in terms of a king with a bow which belongs to Indra (*indradhanús*). Thus the composer metonymically introduces the next input space which is the concept of the god Indra. As I have shown (Jurewicz 2010a: 364), in the ṚV, the concept of Indra is used to conceive the activity of reality within the world and the recipient may evoke this concept here. This concept is used in AVŚ 11.5 (see above, section 2.2.1) with the same meaning. In ŚB 6.1.1.2, the concept of Indra is used to conceive the main breath of reality which, when kindled, kindles other breaths and thus becomes the crucial factor of creation (see chapter 3.2.2). This etymology is well entrenched in the ṚV where Indra, under the influence of Soma, is presented as heated (Jurewicz 2010a: 360–361). We can accept the recipient of AVŚ 15.1.6 could understand the heating of Prajāpati in terms of taking Indra's bow. The image of the king who takes a bow also metonymically activates the royal consecration (Rājasūya). According to its exegesis, the bow given to a king during the consecration is conceived as Indra's bow with which he killed Vṛtra[63]. Thus the next input space is introduced, namely, that of the Rājasūya which, as we will see, will be elaborated by the composer.

[63] Heesterman (1957: 95).

Heesterman (1985: 234, note 89) presents the relationship between Varuṇa and Indra which is realised in the Rājasūya in the following way: Varuṇa loses his *indriyavīrya* which is taken over by Indra who 'is born after disintegration of Varuṇa, at the start of the warrior phase'. Then Varuṇa is born again by the Varuṇapraghāsa rite 'which apparently referred originally to the return of a war band at the end of the hot season' (see also Heesterman 1985c: 136–137). As has already been discussed, a similar relationship between Varuṇa and Indra is already attested in ṚV 10.124 (Jurewicz 2010a), evoked by AVŚ 11.5.7,14 (see section 2.2.1). It is possible that the composer of the *Vrātyakāṇḍa* also refers to this concept. It will be confirmed in that the further stages of creation are conceived in terms of the king's rides.

AVŚ 15.1.7

nī́lam asyodáraṃ lóhitaṃ pṛṣṭhám |

Blue its belly, red (its) back.

The composer conceives Vrātya in terms of a being whose belly is blue and whose back is red. Thus he triggers the recipient to evoke the concept of a fire the flames of which are red while its base is dark. In these terms, the cosmic form of Prajāpati is conceived. Since in the ṚV fire is conceived in terms of a bull, the recipient may use this concept to understand the structure of the world: the earth is conceived in terms of its belly, the sky in terms of its back. The zoomorphic way of thinking about the world is attested in the ṚV (ṚV 10.90, 1.164, see chapters 1.3, 1.6, Jurewicz 2014a) and it is evoked here. In the blend, the lower part of cosmos is the earth and the upper is the sky with the sun. In the Ṛgvedic model of the Wave Of Honey (ṚV 4.58.1), the image of the Somic plant, which grows from the ocean, is built (Jurewicz 2010a). If the recipient evokes this model, he can activate the concept of the earth on the basis of the concept of a blue belly because in ṚV 4.58.1 the concept of the ocean is blended with the concept of the earth. Since in the AVŚ the sun is called *róhita* (see section 2.1.1), the concept of the red back metonymically evokes the sun.

In the next sentence, the composer elaborates this conceptualisation:

AVŚ 15.1.8

nī́lenaivā́priyaṃ bhrā́tṛvyaṃ prórṇoti lóhitena dviṣántaṃ vidhyatī́ti brahmavādíno vadan |

With blue he envelops the hostile cousin, with the red he pierces one hating him (-who knows thus): so say the theologians.

The dangerous power of both spheres of the world is directed towards those who do not possess the correct knowledge. If the recipient elaborates the input space of a king, he would understand those enemies as the king's rivals. It is worth adding that the verb *vṛ-* is used in the ṚV in significant contexts referring to the pre-creative state of the world (Jurewicz 2010a: 324–325, 345). Moreover, this state was conceptually linked to the poets' enemies (Jurewicz 2010a: 72). So it is implied here that enemies are returned to the pre-creative state of the world through the power of its blue sphere. If the recipient understands the verb *prá vṛ-* as expressing covering (as does Whitney), he will understand that Vrātya covers enemies with the soil of the earth.

On the other hand, enemies are killed through red power which is the sun. This agrees with the later Vedic conceptualisation, elaborated especially in the ŚB, of the sun as a dangerous and killing entity.

In the Veda, fire is closely connected with earth (Smith 1994) and is conceived as killing the enemies of the composers, so the recipient may also elaborate this concept in the blend. The sun is conceived as the cosmic form of fire. So in the blend, the recipient may create the image of blazing fire in terms of which the world is conceived which kills what is unwanted within it[64].

The next part of cosmogony (AVŚ 15.2) presents further creation within the world in terms of the riding of a king in four directions (eastern, southern, western, northern). There is a similarity with the pattern of the Rājasūya where the king was supposed to 'mount the quarters of the space' (*digvyāsthāpana*)[65]. The king is followed by a train. The elements of the train are the Sāman-chants together with the gods, other living beings and elements of cosmos specific for them. When he rides to the east, these are the Sāman-chants Bṛhat and Rathaṃtara together with the Ādityas and all the gods (*víśve devā́*). When he rides to the south, these are the Sāman-chants Yajñāyajñiya and Vāmadevya together with a sacrifice, the sacrificer and cattle. When he rides to the west, these are the Sāman-chants Vairūpa and Vairāja together with waters and the king Varuṇa. When he rides to the north, these are the Sāman-chants Śyaita and Naudhasa together with the seven seers and the king Soma. The correct knowledge of the elements of the train causes the agent with the correct knowledge to become the abode of the elements of the train (*priyáṃ dhā́ma bhavati yá eváṃ véda*[66]). The agent of cognition is conceived in terms of the image schema of CONTAINER into which the object of his knowledge enters. This implies transformation of the agent to such an extent that he encompasses

---

[64] ŚB 11.1.6.9 Prajāpati kills the Asuras, see chapter 3.5.2.

[65] Heesterman (1957: 105 ff.).

[66] Whitney (1905, II) in interprets *priyám* as 'dear', however, in the Vedic Sanskrit *priyá* also means 'own' (Mayrhofer 1996: 'lieb, erwünscht, eigen, zu den Eigenen gehörig').

the whole cosmos within himself. Moreover, it is stated that a man, who would speak ill about a Vrātya, who has the correct knowledge, would deprive himself of this world (*ā́ vṛ́ścate yá evám̐ vidvā́ṃsaṃ vrā́tyam upavádati*)[67]. In the light of my interpretation, 'knowing thus Vrātya' refers here not only to a human being, but to reality conceived in terms of Vrātya. The person who speaks ill about Vrātya becomes ontologically empty[68].

In this ride, the king is also accompanied by a prostitute (*puṃścalī́*), a bard (*māgadhá*) and two footmen (*pariṣkandá*). He wears a garment (*vása*), a turban (*uṣṇī́ṣa*) on his hair (*kéśa*), two round ornaments (*pravartá*) and a jewel (*maṇí*). He rides on a chariot fit for untrodden paths (*vipathá*) yoked to two horses (*vipathavāhá*), driven by a charioteer (*sā́rathí*) with a goad (*pratodá*) and preceded by two forerunners (*puraḥsará*). In terms of these elements, various concepts are conceived. Some of them change depending on the direction the king is taking, some do not.

The elements which do not change are as follows: understanding (*vijñā́na*) conceived in terms of the garment, the day (*áhar*) conceived in terms of the turban, the night (*rā́tri*) conceived in terms of the hair, something which is yellow (*hárita*) conceived in terms of two round ornaments (*pravartá*), splendour (*kalmalí*)[69] conceived in terms of the jewel, mind conceived in terms of the chariot, fire and Soma (*mātaríśvan* and *pávamāna*[70]) conceived in terms of the horses, wind (*vā́ta*) conceived in terms of the charioteer, whirlwind/storm (*reṣmán*) conceived in terms of the goad and fame and glory (*kīrtí and yáśas*) conceived in terms of forerunners (*puraḥsará*).

The rest of elements changes depending on the direction the king is taking. When he rides to the east, faith (*śraddhā́*) it is the prostitute, alliance (*mitrá*) is the bard and past and future (*bhūtá* and *bhaviṣyát*) are the footmen. When he rides to the south, the dawn (*uṣás*) is the prostitute, *mántra* is the bard and the new moon and the full moon (*amāvāsyā̀* and *paurṇamāsī́*) are the footmen. When he rides to the west, cheer (*írā*) is the prostitute, laugh (*hása*) is the bard and day and night (*áhar* and *rā́tri*) are the footmen. When he rides to the north, lightning (*vidyút*) is the prostitute, thunder (*stanayintú*) is the bard, and 'what is heard and what is heard of far'[71] (*śrutám* and *víśrutam*) are the footmen.

---

67 For the interpretation of this concept, see below, analysis of the *Vrātyakāṇḍa*, chapter 2.2.2.

68 The same idea is expressed in BU 2.4.6, 4.5.7 according to which everything forsakes a person who does not know thus'

69 The world *kalmalí* appears in the AVŚ only here.

70 Whitney (1905, II) interprets *pávamāna* as 'the 'cleansing' wind'

71 Whitney (1905, II) interprets *śrutám víśrutaṃ ca* as 'what is heard and what is heard abroad'.

The correct knowledge of these elements assures that all them, together with fame and glory, come to the agent of correct knowledge (*aínaṃ kīrtír gachaty ā́ yáśo gachati yá evā́ṃ véda*). The word *yáśas* and *kīrtí* (the meaning of which is synonymous to the meaning of *śrávas*) activate the Ṛgvedic concept of fame which is the supernatural state realised under the influence of Soma. So it is implied that a person who knows the cosmogony will realise the same state.

Reconstruction of the conceptual links between the elements and the directions of the world goes beyond the scope of the present work. Generally speaking, the description can be treated as presenting further creation and organisation of the world. The creative power of reality is conceived in the form of the king and creation in terms of his rides. As far as the cosmos is concerned, space is arranged according to four directions, the divisions of time are created (the dawn, day, night, the new moon and the full moon) as is rain (lightning and thunder). The conditions of sacrifice are also created: the metres, the gods (Ādityas, Viśve Devas, Varuṇa and Soma), the sacrificer, the cattle, the sacred knowledge and the seven seers. Faith and alliance refer to the religious and social aspect of men while the concepts of cheer and laughter evoke the state of satisfaction gained through realisation of those two aspects. The recipient understands that the creation is motivated by cognitive activity just as the king uses his intentions and mind in riding.

The movement of the king and creation of elements are expressed with the verb *ánu ví cal-*. Dore (2015: 50) interprets this verbal form as 'indicating a movement to and from the various directions' and sees it as expressing the wandering lifestyle of the Vrātya. I would like to look at this form slightly differently. The verb *cal-* conveys the meaning of moving and the preposition *ánu* conveys the meaning of following after something. However, the preposition *ví* implies the dispersion of the subject. To the best of my knowledge, the verb *cal-* in its inflected active form is used in the AVŚ only in book 15 (AVŚ 15.2, 15.6, 15.9, 15.4). In three other places, the form *ávicācalā* appears (AVŚ 6.87.1-2, 10.8.4 which are quotations of the ṚV 10.173.1-2, 1.164.48) and which conveys the meaning of stability. Taking into account these usages, the creative activity is seen in terms of shaking; it is possible that the first act of creative movement is repeated here. In AVŚ 15. 2.1-4, the king first stands up (*sá úd atiṣṭhat*) and then proceeds in a direction (*díśam ánu vy àcalat*), followed by the elements created in this stage. The composers of the cosmogonies of the ŚB create the image of Prajāpati who, having created the world, falls apart (with use of the verb *ví sraṃs-*, ŚB 6.1.2.12, 7.1.2.1, see chapter 3.2.2). Seen in this way, creation is motivated by the image schema of VERTICALITY: the king cyclically stands up (*úd sthā-*) and then falls apart (*ánu ví cal-*). In his study on the sources of the king's authority (1985d), Heesterman shows that royal rituals aim at reconciliation two opposing spheres: the one which is settled and domesticated (*grāma*) and that which is alien and wild (*araṇya*). According to him, 'the king must belong to the *grāma*, but his authority must be based on the alien sphere of *araṇya*' (1985: 118). Since the sphere of wilderness is seen as a manifestation of the transcendence[72], the relationship of king's authority with the *araṇya* sphere expresses its transcendent basis. The royal rituals are patterned according to cyclical stages of king's symbolic raids to the *araṇya* sphere and returns to the *grāma*. As we shall see, the same pattern is elaborated in the *Vrātyakāṇḍa*. Heesterman's interpretation confirms the possibility for understanding the movement of Vrātya expressed by *ánu ví cal-* as the moment when the creative power of reality is in danger. As Heesterman writes, the king's unction 'takes away the god's as well as his human epigone's strength, causing them, like humpty-dumpty, to fall apart' (1985d: 123).

It is worth noting that the appearance of the elements of the manifest aspect is also expressed with use of the verb *ánu ví cal-* which confirms the monistic assumption within the frames of which the creative power of reality and its manifest aspect are the same. The elements of cosmos are created in the act of dispersion. According to Heesterman (1962: 26):

> '[t]he sacrificer, enacting Prajāpati's role, integrates, disintegrates and reintegrates the universe; undergoes conception and birth, but at the same time dies, again to mature towards rebirth; ascends, descends and ascends again. But all the time it is the same sacrificer who undergoes this process in endless repetition'

This sacrificial pattern of disintegration and integration of the manifest aspect of reality is activated by the composer of the *Vrātyakāṇḍa* to conceive creation.

Let me once again refer to Heesterman (1957: 105), who in his description of the rite of mounting the quarters, writes: 'It even seems as though the sacrificer disperses himself to the quarters and is in danger of total dissolution'. He then explains that the meaning of this rite is to evoke the concept of an embryo in terms of which the king is understood. In the frames of this interpretation, the composer of the *Vrātyakāṇḍa* expresses the reflexive character of the creative transformations: reality, conceived in terms of Vrātya, cyclically disperses itself and is reborn again.

From the point of view of the present study, it is important that elements of cosmos which do not change can be interpreted as referring to the stages

72 Already in the ṚV (Jurewicz 2010a).

of supernatural cognition[73]. Within the frames of this conceptualisation, understanding is the starting point of the process. Then day and night are cognised which metonymically evoke the concept of time experienced in everyday life. Next, something which is yellow is cognised which metonymically evokes the concept of the sun[74]. The stage called as splendour may refer to the supernatural state realised when the sun cognised. According to the ṚV, supernatural cognition stops here. The composer of the AVŚ 15, however, presents its further stages. The next stage is called 'mind' (*mánas*). This would imply that the agent reaches a stage which is conceived in terms of a manifestation of the mind of reality. Such a conceptualisation of this stage is presented in ŚB 2.2.4.3 and 10.5.1.1 (see chapters 3.1.1, 3.5.1). Having cognised it, the agent understands the paradoxical nature of reality conceived in terms of Agni and Soma. The next two stages called as wind and whirlwind/storm. Such a conceptualisation could be the basis for understanding of the king's movement in terms of shaking and falling. It most probably refers to the specific experience gained during practice leading to supernatural cognition[75]. The process ends with realising a state of fame and glory which evokes the concept of Somic exultation.

If we analyse the source domains of the stages of the proces, we will see more of its aspects. Cognition begins with the external appearance of the agent evoked by the concept of garment. The concepts of turban and hair metonymically evokes the concept of head. This concept will be elaborated in AVŚ 15.18 where head will be identified with the cosmos. The concept of a round ornament activates conceptualisation of time in terms of a wheel. Activation can be strengthened by the word *pravartá* which comes from the verb *prá vr̥-*, 'to roll or go onwards'. They are two because a chariot has two wheels. In KU 1.4 (see chapter 5.3), a man, who transgresses time, is conceived in terms a charioteer who looks at days and nights in terms of two wheels of a chariot. This state is realised in the borderline sphere of the cosmos. This sphere is conceived in the ṚV in terms of the sun the concept of which is evoked *via* the target domain, *hárita*. The concept of the jewel reinforces the meaning of the sun because it activates the Ṛgvedic metaphor THE SUN IS A PRECIOUS STONE which is also attested in the AVŚ 10.5.20 (see section 2.4). The recipient may infer that now the agent has realised the full knowledge

[73] See Dore (2015) who also interprets the description of the first chapter of the *Vrātyakāṇḍa* as 'transfiguration of the same character' (2015:35) and connects this transfiguration with knowledge.

[74] DEFINING PROPERTY FOR CATEGORY, COLOUR FOR SUBSTANCE (Radden, Kövecses 1999: 35).

[75] It is worth noting that in the description of the afterlife journey of man in JUB 3.21.3-4, the wind, which carries him to the space, is called 'Vrātya' and 'the one Vrātya' (*vrātyo ,sy ekavrātyo*, see chapter 5.2.3).

of the borderline sphere of the cosmos. The next sources domains are the concepts connected with a chariot. Thus the further cognition is conceived in terms of journey on a chariot. The concepts of the charioteer and the goad trigger the recipient to highlight the speed of the horses which may reflect the specific nature of the supernatural cognition. Conceptualisation of supernatural cognition in terms of conquest is attested already in the ṚV (Jurewicz 2010a: 92 ff.) and, as will be shown, the metaphor THE IMMORTAL STATE IS A FOREIGN LAND TO BE CONQUERED is also elaborated in the later Veda (especially KU 1, see chapter 5.3).

In the next passage, the composer further elaborates the source domain of a king (AVŚ 15.3). The king stands erects for a year. The concept of standing erect evokes the concept of ascetic practice (Dore, Pontillo 2013), but it may also evoke the year-long Dīkṣā which the king is supposed to undergo before the unction rite (Heesterman 1957: 63)[76]. Moreover, the rites connected with the preparation of the king for the unction also resemble the Dīkṣā rites (Heesterman 1957: 91). At the end of those rites, the king was made to raise his hands (Heesterman 1957: 96 ff.) and in this position he stood during the unction (Heesterman 1957: 114 ff.). The concept of Dīkṣā highlights the concept of self-restriction in the blend. The concept of a year metonymically evokes the concept of time, and, at the same time, the concept of pregnancy which in cosmogonies lasts one year. Ascetic practice and pregnancy have a common feature which is the heating of a whole man or of an embryo/ nestling. The upright position of the king prompts the recipient to understand that in these terms the further creation of the world is conceived; in the blend, Vrātya, conceived in terms of king, becomes its *axis mundi* (Heesterman 1957: 101, 120).

The next stage of creation is conceived in terms of Vrātya being given a throne by the gods[77]. The four feet of the throne consist of the four seasons and its other elements are elements of sacred speech (Bṛhat, Rathaṃtara, Yajñāyajñiya, Vāmadevya, Ṛk-stanzas, Yajus-formulas, Veda, *bráhman*, Sāman-chant, and Udgītha). Such a conceptualisation of a throne is attested in JB 2.25: during the unction, the sun, conceived in terms of king is seated on the throne composed of parts of the sacred speech (Bṛhat, Rathaṃtara, Vairūpa, Vairāja, Śākvara, Raivata, Ṛk-stanzas, Yajus-formulas, Sāmān-chants,

[76] For the links between Vrātya and Dīkṣita, see also Heesterman (1962).

[77] Witzel (1997: 295-296) writes: 'At this time, there were semi-permanent settlements only (*grāma* "trek, wagon train.") Archaeological evidence indicates that some centres existed, mostly as market places. These, however, are not mentioned in the texts and names of settlements are virtually unknown, except North India in the Middle and late Vedic Period (from Parpola 1988) for the seats of the Kuru lineage in Kurukṣetra, such as Āsandīvant ("having the throne"), or Rohitakakūla.' So it cannot be excluded that a concrete king is also meant here.

Vākovākya, *śrī*)[78]. In a similar way the king's throne is conceived in the Rājasūya as also being constructed from speech (Heesterman 1957: 149).

Conceptualisation of a throne as made of elements of time and speech agrees with the Ṛgvedic concept about their identity in the first stage of creation (ṚV 1.164, see chapter 1.6). The gods are conceived in terms of footmen (*pariṣkandá*), intentions (*saṃkalpá*) are conceived in terms of messengers (*prahayyà*) and all beings are conceived in terms of waiters (*upasád*). In this way, the next stage of creation is expressed: reality, having manifested itself in the cosmos, now manifests in the cosmos as its centre. As Heesterman writes: 'the throne represents the centre, the navel of the earth; from this navel originate the four streams dividing the world in four quadrants' (1957: 149). If we take into account conceptualisation of the sun in terms of the throne, we will see the continuity of tradition. As I have shown, in the Ṛgvedic general model of reality transformation the sun is the source of Soma which flows down to the earth in the form of rain (see Jurewicz 2010a). In ṚV 5.62.7-6, the sun is conceived in terms of a *gárta*, which is placed on the top of the bronze pillar on which sit two kings, Mitra and Varuṇa; from the sun thus conceived rain flows down (ṚV 5.62.7-8, Jurewicz 2010a: 397–399). It will also be shown that the composers of the AVŚ elaborated the concept of the centre of cosmos which can be reached through supernatural cognition (see section 2.5.1) and this concept should also be activated here: in the blend reality, conceived in terms of a king who sits on a throne, is the innermost centre of the cosmos and the sun is its visible sign. If we agree that creation is conceived in terms of supernatural cognition, we can interpret this final stage in terms of realisation of this process.

In AVŚ 15.4-6, the composer further elaborates the input space of a king: the king undertakes a further ride. In these terms, further creation is conceived. In this ride, the king is accompanied by twelve guardians (*goptṛ́*) and twelve attendants (*anuṣṭhātṛ́*) who are created from the six directions of the world: east, south, west, north, Dhruvā and Ūrdhvā (AVŚ 15.4-5)[79]. The guardians are: the months of six seasons and the attendants are the four kinds of Sāman -chants (created from the first four directions[80]), the earth and fire are created

[78] In JB 2.25: *athaiṣaudumbarī rājāsandī | tasyai bṛhadranthantare pūrvau pādau vairūpavairāje aparau śākararaivate anūcyāni ṛcaḥ prācīnam ātānā yajūṃṣi tiraścīnaṃ sāmāny āstaraṇam vākovākyam atīrokā śrīr upabarhaṇam*. For analysis of this passage, see Proferes (2007: 88–90). For identification of the king's throne with *śrī* in the Vedic tradition, see also Gonda (1954: 188, 1969: 45).

[79] One can presume that the last two directions are created when the Vrātya stands erect for a year.

[80] Bṛhad and Rathaṃtara from the east, Yajñayajniya and Vāmadevya from the south, Vairūpa and Vairāja from the west, Śyaita and Naudhasa from the north.

from Dhruvā and the sky and the sun are created from Ūrdhvā. AVŚ 15.5 adds the group of seven attendants who are the archers (*iṣvāsá*) created from intermediate directions (*antardeśā́d*); the last one is created from all the intermediate directions (*sárvebhyo antardeśébhyaḥ*). These are: *bhavá*, *śarvá*, *paśupáti*, *ugrá*, *rudrá*, *mahādevá*, *ī́śāna*. The names of the archers are the same as those mentioned in KB 6.1-9 as being the names of Rudra born from Prajāpati's semen placed in a golden vessel, although in different order and with some slight differences (*bhavá*, *śarvá*, *paśupáti*, *ugró devá*, *mahā́n devá*, *rudrá*, *ī́śāna*, *aśáni*)[81]. ŚB 6.1.3.10-17 also mentions these names as the names of Agni born from Prajāpati (*rudrá*, *sárva*, *paśupáti*, *ugrá*, *aśáni*, *bhavá*, *mahā́n devá*, *ī́śāna*). If the composer of AVŚ 15.5 activates the same concept in the blend, he would create the image of a king with surrounded by fiery warriors. Thus the recipient could identify Vrātya with Agni whose flames are conceived in terms of men (see ṚV 1.164.1, chapter 1.6) or with Rudra who is also surrounded by warriors and has a fiery nature in the ṚV (see Srinivasan 1997: 50ff., 78ff.)[82]. As she writes (ad. KB 6.1-9), Rudra is conceived in terms of the archer, who 'wrathful and impetuous opens the drama of creation' (1977: 78).

Then the composer of the *Vrātyakāṇḍa* states that if one has the correct knowledge of this stage of creation, the elements of the world will serve him and will neither injure him or his folk and cattle. As I have argued, such a conceptualisation of reality that is not hurt by its creations is activated in AVŚ 11.5.15 (see section 2.2.1). It is grounded in the monistic assumption and the recipient understands that correct knowledge of this stage of creation leads man to cognise the unity of reality. This interpretation agrees with the result of knowledge of the first stage of creation which is conceived in terms of becoming an abode of the elements of the world. These elements do not hurt him as though they are present within man they are his part.

In AVŚ 15.6, a further description of a second ride is presented. The king first rides in the Dhruvā and Ūrdhvā directions, then towards the highest direction (*uttamā́ṃ díśam*), towards the lofty direction (*bṛhatī́ṃ díśam*), towards the most distant direction (*paramā́ṃ díśam*), towards an unindicated direction (*ánādiṣṭāṃ díśam*), towards an unreturned direction (*ánāvṛttāṃ díśam*), finally, towards the directions (*díśáḥ*) and all the intermediate directions (*sárvān antardeśā́n*). During this process various specific elements of the world are again created. When king rides towards the Dhruvā, the earth, fire, plants and trees together with everything what is connected with them is created (*táṃ*

81 For these epithets in the Vedic tradition, see Gonda (1976b: 38–40)

82 Agni is identified with Rudra in the exegesis of Agnicayana (ŚB 9.1.1.1, 9.1.2.32, see also 1.7.3.8, 5.2.4.13, 5.3.1.10.

bhū́miś cāgníś caúṣadhayaś ca vánaspátayaś ca vānaspatyā́ś ca vīrúdhaś ca). When the king rides towards the Ūrdhvā, right (*ṛtá*) and truth (*satyá*), the sun, the moon and the asterisms are created (*ṛtáṃ ca satyáṃ ca sū́ryaś ca candráś ca nákṣatrāṇi ca*). When the king rides towards the highest direction, the fourfold Veda is created (*ṛ́caś ca sā́māni ca yájūṃṣi ca bráhma*). When the king rides towards the lofty direction, other texts are created (*itihāsáś ca purāṇáṃ ca gā́thāś ca nārāśaṃsī́ś ca*). When the king rides towards the most distant direction, three sacrificial fires, sacrifice, sacrificer and cattle are created (*āhavanī́yaś ca gā́rhapatyaś ca dakṣiṇāgníś ca yajñáś ca yájamānaś ca paśávaś ca*). When the king rides towards the unindicated direction, the seasons and what is connected with the seasons, the worlds and what is connected with the worlds, the months and the half-months are created (*ṛtávaś cārtavā́ś ca lokā́ś ca laukyā́ś ca mā́sāś cārdhamāsā́ś cāhorātré ca*). When the kings rides towards the unreturned direction, what is bounded and what is unbounded together with the wife of Indra are created (*dítiś cā́ditiś céḍā cendrāṇī́ ca*). When the king rides towards the all directions, the Virāj, the gods and the deities are created (*virā́ḍ ánu vy àcalat sárve ca devā́ḥ sárvāś ca devátāḥ*). Finally, when he rides towards the all intermediary directions, Prajāpati, the most excellent one, the father and the great father are created (*prajā́patiś ca parameṣṭhī́ ca pitā́ ca pitāmaháś ca*). The movement of the king and creation of elements is again expressed with use of the verb *ánu ví cal-*; the moment of the king's raising up is omitted. It is again stated that the person who knows the stages of this ride becomes the abode of the elements created during this process (*priyáṃ dhā́ma bhavati*).

My general claim is that the composer of the *Vrātyakāṇḍa* presents the creation of the world as the creation of two perspectives from which reality can experience itself. This is the reason why creation of the elements of the world is repeated. Firstly, reality creates elements of the world in its cosmic experience which is conceived in terms of the first ride of the king. The last stage of this process is conceived in terms of a king sitting on a throne (AVŚ 15.3). Thus reality manifests the innermost essence of the cosmos. In terms of the second ride, reality experiences its manifest aspect from this point of view. Although it is not expressed by the composer explicitly, I would argue that reality is manifest as the innermost essence of cosmos within a prototypical man, also called Vrātya[83].

There are two general differences in the description of these two kinds of experience. Firstly, in the second ride a smaller group of attendants is presented which may imply that now the concept of a practice done in seclusion is

[83] The AU is clear about that, see chapter 4.1.3.

activated. Secondly, the directions in which the king rides are not the directions known from the everyday experience mentioned in the descriptions of the first ride. As I have mentioned above, having ridden in the direction of the Ūrdhvā (AVŚ 15.4.6), the king rides towards the Dhruvā (AVŚ 15.6.1). This word has two meanings, namely, the polar star and the point under a man's feet[84]. Taking into account the meaning of the polar star, I would argue that the intention of the composer is to create the image of climbing the *axis mundi* to the highest point of the sky. This is the common image to conceive of the supernatural states in the ṚV where the aim of the journey is the sun in zenith (see Jurewicz 2010a). If *dhruvā́* refers to the point under a man's feet, this would imply the journey downwards towards the pre-creative form of the world conceived in terms of night; the movement upwards is then realised in the morning (see Kuiper 1962, 1964, 2010a: 405). Both meanings of the word *dhruvā́* can be evoked if the recipient understands the concept of a standing king as the source domain for the *axis mundi* which joins the highest and the lowest points of the cosmos.

The concept of the movement upwards is also evoked *via* the next directions the king takes (*ūrdhvā́*, *uttamā́*, *bṛhatī́* and *paramā́*). Then the king reaches the direction which is 'unindicated' (*ánadiṣṭā*), i.e. it cannot be understood by everyday categories and the recipient may presume he is lost. Having gone further, the king reaches the direction from which there is no return (*ánāvṛttā*) and he fears that he would not return from there (*táto nā́vartsyánn amanyata*). If we take into account the cosmogonies of the ŚB (see chapter 3), we will see that the description of AVŚ 15.6.7 agrees with the pattern that is presented there. As already mentioned, the composers of the ŚB always describe a moment when Prajāpati loses contact with his manifestations and looks for the way to confirm his identity with them. The same is implied here. In the blend, the creative power of reality now conceived in terms of reality manifest in man at some point loses contact with its manifestations. As in the ŚB, when this moment is overcome, Vrātya reaches the whole universe evoked by the concepts of the directions (*diśáḥ*) and intermediate directions (*sárvān antardeśā́n*). I am tempted to think that the intention of the composer is to imply that reality, manifest in the form of man who lives on earth, realises ontic identity with its manifestation in the form of Vrātya sitting on the throne the visible sign of which is the sun.

If we accept this interpretation, we can see the stages of the process described in AVŚ 15.5-6 in the following way. Each act of creation results in creation of a sphere of the world which can be experienced by the agent.

[84] For interpretation of Dhruvā, see Gonda (1965), Bodewitz (2000a).

In the blend, the king's ride towards Dhruvā is the source domain to conceive reality in the form of man which creates the earth for himself. The king's ride towards Ūrdhvā is the source domain to conceive reality in the form of man which creates the sky for himself. The king's ride towards the highest and lofty directions is the source domain to conceive reality which experiences the world in its primeval form of speech[85]. The king's ride towards the most distant direction is the source domain to conceive reality in the form of man which experiences the world in terms of sacrificial activity. The king's ride towards the unindicated direction is the source domain to conceive reality in the form of man which goes beyond time which is the crucial moment in liberating practice (see chapters 4.4, 5.3). The king's ride towards the unreturned direction is the source domain to conceive reality in the form of man which experiences itself as manifest and bounded (*díti*) and unmanifest and unbounded (*áditi*). In this stage, the first creative principle, conceived in terms of Indra who kindles breaths (*índha*), is cognised. In terms of the ride to the all directions, reality, in the form of man, is manifest in the form of Virāj with all the gods; as we remember, the concept of Virāj is used to denote the intermediate sphere between manifestations of reality in the *Puruṣasūkta* (see chapter 1.3) and in AVŚ 11.5.16 (see section 2.2.2). It is worth adding that in BU 4.2.2-3 (see chapter 4.4.2.2) liberating cognition is conceived in terms of the sexual act between the man in the right eye, called *índha*, and his wife present in the left eye, called *virā́j*. It is possible that here we find one of the roots of this conceptualisation.

In the description of the last stage, several names of reality are mentioned. The first pair are *prajā́pati* and *parameṣṭhín*. As we remember, the generative power of reality incited by Vrātya is conceived in terms of *prajā́pati* in AVŚ 15.1.1. On the other hand, in AVŚ 11.5.7 *parameṣṭhín* qualifies *prajā́pati*. Notwithstanding the relationship between these two concepts, we can assume that in this stage reality, in the form of man, experiences its creative power and its unity with itself. The composer mentions also a father and a great-father. On this basis, the recipient may understand that the afterlife is meant here in which the deceased meets his ancestors (see chapter 5.1.2). Already in the ṚV, the supernatural state and the state after death are conceived as the same (ṚV 10.14.18, see Jurewicz 2010a). Since, in the early Veda, it is impossible to cognise reality in its unmanifest aspect, the description stops here. However, it can be seen that the borderline sphere of cosmos is elaborated in more detailed way than in the ṚV.

85 For the first form of reality as the speaking form, see ŚB 6.1.1. (see chapter 3.2.2).

AVŚ 15.7.1

sá mahimā́ sádrur bhūtvā́ntaṃ pṛthivyā́ agachat sá samudró 'bhavat |

This greatness, becoming sessile (?), went to the end of the earth; it became ocean.

The subject of the sentence is 'greatness', *mahimán*. As I have shown, the term *mahát* is used in the AVŚ in reference to the manifestation of reality as great. In this way, it is implied that reality, in the form of man, cognises the greatness of its cosmic manifestation and becomes one with it. This is conceived in terms of the king who in his ride reaches the end of his kingdom. The use of *mahimán* in the present context foreshadows the later usage of the compound *mahātman* to denote the liberated man whose self, *ātmán*, became great – as great as the manifest aspect.

The word *sádru* evokes the concept of stability; the recipient can elaborate the input space of a king who, after a long journey around the world, sits on his throne and takes rest. Since the pre-creative state of the world is conceived in terms of the state of lack of stability (Jurewicz 2010a: 2010a: 349–350), the recipient may understand that in this stage of creation primeval stability is regained. This is consistent with the concept of the shaking movement of the king in terms of which the subsequent stages of cognition are seen in AVŚ 15.2 and in AVŚ 15.4-6.

The concept of the ocean (*samudrá*) evokes the concept of water (*salilá*, *ā́pas*) in terms of which the pre-creative state of the world is conceived (see Jurewicz 2010a: 48-49, ŚB 11.1.6.1, see chapter 5.5.2, AU 1.1.2, 1.2.1, see chapter 4.1.3). So the intention of the composer of AVŚ 15.7.1 is to imply that reality in the form of man reaches a very subtle state of awareness in which it can realise its unity with the pre-creative state of the world just before its creation.

It is worth noting that in BU 4.3.31 (see chapter 4.4.1) the concept of water is used in reference to the liberated state when the agent cognises the unity of reality (*salilá éko draṣṭā́dvaito bhavaty eṣá brahmalokáḥ*). The composer of the BU also elaborates the concept of a king who is visits his kingdom and is greeted by his subjects; in these terms the relationship between the innermost self, *ātmán*, and breaths are conceived (BU 2.1.18, see chapter 4.4.2.2). As we will see, the concept of *prāṇá* is introduced by the composer of AVŚ 15.15-17 (see below); it will also be elaborated in some cosmogonies of the ŚB (especially 6.1.1, see chapter 3.2.3). In this way, we can trace back the continuity of tradition as far as the breath practice is conceived: it begins already in the AVŚ (it is also attested in AVŚ 11.4, see section 2.1.2).

AVŚ 15.7.2-5

táṃ prajā́patiś ca parameṣṭhī́ ca pitā́ ca pitāmahā́ś cā́paś ca śraddhā́ ca varṣáṃ bhūtvā́nuvyàvartayanta | (2)
aínam ā́po gachaty aínaṃ śraddhā́ gachaty aínaṃ varṣáṃ gachati yá eváṃ véda | (3)
táṃ śraddhā́ ca yajñáś ca lokáś cā́nnaṃ cānnā́dyaṃ ca bhūtvā́bhiparyā́vartanta | (4)
aínaṃ śraddhā́ gachaty aínaṃ yajñó gachaty aínaṃ lokó gachaty aínam ánnaṃ gachaty aínam annā́dyaṃ gachati yá eváṃ véda | (5)

After it, turned out both Prajāpati and the most exalted one, and the father and the grandfather, and the waters and faith, becoming rain. (2)
To him come waters, to him cometh faith, to him cometh rain, who knoweth thus. (3)
Unto it, turn about both faith and sacrifice and world and food and food-eating, coming into being. (4)
To him cometh faith, to him cometh sacrifice, to him cometh a world, to him commeth food, to him commeth food-eating, who knoweth thus. (5)

In AVŚ 15.7.2, the highest elements of the manifest aspect (*prajā́patiś ca parameṣṭhī́ ca pitā́ ca pitāmahā́ś ca*) together with waters (*ā́pas*), faith (*śraddhā́*) become rain and rolls after (*ánu*) Vrātya in the form of man. This description again prompts the recipient to think about the afterlife state. Firstly, according to the ṚV and the JB, the deceased meets his fathers before his return to the earth (Jurewicz 2008b, 2010a, see chapters 5.1.2). Moreover, as it will be shown, the deceased, burnt on the cremation pyre, assumes either the form of waters (JB 1.45, see chapter 5.1) or of faith (CU, BU, see chapter 4.3.1). Then assuming the form of rain, he comes back to earth (already in the ṚV, Jurewicz 2008b, 2010a: 310 ff.). If the composer of the *Vrātyakāṇḍa* refers to such a conceptualisation of the afterlife, he would now imply that reality in the form of man, having reached the supernatural state conceived as realised on the sun, is reborn on earth. As I have argued, the same conviction is expressed in AVŚ 11.5 (see section 2.2.1). The circular movement evoked by the verb *vṛt-* evokes the concept of a wheel in terms of which time is conceived. The preposition *ví* implies the separated movement of streams of rain.

In AVŚ 15.7.4, the verb *vṛt-* is qualified by prepositions *abhí* and *pári* which imply movement towards and around the object. If the recipient interprets AVŚ 15.7.2 as expressing the rebirth of reality in the form of man, he will now understands that new life on earth is described in this form. The elements which appear are again faith, then sacrifice, worlds, food and the ability to eat food. Faith is the mental attitude necessary for a sacrifice to be effective. Sacrifice is the activity during which man can create a world for himself which is the space of his particular experience; this space is called *lóka* (see BU 1.4.16, chapter 4.1.2). Moreover, sacrifice is conceived in terms of eating (see chapter 3.2.3). So the recipient understands that reality in the form of man, having been reborn, can experience the world again.

In following passages (AVŚ 15.8-9), reality in the form of man creates the social order i.e. the royal class (*rājanyà*) and the people (*víś*) [86]. It is not clear if the fact that the creation of the Brahmin class is not mentioned is a result of it being implicitly assumed that it appeared when reality manifested itself as Vrātya or by the fact that the text is anti-Brahminical and the Vrātya class replaces the Brahmins. This question needs a separate study. The royal class (*rājanyà*) is created when the Vrātya glows or becomes excited (*so 'rajyata*). Then he arises toward (*abhyúdatiṣṭhat*) 'the tribes (*víś*), the kinsmen, food, food-eating' (*sá víśaḥ sábandhūn ánnam annā́dyam abhyúdatiṣṭhat*, AVŚ 15.8). The concept of food and food-eating can be interpret as metonymically evoking the fact that people nourish the royal class. However, it can also be metaphorically interpreted as the source domain for rulership: the royal power is conceived in terms of food-eating while the people are conceived in terms of food (Smith 1994: 46–48).

In AVŚ 15.9, Vrātya is again presented as shakily moving towards the people (*sá víśó 'nu vy àcalat*). The recipient may presume that Vrātya, now in the form of the Kṣatriya, wants to rule the people. The result of this movement is the creation of the assembly, gathering, an army and the strong drink (*sabhā́ ca sámitiś ca sénā ca súrā*) which can be seen as the instruments of rulership.

The next passages of the AVŚ describe the beneficial role of a 'knowing thus Vrātya' who visits a king's house (AVŚ 10–13). It is not surprising because the human Vrātya is the embodiment of reality in the same way as the human Brahmin is the embodiment of *bráhman*. It is a person who re-enacted the creative experience of reality in the form of man. At the same time, these passages can be seen as the reflection of the negotiations between the royal class and priest class which are also attested in the Upaniṣads (Black 2007). This is confirmed in that the Kṣatriya is also a form of Vrātya, so the rules of social manifestation of reality should be settled so that they do not mingle. The difference is that now the concept of the priest class is evoked *via* the concept of Vrātya and not of Brahmin.

The last chapters of the book 15 (14–18) are meant to present how men, here and now, can re-enact creation through liberating cognition and how it can be achieved. In AVŚ 15.14, the next journey is described. In this journey,

---

[86] See the *Puruṣasūkta* (chapter 1.3), BU 1.4.11-13 (chapter 4.1.2).

Vrātya is not accompanied by anyone. Firstly, he goes to the four directions of the world (east, south, west, north). Then he goes towards the Dhruvā. Next, he goes towards cattle (*paśú*), fathers (*pitáras*), men (*manuṣyà*). The next direction is Ūrdhvā. Then Vrātya goes towards gods (*devá*) and offspring (*prajā́*). Finally, he goes towards all the intermediate directions (*sárvān antardeśā́n*).

The movement of Vrātya is again conceived as shaking (*ánu ví cal-*). In each ride a corresponding god appears with an eater (*annādá*); their movement is conceived in the same way. In the east, the troop of Maruts appears with mind (*mánas*) as the eater. In the south, Indra appears with strength (*bála*) as the eater. In the west, king Varuṇa appears with waters (*ā́pas*) as the eater. In the north, king Soma appears with the oblation given by the seven seers (*saptarṣíbhir hutá ā́hutim*) as the eater. When Vrātya comes to the Dhruvā, Viṣṇu appears with Virāj as the eater. When he comes to the cattle, Rudra appears with plants (*óṣadhi*) as the eaters. When he comes to the fathers, king Yama appears with the call *svadhā́* as the eater. When he comes to men, Agni appears with the call *svā́hā* as the eater. When he comes to the Ūrdhvā, Bṛhaspati appears with the call *váṣaṭ* as the eater. When he comes to the gods, Īśana appears with anger (*manyú*) as the eater. When he comes to the offspring, Prajāpati appears with breath (*prāṇá*) as the eater. When he comes to all the intermediate directions, the excellent one (*parameṣṭhín*) appears with *bráhman* as the eater. It is difficult in the present state of research to explain the full meaning of this description, though the main line of reasoning can be reconstructed.

The concept of eater metonymically evokes the concept of eating in terms of which cognition is conceived in the Veda (see chapters 3.2.3). The first eater is the mind (*máno 'nnādáṃ kṛtvā́*, AVŚ 15.14.1) which confirms that a mental activity is being described here. The concept of the Maruts evokes the concepts of wind and storm. The concepts of mind and wind appear in AVŚ 15.2, in the description of creation, which I interpret as referring to the supernatural cognition undertaken by cosmic manifestation of reality. These two concepts are evoked just before the final stage, conceived in terms of fame, is reached. It seems then that in the human dimension, supernatural cognition is performed in reverse order to that of creation. It is conceived in the later thought in this way (ŚB 10.5.3, see chapter 3.5.1, see also chapters 4.4.2.4-5). In ṚV 10.136, hairy men are presented as closely connected with the wind. The concept of wind metonymically evokes the concept of space between the earth and the sky. It is possible that in these terms the first stage of the liberating practice is conceived.

The next two eaters are strength (*bála*) and waters (*ā́pas*)[87]. Strength appears with Indra the concept of which evokes the first creative heating of reality (see AVŚ 15.1, section 2.2.2) which results in the appearance of its fluid aspect evoked by the concepts of waters and Varuṇa. In this way, it is implied that practice is connected with heating and sweating which agrees with its description in other hymns of the AVŚ and ŚB. In the ṚV, the experience of heat and sweating appears under the influence of Soma (Jurewicz 2010a: 193–195).

The next eater is the oblation of the seven seers (*saptarṣíbhir ā́hutim annādī́ṃ kr̥tvā́*, AVŚ 15.14.4). The seven seers are conceptualised in the AVŚ as sitting on the sun (see section 2.5.1.3), so the recipient may presume that man mentally reaches the sun. This is confirmed as in the next stage Vrātya goes towards the Dhruvā and becomes Viṣṇu. In the ṚV, Viṣṇu is conceived as making three steps to zenith and the path he leaves becomes the *axis mundi* (see Jurewicz 2010a: 387 ff.). As I have shown above, the concept of Dhruvā triggers the recipient to create the image of someone who, standing upright, reaches zenith and nadir. The concept of the sun is also activated by the concept of *virā́j* which is the eater in this state (*virā́jam annādī́ṃ kr̥tvā́*, AVŚ 15.14.5). At the same time, in terms of *virā́j*, the intermediate state between aspects of reality is conceived, so the recipient understands that man, having climbed the *axis mundi*, now realises this state.

The next three stages, conceived in terms of reaching cattle, fathers and men (AVŚ 15.14.11,13,15), seems to imply that, in this stages, all kinds of beings, both living and dead, men and animals are cognised. The next stage is conceived in terms of reaching the Ūrdhvā (AVŚ 15.14.17) which again implies movement upwards; in this stage, Vrātya becomes Br̥haspati with the call *váṣat* as the eater. Br̥haspati is the lord of sacred speech which may imply that man reaches the form of the world in the form of speech in the beginning of creation.

The next stage is conceived in terms of approaching the gods (AVŚ 11.15.19) and the offspring. In the state of approaching gods, Īśana appears which is one of the first manifestations of reality (see above AVŚ 15.1.5). The eater is anger, *manyú* (*manyúm annādáṃ kr̥tvā́*), which in the early Veda is the creative and destructive power which makes the world function (see Malamoud 1996a, Jurewicz 2008a). In the state of approaching offspring, Prajāpati appears with breath as the eater (*prāṇám annādáṃ kr̥tvā́*, AVŚ 15.14.21). During these two stages man cognises the beings through which one can obtain immortality: thanks to sacrifices to gods in the supernatural state and thanks to being reborn

[87] *bálam annādáṃ kr̥tvā́* (AVŚ 15.14.2), *apò 'nnādī́ḥ kr̥tvā́* (AVŚ 15.14.3).

in his offspring. At the same time, the recipient may understand that man mentally reaches the borderline sphere of the cosmos conceived in terms of breath which is the basis for creative speech[88].

In the last stage, the excellent one (*parameṣṭhín*, AVŚ 15.14.23) appears and the eater is *bráhman* (*bráhmānnādáṃ kr̥tvā́*, AVŚ 15.14.23). The recipient may understand that Vrātya reaches the most primeval state of reality. In the human agent, reality becomes one with its manifestation in speech.

The description of each state is followed by the statement that one who knows it will be able to eat with the same eater as is created in this state (*annādénā́nnam atti yá evám véda*). It is worth noting here that eaters can be interpreted as fire. Conceptualisation of mind in terms of fire is attested in ŚB 10.5.3 (see chapter 3.5.1). Strength and water can be seen as forms of fire if we agree that they refer to the creative sequence as presented in the general model of reality transformation. The oblation of the seven seers is recitation and speech is conceived in terms of fire, the same is for the calls *svadhā́*, *svā́hā* and *váṣaṭ*. The meaning of the word *virā́j* which is 'shining', can also evoke the concept of fire. Plants are not only food of fire, but also its hiding place (R̥V 2.1.1, Jurewicz 2010a: 124-125), so metonymically can be identified with it. Anger is conceived in terms of fire in the R̥V (see Jurewicz 2008a). The fiery nature of *bráhman* is elaborated in the cosmogonies of the ŚB and the Upaniṣads which see it as the transformation of fire (see especially BU 1.2, 4 chapters 4.1.1-2); its identification with fire is strengthened if one interprets *bráhman* as speech which is the first form of reality. If we take into account that cognitive powers are conceived in terms of gods in the AVŚ, we will get a consistent image of the liberating practice. Man who knows its stages is endowed with supernatural cognitive abilities conceived in terms of gods the activity of which is conceived in terms of burning.

In the next three chapters (AVŚ 15.15-17), the composer describes three breaths (*prāṇá*, *apāná*, *udāná*) of Vrātya, each of them is divided into seven breaths (*ūrdhvá*, *práuḍha*, *abhyū̀ḍha*, *vibhū́r*, *yóni*, *priyá*, *áparimita*)[89]. Breaths are identified with the seven elements of the cosmos (fire, the sun, the moon, the wind, waters, cattle, and offspring), with the seven elements connected with sacrifices (the days of full moon, of moon's quarter and of new moon, faith, *dīkṣā́*, sacrifice and sacrificial fee, *dákṣinā*) and with the spatio-temporal structure of the cosmos (earth, space, sky, constellations, seasons, what is connected with seasons and year). In this way, it is implied that mental practice

---

88 Such a conceptualisation of breath is elaborated in ŚB 6.1.1.1 where breath is the first form of reality during creation (see chapter 3.2.3).

89 See ŚB 6.1.1.1 where the first stage of creation is conceived in terms of seven breaths (see chapter 3.2.3).

consists in the practice of breaths and that the aim of this practice is to realise one's identity with reality.

AVŚ 15.17.8-10

samānám ártham pári yanti devā́ḥ saṃvatsarám vā́ etád ṛtávo 'nupáriyanti vrā́tyaṃ ca | (8)
yád ādityám abhisaṃviśánty amāvāsyā̀ṃ caivá tát paurṇamāsī́ṃ ca | (9)
ékaṃ tád eṣām amṛtatvám íty ā́hutir evá | (10)

The gods go about the same purpose; thus verily the seasons go about after the year and the Vrātya. (8)
As they enter together into the sun, just so (do they) also into new-moon and full moon day. (9)
One (is) immortality of theirs: to this effect (*iti*) (is) the offering. (10)

In AVŚ 15.17.8, gods and the seasons are presented as following Vrātya and the year. In these terms, passage of time is conceived to which the manifest aspect is subjected. The composer implies identity of Vrātya and the year; in the same way as Prajāpati in his cosmic manifestation is identified with the year in the ŚB (11.1.6.12, see chapter 3.5.2).

I would interpret the next two sentences (AVŚ 15.17.9-10) as referring to the state after death. The deceased enters the sun and then the moon (see JUB, chapter 5.2.3). Contrary to Whitney, I would interpret *íti* in the third sentence as evoking the well-known knowledge: 'the immortality of men is one'. It is the oblation, *ā́huti*. Man can realise immortality through sacrificial activity during his life. When he dies, he himself becomes *ā́huti* which is poured into the sun to come back to the earth in the form of rain (Jurewicz 2008b, 2010a)[90]. Such a way of thinking about immortality as realised in constant death and resurrection within the manifest aspect is elaborated in the ŚB (see chapter 3.2.3).

The last passage (AVŚ 15.18) identifies parts of the head of Vrātya with parts of cosmos. The right eye is the sun, the left eye is the moon, the right ear is fire, the left ear is wind, nostrils are days and nights, skull-halves are what is bounded (*díti*) and what is unbounded (*áditi*) and the head is the year[91]. Conceptualisation of reality in terms of a head appears already in *Puruṣasūkta* (see chapter 1.3). It will be shown that conceptualisation of the

[90] This concept is elaborated in the later thought, in the model of the Five Fires (see chapters 4.3.1, 5)

[91] AVŚ 15.18: *tásya vrā́tyasya* | (1) *yád asya dákṣiṇam ákṣy asáu sá ādityó yád asya savyám ákṣy asáu sá candrámāḥ* | (2) *yò 'sya dákṣiṇaḥ kárṇo 'yáṃ só agnír yò 'sya savyáḥ kárṇo 'yáṃ sá pávamānaḥ* | (3) *ahorātré nā́sike dítiś cā́ditiś ca śīrṣakapālé saṃvatsaráḥ śíraḥ* | (4) *áhnā pratyáṅ vrā́tyo rā́tryā prā́ṅ námo vrā́tyāya* | (5)

manifest aspect of reality in terms of a head is also elaborated in ŚB 6.1.1 (see chapter 3.2.2). The manifest aspect is conceived as a year which is the reason why the head of Vrātya is identified with year in AVŚ 15.18. At the same time, since man is also called Vrātya in this cosmogony, the recipient understands that the final stage of breath practice leads man to his head through which he can finally identify himself with what is created. This agrees with the general concept of creation, proposed in the Veda, which is conceived in terms of image schema of VERTICALITY[92]. Since liberating cognition re-enacts creation, it is conceived in terms of upward movement. In the last sentence, it is said that Vrātya 'with the day is westward, with the night eastward' (*áhnā pratyáṅ vrā́tyo rā́tryā prā́ṅ*, AVŚ 15.18.5). The description refers the movement of the sun: during the day it goes to the west, during the night it goes to the east under the earth in order to rise again in the east (AVŚ 11.4.22 see section 2.5.1.2). The recipient can understand that the final aim of liberating practice is conceived in terms of the identification of man with the sun and that immortality is conceived in terms of the sun's constant movement.

*

From what has been shown above the conceptualisation of cosmogony, of the world's functioning and of the role of man agrees with the way it is conceived in the Veda. During creation reality manifests its freedom and ability to limit itself within its manifest aspect. In the *Vrātyakāṇḍa*, it is presented as taking place in two main phases: firstly, reality manifests itself in the cosmos, then in a prototypical man[93]. Its third phase takes place when a particular human being performs a breath practice which leads to liberation. All three manifestations are called Vrātya which implies the monistic assumption. The three stages of creation are conceived in terms of the raid of a king during which parts of the cosmos are created again and again. The particular stages of three trips elaborated in the source domain differ, but their general scenario is the same. It seems that the intention of the composer is to present these processes as the creation of new perspectives of experience: in the first stage, reality experiences itself in the cosmos, in the second, it experiences itself in man generally and in the third, it experiences itself in concrete men undertaking liberating breath practice. In all creative stages, the movement of reality is conceived as shaking (*ánu ví cal-*) which can be interpreted as the result of Somic exultation or of breath practice or both.

92 Its specific source domains are the sunrise in the ṚV , see Jurewicz (2010a) and the growth of man in the ŚB, see chapter 3.5.2.

93 This conceptualisation will be continued in the AU (see chapter 4.1.3).

From the point of view of the present book, it is important to note the general and abstract exposition of this content. The stages of creation are evoked in a concise, metonymical way, as if the composer assumed the shared general knowledge about them and did not feel obliged to refer to it in more detail. Conceptualisation of creation and liberation in terms of a king's activity shows the change in social conditions which is also reflected in the Upaniṣads. At the same time, the description is more detailed as far as the elements of the comos are concerned. The borderline sphere of the cosmos is also presented more precisely in comparison with the ṚV. It may be inferred then that the range of the supernatural cognition was enlarged in times of the AV. This could be caused by the influence of breath practice connected with recitation.

I am aware that my interpretation does not solve all the problems of AVŚ 15. It is important, however, that it is composed in such a way that its main line of reasoning can be analysed and understood within the frames of the Brahminical context. The general conceptualisation of creation in terms of men who perform ritual activity, agrees with the conceptualisation presented in AVŚ 11.5 the composer of which conceives creation in terms of becoming a Vedic student. The general difference between the concepts of creation presented in these two hymns is that the composer of AVŚ 11.5 presents only manifestations of reality within its manifest aspect. The composer of the *Vrātyakāṇḍa* expands his exposition and presents prototypical human activity of reality and the way it is realised by particular men.

Before I continue, I would like to draw attention to another possibility for interpreting the concept of Vrātya. According to the *Baudhāyana Śrautasūtra* 18.24: 271.7, the bow of Vrātya corresponds to the stick (*daṇḍá*[94]) of the man undergoing initiation (*dīkṣitá*)[95]. In his study (1962), Heesterman has shown many other similarities between Vrātya and Dikṣita. The stick is also the emblem of human kings and of king Yama who personifies death. As Malamoud argues: 'Les rois humaines sont des répliques, nécessairement réduites el limiteés, du roi Yama' (Malamoud 2002b: 28). As already mentioned, Heesterman (1985d) sees the roots of a king's authority in the alien and wild sphere (*araṇya*) which is outside the sphere which is settled and domesticated (*grāma*). On the philosophical level, the division between *grāma* and *araṇya* corresponds to the division between *sát* and *ásat*, between the manifest aspect of reality where life and cognition is possible and its unmanifest aspect incognisable and bringing death.

94 For the meaning of *daṇḍá* in Vedic ritual and the Indo-European roots of this concept, see Gonda (1969: 22 ff.), Minkowski (1991: 141 ff.).

95 Hauer (1927: 193), Heesterman (1962: 13).

Seen within these frames, Vrātya can be interpreted as the first form of reality manifest during creation and conceived in terms of death; this conceptualisation of creation will be elaborated in the ŚB. The free movement of Vrātya agrees with the Vedic conceptualisation of the pre-creative state of the world as unstable[96]. In the analysis of the Ṛgvedic concept of enemies (Jurewicz 2010a), I have shown their features among which are the lack of life and bringing death. I have also argued that the Absolute is conceived in terms of the Other, fascinating and dangerous at the same time. In the ṚV, the dangerous aspect of reality, conceived in terms of the Other, is cyclically repelled (Jurewicz 2010a).

It is possible that the recipient of the *Vrātyakāṇḍa* is expected to identify the concept of the bow of Indra (*indradhanús*), taken by Vrātya, with *daṇḍá*. *Daṇḍá* also means 'weapon' already in the AVŚ and in ŚB (Minkowski 1991: 150). On this basis, the recipient could understand the concept of Vrātya elaborated as a source domain for the dangerous aspect of reality which manifests itself during creation. This concept is blended with the concept of the king, embodiment of death in society, who is initiated in the ritual of the Rājasūya to be able to perform his role (Heesterman 1957). Contrary to the ṚV, the dangerous aspect of reality, conceived in terms of the Other, is now introduced within the frames of the cosmos and society and pacified through royal ritual. As we will see, the role of ritual is seen in the same way in the cosmogonies of the ŚB.

2.2.3. Man is still the measure of all things

In two hymns (10.2, 11.8), the composers of the AVŚ present conceptualisation of reality in terms of man conceived more generally than in AVŚ 11.5 and AVŚ 15. As already mentioned, the description presented in these hymns is much more detailed than in the *Puruṣasūkta*. Various parts of human body are mentioned[97]. Such a detailed analysis of the structure of man is new in Vedic thinking. The concept of man refers to both to a particular human being and to the cosmos conceived in terms of man. That the hymns also describe the cosmos seen in terms of man is attested in AVŚ 10.2.18

---

[96] ṚV 7.104.3, see also the description of the world which shakes when Indra is born (Jurewicz 2010a: 341).

[97] AVŚ 10.2 enumerates ankles, knee-caps, shanks, knee joints (AVŚ 10.2, 2) arms and shoulders on the trunk (AVŚ 10.2.5), seven apertures in the head (the ears, the nostrils, the eyes, the mouth, AVŚ 10.2.6). AVŚ 11. 8 enumerates the two thighs and feet, the two knee-caps, the head, the two hands, the mouth, the ribs, the two nipples, the two flanks (10.8.14) tongue, and neck and the vertebrae (10.8.15), the hair, bone, sinew, and marrow (11.8.11).

where man is presented as covering the earth, encompassing the sky and surpassing the mountains[98].

Creation is seen, according to earlier tradition, as self-transformation: this is expressed as the self-birth of particular gods. In AVŚ 11.8.9cd, the concept of the birth of the father in his own son is used: Tvaṣṭar and the Creator (*dhātṛ́*) are presented as born from themselves (*tváṣṭā ha jajñe tváṣṭur dhātúr dhātā́jāyata*). In this way, the composer activates the model of the Child Of The Waters (see ṚV 1.164, chapter 1.6). At the same time, creation consists of the disappearance of the creative power of reality from the cosmos and its coming back in the form of various gods[99]. The idea that reality leaves its creation and comes back is expressed already in the *Puruṣasūkta* (see chapter 1.3), it is also implied by the model of Footprints Of Viṣṇu (Jurewicz 2010a: 388–389). It will be continued in later cosmogony (see chapters 3.5.3, 4.1.2, 4.1.3). In terms of gods, various human cognitive activities, emotions and states are conceived (AVŚ 11.8.19, 24)[100] and this conceptualisation will be elaborated in the later thought (AU, see chapter 4.1.3). As already shown, it can be activated in the description of creation as transformations of Vrātya (see 2.2.2). Conceptualisation of human faculties in terms of gods is new and here we should look for the roots of the later usage of the word *devátā* in reference to senses.

Thus reality exists in two aspects: as unmanifest outside the cosmos and as manifested, divided into various gods, inside the cosmos conceived in terms of man. At the same time, we can see the efforts to create a general term for the creative power of reality, *saṃdhā́*. It is so general that it is impossible to decide if it is conceived in terms of a person or not[101]. Another general word used to express the gods as the creative principle is *samsíc* (AVŚ 11.8.13). This word implies conceptualisation of creation in terms of pouring a liquid and is elaborated in AVŚ 10.7.28 (see section 2.2.4).

The composers of AVŚ 10.2 and AVŚ 11.8 rarely express the fiery character of the cosmos explicitly. However, there are some stanzas which allow us to presume that creation of the cosmos is performed by Agni and is its manifestation. Let us consider the following stanza:

---

98 AVŚ 10.2.18: *kénemā́ṃ bhū́mim aurṇot kéna páry abhavad dívam | kénābhí mahnā́ párvatān kéna kármāṇi púruṣaḥ ||*

99 The god/gods go out: AVŚ 11.8.10, 11; 10.2.8. The god/gods come in: AVŚ 11.8.13, 18

100 AVŚ 11.8.19: *svápno vái tandrī́r nírṛtiḥ pāpmā́no nā́ma devátāḥ | jarā́ khā́latyaṃ pā́lityaṃ śárīram ánu prā́viśan ||* AVŚ 11.8.24: *ānandā́ módāḥ pramúdo 'bhīmodamúdaś ca yé | hasó naríṣṭā nṛttā́ni śárīram ánu prā́viśan ||*

101 AVŚ 11.8.15: *śíro hástāv átho múkhaṃ jihvā́ṃ grīvā́ś ca kī́kasāḥ | tvacā́ prāvṛ́tya sárvaṃ tát saṃdhā́ sám adadhān mahī́ ||*. AVŚ 11.8.16: *yát tác chárīram áśayat saṃdháyā sáṃhitaṃ mahát | yénedám adyá rócate kó asmin várṇam ā́bharat ||*

AVŚ 11.8.31

sū́ryaś cákṣur vā́taḥ prāṇáṃ púruṣasya ví bhejire |
áthāsyétaram ātmā́naṃ devā́ḥ prā́yachann agnáye ||

The sun and the wind shared Man's sight and breath (respectively). Then his other (or the rest of his) Self (*ātman*) the gods gave to fire. (Edgerton 1965)

As I have shown elsewhere, the semantic range of the word *ātmán* in the ṚV includes everything which constitutes its essence: the visible body and the innermost element without which an entity would not be itself (Jurewicz 1997, see section 4.1.2-3). The eye is identified with the sun already in the ṚV, the same for breath and wind (ṚV 10.90.13, 10.16.3). I would argue that the other self, *ātmán*, of fire is the cosmos conceived in terms of man and a particular man[102]. Within the frames of this conceptualisation, the unmanifest aspect is conceived in terms of fire. The same hymn presents the cosmos as shining and lying in waters:

AVŚ 11.6.16

yát tác chárīram áśayat saṃdháyā sáṃhitaṃ mahát |
yénedám adyá rócate kó asmin várṇam ā́bharat ||

That great body which lay here, combined by the Combination (or Combiner), who brought into it the colour, by which it is resplendent here today? (Edgerton 1965)

AVŚ 11.8.34

apsú stīmā́su vṛddhā́su śárīram antarā́ hitám |
tásmiṃ chávó 'dhi antarā́ tásmāc chávó 'dhy ucyate ||

In waters that are sluggish, old (stale?), the body is deposited. Within it there is strength (*śavaḥ*); therefore it is called a corpse (*śavaḥ*). (Edgerton 1965)

These stanzas present the image of a shining body which lies in waters. This image may prompt the recipient to evoke the metaphoric model of Child Of The Waters with Agni as a child. The relationship between waters and Agni is conceived in terms of general domain of Procreation; Agni is the husband and the son of waters and identified with waters. The image of a shining man lying in the waters can be seen as an elaboration of this way of thinking. Man (be it cosmos or particular man) is the other self of Agni conceived as the husband and the son of waters through which Agni can see

[102] See BU 1.2.3, analysed in chapter 4.1.1.

and experience itself. Conceptualisation of the world and man as a means of cognition and as experience of reality is, as I have shown, already present in the ṚV (see Jurewicz 2010a) and will be developed in later thought.

2.2.4. The concept of the pillar (*skambhá*)

AVŚ 10.7-8 propose yet another way of describing the relationship between the unmanifest and manifest aspects of reality: it is conceived in terms of the pillar (*skambhá*), the manifest aspect is but part. In the ṚV, Agni is conceived in terms of a tree (2.35.8, 1.164.22-24) which constitutes a pillar identical with the world (see Jurewicz 2010a: 304-305). This is an example of a metonymy which identifies the essence (conceived here in terms of the pillar) of the world with the world itself; the same metonymy motivates identification of the sun with the world (see below, section 2.5.3).

Time with its division, space and the elements of the world are presented as being within the pillar (AVŚ 10.7.5-6, 10.7.2-3, 12). Thus understood, the pillar corresponds to the unmanifest aspect. AVŚ 10.8.2 and 10.7.35 declare that the pillar supports the earth and the sky and makes them firm together with the space; all living beings are in the pillar. At the same time, the pillar has entered the worlds which implies its presence within it (AVŚ 10.7.8, 9, 35). In this way, the composer implies that reality in both aspects is conceived in terms of the pillar. The composer of AVŚ 10.7.8-9 conceives the world with its spatio-temporal division as part of the pillar, divided into a thousand parts, which implies that the unmanifest aspect is conceived in terms of the whole pillar.

At the same time, the composers of AVŚ 10.7-8 create a blend in which the pillar is identified with man (*púruṣa*, AVŚ 10.7.15)[103]. Thus the pillar is conceived as alive. The next input space is the concept of reality. The generic space is the image schema of VERTICALITY. This blend is further proof of an intention to create a coherent philosophical apparatus and to subsume various concepts under one. Moreover, identification of the pillar with man allows the composer to precisely express the order of the world: in the blend, the elements of the world are conceived in terms of parts of the human body identified with the pillar[104].

---

103 Srinivasan (1997: 35) interprets human features of the pillar as 'traces of anthropomorphism'. Such a concept as a pillar is the result of blending two philosophical concepts (*skambhá* and *púruṣa*) in order to make an even more general and abstract concept which encompasses within its range both of them.

104 AVŚ 10.7.18: *yásya śíro vaiśvānarás̒ cákṣur áṅgirasó ,bhavan | áṅgāni yásya yātávaḥ skambháṃ táṃ brūhi katamáḥ svid evá sáḥ* || AVŚ 10.7.19: *yásya bráhma múkham āhúr*

The following stanza is the example of incorporation of the Ṛgvedic concepts into the frame of the pillar concept:

AVŚ 10.7.28

hiraṇyagarbhám paramám anatyudyáṃ jánā viduḥ |
skambhás tád ágre prā́siñcad dhíraṇyaṃ loké antarā́ ||

Men recognise the 'golden germ' as the supreme, which no words can surpass; the Support in the beginning poured forth that gold within the world. (Edgerton 1965)

The term 'golden embryo' (*hiranyagarbhá*) is used in ṚV 10.121.1. In ṚV 10.121.7, the embryo is presented as being in waters. This image is the elaboration of the philosophical model of Child Of The Waters. This model is evoked here by the concept of an embryo and, metonymically, by the golden colour which is the colour of Agni, the child in the model (Jurewicz 2010a: 302 ff.). The recipient is prompted to imagine the world in terms of an embryo in the womb; the embryo has a golden colour and probably already has the shape of human being. The womb filled with amniotic fluid corresponding to the unmanifest aspect.

Verses *c–d* present the pillar as reality and its creative activity is presented in an image of gold being poured. In this way, the composer evokes the concept of the purification of gold during which heated gold is poured and becomes solidified[105]. The next input spaces are the concepts of the sunrise and reality. The generic space is the image schema of VERTICALITY. In the blend, sunshine is conceived in terms of a flowing stream of gold which appears in a dark vessel; the dark vessel corresponds to the nocturnal sky. In the ṚV, the domain of purification of gold is also used to express thinking (Jurewicz 2010a: 181), so the blend can also be enriched with this concept. In ŚB 6.1.1.15 (see chapter 3.2.2) and ŚB 6.1.3.6 (see chapter 3.5.1), the creation of the earth is conceived in terms of recitation which in turn is conceived in terms of the purification of gold. Since cognition is verbalised in sacred speech, the recipient may also activate this input space in AVŚ 10.7.28cd. Reality, which creates the sun, is conceived in terms of a pillar which, in turn, is conceived as a conscious agent.

That creation is conceived in terms of a cognitive act is confirmed by the following stanza in which the pillar is seen as the source and material of sacred speech:

---

jihvā́ṃ madhukaśā́m utá | virā́jam ū́dho yásyāhúḥ skambháṃ táṃ brūhi katamáḥ svid evá sáḥ || AVŚ 10.7.9c adds to the blend the next input space which is a cow, evoked metonymically by the word *ū́dhar*, 'udder'.

105 This concept as the source domain for creation is elaborated in ŚB 6.1.3, see chapter 3.2.2.

AVŚ 10.7.20

yásmād ṛ́co apā́takṣan yájur yásmād apā́kaṣan |
sā́māni yásya lómāny atharvāṅgiráso múkhaṃ
skambháṃ táṃ brūhi katamáḥ svid evá sáḥ ||

From whom they chopped off the verses, from whom they scraped off the liturgical formula, of whom the chants are the bodily hairs, the Atharvans-and-Aṅgirases the mouth; declare that Support: which one of all, pray, is he? (Edgerton 1965)

The composer of the stanza creates an integration network with the following input spaces: the first is the concept of pillar, the second the concept of man and the third the concept of speech divided into the four Vedas metonymically evoked by the types of the Vedic stanzas. The generic space is the image schema of VERTICALITY. The creation of the ṚV and the YV elaborates the concept of the pillar: the creation of the ṚV is conceived in terms of carving or chopping while the creation of the YV is conceived in terms of scraping. Creation of the YV and AV elaborates the concept of man and constitute its hair and mouth. In the blend, speech comes from the pillar. The consistency of the blend is reinforced in that creation of hymns is conceived in terms of carving/chopping in the ṚV (ṚV 10.81.4, 1.164.23, 41, see sections 1.4, 1.6). AVŚ 10.7.32-34 implies that the pillar is identified with *bráhman*, the power of the sacred word and the sacred word itself: according to these stanzas, *bráhman* is the world and, as it has been shown earlier, the pillar is also the world[106].

2.3. Fire as the essence of reality

In AVŚ 12.1.19-21, it is explicitly stated that the essence of reality is conceived in terms of fire. Such is the exegetic function of the AV:

AVŚ 12.1.19-21

agnír bhū́myām óṣadhīṣv agním ā́po bibhraty agnír áśmasu | agnír antáḥ púruṣeṣu góṣv áśveṣv agnáyaḥ || (19)

[106] AVŚ 10.7.32: *yásya bhū́miḥ pramā́ntárikṣam utódáram | dívaṃ yáś cakré mūrdhā́naṃ tásmai jyeṣṭhā́ya bráhmaṇe námaḥ ||*
AVŚ 10.7.33: *yásya sū́ryaś cákṣuś candrámā́ś ca púnarṇavaḥ | agníṃ yáś cakrá āsyàṃ tásmai jyeṣṭhā́ya bráhmaṇe námaḥ ||*
AVŚ 10.7.34: *yásya vā́taḥ prāṇāpānaú cákṣur áṅgirasó 'bhavan |díśo yáś cakré prajñā́nīs tásmai jyeṣṭhā́ya bráhmaṇe námaḥ ||*

agnír divá ā́ tapaty agnér devásyorv àlntárikṣam | agníṃ mártāsa indhate havyavā́haṃ ghṛtapríyam || (20)
agnívāsāḥ pṛthivy àsitajñū́s tvíṣīmantaṃ sáṃśitaṃ mā kṛṇotu || (21)

Fire is in the earth, in the herbs; the waters bear Fire, fire is in the stones; Fire (of digestion) is within men; in cattle and horses are Fires.
Fire (as sun) glows from the sky; the broad atmosphere is god Fire's (as lightning).
Mortals kindle Fire (of sacrifice), the bearer of oblation, who loves ghee.
Let earth, fire-clad, black-kneed, make me brilliant, sharp. (Edgerton 1965)

According to AVŚ 12.1.19, fire is omnipresent, it is in the earth, in plants, in waters, in stones, within living beings: men, cattle and horses. Thus described, fire is the essence of everything that exists. In AVŚ 10.8.39, fire is presented as being between the earth and the sky. AVŚ 12.1.20 describes the cosmic and ritual activity of fire in its solar and rainy aspects. In its solar aspect, it shines from the sky. In its rainy aspect, it is present in the space between the earth and the sky. It is kindled by human beings in order to bring oblations as the terrestrial fire. AVŚ 12.1.21 creates a beautiful image of the earth which is clothed in fire with black knees. The earth is conceived in terms of a woman and fire in terms of her robe which burns her and thus makes her visible. If the recipient imagines the earth in this way, he will understand that the earth is identical with fire and that her knees correspond to the lower part of fire which is dark of ember. Black knees of the earth can also correspond to the black path left by fire (ṚV 2.4.6.c, 6.10.4.b).

In verse *b* of AVŚ 21.1.21, the poet asks the earth to make him brilliant and sharp. Sharpening is the source domain for cognition conceived as performed under the influence of fire which is kindled in the human being thanks to drinking Soma (Jurewicz 2010a: 266–267), so the poet asks the earth to arouse cognition in him. Then the poet will become brilliant thanks to the internal heat. The power of the earth to cause cognition comes from her fiery nature.

2.4. Ṛgvedic concepts reconsidered

In this section, I will analyse AVŚ 2.1.1-2 which is an attempt to express the philosophical content with the aid of abstract and general language already created in the ṚV[107]. Already Bhattacharya (1977) has presented how the composers of the AVŚ used the Ṛgvedic imagery to present their views. He shows that the reconstruction of the logic of the experience evoked by

[107] I discuss this problem in more detail in Jurewicz (2016b).

the composers is necessary to understand the content of a given stanza. He writes: 'There is no generally accepted methodology for deciphering such complex symbols, though many renowned scholars have devoted themselves to this study (Bhattacharya 1977: 5)[108]. The cognitive tools used in this study can be proposed as such a methodology as it allows symbols to be deciphered with use of models that reveal the general conceptual mechanisms of human thinking.

The composer of AVŚ 2.1 begins with a description of the first creative and cognitive act of reality:

AVŚ 2.1.1

venás tát paśyat paramáṃ gúhā yád yátra víśvaṃ bhávaty ékarūpam |
idáṃ pṛ́śnir aduhaj jāyamānāḥ svarvído abhy ànūṣata vrā́ḥ ||

Vena saw that highest that was in secret, in which this All becomes of one form. This the varicoloured (cow) milked (out). Being born, the heaven-winning (or, -knowing) females shouted (for joy). (Edgerton 1965)

Verses *a – b*: *venás tát paśyat paramáṃ gúhā yád yátra víśvaṃ bhávaty ékarūpam*

In the AVŚ, the noun *vená* is seldom used, though its full analysis would go beyond this present study. The noun *vená* is used in philosophical contexts in AVŚ 4.1.1 (=AVŚ 5.6.1) and in AVŚ 20.25.5 which is a quotation from ṚV 1.83.5. In AVŚ 4.1.1 (=5.6.1), *vená* refers to a form of reality which appears at the beginning of creation. In AVŚ 20.25.5, *vená* is identified with the sun created by Atharvan. The word *vená* is used in a more concrete context to denote a longing of which the protagonist does not wish to be deprived (AVŚ 16.3.2a: *rujáś ca mā venáś ca mā́ hāsiṣṭām*).

On the other hand, the verb *ven-* denotes the longing of a consecrated king who should abandon it (AVŚ 4.8.2ab: *abhí préhi mā́pa vena ugráś cettā́ sapatnahā́*). In AVŚ 18.3.66, the activity expressed with the verb *ven-* is performed in the heart which implies its cognitive dimension (AVŚ 18.3.66b: *hṛdā́ vénanto abhyácakṣata tvā*). ṚV 9.97.22a sheds more light about the nature of the feeling expressed with the use of the verb *ven-* in the sentence: *tákṣad yádī mánaso vénato vā́g*. In their translation, Jamison, Brereton (2014) interpret this sentence as 'when the speech from the mind of the seeker fashioned

108 He gives as an example the study of Gonda (1959b) who argues 'the choice of epithets in the ṚV has not much to do with metrical necessities or individual fancies of poets, but is necessary for making the description more meaningful' (Bhattacharya 1977: 5-6). Bhattacharya (1977: 6) argues that '[i]mageries, anthropomorphic or zoomorphic figures, also can be viewed in the same way'.

him'.[109] However, both Grassmann (1999[1873–1875]) and Lubotsky (1997) interpret the form *vénatas* as a participle of the verb *ven-*, as in ṚV 1.86.8c (*vidā kāmasya vénataḥ*). Thus interpreted *vénatas* qualifies *mánas* which gives another possible translation: 'when the speech from the seeking mind fashioned him'. In this case, the verb *ven-* would mean the activity of a mind before speech appears. It is desired by some (AVŚ 16.3.2) and should be abandoned by others (AVŚ 4.8.2).

The recipient of AVŚ 2.1.1.a can evoke both meanings of *vená* which are 'longing' and 'a man who longs (the seer)'. This is the first input space of the conceptual network. The second input space is reality. The generic space is concept of transformation. If the recipient highlights the meaning of longing in the blend, he will understand the beginning of creation in abstract terms. The concept of longing will lead his mind to the concept of conscious reality. If he evokes the meaning of seer, he will understand reality in the beginning of creation in the more concrete terms of a seer. Taking into account that the activity called with the verb *ven-* is the activity of the heart (AVŚ 18.3.66) and the mind (ṚV 9.96.22), the recipient can understand that reality in the beginning of creation is conceived in terms of thinking and longing for an object of its thought. This is reinforced by the concept of seeing (*paśyat*) in terms of which cognition is universally conceived (Sweetser 1990).

Then the composer describes the object. It is 'the highest' and what 'lies in secret' (*paramáṃ gúhā yád*). Such a qualification of the object may prompt the recipient to evoke the Ṛgvedic concept of the highest track (*paramá padá*). In the ṚV, the highest track belongs to Viṣṇu or Agni (Viṣṇu 1.22.20-21, Viṣṇu 1.154.5, 6, Agni 1.72.2, 4). The track is hidden and people look for it (ṚV 5.15.5cd: *padáṃ ná tāyúr gúhā dádhāno mahó rāyé citáyann átrim aspaḥ*, see also ṚV 1.65.1). The highest track of Viṣṇu is identified with the sun in zenith. So activation of the Ṛgvedic concepts may make the recipient understand *paramáṃ gúhā yád* as the sun in zenith. The concept of sunrise is the next input space of the conceptual network.

The formulation of the AVŚ is more general than that of the ṚV because the Ṛgvedic poets prompt the recipient to reconstruct the whole experience which is walking along the path made by the tracks of a man (in case of the highest track of Viṣṇu) or of a lost calf (in case of the highest track of Agni). The recipient of the AVŚ is not expected to do so. He is rather prompted to evoke the concept of a sphere which is not explicitly named, but only implicitly evoked *via* the adnominal qualifiers *paramáṃ* and *gúhā*. It is only the Ṛgvedic background which makes him to think about the noun *padá* and its meanings.

---

[109] *Vená* refers to the seers who press Soma in ṚV 9.64.21, 9.73.2, 9.85.10, 11.

Within the frames of this background, reality sees the object of its cognition which is the sun in zenith. Since the logic of everyday experience implies that the sun, before it reaches zenith, rises in the morning, the recipient can understand the first creative act of reality in terms of sunrise.

The meaning of sunrise is clearer in AVŚ 4.1.1[110]. Its composer presents the sacred word (*bráhman*) as born in the east (*purástād*) and being disclosed by Vena from the shining boundary. This description may refer to the early morning where the shine of the rising sun appears at the eastern part of the sky in the form of a narrow line. The sacred word (*bráhman*) is born from it and is conceived in terms of the rising sun. In verse *c*, the composer elaborates the scenario of the sunrise to express further creation: Vena discloses its lowest and highest forms. In this way, the upwards movement of the sun is evoked. Its light illuminates the earth, then the space and the sky. Since these forms belong to Vena, the recipient understands that the world is its manifest aspect.

In verse *d*, Vena is presented as disclosing the womb of the existent and of the non-existent (*satáś ca yónim ásataś ca ví vaḥ*). Thus it is conceived in terms of midwife who takes the new-born child from its mother's womb. In the same way, the poets in ṚV 10.129.4 are presented as conceived when they find the kinship of the existent within the non-existent (*sató bándhum ásati nír avindan*). The existent (*sát*) is the manifest aspect of reality and the non-existent (*ásat*) is its unmanifest aspect. The sun is their womb in that its diurnal path marks the borderline between them. The activity of Vena is conceived in terms of unclosing. To unclose anything is to see it; thus the composer of AVŚ 4.1.1 also implies conceptualisation of creation in terms of seeing, so cognising.

Let us come back to AVŚ 2.1.1. In verse *b*, the composer qualifies *paramáṃ gúhā yád* as the place where 'all becomes of one form' (*yátra víśvaṃ bhávaty ékarūpam*). This is again a very general description. It allows the composer to express the unity of the manifest aspect of reality. Similar formulations of monistic assumption are present in the ṚV 1.164.46.c (*ékaṃ sád víprā bahudhā́ vadanti*) or ṚV 8.58.2d (*ékaṃ vā́ idáṃ ví babhūva sárvam*).

However, the context of both Ṛgvedic formulations is more concrete. ṚV 1.164.46 evokes the names of various gods which should be subsumed under one while ṚV 8.58.2 describes fire, the sun and the dawn which are one but, at the same time, dispersed in the manifold world. On the other hand, the reference to ṚV 1.164.46 confirms the interpretation that it is the sun that is recognised by Vena because the one name under which the names

[110] AVŚ 4.1.1: *bráhma jajñānáṃ prathamáṃ purástād ví sīmatáḥ surúco vená āvaḥ | sá budhnyà upamā́ asya viṣṭhā́ḥ satáś ca yónim ásataś ca ví vaḥ ||*

of various gods can be subsumed is the sun conceived in terms of the divine bird (ṚV 1.164.46b: *átho divyáḥ sá suparṇó garútmān*).

So in the first hemistich, the composer presents reality which is conceived in abstract terms as longing or in more concrete terms as a longing seer. It cognises the sphere where everything becomes one. Taking into account the monistic assumptions of the ṚV, we can presume that reality cognises this sphere in itself. In the blend, reality splits itself into the subject of cognition and the object as takes place in self-cognition. Although the object is already discerned, its internal structure and elements are indiscernible: everything has one form. This state of creation corresponds to the second stage of creation presented in ṚV 10.129 and conceived in terms of darkness hidden by darkness (*táma āsīt támasā gūḷhám ágre*, Jurewicz 2010a: 44 ff., 58). The difference with the Ṛgvedic conceptualisation is that the composer of AVŚ 2.1elaborates the concept of light. The object is conceived in terms of the sun, the subject is presented as seeing and seeing needs light to be fulfilled.

Verses *c–d*: *idáṃ pṛ́śnir aduhaj jāyamānāḥ svarvído abhy ànūṣata vrā́ḥ*

Verse *c* is adeptly constructed. Let us imagine how it could be understood when it is heard by a recipient. Firstly, he hears *idáṃ* which may lead his mind to *paramáṃ gúhā yád* from the previous verse which refers to the sphere where everything becomes one i.e. to the object of cognition.

Then comes the word *pṛ́śni*. This word is used in AVŚ 10.5.20 where it qualifies the heavenly stone which is in waters: *yó va āpo 'pā́ṃ áśmā pṛ́śnir divyó 'psv àntár yajuṣyò devayájanaḥ*. In a similar collocation *pṛ́śni* is used in ṚV 5.47.3 to denote the sun (*mádhye divó níhitaḥ pṛ́śnir áśmā ví cakrame rájasas pāti ántau*). Taking into account the Ṛgvedic background, the recipient may understand that *pṛ́śni* refers here to the sun in zenith evoked in verse *b*. His interpretation is confirmed as the word *pṛ́śni* in masculine is used in the ṚV to denote the bull in terms of which the sun is conceived[111]. Thus the composer activates the next input space of the conceptual network which is the concept of a bull.

The next word, *aduhat*, activates the meaning of rain because in the ṚV raining is conceived in terms of milking (ṚV 9.66.30, Jurewicz 2010a: 163). Such a conceptualisation agrees with the general model of reality transformations according to which rain appears from the sun. The concept of rain is the next input space of the conceptual network created by the composer. Cosmic transformations are manifestation of internally contradictory reality which

[111] ṚV 4.3.10d: *vṛ́ṣā śukráṃ duduhe pṛ́śnir ū́dhaḥ*. It is the description of Agni in its solar form.

alternatively reveals its aspects. In AVŚ 2.1.1, these transformations are also conceived as a reflexive process the subject (*pṛ́śni*) and object (*idáṃ*) being the same.

The word *pṛ́śni* in feminine is used in the ṚV to refer to the dappled cow which is the mother of the Maruts who bring rain[112]. Activation of this meaning confirms the meaning of rain. At the same time, it allows the recipient to understand the scenario in terms of which the creative process is now conceived. Now, the subject is conceived in terms of a cow. If the recipient activates the meaning of the verb *duh-*, which is 'to milk', he will understand the process in terms of a cow that milks the sun. Since milk is identified with semen in the early Veda, the recipient may understand this process as inseminating the cow. Origination of rain is conceived in these terms. The verb *duh-* can also be interpreted as 'to give milk'. In this case, the recipient would understand the sun in terms of a calf suckling its mother. Thus the composer enlarges the input space of a bull with concept of cow and its calf. As has been shown, the Ṛgvedic poets (ṚV 1.164, see chapter 1.6) use the experience of cowherding to conceive sunrise: the cow leaves its calf and its calf follows it along the track the cow leaves. In this way, the possibility to activate the concept of track (*padá*) in the context of AVŚ 2.1.1b is reinforced.

The possibility of this twofold interpretation is well grounded in the ṚV the composers of which expressed the internally contradictory activity of reality in the model of Child Of The Waters. This model is the next input space of the complex conceptual network created by the composer. As has been many times stated, within the frames of this model, the male element is both a father, who inseminates the female element, and a son, which is subsequently born. In the blend, the recipient of AVŚ 2.1.1 can unfold it and conceive the rising sun as a new born calf and the sun in zenith as an adult bull. Thanks to that, he will understand sunrise in terms of a calf which follows the tracks of its mother and runs upwards and during that time grows. The same scenario is elaborated in ṚV 1.164 (see chapter 1.6).

Then comes the participle *jā́yamānāḥ*. In his translation, Whitney proposes emendation of *jā́yamānāḥ* to *jā́yamānā*. In this case, the participle qualifies *pṛ́śni*. The cow is valuable only when it gives milk. We could say that giving milk is the essence of a cow and that it is born when it begins to give milk.

The emendation of Whitney can be supported as the phrase *idáṃ pṛ́śnir aduhaj jā́yamānāḥ* appears in the ṚV 10.61.19d with one change: the word *pṛ́śni* is replaced by the word *dhenú*. In the preceding stanza, the seer

---

[112] E.g. ṚV 2.34.2, 5.52.16. In both the ṚV and AVŚ the Maruts are called *pṛ́śnimātaraḥ*.

Nābhānediṣṭha is presented whose mental activity is expressed with use of the verb *ven-* (ṚV 10.61.18b: *nā́bhānédiṣṭho rapati prá vénan*). He looks for the highest navel (*nā́bhiḥ paramā́*) and asks if it belongs to him or someone other (ṚV 10.61.18c: *sā́ no nā́bhiḥ paramā́ asyá vā gha*). So, the composer of ṚV 10.61 creates a similar cognitive situation as the composer of AVŚ 2.1.1, although he begins from the point of view of the human subject. The next stanza of ṚV 10.61 is interpreted as expressing the answer of Agni who presents to the seer his navel and his abode, and describes himself as the whole (*ayám asmi sárvaḥ*). It follows from the next stanzas of the hymn that Agni is the main object of the supernatural cognition described in the hymn. So if the recipient activates ṚV 10.61.18-19, he will already know that reality is conceived in terms of fire.

The concept of a cow may also prompt him to activate conceptualisation of speech in terms of a cow (e.g. ṚV 8.100.11). Then he will understand that the cognitive activity of reality is fulfilled in that reality is able to express its nature in speech[113]. Speech is conceived in terms of a cow being impregnated by a bull and feeding a calf. Within the frames of this conceptualisation, speech comes from the sun and is strengthened by it.

Then the recipient hears the last verse: *svarvído abhy ànūṣata vrā́ḥ*. The phrase *abhy ànūṣata vrā́ḥ* appears in ṚV 4.1.16 and 10.123.2. In both cases, the context is the description of the culmination of the morning when the light of the rising dawn and sun is joyously invited by men conceived in terms of cows bellowing in the morning. The form *jā́yamānāḥ* refers to *vrā́*: men are born at sunrise. This conforms to Ṛgvedic thinking of night as a state of lack of life (Jurewicz 2010a: 111–112).

Qualification of *vrā́* as *svarvíd* allows the recipient to understand that men are presented as cognising under the influence of Soma. Whitney and Edgerton interpret *svàr* as 'heaven', but this word very often means the sun in the early Veda. The second part of the compound, *-vid*, can mean both 'knowing' and 'finding'. The compound *svarvíd* is used in the ṚV in reference to the gods[114] and their chariots[115], but most often in reference to exulting streams of Soma[116]. In two places, it refers to people under influence of Soma (ṚV 9.94.2, 9.97.39). As I have argued (Jurewicz 2010a), people under the influence of Soma mentally reached the sun. Qualification of troops of men as *svarvíd* in AVŚ 2.1.1d may refer to this state. They are born not

---

[113] Speech is explicitly mentioned in AVŚ 4.1.2.

[114] E.g. ṚV 1.52.1, 3.51.2, (Indra), 3.3.5, 10, 3.26.1, 10.88.1 (Agni), 10.65.14 (All Gods), 10.107.4 (Vāyu).

[115] ṚV 2.23.3, 7.67.3.

[116] E. g. VV 8.48.15, 9.8.9, 9.21.1, 9.84.5, 9.101.10, 9.106.1,9, 9.108.2, 9.109.8

only because the sun has risen, but because they have become exulted. The concept of men cognising under the influence of Soma is the next input space of the blend. In the blend, they share in speech that is created by the longing of reality.

We can conclude that the composer of AVŚ 2.1.1 presents the creation of the world and then the role of men in it. Reality is conceived in terms of a longing seer who cognises in himself a sphere identified with the sun in zenith from which rain appears. The first human seers are created in this process and they realise the unity of reality having reached the sun. The language is so general that it is possible to express the whole cosmologic model in a very concise way. The experience is evoked only by the verb *aduhat*. At the same time, the description is so construed that the recipient is prompted to think about relevant passages of the ṚV. These passages prompt him to create the complex blend which will allow him to make sense of the stanza. This blend is also the conceptual framework on which the meaning of the next stanzas of the hymn is built.

In the next stanza, the composer of the hymn seeks the same vision, i.e. the primeval vision of reality:

AVŚ 2.1.2

prá tád voced amṛ́tasya vidvā̃n gandharvó dhā́ma paramáṃ gúhā yát |
trī́ṇi padā́ni níhitā gúhāsya yás tā́ni véda sá pitúṣ pitā́sat ||

Let the Gandharva, who knows the immortal, declare this highest station, which is in secret. Three quarters of it are set down in secret. He who knows this this shall be the Father's Father. (Edgerton 1965)

Verses *a – b*: *prá tád voced amṛ́tasya vidvā̃n gandharvó dhā́ma paramáṃ gúhā yát*

The full analysis of the meaning of the word *gandharvá* in the ṚV and AVŚ would go beyond the scope of the present study[117]. I will limit myself to contexts which are relevant for my argument. In ṚV 9.85.12 and 9.86.36, *gandharvá* is presented as perceiving forms and men (ṚV 9.85.12: *rūpā́ praticákṣāṇo* ; ṚV 9.86.36: *nṛcákṣas*). In ṚV 10.123.4, *gandharvá* finds the immortal names (*vidád gandharvó amṛ́tāni nā́ma*) while, in ṚV 10.123.7, it knows its own names (*nā́ma janata priyā́ṇi*). In ṚV 10.139.5, it is presented as the one who impels thoughts and who helps human thoughts (*dhíyo hinvānó dhíya ín no avyāḥ*). The word *gandharvá* is also used in reference to Soma which gives cognitive abilities to those who drink it (ṚV 9.85.12, 9.86.35, 36).

[117] See Kuiper (1992, 1996), Witzel (2004).

Moreover, *gandharvá* is presented as being in the sky (ṚV 9.85.12, 10.123.7: *ádhi nā́ke asthād*; ṚV 9.86.35: *gandharvám divyám*; ṚV 10.139.5: *divyó gandharvó*), as shining and illuminating the world (ṚV 9.85.12: *bhānúḥ śukréṇa śociṣā ví adyaut prā́rūrucad ródasī*) and as measuring space between the earth and the sky (ṚV 10.139.5: *rájaso vimā́naḥ*). According to ṚV 10.123.7, it stands high in the sky (*ūrdhvó gandharvó ádhi nā́ke asthāt*)[118] while, in ṚV 10.139.5, it is qualified as heavenly and measures space (*divyó gandharvó rájaso vimā́naḥ*). This allows the recipient to understand *gandharvá* as the sun.

So, taking into account the Ṛgvedic background, the recipient can elaborate the input space of cognition and understand the word *gandharvá* as the name of a mysterious power of reality which gives the power of supernatural vision during which 'what is immortal' (*amṛ́ta*) can be cognised. Conceptual links between *gandharvá* and the sun are consistent with the outcome of the previous stanza where speech, conceived in terms of cow, is presented as coming from the sun. Conceptual links between *gandharvá* and Soma imply that this power is realised in men under the influence of Soma. The composer wants to become of them who 'find' or 'cognise' the sun (*svarvíd*). If the recipient conceives reality in more concrete terms of the seer, he will understand that the composer wants to realise the same creative cognition as takes place *illo tempore*.

In verse *b*, the object of the knowledge gained in the supernatural cognition is qualified as the 'highest abode that is in secret' (*dhā́ma paramáṃ gúhā yát*). The similarity of this expression with the expression *paramáṃ gúhā yád* (AVŚ 2.1.1b) allows the recipient to infer that *gandharvá* knows the same as that which is known by reality called *vená* at the beginning of creation and is now supposed to proclaim it to the composer. It is also possible that the intention of the composer is to evoke the Ṛgvedic expression *amṛ́tasya dhāman* used in the ṚV (9.94.2a, 9.97.32b) to denote the highest parts of the world illuminated by Soma and opened for those who are exulted with it.

Verses *c–d*: *trī́ṇi padā́ni níhitā gúhāsya yás tā́ni véda sá pitúṣ pitā́sat*

The concept of three hidden tracks evokes ṚV 1.164.45 which presents the concept of speech the larger part of which is hidden and only one part of which can be expressed in everyday words (see chapter 1.6). The recipient can presume that the tracks form a path. If one of them is known, there is a chance that it will lead man to the next hidden tracks. As pointed out, the

[118] This hymn is devoted to Vena.

first stanza prompts the recipient to create the image of a path along which the sun rises. Now, he can conceive the cognition realised by the composer in the same way, as following the path of the rising sun. If the recipient activates the concept of speech divided into four parts, he will understand that the secret highest sphere of the world can be cognised when the secret parts of speech are cognised.

The possibility of cognition of three hidden tracks is stated by the composer of AVŚ 2.1.2d: the person, who knows them, will become 'father of the father'. Thus the composer introduces the next input space of the blend which is the relationship between father and his son. In the ṚV, the relationship between the teacher and the pupil is conceived in terms of the relationship between a father and a son. The phrase *sá pitúṣ pitā́sat* is used in ṚV 1.164.16 (*kavír yáḥ putráḥ sá īm ā́ ciketa yás tā́ vijānā́t sá pitúṣ pitā́sat*) in the same context of supernatural cognition (see chapter 1.6). The concept of father and son is also evoked in ṚV 1.164.22 where supernatural knowledge is conceived in terms of climbing a tree on the top of which is the sweet berry (*píppala*) is in terms of which the sun is conceived (see chapter 1.6[119]). The person, who does not reach the berry, does not know the father. So, the recipient can understand that the person, who knows the highest secret part of speech and of the world, will surpass his teacher. If the recipient activates ṚV 1.164, he will understand supernatural cognition of the composer as following the path of the rising sun now conceived in terms of climbing a tree.

Moreover, the relationship between the father and the son is also used to conceive the relationship between the unmanifest and manifest aspect of reality in the ṚV (see chapter 1.6[120]). Such a conceptualisation is implied by the model of Child Of The Waters which presents the monistic and paradoxical relationship between two aspects of reality in terms of an incestuous relationships between a father and his daughters and between a son and his mothers.

The unity of reality is emphasised in that a father was seen as essentially identical with his son. So the recipient understands that a person who knows the hidden tracks of speech revealed to him by the cognitive power of reality (*gandharvá*) will not only surpass his teacher, but will attain the unmanifest aspect of reality. According to the model of Child Of The Waters, Agni is the son which is born in waters yet, in ṚV 6.16.35a, he is also presented as his own grand-father (*gárbhe mātúḥ pitúṣ pitā́*). Thus the composer implies yet again that in supernatural cognition it is Agni that is cognised.

In the next stanzas, the composer presents the recognition of reality as Agni present in the cosmos and in cognising man (Jurewicz 2016b). He

[119] See also Jurewicz (2010a: 304–305).
[120] See also Jurewicz (2010a): 249–250.

creates this meaning prompting the recipient to activate the ṚV. He does this in several ways. He quotes Ṛgvedic stanzas and phrases. He also activates Ṛgvedic concepts not literally, but in such a way that the recipient is made to think about them. The structure of the hymn also patterns the structure of those composed by the Ṛgvedic poets (especially ṚV 6.9, see Jurewicz 2016b).

The conceptual network he creates consists of concepts well entrenched in the ṚV. The input spaces are the concepts of man who cognises under the influence of Soma, sunrise, rain and reality. The next input spaces are concepts which give topology and scenario to the content of the blend. These are concepts connected with cowherding (bull, cow, calf and their activity) and familial relationships (father and son). The next input space is the abstract model of Child Of The Waters. In the blend, cognitive and creative processes are conceived in these terms. The generic space is the concept of transformation.

Similarly to the ṚV, this blend is not expressed in words. However, it has been shared within the minds of the composers of the Veda to form the conceptual framework for their thinking. This common conceptual heritage is one of the important factors facilitating creation of abstract and general concepts. The composer could expect that his recipients would metonymically unfold it to create a consistent meaning for his exposition. In order to activate the blend, the composer uses adjectives which metonymically prompt the recipient to look for the nouns to which they refer (*paramá*, *gúhā*, *víśva*, *ékarūpa*, *pṛ́śni*, *amṛ́ta*). He also elaborates polysemy of words (*pṛ́śni*) and whole phrases (*idáṃ pṛ́śnir aduhaj jāyamānāḥ svarvído abhy ànūṣata vrā́ḥ*). These adjectives become the abstract and general concepts.

The composer also uses nouns with an abstract and general meaning. These are *vená* and *gandharvá*. As has been stated, *vená* can be understood as cognitive longing (abstract meaning) and as longing seer (more concrete meaning). This twofold meaning of this word allows the recipient to build the abstract concept of cognising reality and, at the same time, to understand reality in terms of a cognising seer. Activation of the latter meaning facilitates conceptual identification of a cognising human being with reality. Activation of the former meaning facilitates conceptual transfer from the concrete level to the most abstract.

The word *gandharvá* can be understood in a similar way. On more concrete level, it is a personification of the power of supernatural cognition, on more abstract level, it is this power. Thus the recipient can choose the way he runs the blend. He may elaborate the images in order to understand and experience the supernatural state. He also may conceive the content in a more abstract philosophical way.

2.5. Experience in philosophy

In the previous sections, I have presented how abstract and general concepts were created in the process of blending features of Agni with other concepts, how the Ṛgvedic conceptualisation of reality in terms of man was elaborated in the AVŚ and how the general and abstract concepts, already created in the ṚV, were developed in the AVŚ on the basis of an assumption of the fiery nature of reality. Now, I will discuss another way of creating philosophical language which is the use of concept closely connected with experience, but transformed in such a way that they can express abstract and general content. These are a stronghold, a chariot and its wheel, a vessel, a lotus, reed, a tree and a wild goose. These concepts are often blended with other concepts in order to give deeper insight into the content expressed by them.

2.5.1. A stronghold, the wheel of a chariot and a vessel

The first group of concepts are a stronghold, the wheel of a chariot and a vessel[121]. The experiential connection between them comes from the experience of war during which strongholds were conquered by warriors riding on chariots and the riches were won and probably kept in vessels (see Jurewicz 2010b). This scenario is elaborated in a creative way to express the relationship between aspects of reality.

2.5.1.1. Stronghold

I will begin with a description which elaborates the concept of a stronghold and a chariot.

AVŚ 10.2.29-33

yó vaí tā́ṃ bráhmaṇo védāmṛ́tenā́vṛtāṃ púram |
tásmai bráhma ca brāhmā́ś ca cákṣuḥ prāṇáṃ prajā́ṃ daduḥ || (29)
ná vaí tám cákṣur jahāti ná prāṇó jarásaḥ purā́ |
púraṃ yó bráhmaṇo véda yásyāḥ púruṣa ucyáte || (30)
aṣṭā́cakrā návadvārā devā́nāṃ pū́r ayodhyā́ |
tásyāṃ hiraṇyáyaḥ kóśaḥ svargó jyótiṣā́vṛtaḥ || (31)
tásmin hiraṇyáye kóśe tryàre trípratiṣṭhite |
tásmin yád yakṣám ātmanvát tád vaí brahmavído viduḥ || (32)
prabhrā́jamānāṃ háriṇīṃ yáśasā saṃpárīvṛtām |
púraṃ hiraṇyáyīṃ bráhmā́ viveśā́parājitām (33)

[121] I have discussed the concept of stronghold in Jurewicz (2010b).

> Verily, who knows that citadel of *bráhman*, covered over with immortality, to him *bráhman* and the (powers?) of *bráhman* grant sight, life-breath, offspring.
> Verily, the sight does not leave him, nor life-breath, before old age, who knows the citadel of bráhman, from which Man is (so) called.
> The impregnable citadel of the gods has eight circles, nine doors. In it is a golden treasure-chest, heavenly, enveloped in in light.
> In this golden treasure-chest, which has three spokes and is triply based – the prodigy in it which consists of Self (*ātmán*), that verily *bráhman*-knowers know.
> *Bráhman* has entered into this shining, yellow, golden, impregnable citadel, which is all enveloped in glory.(Edgerton 1965)

The stanzas create an image of a shining, golden stronghold (*prabhrā́jamānāṃ háriṇīṃ yáśasā saṃpárīvṛtām / púraṃ hiraṇyáyīṃ*). Such a qualification of a stronghold allows the recipient to understand that in its terms the sun is conceived. This interpretation is confirmed in that the concept of *yáśas*, 'glory', belongs to the complex concept of fame to which concepts of *śrī́*, *śrávas*, *yáśas* and *ksatrá* also belong (see chapter 1.7). It is state of light, immortality and dominion realised under the influence of Soma in the sun.

The stronghold is endowed with 'eight circles' or wheels (*aṣṭā́cakrā*) which evokes another Vedic conceptualisation of the sun in terms of a chariot or its wheels[122]. Thus the recipient is invited to create a blend with a chariot as its next input space; here, the experience is transformed because the Vedic chariots had two wheels (Sparreboom 1985). At the same time, the stronghold has 'nine doors' (*návadvārā*) which is the reason for the name 'man' (*púruṣa*) because a human male body has nine openings conceived, within the frames of this conceptualisation, in terms of doors. The generic space is the image schema of CONTAINER.

In the blend, the image is of a blazing stronghold identified with the sun and a chariot. The human body is the next input space of the blend. The stronghold is called invincible (*ayodhyá*, *áparājitā*) as are the strongholds in the ṚV which protect the poets[123].

The stronghold contains a 'treasure-chest' as Edgerton (1965) translates the word *kóśa*. As already mentioned, in the ṚV, this word denotes a bucket which can be filled with water or riches. The sun is conceived in the ṚV in terms of the golden bucket, so the contents of the stronghold can be understood as the sun[124]. The idea of the sun is also evoked *via* qualification

---

[122] It is impossible to reconstruct the meaning of the number eight evoked in this context, see also below, analysis of AVŚ 11.4.22

[123] According to Rau (1976), the synonyms of the term *púr* are (among other) *kṛcchrá*, 'a place difficult to reach' and *durgá*, 'inaccessible place in the mountains'.

[124] Jurewicz (2006, 2010a: 163).

of *kóśa* as golden, heavenly[125] and enveloped in in light (*hiraṇyáyaḥ kóśaḥ svargó jyótiṣā́vr̥taḥ*). It is also evoked by the expression 'three spokes' (*tryàre*) which metonymically activates conceptualisation of the sun in terms of a wheel. The recipient will grasp the skilfulness of this description when he realises that in the ṚV the word *kóśa* is sometimes used to denote the body of the chariot[126]: in the blend, the recipient may create a clear image of a shining chariot which corresponds to the stronghold while its body corresponds to the treasure. Identification of the stronghold and the bucket (*kóśa*) with the sun is again motivated by metonymic identification of container and its contents.

In the bucket, there is a mysterious being which 'consists of self' (*yakṣám ātmanvát*). We can see that the concentric structure is the same as in the ṚV (see Jurewicz 2010a: 94): in the stronghold, there is a bucket which corresponds to the treasure-chest, in the bucket, there is the mysterious being (*yaksá*), i.e. the treasure. Such a division of reality implies that between its unmanifest and manifest aspects there is a third sphere which can be seen as the borderline sphere of the cosmos reached in cognition. If the recipient understands *kóśa* as the body of the chariot, the mysterious being which is inside *kóśa* can be understood in terms of a charioteer[127]. To conceive the innermost contents of the stronghold in terms of a man is to strengthen the identity between the mysterious being and the stronghold in the terms of which the human body is conceived.

As stated, in early Vedic thought *ātmán* denotes everything which makes reality and the human being a consistent whole: it refers either to their essence or to their external perceptible manifestation which is the cosmos and the human body. So *ātmán* in *yakṣám ātmanvát* can be both, either the essence of the mysterious being or its hiding places which are the bucket and the stronghold.

The adeptness of the composer is amazing. He creates a complex blend to express the structure of reality. The generic space of this blend is the image schema of CONTAINER. In the blend, a concentric structure is created. Its outer layer is conceived in terms of a stronghold, the human body and a chariot. The middle layer is conceived in terms of a bucket and the body of the chariot (*kóśa*). Its innermost part is conceived in terms of a being which can

---

125 Whitney (1905, II: 571) renders the etymological meaning of *svargá* which is 'heaven-going' and which even more clearly evokes the concept of the sun.

126 ṚV 8.208, 8.22.9, see also Macdonnell, Keith (1967).

127 Here we find probably the earliest roots of the later conceptualisation of the Self (*ātman*) in terms of a charioteer (see e.g. KU 3.4-6 and Kr̥ṣṇa as the charioteer of Arjuna).

be understood as a charioteer. At the same time, we can see a tendency to identify the layers of the structure; thus the monistic assumption is expressed.

The stronghold belongs to *bráhman* (*púraṃ yó bráhmaṇo véda*) and *bráhman* enters it (*púraṃ hiraṇyáyīṃ bráhmā́ viveśā́parājitām*). Thus the concept of the conquest of a stronghold is introduced to express cognition: *bráhman* as a cognising agent enters the stronghold it possesses. The recipient can presume that, in this cognitive act, *bráhman* recognises its identity with the contents of the stronghold. Since in the stronghold, there is a being with *ātmán* and since the word *ātmán* can refer to all of reality, *bráhman* recognises its identity with itself. Here we can see one of the roots of the Upaniṣadic identifications of *bráhman* with *ātmán*.

According to the description, if one knows the stronghold, one will reach old age in health (*ná vaí tám cákṣur jahāti ná prāṇó jarásaḥ purā́ | púraṃ yó bráhmaṇo véda*). On the basis of the metaphorical conceptualisation of cognition in terms of seeing, we can presume that the ability to see is the ability to cognise. Such an effect of cognition of the stronghold takes from Ṛgvedic images of a copper stronghold which contains Soma the necessary factor of cognition and immortality. The coherence of this conceptualisation of a stronghold agrees with the conceptualisation of Sarasvatī in terms of a copper stronghold (ṚV 7.95.1, see chapter 1.6). At the same time, they prepare the ground for Upaniṣadic thinking about liberating cognition conceived in terms of the cognition of a stronghold (see chapter 4.4.2.4). In the ṚV, the superhuman results of conquest of the stronghold are only implied, in the AVŚ, they are explicitly stated, although the desired state is still conceived as lasting only as long as one's life.

The concept of the stronghold is introduced in the following way:

AVŚ 10.2.26-28

mūrdhā́nam asya saṃsī́vyā́tharvā hṛ́dayaṃ ca yát |
mastíṣkād ūrdhváḥ práirayat pávamānó 'dhi śīrṣatáḥ || (26)
tád vā́ átharvaṇaḥ śíro devakośáḥ sámubjitaḥ |
tát prāṇó abhí rakṣati śíro ánnam átho mánaḥ || (27)
ūrdhvó nú sṛṣṭā́3s tiryáṅ nú sṛṣṭā́3s sárvā díśaḥ púruṣa ā́ babhūvā́3m̐ |
púraṃ yó bráhmaṇo véda yásyāḥ púruṣa ucyáte || (28)

Atharvan, having sewed up his (Man's) head and his heart, as a wind rising up, expelled (it) from his brain, out of his head. (26)
Verily that head of Atharvan (is) a treasure-chest of the gods, well closed together. That head the life-breath (*prāṇá*) guards, also food and the thought-organ. (27)
What was created above? Or what was created crosswise? Did Man come to be in all directions? – He who knows the citadel of the *bráhman*, from which Man is (so called). (28) (Edgerton 1965)

In his translation, Whitney (1905: 571) writes that 'the whole sense (of AVŚ 10.2.26, JJ) is extremely obscure'. I agree that not everything can be explained in the present stage of the research. However, these three stanzas seem to refer to a breath practice. The top of man's head which is sewed (AVŚ 10.2.26a) refers to the place which, according to the AU, is the place through which reality, called *ātmán*, enters the cosmos and man (see chapter 4.1.3). In AVŚ 10.2.26cd, the concept of wind is evoked. The wind expels something upwards the man's brain and out of his head. Although it is not clear what is expelled, the recipient may presume that the wind opens the closed cranial bones of man's skull.

In AVŚ 10.2.27ab, the head of Atharvan is called the 'treasure-chest of the gods' (*devakośá*). Since in the previous stanza Atharvan is presented as the agent of activity, the recipient understands that the composer describes reflexive activity: Atharvan manipulates on his own head, closing something in it. As we have seen, the treasure-chest is identified in the next stanzas of the hymn with the stronghold. The concept of stronghold is also activated here *via* the concept of guarding: the composer states that the treasure-chest is guarded by breath (*prāṇá*, AVŚ 10.2.27c). The breath also guards food (*ánna*) and mind (*mánas*, AVŚ 10.2.27d). The whole body of man is also conceived in terms of stronghold (this meaning is also activated in the AVŚ 10.2.28cd). The physical and mental life of man is conceived in terms of guarding the food and the mind by breath. Such a conceptualisation refers to the experience: one has to be alive to be able to eat and think. The concept of life is evoked metonymically *via* the concept of breath.

At the same time, the concept of mind introduces the mental activity which leads to the opening of the cranial bones. This can be inferred from the next stanza (AVŚ 10.2.28ac) where questions appear as it is usually done in the early Veda to present supernatural cognition[128]. Thus breath, which guards the mind, has two meanings. The first one is the meaning is supporting everyday mental activity. The second one is the meaning of the force which is able to convey the supernatural cognition. It corresponds to wind (AVŚ 10.2.26cd) and the recipient may understand that the supernatural cognition leads one to realise identity of man and cosmos. The question, which appears in AVŚ 10.2.28c (*sárvā díśaḥ púruṣa ā́ babhūvā́3m̐*), confirms this interpretation.

It can be seen then that the concept of stronghold is not only created in rational analysis, but also in the experience of a breath practice. As it will be shown, its influence on the creation of philosophical concepts is also attested in the Upaniṣads. The concept of the stronghold, firmly closed, within which

[128] See e.g. ṚV 10.129.5 where *pluta* is also used: *adháḥ svid āsī́3d upári svid āsī3t* in a similar context of cognition.

the mysterious being (*yakṣám ātmanvát*) resides can be seen as the source domain of the agent in the everyday subjective-objective cognition. Everything which his outside the stronghold is the object of its cognition. The realisation of the unity of reality is conceived in terms of opening of the stronghold thanks to the wind which in the micro-scale is breath.

2.5.1.2. Wheel of a chariot

The next concept used in philosophy is the concept of a wheel. It is already used in ṚV 1.164 to express the temporal structure of the world (see chapter 1.6). In the AVŚ, it becomes an independent philosophical source domain used to express the relationship between two aspects of reality: unmanifest and manifest. This conceptualisation highlights the temporal nature of the creation and identifies reality with time (see section 2.1.3). Another basis is the conviction that temporal character of creation visibly manifests itself in the movement of the sun in the sky. A further basis is the metaphorical mappings: THE SUN IS THE CHARIOT, THE SUN IS A WHEEL. The final result is the philosophical metaphor: TIME IS A WHEEL.

AVŚ 11.4.22

aṣṭā́cakraṃ vartata ékanemi sahásrākṣaraṃ prá puró ní paścā́ |
ardhéna víśvaṃ bhúvanaṃ jajā́na yád asyārdháṃ katamáḥ sá ketúḥ ||

It rolls with eight wheels, a single rim, a thousand sounds (or syllables), up in the east, down in the west. With a half it created the whole world; its (other) half, what is the distinguishing mark (thereof)? (Edgerton 1965)

The experience is transformed here to express the metaphysic content. Verse *a* creates the image of a chariot or a cart which has eight wheels. Notwithstanding whether or not such chariots or carts were really used in times of the AVŚ, the recipient immediately sees that he is not expected to reconstruct anything real because the eight wheels have one rim. Probably the eight wheels correspond to a division of time which it is now impossible to reconstruct.

The image of the wheel is elaborated in verse *b*. It is described as rising up in the east and going down in the west[129]. This formulation triggers the recipient to activate the metaphor TIME IS A WHEEL. The movement of the wheel is inferred on the basis of the daily movement of the sun. Within the frames of this conceptualisation, the sun can be seen as a shining nail fixed on an

---

[129] For such a conceptualisation of the sun in the Veda, see Parpola (2005).

invisible rim of a wheel which moves over the earth during the day and beneath it during the night.

According to verse *c*, the wheel created the whole world with its half. The recipient may presume that this is the half which rises up in the east and down in the west, i.e. which is above the earth. Thus the input space of creation is activated; in the blend, the daily movement of the sun is identified with creation. The other part, which is when the sun is invisible at night, corresponds to the unmanifest aspect devoid of any sign (see ṚV 10.129).

The next input space of the blend is speech evoked by the compound *sahásrākṣara*. This compound is used in ṚV 1.164.41 where it qualifies reality conceived in terms of a female buffalo (see chapter 1.6). In terms of the buffalo-cow, sacred speech is conceived, which *in illo tempore* is expressed as if "all together", without division into words and syllables (Jurewicz 2010a: 86ff, , 2012a). It is worth noting that the concept of a wheel seems to be less complex than the concept of the female buffalo and this is further evidence for the tendency to create a more abstract philosophical apparatus. In the blend, reality, conceived in terms of a wheel, is identified with time and speech of which only half manifests itself[130] and thus the world is created. The generic space of this blend is the image schema of SELF-MOTION.

The following stanza presents a similar vision; the second half is the same as in the previous stanza, but the wheel is not explicitly mentioned:

AVŚ 10.8.13

> *prajā́patiś carati gárbhe antár ádṛśyamāno bahudhā́ ví jāyate |*
> *ardhéna víśvaṃ bhúvanaṃ jajā́na yád asyārdhám̐ katamáḥ sá ketúḥ ||*
>
> The Lord of Creatures (Prajāpati) moves within the womb; not being seen, he (yet) is manifoldly born. With half (of himself) he created the whole world; the (other) half of him, what is the distinguishing mark (of it)? (Edgerton 1965)

The description activates the model of Child Of The Waters with Prajāpati as the child. Prajāpati is unseen because he is unmanifest, but he is born manifoldly because he is also the manifest aspect. The opposition between the two aspects is conceived in terms of halves of Prajāpati. The second hemistich prompts the recipient to think about AVŚ 11.4.22 and to blend the image of the wheel with the sun with the image of Prajāpati within the womb; in the blend, Prajāpati corresponds to the sun. The generic space of the blend is image schema of SELF-MOTION.

---

130 Compare ṚV 1.164.45 where only one fourth of the language is revealed, see chapter 1.6.

Conceptualisation of reality in terms of a wheel allows the composer to express the dynamic character of reality even in its unmanifest aspect. Such a conceptualisation of reality is unusual in Indian philosophy which in most cases assumes the dynamic nature of the manifest aspect of reality while the unmanifest aspect is assumed static. The dynamic character of the whole of reality is also implied by the conceptualisation of reality in terms of time (see section 2.1.3) and in terms of speech evoked by AVŚ 11.4.22. However, it can also be supposed that the part of reality conceived in terms of the invisible part of the wheel is the borderline sphere of the manifest aspect while the unmanifest aspect is conceived in terms of everything which is beyond the wheel. As I have argued, the existence of this sphere is implied by the concentric structure of reality.

2.5.1.3. Vessel

There is another source domain which is used to create a similar concept of the manifest aspect conceived in terms of a half of a circle. It is a vessel which is turned upside-down. This concept is used in AVŚ 19.53.3 (*pūrṇáḥ kumbhó 'dhi kālá ā́hitas*) to express the diurnal cycle of the sun caused by the influence of time (see section 2.1.3). The stanza quoted below presents the same vision of the cycle. At the same time, it is construed in such a way that the recipient can conceive not only the sun, but also the sky in terms of a vessel:

AVŚ 10.8.9

tiryágbilaś camasá ūrdhvábudhnas tásmin yáśo níhitaṃ viśvárūpam |
tád āsata ṛ́ṣayaḥ saptá sākáṃ yé asyá gopā́ maható babhūvúḥ ||

A bowl with orifice sideways, bottom-side up – in it is deposited glory of all forms; there sit together the seven seers, who have become the keepers of it, the great one[131].

In the ṚV, the concept of a vessel is used to conceive the sun (Jurewicz 2010a: 164 ff.). In the frames of this conceptualisation, the sun is conceived in terms of a vessel, most often called *kóśa*, which rises up in the morning up to zenith where it is turned upside-down so that Soma which fills it can pour out. This concept is also elaborated in AVŚ 19.53.3 (see section 2.1.3). In the AVŚ 10.8.9.a, the sky as a whole is conceived in terms of bowl which is justified by the metonymic identification the sun with the sky that is already

[131] Edgerton (1965: 99) writes: '8 and 9, too obscure to interpret'.

present in the ṚV[132]. At the same time, 'the seven seers' are the seven stars of the Great Bear (Ursa Maior, verse *c*, Witzel 1984: 225, Brereton 1991), so it turns out that a general model is created here that also encompasses the nocturnal sky.

According to verse *b*, glory is placed in the vessel. The concept of *yáśas* metonymically evokes the Ṛgvedic concept of fame understood as the supernatural state realised thanks to Somic exultation (see chapter 1.7)[133]. This state is realised by the seven seers who are those who reached the sun in the first cosmogonic sacrifice and their activity should be repeated by later generations. If the recipient evokes the Vedic conceptualisation of the head in terms of a vessel (see Jurewicz 2010a), he will understand the seven seers as the seven openings of the head[134]. Thus he will enrich the blend with the input space of a human head, probably with an open mouth turned down (ṚV 10.90.1, chapter 1.3) in terms of which the cosmos is conceived.

In verse *d*, the seers are presented as 'the guardians of the great one' (*gopā́ maható*). As I have shown, in the AVŚ, the concept of greatness is used to conceive the first manifestation of reality which can be measured as great. So the recipient understands that the seers in their supernatural cognition have reached this state. The fact that they are guardians implies that, in their cognition, they keep aspects of reality apart (see AVŚ 11.5.8, 10 section 2.2.1).

Thus the composer creates a blend the input spaces of which are a vessel upside-down, a human head, the cosmos and sacrifice. The generic space is the image schema of a CONTAINER. In the blend, the cosmos is conceived in terms of a vessel and a human head. Within the frames of this conceptualisation, change is a feature only of the manifest aspect, as we do not know anything about the unmanifest aspect except it being implied that this aspect is conceived in terms of a human body.

---

132 For analysis of the word *svàr*, see Renou (1965).

133 *Yáśas* is qualified as *viśvárūpa* which Brereton (1991: 4) interprets as activating the concept of the nocturnal sky conceived in terms of the bowl decorated with stars. However, the compound *viśvárūpa* is used in the philosophical contexts of the early Veda mostly in reference to the sun (see chapter 1.6 ad 1.164.9).

134 For this conceptualisation, see also ŚB 6.1.1.1 (chapter 3.2.2) and BU 2.2 (see chapter 4.4.2.2). According to Brereton (1991: 4), this stanza 'carries no suggestion that the sages are the vital functions', but on my view the conceptualisation of head in terms of vessel was already well entrenched.

2.5.2. Lotus, reed and tree

The next set of concepts which became source domains for philosophical concepts are connected with plants or their parts. The first one is a lotus.

2.5.2.1. Lotus and reed

The concept of lotus is elaborated in the following way:

AVŚ 10.8.43

puṇḍárīkaṃ návadvāraṃ tribhír guṇébhir ā́vr̥tam |
tásmin yád yakṣám ātmanvát tád vaí brahmavído viduḥ ||

The lotus with nine gates, covered over with three strands – the prodigy in it which consists of Self (*ātman*), that verily *bráhman*-knowers know. (Edgerton 1965)

The stanza builds a conceptual network which consists of several input spaces. The first is the concept of a lotus. The lotus is described as having nine gates which prompts the recipient to metonymically create the input spaces of a stronghold (*via* the concept of 'gates') and the man (*via* the concept of 'nine', see section 2.5.1.1).

The concept of three strands (*guṇá*), so important for later thought, here seems not to evoke its later meaning of the three attributes of creation, but rather refers to its literal meaning of a strand and to concepts of *tantú*, and its synonyms, like *raśmí*. In ṚV 10.30.9, the compound *tritántu* appears in a context that allows this compound to be understood as referring to the sun. This stanza is an invocation to rivers that are asked to bring a wave. Verses *a–c* qualify the wave as giving exultation (*matsará*), as dripping honey (*madacyút*) and as a draught for Indra (*indrapā́na*). The recipient can, on this basis, metonymically evoke the concept of Soma. According to verse *c*, the wave is born from a cloud (*nabhojā́*) and in verse *d* it is called a spring (*útsa*). Such a qualification of the wave evokes the concept of the sun which is the source of rain[135]. The concept of the sun is also evoked by the way its movement is expressed: as going around (*pári*) and expanding (*ví*) which evokes the circular movement of the sun and the way its light is dispersed in the air (ṚV 10.140.2). It is not easy to reconstruct the experience which motivates the use of *tritántu* in this context. One could argue that this is a reference to a real well which, as it seems, was endowed with leather strips (ṚV 10.101.5-6).

---

[135] The SUN IS A SPRING is a variant of metaphor THE SUN IS A VESSEL FILLED WITH LIQUID (Jurewicz 2010a)

It is possible then that the poet of AVŚ 10.8.43, in his description of a lotus covered with three strands (*tribhír gunébhir ā́vrtam*), also prompts the recipient to activate the concept of spring or a well endowed with strips in terms of which the sun as the source of rain is conceived. And the use of the word *guṇá*, instead of *tantú* or *raśmí*, is an important lexical root for the later use of *guṇa* in purely philosophical contexts.

So in the blend, the lotus corresponds to the stronghold and to man. Activation of these concepts is strengthened in that the second hemistich of the stanza is identical with AVŚ 10.2.32 analysed above (see section 2.5.1.1). If the recipient thinks about this stanza, he will identify the lotus with the bucket which is inside the stronghold and which contains *yakṣám ātmanvát*. This identification is justified by the metonymic identification of the symbols of darkness with the symbols of light that is discussed elsewhere (Jurewicz 2010a) or, putting things more generally, by the metonymy CONTAINER FOR CONTENT/CONTENT FOR CONTAINER; the image schema of CONTAINER constitutes the generic space of the blend. We can clearly see the effort of the Atharvavedic poets to identify various metaphors in order to create a coherent apparatus for the expression of metaphysical theory.

This tendency can also be seen in the following stanza:

AVŚ 10.8.34

> *yátra devā́ś ca manuṣyā̀ś cārā́ nā́bhāv iva śritā́ḥ |*
> *apā́ṃ tvā púṣpaṃ pṛchāmi yátra tán māyáyā hitám ||*
>
> In which gods and men are set like wheel-spokes in the nave – I ask you that in which the flower (offspring) of the (cosmic) waters was placed by superhuman power. (Edgerton 1965)

The recipient is triggered to create a conceptual network the input spaces of which are the concepts of a wheel, of a flower which grows from water, of gods, of men and of reality. In the blend, the gods and men are identified with the spokes of the wheel. Interestingly, the threefold structure is implied again here because the concept of the wheel metonymically evokes the concept of the chariot. The flower corresponds to the wheel and waters correspond to the chariot. In terms of flower and wheel, the manifest aspect is conceived, in terms of waters and chariot, the unmanifest aspect. The image of a plant which grows from water evokes the Ṛgvedic model of the Wave Of Honey where the wave is identified with the Somic plant growing from water (ṚV 4.58.1, see Jurewicz 2010a: 227 ff.). The image schema of CONTAINER is the generic space of this conceptual network.

Another variation of the philosophical metaphor which uses the image of a plant in order to express what is manifest is presented in the following stanza:

AVŚ 10.7.41

> *yó vetasáṃ hiraṇyáyaṃ tiṣṭhantaṃ salilé véda |*
> *sá vaí gúhyaḥ prajā́patiḥ ||*
>
> Who knows the golden reed that is located in the sea, he verily is the secret Lord of Creatures. (Edgerton 1965)

The word *vetasá* is used in ṚV 4.58.5d where the poet presents himself as gazing at the streams of clarified butter and when the main current seems to transform itself into the golden reed. The hymn identifies streams of butter with waters and builds the same image as is built in AVŚ 10.7.41: of a golden reed appearing in water. In ṚV 4.58, the image of the golden reed which appears in the streams of butter is used to express the vision of reality which manifests itself as Soma and then as Agni. Seen against this Ṛgvedic background, AVŚ 10.7.41can be understood as describing a vision the result of which is Prajāpati. This stanza shows a redefinition of the Ṛgvedic philosophical apparatus in the frames of new thought where Prajāpati becomes a more important concept.

2.5.2.2. Tree

Another kind of plant evoked in this metaphor is that of a tree:

AVŚ 10.7.38

> *mahád yakṣáṃ bhúvanasya mádhye tápasi krāntáṃ salilásya pṛṣṭhé |*
> *tásmin chrayante yá u ké ca devā́ vṛkṣásya skándhaḥ parita iva śā́khāḥ ||*
>
> A great prodigy, in the midst of cosmos, strode in (religious) fervour (or, in the heat) on the back of the ocean; in it are set whatsoever gods there are, like branches round bout the trunk of the tree. (Edgerton 1965)

The input spaces of the blend are the concepts of a heated mysterious being which makes steps and appears in waters, the cosmos, the gods and a tree. The generic space is the image schema of SELF-MOTION. In the blend, the trunk of the tree corresponds to the world and branches of the tree correspond to the gods while the tree grows from water. The structure is as follows: water corresponds to what is unmanifest, branches to what is manifest and the mysterious being to the trunk. In the ṚV, Agni is presented in the form of tree (see Jurewicz 2010a) while ṚV 1.164.20-22 builds an image of a fiery tree (see chapter 1.6). The same image is built here because the mysterious being manifests itself in heat; the recipient may presume that branches of tree are identified with dishevelled flames of fire. The mysterious being is presented as making steps which evokes the model of Footprints Of Viṣṇu in terms of which creation and appearance of the morning light is conceived in the ṚV (see Jurewicz 2010a: 386 ff.). It is worth noting, however, that concept of moving may also evoke the first act of manifestation of reality conceived in these terms (see sections 2.2.1-2).

The concept of a mysterious being (*yaksá*) appears in the stanzas already discussed: AVŚ 10.2.32 (see section 2.5.1.1) and 10.8.43 (see section 2.5.2.1). I would draw attention to the coherence of usage of source domains that allow for the creation of a consistent metaphysics and of an apparatus to express it. In order to reconstruct this process, we have to create a large conceptual network that consists of the content of these three stanzas. Let us reconstruct its input spaces. These are:

1. a stronghold with a bucket inside it (evoked *via kóśa*, AVŚ 10.2.32a and *via* concept of gate in AVŚ 10.8.43a)
2. a chariot with a wheel (evoked by in AVŚ 10.2.32b, 11.4.22a, 10.8.34b)
3. a flower (evoked by AVŚ 10.8.43a, 10.8.34c)
4. a human body (evoked by AVŚ 10.8.43a)
5. a tree (evoked by AVŚ 10.7.38)
6. a mysterious being in a bucket (AVŚ 10.32.2), in a flower (AVŚ 10.8.43) and identified with the trunk of a tree (AVŚ 10.7.38)

In the blend, a bucket, a wheel, a flower, a human body and the branches of a tree are identified and refer to the manifest aspect. A stronghold, a chariot and waters refer to the unmanifest aspect. A mysterious being that possesses himself (*ātmanvát*) is in the bucket and is identified with the nave of a wheel and the trunk of a tree. It is the most mysterious element of the world which cannot be seen by the everyday eye, but only by those who are somehow prepared. In this way, the ground for the concept of *ātman* as the invisible and absolute self of the world and man is prepared. The generic space are images schemas of SELF-MOTION and CONTAINER.

2.5.3. Wild goose

The last concept that serves as the source domain for philosophy is the concept of a wild goose (*haṃsá*). Let us consider the following stanza:

AVŚ 10.8.18, 13.2.38, 13.3.14

sahasrāhṇyáṃ víyatāv asya pakṣaú hárer haṃsásya pátataḥ svargám |
sá devā́nt sárvān úrasy upadádya saṃpáśyan yāti bhúvanāni víśvā ||

> A thousand days' journeys are spread out the two wings of the yellow wild goose[136] flying to heaven. He, taking in his bosom all the gods, moves inspecting all the worlds. (Edgerton 1965)

The first input space of the integration network created in the stanza is a flying wild goose. It is qualified as 'yellow', *harí*, which evokes the metaphoric conceptualisation of the sun in terms of a bird[137]. The sun is the second input space. Since the goose flies up to the sky, the recipient understands that, in the blend, the sun rises. The next input space is time divided into a thousand days. The generic space is the image schema of SELF-MOTION. It seems that the intention of the poet is to create the image of the wild goose whose extended wings are the past and future divided into a thousand days. This image is based on the conceptualisation of time in terms of space: we can measure the past and the future by measuring the length of wings of the goose. Thus it turns out that in terms of goose not only the sun is conceived, but also the whole spatiotemporal world; this is the next input space.

Verses *c–d* present the wild goose as having all gods in its breast and as viewing all worlds. The whole of reality is the next input space. In the blend, the breast of the goose corresponds to the world where the gods are while the goose corresponds to all reality.

The composer seems to iconically reflect the stages of supernatural cognition: the poet sees the sun and while meditating on it sees the manifest aspect of reality and then realises that the manifest aspect is but part of all reality. As it will be shown, the meditation on the sun is an important stage of the liberating process accompanied with breath practice described in the Upaniṣads (see chapter 4.4). So the stanza is one of the proofs that this practice had already began in the times of the AV.

The word *haṃsá* is not often used in the ṚV, but the contexts of its usage are significant. It is used in reference to real animals (e.g. ṚV 1.163.10, 2.34.5, 3.8.9). As the source domain for other concepts, *haṃsá* is used in ṚV 1.65.9 where it is used to denote Agni who breaths in waters (*śvásiti apsú haṃsó ná sī́dan*) and in ṚV 10.124.9, to denote Indra who moves in 'heavenly waters' as the sun[138]. So we can see that already in the ṚV the concept of the wild goose was a source domain for the sun and for the whole manifest aspect. Both Ṛgvedic stanzas evoke the model of the Child Of Waters: in ṚV 1.65.9,

---

136 Edgerton (1965): 'Swan'.

137 We can see how the experience is transformed in order to express philosophical though: in ṚV 7.59.7b, wild gooses have dark back.

138 ṚV 10.124.9: *bībhatsū́nāṃ sayújaṃ haṃsám āhur apā́ṃ divyā́nāṃ sakhiyé cárantam* | *anuṣṭúbham ánu carcūryámāṇam índraṃ ní cikyuḥ kaváyo manīṣā́* ||

the child corresponds to the manifest aspect of reality and, in ṚV 10.124.9, to the sun. The AVŚ enlarge the semantic range of this concept to all reality. The use of the same concept to express the sun, the manifest aspect and all reality is motivated by the metonymy which identifies the symbols of darkness with the symbols of light and at the same time, allows the poet to express the monism of reality.

The conceptualisation of the creation in terms of the wild goose is also evoked also in the following stanza:

AVŚ 11.4.21

ékaṃ pā́daṃ nót khidati salilā́d dhaṃsá uccáran |
yád aṅgá sá tám utkhidén naívā́dyá ná śváḥ syāt |
ná rā́trī nā́haḥ syān ná vy ùchet kadā́ caná ||

When as a wild goose[139] he arises from the see, he does not withdraw his one foot. If he were to withdraw that, there would be no today and no tomorrow at all; there would be neither night nor day, and it would never dawn. (Edgerton 1965)

The composer builds his image from the everyday life experience of a wild goose which rises from water, but immediately transforms it in such a way that it could express philosophical thought: contrary to common everyday experience one foot of the goose remains in water. In terms of water, the unmanifest aspect is conceived while the manifest aspect is conceived in terms of the wild goose. Thus the second input space of the integration network is created which is reality divided into two aspects. In the blend, the leg which remains in water corresponds to the link between the manifest and unmanifest aspects. Such a conceptualisation is similar to that of the *Nāsadīyasūkta* where the poets are conceived in terms of midwives who find the umbilical cord (*bandhú*) which links the unmanifest (*ásat*) sphere with the manifest (*sát*) one (Jurewicz 2010a: 52–53).

At the same time, the leg that is in water can also be seen as the *axis mundi*. In the same way, the *axis mundi* is conceived in the *Puruṣasūkta*: as one leg of reality while three legs are hidden (see chapter 1.3, see also ṚV 1.164.6-7, chapter 1.6). So we can see that the target domain expressed by the image of a goose not taking out one leg from water is well entrenched in earlier thought: this is reality divided into two aspects of which one is unmanifest and the other the world; both aspects are ontologically the same.

The composer of AVŚ 11.4.21 expresses this target domain with a new metaphor and thus creates a new language probably more meaningful for

139 Edgerton (1965): 'Swan'.

his recipients. Like the composer of ṚV 4.58.1, he not only expresses the ontic relationship between two aspects (THE UNMANIFEST ASPECT IS WATER, THE MANIFEST ASPECT IS THE GOOSE, THE LINK BETWEEN TWO ASPECTS IS GOOSE'S LEG), but also the structure of the world (THE UNMANIFEST ASPECT IS WATER, *AXIS MUNDI* IS GOOSE'S LEG, THE SUN IS THE GOOSE).

In both cases, we are not surprised that if the goose takes its leg out of water, there would be no time divisions at all. In the first case, this would mean would mean that the link between the manifest and unmanifest aspect would break and both aspects would become the same. This would mean the end of the world and of time. In the second case, this would mean that the essential ontological and invisible link which supports the sun in the sky[140] would break and thus the day and night, the sky and the earth would become one. This would finally lead to the end of the world too.

2.6. Towards abstraction

In this section, I will discuss more general and abstract descriptions of reality that are used in later thought. Firstly, I will discuss the source domain of 'the full' (*pūrṇá*) which comes from the experience, but it is already an abstraction from the everyday concept of a vessel filled with water (section 2.6.1). In the next section, I will the discuss the source domain of killing that will become one of the main metaphors in the Brāhmaṇas (section 2.6.2). The next two sections are devoted to the abstract concepts of *sát/ásat* and *ātmán/bráhman* and the way that monism and the internal contradiction of reality is expressed (sections 2.6.3, 2.6.4)

2.6.1. The concept of the full (*pūrṇá*)

AVŚ attests attempts to create an abstract concept which could express the essence of reality which creates the world out of itself and is not affected by creative changes. Such a concept is the concept of 'the full', *pūrṇá*. I will begin with an analysis of selected stanzas of AVŚ 10.8.

AVŚ 10.8.14

ūrdhváṃ bárantam udakáṃ kumbhénevodahāryàm |
páśyanti sárve cákṣuṣā ná sárve mánasā viduḥ ||

Him who carries water upward, like a woman carrying water in a jar; all see with their eye; not all know (him) with their mind. (Edgerton 1965)

---

[140] See ṚV 4.13.5, 4.14.5.

The composer creates the image of a woman who draws water from a well in a vessel. This is the source domain of the description. The target domain is the functioning of the cosmos. In the early Veda, the sun is conceived in terms of a vessel filled with water which is the source domain for rain originating from the sun (Jurewicz 2010a: 165–166). The sunrise is conceived in terms of lifting of the vessel from a well while raining is the pouring of the contents of the vessel which takes place when the sun reaches zenith. This metaphor is evoked by the composer and the agent who causes the sunrise is conceived in terms of a water carrier. In this way, he expresses that everyone sees how the sun rises, but not everyone understands who causes this process.

AVŚ 10.8.15

dūré pūrṇéna vasati dūrá ūnéna hīyate |
mahád yakṣáṃ bhúvanasya mádhye tásmai balíṃ rāṣṭrabhŕ̥to bharanti ||

Afar he dwells with the full, afar he is freed from the deficient – the great Prodigy in the middle of the universe; to him the rules of kingdoms bring tribute. (Edgerton 1965)

This stanza presents the absolute essence of the world. It is conceived in terms of a mysterious being. On the one hand, it is transcendent (he dwells 'afar', *dūré vasati*), on the other hand, it is immanent (he is 'in the middle of the universe', *bhúvanasya mádhye*). In its transcendent aspect it is perfect which is expressed literally ('he is freed from the deficient', *ūnéna hīyate*) and in terms of metaphor 'he dwells with the full'. Since according to the next stanza, the sun rises out of it and sets in it [141], the recipient understands that it is the agent of the sunrise mentioned in the previous stanza (AVŚ 10.8.14). As the mysterious being is presented as receiving tribute the recipient may infer that it is Agni because in the ṚV it is Agni who receives tribute (ṚV 1.70.9, 5.1.10).

So, it seems that the AVŚ enlarges the meaning of the concept of the golden bucket so that it could be used to express the relationship between the manifest and the unmanifest. We can witness the same strategy in case of a bowl on which the seers sit (see section 2.5.1.3). The ummanifest aspect is conceived in terms of a full vessel while the manifest is the sphere where there is tension between fullness and emptiness expressed by the image of a vessel which is dragged out, emptied and again filled with water. The visible manifestation of this tension is the movement of the sun.

---

141 AVŚ 10.8.16:
yátaḥ sū́ryaḥ udéty ástaṃ yátra ca gáchati tád evá manye 'háṃ jyeṣṭháṃ tád u nā́ty eti kíṃ caná ||

The following stanza is evidence for further abstraction in thinking:

AVŚ 10.8.29

> *pūrṇā́t pūrṇám úd acati pūrṇáṃ pūrṇéna sicyate |*
> *utó tád adyá vidyāma yátas tát pariṣicyáte ||*
>
> From the full he ladles out the full; the full is poured out by the full; would that we might know today that, from which that is poured out. (Edgerton 1965)

The recipient can interpret *pūrṇá* as the noun denoting the state of being full in general and does not have to evoke metonymically the target concept (a full vessel) in order to understand the perfectness of reality in both aspects: transcendent, on the one hand, and immanent on the other[142]. On the basis that they are conceived in the same way, the recipient infers that they are ontologically the same.

However, the context may still prompt the recipient to evoke the target concept of the metonymy which is a full vessel and the concept of pouring water[143]. If he does, he will conceive creation in terms of the pouring of water from a vessel. Activation of this source domain enables the recipient to understand the paradoxical nature of creation. From everyday experience he knows that when a vessel is full water is not flowing and when water begins to flow a vessel will become empty. Here, however, notwithstanding how much water will flow out, the vessel is always full. Both aspects of reality are conceived in terms of being full and the difference between them consists in the conceptualisation of the immanent aspect as fullness which flows and the conceptualisation of the transcendent aspect as fullness which does not flow.

The concept of the inexhaustible fullness which flows is a very good concept for the monistic vision of reality which is not concerned by any change which takes place within it. Within the frames of this conceptualisation, even if it pours itself totally it still remains whole. Such a reality is absolute reality. The difference with the European concept of the Absolute is that while in early Indian thought it can also manifest as changing, in European thought one of the most essential attributes is permanence. The manifest aspect is conceived in terms of fullness, but this fullness constantly moves in order to fill the gap which appeared during creation. This is expressed in terms of a vessel which is cyclically filled and poured. When it rises up from the earth, it empties,

---

[142] In the same way as he does not have to evoke the target concept in the previous stanza.

[143] This concept is also evoked metonymically A VESSEL FOR POURING WATER FROM IT (an instantiation of metonymy INSTRUMENT FOR ACTION, Radden, Kövecses 1999: 37).

so it has then to be again filled by rain. The tension between fullness and emptiness constitutes the world[144].

We can see the change by comparing this with the ṚV. In the AVŚ, the state of being full is not the source domain for conceptualisation of the sun, but of the unmanifest aspect of reality which is beyond the sun. This conviction is implicitly present in the ṚV in the image of the sun which is the opening in the sky made by Viṣṇu who left the world through it (see Jurewicz 2010a: 392). At the same time, the concepts which refer to experience are still activated by the composer in order to convey more meaning. Using the terms that Heine coined in his explanation of the process of grammaticalisation (Jurewicz 2014a), we have a bridging context here when the abstract meaning is already present, but the concrete meaning still plays a role in understanding a concept. The further step towards abstraction will be taken in BU 5.5.1 (see chapter 4.2.2).

Finally, I would add that conceptualisation of reality in terms of water and its flowing is attested already in ṚV 1.164.41-42 the composer of which uses the concept of flowing which does not flow (*tátaḥ kṣarati akṣáram*) and then conceptualises the transformations of reality in terms of water circulation (see chapter 1.6).

2.6.2. The concept of killing

The source domain of killing will be one of the main concept used in the metaphysical thought of the ŚB. In the AVŚ, it is activated in the following stanza:

AVŚ 10.8.24

śatáṃ sahásram ayútaṃ nyàrbudam asaṃkhyeyáṃ svám asmin níviṣṭam |
tád asya ghnanty abhipáśyata evá tásmād devó rocat eṣá etát ||

A hundred, a thousand, a myriad, a hundred million – innumerable is the property that it entered into him. This of him they destroy, even as he looks on, (yet) on that account this god finds that pleasurable. (Edgerton 1965)

The stanza presents reality divided into two aspects unmanifest and manifest. This is conceived in several ways. The first way of conceptualisation is division between what is innumerably divided (*śatáṃ sahásram ayútaṃ*

[144] This concept will be motivate thinking of the composers of the ŚB who present the manifest aspect as constantly dying and resurrecting, see chapter 3.2.3.

nyàrbudam asaṃkhyeyáṃ) and what is not. The second way is division into the possessed and the owner (*svám, tád asya*). Such a conceptualisation already appears in the AVŚ 11.8.31 where the world is conceived as the self, *ātmán*, of Agni (see section 2.2.3); it will be developed in the Upaniṣads. The third way of conceptualisation is the division between what is killed and what kills (activated by the verbal form *ghnanti*) and what is not killed. In the blend, the undivided and perceiving owner who is beyond killing corresponds to the unmanifest aspect of reality, what is possessed, what is divided, killed and perceived corresponds to its manifest aspect. The unmanifest aspect perceives the manifest aspect in its transformation. However, it may also be presumed that the aspect of reality which is presented as watching is the borderline sphere of the cosmos and that reality as the whole is conceived as being beyond its manifestation. In this case, its manifestation is conceived in terms of subjective-objective activity.

Whitney (1905) translates *rócat* (verse *d*) as 'shines', Edgerton (1965) as 'finds that pleasurable'. If we accept Whitney's interpretation, we could understand shining literally as the power of the sun which comes from the unmanifest aspect and, metaphorically, as the power of cognising. Edgerton's interpretation allows the recipient to evoke the concept of eating. The concept of eating involves the concept of killing and of taking pleasure. One cannot exclude that the concept of a performance is also evoked here. In this case, the manifest aspect of reality would be conceived in terms of a scene on which actors play and the unmanifest aspect would be conceived in terms of the audience; the actors and the audience are the same. Such a conceptualisation would anticipate later thinking about creation in terms of God's play (*krīḍā*, *līlā*, see also chapters 3.5.2, 4.1.2).

The generic space of the conceptual network created in this stanza is not easy to be reconstructed. I would argue that it is the general domain of Cooking which will be elaborated in the ŚB (see chapter 3.2.3). Its scenario includes looking for food, possessing something which will become food, killing it, dividing it and taking pleasure from its eating. If the concept of performance is also one of the input spaces, this would mean that the conceptualisation of aesthetic pleasure as eating is already attested here. As Malamoud (2005c) has shown, the concept of Vedic animal sacrifice betrays similarities with the concept of performance. Sacrifice is conceived in terms of eating which is a specific instantiation of the general domain of Cooking. Thus the meaning of sacrifice could come from this input space and highlight its semantic aspect of performance.

2.6.3. The concepts of *sát* and *ásat*

In the AVŚ, the words *sát* and *ásat* are used in the same way as they are used in the RV: *ásat* refers to the unmanifest aspect and *sát* to the manifest.

AVŚ 10.7.21

asaccākhā́ṃ pratíṣṭhantīṃ paramám iva jánā viduḥ |
utó sán manyanté 'vare yé te śā́khām upā́sate ||

A branch of non-existent, which (branch) stands forth, people know as seemingly the supreme thing. Inferior folk, who revere your branch, think of it also as the existent. (Edgerton 1965)

The stanza belongs to the hymn which elaborates conceptualisation of reality in terms of a pillar (*skambhá*, see section 2.2.4). Here, the pillar is identified with a tree with an extended branch. It is implied that reality is conceived in terms of the whole tree while its manifest aspect is conceived in terms of the branch. The whole tree is called *ásat*, 'non-existent', which agrees with the conceptualisation of the whole of reality as uncognisable and hence non-existent. In verse *b*, the composer states that people conceive it as supreme.

However, there are people who worship the branch and conceive it as the existent (*sát*, verses *c–d*). Such people are called 'lower' or 'inferior', *ávara*. They reduce the whole of reality to its manifest aspect and they do not recognise anything beyond that aspect similarly to people described in the ṚV who claim that there is no Indra (ṚV 2.12.5, 8.100.3).

AVŚ 10.7.25

bṛhánto nā́ma té devā́ yé 'sataḥ pári jajñiré |
ékaṃ tád áṅgaṃ skambhásyā́sad āhuḥ paró jánāḥ ||

Great, to be sure, are called those gods who were born out of the non-existent. That non-existent people declare to be a single member of the Support which is beyond. (Edgerton 1965)

According to the first hemistich, the gods are born from the non-existent (*ásat*). It is again implied that all reality is conceived in these terms: the gods, as the part of manifest aspect, appear from what is unmanifest. In the second hemistich, however, the term *ásat* is attributed to one member (*áṅga*) of the pillar and this member is beyond (*parás*). According to the logic of the image created in AVŚ 10.7.21 (see above), a member of the pillar that is identified with the tree should be its branch. If this is the intention of the poet, then we understand that the hemistich expresses the monistic assumption according to which the manifest aspect is ontologically the same as the unmanifest and as such can also be called *ásat*. The same paradoxical situation is expressed by the composer of the *Nāsadīyasūkta* when he uses the ambiguous expression *tuchyénābhú ápihitaṃ yád ā́sīt* which allows the recipient to understand that the manifest aspect does not exist (*ābhú*) and is about to exist (*ābhū́*, see Jurewicz 2010a: 49–50). So people described in the previous stanza commit a double mistake: not only do they fail to recognise the unmanifest aspect of reality, but they think about the manifest as only existent, *sat,* while it contradictory nature means it is existent and yet non-existent.

According to AVŚ 10.7.10c, *sát* and *ásat* are within the pillar (*ásac ca yátra sác cāntá*). In the *Nāsadīyasukta*, the pre-creative stage of reality is presented as the state when there is neither *sát* nor *ásat*. During creation, both are created: the unmanifest aspect is called *ásat*, the manifest one is called *sát*. We can interpret AVŚ 10.7.10c in the same way. The whole of reality, conceived in terms of a pillar, includes what is unmanifest (*ásat*) and what is manifest (*sát*).

2.6.4. The concepts of *ātman* and *bráhman*

The terms *ātmán* and *bráhman* are crucial in later metaphysics. The analysis of their usage in the AVŚ allows us to reconstruct the development of their meaning towards abstract concepts that denote aspects of reality. In the AVŚ, as in the ṚV, the word *ātmán* denotes the self understood as everything which makes an entity itself. The usage of this word in philosophical contexts can be treated as the conceptual bridge towards later thought. I have already discussed AVŚ 11.8.31 where the word *ātmán* is used to denote the manifest aspect of reality conceived in terms of fire (see section 2.2.3). It is conceived in BU 1.4.10 (see chapter 4.1.2) in the same way.

The use of the form *ātmanvánt* (10.2.32, 10.8.43, see sections 2.5.1.1, 2.5.2.1) is one of the important steps towards the later concept of *ātmán*. As I have shown, the whole structure of reality presented in these hymns is as follows: water/stronghold – lotus/bucket – mysterious being which possesses self. Taking into account the holistic meaning of the word *ātmán*, we can understand that the word *ātmán* in the compound *ātmanvánt* either denotes the invisible internal essence of the mysterious being or everything which is outside it and which can be included as its self. If we remember that AVŚ 11.8.31 uses this word to denote the cosmos, then we can activate the meaning of the cosmos here and understand it as the self of the mysterious being.

In AVŚ 10.8.44, the word *ātmán* is used in a very abstract way similar to those in the Upaniṣads. In the first hemistich, it is presented as the desireless, immortal and self-existent essence (*akāmó dhī́ro amṛ́taḥ svayaṃbhū́*). The only clear reference to experience can be detected in the qualification of *ātmán* as *rásena tṛptó*, 'satiated with essence'. The word *rása* could metonymically evoke the concept of Soma and exultation, but this activation is not necessary in order to understand that *ātmán* is self-content. This is immediately confirmed by the next qualification that it is deprived of any deficiency (*ná kútaś canónaḥ*). The word *tṛptá* also evokes the metaphor of 'the full' in its abstract meaning to denote the perfect wholeness of reality. The recipient may activate the concept of a sentient being which, having been thirsty, is now filled with water or Soma or some other fluid. However, it is not necessary in the abstract context of the stanza. The description of *ātmán* is continued in verse *d*. It is presented as 'wise' (*dhī́ra*) which also can be understood in the abstract meaning of omniscient reality. Its qualification as 'ageless young' (*ajáraṃ yúvānam*) can be understood as expressing its internal contradictoriness (see below, section 2.6.5). According to verse *c*, the person who understands *ātmán* in such a way is not afraid of death (*tám evá vidvā́n ná bibhāya mṛtyór ātmā́naṃ*) which again agrees with the Upaniṣadic way of thinking about the ontic results of cognition; it is important to note that this is already assumed in the RV.

In the AVŚ, the word *bráhman* begins to denote something more than powerful word as well as the power of such a word and in many contexts it acquires the meaning of an ontic entity. However, it has been shown that in AV 10.2.26-28 this word is used in the context of breath practice as a powerful factor which transforms a cognising man. The ontic dimension of this word is also attested in this hymn. In AVŚ 10.2.25, *bráhman* denotes a factor of creation thanks to which the earth, the sky and the space between them is arranged[145]. This cosmogonic context opens the way to its meaning as the most primeval reality which creates everything that exists.

The shift in meaning of the word *bráhman* can also be seen in the stanzas which imply the identity of *ātman* and *bráhman*. It is again implied by AVŚ 10.2. In AVŚ 10.2.32, it is said that the mysterious being which possesses self (*yakṣám ātmanvát*) is known by those who know *bráhman* which means that if one knows *bráhman*, one knows *ātmán* too (see section 2.5.1.1). It is also implied in that *bráhman* is presented as being inside the stronghold

---

145 AVŚ 10.2.25: *bráhmaṇā bhū́mir víhitā bráhma dyaúr úttarā hitā́ | bráhmedám ūrdhváṃ tiryák cāntárikṣaṃ vyáco hitám ||*

which is identified with a human being (AV 10.2.33). In section 2.5.1.1, I have interpreted the entrance of *bráhman* to the stronghold as the source domain for cognition, but the intention of the composer could also be to construe an ontological statement about the presence of *bráhman* within man. The presence of *bráhman* within the human body is explicitly expressed in AV 11.8.30c (*śárīraṃ bráhma prā́viśac*). At the same time, in AV 11.8.32ab *bráhman* is identified with man (*tásmād vaí vidvā́n púruṣam idáṃ bráhméti manyate*). If we remember that the cosmos is conceived in terms of a stronghold, then we will be able to reconstruct the monistic assumption according to which the whole of creation (man and cosmos) is identified with *bráhman*. The ontic presence of *bráhman* within man is strengthened by its meaning of the sacred speech which is realised during recitation connected with breath. It can be seen that the ontic meaning of *bráhman* is created not only in rational analysis, but is also grounded in experience. However, this topic needs a separate research which goes beyond the scope of the present study.

2.6.5. Monism and internal contradictions

The monistic assumption is expressed explicitly in some stanzas of the AVŚ. In AVŚ 10.8.11, reality is presented as one and, at the same time, as 'having all forms' (*viśvárūpa*). In its multiform aspect, reality manifests itself as everything that moves, blinks, breathes and does not breath. Reality, having combined (*saṃbhū́ya*) its forms, sustains the earth. Thus the concept of one reality which is manifests as the world is created.

The relationship between the unmanifest and manifest aspects of reality is conceived in following way:

AVŚ 10.8.12

anantáṃ vítataṃ purutrā́nantám ántavac cā sámante |
té nākapāláś carati vicinván vidvā́n bhūtám utá bhávyam asya ||

The infinite is extended in many places; the infinite and the finite, having a common end (limit, border). The guarding of the firmament moves discriminating these two, he who knows of what it has been and what is to be. (Edgerton 1965)

The concept of what is infinite refers to the unmanifest aspect of reality, the concept of finite refers to the manifest one. They are presented as having a common end. In this way, the most mysterious sphere of reality is described, which is the passage between its aspects, and which is impossible to understand using categories from everyday life. This is the borderline sphere of the cosmos.

On the one hand, it unites two aspects and, on the other, it divides them and, as we may presume, prevents them from mingling which would cause the destruction of the world[146]. In verse *c*, a guardian of the sky (*nākapālá*) is mentioned which can be interpreted as the sun circulating along this borderline and being visible to the poets. This also is the reason that it knows everything what is in the past and in the future. One can presume that this knowledge can be gained by those who reach the sun in supernatural cognition.

Reality which partly manifests itself is internally contradictory. It is expressed in several stanzas of the AVŚ. In AVŚ 10.8.6ab, the internal contradiction is expressed in that the 'great footprint' (*mahát padám*) is called manifest and hidden at the same time (*āvíḥ sán níhitaṃ gúhā járan nā́ma mahát padám*). The 'great footprint' is here an abstract notion which denotes the unmanifest aspect in which the manifest aspect is established. It is hidden because not all reality manifests itself in the creative act and, at the same time, it can be perceived through its moving manifestations. In AVŚ 10.8.25, reality is presented as finer than a hair and invisible while, at the same time, encompassing more than the whole universe; such a way of description foreshadows later Upaniṣadic conceptualisations of reality[147]. In AVŚ 10.8.23ab, reality is called eternal and yet ever new (*sanātánam enam āhur utā́dyá syāt púnarṇavaḥ*). It is eternal because it is unmanifest, it is ever new because it manifests itself in the world with its temporal cycle of days and nights. The multiple internal contradiction of one reality which manifests itself in various forms is also expressed in terms of various sexes, ages and family relationships which coexist together. In AVŚ 10.8.27-28ab, reality is called a woman, a man, a boy, a girl, an old person and a person just born.

The next stanza of this hymn evokes the model of Child Of The Waters in order to express the internal contradictory nature of reality:

AVŚ 10.8.28

utaíṣāṃ pitótá vā putrá eṣām utaíṣāṃ jyeṣṭhá utá vā kaniṣṭháḥ |
éko ha devó mánasi práviṣṭaḥ prathamó jātáḥ sá u gárbhe antáḥ ||

He is both their father and their son; he is both the oldest and the youngest of them; the sole god that is entered into thought, born the first, is (yet) still within the womb. (Edgerton 1965)

---

146 This is elaborated in the Upaniṣads with use of the concept of *setu*, see BU 4.4.22 (4.2.2), CU 8.4.1 (chapter 4.4.2.4).

147 AVŚ 10.8.25: *bā́lād ékam aṇīyaskám utaíkaṃ néva dṛśyate* | *tátaḥ páriṣvajīyasī devátā sā́ máma priyā́* ||

The model of Child Of The Waters is evoked by the concept of the womb and by the reflexive nature of reality conceived in terms of a father and a son; the recipient understands in this context that the pronoun *eṣām* refers to waters. The womb is identified with the mind which implies the cognitive dimension of manifestation. Reality manifests itself in the mind and is both externalised (as, the recipient may presume, in speech), so it is the first born (*prathamó jātáḥ*) and yet still present in the mind (*sá u gárbhe antáḥ*).

2.6.6. The direct cognition of reality

The AVŚ attests the possibility of the direct cognition of reality. The positive results of such a cognition are the same as the results of drinking Soma described in the ṚV (see Jurewicz 2010a: 171 ff.): the subject obtains the ability to see, longevity and offspring (AVŚ 10.2.29-30) and, according to AVŚ 10.8.44, thanks to true cognition he will not be afraid of death. In AVŚ 10.7.29-30, the word *pratyákṣa* is used to express the direct character of cognition[148]. Such a cognition transforms the cognising subject into the object of his cognition which is expressed by the word-play on the words *bráhman* (the object) and *brahmán* (the cognising subject) – the difference between them is a difference of accent:

AVŚ 10.7.24

yátra devā́ brahmavído bráhma jyeṣṭhám upā́sate |
yó vaí tā́n vidyā́t pratyákṣaṃ sá brahmā́ véditā syāt ||

In which the *bráhman*-knowing gods recognise the supreme *bráhman* (neuter) – he verily knows them face to face, would be a priest (masculine) that knows. (Edgerton 1965)

The word *pratyakṣa* is used in later philosophy as the means of true knowledge accepted by all the schools of classical philosophy (Darśanas). The Vedic roots of classical Indian philosophy are again confirmed.

2.7. Conclusion

The philosophers of the AVŚ continue the efforts to name aspects of Agni and to treat them as the ultimate essence of reality identical with that reality. As I have shown, this process had already began in the ṚV. On the

[148] AVŚ 10.7.29c: *skámbha tvā́ veda pratyákṣam*; AVŚ 10.7.30c: *índraṃ tvā́ veda pratyákṣaṃ*.

one hand, this effort leads to a description of reality with the use of more abstract notions (REALITY IS BREATH, REALITY IS TIME). On the other hand, this facilitates the description of reality in terms of concepts which come from everyday life experience (REALITY IS THE SUN, REALITY IS MAN, REALITY IS PILLAR). The tendency to describe reality in abstract notions is realised in its qualifications as *sát*, *ásat*, *ātmán*, *bráhman*, the full (*pūrṇá*). The tendency to describe reality in concrete concepts is realised in the descriptions of reality in terms of a wild goose, a stronghold, a lotus, a flower, a tree, a pillar, a wheel, a chariot, a treasure-chest and in the relationship between aspects in terms of killing.

I have shown that the use of concepts that refer to everyday experience does not exclude the ability for abstract and general thinking. It is often necessary to transform the way of thinking about experience if the concept is to be used as the source domain for philosophical thought. The source domains are selected and transformed very carefully in order to express the target domain which is reality conceived as having two aspects, unmanifest and manifest or, more specifically, as having a three-layered concentric structure with an intermediate borderline sphere. This is the most mysterious sphere on the border between manifestation and the lack of manifestation. This concept will be elaborated in the Upaniṣadic description of liberating cognition. The AVŚ attest the beginnings of a new way that leads to supernatural cognition which is recitation connected with a breath practice. This practice will also be developed in the Upaniṣads.

All the concepts that serve as the source domain for the conceptualisation of the world are dynamic entities (chariot and its wheel) and alive (plants and the wild goose). These features are transferred to the target domain and allow for conceptualisation of the world as dynamic and living. It is worth adding that some of the concepts analysed here will remain important source domains in later thought as well, although their target domains will be changed or narrowed. In the Upaniṣads, man and the cosmos is conceived in terms of a stronghold, the world and the soul in terms of a lotus and the soul in terms of a wild goose (see section 2.5). The Atharvavedic hymns are the earliest testimony for the philosophical usage of these concepts.

As far as metaphysics is concerned, the composers of the AVŚ continue Ṛgvedic thought and assume the monistic character of reality which, in course of creation, divides itself into two aspects: unmanifest and manifest. In this act, it manifests its internal contradiction. The world is the self of reality which wants to cognise and act. The conceptualisation of reality in terms of fire is still motivating and elaborated. As it will be shown, such a conceptualisation will be continued and elaborated although the source domain of fire will slowly lose its importance in the Upaniṣads.

The supernatural cognition is still realised under the influence of Soma. However, its range is expanded in that the borderline sphere of cosmos is more elaborated and there are attempts to describe the unmanifest aspect of reality. Some hymns of the AVŚ, and, especially, the *Vrātyakāṇḍa,* attest conceptualisation of creation in terms of supernatural cognition. The way the cognition is described implies that its stages were better known for the composers and that it was also influenced by an additional practice which I identify as breath practice connected with recitation.

Chapter Three

The *Śatapatha Brāhmaṇa*

Traditional Indology does not treat the Brāhmaṇas as a source of philosophy. As we remember, Max Muller called them the 'twaddle of idiots' and for a long time his opinion has been the prevailing and unquestioned assumption of many Indologists[1]. In this chapter, I will show that the philosophers who composed the ŚB in fact presented a coherent vision of the world. They also developed earlier thought. Philosophical thinking can be found in the cosmogonies that explain the reason for performing ritual. The idea that cosmogony is both a description of how the world functions and directs how a human being should behave comes from the ṚV (see Jurewicz 2010a). As Hayakawa writes, 'the *modus operandi* of the ritualists found its own way from myths towards philosophy' (2014: 106)[2].

Philosophical issues are presented in the cosmogonies that belong to the part of the Brāhmaṇas called *arthavādas* explaining the meaning of rituals and their beneficial results. Malamoud (1996b: 29–30) comments:

---

1 For survey of the opinions of Western scholars about Brāhmaṇas, see Smith (1989: 32 ff.), O'Flaherty (1987: 3 ff.).

2 The research done by Hayakawa (2014) on the meanings of terms Agni Vaiśvānara and Agni Jātavedas in the ṚV confirms the outcomes presented in Jurewicz (2010a), both in terms of metaphysical assumptions according to which circulation of fire constitutes the basis for existence of the world and in terms of tendency to abstraction (according to him the noun *agní* used without attributes refers generally to all its manifestations. He also argues that the form under which Agni comes to the earth is conceived in terms of the sperm of the sun. This also agrees with the reconstruction of cosmic cycle (Jurewicz 2010a) according to which Agni comes to earth in the form of Soma and rain, which are conceived in terms of semen in the ṚV.

> it is this husk of *arthavādas* that become the flesh and blood of the broader tradition: it is by virtue of these accretions, tagged as *arthavādas*, that the Brāhmaṇas truly stand as theological works, since *arthavādas* which furnish justifications for the rite by placing the ritual present in relationship to a mythical past, and to the perspective of an eternity which lies beyond, by relating circumscribed act to the cosmic whole.

According to Bhattacharya, there is a close link between the cosmogonies and ritual practice:

> Rituo-philosophical unity as understood here does not mean that every mantra has a ritual use but that the philosophy of every mantra has got a ritual expression, that the Vedic rituals are arranged according to the cosmogonic ideas expressed in the Vedic mantras. To be more clear, the various rituals, in general, are representations or dramatisations of the process of becoming (cf., *jātavidyā*, ṚV 10.71.11) theoretically stated in the Saṃhitās, mostly, in the *Ṛgveda* and the *Atharvaveda.* (1977: 2)

The philosophers of the ŚB continued Ṛgvedic metaphysics in that they conceived reality in terms of cognising man and in terms of fire. However, they elaborated these concepts in a very detailed way especially in the cosmogonies explaining Agnihotra and Agnicayana. The main assumption is that reality manifests itself as dying and resurrecting thanks to sacrifice. The main pattern of the cosmogonies presented in the ŚB continues and develops a pattern originally coined in the *Puruṣasūkta.* This can be explained in that its composers focused mainly on the metaphysical role of man within the manifest aspect that is realised during ritual.

The main problem of the philosophy in the ŚB is the nature of death: its metaphysical sense and how it can be escaped thanks to the ritual activity[3]. As Heesterman writes:

> Man's manipulation of the contradictory but insoluble link of life and death requires an endless concatenation of sacrifice to play around the problem of death. (1993: 38–39)[4]

The model for human activity is the creative activity of reality. Human life becomes meaningful when it repeats this activity in ritual. This is a great

---

[3] This may be caused by the experience characteristic for that time. According to Witzel (1995c: 15): 'Next to sons, rain, cattle, long life (*āyus*) it is a prolonged (theoretically, but only by exception, eternal) stay in heaven that one strives for, after a stint on earth characterised by constant strife and frequent hunger, as has been described in detail by W. Rau' (Rau 1957).

[4] See also Levi (1898: 23 ff.), O'Flaherty (1985: 20 ff), Smith (1989: 54 ff.).

change compared to the ṚV where the problem of death is not the main focus. In the ṚV, the fear of death is overcome in Somic exultation gained during sacrifices; immortality equals to one hundred years. When a man dies, he reaches the same place and realises the same state as the state realised during the sacrifices performed in his life. Man is finally reborn among his relatives (Jurewicz 2008b, 2010a). Here death and resurrection, re-enacted in ritual, is the basis for metaphysical thinking.

The cosmogonies of the ŚB create complex blends, which present philosophical content with the aid of concepts coming from everyday experience, so that the recipient can use their images and logic to understand abstract content. The most abstract input space of the blends is reality conceived as free and internally contradictory. The second input space is the concept of Prajāpati. The creative power of reality is conceived in these terms and this concept imparts the meaning of creation of the world to the blends. This concept is already metaphoric because Prajāpati is conceived in terms of man who performs an activity during which he toils and heats up.

In most cosmogonies, the composers of the ŚB begin with a description of Prajāpati and his wish to create the world. This stage of creation corresponds to the stage that, in the *Nāsadīyasūkta*, is presented as the manifestation of That One conceived as internally contradictory (*ā́nīd avātáṃ svadháyā tád ékaṃ tásmād dhānyán ná paráḥ kíṃ canā́sa*, Jurewicz 2010a: 46–48). Since, according to this hymn, reality in its pre-creative state cannot be conceived and expressed in words, the decision to omit this state in cosmogonic description is reasonable.

The composers of the ŚB, having introduced the concept of Prajāpati, can present the creative process in human scale. Moreover, since the aim of cosmogonies is to not only present metaphysical reasons for ritual, but also why it must be correctly performed, the concept of Prajāpati allows the composers to explain the role of man in clear terms as re-enacting the creative activity of Prajāpati. The concept of reality is too abstract for this aim. Finally, the concept of Prajāpati allows the composers of the ŚB to activate various emotions which are important if the ritual is to be an activity which takes over the whole human being and not a mere mechanical performance[5]. Within a monistic frame, the creative power of reality called Prajāpati transforms itself into the world. Because of that, the concept of Prajāpati is also used to denote the whole manifest aspect of reality. The next input space is the concept of

[5] As Sweetser (2000), Sørensen (2007) have shown, the mental efficacy of ritual lies in the human ability to create conceptual blends that, in turn, are the basis for emotions felt in fictive situations.

ritual and then the concept of cosmos in its spatio-temporal functioning which is elaborated in many cosmogonies.

The other input spaces are the general domain of Cooking and of Procreation. The former includes the scenario of feeling unwell because of hunger, the preparation of food, its cooking, eating and digesting. It also conveys the meaning of transformation and perfection which in the ṚV is expressed by the general domain of Cleansing By Heat. In some cosmogonies, the domain of Cleansing By Heat is activated independently. In addition, the general concept of heating is activated without evoking the whole scenario of the general domain of Cooking. They can be input spaces or the generic space of the blends.

The general domain of Procreation is elaborated by the composers of the ŚB who introduce the next stages of this scenario which is the feeding of a child and its growth. We have seen an elaboration of this domain already in the *Puruṣasūkta* (see chapter 1.3) and in the *Vrātyakāṇḍa* (see chapter 2.2.2). This input space is coherent with conceptualisation of the creative power of reality in terms of Prajāpati. As we have seen, this concept in the AVŚ is closely connected with generation and in its terms the manifestation of the generative power of reality is conceived (see chapter 2.2.2).

The general domains just mentioned are realised in cosmogonies in their specific instantiations which allow the composers to express subtle aspects of the process of creation. On the more abstract level, they give coherence to the blends and allow the recipient to recognise the common pattern of various cosmogonic descriptions.

The generic space of most of the blends is the concept of transformation under the influence of heat. This concept is a common feature of all activities and processes activated in the input spaces. In the case of the general domain of Cooking, hunger is conceived in terms of fire that is present in the human organism and can destroy it. Looking for food needs effort which causes internal heat. Preparation of food involves heating, so eating and digesting are also conceived in these terms (Malamoud 1996b, Patton 2005: 92–93, 101–108)[6]. In the case of the general domain of Procreation, the sexual act gives a sensation of heat and the development of the embryo is conceived in terms of it being heated within the womb or the egg while delivery heats a mother. The pivotal moment of ritual is cooking the oblation. Conceptualisation of

[6] As it is shown by cognitive research, an important source for choosing the source domain in conceptual metaphor is correlation in experience, e.g. conceptualisation of affection in terms of warmth is motivated by the early experience of an infant which is hugged by its caretaker (Kövecses 2011[2006]: 178–179).

creation in these terms is grounded in the Ṛgvedic conceptualisation of reality in terms of fire (Jurewicz 2010a).

During the time of the ŚB, Soma was lost and only occasionally it could it be bought during some rituals[7]. Here we should look for experiential reasons for the metaphysical concept of hunger and fear: the thinkers of the Brāhmaṇas wanted to realise Somic exultation without Soma. Conceptualisation of Prajāpati in terms of someone who toils and heats himself seems to attest efforts to achieve the first stage of Somic influence which was experienced as heat (Jurewicz 2010a: 193–194). In most cases, we do not know to what kind of activities the composers were referring, but it can be inferred that the activities were exhausting and sometimes led to the death of the agent. Another kind of activity attested in the ŚB that provides experiential grounds for the conceptualisation of Prajāpati is the recitation of the Veda and a breath practice connected with it. Accounts in the ŚB imply that it involved the experience of heat.

Cavallin (2011: 142 ff.) argues that identification of breath (*prāṇá*) with the wind in the Brāhmaṇas of the ṚV (*Aitareya* and *Kauṣītaki*) is based on the experience of respiration and recitation. The early origins of breath practice have also been analysed by Blezer (1992). He claims that 'the term *ātmán* was secondarily connected with the speculations concerning the cultic fire' (1992: 22). My analysis will show that the early breath practices were closely connected with speculations around ritual which were based on the identity of *ātmán* built in ritual and inside the sacrificer.

I will divide this chapter as follows. Firstly, I will discuss the general nature of the creative act and its metaphysical implications presented in ŚB 2.2.4 (section 3.1.1). Then I will discuss the way reality is present within his manifest aspect and the role of men (sections 3.2, 3.3, and 3.4). Finally, the cognitive nature of the activity will be presented (section 3.5) and abstract concepts (*ātmán*, *bráhman*, *sát*, *ásat*, section 3.6). I hope to show that the metaphysical theory is unique in some of its solutions.

In the present book, the main source is the ŚB because the cosmogonies presented by its composers are the most numerous and most rich of all the Brāhmaṇas[8]. However, the cosmogonies of all the Brāhmaṇas need a thorough investigation in order to finally reconstruct the way of thinking of their composers.

The quotations from the *Śatapathabrāhmaṇa* are from Titus Text Database and Weber (1885) and translations are by Eggeling (1882, 1885, 1894, 1897, and 1900).

---

7 For description of buying of Soma in the Agniṣṭoma, see Caland, Henry (1906).

8 Another Brāhmaṇa, which presents many elaborated cosmogonies, is JB.

3.1. The creation of the world

In this section, I will first discuss the cosmogony presented in ŚB 2.2.4 which presents a metaphysics that is unique not only in the Vedic thought, but in all of early Indian philosophy. As will be shown, this cosmogony forms the philosophical background not only for the Agnihotra[9], but also for the whole ritual described in the ŚB. This philosophical paradigm is universal and can be used to explain other rituals. In the following section, I will outline the cosmogony which explains the Dàrśapūrṇamāsa[10] (see section 3.1.2), though the cosmogonic pattern presented in ŚB 2.2.4 is also relevant.

3.1.1. Reality is death

The cosmogony analysed in this chapter explains the metaphysical grounds for performing the ritual of Agnihotra which should be performed every day, in the morning and in the evening, by the males of the three higher states. Generally speaking, it is ritualising the everyday occupation of a cowherd who has to milk his cows twice a day and cook the milk so that it does not curdle. During Agnihotra a special Agnihotra cow was milked, the milk was boiled on the householder's fire (*gārhapatya*) and then two oblations of it were poured on the oblationary fire (*āhavanīya*). I will show that the metaphysics providing the rationale for this simple performance is very complex and exceptionally bold in its solutions.

ŚB 2.2.4.1

prajā́patir ha vā́ idám ágra éka evā̀sa | sá aikṣata kathám̐ nú prájāyeyéti sò 'śrāmyat sá tápo 'tapyata sò 'gním evá múkhāj janayā́m̐ cakre tád yád enam múkhād ájanayata tásmād annādò 'gníḥ sá yó haivám etám agním annādám̐ védānnādó haivá bhávati |

Prajāpati alone, indeed, existed here in the beginning. He considered, 'How may I be reproduced?' He toiled and performed acts of penance. He generated Agni from his mouth; and because he generated him from his mouth, therefore Agni is a consumer of food: and, verily, he who thus knows Agni to be a consumer of food, becomes himself a consumer of food.

---

[9] For Agnihotra, see Dumont (1939), Bodewitz (1973, 1997a).

[10] For Darśapūrṇamāsa, see Rustagi (1981). For the description of Vedic sacrifices, see Kane (1968–1975).

Reality in the first creative stage is called Prajāpati. Prajāpati is presented as one and identical with *idám* which refers to the world. Thus the recipient can understand that it was impossible to discern reality in its unmanifest aspect from the world which in turns means that there was no world at all.

The desire for creation is conceived in terms of a desire to have children. Since there is nothing other than the one reality, Prajāpati may only act on himself. He is presented as heating himself and toiling. Such a description evokes the Ṛgvedic descriptions of the poets who toil while they kindle Agni and heat themselves having drunk Soma (see Jurewicz 2010a: 264 ff.). As already mentioned, in the times of the ŚB, Soma was not in use, so we can presume that the source domain of this description is a kind of effort which is tiresome, which heats its agent and which leads to a change of consciousness[11].

Having heated and toiled, Prajāpati gives birth to fire which comes from his mouth. This image is the source of various concepts. Firstly, it can evoke the concept of vomiting. The conceptualisation of creation in terms of vomiting implies that Prajāpati during creation manifests himself or rather his essence. As we will see the concept of a man who excretes through the openings of his body is evoked in the cosmogonies of the ŚB (see section 3.2). It is elaborated in detail in the description of the Sautrāmaṇī sacrifice (ŚB 12.7.1) where Indra is presented as having drunk Soma by force and then excreting it through his whole body. According to ŚB 12.7.2.1-2, the same happens to a person who is purged by Soma either upwards (vomiting) or downwards (diarrhoea). As I have argued, the composer of the *Nāsadīyasūkta* evokes the concept of drinking Soma in his description of the first stage of creation to express manifestation of That One in the cognitive act (see Jurewicz 2010a: 325–327). If the recipient activates this concept in the frames of the cosmogonies of the ŚB, he would understand that the first manifestation of reality is conceived in the same way. However, the results of drinking are totally opposed to those described in the ṚV (see below and next sections).

Secondly, the fact that fire is born from his mouth metonymically prompts the recipient to evoke the concept of blowing, which, in turn, evokes the concept of producing fire with a fire-drill[12]. When fire appears, heat and light also appear making it possible to cook and to see. The concept of producing fire in a fire-drill also evokes the concept of wind: during kindling with a fire-drill blowing is necessary and the concept of wind can be evoked based on metaphor WIND IS A BLOWING PERSON. The concept of wind metonymically evokes the concept of movement (ACTION FOR AGENT), and confirms that space

[11] Such techniques are attested among shamans (Winkelman 2006: 143).

[12] Metonymy MEANS FOR ACTION, MOUTH FOR PRODUCING FIRE IN FIRE-DRILL.

between the earth and the sky appears because this space is the settlement of wind (metonymy PLACE FOR INHABITANTS).

On the other hand, the concept of fire evokes the concept of speech *via* metaphor SPEECH IS FIRE. In addition, since hunger is conceived in the Veda in terms of fire the recipient may understand that Prajāpati is hungry.

Finally, the verbal form *janayā́ṃ cakre* ('generated') triggers the recipient to understand creation in terms of giving birth. ŚB 2.2.4.7 suggests that the sacrificer, to save himself from death, should generate in himself the same power of giving birth (*prájāti*) as Prajāpati did *in illo tempore*. Prajāpati is conceived as an androgyne and he activates his female aspect in order to create. Identity of mouth and vagina is expressed explicitly in BU 1.4.6 (see chapter 4.1.2)

The recipient is supposed to create a blend of the following input spaces. The first input space is a man who kindles fire and blows on it, the second is a woman who gives birth to a baby. These are two input spaces come from everyday experience and give structure and topology to other spaces. The next input spaces are the concepts of a vomiting man who then feels hunger and a man who recites the Veda and of Prajāpati. The most abstract input space of the blend is the concept of reality. The generic space is the concept of transformation under the influence of heat. In the blend, Prajāpati is a woman who gives birth to a baby and, at the same time, he is a man who kindles fire blowing it from his mouth and who then externalises himself in speech. If the recipient evokes the Ṛgvedic cosmogonies, which see creation of the world in terms of the sunrise (see Jurewicz 2010a), he may add this concept as the source domain. He may also evoke the description of ŚB 1.4.1.22-23 which presents creation of the space between the earth and the sky as thanks to breathing with three syllables and, according to the ṚV, this space is created during sunrise. Finally, since cognition is conceived in terms of seeing and seeing is possible when there is light, the recipient may create the next input space which is a cognising man.

Creation is seen as self-transformation thanks to the input space of a vomiting and hungry man: Prajāpati reveals a part of himself, i.e. transforms a part of himself into fire and speech and into the most basic outline of the world. It should be noted that, if fire appears, the recipient can think that the earth appears too because fire is conceptually connected with earth in the Veda (Smith 1994)[13]; the existence of the earth is mentioned explicitly further on (ŚB 2.2.4.3). Thus three spheres of the future world appear but, as

[13] Fire and the earth can be seen as two aspects of the form of the cosmos which, in creation, becomes the basis for further creation (see sections 3.2.2-3) and the basis for living beings.

the composer will show later, they are present only potentially. The creative activity is understood as a cognitive activity.

Fire is called 'consumer of food' (*annādá*) based on the metonymy MEANS FOR ACTION[14] (MOUTH FOR EATING); the mouth, with which food is eaten by living beings, is the most essential part of the body.

ŚB 2.2.4.2-3

tád vā́ enam etád ágre devā́nām ajanayata tásmād agnír agrír ha vaí nā́maitád yád agnír íti sá jātaḥ pū́rvaḥ préyāya yó vaí pū́rva ety ágra etī́ti vai tám āhuḥ só evā̀syāgnítā (2)
sá aikṣata prajā́patiḥ | annādám̐ vā́ imám ātmáno 'jījane yád agním̐ ná vā́ ihá mád anyád ánnam asti yám̐ vā́ ayám̐ nā̀dyād íti kālvālī́kṛtā haivá tárhi pṛthivy ā̀sa naúṣadhaya āsur ná vánaspatayas tád evā̀sya mánasy āsa | (3)

He thus generated him first (*agre*) of the gods; and therefore (he is called) Agni, for *agni* (they say) is the same as *agri*. He, being generated, went forth as the first (*pū́rva*); for of him who goes first, they say that he goes at the head (*agre*). Such, then, is the origin and nature of that Agni. Prajāpati then considered, 'In that Agni I have generated a food-eater for myself; but, indeed, there is no other food here but myself, whom, surely, he would not eat.' At that time this earth had, indeed, been rendered quite bald; there were neither plants nor trees. This, then, was weighed on his mind.

As I have shown elsewhere, the explanation of the name of fire, as he who goes as the first, is well entrenched in the Ṛgvedic thought according to which its precedence is its main attribute (Jurewicz 2016c). For the present investigation it is important that fire is also conceived as the consumer of food, so it necessarily needs food to exist. The earth is presented as devoid of trees and plants which are the natural fuel for fire. The conceptual link between fire conceived in terms of a consumer of food and plants is the metaphor BURNING IS EATING. The metaphor PLANTS ARE HAIR OF THE EARTH[15] is the conceptual basis for the qualification of the earth as *kālvālī́*, i.e. 'bald' as the earth is conceived in terms of a human being, more specifically in terms of a new born baby who is typically bald. If the recipient elaborates the input space of giving birth, he may refer to his own experience when he has to take care of a new-born child who is hungry and which cries of hunger and for whom – being a male – he does not have food.

However, at the same time, the recipient understands that it is Prajāpati who is hungry because Agni is the manifestation of the essence of Prajāpati.

[14] Radden, Kövecses (1999: 37).
[15] Based on metaphor THE EARTH IS A BEAUTIFUL WOMAN.

Therefore, the concept of fire which comes from Prajāpati's mouth metonymically evokes the concept of hunger; this is additionally justified by the Vedic belief that fire is present in the bellies of living beings and makes digestion possible[16]. On the most abstract level, the creation of fire thus understood as the creation of a void within the entirety of reality[17]. The void is the place for the future world that will be the bald earth. This way of thinking of the initial state of the world corresponds to the stage of creation which the *Nāsadīyasūkta* describes as the stage when the void (*tuchyá*) is surrounded *ābhú* ('what is not') which is 'about to be' (*ābhū́*)[18].

In such a situation the only possible food is Prajāpati himself. Thus creation is an act that is dangerous to reality which can be destroyed by its own manifestation. There are two possible interpretations of this fact. Either the reality described here cannot be called the Absolute because it is not omnipotent and eternal. Alternatively – and this is interpretation for which I would opt – reality can be called the Absolute, but the concept of the Absolute of the Veda is different to the European concept of the Absolute. Its most important attribute is freedom. Here, this attribute is taken in the most serious way as it is implied that the Absolute is so free that it can – if it wants – annihilate itself. In other words, the Absolute can commit suicide.

In his book *Horror Metaphysicus*, Kołakowski (1990) construes a synthesis of philosophical investigation on the Absolute in the main stream of European thought. On this basis, he proposes a definition of the Absolute as something whose non-existence is a logical and ontic contradiction. Such a definition of the Absolute is deeply grounded in the Judeo-Christian background; one of the first definitions of the Yahweh is that given to Moses: 'I am who I am' (*Exodus* 3:14). The Absolute is something which exists necessarily and from that attribute other attributes of the Absolute can be logically deduced as self-sufficiency, permanence, uniqueness, pure actuality, timelessness, lack of complexity.

In Vedic thought, as in European thought, the Absolute is reality which exists out of itself and which is the basis for all contingent beings. However,

---

16 This belief is present until today (Khare 1976: 120, note 1).

17 In the same way, Parmenides conceived the ontological void. As Havelock (1983: 31–32) writes: 'The words *empleon* and *epideues*, used by Parmenides to describe that 'all of the "is" is "filled up" (*empleon*) with "what is" (B6.24) and that it is "not shorting of anything (*epideus*) (B 8.23)' are used by Homer in the context so of a physical sense of being filled with food. This experience can be also traced back in semantic development of The Void.' It is worth noting that the concept of the void as the first creation of God is present in the Cabala of Isaac Luria (Scholem 1969[1960]).

18 The paradox of the existence and non-existence of the future world is conceived in the AVŚ with aid of the metaphor of the full (see chapter 2.6.1): the full flows from the full which is at the same time empty.

not all the attributes ascribed to the absolute by Judeo-Christian theologies hold here. In the Veda, the Absolute is internally contradictory[19] which means that it cannot be defined as lacking complexity. It manifests itself in its opposites: one becomes many, immovable becomes movable, omnipotent becomes limited, omniscient is being deprived of knowledge and also cognising. In addition, as can be inferred from the present description in the ŚB, it can manifest its opposite in the ultimate way, i.e. it can deny its own existence and annihilate itself. Therefore, it does not exist necessarily. Such a concept of the Absolute can be defended only if we accept that freedom is its most important attribute and all other attributes logically follow from it: if the Absolute does not want to be the Absolute, it is free enough not to be. Its internal contradiction is also the result of this basic attribute: if the Absolute is free, all ontic possibilities are potentially present in it.

The final sentence of the passage states that in this stage of creation 'this, then, was in his mind' (*tád evā̀sya mánasy āsa*). In this way, the cognitive principle of creation is expressed. Since the appearance of fire can be understood as the appearance of speech, the recipient can now understand that manifestation in speech has not yet been fully realised.

And the ultimate annihilation of the Absolute almost happens. Fire attacks Prajāpati:

ŚB 2.2.4.4

áthainam agnír vyā́ttenópaparyā́vavarta | tásya bhītásya svó mahimā́pacakrāma vā́g vā́ asyá svó mahimā́ vā́g asyā́pacakrāma sá ātmánn evā́hutim īṣe sá údamr̥̥ṣṭa tád yád udámr̥̥ṣṭa tásmād idáṃ cālómakam idáṃ ca tátra viveda ghr̥̥tāhutíṃ vaivá payāhutíṃ vobháyaṃ ha tv èvá tát páya evá |

Thereupon Agni turned towards him with open mouth; and he (Prajāpati) being terrified, his own greatness departed from him. Now his own greatness is his speech: that speech of his departed from him. He desired an offering in his own self, and rubbed (his hands); and because he rubbed (his hands), therefore both this and this (palm) are hairless. He then obtained either a butter-offering or a milk-offering; but, indeed, they are both milk.

Reality is internally contradictory and it has two powers. One is creative power which manifests itself in Prajāpati's multiplication described in the first sentence (ŚB 2.2.4.1). Its second power is that which manifests itself in the possibility of destruction. Creation can also be seen as destruction: reality begins to manifest itself, so it partially destroys its unmanifest form.

[19] Agni which has Somic aspect That One which breathes without breath, see Jurewicz (2010a).

However, reality does not want to be annihilated totally. Prajāpati himself is terrified by the eruption of his own destructive power. It turns out that creation is unpredictable for reality itself. What does it mean? Wasn't it omniscient before creation? Didn't it know that it can be dangerous to itself? Or maybe it has lost its omniscience when it began to manifest itself in its opposition? In other words, is it now really not knowing and unpredictable of itself? This would be the highest realisation of its freedom. Or, maybe reality only plays and creates tension to see whether the play will succeed or not? In the same way, we can interpret the final question of the *Nāsadīyasukta:* whether *ádhyakṣa* in the highest heaven knows its manifestations or not?

What is more, Prajāpati becomes frightened. It seems that reality begins creation not only to deny its own attributes, but also to experience emotions such as fear. This emotion causes further negation of the omnipotence of reality because when Prajāpati becomes frightened his own greatness (*mahimán*) departs from him. As I have shown, the concept of greatness is used by the composers of the AVŚ to denote the first manifestation of reality which can be measured (see chapter 2.2.2). It is possible that the recipient is prompted to activate this concept based on the description of the bald earth. The recipient can also presume that the greatness manifests itself in speech which appeared in the first moment of creation. This would mean that reality draws back to its unmanifest state, but that this state differs from the state before creation. The annihilating void, ready to destroy everything around it, is already created; this void is conceived in terms of fire and a hungry baby.

If the recipient elaborates the input space of kindling fire, he will understand the annihilation of reality in terms of burning its unmanifest aspect. If the recipient elaborates the concept of a hungry baby, he may create even a more terrifying image. He may understand that the birth-giving was not fully successful and that the baby remains within the womb of reality[20]. The baby cannot be fed from the breast, so it will eat the flesh of its parent. In both cases, the void, having annihilated its unmanifest source, will also annihilate itself. Thus reality would be totally annihilated and the state after its annihilation is impossible to be imagined and conceived.

But, for the moment there is Prajāpati and the void which should be filled with being. And Prajāpati wants to fill the void which is expressed as desire to find an oblation. Thus the next input space is introduced which is sacrifice. The Vedic concept of the sacrifice is a blend of three input spaces: feeding (input space 1), keeping fire (input space 2) and a sacrificial act (input

[20] The same intuition is expressed in ŚB 11.1.6.2 which describes Prajāpati floating in the half-open egg (see section 3.5.2).

space 3). In the blend, oblation is put into fire (input spaces 2+3) in order to feed the gods (input space 1). The generic space of this blend is the concept of transformation under the influence of heat. So the recipient can conceive the desire of filling the void in terms of keeping a fire and feeding a new born baby. Prajāpati wants to find the oblation in himself (*ātmáni*) because there is nothing else beyond reality and creation is self-transformation.

This stage of creation is conceived in terms of kindling fire. If the recipient elaborates this scenario within the frames of cosmogony, he will understand it in terms of kindling fire in order to warm milk for a baby and to sacrifice. Prajāpati rubs his hands so vigorously that his palms become hairless. Thus it is implied that Prajāpati is conceived as a hairy being and the recipient may create an image of an androgynous monster[21]. If this is the form which reality assumes in the first stage of creation, it is not surprising that he is afraid of himself.

Prajāpati creates milk which is metonymically identified with clarified butter (metonymy EFFECT FOR CAUSE). So his next manifestation is conceived in terms of milk. Thus reality manifests its internal contradictory essence conceived as fiery and milky. The scenario of creation agrees with the Ṛgvedic model of reality transformations according to which reality alternatively manifests itself in its fiery and liquid (Somic) forms. The internal contradiction of creation is also expressed in that reality alternatively manifests its creative and destructive powers: the first manifestation of fire is creative, then it turns out to be destructive (on the basis of the ambivalence of fire) and then, again, it is creative (milk is life-giving food).

ŚB 2.2.4.5

sā́ hainaṃ nā̀bhirādhayā́ṃ cakāra | keśamiśrèva hāsa tā́ṃ vyaùkṣad óṣaṃ dhayéti táta óṣadhayaḥ sámabhavaṃs tásmād óṣadhayo nā́ma sá dvitī́yam údamṛṣṭa tátrā́parām ā́hutiṃ viveda ghṛtāhutíṃ vaivá payāahutíṃ vobháyaṃ ha tèvá tát páya evá |

This (offering), however, did not satisfy him, because it had hairs mixed with it. He poured it away (into the fire), saying, 'Drink, while burning (*oṣaṃ dhaya*)!' From it plants sprang: hence their name 'plants (*oṣadhayaḥ*).' He rubbed (his hands) a second time, and thereby obtained another offering, either a butter-offering or a milk-offering; but, indeed, they are both milk.

The logic of the input spaces activated earlier is elaborated. The milk which has been poured in the fire is mixed with hair. On the basis of his everyday

---

21 Conceptualisation of the first manifestation of reality in terms of a monster is attested already in *Puruṣasūkta* (10.90.1, see chapter 1.3).

knowledge, the recipient understands that hair comes from the Prajāpati's palms when he kindles fire with sticks. Milk mixed with hair is not only disgusting, but the act of pouring such milk into fire is ritual transgression: hair is impure and the oblation poured into fire is also impure.

This fact can be interpreted in two ways. On the one hand, it can be seen as the continuation of the state of a lack of creative power caused by fear: in this state, reality cannot control its own action. On the other hand, it can be interpreted as a manifestation of freedom and an ability to commit transgressions. Reality is so free that it can do anything and break any rule known from everyday life experience[22]. The recipient may also presume that, in this way, a negative example is created for further creation that should be avoided.

This transgression has cosmogonic results. Plants appear which are the food of fire. So it can partly be fed and what is needed now is sacrificial food which will appear later. This image has yet more meaning as if the recipient activates the metaphor PLANTS ARE HAIR OF THE EARTH, he will understand that the earth now is no longer bald. The next metaphor THE EARTH IS A BEAUTIFUL WOMAN will allow him to elaborate the input space of the general domain of Procreation and interpret the act of pouring milk as an act of incest with the earth which is conceived as Prajāpati's daughter (SEMENIS MILK). This act of incest, which is sinful, causes the recipient to think about the earth in terms of an adult woman and not a small girl; her hair is the visible sign of her sexual maturity. If the recipient accepts that Prajāpati commits this sin *via* his form of fire[23], he will also understand that fire is now conceived not in terms of a little baby, but in terms of an adult man. It is worth adding that Christian thought also introduces the concept of sexual maturity in its cosmogonic description, but it is caused by the intervention of the devil. In the ŚB, it is caused by reality itself which is so free that it can commit even the most heinous crimes. One could also presume then that the form of Agni is the fearful form of this crime and a revenge for it[24]. Moreover, a crime which violates the most basic social rules reintroduces the pre-creative state of a lack of order and a lack of rules. So reality remains in its internally contradictory state: creation continues and is stopped at the same time. The composer of the cosmogony elaborates the logic of the input space in such

---

[22] In the same way, the creative act of Indra who kills Vṛtra is interpreted in *Taittirīya Saṃhitā* 2.14.12 as a transgressive act during which a Brahmin, Viśvarūpa, is killed.

[23] In ŚB 6.1.2.6-9 Prajāpati is presented as performing a sexual act with speech (*vā́c*) in his form of mind (*mánas*).

[24] Already ṚV 1.32.14 mentions the avenger of Vṛtra who threatens Indra. In *Taittirīya Saṃhitā* 2.14.12, Vṛtra is the embodiment of such an avenger for the crime of killing Viśvarūpa.

an effective way that he can trigger the recipient's understanding of the most subtle philosophical matters.

On the basis of this logic, the recipient may also presume that Agni is still hungry because it is not satisfied with the oblation mixed with hair. The sentence is construed in such a way that one can understand that either Agni or Prajāpati is not satisfied; actually both interpretations are correct because Prajāpati and Agni are the same. So Prajāpati continues creation which is vow conceived in terms of kindling fire. Milk now appears that is clean.

ŚB 2.2.4.6

sā́ hainam abhirādhayā́ṃ cakāra | sá vyácikitsaj juhávānī3 mā́ hauṣā3m íti táṃ svó mahimā̀bhyùvāda juhudhī́ti sá prajā́patir vidā́ṃ cakāra svó vaí mā mahimā̀héti sá svāhéty evā̀juhot tásmād u svāhéty evá hūyate táta eṣá údiyāya yá eṣá tápati táto 'yám prábabhūva yò 'yám pávate táta evā̀gníḥ párāṅ paryā́vavarta |

This (offering) then satisfied him. He hesitated: 'Shall I offer it up? shall I not offer it up?' he thought. His own greatness said to him, 'Offer it up!' Prajāpati was aware that it was his own (*sva*) greatness that had spoken (*āha*) to him; and offered it up with '*Svāhā!*' This is why offerings are made with '*Svāhā!*' Thereupon that burning one (viz. the sun) rose; and then that blowing one (viz. the wind) sprang up; whereupon, indeed, Agni turned away.

Prajāpati hesitates whether he should offer the oblation or not. There are two possibilities for interpretation of this fact. According to the first possibility, reality is not threatened by death. In everyday life, when someone is in danger of death, he immediately grasps at any chance of rescue. On the other hand, one could say that Prajāpati is still so helpless and out of control that he is not able to act at all.

Anyway, after a moment of hesitation, the power comes back which manifests itself in speech and in an ability to decide. Prajāpati pours milk into the fire saying *svā́hā*. It is possible that this formula should be interpreted literally: Prajāpati approves the way he speaks.

Creation is then continued with the appearance of the sun and wind. The concepts of the sun and the wind are metonymically evoked *via* the concepts of their abodes (metonymy PLACE FOR INHABITANTS): the sky and the space between it and the earth (the earth with fire having been created earlier see ŚB 2.2.4.3)[25]. Thus the cosmos becomes divided into three spheres. And fire becomes satisfied and turns away. If the recipient elaborates the input space of the general domain of Procreation, he will conceive of fire in terms of

[25] Metonymy INHABITANTS FOR PLACE (Radden, Kövecses 1999). The sun and the wind are conceived anthropomorphically, as inhabitants of the sky and the space.

a child which goes to sleep having properly eaten. One gets an impression of relaxation after a great fear.

So the composer builds his description in such a way that he triggers in the minds of the recipient a very complex blend. The input spaces are: the concepts of man who produces fire, of a man who recites Veda, of sacrifice, of the cosmos and of reality. The next two input spaces are the general domain of Procreation in its specific instantiation of a birth of a baby and the general domain of Cooking in its specific instantiation of a hungry man who looks for food. The generic space is the concept of transformation under the influence of heat. In the blend, the sacrifice is seen as a safe act of self-eating. Reality manifests itself as the eater (fire, child) and as food (milk). Thanks to that it can safely manifest as the cosmos. Milk is its substitute which is offered to the eating manifestation of reality. Thus reality manifests its self-contradictory and free nature.

Whatever Prajāpati did in the beginning, the same should be repeated by men. The concept of what happens here and now is the next input space of the blend. The sacrificer himself is supposed to create a blend in his mind when performing the Agnihotra. Within its frame, each time when he pours milk into fire with the cry *svā́hā*, he redeems himself from death which threatens him all the time with a mouth that is ready to devour him as Agni, once released, is always present and always hungry and looking for food. Its constant presence conditions the existence of world. If Agni is fully satiated, the world would cease to exist. In the same way, man redeems himself in other sacrifices – be it a Soma sacrifice, an animal sacrifice or a sacrifice during which a cake is offered. Finally, the same redemption takes place during Antyeṣṭi (see section 3.1.1). The difference is that during Antyeṣṭi the substitute of man is given to Agni which is his own body burnt on the cremation pyre.

The imperative to repeat the creative activity of reality is the general social rule in the ŚB. It is often expressed in the general paradigm of a fight between the gods and the Asuras which allows the composer to describe details of the ritual performance settled by the activity of the gods *in illo tempore*. Such descriptions prompt the recipient to create a conceptual network the main input spaces of which are the mythological framework of the gods and the Asuras and the ritual activity of a sacrificer. The full analysis of these cosmogonies goes beyond the scope of this study, but I will analyse one example which has important ontological assumptions. The following cosmogony belongs to the cosmogonies explaining the Darśapūrṇamāsa, though it is so general that it is not necessary to refer to the details of this sacrifice in order to understand the conceptualisation of creation.

ŚB 11.1.8.1-2

> *devā́ś ca vā ásurā́ś ca | ubháye prājāpatyā́ḥ paspṛdhire tátó 'surā atimānénaiva kásmin nú vayáṃ juhuyāméti svéṣv evā̀syèṣu júhvataś cerus tè 'timānénaivá párābabhūvus tásmān nā́timanyeta parābhavásya haitán múkhaṃ yád atimānáḥ* | (1)
> *átha devā́ḥ | anyò'nyásminn evá júhvataś cerus tébhyaḥ prajā́patir ātmā́nam prádadau yajñó haiṣām āsa yajñó hí devā́nām ánnaṃ* (2)

Now, the gods and the Asuras, both of them sprung from Prajāpati, once strove together. Then the Asuras, even through arrogance, thinking, 'Unto whom, forsooth, should we make offering?' went on offering into their own mouths. They came to naught, even through arrogance: wherefore let no one be arrogant, for verily arrogance is the cause of ruin. But the gods went on offering unto one another.

The gods and the Asuras are called sons of Prajāpati. Since the son is identical with his father, the gods and Asuras can be treated as two parts of Prajāpati being the creative power of reality which manifests itself in its two opposing aspects. The network created by the composer consists of the following input spaces: the Daivāsura myth, the general domain of Cooking in its specific realisation of eating and feeding and the concept of reality. The generic space is the concept of transformation under the influence of heat. The Asuras are presented as feeding themselves and the gods are presented as feeding each other. The Asuras perish, the gods obtain Prajāpati.

In the blend, reality divides itself into two parts, conceived in terms of its offspring. The recipient can understand that it tries various possibilities of manifestation to finally find a possibility which allows for its safe manifestation. When reality manifests as the Asuric offspring of Prajāpati, it commits a mistake whereas, when it manifests as the gods, it finds a safe way to manifest. While in ŚB 2.2.4, reality is threatened by the death through annihilation, here it is threatened by the annihilation of excessive existence. Both threats are conceived in terms of eating as in the first case, reality will be eaten while in the second, it will be overeaten. The logic of the input space of the general domain of Cooking prompts the recipient to understand that excessive existence finally leads to annihilation, but now through an explosion. Moreover, in this way, the implications of the monistic assumption are expressed. If reality is only one, it cannot accept more and it has to give away a part of itself in order to create a void that will accept back part. In the cosmogonies of the ŚB, the act of creation of the void is conceived in terms of excretion or vomiting.

ŚB 11.1.8.3-4a

sá devébhya ātmā́nam pradā́ya | áthaitám ātmánaḥ pratimā́m asṛjata yád yajñám
tásmād āhuḥ prajā́patir yajñá íty ātmáno hy ètám pratimā́m ásṛjata | (3)
sá eténa yajñéna | devébhya ātmā́naṃ nírakrīṇīta (4)

Prajāpati gave himself up to them, and the sacrifice became theirs; for, indeed, the sacrifice is the food of the gods. Having given himself up to the gods, he created that counterpart of himself, to wit, the sacrifice: whence people say, 'The sacrifice is Prajāpati;' for he created it as a counterpart of himself. By this (Full and New-moon) sacrifice he redeemed himself from the gods.

In the blend, the gods consume Prajāpati. As it will be shown, during creation Prajāpati becomes the cosmos (see ŚB 7.1.2.6, section 3.2.3). The recipient understands that the gods have access to the whole manifest aspect of reality. They have it because they repeat the first creative act of reality which consists of creation of a void which is conceived in terms of feeding one another. Then the composer says that they obtain the sacrifice because sacrifice is the food of the gods. This sentence is motivated by metonymies. Identification of Prajāpati with sacrifice is motivated by metonymy ACTION FOR AGENT. As it has already been stated, sacrifice is the safe way for the manifestation of reality performed by Prajāpati. Having consumed Prajāpati, the gods participate in this activity. Identification of the sacrifice with the food of gods is motivated by the metonymy RESULT FOR ACTION: the most important result of the sacrifice is to create food for the hungry part of Prajāpati which is the manifest representation of the pre-creative void. Within the frames of ritual, Prajāpati eats the food through the gods. The concept of sacrifice is the next input space of the network created by the composer of the cosmogony.

The sacrifice is called the *ātmán* of Prajāpati. As has been shown, the use of the word *ātmán* to denote the manifestation of reality is attested already in the AVŚ 11.8.31 (see chapter 2.6.4). Sacrifice is also called his replica, *pratimā́*. The word *pratimā́*, literally 'the corresponding measure' (Malamoud 2002a: 21), is used in ṚV 10.130.3 (*kā́sīt pramā́ pratimā́ kíṃ nidā́nam*) in a hymn which describes the cosmogony as the creation of sacrifice. The sacrifice is conceived in terms of measuring of what is unmanifest; thus the umanifest is put into manifest frames. Thus the manifest part of reality can be measured as great. Metonymies INSTRUMENT FOR ACTION, ACTION FOR AGENT motivate the identification of Prajāpati with *pratimā́*. The sacrifice is an activity which allows reality to manifest itself safely in successive acts of giving itself away and obtaining itself back. It is conceived in terms of giving a part of itself to its destructive part. It is worth noting that the metonymy PART OF A THING FOR THE WHOLE THING (Radden, Kövecses 1999: 31) provides the ground for the thinking the substitute of the sacrificer is to be taken for the whole sacrificer.

Now, the next input space is introduced which is man:

ŚB 11.1.8.4b-5

sá yád vratám upaíti yáthaivá tát prajā́patir devébhya ātmā́nam prā́yachad evám evaìṣá etád devébhya ātmā́nam práyachati (...) (4)
átha yád yajñáṃ tanuté | yajñénaivaìtád devébhya ātmā́naṃ niṣkrīṇīte yáthaiva tát prajā́patir nirákrīṇīta (5)

Now when he (the Sacrificer) enters on the fast, he thereby gives himself up to the gods, even as Prajāpati thereby gave himself up to the gods. . (...) And when (on the following day) he performs the sacrifice, then he redeems himself by sacrifice from the gods, even as Prajāpati thereby redeemed himself.

Man in micro-scale realises the cosmogonic activity of Prajāpati[26]. His hunger, which he experiences during a fast, realises creation of a place for the future world. Since hunger is conceived in terms of fire, the recipient can create the image of a hungry man as Prajāpati *in illo tempore* as described in ŚB 2.2.4.1 (and in other cosmogonies, see section 3.2.1-2). He can also understand that the sacrificer is the incarnation of Prajāpati in the beginnings of his creative activity. On the most general level, man ritually re-enacts the creation of the void. At the same time, the mouths of the gods are conceived in terms of fire (ŚB 7.1.2.4, see section 3.2.2), so the recipient may understand that when a sacrificer is hungry during fasting, he is eaten by the gods. When man pours an oblation into a fire, he obtains himself back as he eats the remnants of the sacrifice and he thus redeems himself from the gods and regains his fullness as Prajāpati did *in illo tempore*[27]. On the most general level, he ritually re-enacts the manifestation of reality which, within the frames of its manifest part, constantly creates a void filled with itself. The concept of sacrifice allows the composer to express the reflexive nature of this process because the objects, which constitute oblation, belong to the sacrificer. In this way, he gives away not only his own flesh, while he is hungry during the fast, but also his possession. When he eats the remnants, his possession comes back to him in the most intimate way: it becomes his body.

---

26 As Heesterman shows, sacrifice is self-sacrifice (1987, 1993: 165 ff.)
27 For the redemption theory in the Vedic ritual, see Thite (1975: 144–145). For creation of various substitutes of the sacrificer conceived as his self, ātmán, see Malamoud (2005a).

3.2. Death in creation

The cosmogonies, discussed in this section, differ from ŚB 2.2.4. They present the moment when creation breaks down and present it in a similar way: either Prajāpati is threatened by death or he actually dies. However, he does not lose his power and although, in some cosmogonies, he is not immediately successful in solving the problem, it is not implied that reality in its unmanifest aspect is threatened.

I will firstly discuss cosmogonies which present the death of Prajāpati manifest in its creatures (see section 3.2.1), then cosmogonies which present his own death (see section 3.2.2). This will lead me to an analysis of the complex metaphysics of death elaborated by the composers of the ŚB who see it as the indispensable price for the manifestation of self-contradictory reality (see section 3.2.3). Thus understood, death plays an ontic role as a constituent part of the world and endows human life with profound sense because, thanks to its existence, men can participate in the creative transformation of reality (see section 3.3-4).

3.2.1. Reality dies through his creatures

The cosmogonies analysed in this section (ŚB 2.5.1 and 3.9.1) explain the Caturmāsya and Agniṣṭoma rituals[28]. Again, they are so general that it is not necessary to refer to the ritual themselves in order to understand them.

ŚB 2.5.1.1

prajā́patir ha vā́ idam ágra éka evā̀sa | sá aikṣata kátham nú prájāyeyéti sò 'śrāmyat sá tápo 'tapyata sá prajā́ asṛjata tā́ asyá prajā́ḥ sṛṣṭā́ḥ párābabhūvus tā́nīmā́ni váyāṃsi púruṣo vaí prajā́pater nédiṣṭhaṃ dvipā́d vā́ ayám púruṣas tásmād dvipā́do váyāṃsi |

Verily, in the beginning, Prajāpati alone existed here. He thought within himself, 'How can I be propagated?' He toiled and heated himself[29]. He created living beings. The living beings created by him passed away: they are those birds. Now man is the nearest to Prajāpati; and man is two-footed: hence birds are two-footed.

The beginnings of creation are conceived in the same way as in ŚB 2.2.4. Reality in its manifestation of Prajāpati wants to multiply itself which

[28] For the Caturmāsya see, Thite (1975: 55 ff.), for the Agniṣṭoma see Caland, Henry (1906).
[29] Eggeling (1885) adds: '(practised austerities)'.

is conceived in terms of the desire to procreate. The conceptual network consists of the following input spaces. These are the concepts of Prajāpati, of a man who toils and heats, of a bird which broods an egg, the general domain of Procreation and the concept of reality[30]. The generic space is the concept of transformation under the influence of heat. In the blend, Prajāpati is a bird brooding on its eggs.

The concept of birds may trigger the recipient to evoke the concept of a golden wild goose in terms of which the sun and the world was conceived already in the AVŚ (see chapter 2.5.3). The recipient can also metonymically evoke the concept of the sky the outline of which is created in this stage of creation[31]. Thus he will activate the concept of the world divided into three spheres the appearance of which is the aim of creation. Then, the composer explains the identity of the Prajāpati's manifestation, conceived in terms of birds, with Prajāpati himself. It is based on a similarity in structure: men and birds have two legs and the recipient infers that, since man is the nearest to Prajāpati, birds are the nearest to him too. On this ground, the recipient can understand that Prajāpati's death is conceived in terms of the death of birds.

The composer conceives the moment when creation is interrupted in terms of the death of birds. However, in this state reality in its unmanifest aspect is not threatened by any danger. Death occurs within its manifest aspect conceived in terms of the death of living beings. In this way, reality manifests its internal contradictoriness: in its unmanifest aspect it can be conceived as alive, but in its manifest aspect it does not live.

ŚB 2.5.1.2

sá aikṣata prajā́patiḥ | yáthā nv èvá puraikó 'bhūvam evám u nv èvā́py etárhy éka evā̀smī́ti sá dvitī́yāḥ sasṛje tā́ asyá páraivá babhūvus tád idáṃ kṣudráṃ sarīsṛpáṃ yád anyát sarpébhyas tṛtī́yāḥ sasṛja íty āhus tā́ asyá páraivá babhūvus tá imé sarpā́ |

Prajāpati thought within himself, 'Even as formerly I was alone, so also am I now alone.' He created a second (race of beings); they also passed away: they are those small crawling reptiles other than snakes. He created a third (race), they say; they also passed away: they are those snakes.

30 Kaelber 1975: 359 'In case of biological generation *tapas* invariably refers to the heat of 'brooding' or 'maturing' as with egg'.

31 Metonymy INHABITANTS FOR PLACE (BIRDS FOR THE SKY).

The next stage of creation is conceived in terms of the birth of snakes which, similarly to birds, are born from eggs. The remaining input spaces of the conceptual network are the same. While the recipient may understand birds as the form of reality that is closest to it, snakes, being born on earth, can be understood as its form which is totally opposed to it. On the other hand, their affinity is implied in that both birds and snakes are born from eggs. In ŚB 1.6.3.8, the snake Vṛtra is identified with Agni filled with Soma and the identification of Agni with Prajāpati is stated in many places of the ŚB[32]. On this basis, the recipient may understand that this opposite form of reality is at the same time identical with it. The concept of snakes metonymically evoke the concept of earth[33]. Thus it is implied that the earth is outlined in this stage of creation.

Then the snakes die. In the blend, creation is interrupted. The next stage of creation is conceived in terms of the creation of small, creeping animals. The phrase *kṣudráṃ sarīsṛpáṃ* is used in ŚB 1.5.3.11 to denote animals which shrink during the summer and winter and when rains come grow and look for food. The concept of rain metonymically evokes the concept of the space between the earth and the sky which, as we can presume, is outlined in this stage of creation. Creation is again interrupted conceived in terms of the death of created beings.

Manifestation of Prajāpati in three kinds of creatures can be variously interpreted. On the one hand, it can be interpreted as consecutive attempts of reality to manifest itself. Each attempt ends with failure which poses the same questions as in case of ŚB 2.2.4: either reality is itself unpredictable in its creative activity or it is so free that it can commit mistakes. On the other hand, manifestation in various beings can be interpreted as the manifestation of three aspects of the manifest form of reality. When it assumes the form of birds, it manifests it ontic identity with itself and, when it assumes the form of snakes, it manifests its opposing form. The form which creeps can be interpreted as the manifestation of the possibility to unite opposing forms of reality. In this way, their ontic identity is confirmed.

In the next passage, the recipient is expected to activate the concept of a human being who loses her children. On the basis of general knowledge and experience, he can activate the emotions of loss and despair. In these terms, further creation is conceived.

---

32 Agni is called snake (*áhi*) in ṚV 1.79.1 See Coomaraswamy (1935: 395).

33 Metonymy INHABITANTS FOR PLACE (SNAKES FOR THE EARTH).

ŚB 2.5.1.3

só 'rcañ chrā́myan prajā́patir īkṣā́ṃ cakre | katháṃ nú me prajā́ḥ sṛṣṭā́ḥ párābhavantī́ti sá haitád evá dadarśānaśanátayā vaí me prajā́ḥ párābhavantī́ti sá ātmána evā́gre stánayoḥ páya āpyāyayā́ṃ cakre sá prajā́ asṛjata tā́ asyá prajā́ḥ sṛṣṭā́ stánāv evā̀bhipádya tā́s tátaḥ sámbabhūvus tā́ imā́ áparābhūtaḥ |

While praising and heating himself[34], Prajāpati thought within himself, 'How comes it that the living beings created by me pass away?' He then became aware that his creatures passed away from want of food. He made the breasts in the fore-part of himself teem with milk[35]. He then created living beings; and by resorting to the breasts, the beings created by him thenceforward continued to exist: they are these (creatures) which have not passed away.

The activity of man, in terms of which creative activity of reality is conceived, is now expressed by the verb *arc-*, 'to sing, to shine'[36] and by the verb *śram-*. The cognitive dimension of creation is explicitly expressed: Prajāpati thinks how further creation is possible. And the way of solving the problem is the same as in ŚB 2.2.4: Prajāpati creates milk with which he may feed the future beings. Thus the conceptual network is enriched with the concept of woman. In the blend, Prajāpati transforms himself from a man into a woman who gives birth to children and feeds her children from the breast. If the recipient elaborates this input space, he can feel the emotions of happiness and relief. The androgynous character of Prajāpati is here expressed even more strongly than in ŚB 2.2.4: not only he is able to give birth, but he also has breasts with milk. However, the structure of the world which is the target domain of this description is still the same: the world is divided into two aspects living and dying conceived in terms of an eater and its food. Since the offspring is the same as his father, we understand that it is Prajāpati who dies when he creates the world and he then resurrects[37]. Thus reality can manifests its internally contradictory nature.

34 Eggeling (1882): 'practising austerities'.

35 Eggeling (1882) interprets that breasts belong to the creatures: 'he made the breasts in the fore-parts of [their] body teem with milk', ŚB in the Kānva recension is even more explicit in that the breasts belong to Prajāpati and reads: *ātmány evā́gre*.

36 Analysis of the verb *arc-* see BU 2.1, chapter 4.1.1.

37 At the same time, the root *pyā-* evokes the process of swelling of Soma (ṚV 1.91.16, 17, 18, 9.67.28, 10.85.5). If the recipient activates identity between Prajāpati and Agni, he will see that the creative process agrees with the Ṛgvedic general model of reality transformation

ŚB 3.9.1-2

prajā́patir vaí prajā́ḥ sasṛjānó riricāná ivāmanyata tásmāt párācyaḥ prajā́ āsur nàsyá prajā́ḥ śriyè 'nnā́dyāya tasthire | (1)
sá aikṣatā́rikṣy áham | *ásmā u kā́māyā́sṛkṣi ná me sa kā́maḥ sámārdhi párācyo mát prajā́ abhūvan ná me prajā́ḥ śriyè 'nnā́dyāyāsthiṣatéti* | (2)

Now Prajāpati (the lord of creatures), having created living beings, felt himself as it were exhausted. The creatures turned away from him; the creatures did not abide with him for his joy and food. He thought within him, 'I have exhausted myself, and the object for which 1 I have created has not been accomplished: my creatures have turned away from me, the creatures have not abode with me for my joy and food.'.

This cosmogony begins with the description of Prajāpati who feels empty. Since the next sentence presents the creatures as deprived of food, the recipient can evoke the concept of eating and digesting and understand creation in terms of excretion. Conceptualisation of living beings in these terms is implied by most of cosmogonies of the ŚB and is explicitly attested in the ŚB 10.1.3.1-2, 10.4.2.2-3 (see section 3.2.3), although it is never elaborated further by the authors. In all cases, what is highlighted as the result of excretion is the feeling of being empty which, within the frames of the source domain, should be understood as being hungry. A hungry parent cannot feed her offspring and the recipient understands that the offspring dies. So the composer may generally conceive the first creative act of reality in terms of its death in its manifest aspect.

The creatures are also presented as being beyond the excellence (*śrī́*) of Prajāpati. The concept of *śrī́* evokes the Ṛgvedic concept of fame referred to by words *śrī́*, *śrávas*, *yáśas* and *ksatrá* (see chapter 1.7). As I have shown, the sun is metonymically identified with the whole manifest aspect in the AVŚ. The fact that the creatures are beyond excellence (*śrī́*) implies that they are not yet manifest. Thus they are in a state of internal contradiction: they already exist, but they are at the same time absent. Since, according to the general knowledge activated by the source domain, an offspring is identified with its parent the recipient understands that it is reality which manifests itself in this contradictory form. The *Nāsadīyasūkta* describes this stage of creation as void (*abhú*) and what is about to be (*abhū́*). But, contrary to the *Nāsadīyasūkta*, in the ŚB, the internally contradictory image of dying creatures means that creation is interrupted.

The logic of the concept of a hungry living being hungry implies two possibilities. If there is no food, the eater is threatened by death. In the blend, it is either reality or its manifest aspect. ŚB 2.2.4 elaborates the first possibility and ŚB 2.5.1 and 3.9.1 the second. In both cases, there is a moment during the creative process when reality fails to manifest.

As argued above, this moment does not mean that reality cannot be seen as the Absolute. The main attribute of the Absolute in the ŚB is freedom which allows for its partial manifestation as its own opposition. This manifestation is conceived in terms of death. The cosmogonies analysed here do not use the abstract concept of death (*mr̥tyú*)[38], but if the recipient evokes it metonymically, on the basis of concrete concept of dying creatures evoked by the source domain, he will see that death has an extremely important role in this philosophy. On the one hand, both the absence of cosmos and the first appearance of cosmos are conceived in its terms. On the other hand, death, as the manifestation of absence of the cosmos, is the manifestation of the Absolute: it is manifestation of the state when there is no cosmos as in the pre-creative state when only unmanifest reality exists. Moreover, death is a manifestation of the destructive power of the Absolute. Thus understood, death is the manifestation of Absolute's ability for self-annihilation and also the manifestation of the state totally opposed to the Absolute[39]. In his essay, Malamoud (1996c) shows the ritual realisation of the paradoxical concept of Absolute which is fullness and emptiness at the same time. He writes:

> And, when we look at the places in which the Absolute reveals itself (in ritual – JJ) and the paths that lead to it, it becomes apparent that it is nothing other than the void: the signs of its plenitude are the break, the hole, the cavity, the cope of heaven, the space between the earth and the celestial vault, so many empty spaces (…). Every fissure is an abyss, and the abyss, even if it retains a certain element of its demarcating function as a break, is the vessel of the Absolute. (1996c: 70)

This shows that the search for meaning was the basic intellectual motivation of the composers of the Brāhmaṇas and it comprehended not only theory, but also practice. Moreover, the concepts they tried to put in ritual practice are extremely abstract. Identification of the Absolute manifesting in the cosmos as death is also confirmed by the research of Bodewitz (1999b) who shows that the concept of pit is connected with the concept of netherworlds[40].

---

38 Which is used in later parts of the ŚB, e.g.10.1.3, 10.4.3, see sections 3.2.2, 3.3.

39 Such a concept of the Absolute can be seen as the sophisticated metaphysical interpretation of unity of sacrum and violence analysed by Girard (1993[1972]). For analysis of the early Indian tradition within the frames of Girard's theory, see Collins (2014). For the possibility of use of Girard's theory in the analysis of the problem of sacrificial substitute in Vedic ritual (and other theories), see Smith, Doniger (1989).

40 For his analysis of concepts of the yonder world in the Veda, see also Bodewitz (1999a, 2002a). In Bodewitz (2000b), he analysis the concept of distance (*parāvát*) in the Veda in

It is also worth noting that the language of ŚB 3.9.1 is more abstract than that of ŚB 2.5.1. The general domain of Cooking in its specific realisation of excretion and eating is evoked only *via* the general expression that the creatures are deprived of food. The composer elaborates another more abstract concept which is the image schema of a CONTAINER in terms of which Prajāpati's hungry belly is conceived. In the blend, the place for the future world is conceived in these terms. Death of the creatures is conceived in terms of going beyond the container[41]. When Prajāpati eats and food appears in his belly, living beings will be created. This is conceived in terms of their return to the container which is explicitly expressed in the cosmogony.

The conceptual network created in this cosmogony is simpler than in the previous one (ŚB 2.5.1.1-3). The input spaces of birds, of snakes and of creeping beings, which need to be fed, are reduced in the second cosmogony to the general domain of Procreation with its specific realisation of giving birth and feeding offspring. The next input spaces are the concepts of Prajāpati and of reality. The first cosmogony highlights the appearance of its three spheres and the second cosmogony highlights the concept of the sun in terms of which the world is conceived in the blend. The generic space is the concept of transformation under the influence of heat.

3.2.2. Death of reality within the manifest aspect of reality

In the previous section, I have discussed cosmogonies which present the death of Prajāpati when he manifests himself in his creatures. In many places in the ŚB, however, it is stated that Prajāpati dies in the cosmos himself. In these contexts, the word *prajā́pati* is the name of the creative power of reality and of the cosmos conceived in terms of man. This conceptualisation is presented in the most detailed way in cosmogonies that explain the Agnicayana[42]. While the Agnihotra can be seen as the ritualised activity of a cowherd, the Agnicayana can be seen as a ritualised preparation of a hearth for a fire. It was a long and complex ritual which took twelve days to perform and the preparations before the ritual lasted a year. For the present investigations, two of its elements are

---

terms of which the yonder world is conceived. Such a conceptualisation is based on CENTRE-PERIPHERY image schema and confirms the early Vedic division of cosmos into *sát* and *ásat*. Within the frame of this conceptualisation, *ásat* is the unmanifest sphere where the beings not wanted by the Aryan society are placed (or are expected to be placed), the dead included.

41 More universal metaphor: LIFE IS BEING HERE, DEATH IS GOING AWAY (e.g. attested in English 'He passed away').

42 For Agnicayana, see Staal (1983).

the most relevant: the altar was built of bricks, it had the form of a bird[43] and the ritual included an animal sacrifice.

I will now analyse the initial cosmogony explaining the Agnicayana which begins with the description of the earliest stage of creation before the creative power of reality appears.

ŚB 6.1.1.1

ásad vā́ idám ágra āsīt | tád āhuḥ kíṃ tád ásad āsīd íty ṛ́ṣayo vā̆vá te 'gre 'sad āsī́t tád āhuḥ ké tá ṛ́ṣaya íti prāṇā́ vā ṛ́ṣayas té yát purā̆smā́t sárvasmād idám ichántaḥ śrámeṇa tápasā̆riṣaṃs tásmād ṛ́ṣayaḥ |

Verily, in the beginning there was here the non-existent. As to this they say, 'What was that non-existent?' The Rishis, assuredly, it is they that were the non-existent. As to this they say, 'Who were those Rishis?' The Rishis, doubtless, were the breaths[44]: inasmuch as before (the existence of) this universe, they, desiring it, wore themselves out (*riṣ-*) with toil and heat[45], therefore (they are called) Rishis (*ṛṣayaḥ*).

The first form of the world is called non-existent (*ásat*). In this way, it is implied that the first manifestation of reality is conceived in terms of its absence, which can be interpreted in terms of a void. Contrary to the cosmogonies discussed till now, which express the concept of the primeval void with more concrete source domains (such as hungry fire or dying creatures), here the abstract notion, *ásat*, is used. Such a use of the word *ásat* agrees with the general cosmogonic pattern of the early Veda (Jurewicz 2010a: 52–53).

But, as previously argued, in the early Veda *ásat* does not mean a total void, but rather a state which is contrary to being here and now within the frames of manifestation. In the ṚV, such a state is not defined. In ŚB 6.1.1.1, it is implied that it can be defined because the question about the nature of the non-existent is posed. The answer is that the seers were the non-existent. This answer is consistent with early Vedic thought in which the creative power of reality is conceived in terms of a human or divine (*devá*) form[46]. The recipient may also understand that reality, having created space for the future world in itself (*ásat*), immediately wants to manifest itself within its frame. The multiplicity of the seers implies that reality splits itself into parts. The number of the seers is not mentioned here, but on the basis of general knowledge the recipient can understand that the seven seers are meant.

43 There were also other forms of the altar, but the form of the bird is analysed in the ŚB.
44 Eggeling (1894): 'vital airs'.
45 Eggeling (1894): 'austerity'.
46 This is an instantiation of the more universal way conceptualisation of cognitive faculties in terms of men ('The Society of Mind metaphor', Lakoff, Johnson 1999: 410 ff.)

The concept of the seven seers may trigger the recipient to activate the concept of a head (Mitchiner 1982: 285–287). As has been shown, seven openings of head (two eyes, two ears, two nostrils and mouth) are identified with seers in the AVŚ (see chapter 2.5.1.3)[47]. If the recipient evokes this blend in the context of ŚB 6.1.1.1, he will understand that the first form of the world is conceived in terms of a cognising head.

Moreover, the concept of head evokes the general domain of Procreation which endows the creative process with a more precise scenario. Within the frames of this conceptualisation, the stage called *ásat* is conceived in terms of the state just before a delivery when the child is still hidden within its mother's womb. The first manifestation of reality is conceived in terms of the child's head emerging from the womb during delivery. Then the entire child appears which agrees with the metonymic thinking HEAD FOR A PERSON, PERSON FOR A HEAD.

The concept of birth-giving may lead the recipient to the ṚV the composers of which conceive the sunrise in terms of delivery: it was believed that the sun during the night is present in fire burning on earth. In this state, it was conceived in terms of the head of a child which will be born in the morning (Jurewicz 2010a: 139–141). If the recipient introduces the concept of sunrise to the blend created by the composer of ŚB 6.1.1, he will understand that the first form of reality is conceived not only in terms of the head, but also in terms of the sun in the form of burning a fire on earth.

The input spaces of the conceptual network are as follows: the concept of seven seers who cognise, the sunrise and the concept of reality. The next input space is the general domain of Procreation. The input space of the sunrise activates the concept of the world subject to the power of time. The generic space is the concept of transformation under the influence of heat. In the blend, creation is cognitive activity conceived in terms of birth-giving. The first form of reality is fire which is transformed into the sun. The input space of seers also makes the recipient understand the seven seers as flames of fire (in the same way as the Aṅgirases are conceived in the ṚV, see Jurewicz 2010a: 270 ff.). The input space of seven seers metonymically imparts to the blend the meaning of recitation of sacred speech (AGENT FOR ACTIVITY). In these terms, creation of the world is also conceived in the blend. This conceptualisation is coherent with the scenario of delivery according to which the new-born child cries and with the metaphoric conceptualisation of speech in terms of fire.

In the next sentence, the seers are called breaths (*prāṇá*). Thus the seers are metonymically reduced to the essence which makes them live. Moreover,

[47] See also BU 2.2.3-4 (analysed by Brereton 1991 and Gren-Eklund 1978).

conceptualisation of this state of creation in terms of breath attests that some sort of breath practice, connected with recitation, was common enough to become a meaningful source domain for the conceptualisation of creation[48]. As I have shown, this concept is already activated in the cosmogonic descriptions of the AV.

The concept of breath allows the recipient to elaborate the input space of fire based on metonymy (blowing was necessary to produce fire with the aid of fire-drill) and based on metaphor (breath is metaphorically conceived in terms of fire). In the blend, seers are fire which makes the etymological explanation of the word *ṛ́ṣi* fully coherent. The seers are those who suffer because of toil (*śráma*) and heat (*tápas*). Kindling of fire with the aid of a fire-drill was very tiresome and caused its agent to be heated. Moreover, in the ṚV, the activity of fire is conceived in terms of toiling (Jurewicz 2010a: 267 ff.); on this basis, the identity of the seers and fire is also built. The etymology of their name refers to their essence: they are conceived in terms of living burning entities. The recipient may elaborate the blend and create the image of a head the openings of which begin to burn. In these terms, cognition is conceived and may be specified as smelling, speaking, seeing, hearing, thinking (Blezer 1992: 24[49]). I would see this description as one of the earliest accounts of use of the concept of breath in reference to the cognitive powers; this use is common in the Upaniṣads.

Conceptualisation of the seers as burning is confirmed in the following sentences of the cosmogony:

ŚB 6.1.1.2

sá yò 'yám mádhye prāṇáḥ | eṣá evéndras tā́n eṣá prāṇā́n madhyatá indriyéṇainddha tásmād índha índho ha vaí tám índra ity ā́cakṣate paró 'kṣam paró 'kṣakāmā hí devā́s tá iddhā́ḥ saptá nā́nā púruṣān asṛjanta |

This same breath[50] in the midst doubtless is Indra. He, by his power (*indriya*), kindled those (other) breaths[51] from the midst; and inasmuch as he kindled (*indh*), he is the kindler (*indha*): the kindler indeed, him they call 'Indra' mystically (esoterically), for the gods love the mystic. They (the breaths[52]), being kindled, created seven separate men[53].

[48] For the interiorisation of the Agnihotra ritual, see Bodewitz (1973).
[49] For the analysis of *prāṇás* as psychic and cognitive forces, see Bakker 1982.
[50] Eggeling (1894): 'vital air'.
[51] Eggeling (1894): 'vital airs'
[52] Eggeling (1894): 'the vital airs'
[53] Eggeling (1894): 'persons'.

The main breath is the breath which ensures living[54]. It is conceived as a special power which kindles the seers, the head in the blend. The main breath is identified with Indra which allows the recipient to activate the next input space, i.e. the Ṛgvedic concept of this god. In the ṚV, Indra drinks Soma and, filled with it, is able to act and to kill Vṛtra. Indra is the only god in the ṚV who is called *sómya*. It is caused in that Soma transforms Indra from a warrior into a seer thanks to which he has not only killing power, but also creative power (Jurewicz 2010a: 342). Soma is the essence of Indra (*ātmā́ yajñásya*, ṚV 9.2.10, 9.6.8), so the concept of Indra can function as a metonymic vehicle which activates the concept of Soma. According to the ṚV, Soma has the power to enkindle the person drinking it (ṚV 8.48.6a: *agníṃ ná mā mathitáṃ sáṃ didīpaḥ*, Jurewicz 2010a: 193–194). On this basis, the recipient will understand why the main breath is called Indra: it is the embodiment of the power of Soma conceived in terms of enkindling. In the blend, cognitive powers of reality, conceived in terms of seers, heat themselves (they become 'cooked', ṚV 9.83.1d) and then they are filled with Soma which enables them to cognise. The recipient may elaborate the blend and create the image of the head from each opening of which a flame appears which has form of a man who cognises[55]. This again agrees with metaphoric conceptualisation of the cognitive faculties in terms of man[56].

ŚB 6.1.1.3

> *tè 'bruvan | ná vā́ itthám̐ sántaḥ śakṣyāmaḥ prájanayitum imā́nt saptá púruṣān ékam púruṣaṃ karavāméti tá etā́nt saptá púruṣān ékam púruṣam akurvan yád ūrdhváṃ nā́bhes taú dvaú samaúbjan yád ávāṅ nā́bhes taú dvaú pakṣáḥ púruṣaḥ pakṣáḥ púruṣaḥ pratiṣṭhaíka āsīt |*
>
> They said, 'Surely, being thus, we shall not be able to generate: let us make these seven men[57] one man!' They made those seven men one man: they compressed two of them (into) what is above the navel, and two of them (into) what is below the navel; (one) man was (one) wing (or side), (one) man was (the other) wing, and one man was the base (i.e. the feet)

---

54 According to ŚB 7.1.2.1, when this breath comes out from Prajāpati, he falls (see section 3.2.2).

55 It is worth noting that during recitation of Sāmidhenī verses not only fire, but also parts of the priest are kindled which are: three breaths (*prāṇá, apāná, udāná*), hearing (*śrótra*), speech (*vā́c*), mind (*mánas*), seeing (*cákṣus*), then the *madhyamá prāṇá*, then the penis (*śiśná*) and, finally, the whole person who blazes from the nails to the hair (*sárvam ātmā́naṃ sáminddha ā́ nakhebhyò 'tho lómabhyaḥ*, ŚB 1.4.3.10).

56 This is a more general conceptualisation (Lakoff, Johnson 1999: 410–414).

57 Eggeling (1894): 'persons'.

The seers, in order to create, have to unite themselves into one. Thus the concept of ensemble activity is evoked which makes action more effective. When the recipient highlights the input space of cognition, he will understand that it cannot be performed by each faculty separately. Conceptualisation of cognition in terms of human activity allows the author of the cosmogony to express intentionality. In the blend, cognitive faculties unite and become one cognitive subjective power which is able to cognise and create. The head becomes the whole body conceived in terms of a flying man. In these terms, the first manifestation of reality is conceived with its body composed of burning breaths. Moreover, since society is conceived in terms of the human body already in the ṚV (see chapter 1.3), the recipient may enrich the conceptual network with this concept as well.

ŚB 6.1.1.4

átha yaìtéṣāṃ saptā́nām púruṣāṇāṃ śrī́ḥ | yó rása ā́sīt tám ūrdhváṃ samúdauhaṃs tád asyá śíro 'bhavad yáchrīyaṃ samudaúhaṃs tásmāchíras tásminn etásmin prāṇā́ aśrayanta tásmād vevaìtáchírò 'tha yát prāṇā́ áśrayanta tásmād u prāṇā́ḥ śriyaú 'tha yát sárvasminn áśrayanta tásmād u śárīram |

And what excellence, what life-sap (*rasa*) there was in those seven men, that they concentrated above, that became his head. And because (in it) they concentrated the excellence (*śrī*), therefore it is (called) the head (*śiras*). It was thereto that the breaths resorted (*śrī*): therefore also it is the head (*śíras*). And because the breaths did so resort (*śrī*) thereto, therefore also the breaths[58] are elements of excellence (*śrī*). And because they resorted to the whole (system) therefore (this is called) body (*śarīra*).

The composer presents the creation of the head of the flying man. Its creation is conceived in terms of image schema of VERTICALITY which is the next input space of the conceptual network. The excellence of the seers (*śrī́*), identified with essence (*rása*), is pushed up to create the head. The concept of *śrī́* evokes the Ṛgvedic concept of fame expressed by the words *śrī́*, *śrávas*, *yáśas* and *ksatrá* conceived as being realised under the influence of Soma in the sun (see chapter 1.7). As I have shown, this concept has a feature of fluidity. In the present context, the recipient is prompted to conceive this fluidity as Soma because the word *rása* is used in reference to it in the ṚV (e.g. 9.6.6a, 9.14.3a, 9.16.1b, 9.23.5b, 9.38.5a, 9.47.3a, 9.61.17a, 9.61.18a). The literal meaning of the word *rása* may evoke the recipient to activate the image of drinking sap. In the ṚV, people exulted with Soma are presented as drinking Somic juice purified in the sun. If the recipient of the ŚB activates

[58] Eggeling (1894) adds: '(vital airs, and their organs)'.

this conceptualisation, he would understand that now the possibility for the supernatural state is created within the world. At the same time, the creation of the head can be conceived in terms of drinking sap: the head appears when it performs its main activity, from the point of view of everyday life, of eating and drinking while, from the point of view of supernatural cognition, it appears when cognition is performed by the mind.

If the recipient elaborates the input space of the sunrise, he will create an image of its rising in the morning. If he elaborates the input space of cognition, he will understand that the seven seers perform it under the influence of Soma which is their essence. In the blend, this essence is located in the sun and in the head of the flying man. This is why the word *śíras* is explained as the part of the body the essence of which is *śrī́*.

Moreover, as it has been shown, the concept of *śrī́* is also connected with the concept of *ksatrá*, royal rule[59]. In this way, the composer would imply that within the frames of the social order now created, the Kṣatriya comes from the Brahmin. Such a conceptualisation agrees with classification of the parts of day according to which the Brahmin corresponds to morning and the Kṣatriya to midday (Smith 1994: 66, *passim*). In the blend, the sunrise is also the creation of the social order.

The next etymology of the word *śíras* explains its meaning as the place where breaths find their support (*áśrayanta*). Here, the composer again seems to refer to a breath practice: the head gives support to breaths because it is the locus of speech. The supernatural effects of this practice are implied in that breaths are presented as being 'in the excellence' (*śriyaú*). Thus it is implied that the state realised thanks to a breath practice connected with recitation is conceived in the same terms as the state gained in Somic exultation, i.e. as realised on the sun[60]. The third etymology is that of the word *śárīra*: the body is called in this way because breaths find their support in it. This means that body of the flying man is permeated by breaths.

As I have argued above, all the processes described by the cosmogony take part in the head. In this way, the composer implies that creation is a cognitive process. Since, in terms of the body society is conceived, the recipient may understand that it is also created now.

Conceptualisation of the manifest aspect of reality in terms of the head elaborates earlier thinking presented in the *Puruṣasūkta* (see chapter 1.3) which presents the conceptualisation of the manifest aspect in terms of an open mouth. The composer of the present cosmogony highlights the cognitive abilities of the head. Thus he prompts the recipient to understand that reality

---

[59] For this meaning of *śrī́* in the Brāhmaṇas, see Gonda (1954: 188 ff.)

[60] This is confirmed in the Upaniṣads, see chapter 4.

thinks about itself and creates its own replica within its own head. It is important to note, however, that the meanings of the head and the body are now reversed: while from the perspective of all reality the head corresponds to the manifest aspect, within its manifest aspect the head, which is the sun reached in supernatural cognition, corresponds to what is unmanifest.

In the next two sentences (ŚB 6.1.1.5-7), the manifest part of reality is called *púruṣa prajā́pati* which highlights its conceptualisation in terms of man. The recipient understands that the creative power of reality is finally created. It will convey further creation. The ritual form of Prajāpati is the fire altar. Thus the next input space, i.e. the concept of Agnicayana, is introduced.

ŚB 6.1.1.8

sò 'yám púruṣaḥ prajā́patir akāmayata | bhū́yānt syām prajāyeyéti sò 'śrāmyat sá tápo 'tapyata sá śrāntás tepānó bráhmaivá prathamám asr̥jata trayóm evá vidyā́ṃ saìvāsmai pratiṣṭhā́bhavat tásmād āhur bráhmāsyá sárvasya pratiṣṭhéti tásmād anū́cya prátitiṣṭhati pratiṣṭhā́ hy èṣā́ yád bráhma tásyām pratiṣṭhā́yām prátiṣṭhito 'tapyata |

Now this man[61] Prajāpati desired, 'May I be more (than one), may I be reproduced!' He toiled, he heated himself[62]. Being worn out with toil and austerity, he created first of all the *Brahman* (neut.), the triple science. It became to him a foundation: hence they say, 'the *Brahman* (Veda) is the foundation of everything here.' Wherefore, having studied (the Veda) one rests on a foundation; for this, to wit, the Veda, is his foundation. Resting on that foundation, he (again) heated himself[63].

Reality, in the form of Prajāpati, repeats its first creative manifestation conceived in terms of the exhausting toil that causes heat. The result of the creative activity is *bráhman* defined as the triple science (*trayī́ vidyā́*). From that, the recipient understands that Prajāpati recites three Vedas. The recipient understands that speech, in the form of which reality has manifested itself in the beginning of creation, is now ordered in three parts and becomes sacred speech, *bráhman*.

Then the composer states that *bráhman* becomes the foundation of Prajāpati. In the ŚB, the earth and the lower part of the body of Prajāpati are conceived in terms of foundation (see ŚB 6.1.1.15, 7.1.2 .1-4, section 3.2.3). The recipient can elaborate the concept of giving birth and activate its whole scenario: a child cries when it born, then it grows and stands speaking more and more[64]; then it learns sacred texts. The image schema of VERTICALITY gives

61 Eggeling (1894): 'Person'.
62 Eggeling (1894): 'practised austerity'.
63 Eggeling (1894): 'practised austerity'
64 This concept is elaborated in detail in ŚB 11.1.6, see section 3.5.2.

coherence to the structure of the cosmos, society and man and allows for the evaluation of its parts (BETTER IS UP, WORSE IS DOWN). The general domain is that of Procreation in its specific realisation of the concept of a child whose body grows to adulthood. In the beginning of the process, the head appears first, and then it rises up along the vertical axis and becomes the highest part of the body. In the blend, the earth, which is identical with the rising sun, is the foundation of the cosmos as the Brahmin is the foundation of other social classes (see also BU 1.4.11, see chapter 4.1.2)[65]. The movement of the rising sun splits the earth into itself and the sun which rises up. In society, the Brahmin becomes the highest social class and his priority is implied by his identification with the head. The image schema of VERTICALITY also gives coherence to the conceptualisation of the consecutive stages of creation which are conceived in general terms of an upward movement. The process described in this passage repeats the pattern of the process described in the previous passages where creation is conceived in terms of the essence of the seers which flows up and becomes the head.

In the last sentence of the passage, Prajāpati is presented as heating himself on this foundation. In the blend, the recipient is expected to activate the complex meaning of sacred speech. It is the foundation of Prajāpati because it is his legs and the earth, and because it is his head. The manifest aspect is conceived in terms of man who, burning with breath, recites the Veda.

ŚB 6.1.1.9

sò 'pò 'sṛjata | vācá evá lokā́d vā́g evā̀sya sā̀sṛjyata sèdáṃ sárvam āpnod yád idáṃ kíṃ ca yád ā́pnot tásmād ā́po yád ávṛṇot tásmād vā́ḥ |

He created the waters out of Vāc (speech, that is) the world; for speech belonged to it: that was created (set free). It pervaded everything here; and because it pervaded (*āp*) whatsoever there was here, therefore (it is called) water (*āpas*); and because it covered (*vār*), therefore also it (is called) water (*vār*).

The sequence of creation is the same as in ŚB 2.2.4: after the stage conceived in terms of heat comes the stage of fluid. Water is presented as coming from Prajāpati's speech which is identified with the world, *loká*. The

65 It is worth noting that the general domain of Cooking is used to conceive relationship between the social classes and their mutual dependence. As Smith (1994: 46–48) shows, the Brahmins are those who 'eat' Kṣatriyas, but they are not to be 'eaten'. The Kṣatriyas 'eat' the Vaiśyas. For this metaphor, see also Mus (1968). Such a conceptualisation also implies the cognitive meaning of the general domain of Cooking where the subject is conceived in terms of the eater and the object in terms of food, see section 3.3.

recipient is triggered to highlight the meaning of space (Gonda 1966)[66] and to create the image of an open mouth from which water flows. Thus the concept of vomiting is implied just as it is implied in in ŚB 2.2.4 (see section 3.1.1). Water reaches everywhere and covers everything. This is the essence of water which is expressed by its names *ā́pas* and *vā́r*. The recipient may elaborate the images activated by definitions of water. The image of water which reaches everywhere may prompt him to think about a flood which covers the earth with irresistible power. Within the frames of this conceptualisation, he may understand Prajāpati now loses control over his creative activity which is conceived in terms of drowning. The concept of covering metonymically activates the concept of losing the ability to see (LACK OF COGNITION IS IMPOSSIBILITY TO SEE).

Then Prajāpati wants to overcome the state of lack of control and the inability to see and to confirm his identity with what was diffused from him (ŚB 6.1.1.10). He is presented as entering water together with the triple science. Since Prajāpati is conceived as a male and the triple science (*trayī́ vidyā́*) as female, the recipient can activate the sexual act between these two forms of Prajāpati. It is worth noting that triple science is identified with water in the previous passage (ŚB 6.1.1.9). Thus the female element of Prajāpati is conceived in terms of his wife and his mother. Such a conceptualisation agrees with conceptualisation of reality conceived with aid of the model of Child Of The Waters. At the same time, in the ŚB, the verbalisation of speech is conceived in terms of a sexual act between mind and speech (see section 3.5, Jurewicz 2012b), so the recipient understands that Prajāpati can be born from waters only when he cognises himself. The coherence of thinking of the composer is strengthened in that, in the ŚB, mind is conceived in terms of fire (10.5.3, see section 3.5.1) and speech, as we have just seen, in terms of water.

The sexual act results in the appearance of an egg. Such a conceptualisation is coherent with the conceptualisation of Prajāpati as a flying man, i.e. an entity which unites human and avian features. The concept of bird is the next input space of the blend and it is elaborated by the composer: Prajāpati is conceived in terms of a bird which broods an egg. A nestling is again the triple science called *bráhman*, metonymically identified with the mouth of Prajāpati[67]. In the blend, the mouth is identified with an egg; such a conceptualisation of creation will be elaborated in the AU (see chapter 4.1.3). If the recipient elaborates the scenario of birth, he will again conceive this phase of creation

---

[66] As it will be argued, in the early Upaniṣads the term *loká* is often means 'space of experience' (see chapter 4.1.2).

[67] Metonymy MEANS FOR ACTION (Radden, Kövecses 1999: 37). For conceptual connections between the sexual act, brooding an egg and *tapas* (heat), see Kaelber (1975).

of terms of a crying baby. The fact that speech is born from itself agrees with the Vedic belief that a parent is reborn in his offspring. On this basis, the recipient understands that Prajāpati himself is reborn as the sacred speech, *bráhman*. Moreover, conceptualisation of speech in terms of fire, activated *via* qualification of the learned person as *agníkalpa*, allows the recipient to activate the image of fire appearing in waters used in the model of Child Of The Waters. We can see, then, that Ṛgvedic thinking still motivates the thought of the composers of the Brāhmaṇas. At the same time, the input space of speech allows the recipient to elaborate the concept of cognition and to understand that Prajāpati recognises his identity with his transformations.

In the blend, created in the next passage of the cosmogony (ŚB 6.1.1.11), the elements of the egg become elements of the manifest aspect of reality. Agni is the nestling and the definition of its name is the same as in ŚB 2.2.4: Agni's nature is that it is created as the first (*agrí*) of all beings (see section 3.1.1). The yellow, evoked here by the concept of tear (*áśru*), probably because of the similarity of their form becomes the horse (*áśva*)[68]. The ass (*rā́sabha*), the nature of which is defined as 'roaring' (*ras-*), is created from the white which flows out together with the yellow. It is also possible that another phonetic similarity is activated here (although not mentioned by the composer) between *rā́sabha* and *rása*. In the ṚV, *rása* often refers to Soma and Soma is metaphorically identified with semen which looks similar to the white of an egg. The white which adheres to the shell becomes the he-goat. These three animals (the horse, the ass and the he-goat, are used in the Agnicayana during preparation of lump of clay for the first brick of the altar and the fire pan (*ukhā́*) (Thite 1975: 184). The shell becomes the earth.

In the blend, the recipient may conceive this stage of creation in terms of the flight of a nestling. According to the Ṛgvedic general model of reality transformation, fire becomes the sun from which rain appears. Here, the concept of the sun is metonymically evoked by the colour yellow (DEFINING PROPERTY FOR CATEGORY[69]) and metaphorically by the concept of the horse (THE SUN IS A HORSE). The concept of rain can be evoked *via* the concept of crying or roaring (*ras-*) which also appears in descriptions of raining (verbs *rud-*, *krand-*). As we have seen, in the descriptions of the AVŚ, rain was seen as life-giving; we could say that the earth is created after rain because it is only then that it becomes covered by plants.

It is also important to add that the word *ajá* means also 'unborn'. Activation of this meaning highlights the monistic assumption according to which the unmanifest and unborn aspect appears as manifest. Moreover, as we have

[68] For the explanation of this definition, see also Witzel (1979)

[69] In its instantiation COLOUR FOR SUBSTANCE.

seen, the first creation of Prajāpati is *bráhman*, the triple science, which is manifestation of the unborn reality in speech. *Brahman* is seen as the foundation (*pratiṣṭhā́*) for further creation. The earth is conceived in the same way (ŚB 6.1.1.15, see below). Therefore, we can see conceptual coherence between the he-goat and the earth based on polysemy of the word *ajá*.

ŚB 6.1.1.12

sò 'kāmayata | ābhyò 'dbhyó 'dhīmā́m prájanayeyam íti tā́ṃ saṃkḷ́śyāpsú prā́vidhyat tásyai yáḥ párāṅ ráso 'tyákṣarat sá kūrmò 'bhavad átha yád ūrdhvám udaúkṣyatedáṃ tád yád idám ūrdhvám adbhyó 'dhi jā́yate sèyáṃ sárvāpá evā̀nuvyaìt tád idám ékam evá rūpáṃ sámadṛśyatā́pa evá |

He desired, 'May I generate, this (earth) from these waters!' He compressed it and threw it into the water. The juice which flowed from it became a tortoise; and that which was spirted upwards (became) what is produced above here over the waters. This whole (earth) dissolved itself all over the water: all this (universe) appeared as one form only, namely, water.

From that Prajāpati wants to create earth the recipient understands that in the preceding stage he did not succeed. It can be also inferred on the basis of the source domain which presents the flight of a nestling. Such a flight cannot be success and usually ends with death. Contrary to the description of ŚB 2.2.4, this stage of creation, conceived in terms of the death of creation, is not dangerous either for all of reality or for Prajāpati.

Now, Prajāpati is presented as compressing the shell so strongly that liquid flows out of it and he throws the shell into water. Since the living being is conceived in terms of a container filled with fluid already in the ṚV (Jurewicz 2010a: 314, 419), the recipient may understand that the nestling is still in the shell and that fluid is the life of a nestling which has gone. Thus the experience is transformed in the same way as it is transformed in ŚB 2.2.4 where the image of a half-born embryo is activated in the source domain (see section 3.1.1). At the same time, the word *rása* is used earlier in the cosmogony (ŚB 6.1.1.4) in reference to the excellence (*śrī́*) of the manifest aspect of reality which is placed in the head identified with the sun. If the recipient activates this conceptualisation, he will understand that Prajāpati wants to repeat this phase of creation. Since the word *rása* activates the concept of Soma, it is implied that Prajāpati wants to realise a state of omniscience which will allow him to confirm his identity with the unmanifest aspect of reality. However, he fails as the nestling fails in its flight.

The liquid which flows from the shell is divided according to its movement: one part flows out (*áti*) beyond (*párañc*) the shell and one part rises upwards (*ūrdhvám*). The former part becomes the tortoise and the latter becomes everything which is born above waters. It is important to note that tortoises are also born of eggs which make the description coherent with the preceding stage of creation conceived in terms of brooding a nestling. If the recipient activates the input space of the Agnicayana, he will understand the meaning of the tortoise. In the Agnicayana, a living tortoise was buried under the altar; its meaning is explained in ŚB 7.5.1.1-11 with use of this part of the cosmogony. When the Adhvaryu places the tortoise under the altar, he fills the altar with sap, *rása* (ŚB 7.5.1.1). The concept of the fire altar which becomes filled with the sap together with the metonymy CONTENT FOR CONTAINER allows the composer to identify the tortoise which is the sap filling the whole altar. Since the altar is the ritual representation of the world and Prajāpati, the tortoise is identified with the world and Prajāpati. So the recipient of the cosmogony understands that the creation of the tortoise is creation of the world and Prajāpati. According to ŚB 7.5.1.2, the lower shell of the tortoise becomes the earth while the upper shell becomes the sky. We can presume that when Prajāpati throws the shell into water, it is broken into two halves. In ŚB 7.5.1.6, the tortoise is identified with the sun. It is placed with head towards the west because the sun goes towards the west. Taking this into account, we can understand that separation of the earth and the sky, conceived in terms of two shells, results in sunrise. Identification of the tortoise with the sun is metonymic, in the same way as the world is identified with the sun in the AVŚ (see chapter 2.5.3). In ŚB 7.5.1.7, the tortoise is identified with breath (*prāṇó vaí kūrmáḥ*). The composer of ŚB 7.5.1.7 gives an explanation of this identification: the breath makes (*karóti*) all the beings (*prāṇó hīmā́ḥ sárvāḥ prajā́ḥ karóti*). Within the frames of the cosmogony presented in ŚB 6.1.1.12, such identification is fully justified because, as it has been stated, in this stage of creation reality manifests itself in the form of breath and speech. Therefore, the recipient understands that Prajāpati has created the cosmos with the sun conceived in terms of a living being[70]. It should be noted that on the most general level the patterns of creation is the same: creation of the cosmos is creation of sunrise.

In the next sentence of ŚB 6.1.1.12, it is said that the earth followed waters and dissolved in it (*ánuvyait*). In this way, the composer implies that creation does not succeed because the aim of Prajāpati's activity is creation of the earth. The recipient may understand this moment in terms of the death of a living being. Contrary to ŚB 2.2.4, this stage is not dangerous for reality

---

[70] In ŚB 7.5.1.5, the meaning of the word *kūrmá* is explained with reference to the cosmogony presented in ŚB 6.1.1.12: the tortoise is the form assumed by Prajāpati when he created living beings: *sá yát kūrmó nā́ma etád vaí rūpáṃ kr̥tvā́ prajā́patiḥ prajā́ asr̥jata yád ásr̥jatā́karot tád yád ákarot tásmāt kūrmáḥ*| For the meaning of tortoise in Vedic ritual, see Arole (1987), Patyal (1978–79).

in its unmanifest aspect; the description is similar to those which evoke the concept of death of Prajāpati's offspring (see section 3.2.1). The manifest aspect acquires one form that of waters (*evā̀nuvyaìt tád idám ékam evá rūpáṃ sámadr̥śyatā́pa evá*). ŚB 7.5.1.5 explicitly states that the tortoise is identical with Prajāpati, so the recipient of ŚB 6.1.1.12 can understand that, in this stage, Prajāpati again becomes unrecognisable to himself which is conceived in terms of dissolving of the tortoise in water.

It is worth noting how the composer uses general knowledge which is shared within his linguistic community the activation of which will allow the recipient to complete the meaning of the description. According to everyday experience, a nestling emerges from an egg. This experience is used in conceptualising the creation of the world: the lower shell is the earth, the upper the sky (CU 3.19). In the present description (ŚB 6.1.1.11), the shell becomes the earth and the sky is not mentioned. In this way, the meaning of unsuccessful creation is strengthened. According to ritual knowledge, the earth and the sky are conceived in terms of parts of a tortoise (ŚB 7.5.1.2, see above). Nevertheless, the tortoise is dissolved in water and thus the meaning of unsuccessful creation is again strengthened.

As has been mentioned above, the sacrificer realises the creative activity of Prajāpati in ritual. The act of building a sacrificial self is regarded as a 'work of art' (*śilpa*[71]). On this basis, the recipient may understand creation in terms of artistic creation with all the emotions which appear during this process. Thus the conceptual network will be enriched with this concept. In the blend, when clay is dissolved in water, Prajāpati is disappointed and upset.

ŚB 6.1.1.13

sò 'kāmayata | bhū́ya evá syāt prajāyetéti sò 'śrāmyat sá tápo 'tapyata sa śrāntás tepānáḥ phénam asr̥jata sò 'ved anyád vā́ etád rūpám bhū́yó vaí bhavati śrā́myāṇy evéti sá śrāntás tepānó mŕ̥daṃ śúṣkā́pamū́ṣasikatā́ṃ śárkarām áśmānam áyo híraṇyam óṣadhivanaspaty àsr̥jata ténemā́m pr̥thivī́m prā́chādayat |

He desired, 'May it become more than one, may it reproduce itself!' He toiled and heated himself[72]; and worn out with toil and heat[73], he created foam. He was aware that 'this indeed looks different, it is becoming more (than one): I must toil, indeed!' Worn out with toil and heat[74], he created clay, mud, saline soil and sand, gravel (pebble), rock, ore, gold, plants and trees: therewith he clothed this earth.

---

71 Smith (1985: 80, 1989: 101): 'The sacrificer "fashions" (*saṃskurute*) his own self in a rhythmical way (*chandomaya*) through the ritual chants likened to seeds being poured into the womb'. See also Malamoud (2005a).

72 Eggeling (1894): 'practised austerity'.

73 Eggeling (1894): 'austerity'.

74 Eggeling (1894): 'austerity'.

This stage of creation is again conceived in terms of a toiling and heating man. Prajāpati is presented as creating foam[75]. The recipient can understand that Prajāpati's sweat is conceived in these terms. He may also activate the concept of boiling water which bubbles. In ṚV 10.67.7, cognition is conceived in terms of boiling milk which becomes the sweat of the Aṅgirases (Jurewicz 2010a: 382). Then Prajāpati sees that his form is different to his previous form and realises that creation goes on. The input space of human creativity allows the recipient to enrich the blend with the emotions of happiness and excitement which are felt when an agent sees that he has succeeded. The foam, constantly heated, transforms itself into more and more solid forms[76]. Finally, trees and plants appear which cover the shell. In the blend, the recipient understands that now the earth is created.

The description ends in the following way:

ŚB 6.1.1.15

ábhūd vā́ iyám pratiṣṭhéti | tád bhū́mir abhavat tā́m aprathayat sā́ pṛthivy àbhavat sèyáṃ sárvā kṛtsnā́ mányamānāgāyad yád ágāyat tásmād iyáṃ gāyatry átho āhur agnír evā̀syai pṛṣṭhé sárvaḥ kṛtsnó mányamāno 'gāyad yád ágāyat tásmād agnír gāyatrá íti tásmād u haitád yáḥ sárvaḥ kṛtsnó mányate gā́yati vaivá gīté vā ramate |

'This (earth) has indeed become (*bhū-*) a foundation!' (he thought): hence it became the earth (*bhūmi*). He spread it out (*prath-*), and it became the broad one (or earth, *pṛthivī*). And she (the earth), thinking herself quite perfect, sang; and inasmuch as she sang (*gā-*), therefore she is Gāyatrī. But they also say, 'It was Agni, indeed, on her (the earth's) back, who thinking himself quite perfect, sang; and inasmuch as he sang (*gā-*), therefore Agni is Gāyatra.' And hence whosoever thinks himself quite perfect, either sings or delights in song.

The essence of the earth is expressed in its names. The name *bhū́mi* comes from *abhūd*, 'it became'. Eggeling interprets the sentence *ábhūd vā́ iyám pratiṣṭhā́* as a quotation of Prajāpati's thought, though I would argue that it is meant to evoke a conventional saying which expresses the shared knowledge of the community of the composer. The name *pṛthivī́* comes from the verb denoting its extension (*prath-*). The name *gāyatrī́* comes from the fact that it sings (*gai-*). The earth is conceived in terms of a beautiful woman who sings knowing that she is perfect. The beauty of the earth is not surprising when one takes into account that it is golden. The input space of human creativity allows the recipient to feel happiness and fullness as it is felt when a beautiful

---

75 This cosmogony will be elaborated in ŚB 6.1.3, see section 3.5.1.

76 This will be elaborated later, in ŚB 6.1.3, see section 3.5.1.

object is created. From the fact that it is covered with plants, and on the basis of the metaphor PLANTS ARE HAIR OF THE EARTH, the recipient understands that the earth is conceived in terms of an adult woman (see section 3.1.1). Fire, which is created as the first of beings (see ŚB 2.2.4.1, 6.1.1.11, see sections 3.1.1, 3.2.2), is here conceived in terms of a perfect male who also sings. Cohabitation of the earth and fire is conceived in terms of a sexual act that takes place on the back of the earth.

In the blend, reality finally manifests its dual nature conceived in terms of the earth and fire. In this stage of creation, reality in its manifest aspect, conceived until now in terms of a man who breaths and recites, becomes visible. Putting this in Vedic terms, the previous stages were the creation of its name (*nāman*), now, the creation of form (*rūpa*) is to be described.

In the following passages, the composer describes the creation of parts of the cosmos and the corresponding deities (ŚB 6.1.2.1-9). The consecutive stages of creation are conceived in terms of sexual acts between two opposing aspects of reality manifested in creation. The composer again elaborates the input space of hatching a bird and in each act a male nestling is born. The first stage is conceived in terms of a sexual act between fire and the earth from which the wind is born, the second stage is a sexual act between the wind and the space from which the sun is born and, in a further sexual act, between the sun and the sky, the stars are born. Other elements of cosmos are created at the same time.

The creation of groups of deities (Vasus, Rudras, Ādityas) is conceived in terms of a sexual act between mind and speech (ŚB 6.1.2.6-9). Now, only the input space of human birth is elaborated while the internally opposed nature of reality is conceptualised in terms of an androgyne: Prajāpati becomes pregnant with drops which correspond to embryos. The identity of Prajāpati and the gods is implied not only by the belief that the parent is reborn in his offspring, but because Prajāpati says that he wants to create creatures that will belong to him (ŚB 6.1.2.5: *tā́ḥ prajā́ḥ sṛjeya yā́ ma eṣú lokéṣu syū́r íti*). The cognitive dimension of creation is evoked by the concepts of mind and speech: in terms of sexual act between them the verbalisation of thought is conceived in the Veda (see section 3.5, Jurewicz 2012b).

ŚB 6.1.2.11

átho āhuḥ | prajā́patir evèmā́ṃ lokā́nt sṛṣṭvā́ pṛthivyā́m prátyatiṣṭhat tásmā imā́ óṣadhayó 'nnam apacyanta tád ā́śnāt sá garbhy àbhavat sa ūrdhvébhya evá prāṇébhyo devā́n ásṛjata yé 'vāñcaḥ prāṇā́s tébhyo mártyāḥ prajā́ ity ato yatamathā́sṛjata táthāsṛjata prajā́patis tv èvèdáṃ sárvam asṛjata yád idáṃ kíṃ ca |

> And so they say, Prajāpati, having created these worlds, was firmly established on the earth. For him these plants were ripened into food: that he ate. He became pregnant. From the upper breaths[77] he created the gods, and from the lower breaths[78] the mortal creatures.' In whatever way he created thereafter, so he created; but indeed it was Prajāpati who created everything here, whatsoever exists.

The earth in its visible form becomes the firm foundation of Prajāpati. Prajāpati is presented as eating plants. The concepts of cooking and eating metonymically evoke the scenario within the frame of which plants grow and become edible[79]. In this way, it is implied that time is created whose influence, in the ŚB, is conceived in terms of cooking (Jurewicz 2014b). The fact that Prajāpati becomes pregnant, having eaten plants, implies that eating plants leads to conception. This is elaborated in the so-called model of the Five Fires (see chapters 4.3.1, 5.1) according to which the deceased are reborn in plants. This account in the ŚB already attests this belief.

The creation of gods and mortals is conceived in terms of the transformation of breaths of Prajāpati: the upper are transformed into gods, the lower are transformed into mortals. The logic of the scenario of breathing implies that he emits breath from the openings of his body. As already said (see above, ŚB 6.1.1.1), seers identified with breaths can be understood as cognitive faculties, i.e. seeing, hearing, smelling, tasting and speaking. These breaths form the gods so, we could say, that the gods are their visible form. Mortals are created from breaths from the lower part of the body, i.e. the penis and the anus. Conceptualisation of breaths as cognitive faculties is the reason why procreation and excretion are included among the cognitive faculties in the Upaniṣads[80]. In ŚB 11.1.6.9, negative evaluation of the beings created from the lower breaths appears (see section 3.5.2) which is not attested in ŚB 6.1.2.11.

The last sentence of the passage can be interpreted as the composer not wanting to enumerate all further stages of creation contrary to the later thought, which devotes a lot of space to this topic[81]. In this respect, the cosmogonies of the ŚB are more abstract and general than the cosmogonies presented in the Smṛti texts. The composers of the ŚB focus on its most important aspects. They try to explain what happens in the most mysterious stages of

---

77 Eggeling (1894): vital airs'.

78 Eggeling (1894): vital airs'.

79 Metonymy THE INITIAL PHASE OF THE PROCESS FOR THE WHOLE PROCESS (Radden, Kövecses 1999).

80 See AU, chapter 4.1.3. Here I would see the roots of the concept of the senses of action (*karmendriya*) which include procreation and excretion. See Bakker (1982).

81 See e.g. *Manusmṛti* 1 and Purāṇic cosmogonies (Biardeau 1981).

the beginning of existence of the world, and how it influences human life, without going into a multitude of detail about the perceptible world. This seems to be less important than the next stage of creation which is conceived in terms of death of Prajāpati:

ŚB 6.1.2.12

sá prajā́ḥ sṛṣṭvā́ | sárvam ājím itvā́ vyásraṃsata tásmād u haitád yáḥ sárvam ājím éti vy èvá sraṃsate tásmād vísrastāt prāṇó madhyatá údakrāmat tásminn enam útkrānte devā́ ajahuḥ |

Having created creatures he, having run the whole race, became relaxed; and therefore even now he who runs the whole race becomes indeed relaxed. From him being thus relaxed, the breath[82] went out from within. When it had gone out of him the gods left him.

Now the composer activates the next input space of the conceptual network created by the composer of the cosmogony which is the concept of a runner who is so tired after a long run that he dies. In these terms, Prajāpati is conceived: his breath has expired and the gods leave him. Since the breath goes from Prajāpati's centre (*madhyatáḥ*), the recipient understands that the breath it is the main breath which, at the beginning of creation, enkindled other breaths (*mádhya prāṇá*, ŚB 6.1.1.2, see above). Breath is connected with speech, so it is implied that Prajāpati loses his ability to speak. The recipient understands that the gods which leave Prajāpati are the gods which are forms of his upper breath. Since the breaths can be interpreted as cognitive faculties, the recipient may infer that Prajāpati loses his cognitive abilities. And since presence of breath in the body is the sign of life the recipient understands that Prajāpati dies. If he elaborates the input space of human creativity, he could understand Prajāpati in terms of a casing which is now empty and is therefore finished[83]. We could say that, although Prajāpati preserves his form (*rūpa*), he has lost his name (*nāman*). Thus the creative transformations of reality lose their meaning. The image schema of VERTICALITY gives coherence to the blend in that all the processes are conceived as a downwards movement.

The following cosmogony gives more details as to how we should understand the death of Prajāpati:

[82] Eggeling (1894): 'vital air'.

[83] Maybe the term *mártyaḥ kuṇapó* used in ŚB 6.2.1.9 refers to that form to denote the form of Prajāpati built of the non-cooked torsos of animals (see Jurewicz 2015b, 2016e).

ŚB 7.1.2.1

prajā́patiḥ prajā́ asṛjata | sá prajā́ḥ sṛṣṭvā́ sárvam ājím itvā́ vyásraṃsata tásmād vísrastāt prāṇó madhyatá údakrāmad áthāsmā́d vīryàm údakrāmat tásminn útkrānte 'padyata tásmāt pannā́d ánnam asravad yác cákṣur adhyáśeta tásmād asyā́nnam asravan nò hehá tárhi kā́ caná pratiṣṭhā̀sa |

Prajāpati produced creatures. Having produced creatures, and run the whole race, he became relaxed. From him, when relaxed, the breath[84] went out from within: then his vigour went out of him. That having gone out, he fell down. From him, thus fallen, food flowed forth: it was from that eye on which he lay that his food flowed. And, verily, there was then no firm foundation whatever here.

Prajāpati falls down and his main breath departs. In the ṚV, *vīryà* is an abstract noun which signifies 'the ideal of manhood'[85]. At this point, the recipient is expected to evoke metonymically the penis which is the most important physical sign of manhood with one of its primary characteristics being its vertical movement. This image schematic understanding of *vīryà* is activated in ŚB 6.1.1.6 where the composer says that it is the *vīryà* of the fire-altar which makes its wings and tail to rise 'as man enlarges himself by one man' (*átha yád ékena púruṣeṇātmā́naṃ vardháyati téna vīryèṇāyám ātmā́ pakṣápuchā́ny údyachati*). The name *púruṣa* here seems to metonymically refer to the penis which ensures enlargement of man through his offspring. Activation of this concept in the context of ŚB 7.1.2.1 prompts the recipient to create the image of a penis which collapses after ejaculation. This interpretation ties in with creation being seen in terms of a sexual act. Loosing *vīryà* understood as both an abstract power and a penis implies that Prajāpati collapses. The food which flows from Prajāpati are the plants he ate to create gods and mortals (ŚB 6.1.2.1[86]). Thus the composer creates a very suggestive image of a dead body from which internal fluids flow.

There are also cosmogonies which do not describe the death of Prajāpati in his manifest part, but examine his fear of death. Let us consider the following passage:

---

84 Eggeling (1894): 'vital air'.

85 Whitaker (2011: 4, 59–61).

86 Cosmogony of ŚB 7.2.1 is interpretation of ŚB 6.1.2.12, as ŚB 6.1.3 (see section 3.5.1) is interpretation of ŚB 6.1.1.13.

ŚB 10.1.3.1-2

prajā́patiḥ prajā́ asr̥jata | sá ūrdhvébhya evá prāṇébhyo devā́n ásr̥jata yé 'vāñcaḥ prāṇā́s tébhyo mártyāḥ prajā́ áthordhvám evá mr̥tyúm prajā́bhyo 'ttā́ram asr̥jata | (1)
tásya ha prajā́pateḥ | ardhám evá mártyam ā́sīd ardhám amŕ̥taṃ tád yád asyá mártyam ā́sīt téna mr̥tyór abibhet | (2)

Prajāpati created living beings. From the upper breaths[87] he created the gods, and from the lower breaths[88] the mortal beings; and above the (mortal) beings he created Death as their consumer. Now, one half of that Prajāpati was mortal, and the other half immortal: with that part of him which was mortal he was afraid of death.

As in ŚB 6.1.2.11, this stage of creation is conceived in terms of the transformation of the breaths of Prajāpati: the upper breaths are transformed into gods and the lower breaths into mortal beings. Eggeling adds in brackets that death is above mortal beings. However, Prajāpati is conceived in terms of man and his head is the source domain for the sun. As it has been shown in ŚB 6.1.1.4, the sun, identified with the head, is the place where the immortal state is realised thanks to supernatural cognition. At the same time, as will be shown in the ŚB, the evaluation of the sun changes and its dangerous, killing aspect is highlighted. The sun is still identified with fire, but it is now conceived in terms of fire which brings death. Within the frame of this conceptualisation, death, conceived in terms of a head and the sun, is above gods and mortals.

*

Creation in the ŚB is understood as a process in which the ambivalent nature of reality manifests itself. It is expressed in the manifestation of its creative and destructive powers. The destructive power, manifest as death, is constantly present in the world. Its presence is conceived in terms of the sun identified with the head of Prajāpati. The gods who are his upper breaths are the agents through which death can kill. The mortals who are his lower breaths are those who are subject to death. On the more general level, the manifestation of reality as death can be seen as having two aspects. One is the power to kill[89].

[87] Eggeling (1897): 'out- (and in-) breathings'.
[88] Eggeling (1897): 'downward breathings'.
[89] Fauconnier, Turner (1993: 292-295), in their analysis of the blend The Grim Riper, argue that one of its input space is Death understood as the Empty General Cause which is the reason for itself ('If we ask "What caused this death?" and receive answer "Death", we do not think our question has been answered').

The second is the ability to be killed which is marvellous if we take into account that this is an ability of the Absolute. Taking this into account, we could say that when the Absolute manifests itself, it manifests as death.

3.2.3. Reality resurrects in its manifest aspect

The resurrection of reality in the world is generally conceived in terms of eating[90]. Let us consider the following passage:

ŚB 10.4.2.2-3

sò 'yáṃ saṃvatsaráḥ prajā́patiḥ | sárvāṇi bhūtā́ni sasṛje yác ca prā́ṇi yác cāprāṇám ubháyān devamanuṣyā́nt sá sárvāṇi bhūtā́ni sṛṣṭvā́ riricāná iva mene sá mṛtyór bibhayā́ṃ cakāra | (2)
sá hekṣā́ṃ cakre | katháṃ nv áhám imā́ni sárvāṇi bhūtā́ni púnar ātmánn ā́vapeya púnar ātmán dadhīya katháṃ nv àhám evaìṣā́ṃ sárveṣām bhūtā́nām púnar ātmā́ syām íti | (3)

This Prajāpati, the year, has created all existing things, both what breathes and the breathless, both gods and men. Having created all existing things, he felt like one emptied out, and was afraid of death.
He bethought himself, 'How can I get these beings back into my self[91]? how can I put them back into my self[92]? how can I be again the self[93] of all these beings?'

Prajāpati is presented as feeling empty after the creation of all beings. Such a description evokes the image of a man who excretes causing him to be so hungry that he is afraid of death; the concept of hunger is metonymically evoked by the concept of emptiness felt by Prajāpati. So the general domain of Cooking, in its specific instantiation of being hungry, is the first input space of the conceptual network created in this passage. The next are the concept of Prajāpati and the concept of reality. The generic space is the concept of transformation.

Prajāpati wants to eat and to build himself a body from the eaten food. The food becomes his own self. In the blend, Prajāpati creates creatures from himself and then wants to reabsorb them. He does not want to annihilate them, but wants to manifest himself through them and thus confirm his identity with them. The pattern of creation is always the same: the first manifestation of

---

[90] I also discuss this problem in Jurewicz (2016f).
[91] Eggeling (1897): 'body'.
[92] Eggeling (1897): 'body'.
[93] Eggeling (1897): 'body'.

reality is death in its killing aspect which is conceived in terms of an eater who dies of hunger (or almost dies); thus reality manifests its ability to be killed.

According to the main cosmogony explaining the Agnicayana, presented in the beginning of the sixth book of the ŚB and analysed in the previous section, although Prajāpati dies in his manifests aspect, he preserves his omnipotence which allows him to ask Agni to restore him which Agni does:

ŚB 6.1.2.13

sò 'gním abravīt | tvám mā sáṃdhehī́ti kíṃ me táto bhaviṣyatī́ti tváyā mā́cakṣāntai yó vaí putrā́ṇāṃ rā́dhyate téna pitáram pitāmahám putrám paútram ā́cakṣate tváyā mā́cakṣāntā átha mā sáṃdhehī́ti tathéti tám agníḥ sámadadhāt tásmād etám prajā́patiṃ sántam agnír ity ā́cakṣata ā́ ha vā́ enena pitáram pitāmahám putrám paútraṃ cakṣate yá eváṃ véda |

He said to Agni, 'Restore me!' – 'What will then accrue to me?' said he. – 'They shall call me after thee; for whichever of the sons succeeds (in life), after him they call the father, grandfather, son, and grandson: they shall call me after thee,- -restore me, then!' – 'So be it!' so (saying) Agni restored him: therefore, while being Prajāpati, they call him Agni; and verily, whosoever knows this, after him they call his father, grandfather, son, and grandson.

From the fact that Agni still exists, the recipient understands that, in the stage of creation described in terms of the death of Prajāpati, the manifest aspect withdraws itself to the stage when only Prajāpati and fire are present. This stage is most explicitly described in ŚB 2.2.4 (see section 3.1.1), but in ŚB 6.1.2.13 the presence of Agni does not threaten Prajāpati, but saves him from annihilation. Prajāpati asks fire to burn him. The image of the dead body put into a fire evokes two concepts. The first is preparation of food (secular and ritual) and the second is cremation. In the blend, Prajāpati is transformed and enlivened as food is enlivened in the body of the eater and as the dead body is enlivened thanks to the heat of the cremation fire (Jurewicz 2010a: 292 ff.). These activities are internally contradictory as they destroy one form (the dead body) in order to create a new one. Both processes, digesting and cremation of the body, are conceived in terms of cooking in the Veda (Malamoud 1996b: 42), so the latter concept can also be seen as the elaboration of the general domain of Cooking. The monistic relationship between reality and creation is conceived in terms of the relationship between male parents and their male offspring and by the name Agni being shared by the generations. Fire is therefore presented (contrary to ŚB 2.4.4) as having a life-giving nature that transforms the dead body into food and the dead person into the Father (Jurewicz 2010a: 292 ff.). The monistic assumption allows the recipient to understand that in the blend Prajāpati is not only food, but also the eater.

This source domain is elaborated in the following cosmogony the beginning of which has also been analysed earlier (see section 3.2.2):

ŚB 7.1.2.2-4

té devā́ abruvan | ná vā́ itò 'nyā́ pratiṣṭhā̀stīmám evá pitáram prajā́patiṃ sáṃskaravāma saìvá naḥ pratiṣṭhā́ bhaviṣyatī́ti | (2)
tè 'gním abruvan | ná vā́ itò 'nyā́ pratiṣṭhā̀sti tváyīmám pitáram prajā́patiṃ sáṃskaravāma saìvá naḥ pratiṣṭhā́ bhaviṣyatī́ti kím me táto bhaviṣyatī́ti | (3)
tè 'bruvan | ánnaṃ vā́ ayám prajā́patis tvánmukhā etád ánnam ádāma tvánmukhānāṃ na eṣó 'nnam asad íti tathéti tásmād devā́ agnímukhā ánnam adanti yásyai hí kásyai ca devátāyai júhvaty agnā́v evá juhvaty agnímukhā hí tád devā́ ánnam ákurvata | (4)

The gods spake, ,Verily, there is no other foundation than this: let us restore even him, our father Prajāpati; he shall be our foundation.' They said unto Agni, 'Verily, there is no foundation other than this: in thee we will restore this our father Prajāpati; he shall be our foundation.' – 'What will then be my reward?' said he. They spake, 'This Prajāpati is food: with thee for our mouth we will eat that food, and he (Prajāpati) shall be the food of us, having thee for our month.' He said, 'So be it!' Therefore the gods eat food with Agni as their mouth; for to whatsoever deity men offer, it is into Agni that they offer, since it is with Agni for their mouth that the gods thus took in the food.

Contrary to the previous cosmogony where Prajāpati is engaged in his own resurrection, here the gods are presented as a manifestation of his cognitive power. The composer creates the following conceptual network. The first input space is concept of cremation which can be seen as an elaboration of the general domain of Cooking. The next input spaces are concepts of Prajāpati and of reality. The generic space is the concept of transformation under the influence of heat. In the blend, Prajāpati lies dead and gives no foundation to the gods who are personifications of the cognitive powers of Prajāpati located in the head and who want to eat[94]. Since cognition is conceived in terms of eating, the recipient can activate this concept as the next input space of the blend. The gods look for the head through which they could not only eat, but also cognise. The recipient can imagine a frightened hungry power looking for food. The food will be the dead body of Prajāpati which will be cooked and eaten by the head. In this way, the head will endow itself with body as we do in in everyday eating.

---

[94] See above, section 3.2.2. This motive is elaborated in the cosmogony of the AU, see chapter 4.1.3.

ŚB 7.1.2.6

táṃ devā́ agnaú prā́vṛñjan | tád yá enam právṛktam agnír ā́rohad yá evā̀smā́t sá prāṇó madhyatá udákrāmat sá evaìnaṃ sá ā́padyata tám asmínn ádadhur átha yád asmā́d vīryàm udákrāmat tád asmínn ádadhur átha yád asmā́d ánnam ásravat tád asmínn ádadhus táṃ sárvaṃ kṛtsnáṃ saṃskṛ́tyordhvám údaśrayaṃs tád yáṃ tám udáśrayann imé sá lokā́ḥ |

The gods heated him in the fire; and when the fire rose over him thus heated, that same breath[95] which had gone out from within him came back to him, and they put it into him; and the vigour which had gone out of him they put into him; and the food which had flowed from him they put into him. Having made him up entire and complete, they raised him (so as to stand) upright; and inasmuch as they thus raised him upright he is these worlds.

Prajāpati is enlivened thanks to the cremation fire and having eaten himself through his cognitive manifestations[96]. In the blend, reality manifests itself in parts of the body of Prajāpati and becomes the cosmos. It is presented in the next passages: the head of Prajāpati is the sky, his eyes are the sun, the moon, the torso is the space between the sky and the earth, and the feet are the earth (ŚB 7.1.2.7-8). The image schema of VERTICALITY is introduced as the next input space which gives coherence to the description: the creation of the cosmos is conceived in terms of an upward movement.

Such a conceptualisation of creation allows the composers of the ŚB to conceive the organisation of Prajāpati in time and in terms of the general domain of Cooking:

ŚB 10.4.2.19

eṣá vā́ idáṃ sárvam pacati | ahorātraír ardhamāsaír mā́sair ṛtúbhiḥ saṃvatsaréṇa tád amúnā pakvám ayám pacati pakvásya paktéti ha smāha bhā́radvājo 'gním amúnā hí pakvám ayám pácatī́ti |

That one (the sun) bakes everything here, by means of the days and nights, the half-moons, the months, the seasons, and the year; and this (Agni, the fire) bakes what is baked by that one: 'A baker of the baked (he is),' said Bhāradvāja of Agni; 'for he bakes what has been baked by that (sun).'

---

95 Eggeling (1894): 'vital air'

96 I am also tempted to think that the recipient is invited to create one more input space which is producing fire in the fire drill when blowing with blowing: the Prajāpati is blown up and because of that he can stand up. Such a concept is evoked in ŚB 1.4.1.23 where the gods create the earth and the sky in the act of blowing. A living being is conceived in the Veda in terms of a gourd filled with liquid, e.g. Vṛtra when killed is compared to a conflated gourd (ŚB 1.6.3.16, Jurewicz 2010a: 314, 419)

The first input space of the conceptual network created by this passage is the general domain of Cooking in its specific realisation of baking food with fire. The second input space is the concept of the movement of the sun in the sky. The third is the concept of time metonymically evoked by the concept of time divisions (days, nights, half-moons, moons, the seasons and the year). The generic space is the concept of transformation under the influence of heat. In the blend, the divisions of time are conceived in terms of fuel[97] and/or teeth because it is said that the sun cooks everything with their aid. If time divisions are fuel/teeth, the passage of time is conceived in terms of cooking. If divisions of time are conceived as teeth, the passage of time is conceived in terms of eating and digesting. Thus the earthly fire transforms what has been already transformed by time. Because of that it is called 'a baker of the baked' (*pakvásya paktṛ́*). We could say that time is a realisation of the way reality manifests itself in the cosmos in a round of constant killing, dying and resurrection and the movement of the sun is the visible sign of this manifestation. According to Schayer (2012[1938]), time in Vedic philosophy is conceived as substance, though his interpretation obscures the dynamic nature of the manifest aspect which manifests itself in time. Conceptualisation of reality as manifesting in time goes back to ṚV 1.164 (see chapter 1.6) and AVŚ 19.53 (see chapter 2.1.3).

It is worth noting that on a deeper level all the elements of the cosmos are fire: the sun is identified with fire as is the earth because fire is connected with earth (ŚB 6.1.1.15, see section 3.2.2). The cooking power in terms of which the cosmic activity of reality is conceived is fire too, while time divisions are conceived in terms of fuel. The conceptualisation of reality in terms of death also highlights its fiery character because fire has a killing aspect which is highlighted in the ŚB. In the blend, the cosmos is conceived in terms fire which kills, cooks and eats itself.

Conceptualisation of the manifest aspect of Prajāpati in terms of the general domain of Cooking allows the composer to express very subtle metaphysics. The manifest aspect is the manifestation of death understood as mortality on the earth conceived in terms of food with the killing power located in the sun conceived in terms of an eater. It is important to note that the death ensures life: firstly, the killing power can live only thanks to that it is able to kill and, secondly, it ensures life on earth.

If we try to express the process of manifestation of Prajāpati in the cosmos in more general terms, we could say as follows. In the creative act, reality disintegrates itself in its manifest aspect and this stops creative movement.

---

[97] As it is in the *Puruṣasūkta*, see chapter 1.3.

This creative phase is conceived in terms of dying. Then reality sets itself into motion again and unites the disintegrated elements conceived in terms of cooking and digesting. In this way, reality manifests itself as death and as a power which annihilates and which can be annihilated. The movement that unites the disintegrated elements involves spatial and temporal division. Thus death ensures the preservation of the ontic unity of reality within its manifest aspect.

In course of development of Indian philosophy, the active, killing aspect of death has been forgotten. Philosophers were less concerned by the fact that the death has ontological meaning as an active power without which the word would not exist. They focused more on the sad destiny of those who are supposed to die which, strengthened by the Buddha's theories, led to the pessimistic evaluation of the world as a place where sentient beings constantly die. Putting this change in terms of the general domain of Cooking, we could say that the eater was lost and only the food remained.

3.3. The necessity and significance of death for mortals

In this section, I will discuss the role of living beings in the manifest aspect of reality. The sense of death of mortals is explained by ŚB 10.4.3 in the following way:

ŚB 10.4.3.1

eṣá vaí mr̥tyúr yát saṃvatsaráḥ | eṣá hí mártyānām ahorātrā́bhyām ā́yuḥ kṣiṇoty átha mriyante tásmād eṣá evá mr̥tyuḥ sá yó haitám mr̥tyúṃ saṃvatsaráṃ véda ná hāsyaiṣá purā́ jaráso'horātrā́bhyām ā́yuḥ kṣiṇóti sárvaṃ haivā́yur eti |

The Year, doubtless, is the same as Death; for he it is who, by means of day and night, destroys the life of mortal beings, and then they die: therefore the Year is the same as Death; and whosoever knows this Year (to be) Death, his life that (year) does not destroy, by day and night, before old age, and he attains his full (extent of) life.

The description begins with the identification of death with a year. The input spaces of the conceptual network are as follows: the first is the concept of time metonymically evoked by the concept of a year[98], the second is the concept of death in its two aspects (the active, killing one and the passive,

[98] In the same way the concept of autumn in Sanskrit metonymically evokes the concept of year, the same is in Polish where the concept of year is metonymically evoked by the concept of summer or, more rarely, of spring.

dying one) and the third is living beings. The generic space is concept of transformation under the influence of heat. In the blend, death is time and the cosmos dynamically conceived[99]. In the next passage (ŚB 10.4.3.2), death is called *ántaka*, 'ender', which highlights the destructive power of time.

ŚB 10.4.3.3

té devā́ḥ | etásmād ántakān mṛtyóḥ saṃvatsarā́t prajā́pater bibhayā́ṃ cakrur yád vaí nó 'yám ahorātrā́bhyām ā́yuṣó 'ntaṃ ná gáched íti |

The gods were afraid of this Prajāpati, the Year, Death, the Ender, lest he, by day and night, should reach the end of their life.

Now, the concept of Prajāpati is introduced as the next input space of the conceptual network. In the blend, Prajāpati is identified with death. The next input space is reality in its manifest aspect. The gods, who are the manifestation of the cognitive powers of reality are afraid of death (ŚB 10.1.3.1-2, see section 3.2.3). So they perform various sacrifices: Agnihotra (*agnihotrá*), the New and Full-moon sacrifices (*darśapūrṇamāsá*), the Seasonal offerings (*cāturmāsyá*), the animal sacrifice (*paśubandhá*), the Soma-sacrifice (*saumyá adhvará*), but they are still not immortal (ŚB 10.4.3.4). The concept of sacrifice is the next input space of the conceptual network. It is a safe way for reality to manifest as it dies and is then resurrected. According to ŚB 7.1.2.2-4 discussed above (see section 3.2.3), during sacrifice the gods eat with fire as their mouth. Thus the recipient can activate the next input space which is the general domain of Cooking. In the blend, the gods are expected to eat the sacrificial oblations and thus become full and immortal. Thanks to that reality will continue its manifestation. However, the gods fail in their attempts to become immortal as they do not eat enough and are still hungry. In this way, they repeat the situation of Prajāpati who, *in illo tempore*, commits mistakes before he finds the safe way for manifesting within the cosmos.

Finally, the gods try to create fire in the Agnicayana and, after some mistakes, they manage to do so (ŚB 10.4.3.5-8). Since the layers of the altar correspond to the layers of cosmos (the earth, the space, the sky and two intermediate layers between the earth and the space and between the space and the sky), the gods, having built the altar, get access to the sun where they become the eaters and thus gain immortality. Realisation of the immortal state is conceived in terms of the image schema of VERTICALITY and conceived in terms of a movement upwards. The image schema of VERTICALITY is the next input space of the conceptual network.

[99] In ŚB 10.4.2.2 Prajāpati himself is called year (Levi 1989: 16, see also section 3.5.2).

However, accordingly to the logic of this image schema, the earth will become empty and there will be no food for the eaters: for the gods or for reality which manifests itself as death. When there are no mortal beings active, death is in danger too:

ŚB 10.4.3.9

sá mṛtyúr devā́n abravīt | itthám evá sárve manuṣyā̀ amṛ́tā bhaviṣyanty átha kó máhyam bhāgó bhaviṣyatī́ti té hocur nātó 'paraḥ káścaná sahá śárīreṇāmṛ́to 'sad yadaìvá tvám etám bhāgáṃ hárāsā átha vyāvṛ́tya śárīreṇāmṛ́to 'sad yò' mṛtó 'sad vidyáyā vā kármaṇā véti yád vaí tád ábruvan vidyáyā vā kármaṇā véty eṣā́ haivá sā́ vidyā yád agnír etád u haivá tát kárma yád agníḥ |

Death spake unto the gods, 'Surely, on this wise all men will become immortal, and what share will then be mine?' They spake, 'Henceforward no one shall be immortal with the body: only when thou shalt have taken that (body) as thy share, he who is to become immortal either through knowledge, or through holy work, shall become immortal after separating from the body.' Now when they said, 'either through knowledge or through holy work,' it is this fire-altar that is the knowledge, and this fire-altar that is the holy work.

If men repeat the deed of the gods and build an altar which gives them access to the sky, they will become immortal and also become eaters without food. In that case, either death, in terms of which the manifest aspect is conceived, will die or it will attack the unmanifest aspect of reality. So the part of man which is the body will become the food of death and only the other part of man will become immortal.

As the cosmogony says, immortality can be gained 'either through knowledge or through holy work' (*vidyáyā vā kármaṇā*). Therefore, according to the composers of the ŚB, immortality is gained not only thanks to the fire of cremation after the sacrificer's death as implied in the ṚV[100], but also thanks to the fire of sacrifices performed during life with proper knowledge. Such knowledge concerns the meaning of ritual. We can presume that rituals performed without this knowledge are useless. The composer of this passage metonymically reduces both knowledge and sacrifice to the fire-altar. Thus he abrogates the alternative expressed in the previous sentence by the copula *vā*. In this way, he implies that mental activity should accompany bodily activity. The Upaniṣadic tradition will elaborate this alternative further. In my view,

100 In the ṚV, the properly performed cremation seems to be the most important factor for gaining immortality in the sun; although once the concept of 'the sacrifices and good deeds', *iṣṭāpūrtá* (ṚV 10.14.8) is mentioned as something which accompanies the deceased too; there is also a mention about 'the world of those who are doing good deeds' (ṚV 10.14.6). For this problem see chapter 5.

the composers of the ŚB are obsessed with their search for the meaning of their ritual activity without which it would be nonsensical[101]. *Evaṃvíd*, the person who 'knows in this way', is a conscious agent of this activity and the ideal for the composers of the Brāhmaṇas.

The role of deeds and knowledge which should go together is explained in the following passage:

ŚB 10.4.3.10-11

té yá evám etád vidúḥ | yé vaitát kárma kurváte mṛtvā́ púnaḥ sámbhavanti té sambhávanta evā̀mṛtatvám abhisámbhavanty átha yá evám ná vidur yé vaitát kárma ná kurváte mṛtvā́ púnaḥ sámbhavanti tá etásyaivā́nnam púnaḥ-punar bhavanti | (10)
sa yád agníṃ cinuté | etám evá tád ántakam mṛtyúṃ saṃvatsarám prajā́patim agním āpnoti yáṃ devā́ ā́pnuvann etám úpadhatte yáthaivaìnam adó devā́ upā́dadhata | (11)

And they who so know this, or they who do this holy work, come to life again when they have died, and, coming to life, they come to immortal life. But they who do not know this, or do not do this holy work, come to life again when they die, and they become the food of him (Death) time after time. (10)
But when he builds the fire-altar, he thereby gains Agni, Prajāpati, the Year, Death, the Ender, whom the gods gained; it is him he lays down even as the gods thus laid him down. (11)

Those who perform ritual deeds with knowledge of their meaning come to the sun and eat food forever. They do not come back as rain to earth as in the ṚV (Jurewicz 2008b, 2010a: 310 ff.). Those who do not know and who do not ritually act return to become the food of death and we can assume that their form is rain. Thus the way to a belief in rebirth conceived in terms of the two paths of the deceased is opened and it is based on earlier elaborations about man's posthumous destiny. However, the concept of immortality remains in accordance with earlier tradition: man escapes death as long as possible by redeeming himself with a sacrificial substitute and understanding the nature of reality[102]. He lives his whole life and does not die too early.

---

[101] As Minkowski (1992: 35) writes: 'yajñas mean something'. Since Staal's famous paper about the meaninglessness of ritual (1979) much work has been done which challenges his argument. In her book, Patton (2005) has proved the validity of her two basic assumptions: '(1) that mantras have some semantic content, even if it is only in terms of a single word association; and (2) that some imaginative world is built in juxtaposing, or metonymically linking, ritual poetic word and ritual action' (2005: 59). See also Witzel (1992), Hayakawa (2014), Jurewicz (2016d).

[102] For the problem of the sacrificial substitute in Vedic ritual, see Smith, Doniger (1989).

The structure of man reflects the structure of the world conceived in terms of the human body. While his body is mortal, his head is immortal because in the head excellence, *śrī́*, is present (see above, section 3.2.2)[103]. The body is food and the head is the eater. When a man dies, death takes only his mortal part, i.e. his body burnt in the cremation fire which then becomes his substitute. His head, filled with the fiery essence, unites with the cosmic head which is the sun.

3.4. The creation of the immortal part of man. The verb *sáṃ kr̥-*

The problem how the immortal self of sacrificer is created in ritual action has been discussed by Smith (1989[104]), Fuiji (2011). Proferes (2007) analysed this problem by focusing on the social dimension of this process. Whitaker (2011: 17) argues that '[r]itualisation constitutes a direct means to manipulate the representations, conduct, and politics of a symbolically defined social body and the body of society at large'. He sets out how masculinity is socially and ritually built by the Ṛgvedic ritual practitioners. One cannot exclude the possibility that the concept of construction of the ritual self in the Brāhmaṇas has its roots in the Ṛgvedic concepts and practices described by Whitaker.

In this section, I will analyse the selected usages of the verb *sáṃ kr̥-* with the word *ātmán* as its direct object in the cosmogonic and ritual contexts of the Agnicayana ritual in the ŚB[105]. My analysis will allow me show that this process is conceived in terms of heating under the influence of fire which can be seen, on a more general level, as the tempering of the sacrificer. Such a conceptualisation is consistent with the Vedic assumption that the sacrificer reaches the sun during his life and after death so his self should be resistant to heat. At the same time, the consistent use of the verb *sáṃ kr̥-* with *ātmán* as the direct object is the proof of the creation of general and abstract term for creative and ritual activity. It is on this basis that the Upaniṣadic philosophers built their concept of *ātmán*.

The main input spaces of the conceptual network created in these descriptions are as follows: the concept of the Agnicayana ritual, the concept of creation of the immortal self of the sacrificer, the concepts of Prajāpati

[103] Because of that Prajāpati has to cook the torsos of the animals in order to make them immortal and does not have cook their heads, see ŚB 6.2.1.9 (see Jurewicz 2015b, 2016e).

[104] For this see also analysis of ŚB 10.6.1, chapter 3.5.1.

[105] For the use of the *verb saṃ kr̥-* in Vedic cosmogonies and its meaning, see Smith (1989: 62–63, 91 ff., 101 ff.)

and of reality. The generic space is the concept of transformation under the influence of heat.

I will begin with ŚB 10.4.2.2-3, quoted above (see section 3.2.3) which presents Prajāpati as a hungry man afraid of death. Having created all beings, he wants to transform them into his own self, *ātmán*, conceived in terms of their being eaten. The composer then presents how Prajāpati attempts to realise his wish which is conceived in terms of his successive divisions into bricks in accordance with the divisions of time. At the end of this phase, Prajāpati sees all beings in the form of the triple knowledge, the Veda:

ŚB 10.4.2.21

átha sárvāṇi bhūtā́ni páryaikṣat | sá trayyā́m evá vidyā́yāṃ sárvāṇi bhūtā́ny apaśyad átra hí sárveṣāṃ chándasām ātmā́ sárveṣāṃ stómānāṃ sárveṣām prāṇā́nāṃ sárveṣāṃ devā́nām |

He then looked round over all existing things, and beheld all existing things in the threefold lore (the Veda), for therein is the self[106] of all metres, of all stomas, of all breaths[107], and of all the gods.[108]

Reality splits itself into the agent and object: Prajāpati is the agent and speech is the object. The Veda is called *ātmán*, the self, of everything that exists. In this way, reality repeats its first manifestation conceived in terms of breathing and speaking seers within its manifest aspect; in this stage of creation the manifestation of its subjective cognitive power is called Prajāpati.

Now, the verb *sáṃ kr̥-* with *ātmán* as the direct object is used in order to express the wish of Prajāpati to recognise his own identity with his speaking self, *ātmán* that potentially contains all beings:

ŚB 10.4.2.22

sá aikṣata prajā́patiḥ | trayyā́ṃ vā́vá vidyā́yāṃ sárvāṇi bhūtā́ni hánta trayóm evá vidyā́m ātmā́nam abhisaṃskarávā íti |

Prajāpati bethought himself, 'Truly, all existing things are in the threefold lore: well, then, I will construct for myself[109] so as to contain the whole threefold lore.'

The phrase *átmā́naṃ sáṃ kr̥-* is used to express how this recognition is realised:

106 Eggeling (1897): 'body'.
107 Eggeling (1897): 'vital airs'.
108 The last sentence of this passage will be analysed in section 3.6.
109 Eggeling (1897) adds: 'a body'.

ŚB 10.4.2.26

sá esú triṣú lokéṣūkhā́yām | yónau réto bhūtám ātmā́nam asiñcac chandomáyaṃ stomamáyam prāṇamáyaṃ devatāmáyaṃ tásyārdhamāsé prathamá ātmā́ sámaskriyata dávīyasi páro dávīyasi páraḥ saṃvatsará evá sárvaḥ kṛtsnáḥ sámaskriyata |

Into these three worlds, (in the form of) the fire-pan, he (Prajāpati) poured, as seed into the womb, his own self made up of the metres, stomas, breaths[110], and deities. In the course of a half-moon the first self[111] was made up, in a further (half-moon) the next (self[112]), in a further one the next, – in a year he is made up whole and complete.

The cosmogony uses the general domain of Procreation in its specific realisation of the sexual act to conceive the act of recognition of the unity of subjective and objective aspects of reality. The conceptual network consists of the following input spaces. The first one is the general domain of Procreation in its specific realisation of a sexual act. The next are the concepts of Prajāpati and reality. The next input space is the concept of the ritual of Agnicayana. It is activated by the concept of a fire pan (*ukhā́*) which was prepared from clay and filled with fire. The generic space is the concept of transformation under the influence of heat. In the blend, the empty fire pan represents the emptiness felt by Prajāpati. Prajāpati is presented as filling the pan with his own self metonymically identified with semen. In the blend, reality fills its empty manifest aspect with itself. Since in terms of the sexual act, thinking is conceived in the ŚB (see sections 3.2.2, 3.5, Jurewicz 2012b), the recipient understands that reality in its subjective manifestation (Prajāpati) understands its own creative speech and manifests in it. The ontic dimension of this manifestation is based on the assumption that the parent is reborn in his offspring. This stage of creation can be labelled as the creation of names (*nāman*).

Now Prajāpati constructs the manifest self of reality which is the world visible in forms (*rūpa*). Its construction is conceived in terms of the construction of the bricks of a fire altar in accordance to the division of time which are in this very moment created:

ŚB 10.4.2.27

evám etā́ṃ trayī́ṃ vidyā́m ātmánn ā́vapatātmánn akuruta só 'traivá sárveṣām bhūtā́nām ātmā̀bhavac chandomáya stomamáyaḥ prāṇamáyo devatāmáyaḥ sá etanmáya evá bhūtvòrdhvá údakrāmat |

[110] Eggeling (1897): 'vital airs'.
[111] Eggeling (1897): 'body'.
[112] Eggeling (1897): '(body)'.

In this manner he put this threefold lore into his own self, and made it his own; and in this very (performance) he became the self[113] of all existing things, (a self)[114] composed of the metres, stomas, breaths[115], and deities; and having become composed of all that, he ascended upwards.

In the blend, the manifest aspect of reality is the cosmos subjected to the power of time conceived in terms of the fire altar.

Creation of the self of reality is also conceived in terms of giving food to Prajāpati; the verb *sáṃ kr̥-* is used in reference to restoration of Prajāpati:

ŚB 10.4.1.1

prajā́patiṃ vísrastam | yátra devā́ḥ samáskurvaṃs tám ukhā́yāṃ yónau réto bhūtám asiñcan yónir vā́ ukhā́ tásmā etát saṃvatsaré 'nnaṃ sámaskurvan yò 'yám agníś citás tád ātmánā páryadadhus tád ātmánā párihitam ātmaìvā̀bhavat tásmād ánnam ātmánā párihitam ātmaìvá bhavati |

When the gods restored the relaxed Prajāpati, they poured him, as seed, into the fire-pan (*ukhā*) as the womb, for the fire-pan is a womb. In the course of a year they prepared for him this food, to wit, the fire-altar built here, and enclosed it in itself[116]; and, being enclosed in itself[117], it became itself[118]; whence food, when enclosed in oneself[119], becomes oneself[120].

The composer elaborates the general domain of Procreation with a focus on the phase of pregnancy. As an embryo is fed in the womb of his mother during a year (symbolic interval of time of pregnancy), in the same way Prajāpati is fed by the gods. Within the frames of this conceptualisation, the gods are the embodiment of the subjective power of reality and its killing aspect. At this moment, Prajāpati is a manifestation of the ability of reality to be subject to death. When he is restored, he will become the manifestation of death in both of its aspects: the gods will enter his head and become the embodiment of the killing power of reality, while the lower parts of reality will become the embodiment of the power of reality to be killed.

---

113 Eggeling (1879): 'body'.
114 Eggeling (1879): 'body'.
115 Eggeling (1870): 'vital airs'.
116 Eggeling (1879): 'in a body'.
117 Eggeling (1879): 'in a body'.
118 Eggeling (1879): 'the body itself'.
119 Eggeling (1879): 'in a body'.
120 Eggeling (1879): 'the body itself'.

The word *ātmán* as direct object of *sáṃ kṛ-* also denotes the fire altar that is constructed in ritual. The fire altar is conceived in terms of a living entity with a head which should be united to the body:

ŚB 9.3.1.6

śíra evá dyaúḥ | nákṣatrāṇi kéśās tád etád víśvaṃ cákṣur evā̀dityáḥ sá náras tád avástāchīrṣṇó bhavaty avástād dhí divá ādityás tád asyaìtáchiro vaiśvānará ātmā̀yám agníś citá ātmā́nam evā́syaitát saṃskṛ́tya śíraḥ prátidadhāti |

The sky is the (upper part of the) head, and the stars are the hair; it is the All, and Āditya (the sun) is the eye, he is the man: it is in the lower part of the (upper) head, for the sun is below the sky. Vaiśvānara is the head thereof, and this built-up Agni (the altar) is himself[121]: thus, having completed himself[122], he restores the head thereto.

The fire altar is conceived in terms of a living body with all its details, it has arms, thighs, torso and ribs:

ŚB 8.1.4.3

sá eṣá paśúr yád agníḥ | só 'traivá sárvaḥ kṛtsnáḥ sáṃskṛtas tásya yā́ḥ purástād upadádhati taú bāhū́ átha yā́ḥ paścā́t té sakthyā̀v átha yā́ mádhya upadádhāti sá ātmā́ tā́ retaḥsícor vélayópadadhāti pṛṣṭáyo vaí retaḥsícau mádhyam u pṛṣṭáyo madhyató hy áyám ātmā́ sarváta úpadadhāti sarváto hy àyám ātmā́ |

Now that Agni (the altar) is an animal, and (as such) he is even now made up whole and entire, – those (bricks) which he lays down in front are his fore-feet, and those behind are his thighs; and those which he places in the middle are that self[123] of his. He places these in the region of the two *retaḥsic* (bricks), for the retaḥsic are the ribs, and the ribs are the middle, and that self[124] is in the middle (of the limbs). He places them all round, for that self[125] extends all round.

In the ritual, man is re-enacting the creative activity of reality which is conceived as transformations of Prajāpati. The activity of Prajāpati is a pattern for man because, as I have mentioned, the concept of ambivalent reality is too abstract to be such a pattern. The most important aim of the construction of the fire altar is to create an immortal self, *ātmán*, for the

---

121 Eggeling (1879): 'the body'.
122 Eggeling (1879): 'his body'.
123 Eggeling (1897): 'body'.
124 Eggeling (1897): 'body'.
125 Eggeling (1897): 'body'.

sacrificer. The cosmogonies express its creation in exactly the same way as they describe creation:

ŚB 10.4.2.29 (compare ŚB 10.4.2.26)

sá yád agníṃ ceṣyámāṇo dī́kṣate | yáthaiva tát prajā́patir eṣú triṣú lokéṣūkhā́yāṃ yónau réto bhūtám ātmā́nam ásiñcad evám evaiṣá etád ātmā́nam ukhā́yāṃ yónau réto bhūtáṃ siñcati chandomáyaṃ stomamáyam prāṇamáyaṃ devatāmáyaṃ tásyārdhamāsé prathamá ātmā́ sáṃskriyate dávīyasi páro dávīyasi páraḥ saṃvatsará evá sárvaḥ kṛtsnáḥ sáṃskriyate |

Now when he (the Sacrificer), being about to build an altar, undergoes the initiation-rite, – even as Prajāpati poured his own self, as seed, into the fire-pan as the womb, – so does he pour into the fire-pan, as seed into the womb, his own self composed of the metres, stomas, breaths[126], and deities. In the course of a half-moon, his first self[127] is made up, in a further (half-moon) the next (self[128]), in a further one the next, – in a year he is made up whole and complete.

ŚB 10.4.1.2 (compare ŚB 10.4.1.1)

táthaivaìtád yájamānaḥ | ātmā́nam ukhā́yāṃ yónau réto bhūtáṃ siñcati yónir vā́ ukhā́ tásmā etát saṃvatsaré 'nnaṃ sáṃskaroti yò 'yám agníś citás tád ātmánā páridadhāti tád ātmánā párihitam ātmaìvá bhavati tásmād ánnam ātmánā párihitam ātmaìvá bhavati |

In like manner does the Sacrificer now pour his own self[129], as seed, into the fire-pan as the womb, for the fire-pan is a womb. In the course of a year he prepares for it[130] this food, to wit, the fire-altar here built, and enclosed it in himself[131]; and, being enclosed in himself[132], it became himself[133]; whence food, when enclosed in oneself[134], becomes oneself[135].

The act of bringing waters is a ritual manifestation of uniting the head of the sacrificer's head to his *ātmán*:

126 Eggeling (1897): 'vital airs'.
127 Eggeling (1897): 'body'.
128 Eggeling (1897): '(body)'.
129 Eggeling (1897) adds: '(or body)'.
130 Eggeling (1897) adds: '(this self)'.
131 Eggeling (1879): 'in a body'.
132 Eggeling (1879): 'in a body'.
133 Eggeling (1879): 'the body itself'.
134 Eggeling (1879): 'in a body'.
135 Eggeling (1879): 'the body itself'.

ŚB 11.2.6.1 (compare ŚB 9.3.1.6)

śíro ha vā́ etád yajñásya yát práṇītāḥ | sá yát práṇītāḥ praṇáyati śíra evaìtád yajñásya sáṃskaroti sá vidyāchíra evá ma etát sáṃskriyata íti |

The Praṇītā water, doubtless, is the head of the sacrifice; and when he leads forward the Praṇītā water, it is the head of the sacrifice he thereby forms, and he should know that it is that head of his own that is then being formed.

In this passage, the word *ātmán* is not used, but there is no doubt that the head of the sacrificer is meant when the ritual act of bringing water is performed. I am tempted to think that the phonetic similarity between the words *práṇītā* and *prāṇás*, breaths, which are located in the head of Prajāpati, gives additional rationality to the description.

Besides the fire altar, there is another ritual manifestation of the *ātmán* of the sacrificer: it is the sepulchral tomb built for the sacrificer after his death. It should be built in the same way as the fire altar was built during his life:

ŚB 13.8.1.17

athā́ta āvṛ́d evà | agnividháyāgnicítaḥ śmaśānáṃ karoti yád vaí yájamāno'gníṃ cinutè 'múṣmai tál lokā́ya yajñénātmā́naṃ sáṃskuruta etád u ha yajñíyaṃ karmā́saṃsthitam ā́ śmaśānakaraṇā́t tád yád agnividháyāgnicítaḥ śmaśānáṃ karóty agnicityā́m evá tát sáṃsthāpayati |

Now as to the order of procedure. For an Agnicit (builder of a fire-altar) one makes the tomb after the manner of the fire-altar; for when a Sacrificer builds a fire-altar he thereby constructs for himself by sacrifice a (new) self[136] for yonder world; but that sacrificial performance is not complete until the making of a tomb; and when he makes the tomb of the Agnicit after the manner of the fire-altar, it is thereby he completes the Agnicityā.

The composer explicitly states that the performance of Agnicayana is fully completed only when the tomb is built. He implies, then, that the afterlife state of man depends on the ritual performed after his death. I will discuss this topic in chapter 5.

Construction of the ritual self of the sacrificer needs a safe place:

---

136 Eggeling (1900): 'body'.

ŚB 10.2.5.1

athā́taś cáyanasyaivà | antaròpasádau cinoty etád vaí devā́ abibhayur yád vaí ná imám ihá rákṣāṃsi nāṣṭrā́ ná hanyur íti tá etā́ḥ púro 'paśyann upasáda imā́n evá lokā́n imé vaí lokā́ḥ púras tā́ḥ prā́padyanta tā́ḥ prapadyā́bhaye 'nāṣṭrá etám ātmā́naṃ sámaskurvata táthaivaìtád yájamāna etā́ḥ púraḥ prapadyā́bhaye 'nāṣṭrá etám ātmā́naṃ sáṃskurute |

Now as to the building itself. He builds between the two (performances of the) Upasads. For at that time the gods were afraid lest the fiends, the Rakṣas, should destroy that (self[137]) of theirs (built) there. They saw these strongholds, the Upasads, to wit, these worlds, for these worlds are indeed strongholds. They entered them, and having entered them, they completed that self[138] in a place free from danger and devilry; and in like manner does the Sacrificer now, after entering these strongholds, complete this self[139] in a place free from danger and devilry[140].

In this passage, the creation of the sacrificer's *ātmán* is conceived in terms of the creation of strongholds which guard the sacrificer from evil. As I have shown elsewhere, the concept of conquering a stronghold is used as the source domain for a spiritual process already in the ṚV (Jurewicz 2010b). Within the frames of this conceptualisation, it is in the stronghold that the precious object is hidden which is the self of man transformed under the influence of Soma. This concept is elaborated in the AVŚ (see chapter 2.5.1) and will be further elaborated in the Upaniṣads (see chapter 4.4.2.4). This fact attests the continuity of philosophical tradition as far as metaphoric philosophical concepts are concerned. The composer of ŚB 10.2.5.2 evokes this conceptualisation. He puts it within the frames of a fight between the gods and evil beings (*rákṣas*). In the blend thus enriched, the performance of Upasads is identified with the creation of worlds conceived in terms of building strongholds with the sacrificer identified with the gods. Within the strongholds thus built, he can safely built his precious immortal self. The fact that the worlds are built 'in front' (*purástāt*) also attests the continuity of tradition. In the ṚV, the world is conceived as a dynamic whole which develops eastwards; east is in front of the agent (Heesterman 1983, Jurewicz 2010a: 128 ff.). Evil beings, like Rakṣases, remain beyond the world which also accords with Ṛgvedic thinking (Jurewicz 2010a: 65 ff.).

---

137 Eggeling (1897): 'Agni's body'.
138 Eggeling (1997): 'body'.
139 Eggeling (1997): 'body'.
140 See also ŚB 7.4.1.33, 10.2.5.2.

The sacrificer should be careful when he constructs his *ātmán* and that he should use only perfect bricks:

ŚB 8.7.2.16

ná binnā́ṃ ná kṛṣṇām úpadadhyāt | ā́rchati vā́ eṣā́ yā́ bhidyáta ā́rtam v etád rūpáṃ yát kṛṣṇáṃ néd ā́rtam ātmā́nam abhisaṃskarávā íti nā́bhinnām párāsyen néd ánārtam ātmáno bahirdhā́ karávāṇī́ti |

Let him not lay down either a broken (brick) or a black one; for one that is broken causes failure, and sickly is that form which is black: 'Lest I should make up a sickly self[141],' he thinks. Let him not throw aside an unbroken (brick), lest he should put what is not sickly outside the self[142].

Conceptualisation of *ātmán* in terms of the content of a stronghold implies that it is seen as a precious treasure. Together with the prescription to use only perfect bricks, it activates the concept of human artistic creativity in terms of which manifestation of reality and the ritual process are conceived.

The correspondence between the activity of Prajāpati and the sacrificer is even stronger. As I have already shown, the cosmos is the visible self of reality and is manifest in sacred speech. The same is for the sacrificer. As did Prajāpati in constructing a fire altar, the sacrificer constructs his immortal self made of the sounds of sacred speech[143]:

ŚB 10.5.1.5

sā́ vā́ eṣā́ vā́k tredhā́ vihitā́ | ṛ́co yájūṃṣi sā́māni máṇḍalam evā́ṛ́co 'rciḥ sā́māni púruṣo yájūṃṣy áthaitád amṛ́taṃ yád etád arcír dī́pyata idáṃ tát puṣkaraparṇáṃ tád yát puṣkaraparṇám upadhā́yāgníṃ cinóty etásminn evaìtád amṛ́ta ṛṅmáyaṃ yajurmáyaṃ sāmamáyam ātmā́naṃ sáṃskurute sò'mṛ́to bhavati |

This speech, indeed, is threefold – the Ṛk-verses, the Yajus-formulas, and the Sāman-tunes the Ṛk-verses are the orb, the Sāman-tunes the light, and the Yajus-formulas the man (in the sun); and that immortal element, the shining light, is this lotus-leaf: thus, when he builds up the Fire-altar after laying down the lotus-leaf, it is on that immortal element that he builds for himself[144] consisting of the Ṛk, the Yajus, and the Sāman; and he becomes immortal.

141 Eggeling (1897): 'body'.

142 Eggeling (1897): 'body'.

143 For construction of self made of words and poetic metres, see Malamoud (2002a), Malamoud (2005a).

144 Eggeling (1897) adds: 'a body'.

The input spaces of the blend are the Veda, the sun and the ritual action of the sacrificer. In the blend, the Ṛk-stanzas are the orb of the sun, the Sāman-chants are its light and the Yajus-formulas are man in the sun. The lotus-leaf is the immortal light in the sun and this light is the basis for the altar and for the sacrificer's *ātmán*. It is implied that when the construction of the altar begins, the sacrificer is conceived as being in the sun and all transformations leading to the creation of the immortal self take place there. The self is composed of the sounds of sacred speech which implies an internal transformation connected with breath and recitation. The concept of a man in the sun will be used in the Upaniṣadic descriptions of a breath practice which leads to liberating knowledge. We can see just how strongly Upaniṣadic philosophical thought is entrenched in earlier thinking.

In another part of the ŚB, which does not belong to the Agnicayana ritual, though worth mentioning in the present discussion, it is said that the immortal *ātmán* of the sacrificer is built by the priests as in cosmogonies the gods created Prajāpati's *ātmán*:

ŚB 4.3.4.5

> *tā vā́ etā́ḥ | ṛtvíjām evá dákṣiṇā anyáṃ vā́ etá etásyātmā́naṃ sáṃskurvanty etáṃ yajñám ṛṅmáyaṃ yajurmáyaṃ sāmamáyam āhutimáyaṃ sò 'syā̀múṣmiṃ loká ātmā́ bhavati tád yé mā́jījanantéti tásmād ṛtvígbhya evá dákṣiṇā dadyān nā́nṛtvigbhyaḥ |*
>
> But it is to the officiating priests, forsooth, that these gifts of his belong, for they prepare him another self, to wit, this sacrifice, consisting of Ṛk and Yajus and Sāman and oblations, that becomes his self in yonder world: 'It is they that have generated me,' from this (consideration) he should give the gifts to officiating priests and not to non-officiating.

The role of the sacrificer and the priests in ritual activity is patterned after the cosmogonic theories described above according to which Prajāpati dies in creation and is restored by the gods to become the cosmic manifestation of aspects of reality, i.e. of its killing aspect and the aspect which is able to be killed. In the same way, the sacrificer's self dies during initiation (*dīkṣā́*). Thus the ability of reality to be killed is re-enacted in a micro-scale. Then the immortal self is restored by the priests and it becomes the manifestation of the killing aspect of reality, while the body of the sacrificer is the manifestation of its dying aspect (see section 3.2.3).

The following paragraph explicitly states that the sacrificer reaches the sky when he places the bricks called *nākasád*, 'living in the sky', in the fifth layer of the altar:

ŚB 8.6.1.1

nākasáda úpadadhāti | devā́ vaí nākasádó 'traiṣá sárvo 'gniḥ sáṃskṛtáḥ sá eṣó 'tra nā́kaḥ svargó lokás tásmin devā́ asīdaṃs tád yád etásmin nā́ke svargé loké devā́ ásīdaṃs tásmād devā́ nākasádas táthaivaìtád yájamāno yád etā́ upadádhāty etásminn evaìtán nā́ke svargé loké sīdati |

He lays down the Nākasads (firmament-seated bricks): the firmament-seated ones, assuredly, are the gods. In this (layer) that whole fire-altar becomes completed, and therein these (bricks are) the firmament (*nāka*), the world of heaven: it is therein that the gods seated themselves; and inasmuch as the gods seated themselves on that firmament, in the world of heaven, the gods are the firmament-seated. And in like manner does the Sacrificer, when he lays down these (bricks), now seat himself on that firmament, in the world of heaven.

Placing the bricks is the ritual manifestation of the moment when the construction of the immortal self of the sacrificer commences. It begins with placing a lotus-leaf under the altar which, as I have argued, is the manifestation of the beginning of the internal transformations of the sacrificer conceived in terms of being in the sun. When the *nākasád*-bricks are placed, the self of the sacrificer lives in the sky like the gods. As I have shown, the final stage of Somic exultation is conceived in the ṚV as taking place in the sun under the heating influence of Soma which fills the sun. This concept is now reinterpreted within ritual frames, but it preserves its main scenario. Since Soma is lost its influence, is replaced by the influence ritual activity accompanied by recitation and breath practices. And, contrary to the ṚV, the inner spiritual transformation is externalised in that its stages can be perceived while the altar is built. The composers of the Upaniṣads will again interiorise this transformation.

The context of cosmogonies, which use the verb *sáṃ kṛ-*, allows me to reconstruct its semantic range. Eggeling translates this verb in various ways: 'to construct', 'to make up', 'to prepare', 'to complete', 'to encompass', 'to build'. His translations highlight the meaning of composing an object which is to be done perfectly. The idea of perfectness is also expressed in that the bricks used for making ritual *ātmán* should be flawless. However, the composers of the ŚB, in their cosmogonic descriptions, also activate the concepts of heating, insemination, pregnancy and feeding. All these activities are seen as transformation under the heat of fire. Therefore, I would argue that, on a more general level, the verb *sáṃ kṛ-* conveys the meaning of transformation under the influence of heat. As I have shown, the general domain of Cleansing By Heat is an important source domain in the ṚV for various processes such as creation, kindling fire, purification of Soma and cognition

(Jurewicz 2010a). I have also shown that this general domain is expressed *via* its various specific realisations such as grooming a horse, clarification of butter, sharpening, anointing with balm, licking, purification of gold and sweating. In the ŚB, this domain is activated mostly *via* the verb *tap-* and *śram-*, but also *via* more concrete concepts, such as those mentioned above (ŚB 6.1.3, see section 3.5.1).

There is one more concrete concept which seems to be evoked by the composers of the ŚB in order to conceive creation of the sacrificer's *ātmán* when they use the verb *sáṃ kṛ-*. This is the concept of tempering[145]. It fits well within the frames of the ritual assumptions of the ŚB. During his life, man is supposed to create his *ātmán* in the sun. It is created in ritual. Each sacrifice strengthens his solar self *ātmán*. When man dies, he finally unites with his solar self. Because of that, the composers of the ŚB say that the afterlife state depends on deeds. Conceptualisation of the creation of *ātmán* in terms of tempering highlights its resistance to the fiery power of the sun which is not able to destroy it. Those deceased who do not possess knowledge about themselves can only see their *ātmán* just before its destruction by the sun (see chapter 5.1, 5.2). Thus it is implied that ritual activity is only a part of spiritual transformation. Its counterpart is knowledge which is realised in breath practices and recitation. Since breath and speech are conceived in terms of fire, the recipient can also understand their influence in terms of tempering. If the recipient enriches the conceptual network with this input space, he will understand that the self of the sacrificer is fully resistant to the power of the sun only when it is tempered by ritual acts and spiritual practice. If one of them is lacking, the self will be destroyed and it will become 'a mortal carcass' (*mártya kuṇapó*, ŚB 6.2.1.9, see Jurewicz 2015b, 2016e).

*

The expression *ātmā̆nam sáṃ kṛ-* is consequently used in the ŚB in reference to the creative activity of Prajāpati and the ritual activity of man. Both processes are conceived in the same way. Reality firstly manifests itself in breath and speech (the stage of *nāman*) and, then, in the visible cosmos (the stage of *rūpa*). This is conceived in terms of the creation of Prajāpati's self *ātmán* which is, in turn, conceived in terms of building the fire altar. The sacrificer does the same. He constructs his visible self, his *ātmán*, while he constructs the fire altar (the stage of *rūpa*) and, at the same time, he

[145] The metaphor CREATION OF THE IMMORTAL SELF IS PURIFICATION OF GOLD is activated in JB 1.47, see chapter 5.1.2.

constructs his invisible self, his *ātmán* composed of the sounds of the Veda (the stage of *nāman*).

Putting this in more general terms, we could say that inconceivable and inexpressible reality creates its *ātmán* in order to manifest itself in space and time. Its immortality realises itself in the constant change of life and death. The immortality of the sacrificer is realised thanks to his *ātmán* created in the ritual. He rescues his part made of the sounds of the Veda from death which will consume only his visible part.

In the ŚB 2.2.4, the first manifestation of reality is conceived in terms of Prajāpati who creates fire. In ŚB 6.1.1.1, this first manifestation is conceived as the appearance of speaking and of shining breaths (see section 3.2.2). The descriptions of the next stages of creation implies that these stages are conceived as transformations of fire. Their composers evoke the concepts of heating, burning in fire, insemination, pregnancy, eating, sweating and purifying gold (for the last two concepts, see section 3.5.1). Transformations of the sacrificer are conceived in the same way: he breathes, speaks, inseminates, eats, and in this way builds his *ātmán* in the sense of his outward appearance. In his sacrificial activity, he also builds his immortal *ātmán* under the influence of heat caused by breath and recitation. This is the reason why the fire altar in the Sanskrit original is simply called 'fire'. It is the ritual manifestation of the burning aspect of reality and of the burning self of the sacrificer.

The concept of *ātmán* understood in this way is the starting point of the Upaniṣadic thinkers about *ātmán* as the whole of reality and its innermost essence. Moreover, this concept of *ātmán* is referred to by the Buddha in his *pratītyasamutpāda* in its first two links: *avijjā* (*avidyā*) and *saṃkhāra* (*saṃskāra*)[146]. According to the *pratītyasamutpāda*, the lack of knowledge conditions mental formations or volitional disposition (as the word *saṃkhāra* is usually translated). My claim is that the Buddha was referring to Vedic ritual thinking and practice[147]. In the descriptions of the Agnicayana, the possibility of re-enacting creation is conditioned not only by the correct performance of the ritual, but also by the knowledge of the sacrificer. The Buddha seems to say that it is not knowledge, but a lack of knowledge (*avijjā*) which is the

146 As far as I know, the word *saṃskāra* is not used in the Vedic texts (the nominal form of the *sáṃ kr̥-* is *sáṃskr̥ti*, ŚB 4.2.1.17, 7.4.1.14, 8.3.4.11). It probably came back from the Buddhism to the later Hinduism to denote ritual ceremonies which should be performed by the members of three upper social classes in the crucial moments of their life. The concept of heating is not highlighted, however, it can be reconstructed by the way the *saṃskāras* are described. The analysis of this problem goes beyond the scope of the present work (see Smith 1985: 81 ff., 1989: 90 ff.).

147 Blanchard (2012), Jurewicz 2005[2000].

condition of *saṃkhāra*. It is a lack of knowledge which makes people build a fire altar and believe it is the *ātmán* of reality and of the sacrificer.

As Hamilton writes: 'the fact that the Pāli term (as a past participle, *saṃkhata*) also means 'constructed' or 'made' refers to the fact that all of the factors of experience are constructed or made *like that* by our cognitive process' (Hamilton 2000: 109). Just as Prajāpati creates the world to experience it, similarly the sacrificer creates the world for himself as if from the beginning. In his analysis of the meaning of the Vedic concept of *loká*, Gonda (1966) sees its roots in the Ṛgvedic experience of looking for new lands. The conquest of a new land is its creation from the beginning, according to the needs of the conquerors. This involves a new experience for them. According to Gonda, in the early Vedic texts *loká*

> 'is a position or situation which from the point of view of religion and view of life is important, safe, stable and steady, a resting-place in universal extensity towards which man directs himself. That is why I have my doubts about the correctness of the translation "world"' (1966: 35).

In his definition, Gonda still assumes the ontological dimension of this concept which is followed by Smith who sees *loká* as '"world" in the sense of an ontological condition or status' (1989: 103). The etymology of this word, which is Indo-European **loukos*, 'bright open space, clearing', activates the meanings of light, of possibility to see and to move in an unconstrained way[148]. As I have shown, these are features of the supra-natural state gained thanks to Soma as presented in the ṚV (Jurewicz 2010a). So I would argue that primarily *loká* is space of experience of an individual sacrificer who is able to make it his own self, *ātmán*, and thus realise supra-natural state thanks to ritual process[149]. The ontological status of this state is the result of cognitive process and it is this very ontological status which is denied by the Buddha in his link *saṃkhāra*.

Finally, I would add that the use of the same phrase *átmānaṃ sáṃ kṛ-* to denote creative and ritual processes and the use of the word *agní* in reference to a fire altar is important proof of the tendency for abstraction and generalisation. The composers of the ŚB could be sure that when they used them, their recipients would immediately unfold the cosmogonical, cosmological and teleological knowledge which made their life meaningful.

[148] Mayrhofer (1996), Gonda (1966: 7 ff.), Malamoud (2005b: 88).

[149] For the meaning of *loká* as the space of experience of reality see chapter 4.1.2.

3.5. The cognitive character of the creative process

In this section, I will discuss the conceptualisation of creation in terms of cognition. This way of thinking about creation is attested already in the ṚV (Jurewicz 2010a). In the ŚB, the use of the verbs 'to think' (*īkṣ-*) and 'to desire' (*kam-*), betrays the conceptualisation of the beginnings of creation in terms of human mental activity. The cognitive nature of creation is expressed explicitly in ŚB 2.2.4 (analysed above, see section 3.1.1), where the description of the first state of creation, conceived in terms of the lack of food for fire, is presented as taking place in the mind of Prajāpati (*tád evā̀sya mánasy āsa*, ŚB 2.2.4.3). This implies the cognitive nature of the whole process. In the frames of this conceptualisation, the pre-creative state is the state when the subjective cognitive power of reality is already manifested in speech (conceived in terms of fire), but there is no object which could be cognised by it. It exists only potentially conceived in terms of the bare earth.

In the previous sections, I have discussed the general domain of Cooking which allows the composers of the ŚB to conceptualise the manifestations of reality in the world as the death and resurrection of Prajāpati. I have also argued that cognition undertaken by reality within its manifest aspect is conceived in terms of eating. Within the frames of this conceptualisation, the cognising subject is conceived in terms of the eater, the object of cognition is conceived in terms of food and the act of cognition in terms of eating. The logic of the source domain, which is the creation of the body of the eater, allows the composers to express the reflexive character of cognition during which the subject cognises its identity with the object. In this way, they can preserve the monistic nature of reality which in its manifest aspect cognises and realises its ontic unity. The general domain of Cooking will be elaborated in the Upaniṣad in reference to subjective-objective cognition which is characteristic for the manifest aspect of reality and which is different from liberating cognition (see chapter 4.1.3).

The next source domain used in by the composers of the ŚB to conceive cognition is the general domain of Procreation (section 3.5.3). Conceptualisation of creation in terms of the sexual act is activated in all Vedic thought and is already in the ṚV. The subject is conceived in terms of a male, the object in terms of a female and the act of cognition in terms of the sexual act. The externalisation of thought in speech is conceived in these terms: mind is a male and speech is a female, so when they sexually unite, thought is expressed conceived in terms of an offspring identical with its parent (see section 3.2.2, Jurewicz 2012b). There is a similarity between the concept of eating and the concept of the sexual act in that they lead, at least partially, to identification of subject and the object. While the general domain of Cooking highlights the horrifying and destroying aspect of sacrum, the general domain of Procreation highlights its life-giving and creative aspect. This general domain is elaborated by the composers of the Upaniṣads: the concept of the sexual act is used to conceive subjective-objective cognition, while the concept of orgasm is used to conceived of the ultimate happiness realised in liberating cognition (see chapters 4.4.2.3, 4.4.2.5).

Conceptualisation of cognition in terms of seeing is quite widespread among the Indo-European community (Sweetser 1990). This conceptualisation is attested in the ŚB by the use of the verb *dr̥ś-* in reference to a cognitive act, for example ŚB 2.5.1.3 (see section 3.2.1). In ŚB 10.4.2.21 (quoted above, see section 3.4), Prajāpati is presented as seeing his creation in the triple Veda. The concept of light which is elaborated by the composers of the ŚB to conceive the beginnings of creation and the creative activity is also based on the metaphor COGNITION IS SEEING because light is a necessary condition for seeing. This conceptualisation is elaborated in all Indian philosophy[150].

Generally speaking, it could be said that, in the earlier cosmogonies of ŚB, the cognitive character of the creation is expressed mostly with use of metaphors while the later cosmogonies are more explicit. I will first analyse the main metaphors in terms of which creative cognition is conceived in the ŚB and I will then show how this conceptualisation is expressed in more direct ways.

3.5.1. Cognition as cleansing and heating

In this section, I analyse how cognition is conceived in terms of a general domain which comes from the R̥V, i.e. Cleansing By Heat. As argued above, the thinkers of the ŚB seek to repeat the Somic experience without Soma trying to find other methods of gaining supernatural cognition. In their search, they practiced activities which resulted in the heating of the body. These activities are reflected by the formula which begins cosmogonies (*sò 'śrāmyat sá tápo tapyata*). Sometimes these activities can be reconstructed, for example ŚB 6.1.1.12 which evokes the concept of a tired runner (see section 3.2.2). The specific domain evoked by the general domain of Cleansing By Heat is no longer clarification of butter (as it is in the RV), but other cleansing processes under the influence of heat such as sweating, boiling water, boiling milk and the purification of gold[151].

---

[150] For the use of this metaphor by Descartes, see Lakoff, Johnson (1999).

[151] For the production of gold in the Vedic India, see Rau (1974).

ŚB 6.1.3.1

> *prajā́patir vā́ idám ágra āsīt | éka evá sò 'kāmayata syām prájāyeyéti sò 'śrāmyat sá tápo 'tapyata tásmāc chrāntā́t tepānā́d ā́po 'sṛjyan tát ásmāt púruṣāt taptā́d ā́po jāyante |*
>
> Verily, Prajāpati alone was here in the beginning. He desired, 'May I exist, may I reproduce myself!' He toiled, he practised austerity (or, became heated). From him, worn out and heated, the waters were created: because of that from that heated Person the waters are born.

The main input spaces of the conceptual network created in the first sentence of this cosmogony are the same as always. They are concepts of Prajāpati, of a man who toils and sweats and reality. The generic space is the general domain of Cleansing By Heat. In the blend, Prajāpati who wants to multiply himself toils and heats himself up. In this way, reality manifests its fiery aspect. Then its liquid aspect is manifested conceived in terms of waters. It is worth noting that the composer himself reveals the source domain in terms of which creation is conceived: it is sweating after a heavy effort which could be the practices performed in order to get to a supernatural state of consciousness. In the frames of cosmogony, the activity of Prajāpati is the model for other activities and an explanation of human behaviour. In the blend, sweat is identified with water which is its next input space. Thus the recipient may activate earlier descriptions of creation in which the primeval state of the future world is conceived in terms of water (as in the *Nāsadīyasūkta*, Jurewicz 2010a: 48–49).

Creation is conceived in terms of further heating of the sweat of Prajāpati:

ŚB 6.1.3.2

> *ā́po 'bruvan | kvà vayám bhavāméti tápyadhvam íty abravīt tā́ atapyanta tā́ḥ phénam asṛjanta tásmād apā́ṃ taptā́nām phéno jāyate |*
>
> The waters said, 'What is to become of us?' 'Ye shall be heated,' he said. They were heated; they created foam: hence foam is produced in heated water.

The composer elaborates the input space of water and creates the image of boiling water which makes bubbles. The recipient may introduce one more input space which is the concept of milk because milk, when boiled, produces more foam than water. The concept of milk is easily evoked on the basis of the general knowledge of cosmogonies which often conceive the liquid aspect of Prajāpati in terms of milk (e.g. ŚB 2.2.4, 2.5.1.3, see sections 3.1.1,

3.2.1)[152]. The recipient well versed in the Veda can also activate the image of the Aṅgirases sweating with hot milk, evoked in ṚV 10.67.7. The foam is heated and the blend is elaborated:

ŚB 6.1.3.3

phénò 'bravīt | kvā̀hám bhavānī́ti tápyasvéty abravīt sò 'tapyata sá mŕ̥dam asr̥jataitád vaí phénas tapyate yád apsv ā̀véṣṭamānaḥ plávate sá yadòpahanyáte mŕ̥d evá bhavati |

The foam (m.) said, 'What is to become of me?' – 'Thou shalt be heated!' he said. It was heated, and produced clay; for indeed the foam is heated, when it floats on the water, covering it; and when one beats upon it, it indeed becomes clay.

Now, the blend is enriched with the next input space of clay. The concept of heating comes from the input space of boiling water and milk and the concept of solidification comes from the input space of milk: in the blend, the sweat of Prajāpati is milk which is beaten in order to get cream[153] and cream is identified with clay. At the same time, clay is soil mixed with water so the consistency of the blend, which identifies sweat with water, is also based on the experience.

The next stages of cosmogony are conceived in the following terms. The clay heats itself and becomes sand (ŚB 6.1.3.4). In his explanation, the composer introduces the next input space: it is a field which is ploughed and this way heated: in the blend, the clay (which is the transformation of Prajāpati's sweat) becomes sand. Then sand becomes pebbles, pebbles become stones, stone become iron and iron becomes gold (ŚB 6.1.3.5). The way of their transformation is not specified except for gold, the purification of which is metonymically evoked *via* the concept of blowing (verb *dham-*). The logic of the input spaces of boiling water and milk allows the recipient to assume that these are also transformation under the influence of heat[154]. It could be said that ploughing also makes the earth warm and clean in that sense that it can be used for cultivation. The description clearly shows that the composer was aware of the difference between iron ore and gold ore because in his experiential explanation he says that heated ore is similar to gold; it does not become gold. In the blend, the concept of cleaning under the influence

---

152 See ṚV 10.68.7 (Jurewicz 2010a: 382–383). The same blend is created in the *amr̥tamanthana* description where the water of the ocean is conceived as milky. For Ṛgvedic roots of this myth, see Lidova (1994).

153 See BU 1.2.3, see chapter 4.1.1.

154 It is difficult to say if the composers of the ŚB really thought that iron becomes from the sand, but surely they wanted to present this process as such.

of heat is elaborated: cleaning causes the appearance of a shining and liquid substance which finally becomes solid. In these terms, creative changes are seen as the transformation of the sweat of Prajāpati.

The next two sentences of the cosmogony allow the recipient to understand the epistemological and ontological effects of creation:

ŚB 6.1.3.6-7

> *tád yád asr̥jyatā́kṣarat | tád yád ákṣarat tásmād akṣáraṃ yád aṣṭáu kr̥tvó 'kṣarat saìvā̀ṣṭā́kṣarā gāyatry àbhavat* | (6)
> *ábhūd vā́ iyám pratiṣṭhéti | tád bhū́mir abhavat tā́m aprathayat sā́ pr̥thivy àbhavat* | (7)
>
> Now that which was created was flowing; and inasmuch as it was flowing (*akṣarat*), a syllable (*akṣara*) resulted therefrom; and inasmuch as it flowed eight times, that octosyllabic Gāyatrī was produced[155] (6)
> This has indeed become (*bhū*) a foundation (resting-place),' so he thought: whence it became the earth (*bhūmi*). He spread it out (*prath*): it became the broad (earth, *pr̥thivī*). (7)

The heated gold is liquid and it flows before it becomes solid. If the recipient elaborates the input space of boiling milk, he can conceive this stage of creation in terms of the clarification of butter the final form of which is similar to purified gold. The composer builds a metaphor which allows for the conceptualisation of the *Gayatrī*-stanza in terms of heated gold: each syllable is conceived in terms of one flow of a golden stream[156]. Such a conceptualisation of the creation of speech is justified within the light of the earlier thought which conceives cognition in terms of the general domain of Cleansing By Heat and in terms of the appearance of fluid (Jurewicz 2010a). The blend created by the composer is now is enriched with the input space of cognition and speech and the recipient can create the image of a person who heats up in order to obtain supernatural cognition and the ability to produce speech so excellent that it can be conceived in terms of streams of gold.

The general process presented in the blend is transformation of something that is liquid, conceived in terms of water, into something that is solid conceived in terms of gold. The crucial role of cognition in creation of the world can be clearly seen: cognition, conceived in terms of the general domain of Cleansing By Heat which is the generic space of the blend, is the underlying motive of creation and the earth is the form of speech.

---

[155] I analyse this passage of the ŚB and *aksára* as philosophical notion in Jurewicz 2012.
[156] Speech is conceived in terms of gold already in AVŚ 10.7.28 (see chapter 2.2.4).

The composer of the next cosmogony (ŚB 10.5.3) creates a conceptual network consisting of two main input spaces. The first is the concept of cognition and the second the concept of reality. The generic space is transformation under the influence of heat. In the blend, transformations of reality are seen as cognitive and are conceived in terms of heating. The meaning of the generic space is introduced into the blend (Turner 1996) and the process described in the blend is conceived in abstract terms. However, in order to understand the logic of the process, the recipient is expected to elaborate the abstract input space of cognition in more concrete terms of a cognising man.

ŚB 10.5.3.1-2

nèva vā́ idám ágre 'sad ā́sīn nèva sád āsīt | *ā́sīd iva vā́ idám ágre nèvā́sīt tád dha tán mána evā̀sa* | (1)
tásmād etád ṛ́ṣiṇābhyánūktam nā́sad āsīn nò sád āsīt tadā́nīm íti nèva hí sán máno nèvā́sat | (2)

Verily, in the beginning this (universe) was, as it were, neither non-existent nor existent; in the beginning this (universe), indeed, as it were, existed and did not exist: there was then only that Mind.
Wherefore it has been said by the Ṛṣi (*Ṛg-veda* X, 129, 1), 'There was then neither the non-existent nor the existent; for Mind was, as it were, neither existent nor non-existent.

The cosmogony is the exegesis of the *Nāsadīyasūkta*. Although the composer accepts that reality in the pre-creative state is inexpressible, he tries to construe a positive claim about this state (similarly to ŚB 6.1.1.1). The only possible thing which can be said about reality in its pre-creative state is that it is mind. Conceptualisation of reality in terms of mind betrays a tendency for abstraction. The way to this abstract notion can be reconstructed in the following way. The first step is the metaphoric conceptualisation of reality in terms of man (REALITY IS A MAN, see *Puruṣasūkta*, chapter 1.3). Thinking is the essential feature of man and it takes place in mind. This fact is the reason for the metonymy MIND FOR HUMAN BEING[157]. Then the concept of the mind becomes a metaphor for reality (REALITY IS MIND).

---

[157] A specific instantiation of the general metonymy DEFINING PROPERTY FOR CATEGORY (Radden, Kövecses 1999: 35).

ŚB 10.5.3.3

tád idám mánaḥ sṛṣṭám āvír abubhūṣat | níruktataram mūrtátaraṃ tád ātmā́nam ánvaichat tát tápo 'tapyata tát prā́mūrchat tát ṣáṭtriṃśataṃ sahásrāṇy apaśyad ātmáno 'gnī́n arkā́n manomáyān manaś cítas té mánasaivā́dhīyanta mánasācīyanta mánasaiṣú gráhā agṛhyanta mánasāstuvata mánasāśaṃsan yát kíṃ ca yájñe kárma kriyáte yát kíṃ ca yajñíyaṃ kárma mánasaiva téṣu tán manomáyeṣu manaścítsu manomáyam akriyata tád yát kíṃ cemā́nibhūtā́ni mánasā saṃkalpáyanti téṣām evá sā́ kṛ́tis tā́n evā́dadhati tā́ṃś cinvanti téṣu gráhān gṛhṇanti téṣu stuvate téṣu śaṃsanty etā́vatī vai mánaso víbhūtir etā́vatī vísṛṣṭir etā́van mánaḥ ṣáṭtriṃśat sahásrāṇy agnáyo'rkā́s téṣām ékaika evá tā́vān yā́vān asaú pū́rvaḥ |

This Mind, when created, wished to become manifest, – more defined, more substantial: it sought after a self[158]. It practised austerity: it acquired consistency. It then beheld thirty-six thousand Arka-fires of its own self, composed of mind, built up of mind: mentally alone they were established (on sacrificial hearths) and mentally built up; mentally the cups (of Soma) were drawn thereat mentally they chanted, and mentally they recited on (near) them, – whatever rite is performed at the sacrifice, whatever sacrificial rite there is, that was performed mentally only, as a mental performance, on those (fires or fire-altars) composed of mind, and built up of mind. And whatever it is that (living) beings here conceive in their mind that was done regarding those (mental Agnis): – they establish them (on the hearths) and build them up (as fire-altars); they draw the cups for them; they chant on (near) them and recite hymns on them, – of that extent was the development of Mind, of that extent its creation, – so great is Mind: thirty-six thousand Arka-fires; and each of these as great as that former (fire-altar) was.

The generic space of heating is evoked *via* concepts of heating (*tát tápo 'tapyata*) and the concept of *mūrch-* which denotes solidification under the influence of heat[159]. Conceived in this way, mind acquires the form which can be cognised by itself: the form that is possible to be seen is conceived in terms of thirty six thousand fires in which the sacrifice of Soma is performed. If the recipient metonymically activates conceptualisation of the manifest aspect of reality in terms of man (MIND FOR HUMAN BEING), he can create the image of a shining man inside of whom mental cognition takes place. In the frames of this conceptualisation, the number 36 000 is a symbolic number for years for the ideal life of this manifestation, which is one hundred years each of 360 days.

The fires are presented as performing sacrifice and receiving oblations. Thus the input space of sacrifice, which is performed by beings, is activated. The sacrifice consists of pouring oblation into fire which is conceived in

---

158 Eggeling (1897) adds: '(body)'

159 Used in AU 1.1.2, see chapter 4.1.3.

the ŚB in terms of eating[160]. Since cognition is also conceived in terms of eating, the recipient can understand the activity of fires as cognition. This meaning is strengthened by the fact that fires transform mind in the blend. The general formulation 'beings' (*bhūtā́ni*) implies that functioning of the cosmos is conceived in terms of sacrifice which is expressed explicitly by the model of the Five Fires (*pañcāgnividyā*, see chapter 4.3.1).

In the same way, mind transforms itself into speech (*vā́c*), speech into breath (*prāṇá*), breath into sight (*cákṣus*), sight into hearing (*śrótra*), hearing into deed (*kárman*) and deed into fire (*agní*). Such a conceptualisation of creation is motivated by metonymic thinking: in consecutive states of creation, reality is thought of in terms of man performing an activity evoked by its salient factor, i.e. the faculty which enables its performance.

Thus reality manifests itself in forms which are more and more cognizable and which are its self, *ātmán*. The mental form is the form which thinks and can be thought about. The verbal form is the form which speaks and can be spoken about. But speech involves the hearer, so the recipient may presume that, during its manifestation in verbal form, reality in its manifest aspect divides itself into two and creates the form to which it can speak. The next form breathes which implies that it is the form which is alive. Since life presupposes death, the recipient can understand that death is also created in this stage of creation. The visible form is the form which sees and can be seen. The audible form is the form which hears and can be heard. Both forms presuppose the existence of an object which can be seen and heard. The form called 'deed' (*kárman*) is the form which acts and which creates objects. The fiery form is the form which burns and is burnt. In other words, reality, in its manifest aspect, begins to think about itself, to speak about itself, to live and to die, to see itself, to hear itself, to act upon itself and to burn itself. It order to perform these activities, it divides itself into a cognising subject (one who thinks, speaks, breathes, sees, hears, moves and burns) and an object which is cognised (which can be thought about, verbalised, which is alive and dead at the same time, visible, audible, expressed in deed and burnt). The aim of this cognitive process is to recognise itself. The reflexive character of creation is explicitly expressed by the cosmogony (*tád ātmā́nam ánvaichat*). The fact that creation ends when reality manifests itself as fire implies that reality is conceived in these terms. The recipient may presume that reality has found the form which most perfectly expresses its essence, hence creation is finished. We can clearly see that conceptualisation of reality in terms of fire is still assumed by the composers of the ŚB.

---

[160] ŚB 2.2.4, see section 3.1.1, BU 1.4, see chapter 4.1.1.

The recipient may also activate the next input space of the conceptual network which is a particular man who is expected to re-enact creation in ritual. Just as reality manifests itself as burning, so men who perform sacrifices burn with *tápas* created in *dīkṣā́* and with breath practice and recitation. They thereby realise in micro-scale the monism of reality. Conceptualisation of the manifest aspect of reality in terms of man strengthens the coherence of this interpretation.

The sequence of the first stages of creation reflects breath practice: man heats himself, thinks, expresses his thoughts in the sounds of the Veda and at this very moment begins to breath. The appearance of sight probably refers to the experience of the internal heat which can be perceived as light enabling the agent to see. Recitation makes the agent hear the sounds as if inside him. Then he begins to act according to the words he recites, i.e. kindles fire and sacrifices. This cosmogony is an important stage in the development of the meaning of the word *tapas* towards the meaning of 'ascesis' understood as the mental effort leading to the experience of reality and in which real heat is not necessary.

Moreover, if we reverse the sequence of the stages of manifestation, we get a similar sequence to the Upaniṣadic descriptions of liberating experience (see chapters 4.4.2.4, 4.4.2.5). The process begins with fire which is an outside object on which cognition can focus in order to understand that fire is the essence of everything that exists and that reality is fire too[161]. At the same time, the concept of fire activates the concept of ritual which is an outside activity enabling the performer to experience his identity with Prajāpati (Jurewicz 2014b). In the following stages, the mental focus of the practitioner is internalised: it begins with activity of the body, then sensual perception, hearing and seeing, comes, then breathing, speaking and thinking. Viewed in this way, the ritual is an activity which not only deals with external objects, but also embraces deeper and deeper states of oneself. This agrees with the way the ritual of Agnicayana is understood. The present description goes even further: the sacrifice can be performerd, while man thinks. It is explicitly expressed in the following passage:

ŚB 11.2.6.13

tád āhuḥ | ātmayājī́ śreyā́3n devayājī́3 íty ātmayājī́ti ha brūyāt sá ha vā́ ātmayājī́ yó védedám me 'nenā́ṅgaṃ saṃskriyáta idám me'nenā́ṅgam úpadhīyata íti sá yathā́his tvacó nirmucyétaivám asmā́n mártyāchárīrāt pāpmáno nírmucyate sá ṛṅmáyo yajurmáyaḥ sāmamáya āhutimáyaḥ svargáṃ lokám abhisámbhavati |

---

[161] See ṚV 1.164.1, chapter 1.6.

> As to this they ask, 'Who is the better one, the self-offerer, or the god-offerer?' Let him say, 'The self-offerer;' for a self-offerer, doubtless, is he who knows, 'This my (new) body is formed by that[162], this my (new) body is procured thereby.' And even as a snake frees itself from its skin, so does he free himself from his mortal body, from sin; and made up of the Ṛk, the Yajus, the Sāman, and of offerings, does he pass on to the heavenly world.

The concept of self-offering is grounded in a breath practice which leads to cognition conceived in terms of sacrificial eating. As reality, in the form of Prajāpati, heats itself and creates its speaking and breathing form, in the same way man heats himself and creates his immortal self (see section 3.4). This experience is the base for the Upaniṣadic search of *ātmán* and for the philosophical apparatus created during this search which was adequate to express the states realised during liberating cognition. Without the mental effort attested in the Brāhmaṇas, the philosophers of the Upaniṣads would never have achieved their aim[163].

3.5.2. Creation as agreement. The concept of *māyā*

The cognitive character of the creation can also be seen in the following cosmogony. The input spaces of the conceptual network are the general domain of Procreation, the concept of Prajāpati, the concept of the cosmos in its spatio-temporal functioning and the concept of reality. The generic space is transformation. The general domain of Procreation includes brooding an egg, human pregnancy and a child's development. The earliest stages of creation are conceived in terms of the former and the later in terms of the latter. Moreover, the composer takes into account not only the physical, but also the cognitive development of a child. This allows him to enrich the conceptualisation of creation with concepts of giving names and agreement. However, contrary to ŚB 11.2.3, which will be discussed in the next section (3.5.3), the cognitive dimension of creation is conceived metaphorically.

162 Eggeling (1900) adds: 'body of Yajña, the sacrifice'.

163 The text anticipates the conceptualisation of the sacrifice in the *Bhagavadgītā* according to which every deed, be it external or internal, is sacrifice.

ŚB 11.1.6.1

ā́po ha vā́ idám ágre salilám evā̀sa | tā́ akāmayanta katháṃ nú prájāyemahī́ti tā́ aśrāmyaṃs tā́s tápo'tapyanta tā́su tápas tapyámānāsu hiraṇmáyam āṇḍáṃ sámbabhūvā́jāto ha tárhi saṃvatsará āsa tád idáṃ hiraṇmáyam āṇḍáṃ yā́vat saṃvatsarásya vélā tā́vat páryaplavata |

Verily, in the beginning this (universe) was water, nothing but a sea of water. The waters desired, 'How can we be reproduced?' They toiled and performed fervid devotions, when they were becoming heated, a golden egg was produced. The year, indeed, was not then in existence: this golden egg floated about for as long as the space of a year.

The first manifest form of reality is conceived in terms of water. Such a conceptualisation brings the recipient's mind to the third stage of creation of the *Nāsadīyasūkta* (*apraketáṃ saliláṃ sárvam ā idám*)[164]. This association is justified as the next stage is conceived in terms of the appearance of a golden egg which corresponds to the fourth stage of creation (*tuchyénābhú ápihitaṃ yád ā́sīt tápasas tán mahinā́jāyataíkam*).

The concept of the golden egg is already a blend. Its input spaces are evoked as follows. The first, evoked *via* the concept of egg, is the concept of brooding (the specific realisation of the general domain of Procreation). The second, evoked *via* the concept of gold, is the production of gold. The third, evoked on the basis of the golden colour, is the sun. All the input spaces are evoked metonymically[165] and their elements are expected to be transferred to the blend. Within it, the creative transformation of reality in this stage are conceived in terms of brooding, producing gold and the sunrise. The consistency of the network can be seen in that all these processes involve heating. However, the wording of the cosmogony is quite abstract and the recipient does not have to activate all those processes in order to understand the general meaning of the passage according to which reality, in its creative activity, heats itself and transforms part into a shining, round form which is potentially the world. As we will see, input spaces of the sunrise and of the general domain of Procreation will be elaborated in the later passages of cosmogony, though not the input space of producing gold.

---

[164] For water mythology in the Laurasian mythology, see Witzel (2012: 112 ff.). For classification of waters in the Veda, see Bodewitz (1982).

[165] RESULT OF ACTION FOR ACTION (EGG FOR HATCHING, GOLD FOR PURIFICATION OF GOLD, APPEARANCE OF THE BABY'S HEAD DURING THE DELIVERY FOR DELIVERY), DEFINING PROPERTY FOR CATEGORY (GOLDEN COLOUR FOR THE SUN, Radden, Kövecses (1999)).

The composer states that time did not exist in this stage of creation and that the golden egg floated during a year. A year is a symbolic measure of pregnancy in the Veda (ŚB 11.1.6.2 below, see also BU 1.2.4, chapter 4.1.1) and, on this basis, the recipient may enrich the blend with this concept. At the same time, a year is the time for a full turn of the sun. The recipient then understands that the first general measure of time is created and it corresponds to the first creative change which happens at this stage of creation. Thus the input space of a world subjected to time is activated. This is the stage when it exists as a potential. Its actualisation is described in the following way:

ŚB 11.1.6.2

tátaḥ saṃvatsaré púruṣaḥ samábhavat | sá prajā́patis tásmād u saṃvatsará evá strī́ vā gaúr vā váḍabā vā víjāyate saṃvatsaré hí prajā́patir ájāyata sá idáṃ hiraṇmáyam āṇḍáṃ vyárujan nā́ha tárhi kā́ caná pratiṣṭhā̀sa tád enam idám evá hiraṇmáyam āṇḍáṃ yā́vat saṃvatsarásya vélā́sīt tā́vad bíbhrat páryaplavata |

In a year's time a man, this Prajāpati, was produced therefrom; and hence a woman, a cow, or a mare brings forth within the space of a year; for Prajāpati was born in a year. He broke open this golden egg. There was then, indeed, no resting-place: only this golden egg, bearing him, floated about for as long as the space of a year.

The composer explicitly activates the input space of pregnancy and, similarly to ŚB 6.1.3 (see above), he refers to the experience motivating the conceptualisation of creation. In the blend, a Prajāpati is born who is conceived in terms of a blended concept of bird and man. Again, similarly to ŚB 6.1.3, everyday life experience becomes the result of the first creative activity as the pregnancy of women, cows and mares lasts one year.

Then the composer says that there is was no foundation. In the ŚB, the feet and the earth are treated as the foundation of Prajāpati (ŚB 6.1.1.3, 15, section 3.2.2, ŚB 7.1.2.7-8, see section 3.2.3). The recipient can therefore create the image of a nestling which, in a half-broken egg, pokes out its head. He can also understand this stage of creation in terms of a little baby who cannot walk. In ŚB 2.2.4, a grim image of an unsuccessful delivery is created of a baby whose head has emerged from his mother's womb, but who is stuck and is therefore unable or unwilling to emerge fully (see section 3.1.1). The composer implies, in this way, that the destructive power of reality, conceived in terms of the hungry eater, is dangerous for itself. However, it seems that, contrary to ŚB 2.2.4, here, reality is not threated by the appearance of the eater and is just a stage of creation.

ŚB 11.1.6.3-5

sá saṃvatsaré vyā́jihīrṣat | sa bhū́r íti vyā́harat sèyám pṛthivy àbhavad bhúva íti tád idám antárikṣam abhavat svàr íti sā̀saú dyaúr abhavat tásmād u saṃvatsará evá kumāró vyā́jihīrṣati saṃvatsaré hí prajā́patir vyā́harat | (3)
sá vā́ ékākṣarad vyakṣarā́ṇy evá | prathamáṃ vádan prajā́patir avadat tásmād ékākṣarad vyakṣarā́ṇy evá prathamáṃ vádan kumāró vadati | (4)
tā́ni vā etā́ni páñcākṣárāṇi | tā́n páñca rtū́n akuruta tá imé páñca rtávaḥ sá evám imā́ṃ lokā́n jātā́nt saṃvatsaré prajā́patir abhyúdatiṣṭhat tásmād u saṃvatsará evá kumāra úttiṣṭhāsati saṃvatsaré hí prajā́patir udátiṣṭhat | (5)

At the end of a year he tried to speak. He said *'bhūḥ'*: this (word) became this earth; '*bhuvaḥ*': this became this air; '*svaḥ*': this became yonder sky. Therefore a child tries to speak at the end of a year, for at the end of a year Prajāpati tried to speak. (3)
When he was first speaking Prajāpati spoke (words) of one syllable and of two syllables; whence a child, when first speaking, speaks (words) of one syllable and of two syllables. (4)
These (three words consist of), five syllables: he made them to be the five seasons, and thus there are these five seasons. At the end of the (first) year, Prajāpati rose to stand on these worlds thus produced; whence a child tries to stand up at the end of a year, for at the end of a year Prajāpati stood up. (5)

Now, the composer elaborates the input space of the general domain of Procreation: a child, has been born, grows and begins to speak. The halves of the egg and the space between them are named. Since cognition results in being, naming parts of the egg causes creation of the world. It can be presumed that not only spatial organisation of the world takes place in this stage. Prajāpati stands up, which means he now has a foundation, and his upward movement breaks the egg and creates its parts. The concept of movement activates the concept of time which has already been created in its form of a year. The composer now elaborates the input spaces of a growing baby and of reality manifesting itself as the spatio-temporal cosmos. In the blend, Prajāpati says *bhū́ḥ* and thereby gains both his legs and his foundation which is the earth. He then says *bhúvaḥ* and rises up which creates both his torso and space. Finally, he says *svàḥ* and stands up thereby creating his head and the sky with the sun. The recipient may also activate the input space of the sunrise and see the process of creation in terms of the rising sun. Thus the cosmos is divided into three spatial spheres and three parts of time, most probably the spring, summer and autumn (see ṚV 10.90.6, see section 1.3).

ŚB 11.1.6.6

sá sahásrāyur jajñe | sá yáthā nadyaí pārám parāpáśyed eváṃ svasyā́yuṣaḥ pārám párācakhyau |

He was born with a life of a thousand years: even as one might see in the distance the opposite shore, so did he behold the opposite shore (the end) of his own life.

The composer elaborates the scenario of human development: Prajāpati, conceived now in terms of an adult person who is able to stand, looks down at his own feet. The second input space of the network is the cosmos. In the blend, the head of Prajāpati is the sun and his feet are the earth. The composer introduces the concept of a river. It can be seen as an elaboration of the input space of waters in terms of which the first form of reality is conceived (ŚB 11.1.6.1). Now, water assumes the form of a river. It is worth mentioning that the creation of a river in the sky is presented in ṚV 1.164.25 (see chapter 1.6). Again one sees the continuity of tradition. The difference here lies in topology as in the ṚV the river flows downwards while in ŚB 11.1.6.6 it is a conceptualisation of the space between the earth and the sky. In the blend, the body of Prajāpati, covered by a river, is the *axis mundi* delineated by the rising sun. If the space between the earth and the sky is conceived in terms of a river, the *axis mundi* is a ford enabling human beings to cross to the other side. Here I would see the source of the later use of the name *tīrtha* to denote a sacred place: it is the place where a ford to heaven begins.

The life of Prajāpati will last a thousand years. The recipient thus infers that immortality is included within the cosmos. At the same time, Prajāpati looks down at his feet which is the earth on which mortal beings live and sees the end of his own life. We may presume that he is afraid of death, although here this is not expressed specifically as in other cosmogonies.

ŚB 11.1.6.7-8

só 'rcañ chrā́myaṃś cacāra prajā́kāmaḥ | sá ātmány evá prájātim adhatta sá āsyènaivá devā́n asṛjata té devā́ dívam abhipádyāsṛjyanta tád devā́nāṃ devatváṃ yád dívam abhipadyā́sṛjyanta tásmai sasṛjānā́ya dívevāsa tád vevá devā́nāṃ devatváṃ yád asmai sasṛjānā́ya dívevā́sa | (7)
átha yò 'yám ávāṅ prāṇáḥ | ténā́surān asṛjata tá imā́m evá pṛthivī́m abhipádyāsṛjyanta tásmai sasṛjānā́ya táma ivāsa | (8)

Desirous of offspring, he went on singing praises and toiling. He laid the power of reproduction into his own self. By (the breath of) his mouth he created the gods: the gods were created on entering the sky; and this is the godhead of the gods (*deva*) that they were created on entering the sky (*div*). Having created them, there was, as it were, daylight for him; and this also is the godhead of the gods that, after creating them, there was, as it were, daylight (*diva*) for him. (7) And by the downward breathing he created the Asuras: they were created on entering this earth. Having created them there was, as it were, darkness for him. (8)

This stage of creation is expressed by the verb *arc-* which means 'to sing' and 'to shine'. The recipient understands that Prajāpati is conceived in terms of a man who is toiling and heats himself during recitation. The form *só 'rcañ chrā̆myaṃś cacāra* conveys the meaning of an activity which is performed for a long time and involves movement. It probably reflects some practices which led to mental transformations. The result of this activity is the manifestation of Prajāpati's androgynous nature: he becomes able to give birth. In this way, the ambivalent essence of reality is expressed.

The appearance of the gods and the Asuras is the result of reality realising its cognitive abilities. The network now consists of five input spaces. The first is a woman giving birth; this concept is an elaboration of the general domain of Procreation. The second is a man who cognises or does not cognise. This input space can be seen as the elaboration of the general domain of Procreation in its specific realisation of a child's development. Now, the child, as an adult, tests his cognitive abilities. One could argue that he also tests his possible human forms and realises that he can be both man and woman. In this way, the internally contradictory character of reality is manifest. The third input space are the concepts of the gods and the Asuras, the fourth is the cosmos and the fifth is the concept of reality. In the blend, the creation of the gods and the Asuras is conceived in terms of birth-giving and is seen as a result of a cognitive process. When Prajāpati sees and cognises, his head is active and he gives birth to the gods from his mouth. When Prajāpati does not see and cognise, his lower part is active and he gives birth to the Asuras from his lower breath. The gods are in the sky where the sun is, identical with Prajāpati's head, and this is that part of him which sees and cognises. The Asuras are on earth identified with Prajāpati's feet which cannot see and cognise and this is the part of Prajāpati where consciousness is lost. The identification of the mouth with a womb (ŚB 2.2.4, see section 3.1.1, BU 1.4.6, see chapter 4.1.2) gives coherence to an image of Prajāpati conceived as giving birth from his upper and lower parts. At the same time, this image may trigger the recipient to activate the image of a man emitting internal fluids from openings of his body.

We can see that, although the main scenario of creation is the same as in earlier cosmogonies, different aspects are highlighted. In the earlier cosmogonies, the composers elaborate the general domain of Cooking. The grim nature of eating, which is connected with killing, is transferred into the blend and elaborated thus grounding the conceptualisation of the world's existence as a manifestation of death. In ŚB 11.1.6, the concept of cognition is the main source domain for the conceptualisation of creation. Cognitive activity does not involve emotions, at least they are not elaborated in the context of this cosmogony. The nature of subjective-objective cognition is such that it needs differentiation of the cognising subject and an object which does not cognise, but is cognised. There is nothing frightening as the structure of the cosmos is but a manifestation of the cognitive abilities of reality. The Upaniṣadic thinkers will continue this way of thinking about creation.

ŚB 11.1.6.9

sò 'vet | pāpmā́naṃ vā́ asṛkṣi yásmai me sasṛjānā́ya táma ivā́bhūd íti tàṃs táta evá pāpmánāvidhyat té táta evá párābhavan |

He knew, 'Verily, I have created evil for myself since, after creating, there has come to be, as it were, darkness for me.' Even then he smote them with evil, and owing to this it was that they were overcome[166].

In the ŚB, the word *pāpmán* means not only evil, but also death (ŚB 8.4.2.1-14, 8.4.3.1, 10.4.4.1, 14.4.1.11). If the recipient activates the latter meaning, he will understand that when Prajāpati creates the Asuras, his lower part dies. Since the Asuras are created with the lower breath of Prajāpati, we can see why, in AU 1.3.10, the breath called *apāná* is connected with death (see chapter 4.1.3). If the recipient highlights the meaning of *pāpmán,* which is evil, he will see that the creation of the Asuras in this way introduces an evaluation as Prajāpati qualifies his own death as something unwanted. Such an evaluation appears for the first time in the ŚB and is, possibly, one of the Vedic sources for the later evaluation of the lower part of the body as unclean. It agrees with the universal evaluation of the image schema of VERTICALITY according to which downwards is evaluated negatively (Krzeszowski 1997).

In this way, the concept of the creative mistake is introduced, though, contrary to the earlier cosmogonies, creation is not interrupted. And, again there is no fear. Prajāpati is presented as piercing the Asuras with evil/death. Thus he confirms his own partial mortality and kills the creatures identified with his feet. In this way, the world is arranged into what will be mortal and what will be immortal. Prajāpati is conceived in terms of man who is aware of his cognitive activity, can name and evaluate it.

The death of the mortal part of Prajāpati will be realised as long as reality manifests itself in the cosmos: the head will constantly kill the feet, the sun will kill those who live on the earth and the gods will kill the Asuras. When Prajāpati kills the Asuras, he shows how to be a subject and not an object, how to kill and not to be killed, how to behave like a god and not like an Asura.

---

[166] For the interpretation of *iva* see Brereton (1982).

Thus, the creative mistake can be seen as an example of the activity which should be realised by men during ritual. Men, who live on earth, should not remain on it and should die. They should go up to the sun in sacrifices in order to obtain immortality. On a more general level, death is the manifestation of the ability of reality to be cognised by itself through its manifestations.

ŚB 11.1.6.9cd-10

tásmād āhur naìtád asti yád daivāsurám̐ yád idám anvākhyā́ne tvad udyáta itihāsé tvat táto hy èvá tā́n prajā́patiḥ pāpmánāvidhyat té táta evá parā́bhavann | (9) *íti tásmād etád ŕ̥ṣiṇābhyánūktamná tvám̐ yuyutse katamác canā́har ná te 'mítro maghavan káś canāsti māyét sā́ té yā́ni yuddhā́ny āhur nā̀dyá śátrum̐ ná nú purā́ yuyutsa íti* | (10)

Whence people say, 'Not true is that regarding (the fight between) the gods and Asuras which is related partly in the tale and partly in the legend; for it was even then that Prajāpati smote them with evil, and it was owing to this that they were overcome.'
Therefore it is with reference to this that the Ṛṣi has said (9), 'Not for a single day hast thou fought, nor hast thou any enemy, O Maghavan illusion is what they say concerning thy battles; no foe hast thou fought either to-day or aforetime.' (10)

In this passage, the composer reinterprets ṚV 10.54.2[167] and the motive for the fight between Indra and Vr̥tra within the general frame of the fight between the gods and the Asuras and within the specific frame of the cosmogony. Indra and the gods are the head of Prajāpati, i.e. the part that kills and cognises while Vr̥tra and the Asuras are the feet of Prajāpati, i.e. the part that is killed and cognised[168].

As I have argued, in the ṚV, the word *māyā́* (translated by Eggeling as 'illusion') is used in contexts which highlight the meaning of the power of reality to manifest itself in alternate transformations of fiery and liquid aspects and thus sustain the existence of the world. This power is conceived in terms of a wondrous activity (Jurewicz 2010a: 403)[169]. In the context of the present cosmogony, I would understand the concept of *māyā́* as the power of reality to make an agreement with itself about the way it will manifest. The immortal status of the gods and the mortal status of the Asuras is only provisional in that it is limited to the manifest aspect. Moreover, the death of the Asuras is not ultimate as they will be reborn again and again in order

[167] ṚV 10.54.2 *yád ácaras tanúvā vāvr̥dhānó bálānīndra prabruvāṇó jáneṣu* | *māyét sā́ te yā́ni yuddhā́ni āhúr nā́dyá śátrum̐ nanú purā́ vivitse* ||

[168] For the reinterpretation of the mythical stories, see Witzel (1987a).

[169] For analysis of meaning of *māyā́* in the ṚV, see Gonda (1959a).

to be killed[170]. Without an object to be killed, reality would be annihilated. Reality manifests its immortality in constant death and resurrection within a world subjected to the power of time. But, in the context of the present cosmogony, death and life have another and deeper meaning as they are manifestation of the cognitive abilities of reality to realise itself in subjective-objective cognition.

The next passage of the ŚB (ŚB 11.1.6.11) expresses the temporal dimension of the relationship between the gods and the Asuras: the state, in which Prajāpati creates the gods, is day and the state, in which he creates the Asuras, is night. On the basis of the nature of the act of self-cognition, the recipient understands that the gods and the Asuras cyclically become one and lose their distinctive features such as immortality and mortality. They then again separate into two distinct aspects and their features will be realised till the next act of union comes. Reality in its unmanifest aspect is not influenced by these changes: it has no foes because it is one.

ŚB 11.1.6.12

sá aikṣata prajā́patiḥ | sárvaṃ vā́ atsāriṣaṃ yá imā́ devátā ásṛkṣīti sá saṃvatsarò 'bhavat saṃvatsaró ha vaí nā́maitád yát saṃvatsará íti sá yó haivám etát saṃvatsarásya saṃvatsaratvā́ṃ véda yó hainam pāpmā́ māyáyā tsárati ná hainaṃ sò 'bhíbhavaty átha yám abhicáraty abhí haivàinam bhavati yá evám etát saṃvatsarásya saṃvatsaratvā́ṃ véda |

Prajāpati bethought himself, 'Everything (*sarva*), indeed, I have obtained by stealth (*tsar*) who have created these deities:' this became the '*sarvatsara*,' for '*sarvatsara*,' doubtless, is the same as '*saṃvatsara* (year).' And, verily, whosoever thus knows '*saṃvatsara*' to be the same as '*sarvatsara*,' is not overcome by any evil which, by magic art, steals upon him (*tsar*); and whosoever thus knows '*saṃvatsara*' to be the same as '*sarvatsara*,' overcomes against whomsoever he practices magic art.

In his explanation of the essence of the year, the composer creates an image of a living being that sneaks secretly towards something or someone. Most probably, this living being is a snake which creeps towards its prey. This image becomes the next input space of the blend created in this cosmogony. Prajāpati calls himself year and the year is identified with death (see ŚB 10.4.3.1-2, section 3.3). The concept of a year metonymically evokes the concept of time. Metonymy HEAD FOR A PERSON motivates the etymology of the word *saṃvatsara*: Prajāpati is identified with the activity of his head conceived in terms of sneaking in order to kill. In this way, the ontological dimension

[170] Compare the despair of the death which will not have food, ŚB 10.4.3.9, see section 3.3.

of agreement (*māyā́*) is highlighted. In the blend, the influence of time is conceived in terms of killing. On the cosmic level, the death of the Asuras is not ultimate. On the level of mortal beings, however, death is real and is a result of the temporal existence of the world.

The composer states that a person who knows the secret essence of reality expressed by the name *samavatsará* is not overcome by *māyā́*, the evil which creeps stealthily to kill him (*yó hainam pāpmā́ māyáyā tsárati*). Man is a part of reality destined for godly status. If he knows that death is but a manifestation of reality, which agrees with itself to limit itself within the frames of the spatio-temporal world and can use its agreement for its own benefit, he can become god and kill the evil.

ŚB 11.1.6.13

> *sá aikṣata prajā́patiḥ | imáṃ vā ātmánaḥ pratimā́m asṛkṣi yát saṃvatsarám íti tásmād āhuḥ prajā́patiḥ saṃvatsará íty ātmáno hy ètám pratimā́m ásṛjata yád vevá cáturakṣaraḥ saṃvatsaráś cáturakṣaraḥ prajā́patis téno haivā̀syaiṣá pratimā́ |*
>
> Prajāpati bethought himself, 'Verily, I have created here a counterpart of myself, to wit, the year;' whence they say, Prajāpati is the year;' for he created it to be a counterpart of himself: inasmuch as '*saṃvatsara* (year),' as well as Prajāpati,' consists of four syllables, thereby it (the year) is a counterpart of him.

Prajāpati calls the the year the replica (*pratimā́*) of himself (*ātmán*). In ŚB 11.1.8.3-4, the replica of Prajāpati is identified with sacrifice which is the activity which allows reality to manifest in a safe way (see section 3.5.2). The essence of sacrifice is to kill a substitute of the sacrificer who in this way saves himself from death. To call a year the replica of Prajāpati is to highlight the killing dimension of ritual which is realised by the sacrificer. The sacrificer participates in death which, as argued above, is a manifestation of the Absolute.

The correspondence between Prajāpati and a year is based on the abstract correspondence of the numbers of syllables in the words *prajāpati* and *saṃvatsará*. In ŚB 6.1.1, Prajāpati is the form of reality which appears when it unites its cognitive powers conceived in terms of seers and breaths. I have shown that the earliest transformation of reality are conceived as manifestation of speech. Taking this into account, the recipient may create a general scenario of creation: in the first stage, it utters the word *prajāpati* and, in the second, *saṃvatsará*. When it utters *prajā́pati*, it manifests itself in speech and, when, it utters *saṃvatsará* it manifest itself in time. The world is a manifestation of both. As we remember, the same blended concept of speech and time is used to conceptualise the world in ṚV 1.164 (see chapter 1.6). Speech can exist only in time, so the appearance of the latter is a necessary condition for the appearance of the former.

*

The composer of ŚB 11.1.6 begins his cosmogony with the stage conceived in terms of waters desirous of multiplying itself. This stage corresponds to the third stage of creation in the *Nāsadīyasūkta*. Since speech is conceived in terms of flowing water in the Veda (see chapter 1.6, Jurewicz 2010a: 85 ff., 379), it is also possible that this stage should be understood as the stage in which reality manifests itself in speech. Conceptualisation of speech in terms of a woman allows the recipient to imagine this stage more precisely in terms of a pregnant woman. Metonymically, the concept of pregnancy is activated *via* the concept of water and, as I have shown, is further elaborated by the composer of the cosmogony. If the recipient thinks about ṚV 1.164, he may understand the conceptualisation of this stage in terms of a mother. In the ṚV, she is identified as Aditi and Sarasvatī whereas here she is conceived in a more abstract way. In the next stage, conceived in terms of the appearance of golden egg, time is created and its concept is activated *via* the concept of year. Moreover, the logic of the general domain of Procreation allows the recipient to understand that Prajāpati is already within the egg. This sequence of creation is expressed in ŚB 11.1.6.13 as a sequence of words: the first is the word *prajā́pati* and the second is *saṃvatsará*. The fourfold division of both words evokes the fourfold division of speech in ṚV 1.164.45. The sequence of the following stages is the same: firstly, Prajāpati is born and then he utters the words *bhū́ḥ*, *bhúvaḥ* and *svàḥ* which correspond to the spatio-temporal division in the cosmos. Thus speech and time are divided into parts which give access to the whole manifest aspect of reality.

We can see the continuity of tradition at a conceptual level. The term 'speech' (*vā́c*) is used by the composer of ṚV 1.164, but the term 'time' (*kālá*) is not used, though the concept is evoked metonymically and metaphorically. In ŚB 11.1.6, the term *kālá* is also not used, but is evoked metonymically by the concept of a year while the concept of speech is evoked metonymically, *via* the words spoken by Prajāpati. In spite of that, both texts are created in such a way that the recipient can evoke these concepts and analyse the nature of their designates and the relationship between them.

The composer of ŚB 11.1.6 tries to put the concept of creation in a clear scenario recruited from the input space of the general domain of Procreation. Creation is conceived in terms of pregnancy and of the development of a human being. The composer especially elaborates the concept of the development of man and its cognitive dimension. This allows him to conceive creation in terms of subjective-objective cognition and in terms of agreement. The general domain of Procreation includes also the concept of feeding, an embryo and a child. Thanks to that, the composer can coherently introduce within the cosmogony a metaphoric conceptualisation of cognition in terms of eating. In his exposition, the composer also redefines the Daivāsura myth and puts it in the frames of his general metaphysical assumptions according to which creation is the manifestation of death. Moreover, he quotes the ṚV in order to support his assumption (ŚB 11.1.6.10). In ŚB 11.1.6.13, he evokes the conceptualisation of speech and time that is presented in ṚV 1.164. Thus he construes an abstract summary of the content of cosmogony which reduces the process described within it to the manifestation of speech and time. The same conceptualisation is attested in ŚB 6.1.1 the composer of which divides the creative process into a stage of name (*nāman*) and a stage of form (*rūpa*, see section 3.2.2). It is worth noting that in BU 1.4.7, the form (*rūpá*) is identified with action (*kárman*, see chapter 4.1.2) and action, similarly to speech, can occur only in time.

3.5.3. Creation as giving names and assuming forms

The cognitive dimension of creation is explicitly expressed in the cosmogonies which present it as the process during which reality acquires a different shape and name.

ŚB 11.2.3. begins its cosmogony with the formula which calls reality *bráhman* as it will be called in the later philosophy[171]. As we have seen, in the earlier ŚB, the word *bráhman* is mainly used to denote sacred speech conceived as the foundation of Prajāpati. In the cosmogonic blends, it is identified with the earth. Such a use implies its ontological meaning. A further possible reason for this meaning is grounded in the general Vedic assumptions about the ontic dimensions of cognitive activity. Sacred speech is realised ontologically. Another reason is the assumption about the unity of reality. Thus the word used to denote sacred speech can be used to denote the unmanifest aspect of reality too. The conceptual roots of this semantic transformation of the word *bráhman* can be seen in ṚV 1.125 where reality is conceived as speech (see chapter 1.2, see also ṚV 1.164, chapter 1.6).

[171] ŚB 11.2.3.1-2: *bráhma vā́ idam ágra āsīt | tád devā́n asṛjata tád devā́nt sṛṣṭvaìṣú lokéṣu vyā̀rohayad asmínn evá lokè'gním vāyúm antárikṣe divy èvá sū́ryam | átha yé 'tha ūrdhvā́ lokā́ḥ | tád yā́ áta ūrdhvā́ devátās téṣu tā́ devátā vyā̀rohayat sá yáthā haivèmá āvír lokā́ imā́ś ca devátā evám u haivá tá āvír lokā́s tā́ś ca devátā yéṣu tā́ devátā vyā̀rohayat |*

In ŚB 11.2.3.1, reality is presented as creating three gods Agni, Vāyu and Sūrya. It makes them present in the three spheres of the created world: the earth, the space and the sky. Creation of three spheres is not mentioned, but it is implied by the logic of the cosmogonic formula: if *bráhman* in the beginning is 'this' world, this means that in the beginning there was no world at all because everything was identical with *bráhman*. Creation of the world is thus implicitly assumed. The composer also mentions higher worlds with their deities. Having created the cosmos, reality withdraws itself from its creation which is conceived in terms of the image schemas of VERTICALITY and of CONTAINER: it goes up to the sphere which is beyond what is manifest[172].

Then reality wants to come back to what is manifest (*átha bráhmaivá parārdhám agachat tát parārdhám gatvaìkṣata katháṃ nv ìmā́ṃ lokā́n pratyáveyām íti*). It can be assumed that reality wants to come back in order to confirm its identity with its manifest aspect and, at the same time, to continue creation. This act is presented in the following way:

ŚB 11.2.3.3

> *tád dvā́bhyām evá pratyávaid | rū́péṇa caivá nā́mnā ca sá yásya kásya ca nāmā́sti tán nā́ma yásyo ápi nā́ma nā́sti yád véda rūpéṇedáṃ rūpám íti tád rūpám etā́vad vā́ idáṃ yā́vad rūpáṃ caivá nā́ma ca |*
>
> It then descended again by means of these two – Form and Name. Whatever has a name, that is name; and that again which has no name, and which one knows by its form, 'This is (of a certain) form,' that is form: as far as there are Form and Name so far, indeed, extends this (universe).

The cognitive dimension of this creative stage is activated by the concept of name, *nā́man*. Such a conceptualisation can be seen as a further elaboration of the general domain of Procreation the scenario of which presupposes that a new-born child is given a name. However, the composer expands everyday experience in order to explain the creative activity of reality: names and forms are seen as general means to cognise the world. If the world is the manifest aspect of reality, then names and forms are the means to cognise it. The image schemas of VERTICALITY and of CONTAINER are again exploited and the ontic presence of *bráhman* within the world is conceived in terms of its descent into a container. So the conceptual network created in this cosmogony is as follows. The first input space is the general domain of Procreation in its specific realisation of giving name to a new born child. The second input space

---

[172] In the *Puruṣasūkta*, reality is presented as cyclically going out from its manifest aspect and coming back there (see chapter 1.3). In the AVŚ, the gods-creators come out from the cosmos conceived in terms of a man and come back there (see chapter 2.2.3).

is the concept of cognition. The third is the concept of reality. The following input spaces are the images schemas of VERTICALITY and of CONTAINER. The generic space is the concept of transformation. In the blend, reality gives names to itself and assumes forms corresponding to those names. Thus the world is created. The ability to assume forms according to names is based on the assumptions of the ontic results of cognition and of the unity of reality. It is speech which names objects. Within the frames of this assumption, objects appear as perceptible manifestations of speech. The name of reality which is *bráhman*, sacred speech, is fully justified in this context.

*

The wording of this cosmogony is very abstract in comparison with the cosmogonies so far analysed. The recipient is not expected to evolve the scenario of the general domain of Procreation and simply needs to activate one stage which is the giving of a name. A further basis for his reasoning is the general Vedic assumption that cognition has its results in being. The world is generally conceived as names and forms of reality. Such its conceptualisation will be elaborated in the Upaniṣads.

The composer profiles the blend in such a way that the role of image schemas in conceptualisation of the process is highlighted. This allows the composer to present the process in simple terms of movements out/up and in/down. The conceptualisation of creation in terms of giving names and the assumption of forms by reality and the use of image schemas is an important step towards a more abstract way of conceiving and expressing metaphysics.

3.5.4. Creation as division into truth and untruth

The cognitive motive of creation is also explicitly expressed in ŚB 9.5.1 which presents creation as the division of truth and untruth conceived as ontological concepts. The frame of the cosmogony is constituted by the Daivāsura myth. The gods and the Asuras are the offspring of Prajāpati. They are mingled together and are the same because they speak both truth and untruth (ŚB 9.5.1.12). This can be interpreted as the pre-creative state of the world, being the state when cognition is impossible because of the impossibility of discerning what is true and what is false[173]. Then the gods obtain truth and the Asuras obtain untruth (ŚB 9.5.1.13-14).

[173] In the same way it is conceived in ṚV 10.129.1 (Jurewicz 2010a: 45–46).

The division into truth and falseness renders cognition possible. The gods and the Asuras are manifestation of the cognising and non-cognising aspects of reality within its manifest part. The gods are the manifestation of the head which has ability to cognise the truth. The Asuras are the manifestation of the feet which do not cognise, so they are the embodiment of untruth. Truth and untruth are understood ontologically. At the same time, they are ethical notions. The activity of the gods is a normative for human beings, while the activity of the Asuras is an anti-norm. Men should behave accordingly to truth which can be realised in Prajāpati's head, i.e. on the sun. This can be reached in sacrificial activity. While in the earlier ŚB, the eating ability of the head was highlighted, here, as in ŚB 11.1.6, its cognising ability is highlighted. The sacrificer becomes one of the gods who are Prajāpati's head which cognises.

It is worth noting that true activity does not mean that deception is forbidden. The composer of ŚB 9.5.1 continues his description by presenting the gods who, having gained the truth, perform the sacrifice and arrange the world, but when the Asuras approach, they stop doing that and pretend that they are doing something else (ŚB 9.5.1.19-26). In ŚB 2.1.2, when the Asuras build the fire altar, Indra, disguises himself as a Brahmin, inserts his brick and then, when the altar is almost finished, takes away the brick causing the altar to fall down.

It is worth noting that there is at least one human activity which allows its participants to cheat. It is play. So maybe one should not judge the god's deceit as moral corruption, but rather as proof that creation was also conceived in terms of play? My interpretation of *māyā́* as the agreement which reality realises within its manifest aspect may also confirm that the concept of play could motivate thinking about creation[174].

Notwithstanding the possibility of this interpretation, it can be concluded that during ritual, man behaves truly when he confirms the real state of affairs. In order to perform sacrifices accordingly to the real state of affair, one should know how things are. Not only activity is important, but also knowledge about the activity and the world. This knowledge is secret (*paróksa*) and consists of the knowledge of the meaning of ritual. A man 'who knows in this way' (*evaṃvíd*) understands that sacrifice is a model of reality and is identical with it. He also understands that sacrifice operates on both a micro- and a macro-scale and can disturb the subtle structure not only of the cosmos, but of what is unmanifest.

[174] For elements of drama in the Vedic ritual, see Malamoud (2005c).

3.6. The concepts of *ātmán*, *bráhman*, *sát*, *ásat*

The analysis till now shows that the word *ātmán* in the ŚB is used in the following way. It denotes the manifest aspect of reality conceived in terms of Prajāpati who realises the safe way of manifestation which prevents reality from annihilation. Since the manifest aspect is conceived dynamically and its transformations are conceived in terms of sacrifice, the word *ātmán* is also used metonymically in reference to the sacrifice. It is also used in reference to man's self in the sense of his outward appearance and his essence. Finally, the word *ātmán* is used in reference to the fire altar which is the ritual manifestation of Prajāpati and the sacrificer. There is no doubt that the Upaniṣadic use of the word *ātmán* in reference to the whole of reality, its manifest aspect and its innermost essence, is deeply entrenched in its usage in the ŚB (see Jurewicz 1997).

In the earlier ŚB, the word *bráhman* is used in reference to sacred speech, i.e. the Veda which is conceived ontologically as the foundation for everything which is manifest. In the later ŚB, this word is used in reference to reality during its creative act and, in this context, can be interpreted as referring to the whole of reality.

The word *ásat* is used in reference to the pre-creative state of the world conceived in terms of the void which in some contexts is conceived in terms of a hungry belly (see ŚB 6.1.1.1, chapter 3.2.2). In the following passage, a definition of *sát* is presented:

ŚB 10.4.2.21

átha sárvāṇi bhūtā́ni páryaikṣat | sá trayyā́m evá vidyā́yāṃ sárvāṇi bhūtā́ny apaśyad átra hí sárveṣāṃ chándasām ātmā́ sárveṣāṃ stómānāṃ sárveṣām prāṇā́nāṃ sárveṣāṃ devā́nām etád vā asty etád dhy àmŕ̥taṃ yád dhy àmŕ̥taṃ tád dhy ásty etád u tád yán mártyam |

He then looked round over all existing things, and beheld all existing things in the threefold lore (the Veda), for therein is the self[175] of all metres, of all stomas, of all breaths[176], and of all the gods: this, indeed, exists, for it is immortal, and what is immortal exists; and this (contains also) that which is mortal.

The composer calls the manifestation of reality in the triple Veda as that which exists (*etád vā asti*). According to the next sentence, what exists is immortal (*yád dhy àmŕ̥taṃ tád dhy àsty*). We can understand then that immortality is a necessary feature of existence. Since the pronoun *eta* means

[175] Eggeling (1897): 'body'.
[176] Eggeling (1897): 'vital airs'.

'this here', the sentence *etád u tád yán mártyam* seems to define the mortality of the world. It is therefore implied that it is non-existence (*ásat*). This assumption will become explicit in the Upaniṣads (CU 6.2.1-2, see chapter 4.1.4). The definition betrays a shift of meaning in comparison with the ṚV where *sát* refers to manifest aspect of reality and *ásat* to its unmanifest aspect.

3.7. Conclusion

The composers of the ŚB conceive reality as internally contradictory. Its activity is also internally contradictory. In the first act of its manifestation, reality annihilates itself within limited frames. The annihilation is conceived in terms of the death of hunger and a place for the future universe is conceived in terms of a hungry belly. Further creation is conceived in terms of eating and digesting: thus the cosmos appears. Its creative power is conceived in terms of a man called Prajāpati identical with the cosmos. His head is the sun and his feet are the earth. Mortal livings who live on earth are eaten by the immortal upper sphere of Prajāpati.

Conceptualisation of the cosmos in terms of man allows the composers of the ŚB to present in a precise way the relationship between immortality and mortality within the manifest chapter of reality. The head, in terms of which the sun is conceived, marks the borderline sphere of the cosmos. It is the manifestation of death, the annihilating power of reality that is always present within the world and which has to be constantly pacified. It is pacified in ritual and eats the oblation through the gods who are the upper breaths of Prajāpati. His lower breaths are the mortals among which men are the only sentient beings who can sacrifice, i.e. to repeat the creative act conceived in terms of killing and eating. The general domain of Cooking allows the composers of the ŚB to present very subtle metaphysical issues.

The ŚB creates a sophisticated metaphysics of death. It is a manifestation of reality. It is also understood as internally contradictory. On the one hand, it is the active destroying force which manifests itself in the movement of the sun which is the visible sign of the passing of time. It is the part of reality which realises itself in killing and being immortal. It manifests itself on the sun. On the other hand, death is what is mortal and is liable to destruction. It is this part of reality which realises itself in dying and manifests itself on earth. Manifestation in death thus understood allows reality to preserve its most important attribute which is freedom. It cannot be excluded that the concept of reality which constantly dies and is born in its creation is motivated by the belief in the rebirth of human beings within their family.

The general pattern of creation agrees with that of the *Nāsadīyasūkta*.

1. the pre-creative state of reality – though this state is not described as such in the ŚB
2. Prajāpati is one / wants to create / heats and toils = the first stage when That One manifests itself
3. manifestation of Agni / of eater / death of what is created / hunger of Prajāpati / of what is created / death of Prajāpati = the second stage conceived in terms of the darkness (the pre-creative state of the world)

Then creation is stopped and the pre-creative state comes back, but only within the sphere which will become the future world.

4. the fluid form of Prajāpati appears (milk, water, semen) = the third stage conceived in terms of water
5. Prajāpati manifests himself as the cosmos / Golden Egg = the fourth stage when Agni manifests himself as the cosmos
6. Prajāpati desires to have children, to become greater, heats himself again = the fifth stage which is the manifestation of desire
7. the activity of gods / creation of the earth and the sky = the sixth stage which is the activity of the poets.

Cosmogonies of the ŚB, in most cases, begin with a description of the first stage of creation. Their composition depends on the explanation of ritual and does not necessarily reflects different views about the creation of the world. In all cosmogonies, sacrifice is seen as the way to ensure the safe manifestation of reality in death. Prajāpati gives to his eating part (Agni) a substitute of himself (oblation) and thus reality dies only in the part in which it can be safely done. In a micro-scale, sacrifice ensures long life to men because they re-enact the creative activity of Prajāpati: they give a substitute for their eating part. Since sacrifice is conceived as a model of the universe and identical with it, men take part in cosmic transformations of reality and support its manifestations.

The structure of man reflects the structure of the cosmos. His head is immortal and the body is mortal. Men escape death thanks to the sacrificial substitutes and to their proper understanding of reality. Thanks to that, a man does not die before his time. Moreover, during sacrifices, man builds his immortal self *ātmán* in himself and on the sun. When he dies, death takes the share which belong to it, i.e. the body, and the head goes to the head, i.e. the sun[177].

---

[177] In JB 1.18 (chapter 5.1.1).

The composers of the ŚB also elaborate the Ṛgvedic metaphysics in their assumption about the fiery nature of reality. In some cases, they explicitly quote the Ṛgvedic stanzas in order to explain their meaning. They also use the concepts coined by the poets. The most important is the concept of *śrī́*: it activates the Ṛgvedic concept of fame realised in the sun (see chapter 1.7).

The cognitive character of creation is also continued and elaborated in the ŚB. In the earlier parts of the ŚB, is it conceived in terms of the general domain of Cooking (in its specific realisation of eating) and in Procreation (in its specific realisation of the sexual act). Later parts express it explicitly. In some cosmogonies the composers of the ŚB seem to aim at triggering emotional reactions in recipients: fear and helplessness when creation fails and hope, excitation and happiness when it continues. In this way, they imply that reality also manifests itself in order to experience emotion. This way of thinking about creation will be elaborated in the Upaniṣads (BU 1.4.1-6, see chapter 4.1.2).

The cosmogonies of the ŚB attest the efforts of their composers to experience the supernatural cognition without the aid of Soma. These efforts consisted on toiling and heating thanks to specific activities, such as the excessive run. The influence of breathing and recitation is also attested in the ŚB. There are cosmogonical concepts which are motivated by these practices; the sequence of creative stages also reflects them (ŚB 6.1.1, 10.5.3).

The process of the gradual abstraction of thinking can also be seen in the ŚB. In its later parts, the concept of Prajāpati is replaced by more abstract concepts such as water, mind (*mánas*) and finally *bráhman*. The fact that the cognitive nature of creation is more and more explicit is also proof of abstraction. The cognitive character of creation weakens the dramatic character of earlier concepts of creation which conceives it in terms of death.

Cognition is also an essential factor for the proper performance of ritual. The composers of the ŚB are obsessed not only with explaining the meaning of detail, but explaining its overall metaphysical sense. The ritual must be meaningful for those who perform it. The person called *evaṃvíd*, 'he who knows in this way', is more than an expert of correct performance. He is the one who understands the mystery of reality in theoretical and practical aspects. Thus knowledge makes his life meaningful.

Ability to create ritual can be seen as another example of the human ability to create general and abstract concepts not expressed in language. As Cavallin argues:

> 'There is a close connection between stylised theatrical *dramatis personae* and the ritual person; they share this tendency to abstraction, of moving away from a particular context, a definite position in time and space, and striving toward an intersubjective world of abstract notions, social roles, and norms'.
> (2013: 25–26)

Cavallin's claims are congruent with the description of the sacrifice in the Brāhmaṇas as being a model of reality and identical with it. As a model, Vedic sacrifice reduced the world's complexity into a manageable form which is the next proof of the ability for abstraction and generalisation.

Chapter four

The Upaniṣads

The source for the analysis in this chapter are selected parts of the oldest Upaniṣads composed in prose, namely the BU, the CU, the AU, the TU and the KU which predate the Buddha (Olivelle 1998: 12–13, Angot 2007, I: 87 ff.). I have chosen those passages of the Upaniṣads which are relevant for my topic, i.e. which allow me to show how early Indian thought transformed earlier tradition and elaborated it in new directions.

The Upaniṣadic philosophers change the topic of philosophical interest. Cosmogony is not the main subject as in the earlier Vedic texts. They are mainly concerned with the situation of human beings in the world, during life and after death, and the problems connected with accessing the unmanifest aspect. During creation not only cosmic but also social rules are settled which attests a change in cultural experience and earlier concepts are now redefined to meet new needs.

The composers of the Upaniṣads analysed in this chapter continue the breath practices attested already in the ŚB that, in the later Upaniṣads influenced by Buddhist practice, will be called *yoga*. The efforts attested by the ŚB to reach the state after Soma without Soma were more and more successful. People had found the way to a state of supernatural consciousness that could be experienced and theoretically described and analysed. However, there is a difference between the state gained through Soma and through breath practices in that the latter includes the former and it also permits one to realise a state of bliss thanks to mental contact with the unmanifest aspect. The assumption of the ontological dimension of cognition allows the composers to claim that knowledge of reality transforms ontologically a cognising agent. Breath practice triggers a blend in the minds of its practitioners thanks to which man feels identical with the cosmos and with reality.

The way abstract concepts are built can be reconstructed with the aid of cognitive linguistics tools. In many cases, the abstract concepts are construed in the same way as in earlier philosophy: the vehicle of metonymies and the source domains of metaphors become independent concepts which blend the salient features of their target domains. In some cases, the recipient is expected to activate only the logic of the image schemas (VERTICALITY, CONTAINER, CENTRE-PERIPHERY, SOURCE-PATH-GOAL) without reference to other more specific input spaces of the blend. In other cases, the vehicles of metonymies become abstract concepts and are separated from their target domains.

The general domains become of much less importance. In the earlier thought, their scenario was activated in various ways to express subtle aspect of the processes described in the blends. Moreover, they were often elaborated in a description of the process. It is rarely the case in the Upaniṣads. Even if they are activated in their specific realisations the recipient is not expected to unfold its scenario and evolve it during the description of the process.

The Upaniṣadic composers evoke the general domain of Cooking in its specific realisation of eating, the general domain of Procreation in its specific realisation of sexual act and the general domain of Cleansing By Heat in its specific realisation of transformation of milk to produce cream, butter or gold[1]. On the other hand, the Upaniṣadic philosophers introduce new experiential concepts in their metaphysical conceptualisations. They also elaborate the concept of a king which is used in the *Vrātyakāṇḍa* to conceive creation (see chapter 2.2.2). The relationship between a king and his subjects is used to conceive the relationship between the innermost self of man and his breaths while the concept of entering a palace is used to conceive liberating practice[2].

As we will also see, the composers of the Upaniṣads refer to and elaborate earlier thought. Even the parts which seem to be more abstract are deeply immersed in the philosophical investigation of the ṚV, the AVŚ and the ŚB.

The chapter is divided into five sections. In the first section (4.1), I will discuss cosmogonies presented in BU 1.2 (section 4.1.1), in BU 1.4 (section 4.1.2-3), in the AU (section 4.1.4) and in CU 6.1-7 (section 4.1.5) which are very good examples of how abstract concepts and language are created based

---

1 Another specific realisation of the general domain Cleansing By Heat is concept of salt transformations analysed by Slaje (2001a, 2001b, 2002).

2 For conceptualisation of breath in terms of king in the early Vedic texts, see Bodewitz (1992). For the use of concept of kinship as the source domain of spiritual freedom, see Proferes (2007).

on earlier tradition. In this section, the problem of the real character of the manifest aspect of reality will be discussed (4.1.6).

The second section (4.2) is devoted to ontology. I will discuss the cognitive nature of the manifestations of reality and the ways they are described. In the following section (4.3), the role of human being will be discussed. In this section, the model of the Five Fires and the path of gods (*devayāna*) and path of fathers (*pitṛyāna*) presented in BU 6.2.9-16 and CU 5.4-10 (section 4.3.1) will be considered. I interpret two paths as the realisation of the two aspects of reality: the manifest aspect is realised on the path of fathers, the unmanifest aspect is realised on the path of gods. Thus human existence and death has its ontological value. I also show the role of the earlier conceptual background in the creation of these concepts. Finally, I will discuss CU 4.11.15 (section 4.3.2). Its composer presents breath practice which leads to the realisation of the unity of man with the unmanifest aspect conceived in terms of walking along the path of gods (*devayāna*).

In the final section (4.4), liberating cognition will be discussed. Firstly, the nature of the liberated state will be presented as consisting in the suspension of the subjective-objective cognition characteristic for the manifest aspect of reality (section 4.4.1, see also Jurewicz 1994). Its climax is the realisation of the unity of reality when absolute omniscience and freedom are gained. In the following sections (4.4.2.1-4), ways of achieving liberating cognition will be analysed. I focus on the problem as to how liberating cognition is realized in breath practice and show the common assumptions which betray the shared knowledge about the practice and its aim. At the same time, the process of abstraction in thinking can be seen which finds its culmination in TU 2.1-5 (section 4.4.2.5).

The quotations are from the Titus Text Database[3]. In case of the BU, I have followed the edition of Olivelle (1998). Translation is by Olivelle (1998)[4].

4.1. Cosmogony

As already mentioned, cosmogony is not the main topic of the Upaniṣads. There are, however, some more detailed accounts about creation in the BU, AU and CU. I will begin with the cosmogonies of the first chapter of the

---

3 http://titus.uni-frankfurt.de/texte/etcs/ind/aind/ved/rv/upanisad/aitup/aitup.htm; http://titus.uni-frankfurt.de/texte/etcs/ind/aind/ved/yvw/upanisad/bau/bau.htm; http://titus.uni-frankfurt.de/texte/etcs/ind/aind/ved/sv/upanisad/chup/chup.htm; http://titus.uni-frankfurt.de/texte/etcs/ind/aind/ved/yvs/upanisad/taittup/taitt.htm

4 For another recent translation of Upaniṣads, see Roebuck (2000).

BU (1.2, 1.4). Their composers elaborate the cosmogonies of the ŚB which is not surprising taking into account that it is included in the ŚB as its final section[5]. At the same time, they aim to make earlier concepts more abstract and general. They also redefine the concept of *ātmán* as the unifying principle of reality. The composer of BU 1.4 also enriches his exposition with ethical perspective based on unity of *ātmán*. The redefition of this concept can also be seen in the cosmogony of the AU. Its composer elaborates the conceptualisation of reality in terms of man and the Atharvavedic concept of reality as the innermost essence of the cosmos and man. The composers of BU 1.4 and AU highlight the meaning of the word *loka* as the space of experience realised by reality in creation and by man in ritual and liberating cognition. I will conclude with the analysis of the cosmogony presented in CU 6.1-7. This cosmogony is an attempt to redefine earlier concepts about creation in more abstract and general way.

4.1.1. The continuity of tradition (*Bṛhadāraṇyaka Upaniṣad* 1.2)

The composer of BU 1.2 mostly elaborates the general domain of Cooking in its specific realisation of the preparation of food and its eating.

BU 1.2.1

> *naìvèhá kíṃ canā́gra āsīt | mṛtyúnaivèdám ā́vṛtam āsīd aśanāyáyā | aśanāyā́ hí mṛtyúḥ | tán máno 'kurutātmanvī́ syām íti | só 'rcann acarat | tásyā́rcata ā́po 'jāyantā́rcate vaí me kám abhūd íti | tád evā̀rkyàsyārkatvám̥ | kám̐ ha vā́ asmai bhavati yá evám etád arkyàsyārkatvám̥ véda | ā́po vā́ arkás*[6]|
>
> In the beginning there was nothing here at all. Death alone covered this completely, as did hunger; for what is hunger but death? Then death made up his mind: 'Let me equip with myself[7] (*ātman*)'. So he undertook a liturgical recitation (*arc*), and as he was engaged in liturgical recitation (*arc*), water (*ka*) sprang from him. And he thought: 'While I was engaged in liturgical recitation water sprang up from me.' That is what gave the name to and discloses the true nature of the recitation (*arka*). Water undoubtedly springs for him knows the name and nature of recitation in this way. So, recitation is water.

The opening sentence of the cosmogony describes the stage of creation which in the *Nāsadīyasūkta* is the second stage expressed by the phrase

---

5 Olivelle (1998:29).

6 In the TITUS version (titus.uni-frankfurt.de/texte/etcs/ind/aind/ved/yvw/upanisad/bau/bau.htm) the last sentence is the first sentence of BU 1.2.2. I follow Olivelle (1998) here.

7 Olivelle (1998): 'a body'.

táma āsīt támasā gūḷhám ágre ('Darkness was hidden by darkness in the beginning'). In the ŚB, this stage is expressed by the formula *prajā́patir ha vā́ idám ágra éka evā̀sa* ('Verily, in the beginning, Prajāpati alone existed here). The composer of the BU evokes this formula but replace the noun *prajāpati* with the noun *ásat*. Thus he evokes the beginning of ŚB 6.1.1.1 *ásad vā́ idam ágra āsīt* ('Verily, in the beginning there was here the non-existent', see chapter 3.5.1). However, he expresses this stage of creation in slightly different terms because it metonymically activates the concept of the world (*via* the word *ihá*) which is already created and there is nothing. One can presume that the world remains in the contradictory state as both existing and non-existing at the same time.

In the next sentence, the world is covered by death which is hunger. The composer continues the metaphysical assumptions of the ŚB according to which reality manifests itself as death. Identification of death with hunger evokes ŚB 2.2.4 (see chapter 3.1.1) which creates the image of a hungry fire which threatens Prajāpati with death. If the recipient activates ŚB 6.1.1, he may also evoke the concept of breath (*prāṇá*) which is conceived in terms of fire. Death in its killing power is conceived in these terms (see also ŚB 2.2.4, see chapter 3.1.1). The input spaces of the blend are: the abstract concept of death, the concept of a hungry living being which is an instantiation of the general domain of Cooking, the concept of fire, the cosmos and reality. However, the wording of cosmogony is so abstract that the recipient is not necessarily expected to run the blend in all its details. The general meaning of the blend is the conception of a place for the future world which appears when reality withdraws itself. The generic space is the concept of transformation.

Then, reality wants to return to this aspect of itself from which it has withdrawn. This is expressed in the phrase 'I want to have myself' (*tán máno 'kurutātmanvī́ syām íti*). As has been shown, death in the ŚB is understood as the ability of reality to kill and to die (see chapter 3.3). Reality, having manifested its ability to die, now manifests its ability to kill which will result in its manifestation. This cosmogonic stage is conceived in terms of a hungry person who wants to eat and thus build his body (see chapter 3.2.3). The recipient may also refer to the ritual during which the immortal self *ātmán* of the sacrificer is created that is made of the sounds of the Veda (see chapter 3.4) and conceive of creation in these terms. The concept of ritual is the next input space of the conceptual network and will be elaborated in further sentences of the cosmogony. The phrase *máno 'kuruta* allows the recipient to understand that the hungry being, in terms of which death is conceived, is a cognising being. In the blend, reality thinks about itself and splits itself into the subject (the thinking 'it') and the object ('self' about which 'it' thinks). This process is conceived in terms of a division into an eater and food.

The verb *arc*-, translated by Olivelle as 'liturgical recitation', literally means 'to shine' and 'to sing' (see ŚB 2.5.1.3, see chapter 3.2.1, 11.1.6.7-8, and see chapter 3.5.2). Activation of the literal meaning of this verb allows the recipient to elaborate the input spaces of fire and a cognising hungry being. In the blend, cognition is verbalised in speech conceived in terms of fire. Moreover, if the recipient activates the literal meaning of the verb *arc*-, he will also see the next stage of creation as the logical consequence of the previous one. According to the general model of reality transformation, Agni manifests its liquid aspect conceived in terms of Soma. As I have shown, this model is elaborated in the cosmogonies of the ŚB and this stage of creation, conceived in terms of Soma in the ṚV, is conceived in terms of a heated, tired man who sweats. The concept of sweat is activated *via* the concept of water with both concepts being identified in ŚB 11.1.6.1 (see chapter 3.5.2). If, in the blend, the recipient conceives death in such terms, the etymology of *ká* becomes fully justified. Contrary to Olivelle, I would read the word *ká* as 'pleasure'[8]. Sweat, or more generally water, is pleasant for a heated man and this experience is evoked here to become the experiential basis for a definition of *arká*: this is heat which becomes pleasant sweat/water.

In the last sentence of the passage, the cause (heat) and the effect (water) are metonymically compressed (*ā́po vā́ arkás*). At the same time, the internally contradictory character of reality is expressed. It is conceived in terms of the opposing concepts of light/fire and water similarly for Agni in the ṚV.

BU 1.2.2

tád yád apā́m̐ śára ā́sīt tát sámahanyata | sā́ pṛthivy àbhavat | tásyām aśrāmyat | tásya śrāntásya taptásya téjo ráso níravartatāgníḥ |

Then foam that gathered on the water solidified and became the earth. Death toiled upon earth. When he had become worn out by toil and hot with exertion, his heat – his essence – turned into fire.

This stage of creation is conceived in terms of the production of cream by churning. This is the next input space of the conceptual network. Now, sweat, in this blend, is conceived in terms of milk[9]. Churning is an activity which consists of heating which leads to the consolidation of milk into cream. This

[8] The author of the BU refers here to ŚB 10.6.2.5-7 where the world is conceived in terms of *arká*; the meaning of joy is very clear there, see section 4.4.2.1. For the meaning of *kám* as joy see also ŚB 10.6.1 analysed below (section 4.4.2.1).

[9] Such a conceptualisation is already attested in the ṚV 10.67.7 (Jurewicz 2010a: 282–283).

is a specific realisation of the general domain of Cleansing By Heat which in the ṚV is mostly used in its realisation of the clarification of butter (Jurewicz 2010a). In the later Veda, other processes are added the most important of which is the purification of gold (AVŚ 10.7.28, see chapter 2.2.4, ŚB 6.1.3, see chapter 3.5.1). In BU 1.2.2, the earth is conceived in terms of cream. The recipient may presume that earth metonymically evokes the concept of the future world similarly to the cosmogonies of the ŚB. If the recipient elaborates the input space of fire, he may understand the process described in this passage in terms of kindling fire. The similarity of movement during this activity and churning butter strengthens the coherence of this interpretation.

The earth becomes the foundation for further creative activity (ŚB 6.1.1.3, 15, section 3.2.2, ŚB 7.1.2.7-8, see chapter 3.2.3). It is conceived in terms of heating: reality, conceived in terms of personified death, toils and heats itself. The result is internally contradictory as two aspects of reality are mentioned, the fiery (*téjas*) and the liquid (*rása*). The sequence of words *téjas* and *rása* iconically reflects the sequence of creation: manifestation of the fiery aspect precedes the manifestation of the liquid aspect. In the blend, reality manifests as Agni. If the recipient elaborates the input space of fire, he can create an image of a blazing fire in the blend. If he elaborates the input space of a hungry being, he will understand that the eater is ready to prepare food. If he highlights the cognitive abilities of this being, he can imagine death as a burning seer (see ŚB 6.1.1.1, chapter 3.2.2).

The sentence *téjo ráso nírava rtatāgníḥ* is constructed in such a way that the recipient may understand that Agni consists of both aspects, the fiery and the liquid. Thus reality manifests its internal contradictory nature. This stage corresponds to the fourth stage of creation of the *Nāsadīyasūkta*.

BU 1.2.3

sá tredhā̀tmā́naṃ vyàkurutādityáṃ tṛtī́yaṃ vāyúṃ tṛtī́yam̐ | sá eṣá prāṇás tredhāvihitáḥ | tásya prā́cī dík śíro 'saú cāsaú cermā́v | áthāsya pratī́cī dík púccham asaú cāsaú ca sakthyaù | dákṣiṇā códīcī ca pārśvé | dyaúṣ pṛṣṭhám antárikṣam udáram iyám úraḥ | sá eṣò 'psú prátiṣṭhito | yátra kvà caíti tád evá prátitiṣṭhaty eváṃ vidvā́n |

He divided himself[10] (*ātman*) of his into three – one third became the sun and another the wind. He is also breath divided into three. His head is the eastern quarter, and his two forequarters are the southeast and the northeast. His tail is the west, and his two hindquarters are the south west and the northwest. his flans are the south and the north, His back is the sky; his abdomen is the intermediate region; and his chest is this earth. He stands firm in the waters. A man who knows this will stand firm wherever he may go.

[10] Olivelle (1998): 'this body'.

The self of reality is divided into three to become the cosmos. The earth with fire has already been created and now the next two parts are created which are space with wind and the sky with the sun. The concepts of space and the sky are evoked metonymically *via* the concept of the wind and the sun (INHABITANTS FOR PLACE). The upward direction of the creation agrees with the creative model elaborated in the ŚB conceived in terms of the image schema of VERTICALITY. At the same time, this stage corresponds to the sixth stage of creation in the *Nāsadīyasūkta* during which the cosmos is created divided into three parts (see Jurewicz 2010a: 53–55).

The cosmos is conceived in terms of a living being the concept of which is metonymically evoked *via* the concept of breath, *prāṇá*. At the same time, this qualification confirms its fiery nature because breath is conceived in terms of fire in the Veda. In order to conceive the cosmos, the composer enriches the conceptual network with the input space of a bird activated by the concept of tail and by the earlier conceptualisation of the cosmos in terms of a flying bird that is ritually realised in the Agnicayana ritual (see chapter 3.2.2). In the blend, the cosmos, conceived in terms of a flying man, lies in water and is directed eastwards and it is in terms of parts of the body that parts of the cosmos are conceived. Everything what happens thereafter takes place within the cosmic body of reality.

Thus reality fulfils its desire to have its 'self' (*ātmán*) and fills the primeval void. Taken against the earlier cosmogonies of the ŚB, we could say that death is overcome and reality resurrects within its manifest aspect and becomes his own replica (*pratimā́*). The composer takes the ritual concepts out of their context. They become source domains for thinking about the cosmos. This is further proof of the tendency for abstraction.

The water, on which the body lies, can be interpreted as either the unmanifest aspect of reality or as the borderline sphere of the cosmos the concept of which will be elaborated in the descriptions of breath practice (see section 4.4).

BU 1.2.4

sò 'kāmayata dvitī́yo ma ātmā́ jāyetéti | sá mánasā vā́caṃ mithunám̐ sámabhavad aśanāyā́ṃ mṛtyúḥ | tád yád réta ā́sīt sá saṃvatsarò 'bhavan | ná ha purā́ tátaḥ saṃvatsará āsa | tám etā́vantaṃ kālám abibhar yā́vānt saṃvatsaráḥ | tám etā́vataḥ kālásya parástād asṛjata | táṃ jātám abhivyā́dadāt | sá bhā́ṇ akarot | saìvá vā́g abhavat |

The death had this desire: 'Would my second self[11] (*ātman*) were born for me!' So, by means of his mind, he copulated with speech, death copulated with hunger.

[11] Olivelle (1998): 'that a second body'.

> Then the semen he emitted became a year. The year simply did not exist before this. He carries him for as long as a year, at the end of which he gave birth to him. As he was born, death opened his mouth to swallow him, He cried: '*bhāṇ*!' That is what became speech.

This passage recruits from concepts of the earlier cosmogonies of the ŚB, but, at the same time, it is an attempt to put their content in one general and simple scenario. Reality, having created the cosmos conceived as its own self, wants to create a second self which will enable it to act in its manifest form. Within the frames of the input space of a hungry cognising being, the eater is looking for food. Thus the composer continues the earlier conceptualisation of creation presented in the ŚB.

The cognitive dimension of creation is conceived in terms of a sexual act between mind and speech elaborated already in ŚB 6.1.2.6-9 (see chapter 3.2.2). Here mind is identified with death and speech with hunger. Thus the conceptual network is enriched with the next input space. It is the general domain of Procreation in its realisation of the sexual act between male and female. In the blend, reality performs cognitive activity during which it expresses itself in speech. It is conceived in terms of the birth of a child which is the second self (*ātmán*) of reality and identical with it.

The child is identified with the year[12]. The sentence *yád réta ā́sīt, sá saṃvatsarò 'bhavat* metonymically compresses the beginning of the pregnancy (insemination) with the time it lasts (a year) and with a child which is the effect of insemination. The concept of a year metonymically evokes the concept of time. The composer preserves the metaphysical assumption expressed already in ṚV 1.164 according to which reality manifests itself in speech and time (see chapter 1.6).

In the next passage, the composer elaborates the general domain of Procreation in the same way as it is elaborated in some cosmogonies of the ŚB: it is the relationship between a father and a child who is afraid of him (ŚB 6.2.1[13]). Manifestation of the killing power of reality is conceived in terms of a father who can eat his child; its ability to die is conceived in terms of a child who can be killed. In the blend, the child shouts *bhā́ṇ* because it is afraid of death. The composer states that in this way speech appears. The conceptual ground for this thinking is metonymic: from one sound all speech appears. It is worth noting that speech has already been mentioned in BU 2.1.1 as a creative factor. If the recipient activates ṚV 1.164, he will

---

[12] Like Prajāpati in the ŚB, e.g. 10.4.2.2.

[13] See *Tāṇḍya Mahābrāhmaṇa* 21.1.2 (Lévi 1898: 25). See Jurewicz (2015b, 2016e).

understand that now everyday speech is created conceived as a footprint of all speech (see chapter 1.6).

BU 1.2.5

sá aikṣata yádi vā́ imám abhimaṁsyé kánīyó 'nnaṃ kariṣya íti | sá táyā vācā́ ténātmánedáṁ sárvam asṛjata yád idáṃ kíñcárco yájūṁṣi sā́māni chándāṁsi yajñā́n prajā́ṃ paśū́n | sá yád-yad evā́sṛjata tát-tad áttum adhriyata | sárvaṃ vā́ attī́ti tád áditer adititvám | sárvasyāttā́ bhavati sárvam asyā́nnaṃ bhavati yá evám etád áditer adititvā́ṃ véda |

Death reflected: 'If I kill him, I will only reduce supply of food'. So, with that speech and himself[14] (*ātman*) he gave birth to this whole world, to everything that is here – Ṛgvedic verses, Yajurvedic formulas, Sāmavedic chants, meters, sacrifices, people and animals. He began to eat whatever he gave birth to, 'He eats (*ad*) all' it is this that gave the name to and discloses the true nature of Aditi. When someone comes to know the name and nature of Aditi, he becomes the eater of this whole world, and this whole world becomes his food.

According to the pattern of earlier cosmogonies of the ŚB, the dangerous power of reality needs something which could pacify it and which is conceived in terms of food. In the cosmogonies, Prajāpati is presented as committing mistakes before he finds a safe way of manifestation in dying and resurrection through sacrifice. Either he dies (see chapter 3.2.2), or his creation dies of hunger (see chapter 3.2.1), or he is in danger of annihilation in his unmanifest aspect (see chapter 3.1.1). Here, reality immediately realises that a sacrificial structure is needed in order that it could safely manifest itself. It creates everything that is needed to perform ritual: three Vedas and various sacrifices, men and animals.

This stage of creation is again conceived in terms of a sexual act. The couple is speech and the self (*ātmán*) of reality. The recipient may presume that *ātmán* is identified with mind (*mánas*) which is conceived in male terms in the description of the previous stage (BU 1.2.4). In ŚB 11.2.3 (see chapter 3.5.3), reality called *bráhman* enters its creation with name and form; in the same way creation is conceived in BU 1.4.7 (see below, section 4.1.2) and in CU 6.3.2.3 (see section 4.1.4). I would therefore argue that the recipient of BU 1.2.5 is also expected to activate a similar way of thinking about creation: reality gives names to itself and assumes a form adequate to the name.

The next phase of creation is conceived in terms of eating as in earlier parts of the ŚB: whatever is created is eaten by reality. So reality dies as food and resurrects as the eater. In this way, it realises its two creative powers: the

---

14 Olivelle (1998): 'that body'.

power to kill and the power to be killed. This constant dying and resurrection, conceived in terms of eating, is the essence of infinity (*áditi*) which is realised by reality within its manifest aspect. In this way, the manifestation of reality is conceived in the ŚB (see chapter 3.2.3). At the same time, since cognition is conceived in terms of eating, the recipient understands that reality cognises itself in its manifest forms. The name *áditi* again brings the recipient's mind back to ṚV, namely to ṚV 10.72 and ṚV 1.164, the composers of which call reality in its unmanifest aspect with this name (see chapter 1.6). The definition of *áditi* given in BU 1.2.5 is an abstract definition based on earlier thought.

The composer then states that the person who knows this definition is the eater of the whole world and everything becomes his food. In these terms, human immortality is conceived as man will be like death itself, always killing and never killed[15]. This agrees with what is implied in the earlier cosmogonies of the ŚB, that the only way for reality to manifest its immortality is to die and resurrect constantly (see chapter 3.2.3).

BU 1.2.6

> *sò 'kāmayata bhū́yasā yajñéna bhū́yo yajeyéti | sò 'śrāmyat sá tápo 'tapyata | tásya śrāntásya taptásya yáśo vīryàm údakrāmat | prāṇā́ vaí yáśo vīryàṃ | tát prāṇéṣū́tkrānteṣu śárīram̐ śváyitum adhriyata | tásya śárīra evá mána āsīt |*
>
> Then death had this desire: 'Let me make an offering once more, this time with a bigger sacrifice'. So he strenuously toiled and fiercely exerted himself. When he had become worn out by toil and hot with exertion, his splendour – his vigour – departed from him. Now, splendour – vigour – consists of the vital breaths. So, when his vital breaths had departed, his corpse began to bloat. His mind, however, still remained within his corpse.

The composer presents death who wants to make one more offering, so it toils and heats, but now it loses its splendour (*yáśas*) and its vigour (*vīryà*) which are identified with its breath (*prāṇá*). This description again evokes earlier thought. The concept of *yáśas* evokes the Ṛgvedic concept of fame realised thanks to influence of Soma in the sun (see chapter 1.7). In ŚB 7.1.2.1, a similar image is created to conceive this stage of creation: Prajāpati is presented as losing his breath (*prāṇá*), virility (*vīryà*) and falling down; then he loses his food (*ánna*, see chapter 3.2.2). The recipient understands that reality tries once again to manifest itself and dies losing its cognitive abilities. Death of death is an impossible situation which expresses in the blend the contradictory nature of the creative process. It also expresses the ability of

[15] This is expressed in the *pitṛyāna* path, see section 4.3.1.

reality to submit itself to the rules of its manifest aspect. In this way, the oblation of all sacrifices will be created.

On the other hand, the composer explicitly says that the death of reality within its manifest aspect is not total death: something of it is still alive, i.e. its mind or thought which remains in its body (*tásya śárīra evá mána āsīt*). In BU 1.2.1, the mind or the thought of reality is the first impulse which incites creation of itself. The recipient may presume that the part of reality, which is able to think and convey further creation, has not disappeared[16]. That it is the same part is confirmed in the next passage of the cosmogony according to which reality again wants to create itself. Since the creative factors of reality are mind and speech (BU 1.2.4), the recipient may also interpret this stage of creation as the stage in which speech is lost (like in ŚB 2.2.4.1-3, see chapter 3.1.1).

BU 1.2.7a

sò 'kāmayata médhyaṃ ma idám̐ syād ātmanvy ànéna syām íti | tátó 'śvaḥ sámabhavad | yád áśvat tán médhyam abhūd íti | tád evā̀śvamedhásyāśvamedhatvám | eṣá ha vā́ aśvamedhám̐ veda yá enam eváṃ véda | tám ánavarudhyevāmanyata | tám̐ saṃvatsarásya parástād ātmána ā́labhata | paśū́n devátābhyaḥ prátyauhat | tásmāt sarvadevatyàṃ prókṣitaṃ prājāpatyám ā́labhante |

Then he had this desire: 'I wish that this corpse of mine would become fit to be sacrificed so I could equip me with myself[17] (*ātman*)'. Then that corpse became a horse. 'Because it bloated (*aśvat*), it became fit to be sacrificed (*medhya*)' – that is what gave the name to it and discloses the true nature of the horse sacrifice (*aśvamedha*). Only a man who knows the horse sacrifice in this way truly understands it.

Death believed that the horse was not to be confined in any way. At the end of one year, he immolated it as a sacrifice to himself, while he assigned the other animals to the gods. That is why people, when they immolate the horse consecrated to Prajāpati, regard it as an offering to all the gods.

Reality wants to transform the dead part of itself into something fit for sacrifice (*médhya*). The recipient is triggered to activate the general domain of Cooking in its specific realisation of the preparation of raw meat under the influence of fire. Thus the dead corpse will be transformed into something that can be eaten. It becomes a horse which is free for one year.

[16] In the earlier cosmogonies this part of reality is conceived in terms of the seers or the gods conceived anthropomorphically. Its conceptualisation in terms of mind and death is the next proof for abstraction.

[17] Olivelle (1998): 'get myself a living body'.

The concept of a year activates the general domain of Procreation in its specific realisation of pregnancy and birth giving. The coherence of this activation is strengthened as the development of the embryo is conceived in terms of its heating. Since in ŚB 11.1.6 the development of a child is conceived as occurring in sequence of years, the recipient can also activate this concept. The freedom of a horse can refer to the period of childhood. The concept of free movement of the horse is meant to evoke the concept of the freedom of reality which is realised within its manifest aspect.

If the recipient elaborates the scenario of the general domain of Cooking, he can create the image of an animal which runs away from those who want to kill it. Within the frame of the monistic assumption, the body of reality is identical with itself, so the recipient understands that reality assumes a form which runs away or hides from itself. Such a conceptualisation of creation is elaborated in ŚB 6.2.1 where Agni, because of fear that Prajāpati would kill him, assumes the form of five animals and thus hides against Prajāpati (Jurewicz 2014b). It is also elaborated in BU 1.4.5 (section 4.1.2) and in the AV (section 4.1.4). The recipient may understand that the horse grows in order to become fit for being eaten. The meaning of growing is expressed *via* the verb *áśvat*. This word also highlights the gruesome aspect of the process which is the swelling of the dead body. Creative transformations of reality within its manifest aspect are conceived in the blend in these contradictory terms.

The concept of year also metonymically evokes the concept of time and the recipient may understand that time is again measured with its main measure, now within the ritual context. This metonymic association is strengthened as the sun is conceived in terms of the horse and the horse's run for one year is the source domain for the sun's movement throughout the year. Thus the creative activity of reality is realised in the cosmos.

Then the essence of the Aśvamedha sacrifice is defined. It is a horse (*áśva*) which has grown (*aśvat*) and thanks to that became fit for sacrifice (*médhya*). The basis for this explanation is the general domain of Cooking because the dead body become 'fit for sacrifice' (*médhya*) only when is cooked. The dynamic aspect of sacrifice as action is implied in that the horse has been running for one year and during his run it grew. This activity of reality will be re-enacted by men in the frames of this sacrifice[18].

According to BU 1.2.6, when the horse becomes fit for sacrifice, it is killed, cooked and eaten. This sacrificial scenario is metonymically evoked

---

[18] For Aśvamedha see Dumont (1927), see also Talbot (1995).

via its initial phase which is catching a sacrificial animal[19]. The horse is the oblation for reality while other animals are the oblations for the gods. But in the last sentence it is said that the horse, which is consecrated to Prajāpati, can be regarded as an offering to all the gods. In this way, the composer, for the first time, introduces the name of the creative power of reality used in the ŚB and other Brāhmaṇas. This concept becomes here the general concept which includes all other killing manifestations of reality. Thus reality realises identity with its whole manifest aspect. It also realises the identity between its subjective powers conceived in terms of various eaters and their objects conceived in terms of various animals which are the food of the eaters. The men will re-enact this primeval sacrifice of reality in rituals.

BU 1.2.7b

eṣá vā́ aśvamedhó yá eṣá tápati | tásya saṃvatsará ātmā́ | ayám agnír arkáḥ | tásyemé lokā́ ātmā́nas | tā́v etā́v arkāśvamedhaú | sò púnar ékaivá devátā bhavati mṛtyúr | evā́pa punarmṛtyúṃ jayati | naìnaṃ mṛtyúr āpnoti | mṛtyúr asyātmā́ bhavaty | etā́sāṃ devátānām éko bhavati yá evám̐ véda |

The sun that shines up there, clearly, is a horse sacrifice; the year is its body (*ātman*). The fire that burns down here is the ritual fire; these worlds are its body. Now, there are these two: the horse sacrifice and the ritual fire (*arka*). Yet they constitute in reality a single deity – they are simply death. (Whoever knows this) averts repeated death – death is unable to seize him, death becomes his very body (*ātman*) and he becomes one of these deities.

In the first sentence, the composer identifies Aśvamedha sacrifice with the sun. This identification is based on metaphor THE SUN IS A HORSE. The year is called the self (*ātmán*) of reality visible in the sun. It agrees with conceptualisation of its appearance in terms of the general domain of Procreation which implies the identity of the parent and his son.

In the next sentence, fire is called *arká*. This identification fully agrees with the definition of *arká* presented in BU 1.2.1 according to which it is heat which becomes pleasant sweat or water. Thus it conveys the meaning of fire as internally contradictory: it has fiery and fluid aspects. Reality thus conceived manifests in ritual fire. The self (*ātmán*) of reality visible in fire are the worlds (*loká*). Thus the word *ātmán* is used in reference to the cosmic manifestation of reality which is the sun and to its manifestation in earthly fire. In this way, the composer implies their identity realised in the spatio-temporal cosmos. The concept of time is evoked metonymically by the concept

---

[19] THE INITIAL PHASE OF THE PROCESS FOR THE WHOLE PROCESS (Radden, Kövecses 1999). See also AU 1.3 (see section 4.1.3).

of a year, the concept of space is evoked by the concept of *loká*. The year is marked by the full turn of the sun. Its ritual manifestation is the free movement of the sacrificial horse. In this way, the dynamism of the manifest aspect of reality is conceived and expressed, and the sacrificial context endows this concept with the concept of killing and resurrection: while the sun moves, it is cyclically eaten by the killing power of reality in order to become its self, its *ātmán*, again and again. This ontological situation of reality within its manifest aspect is re-enacted in the ritual of Aśvamedha.

The identity of the manifest aspect of reality is expressed explicitly in the next sentence in which the composer states that *arká* and Aśvamedha are the same, i.e. death. It is worth adding that the identification of fire and *arká* fully agrees with the initial description of the cosmogony where creative transformations of reality are conceived as transformation of personified death which heats, sweats and becomes fire (BU 1.2.1). The manifestation of reality and its agency in the cosmos is conceived in terms of death which creates itself (*ātmán*) in cosmic and human dimensions.

At the end, it is stated that man who understands this can overcome death. Death becomes his self, *ātmán*. In this way, it is implied that he reaches beyond the manifest aspect and realises the state described in the first passage of cosmogony. Through his cognitive and ritual activity, reality can manifest itself and experience its various forms. In the micro-scale, he performs creative activity as if from the beginning. The role of man thus understood will be elaborated in other cosmogonies of Upaniṣads.

As it can be seen, it is impossible to understand this cosmogony of the BU without the reference to earlier cosmogonies of which this description makes an abstraction. Only the logic provided by the source domains used in the earlier cosmogonies makes this text intelligible.

4.1.2. The redefinition of the concept of *ātmán* (*Bṛhadāranyaka Upaniṣad* 1.4)

BU 1.4 consists of several cosmogonies. All of them begin with the Brāhmaṇic formulas *X idám ágra āsa*. However, *X* is not Prajāpati but *ātmán* or *bráhman*. Its aim is to incorporate the earlier metaphysical and ethical ideas into the new way of thinking. I will show that the meaning of *ātmán* still preserves the Vedic meaning of the whole and its essence but, at the same time, there are attempts to redefine and enlarge this meaning. The composer elaborates the general domain of Procreation in its specific realisation of the sexual act.

BU 1.4.1

> *ātmaivèdám ágra āsīt púruṣavidhaḥ | sò 'nuvīkṣya nānyád ātmáno 'paśyat | sò 'hám asmī́ty ágre vyā́harat | táto 'haṃ nā́mābhavat | tásmād ápy etárhy ā́mantrito 'hám ayám íty evā́gra uktvā́thānyán nā́ma prábrūte yád asya bhávati | sá yát pū́rvo 'smāt sárvasmāt sárvān pāpmána aúṣat tásmāt púruṣa | óṣati ha vaí sá táṃ yò 'smāt pū́rvo búbhūṣati yá eváṃ véda |*
>
> In the beginning this world was just self[20] (*ātman*) shaped like a man. He looked around and saw nothing but himself. The first thing he said was, 'Here I am!' and from that the name 'I' came into being. Therefore, even today when you call someone, he first says, 'It's I,' and then states whatever other name he may have. That first being received the name 'man' (*puruṣa*), because ahead (*pūrva*) of all this he burnt (*uṣ*) all evils. When someone knows this, he churns up anyone who may try to get ahead of him.

The cosmogony begins with the stage of creation when reality manifests itself in itself, *ātmán*, conceived in the form of man who cognises himself. The conceptual network consists of the concepts of self-cognising man and reality. The generic space is the concept of self-cognition. This corresponds to the first stage of creation in the *Nāsadīyasūkta* conceived as the manifestation of That One which is a manifestation of the uniqueness of reality (Jurewicz 2010a: 46–48).

The blend is run by the composer in the following way: man looks around and sees that there is no one except himself. In these terms, the realisation of the unity of reality is conceived. Then man calls himself with the name "I" (*áham*). This is the name of reality and in this way the future division into subject and object is outlined. In the *Nāsadīyasūkta*, this stage of creation is conceived in terms of darkness hiding darkness. It is worth remembering that in the ṚV the concept of darkness metonymically evokes the concept of night which is the state during which cognition is impossible (see Jurewicz 2010a: 109–110). The impossibility to cognise is also implied here because reality cannot cognise anything else beyond itself. Similarly to the cosmogonies of the ŚB, the experience which motivates thinking of creation is revealed and presented as its result (see ŚB 6.1.3, chapter 3.5.1, ŚB 11.1.6, chapter 3.5.2).

At the end of the passage, the etymology of the word *púruṣa* is given which is different from that given in AVŚ 10.2.30 (see chapter 2.5.1). The essence of *púruṣa* is burning everything that is in front of him. Thus the fiery nature of reality is expressed and the recipient may construe the image of a human being with an open mouth filled with fire similar to that in ŚB 2.2.4 (see chapter 3.1.1). However, the change in thinking about cosmogony is clear

[20] Olivelle (1998): 'a single body'.

as here, contrary to ŚB 2.2.4, the cognitive character of creation is highlighted with the fiery essence of reality only implied in the definition of *púruṣa*. The concept of fire is the next input space of the conceptual network. The coherence of the blend is preserved thanks to the metaphoric conceptualisation of cognition in terms of heating (ŚB 10.5.3, see chapter 3.5.1). The concept of a particular man, the recipient of the cosmogony, is the next input space of the blend.

BU 1.4.2

sò 'bibhet | tásmād ekākī́ bibheti | sá hāyám īkṣā̆ṃ cakre yán mád anyán nā̆sti kásmān nú bibhemī́ti | táta evā̆sya bhayáṃ vī̀yāya | kásmād dhy ábheṣyad | dvitī́yād vaí bhayáṃ bhavati |

He[21] became afraid; therefore, one becomes afraid when one is alone. Then he thought to himself: 'Of what should I be afraid, when there is no one but me?' So his fear left him, for what he was going to be afraid of? One is, after all, afraid of another.

The composer further runs the blend: the man, having realised that he is alone, becomes afraid. In these terms, the next creative stage is conceived. Here we again have an echo of ŚB 2.2.4 and other cosmogonies of the ŚB which present the fear of Prajāpati because of the possibility of death (see chapter 3.1.1). However, there is no real danger and creation is fully under control. Reality realises again its own uniqueness and its fear disappears.

BU 1.4.3

sá vaí naìvá reme | tásmād ekākī́ ná ramate | sá dvitī́yam aicchat | sá haitā̆vān āsa yáthā strīpumā̆ṁsau sampáriṣvaktau | sá imám evā̆tmā̆naṃ dvedhā̆pātayat | tátaḥ pátiś ca pátnī cābhavatāṃ | tásmād idám ardhabr̥galám iva sva íti ha smāha Yā̆jñavalkyaḥ | tásmād ayám ākāśáḥ striyā̆ pūryáta evá | tā̆ṁ sámabhavat | táto manuṣyā̀ ajāyanta |

He found no pleasure at all: so one finds no pleasure when one is alone. He wanted to have a companion. Now he was as large as a man and a woman in close embrace. So he split (*pat*) himself[22] into two, giving rise to husband (*pati*) and wife (*patnī*). Surely this is why Yājñavalkya used to say: 'The two of us are like two halves of a block.' The space here, therefore, is completely filled by the woman. He copulated with her, and from their union human beings were born.

The lack of an object causes not only a lack of fear but also a lack of any subjective-objective relationships, not only negative (metonymically

[21] Olivelle (1998): 'That first being'.
[22] Olivelle (1998): 'his body'.

evoked by the concept of fear), but also positive (metonymically evoked by the concept of pleasure). The motive for creation is conceived not only in terms of man's need to cognise, but also in terms of man's need to experience various emotions[23].

In the description of the further stages of creation, the composer introduces the general domain of Procreation in its specific realisation of a sexual act. The generic space of the blend now created is the concept of transformation with cognition as one of its input spaces. The manifest aspect is conceived in terms of a pair 'in close embrace' (*strīpumā̃ṁsau sampáriṣvaktau*). This expression also evokes the Ṛgvedic conceptualisation of the nocturnal state in terms of the sexual act; within the frame of this conceptualisation, the sky is man and earth is woman (see Jurewicz 2010a). So the recipient may activate this concept too as the next input space of the conceptual network. At the same time, the word *etā́vant* evokes the concept of dimension. As I have shown, the concept of greatness (*mahát*, see chapter 2.2.2) is used in the AVŚ in order to express the stage of creation when the future world becomes possible to be measured. The composer of the BU evokes the same concept. At the same time, the creative order of the *Nāsadīyasūkta* model is preserved. The scenario of the general domain of Procreation allows the recipient to activate the concept of future pregnancy and a womb filled with amniotic fluid which is metonymically evoked in the Veda *via* the general concept of waters. Thus the third stage of creation conceived in terms of flood, *salilá*, is evoked.

Creation of the earth and the sky is conceived in terms of splitting of a pair after the sexual act; the sky is conceived in terms of a husband (*páti*) and the earth in terms of a wife (*pátnī*). Moreover, the separation of two parts of reality in its manifest aspect results in the creation of space which agrees with the earlier cosmogonies that present the act of creation as the creation of space which is to be filled by reality. The space is filled with the female aspect of reality and this results in the creation of human beings. The difference from earlier cosmogonies is that space is created within the manifest aspect and is not a place for the future world.

At the same time – and this is also new in this cosmogony in comparison with earlier thought – social rules are settled in the creative act: the husband and wife are two halves of a whole which implies that marriage should not be broken[24].

[23] Already in ŚB 6.1.1, see chapter 3.2.2.

[24] Conceptualisation of marriage in terms of a whole is well grounded in European culture: 'For example, marriage is understood as the creation of a family (a whole) with spouses as parts. Divorce is thus viewed as *splitting up*.' (Lakoff 1987: 273–274).

BU 1.4.4

sò heyám īkṣā́ṃ cakre katháṃ nú mātmána evá janayitvā́ sámbhavati | hánta tiró 'sānī́ti | sā́ gaúr ábhavad vṛṣabhá ítaraḥ| tā́ṁ sám evā̀bhavat| táto gā́vo 'jāyanta | váḍavétarā́bhavad aśvavṛ̥ṣá ítaraḥ | gardabhī́tarā gardabhá ítaraḥ | tā́ṁ sám evā̀bhavat | táta ékaśapham ajāyata | ajétarā́bhavad bastá ítaraḥ | avír ítarā meṣá ítaraḥ | tā́ṁ sám evā̀bhavat | táto 'jāváyo 'jāyanta | evám evá yád idáṃ kíñca mithunám ā́ pipī́likābhyas tát sárvam asṛjata |

She then thought to herself: 'After begetting me from himself[25] (*ātman*), how could he copulate with me? I Know – I'll hide myself'. So she became a cow. But he became a bull and again copulated with her. From their union cattle were born. Then she became a mare, and he a stallion; she became a female donkey, and he, the male donkey. And again he copulated with her, and from their union one-hoofed animals were born. Then she became a female goat, and he, a male goat; she became a ewe and he, a ram. And again he copulated with her, and from their union goats and sheep were born. In this way he created every male and female pair that exists, down to the very ants.

The conceptual network is enriched with the input space of hide-and-seek. This concept has already been used in the ŚB 6.2.1: Agni hides from Prajāpati in five animals and is finally found in them. The motive for that play is that Agni is afraid that Prajāpati will kill and eat him[26]. In the BU, the female part of reality is also afraid of the male part but the motive is different. It is conceived in terms of a fear of transgressing social rules which are the rules that prohibit incest. In earlier cosmogonies of the ŚB, the concept of an incestual sexual act is used to express the multiplication of reality, but it is not evaluated and can be seen as the expression of freedom of reality conceived in terms of the transgression of social rules. Here incest is evaluated negatively which can be interpreted as setting those social rules. Nevertheless, the creative activity is still seen in these terms which can therefore be interpreted as expressing the freedom of reality.

The input space of hide-and-seek allows the composer to conceive and express the cognitive dimension of creation in the blend[27]. Reality, within its manifest aspect, hides itself from itself by assuming a female form and then again recognises itself. The act of recognition gives pleasure to reality and it is conceived in terms of the pleasure experienced during the sexual act. The recognition has ontic results which are forms of reality that are able to repeat its creative act. We should notice that eating and the sexual act are similar in

---

25 Olivelle (1998): 'his own body'.

26 See also Lévi (1898: 25).

27 The cognitive meaning is more explicitly expressed in *Vādhūlasūtra* (4.30) where the participants are Prajāpati in the form of sacrifice (*yajña*) and speech (*vāc*, Parpola 1992).

that in both there is a division between two opposing living agents and that the result of both activities is the disappearance of this division (in the act of eating it is literal disappearance, and in the sexual act it is a realisation of the closest unity possible between two living beings). Finally, both activities give pleasure to its agents. Concepts of both activities are used in the Veda in order to express creation. However, in the Upaniṣads, the metaphor of eating loses its importance. This may be connected with the fact that at the time of the Upaniṣads the life-giving character of sacrifice was less clear for the actual recipient[28].

The concept of hide-and-seek play also allows the composer to express other aspects of creation. First are the emotions which are connected with the presence of the second and the division into subject and object. They are impossible – as it is clearly stated by the cosmogony – when one is alone. Fear and pleasure are emotions which are felt during hide-and-seek: the one who looks fears that he will not find the hidden one and is happy when it happens, the one who is hidden fears that she will be found and is happy as long as she is not found. The sexual act which is the result of finding brings happiness to both agents. The concept of a reality who wants to create conditions which enable it to realise interpersonal relationships displays some similarities with the modern philosophy of dialogue[29]. Creation is the creation of the Other which reality desires in order to recognise its own identity. But, before identity is recognised, reality experiences various emotions, both negative and positive, as does the agent of a meeting when hiding and looking for the hidden[30].

In his famous book *Homo ludens*, Huizinga (1985[1939]) proposes a definition of play which fits very well to the concept of creation presented in BU 1.4. Firstly, play needs the free activity of an agent and is autotelic being undertaken only for the pleasure of its agents. Freedom then is the main attribute of reality conceived in terms of such a player and the only motive for creation of the world is creation itself: reality does not create the world *for* something else or *because of* something other than its own manifestations in the world. Secondly, play needs a separate place and time to be performed. The playground is the manifest aspect of reality and a year, created in the very beginning of creation, is the time of its play. Thirdly, play needs rules which are accepted freely by its participants, but then they must be obeyed

[28] It may be connected with a general improvement of the way of living (Witzel 1997).
[29] Jurewicz (2013b).
[30] This dialogical character of God's activity is later practically realised in the Bhakti movement where the relationship between the God and his devotee is conceived. At the same time, this can be seen as the elaboration of the Ṛgvedic general domain of Finding The Hidden.

without exception. The manifest forms of reality, namely, human beings and everything that lives in pair 'down to the very ants', are, as we can assume, acquired freely, but then there is no possibility to change them at least within one life[31]. As Malamoud (2005c) shows, there are elements of drama in the Vedic ritual. One could say that the essence of ritual is pretending to be someone other than who one is in everyday life and that this is the essence of theatre and of creation in the Vedic cosmogonies. It cannot be excluded then that the intention of the composer of BU 1.4 is to evoke a more general concept of play *via* the concept of hide-and-seek.

BU 1.4.5

sò 'ved ahám̐ vā̆vá sŕ̥ṣṭir asmy ahám̐ hìdám̐ sárvam ásr̥kṣīti | tátaḥ sŕ̥ṣṭir abhavat | sŕ̥ṣṭyām̐ hāsyaitásyām̐ bhavati yá evám̐ véda |

It then occurred to him: 'I alone am the creation, for I created all this'. From this 'creation' came into being. Anyone who knows this prospers in this creation of this.

Having acquired various manifest forms, reality now cognises its whole manifest aspect because it does not lose control in its creation. This is contrary to human beings which will be elaborated in later philosophy (Jurewicz 1994).

The initial part of the cosmogony analysed so far elaborates the conceptualisation of creation in terms of human relationships. The further description introduces other source domains some of which continue earlier thinking while others are new. The composer, on the one hand, elaborates earlier thought and puts it in more abstract terms while, on the other, he introduces new ideas, both metaphysical and social, and tries to reconciliate them with earlier thinking.

BU 1.4.6

áthéty abhyàmanthat | sá múkhāc ca yóner hástābhyām̐ cāgním asr̥jata | tásmād etád ubháyam alómakam antaratáḥ | alómakā hí yónir antaratáḥ | tád yád idám āhur amúm̐ yajāmúm̐ yajéty ékaikam̐ devám etásyaivá sā́ vísr̥ṣṭir | eṣá u hy èvá sárve devā́ḥ | átha yát kíñcedám ārdrám̐ tád rétaso 'sr̥jata | tád u sóma| etā́vad vā́ idám̐ sárvam ánnam̐ caivā̀nnādáś ca| sóma evā́nnam agnír annādáḥ | saìṣā́ bráhmaṇó 'tisr̥ṣṭiḥ | yác chréyaso devā́n ásr̥jatā́tha yán mártyaḥ sánn amŕ̥tān asr̥jata tásmād átisr̥ṣṭiḥ | átisr̥ṣṭyām̐ hāsyaitásyām̐ bhavati yá evám̐ véda |

Then he churned like this and, using his hands, produced fire from his mouth as from a vagina. As a result the inner sides of both these – the hands and the mouth – are without hair, for inside of the vagina is without hair. 'Sacrifice to this god. Sacrifice to that god' – people of say these things but in reality each

[31] For the elaboration of this metaphor in the later thought, see Jurewicz (1994).

> of these gods is his own creation, for he himself is all these gods. From his semen, then he created all that is moist here, which is really Soma. Food and eater – that is the extent of this whole world. Food is simply Soma, and the eater is fire. This is brahman's supercreation. It is a supercreation because he created the gods, who are superior to him, and, being a mortal himself, he created the immortals. Anyone who knows this stands within this supercreation of his.

The composer elaborates the input spaces of the concept of fire and the general domain of Procreation. He also triggers the recipient to activate the description of ŚB 2.2.4 which presents Prajāpati, who fears Agni because Agni wants to eat him, as creating an oblation of milk with aid of churning (see chapter 3.1.1). As I have argued, the creation of milk can also be understood as the creation of semen. In this way, the androgynic nature of reality is conceived. In the BU, this scenario is compressed into a simple image of the creation of fire from a mouth and a vagina with use of hands. Since speech is conceived in terms of fire, the recipient may elaborate the input space of cognition and understand that reality verbalises its cognition.

The blend is enriched with the next input space which is sacrifice activated metonymically by the concept of oblation. It is Soma which represents everything which is moist in the cosmos. The coherence of the blend is strengthened by the metaphoric conceptualisation of Soma in terms of semen and, in the blend, the recipient may understand Soma in these terms. Thus the composer activates the Ṛgvedic general model of reality transformation and reinterprets it as a relationship between an eater and food[32]. If the recipient activates the input space of cognition, he can apply the model to the subjective-objective relationship. In this way, the complex dynamism of the manifest aspect is conceived in terms of an abstract relationship which refers to any processes that take place in the world. Since this relationship is realised in sacrificial activity, the sacrifice can be seen as the multimodal expression of this abstract model. This model is also elaborated in the model of the Five Fires' (*pañcāgnividyā*, see section 4.3.1) where the processes which take place within the world are seen in terms of the interaction between fire and oblation.

This stage of creation is called *átisṛṣṭi*, 'supercreation'. The reason it is called such is explained by the composer as reality, being dead, created immortal gods. Again this can be understood only against the earlier background of the ŚB which conceives cosmogonic activity in terms of Prajāpati's death who resurrects as immortal. The means of this process is sacrifice. Thus the division between what is mortal and what is immortal appears within the manifest aspect of reality.

---

[32] See ŚB 10.6.2.1, see section 4.4.2.1.

The upward movement of creation is preserved, but is evoked in a schematic way *via* the preposition *áti*. Thus the image schema of VERTICALITY is introduced as the next input space of the conceptual network. The recipient can infer that the first phase of creation (which could be called *sṛ́ṣṭi*) is conceived in terms of the death of reality within its manifest aspect, its lack of cognition and its feeling of unhappiness. In the second phase (*átisṛṣṭi*), reality regains life, cognition and happiness within its manifest aspect and realises it in subjective-objective relationship. The image schema of VERTICALITY is used in ŚB 6.1.1.4 to conceive the possibility for creating supernatural knowledge (see chapter 3.2.2) and the recipient may also interpret the description in this way. This interpretation is confirmed in that the word *átisṛṣṭi* refers to the stage when Agni and Soma, which are the basic conditions of ritual, are created and supernatural knowledge can be realised only within its frames.

Contrary to earlier descriptions, the creative process is all the time under the control of reality. Its identity with its creation is explicitly said: although during sacrifices various gods are worshipped they are all identical with reality (*eṣá u hy èvá sárve devā́*).

BU 1.4.7

tád dhedáṃ tárhy ávyākṛtam āsīt | tán nāmarūpā́bhyām evá vyā́kriyatāsaú nā́māyám idám̐rūpa íti | tád idám ápy etárhi nāmarūpā́bhyām evá vyā́kriyata asaú nā́māyám idám̐rūpa íti | sá eṣá ihá práviṣṭa ā́ nakhāgrébhyo yáthā kṣuráḥ kṣuradhāné 'vahitaḥ syā́d, viśvambharó vā viśvambharakulāyé | táṃ ná páśyanty | ákṛtsno hí sáḥ | prāṇánn evá prāṇó nā́ma bhávati vádan vā́k páśyaṃś cákṣuḥ śṛṇvā́ñ chrótraṃ manvānó mánaḥ | tā́ny asyaitā́ni karmanāmā́ny evá | sá yó 'ta ékaikam upā́ste ná sá veda | ákṛtsno hy èṣó 'ta ékaikena bhávati | ātméty evópāsītā | átra hy èté sárva ékaṃ bhávanti | tád etát padanī́yam asya sárvasya yád ayám ātmā́ | anéna hy ètát sárvaṃ véda | yáthā ha vaí padénānuvindéd evám kīrtím̐ ślókaṃ vindate yá eváṃ véda |

At that time this world was without real distinctions; it was distinguished simply in terms of name and visible appearance – 'He is so and so by name and has this sort of an appearance.' So even today this world is distinguished simply in terms of name and visible appearance, as when we say, 'He is so and so by name and has this sort of an appearance'. Penetrating this body up to the very nailtips, he remains there like a razor within a case or a termite within a termite-hill. People do not see him, for he is incomplete as he comes to be called breath when he is breathing, speech when he is speaking, sight when he is seeing, hearing when he is hearing, and mind when he is thinking. These are only names of his various activities'. One should consider them as simply his self (*ātman*), for in it all these become one. The same self (*ātman*) is the trail to this entire world, for by following it one comes to this entire world, just as by following their tracks one finds (the cattle). Whoever knows this finds fame and glory.

In the previous chapter, I discussed ŚB 11.2.3 where reality, called *bráhman*, creates the world and then leaves it in order to come back and recognise it with aid of names and forms (see chapter 3.5.3). Its composer elaborates the image schemas of VERTICALITY and CONTAINER. The use of the word *átisr̥ṣṭi* in the previous passage of the BU evokes the same way of thinking of creation. At the same time, its use shows a further tendency to abstraction: in the ŚB this stage of creation is conceived in the anthropomorphic terms of a person who leaves a container. In BU 1.4.7 it is expressed *via* image schema of VERTICALITY.

In this stage, reality reverts to its manifest aspect and recognises it with aid of name and form in the same way as it is presented in ŚB 11.2.3. This cognitive activity has ontological results: reality gives names and forms to itself and thus transforms itself into its manifest aspects. The process is conceived in terms of entering a container, but here the container is conceived in terms of man because the composer says that reality penetrates its manifest aspect 'up to the nailtips' (*ā́ nakhāgrébhyo*). The general way of expression allows the recipient to presume that it penetrates every human being in the same way.

Then the way that reality transforms itself into its manifest aspect with the aid of name and form is explained: it undertakes various cognitive activities and gives names to them. When it speaks, it calls itself speech; when it sees, it calls itself sight; when it hears, it calls itself hearing; when it breathes, it calls itself breath; when it thinks, it calls itself mind. As we can see, the form (*rūpá*) is identified here with an activity (*kárman*). These transformations are seen as real. However, reality should not be seen separately in each activity, it can only be cognised as performing all these activities simultaneously[33]. Only then does it becomes full and complete. Man is expected to know all its names and forms and then he will know the whole manifest aspect which is self, *ātmán*, of reality as stated in the beginning of the cosmogony.

This passage can also be seen as an attempt to express creation in a more abstract way to that previously attested in the ŚB. The earlier descriptions use the general domain of Procreation in its specific realisation of the sexual act as the source domain of verbalisation of thoughts with its ontic result. Here, this source domain disappears and only its target domain is elaborated.

However, the last sentence brings the recipient back to the R̥gvedic concept of following cattle's footprint in terms of which creation of fire and

[33] It is expressed already in ŚB 6.1.1.3 which presents unification of breaths (see chapter 3.2.2).

cognition is conceived (Jurewicz 2010a). In BU 1.4.7, *ātmán* is seen as the object which should be followed by its footprints. The conceptualisation of *ātmán* as fiery (BU 1.4.1, see section 4.1.1) is also coherent with Ṛgvedic thought and allows the recipient to create the image of fire which leaves a black track when it burns everything that is in front of it. Since *ātmán* is the whole manifest aspect, when man knows it he knows everything that is manifest.

The final result of following footprint is also conceived in the Ṛgvedic terms: this is fame (*kīrtí*) and *ślóka* (translated by Olivelle as 'glory'). The composer again evokes the Ṛgvedic concept of fame which is the supernatural state in which man, under the influence of Soma, gains immortality and could be heard by everyone[34]. Although the word *kīrtí* is used only once in the ṚV (10.54.1), the meaning of fame is present is the semantic range of the Ṛgvedic concept conveyed by the words *śrī́*, *śrávas*, *yáśas* and *kṣatrá* (see chapter 1.7). In this way, the new idea that *ātmán* is everything that is manifest is put within the frame of the oldest parts of tradition. The next passage emphasises that *ātmán* is dear to every human being:

BU 1.4.8

> *tád etát préyaḥ putrā́t préyo vittā́t préyo 'nyásmāt sárvasmād ántarataraṃ yád ayám ātmā́ | sá yò 'nyám ātmánaḥ priyáṃ bruvāṇáṃ brūyā́t priyáṁ rotsyatī́tīśvaró ha táthaivá syād | ātmā́namevá priyám úpāsīta | sá yá ātmā́nam evá priyám upā́ste ná hāsya priyáṃ pramā́yukaṃ |*
>
> This innermost thing, this self (*ātman*) – it is dearer than a son, it is dearer than wealth, it is dearer than anything else. If a man claims that something than his self is dear to him, and someone were to tell him that he will lose what he holds dear, this is liable to happen. So a man should regard only his self as dear to him. When a man regards only his self as dear to him, what he holds dear will never perish.

As I have already argued, the aim of creation is the appearance of subjective-objective relationship in its cognitive and emotional dimensions. The division into names and forms creates diversity which should be overcome not only in the act of recognition of the underlying unity but also in the act of love. This agrees with the conceptualisation of the earlier stages of creation in terms of the amorous hide-and-seek play and will be further discussed by Yājñavalkya in his talk with Maitreyī.

[34] The sound of the sun is called ślóka in the RV, see chapter 1.7.

BU 1.4.9-10a

tád āhur yád brahmavidyáyā sárvaṃ bhaviṣyánto manuṣyā̀ mányante | kím u tád bráhmāved yásmāt tát sárvam ábhavad íti | (9)
bráhma vā́ idám ágra āsīt | tád ātmā́nam evā̀ved | ahám bráhmāsmī́ti | tásmāt tát sárvam abhavat | tád yó-yo devā́nāṃ pratyábudhyata sá evá tád ábhavat | táthárṣīṇām | táthā manuṣyā̀ṇām| tád dhaitát páśyann ṛ́ṣir Vāmádevaḥ prátipede | ahám mánur abhavaṁ sū́ryaś céti | tád idám ápy etárhi yá eváṃ védāhám bráhmāsmī́ti sá idáṁ sárvaṃ bhavati | (10)

Now, the question is raised: 'Since people think that they will become the Whole by knowing *brahman*, what did *bráhman* know that enabled it to become the Whole?' (9)
In the beginning this world this world was only *bráhman*, and it knew only itself (*ātmán*), thinking: 'I am *bráhman*.'. As a result, it became the Whole. Among the gods, likewise, whosoever realised this, only they became the Whole. It was the same also among the seers and among humans.
Upon seeing this very point, the seer Vāmadeva proclaimed: 'I was Manu, I was the sun.' This is true even now. Of a man knows 'I am *bráhman*' in this way, he becomes this whole world. (10)

BU 1.4.9 attests the search for rationalisation of the knowledge about reality which is called *bráhman* and which can be realised through cognition. The tacit assumption expressed here is that man repeats the activity of reality as expressed explicitly in many places in the ŚB. The answer is that *brahman* just knew itself (*ātmā́nam*) and thus he became the whole. Since, in the cosmogony that is presented in BU 1.4, the word *ātmán* refers to the manifest aspect of reality conceived in terms of man, the recipient can understand that the first three sentences of BU 1.4.10 are a concise version of cosmogony. Reality called *bráhman* perceives itself (*ātmā́nam*) and this self becomes its manifest aspect with which *bráhman* asserts its identity and thus regains its wholeness split in the creative cognitive act. This creative activity of *bráhman* is the rule for gods, seers and men who should know themselves as the one with reality; only then do they become the whole.

We again witness the tendency for abstraction: creation is presented in terms of self-cognition. Its composer does not activate the complex experiential processes as it is in the initial passages of the cosmogony. The conceptual network is again reduced to two input spaces: the concepts of reality and of man with self-cognition as their generic space.

At the same time, the composer grounds this abstract exposition in the RV: he quotes ṚV 4.26.1 which, as tradition claims, was composed by Vāmadeva Gautama. In this hymn, the poet in Somic exultation realises his identity with Indra[35]. Thus the composer of the BU implies that the state realised in the times of the ṚV thanks to Soma[36] can be gained thanks to a knowledge of *bráhman*.

BU 1.4.10b

tásya ha ná devā́ś canā́bhūtyā īśate | ātmā́ hy èṣā́ṁ sá bhávati | átha yò 'nyā́ṃ devátām upā́ste 'nyò 'sā́v, anyò 'hám asmī́ti, ná sá veda | yáthā paśúr evám̐ sá devā́nāṃ | yáthā ha vaí bahávaḥ paśávo manuṣyàṃ bhuñjyúr evám ékaikaḥ púruṣo devā́n bhunakti | ékasminn evá paśā́v ādīyámāné 'priyaṃ bhavati kím u bahúṣu | tásmād eṣāṃ tán ná priyáṃ yád etán manuṣyā̀ vidyúḥ | (10)

Not even the gods are able to prevent it, for he becomes their very self (*ātman*). So when a man venerates another deity, thinking, 'He is one, and I am another,' he does not understand. As livestock is for men, so he is for the gods. The loss even a single head of livestock is painful; how much more if many are lost. The gods, therefore, are not pleased at the prospect of man coming to understand this.

In this passage, the composer states that a man who cognises himself as *bráhman* is stronger than gods because, as it is said, gods become his self *ātmán*. This statement agrees with what has been presented in the cosmogony: the manifest aspect of *bráhman* is called his self, *ātmán*, and gods are created within it. As gods are the self, *ātmán*, of *bráhman*, they become the self, *ātmán*, of the knowing man in the same way.

Then the composer states that if one venerates another deity (*devátā*) as separate from himself, he does not know the truth. The word *devátā* is used in the AU in reference to cognitive powers of reality which are performed by agents personified as gods (see section 4.1.3). It is possible that this is the meaning of the word here too. It is consistent with the conceptualisation of the manifest aspect of reality in terms of various cognitive activities described in BU 1.4.7. Truth can be cognised if one understands all these activities as performed simultaneously. The same conviction is expressed already in ŚB 6.1.1.3 where breaths cannot perform their activity if they are separated (see chapter 3.2.2).

The relationship between the gods and men is conceived in terms of the relationship between a cowherd and his cattle: the gods are conceived in terms of the cattle-owners and the sacrificer in terms of the cattle. The roots of this conceptualisation can be found already in the ṚV. Cattle is used in

---

[35] I would follow the Anukramaṇī's interpretation, contrary to Jamison, Brereton (2014: 600).

[36] See ṚV 4.26.7: *ādā́ya śyenó abharat sómaṃ sahásraṃ savā́m̐ ayútaṃ ca sākám | átrā púraṃdhir ajahād árātīr máde sómasya mūrā́ ámūraḥ* || This stanza is fully quoted by AU 2.5.6, see section 4.1.3.

sacrifices which are conceived in terms of eating the oblation. Moreover, in the ŚB, power is conceived in terms of eating: the ruler is the eater and the ruled the food (Smith 1994: 46–48). It is implied then that when man venerates the gods thinking that they are different from him man becomes the food of gods. This agrees with the general cosmological thinking of the ŚB which conceives of the gods, who are in the sun, in terms of eaters and everything that is on the earth together with men in terms of their food (see chapter 3.3). Such a conceptualisation is elaborated in the description of the path of the fathers (*pitṛyāna*) in the BU and CU (see section 4.3.1).

But if man knows *bráhman*, he becomes *bráhman* and as *bráhman* he contains everything, including the gods, within himself because the gods who are of the manifest aspect become his *ātmán* too. The composer shows compassion towards the gods: he elaborates the source domain of the cattle-owner who is unhappy if he loses even one animal from his herd. Similarly, the gods are unhappy when men realise the truth.

The next passage (BU 1.4.11-15) presents the creation of the essence of the four social states. This concept is the next input space of the conceptual network created in the cosmogony. The creation of social states is expressed in the same way as creation of the world in ŚB 10.4.2 where Prajāpati, in his attemptions to manifest himself (*ví bhū-*), divides himself into more and more parts, but does not succeed until he reaches a certain number which corresponds to the divisions of time and numbers of bricks in the fire altar.

In BU 1.4.11, reality firstly creates the royal power, *ksatrá*, together with the gods who are conceived as rulers among the gods. Creation of the royal power is again conceived with aid of image schema of VERTICALITY (*áti sṛj-*). This image is also used to explain the relationship between the Brahmin and the Kṣatriya during the Rājasūya sacrifice when the Brahmin seats below the Kṣatriya. As I have argued (Jurewicz 2010a: 249–250), this sacrificial arrangement reflects the metaphysical assumption implied by the model of the Wave Of Honey according to which Soma is born from Agni. This relationship is conceived in terms of raising a wave of honey identical with the Somic stalk from the ocean. In BU 1.4.1, *ātmán* is conceived as fiery and the cosmogony identifies it with *bráhman* which in this context is understood as the priestly power. From it royal power is created. The word *átisṛṣṭi* now refers not to the philosophical model of the world's functioning in general sacrificial terms, but to the social model which will enable the realisation of sacrifice and thus the world's functioning. Within its frames, the social rule are settled: the Kṣatriya is subordinated to Brahmin who is conceived as Kṣatriya's womb conceived as his source and his final goal just as the wave will fall down and as the rain will come back to the earth from the sun.

But reality still cannot fully manifest itself, so it creates the essence of the Vaiśyas (*víś*) with the gods who are listed in groups. Then it creates the essence of the Śūdra class (*śaúdra*) together with the god Pūṣan because he nourishes this world (BU 1.4.12-13). Creation of these two essences is expressed with the verb *sṛj-* without the preposition *áti*. The explanation of the type of gods created with the essences of the classes implies their social function: the Kṣatriyas rule, the Vaiśyas live in groups and the Śūdras nourish other classes. Since in BU 1.4.6 the word *átisr̥ṣṭi* is used to describe the moment when reality regains life, cognition, happiness and immortality within its manifest aspect, the recipient may presume that within the social sphere this state is realised by the two upper classes that have full access to ritual.

Reality still cannot fully develop and it finally 'over-creates' (*áti sr̥j-*) dharma (*dhárma*) which is called his better form (BU 1.4.14). Dharma settles the rules between people so that the weak ones can feel safe. It is identified with truth (*satyá*). We should remember that truth is conceived ontologically in the Vedic thought, so to call *dhárma* 'truth' is to see it as the state of affairs. The truthfulness of dharma, seen within the input space of play, can be interpreted as the inevitability of the rules of play. We witness here the beginnings of another aspect of freedom which will be developed in later Indian thought: freedom is not only the ability and possibility to do whatever one wants but also the ability to obey rules which are freely accepted[37]. The image schema of VERTICALITY strengthens the meaning of power inscribed in the concept of *dhárma* because it allows power to be conceived in terms of what is up.

According to the next passage (BU 1.4.15), *bráhman* becomes fire among the gods, Brahmin among the Brahmins, Kṣatriya among the Kṣatriyas, Vaiśya among the Vaiśyas, Śūdra among the Śūdras. The unity of reality between its unmanifest aspect and its social manifestation is realised *via* particular members of the different social classes. In this way, the concept of reality as the innermost essence of cosmos and man is introduced. Here this essence is called *bráhman*. Thus it is implied that the essence is reality in its unmanifest aspect. This concept will be especially elaborated in the AU (see section 4.1.3).

In the next sentences of BU 1.4.15, the composer states that people look for the world (*loká*) for themselves in fire among the gods and in the Brahmin among the people. In the ṚV, the word *loká*, often qualified as broad (*urú*, Gonda 1966), is used in reference to the created world, i.e. to the manifest aspect called *sát*. And this meaning should be evoked here: *ātmán* is the whole manifest aspect for men in the same way as it is for *bráhman* in BU 1.4.10.

37 See Jurewicz (1994).

In the next passage of BU 1.4.15, the composer states that one should know one's world because if one dies without knowing, it one will not reach it[38]. The situation of such a man is compared to a person who does not know the Veda or does not perform rituals. And even great and holy rites will not help in his difficult afterlife situation. This statement betrays the conviction that traditional knowledge and ritual are not sufficient to get happiness after death which contrasts to earlier thought which assumed that the correct performance of rituals with their correct knowledge ending with properly performed cremation is enough for that aim. But when man realises his identity with reality, not only will those deeds performed during his life not vanish, but he himself will become one with reality able to create anything from his own self, *ātmán* (in the same way as reality which creates from its self, *ātmán*, everything what live in pairs down to the ants).

The concept of *ātmán*, identified with *loká*, is further elaborated (BU 1.4.16)[39]. *Ātmán* becomes the world (*loká*) for all beings. It is realised by man when he, knowing that *ātmán* is the world, performs rituals. He becomes the world (*loká*) for the gods when he performs sacrifices for the gods, he becomes the world (*loká*) for fathers in oblations to the ancestors and in begetting children, he becomes the world (*loká*) for human beings in providing them with food and shelter, he becomes the world (*loká*) for cattle in their good treatment, finally, he becomes the world (*loká*) for wild animals down to the ants when giving them shelter.

Here we have a redefinition of sacrifice which is seen not only as performing ritual in a correct way, but also as being kind to all sentient beings. And since man becomes *ātmán* of reality, thanks to his knowledge, the recipient can understand that all beings can realise their identity with it thanks to human activity. The idea that the world (*loká*) can be constructed is expressed in JB 1.46 (see chapter 5.1.1) where the afterlife of man is conceived in terms of the creation of a world for him[40]. In BU 1.4.16, the various beings conquer their *loká* through the activity of the sacrificer who, as is said, becomes *loká*

---

38 *átha yó ha vā́ asmā́l lokā́t svám̥ lokám ádr̥ṣṭvā praíti sá enam ávidito ná bhunakti yáthā védo vā́nanūkto 'nyád vā kármā́kr̥tam | yádi ha vā́ ápy ánevam̥vin mahat púṇyam̥ kárma karóti tád dhāsyāntatáḥ kṣī́yata evá | ātmā́nam evá lokám úpāsīta| sá yá ātmā́nam evá lokám upā́ste ná hāsya kárma kṣīyate | asmā́d dhy èvā̀tmáno yád-yat kāmáyate, tát-tat sr̥jate |*

39 *átho ayám̥ vā́ ātmā́ sárveṣām̥ bhūtā́nām̥ lokáḥ | sá yáj juhóti yád yájate téna devā́nām̥ lokáḥ | atha yád anubrūté ténárṣīṇām | átha yát prajā́m iccháte yát pitŕ̥bhyo niprṇā́ti téna pitr̥̄́ṇā́m | átha yán manuṣyā̀n vāsáyate yád ebhyó 'śanam̥ dádāti téna manuṣyā̀ṇām | átha yát paśúbhyas tr̥ṇodakám̥ vindáti téna paśūnā́m̥ | yád asya gr̥héṣu śvā́padā váyām̐sy ā́ pipī́likābhya upajī́vanti téna téṣām̥ lokó | yáthā ha vaí svā́ya lokā́yā́riṣṭim icchéd evám̐ haivam̥víde sarvadā́ sárvāṇi bhūtā́ny áriṣṭim icchanti | tád vā́ etád viditám̥ mīmām̐sitám |*

40 *so 'sya lokaḥ punar utthāyai bhavati*, see also JB 1.245: *kl̥ptam̥ ha vai lokam̥ yajamāno 'bhijayate.*

for them. Such a conceptualisation allows the composer to express their active role in this process. At the same time, the sacrificer is also active. Taking into account that everything is *ātmán*, the recipient understands that it is *ātmán* who acts on himself during ritual just as he acts on himself in *illo tempore*. The word *loká*, in this context, could be understood as referring to the levels of *ātmán*'s experience who creates the world for himself in every sentient being thanks to ritual broadly understood. On the highest conceptual level, it is reality which engages itself in subjective-objective experience.

The final passage (BU 1.4.17) begins with a cosmogony which is a realisation of the subjective-objective relationships on the micro-scale from the perspective of an individual agent, called also *ātmán*, who wants to have wife, children, riches and the possibility to perform deeds. Only when man realises all these desires, can he feel complete. Then a conceptual network is created: the first input space is the manifest aspect conceived in terms of the self of reality (*ātmán*), the second input space is the sacrificer and the third is the internal and external cognitive powers of mind (*mánas*), speech (*vā́c*), vital breath (*prāṇá*), sight (*cákṣus*), hearing (*śrótra*) and *ātmán* (here the meaning of the whole organism which enables cognition is highlighted). In the blend, the sacrificer, in the form of *ātmán*, becomes the mind, wife becomes speech, offspring becomes vital breath, sight becomes human wealth (because it is gained with the eye), hearing becomes divine wealth (because it is heard through the Vedas) and man's deeds become *ātmán* because one acts with his own body (*ātmán*). The state realised in the blend is called completeness (*kṛtsnátā*). The composer does not explain why the wife is identified with speech and offspring with breath probably because these identifications are well entrenched in the Vedic thought. The concept of woman is a conventionalised source domain for the conceptualisation of speech. Offspring is breath because in offspring the man is reborn (see AU 2.1, section 4.1.3), so through his offspring he regains his life metonymically evoked by the breath. Although the word *loká* is not used here, the human level of experience is described: each man during his life creates a world for himself as *ātmán* did *in illo tempore*.

This conceptual blend brings the recipient's mind back to earlier thought and, at the same time, it opens the way to the new trends in philosophy. The cognitive powers enumerated in the second input space are the same as those enumerated in ŚB 10.5.3. Its composer identifies all reality with the mind which transforms itself into speech, then, into breath, into sight, into hearing, into deed and, finally, into fire (see chapter 3.5.1). The BU fuses the last two into one called *ātmán*. We can presume that the most external layer of fire is reduced to *ātmán* because the description of the BU is taken from the analysis of the Agnicayana and its composer aims to use sacrificial concepts in order to express ontological and ethical issues seen more generally. At the same time, the identity of manifestations is preserved. In the ŚB, mind, which is fiery, finally manifests itself as fire. In the blend created by the composer of the BU, *ātmán*, identified with the mind, finally manifests itself as *ātmán* doing deeds.

The concept of fullness (*kṛtsnátā*) brings the recipient's mind to the earlier description in BU 1.4.10 where *bráhman* is presented as being divided in his names and active forms which are breathing, speaking, seeing, hearing and thinking. *Ātmán* is incomplete within those activities taken separately, but becomes complete, when they are seen together. In the context of this passage, the recipient can understand that *ātmán* in BU 1.4.17 is seen as the agent who performs deeds because *ātmán* is the whole which includes the five cognitive elements and the body of the agent.

At the same time, this passage is evidence for the interiorisation of the sacrifice and for the possibility to perform it when one thinks, breaths, sees and hears; in this case, deeds would be deeds that lead to supernatural cognition.

*

The broad meaning of the word *ātmán*, which in the Veda means everything that constitutes the individual character of an entity, its outward appearance and internal essence (see Jurewicz 1997), allows the composer of BU 1.4 to express his philosophical concepts. He can say explicitly what was implied by the earlier thought and redefine it according to the conceptual needs of his recipients. In the beginning of this cosmogony, the word *ātmán* refers to reality who realises its cognitive abilities. It divides itself into names and active forms and becomes hidden but should be understood and loved as one. The positive emotional aspect is highlighted because this is the motive for the successful manifestation of reality. Then the concept of *bráhman* is introduced which refers to the unmanifest aspect of reality which cognises itself (*ātmā́nam*) and thus becomes the world. Everything which is in the world is *bráhman*'s self, *ātmán*, which is the same as *loká*, the world itself.

Then various levels of *ātmán*'s experience are discussed. This experience consists in the realisation of the unity of *ātmán* by particular living manifestations of *bráhman* (gods, ancestors, men, animals). It is realised in the activity of the sacrificer. The unity of reality, implied in the ṚV in its sophisticated conceptual edifice, is now explicitly stated and emphasised as the basis for a happy life here and in the afterlife.

The final passage (BU 1.4.17) redefines the concept of *ātmán*. In the first half, it is understood as reality in its manifest form of the individual human being who wants to realise positive, subjective-objective relationship with other manifestation of the world. This is in accord with earlier Brāhmaṇic ethics. And this ethics is then reinterpreted in order to create a link between the earlier sacrificial practices and the contemporary pre-yogic practices. Because of this, the composer concludes that the activity described in the blend is the fivefold sacrifice, the fivefold sacrificial animal and the fivefold human being. The reason for this explanation is that everything in the world which is *ātmán*, the self of reality, is fivefold: it consists of power of thinking, speaking, breathing, seeing and hearing. *Ātmán* here still preserves its meaning of the whole (together with the outward appearance) and the essence of this whole. What is new is its usage in reference to the whole cosmos seen as the self of whole of reality called *brahman*.

We can also see the tendency to abstraction and the change of interest in comparison with earlier thought. The rich cosmogonic blend is narrowed in BU 1.4.10 and the composer focuses on the situation of man in the cosmos identified with reality and his ontological, epistemological and ethical role. In this simple blend, the generic space is cognition and, in the blend, cognitive transformations have their result in being.

4.1.3. Reality and manifestations of *ātman* in the *Aitareya Upaniṣad*

This cosmogony can be seen as the first clear Upaniṣadic testimony of the usage of the concept of *ātman* as the essence of the cosmos and of man identical with reality. As I have shown, this usage is already foreshadowed in the AVŚ (see chapter 2.5.1.1). The composer of the AU also elaborates the concept of the cosmos seen in terms of man (BU 1.2.3, section 4.1.1) which will be continued in later philosophy in greater detail. At the same time, he follows the main Vedic cosmogonic pattern.

AU 1.1.1-2.

ātmā vā idam eka evāgra āsīt | nānyat kiñcana miṣat | sa īkṣata lokān nu sṛjā iti | (1)
sa imāṃl lokān asṛjata | ambho marīcīr maram āpaḥ| ado 'mbhaḥ pareṇa divam| dyauḥ pratiṣṭhā | antarikṣaṃ marīcayaḥ| pṛthivī maraḥ | yā adhastāt tā āpaḥ | (2)

In the beginning this world was the self (*ātman*), one alone, and there was no other being at all that blinked an eye. He thought to himself: 'Let me create the worlds'. (1)
So he created these worlds – the flood, the glittering specks, the mortal and the waters. Now, the flood is up there beyond the sky, and its foundation is the sky. The glittering specks are the intermediate world. The mortal is the earth, and what is underneath are the waters. (2)

The cosmogony begins in the same way as BU 1.4 using the Brāhmaṇic formula *X idám ágra āsa*. The difference with BU 1.4 lies in that in this cosmogony nothing is said about *ātman* in the first sentence except that it is one. It is possible that the intention of the composer is to enlarge the meaning of this word towards the unmanifest aspect of reality. Conceptualisation of reality in terms of *ātman*, which means the whole and its essence, is very abstract. This is also a blended concept the input space of which are the concept of reality and of self-cognising man. In the blend, the reflexive nature of self-cognition is ascribed to reality. The concept of reflexive action is the generic space of this blend.

The next sentence refers to the lack of anything that blinks. In this way, the composer elaborates the input space of self-cognising man. The concept of blinking activates the concept of seeing (we blink only when we have open eyes). Since cognition is conceived in terms of seeing, the recipient understands that reflexive reality cognises. Moreover, the concept of seeing, taken literally, implies a cognition which needs an object external to the cognising agent. Thus the composer outlines the nature of the future creative process which will be the creation of the possibility of subjective-objective cognition. This creative stage corresponds to the second stage of the *Nāsadīyasūkta* model in which reality cannot yet see the object. The same stage is conceived in terms of man who looks around and does not see anything except himself in BU 1.4.1 (see section 4.1.2). Taking this into account the recipient understands that the concept of *ātman* in the previous sentence is also used to denote the first manifestation of reality.

I would interpret the sentence *ambho marīcīr maram āpaḥ* as expressing the sequence of manifestations of reality undertaken in its cognitive process. Firstly, flood (*ambhas*) appears, then glittering specks (*marīci*), then 'the mortal' (as Olivelle 1998 translates *mara*) and, finally, water (*āpas*). The next sentence expresses the spatial arrangement of these manifestations. The word *ámbhas* is used in the *Nāsadīyasūkta* where the poet, in his description of the pre-creative state of reality, asks if there was water in that state. The stage of creation of *ambhas*, described in the AU, corresponds to the third stage of creation of the *Nāsadīyasukta* which is conceived in terms of flood without any sign (*ápraketam salilám*). This confirms that the word *ātman* used in the first sentence of the description refers to the first stage of creation where reality manifests itself and its cognising power.

Then light is created; the concept of light is metonymically evoked by the expression 'the glittering specks' (*marīci*). This word is used in the ṚV in two late stanzas (10.58.6, 10.177.1). ṚV 10.177.1 creates the image of the seers who follow the tracks of 'the glittering specks' within the ocean. The word *marīci* also metonymically evokes the concept of the sun. The recipient then may create the image of the sun rising from the darkness of the sky conceived in the Veda in terms of the ocean (see Jurewicz 2010a) [41]. The stage of creation described in this way corresponds to the fourth stage of the *Nāsadīyasūkta* model. The general image of reality divided into two aspects is outlined: in terms of water (*ambhas*) the unmanifest aspect is conceived and in terms of light (*marīci*) the manifest.

The next stage of manifestation of reality is conceived in terms of 'the mortal' (*mara*). In this way, the concept of reality which dies in its creation is activated. Then manifestation in waters (*āpas*) takes place. It has been shown that in the ŚB death is conceived in terms of fire which is the first manifestation of reality (see also BU 1.2.1, section 4.1.1). The next manifestation is conceived in terms of the fluid aspect of reality (it can be water, milk or semen). In the general model of reality transformation created in the ṚV, this ambivalence of reality is expressed in alternate creation of fire and Soma. One could presume that this way of thinking about creation also motivates thinking of the composer of the AU who, having presented the creation of death, conceived as fiery, now presents the creation of waters.

If the recipient evokes the meaning of *loka* as a level of experience, he would understand creation in terms of the experience of reality which agrees with the earlier cosmogonic pattern. In the first stage, conceived in terms of water (*ambhas*), reality outlines the object of its cognition which will be the world. In the second stage, it begins to cognise which is conceived in terms of light. The third stage is conceived in terms of its death which may be understood literally in the sense it is understood in the early ŚB (see chapter 3.2.2) or, metaphorically, as the loss of cognitive power as understood in ŚB 11.1.6 (see chapter 3.5.2). The fourth stage, conceived now in terms of waters (*āpas*), is the state when reality recognises its identity with its manifest aspect. Because of that, the composer of the AU uses two Sanskrit words denoting water: the first is meant to evoke the beginnings of creation and the second its last phase. All these phases in AU 1.3 are called *loka*, the levels of various experiences acquired by reality during creation.

The next sentence of the cosmogony presents the spatial arrangement of the manifest aspect of reality. The flood (*ambhas*) is above and beyond the

---

[41] Kulke (1992: 194) quotes ŚB 5.3.4.21 which presents the consecration of the king with glittering specks (*marīci*) 'collected the hollow of the hands and mixed with water'. The sun motes are identified with waters which, according to the model of Child Of The Waters can be seen as mothers of the sun. In ŚB 9.4.1.8, the sun is identified with Gandharva and the sun motes with Apsarases with which the sun unites and thanks to that rises up, most probably as their son.

sky. It corresponds to the borderline sphere of the cosmos. The sky is called the foundation (*pratiṣṭhā*). Olivelle (1998) interprets it as the foundation of the flood ('its foundation is the sky'). I would, however, refer to the cosmogonies of the ŚB where the earth is the foundation of Prajāpati. Thus understood the earth is the first form of reality. The composers of the ŚB evoke the general domain of Procreation in order to explain that the earth is the head of Prajāpati which, when he grows up, become the sun in zenith and the sky (see chapter 3.5.2). This conceptualisation of the sky is activated by the composer of AU 1.2. The sky is the foundation for reality in its creative activity and for men in their liberating cognition. *Mara* ('the mortal') is identified with earth on which mortal beings live (metonymy INHABITANTS FOR PLACE). Below are waters (*āpas*) which can also be interpreted as corresponding to the borderline sphere of the cosmos. The image schema of VERTICALITY, according to which the upwards direction is evaluated positively and the downwards negatively (Johnson 1987), is evoked by the composer of the description as *ado 'mbhaḥ pareṇa divam yā adhastāt tā āpaḥ* implies that man can reach the borderline sphere in two ways. The positive one is conceived as reaching the sun, the negative one is conceived as falling down (see below, AU 1.2.1).

It is important to note that the concepts used in the description are very abstract. The concept of the borderline of the cosmos is conceived in terms of waters. The space between the sky and the earth is metonymically evoked *via* the concept of glittering specks which fill it. The concept of earth is evoked on the basis of the metonymy PLACE FOR INHABITANTS: the inhabitants of the earth are mortal. The word *loka* highlights its spatial meaning, but remains consistent with its interpretation as a level of experience and the general assumption that cognition precedes and creates being. Reality experiences itself and thus creates spaces within which it can continue its experience. The cosmos is the next input space of the blend.

AU 1.1.2

sa īkṣateme nu lokāḥ | lokapālān nu sṛjā iti | so 'dbhya eva puruṣaṃ samuddhṛtyāmūrcchayat |

He further thought to himself: 'Now that these worlds are in place, I had better create their keepers'. From those very waters he drew out and gave a definite shape to a man.

In some cosmogonies of the ŚB, Prajāpati, having created the world, creates the inhabitants of its regions who are the gods connected with earth, space, sky and other parts of the world (e.g. ŚB 6.1.2.5ff, 11.2.3.1-2). The composer of the AU follows this pattern, but elaborates it in a different way.

The verb *mūrch-*, 'to become solid, thicken, congeal', activates the general domain of Cleansing By Heat in its specific realisation of producing butter as the next input of the conceptual network. The concept of drawing out of a man from the waters triggers the recipient to activate the general domain of Procreation in its specific realisation of the birth of man as the next input space. The fact that development of the embryo in the mother's womb is conceived in terms of heating makes the blend more coherent. The verb *mūrch-* is used in ŚB 10.5.3 to denote transformation of reality conceived in terms of mind (see chapter 3.5.1). If the recipient activates this cosmogony, he will see that the transformations of reality conceived in terms of milk are cognitive. Moreover, he will understand that the self-cognition, which is the generic space of the blend, is conceived as self-heating. In BU 1.2.2, the concept of congealing is activated to conceive creation of the earth which becomes the foundation for later creation (see section 4.1.1). In the blend created by the composer of AU 1.1.2, this foundation is conceived in terms of a man made of butter.

It is worth noting that the *Taittirīya Brāhmaṇa* (2.1.2.1-4) presents creation of man from Prajāpati's sweat which is thrown into a fire. There is an experiential link between clarified butter and sweat that both arise under the influence of heat. In Jurewicz (2010a), I have shown that clarification of butter and sweating are the specific domains of the general domain of Cleansing By Heat and are used in conceptualisation of the same processes (e.g. raining, thinking). It is possible that the composer of the AU is evoking this tradition.

The general domain of Procreation endows the blend with the meaning of self-reflexive action. On the most general level, the recipient can understand that reality thinks about itself and its thought becomes man. The input space of production of butter imparts to the blend the bright colour of man.

AU 1.1.3

tam abhyatapat | tasyābhitaptasya mukhaṃ nirabhidyata yathāṇḍam mukhād vāk vāco 'gniḥ |

He incubated that man. From that man so incubated mouth was hatched like an egg; from the mouth sprang speech, and from speech, fire.

The composer elaborates the input space of the general domain of Procreation and specifies it as the brooding of an egg and hatching a nestling[42].

[42] The recipient may also introduce a new input space which is making holes in an effigy through which it can cognise (see AVŚ 10.2.6, chapter 2.2.3.). It is worth noting that in later

The creation of the mouth is conceived according to the logic of the scenario of incubation: an egg is finally broken and a nestling emerges[43]. In a similar way, the mouth is created from which emerges speech and fire. In the blend, reality, conceived as its own self *ātman* in the form of man, becomes able to speak; the metaphoric conceptualisation of speech in terms of a flying bird is implied (see chapter 3.2.1). From speech appears fire which is motivated by the metaphoric conceptualisation of speech in terms of fire[44].

Then the subjective powers are created. Their order of creation is presented as follows. Firstly, the instruments of cognition are created: mouth (*mukha*), nostrils (*nāsike*), eyes (*akṣiṇī*), ears (*karṇau*), skin (*tvac*), heart (*hr̥daya*), navel (*nābhi*), penis (*śiśna*). Similarly to the earlier stage, the creation of these powers is conceived in terms of brooding and hatching a nestling. From the instruments of cognition the powers of cognition are created, conceived in terms of a nestling which hatches from a broken egg: speech (*vāc*), out-breath (*prāṇa*), sight (*cakṣus*), hearing (*śrotra*), hair (*lomāni*), mind (*manas*), in-breath (*apāna*), semen (*retas*). From the powers of cognition the guardians of the cognitive instrument are created: fire (*agni*), the wind (*vāyu*), the sun (*āditya*), the quarters (*diśaḥ*), plants and trees (*oṣadhivanaspatayaḥ*), the moon (*candramās*), death (*mr̥tyu*), the waters (*āpas*). If the recipient follows the logic of hatching elaborated in this passage, he will understand the guardians in terms of birds which fly in various directions to find a suitable abode. Within the frames of this conceptualisation, the cosmos is a tree. This way of thinking about the cosmos is well entrenched in the Vedic thinking as the AVŚ identifies a tree with man in terms of which the cosmos is conceived (see chapters 2.2.4). If the concept of a tree is introduced as its next input space, it will impart to the blend a clear topology.

We can also see the continuation of the Atharvavedic way of thinking in that the psycho-physiological activity of the cosmos is guaranteed by the gods present in its respective parts (AVŚ 11.8.19, 24, see chapter 2.2.3). The concept of guardians of the worlds (*lokapāla*) can be explained if one interprets *loka* as the level of experience. Within the frames of this interpretation, a guardian is a manifestation of the subjective aspect of reality which can use the cognitive

Hinduism images of gods are called *mūrti*. One cannot exclude that the roots of this are already found here.

43 Well entrenched in the ŚB, see chapter 3.2.2.

44 The image is similar to ŚB 2.2.4.1, but it deconstructs the blend created there and presents the process of creation in linear sequence: from mouth appears speech, from speech, fire, whereas in the ŚB the image is holistic and the recipient is expected to evoke the concept of speech on the basis of the concept of fire. Such a linear analytic sequence is also proof of the creation of a philosophical language.

ability realised by the instrument and thus experience itself in various ways. Fire is the manifestation of the ability to be a speaking agent that can use speech realised by the mouth. Wind is the manifestation of the ability to be a breathing agent that can use out-breath realised through the nostrils. It should be noticed that an out-breath is an inseparable element of speech as one cannot speak if one does not also breath out.[45] The sun is the manifestation of an ability to be a seeing agent that can use sight realised by the eyes. The quarters are a manifestation of an ability to be a hearing agent that can hear through the ears. Plants and trees cover the agent with skin which can realise his power through bodily hair. The moon is the manifestation of an agent's ability to think and feel using his mind located in the heart. Death is the manifestation of an agent's ability to kill and to be killed using an in-breath through the navel. Killing is specified here as eating[46]. In-breath metonymically evokes the concept of eating on the basis of the image schema CENTRE-PERIPHERY: in both cases something that is outside the agent is absorbed by him. The navel metonymically evokes the whole belly. Finally, waters are the power of the agent to procreate realised through the penis by semen.

Thus reality manifests itself in the world when it speaks, breathes, sees, hears, touches, cognises, feels, kills (eats) and procreates. In this way, it creates various *lokas* for itself, i.e. various levels of spaces of possible experience. The sequence of the first five activities agrees with ŚB 10.5.3 (see chapter 3.5.1). Touch realised through skin evokes the concept of the whole body covered with skin. The deeds of reality which are conceived in the ŚB in terms of fire are, in the AU, specified as thinking and feeling, killing (eating) and procreation.

At the same time, it is implied that all human activity can be seen as cognitive and a manifestation of the activity of reality. There is no evaluation of this activity (contrary to ŚB 11.1.6.9, see chapter 3.5.2). The concept of purity of the higher part of the body is not attested here, just the opposite. The following passages of the cosmogony will show that it is the lower part of the body which is the most efficient in realising reality's will to create. The ancient Upaniṣadic thinkers conceive man as a whole which cannot be divided into better and worse parts. The image schema of VERTICALITY is elaborated together with the CENTRE-PERIPHERY image schema. The sequence of creation of subjective powers begins with the head, then the whole body (skin) and then the lower parts of the cosmic self of reality.

---

45 At least as far as the Indo-European languages are concerned.

46 In-breath is connected with death also in the earlier thought: the Asuras, who are identified with death, are created from in-breath, see ŚB 11.1.6.8, chapter 3.5.2.

AU 1.2.1

> *tā etā devatāḥ sr̥ṣṭā asmin mahaty arṇave prāpatan | tam aśanāpipāsābhyām anvavārjat | tā enam abruvann āyatanaṃ naḥ prajānīhi | yasmin pratiṣṭhitā annam adāmeti |*
>
> Once these deities were created, they fell into this vast ocean here. It afflicted him with hunger and thirst. Those deities then said to him: 'Find us a dwelling in which we can establish ourselves and eat food'.

The word 'deities' (*devatā*) refer to the guardians of the experience of reality mentioned in the previous passage. The description presents the moment when creation fails. The recipient can infer this on the following basis. Firstly, the vast ocean (*arṇava*) can be treated as synonymous to the terms used in AU 1.2 to denote the borderline of the cosmos, i.e. *ambhas* and *āpas*[47]. Secondly, within the frames of the image schema of VERTICALITY, the unwanted process, death included, are conceived in terms of the movement down, so the recipient may understand that *arṇava* corresponds to *āpas* which are below the earth. Thirdly, the deities are hungry and on this basis the recipient can create the image of a body that falls because of hunger (as in ŚB 7.1.2.1, see chapter 3.2.2). Thus the composer activates the general domain of Cooking in its specific instantiation of being hungry as the next input space of the blend. Fourthly, the concept of the abode (*āyatana*) in which the deities could establish themselves and eat food corresponds to the concept of *pratiṣṭhā* in the ŚB which is needed by Prajāpati in order to perform further creation (see chapter 3.2.2)[48].

In the blend, the general image is as follows: the subjective cognitive abilities that are manifest in the parts of the cosmos fail to perform their activity not only because they have no object, but also because they need to be manifest in proper subjects which can cognise the object. For as long as they are manifest in the cosmos, they are their own object as there is no division between the subject and the object. This division is a necessary condition to perform subjective-objective cognition. Creation of the abode will create a subject in which the cognitive subjective powers will cognise everything that is outside the abode.

[47] In the AVŚ, the expression *mahát arṇavá* is used in the following contexts. In AVŚ 11.8.2, 6 it is used in reference to the sphere where heat (*tápas*) and deed (*kárman*) are placed. In AVŚ 13.1.26, is used in reference to the sphere from which the sun rises. In AVŚ 1.10.4, it is used in reference to the state which is realised because of Varuṇa's wrath. Such a use of this expression implies that it refers to the spheres which are at the verge of what is manifest, conceived in terms of night and sin (see Jurewicz 2010a).

[48] For the meaning of the word *āyatana* see Gonda (1975c).

The creation of the abode is conceived in terms of everyday experience. Reality brings to the guardians a cow and a horse, but they are not satisfied with them. Then it brings them a man (*puruṣa*). The guardians are pleased with him (they call him 'well made', *sukṛta*[49]) and so they enter into their respective abodes. Within the frames of Vedic cosmogony, the recipient may presume that reality itself assumes these forms and that man is its manifestation in which it will be able to fully continue cognition. The fact that the deities are pleased with the last form implies conceptualisation of creation in terms of an activity which brings pleasure.

The order of entrance of cognitive powers into man reverses the creative order: a guardian become a cognitive power and in this form enters an instrument of cognition. Thus fire becomes speech and enters the mouth. The wind becomes out-breath and enters the nostrils. The sun becomes sight and enters the eyes. The quarters becomes body hairs and enters the skin. The moon becomes mind and enters the heart. Death becomes the in-breath and enters the navel. The waters became semen and enter the penis.

On a more general level, it could be said that the cosmos enters man: the respective cosmic guardians become the cognitive powers and the instruments enter man. Thus the guardians acquire an abode in which they can realise their cognitive needs. The ontological identity between the cosmos and man is expressed here. Man has the same cognitive abilities as the cosmos. The human possibility to cognise is based on man's ontological identity with the cosmos.

Since the guardians are presented as hungry (see AU 1.2.1), their entrance into man can also be understood in terms of eating. Man eats the cosmos and thus makes it stand up within the frame of his own body just as in ŚB 7.1.2.6-8 where fire makes Prajāpati stand while it burns him which can also be conceived in terms of eating fire (see chapter 3.2.3). As has been shown, the cosmogonies of the ŚB are focused on the cosmic dimension of creation. Man, conceived as identical with Prajāpati, should repeat his creative activity in ritual, but this fact is just stated. In the Upaniṣads, the level of individual human existence is also analysed. It is already attested in the *Vrātyakāṇḍa* (see chapter 2.2.2). Man is seen as the next manifestation of reality through which it will be able to create the next level of its experience.

---

[49] The word *sukṛta* is used in the descriptions of the afterlife state: the deceased reaches the world of those who have performed good deeds (ṚV 10.16.4cd: *yā́s te śivā́s tanúvo jātavedas tā́bhir vahainaṃ sukṛ́tām ulokám*), his good deeds (*sādhukṛtyā*) are distributed after his death (see JB 1.46, 50, JUB 13.14.6, chapter 5). One cannot exclude that this meaning is also implied here.

AU 1.2.5

tam aśanāpipāse abrūtām avābhyām abhiprajānīhīti te abravīd etāsv eva vāṃ devatāsv ābhajāmy etāsu bhāginyau karomīti | tasmād yasyai kasyai ca devatāyai havir gr̥hyate bhāginyāv evāsyām aśanāpipāse bhavataḥ |

There upon, hunger and thirst told to him: 'Find one for us also'. He told them: 'I give you a share in what belongs to these very deities, and I make you sharers with them'. As a consequence, to whatever deity one may make an offering, hunger and thirst share it with that deity'.

Hunger and thirst metonymically evoke death (CAUSE FOR EFFECT) which is one of the creative experiences of reality. In the ŚB 10.4.3.9, death is afraid that if all creatures are immortal, it will also die (see chapter 3.3). Death's share is the human body. In this way, the composer implies that manifestation of reality in man and the realisation of its identity with the world leads to immortality but, at the same time, it threatens the world with destruction as the world is also constituted by death.

As in the ŚB, the participation of death in the cosmos is seen in terms of a participation in the sacrificial share. In ŚB 2.2.4, death gets sacrificial oblations as a substitute for the sacrificer (see chapter 3.1.1). Thus the sense of the death is expressed in terms of sacrifice and is realised in the sacrifice which involves killing. The concept of ritual is the next input space of the blend.

AU 1.3.1-2

sa īkṣateme nu lokāś ca lokapālāś ca annam ebhyaḥ sr̥jā iti | (1)
so 'po 'bhyatapat | *tābhyo 'bhitaptābhyo mūrtir ajāyata* | *yā vai sā mūrtir ajāyatānnaṃ vai tat* | (2)

He then thought to himself: 'Now that these worlds and their keepers are in place, I had better create food for them'. (1)
So he incubated the waters. When the waters were incubated, there emerged from them something solid. And the solid thing that emerged was food. (2)

From what has been said above, it may be inferred that the guardians of the world are in the cosmos and in man. There are also spaces of experience of reality within its manifest aspect. In order to describe this experience, the composer elaborates the general domain of Cooking. Reality wants to create an object for its subjective manifestations that is both cosmic and human. This object is conceived in terms of food. The concept of food also evokes the concept of killing which is consistent with previous passages of the cosmogony. In the blend, the recipient is given to understand that death obtains its share in the sacrificial activity of reality.

The word *mūrti* comes from the verb *mūrch-* which is used to express creation of the guardians and the cosmos (see above, AU 1.1.3). In this way, the composer evokes the concept of cooking food. The recipient can activate the general domain of Cleansing By Heat and specify this process as the transformation of milk into cream, butter or clarified butter[50]. At the same time, the food is conceived as alive because it runs away (AU 1.3.3-10). The composer again elaborates the earlier descriptions of the ŚB and the moment when creation hides from Prajāpati. It is a play similar to that in ŚB 6.2.1 (where Prajāpati looks for Agni), though contrary to BU 1.4 (see section 4.1.2). It is here conceived in terms of playing tag with life as the stake. The tag runs away and the other players try to catch him. Playing tag is the next input space of the conceptual network. In the blend, reality tries to capture the tag with its cognitive instruments (speech, out-breath, sight, hearing, skin, mind and penis) but it fails[51]. The reason for his failure is explained by the composer as it being impossible to satisfy one's appetite only by speaking about food, breathing upon it, looking at it, hearing about it, touching it, thinking about and having intercourse with it[52]. In the blend, the recipient understands that full cognition needs a proper cognitive faculty.

At the end of this description it is said:

AU 1.3.10

tad apānenājighṛkṣat tad āvayat | saiṣo 'nnasya graho yad vāyuḥ annāyur vā eṣa yad vāyuḥ |

Finally, he tried to capture it with the in-breath and then he managed to consume it. So, the wind is the one that captures food, for the wind (*vāyu*) is the food-finder (*annāyu*).

The food is finally captured by an in-breath which is located in the navel. Its guardian is death which is now identified with the wind. As can be seen from BU 1.2 (see section 4.1.1), death is conceived in terms of fire and wind has previously been identified with fire in the ṚV (Jurewicz 2010a: 265–266). Identification of these two concepts is also attested in the concept of Mātariśvan in the AVŚ (see chapter 2.1.2). Identification of the wind with death *via* the concept of fire makes the description coherent.

50 See BU 1.2.2, see section 4.1.1.

51 BU 1.2.7, see section 4.1.1.

52 Olivelle (1998) translates AU 1.3.9: 'for had he captured it with penis, one would satisfy one's appetite by simply ejaculating food'. But I would argue that here the concept of food as a living being is evoked, specified here as a female with whom a male has sexual intercourse; within the frames of Vedic conceptualisation of sexual activity, male is conceived in terms of the eater and female in terms of food.

In the blend, death is seen here as the price which reality has to pay for its manifestation. This price is paid in ritual: death which occurs within its frames is a manifestation of the creative death of reality; this is the share given to hunger and thirst. Moreover, since subjective-objective cognition is conceived in terms of eating, so death of the tag means that cognition is finally realised. One could wonder if the intention of the composer is not to imply that cognition involves the whole human organism, but rather that it must be done with the use of all cognitive powers and that failure is inherent. It is also possible that in-breath (*apāna*) played an important role in breath practices which led to supernatural cognition and because of that reality finally succeeds with its use. It is worth noting that in BU 2.3 the wind is a cosmic counterpart of breath and both are seen as the starting point of liberating practice which leads to knowledge of the whole of reality (see 4.4.2.2[53]). As we have just seen, wind is connected with in-breath in AU 1.3.10.

And it is the cognitive level which is elaborated in the next passage:

AU 1.3.11

> *sa īkṣata kathaṃ nv idaṃ mad ṛte syād iti| sa īkṣata katareṇa prapadyā iti | sa īkṣata yadi vācābhivyāhṛtaṃ yadi prāṇenābhiprāṇitaṃ yadi cakṣuṣā dṛṣṭaṃ yadi śrotreṇa śrutaṃ yadi tvacā spṛṣṭaṃ yadi manasā dhyātaṃ yadyapānenābhyapānitaṃ yadi śiśnena visṛṣṭam atha ko 'ham iti |*
>
> The he thought to himself: 'How can this possibly carry on without me?' And he thought: 'Through which of these shall I enter?'. He thought: 'If speaking is done through speech; if breathing out is done through the out-breath; if seeing is done through side; if hearing is done through hearing; if touching is done through the skin; if thinking is done through the mind; if breathing (emitting) is done through the in-breath; and if ejaculating is done through the penis – then who am I?'

The composer of AU again implies that reality loses contact with its manifest part and wants to recognise its own identity with it. In other cosmogonies, this creative stage is presented with the use of the image schema of CONTAINER: reality leaves its creation and then comes back with the aid of name and form (ŚB11.2.3, see chapter 3.5.3, BU 1.4.7, see section 4.1.2). In the cosmogony of the AU, this image schema is not elaborated. The composer brings the recipient back to the concept of reality described in the first sentence. It performs subjective-objective cognition on a cosmic and a human level. Now it wants to finally fulfill its creative desire and confirm its identity with its manifest aspect and thus cognise and experience itself through its manifestations. In

---

[53] See also JUB 3.21.2-4, chapter 5.2.3.

other words, it wants to becomes the highest cognitive agent of cosmic and human activity.

AU 1.3.12

sa etam eva sīmānaṃ vidāryaitayā dvārā prāpadyata | saiṣā vidṛtir nāma dvāḥ tad etan nāndanam | tasya traya āvasathās trayaḥ svapnā ayam āvasatho 'yam āvasatho 'yam āvasatha iti |

So he split open the head at the point where the hairs part and entered through that gate. This gate (*dvār*) has the name 'Split' (*vidṛti*), and thus is the heaven of pleasure (*nāndana*). He has three dwellings, three levels of sleep – this is one dwelling, this is another, and this is third.

Reality is presented as splitting a head; the recipient may presume that the skull is parted in the middle of the cranial bones, along the parting[54]. The recipient understands that the composer is evoking the concept of a man in both meanings: as the source domain of cosmos and in its literal meaning of human being. Through this split, reality enters its manifest aspect in both dimensions.

The composer enriches the conceptual network again. The concept of entering man activates the image schema of CONTAINER. The container is metonymically specified as an abode *via* the concept of gate or door (*dvār*). The recipient may understand the abode as a stronghold (as understood in the AVŚ, chapter 2.5.1.1). He may also understand it as a palace the concept of which is elaborated in the Upaniṣads in the descriptions of liberating cognition (BU 4.3.9, see section 4.2.3, KU 1.3-4, see chapter 5.3). It is worth mentioning that the concept of entering a hiding place with the desired goods is already elaborated in the ṚV where the concepts of entering a mountain filled with riches or of conquest of fortresses are used to conceive cognition (Jurewicz 2010a, 2010b). So the composer of the AU activates a source domain which is well-entrenched in Vedic tradition.

The concept of pleasure (*nāndana*) metonymically activates the general domain of Procreation in its specific realisation of the sexual act. This activation is reinforced by the phonetic resemblance between the words *nāndana* and *ānanda*. The Vedic identification of the mouth with a vagina (ŚB 2.2.4, see chapter 3.1.1, BU 1.4.6, see section 4.1.2) gives rational ground for the above description: here the mouth is replaced by the top of the head. The blended

[54] See AVŚ 10.2.26-28, chapter 2.5.1.1. It is also mentioned in TU 1.6.1-2 as the place through which reality manifest in man recognises its identity with itself manifesting in the cosmos (see *Conclusion*, 3).

concept which identifies a vagina with the top of the head allows the composer to express, on the one hand, the cognitive nature of creation and, on the other, to endow this process with the clear logic of the scenario of the general domain of Procreation and the ontic presence of reality within the world. Reality equips itself with itself manifest in the cognising and acting organism, cosmic and human. The meaning of the self-reflexive nature of this act is imparted to the blend by the general domain of Procreation. It is reinforced by the word *ātman* which refers to the whole of reality and its manifest aspect. Now *ātman* becomes the highest cognitive agent of cosmos and man. Moreover, conceptualisation of this stage of creation in terms of the sexual act allows the recipient to understand that reality experiences pleasure and satisfaction, as implied in BU 1.4.4, thanks to the use of the concept of hide-and-seek as the source domain of manifestation of reality in the world (see section 4.1.2).

In the next sentence, the composer elaborates the input space of an abode. The division into three dwellings (*āvasatha*) is evoked. Realisation of the identity of reality is conceived in terms of visiting the three dwellings of the abode. The first dwelling is identified with sleep, the next two are only mentioned. The recipient can understand that they refer to the meditative states which are dreaming sleep and dreamless sleep (BU 2.1, see section 4.4.2.2, BU 4.3, see section 4.4.2.3, CU 8.3, see section 4.4.2.4)[55]. Moreover, the concept of entering a palace is also used to conceive the afterlife state of a man (KU 1.3-4, see chapter 5.3). In this way, the composer implies that realisation of the identity of reality is the same state as that gained after death. This agrees with Ṛgvedic assumptions about the identity of the states gained in Somic exultation and after death, expressed explicitly in ṚV 9.113 (Jurewicz 2010a: 177 ff.). It is also worth adding that in the ṚV the state realised thanks to Soma is also conceived in terms of entering the home of Varuṇa (Jurewicz 2010a: 416-417). This confirms a long conceptual tradition elaborated now in a new context.

So in this passage the composer of the AU creates a complex conceptual network. The first input space is the concept of entering an abode, the second is cognition, the third is reality and the fourth is the general domain of Procreation in its specific realisation of insemination. The generic space is the concept of self-cognition. In the blend, cognition and transformations of reality are conceived in terms of entering an abode and the sexual act. The description of the AU is very abstract as the input spaces are only evoked (*via* the words *dvār*, *āvasatha*, *nāndana*). The recipient may elaborate them

55 Olivelle (1998: 579) also interprets the three chambers in this way.

in the blend in order to understand the activity of reality which in a cognitive act becomes one with itself and is manifest in the world and man. But he may also remain on the level of an image schematic conceptualisation which will allow him to understand this process in simple terms of breaking the boundaries of a container in terms of which the manifest aspect of reality is conceived. The passage from conceptualisation in terms of rich images to conceptualisation in terms of image schematic concepts is an important step towards abstraction which begins in the Upaniṣads.

AU 1.3.13-14

sa jāto bhūtāny abhivyaikhyat kim ihānyaṃ vāvadiṣad iti| sa etam eva puruṣaṃ brahmatatamam apaśyad idam adarśam itī3 |
tasmād idandro nāmedandro ha vai nāma tam idandraṃ santam indra ity ācakṣate parokṣeṇa | parokṣapriyā iva hi devāḥ parokṣapriyā iva hi devāḥ |

After he was born, he contemplated the creatures with the thought: 'Will anyone declare there to be another here?' But he saw only that man, the *brahman*, the utmost, and he said: 'This (*idam*) I have seen (*adarśam*)'. Therefore, he is called 'Idandra'. Now, his name is Idandra; but even though he is Idandra, people cryptically call him Indra, because the gods somehow love the cryptic.

The composer elaborates the input space of general domain of Procreation in its specific realisation of the birth of a baby. In the blend, reality is presented as being born within its manifest aspect in cosmic and human form. From within it performs subjective-objective cognition conceived in terms of seeing. This kind of cognition needs the division into subject and object and reality again looks for the object called *anya*. Olivelle (1998) translates the sentence *kim ihānyaṃ vāvadiṣad* as 'Will anyone declare there to be another here?', but it is constructed in such a way that is it also possible to interpret *anyam* as the nominative. The question would then mean 'Will anything else speak here?'. I think that this equivocality is caused by the fact that the state of final recognition of the unity of *ātman* cannot be expressed in words. Anyway, reality perceives 'that man, the *brahman*, the utmost' (*sa etam eva puruṣaṃ brahmatatamam*[56]). In other words, it perceives itself in the cosmos and in man and realises that there is no other (*anya*) except itself. This recognition is confirmed by the sentence 'This (*idam*) I have seen (*adarśam*)'. Within the frame of conceptualisation of cognition in terms of seeing, the recipient understands that it is in this way that the unity of reality is cognised. If he elaborates the input space of entering a palace, he will conceive this recognition

[56] For various interpretations of the difficult word *tatama*, see Olivelle (1998: 579).

in the following terms: reality, present within the cosmos and with man as their highest cognitive agent, is a king who sits in his palace and sees his kingdom as his own. As I have shown, such a conceptualisation of reality is elaborated already in the *Vrātyakāṇḍa* (see chapter 2.2.2). It will be shown that reality as the highest cognitive agent should be recognised in liberating cognition (see section 4.4.2.1-3).

Reality, who sees itself as one, is called Indra. As the composer explains in secret language the word *indra* means *idandra*: 'This I have seen' (*idam adarśam*). In this way, the composer grounds his exposition in earlier tradition. In ŚB 6.1.1.2, the main breath, which conveys creation, is called Indra and there this word is explained as *índha*, i.e. 'heated up' (see chapter 3.2.2)[57]. Activation of the cosmogony of ŚB 6.1.1 allows the recipient to enlarge the meaning of this passage. As I have argued, the conceptualisation of the beginnings of creation in ŚB 6.1.1 shows that some sort of breath practice, connected with recitation, was common enough to become the source domain for conceptualisation of creation. This practice is evoked here *via* the word *indra* which is the name of the main breath. The composer of the AU explains that the aim of this practice is the realisation of the unity of reality called *ātman*. The input space of entering an abode links this practice with the earliest concepts of reaching a supernatural state which in the ṚV is gained thanks to Somic exultation.

Creation, presented in the first chapter of the AU, is seen as the transformation of reality called *ātman* which endows itself with a body identical with itself also called *ātman*. In the same way, creative activity is conceived BU 1.2. (section 4.1.1). Thus creation is a reflexive process during which reality acts on itself and, at the same time, manifests itself in perceptible form. The composer of the AU then introduces the next stage of manifestation of reality conceived in terms of its birth within the cosmos and man. Thus the meaning of *ātman* as the absolute essence of the manifest aspect and its highest cognitive agent is built. This stage will be elaborated by the Upaniṣadic thinkers who seek a practice which would lead to final liberation.

I would interpret the next chapters of the cosmogony as a continuation of the description of creation seen from the point of view of a particular human being. The composer of the AU conceives this process in terms of three births of *ātman*[58] and skilfully plays with the broad meaning of this word.

The first birth of *ātman* takes place during insemination:

---

57 The concept of Indra also appears in the description of liberating cognition in TU 1.6.1 where its beginnings are conceived in terms of 'the womb of Indra' (*indrayoni*), see *Conclusion*, 3.

58 In JUB 3.8.10-3.9.1.8 the births are interpreted as deaths (see chapter 5.2.3).

AU 2.1

puruṣe ha vā ayam ādito garbho bhavati yad etad retaḥ | tad etat sarvebhyo 'ṅgebhyas tejaḥ sambhūtam ātmany evātmānaṃ bibharti |
tad yadā striyāṃ siñcaty athainaj janayati | tad asya prathamaṃ janma |

At the outset, this embryo comes into being within a man as semen. This radiance gathered from all the bodily parts he bears in himself (*ātman*) as himself (*ātman*). And when a man deposits it in a woman, he gives birth to it. This is his first birth.

The composer begins with the explanation of the relationship between man and his semen. He identifies the embryo with semen, which in earlier thought is identified with father (ŚB 10.4.2.26, section 3.4). Here this concept is evoked implicitly. The embryo and semen are conceived in terms of the radiance (*tejas*) which is gathered from all the parts of a man's body and is kept in it. Such a conceptualisation of semen is well entrenched in the earlier thought where it is conceived in terms of fire. The phrase *ātmany evātmānaṃ bibharti* draws the mind of the recipient not only to a particular father who is reborn in his wife's womb as his own son but also to the agent referred to in AU 1 which is reality called *ātman*. It inseminates woman with itself.

The second birth of *ātman* takes place during birth:

AU 2.2-3

tat striyā ātmabhūyaṃ gacchati yathā svam aṅgaṃ tathā | tasmād enāṃ na hinasti | sāsyaitam ātmānam atra gataṃ bhāvayati | (2)
sā bhāvayitrī bhāvayitavyā bhavati | taṃ strī garbhaṃ bibharti | so 'gra eva kumāraṃ janmano 'gre 'dhi bhāvayati | sa yat kumāraṃ janmano 'gre 'dhi bhāvayaty ātmānam eva tad bhāvayaty eṣāṃ lokānāṃ santatyā evaṃ santatā hīme lokāḥ | tad asya dvitīyaṃ janma | (3)

It becomes one with the woman's self[59] (*ātman*), as if it were a part of her own body. As a result, it does not harm her. And she nourishes this self (*ātman*) of his that has entered her. (2)
As she nourishes him, so he should nourish her. The woman carries him as the embryo. At the beginning, he nourishes the child even before its birth. When he nourishes the child even before its birth, he thereby nourishes himself (*ātman*) for the continuance of these worlds, for it is in this way that these worlds continue. This is his second birth. (3)

Here again the author plays with the meaning of the word *ātman* which allows him to show that the embryo inside the woman's womb is one with her. In the context of the whole Upaniṣad, the recipient understands that reality

[59] Olivelle (1998): 'body'.

enters the woman's body in the form of semen which is identical with it[60]. Thus the composer of the AU explicitly expresses the reflexive character of the creative process. Because the embryo and the woman are the same, the embryo does not harm the woman[61]. I would argue that not only a biological fact is stated. As earlier cosmogonies show, the manifestation of reality can be dangerous to it (see chapter 3.1.1). The recipient can understand that reality can restrain its dangerous aspect and conform to rules set by itself. Thanks to that it does not hurt itself in the form of a woman.

The word *loka* in the sentences *eṣāṃ lokānāṃ santatyai evaṃ santatā hīme lokāḥ* can again be interpreted as a space of experience. Reality, being born from a woman in the form of a particular man, creates a new space for its experience. The spaces for reality's experience are numerous since there are many men and women.

It should be noted that in earlier Vedic accounts of the concepts of three births and deaths of man (JUB 3.8.9-10, 3.9.1-8, see chapter 5.2), the second birth is initiation and not the biological birth which is conceived as the first birth. This fact attests that for the process of one's liberation initiation is not necessary.

The third birth is death and rebirth:

AU 2.4

> *so 'syāyam ātmā puṇyebhyaḥ karmebhyaḥ pratidhīyate | athāsyāyam itara ātmā kṛtakṛtyo vayogataḥ praiti | sa itaḥ prayann eva punar jāyate | tad asya tṛtīyaṃ janma |*
>
> And he – this self (*ātman*) of his – is appointed to carry out the holy rites, while his other self, after it has done all it has to do, becomes old and dies. As soon as he departs from this world, he is born again. That is his third birth.

According to Olivelle (1998), this description refers to the rebirth of the father in the form of his son. However, the use of the verb *prati dhā-* brings the recipient's mind to the ŚB. This verb is used there in very specific contexts. It is most often used in the descriptions of building the fire-altar conceived in terms of restoring Prajāpati's *ātman*. This verb is used in the conventionalised phrase *yad evāsya... asminn etat pratidadhāti*. The composers of the ŚB, with use of this phrase, mention various elements of the altar which correspond

[60] For identity of the embryo with his parents (especially his father), see Smith (1985: 77–78).

[61] The identity of everything is the basis for the ethics which is exposed in BU 1.4.8 (see section 4.1.2). The same is expressed in ŚB 5.4.3.20 in the context of the Rājasūya (see Kulke 1992).

to various parts of Prajāpati[62]. The second use of the verb *prati dhā-* is to express the restoration of head to the body in the context of Agnicayana (ŚB 9.2.1.22, 9.2.3.51, 9.3.1.6), in the context of the story of Dadhyañc who, having had his head cut off by Indra, obtains the horse's head from the Aśvins (ŚB 14.1.1), in the context of Pravargya (ŚB 14.1.3.2, 14.1.3.2, 14.3.1.15, 14.3.1.29). It is also used in reference to the restoration of arms to the body (ŚB 7.4.1.36) or of wings and tails (ŚB 8.7.2.15). Generally speaking, we could say that the verb *prati dhā-* in these contexts express the composition of a whole body called *ātman*. It is explicitly expressed in passages which also use the verb *saṃ kṛ-*, 'to compose, to construct' (ŚB 7.3.1.42, 9.2.3.51, 9.3.1.6 see chapter 3.4).

If the recipient evokes these usages of the verb *prati dhā-*, he will understand the sentence *so 'syāyam ātmā puṇyebhyaḥ karmebhyaḥ pratidhīyate* as expressing the composition of the man's self, *ātman*, during his life. The means of building are his 'holy rites', i.e. his ritual activity. According to ŚB this self, built of Ṛk-stanzas, Yajus-formulas, Sāman-chants and of oblations (*ā́huti*) survives death and becomes immortal (ŚB 4.3.4.5, 10.5.1.5, 11.2.6.13, see chapter 3.4). The recipient may presume that this is the case here too.

Then the composer of the AU mentions 'the other self' (*itara ātman*) which, having performed all the rites, dies and thus death obtains its share as it was appointed during creation. It is, however, implied that this same *ātman* is reborn, so the meaning of the phrase *itara ātman* must be larger than a living body. It is possible that the composer plays with the meaning of the word *ātman* which refers to the whole of human being which gives him individuality, i.e. his outward appearance which is his body and his internal individuality built in ritual. This internal individuality survives death and is reborn again.

Thus the composer of the AU implies that those who perform rituals are reborn and thus they assure continuation of the existence of the worlds (*loka*). If the recipient understands *loka* as the sphere of experience, he will understand that the aim of creation is finally fulfilled: reality can experience itself through its living manifestations thanks to their ritual activity.

The next passages expresses another possible way of experience. The composer begins with the quotation from ṚV 4.27.1:

---

62 ŚB 8.2.1.13, 8.2.1.18, 8.3.1.7, 8.3.2.7, 8.3.2.8, 8.4.1.8, 8.4.2.15, 8.4.2.16, 8.7.1.7, 8.7.2.15, 8.7.3.17.

AU 2.5-6

tad uktam ṛṣiṇā | garbhe nu sann anv eṣām avedam ahaṃ devānāṃ janimāni viśvā | śataṃ mā pura āyasīr arakṣann adha śyeno javasā nir adīyam (5)
iti | garbha evaitac chayāno vāmadeva evam uvāca | sa evaṃ vidvān asmāc charīrabhedād ūrdhvam utkramyāmuṣmin svarge loke sarvān kāmān āptvāmṛtaḥ samabhavat samabhavat | (6)

This very point has been made by the seer:
I knew all the births of these gods, while I was still within the womb.
A hundred iron forts encaged me, then a falcon – swiftly I flew away. (5)
Vāmadeva spoke this way while he was still lying within the womb. Knowing this, he went up after the dissolution of his body and heaving obtained all his desires in the heavenly world up there, became immortal. (6)

The same stanza is evoked by BU 1.4.10 in a context expressing the realisation of the unity of reality (see section 4.1.2). Knowledge of the whole manifest aspect is expressed by the stanza in the first verse: the subject of the hymn knows the births of all the gods which, in the Ṛgvedic context, means omniscience. The composer of the AU emphasises that Vāmadeva has already gained this omniscience in his womb and because of that he could be finally liberated without initiation and Vedic rituals thanks to correct knowledge. This will be elaborated in the last chapter of the AU which I interpret as the exegesis of this Ṛgvedic stanza.

AU 3.1-3a

ko 'yam ātmeti vayam upāsmahe | kataraḥ sa ātmā | (1)
yena vā paśyati yena vā śṛṇoti yena vā gandhāñ jighrati yena vā vācaṃ vyākaroti yena vā svādu cāsvādu ca vijānāti | (2)
yad etad dhṛdayaṃ manaś caitat saṃjñānam ājñānaṃ vijñānaṃ prajñānaṃ medhā dṛṣṭir dhṛtir matir manīṣā jūtiḥ smṛtiḥ saṅkalpaḥ kratur asuḥ kāmo vaśa iti | sarvāṇy evaitāni prajñānasya nāmadheyāni bhavanti | (3)

'Who is this self (*ātman*)?' – that is how we venerate. (1)
Which of these is the self? Is it that by which one sees? Or hears? Or smells odours? Or utters speech? Or distinguishes between what is tasty and what is not? (2)
Is it the heart and the mind? Is it awareness? Perception? Discernment? Cognition? Wisdom? Insight? Steadfastness? Thought? Reflection? Drive? Memory? Intention? Purpose? Will? Love? Desire? But these are various designations of cognition. (3)

The composer begins his exegesis with questions about *ātman*. I would translate the first sentence of the AU in a slightly different way: 'Who is he whom we venerate as *ātman*?'. The next sentences are answers to this question. In AU 3.1, he enumerates five subjective-cognitive functions: seeing, hearing, smelling, speaking and tasting. In the next passage, he lists various kinds of cognition (AU 3.3). This shows that the composer of the AU is well aware of various states of consciousness and that investigation of these states can lead to a cognition of reality called *ātman*. In the last sentence, a general concept of cognition (*prajñāna*) is created which encompasses all cognitive states.

Then *ātman* is identified with *brahman* and then with Indra and Prajāpati (AU 3.3)[63]. The first two identifications with Indra result from the previous passage (AU 3.13) where *indra* is the secret name of *ātman* who, having manifested itself once again within the frames of cosmos and man, recognises its identity with the whole of reality called *brahman*. Identification with Prajāpati allows the composer to ground the concept of cognising *ātman* within the earlier tradition which calls the creative power of reality by this name. Then *ātman* is identified with all gods and all kinds of living beings (AU 3.3)[64].

At the end of the passage the ontic role of cognition (*prajñāna* or *prajñā*) is presented:

AU 3.3b

> *sarvaṃ tat prajñānetram prajñāne pratiṣṭhitam prajñānetro lokaḥ prajñā pratiṣṭhā prajñānaṃ brahma |*
>
> Knowledge is the eye of all that, and on knowledge it is founded. Knowledge is the eye of the world, and knowledge, the foundation. *Brahman* is knowing.

The manifest aspect (*sarvam*) and the worlds (*loka*) are called as 'having the eye of insight' (*prajñānetṛ*). In this way, the composer implies that all the elements of the manifest aspect have the ability to cognise which agrees with the assumption that the manifest aspect is the result of the transformation of the cognising self of reality. The use of the expression *prajñānetṛ* in reference to the manifest aspect of reality confirms the interpretation of this word as the space of experience: the cognising self, within its particular manifestations, creates from the beginning a new possibility to cognise and experience itself.

The manifest aspect is also presented as founded on insight (*prajñāne pratiṣṭhitam*). The concept of a foundation of the manifest aspect of reality as a basis for creation is used in the cosmogonies of the ŚB. In the cosmogony of AU 1, this concept is activated *via* the concept of abode (*āyatana*). Now

---

63 *eṣa brahmā | eṣa indraḥ| eṣa prajāpatiḥ |*

64 *ete sarve devā | imāni ca pañca mahābhūtāni pṛthivī vāyur ākāśa āpo jyotīṃṣīty etānīmāni kṣudramiśrāṇīva bījānītarāṇi cetarāṇi cāṇḍajāni ca jārujāni ca svedajānicodbhijjāni cāśvā gāvaḥ puruṣā hastino yat kiñcedam prāṇi jaṅgamaṃ ca patatri ca yac ca sthāvaram |*

the composer uses this cosmogonic pattern to express the fundamental role of cognition in the manifest aspect.

In the last sentence, the word *brahman* is qualified with the word *prajñāna* which Olivelle translates as 'knowing', but I would argue that the intention of the composer is to convey the same meaning as in the earlier sentences of this passage which is 'insight'. If the recipient understands that the word *brahman* refers the unmanifest aspect of reality (as in BU 1.4.7, see section 4.1.2), he will then understand that insight is its essence too.

The chapter ends in the following way:

AU 3.4

> *sa etena prajñenātmanāsmāl lokād utkramyāmuṣmin svarge loke sarvān kāmān āptvāmṛtaḥ samabhavat samabhavat* |
>
> It is with this self of knowledge that he went up from this world and, having obtained all his desire in the heavenly world up there, became immortal.

The subject of the sentence is not specified. We must take into account that the sentence is almost the same as the sentence which describes the cognition of the Vāmadeva in AU 2.5. The composer, in third chapter of the AU, presents Vāmadeva's liberating knowledge. In this way, he can express that his teaching is consistent with the Ṛgvedic heritage.

At the same time, the pronoun 'he' (*sa*) refers to the main subject of cosmogony which is reality called *ātman* manifesting itself in cognition. On my view, chapters 2 and 3 present two possible ways of manifestation of reality in men. In AU 2.1-4, the composer describes the possibility of its manifestation through the ritual practice of a man. In AU 2.5 and AU 3, he describes the possibility of its manifestation through knowledge. Thus understood, the AU present the afterlife in the same way as in the descriptions of the path of gods (*devayāna*) and the path of fathers (*pitṛyāna*) in the BU and CU (see section 4.3.1).

*

The composer of the cosmogony of the AU elaborates the concept of *ātman* in a new way. He enlarges its meaning to denote, besides its meaning of the manifest aspect, reality in its unmanifest aspect, reality in the first act of creation and reality as the deepest essence of the cosmos and man. This is a new usage of the word *ātman* which is elaborated in other Upaniṣads. The detailed analysis of the manifestation of reality within the cosmos and man with its cognitive dimension is also a new element. The holistic meaning of the word *ātman* as everything that gives individuality to an entity allows the composer to express the reflexive nature of the manifestation of reality. We can also see how the rich cosmogonic blends are reduced to more simple ones when the role of man is described.

At the same time, the cosmogony of the AU is motivated by earlier cosmogonic scenarios. Similarly to the cosmogonies of the BU, many elements of this cosmogony are too elliptic to be fully understood without reference to the cosmogonical patterns of the ŚB and to the ṚV. This elliptic expression is caused by the tendency to create abstract description. The composer could assume that his recipients know the conceptual background well enough to activate it and to understand the meaning he conveyed in more abstract terms.

4.1.4. The levels of experience (*Chāndogya Upaniṣad* 6.1-7)

The cosmogony in CU 6.1-7 is presented by Uddālaka Āruṇi who teaches his son about the knowledge thanks to which what is unheard can be heard, what is unthinkable can be thought of and what is impossible to be recognised can be recognised. The characteristic feature of this cosmogony is its abstract exposition. Its composer also tries to resolve the problem how to understand and express the ontological dimension of reality's transformation.

The cosmogony begins with a passage in which the basic ontological assumptions and terminology used in the further exposition are presented:

CU 6.1.4-6

yathā somyaikena mr̥tpiṇḍena sarvaṃ mr̥nmayaṃ vijñātaṃ syāt | vācārambhaṇaṃ vikāro nāmadheyaṃ mr̥ttikety eva satyam | (4)
yathā somyaikena lohamaṇinā sarvaṃ lohamayaṃ vijñātaṃ syāt | vācārambhaṇaṃ vikāro nāmadheyaṃ loham ity eva satyam | (5)
yathā somyaikena nakhanikr̥ntanena sarvaṃ kārṣṇāyasaṃ vijñātaṃ syāt | vācārambhaṇaṃ vikāro nāmadheyaṃ kr̥ṣṇāyasam ity eva satyam | (6)

'It is like this, son. By means of just one lump of clay one would perceive everything made of clay – the transformation is a verbal handle, a name – which the reality is just this: "It's clay."' (4)
'It is like this, son. By means of just one copper trinket one would perceive everything made of copper – the transformation is a verbal handle, a name – which the reality is just this: "It's copper."' (5)
'It is like this, son. By means of just one nail-cutter one would perceive everything made of iron – the transformation is a verbal handle, a name – which the reality is just this: "It's iron."' (6)

According to the composer, the multiplicity of objects we perceive can be reduced to the basic material from which they are made. On the basis of knowledge of the material from which a particular object is made, one can know everything else that is made from this material: on the basis of a particular lump of clay, one can know everything made of clay, on the basis of a particular copper trinket, one can know everything made of copper and on the basis of a particular iron nail-cutter, one can know everything made of iron. All these examples of transformation are then formulated in a general statement that transformation of the material into particular objects is the process of giving a name. What is real (*satya*) is the material such as clay, copper and iron.

The composer wants to distinguish various levels of experience. On the level of everyday experience, we perceive separate objects. but there is a level of experience where we perceive the material from which the objects are made. Uddālaka does not say that the multiplicity of the objects is unreal or false, he only says that the unity of the material is also real and true. Within the context of the Vedic thinking, words influence the world, transform it and create its elements[65]. So the level of objects created by word is also real. The problem of the real character of the world and its ontic relationship with the unmanifest aspect is discussed in the next passages of the CU which describe cosmogony.

CU 6.2.1-2

sad eva somyedam agra āsīd ekam evādvitīyam | *tad dhaika āhur asad evedam agra āsīd ekam evādvitīyam* | *tasmād asataḥ saj jāyata* | (1)
kutas tu khalu somyaivaṃ syād iti hovāca | *katham asataḥ saj jāyeta* | *sat tv eva somyedam agra āsīd ekam evādvitīyam* | (2)

In the beginning, son, this world was simply what existent – one only, without a second. Now, on this point some do say: 'In the beginning this world was simply what was nonexistent – the one only, without a second. And from what is nonexistent was born what is existent'. (1)
'But, son, how can that possibly be?' he continued. 'How can what is existent be born from what is nonexistent? On the contrary, son, in the beginning this world was simply what is existent – the one, without a second'. (2)

The argument presented by Uddālaka is a redefinition of earlier Vedic thinking. As I have shown, the word *sat* has been used till now in reference to

[65] For interpretation of the phrase *vācārambhaṇam*, see Kuiper (1957), Buitenen (1988c, d). Buitenen (1988c) refers to ṚV (10.72, 10.83, and 10.129) to show how the Upaniṣadic concept is grounded in earlier thought.

the manifest aspect of reality and the word *asat* to the unmanifest. Uddālaka questions this view and his criticism uses common sense: how anything can be created from nothing? So one should assume that *sat*, being, exists before creation[66]. It should be noted that Uddālaka does not challenge the real character of the manifest aspect. He only enlarges the scope of what is real towards the unmanifest aspect. He does this because he knows how to reach and experience this aspect in liberating practice.

The next passages evoke the earlier cosmogonic and cosmologic models but puts them in very abstract terms:

CU 6.2.3-4

tad aikṣata | bahu syāṃ prajāyeyeti | tat tejo 'sṛjata | tat teja aikṣata| bahu syāṃ prajāyeyeti | tad apo 'sṛjata | tasmād yatra kva ca śocati svedate vā puruṣas tejasa eva tad adhy āpo jāyante | (3)
tā āpa aikṣanta | bahvyaḥ syāma prajāyemahīti | tā annam asṛjanta | tasmād yatra kva ca varṣati tad eva bhūyiṣṭham annaṃ bhavati | adbhya eva tad adhy annādyaṃ jāyate | (4)

And it thought to itself: 'Let me become many. Let me propagate myself.' It emitted heat. The heat thought to itself: 'Let me become many. Let me propagate myself'. It emitted water. Whenever it is hot, therefore, a many surely perspires; and thus it is from heat that water is produces. (3)
The water thought to itself: 'Let me become many. Let me propagate myself.' It emitted food. Whenever it rains, therefore, food becomes abundant; and thus it is from water that foodstuffs are produced'[67]. (4)

Reality called *sat* is presented as thinking. This blended concept is motivated by two input spaces. The first one is an abstract concept of reality called *sat*. The second one is the concept of self-cognising man. The generic space is self-cognition. In the blend, the cognitive abilities of man are assigned to reality.

Then heat (*tapas*) is created. This is another abstraction of the Vedic model according to which reality, conceived in terms of man, toils and heats himself. The recipient may evoke all earlier conceptualisations of creation in terms of the general domains of Cooking and Cleansing By Heat. Moreover, since the word *tapas* in the Veda is mostly used to express activity of the fire and the sun, the recipient may evoke these two concepts and the general

[66] We can presume that arguments based on common sense were also used by those who postulated that the unmanifest sphere is untrue and unreal; as everything which is beyond our present experience, be it temporally or spatially, is untrue and unreal.

[67] It should be noted that the mutual relationship between three basic forms reflects the structure of a subjective-objective cognitive act: heat corresponds to the subject, water, as the opposite of heat, to the object and food to the cognitive act.

model of reality transformation established in the ṚV according to which the sun is the cosmic form of fire (see Jurewicz 2010a).

The next stage of creation is conceived in terms of water (*āpas*). Such a sequence also agrees with the general model of reality transformation according to which fire transforms itself into Soma. On the cosmological level, Soma transforms into rain in the sun (Jurewicz 2010a). In the ŚB, Prajāpati, having heated himself, emits his liquid aspect conceived in terms of milk, sweat or semen. The recipient may also evoke the general domain of Cleansing By Heat elaborated in ŚB 6.1.3 (see chapter 3.5.1) and understand this stage of creation in those terms.

The third stage of creation is conceived in terms of food (*anna*). The recipient may metonymically evoke the general domain of Cleansing By Heat in its specific realisation of transformation of milk, *via* the concept of food, and specify it as cream or butter. If he evokes the Ṛgvedic general model of reality transformation, he will understand the coherence of the creative order and its hidden motivation; on the ground of his experience he knows that thanks to rain plants appear and they food. The concept of food metonymically evokes the concept of the eater. In turn, this concept evokes the concept of killing and death. On this basis, the recipient can understand that life and death appear. Finally, in terms of eating, subjective-objective cognition is conceived and the recipient may evoke this target domain and understand that reality now manifests itself in this kind of cognition. The spatial organisation of the world is also implied here because food metonymically evokes concepts of rain and plants and these concepts metonymically evoke the concepts of the space and the earth.

In order to understand the sequence of stages of creation, the recipient may evoke earlier cosmogonic models and blend them with the cosmogonic process presented here. But he is not forced to do so by the composer. He may just remain within the context of the CU and understand the stages of creation as stages of transformation of reality the only attribute of which is thought. Then heat, water and food are just general concepts of the forms of conscious reality assumed by it in this process. It firstly manifests itself as warm and shining, then as fluid and, finally, as food which can be understood as life generally.

Correspondence with the *Nāsadīyasūkta* can be seen in two ways: either the stage of heat corresponds to the first stage of creation and the stage conceived in terms of water corresponds to the third stage of creation (*apraketáṃ saliláṃ sárvam ā idám*) with food to the fourth (*tápasas tán mahinā́jāyataíkam*), or the stage conceived in terms of heat corresponds to the fourth stage of creation, water to the fifth and food to the fourth (Jurewicz 2010a). This double convergence with the scheme of the *Nāsadīyasūkta* confirms the general and abstract character of the CU scheme.

CU 6.3.2-3

seyaṃ devataikṣata hantāham imās tisro devatā anena jīvenātmanā anupraviśya nāmarūpe vyākaravāṇīti | (2)
tāsāṃ trivṛtaṃ trivṛtam ekaikāṃ karavāṇīti |
seyaṃ devatemās tisro devatā anenaiva jīvenātmanā anupraviśya nāmarūpe vyākarot tāsāṃ trivṛtaṃ trivṛtam ekaikām akarot |
yathā tu khalu somyemās tisro devatās trivṛt trivṛd ekaikā b^havati tan me vijānīhīti | (3)

Then that same deity thought to itself: 'Come now, why don't I establish the distinctions of name by entering these three deities here with this living self (*ātman*), and make each of them threefold' (2)
So, that deity established the distinctions of name and appearance by entering these three deities here with this living self (*ātman*), and made each of them threefold'. Learn from me, my son, how each of these three deities becomes threefold. (3)

This stage of creation corresponds to the stage when reality loses contact with its own creation and wants to attest identity of two aspects with the cognitive act of giving names and forms. As we have seen, conceptualisation of creation in terms of giving names is used in the Vedic cosmogonies. The verb *vi ā kṛ-* is used here to denote the cognitive act with the aid of names and forms, it is also used in the BU 1.4.7 in the same context to present reality, called *ātman*, which enters its manifest aspect with names and forms 'up to the nailtips' *ā́ nakhāgrébhyo* (see section 4.1.2). On this basis, the recipient may precise the character of creative stage presented in this passage. He may add the general domain of Procreation as the next input space of the conceptual network. In the blend, reality as thinking is conceived in terms of man, reality as speaking is conceived in terms of woman, verbalisation of its cognition is conceived in terms of the sexual act and the named manifest form of reality is conceived in terms of offspring. The instrumental form *jīvena ātmanā* activates thinking about offspring in terms of the self of the father and strengthens the reflexive nature of the creative process. At the same time, the recipient understands that the manifest aspect of reality is alive. The same conceptualisation is activated in BU 1.2.3 where it is called 'breath' (*prāṇá*, see section 4.1.1).

The unity of reality and its threefold manifestation is also expressed as all of them are called *devatā*[68]. In this way, the composer creates a general

[68] This word is used in the ŚB 11.2.3.2 in a similar context as in the CU. *Bráhman* creates gods (*devá*), Agni, Vāyu and Sūrya and places them in three worlds: Agni on the earth, Vāyu in the space, Sūrya in the sky. And then it is said that the deities (*devátā*) which are above are

description of creation which can be seen as the transformation of one reality which he calls the deity (*devatā*). In the AU, the word *devatā* is used to denote the subjective powers of reality within its manifest aspect. The general use of the word *devatā* in CU 6.2.3 may be seen as an attempt to generally express the subjective power of reality which in the ŚB is expressed with use of the word Prajāpati.

From the final sentence of CU 6.3.3, the recipient understands that the following passages CU 6.4.1-5 describe the division of heat, water and food. They are divided into four luminous entities: fire, the sun, the moon and lightning. The form of their manifestation is called *rūpa*, 'shape' but also 'colour'. The red colour in those four entities is heat, the white colour is water and the black colour is food[69]. Each presentation ends with the same general statement as in the examples given in the beginnings of Uddālaka's teaching: 'the transformation is a verbal handle, a name – which the reality is just this: "It's the three appearances."'[70] (*vācārambhaṇaṃ vikāro nāmadheyaṃ trīṇi rūpāṇīty eva satyam*).

At first glance, it seems that the description is inconsistent. At the beginning of the cosmogony, the forms of reality are three and Uddālaka in CU 6.3.2-3 explicitly states that he will describe how each of those three forms are divided into three. In CU 6.4.1-5, the forms are four. This inconsistency disappears in the next passage of the CU (6.4.6-7) which describes how man can cognise the structure of the manifest aspect of reality. The basic threefold division is inferred on the basis of colours present in the four entities: what is reddish in them is the form of heat, what is whitish in them is the form of water, what is blackish in them is the form of fire and what is as if impossible to be cognised is the combination of those three aspects[71]. Lightning is seen as a combination of the other three forms, namely, the sun, the moon and fire (CU 6.4.7: *yad v avijñātam ivābhūd ity etāsām eva devatānāṃ samāsa*). So the recipient can understand that lightning does not exist independently as do fire, the sun and the moon.

---

placed in the worlds which are above. Then *bráhman* goes away and comes back with aid of name and form (see chapter 3.5.3.). In the ŚB, the word *devátā* is most often used to denote deities venerated in sacrifices, sometimes identified with Agni (e.g. ŚB 4.6.3.2). In the AVŚ, the word *devátā* is used to denote the gods who are present in cosmos and human being as cognitive powers (see chapter 2.2.3). See Kudelska (2009: 27–28).

69 Similar colours are that of the sun (CU 3.1): the red one (*rohita*), the white one (*śukla*), the black one (*kṛṣṇa*), the very black one (*paraḥkṛṣṇa*), and the one that flickers in its middle (*ādityasya madhye kṣobhata iva*).

70 Olivelle (1998).

71 For the meaning of the particle *iva* see Brereton (1982).

Moreover, from the fact that the lightning does not have its ontological correspondent, the recipient may also infer that it is a manifestation of the pre-creative unity of *sat* which becomes possible to be perceived, inferred and experienced within the world when one gains true, liberating knowledge. Such an interpretation of lightning is confirmed as its concept appears in the description of the path of gods (*devayāna*) to denote the last step before the liberated person crosses the boundary between the manifest and the unmanifest aspects (see section 4.3.2)[72].

The argument of Uddālaka can be presented as follows. The process of recognition of the identity between reality and its manifestation consists on giving names (*nāma*) and acquiring forms (*rūpa*). The recipient understands that reality gives names to its manifestations and assumes a form adequate to the name. The forms are metonymically identified with colours. In this way, their visibility is implied because it is impossible to visually perceive a form which has no colour to distinguish it from its environment. Thus, when heat gets its name, it becomes red and thus visible, when water acquires its name, it becomes white and thus visible, and when food acquires its name, it becomes black and thus visible[73]. But these three manifestations of reality, *sat*, do not exist in the world in their pure forms. They mingle together and create fire, the sun, the moon and lightning. Thus fire is threefold and consists of heat, water and food; the same is for the sun, the moon and lightning.

So on the one hand, there is no fire, no sun, no moon that would be ontologically independent from the three manifestations. They are only forms that appeared in the process of naming (*vācārambhaṇam vikāro nāmadheyaṃ*). At the same time, however, they do exist in some way and have their peculiarity expressed by their names (*agnitva*, *ādityatva*, *candratva*, *vidyuttva*). On this cognitive level, the three basic manifestation can only be recognised indirectly *via* inference: a red colour allows people to infer heat, a white colour allows people to infer water, and a black colour allows people to infer food. The lack of subjective-objective cognition allows people to infer lightning. When this peculiarity is removed (*apāgād agner agnitvam*; *apāgād ādityād ādityatvam; apāgād candrāc candratvam*; *apāgād vidyuto vidyuttvam*), only three basic manifestations remain: heat, water and food.

---

72 BU 6.2.15: *ādityắd vaídyutaṃ tắn vaídyutāt púruṣo mānasá étya brahmalokắn gamayati*, CU 5.10.2: *candramaso vidyutam | tat puruṣo 'mānavaḥ | sa enān brahma gamayati | eṣa devayānaḥ panthā iti.* For the meaning of lightning, see also section 4.4.2.4.

73 The correlation between the forms of the sun (red) and moon (white) seems to be natural, black is the form of fire because of its metonymic link with black coals and black roads which are left by it.

Let us return to the first passage of the CU which introduces the metaphysical assumptions and its terminological basis. We can see now that clay, copper and iron correspond to three basic manifestations in the cosmogony and particular objects to their luminous forms. The explanative power comes from the blend. The concept of production of objects is the next input space of the conceptual network created by the composer. The generic space is the concept of transformation. In the blend, production of objects and cosmogony are seen in terms of naming that has ontological results in the same way as the production of objects is the transformation of the material. The input space of production of objects imparts to the blend the concept of real transformation to the blend and the input space of verbalised cognition the concept of giving names.

There is a difference between the first description which presents the examples and the cosmogonic description. The first expresses the process as consisting of two stages: from the material the object is created. The cosmogonic description adds a third level which is reality called *sat*. In the blend, therefore, the objects correspond to the luminous forms and they constitute the level of the transformation (*vikāra*) from the ontological point of view and the level of naming (*nāmadheya*) from the epistemological point of view. The materials (clay, copper, iron) correspond to the three manifestations of *sat* (heat, water, food) and constitute the level called *satya*. Thus the difference between both aspects of reality is expressed with the use of two synonymous words: *sat* and *satya*. Both are real, contrary to earlier thought according to which the unmanifest aspect of reality is called unreal (*asat*)[74]. One could ask about the reality of transformations within the *satya* level, but, as I have argued above, they are as real as the creative power of speech.

As mentioned in the beginning of this section, the aim of the whole exposition is 'to make heard what is not heard, thought what is not thought, recognised what is not recognised'. The composer, having explained transformation of heat, water and food into their colourful forms, concludes that the way of reasoning from forms was known to the rich and learned people of old. In this way, he expresses that the exposition presented here draws upon earlier tradition. We have seen that the cosmogony is based on ancient cosmogonic models, but its composer uses much more abstract terms to express it. He creates the general and abstract concepts of heat, water and food that are manifest in colourful form; the concept of colour and form (*rūpa*) is also abstract and general. The concrete terms appear only when the particular phenomena are created.

74 Not in the ontological sense.

The tendency to general and abstract concepts can also be seen in that the composer uses the terms of *sat* and *satya* in a very coherent way. The term *sat* is used to denote reality and the term *satya* is used to denote its three basic forms that manifest in colours. They are true in the ontological and epistemological sense as they really exist and their recognition is true recognition.

It should be noted that there is an important similarity between this cosmogony and the cosmogony of the AU which is also novel in comparison with earlier thought. The composers of both Upaniṣads see the processes of the world and living entities as the continuation of the creative activity of reality. The presentation of the division in names and forms is preceded by the following sentence:

CU 6.3.1

> *teṣāṃ khalv eṣāṃ bhūtānāṃ trīṇy eva bījāni bhavanty āṇḍajaṃ jīvajam udbhijjam iti* |
>
> There are, as you can see, only three sources from which these creatures here originate: they are born from eggs, from living individuals, or from sprouts.

It is possible to see this sentence as an attempt to look for the roots of living beings in three manifestations of *sat*. The creatures born of eggs are birds which are connected with heat and the sun. The creatures born from living beings are creatures born from pregnant females. They are connected with water *via* concept of amniotic fluid. And the creatures born from sprouts are plants connected with food.

The similarity with the AU can also be seen in that Uddālaka, having presented the cosmic transformations of reality, presents its transformation in a particular man who interacts with the world (CU 6.5). This interaction is conceived in terms of eating. Three basic manifestations of *sat* constitute the human organism which is divided into three: the densest, the medium and the finest parts. Food become feces, flesh and mind. The parts of water become urine, blood and breath (*prāṇa*). The parts of heat are bones, marrow and speech. In order to explain the rational background of his exposition, Uddālaka evokes an example of churned curd: its finest part becomes butter. Thus the recipient is triggered to activate the general domain of Cleansing By Heat in its particular realisation of the transformation of milk. In the blend, the division of the basic manifestations of *sat* in the human organism is conceived in terms of heating. Activation of this domain allows him to understand it as cognitive transformations.

Moreover, if it is possible to cognise the three basic manifestations of reality on the basis of colours of fire, the sun, the moon and lightning, it should also be possible to cognise them on the basis of their manifestation in the human body. In order to prove his thesis that mind is made of food, that breath is made of water and that speech is made of heat, Uddālaka asks his son not to eat for fifteen days (CU 6.7). He can drink as much water as he wants in order not to lose his breath (*prāṇa*) made of water. After fifteen days of fasting, Śvetaketu forgets everything he has learnt. This is because, as Uddālaka explains, he has lost his mind made of food and speech made of heat. He puts his explanation in the frames of earlier tradition and evokes the concept of Prajāpati who is divided into sixteen parts of which the sixteenth is the whole[75]. During his fast Śvetaketu lost one part of himself each day but preserved himself as a whole on the basis of which he can rebuilt himself. This whole is preserved because he preserved his breath. Preservation of breath is important not only because a living being dies when it is lost. The importance of breath also comes from meditative practices on breath which finally lead to recognition of the unity of reality. Viewed in this context, the next exposition of Uddālaka logically follows the cosmogony.

*

Generally speaking, the intention of the composer of CU 6.1-7 is to present various levels of experience. On the level of everyday life experience, what comes through senses is understood as real: we feel the heat of the sun and fire, we see their light, we also see moon and lightning and we interact with various kinds of beings. We are not interested in their components or origin. In the same way, in the ṚV and ŚB, the word *sát* refers to the manifest aspect of reality because it can be perceived and experienced. However, the philosophers of the Upaniṣads, contrary to their earlier Vedic predecessors, have found a way to the ummanifest aspect of reality which gives them access to another kind of experience. On this level, the real character of everyday life experience is not abolished but is rather enriched with underlying meaning. Within its frames, the real character of the manifest aspect turns out to be dependent on the real character of transformations of the unmanifest aspect.

---

75 In BU 1.5.14, Prajāpati is called year and is divided into sixteen parts, of which fifteen are nights and the sixteen is constant (such a conceptualisation is the result of a blend the input spaces of which are Prajāpati, the yearly movement of the sun, and the monthly movement of the moon). A man who knows this is Prajāpati, the year: his fifteen parts are his wealth, his sixteen parts are his *ātmán*, not only the body, as Olivelle interprets it (1988), but also he as a whole. This relationship between man and his wealth is also conceived in terms of a wheel: the wealth is its rim, *ātmán* is *nábhya*, i.e. the part connected with the axle.

4.1.5. Reality really transforms itself. *Sat, tyam* and *satyasya satyam*

In this section, I will discuss other ways in which the Upaniṣadic composers try to explain the real nature of creative transformation. I will analyse the semantic play with the word *satya* and the expression *satyasya satyam*[76]. I will discuss selected fragments of the TU, the BU and the CU. The account of KU 1.6 will be discussed later (see chapter 5.3).

TU 2.6.1

> *so 'kāmayata | bahu syāṃ prajāyeyeti | sa tapo 'tapyata | sa tapas taptvā | idaṁ sarvam asṛjata | yad idaṃ kiñ ca | tat sṛṣṭvā | tad evānuprāviśat | tad anupraviśya | sac ca tyac cābhavat | niruktaṃ cāniruktaṃ ca | nilayanaṃ cānilayanaṃ ca | vijñānaṃ cāvijñānaṃ ca | satyaṃ cānṛtaṃ ca satyam abhavat |*
> *yad idaṃ kiñca | tat satyam ity ācakṣate |*

> He had this desire: 'Let me multiply myself. Let me produce offspring'. So he heated himself up. When he had heated himself up, he emitted this whole world, everything that is here. After emitting it, it entered that very world. And after entering it, he became in turn Sat and Tyat, the distinct and the indistinct, the resting and the never resting, the perceived and the nonperceived, the real (*satya*) and the unreal (*anṛta*). He became the real, everything that is here; that is why people call all this Sat.

Reality in its pre-creative state is not mentioned here and the cosmogony begins with the description of its creative desire. Creation is presented accordingly to the general Vedic model and it is conceived in terms of heating man. Then reality is presented as entering its creation. The recipient, on the basis of his knowledge about Vedic cosmogonies, may presume that reality before its entrance loses contact with its manifest part[77]. As we have seen from other cosmogonies, that act that confirms that the unity of reality is conceived in terms of eating and of giving names and forms. Here this act is expressed in an abstract way with the use of the image schema of CONTAINER with it being merely stated that reality enters the world. As a result reality is divided into two parts called *sat* and *tyam*. As the recipient may presume, *sat* refers to the part which is distinct (*nirukta*), resting (*nilayana*), aware (*vijñāna*) and real (*satya*), *tyam* to the part which is indistinct (*anirukta*), never resting (*anilayana*), not aware (*avijñāna*), and unreal (*anṛta*). So, as a whole, the manifest aspect is *satyam* consisting of two opposing parts. The aspect called

[76] See also Buitenen (1988b).
[77] Metonymy THE INITIAL PHASE OF THE PROCESS FOR THE WHOLE PROCESS (Radden, Kövecses 1999).

sat can also be interpreted as the subjective aspect and the aspect called *tyam* the objective aspect.

At the same time, one can understand this division as the division into what is manifest and what is unmanifest. According to another cosmogony of the TU, the pre-creative state is the nonexistent (*asad vā idam agra āsīt | tato vai sad ajāyata*, 2.7.1[78]). So the recipient of TU 2.6.1 can also understand the division into *sat* and *tyam* as being in accord with earlier tradition where the unmanifest aspect is called *tyam* and the manifest *sat*. Qualification of the unmanifest aspect as unresting agrees with earlier cosmogonies according to which creation makes stable that which is unstable. It is also possible that the ambiguity is deliberate and that the intention of the composer is to bring together two traditions of use of the word *sat,* the earlier of which refers it to the manifest aspect of reality and the new one which refers to the unmanifest aspect.

The same play with the word *satya* is attested in BU 2.3. Here the aspect called *sat* is the aspect which has a fixed shape (*mūrta*), is mortal (*martya*) and is stationary (*sthita*). The aspect called *tyam* does not have a fixed shape (*amūrta*), is immortal (*amṛta*) and is in motion (*yat*, BU 2.3.1). Such a qualification of the aspects is ambiguous. Taking into account that the aspect called *sat* is qualified as mortal, one could infer that *sat* refers to the manifest aspect. This is confirmed in that it *mūrta* comes from the root *mūrch-*, 'to congeal', used in cosmogonies to express the process of creation (ŚB 10.5.3, see chapter 3.5.1 and AU 1.1.2, see section 4.1.3). Here this word is abstract and the recipient is not expected to evoke concrete experience. On the other hand, the aspect called *tyam* is qualified as immortal (*amṛta*) and without a fixed shape (*amūrta*) which implies that it refers to the unmanifest aspect. The last pair are opposites in that the aspect *sat* is in motion (*yat*) and the aspect *tyam* is stationary (*sthita*). Similarly to TU 2.6, such thinking of the composer may be motivated by earlier thought according to which the unmanifest aspect of reality is unstable. But it may also imply that the qualification of *sat* and *asat* can refer to both aspects of reality.

The expression *satyásya satyám* is also used in BU (2.1.20) at the end of the teaching given by king Ajātaśatru to a learned Brahmin Dṛptabālāki Gārgya:

> *sá yáthorṇavā̆bhis tántunoccáred, yáthā agnéḥ kṣudrā̆ viṣphuliṅgā vyuccáranty evám evā̀smād ātmánaḥ sárve prāṇā̆ḥ sárve lokā̆ḥ sárve devā̆ḥ | tásyopaniṣát satyásya satyám iti | prāṇā̆ vaí satyám̥ téṣām eṣá satyám |*

[78] For analysis of this cosmogony, see section 4.4.2.5.

> As a spider sends forth its thread, and as tiny sparks spring forth from a fire, so indeed do all the vital breaths, all the worlds, all the gods and all beings spring from this self (*ātman*). Its hidden name (*upaniṣad*) is 'The real of the real'; for the real are breaths, and he is the real of breaths[79].

The unmanifest aspect of reality is called *ātmán* and 'the real of the real' (*satyásya satyám*). Its manifestation is conceived in terms of the activity of a spider which produces its web and of fire which creates sparks. The composer has chosen these concepts as the input spaces of his conceptual network in order to express the ontic identity between both aspects of reality. As a spider-web and sparks are identical with spider and with fire in that they are originate from them and their material is the same, in the same way the manifest aspect is produced from reality and constitutes its part being the same yet separated. Here *ātmán* is identified with breaths the practice of which will lead man to cognise the unity of all reality.

The play with the word *satya* also appears in CU 8.3. The passage which I now analyse comes after the description of the liberated man who can create anything he wants by his intention; thus his desires become real. The explanation is also placed within the context of liberating practice. At the end of his description (CU 8.3.4-5), the composer states that the name of *brahman* is 'real' (*satya*). The word has three syllables: *sa*, *ti* and *yam*. Syllable *sat* is the immortal, syllable *ti* is mortal while syllable *yam* joins those two together. The recipient understands that *sat* refers to the unmanifest aspects of reality and *ti* to the manifest aspect. In a monistic vision of the world, there must be an ontological link between two aspects of reality and it is referred to by the syllable *yam*. It designates the most borderline sphere between the manifest and the unmanifest aspects[80]. Then the composer explains the reason why *yam* can refer to this sphere: because by it one can join them (*yad anenobhe yacchati tasmād yam*). The subject of this sentence is not specified. In my view, it refers to reality itself which thus manifests its unity. This is the ontological meaning of *yam*. Secondly, it refers to a human subject who, thanks to his cognition, can realise in the micro-scale this unity. Such an understanding of *yam* foreshadows the later definition of the word *yoga* which is explained in the same way as an activity which joins[81].

---

79 Olivelle (1998): 'for the real consists of the vital functions, and the self is the real behind the vital functions'.

80 For the concept of *setu*, see also sections 4.2.2, 4.4.2.4.

81 *Maitrāyaṇī Upaniṣad* 6.25: *evaṃ prāṇam athoṃkāraṃ yasmāt sarvam anekadhā | yunakti yuñjate vāpi tasmād yoga iti smṛtaḥ ||*

*

The uses of the words *satya* analysed above betray a tendency to present in abstract terms the ontological relationship between the unmanifest and the manifest aspects of reality. The real character of the manifest aspect is not denied though its ultimate foundation is even more real. This is new in the Vedic philosophy. The philosophers of the ṚV, AVŚ and the ŚB limited their range of philosophical investigation to what is manifest (*sat*) and can therefore be defined and experienced. The unmanifest aspect is beyond any possibility to be cognised and verbalised and can be qualified only as *ásat* (in opposition to *sat*), or as neither *sat* nor *asat* (in the pre-creative state when there is no point of reference for cognition). In the time of the Upaniṣads, the search for achieving an experience, similar to that realised in Somic exultation, has not only succeeded but had led the philosophers further than was possible with the use of earlier methods. The cognition of the whole of reality is based on breath practice although in the passages analysed so far it is not explained how it is done. This practice opens the way to later yogic practice but, as I have shown, it is deeply grounded in the earlier search for supernatural states that are to be gained within the frames of the human body.

4.2. Ontology

From what has been said above, the basic ontological assumptions of the Upaniṣadic philosophers can be seen. The relationship between two aspects of reality is explicitly seen as cognitive and their unity is defined. The cognitive nature of the transformations of reality allows the composer to preserve the monistic assumption and the real nature of transformations of reality discussed in the previous section. At the same time, the coexistence of oneness and multiplicity results in the internal contradictoriness of reality.

4.2.1 The cognitive relationship between aspects of reality

In the creative act, reality divides itself into two aspects: the unmanifest and the manifest, which are ontologically the same. The monistic assumption is explicitly expressed e.g. by Yājñavalkya in BU 4.4.19[82]. The relationship between the two aspects is cognitive: the unmanifest aspect cognises the

[82] *mánasaivā̀nudraṣṭávyaṃ nèhá nā́nāsti kíṃ caná | mṛtyóḥ sá mṛtyúm āpnoti yá ihá nā́neva páśyati ||*

manifest one. It is expressed in most concise way in BU 1.4.10: reality called *bráhman* cognises itself (*ātmā́nam*) and thus becomes everything (see section 4.1.2). This creative moment is the moment of separation of the subject of cognition which is *bráhman* and the object which is *bráhman* perceived by itself and called *ātmán*. The BU follows the *Nāsadīyasūkta*'s concept of creation as self-cognition and expresses it explicitly. *Bráhman* is the unmanifest aspect of reality, the manifest aspect of reality, its perceived self and the object of its cognition. Then identity is confirmed and, as the cosmogony says, *bráhman* becomes everything.

In order that creation could develop further, reality repeats its cognitive split within its manifest aspect into subject and object. The cosmogonies of the ŚB and the BU express this conviction in terms of the general domains of Procreation and Cooking, but some express it more explicitly as giving names and forms to what is manifest (ŚB 11.2.3, see chapter 3.5.3, BU 1.4.7, see section 4.1.3, CU 6.2.3-4, see section 4.1.4).

The cognitive character of this stage of creation is most explicitly expressed in the cosmogony of the AU (see section 4.1.3). It presents the manifestation of the subjective and objective powers within the world. It also presents the final manifestation of *ātman* within the cosmos and man. This is the most mysterious aspect of creation because the *ātman* is unmanifest and yet manifest. It is implied, then, that reality functions in four aspects. Two aspects are unmanifest: one of them is the aspect beyond any manifestation and the second is within manifestation as the conscious factor of the cognising activity of reality. The manifest aspects of reality are the cosmos and man. All of them are called *ātman*[83]. While in the ŚB, the main reason for creation is the will of reality to manifest its ability to live (so to kill) and die, in the Upaniṣads it is his will to cognise himself in subjective-objective cognition[84]. The AU presents *ātman* which is born within himself, i.e. as the world and man, and, then looks at itself as if from the other side from within its manifestation. He sees itself as manifest and unmanifest and confirms its identity not from the outside of creation, but from the inside, using the subjective-objective powers to cognise its manifestations while, at the same time, being beyond their range. This internal unmanifest aspect is the self of man and the world.

This structure of reality is described by the CU in the following way:

---

[83] The later Upaniṣads will call *ātman aṅguṣṭhamātrapuruṣa* (*Kaṭha Upaniṣad* 4.12, 6.17, *Śvetāśvatara Upaniṣad* 3.13).

[84] As I have shown, cognitive reason is also present there, but not so much highlighted (see chapter 3.5).

CU 3.12.6-9

tāvān asya mahimā tato jyāyāṃś ca puruṣaḥ |
pādo 'sya sarvā bhūtāni tripād asyāmṛtaṃ divīti | (6)
yad vai tad brahmetīdaṃ vāva tad yo 'yaṃ bahirdhā puruṣād ākāśaḥ | yo vai sa bahirdhā puruṣād ākāśaḥ || (7)
ayaṃ vāva sa yo 'yam antaḥ puruṣa ākāśaḥ | yo vai so 'ntaḥ puruṣa ākāśaḥ | (8)
ayaṃ vāva sa yo ayam antarhṛdaya ākāśaḥ | tad etat pūrṇam apravarti |
pūrṇam apravartinīṃ śriyaṃ labhate ya evaṃ veda | (9)

Such is his greatness – even greater than that is that person.
One quarter of him are all creatures, three quarters the immortal in heaven. (6)
And take what people call '*brahman*' – clearly, it is nothing but this space here outside a person. And this space outside a person – (7)
clearly, it is the same as this space here within a person. (8)
And this space here within a person – clearly, it is the same as this space here within the heart; it is full and nondepleting. Anyone who knows this obtains full and nondepleting prosperity. (9)

The description begins with the stanza from the *Puruṣasūkta* (10.90.3). In this hymn, reality and its manifest aspect is conceived in terms of a man (see chapter 1.3). The commentary of the CU is an attempt to incorporate the new metaphysics within the frames of tradition. The space which is outside the person (*puruṣa*) is called *brahman*. This space can be understood in the following way. Firstly, if *puruṣa* refers to cosmos conceived in terms of man, then the space which is outside *puruṣa* is the unmanifest aspect of reality. Secondly, if *puruṣa* refers to man, then the space which is outside *puruṣa* is the cosmos. Thirdly, if *puruṣa* refers to the inner self of man, then the space which is outside *puruṣa* is the human body. *Brahman* thus conceived is then identified with the space within man and with the space in man's heart. Thus, in a very abstract and general way, the unity of the four aspects of reality is expressed.

Then the composer says that the space which is outside the person is the same as the space within the person. And this space is the space within the heart. Thus he narrows the meaning of *puruṣa* to the meaning of man. This space is full and immovable. As it will be shown, the concept of the full (*pūrṇa*) is used in the Upaniṣads in an abstract way to express reality as not being affected by its manifestation (see section 4.2.2[85]). This absolute state is realised by those who know reality.

I would draw attention to the point that notwithstanding the abstract character of this description, the composer recruits from spatial concepts to

[85] For the concept of *pūrṇá* in AVŚ see chapter 2.6.1.

conceive reality. The recipient is prompted to activate the image schema of CONTAINER and the conceived aspects of reality in terms of containers which contain one another. Within the frames of this metaphor, the unmanifest aspect is a container which contains its manifest aspect and this in turn contains man with the unamanifest aspect as his content.

The description of CU 3.12.6-9 is also a description of the stages of liberating cognition which begins with cognition of one's innermost self[86]. Firstly, the unity of reality is expressed in a general and abstract way. This assumption provides a basis for liberating cognition as since the structure of man reflects the structure of reality, cognition of oneself leads to cognition of the whole of reality. In the description of the result of liberating cognition, the word *śrī*, 'excellence', (translated by Olivelle as 'prosperity') is used. In this way, the composer evokes the Ṛgvedic concept of fame which is the supernatural state expressed in the ṚV with use of words *śrī́*, śrávas, *yáśas* and *ksatrá* (see chapter 1.7). Thus he puts the state described by him within the frame of earlier tradition.

If all aspects of reality are ontologically the same, the difference between them is that the unmanifest aspect is beyond subjective-cognitive cognition, while in the manifest aspect subjective-objective cognition takes place in cosmic and human dimensions. When Uṣasta Cākrāyaṇa asks Yājñavalkya about *ātmán*, Yājñavalkya answer's him thus:

BU 3.4.1

> *ná dṛ́ṣṭer draṣṭā́raṃ paśyeḥ | ná śrúteḥ śrotā́raṁ śṛṇuyāḥ | ná matér mantā́raṃ manvīthāḥ | ná vijñāter vijñātā́raṃ víjānīyāḥ | eṣá ta ātmā́ sarvāntaráḥ | áto 'nyád ā́rtam |*
>
> 'You can't see the seer who does the seeing; you can't hear the hearer who does the hearing; you can't think of the thinker who does the thinking; and you can't perceive the perceiver who does the perceiving. The self within all is the self of yours. All else besides this is grief!'

Ātmā́ sarvānantará is reality in its unmanifest aspect present within its manifest appearance. It renders possible subjective-cognitive cognition: seeing, hearing, thinking, perceiving. We could say that reality cognises with the aid of its subjective-objective instruments only its manifest aspect. Reality in its unmanifest aspect cannot be cognised this way. For that, a cognition that is different from subjective-objective cognition is needed.

---

86 For this passage and its context, see section 4.4.2.1.

Reality as the factor of consciousness is called 'the perceiver of everything' (*sárvānubhū*, BU 2.5.19). In this function, it is called by Yājñavalkya in the following way:

BU 3.8.11

tád vā́ etád akṣáram Gārgy ádr̥ṣṭam draṣṭrā́śrutam śrotrámatam mantrávijñātam vijñātŕ̥ | nā̀nyád ato asti draṣṭŕ̥| nā̀nyád ato asti śrotŕ̥ | nā̀nyád ato asti mantŕ̥ | nā̀nyád ato asti vijñātŕ̥ | etasmin nú khálv akṣáre Gārgy ākāśá ótaś ca prótaścéti |

This is the imperishable, Gārgī, which sees but can't be seen; which hears but can't be heard,; which thinks but can't be thought of; which perceives but can't be perceived. Besides this imperishable there is no one that sees, no one that hears, no one that thinks and no one that perceives. On this very imperishable, Gārgī, space is woven back and forth.'

Reality is imperishable (*akṣárá*[87]) and is called with the names of subjective powers, seer, hearer, thinker and perceiver. At the same time, the composer states that it cannot be cognised as the object of those acts. The recipient then can infer that reality renders possible subjective-cognitive acts without being involved in those processes. The last sentence is a further example of how the earlier thinking motivates the thinking of the Upaniṣadic philosophers. Within reality there is a space (*ākāśá*). The concept of space evokes the cosmogonies of the ŚB which present the creation of a space within Prajāpati. This space is conceived in terms of hunger or death; here this source domain is not activated. At the same time, the composer seems to evoke the source domain of the earliest source, i.e. R̥V, which conceives creation in terms of weaving (Jurewicz 2010a: 117–118, 249–250, 412). He refers not only generally to this concept, but also more specifically to R̥V 10.130 where the creation of the world is conceived in terms of the creation of sacrifice which, in turn, is conceived in terms of weaving. The second hemistich of the last verse of R̥V 10.130.1 creates a similar image of weaving: 'They sit at the warp saying, 'Weave forth, weave back'[88] (*imé vayanti pitáro yá āyayúḥ prá vayāpa vayéti āsate taté*). In BU 3.8.11, the recipient is not expected to elaborate this source domain, but, if he does, he will see the creation of space in terms of fixing threads on a loom and weaving. I would argue that the composer of the BU intentionally evoked here this old source domain in order to express the links between his teachings and tradition.

[87] For the beginnings of this concept, see chapter 1.6. See Jurewicz (2012a). See also BU 5.1.1, discussed below in this section.

[88] Jamison, Brereton (2014).

A similar mixture of abstract and metaphorical thinking in the description of reality that evokes earlier tradition is attested in the sentence preceding Yājñavalkya's exposition quoted above:

BU 3.8.8

sá hovācaitád vaí tád akṣáraṃ Gārgi brāhmaṇā́ abhívadanty ásthūlam ánaṇv áhrasvam ádīrgham alóhitam asnehám acchāyám atamò 'vāyv ànākāśám asaṅgám arasám agandhám acakṣúṣkam aśrotrám avā́g amanò 'tejáskam aprāṇám ámukham amātrám | ná tád aśnāti kiṃ cana | ná tád aśnāti káścaná |

He replied: 'That, Gārgī, is imperishable, and Brahmins refer to it like this – it is neither coarse, not fine; it is neither short nor long; it has neither blood not fat; it is without shadow or darkness; it is without air or space; it is without contact; it is without it has not taste or smell; it is without sight or hearing it is without speech or mind; it is without energy, breath, or mouth; it is beyond measure, it has nothing within it or outside of it does not eat anything, and no one eats it.'

The description begins with an abstract apophatic description of reality in its unmanifest aspect again qualified as imperishable (*akṣárá*). However, in the last sentence the concept of eating is evoked. Since in these terms subjective-objective cognition is conceived, the recipient understands that reality in its unmanifest aspect cannot be grasped by this kind of cognition. Interestingly enough, the *Mādhyandina* recension of the BU accepts the version *ná tád aśnoti káṃ caná ná tád aśnoti káś caná*, 'nothing he reaches and no one reaches him'. It is possible that for the composers of this version the concept of eating was too concrete to be used in such an abstract description and because of that they used the image schematic concept of reaching a container which seems to be more abstract and general. I would argue, however, that the composer used this concept intentionally to show that the impossibility of understanding reality with the aid of subjective-objective cognition is not a new problem although expressed with new language.

4.2.2. Ways of description of reality

As in earlier thought, the monistic assumption of the philosophy causes the internal contradictoriness of reality. Reality is all the elements of the world, even those in opposition, but at the same time, it is none of them and it is described in two ways that reflect its contradictory nature. On the one hand, in its unmanifest aspect, reality is described in an apophatic way as being neither this nor that, e.g.:

BU 4.4.25

sá vā́ eṣá mahā́n ajá ātmā̀járo 'máro 'mṛ́to 'bháyo bráhma |

And this is the immense and unborn-self, unaging, undying, immortal, free from fear – the *brahman*.[89]

Yet, on the other hand, in its manifest aspect reality is the world and it is described positively as this and that:

BU 4.4.5

sá vā́ ayám ātmā́ bráhma vijñānamáyo manomáyo prāṇamáyaś cakṣurmáyaḥ śrotramáyaḥ pṛthivīmáya āpomáyo vāyumáya ākāśamáyas tejomáyo 'tejomáyaḥ kāmamáyo 'kāmamáyaḥ krodhamáyo 'krodhamáyo dharmamáyo 'dharmamáyaḥ sarvamáyaḥ |

Clearly, this self is *brahman* – this self that is made of perception, made of mind, made of sight, made of breath, made of hearing, made of earth, made of water, made of wind, made of space, made of light and lightless, made of desire and desireless, made of anger and angerless, made of the righteous and the unrighteous; this self is made of everything.

The beginning of the passage evokes the creative process during which reality, called here *ātmán*-bráhman, transforms itself into the highest cognitive power called *vijñā́na*, then into mind and then into other cognitive faculties: seeing, breathing and hearing. This description seems to be an elaboration of ŚB 10.5.3 that describes transformations of the mind although the number of the phases though their order is slightly different (see chapter 3.5.4)[90]. Then *ātmán-bráhman* transforms itself into manifest forms of the world (earth, water, wind, and space). The recipient understands that the cognitive powers of reality acquires an organism which will enable it to perform subjective-objective cognition (similarly to the AU, see section 4.1.3). As the cosmos, reality manifests in its opposing elements: light and darkness, positive and negative emotions and their lack and finally *dhárma* and *ádharma*. According to BU 1.4.14, *dhárma* is a form (*rūpá*) of reality that is created in order to guard the weaker from the stronger (see section 4.1.2). It is identified with truth or reality, *satyá*. It is implied then that reality is also a lack of this

[89] See also BU 4.2.4, 4.4.22 discussed below. For the meaning of the formula *néti néti*, see Slaje (2010).

[90] ŚB 10.5.3 enumerates six transformations of the mind in the following order: speech, breath, sight, hearing, deed and fire, see chapter 3.5.1.

form, so the recipient understands that the superiority of the stronger over the weaker is morally equivocal[91].

A clear example of a contradictory description of reality is the teaching of Śāṇḍilya (CU 3.14[92]). As the self of man reality is smaller than anything that is manifest, as the unmanifest aspect beyond creation it is larger than the world. As the manifest aspect it contains everything in the world: all actions, all desires, all smells and all tastes[93].

In order to express the contradictory nature of reality, the composer of the BU 5.1.1 further elaborates the Atharvavedic concept of the full (see chapter 2.6.1):

BU 5.1.1

pūrṇám adáḥ pūrṇám idáṃ pūrṇā́t pūrṇám údacyate |
pūrṇásya pūrṇám ādā́ya pūrṇám evā́vaśiṣyate | 5.1.1

The world there is full; The world here is full;
Fullness from fullness proceed. After taking fully from the full, it still remains completely full.

The composer of the BU, similarly to the composer of the AVŚ, activates the concept of pouring water from a bucket to conceive the creation of the world. The unmanifest aspect is conceived in terms of a vessel full of fluid and creation in terms of fluid which flows out of it. The wording is very abstract and the source domain is only evoked *via* the word 'full', *pūrṇá*. However, the recipient has to evoke the experience which is then violated. The meaning is conveyed thanks to this violation. In everyday experience, when water is poured out of a full vessel, the vessel empties. In the target domain, it does not happen and the unmanifest aspect remains full. Such a conceptualisation of creation expresses the real character of the creative transformations of reality. It also expresses the fact that creation does not influence reality which is not changed in any respect because of its creation. Creation does not affect reality in any way. At the same time, its manifestation, also conceived in terms of the full, has the same nature: it is its perfect manifestation identical with him. As I have shown elsewhere (Jurewicz 2012a), while reality in its unmanifest aspect is fullness that does not flow, its creation is fullness that flows.

---

[91] This description is also discussed in section 4.4.2.3.

[92] This teaching will be discussed at length in section 4.4.2.1.

[93] CU 3.14.3: *eṣa ma ātmā antarhṛdaye aṇīyān vrīher vā yavād vā sarṣapād vā śyāmākād vā śyāmākataṇḍulād vā* | *eṣa ma ātmā antarhṛdaye jyāyān pṛthivyā jyāyān antarikṣāj jyāyān divo jyāyān ebhyo lokebhyaḥ* | CU 3.14.4: *sarvakarmā sarvakāmaḥ sarvagandhaḥ sarvarasaḥ sarvam idam abhyatto 'vākyanāvākya eṣa ma ātmā antarhṛdaye* | *etad brahma* |

The following passage of the BU, put in the mouth of Yājñavalkya, elaborates the image of flowing water as the source domain for the conceptualisation of the relationship between two aspects of reality. Its composer begins with the abstract description of reality present within the man as the factor of cognition (*vijñā́na*) and then elaborates the image of a dike:

BU 4.4.22

sá vā́ eṣá mahā́n ajá ātmā́ yó 'yám vijñānamáyaḥ prāṇéṣu | yá eṣò 'ntár hṛ́daya ākāśás tásmiñ chete sárvasya váśī sárvasyéśānaḥ sárvasyā́dhipatiḥ | esá ná sādhúnā kármaṇā bhū́yān nò evā̀sādhúnā kánīyān | eṣa sarveśvara | eṣá bhūtādhipatír | eṣa bhūtapāla | sá sétur vídharaṇa eṣā́ṃ lokā́nām ásaṃbhedāya |

This immense, unborn self is none than the one consisting of perception here among the breaths[94] (*prāṇa*). There, in that space within the heart, he lies – the controller of all, the lord of all, the ruler of all! He does not become more by good actions or in any way less by bad actions He is the lord of all! He is the ruler of creatures! He is the guardian of creatures! He is the dike separating these worlds so they would not mingle with each other.

Reality is present in its manifest aspect as its own self, but its presence does not influence it in any respect. As BU 4.4.5 states, reality is *dhárma* and *ádharma* when it manifests in the world (see above) but, according to BU 4.4.22, its unmanifest aspect is above moral evaluation. It is explicitly expressed by Yājñavalkya that good and bad deeds do not affect it because it is self-sufficient. The concept of the dike, introduced in the final sentence, is motivated by the metaphor of the full in terms of which self-sufficiency of reality is conceived. Here reality is conceived in terms of a dike that separates two water receptacles in terms of which both its aspects are conceived. The logic of the experience is again violated because in everyday life experience a dike is something different from the receptacles it separate, but in the target domain reality is the same with its aspects. The dike is the source domain for conceptualisation of this sphere of reality which separates and, at the same time, links both its aspects[95]. This is the most difficult problem for the monistic theories: what happens at the very verge between manifest and unmanifest aspects? How should it be conceived? When does unmanifest "finish" and manifest "begin"? As it has been shown, the composers of the Upaniṣads elaborate the image schema of CONTAINER in their description

---

[94] Olivelle (1998): 'vital functions'.

[95] In the *Nāsadīyasūkta* this link is conceived in terms of kinship (*bándhu*, Jurewicz 2010a: 52).

of the relationship between aspects of reality, but the concept of container implies fixed boundaries. Therefore, the recipient has to violate the logic of everyday experience and to imagine a container that, at the same time, is not a container. As will be shown, Yājñavalkya devotes much time analysing the mysterious borderline sphere between the two aspects which can be experienced in liberating cognition (see section 4.4.2.3).

The concept of a dike is also used as the source domain to conceive the borderline sphere between the two aspects of reality in CU 8.4. As in BU 4.4.22, the dike is presented as a divider which keeps the worlds apart so that they do not mingle together (*atha ya ātmā sa setur dhṛtir eṣāṃ lokānām asaṃbhedāya*, CU 8.4.1). Time cannot influence it, neither can death and sorrow or good and bad deeds because the unmanifest aspect, called here *brahman*, is beyond any evil. The borderline sphere between the two aspects, conceived in terms of a dike, is identified with *ātman* the cognition of which make that 'a blind turns out not to be blind, wounded, not to be wounded, sick, not to be sick' (CU 8.4.2[96]). The passage from the manifest aspect to the unmanifest is conceived in terms of passage from night to day (CU 8.4.2). The passage results in complete freedom which is conceived in terms of free movement according to one's will (CU 8.4.3[97]). Thus the composer creates a conceptual network. The first input space is the concept of two receptacles of water divided by a dike. The second input space are the concepts of night and morning. The third input space is liberating cognition. The generic space is the concept of transition. In the blend, liberating cognition is conceived in terms of swimming across the receptacle and thus going beyond the darkness of the night to the eternal light. It is worth mentioning that in BU 4.3.9 (see section 4.4.2.3), the borderline state between the two aspects of reality is called *sándhya* which is also the term used in reference to the break of the day and twilight. Such a conceptualisation of this sphere strengthens the coherence of the blend. It is possible that this blend is the one to be evoked during the morning bath in a river (Glucklich 1994: 82–85)[98].

---

96 CU 8.4.2: *tasmād vā etaṃ setuṃ tīrtvā andhaḥ sann anandho bhavati | viddhaḥ sann aviddho bhavati | upatāpī sann anupatāpī bhavati | tasmād vā etaṃ setuṃ tīrtvā api naktam ahar evābhiniṣpadyate | sakṛd vibhāto hy evaiṣa brahmalokaḥ |*

97 CU 8.4.3: *tad ya evaitaṃ brahmalokaṃ brahmacaryeṇānuvindanti teṣām evaiṣa brahmalokaḥ | teṣāṃ sarveṣu lokeṣu kāmacāro bhavati |*

98 For analysis of CU 8.1-12, see section 4.4.2.4.

4.3. The role of man

The Upaniṣads begin to analyse in detail the role of human beings. They continue earlier thinking, but also open new ways. Generally speaking, the two-aspect character of reality is also realised by human beings who after death either join the manifest or the unmanifest aspect.

4.3.1. Men create reality. The model of the Five Fires and the two afterlife paths

The model of the Five Fires (*pañcāgnividyā*) is presented in BU 6.2.9-16 and CU 5.4-10. It is another example of tendency to create abstract and general models but, as I will show, it is deeply entrenched in the efforts of the earlier thinkers beginning from the Ṛgvedic ones[99]. Since I have discussed this problem in detail elsewhere (Jurewicz 2004), I will limit myself to the most important conclusions of my earlier research. The complex functioning of the world and men is reduced to several simple processes. The functioning of the world is reduced to the shining of the sun, raining and the growing of eatable plants. The human processes are eating and procreation. These processes undergo further reduction in that they can be conceived as sacrifice in which oblation is poured into fire. In this way, the world's functioning is conceived in BU 1.4.6 (*etā́vad vā́ idáṁ sárvam ánnaṃ caivā̀nnādáś ca | sóma evā́nnam, agnír annādáḥ*, see section 4.1.2). In each sacrifice, the oblation for the next sacrifice appears. Thus the process is uninterrupted.

So on the most general level, the manifest aspect can be expressed in simple terms of sacrifice constantly performed. Since the sacrifice is the burning of oblation, the recipient can understand the functioning of the manifest aspect in terms of burning. In this way, the Upaniṣads continue the basic Vedic assumption about fire as the essence of what exists.

This assumption is explicitly expressed in the description of cremation in BU 6.2.14. A man remains alive as long as he lives and when he finally dies:

---

[99] For detailed analysis of particular concepts and relationships between the Upaniṣadic versions of *pañcāgnividyā* and the version in JB, see Schmithausen (1994) and Hayakawa (2014). Notwithstanding the differences between the versions of the model, they generally present the same cosmologic content as that in which I am most interested. For a more general survey of the earlier roots, see Schmithausen (1993/1994), Bodewitz (1996a), Butzenberger (1996, 1998), and Gotō (2005).

> *áthainam agnáye haranti | tásyāgnir evā̀gnír bhavati samít samíd dhūmó dhūmò 'rcír arcír áṅgārā áṅgārāviṣphulíṅgā viṣphulíṅgās | tásminn etásminn agnaú devā́ḥ púruṣaṃ juhvati | tásyā ā́huteḥ púruṣo bhā́svaravarṇaḥ sáṃbhavati |*
>
> [T]hey offer him in the fire. Of that fire, the fire is the fire itself; the firewood is the firewood; the smoke is the smoke; the flame is the flame; the embers are the embers; and the sparks are the sparks. In that very fire gods offer man, and from that offering springs a man of brilliant colour.

CU 5.9.2 present this identity of man with fire in a less explicit way:

> *taṃ pretaṃ diṣṭam ito 'gnaya eva haranti yata eveto yataḥ saṃbhūto bhavati |*
>
> When he has departed, when he has reached his appointed time – they take him from here to this very fire, from which he (sprang and) from which he (now) becomes (again).

My interpretation of the last part of this sentence is based on earlier interpretations of the relationship between man and fire. In his exegesis of Agnihotra, the composer of ŚB 2.3.3.3 states that man supports fire during his life and fire supports man after his death. The same idea is expressed by JB 1.1-2 in the exegesis of Agnyādhāna. This relationship is conceived in terms of their mutual birth: man and fire are both father and son. Taking into account the Vedic assumption about fire as the essence of reality and the assumption that the father is identical with his son, the recipient understands that cremation fire and the deceased are the same. The way of presentation in the CU (even in its wording) is more similar to the earlier presentations of this issue than the BU's presentation. On the other hand, it is less explicit because the idea of identity between man and cremation fire is to be inferred metonymically (FATHER FOR SON, SON FOR FATHER) and on the basis of the general knowledge of the recipient.

The conceptual network created by the composers of the BU and the CU to conceive the afterlife described in the next passage is as follows. The first input spaces are the concepts of the deceased which includes his previous life and the concept of reality. The next input spaces are two image schemas: SOURCE-PATH-GOAL and VERTICALITY. The input space that follows is the image schema of CAUSE-EFFECT[100]. In the blend, people are divided into two kinds and follow two different paths according to their activity during life. In their afterlife, reality realises both its aspects: the unmanifest one is realised by those who follow the path of gods while the manifest one is realised by those who follow the path of their fathers.

[100] For this image schema, see Zelinsky-Wibbelt (2000: 274–275).

According to BU 6.3.15, the first kind of people are those 'who know this, and the people there in the wilderness who venerate truth as faith' (*yé cāmī́ áraṇye śraddhā́ṁ satyám upā́sate*). According to CU 5.10.1, they are those 'who know this and the people here in the wilderness who venerate thus: "Austerity is faith"' (*ye ceme araṇye śraddhā tapa ity upāsate*). As we can see, the conditions which make realisation of this afterlife situation possible are not just right knowledge and renunciation of society. It is also the faith, *śraddhā*, of the deceased understood as truth or real (*satyá*, the BU) or austerity (*tapas*, CU). The word *śraddhā* is used in JUB 3.11.7 to refer to the faith of those who remain on earth and whose ritual activity enables the deceased to successfully realise his afterlife destiny (see chapter 5.2). In JB 1.47-49, it is implied that the liberating path is acquired by those for whom the cremation rite is properly performed (see chapter 5.1.2). The same is implied already in the ṚV (Jurewicz 2008b, 2010a).

In the model of the Five Fires presented in the BU and the CU, faith is the first oblation poured into the sun (see Jurewicz 2004). Although the composers of the BU and the CU leave this concept in their model, they seem to say that there are people who do not need the faith of their relatives and the rituals performed by them in order to be successful after death. They redefine this concept. Faith of those who will be liberated concerns their true cognition of reality (metonymically evoked by the word *satyá*[101]) and austerity (*tapas*). Thus the composer redefines the concept of faith, *śraddhā*, of those who are liberated. We may presume that others merely understand *śraddhā* as faith in the power of rituals as understood in earlier thought. The new understanding of the concept of *śraddhā* is the most important difference between the two kinds of people described in the BU and the CU.

Those people follow the path of gods (light of fire, day, the fortnight of the waxing moon, the six months when the sun moves north). Then BU 6.2.15 enumerates the world of the gods (*devaloká*), the sun (*ādityá*) and the region of lightning (*vaídyuta*). The CU 5.10.2 enumerates a year (*saṃvatsara*), the sun (*āditya*), the moon (*candramas*) and lightning (*vidyut*). The exposition of the CU is similar to the description in JUB 3.28.1-2 where the sun and the moon are presented as the spheres reached by the deceased between which he freely wanders (see chapter 5.2.3). The composer of the CU does not mention the concept of wandering and he seems to see the moon as the highest sphere of the manifest aspect. In the BU, this sphere is conceived as the sun. This

[101] Taking into account that the composer of BU 2.1.20, in his analysis of the word *satyá*, describes liberating practice (see section 4.4.2.2), one can presume that this practice is also evoked here.

ultimate sphere can be interpreted as the borderline sphere between the two aspects of reality. The passage between the manifest and unmanifest aspects is conceived in terms of reaching lighting (the CU; *vidyut*) and the region of lightning (the BU: *vaídyuta*). As I have already argued, the concept of lightning appears in contexts which imply that it was the source domain for conceptualisation of the moment liberating cognition is gained (for that see section 4.4.2.4).

Then, according to BU 6.2.15, the deceased meets a man that consists of mind (*mānasó púruṣa*). I would argue then that this concept is the source domain for the most primeval manifestation of reality which thinks about itself in terms of man. My assumption agrees with the general thinking of the Vedic philosophers about creation in terms of a cognitive act. It is possible that the composer of the BU evokes here ŚB 2.2.4.3 which presents the first stage of creation as taking place in the mind of reality (*tád evā̀sya mánasy āsa*). This stage of the afterlife in the CU is conceived in terms of a man who is qualified as not human (*puruṣo 'mānava*). It may be inferred that the most primeval manifestation of reality is conceived in terms of man but the composer stresses the metaphoric character of this conceptualisation by qualifying it as 'not human'. In this way, he also can express the internally contradictory character of the first manifestation of reality.

The goal of the path is called by the composer of the BU 'the worlds of *bráhman*' (*brahmaloká*) where a deceased stay forever and does not return. In these terms, the unmanifest aspect is conceived. If the recipient interprets the word *loká* as the sphere of experience, he would understand that the range of the experience of those people is *bráhman*, i.e. the whole of reality. In the CU, the goal is generally conceived as *brahman*. This Upaniṣad also uses the word *devayāna* to name this afterlife situation[102].

The second kind of people is presented by BU 6.3.16 as those 'who win heavenly worlds… by offering sacrifices, by giving gifts, and by performing austerities' (*átha yé yajñéna dānéna tápasā lokāñ jáyanti | té dhūmám abhisáṃbhavanti*). As I have discussed, the realisation of human goals is conceived in the Veda in terms of winning a space where life is possible (see Jurewicz 2010a). In these terms, the composer of the BU conceives the afterlife lot of the second kind of people. Sacrifices (*yajñá*), gifts (*dāná*) and austerities (*tapas*) are the means for reaching this goal. These means are in opposition to the means which lead to the first path which is veneration of truth as faith. The recipient can understand that this is ritual Vedic activity of which austerity is a part.

[102] The earlier usages of the word *devayāna* are discussed by Killingley (1997).

According to CU 5.10.3, they are those who are 'here in villages' and 'who venerate thus: "Gift-giving is offerings to gods and to priests"' (*atha ya ime grāma iṣṭāpūrte dattam ity upāsate*). The CU is more archaic here than the BU. Its composer uses the Ṛgvedic concept *iṣṭāpūrta* (ṚV 10.14.8) in which the deceased is supposed to meet his fathers and Yama again on the sun. The composer of the CU redefines this Ṛgvedic concept as gift-giving (*datta*). In this way, he evokes the description of the afterlife presented in JB 1.46 where the deceased who follows the first path is finally reborn in the form which is 'won by his gifts'[103] (*dānajita*, see chapter 5.1.1). It is possible that *datta* refers to the *dakṣinā*, the priests, as in the JB. On this basis, the recipient understands that people who give such gifts perform Vedic rituals[104].

Other people follow the path of the fathers (smoke of fire, night, the fortnight of the waning moon, the six months when the sun moves south). Then, according to the BU, they reach the world of fathers (*pitṛloká*) and the moon (*candrá*). The composer of the CU explicitly states that they do not reach the year. Since the yearly movement of the sun was conceived in the Veda as marking the borderline of the cosmos which separates the manifest aspect subjected to time and the unmanifest aspect which is timeless (KU 1.4, see chapter 5.3), it is implied that the deceased do not go beyond the range of time (see chapter 5.1.1, 5.2.2). Then the stages are the world of fathers (*pitṛloka*), space (*ākāśa*) and the moon (*candramas*).

According to the BU, the stages back are the following: from the moon the dead reach the space (*ākāśá*), then wind (*vāyú*), then rain (*vṛṣṭí*) and then the earth (*pṛthivī́*). Then they become food and they are 'poured' into 'the fire of man' and are born in 'the fire of woman' (*té púnaḥ puruṣāgnaú hūyante táto yoṣāgnaú jāyante*). The recipient understands that they are eaten by men to become semen which is then inseminated in a woman's womb. Thus they circle around between existence and death (*tá evám evā̃nupárivartanté*).

The description of the CU is more detailed. The first stages are the space (*ākāśa*) and wind (*vāyu*). Then the origination of rain is presented as the next stages of the afterlife path. These are smoke (*dhūma*), cloud (*abhra*) and rain cloud (*megha*). The next stages are various plants rice and barley, plants and trees, sesames and beans (*vrīhiyavā oṣadhivanaspatayas tilamāsā*). The composer of the CU emphasises that it is very difficult to get out of this stage, but those who manage to do so become food (*anna*) of men and their semen (*retas*) and they become again (*tad bhūya eva bhavati*).

The composer of the BU calls people who are reborn 'those who rise up once again to the worlds' (*lókān pratyuthāyínas*). Olivelle in his translation

---

103 JB 1.45: *sa yo hāsya dānajito loko bhavati tasmin niramate* |

104 THE FINAL PHASE OF THE PROCESS FOR THE WHOLE PROCESS (Radden, Kövecses 1999).

interprets it as '(heavenly) worlds' but it has been shown that in the early Upaniṣads this word had a wider meaning. The recipient can understand this phrase as expressing the idea that the deceased rise up again to various kinds of experience in the manifest aspect. JB 1.46 presents the deceased who is reborn in a similar way: *so 'sya lokaḥ punar utthāyai bhavati* ('that it for him the world in which he resurges').

As I have shown elsewhere (Jurewicz 2004), the successive processes expressed by the *pañcāgnividyā* correspond to the successive stages of the afterlife. I will shortly repeat my arguments. The last two processes presented in the *pañcāgnividyā*, which are eating and procreation, are explicitly presented as the same in both Upaniṣads. The identity of the deceased coming back to the earth with the rain is already attested in the ṚV (see Jurewicz 2010a: 310 ff.). The identity of the deceased placed on the cremation pyre with Soma is also attested in the ṚV (Jurewicz 2008b, 2010a: 294). The Upaniṣadic account also confirms this identity. In BU 6.2.16, the gods say to the deceased as they say to the King Soma 'increase, decrease' (*tā́ṁs tátra devā́ yáthā sómaṁ rā́jānam ā́pyāyasva ápakṣīyasvéty*), so it is implied that the deceased is conceived in these terms. The composer of the BU activates the metonymy PLACE FOR INHABITANTS which allows him to identify the deceased with the moon and thus with Soma. In CU 5.10.4, the moon is called the king Soma (*eṣa somo rājā*). Here it is implied that the deceased becomes one with the moon[105]. According to both Upaniṣads, the deceased is eaten by the gods in this stage. This evokes the descriptions of the ŚB which present mortal beings on earth as eaten by the gods in the sun. This concept is transformed here to conceive the afterlife situation. It is also possible that the composer of the BU refers to the concept of repeated death (*punarmṛtyu*): the deceased is supposed to increase and decrease cyclically which refers to the phases of the moon. The moment of being eaten is conceived in terms of interlunar[106].

The identity of faith with the deceased is confirmed in JUB 3.11.5 where it is said the deceased becomes the faith of his relatives (see chapter 5.2). It seems that this concept remained although its conceptual basis is already lost. The conceptual link between Parjanya and the gods is not strongly attested. The conviction that plants are gods's wives may imply identity of gods with Parjanya who inseminates plants (already in ṚV 5.83.1,7,9)[107].

---

105 Identification of the deceased with the celestial body which he reaches is expressed in JB 1.50: *sa evam etat tredhā vibhajyaitasya salokatām apyeti ya eṣa tapati* (see chapter 5.1.2).

106 The same concept is evoked by ŚB 2.3.3.8.

107 For metaphor RAINING IS INSEMINATION (see chapters 1.6, 2.2.1). For connection between Parjanya and the moon see Gonda (1986).

It is also possible that the concept of Parjanya as the representative of the gods is introduced here to activate the recipient's thinking about the rain as the form in which the deceased returns to the earth. In the version of the model of the Five Fires presented in JB 1.45 (see chapter 5.1), *parjanya* is replaced by *stanayitnu*, thunder. It is possible that the concept of thunder is meant to metonymically activate the concept of Indra whose weapon is *vájra*, a thunderbolt. Since Indra is conceived as the king of the gods, it can be argued that the concept of gods is introduced in the account of the BU and the CU on this metonymic basis.

Bodewitz (1997b) treats cremation as the sixth sacrifice. However, within the frames of the earlier background, attested already in the ṚV, cremation is the first cosmic sacrifice: the deceased, placed on the creation pyre, becomes the oblation to the fire and to the sun in the form of water or faith, *śraddhā* (see Jurewicz 2004).

In this way, the deceased become material of the world. They constitute the oblation for its destroying and life-giving creative power conceived in terms of fire. This process is conceived in terms of sacrifice which consists of pouring oblation (conceived in terms of food) into fire (conceived in terms of eater). Such a worldview is presented already in the ŚB (see chapter 3.1.1) and the authors of the Upaniṣads develop it in more detail.

The sense they give to death is the same as in earlier thought: death is life-giving. The sun shines when it kills men that are burnt on the pyre. Rain falls when the deceased are killed by the gods on the moon. The earth gives birth to plants that have killed the deceased in their form of rain. Semen arises in man when he kills the deceased in plants. The woman gives birth to man having accepted the deceased in the form of semen. As will be shown, the act of insemination is also seen as death in the JUB 3.8.10-3.9.1 (see chapter 5.2). It should be noted that all the forms of the deceased are life-giving. Soma gives health and immortality, rain gives water and renders possible the growth of plant, food supports life and from semen life is born.

At the end of the description of the *pitṛyāna* path, the composer of the CU presents two possibilities for rebirth. Those whose behaviour is pleasant are reborn in a pleasant womb as a member of one of the three higher social class. Those whose behaviour is foul are born in foul wombs as dogs, pigs or outcastes. The possibility of rebirth as a member of Brahmana and Kṣatriya class is also stated in JUB 3.28.4 where it happens according to the wish of the deceased (see chapter 5.2.3). According to the composer of the CU, the kind of birth depends on deeds performed in the previous life.

There is a third kind of beings that leads a very mean life:

BU 6.2.16

atha yá etaú pánthānau ná vidúḥ té kīṭā́ḥ patáṅgā yád idáṃ dandaśū́kam |

Those who do not know these paths, however, become worms, insects, or snakes'.

CU 5.10.8

athaitayoḥ pathor na katareṇacana tānīmāni kṣudrāṇy asakṛdāvartīni bhūtāni bhavanti jāyasva mriyasveti |

Then there are those proceeding on neither of these two paths – they become the tiny creatures revolving here ceaselessly. 'Be born! Die!' – that is a third state.

The difference between the third kind of beings and men on the *pitṛyāna* path is as follows. Men do not die, but they live as forms of the world as part of its life-giving processes. This is implied by the logic of the scenario of sacrifice in terms of which the process is conceived. The conviction that the oblation does not die appears already in the RV[108]. Other creatures are constantly born and die. Their life is meaningless. It is possible that the word *kṣudrāṇi* metonymically evokes little beings (*kṣudráṃ sarīsṛpám*, ŚB 1.5.3.11, see chapter 3.2.1) which look for food during rains which implies that they are constantly hungry. The composer of the CU had in mind those kind of creatures and thus he could express that their life is miserable and full of suffering.

*

My general conclusion is that according to the BU and the CU, the aim of man is to realise both aspects of reality. The unmanifest aspect is realised by those who go beyond it, the manifest aspect is realised by those who remain in it thanks to a proper life and a proper death. The composers of the ṚV, the AVŚ and the ŚB are interested in human activity that is concentrated within the manifest aspect. The composers of the Upaniṣads enlarge the range of their philosophical investigation and are also interested in what happens with those who go beyond this aspect and how to reach there. The ethics of the Smṛti period will try to harmonise these two ways within one human life and the postulate four stages of life (Olivelle 1993, Jurewicz 1994).

The composers of the CU and the BU develop earlier thought and put it in abstract terms in BU 1.4.6 where the manifest aspect is reduced to Agni and Soma, fire and oblation (see section 4.1.2). Such a conceptualisation of

108 ṚV 1.162.21ab: *ná vā́ u etán mriyase ná riṣyasi devā́m̐ id eṣi pathíbhiḥ sugébhiḥ*. See also Thite (1975).

the cosmos is based on the Ṛgvedic general model of reality transformation which is now verbalised and elaborated in a way that it could be used within the new metaphysical frames.

In their exposition, the composers of the BU and the CU also evoke particular Vedic beliefs and the way they are expressed, but do so in a different way. The composer of the BU conceives the sun as the borderline sphere between aspects of reality which agrees with the Ṛgvedic conceptualisation of the highest heaven (*paramá vyòman*). He also evokes the concept of people who are reborn as 'raising up to the worlds' (*lókān pratyuthāyínas*) which is also elaborated in JB 1.46 (*so 'sya lokaḥ punar utthāyai bhavati*, see chapter 5.1.1). Finally, he evokes the concept of mind in terms of which the first manifestation of reality is conceived.

The exposition of the BU also preserves traditional thinking in that its composer does not explicitly identify the moon with Soma. As I have shown, in the ṚV, Soma is conceived as an aspect of the sun (Jurewicz 2010a). The identity of Soma and the moon was slowly established during the Brāhmaṇas. To the best to my knowledge, in the ŚB, the moon is directly identified with Soma two times (ŚB 2.4.2.7 and 11.1.5.3). In ŚB 4.6.7.12 and 11.1.5.3, it is called the food of the gods while in ŚB 4.6.7.12 it is called the food of the sun. In ŚB 10.4.2.1, a year is identified with Prajāpati and Agni with the moon. In ŚB 6.5.1.1, the moon, identified with Soma, is one of forms of Agni. In ŚB 4.6.7.12, the moon is born from Soma and is called the food of the sun.

The composer of the CU evokes the Ṛgvedic concept of the identity of man with fire. He also highlights the role of *iṣṭāpūrta* and activates the earlier conceptualisation of time in terms of fuel (*saṃvatsara* instead of *pṛthivī*, see ṚV 10.90.6 chapter 1.3, see also chapter 3.2.3). He explicitly describes the influence of deeds performed by men in their previous life elaborating the JUB's account about rebirth as a member of the upper social classes.

On the other hand, his exposition is more analytical than is the exposition of the composer of the BU as far as the stages of the origination of rain are concerned. It is also more explicit in presenting the names of the elements of fires and the oblations in the exposition of the *pañcāgnividyā*: the word *pṛthivī* is used instead of the more archaic but, at the same time, more general expression *ayáṃ lokás*, *vāc* is used instead of 'opened' and *vyātta* is used which triggers the recipient to metonymically activate of the concept of mouth.

In his book (2007: 120), Johannes Bronkhorst claims that the Vedic elements in the Upaniṣadic descriptions of rebirth and karmic retribution are 'no more than an external veneer, a clothing which does not really belong to it'. My analysis shows that the authors of both the BU and CU knew the earlier tradition very well[109]. The descriptions of the *pitṛyāna* path in both Upaniṣads are very similar and the message conveyed by them is the same. To say that the account of the BU has 'something corresponding' (Bronkhorst 2007: 121) to the account of the CU is at least surprising. Neither I can see any implicit 'critical attitude to traditional Vedic learning' as being present in either descriptions (2007: 119). Their composers just describe two possible afterlife situations and do not judge if it is better not to be reborn than to be reborn within the manifest aspect. Finally, I have shown that there are close conceptual links between the model of the Five Fires and the stages of the *pitṛyāna* path which contradicts Bronkhorst's claim that their exposition is proof 'that the earlier Vedic ideas and materials are hooked onto a doctrine with which they are essentially unconnected' (2007: 124).

4.3.2. How to achieve the path of gods (*Chāndogya Upaniṣad* 4.10–15)

In this section, I will analyse CU 4.10-15 in order to show that the concept of path that leads to final liberation after death is attested not only in the teaching of Uddālaka. The context of this exposition is interesting because it evokes the ideas presented in the description of the third path of the deceased (see section 4.3.1) which proves the continuity of tradition. The exposition is presented in the frames of the story about a Vedic student Upakosala Kāmalāyana whose teacher, Satyakāma Jābāla, after twelve years of teaching him and other students permits them to return home but not Upakosala. Then the teacher goes on a journey. (CU 4.10.1-2). Upakosala gets ill and stops eating (CU 4.10.3) which can be interpreted as fasting during initiation (*dīkṣā*). Then he receives teaching from three domestic fires who tell him that *brahman* is breath, joy and space. Upakosala understands that *brahman* is breath but cannot understand how *brahman* can be joy (*kam*) and space (*kham*). The fires tell him that joy and space are the same (*yad vāva kaṃ tad eva kham* | *yad eva khaṃ tad eva kam iti* CU 4.10.5). The first form of the world is conceived in the Veda in terms of space (see chapter 3.1.1). The word *kam* is used in the cosmogony of BU 1.2.1 to denote the first positive experience

[109] It also shows that CU 5.10.7 logically follows earlier tradition and is in accordance with earlier beliefs about the afterlife and it even preserves some of its concepts (most obviously the concept of the moon as the highest sphere of the world). This is against Bronkhorst's claim that CU 5.10.3-6 and CU 5.10.7 'do not fit very well together' (2007: 121). I rather see the reasons for this clear exposition as being generally the more explicit and analytic approach of the CU.

of reality (see section 4.1.1). Since reality is one, both space (*kham*) and joy (*kam*) can be identified with *brahman*.

The fires teach Upakosala about breath and space (*prāṇam ca hasmai tad ākāśam ca ūcuḥ*). The householder's fire (*gārhapatya*) tells him that it is the earth, fire, food and the sun because it is man one sees in the sun. The southern fire (*anvāhāryapacana*) tells him that it is the waters, the quarters, the stars and the moon, because it is man one sees in the moon. The offertorial fire (*āhavanīya*) tells him that it is breath, space, sky, and lightning, because it is man one sees in lightning. As will be shown, in the cosmos, the visible form of *ātman* is conceived in terms of man manifesting in the sun (see section 4.4.2.2). The correct knowledge of the three fires gives knowledge of *ātman* manifest in the cosmos (*eṣa saumya te asmadvidyā cātmavidyā ca*, CU 4.14.2).

Finally, the fires tell Upakosala that he should ask his teacher for the final teaching. The teacher tells Upakosala that the fires have told him about the worlds (*lokān vāva kila somya te avocan*, CU 4.14.3). If the recipient activates the meaning of *loka* as the space of experience, he will understand that Upakosala now knows how to realise all kinds of positive experiences possible in the world evoked by the word *kam* in the beginning of the exposition. The concept of breath, with which *brahman* is identified, metonymically evokes the concept of the breath practice which led to this supernatural experience (see also section 4.4.2.4).

The topic of the teacher's teaching is called *gati*, the final goal, but also the way that leads it (CU 7.14.2). This is the state free from the influence of evil which state is conceived in terms of a leaves of a lotus to which water does not stick[110]. The teacher identifies *ātman* with man which is seen in the eye and defines it as immortal, free from fear and *brahman* (CU 4.15.1)[111]; in the same way Prajāpati began his instruction to Indra and Virocana (CU 8.7.4, see section 4.4.2.4). It is then implied that the knowledge of the whole of reality should begin with one's own self. Then the concept of two paths is introduced along which water or clarified butter flow[112]. Such a conceptualisation of paths brings the mind of the recipient to the Ṛgvedic conceptualisation of rain in terms of clarified butter (see Jurewicz 2010a). Thus he may create the concept of a path between the earth and the sky. This concept will be elaborated in the next paragraph (CU 4.16, see below). *Ātman* is called 'lovely-uniting'

[110] *ahaṃ tu te tad vakṣyāmi yathā puṣkarapalāśa āpo na śliṣyanta evam evaṃvidi pāpaṃ karma na śliṣyata iti* |

[111] *ya eṣo 'kṣiṇi puruṣo dṛśyata eṣa ātmā iti hovāca* | *etad amṛtam abhayam etad brahmeti* | CU 4.15.1.

[112] CU 4.15.1: *tad yady apy asmin sarpir vodakaṃ vā siñcati vartmanī eva gacchati* |

(*samyadvāma*), 'lovely-leading' (*vāmanī*) and 'shining' (*bhāmanī*) which is probably meant to evoke the concept of joy and light experienced during supernatural cognition.

In the next paragraph (CU 4.15.5), the composer presents the *devayāna* path in exactly the same way as it is presented in CU 5.10.1-2. The logic of the description implies that this is the afterlife lot of liberated man. The knowledge given by the fires is the knowledge which leads to cognition of the manifest aspect. This kind of knowledge is gained in traditional ritual activity. The knowledge of *ātman,* presented by the teacher, can be gained in breath practice and leads to the unmanifest aspect. The composer also states that the path described by him can be reached even by those who have not been cremated (*atha yad u caivāsmiñ chavyaṃ kurvanti yadi ca*, CU 4.15.5). This opposes earlier thought in the ṚV and JB where the cremation rite is seen to be a necessary condition for a happy afterlife (see chapter 5.1.2, Jurewicz 2008b, 2010a). It is important to note that here the exposition of the final liberation after death is put in a purely Brahminic context.

This context is elaborated in the next two chapters (CU 4.16-17) where the composer clearly refers to the description of the JUB 3.16-17 concerning the afterlife (see chapter 5.2.2). I will not go into details of this exposition and concentrate upon the similarities between these two accounts. The sacrifice, identified with 'that which purifies' (*eṣa ha vai yajño yo 'yaṃ pavate*, CU 4.16.1) is presented as having two tracks which are mind and speech (*tasya manaś ca vāk ca vartanī*). It is possible that the composer refers here to the two paths mentioned earlier along which water and clarified butter flow (CU 4.15.1). Speech is conceived in terms of water (ŚB 6.1.1.9, see chapter 3.2.2) and cognition is conceived in terms of the clarification of butter (Jurewicz 2010a). Thus the path with water is the path of speech and the path with clarified butter is the path of mind. The same conceptualisation of sacrifice is presented in JUB 3.16.1. Further description also agrees with the JUB: the Brahman-priest constructs the track of sacrifice with his mind and the Hotar, Adhvaryu and Udgatar with their speech; in order to express the role of Brahman the metaphor of a man walking with one leg or a chariot riding on one wheel is introduced (CU 4.16.3-4); JUB 3.16.1 presents it in the same way.

The next paragraph presents creation in terms of heating the worlds from which the essence comes, the final products being *bhūr*, *bhuvaḥ* and *svaḥ* (CU 4.17.1-3). A similar cosmogony is evoked twice in the JUB, in the beginning of the whole text (JUB 1.1) and in the context of dying (JUB 3.15.4-9, see chapter 5.2.3) and in both cases it ends with *oṃ* which is not mentioned in the CU. Then the composer presents the way the Brahman-priest cures the sacrifice if there is a mistake on account of a Ṛk-stanza, of a Yajus-formula and of a Sāman-chant; he does it by pronouncing *bhūr*, *bhuvaḥ* and *svaḥ* respectively (CU 4.17.4-6[113]). The curing activity of Brahman is also conceived in the same terms of binding various substances with aid of heat as in the JUB (3.17.4)[114]. In both texts it is emphasised that the Brahman-priest should be someone who possess true knowledge (CU 7.17.8).

In the JUB, the role of Brahman-priest is presented in order to show that his recitation influences the afterlife situation of man (see chapter 5.2). It is also possible that this is what is meant by the Brahman-priest quoted at the end of description:

CU 5.17.9-10

yato yata āvartate tat tad gacchati | (9) *mānavaḥ* |
brahmaivaika ṛtvik kurūn aśvābhirakṣati | (10)

Wherever it turns, there a human goes. (9)
Alone among the priests, the Brahman protects,
Like a mare, the men of Kuru (10)[115].

Olivelle interprets the subject of the dependent clause in the first hemistich as 'it', adding in his commentary that sacrifice is meant here ('wherever the sacrifice turns', 1988: 553). I would interpret it as referring to the place where a man goes. Thus the hemistichs would express the conviction that man goes to places from which he returns. It is possible that the concept of the rebirth is evoked here. Within the frames of this interpretation, the whole exposition of the role of the Brahman-priest, presented in CU 5.16-17, becomes fully justified. The composer, having presented the role of the liberating knowledge which does not need any ritual, presents the afterlife lot of those who perform rituals. For them a good Brahman-priest is needed[116] because the state of the deceased depends on his activity. It is important to add that, in the JUB, the final liberation is seen in terms of an ability to choose one's future rebirth

---

113 CU 4.17.7: *tad yathā lavaṇena suvarṇaṃ saṃdadhyāt* | *suvarṇena rajataṃ rajatena trapu trapuṇā sīsaṃ sīsena lohaṃ lohena dāru dāru carmaṇā* | CU 4.17.8: *evam eṣāṃ lokānām āsāṃ devatānām asyās trayyā vidyāyā vīryeṇa yajñasya viriṣṭaṃ saṃdadhāti* |

114 CU 4.17.4: *tad yady ṛkto riṣyed bhūḥ svāheti gārhapatye juhuyāt* | *ṛcām eva tadrasenarcāṃ vīryeṇarcāṃ yajñasya viriṣṭaṃ saṃdadhāti* | CU 4.17.5: *atha yadi yajuṣṭo riṣyed bhuvaḥ svāheti dakṣiṇāgnau juhuyāt* | *yajuṣām eva tadrasena yajuṣāṃ vīryeṇa yajuṣāṃ yajñasya viriṣṭaṃ saṃdadhāti* | CU 4.17.6: *atha yadi sāmato riṣyet svaḥ svāhety āhavanīye juhuyāt* | *sāmnām eva tad rasena sāmnāṃ vīryeṇa sāmnāṃ yajñasya viriṣṭaṃ saṃdadhāti* |

115 For interpretations of the second stanza see Olivelle (1998: 552).

116 CU 4.17.10: *evaṃvid dha vai brahmā yajñaṃ yajamānaṃ sarvāṃś cartvijo 'bhirakṣati* | *tasmād evaṃvidam eva brahmāṇaṃ kurvīta nānevaṃvidaṃ nānevaṃvidam* |

(see chapter 5.2.3). Thus the teaching of Satyakāma Jābāla turns out to be a reinterpretation of the JUB's account of afterlife within the frames of new possibilities gained thanks to liberating breath practice.

*

My main conclusion from the analysis of the Upaniṣadic passages connected with the belief in rebirth is that there is no doubt that their composers knew earlier tradition very well and referred to it. This is further proof that the relationship between the Upaniṣads and the Brāhmaṇas is very complex and that it does not consist on simple inserting some passages as assumed by Bronkhorst and other scholars (Bodewitz 2007, Gotō 1996) but on the conscious analysis of tradition and its reinterpretation. In order to look for the meaning of the Upaniṣadic concepts, one has to analyse the full context in which they were presented, not only passages taken from it. One should also take into account earlier tradition which seems to be a constant point of reference for the Upaniṣadic thinkers.

Although the concepts of the paths of fathers and of gods are proof of the attempts to incorporate the earlier metaphysical background into the new frames, the teaching of Satyakāma Jābāla shows that the main focus of the Upaniṣadic composers was on how to reach the unmanifest aspect and become finally liberated. This will be topic of the next chapter.

4.4. Liberating cognition

In this section, I will analyse the nature of the liberating cognition presented in the early Upaniṣads. It will be shown that the Upaniṣadic thinkers refer to breath practice which is not connected so much with ritual as it had been during the time of the Brāhmaṇas. It will be also shown that this practice allows its agent to realise his identity with the whole reality and it is an important source for understanding the world and philosophical concepts. The Upaniṣadic thinkers devote much space to describing the goal of this practice but there are accounts which analyse the stages realised during this practice. I will analyse selected expositions of the BU, the CU and the TU. The lists of identifications of *ātman* with elements of the cosmos, presented in many chapters of the BU and the CU, can also be interpreted as referring to the stages of liberating cognition, but analysis of this topic would go beyond the scope of the present research. Contrary to the later Upaniṣads, we will not find here much specific information as to how this practice should be performed. It could mean either that it was too obvious to be explicitly analysed or that it was a secret, or the thinkers were still searching for the best way of practice.

4.4.1. The state gained in liberating cognition

The aim of liberating cognition is to go beyond everyday subjective-objective cognition and to become aware of the unmanifest aspect of reality, the conscious factor of this cognition which gives cognitive access to the whole of reality. Ganeri (2007: 35) proposes to understand the liberation as 'catching' the self 'in its activity of sensing and thinking'. He writes:

> 'the self is caught in the phenomenological quality of thinking, in the flavour of experience of "what it is like" to think.'

Man is supposed to allow the reality that is present in himself to see itself "from the other side" as described in the cosmogony of the AU (see section 4.1.3), or to see itself in another being as it is described in the cosmogony of the BU 1.4 (see section 4.1.2). Although subjective-objective cognition is suspended the state of liberating cognition is a state of awareness. Yājñavalkya, in his discussion with Janaka which will be discussed at length below (see section 4.4.2.3), presents this state in the following way:

BU 4.3.23

> *yád vaí tán ná páśyati páśyan vaí tád ná paśyati | ná hí draṣṭúr dṛṣṭér viparilopó vidyáté 'vināśitvāt | ná tú tád dvitī́yam asti táto 'nyád víbhaktaṃ yát páśyet |*
>
> Now, he does not see anything here; but although he does not see, he is quite capable of seeing, for it is impossible for the seer to lose his capacity to see, for it is indestructible. But there isn't a second reality here that he could see as something distinct and separate from himself[117].

In order to explain the state of liberating cognition, the composer creates an internally contradictory sentence that when the liberated person does not see he sees. One could argue that such a contradictory statement is caused by lack of proper philosophical apparatus, but it is created intentionally because the liberated person realises the pre-creative contradictoriness of reality. Then the contradictoriness of the sentence is resolved: it said that the capacity to see cannot be lost 'because of indestructibility' (*avinaśitvāt*). The recipient

---

[117] The context of this description will be discussed in section 4.4.2.3.

understands that in the liberated state the ability to see is preserved although does not have to be used by the one liberated. The recipient may even presume that the liberated person can choose if he wants to see, or not, even when he has his eyes open. In his translation, Olivelle decided that indestructibility refers to the capacity of seeing, I would argue, however, that it rather refers to the indestructibility of the pre-creative reality. In this state, its unity is realised so subjective-objective cognition is not needed. But it still remains in its potential form.

Then other kinds of subjective-objective cognition are enumerated: smelling, tasting, speaking, hearing, thinking, touching, perceiving (knowing). Though they are suspended, yet the conscious power which enables those acts in everyday experience is all the time active because it, or rather its agent, is indestructible. Finally, the conditions for the occurrence of subjective-objective cognition are summarised:

BU 4.3.31-32

yátra vā́ anyád iva syāt tátrānyò 'nyát paśyed anyò 'nyáj jighred anyò 'nyád rasayed anyò 'nyád vaded anyò 'nyác chṛṇuyād anyò 'nyán manvītā 'nyò 'nyát spṛśed anyò 'nyád vijānīyāt | (31)
salilá éko draṣṭā́dvaito bhavaty | *eṣá brahmalokáḥ samrāṭ* | (32)

When there is some other thing, then the one can see the other, the one can smell the other, the one can taste the other, the one can speak to the other, the one can hear the other, the one can taste the other, the one can speak to the other, the one can hear the other, the one can think of the other, the one can touch the other, and the one can perceive the other. (31)
He becomes the one ocean, he becomes the sole seer! This, Your Majesty, is the world of *brahman*.' (32)

In the creative process, reality transforms itself into something different yet the same with itself. Then, within the manifest aspect, reality transforms itself again into subject and object and begins to experience itself as something different. The word *iva*, which Brereton (1982) understands as expressing indefiniteness, grasps the nature of creation within the frame of the monistic assumption. However, the aim of this creative experience of reality is to finally confirm its identity with both the subject and the object. As we can presume, on the basis of the cosmogonies, it is done on the macrocosmic scale all the time. In microcosmic scale, it should be done by the liberated person.

The state during which primeval unity is regained is conceived here in terms of flood. The concept of flood without any sign is already used in the *Nāsadīyasūkta* in a conceptualisation of the first form of the world which potentially exists, but, at the same time, does not differ from reality and is within itself (10.129.03b *apraketáṃ saliláṃ sárvam ā idám*, Jurewicz 2010a: 48–49). Conceptualisation of the liberated state in terms of the ocean conveys the same meaning: the lack of differentiation into subject and object and the potentiality to return once again back to duality. The word *iva* may evoke the experience at night which is evoked by the *Nāsadīyasūkta* description when one can see something in the darkness although one does not know exactly what this is (10.129.03a *táma āsīt támasā gūḷhám ágre*). The recipient can also activate conceptualisation of the borderline sphere between the two aspects of reality in terms of a dike (*setu*, BU 4.4.22, see section 4.2.2, CU 8.4.2, see section 4.2.2) and a more abstract conceptualisation of reality in terms of the full (*pūrṇa*, see chapter 2.6.1, BU 5.1.1, see section 4.2.2). Thus he may conceive the moment of liberation in terms of reaching the ocean the shores of which are invisible.

In this state, categories known from the everyday experience, including moral ones both positive and negative, loose their meaning:

BU 4.3.22

átra pitā́pitā bhavati mātā́mātā lokā́ álokā devā́ ádevā védā ávedāḥ | átra stenó 'steno bhavati bhrūṇahā́bhrūṇahā cāṇḍāló 'caṇḍālaḥ paulkasó 'paulkasaḥ śramaṇó 'śramaṇas tāpasó 'tāpasáḥ | ánanvāgataḥ púṇyenā́nanvāgataḥ pāpéna | tīrṇó hí tadā́ sárvāñ śókān hŕ̥dayasya bhavati |

Here a father is not a father, a mother is not a mother, worlds are nor worlds, gods are not gods, and Vedas are not Vedas. Here a thief is not a thief, an abortionist is not an abortionist, an outcaste is not an outcaste, a pariah is not a pariah, a recluse is not a recluse, and an ascetic is not an ascetic. Neither the good nor the bad follows him, for he has now passed beyond all sorrows of the heart.

Taking into account the fact that the experience of emotions is the motive for creation, the recipient can understand that they do not disappear. They are now experienced from the unmanifest perspective and grounded in the recognition of the unity of reality. Because subject and object become one in this state, the natural love for oneself is the basis for love for other beings and objects such as love for family, desire for wealth and power and longing for the gods. This is already mentioned in BU 1.4.8 (*tád etát préyaḥ putrā́t préyo vittā́t préyo 'nyásmāt sárvasmād ántarataraṃ yád ayám ātmā́. (...) ātmā́nam evá priyám úpāsīta*, see section 4.1.2), but is fully developed by Yājñavalkya who teaches his wife Maitreyī (BU 2.4, 4.5)[118]. When one realises oneness of himself (or herself as implied by the teaching of Yājñavalkya given to

[118] For interpretation of the form *párādāt*, see Brereton (1996).

Maitreyī) with reality, one repeats in micro-scale the creation described in BU 1.4.17 where *ātmán* becomes whole when he has wife, children, wealth and can act (see section 4.1.2).

Then the composer states that when one recognises an object as different from oneself, one is deprived of it. The object forsakes the subject and the epistemological state becomes ontological. And, since the subject is the same as the object, the subject that does not know the object is deprived of himself and becomes empty. In terms of earlier thought, in this state, man becomes like Prajāpati attacked by fire or dying of hunger. When one knows everything, one knows oneself and becomes everything that exists.

4.4.2. The nature of liberating cognition and its stages

It seems that the way towards mystic experience gained without Soma had already been forged by the time of the early Upaniṣads. There are passages which show that there were people who were able to successfully reach supernatural consciousness[119].

A full analysis of this problem would need separate research, so here I will limit myself to five accounts which are the clearest in this respect. The first account is the teaching of Śāṇḍilya (CU 3.14), the second is the debate between Ajātaśatru and Dṛptabālāki Gārgya (BU 2.1), the third is the debate between Yājñavalkya and Janaka (BU 4.3-4), the fourth is the teaching of Prajāpati (CU 8.1-12) and the fifth is the doctrine of five states of *ātman* (TU 2.1-5).

4.4.2.1. Tradition reworked (*Chāndogya Upaniṣad* 3.1-14 and *Śatapathabrāhmaṇa* 10.6.3)

I will begin my analysis of liberating cognition with the teaching of Śāṇḍilya (CU 3.14) and will read it in its larger context. I will take into account not only earlier chapters of the CU (CU 3.12-13) but also the teaching and its context which is presented in ŚB 10.1.3. My analysis will allow me to discuss three issues. Firstly, the continuity of tradition as far as breath practice is concerned. Secondly, how tradition is consciously reframed in order to present new ideas. Thirdly, a reconstruction of the main stages of the liberating process described in the Upaniṣads composed before the Buddha.

119 Even the way Yājñavalkya presents his theory to Maitreyī seems to reflect efforts to make her meditate. The text quietly repeats the same stanzas, changing only selected words in the way that could incite the calmness and concentration necessary to reach the supernatural state of consciousness.

The teaching of Śāṇḍilya begins with a statement about the unity of reality called *brahman* (CU 3.14.1):

CU 3.14.1

> *sarvaṃ khalv idaṃ brahma tajjalān iti śānta upāsīta | atha khalu kratumayaḥ puruṣo yathākratur asmiṃl loke puruṣo bhavati tathetaḥ pretya bhavati | sa kratuṃ kurvīta |*
>
> *Brahman*, you see, is this whole world. With inner tranquillity, one should venerate it as *jalān*. Now, then, man is undoubtedly made of resolve. What a man becomes on departing from here after death is in accordance with his resolve in this world. So he should make this resolve:

In the present state of research, the exact meaning of the hapax *jalān* is difficult to reconstruct (Olivelle 1998: 544). I will propose a tentative interpretation below. Man is presented as *kratumaya* 'made of resolve'[120]. The same conviction is presented by Yājñavalkya in BU 4.4.5 in a more analytical way (see section 4.4.2.3). In the ṚV, the word *krátu* means 'volition, will' (Reat 1990: 135). This word is used with the same meaning in many places of the ŚB which defines *krátu* in the following way: 'whenever he desires anything in his mind, as "Would that this were mine! I might do this!" that is will'[121] (*sá yád evá mánasā kāmáyata idám me syād idáṃ kurvīyéti sá evá krátur*, ŚB 4.1.4.1). In the earlier Veda, the word *krátu* also means 'rite'. As we will see, this dual meaning is preserved in the teaching of Śāṇḍilya presented in ŚB 10.1.3.1. In the CU, however, the composer narrows this meaning in his prescription expressed in the last sentence of the passage to 'make the resolve' (*sa kratuṃ kurvīta*). The content of the resolve is presented in the next passage of the CU and the recipient understands that *kratu* here means mental activity.

CU 3.14.2

> *manomayaḥ prāṇaśarīro bhārūpaḥ satyasaṃkalpa ākāśātmā sarvakarmā sarvakāmaḥ sarvagandhaḥ sarvarasaḥ sarvam idam abhyatto 'vāky anādaraḥ |*
>
> (This self (*ātman*) of mine that lies within my heart –) it is made of mind, breaths[122] are its physical form; luminous is its appearance; the real is its intention; space is its essence (*ātman*); it contains all actions, all desires, all smells, and all tastes; it has captured this whole world; it neither speaks nor pays any heed.

---

120 Thus Olivelle (1998).
121 Eggeling (1885): 'intelligence'.
122 Olivelle (1998): 'the vital functions'.

Qualification of *ātman* as composed of mind (*manomaya*) highlights its cognitive essence. The recipient may activate the cosmogony of ŚB 10.5.3 where reality in its pre-creative state is conceived in terms of mind (see chapter 3.5.1). Thus he will understand that the unmanifest aspect of reality is present in him. In the cosmogony of the AU, reality finally manifests itself in man and the cosmos as their innermost essence in order to cognise itself from within its manifestation. It is the highest cognitive agent which should be recognised in liberating cognition. In the description of liberating cognition in the BU (2.1, 4.3-4, see sections 4.4.2.2-3), *ātman*, as the highest cognitive agent, is qualified as composed of perception (*vijñānamáya*).

Qualification of *ātman* as 'made of breaths' (*prāṇaśarīra*) refers to the immortal self of the sacrificer built of sounds of the Veda during ritual and recitation connected with breath practice described in the ŚB. Its form is light (*bhārūpa*) which is the form under which reality manifests itself during liberating cognition. The compound *ākāśātman*, taken against the earlier background, can be understood as activating the initial creative stage when reality withdraws itself in order to create a place for the future world[123]. In the ŚB, this place is most often conceived in terms of a hungry belly while in BU 1.2, it is conceived in terms of death. Within the frame of this conceptualisation, reality manifests its ability to die and thus creates a void within itself. Then it manifests its ability to kill thanks to which it will have 'self', *ātman*. The recipient CU 3.14.2 understands that *ātman* described in this creative stage is reality in its unmanifest aspect: the self of reality is space which means that it is still empty. In this context, the reflexive nature of creation is highlighted thanks to *ātman* also being the subject of the sentence. The compound *ākāśātman* allows the recipient to understand reality as being divided into its unmanifest self, *ātman*, and into its self, *ātman*, which is not yet present but which already is. The same paradoxical situation is presented in the *Nāsadīyasūkta* with the use of the equivocal sentence *tuchyénābhú ápihitaṃ yád ā́sīt*.

The compounds *sarvakarman* and *sarvakāma* express the agency of reality within its manifest aspect: it is the agent of all actions and all desires. The next two compounds, *sarvagandha* and *sarvarasa* metonymically activate the conceptualisation of subjective-objective cognition in terms of eating. As food is firstly smelled and then tasted, in the same way the object of cognition is first perceived and then cognised. Thus the space (*ākāśa*) within it is filled with the cosmos which becomes the perceptible self, *ātman*, of reality. At the

---

[123] See BU 3.8.11, section 4.2.1.

same time, reality in its unmanifest aspect is beyond speech (*avākin*) and not influenced by anything that happens in its manifestations (*anādara*).

In the next passage, *ātman*, as the highest cognitive agent of cosmos and man, is presented as smaller than the smallest seed yet greater than all the worlds:

CU 3.14.3

eṣa ma ātmā antarhṛdaye 'ṇīyān vrīher vā yavād vā sarṣapād vā śyāmākād vā śyāmākataṇḍulād vā |
eṣa ma ātmā antarhṛdaye jyāyān pṛthivyā jyāyān antarikṣāj jyāyān divo jyāyān ebhyo lokebhyaḥ |

This self (*ātman*) of mine that lies within my heart – it is smaller than a grain of rice or barley, smaller
than a mustard seed, smaller even than a millet grain or a millet kernel; but it is larger than the earth,
larger than the intermediate region, larger than the sky, larger even than all these worlds put together.

The first set of qualifications refers to the innermost self of man and the second to the unmanifest aspect. Man, having cognised his self, will realise his unity with the whole of reality. In CU 3.14.4, *ātman* is identified with *brahman* (*eṣa ma ātmā antarhṛdaye | etad brahma*). In this concise way, it is implied that man in his liberating cognition repeats the creative cognition of reality described in the AU (see section 4.1.3) which, having manifested itself in the cosmos and man, sees itself as *brahman*. The recipient is prompted to activate the image schema of CONTAINER and to conceive the relationship between aspects of reality in these terms: man is conceived in terms of a container with the *ātman* present within his self as his content. Reality in its unmanifest aspect is conceived in terms of a container the content of which is the cosmos. This conceptualisation is elaborated in CU 3.12.6-9 (see below) and I will show that this chapter should be interpreted as providing the context for the teaching of Śāṇḍilya.

So let us look now at this context. The analysis of the full chapter would go beyond the scope of the present work, so I will focus on the two proceeding chapters. The whole book begins with a statement that the sun is the honey of the gods (*asau vā ādityo devamadhu*)[124]. Such a conceptualisation of the sun agrees with the Ṛgvedic general model of reality transformation according to which the sun is filled with Soma which, in the ṚV, is also called honey (*mádhu*). In CU 3.1.1-5, the analysis of the sun, conceived in terms of the

124 For *madhuvidyā* see also BU 2.5.

experience connected with production of honey, is presented. The concepts of the sun and of producing honey are the input spaces of the blend. The generic space is the concept of transformation.

In the blend, the crossbar (probably the branch of a tree on which the comb is hanging) is identified with the sky, the hive (or maybe the comb) with the space between the earth and the space between the earth and the sky (*antarikṣa*) and the larvae with glittering specks (*marīci*, CU 3.1.1). The honey cells are identified with the rays of the sun divided according to the five direction of the world (the cardinal directions and the upward direction, *ūrdhva*). The bees are identified as the Ṛk-stanzas, Yajus-formulas, Sāman-chants, the Atharva and Angirasa formulas and *ādeśas* which is translated by Olivelle (1998) as 'secret rules of substitution'. The flowers are identified with the corresponding texts (ṚV, YV, SV, AV) while the fifth is *brahman*. Thus, the blend is enriched with the next input space which is the concept of recitation of the Veda. The texts are called immortal waters (*amṛtā āpas*[125]) which implies that they are also identified with honey. This agrees with the conceptualisation of the sun as the source of Soma and the general model of reality transformation according to which rain appears from the sun. At the same time, the composer redefines this model according to contemporary experience. Just as Soma gave supernatural cognition, so in the times of the Upaniṣads the recitation of the Vedas and *brahman* leads to supernatural cognition.

Then the elements of the texts (Ṛk-stanzas, Yajus-formulas, Sāman-chants, Atharva and Angirasa formulas and the secret rules conceived in terms of bees) are presented as heating the corresponding texts. The concept of heating activates the general domain of Cleansing By Heat. The full reconstruction of the meaning of the passage would need more research on honey production in ancient India. However, the general aim of the process is to obtain a clear, bright substance which makes it similar to other specific domains of the general domain of Cleansing By Heat (Jurewicz 2010a). The traditional way of obtaining honey in India includes the use of a smoker to produces smoke which is meant to pacify bees, but it also activates the concept of heating. Then the comb is cut and squeezed. Honey is purified with aid of a cloth through which it is squeezed for a second time[126]. These two phases (squeezing and purification) are similar to the phases for the preparation of Soma.

---

[125] The composer of the CU may also evoke here the concept of immortality and water (*amṛtam āpas*) which is the first oblation poured into the sun in the model of the Five Fires presented in the JB 1.45 (see chapter 5.1).

[126] https://www.youtube.com/watch?v=j1xDKrR4pkY: https://www.youtube.com/user/WildFilms India. I am grateful to my student, Miss Magdalena Staszczak, for drawing my attention to this film.

The process of heating of the texts results in the appearance of states called *yaśas, tejas, indriya, vīrya, annādya and rasa*[127]. As already shown, these terms are used in the earlier Veda to express the supernatural state. The concept of glory, *yaśas* evokes the Ṛgvedic concept of fame (see chapter 1.7). The concept of fiery energy, *tejas*, activates the concept of being heated thanks to Soma or to the practice evoked in the ŚB. The concept of the power of Indra, *indriya*, evokes the concept of the main breath heating other breaths on the basis of its essence which is *índha* (ŚB 6.1.1.2, see chapter 3.2.2). The concept of virility, *vīrya*, evokes the power of Prajāpati to stand after resurrection in fire (ŚB 7.1.2, see chapter 3.2.3). The concept of food, *annādya*, also evokes cosmogonies of the ŚB which are generally conceived in terms of its creation. The concept of sap, *rasa*, not only agrees with such conceptualisation of creation, but also with the source domain: food is valuable thanks to its nutritious essence. This word appears in ŚB 6.1.1.3 in the description of the creation of a possibility to realise a supernatural state. It can be seen that the composer of the CU recruits from the earlier conceptual tradition. One can argue that it was so well known that it was enough for him just to mention the names of the crucial concepts to be sure that his recipients metonymically unfolded their full meaning.

The next stage of the process described by the composer of the CU agrees with the general model of reality transformation according to which heating results in the appearance of fluid. All these states are presented as flowing out (*tad vyakṣarat*). The verb *kṣar-* in the context of creation is used already in ṚV 1.164.41(*tátah kṣarati akṣáram*, see chapter 1.6) to present the manifestation of reality conceived in terms of speech. In the ŚB 6.1.3.6-7, it is used to describe creation of earth conceived in terms of Gāyatrī-stanza (see chapter 3.5.1). These states form (*rūpa*) the sun: the red (*rohita*), the white (*śukla*), the black (*kr̥ṣṇa*), the very black (*paraḥkr̥ṣṇa*) and that which flickers in its middle (*ādityasya madhye kṣobhata iva*)[128]. This analysis of the sun reflects the meditation on it attested already in the AVŚ (see chapter 2.5.3). Moreover, it agrees with the Ṛgvedic cosmology that sees the sun as filled with fluid which is Soma in times of the ṚV and with honey identified with the 'sap of the sap' (*rasānāṃ rasāḥ*) and 'immortal of immortal' (*amr̥tānām amr̥tāni*) in the CU[129]. Recitation of the Veda replaces Somic exultation. Since no agent is mentioned so far, the recipient understands that the composer

---

127 CU 3.1.3, 3.2.2, 3.3.2, 3.4.2, 3.5.2: *tasyābhitaptasya yaśas teja indriyaṃ vīryam annādyaṃ raso 'jāyata |*

128 CU 3.1.4, 3.2.3, 3.3.3, 3.4.3, 3.5.3.

129 CU 3.5.4: *te vā ete rasānāṃ rasāḥ | vedā hi rasāḥ | teṣām ete rasāḥ | tāni vā etāny amr̥tānām amr̥tāni | vedā hy amr̥tāḥ | teṣām etāny amr̥tāni |*

describes creation of the world conceived in terms of recitation which, in turn, is conceived in terms of production of honey.

In the next passages (CU 3.6-10), the composer describes the groups of gods who are active thanks to sap, *rasa*, also called 'immortal' (*amṛta*[130]). They are present in the respective forms of the sun. Conceptualisation of the gods as being on the sun continues earlier thinking. The gods are presented as being sated just by looking at the sap as they do not eat it neither do they drink. In this way, the composer activates conceptualisation of subjective-objective cognition and elaborates it. The recipient may infer that everyday life cognition is conceived in terms of eating and drinking food whereas supernatural cognition is conceived in terms of seeing.

In CU 3.6-11, the composer describes supernatural cognition as being realised in the sun by men. In this cognition, man gradually cognises the earth, the space and the sky (metonymically activated *via* the concepts of *agni*, *indra* and *āditya*, CU 3.6-8). Then he reaches the state which is realised on the borderline sphere between aspects of reality. This sphere is metonymically activated *via* the concepts of *Soma* (CU 3.9.9). The next stage is the beginning of being aware of the unmanifest aspect which will also come to an end (CU 3.10). In CU 3.11, the composer presents the state of final liberation which is realised when man mentally goes above zenith (*atha tata ūrdhva udetya naivodetā nāstam etaikala eva madhye sthātā*).

Each passage of CU 3.6-11 ends with the statement that men who understands the cognition of the respective gods will have power over them. The power over respective gods is limited. In the first two stages, it lasts as long the sun rises in the east to set in the west. In the third stage, it lasts as long the sun rises in the west to set in the east. In the fourth stage, it lasts as long as the sun rises in the north to set in the south. In the fifth stage, it lasts as long as the sun rises in zenith to set in the nadir. The way the intervals of the rulership are presented imply that man, during his meditation, reverses time[131].

In the fifth stage, man reaches the state when the sun never rises or sets and time is suspended (CU 3.11.1: *atha tata ūrdhva udetya naivodetā nāstam etaikala eva madhye sthātā*). The way to this state is knowledge

---

[130] Olivelle (1998) translates *amṛta* as 'nectar'. This translation hides the connection of this passage with the ṚV.

[131] CU 3.8.4: *sa yāvad ādityo dakṣiṇata udetottarato 'stam etā dvis tāvat paścād udetā purastād astam etādityānām eva tāvad ādhipatyaṃ svārājyaṃ paryetā* | CU 3.9.4: *sa yāvad ādityaḥ paścād udetā purastād astam etā dvis tāvad uttarata udetā dakṣiṇato 'stam etā marutām eva tāvad ādhipatyaṃ svārājyaṃ paryetā* || CU 3.10.4: *sa yāvad āditya uttarata udetā dakṣiṇato 'stam etā dvis tāvad ūrdhvam udetārvāg astam etā sādhyānām eva tāvad ādhipatyaṃ svārājyaṃ paryetā* | I am grateful to my student, Miss Weronika Wysocka, for drawing my attention to this issue.

of *brahmopaniṣad*, i.e. the hidden teaching on *brahman*. This is the most basic context of the teaching of Śāṇḍilya who begins with the statement that '*brahman* is this whole' (*sarvaṃ khalv idaṃ brahma tajjalān iti śānta upāsīta*).

Then the composer identifies the manifest aspect of reality with the Gāyatrī-stanza and with speech (CU 3.12.1)[132]. As shown, in the cosmogonies of the ŚB, the word *brahman* is used in reference to the sacred speech which becomes the foundation for Prajāpati and is identified with the earth. In ŚB 6.1.1.15, the earth is identified with the Gāyatrī-stanza at the end of creation (see chapter 3.2.2). The composer continues this way of thinking and identifies the Gāyatrī-stanza with the earth (CU 3.12.2[133]). The explanations for these identifications are based on ŚB 6.1.1.15.The identification of the Gāyatrī-stanza with speech is based on the phonetic similarity between the words *gāyatrī* and *gāyati* (CU 3.12.1) and identification with the earth is based on the fact that both are foundations for creation (CU 3.12.2). The composer also adds a new explanation for identification of the Gāyatrī-stanza with speech which is based on phonetic similarity between *gāyatrī* and *trāyate* which means 'to protect, to rescue from' (CU 3.12.1). Taking into account the role of sacred speech presented in earlier passages of the CU, this explanation is fully justified. We can clearly see that in these sentences the composer refers to the concept of *brahman* as conceived in the ŚB.

Then he elaborates this concept in a new way. He says that the earth is the same as the body of man (*puruṣa*, CU 3.12.3)[134]. The use of the word *puruṣa* allows him to simultaneously activate the concepts of the cosmos and of man. Just as entire creation rests on the earth, in the same way breaths (*prāṇa*) rest on the body. They also rest on the heart which is within man[135]. Thus the composer metonymically introduces the concept of breath practice which will be described in the next chapter. He also states that neither creation nor breaths extend beyond the earth and the body[136]. The recipient may presume that the composer now refers to the shared knowledge about the everyday functioning of living beings.

In CU 3.12.5, the composer presents the Gāyatrī-stanza as having four quarters and six types (*catuṣpadā ṣaḍvidhā*). To explain this, he quotes ṚV 10.90.3 (see chapter 1.3). I have already discussed the following passages of

[132] *gāyatrī vā idaṃ sarvaṃ bhūtaṃ yad idam kiñca | vāg vai gāyatrī |*

[133] *yā vai sā gāyatrīyaṃ vāva sā yeyaṃ pṛthivī | asyāṃ hīdaṃ sarvaṃ bhūtaṃ pratiṣṭhitam |*

[134] CU 3.12.3: *yā vai sā pṛthivīyaṃ vāva sā yad idam asmin puruṣe śarīram | asmin hīme prāṇāḥ pratiṣṭhitāḥ |*

[135] CU 3.2.4: *yad vai tat puruṣe śarīram idaṃ vāva tad yad idam asminn antaḥ puruṣe hṛdayam | asmin hīme prāṇāḥ pratiṣṭhitāḥ |*

[136] CU 3.12.2, 3.12.3, 3.12.4: *etad eva nātiśīyante |*

CU 12.6-9 (see section 4.2.1), so now I will only highlight their role in the whole context.

Firstly, I would like to point out that the concept of speech divided into four parts is also presented in ṚV 1.164.45 (se section 1.6). As we remember, both stanzas present the manifest aspect of reality with its borderline sphere. Secondly, conceptualisation of the Gāyatrī-stanza as sixfold may also activate earlier thinking. In ŚB 11.4.4.1 six doors which leads to *brahman* are mentioned (*ṣaḍḍha vai brahmaṇo dvāro*). As we will see, this Brāhmaṇa is also evoked in the next chapter of the CU (3.13 see below). Thus the composer implies that the unmanifest aspect of reality can be recognised thanks to knowledge of *brahman* which is conceived in terms of opening his gates.

Then the composer redefines the relationship between body, breaths and heart in the light of his new interpretation of *brahman. Brahman* is identified with the space which is outside and inside the cosmos, man and his heart. As present in the heart, *brahman* is qualified as 'full and nondepleting' (*pūrṇam apravarti*)[137]. This is a new understanding of *brahman.*

In CU 12.6-9, the exegesis of *Puruṣasūkta* is presented which uses the word *ātman* as meaning everything that is beyond and within man (*puruṣa*): the cosmos and man (for analysis see section 4.2.1). In the last sentence of his exposition, the composer introduces the concept of space of the heart (*antar hṛdayākāśa*) in which *ātman*, qualified as full and non-depleting (*pūrṇam apravarti*), resides.

Thus the composer presents a new interpretation of *brahman* as identified with the innermost self of man and cosmos. The word *ātman* is not used here, but the recipient may easily evoke it. The recipient also understands that even the knowledge of *brahman* realised in the middle of the sun will not allow man to understand *brahman* in its new meaning and to finally liberate himself. At the same time, however, the composer presents the results of this new knowledge in Ṛgvedic terms of inexhaustible fame:

CU 3.12.9

pūrṇam apravartinīṃ śriyaṃ labhate ya evaṃ veda |

Anyone who knows this obtains full and nondepleting excellence[138].

---

[137] CU 3.12.7-9 *yad vai tad brahmetīdaṃ vāva tad yo 'yaṃ bahirdhā puruṣād ākāśaḥ* | *yo vai sa bahirdhā puruṣād ākāśaḥ* | (7) *ayaṃ vāva sa yo 'yam antaḥ puruṣa ākāśaḥ* | *yo vai so 'ntaḥ puruṣa ākāśaḥ* | (8) *ayaṃ vāva sa yo 'yam antarhṛdaya ākāśaḥ* | *tad etat pūrṇam apravarti* | (9)

[138] Olivelle (1998): 'prosperity'.

Thus he implies that new concepts can be inscribed into earlier theories and their knowledge brings the same results as Somic exultation. He does not reject earlier tradition but enriches it. From the previous passages it is clear that knowledge of the Vedas and their hidden teaching is indispensable for liberation. However, present practice allows man to cognise and experience more. Traditional knowledge of *brahman* brings man to the borderline sphere between aspects of reality conceived in terms of the sun. The new knowledge of *brahman* will lead man to the unmanifest aspect which is conceived as being beyond zenith.

In the next chapter (3.13), the composer describes how the new knowledge of *brahman* can be realised. He presents five canals of the heart. The canals are oriented according to the directions of the world (eastern, southern, western, northern and the *ūrdhva* direction CU 3.13.1-6). He identifies the five breaths with cognitive abilities and parts of the cosmos. The eastern canal is identified with *prāṇa*, sight and the sun. The southern canal is identified with *vyāna*, hearing and the moon. The western canal is identified with *apāna*, speech and fire. The northern canal, *samāna* with mind and rain. The upper canal (*ūrdhva*) is identified with *udāna*, wind and space. The orientation of the canals according to directions of the world allows the composer to trigger the blend in which the heart of cognising man is the cosmos. Its input spaces are the concepts of the cosmos and of man while the generic space is the image schema of CONTAINER. The compound *devasuṣi*, 'canals of the gods', activates conceptualisation of the cosmic cognitive powers of reality in terms of gods (see AU, section 4.3.1).

Each breath together with the corresponding parts of the cosmos has an abstract form under which it should be venerated: *tejas* and *annādya* (splendour and food), *śrī* and *yaśas* (excellence and glory), *brahmavarcas* and *annādya* (lustre of *brahman* and food), *kīrti* and *vyuṣṭi* (fame and beauty), *ojas* and *mahas* (might and greatness). Such qualifications of the forms of breaths is grounded in earlier tradition. The nouns *śrī*, *yaśas*, and *kīrti* activate the Ṛgvedic concept of fame in terms of which a state of immortality, realised under the influence of Soma, is conceived (see chapter 1.7). The concept of greatness (*mahas*) is used in cosmogonies to denote the first manifestation of reality conceived as being possible to be measured (see chapter 2.2.2). In the description of the CU, the noun *mahas* appears together with the direction of *ūrdhva* which is reached in the beginning of supernatural cognition (see also chapter 2.2.2). The fact that most of the nouns connected with the four main directions activate the concept of light is the reason why in the definition of *ātman* given in the next chapter it is qualified as 'having form of light' (*bhārūpa*). The agent who recognises these forms becomes one with them.

If the recipient runs the blend, he will understand what practice looks like. Man faces east. He mentally concentrates on forms of reality and breaths in a proper way. I am tempted to think that the concept of food under which the eastern and western canal are conceived is grounded in experience: man eats food with his face which is directed towards the east and excretes with his anus which is directed towards the west.

Then the canals are called 'men of *brahman*, guardians of the gates to the heavenly world' (*te vā ete pañca brahmapuruṣāḥ svargasya lokasya dvārapāḥ*, CU 3.13.6). The concept of guardians of the gate activates conceptualisation of subjective-objective cognition in terms of entering an abode. It is activated in the cosmogony of AU 1.3.14 (see section 4.1.3) and is elaborated in the description of the afterlife state in KU 1.3-4 (see chapter 5.3). The conceptualisation of canals in terms of guardians agrees with its qualification as 'canals of the gods' (*devasuṣi*); as we remember, in the AU, the cognitive powers of reality are conceived in terms of guardians (*lokapāla*). The experience realised during breath practice is conceived in terms of making the guardians open the way to the abode they guard. Thus the unmanifest aspect of reality, manifest as the innermost self of man, recognises its identity with parts of its cosmic manifestation. This agrees with the cosmogony of the AU the composer of which presents reality as manifesting in man in order to cognise itself from there; he will understand that liberating cognition is the process which allows reality to do so. Simultaneously, in this way, man reaches a new cognitive perspective which is that of the unmanifest aspect.

It can also be seen that liberating practice is performed in the opposite order to creation. In the AU, reality enters man and the cosmos and manifests as their self, *ātman*. Now man allows *ātman* to expand from his heart. The canals are opened thanks to proper breathing. In the first stage of practice, the identity of *ātman* with the human organism is realised and in the second stage his identity with the cosmos. Thus the unity of the manifest aspect of reality is realised in the cognition of a particular human agent.

The concept of gate which is opened in human activity is evoked in ŚB 11.4.4 the composer of which mentions six gates to *bráhman* (*bráhmano dvā́ra*). These are fire, wind, the waters, the moon, lightning, and the sun. They are realised depending on the way an oblation is cooked. If the composer of the CU refers to this concept, he could present the breath practice in ritual terms and show that it leads to the same goal as earlier ritual practice. Both texts formulate the goal in the same way – as the heavenly world (*svarga loka*).

Then the composer states:

CU 3.13.7a

atha yad ataḥ paro divo jyotir dīpyate viśvataḥ pṛṣṭheṣu sarvataḥ pṛṣṭheṣv anuttameṣūttameṣu lokeṣv idaṃ vāva tad yad idam asminn antaḥ puruṣe jyotiḥ |

Now, far above here the light that shines from heaven on the back of everything, on the back of all things, in the very highest of the high worlds – it is clearly the same light here within a man.

The concept of the sun is again activated. Taken against the earlier chapters of the CU (3.1-10) the present description redefines them. The number of breaths is the same as the number of sets of rays of the sun and the order of directions of the world is also the same. The recipient may presume that breath practice leads to the borderline of the cosmos similarly to the knowledge that is described in the previous chapters. It is difficult to state whether the composer wants to replace traditional knowledge with the new practice or the breath practice refers to a process which is further realised in the sun.

The composer conceives the sun as being on the back of everything. Such a conceptualisation evokes the zoomorphic conceptualisation of the cosmos attested in the ṚV the source domain of which is the concept of a bull or a horse (see Jurewicz 2014a). The sun marks the borderline sphere between the two aspects of reality. This sphere is the starting point for recognition of its unmanifest aspect. In ŚB 11.4.4.7, which describes the doors of *bráhman*, the sun is the most important door which enables realisation of the full unity of the sacrificer with *bráhman*. This light is also present in the heart of man and the recipient understands that supernatural cognition begins with cognition of the space within it. According to CU 3.12.9, this space is *brahman*. It is worth noting that the last chapter of this book begins with the explicit statement that *brahman* is the sun (*ādityo brahmety ādeśaḥ*, CU 3.19.1[139]).

Now the composer describes how it can be cognised experientially:

CU 3.13.7b-8

tasyaiṣā dṛṣṭiḥ | (7)
yatraitad asmiñ charīre saṃsparśenoṣṇimānaṃ vijānāti | *tasyaiṣā śrutir yatraitat karṇāv apigṛhya ninadam iva nadathur ivāgner iva jvalata upaśṛnoti* | *tad etad dṛṣṭaṃ ca śrotaṃ cety upāsīta* | *cakṣuṣyaḥ śruto bhavati ya evaṃ veda ya evaṃ veda* (8)

We see it (7) when, on touching the body, we feel the warmth within it. We hear it when, as we press our ears shut, we hear something like the hum and noise of a blazing fire. One should venerate this light as something seen and heard. Anyone who knows this will become handsome and famous. (8)

139 It is followed by a cosmogony which is closely based on the earlier ones to explain, in ancient terms, the new concepts.

At the end of his exposition the composer presents the physical outcome of experiential recognition of *brahman* within one's organism. It is recognised as fire is recognised: by the heat of the body and a sound similar to the sound of fire. This is proof that conceptualisation of reality in terms of fire still motivates the way of thinking of the Upaniṣadic philosophers. It may also be a description of the experience felt during breath practice during which the body becomes heated.

The teaching of Śāṇḍilya is the next chapter of the CU (3.14). Seen within context the teaching explicitly specifies the final goal of cognition realised in breath practice which is the unmanifest aspect of reality. It also concisely resumes liberating cognition which begins with the recognition of reality within one's heart and ends with the recognition of its manifest aspect. Within the frames of the earlier thinking, it was impossible to go beyond the limits of the body and the world (CU 3.13.2-4). The new thinking allows for that that to happen.

As has been noticed by scholars (Gotō 1996, Bronkhorst 2007) the teaching of Śāṇḍilya also appears in ŚB 10.6.3. Bronkhorst (2007: 125–126) quotes Gotō (1996) who concludes his argument saying that the passage of the CU concerning *ātman*, conceived in terms of the immortal essence of man, was somehow inserted into the ŚB.

I will now analyse ŚB 10.6.3 to show that it was the composers of the CU who used this description and reframed it to present their own views. Moreover, this analysis will allow me to propose a possible solution to the problem of how to interpret *tajjalān* in the CU[140].

ŚB 10.6.3.1-2a

satyám bráhmety úpāsīta | átha khálu kratumáyo 'yám púruṣaḥ sá yā́vatkratur ayám asmā́l lókāt praíty evaṃkratúr hāmúṃ lokám prétyābhisámbhavati | (1) *sá ātmā́nam úpāsīta | manomáyam prāṇáśarīram bhā́rūpam ākāśā́tmānaṃ kāmarūpíṇam mánojavasaṃ satyásaṃkalpaṃ satyádhṛtiṃ sárvagandhaṃ sárvarasaṃ sárvā ánu díśaḥ prábhūtaṃ sárvam idám abhyā̀ptám avākkám ánādaraṃ* | (2)

Let him meditate upon the 'true *Brahman*.' Now, man here, indeed, is possessed of understanding, and according to how great his understanding is when he departs this world, so does he, on passing away, enter yonder world. (1).
Let him meditate on the Self, which is made up of intelligence, and endowed with a body of spirit, with a form of light, and with an etherial nature, which changes its shape at will, is swift as thought, of true resolve, and true purpose, which consists of all sweet odours and tastes, which holds sway over all the regions and pervades this whole universe, which is speechless and indifferent (2) (Eggeling 1897)

[140] For discussion of the meaning of *jalān* see Olivelle (1998: 544).

The description of the relationship between man and action (ŚB 10.6.3.1) is conceived in the same way as in the CU. The initial description of *ātmán* is also similar. The composer of the ŚB presents it as ruling all the regions (*sárvā ánu díśaḥ prábhūtam*) and pervading the world (*sárvam idám abhyā̀ptám*). Thus he activates the conceptualisation of *ātmán* in terms of a king. In his description, the composer of the CU omits the phrases which activate the source domain of a king (*sárvā ánu díśaḥ prábhūtam*), but elaborates the source domain of eating activated by the earlier compounds (*sárvagandha* and *sárvarasa*). This can be seen as one of the proofs that the composer of the CU reframed the text of the ŚB to try and make his description conceptually more coherent within the frame of his own exposition.

ŚB 10.6.3.2b

> *yáthā vrīhír vā yávo vā śyāmā́ko vā śyāmākataṇḍuló vaivám ayám antárātman púruṣo hiraṇmáyo yáthā jyótir adhūmám evám̐ jyā́yān divó jyā́yān ākāśā́j jyā́yān asyai pṛthivyaí jyā́yānt sárvebhyo bhūtébhyaḥ |*
>
> [E]ven as a grain of rice, or a grain of barley, or a grain of millet, or the smallest granule of millet, so is this golden Puruṣa in one's self[141]; even as a smokeless light, it is greater than the sky, greater than the ether, greater than the earth, greater than all existing things. (Eggeling 1897)

The general concept of *ātmán* presented by the composer of the ŚB agrees with the concept presented in the CU. *Ātmán* is present in the heart of man and surpasses the whole cosmos. However, the way it is presented is different. The composer of the ŚB conceives reality manifest in the heart of man in terms of a golden man (*púruṣo hiraṇmáyo*). Within the context of the ŚB, the concept of the golden man activates the concept of the Agnicayana ritual during which a figure of man made of gold was buried under the altar. In this way, the composer states that ritual has its internal dimension of cognition of reality and of transformation of sacrifice. He then creates the image of a smokeless light which draws the recipient's mind to the model of Child Of The Waters where Agni is presented in the same way (Jurewicz 2010a: 208). Since, in the ṚV, cognition of Agni as the essence of reality is realised under the influence of Soma, the composer may be implying that the results of ritual activity are the same. As we have seen the composer of the CU does not want to refer to ritual; in his exposition the word *kratu* means only mental activity. So he replaces these two qualifications of *ātman* with the general description *eṣa ma ātmā antarhṛdaye*.

[141] Eggeling (1897): 'heart'.

The description of *ātmán* in the ŚB 10.6.3.2 also allows me to propose a possible interpretation of *tajjalān* in CU 3.14.1. The composer of the ŚB first presents *ātmán* as smaller than anything in the world. Then in the form of golden man, then in the form of smokeless light, then as greater than parts of the cosmos and then as greater than the whole cosmos. This sequence iconically reflects the sequence of stages of supernatural cognition. Reality is first recognised within the heart of the cognising man, then it assumes specific forms that turn out to be greater than its manifest aspect. The reference to the ṚV confirms the meaning of supernatural cognition. The model of Child Of The Waters is used to conceive the content of the cognition performed under the influence of Soma. This model is evoked in ṚV 4.48.8-9 in the last stage of the vision of the poet (Jurewicz: 2010a: 240 ff.). Before this stage, the stage conceived in terms of a golden reed (*hiraṇyáya vetasá*) is described. It is possible that the stage conceived as a golden man in the ŚB corresponds to that stage.

As I have argued above, the metaphysical novelty of the Upaniṣadic practice is the recognition of the unmanifest aspect of reality. And this is concisely expressed by the phrase *tajjalān* on the basis of phonetic similarity between *jalān* and *jyā́yān*. The definitions based on phonetic similarity, so widespread in the Brāhmaṇas, are proof that it was one of the important factors in the creation of meaning in the Veda. If my interpretation is correct, then the expression *tajjalān* is meant to evoke the meaning 'greater than this' where *tad* can refer to the manifest aspect of reality (*sarvam idam*) identified with *brahman* in CU 3.14.1. The earlier context of this Upaniṣad allows me to argue that the composer activates the earlier Vedic use of the word *bráhman* which is sacred speech and then conceptualises the manifest aspect of reality in these terms. Thus the meaning of the first sentence of Śāṇḍilya's teaching in the CU is that all this world is *brahman*. Someone who is quiet should venerate it as it is greater than this because *brahman* is also the unmanifest aspect of the reality.

The second concept which can be activated on the basis of phonetic similarity is the concept of water, *jala*. As we have seen, the concept of water is extensively elaborated by the Vedic thinkers. It is also elaborated by the composer of the CU in earlier chapters: creation of the forms of the sun is conceived in terms of flowing out (*tad vyakṣarat*) while *brahman*, present within the space of man's heart and identical with the whole reality, is qualified as full *pūrṇa* (CU 3.13.7).

So my tentative interpretation of the expression *tajjalān* is as follows. This expression activates a blended concept. Its first input space is the concept of reality. Its second input space is the concept of cognising man. Its third input space is the image schema of CONTAINER. Its fourth input space is the concept of water. The generic space is the concept of transformation. In the blend, reality in its manifest aspects is conceived in terms of flowing water which overflows its container, while the adjacent containers that are taking the overflow are conceived in terms of the heart of man, his organism and the cosmos. This process takes place when man undertakes liberating cognition. Conceptualisation of speech in terms of water strengthens the coherence of the blend. In ṚV 4.58.5-7, thoughts are conceived in terms of streams of clarified butter identified with streams of Soma and streams of water (Jurewicz 2010a: 238 ff.). These liquid substances are presented as flowing rapidly which implies quickness of thinking. The recipient may also elaborate in the blend the image of a dike in terms of which the borderline sphere between the two aspects of reality is conceived in BU 4.4.22 and CU 8.4.2 (see sections 4.2.2, 4.4.2.4). The cognition of the unity of the manifest aspect is conceived in terms of rapidly flowing water which reaches a dike which it overwhelms thanks to its speed. Then the unmanifest aspect of reality is cognised conceived in terms of the second container. In BU 4.3.32, this aspect is conceived in terms of a flood (*salilá*) and the recipient may also activate this concept in order to understand the difference between the two aspects of reality. Putting this in other terms which also use the concept of water, in his cognition of the manifest aspect man cognises that reality is full (*pūrṇa*) and does not flow and, at the same time, it flows (*tátaḥ kṣarati akṣáram*, ṚV 1.164.41, see chapter 1.6). In the moment of liberation, he reaches not flowing fullness. Thus the new teaching leads to a transgression of the world and the body which was impossible within earlier frames. At the same time, we can see that its beginnings are attested in ŚB 10.1.3 which puts this fact more clearly than does the corresponding Upaniṣadic version.

Now let us look on the context of the teaching of Śāṇḍilya in the ŚB. Two earlier chapters in the ŚB (10.6.1.1-2) describe a debate about Agni as belonging to all men (*vaiśvānara*) between five Brahmins (Satyayajña Pauluși, Mahāśāla Jābāla, Buḍila Āśvatarāśvi, Indradyumna Bhāllaveya, and Jana Śārkarākṣya) who come to the house of King Aruṇa Aupaveśi. Each of them defines Agni Vaiśvāra differently: as the earth (*pṛthivī́*), water (*ā́pas*), space (*ākāśá*), wind (*vāyú*), the sun (*ādityá*), and sky (*dív*). The king answers that they know only aspects of Agni Vaiśvānara, namely, its feet (*pā́dau*), its bladder (*vastí*), its body (*ātmán*), its breath (*prāṇa*), its eye (*cákṣus*) and its head (*mūrdhán*). Then he points at parts of his own head and identifies aspects of Vaiśvānara with them (ŚB 10.6.1.11). The head is identified with the Vaiśvānara of pre-eminence (*atiṣṭhā́*), the eyes with the Vaiśvānara of Soma's splendour (*sutáteja*), the nostrils with the Vaiśvānara of diverse courses (*pṛ́thagvartman*), the space in the mouth with the Vaiśvānara of Plenteous (*bahulá*), the saliva with the Vaiśvānara of Wealth (*rayí*) and the chin with the Vaiśvānara of Foundation (*pratisthā́*).

Conceptualisation of Agni Vaiśvānara in terms of parts of a head activates cosmogonies the composers of which elaborate parts of a head to conceive the manifest aspect of reality (*Puruṣasūkta*, see chapter 1.3, ŚB 6.1.1 see chapter 3.2.2). The justness of this activation is confirmed as Agni Vaiśvānara, identified with parts of the human body, is called man (*púruṣa*), a form of man (*púruṣavidha*[142]) and as present in man. He who knows this conquers death and attains all life (ŚB 10.6.1.11). Moreover, the composer states that Agni Vaiśvānara does not hurt man who knows him. As it has been shown, such a conceptualisation of reality is elaborated in the AU and BU and is based on the monistic assumption. At the same time, the conceptualisation of Agni Vaiśvānara in terms of parts of a head reduces the whole human organism to his head which can be seen as the starting point of liberating practice (similarly as in BU 2.2.2 the human organism is reduced to the eye, see below, section 4.4.2.2).

In the next chapter, the composer creates three abstract models of the world, man and ritual activity (ŚB 10.6.2). The first is the model of the eater and food. The food, when eaten, becomes the eater (ŚB 10.6.2.1). In the ritual dimension, fire is conceived in terms of the eater and oblations are conceived in terms of food (ŚB 10.6.2.2). In the cosmic dimension, the sun is conceived in terms of the eater and the moon is terms of food (ŚB 10.6.2.1). In the human dimension, breath (*prāṇa*) is conceived in terms of the eater and food is the food. The relationship between the eater and the food is seen in terms of assignment. This meaning is built on the phonetical similarity between the words *ā́huti* and *ā́hiti* which is the noun created from the verb *ā́ dhā-* 'to give, supply, lend, deliver, to assign'.

The second model is the model of *arká*. In the ritual dimension, fire is conceived in terms of *arká*, and its oblations are conceived in terms of its joy (*kám*, ŚB 10.6.2.5). In the cosmic dimension, the sun is conceived in terms of *arká* and the moon in terms of its joy (ŚB 10.6.2.6). In the human dimension, breath (*prāṇá*) is conceived in terms of *arká* and food in terms of its joy (ŚB 10.6.2.7).

Eggeling interprets the noun *arká* as a fire's flame, but it has a larger meaning here. The composer of the ŚB conceives the relationship between *arká* and *kám* in terms of pleasure which is realised by fire when it receives oblation, by the sun thanks to the moon and by the breath when it gets food.

---

142 The compound *púruṣavidha* is used in the cosmogony of BU 1.4 (see section 4.1.2) which again shows conceptual closeness between thought of the ŚB and that of the early Upaniṣads.

In my analysis of BU 1.2, I have argued that, if the recipient evokes the literal meaning of the verb *arc-* from which the noun *arká* comes, which is 'to shine' and 'to sing', he would understand this noun as referring to ritual recitation which gives heat and causes sweating and that sweating, when one is hot, is pleasant (see chapter 4.1.1). The same meaning can be evoked here. The fire is hot and the oblations can be seen as cooling it. Similarly, the sun is hot and the cooling light of the moon is a pleasure for it. Hunger is conceived in terms of fire and it is cooled by food. At the same time, the composer triggers the recipient to evoke the concept of eating in in his explanation of the human dimension. In this way, the model of *arká* is identified with the model of the eater and food explained in ŚB 10.6.2.2-4).

The third model is the model of *ukthá*, part of the Sāman-song. In the ritual dimension, fire is *úk* and oblations are *thám* (ŚB 10.6.2.8). In the cosmic dimension, the sun is *úk* and the moon is *thám* (ŚB 10.6.2.9). In the human dimension, breath is *úk* and food is *thám* (ŚB 10.6.2.10). The relationship between *úk* and *thám* is seen in terms of the image schema of VERTICALITY activated on the basis of the phonetical similarity between *ukthá* and *úttiṣṭhati*.

The three models encompass the ways in which the human self, *ātmán*, is built. The first model explains the creation of the physical *ātmán* and the second two the creation of the ritual *ātmán*. The word *arká* activates ritual heating recitation. The meaning of recitation is also activated by the word *ukthá*. Since the word *arká* is a noun derivative from *arc-* from which the noun *ṛc* comes, the recipient may also understand that the *arká* model refers to the recitation of Ṛk-stanzas. The *ukthá* model refers to the recitation of the Sāman-songs. The instrument which enables man to eat and recite is the mouth. This agrees with the earlier identification of Agni Vaiśvānara with parts of the head.

Thus man (*púruṣa*) is like fire, like *arká* and like *ukthá* (*sá eṣò 'gnivídho 'rkávidha ukthávidho yát púruṣaḥ*). In the ŚB, the general noun *púruṣa* refers to reality, to Prajāpati, to the fire altar (ŚB 6.1.1.5-7, see chapter 3.2.2) and to the sacrificer. On this basis, the composer can expect that the recipient will understand the unity of reality realised during the ritual activity of man.

The teaching ends with a general description of the world's functioning which begins with breath: breath kindles fire, fire kindles wind, wind kindles the sun, the sun kindles the moon, the moon kindles the stars and the stars kindle lightning (ŚB 10.6.2.11). The world's functioning is thus conceived in terms of kindling fire as in the model of the Five Fires. The concept of breath metonymically activates the concept of breath practice. The composer implies that the world depends on man's breathing just as it depends on Prajāpati's breathing in ŚB 2.2.4 (see chapter 3.1.1). Thus breath practice transforms man into Prajāpati. The framework of the Agnicayana ritual justifies this interpretation. Moreover, the recipient understands that, during this process, man experiences his identity with the whole cosmos up to the borderline sphere of the cosmos. This sphere is conceived in terms of lightning. It will be shown that, in the Upaniṣads, the moment of liberating cognition which opens the way to the unmanifest aspect is conceived in terms of lightning (see section 4.4.2.4).

Within this context, ŚB 10.6.3 can be seen as a redefinition of the concept of *ātmán*. In the teaching of Aruṇa Aupaveśi, the word *ātmán* is used only once to denote the torso of Agni Vaiśvānara (ŚB 10.6.1.6[143]). In ŚB 10.6.3, the word *ātmán* is used to denote the totality of Agni which should be cognised. It is worth noting that in the exegesis of the Agnicayana ritual the word *ātmán* is similarly used to denote both the torso of the fire altar and the whole altar. As we have seen, liberating cognition is conceived in terms of overflowing containers that fill adjacent containers. The recipient can understand that *ātmán*, which is smaller than anything in the world, is present in his torso. The final aim of ritual recitation and breath practice is to understand *ātmán* as greater than its manifest aspect and to expand the meaning of this word to all reality. I would argue that Aruṇa Aupaveśi is still the subject of the teaching presented in ŚB 10.6.3. It is put in the mouth of Śāṇḍilya in order to evoke another authority to strengthen the power of his argument[144].

In the CU, the same story about a debate appears in 5.11.24 immediately after the description of the model of the Five Fires and the paths of afterlife. The names of the Brahmins change to an extent (Prācīnaśāla Aupamanyava, Satyayajña Pauluṣi, Indradyumna Bhāllaveya, Jana Śārkarākṣya and Buḍila Āśvatarāśvi) and the context of the debate is more complex: they first want to be taught by Uddālaka Āruṇi who, not sure of his knowledge, takes them to king Aśvapati Kaikeya who accepts them as his officiating priests (see Black 2007: 112–114). The topic of the debate is *ātman-brahman* (CU 5.11.1: *ko na ātmā kiṃ brahmeti*) which is then qualified as *vaiśvānara* by all the Brahmins (CU 5.12.1, 5.13.1, 5.14.1, 5.15.1, 5.16.1, 5.17.1) and by the king himself (CU 5.18.1, see below). This qualification shows the close conceptual links with ŚB 10.6.1.1. The debate is presented in the same way with the Brahmins knowing only aspects of *ātman*. The elements identified with *ātman* are the same as in the ŚB 10.6.1, although the order of their enumeration is different. The composer of the ŚB elaborates the image schema of VERTICALITY (earth,

[143] As in the exegesis of the Agnicayana (ŚB 6.1.1.6, see chapter 3.2.2).

[144] As Black (2007: 34) argues, 'Śāṇḍilya is one of the first Brahmins in Vedic literature that becomes known primarily as a teacher rather than as a ritualist'.

water, space between the earth and the sky, wind and the sun). The sequence presented by the composer of the CU is as follows: the sky, the sun, wind, the space and water. Qualification of the elements identified with *ātman* in most cases is the same. Then the composer of the CU identifies the elements mentioned by the Brahmins with parts of the body; he does not state explicitly that the king identifies them himself as in ŚB 10.6.1.11. Contrary to the ŚB, he does not limit himself to the head, but includes other parts of the body and three sacrificial fires (CU 5.18.2)[145].

The composer concludes:

CU 5.18.1

tān hovāca | ete vai khalu yūyaṃ pṛthag ivemam ātmānaṃ vaiśvānaraṃ vidvāṃso 'nnam attha | yas tv etam evaṃ prādeśamātram abhivimānam ātmānaṃ vaiśvānaram upāste sa sarveṣu lokeṣu sarveṣu bhūteṣu sarveṣv ātmasv annam atti |

Then he said to them: 'You who know this self here, the one common to all men, as somehow distinct – you eat food. But when someone venerates this self here, the one common to all men, as measuring the size of a span and yet as beyond all measure, he eats food within all the worlds, all the beings and all the selves.

In the first sentence, the composer activates the concept of eating. In these terms, partial subjective-objective cognition is conceived. Then he says that *ātman vaiśvānara* should be venerated as measuring the size of a span (*prādeśamātra*). Generally, a span is the distance between the thumb and the forefinger. The man who does this is conceived in terms of someone who eats food in all worlds, all beings and all selves. Such a conceptualisation directs the recipient's mind to the cosmogonies of the ŚB which present Prajāpati as creating the cosmos conceived in terms of his self which is built thanks to eating. The wording may even prompt him to activate ŚB 10.4.2.21-22, 26 (see chapter 3.4). We could say that the Upaniṣadic exposition of the results of proper cognition of *ātman* is more Brāhmaṇic than the corresponding exposition of the ŚB:

ŚB 10.6.1.10

tā́n hovāca eté vaí yūyám pṛ́thag vaiśvānarā́n vidvā́ṃsaḥ pṛ́thag ánnam aghasta prādeśamātrám iva ha vaí devā́ḥ súviditā abhisámpannās táthā tú va enān vakṣyāmi yáthā prādeśamātrám evā̀bhisampādayiṣyāmī́ti |

---

145 CU 5.18.2: *tasya ha vā etasyātmano vaiśvānarasya mūrdhaiva sutejāś cakṣur viśvarūpaḥ prāṇaḥ pṛthagvartmātmā saṃdeho bahulo bastir eva rayiḥ pṛthivy eva pādāv ura eva vedir lomāni barhir hṛdayaṃ gārhapatyo mano 'nvāhāryapacana āsyam āhavanīyaḥ |*

> He said to them, 'Ye then, knowing different Vaiśvānaras, have been feeding on different kinds of food; but verily, the well-beknown gods have attained, as it were, the measure of a span; but I will so tell them unto you that I shall make them attain no more nor less than the measure of a span.

Partial subjective-objective cognition is conceived in terms of eating in the same way as in the CU. Both expositions agree that reality is conceived as having the measure of a span (*prādeśamātram*). According to Coomaraswamy (1946: 146), '*[p]rādeśa* is a measured or indicated field or extent, situation or predicament; a 'span' not of fixed value but to be understood according to the context'. It is used in a few places in the ŚB in reference to ritual measuring[146]. In ŚB 7.5.1.14, the compound *prādeśamatrá* is used to qualify Viṣṇu who, when he was an embryo, was a span long, but then became as great as the whole cosmos. In another place, where the myth of the boar Emūṣa is evoked, the earth, before being dug up by Emūṣa, is qualified as 'a span long' (*prādeśamatrá*). Since the essence of earth is breadth (see ŚB 6.1.1.15, chapter 3.2.2), the recipient understands that the earth expands in order to become itself. In these contexts, the use of *prādeśamatrá* implies the potential expansion of what is just a span's width. This concept is evoked in the CU by the word *abhivimāna*. Thus the account of the CU looks like an exegesis of the account of the ŚB the composer of which did not feel the necessity to express the concept explicitly.

Then the king described in the ŚB states that he will explain how to cognise Agni who has the measure of a span (*táthā tú va enān vakṣyāmi yáthā prādeśamātrám evàbhísampādayiṣyāmī́ti*, ŚB 10.6.1.10). I would interpret *evá* differently to Eggeling. In my view, the intention of the composer is to emphasise that now the knowledge of reality present within man will be explained. This is fully justified within the context of the whole chapter of the ŚB which ends with teaching about *ātmán* as being present in man and yet greater than all creation. It is important to note that the composer of ŚB 10.6.3 having presented *ātmán* in its unmanifest aspect calls it 'the self of the breath' (*sá prāṇásyātmā́, ŚB* 10.6.3.2). He is pointing out that *ātmán* in his potentiality can be reached through breath practice. This breath practice is described in the preceding chapter of the ŚB (10.6.2), discussed above.

The composer of CU 5 also presents a breath practice but does it differently to the composer of the ŚB. He redefines the way the Agnihotra ritual should be performed (CU 5.19-23)[147]. The redefinition is based on the identification of offering an oblation with breaths: *prāṇa*, *vyāna*, *apāna*,

---

[146] E.g. ŚB 3.5.4.5, 6.3.1.33. Is it the source of the concept of *ātman aṅguṣṭhamātra*?

[147] Bodewitz (1973: 264–269, 213–343).

samāna and *udāna*. Each act of oblation satisfies (*tṛpyati*) the corresponding parts of the cosmos. The first oblation by satisfying *prāṇa* satisfies: sight, the sun, the sky and everything below them. It is important to add that the first oblation is identified with the eating of food by the sacrificer. Then the four other breaths are satisfied corresponding to the four oblations given in the morning and evening Agnihotra. The satisfaction of *vyāna* satisfies: hearing, the moon, the quarters, and whatever is below them. The satisfaction of *apāna* satisfies: speech, fire and the earth with everything what is above them. The satisfaction of *samāna* satisfies: the mind, the rain and lightning with everything that is above them. The satisfaction of *udāna* satisfies: the wind and space with everything that is above them. Thus the composer of the CU reinterprets Agnihotra as breath practice.

*

So the state of affairs is as follows. In the ŚB, there are three chapters I would treat as one teaching. In the first, a discussion about Agni Vaiśvānara is presented (ŚB 10.6.1). The next presents a possibility for gaining knowledge within the frames of ritual including recitation of the Veda and breath practice (ŚB 10.6.2). The third presents the teaching of Śāṇḍilya (ŚB 10.6.3). The qualification of *ātmán* as the self of the breath (*prāṇásyātmā́*) unites this teaching with the preceding chapters.

In the CU, the discussions about *ātman* qualified as *vaiśvānara* and a breath practice which leads to its cognition are presented separately (CU 5.11-24). It is preceded by the description of the model of the Five Fires and two possible afterlife states. It is worth noting that the description of this model and of the two possible afterlife states is presented in the context of the exegesis of the Agnihotra in the JB also (see chapter 5.1). Qualification of *ātman* as *vaiśvānara* is also influenced by the exposition in the JB 1.46 because the composer of the JB calls 'fire' in the model of the Five Fires *agni vaiśvānara* (see chapter 5.1).

The teaching of Śāṇḍilya appears in CU 3.14 after the presentation of a breath practice. It commences with the metaphysic assumption of the unity of reality (CU 3.1-11) and ends with experiential ways for gaining cognition of *ātman* (CU 3.12-13). It is important to note that breath practice is generally seen in the same way in both chapters of the CU (3.13 and 5.19-23). The sequence of breaths is the same and the elements of the cosmos satisfied in this process thanks to satisfaction of breaths are the same too. This fact can be seen as proof that the composers of the CU saw the conceptual links between these two expositions although they separated them. At the same time, the composer of CU 5.17-22 evokes the concept of eating as the conceptual basis for the breath practice identified with the Agnihotra. This conceptualisation is close to that of ŚB 10.6.2 where cosmic and human transformations are expressed in the model of the eater and the food. This all leads to me conclusion that it is the composer of the CU who refers to the ŚB rather than the opposite.

If we accept the views of Gotō and Bronkhorst, that teaching of Śāṇḍilya in the ŚB is an insertion, this would not solve the problem of the origin of the earlier two chapters of the ŚB (10.6.1-2) which display a striking correspondence with the CU (5.13-18). Have the composers of the ŚB inserted them as well and, if they did, what could be the reason?

Therefore, my conclusion is that the composers of the CU knew well the earlier material and used it their expositions. The reasons for the composers of the CU divided the teaching of the ŚB into two parts are not clear in the present state of research. There is no doubt, however, that they wanted to redefine ritual practice in the light of new ways of cognition of reality and its understanding. My analysis also shows that it is impossible to fully understand the teaching of the Upaniṣads without knowledge of earlier tradition because its composers constantly refer to that earlier tradition.

*

On the basis of the above analysis, the basic stages of liberating practice can be reconstructed. In the first stage, man recognises the identity of his innermost self in its unmanifest aspect with his organism. In the second stage, he recognises its identity with the cosmos and reaches the borderline sphere between the two aspects. Then he finally recognises the unity of all reality. The sequence of liberating cognition is in reverse order to the sequence of creation. The state realised in liberating cognition is the same state as that realised after death which agrees with earlier conceptualisations of Somic exultation. Liberating cognition is realised in a breath practice. As we will see other composers of the Upaniṣad generally see liberating cognition in the same way.

4.4.2.2. How the unmanifest can be seen (*Bṛhadāranyaka Upaniṣad* 2.1-3)

The composer of this chapter begins with a description of the context of the debate. Dṛptabālāki Gārgya, a Brahmin, comes to the king of Kāśi, Ajātaśatru, and wants to teach him *brahman* (for a very similar story, see KU 4). Ajātaśatru promises Dṛptabālāki a thousand cows for that (see Black

2007: 119–120, 127–129). Dṛptabālāki then consecutively identifies *brahman* with man (*púruṣa*) in the sun (*ādityá*, BU 2.1.2), in the moon (*candrá*, BU 2.1.3), in lightning (*vidyút*, BU 2.1.4), in space (*ākāśá*, BU 2.1.5), in the wind (*vāyú*, BU 2.1.6), in fire (*agní*, BU 2.1.7), in waters (*ā́pas*, BU 2.1.8), in a mirror (*ādarśá*, BU 2.1.9), with a sound that one hears behind him when he walks (*yá evā̀yáṃ yántaṃ paścā́c śábdo 'nūdéty*, BU 2.1.10), with a man in quarters (*dikṣú púruṣa*, BU 2.1.11), with a man composed of shadow (*chāyāmáyah púruṣa*, BU 2.1.12) and finally with man in one's self (*ātmáni púruṣa*, BU 2.1.13) understood here as the human organism. Such partial knowledge reminds the recipient of the partial knowledge of Agni Vaiśvānara described in ŚB 10.6.1.1-2 (see section 4.4.2.1).

The concept of a man in parts of the cosmos is used to conceive the form of *ātmán* that can be perceived in its manifest aspect during breath practice. Conceptualisation of these forms in terms of a man allows the composer to convey the meaning of self-cognition: as one sees oneself in the eye of others in a similar way one can see oneself in parts of the cosmos (see sections 4.3.2, 4.4.2.4). The aim of liberating cognition is to find a manifestation of reality which leads the agent to recognise himself in it as a whole.

For Ajātaśatru, the forms enumerated by Dṛptabālāki are not forms of *bráhman*, of all reality, and give only partial cognition and partial success. Identification of *bráhman* with a man in the sun leads only to a conceptualisation of reality in terms of a king (BU 2.1.2[148]) based on metaphor THE SUN IS A KING. Its identification with a man in the moon leads to its conceptualisation in terms of Soma (THE MOON IS SOMA, BU 2.1.3[149]). Identification with lightning is its conceptualisation in terms of something radiant (BU 2.1.4[150]) based on the metonymy COLOUR FOR SUBSTANCE[151]. Identification with a man in space is its conceptualisation in terms of the full and immovable (BU 2.1.5[152]) which is the way reality is conceived in BU 5.1.1 (see section 4.2.2). Identification with a man in the wind is its conceptualisation in terms of Indra Vaikuṇṭha and his invincible weapon (BU 2.1.6) which we may presume is his thunderbolt, *vájra*[153]; Indra is a god of wind. Identification with a man in fire is its conceptualisation in terms of something which is irresistible (*viṣāsáhi*, BU 2.1.7[154]) based on the metonymy FEATURE FOR AN OBJECT.

[148] BU 2.1.2: *atiṣṭhā́ḥ sárveṣāṃ bhūtā́nāṃ mūrdhā́ rā́jéti vā́ ahám etám úpāsa íti*|

[149] BU 2.1.3: *bṛhán pā́ṇḍaravāsāḥ sómo rā́jéti vā́ ahám etám úpāsa íti.*

[150] BU 2.1.4: *tejasvī́ti vā́ ahám etám úpāsa íti* |

[151] An instantiation of metonymy DEFINING PROPERTY FOR CATEGORY (Radden, Kövecses 1999: 35).

[152] BU 2.1.5: *pūrṇám ápravartī́ti vā́ ahám etám úpāsa íti* | (see CU 3.12.9)

[153] BU 2.1.6: *índro vaikuṇṭhó 'parājitā sénéti vā́ ahám etám úpāsa íti* |

[154] BU 2.1.7: *viṣāsáhir íti vā́ ahám etám úpāsa íti* |

Identification with a man in waters leads to the conceptualisation of reality as the resemblance one sees when one sees oneself reflected in the water (BU 2.1.8[155]). Identification of *bráhman* with a man in a mirror leads to the conceptualisation of reality as shining; the probable reason being that a mirror should be bright in order to reflect anything (BU 2.1.9[156]).

At the same time, this set of comparisons seems to activate the stages of liberating cognition. The first two are conceived in the same way as in BU 2.3.6 where reality is conceived in terms of a king and in terms of Soma. The concept of lightning evoked in the third comparison can be seen as a source domain for the beginning of supernatural cognition. In this stage of cognition, reality is conceived in terms of something which is immovable and full. This concept may lead the recipient to conceive this stage of cognition in terms of 'unmarked flood' (*ápraketam salilám*, ṚV 10.129.3b). In order to recognise it, the subject activates the main breath which is conceived in terms of at the beginning of creation in ŚB 6.1.1.2 (see chapter 3.2.2). Then reality is conceived in terms of fire. In the final two conceptualisations, the subject realises his identity with reality. Yet they retain the division into subject and object which is implied by the concept of looking at oneself in water and in a mirror. It is worth noting that the last two identifications are evoked in CU 8.7 at the beginning of teaching of Prajāpati when Indra and Virocana receive false knowledge of *ātman* as their outward appearance (see section 4.4.2.4).

Then the composer of BU 2.1 describes further stages of liberating cognition. This exposition can be seen as an attempt to define the subtle stages just before subjective-objective cognition is suspended. Identification of *bráhman* with the sound of someone who walks behind is interpreted by Ajātaśatru as its conceptualisation of life (BU 2.1.10[157]). This conceptualisation evokes the definition of *ātmán* the knowledge of which fills the agent with fire so that he can burn everything that is in front of him (BU 1.2.1, see section 4.1.1). The concept of fire is evoked *via* the concept of *ásu*, 'life' but also 'breath' which is conceived in terms of fire already in the RV[158]. Identification of *brahman* with man in quarters is interpreted by Ajātaśatru as its conceptualisation in terms of an inseparable companion (BU 2.1.11)[159]. We can see that the concept of the second is still present in these stages of liberation. This concept is also present in the identification of *brahman* with

[155] BU 2.1.8: *pratirūpá íti vā́ ahám etám úpāsa íti* |
[156] BU 2.1.9: *rociṣṇúr íti vā́ ahám etám úpāsa íti* |
[157] BU 2.1.10: *asúr íti vā́ ahám etám úpāsa íti* |
[158] Fire has breath (*ásu*) in ṚV 10.12.1.
[159] BU 2.1.11: *dvitī́yo 'napagá íti vā́ ahám etám úpāsa íti* |

shadow (BU 2.1.12[160]) because a shadow can be seen as someone other who never leaves man. This identification is interpreted by Ajātaśatru as its conceptualisation in terms of death. Death is conceived as the shadow of reality and is identified with Agni in the ṚV (Jurewicz 2010a: 327–329). The identification of *bráhman* with a man in a human organism leads to its conceptualisation as an agent possessing the body (BU 2.1.13[161]). The recipient is prompted to evoke BU 1.2.1 where the beginnings of creation are conceived in terms of death which wants to possess itself (*tán máno 'kurutātmanvī́ syām íti*, see section 4.1.1). The concept of the other is still preserved in this stage of liberating cognition.

As we can see, all the conceptualisations of reality recognised by Dṛptabālāki, given by Ajātaśatru, are entrenched in Vedic thinking. It seems as if Dṛptabālāki is lost in his practice and is trying to concentrate upon various forms of the manifest aspect of reality without being able to realise cognition of the whole.

Then the practice which leads to the true cognition of reality is presented. Ajātaśatru takes Dṛptabālāki by his hand and they approach a sleeping man. Firstly, Ajātaśatru tries to wake him up by calling him with one of names mentioned by Dṛptabālāki: 'Soma, great king dressed in white' (*bṛhán pā́ṇḍaravāsaḥ sóma rājan*, BU 2.1.15), but the man does not wake up. Putting this in cognitive terms, we could say that Ajātaśatru builds a multimodal metaphor[162]. A sleeping man is the source domain for man in terms of which reality as a whole is conceived. Its presence before the liberation of a particular human being is conceived in terms of its sleep. The source domain is expressed *via* visual and verbal signs. Ajātaśatru shows that it is impossible to cognise reality with aid of the names Dṛptabālāki has mentioned. Then the king touches the man and he wakes up. In this way, he presents effective meditative practice conceived in terms of touching.

I would like to note that a similar conceptualisation can be activated in the description of the debate between Yājñavalkya and Jāratkāva Ārtabhāga (BU 3.2.13). Jāratkāva asks Yājñavalkya what happens to a man when he dies and all elements of his body resolve in elements of the cosmos (*kvā̀yáṃ tadā́ púruṣo bhavatī́ty*). Yājñavalkya takes Jāratkāva by the hand and they leave the assembly. The topic there is action (*kárman*) and it is rendered by the composer in the following sentence: a man becomes good by good deeds, evil by evil deeds (*púṇyo vaí púṇyena kármaṇā bhavati pā́paḥ pā́penéti*). This is a very general statement which can be applied not only to man's situation

[160] BU 2.1.12: *mṛtyúr íti vā́ ahám etám úpāsa íti* |
[161] BU 2.1.13: *ātmanvī́ti vā́ ahám etám úpāsa íti* |
[162] For multimodal metaphor, see Forceville, Urios-Aparisi (2009).

after death but also to his life[163]. The fact that Yājñavalkya teaches Jāratkāva about the influence of action on man in secret may imply that a new teaching is introduced[164], but, even if it is the case, the nature of this novelty does not lie in the fact that action influences man after death. In this context, it is rather a universal conviction that a man's afterlife depends on what he has done during his life which is a position shared by the earlier Vedic people.

What is more important, in my view, is that Yājñavalkya takes Jāratkāva by the hand. It is possible that the concept of touching is used here to activate the multimodal metaphor of liberating cognition as it is activated in the description of the teaching of Ajātaśatru (BU 2.1.15). This may imply that the teaching concerns liberating cognition. In this way, the composer could imply that the state after death is the same as the state of liberation. Since such a conviction has already been expressed in the ṚV (Jurewicz 2010a: 295), it is not new. It is also important to note that the composer of BU 3.2.13 not only states that Yājñavalkya and Jāratkāva were talking about action (*kárma haivá tád ūcatuḥ*) but states they praised it (*kárma haivá tát práśaṁsatuḥ*). The verb *śaṃs-* is used in the ṚV to express the extolling of gods with hymns. It is used with the preposition *prá* in various contexts but most often the object is Agni. If the recipient takes this into account and activates ŚB 10.5.3 where the two final stages of manifestation of fiery reality are called 'deed' (*kárman*) and 'fire' (*agní*, see chapter 3.5.1), he may understand that Yājñavalkya and Jāratkāva are talking about the ritual of building a fire altar. According to the exegesis of Agnicayana presented in the ŚB, the aim of this ritual is the construction of the immortal self of the sacrificer which allows him to survive death. Thus the teaching of Yājñavalkya is not new in this respect either. I would rather interpret Yājñavalkya's formulation as further proof of the creation of abstract and general language in the early Upaniṣads: all kinds of action are seen as influencing the agent. The novelty of Yājñavalkya's teaching may lie in the scope of knowledge gained in liberation which encompasses the unmanifest aspect of reality and thanks to which one is not reborn again. This can be inferred on the basis of his further teaching presented in the fourth book of the BU which presents the problem of the influence of action on the afterlife lot within an overall metaphysical context (see section 4.4.2.3).

Let us come back to BU 2.1. In following passages (BU 2.1.16-19), the composer elaborates the concept of sleep in terms of which the presence of unmanifest reality within a particular man is conceived. The highest agent of human cognitive powers is called 'man made of perception' (*vijñānamáya*

163 There is nothing about 'vicissitudes of the dead person' to which Bronkhorst refers (2007: 122).

164 It is interpreted in this way by Bronkhorst (2007).

púruṣa) present in the space of the heart[165]. In my view, this is *ātman* described in the AU as being born in the cosmos and in man and it is identified with insight, *prajñāna*, and *brahman* (see section 4.3.1). Sleep is the state when the subjective-objective faculties of cognition (breath, speech, seeing, hearing and mind) are suspended. The lack of outwards perception is explained in that the highest cognitive agent's awareness of the senses is integrated with his own awareness and he is composed only of it (*tád eṣā́ṃ prāṇā́nāṃ vijñā́nena vijnā́nam ādā́ya*).

The situation of the highest cognitive agent, in the state of dreaming sleep, is then presented:

BU 2.1.18

> *sá yátraitát svapnyáyā cárati té hāsya lokā́ḥ | tád utèvá mahārājó bhávaty evá mahābrāhmaṇáḥ | utèvoccāvacáṃ nígacchati | sá yáthā mahārājó jā́napadān gr̥hītvā́ své janapadé yathākāmáṃ parivártetaivám evàiṣá etát prāṇā́n gr̥hītvā́ své śárīre yathākāmáṃ párivartate |*
>
> Wherever he may travel in his dreams, those regions become his worlds. He may appear to become a great king or an eminent Brahmin, or to visit the highest and the lowest regions. Just a great king, taking his people with him, may move around in his domain at will, so he, taking the breaths[166] with him, moves around his body at his will.

The highest cognitive agent is conceived in terms of a king who has control of his subjects and because of that can move freely around his kingdom. In the same way, cognitive faculties are under the control of the highest agent which gives it the experience of freedom. The word *loká* refers to the spaces of experience created by the highest cognitive agent. This state corresponds to the state gained under the influence of Soma; as I have shown the experience of freedom and creativity was one of the most important feature of this state (see Jurewicz 2010a: 177 ff.).

Then the experience of dreamless sleep is discussed. In this state cognition is suspended and the subject does not cognise anything (*átha yadā́ súṣupto bhávati yadā́ ná kásya caná véda*, BU 2.1.19). This state is conceived in the same way in CU 8.6 (see section 4.4.2.4). Through the seventy-two thousands veins the highest cognising agent enters the part of the heard called *purītát* (pericardium) and rests there. The verb *práti áva sr̥p-* evokes the conceptualisation of the agent, in this state, in terms of a snake which creeps to its hiding place. The concept of a snake is used in the earlier Veda

[165] Compare BU 4.4.5, BU 4.4.22, see section 4.2.2.
[166] Olivelle (1998): 'vital functions'.

to conceive fire (Coomaraswamy 1935, Jurewicz 2010a: 346) and Prajāpati in his dangerous, killing form of time (see chapter 3.3). The preposition *práti* implies a movement back. The recipient may presume that in these terms the suspension of awareness is conceived. The composer elaborates the image schema CENTRE-PERIPHERY; the suspension of cognition is conceived in terms of a movement towards the centre. The application of this schema allows the composer to imply that the suspension of cognition is reversible. This state is conceived in erotic terms of an orgasm (*ānandá*) which again evokes Somic exultation, the description of which uses the word *ānandá* (ṚV 9.113 11[167]). Such a conceptualisation is a usually evoked in Upaniṣadic descriptions of the state of final cognition (Olivelle 1997). The composer emphasises that this state is not only happiness but also a state in which the agent is indifferent to outside experience.

Although the next two chapter of the BU (2.2-2.3) are not explicitly presented as the continuation of the dialogue between Ajātaśatru and Dṛptabālāki, I would treat them as a continuation of the topic presented in BU 2.1. Their composer describes the liberating process, which leads to realisation of three stages of *ātmán*, in a more detailed way. BU 2.2 has already been analysed by Brereton (1991) and Gren-Eklund (1978). In his interpretation, Brereton reconstructs the meaning of this chapter as describing the macrocosmos and the microcosmos based on the identification of fire and the sun on the one hand and the main breath (*madhyamá prāṇá*) on the other. I am fully convinced by his interpretation, though I would expand it to consider issues connected with the liberating process.

According to Brereton, the composer here creates a complex conceptual network[168]. Its first input space is the human body, its second input space is the cosmos, its third input space is ritual and the cosmic transformations of fire. The generic space is the concept of transformation. In the blend, elements of all the input spaces are identified. The next input space is the concept of a horse activated *via* the words *śíśu*, *adhāna*, *sthūṇá* and *dā́ma* which can be interpreted as a horse's bridle, the rope which holds the calf/ foal and a hitching post. These words also strengthen the input space of the transformation of fire, Brereton (1991: 9). In the blend, all transformations are conceived in terms of the growth of a foal.

In my view, the chapter also describes the meditative process. The concept of a child, evoked in BU 2.2.1 *via* the word *śíśu*, is the source domain for conceptualisation of the beginning of the process which, as a whole, is

---

[167] For the history of the semantic changes of the word *ānanda* and its experiential motivation, see Olivelle (1997).

[168] He does not use cognitive linguistic methodology.

conceived in terms of the growth of a child. The general meaning of the word *śíśu* also allows the recipient to activate the meaning of a foal. In the blend, the main breath is conceived in terms of a foal which it is possible to harness. Thus the composer implies that meditation can be controlled. It is possible to harness it so as to control it. Such a conceptualisation of mental practice can be seen as the as one of the earliest Upaniṣadic sources of the use of the term *yoga* for meditation.

The next passage describes the homology between parts of the eye, the gods and cosmic elements. In the blend, the input space of human body is reduced to the eye which can be understood as the starting point of the meditative process. This is explicitly stated in the next chapter (BU 2.3 see below) the composer of which presents the concept of man in the right eye understood as the visible form of *ātmán* in man. Its cosmic counterpart is the sun.

In BU 2.2.3 a stanza is quoted which in its first three verses repeats (with some slight changes) AVŚ 10.8.9 (see chapter 2.5.1.3). Their composer creates the image of a bowl turned upside down in which 'glory of all forms' (Whitney 1905) or 'dazzling splendour' (Olivelle 1998) is placed (*tásmin yáśo níhitaṃ viśvárūpam*). The seven seers sit in it. As I have argued, the stanza presents the supernatural state realised by the seven seers conceived as realised on the sun; the possibility to interpret the seven seers as the stars of Ursa Maior enlarges the model of the cosmos and the human activity created by the composer. Thus the composer of BU 2.3.3 presents the aim of the practice he describes and implies that it is the same as in earlier tradition.

However, in his commentary he interprets the bowl as the head and *yaśas* as breaths (*prāṇa*); in the same way he interprets the seers. To the best of my knowledge, identification of *yaśas* with breaths is new. It is based on the metonymy RESULT OF ACTION (*YAŚAS*) FOR MEANS OF ACTION (*PRĀṆA*)[169]. On the other hand, the seers are identified with breaths in ŚB 6.1.1.1 (see chapter 3.2.2, Brereton 1991). This identification, based on the same metonymy, focuses the recipient's mind on breath practice as the way for realisation of the supernatural state when Soma is not in use.

The last verse of the stanza mentions the eighth element which is speech joined with brahman (*vā́g aṣṭamī́ bráhmaṇā saṃvidānā́*). Brereton (1991) sees here a possible reference to ṚV 1.164.15 (see chapter 1.6). It is also possible that ṚV 10.72.8-9 is activated here where Aditi is presented as going to the gods with her seven sons with the eight becoming the dead-egg from which men will be born (see chapter 1.5). Within the frame of this conceptualisation, speech is the means for men to reach *bráhman* in the supernatural state. The

[169] This kind of metonymy is not attested in Radden-Kövecses (1999).

identification of this state with *bráhman* is elaborated in CU 3.1-14 analysed above (see section 4.4.2.1).

The composer quotes the AVŚ in order to place the new practice he describes within the frames of tradition. He wants to present the final goal of this practice as being the same as the goal realised thanks to Soma. Instead of Soma, man is now endowed with speech and breath which can lead him to cognition of his innermost self which is identical with the whole of reality.

In the next chapter (BU 2.3), the composer further elaborates the breath practice which leads to supernatural cognition. He begins playing with the word *satyá* which has already been analysed (see section 4.1.5). It will be recalled that this play is also elaborated by Ajātaśatru (BU 2.1.20) which supports my view that BU 2.2-3 continue the topic analysed in BU 2.1. In BU 2.3.2, the composer continues the play and uses the words *sát* and *tyám* in reference to the cosmic and human dimensions within the world (*rása*, BU 2.3.2). In the cosmic dimension, the word *sát* refers to everything that is different from wind and the space between the earth and the sky, its essence is the sun. The word *tyám* refers to wind and the space between the earth and the sky and its essence is man within the sun's orb (BU 2.3.3). In the human dimension, the word *sát* refers to everything which is different from breath (*prāṇá*) and the space within the body; its essence is the eye (BU 2.3.4). The word *tyám* refers to breath and space; its essence is the man within the right eye (BU 2.3.5). Again the word *sat* is connected with what moves. It can be motivated by earlier cosmogonies but also by the fact that wind and breath move. In the context of this passage, *satyá* refers to the manifest aspect.

In the next passage (BU 2.3.6), the composer states that the form (*rūpá*) of man within the sun's orb and within the right eye is like 'a golden cloth, or like a white wool, or a red bug, or a flame, or a white lotus, or a sudden flash of lightning'[170]. Almost all these qualifications are well entrenched in Vedic tradition, both earlier and contemporary, and evoke source domains in terms of which *ātmán* as the innermost self of man is conceived[171]. The concept of a rich (golden or coloured with saffron) cloth metonymically evokes the concept of a king and metaphorically the concept of *ātmán* (ĀTMAN IS A KING). The concept of white wool evokes the concept of the sheep wool strainers in which Soma was purified. The concept of strainer metonymically evokes the process of purification of Soma and this concept evokes the concept of cognition realised under the influence of Soma. As I have shown, the composers of the

[170] BU 2.3.6: *tásya haitásya púruṣasya rūpáṃ yáthā māhārajanáṃ vā́so yáthā pāṇḍvā́vikaṃ yáthendragopó yáthāgnyarcír yáthā puṇḍárīkaṃ yáthā sakŕ̥d vidyuttáṁ* |

[171] The concepts of wind, rain-cloud, lightning and thunder are mentioned in the context of liberating cognition gained in the fourth state of *ātman* in CU 8.12.2 (see section 4.4.2.4).

BU identify their mental practices with exultation[172]. The word *indragopá* can also mean fire-fly and I would interpret it in such a way taking into account that flames of fire are the next concept evoked by the composer from which sparks fly similar to fire-flies[173]. Since the ṚV the concept of fire has been a conventionalised source domain for the conceptualisation of reality. The concept of a lotus is used to conceptualise the manifest aspect of reality in the AVŚ and describes the mysterious being which consists of self (*yakṣám ātmanvát*, see chapter 2.5.2.1). The concept of lightning activates cognition of the unmanifest aspect. Moreover, conceptualisation of *ātmán* as fiery is preserved in some passage of the Upaniṣads (BU 1.2.1, see section 4.1.1, CU 3.13.7-8, see section 4.4.2.1).

The stages which lead to supernatural cognition are mentioned here: firstly, *ātmán* appears in a golden shining form, then the state conceived as characteristic for Somic exultation is experienced which, within the present context, leads to the perception of *ātmán* as dispersed flashes of fire. They finally unify in one flame to become the white lotus[174]. The recipient may also assume that all these forms have the form of man.

The passage from the manifest aspect of reality into its unmanifest aspect is then conceived in terms of a flash of lightning. This image is again evoked by the composer at the end of his description: 'when a man knows this, his excellence (*śrī́*) unfolds like a sudden flash of lightning'[175]. The concept of *śrī́* brings the mind of the recipient to the Ṛgvedic concept of fame realised in Somic exultation in the sun (see chapter 1.7) and he can understand that knowledge of what is *sát* and *tyám* leads to the same state.

Supernatural cognition described in BU 2.3 is realised in breath practice and the definitions of *sát* and *tyám* are based on it. The concept of man in parts of the cosmos and in a man's eye is used in the Upaniṣads as the source domain for conceiving *ātman*'s presence in the cosmos and in man; their identity is the starting point for recognising the ontic unity of reality (see sections: 4.3.2, 4.4.2.2, 4.4.2.4). The possibility for perceiving the unmanifest aspect within its manifestation is attested already in AVŚ in the conceptualisation of the sun (see chapter 2.5.3).

The man in the right eye, called the essence (*rása*) of *tyám*, is the visible form of *ātmán* (see CU 8.7.4, section 4.4.2.4). One can perceive it in the

---

172 It may also refer, on the basis of similarity between color and texture of sheep wool and a spider's web, to the latter, see BU 2.1.20, analysed below.

173 The image of sparks bursting from fire is used in BU 2.1.20 analysed below.

174 A similar sequence is presented in ṚV 4.58 where the shining streams of butter become the golden reed which finally appears to be Agni.

175 BU 2.3.6: *sakṛdvidyuttèva ha vā́ asya śrī́r bhavati yá evám̐ véda.*

eyes of others[176], but in order to experience it as one's own eye one has to concentrate on one's own breathing (*prāṇá*) which is called *tyám*. The form *tyám* is the second part of the word *satyám* and metonymically triggers the listener to look for its beginning which is *sát*. In that way, man will look for what corresponds to *sat* within him which is the rest of his body. And since he knows the cosmic meanings of *tyám* and *sát*, which are wind, space, and everything that is beyond them, he will be able to enlarge the knowledge of himself towards the cosmos.

The crucial aspects of *tyám* and *sát* (the man in the sun and the sun, the man in the eye and the eye) are called *rása* in BU 2.3. This word is used in ŚB 6.1.1.4 where it denotes the most excellent part of the seers, identified with breaths, which rises to become the sun and head of Prajāpati (see chapter 3.2.2). Thus the possibility of supernatural cognition is created. As I have argued, the recipient of ŚB 6.1.1 may evoke the image of drinking sap. It is also used to conceive the way the head is created. So the recipient of the BU can create a conceptual network the input spaces of which are: the concept of reality, the concept of a breathing man and of a drinking man. The generic space is the concept of transformation. In the blend, the cognition of reality is conceived in terms of drinking or sucking sap, *rasa*, and is realised in breathing.

In the first stage of practice, man has to concentrate on his breath to reach everything different from it. Simultaneously, we may presume, he has to concentrate on wind in order to reach everything that is different from it. Thus he will encompass with his cognition the aspect called *tyám* and *mūrtám*. Then he should concentrate on the essence of the aspect *tyam* which is man in the right eye and man in the sun. This cognitive concentration will lead to the essence of *sat* which is the eye and the sun. It may be presumed that in this way man cognises his own identity with the manifest aspect. He will acquire full knowledge of what is called *satya* which will bring him the state of excellence (*śrī́*). The word *śrī́* is also used in ŚB 6.1.1.4 to denote a state identified with *rása* of the breaths (see chapter 3.2.2). Moreover, this word activates the Ṛgvedic concept of fame understood as the supernatural state gained under the influence of Soma. Thus the composer of the BU entrenches his teaching in early tradition and implies that breath practice leads to the same state as Somic exultation.

The description ends with an apophatic description of *ātman*:

---

[176] See Magnone (2015).

BU 2.3.6

áthā̆ta ādeśá néti néti | ná hy ètásmād íti néty anyát páram asty | átha nāmadhéyaṁ satyásya satyám íti | prāṇā́ vaí satyám̥ | téṣām eṣá satyám.

Here, then, is the rule of substitution: 'not-, not-,' for there is nothing beyond this 'not'. And this is the name – 'the real of the real,' for the real are breaths, and he is the real of breaths[177].

The final state realised in liberating practice is called *satyásya satyám*: 'the real of the real' or 'truth of the truth'. The process of cognitive transition from the manifest aspect to the unmanifest one is not described by the composer probably because it cannot be expressed in language. It is also possible he wants to show that liberating practice with breath leads further than Somic exultation which led only to cognition of the manifest aspect.

The composer tries to express the real nature of both aspects of reality: the manifest is called real, but the unmanifest is more real than it is. In this abstract way the composer of the BU formulates the ontic relationship between aspects of reality. And, in a concise way, he again points out the way to cognise this. Breaths are called *satyá*. This is a metonymic compression of cause and effect: practice on breaths leads to an understanding of reality (CAUSE FOR EFFECT) which is the real foundation of everything that exists.

*

Let me resume the main content of BU 2.1-3. In the first chapter, the composer, having described partial cognition of reality, presents the possibility of its full knowledge. This is conceived in terms of sleep. The way how this state can be achieved is presented in the next two chapters. The second chapter emphasises possibility to control the process based on breath practice. The third chapter elaborates the abstract concept of *satyá* which is the theoretical frame of the structure of reality and, at the same time, the basis for practice. Unmanifest reality can paradoxically be seen in its manifestations and thanks to that man can realise its unity himself. Conceptualisation of reality in terms of *satyá*, a concept which can be rationally analysed as composed of two parts allows the composer to show rational nature of the liberating process. As the whole word can be inferred on the basis of its final part, in the same way the existence of the unmanifest aspect can be rationally inferred on the basis of what is manifest. At the same time, this rational process overwhelms the whole man through breath practice to become practical confirmation of this theoretical truth.

177 Olivelle (1998) translates *prāṇa* as 'vital function'.

4.4.2.3. Who sleeps and who does not (*Bṛhadāranyaka Upaniṣad* 4.3-4)

This exposition is presented within the frames of the debate between Janaka, the king of Videha and Yājñavalkya, the Brahmin philosopher. Yājñavalkya visits Janaka, but does not want to teach him (*sá mene: ná vadiṣya íti*, BU 4.3.1). But then they begin to talk about Agnihotra and Yājñavalkya grants Janaka a wish; he can ask him anything he wants (BU 4.3.1). The topic of Agnihotra is not accidental. As will be shown, within the frame of this sacrifice, the issues of death are discussed in the JB (see chapter 5.1). And this issue will also be discussed here.

The question Janaka asks in this section is formulated as 'What is the source of light for a person here?'[178] (*kímjyotir ayáṃ púruṣa íti*, BU 4.3.2). This question is very general. The word *púruṣa* can refer to a man but also to the whole of reality and its perceptible forms in its manifest aspect. In the beginning of his teaching, Yājñavalkya elaborates the first meaning of this word. The light is the sun, the moon and fire because thanks them a man can act (BU 4.3.2-4). When this light disappears, speech is the light because at night, when it is so dark that it is impossible to discern one's own hand, a man can direct himself hearing the voice of the other (BU 4.3.5).

The composer deliberately introduces the concept of a dark night. The well-versed recipient can activate the cosmogony of the *Nāsadīyasūkta* where the poet conceives the second stage of creation in terms of darkness which, in turn, evokes the concept of night when cognition is impossible (see Jurewicz 2010a). The concept of night evoked by Yājñavalkya can be interpreted as the source domain in terms of which the impossibility to cognise is conceived. As at night one is helped by voices of others in the same way one who does not know anything is helped with the words of Veda.

Then Janaka asks what happens if this light disappears (BU 4.3.6). In this way, he implies that there are situations when the teaching of the Veda is not sufficient. Yājñavalkya answers that then *ātmán* is the light. He understands this word as referring to the whole human organism because he explains that with its aid a man can act[179]. In the same way, the composer of the CU 8.7.1 plays with the word *ātmán* when he begins his teaching (see section 4.4.2.4). Then Janaka asks what is *ātmán* (BU 4.3.7).

The next passage refers to the cognition of *ātmán* who is the highest cognitive agent of reality called 'man composed of perception among the

[178] Olivelle (1998).

[179] BU 4.3.6: *ātmánaivàyáṃ jyótiṣāste pályayate kárma kurute vipáryetī́ti.*

breaths' (*vijñāmáya prāṇéṣu*)[180]. The recipient understands that their cognitive activity is suspended because of the lack of light. The highest cognitive agent is conceived as the inner light within the heart (*hṛdy àntárjyotis*). He is called *samānā́*, uniform[181], and is presented as travelling across both worlds, *loká*, which I interpret as his twofold experience. The recipient can presume that one space of experience is the state when man is awake and the second is the state of dreaming sleep. The activity of the cognitive highest agent is conceived in terms of an activity similar to reflecting and to fluttering (*dhyā́yatīva lelā́yatīva*). The first source domain highlights its cognitive ability and the second evokes its conceptualisation in terms of fire. The highest cognitive agent described here is *ātmán* who is described in the cosmogony of the AU as being born in the cosmos and in man and is identified with insight, *prajñāna*, and *brahman* (see section 4.1.3).

Then it is said:

BU 4.3.7-8

sá hi svápno bhūtvèmáṃ lokám átikrāmati mṛtyó rūpā́ṇi | (7)
sá vā́ ayáṃ púruṣo jā́yamānaḥ śárīram abhisampádyamānaḥ pāpmábhiḥ sáṁsṛjyate | *sá utkrā́man mriyámāṇaḥ* | (8)

When he falls asleep he transcends this world, these visible forms of death. (7) When at birth this person takes on a body, he becomes united with bad things, and when at death he leaves, it behind, he get rid of those bad things. (8)

According to the first sentence, the highest cognitive agent (*vijñānamáya púruṣa*) leaves the world and the forms of death. If the recipient interprets *loká* as the space of experience, he will understand that the highest cognitive agent does not experience himself as dying. In the next sentence, the condition of this experience is presented. The highest cognitive agent experiences himself as dying when he manifests in man at his birth and leaves it during his death. The state when the highest cognitive agent leaves a man's body is conceived in terms of sleep.

---

180 In BU 2.1.16-17, *vijñānamáya púruṣa* is used in the description of the second stage (dreaming sleep).

181 It is also possible that the breath, called *samānā́*, is evoked. It connected with mind and rain (CU 3.13.3, 5.22.1-2). The concept of rain evokes the concept of lightning (CU 5.22.2) connected with liberating cognition. It also evokes the concept of wind and within the frames of the present topic it may be source domain for conceptualisation of free movement between both worlds. However, the conceptual links between the wind and liberating cognition need a separate study.

In the next passage, the composer elaborates the concept of sleep as the source domain for transition of the highest cognitive agent from the body (BU 4.3.9). The state of sleep (*svapnasthā́*) is the intermediate state between two states called 'this place' (*idám*) and 'the other place' (*paralokasthā́na*). The composer refers here to both aspects of reality: 'this place' refers to the manifest aspect and 'the other place' refers to the unmanifest aspect. The composer uses the image schema of CONTAINER to make his description as abstract as possible: both aspects of reality are conceived in terms of the container. Change is conceived in terms of going out and entering containers[182]. The intermediate sphere is conceived as being between them. It corresponds to the borderline sphere between the two aspects of reality. The sleep, in terms of which the state of the highest cognitive agent is conceived here, is dreamless sleep which gives access to a different perception that is only possible when subjective-objective cognition is suspended (see below).

BU 4.3.9a

> *tásmint sándhye sthā́ne tíṣṭhan eté ubhé sthā́ne paśyatīdáṃ ca paralokasthā́naṃ ca | átha yathākrámo 'yáṃ paralokasthā́ne bhávati tám ākrámam ākrámyobháyān pāpmána ānandā́ṁś ca paśyati |*
>
> Standing there in the place where the two meet, he sees both those places – this world and the other world. Now, that place serves as an entryway to the other world, and as he moves through that entryway he sees both the bad things and the joys.

The intermediate state is a conscious state. In this state the highest cognitive agent can cognise both aspects of reality. He is aware of the evil and the bliss he experiences in the manifest aspect. At the same time, the intermediate state is conceived as an entrance to the unmanifest aspect. The recipient is prompted to refer to everyday life experience and create the image of a man who stands at the entrance to an abode. Even if he does not want to enter, he is aware of it. Thus the composer implies that, in the intermediate state, the highest cognitive agent is aware of his unmanifest aspect.

---

182 For the concept of *setu*, see sections 4.2.2, 4.4.2.4.

BU 4.3.9b

> *sá yátra prasvapiti asyá lokásya sarvā́vato mā́trām apādā́ya svayáṃ vihátya svayáṃ nirmā́ya svéna bhāsā́ svéna jyótiṣā prásvapity | átrāyáṃ púruṣaḥ svayáṃjyotir bhavati |*
>
> This is how he dreams. He, having taken[183] material from the entire world and, having destroyed (it)[184] and having measured it (again)[185], he dreams with his own radiance, with his own light. In that this man[186] becomes his own light.

Now the composer presents cognition of the manifest aspect realised by the highest cognitive agent at the borderline sphere. The word *mā́trā* literally means 'measure'. The composer creates the image of a man who measures an object, then folds[187] and measures again. In these terms, the cognitive activity of the highest cognitive agent is conceived. It is worth mentioning that the word *mā́trā* is used in the compound *prādeśamatrá* in ŚB 10.6.1.10 and in CU 5.18.1 to describe *ātman* in his potentiality to expand and manifest himself (see section 4.4.2.1). The concept of measuring is used more generally to conceive creation already in the ṚV, so the recipient may understand that the highest cognitive agent, in his cognition at the borderline sphere, is able to create the world for himself and also destroy it in order to create it once again. Thus he is able to experience and not experience various states. In this activity the cognitive ability of the highest cognitive agent is conceived in terms of his own light (*svayáṃjyotis*).

The next passage (BU 4.3.10) presents the highest cognitive agent of reality as creating chariots, horses and paths, water ponds with lotuses and rivers and all kinds of pleasures. Such a description implies that he is conceived in terms of a rich king who can build a kingdom according to his will. The composer emphasises that in this state all manifestations are created by the cognitive agent and he is called 'the maker' (*sá hí kartā́*).

Then two stanzas are quoted which evoke the conceptualisation of the highest cognitive agent in terms of a wild goose which goes back to the AVŚ (see chapter 2.5.3):

---

183 Olivelle (1998): 'takes'.
184 Olivelle (1998): 'taking them apart on his own'.
185 Olivelle (1998): 'and then on his own putting them back together'.
186 Olivelle 91998): 'person'.
187 The participle *saṃhatya* is used in BU 4.3.19 to express folding of wings.

BU 4.3.11-12:

tád eté ślókā bhavanti |

svápnena śārīrám abhiprahátyā́suptaḥ suptā́n abhicākaśīti |
śúkram ādā́ya púnar áiti sthā́naṃ hiraṇmáyaḥ púruṣa ekahaṁsáḥ || (11)
prāṇéna rákṣann avaraṃ kulāyáṃ bahíḥ kulāyā́d amṛ́taś caritvā́ |
sá īyate 'mṛ́to yatrakāmáṃ hiraṇmáyaḥ puruṣa ekahaṁsáḥ || (12)

Subduing by sleep the bodily realm remaining awake, he contemplates
the sleeping senses. Taking the light, he returns to this place –
The golden person! The single goose! (11)
Guarding by breath the lower nest, The immortal roams outside the nest;
The immortal goes whenever he wants –
The golden person! The single goose! (12)

The manifest aspect is conceived in terms of a lower nest which is guarded by the breaths of the highest cognitive agent (BU 4.3.12a) and which can be left by him (BU 4.3.12b). The concept of nest activates the concept of birds in which breaths are conceived. A similar conceptualisation is implied in AU 1.1.3 (see section 4.1.3) and the recipient may presume that the word *prāṇá* refers to the subjective cognitive abilities of reality[188]. The recipient can create the image of birds guarding their nest in order to understand the relationship between the cognitive activity of reality and its manifest aspect. In this way, the composer implies that the manifest aspect is the result of the subjective-objective activity of reality which is conceived in terms of breathing (see BU 2.1. 20, section 4.4.2.2).

The highest cognitive agent is presented as subduing or overpowering 'the bodily realm' (*śārīrā*) with sleep (BU 4.3.11a). This is consistent with the previous passage (BU 4.3.7) where the moment the body is left by the agent is conceived in terms of sleep. The composer now states that the highest cognitive agent of reality is awake (*ásupta*) and only its subjective-objective abilities are sleeping (*suptá*, BU 4.3.11b). Now the highest cognitive agent is presented as being woken. The recipient may assume that the composer conceives the unmanifest state of reality in these terms. It is the source of all cognitive activities and can observe everything that happens in its manifest aspect (BU 4.3.11b). In this state, it cannot be cognised by its subjective-objective powers. The freedom of the highest cognitive agent is expressed *via* the metaphor FREEDOM IS LACK OF BONDAGE (*sá īyate 'mṛ́to yatrakāmáṃ*, BU 4.3.12c).

---

188 For such a conceptualisation of breaths in the Upaniṣads, see Bakker (1982).

The concept of sleep is elaborated in the following way in order to conceive the cognitive manifestation of reality. In its unmanifest aspect, it is conceived as being awake while at the borderline sphere it is conceived in terms of dreamless sleep. It is worth noting that the composer also activates ŚB 10.6.3.2 where the concept of the golden man (*púruṣa hiraṇmáya*) is used in reference to *ātmán* present in the heart of man (see chapter 3.5.1). Within the frames of the context of the ŚB, this concept evokes the Agnicayana ritual. In the BU, the recipient is not triggered to evoke this concept. On the other hand, the adjective 'golden', *hiraṇmáya*, strengthens the conceptual links with the AVŚ where the goose, in terms of which the manifestation of reality is conceived, is qualified in the same way (see chapter 2.5.3).

The concept of *śúkra* (translated by Olivelle 1998 as 'light'), which is taken by the highest cognitive agent when he returns 'to this place' (4.3.11cd: *śúkram ādā́ya púnar aíti sthā́naṃ*), needs a separate study. Understood as light, the word *śúkra* can be interpreted as the source domain in terms of which the cognitive ability of the highest cognitive agent is conceived. In ŚB 11.5.8.4, the word *śúkra* denotes the essence of three Vedas which is *bhū́r*, *bhúvas* and *svàr*, in JUB 3.15.5-10, this word also denotes also three worlds and three Vedas[189]. *Bhū́r*, *bhúvas* and *svàr* are called 'brightness (*śúkra*) of the threefold knowledge' (Oertel 1896) and are identified with manifest the aspect (*tad dha vai trayyai vidyāyai śukram etāvad idaṃ sarvam*). If the recipient activates this usage of the word *śúkra*, he would understand that the highest cognitive agent assumes the form of the sounds of the Veda while he remains at the borderline sphere between the two aspects of reality. This agrees with the general Vedic cosmogonic pattern. The place when he again goes can be either of these two aspects.

However, it is possible that *śúkra* also activates here the meaning of semen. Thus this hemistich would also refer to rebirth. The word *śúkra* qualifies two oblations of the Agnihotra which circulate around the cosmos (11.6.2. 6-10); this passage is seen as one of the early testimonies of the belief in rebirth (Bodewitz 1996a). Moreover, according to this belief, a dead father becomes semen which transforms into his son[190]. Within the frames of this interpretation, the place reached again by the highest cognitive agent is man. Taking into account that the highest cognitive agent is free, the recipient understand that he is not forced to assume this form and he may act according to his will. My interpretation is confirmed by the next passage (BU 4.3.14) where the

189 IN CU 4.17, the word *rasa* is used.

190 In AU 2.1, the embryo and the semen are conceived in a similar way, as the radiance (*tejas*, see section 4.1.3).

composer begins to describe manifestations of the highest cognitive agent in a particular man (see below).

BU 4.3.13

svapnāntá uccāvacám īyámāno rūpā́ṇi deváḥ kurute bahū́ni[191]|
utèvá strī́bhiḥ sahá módamāno jákṣad utèvā́pi bháyāni páśyan ||

Travelling in sleep to places high and low,
The god creates many a visible form –
now dallying with women, now laughing,
now seeing frightful things.

The composer now presents the experience of reality within its manifest aspect. It is conceived in terms of a dreaming sleeping man. The highest cognitive agent experiences various emotions which again confirms that this is the motive for creation (see BU 1.4, section 4.1.2).

BU 4.3.14

ārāmám asyá paśyanti ná tám̥ paśyati káś canéti |

All they see is his pleasure ground. But him no one sees at all.

The concept of pleasure ground evokes the concept of play in terms of which the creative activity of reality is conceived in BU 1.4 (see section 4.1.2). The manifestations of reality performed in cognitive acts are conceived as mental play. They constitute the cosmos which can be perceived by men but it is impossible to see the highest cognitive agent in everyday cognition. Conceptualisation of creation in terms of play allows the composer to imply that various experiences, described in the previous passage (BU 4.3.13), are not ultimate and happen according to the will of reality.

In the following sentences of BU 4.3.14, the composer introduces the perspective of a particular man. He says that one should not wake up a person who sleeps because it is difficult to cure someone the cognitive agent of whom has not returned (BU 4.3.14). The highest cognitive agent is present within every man. When man sleeps, the highest cognitive agent realises the intermediate state between the manifest and the unmanifest aspect. This state is conceived in terms of his dreamless sleep. But in ordinary sleep man cannot control this process contrary to liberating practice. A sleeping man should not

[191] It is possible that the recipient is expected to activate the Ṛgvedic concept of Indra as changing forms (ṚV 3.53.8ab: *rūpám̥-rūpam maghávā bobhavīti māyā́ḥ kṛṇvānás tanúvam pári svā́m;* 6.47.18a-c: *rūpám̥-rūpam prátirūpo babhūva tád asya rūpám praticákṣaṇāya índro māyā́bhiḥ pururū́pa īyate*).

be woken too suddenly because the highest cognitive agent has to come back from the borderline between the two aspects of reality. If he does not come back, it will be dangerous for a man. He would be in a similar situation as was reality in the beginnings of its creation and would be an empty space not filled with *ātmán*.

Next the composer quotes shared knowledge according to which when man sleeps he is in fact awake because he sees in dream everything that he sees when he is awake (BU 4.3.14). This part of the teaching ends with the sentence *átrāyáṃ púruṣaḥ svayáṃjyotir bhavatī́ty*.

Then Janaka urges Yājñavalkya to teach him more (*áta ūrdhváṃ vimokṣā́ya brūhī́ti*, BU 4.3.15). The shared knowledge quoted by Yājñavalkya is incomprehensible for him in the light of the whole teaching. Till now, the manifestation of reality is conceived in terms of its sleeping and its unmanifest aspect is conceived in terms of being awake. Now, Yājñavalkya implies that there is a possibility to be awake while one is asleep. Moreover, in this state cognition of the whole manifest aspect is possible which is implied by the qualification *svayáṃjyotis* which is used to describe the cognitive activity of the highest cognitive agent at the borderline sphere between the two aspects (BU 4.3.9).

Urged by Janaka, Yājñavalkya continues his teaching. In the next passage (BU 4.3.15), the highest cognitive agent is presented in the following way. Having experienced its various manifestations, good and bad, at the borderline sphere between the two aspects of reality (*etásmint saṃprasā́de ratvā́ caritvā́ dr̥ṣṭvaìvá púṇyaṃ ca pāpáṃ*), he comes back to a dream state. The recipient may presume that the dream state refers now to a particular sleeping man. And that man wakes up. His subjective-objective powers are now active and the highest cognitive agent can experience his manifestations, good and bad, from the point of view of an individual human agent (BU 4.3.16). The composer stresses that in both cases the highest cognitive agent is not influenced by its manifestations and calls him *ásanga* ('nothing sticks to this person')[192].

In this moment, Yājñavalkya again stops and is again urged by Janaka to teach him more (BU 4.3.17). So Yājñavalkya says that man falls asleep again[193]. In the following passages, the situation of the highest cognitive agent, who in a particular man moves between waking state and sleep, is conceived in terms of a large fish which moves between two banks of a river. In the same way the cognitive agent, manifest in a particular man, moves between the state of sleep and state of being awake (BU 4.3.18). The concept of

[192] BU 4.3.15,4.3.16: *sá yád tatra kiñcit páśyaty ánanvāgatas téna bhavati | ásaṅgo hy àyáṃ púruṣa íti |*

[193] BU 4.3.17: *sá vā́ eṣá etásmin buddhānté ratvā́ caritvā́ dr̥ṣṭvaìvá púṇyaṃ ca pāpáṃ ca púnaḥ pratinyāyáṃ pratiyóny ā́dravati svapnāntā́yaivá |*

the wandering of the cognitive agent between those two states evokes the concepts of the deceased in the JUB who wanders between the sun and the moon (see chapter 5.2.3). The composer of the JUB interprets this situation as a manifestation of freedom. Conversely, the composer of the BU implies that this situation can be seen as a kind of bondage – the fish is enclosed between two banks of a river.

Then the composer elaborates the source domain of a bird (BU 4.3.19). Now it is not a wild goose but a bird of prey which, having spent a lot of time in flight looking for food, becomes tired and folds his wings. In the same way, the highest cognitive agent can reach another state which is dreamless sleep. This last state is the state realised at the borderline sphere between the two aspects of reality.

In this way, the composer presents three possible states of the highest cognitive agent within a particular man. They are the waking state, the dreaming sleep and the dreamless sleep. The cognitive agent is either captured between the two first states (as a fish between the banks of a river) or can escape from it (as a bird of prey flies high up) to experience another kind of state. But this liberation depends on a particular man in whom the highest cognitive agent manifests himself: it seems that now he can cooperate with its unmanifest part.

It is important to discern the ways the composer uses the concept of waking state and sleep depending on his perspective. From the perspective of the highest cognitive agent, the unmanifest aspect of reality is conceived in terms of waking state, the manifestation at the borderline sphere is conceived in terms of dreamless sleep and the manifest aspect is conceived in terms of sleeping. From the perspective of the particular man, the three states (the waking state, the dreaming state and the dreamless sleep) are not metaphorical concepts, but describe three possible kinds of experience.

In the next section, the composer describes the veins (*hitā́*). They are also described by Ajātaśatru (BU 2.1.19, see section 4.4.2.2) in the context of dreamless sleep and the recipient may presume that this state is not being described.

BU 4.3.20

tā́ vā́ asyaitā́ hitā́ nā́ma nāḍyò yáthā kéśaḥ sahasradhā́ bhinnás tā́vatāṇimnā́ tiṣṭhanti śuklásya nīlásya piṅgalásya háritasya lóhitasyapūrṇā́ḥ | átha yátrainaṃ ghnántīva jinántīva hastī̀va vicchāyáyati gártam iva pátati yád evá jā́grad bháyaṃ páśyati tád átrā́vidyayā manyate | átha yátra devá iva rā́jevāhám evá idám̐ sárvo asmī́ti manyate sò 'sya paramó lokó |

Now, he has these veins called Hitā. They are as fine as a hair split thousandfold and are filled with white, blue, orange, green and red fluid. Now, when people appear to kill or to vanquish him, when an elephant appears to chase him, or

> when he appears to fail into a pit, he is ignorantly imagining dangers that he has seen while he was awake. But when he, appearing to be a god or a king, thinks 'I alone am this world! I am all!' – that is his highest world.

According to Yājñavalkya, in this state man also experiences dreams but they are only terrifying. If man does not possess the right knowledge, he would take them as a real as in the waking state. Taking this in the background of earlier tradition, man is experiencing the same state as Prajāpati in the beginnings of creation when he is afraid of his own fiery manifestation (ŚB 2.2.4, see chapter 3.1.1). In BU 1.4, the first feeling of reality, called *ātmán* and conceived in terms of man, is fear too; fear only disappears when reality realises that it is alone and there is no other of which to be afraid (see section 4.1.2). I would argue that the composer refers here to the state of consciousness just before liberation when the whole manifest aspect is experienced as terrifying as it was terrifying for reality at the beginning of creation. This state is still the state of duality.

The duality is suspended when man realises that he is one with the whole of reality in the same way as the fear of reality in BU 1.4 disappears when it realises its oneness. The realisation of the state of unity is conceived here in terms of being a god or a king.

In the next passage, the composer describes this state in full detail: it is free from desires, without evil and fear (*tád vā́ asyaitád áticchandā ápahatapāpmā̆bhayáṁ*, BU 4.3.21), and is conceived in terms of sexual act when man embraced by a woman is does not cognise anything else. In the same way, the agent is overwhelmed by his cognising self (*prājñánātmánā*) and does not cognise anything other than himself. The words *prajñāna* are used in AU 3.3 in reference to *brahman* (*prajñānaṃ brahma*) and the manifest aspect is qualified as having an eye of cognition and being founded on it (*sarvaṃ tat prajñānetram prajñāne pratiṣṭhitam*, see section 4.1.3). If the recipient evokes this use, the meaning of unity realised in this state is clearer. In this state, all desires are fulfilled because the agent becomes one with everything; there is no desire for anything and hence no sorrow[194] which comes from frustration when one's desires are not fulfilled. In this state (BU 4.3.22) all everyday concepts lose their meaning: family bonds, ritual concepts, social divisions and moral values.

In the following passages (BU 4.3.23-32), the composer describes the suspension of subjective-objective cognition characteristic for the state of liberation when the cognitive ability is still preserved and which is realised in the state of dreamless sleep. Yājñavalkya ends this part of his teaching

---

194 BU 4.3.22: *etád āptákāmam ātmákāmam akāmáṃ rūpám śokāntaram.*

by describing bliss (*ānandá*) which can be realised in the manifest aspect of reality depending on the state of cognition (BU 4.3.33). The highest bliss is realised in the liberating state when all duality is suspended.

But Janaka wants to know more (BU 4.3.33). And Yājñavalkya is now alarmed that he will have to say everything he knows and, as we remember, he did not want to say anything to Janaka when they began their talk (BU 4.3.1). But he carries on and begins to explain what happens to a man after death and describes rebirth.

The composer again describes the highest cognitive agent who wanders between the dreaming sleep state and the waking state (BU 4.3.34). Then the relationship between the cognitive agent and the body in which it manifests is presented: the body is conceived in terms of a heavy loaded cart (4.3.35[195]). One could presume that the more liberated the agent the more burdensome is his presence within a body especially when the body gets old. It should be noted that the composer does not use the word *ātmán* often in this chapter, although the recipient understands that the whole teaching refers to it (see BU 4.3.6-7). But in this moment the composer does use the word *ātmán* to express the unity of the body, called 'the bodily self' (*śārīrá ātmā́*, Olivelle 1998), and the highest cognitive agent called 'the self of knowledge' (*prajná ātmán*, Olivelle 1998). As we remember, reality manifest in the cosmos and man is qualified in the same way in the AU (see section 4.1.3).

BU 4.3.36

sá yátra aṇimā́naṃ nyéti jaráyā vopatápatā vāṇimānáṃ nigácchati | yáthāmráṃ vodúmbaraṃ vā píppalaṃ vā bándhanāt pramucyáte evám evā̀yáṃ púruṣa ebhyó 'ṅgebhyaḥ sapramúcya púnaḥ pratinyāyáṃ pratiyóny ā́dravati prāṇā̀yaivá |

Now a man grows feeble on account of either old age or sickness. It is like this. As a mango or a fig or a berry detaches itself from its bond[196], so this person frees himself from these bodily parts and rushes along the same path and through the same opening towards breath[197].

I think that the use of the general term bonds (*bándhana*) in the simile is caused by the composer wanting to highlight the conceptualisation of death in terms of liberation from bonds[198]. From that he has just described, liberating cognition the recipient may presume that death is liberating only in the case of

[195] This metaphor is also activated in the context of liberated state by the composer of the CU8.12.3 (see below, section 4.4.2.4).

[196] Olivelle (1998): 'stem'.

[197] Olivelle (1998): 'to a new life'.

[198] In the same way it is conceived in CU 8.12.1-2 (see section 4.4.2.4)

a man who has realised his unity with the whole of reality. Olivelle interprets *prāṇá* in the last sentence as 'new life', but I would argue that the meaning of breath should be activated here. Such an interpretation seems to be more consistent with the further teaching of Yājñavalkya concerning the death of man. In BU 4.3.38, the image of a king surrounded by his servants is used in order to conceive breaths concentrating around the *ātman* of a dying man. The way from the dying body is the same as the way leading to the borderline sphere between the two aspects of reality described earlier.

In BU 4.4.1, the composer continues the description of the dying man. His breaths follow *ātmán* (*sá yátrāyám ātmā́balyaṃ nyétya saṃmohám iva nyéty áthainam eté prāṇā́ abhisamā́yanti*). This agrees with BU 4.3.36, according to which the highest cognitive agent goes towards breath. This also agrees with the earlier thought according to which the part of man which survives death is composed of breaths (see chapter 3.4). Subjective-objective cognition is stopped and man is described with the phrase *ekī́bhavati* which literally means 'he is one'. The departure of the highest cognitive agent is conceived in terms of a flash of light[199]. According to the composer of the BU 4.4.2, he departs through any opening of a man's body; he mentions the head among them. This again agrees with the AU in which the manifestation of reality in the cosmos and in man is conceived in terms of it entering through their head (see section 4.1.3). The highest cognitive agent in this state is described as endowed with perception (*sávijñana*) and he will manifest again in the same state (*sávijñano bhavati sávijñānam evā̀nvávakrāmati*)[200].

The description of BU 4.4.2 ends with a sentence:

> *táṃ vidyākarmáṇī samanvā́rabhete pūrvaprajñā́ ca* |
>
> Then learning and rites, as well as memory, take hold of him.

Thus the afterlife state of the deceased is influenced by his knowledge and the deeds he performed during life. Olivelle translates *pūrvaprajñā́* as 'memory', but I would rather interpret this word as expressing the whole cognitive apparatus preserved after death which is later conceived in terms of a subtle body (*sūkṣmaśarīra*). As it can be shown, the influence of deeds is also described in the JB and the JUB (see chapter 5).

The composer then creates two images in order to conceive the situation of the highest cognitive agent of the deceased described in this part of the

---

199 BU 4.4.2. *tásya haitásya hṛ́dayasyā́graṃ prádyotate | téna pradyoténaiṣá ātmā́ niṣkrāmati | cakṣuṣṭó vā mūrdhnó vānyébhyo vā śarīradéśebhyaḥ |tám utkrā́mantaṃ prāṇò 'nū́tkrāmati | prāṇám anūtkrā́mantaṁ sárve prāṇā́ anū́tkrāmanti* |

200 Olivelle (1998): 'He then descends into a state of mere awareness and develops into one who is thus endowed with awareness'.

teaching. He compares the deceased to a caterpillar which, having left one blade of grass, finds another (BU 4.4.3) and in BU 4.4.4 the deceased is compared to a weaver who, having finished one cloth, creates a new more beautiful. According to Bronkhorst, the latter simile does not fit here because the form of the next rebirth can be 'a lot *less* attractive' than the previous one (2007: 122). It is, however, important to read these similes in the context of the whole exposition. BU 4.4.4 shows that the composer *did* think about better rebirth: it could be 'the figure of a forefather, or of a Gandharva, or of a god, or of Brahma, or else the figure of some other being'[201]. I would argue that the composer of the BU is evoking here the same conceptualisation of the ultimate afterlife state as described in JUB 3.28.1-2: this is a state when the agent can choose the form in which he will be reborn (see chapter 5.2.3). In this context, it is more possible that the phrase *anyéṣāṃ vā bhūtā́nām* ('or else the figure of some other being') would evoke the concept of a pleasant rather than an unpleasant rebirth. Taken account of the JUB, it is rebirth as a Brāhmaṇa or a Kṣatriya than as the womb of a dog, a pig or an outcaste woman who are enumerated by CU 5.10.7 (see section 4.3.1).

Then the composer describes reality which he calls now *ātmán-bráhman* (BU 4.4.5). In its manifest aspect it is composed of perception (*vijñā́na*), of subjective-cognitive faculties (mind, seeing, breath and hearing), of five cosmic spheres (space, wind, fire, water and earth) and then of opposing pairs (light and darkness, positive and negative emotions and their lack and finally *dhárma* and *ádharma*, for its analysis see section 4.2.2). The last opposition implies that good and evil deeds are manifestation of the equivocal moral nature of the unmanifest aspect of reality. Now the composer connects this metaphysical situation with the situation of a human agent:

BU 4.4.5a

tád yád etád idaṃmáyo 'domáya íti | yathākārī́ yathācārī́ táthā bhavati | sādhukārī́ sādhúr bhavati | pāpakārī́ pāpó bhavati | púṇyaḥ púṇyena kármaṇā bhavati pāpáḥ pāpéna |

Hence there is this saying: 'He is made of this. He is made of that.' What a man turns to be depends on how he conduct himself. If his actions are good, he becomes good[202]. If his actions are bad, he becomes bad[203]. A man is good by good action, bad by bad action[204].

---

[201] Olivelle (1998). BU 4.4.4: *návataraṃ kalyāṇátaraṃ rūpaṃ kurute | pítryaṃ vā gāndharváṃ vā daívaṃ vā prājāpatyáṃ vā brāhmáṃ vānyéṣāṃ vā bhūtā́nām |*

[202] Olivelle (1998): 'turn into something good'.

[203] Olivelle (1998): 'turn into something bad'.

[204] Olivelle (1998): turns into something good by good action and into something bad by bad actions'.

As reality in its manifest aspect is 'composed' (*-máya*) of *dhárma* and *ádharma*, in the same way man is 'composed' of his desires which lead him to perform good or bad, dharmic or adharmic, deeds. The assumption of the ontological results of cognitive states is explicitly expressed:

BU 4.4.5b

kāmamáya evā̀yáṃ púruṣa íti | sá yáthākāmo bhavati tátkratur bhavati | yátkratur bhavati tát kárma kuruté | yát kárma kuruté tád abhisáṃpadyate |

And so people say: 'A person here consists simply of desire'. A man resolves in accordance with his desire, acts in accordance with his resolve, and turn out to be in accordance with his action.

Then the composer presents two kinds of dharmic agents. First are those who desire to act. They are reborn to experience the world again and to act (*asmaí lokā́ya kármaṇe*). Another is one without such desires (*akāmá, níṣkāma*) and all his desires are fulfilled at the same time (*āptákāma*). He desires only himself (*ātmákāma*), and then he becomes *bráhman* (*bráhmaiva sán bráhmā́pyeti*). Thus the composer, in a concise way, refers to the two paths presented in BU 6.2.9-16 and in CU 5.4-10, *pitṛyāna* for those who desire to act and *devayāna* for those who desire *ātman*. Bronkhorst (2007: 122) claims that 'here the contexts do not provide any direct references to the journey which a person is supposed to make after death'. However, it is just the opposite. Taken in their full contex, these passages present a consistent teaching about two possible afterlife situations of man grounded in earlier tradition.

Then the composer quotes fourteen stanzas (BU 4.4.8-21). Some of them also appear in the later Upaniṣads (*Kaṭha*, *Kena*, *Īśā*, Olivelle 1988: 520). It is possible that such stanzas, expressing shared knowledge about liberating cognition, were circulating among Vedic people. In the last four passages (BU 4.4.22-25), the composer describes the unmanifest aspect of reality cognised in liberating cognition. It is in the space of man's heart as the highest cognitive agent. It rules over all its manifestation and, at the same time, is independent from them and is not influenced by any moral value nor by unpleasant emotions particularly fear. In its manifestation at the borderline sphere it is conceived in terms of a dike (*sétu*, see sections 4.2.2, 4.4.2.4). The ontic result of the epistemic process is presented in BU 4.4.23 where it is said that man who cognises unmanifest reality becomes similarly independent[205].

[205] BU 4.4.23: *tád etád ṛcā̀bhyùktam eṣá nítyo mahimā́ brāhmaṇásya ná kármaṇā vardhate nò kánīyān | tásyaivá syāt padavittáṃ viditvā́ ná lipyate kármaṇā pāpákenéti |*

The fact that he realises the unity of reality is explicitly stated: he is presented as seeing himself in himself and everything as himself (BU 4.4.23: *ātmány evā̀tmā́naṃ paśyati | sárvam ātmā́naṃ paśyati*). He becomes the subject and the object of his cognition. Then the composer states that he is not burnt by evil but burns all evil (BU 4.4. 23: *naìnaṃ pāpmā́ tapati sárvaṃ pāpmā́naṃ tapati*). Since in the ŚB the word *pāpmán* also denotes death, the recipient may unfold the conceptualisation of death in terms of fire (BU 1.2, see section 4.1.1) and understand that such a person goes beyond the initial creative state conceived as the manifestation of death.

From what has been said above, it can be seen that there is great similarity between the teaching of Ajātaśatru and Yājñavalkya. In both chapters, the situation of the highest cognitive agent is described which is reality present in the cosmos and in man with the agent described in the AU as entering them to see itself from this new perspective. In both Upaniṣads, this agent is called *vijñānamaya.* In both chapters, three states of liberating process are presented: the waking state, dreaming sleep, and dreamless sleep. However, Yājñavalkya adds and elaborates in great detail a fourth state which is seen as the conscious realisation of the unity of reality and which involves the suspension of subjective-objective cognition. Moreover, while Ajātaśatru describes this process from the point of view of a particular man, Yājñavalkya begins his exposition from the perspective of the highest cognitive agent. His manifestations in the cosmos and man are conceived in terms of his sleep, his manifestation at the borderline sphere between the two aspects is conceived in terms of dreamless sleep while the unmanifest aspect of reality is conceived in terms of waking state. Having presented an overall perspective, Yājñavalkya introduces the individual perspective of a particular man whose cognising *ātmán*, during his sleep, wanders through his manifestations. It is implied that within the cosmos only man is able to realise the unity of his cognising agent with the whole of reality which takes place in the fourth state. The composer also seems to imply that during normal sleep one's *ātmán* wanders through his manifestations, but man does not have any control over this process. During liberating practice, man can control this process and lead it towards its unmanifest aspect.

Both teachers, Ajātaśatru and Yājñavalkya, mention veins (*hitā́*) which are concentrated around the heart and within it. The full analysis of this concept would go beyond the scope of the present research. I would, however, like to briefly analyse BU 4.2 which precedes the description of the fourth state of liberation just analysed in order to show that the process of liberation consists of a breath practice grounded in earlier tradition.

In BU 4.2.1, Yājñavalkya asks Janaka if he knows what happens to a man when he leaves the world. The king does not know and Yājñavalkya begins with an explanation of breath practice:

BU 4.2.2-3a

índho ha vaí nā́maiṣá yò 'yáṃ dakṣiṇè 'kṣán púruṣaḥ | táṃ vā́ etám índhaṁ sántam índra íty ā́cakṣate paróksẹṇaivá | paróksạpriyā iva hí devā́ḥ pratyákṣadviṣaḥ | (2)
áthaitád vā́me 'kṣán púruṣarūpam eṣā̀syá pátnī virā́ṭ | (3)

Clearly, the true name of the person in the right eye is Indha. Even though he is really Indha, people cryptically call him 'Indra', because gods in some ways love the cryptic, and despise the plain. (2)
That looks like a person in the left eye, on the other hand, is his wife, Virāj. (3)

In the right eye, there is a visible form of unmanifest reality conceived in terms of man and called *índha* which cryptically means *índra*. The composer evokes here ŚB 6.1.1.2 where the main breath of reality is called *índra* which means *índha* because it kindles other breaths during creation (see chapter 3.2.2). The visible form of unmanifest reality in the left eye is called *virā́j* and is conceived as the wife of Indra. Since *virā́j*, among other meanings, is the name of a metre, the recipient can assume that the composer wants to activate the concept of breath practice. At the same time, his conceptualisation of the visible forms of unmanifest reality in terms of man and woman highlights its contradictory nature. The conceptual network created by the composer consists of the input spaces of the human organism, of reality and of the general domain of Procreation in its specific realisation of the sexual act. The generic space is the concept of transformation.

Then the composer states:

BU 4.2.3b

táyor eṣá saṁstāvó yá eṣò 'ntár hṛ́daya ākāśáḥ | áthainayor etád ánnaṃ yá eṣò 'ntár hṛ́daye lohitápiṇḍaḥ | áthainayor etát prāvaráṇaṃ yád etád antár hṛ́daye jālakám iva | áthainayor eṣā́ sṛ́tiḥ saṃcáraṇī yaìṣā́ hṛ́dayād ūrdhvā́ nā́ḍyùccárati | yáthā kéśaḥ sahasradhābhinná evám asyaitā́ hitā́ nā́ma nāḍyò 'ntár hṛ́daye pratiṣṭhitā́ bhavanti | etā́bhir vā́ etád āsrávad ā́sravati | tásmād eṣá praviviktāhāratara ivaivá bhavaty asmā́c chārīrā́d ātmánaḥ |

Their meeting place is the space within the heart, their food is the red lump in the heart, and their garment is like the meshlike substance within the heart. The path along which they travel is the vein that goes up from the heart. The veins called Hitā that are located in the heart are as fine as a hair split thousandfold.

Along them the sap flows continuously. In some ways, this person eats food that is more refined than does the bodily self (*ātman*).

The composer now runs the blend. Within its frame, everyday cognition is conceived in terms of the separate existence of Indra and Virāj. The beginning of the liberating process is conceived in terms of their meeting in the space within the heart of man. The next stage is conceived with the use of the image schema of VERTICALITY which is the next input space of the blend. Indra and Virāj, united in a sexual act, go upwards along the vein which goes up from the heart. In these terms, the suspension of everyday subjective-objective cognition is conceived. Along the veins a fluid (*āsrávat*) flows. The concept of the fluid (*āsrávat*) evokes the concept of *rása* used in ŚB 6.1.1.4 to conceive the creation of a possibility to realise a supernatural state; the composer of the ŚB also elaborates the image schema of VERTICALITY to conceive this process (see chapter 3.2.2). The recipient can also activate a conceptualisation of the liberating process in terms of drinking sap as evoked in BU 2.3 (see section 4.4.2.2).

The objects of cognition are less real than the objects perceived in the waking state. They are conceived in terms of more refined food. It is possible that this is the fluid which flows along the veins. Thus the conceptual network is enriched with the general domain of Cooking in its specific realisation of eating. This domain is used in earlier thought to express subjective-objective cognition and the recipient can evoke this concept here too. Thus he will understand that in this stage subjective-objective duality is not yet suspended although it is performed in a different way.

Then the composer identifies the breaths with the directions of the world:

BU 4.2.4a

tásya prā́cī dík prā́ñcaḥ prāṇā́ dákṣiṇā díg dákṣiṇāḥ prāṇā́ḥ pratī́cī dík pratyáñcaḥ prāṇā́ údīcī díg údañcaḥ prāṇā́ ūrdhvā́ díg ūrdhvā́ḥ prāṇā́ ávācī díg ávāñcaḥ prāṇā́ḥ sárvā díśaḥ sárve prāṇā́ḥ |

The breaths of this person that are on his front constitute the eastern quarter; the breaths on his right side constitute the southern quarter; the breaths at his back constitute the western quarter; the breaths on his left side constitute the northern quarter; the breaths on his upper side constitute the zenith; the breaths on his bottom constitute the nadir; and all his breaths constitute all his quarters[206].

[206] Olivelle (1998) translates *prāṇa* as 'vital function'. For identification of five breaths with directions, see CU 3.13.1-6 (see section 4.4.2.1).

The concept of breaths metonymically activates the concept of breath practice. Thanks to the use of the general word *púruṣa*, the recipient may understand that the composer refers to the human agent and to the whole of reality the unity of which is realised in breath practice. Identification of breaths with parts of the cosmos is already attested in AVŚ 15.15-17 (see chapter 2.2.2).

Breath practice leads to the unmanifest aspect of reality which is described in the next passage of the BU in an apophatic way:

BU 4.2.4b

sá eṣá néti néty ātmā́ | ágr̥hyo ná hí gr̥hyáte | áśīryo ná hí śīryáte | ásaṅgó na hi sajyate| ásito ná vyáthaté | ná riṣyati |.

About this self (*ātman*) one can say 'not-, not-.' He is ungraspable, for he cannot be grasped. He is undecaying, for he is not subject to the decay. He has nothing sticking to him, for he does not stick to anything. He is not bound; yet he neither trembles in fear nor suffers injury'

This passage is repeated in BU 4.4.22 at the end of Yājñavalkya's teaching. In my view, there is no doubt that this repetition is conscious and that the exposition of the situation of the highest cognitive agent in BU 4.3-44 is meant to give the metaphysical background for the practice and its results that was described earlier.

At the end of the teaching, Yājñavalkya claims that the concept of *ātmán-bráhman* independent from its manifestations was also looked for by Brahmins who practiced 'Vedic recitation, sacrifice, gift-giving, austerity and fasting'[207]. He also mentions ancient (*pū́rve*) people who contested the mainstream tradition and did not want to possess offspring[208]. Then he calls liberated man with the word *muní* (BU 4.4.22: *evá viditvā́ munír bhavati*)[209]. The use of this word brings us back to old practices attested already in R̥V 10.136. These practices must have been well known for the composers of the R̥V because the strength of the Maruts is compared to people who are called *muní* (R̥V 7.56.8). In R̥V 8.17.14, the word *muní* is used in a context which refers to Somic exultation[210]. This is further proof that the Upaniṣadic composers wanted to convince their recipients that the mental results of their practices are the same as those that were gained under the

---

207 BU 4.4.22: *tám etáṃ vedānuvacanéna brāhmaṇā vividiṣánti brahmacaryéna yajñéna dānéna tápasā́nāśakena |*

208 BU 4.4.22: *etád dha sma vaí tát pū́rve vidvā́ṁsaḥ prajā́ṃ ná kāmayante |*

209 In the description of the liberated state in BU 3.5.1 the word *mauná* is used.

210 R̥V 8.17.14 *vā́stoṣ pate dhruvā́ sthū́ṇā áṃsatraṃ somiyā́nām | drapsó bhettā́ purā́ṃ śáśvatīnām índro múnīnāṃ sákhā ||*

influence of Soma and are even better because they lead further. Even if in the ṚV the practices of the people called *muní* have come from the outside of Ṛgvedic society, in the BU they are mentioned as already old and belonging to the Brahminic tradition.

In the next passage, Yājñavalkya quotes a stanza which he calls *ṛc* (*tád etád ṛcā̀bhyùktam*, BU 4.4.23). Although this stanza does not appear in the ṚV, we know that the composer is activating the Ṛgvedic conceptualisation of cognition in terms of the general domain of Finding The Hidden in its specific realisation of Finding Of Hidden Hoofprints/Footprints in order to present liberating cognition (*tásyaivá syāt padavíd*).

*

From what has been shown in this section, it follows that the composers of the Upaniṣads knew the earlier Vedic tradition and that they wanted to introduce their contemporary practice as being within that tradition. The object of this introduction was not a belief in rebirth. It was rather a new practice which was developed by the Upaniṣadic philosophers and which was so efficient that it led further than Somic exultation and prevented from rebirth. The analysis also confirms that philosophical concepts are created in liberating practice.

It is worth noting that while BU 2.1-3 focuses on the way that leads to supernatural cognition, Yājñavalkya in BU 4.3-4 metaphysically grounds this process. He shows in detail how reality manifests in the cosmos and in man and how it can realise its aim which is the recognition of its unity from the perspective of the individual human being. However, this metaphysical description is preceded by the description of practice which leads to realisation of this state and which generally conforms with the description of BU 2.2-3. The difference lies in concepts which are used to conceive the process. The composer of BU 2.3 uses the concept of *satyá*, the composer of BU 4.2 activates the general domains of Cooking and of Procreation in order to explain the nature of liberating cognition. Taken from this perspective BU 2.3 is more abstract than BU 4.2 the composer of which elaborates metaphorical concepts characteristic for earlier tradition. However, the result is described in the same apophatic way in both chapters (BU 2.3.6, BU 4.2.4).

4.4.2.4. Philosophy in practice (*Chāndogya Upaniṣad* 8.1-12)

Before I begin my analysis Prajāpati's teaching, I will devote some words to the preceding chapters of the CU which give the teaching some context. Seen in context, the teaching of Prajāpati is a further attempt to express the concept of liberating cognition as a result of breath practice. It is also an attempt to name its stages which in the teachings presented in the BU are not named.

CU 8.1.1 evokes the conceptualisation of reality in terms of a lotus in a stronghold[211]. A lotus is identified with a dwelling place (*veśman*). It belongs to the *brahman* (*brahmapura*). Within a lotus a small space is present in which there is something which should be known. As I have shown this conceptualisation is elaborated in the AVŚ (see chapter 2.5.2). The composers of the AVŚ use the concept of lotus in two ways: either in reference to the same aspect of reality as a stronghold or in reference to its aspect conceived as being within a stronghold. Within the frame of the latter usage, within the lotus there is a mysterious being which consists of self (*yakṣám ātmanvát*). The composer of CU 8.1.1 proposes a fivefold division conceived in terms of the image schema of CONTAINER: *brahman* – stronghold – lotus = dwelling place – space within it – something in the space. The description is so general that it can refer to the human organism, the manifest aspect of reality or the whole of reality. If the recipient activates the Atharvavedic usage of this metaphor, he would understand that the something present in the space is the innermost self of man, the cosmos and reality. This will be confirmed in CU 8.1.5.

In CU 8.1.2, a question is posed about the content of the space which should be known. In the answer, two spaces are mentioned. The first is that space which contains the earth and the sky, fire and wind, sun and moon, lightning and stars and everything that belongs to it and everything which does not belong to that space. The second one is that space within man's heart which is identical with cosmic space (CU 8.1.3). As I have shown, the creation of space which will be filled is the first creative act of reality (see chapter 3.1.1, section 4.1.1), so the recipient understands that there is a possibility to realise this first creative state of reality. Within the frames of this interpretation, *brahman* corresponds to the unmanifest aspect of reality, a stronghold with a lotus corresponds to the borderline sphere of the manifest aspect, the space within it corresponds to the world and the entity within the space corresponds to the innermost self.

With the next question, a general conclusion is presented: it is said that the stronghold of *brahman* contains the whole world, all beings and all desires. The question is now posed about what remains when old age and death comes (CU 8.1.4). Thus the composer focuses on the human dimension of this general structure. The answer is as follows:

---

[211] CU 8.1.1: *atha yad idam asmin brahmapure daharaṃ puṇḍarīkaṃ veśma daharo 'sminn antarākāsaḥ* |

CU 8.1.4

sa brūyāt | nāsya jarayaitaj jīryati na vadhenāsya hanyate | etat satyaṃ brahmapuram asmin kāmāḥ samāhitāḥ | eṣa ātmāpahatapāpmā vijaro vimṛtyur viśoko vijighatso 'pipāsaḥ satyakāmaḥ satyasaṃkalpaḥ |

That does not age, as this body grows old; That is not killed, when his body is slain, That is the real fort of *brahman*, in it are contained all desires. The self (*ātman*) that is free from evils, free from old age and death, free from sorrow, free from hunger and thirst; the self whose desires and intentions are real.

The recipient understands that the entity which is within the space is the innermost self, *ātman*. Its definition is the same as the definition given later by Prajāpati (CU 8.7.1, see below).

In the next sentence, the composer evokes the image of subjects of a king who can settle anywhere they want provided they do this according to the king's order (CU 8.1.5). Within the frames of this metaphor, *ātman* is conceived as a king and the cognitive faculties of man are conceived as the subjects. Liberated man, led by his innermost unmanifest self, has full control over them and can freely realise his desires and his will to experience anything he wants.

It the next sentence, it is said:

CU 8.1.6

tad yatheha karmajito lokaḥ kṣīyata evam evāmutra puṇyajito lokaḥ kṣīyate |

As here in this world the possession of territory won by action comes to an end, so in the hereafter a world won by merit comes to an end.

I would again interpret the word *loka* as the space for experience: all kinds of experience finally come to an end and then man has a new desire. In the same way, experiences, which gained a man his afterlife thanks to good deeds, also come to an end. Then the composer states that when a man dies without knowing *ātman* and his real desires he is not free (*akāmacāro*), contrary to a man who knows this and is free (*kāmacāra*)[212]. The state of freedom is conceived in terms of the possibility to move without any constraints (FREEDOM IS LACK OF PHYSICAL BONDAGE).

In the next chapter, the composer describes various kinds of desire. He begins as follows:

212 CU 8.1.6: *tad ya ihātmānam ananuvidya vrajanty etāṃś ca satyān kāmāṃs teṣāṃ sarveṣu lokeṣv akāmacāro bhavati | atha ya ihātmānam anivudya vrajanty etaṃś ca satyān kāmāṃs teṣāṃ sarveṣu lokeṣu kāmacāro bhavati |*

CU 8.2.1

yadi pitṛlokakāmo bhavati | saṃkalpād evāsya pitaraḥ samuttiṣṭhanti | tena pitṛlokena sampanno mahīyate |

If such a person desires the world of fathers, by his intention alone fathers rise up. And, securing the world of fathers, he rejoices.

According to the definition of *ātman* given at CU 8.1.5, the desires and intentions of *ātman* are real. The recipient understands that the composer is describing how the reality of it's desires and intentions in various stages of liberating cognition. Interpretation of the word *loka* as a space for experience allows the recipient to understand that liberated man, if he wishes, experiences himself as a father[213]. In this way, he realises his identity with the whole of reality in its experience of being a father. This identity is implied by the participle *saṃpanna* which comes from the verb *saṃ pad-*, 'to meet', but also 'to enter into, to become absorbed'. The real nature of these intentional acts is expressed explicitly: everything man wants comes to being (*samuttiṣṭhati*). As I have mentioned several times, the verb *sam ut sthā-* is used in the JB in collocation with *loka* which is realised after man's death (see chapter 5.1.1), so the way it is used here conforms to its use in earlier tradition. Then other kinds of experience are listed: the experience of being a mother, a brother, a sister, a friend, of having perfumes and garlands, of having food and drink, of singing and listening to music. The description ends with the general statement that liberated man can realise any desire by his intention[214].

According to CU 8.3.1, real desires (*satyāḥ kamāḥ*) are hidden by the unreal (*anṛta*). In order to explain the nature of this hiding, the composer evokes the image of a hidden treasure of gold:

CU 8.3.2

tad yathāpi hiraṇyanidhiṃ nihitam akṣetrajñā upary upari sañcaranto na vindeyuḥ | evam evemāḥ sarvāḥ prajā ahar ahar gacchantya etaṃ brahmalokaṃ na vindanty anṛtena hi pratyūḍhāḥ |

Take, for example, a hidden treasure of gold. People who do not know the terrain, even if they pass right over it time and again, would not discover it. In exactly the same way, all these creatures, even though they go there every day, do not discover the world of *brahman*, for they are led astray by the unreal.

---

213 As I have argued, the same possibility of experiencing reality from various perspectives is expressed already in the *Vrātyakāṇḍa*, see chapter 2.2.2.

214 CU 8.2.10: *yaṃ yam antam abhikāmo bhavati | yaṃ kāmaṃ kāmayate | so 'sya saṃkalpād eva samuttiṣṭhati | tena saṃpanno mahīyate |*

Liberating cognition is conceived here in terms of finding a treasure. This metaphor is already used in the ṚV to express cognition under the influence of Soma (Jurewicz 2010a: 255 ff.). The conceptualisation of *ātman* in terms of gold allows the recipient to understand that it is not enough to find it but one has to practice more having found it just as one has to purify gold having found it (see chapter 3.5.1, see also chapter 5.1.2). But many people are not able to find their innermost self because they are distracted by its multifold manifestations. They will never experience *brahman*, i.e. the unity of reality even if they try to recognise it every day. Such a conceptualisation of *ātman*'s presence agrees with its conceptualisation in terms of sleep presented by Yājñavalkya (see section 4.4.2.3): in its manifestations *ātman* is conceived as sleeping as long as he is cognised by someone who wants that. This state corresponds to the waking state realised in everyday life.

Then the composer explains that one should look for one's innermost self within one's heart (CU 8.3.3). The true meaning of the word 'heart' (*hṛdaya*) is the place where *ātman* is (*hṛdy ayam*). Its knowledge allows man, as Olivelle interprets, to go 'to the heavenly world every single day' (*ahar ahar vā evaṃvit svargaṃ lokam eti*). I would again understand the word *loka* as a space for experience: a man who possesses true knowledge about himself is able to realise the heavenly experience every day. This state correspond to the state of dreaming sleep. The description of this state still presupposes duality. The logic of everyday experience activated by the expression *ahar ahar*, 'every day', implies that liberating activity and its results are repeated in the same way as human activity is interrupted at night and is picked up again in the morning.

CU 8.3.4

> *atha ya eṣa saṃprasādo 'smāc charīrāt samutthāya paraṃ jyotir upasaṃpadya svena rūpenābhiniṣpadyata eṣa ātmeti hovāca | etad amṛtam abhayam etad brahmeti |*
>
> This deeply serene one, after he rises up from this body and reaches the highest light, emerges in his own true appearance – that is the self', he said, 'that is the immortal; that is the one free from fear; that is *brahman*.

The word *saṃprasāda* refers to the state realised by *ātman* at the borderline sphere between its unmanifest and manifest aspects (see BU 4.3.14[215]). The recipient may then presume that the state of dreamless sleep is now presented.

---

[215] In CU 8.11,1 *saṃprasanna* is used in reference to the third state (dreamless sleep), in CU 8.12.3, however, *saṃprasāda* in the description of the moment of liberation.

This description will be repeated and explained in CU 8.12.3 in the description of final liberation (see below). The moment of final liberation of *ātman* comes immediately after it. *Ātman* is freed from the influence of its body and realises his unity with the whole of reality.

In the next paragraph (CU 8.4), the composer analyses the structure of reality conceived in terms of water; the composer elaborates the concept of a dike (*setu*) in terms of which the borderline sphere between the two aspects of reality is conceived (see sections 4.2.2, 4.4.2.4). Within the frames of this conceptualisation, the cognition of *ātman* is conceived in terms of crossing the dike which frees man from any sorrow, death and influence of time and also in terms of the passage from night to day (CU 8.4.1-2)[216]. I would draw attention to the coherence of this metaphor in the early Upaniṣads. It is also used by Yājñavalkya (BU 4.4.22) at the end of his description of the state of final liberation (see section 4.4.2.3).

At the end, the composer repeats that a man who cognises *ātman* realises full freedom and the way leading to this goal is *brahmacarya* the life of a celibate student (CU 8.4.3). Notwithstanding the social circumstances which made the composer identify liberating practice with *brahmacarya*, it will be recalled that this identification agrees with earlier thinking attested in the AVŚ where the concept of Brahmacārin is used to conceive the manifest aspect of reality (see chapter 2.2.1).

In the next paragraph, the composer redefines various holy rites such as sacrifice (*yajña*), the performance of a long sacrifice (*sattrāyana*), a vow of silence (*mauna*) and fasting (*anāśakayana*) and shows that all these rites are the activities of a Brahmācarin who looks for *ātman* (CU 8.5.1-2). The rational ground for these identifications is given in the etymologies of the names of the rites. In this way, the ritual activity of the householder is seen as liberating practice. Now the description of those who leave society is presented:

CU 8.5.3-4

> *atha yad araṇyāyanam ity ācakṣate brahmacaryam eva tat | tat araś ca ha vai ṇyaś cārṇavau brahmaloke tṛtīyasyām ito divi | tad airaṃmadīyaṃ saraḥ | tad aśvatthaḥ somasavanaḥ | tad aparājitā pūr brahmaṇaḥ prabhuvimitaṃ hiraṇmayam* (3) *tad ya evaitāv araṃ ca ṇyaṃ cārṇavau brahmaloke brahmacaryeṇānuvindanti teṣām evaiṣa brahmalokaḥ | teṣāṃ sarveṣu lokeṣu kāmacāro bhavati* | (4)

[216] CU: 8.4.1-2: *atha ya ātmā sa setur dhṛtir eṣāṃ lokānām asaṃbhedāya | naitaṃ setum ahorātre tarato na jarā na mṛtyur na śoko na sukṛtam | sarve pāpmāno 'to nivartante | apahatapāpmā hy eṣa brahmalokaḥ* | (1) *tasmād vā etaṃ setuṃ tīrtvā andhaḥ sann anandho bhavati | viddhaḥ sann aviddho bhavati | upatāpī sann anupatāpī bhavati |tasmād vā etaṃ setuṃ tīrtvā api naktam ahar evābhiniṣpadyate | sakṛd vibhāto hy evaiṣa brahmalokaḥ* | (2)

> And, finally, what people normally call 'the embarking to the wilderness' (*araṇyāyana*) is, in reality, the life of a celibate student. Now, Ara and Ṇya are the two seas in the world of *brahman*, that is, in the third heaven from here. In that worlds are also the lake Airaṃmadīya, the banyan tree Somasavana, the fort Aparājita, and *brahman* golden hall called Prabhu. (3)
> So, only those who, by the life of celibate student, find these two seas, Ara and Ṇya, in the world of *brahman* come to possess that world, and they obtain complete freedom of movement in all the worlds. (4)

There is a similarity between the conceptualisation of the meaning of the word *araṇyāyana* and the third heaven, and the afterlife journey described in KU 1.3 (see chapter 5.3). In both texts, the concepts of a lake and of a tree are used as source domains to conceive supernatural experience although their names are different. Since in the preceding description of the CU (8.1.5), liberating cognition is conceived in terms of conquering land, the recipient can understand that this domain is also evoked here. If the recipient elaborates the source domain of conquering land, he can include the source domain of a dike and see the liberating process in terms of a warrior who crosses a dike between two receptacles of water who then realises that the second receptacle consists of two oceans; he crosses them to finally reach a land with a lake and a tree where there is a stronghold with a golden hall. Such a conceptualisation of the content of a stronghold is implied already in CU 8.1.1 where a lotus is identified with a dwelling place (*veśman*). Within the frames of this conceptualisation, the recipient is prompted to conceive the manifest aspect of reality in terms of the first receptacle of water, the borderline between the aspects in terms of the dike and the unmanifest aspect in terms of the next receptacle of water. The further recognition of *brahman* is then conceived in terms of the final conquest of the land and the stronghold. We can see that the practice of the Upaniṣadic thinkers allows them not only to cognise the unmanifest aspect of reality, but also to understand and express its structure.

However, the source domains used in this conceptualisation are ancient and the composer seems to show that contemporary liberating practice is the same as that described in the AV: he begins his description with the concept of the stronghold of *brahman* and ends with it. The practice is conceived in terms of the practice of Brahmacārin which evokes thinking about the manifest aspect of reality presented in AVŚ 11.5 (see chapter 2.2.1). The name of the banyan which is *somasavana* brings the recipient's mind even further to the RV's conceptualisation of liberating cognition in terms of the conquest of a foreign land and of looking for a treasury.

Next the composer presents aspects of liberating practice (see BU 2.1.19, section 4.4.2.2, BU 4.3.20, section 4.4.2.3). The veins present in the heart of man have the same colours as the sun (CU 8.6.1)[217] and the recipient can presume that concentration on one's heart leads to cognition of the sun which is the visible form of *ātman* within its manifest aspect. This is explicitly said in the next sentence: the rays of the sun pervade both worlds: the one down here and the one up above (CU 8.6.2). The world down here is the manifest aspect and the world above is the borderline sphere between the two aspects. Rays are also present in the veins. The way the rays pervade the manifest aspect is conceived in terms of a long road which links two remote villages. Thus the composer evokes the SOURCE-PATH-GOAL image schema in terms of which liberated cognition is conceived. Man reaches the borderline sphere in sleepless dream; in this state his cognitive abilities are absorbed within the veins (see sections 4.4.2.2, 4.4.2.3). The act of absorption is expressed with use the verb *sṛp-* which evokes the concept of a snake (see BU 2.1.19, section 4.4.2.2) in terms of which the cognitive abilities of man in the dreamless sleep are conceived. In this state, man is not touched by any evil and becomes one with light (*tejasā hi tadā saṃpanno bhavati*, CU 8.6.3). It is implied that realisation of this state is possible during a man's life.

Then the composer presents the death of man during which the highest cognising agent[218] leaves the body through the crown of the head follows the same rays of the sun (CU 8.6.4-5). It is worth remembering that according to AU 1.3.14, this is the place through which reality enters the cosmos and man (see section 4.1.3). Then, sooner that one could think, man reaches the sun which is called the gateway to the farther world open only to those who possess the right knowledge. The composer implies that the syllable *oṃ* should be recited; it is not specified if this has to be done by the dying person or by a priest. However, since in the JUB the recitation of the Udgātar plays an important role in the afterlife state of man, he may be meant here too.

The composer has stated that the world to the unmanifest can be reached only by those who possess true knowledge and this is the topic of the following chapters (CU 8.7-12). Now the composer plays with the wide semantic range of the word *ātman* that refers to everything that makes oneself himself,

---

217 CU 8.6.1: *atha yā etā hṛdayasya nāḍyas tāḥ piṅgalasyāṇimnas tiṣṭhanti śuklasya nīlasya pītasya lohitasyeti | asau vādityaḥ piṅgala eṣa śukla eṣa nīla eṣa pīta eṣa lohitaḥ |*

218 Contrary to teachings of Ajātaśatru and Yājñavalkya, *vijñānamáya púruṣa* is not used here, but the description is so similar to the exposition presented in their teachings that there is no doubt that the composer refers it. This possible interpretation of this difference will be discussed below (ad CU 8.10.1).

beginning with the body and ending with the essence of a person. Taking into account the context of the story, it is clear that philosophical concepts are being built in practice. There is a great consistency in the conceptualisation of the experience realised in breath practice and the stages of liberating practice.

In subsequent chapters, the composer presents the teaching of Indra. The story, within the frames of which this exposition is put, is a story about gods and the Asuras who hear the teaching of Prajāpati about *ātman* and want to cognise it. Prajāpati gives the following definition of *ātman* at the beginning:

CU 8.7.1

ya ātmā apahatapāpmā vijaro vimṛtyur viśoko vijighatso 'pipāsaḥ satyakāmaḥ satyasaṃkalpaḥ so'nveṣṭavyaḥ sa vijijñāsitavyaḥ | sa sarvāṃś ca lokān āpnoti sarvāṃś ca kāmān yas tam ātmānam anuvidya vijānātīti ha prajāpatir uvāca |

The self (*ātman*) that is free from evils, free from old age and death, free from sorrow, free from hunger and thirst; the self whose desires and intentions are real – that is the self that you should try to discover, that is the self that you should seek to perceive. When someone discovers that self and perceives it, he obtains all the worlds, and his desires are fulfilled.

The first sentence of the definition has been presented earlier in CU 8.1.5. *Ātman* is presented as free from evil (*apahatapāpmā*). He is perfect and does not experience any kind of lack caused by hunger or thirst (*vijighatso 'pipāsaḥ*), by the flow of time (*vijaro vimṛtyur*) or by the impossibility of realising one's desires or intentions (*satyakāmaḥ satyasaṃkalpaḥ*). Knowledge of *ātman* thus defined makes man feel all kinds of experience (conceived in terms of conquest of all worlds) and able to fulfil all his desires.

The gods and the Asuras want to know *ātman* thus defined and they send their representatives Indra and Virocana to Prajāpati (CU 8.7). The first teaching of Prajāpati as follows:

CU 8.7.4

tau ha prajāpatir uvāca ya eṣo 'kṣiṇi puruṣo dṛṣyata eṣa ātmeti hovāca | etad amṛtam abhayam etad brahmeti | atha yo ayaṃ bhagavo 'psu parikhyāyate yaś cāyam ādarśe katama eṣa iti | eṣa u evaiṣu sarveṣvannteṣu parikhyāyata iti hovāca |

Prajāpati then told to them: 'This person that one sees here in the eye – that is the self (*ātman*); that is the immortal; that is the one free from fear; that is *brahman*'. 'But then, sir, who is the one that's seen here in the water and here in a mirror?' 'It is the same one who is seen in all these surfaces,' replied Prajāpati.

The expression 'man in the eye' (*akṣiṇi puruṣo*) is used in the context of liberating cognition as its starting point (see CU 4.15.1, section 4.3.2, BU 2.3.5, section 4.4.2.2). On this basis, the recipient may presume that Prajāpati gives the true answer about *ātman* to Indra and Virocana. However, they understand it in another way: as a reflection of a human's figure as in a mirror or in the waters. Therefore, they understand *ātman* as outward appearance. They are not completely wrong in their interpretation because this is also the meaning of the word *ātman*. They go away and Virocana brings the news to the demons and never comes back.

However, Indra notices that the concept *ātman* understood as the outward appearance does not fit the definition given in the beginning by Prajāpati because it is physically imperfect and not, therefore, free from evils such as old age and death, sorrow, hunger and thirst (CU 8.9.1). Moreover, while it is beautiful when beautifully adorned and dressed, it is handicapped when the body is handicapped and it, finally, dies with the death of the body.

So he returns to Prajāpati to learn more and a further definition is given to him. Now *ātman* is defined as the state of consciousness during sleep with dreams. Indra again sees that it does not agree with definition of *ātman* given by Prajāpati because there is no freedom from sorrow in this state. *Ātman* is not influenced by imperfections of the body, but experiences unhappiness and fear in terrifying dreams (CU 8.10.2).

The third definition identifies *ātman* with the state of consciousness in dreamless sleep which again is not sufficient because in this state one is not conscious at all and it is not a state in which one can have real desires and intentions (CU 8.11.1). I would like to point out that, in the preceding chapters of the CU which describe breath practice, the highest cognitive agent is not called *vijñānamaya*, contrary to the teaching of Ajātaśatru and Yājñavalkya that are presented in the BU. It is possible that breath practice led to two kinds of experience realised at the borderline sphere of reality. One gave omniscience about the manifest aspect of reality and the highest cognitive agent called *vijñānamaya*[219] and the second led to the experience of a total lack of any knowledge because of the suspension of subjective-objective cognition.

Finally, the fourth definition is presented:

[219] This experience is also evoked in the TU 2.4.1 (see section 4.4.2.5).

CU 8.12.1-3

maghavan martyaṃ vā idaṃ śarīram āttaṃ mṛtyunā | tad asyāmṛtasyāśarīrasyātmano 'dhiṣṭhānam | ātto vai saśarīraḥ priyāpriyābhyām | na vai saśarīrasya sataḥ priyāpriyayor apahatir asti | aśarīraṃ vāva santaṃ na priyāpriye spṛśataḥ | (1)
aśarīro vāyuḥ | abhraṃ vidyut stanayitnur aśarīrāṇy etāni | tad yathaitāny amuṣmād ākāśāt samutthāya paraṃ jyotir upasaṃpadya svena rūpeṇābhiniṣpadyante | (2)
evam evaiṣa saṃprasādo 'smāc charīrāt samutthāya paraṃ jyotir upasaṃpadya svena rūpeṇābhiniṣpadyate | sa uttamapuruṣaḥ | sa tatra paryeti jakṣat krīḍan ramamāṇaḥ strībhir vā yānair vā jñātibhir vā nopajanaṃ smarann idaṃ śarīram | sa yathā prayogya ācaraṇe yukta evam evāyam asmiñ charīre prāṇo yuktaḥ | (3)

This body, Maghavan, is mortal; it is in the grip of death. So, it is the abode of this immortal and nonbodily self. One who has a body is in the grip of joy and sorrow, and there is no freedom from joy and sorrow for one who has a body. Joy and sorrow, however, do not affect one who has no body. (1)
The wind is without a body, and so are the rain-cloud, lightning, and thunder. There are without bodies. Now, as these, after they rise up from the space up above and reach the highest light, emerge in their own true appearance (2),
in the very same way, this deeply serene one, after he rises up from this body and reaches the highest light, emerges in his own true appearance. He is the highest person. He roams about there, laughing, playing, and enjoying himself with women, carriages, or relatives, without remembering the appendage that is this body. The breath[220] is yoked to this body, as a draft animal to a cart. (3)

This definition of *ātman* agrees with the definition given by Prajāpati at the beginning of his teaching. Firstly, the difference between *ātman* in its meaning of the whole human organism and *ātman* in its meaning as the innermost essence of man is presented: joys and sorrows are connected with the former and not with the latter[221]. The composer introduces the concepts of wind, lightning and thunder in terms of which the moment of getting final cognition of *ātman* should be understood. As those celestial phenomena appear themselves high in the sky, not having any bodily appearance, in the same way *ātman* appears as man's self when the stage of dreamless sleep is overcome. Thus man becomes free from any imperfection that comes from the body: hunger, thirst, fear and death. Then the composer introduces the concept of a king who is happy with his wives and relatives and takes leisure and rides on carriages. In these terms, a state of conscious happiness is conceived when any desire or intention can be immediately fulfilled because there is no mental connection with the body. This concept is used in earlier

---

220 Olivelle (1998): 'lifebreath'.

221 In BU 4.3.36, the relationship between the highest cognitive agent and the body is conceived in terms of bonds (*bándhana*), see section 4.4.2.3.

description of the CU (8.1.6, see above) to express freedom realised thanks to liberating cognition.

The composer of the CU emphasises that this state is reversible in that it is possible to go back to subjective-objective cognition[222]:

CU 8.12.4-5

atha yatraitad ākāśam anuviṣaṇṇaṃ cakṣuḥ sa cākṣuṣaḥ puruṣo darśanāya cakṣuḥ | atha yo vededaṃ jighrāṇīti sa ātmā gandhāya ghrāṇam | atha yo vededam abhivyāharāṇīti sa ātmā abhivyāhārāya vāk | atha yo vededaṃ śṛṇvānīti sa ātmā śravaṇāya śrotram | (4)
atha yo vededaṃ manvānīti sa ātmā | mano 'sya daivaṃ cakṣuḥ | sa vā eṣa etena daivena cakṣuṣā manasaitān kāmān paśyan ramate ya ete brahmaloke | (5)

Now, when this sight here gazes into space, that is the seeing person, the faculty of sight enables one to see. The one who is aware: 'Let me smell this' – that is the self; the faculty of smell enables him to smell. The one who is aware: 'Let me say this' – that is the self; the faculty of speech enables him to speak. The one who is aware: 'Let me listen to this' – that is the self; the faculty of hearing enables him to hear. (4)
The one who is aware: 'Let me think about this' – that is the self; the mind is his divine faculty of sight. This very self rejoices as it perceives with his mind, with that divine sight, these object of desire found in the world of *brahman*. (5)

The acts of seeing, smelling, speaking, hearing and thinking are subjective-objective acts characteristic for the manifest aspect and realised in the waking state and the state of dreams. The unmanifest aspect is realised by reality that wants to perform those acts and that is experienced in the fourth state of consciousness. Thus man in the microscale realises the state of reality for which the world exists in its potential state and that is always possible for to be realised whenever wanted. The ability to begin subjective-objective cognition is conceived in terms of a seeing man (*cākṣuṣaḥ puruṣaḥ*). Such a conceptualisation recruits from the metaphor COGNITION IS SEEING. This term also appears in BU 4.4.1 in the description of the death of man when subjective-objective cognition is suspended[223].

---

222 I do not agree here with Black (2007: 43), according to whom the concept of *ātman* presented by Prajāpati differs from the concept of *ātman* presented by Śāṇḍilya. The idea of liberating cognition which encompasses the whole cosmos is also implicitly expressed in Śāṇḍilya's teaching in his description of *ātman* which is greater than the whole cosmos. Prajāpati is just more explicit in his explanation of this stage of liberating cognition.

223 BU 4.4.1: *sá etā́s tejomātrā́ḥ samabhyā́dádāno hṛ́dayam evā̀nvávakrāmati | sá yátraiṣá cā́kṣuṣaḥ púruṣaḥ párāñ paryā́vártate | áthā́rūpajño bhavati* |

*

Let me now compare the description of the liberating cognition given in the BU (sections 4.4.2.2 and 4.4.2.3) and the CU (section 4.4.2.4). The composer of the CU enumerates four states realised in this cognition as does Yājñavalkya. Ajātaśatru mentions only three and ends with the dreamless sleep seen as the ultimate source of creation. Yājñavalkya analyses the problem of liberation from the point of view of the highest cognitive agent of man and from the point of view of a particular man. The perspective of the highest cognitive agent is elaborated in the cosmogony presented in the AU where manifestation in the cosmos and in man gives reality the possibility of cognising itself from the point of view of its manifestations (see section 4.1.3). In his teaching about the three first states, Yājñavalkya uses metaphors, while the composer of CU 8.7-12 describes them in a short and abstract way. On the other hand, in his description of the fourth state, the composer of CU 8.7.-12 evokes more metaphors than does Yājñavalkya who mostly describes it in general cognitive terms. All three teachings use the concept of sleep in their description of the stages of liberating cognition. The composer of the CU uses the term *ātman* in reference to the highest cognitive agent which, as we have seen, is not often used in the description of the stages of liberating cognition in the BU; it is mentioned in the beginning of the description and in the description of the final state. The use of the word *ātman* allows the composer of the CU to play with its broad meaning in a way that is similar to the composer of the AU (see section 4.1.3).

The descriptions of liberating cognition just analysed are testimonies to systematic practices that leads to supernatural states of consciousness and can be treated as the source of later yogic practices. The waking state is the everyday life during which subjective-objective cognition takes place. The second state of consciousness, conceived in terms of dreaming sleep, is the state during which everyday perception is closed, i.e. the senses do not operate, but the mind is still active and the memory of subjective-objective acts is performed by it and within it. According to CU 8.7-12, the third state of consciousness is the state when subjective-objective perception disappears but the new kind of cognition has not yet arisen. The perspective of the analysis that is elaborated by Yājñavalkya allows me to assume that the total lack of cognition in this state, assumed by the composer of the CU (and also by Ajātaśatru), concerns the human agent but not the highest cognitive agent who is still aware. His awareness is experienced by the human agent in the fourth state when he cognises his identity with the unmanifest aspect that is the source of all cognitive acts. In this state, the agent is aware of subjective-objective acts, but does not identify with the subject or the object.

It should be emphasised that all the composers, in their description of the liberating practice, explicitly evoke earlier tradition. The composer of BU 2.2 quotes Atharvavedic stanza and refers to ṚV. The composer of BU 4.2 evokes the conceptualisation of main breath in terms of Indra attested in the ŚB. The composer of the CU begins his exposition with elaboration of the Atharvavedic concepts of lotus and stronghold. This supports my argument that the Upaniṣadic composers emphasised links with tradition as far as liberating breath practice is concerned.

As I have shown elsewhere (Jurewicz 2010c), the description of the four states of consciousness, taken in reverse order, refers to the creative process. I will briefly recapitulate my argument. The fourth state of consciousness corresponds to the pre-creative state of reality. The third state corresponds to the second state of creation. In the *Nāsadīyasukta*, it is conceived in terms of the darkness hiding the darkness. In the ŚB, it is the moment when Prajāpati dies in his creation (see chapters 3.2.2). In BU 1.2, it is conceived in terms of death and hunger (see sections 4.1.1). In BU 1.4.1, this state is presented as the stage when reality perceives that it is alone, that there is nothing else except it, so it cannot cognise anything other than it (see section 4.1.2). The second state of consciousness corresponds to the state when reality begins to think about its second self manifest in its creation (as in BU 1.4.2-3, see section 4.1.2). The first state corresponds to the state when the second self of reality, which is the world, is created.

4.4.2.5. Abstraction of experience (*Taittirīya Upaniṣad* 2.1-5)

In spite of the use of metaphors in the description of the liberating state of cognition, the whole exposition of CU 8.7-12 is abstract and general. The account of TU 2.1-5 is even more abstract.

TU 2.1.1

satyaṃ jñānam anantaṃ brahma yo veda nihitaṃ guhāyāṃ parame vyoman |
so 'śnute sarvān kāmān saha brahmaṇā vipaściteti ||

tasmād vā etasmād ātmana ākāśaḥ saṃbhūtaḥ | ākāśād vāyuḥ | vāyor agniḥ| agner āpaḥ | adbhyaḥ pṛthivī | pṛthivyā oṣadhayaḥ | oṣadhībhyo 'nnam| annāt puruṣaḥ | sa vā eṣa puruṣo 'nnarasamayaḥ | tasyedam eva śiraḥ | ayaṃ dakṣiṇaḥ pakṣaḥ | ayam uttaraḥ pakṣaḥ | ayamātmā | idaṃ pucchaṃ pratiṣṭhā |

Truth and knowledge, the infinite and *brahman* –
a man who knows them as hidden in the deepest cavity,

> hidden in the highest heaven;
> Attains all his desires, together with the wise *brahman*.
>
> From this very self (*ātman*) did space come into being; from space, air; from air, fire; from fire the waters; from the waters, the earth; from the earth, plants; from the plants, food; and from food, man. Now, a man here is formed from the essence of food. This here is his head; this is his right side; this is his left side; this is his torso (*ātman*); and this is his bottom on which he rests.

The description begins with the definition of *brahman* which is understood as truth, knowledge and infinity. Then the possibility to cognise it is stated: reality thus understood is immanently and secretly present in the cosmos and in man. The composer uses the phrase *paramá vyòman*. This expression is used in the ṚV to denote the borderline sphere of the cosmos (Jurewicz 2010a: 296–298). The recipient may also evoke the concept of looking for hidden treasure in terms of which cognition is conceived in the ṚV (see Jurewicz 2010a: 92 ff.), but it is not necessary to understand the meaning of the sentence *yo veda nihitaṃ guhāyāṃ parame vyoman*. The image schematic logic of the source domain, which is going along a path in order to reach a goal (SOURCE-PATH-GOAL), is fully conflated with the target domain which is cognition and is immediately understood. Thus the abstract concept of cognition is created.

Then the composer presents a cosmogony. Similarly to the AU (see section 4.1.3), the composer of TU calls reality in its creative activity *ātman*. If we see the first five phases of creation from the perspective of later thought, we could say that five great elements (later called *mahābhuta*) appear from *ātman*. However, the sequence of the creative stages is also motivated by the earlier cosmogonies. Reality firstly creates space which is an abstract formulation of the metaphoric conceptualisation of the stage of creation conceived in terms of hunger or death in the ŚB and in BU 1.2 (see chapters 3.1.1, 3.2.1-2, and section 4.1.1). Appearance of wind and fire corresponds to the appearance of breath and speech: reality begins to breath and then fire appears as in ŚB 2.2.4; in terms of fire, speech is conceived (see chapter 3.1.1). As I have previously pointed out, in the Veda the concept of *vāyu* inherits features of fire, e.g. it is conceived as a purifying element (see chapter 2.1.2). According to the scenario of the earlier cosmogonies, the fiery manifestation of reality is followed by a liquid manifestation which is expressed in the TU as the creation of water. Finally, the earth is created which is the foundation for further creation (see ŚB 6.1.1.15, chapter 3.2.2, BU 1.2, section 4.1.1). So the sequence of the stages of creation is motivated by earlier thought, but the composer of the TU expresses them in a more abstract way just mentioning the nouns which name the consecutive stages. In this form, it will be inherited by later Indian philosophy without any change. This form will be taken for granted and treated as obvious. It will not be necessary to evoke its motivating conceptual background in order to understand the process of creation of the great elements (*mahābhūta*) of which the cosmos is composed. This is an example of another way to build abstract concepts: a vehicle of metonymy (like space, wind, fire, water, earth) becomes an abstract concept which can be understood separately from its target domain.

The names of the next stages metonymically evoke the stages of the path of the fathers (*pitryāna*, see section 4.3.1): these are plants, food and man who is the visible form of reality; its *ātman* in the sense of outward appearance. This is further proof that the concepts of stages connected with rebirth were widespread in the times of the Upaniṣads. Similarly to the cosmogony of the AU the aim of man is to make it possible for reality to perceive and experience itself from within its manifestation (see section 4.1.3).

The further exposition is such that the recipient can presume the teacher is pointing at parts of his body in order to explain how the ultimate manifestation of reality in man looks: 'here is his head; this is his right side; this is his left side; this is his torso (*ātman*)[224]; and this is his bottom on which he rests'[225]. The body is called *annarasamaya* which Olivelle translates as 'is formed from the essence of food'[226]. I would enlarge his interpretation as the compound *annarasa* can also be understood as a *dvandva* compound and the word *rasa* refers here to liquid food or more specifically to drinks which, together with food, constitute the body of man.

At the same time, this exposition evokes the concept of building a fire altar in the Agnicayana. So the recipient is prompted to create a blend the input spaces of which are the fire altar and the human body (*ātman*). The concept of *ātman* is already a blend the input spaces of which are a human body, a bird[227] and the cosmos. The ritual input space is needed mainly to endow the blend with the clear logic of the stages of the liberating process. It is conceived in terms of the construction of consecutive selves (*ātman*) of man and does not convey the meaning of a necessity for ritual practice. Other input spaces are the concepts of cognition and of reality. The generic space is the image schema of CONTAINER.

In his further description, the composer elaborates the blend. He presents consecutive *ātman*s which are conceived in terms of the image schema of

---

224 In the same way the word *ātmán* is used in the exegesis of Agnicayana (ŚB 6.1.1.6).

225 *tasyedam eva śiraḥ | ayaṃ dakṣiṇaḥ pakṣaḥ |ayam uttaraḥ pakṣaḥ | ayam ātmā | idaṃ puccham pratiṣṭhā |*

226 See also Angot (2007 I, 400).

227 The word *pakṣa* means also 'wing'

CONTAINER: *ātman*s are inside one another, each of them fills the external one completely and have the form of man (*tenaiṣa pūrṇaḥ*)[228]. Each internal *ātman* is called the embodied self (*śārira ātman*) of the previous one. It is worth drawing attention to the fivefold structure elaborated in CU 8.1.1 with the use of different metaphors (se section 4.4.2.4).

These are *ātman*s made of breath (*prāṇa*), of mind (*manas*), of perception (*vijñāna*) and bliss (*ānanda*). The composer defines their parts (head, right side/wing, left side/wing, torso and bottom/foundation, i.e. legs) according to the nature of the respective *ātman*.

The *prāṇamaya ātman* consists of the out-breath (*prāṇa*), the inter-breath (*vyāna*), the in-breath (*apāna*), space (*ākāśa*) and earth (*pṛthivī*, TU 2.2.1). The *manomaya ātman* consists of the sounds of the Vedas: the Yajus-formulas, the Ṛk-stanzas, the Sāman-chants, the rules of substitution (*ādeśa*) and the Atharva-Aṅgirases (TU 2.3.1). The *vijñānamaya ātman* consists of cognitive faculties and states: faith (*śraddhā*), truth (*ṛta*) and the real (*satya*). The torso is *yoga* which Olivelle translates as 'performance' and the foundation is *mahas* translated by Olivelle as 'celebration' (TU 2.4.1). The *ānandamaya ātman* consists of various kinds of positive emotional experiences such as pleasure (*priya*), delight (*moda*), thrill (*pramoda*), bliss (*ānanda*) and the foundation is *brahman* (TU 2.5.1).

I would argue that the composer of this passage presents the process, although he uses terms which refer to states[229]. As already mentioned the use of such words is a result of the endeavour for abstraction. Thanks to their use, the composer can present more generally the structure of the world and man.

The first stage of the process, called *annarasamaya*, is both the state of everyday activity of a man in the cosmos and a starting point for the liberating process. The second stage, called *prāṇamaya*, refers to breath practice. It is metonymically evoked by the concept of breaths (*prāṇa*, *vyāna* and *apāna*). In this way, the input space of the human body is elaborated. Then the composer elaborates the input space of the cosmos: its torso is space (*ākāśa*) and the earth (*pṛthivī*) is the foundation. In the blend, there is identity between man's body and the cosmos and breath practice leads to cognition of this identity. The correspondence between the torso and space is based on the fact that the torso is the main locus of breaths in the same way that space is the main locus of the wind which is the cosmic counterpart of breath. The correspondence between the feet and the earth is well attested in the earlier texts.

---

[228] TU 2.2.1, 2.3.1, 2.4.1, 2.5.1.

[229] The concept of a process is evoked by the composer in TU 8 in the description of afterlife state, see below.

The use of the word *ātman* in reference to a torso is attested already in the exegesis of Agnicayana ritual in the ŚB (see ŚB 6.1.1.6[230]) Moreover, it seems that the use of the word *ātman* to denote the whole body and its central point which is its torso is not only an intellectual device (motivated by metonymy PART OF A THING FOR THE WHOLE THING/WHOLE FOR A PART OF THE THING) on the basis of which man understands the identity of his central part with the whole body and the cosmos. It may also be of practical use and helps in liberating cognition. In the ŚB, the sacrifice is the *ātman* of Prajāpati seen as the space where he can safely manifest himself and where men could safely realise their identity with reality and its creation (see chapter 3.1.1). In the TU, the torso of man, called *ātman*, becomes a space which gives access to his whole body, to the cosmos and finally to the unmanifest aspect also called *ātman*. The broad meaning of the word *ātman* allows the composer to imply the centrifugal movement from the centre of the body 'up to its nail-tips' (*ắ nakhāgrébhyo*) as BU 1.4.7 puts it (see section 4.1.2) and then a reverse movement towards the centre. Creation and liberation are conceived by the image schema of CENTRE-PERIPHERY which is the next input space of the blend. Creation is the movement towards the periphery while liberation is movement towards the centre. On a more general level, it is the realisation of the identity of *ātman* which means both innermost essence and outward appearance. The essence of man is seen here as located in the torso (*ātman*) and its recognition leads to the recognition of man's self (*ātman*), of the self (*ātman*) of the cosmos and the whole of reality. Putting this in terms of the cosmogony of the AU, in this way man allows the reality that is present in him to look at itself from a different perspective.

The third stage, called *manomaya*, is concentration on mind. The elements of *ātman* mentioned here are the Vedas. In this way, the composer elaborates the ritual input space and evokes the concept of the *ātman* of the sacrificer which is composed of the sounds of the Veda (see chapter 3.4). It is also possible that this reflects the practice of mental recitation (*jāpa*) which is an important element in later yogic practice. This is the moment when the externalisation of speech is not necessary as cognition is realised within the human body and is focused on what is internal.

The fourth stage, called *vijñānamaya*, is the realisation of perception (*vijñāna*). This compound qualifies *puruṣa* (*vijñānamaya puruṣa*) to denote the highest cognitive agent manifesting in the cosmos and in man (BU 2.1.17, 4.3.7); the same meaning is conveyed in BU 4.4.5, 4.4.22 (see sections 4.4.2.2,

---

230 *sá vaí saptapuruṣó bhavati* | *saptapuruṣó hy áyam púruṣo yác catvắra ātmā tráyaḥ pakṣapuchắni catvắro hí tásya púruṣasyātmắ tráyaḥ pakṣapuchắni* |

4.4.2.3)[231] where *ātmán* is called *vijñānamáya*. The composer of the TU uses this compound in the same way: to denote the state reached in the borderline sphere between the unmanifest and manifest aspects of reality.

The aspects of this stage are faith *śraddhā* (head), the right *ṛta* (right side/wing) and the real *satya* (left side/wing). The exact meaning of *śraddhā* is still discussed[232]. As has been shown, in the model of the Five Fires the word *śraddhā* refers to the form of the deceased who are the first oblation poured into the sun. The evidence of the *Kaṭha Upaniṣad*, although later than the TU, but belonging to the same school as the Black YV, reveals that *śraddhā* refers to a state of mind that causes the radical transformation of the agent: having been overwhelmed with *śraddhā*, Naciketas begins his search for liberation[233]. It is worth noting that the words *ṛta*, *satya* and *śraddhā* are used in ṚV 9.113 which describes the supernatural effects of Soma: the truth, the real and faith are spoken by Soma while it is prepared during ritual (ṚV 1.113.4). Since thoughts, which appear under the influence of Soma, are conceived in terms of streams of Soma (Jurewicz 2010a), the recipient of the hymn may understand that that the speech of Soma becomes the speech of the agent who drinks it and who externalises it in his cognition. If the intention of the composer of the TU was to evoke Ṛgvedic thinking, he could imply in this way that the results gained in the process he now describes are the same as the results of drinking Soma by the Ṛgvedic poets. As it has been shown, the composers of the early Upaniṣads wanted their recipient to think so.

In this state, the torso is identified with *yoga* which again implies the central role of the torso, called *ātman*, in the liberating process: this is the place where the agent's activity is performed and concentrated. In the ṚV, this word is used in the compound *yogakṣema* to denote phases of the Aryan life divided into conquest and peace (Oberlies 1998: 333 ff.). Since the Ṛgvedic poets see conquest as an intentional action[234], I would argue the composer of the TU uses the word with this meaning. Contrary to Angot (2007, II 694), however, I would argue that the whole context of the use of the word *yoga* in TU 2.4 can be seen as an important root for the later use of *yoga* in reference to liberating practice. The word *mahas*, which corresponds to a tail, is interpreted by Olivelle as celebration[235]. I would interpret *mahas* in its more literal sense as the greatness in terms of which the first manifestation

---

[231] In BU 4.4.2 *ātmán* of the dying man who leaves his body is called *sávijñāna*.

[232] Hacker (1963), Köhler (1973), Hara (1992).

[233] *Kaṭha Upaniṣad* 1.1: *taṃ ha kumāraṃ santaṃ dakṣiṇāsu nīyamānāsu śraddhāviveśa* | For analysis of *Kaṭha Upaniṣad* against the earlier background, see Smith (2016).

[234] It becomes the source domain for other intentional actions such as creation and cognition, see (Jurewicz 2010a: 128 ff.).

[235] Angot (2007, I, 412) leaves it in original meaning.

of reality are conceived in the AVŚ (see chapter 2.2.2). Here I would look for the use of the word *mahat* to express the last phases of the liberating process in the classical description of yoga.

The fifth stage called *ānandamaya* is the stage of final recognition of the unity of reality. Here the identity of the experience felt in the torso and in the whole state is expressed explicitly: the torso is bliss (*ānanda ātmā*). The words *moda* and *pramoda* which name the left and the right side/wing are almost the same as the words used in ṚV 9.113.11 to describe the state under the influence of Soma. This state is also described as a state where all desires are fulfilled which agrees with the initial definition of *brahman* as the final aim of the process described in the TU 2.1. In this process, *brahman* becomes the foundation of *ātman* which evokes the cosmogony of the ŚB (6.1.1.8) and their understanding of *brahman* as the foundation of Prajāpati (see chapter 3.2.2).

Finally, the head is pleasure (*priya*)[236]. This word appears in the Upaniṣads in important contexts that describe liberation. In BU 1.4.8, it is said that one should understand *ātmán* as being dear to oneself (*ātmán*), in BU 2.4, Yājñavalkya uses this word to explain to Maitreyī that one's love of anything in the world is motivated by the love of oneself (*ātmán*). I would argue then that the head is called in such a way to describe the moment of recognition of one's identity with everything that exists and of the experience of love for everything which is the result of this recognition. Thus the torso becomes filled with bliss, *ānanda*, which explodes into the whole body and the cosmos.

It is important to note that there is a clear correspondence between the processes described by the TU and the processes of liberation described by Yājñavalkya and Prajāpati. The stages called *annarasamaya* and *prāṇamaya* correspond to the waking state. The third state, *manomaya*, corresponds to the state conceived as dreaming sleep when mental cognition takes place without external perception. The state of *vijñāna* corresponds to the state conceived as dreamless sleep. Here we can see the difference in the descriptions of the state just before final liberation is gained. The composer of the CU highlights the decline of everyday cognitive abilities before the agent realises supernatural cognitive ability. The composer of the TU, similarly to the composers of the BU, highlights the awakening of a new cognitive ability that is above everyday subjective-objective cognition. The last stage, called in the TU *ānanda*, corresponds to the fourth stage of *ātman*.

The five states of *ātman* presented in the TU also display a striking similarity with the stages of yoga proposed by Patañjali in his *Yogasūtras*.

---

236 In ṚV 2.20.6cd, the adjective *priyá* qualifies head of the enemy killed by Indra: *áva priyám arśasānásya sāhvā̃ñ chíro bharad dāsásya svadhā́vān.*

The stage called *annarasamaya* can be seen as the state of consciousness that is gained during the practice of sitting, *āsana*: both stages are connected with the physical body. The stage called *prāṇamaya* corresponds to *prāṇayama*, the stage called *manomaya* corresponds to concentration, *dhāraṇa*, and is practice of mind. The stage called *vijñānamaya* can be seen as corresponding to contemplation, *dhyāna*, and is the last state in yoga before meditation, *samādhi*, is realised. The *ānandamaya* state corresponds to *samādhi*. These similarities support my claim that the description of the TU can be seen as the source for the later use of yoga as a technique which leads to liberation.

Similarly, the four states of *ātman* described in the CU and the process described in the TU, in its reversed form, can be treated as cosmogony. The stage of *ānandamaya* corresponds to the unmanifest state of reality. The stage of *vijñānamaya* corresponds to the stage of creation when the subjective power of reality is manifested (the first stage of creation in the *Nāsadīyasūkta*). The stage of *manomaya* corresponds to the stage when thought about the object appears. The *prāṇamaya* and the *annarasamaya* stages are the stages when the object acquires life and body.

This brings us back to the cosmogony of ŚB 10.5.3 the composer of which sees it in terms of the transformation of the mind through speech, breath, sight, hearing, deed and fire (see chapter 3.5.1). Although the sequence of the states is different, there is similarity between the two descriptions in that, as I have shown, the cosmogony of the ŚB sees creation as the creation of the possibility of subjective-objective cognition. The process described in the TU consists in suspending this possibility.

The description of each liberating stage by the TU is preceded a stanza which emphasises the importance of knowledge of its nature. In this way, the composer refers to various practices which lead to a partial knowledge of reality[237]. The descriptions of *ātmans annamaya* and *prāṇamaya* are preceded by stanzas which emphasise the importance of food and breath for living (TU 2.2.1, 2.3.1). Men who venerate food or breath as *brahman* acquire 'all the food' (*sarvam te 'nnam apnuvante*) and live a full life. The description of *ātman manomaya* is preceded by the following stanza:

TU 2.4.1

yato vāco nivartante aprāpya manasā saha |
ānandaṃ brahmaṇo vidvān na bibheti kadācaneti ||

Before they reach it, the words turns back, together with the mind.
One who knows that bliss of *brahman*, he is never afraid.

---

237 As in BU 2.1 (section 4.4.2.2), ŚB 10.6.1.1-2 (section 4.4.2.1), CU 5.11-18, see section 4.4.2.1.

This stanza is repeated at the end of the chapter after the presentation of the whole liberating process (I will return to this below). As I have argued, the stage called *manomaya* corresponds to the state which in the ŚB is realised during ritual when the immortal self of the sacrificer is composed from the sounds of Veda (see chapter 3.4). In this state, words are internalised. This is the state everyday words and everyday thinking cannot grasp. The composer seems to open a way to further processes because, contrary to the description of the first two *ātman*s and of the *ātman vijñānamaya*, he does not show the ontic results of knowledge of the mind as the recipient could expect but rather knowledge of bliss (*ānanda*) which will be described later after the *vijñānamaya* stage. In this way, he implies that ritual practice which ends with the construction of the immortal self, made of the sounds of the Veda, ends here and does not lead to ultimate bliss. It is worth mentioning that in the cosmogony of ŚB 10.5.3 speech is the first perceivable manifestation of mind (see chapter 3.5.1), so the stanza could also refer to this state.

The description of the stage called *vijñānamaya* is preceded by a stanza which present the importance of awareness of sacrifice and deeds; it is not specified if ritual deeds are concerned (thus Olivelle 1998), or deeds understood generally (thus Angot 2007, II: 415: 'actions', TU 2.5.1). It is concluded that a man who knows that *brahman* is *vijñāna* leaves evil in his body and realises all his desires.

The description of the stage called *ānandamaya* follows the description of the *vijñānamaya* stage (TU 2.5.1, see above). Having described it, the composer quotes a stanza according to which men who thinks that *brahman* is nonexistent (*asat*) become nonexistent, men who thinks it as existent (*sat*) become existent (TU 2.6.1)[238]. This stanza introduces the next topic. It is the afterlife state of a man who does not know *brahman* as existent and of a man who knows it (TU 2.6.1). As has been shown, this topic is also discussed in the descriptions of the liberating process in Yājñavalkya teachings (see section 4.4.2.3). As an answer the composer presents another cosmogony which is conceived in terms of the division of reality (called *satya*) into two aspects (called *sat* and *tyam*, see section 4.1.5). Then he supplies his exposition with another cosmogony:

[238] Literally it is said that people think that man who knows *brahman* as existent become existent too: *asann eva sa bhavati asad abrahmeti veda cet | asti brahmeti ced veda santam enaṃ tato vidur iti |*

TU 2.7.1a

asad vā idam agra āsīt | tato vai sad ajāyata | tad ātmānaṁ svayam akuruta | tasmāt tat sukr̥tam ucyata iti | yad vai tat sukr̥tam | raso vai saḥ | rasaṁ hy evāyaṃ labdhvā 'nandī bhavati |

In the beginnings this world was nonexistent, and from it arose the existent. By itself it made itself [239] (*ātman*) for itself; therefore it is called 'well-made'. And precisely because it is well-made, it is the essence, for only when one has grasped that essence does one attain bliss.

This cosmogony begins with an assertion that in the beginning this world is nonexistent which agrees with earlier thinking (ŚB 6.1.1.1, see chapter 3.2.2). As I have argued, the concept of nonexistent (*asat*) is defined in the early Veda from the point of view of an agents' experience in the world. From this point of view, what is beyond the world does not exist because it cannot be experienced and cognised. Then the world becomes existent. Within the frame of the monistic assumption and the cosmogonic model, implicitly accepted by the Vedic authors, the recipient understands that the world called *sat* is the manifest aspect of unmanifest reality. The subject of the next sentence, expressed by the pronoun *tat*, can be the whole of reality and its manifest aspect. Olivelle and Angot interpret the sentence as expressing the fact that reality creates a body for itself. I would add another level to their interpretation which is the reflexive one: reality transforms itself into itself. The use of the verb *sáṃ kr̥-* brings the recipient's mind to its use in the ŚB in reference to composition of self which is full and perfect (see chapter 3.4). Activation of this concept gives rational grounds for the next sentence: reality manifest in its visible form is well-made (*sukr̥ta*). The word *sukr̥ta* evokes the cosmogony of the AU which uses this compound in reference to man which is the best form for the manifestation of the subjective powers of reality (see section 4.1.3). So the recipient can understand that the perfect manifest form of reality is man, i.e. the human being and the cosmos. The exposition of the TU is very abstract and general by comparison with the cosmogony of the AU which presents creation with much detail.

Then the composer says that what is well-made (*sukr̥ta*) is the essence (*rasa*). The word *rasa* is also used in BU 2.3 in the context of a play on the word *satya* (see section 4.4.2.2). In the cosmic dimension, the word *rasa* refers to the sun and man within the sun. In the human dimension, the word *rasa* refers to the eye and to man within the right eye. As I have argued, in this context the word *rasa* refers to the starting point of liberating cognition

239 Olivelle (1998): 'a body'.

which begins in recognising the visible forms of *ātman* in its manifest aspect (*rūpa*) conceived in terms of man (see section 4.4.2.2). The word *rasa* can be understood here in the same way which is confirmed in that the composer says that when one grasps *rasa* one becomes full of bliss (*ānandin*). Thus, in a very concise and abstract way, the composer presents the transformation of reality the final form of which is its visible form within the world. In a similarly concise way, he presents the way of its cognition through its essence. The source domain of drinking sap is not required to understand the meaning conveyed by the composer. However, if the recipient activates it, he will see that the liberating cognition described in the TU leads to the same state as Somic exultation.

TU 2.7.1b

ko hy evānyāt kaḥ prāṇyāt | yad eṣa ākāśa ānando na syāt | eṣa hy evānandayāti | yadā hy evaiṣa etasminn adṛśye 'nātmye 'nirukte 'nilayane 'bhayaṃ pratiṣṭhāṃ vindate | atha so 'bhayaṃ gato bhavati |

Now, who would breathe in, who would breathe out, of that essence were not in space as bliss, for it is that essence that causes bliss. For when a man finds within that invisible, incorporeal (*anātmya*), indistinct, and supportless essence, the fearless state on which to rest, then he becomes free from fear.

Then the composer states that in space there is bliss which is identified with the essence (*rasa*) in the previous sentence. If the recipient activates the source domain of drinking sap, he will see the rationality of this identification: in the source domain drinking sap give pleasure which is experientially experienced. It is implied that this essence is the motive for existence of all living beings metonymically evoked by the concept of breathing out and in. Moreover, this essence is the reason for the bliss reached by those who find support in what is invisible, without *ātman*, indistinct and without fear. The cognition of the blissful essence of reality resulted in a lack of fear. I would enlarge Olivelle's and Angot's interpretation of *anātmya* and see it as referring to unmanifest reality which in its pre-creative is without *ātman*, i.e. its cosmic and human self; during creation reality assumes *ātman* (see *ātmanvī syām*, BU 1.2.1, section 4.1.1). In this way, the composer implies that it is possible to reach a state beyond creation.

Those who are not liberated are full of fear:

TU 2.7.1c

yadā hyevaiṣa etasminn antaraṃ udaram kurute | atha tasya bhayaṃ bhavati | tat tv eva bhayaṃ viduṣo ‹manvānasya |

> When, on the other hand, a man creates a hollow or a fissure within it, then he experiences fear. Now, this is the fear experienced by a man who thinks that he knows.

If the recipients activates the literal meaning of the word *udara*, he will be able to evoke earlier cosmogonies presented in the ŚB (see chapter 3.1.1, 3.2.2-3) and in BU 2.1 (see section 4.1.1) which conceive the initial form of the word in terms of an empty, hungry belly. The logic of this source domain implies the concept of fear because a hungry man feels the fear of death. In this way, the source domain is elaborated by ŚB 2.2.4 where Prajāpati is afraid of fire that is about to kill him (see chapter 3.1.1). The composer of the TU plays with the conceptualisation of the first form of the world: when one cognises it as a space filled with bliss, one is able to cognise the whole of reality and become blissful too. When one cognises it as an empty, hungry belly, one feels fear. This play could be seen as a debate with the earlier tradition attested in the ŚB which conceives of liberation from fear in terms of feeding reality with food during ritual. The composer seems to imply that the ontological gap cannot be overcome thanks to ritual but rather to liberating cognition performed during realisation of the five stages described above. Then man will see himself as the whole of reality and feel no fear because, as BU 1.4.2 says, one is afraid of someone which is different (see section 4.1.2). If someone is everything, and all, there is no reason to be afraid.

In the next stanza, the composer presents fear as the motive for cosmic processes: because of fear the wind blows, the sun rises, fear also is the reason for fire and for Indra and death in the world (TU 2.8.1). The concept of Indra evokes associations with the concept of the main breath which begins creation according to ŚB 6.1.1.2 (see chapter 3.2.2) and with the liberating process (BU 4.2.2, see section 4.4.2.3). In the cosmogonies of the ŚB, the fear of reality is the motive for creation. Reality is afraid of death in its manifestations (see chapter 3.1.1, 3.2.3). However, this fear is overcome in the next stages of creation. On the other hand, the fear of death is the motive for beginning liberating practice the aim of which is to overcome death. Man who does not know will never be liberated from fear. Man who knows will be liberated.

Now the composer presents the experience of bliss which increases according to the sphere of manifestation; the last sphere is the sphere of *brahman* (TU 2.8.1). One could interpret this description as referring to the states realised during breath practice which increase a man's bliss as he realises identity with the whole of reality. Man successively becomes the agent able to experience bliss from his point of view to the final realisation of its universal range. The same concept of increasing bliss realised in the liberated state is presented by Yājñavalkya (BU 4.3.33).

At the end of this description, the composer of the TU concisely presents how to achieve this state after death:

TU 2.8.1

> *sa yaś cāyaṃ puruṣe | yaścāsāv āditye | sa ekaḥ | sa ya evaṁvit | asmāl lokāt pretya | etam annamayam ātmānam upasaṃkrāmati | etaṃ prāṇamayam ātmānam upasaṃkrāmati | etaṃ manomayam ātmānam upasaṃkrāmati | etaṃ vijñānamayam ātmānam upasaṃkrāmati | etam ānandamayam ātmānam upasaṃkrāmati |*
>
> He who is here in a man and he who is there in the sun – they are one and the same. After a man who knows this departs from this world – he first reaches the self (*ātman*) that consists of food, then the self that consists of breath[240], then the self that consists of mind, then the self that consists of perception, then the self that consists of bliss.

The starting point is *ātman* in man which is his innermost self identical with the visible form of *ātman* present in the sun. In this way, the composer explicitly expresses that the sun is the cosmic visible form of *ātman*. After death a man realises the stages of himself he has realised during life. He leaves his body and breath, his cognitive faculty which rendered possible subjective-objective cognition (mind, *manas*) and he leaves a state of awareness to realise the overwhelming bliss of *brahman*. To explain this state, the composer repeats the stanza previously mentioned (TU 2.4.1). Now its content fully agrees with the state: words and thoughts cannot grasp the state of *brahman*'s bliss so fear is dispersed[241]. Moreover, in this state man is not influenced by his previous deeds and does not suffer because of the fact that he did not do good things and did wrong ones (TU 2.9.1)[242]. He is freed not only from these two thoughts, as Olivelle interprets it, but also from these two kinds of deeds.

---

240 Olivelle (1998): 'lifebreath'.

241 Grinshpon (2003) argues that the Upaniṣadic accounts about the beginning of liberating cognition is crisis: 'Upanishadic tales are about men and women in crisis, awakened to their inferiority, the painful consciousness of a gap between (their own) lesser selves and an elusive better self'. (2003: VII). In BU 1.4.2, fear is the first feeling of reality which realises that it is alone (see section 4.1.2). Since liberating process is reverse to creation, one can presume that fear is an important component of this crisis.

242 TU 2.9.1: *etaṁ ha vāva na tapati | kim ahaṁ sādhu nākaravam | kim ahaṃ pāpam akaravam iti | sa ya evaṃ vidvān ete ātmānaṁ spṛṇute | ubhe hy evaiṣa ete ātmānaṁ spṛṇute | ya evaṃ veda |*

4.5. Conclusion

The abstract and general way of expressing philosophical thought in the early Upaniṣad has widely been recognised by scholars. I have shown how this thought is built on the basis of earlier tradition and background[243]. The philosophical thought in those early Upaniṣads could not appear without this background. The reason for the creation of abstract thought is not only the human need for the creation of philosophy. It is also motivated by liberating cognition in which breath practice plays a crucial role.

I have shown that the composers of the cosmogonies of the BU, AU and CU elaborate earlier material and present it in more abstract terms on the one hand and, on the other, add many details which are connected with the development of thought and changes in society. The concept of the innermost self of the cosmos and man understood as the unmanifest aspect of reality present within its manifest aspect is established. Its knowledge becomes the aim of liberating cognition. Liberating cognition involves breath practice and leads to cognition of the unmanifest aspect of reality. The way to get the Somic experience without Soma is found and it leads even further than was possible with its use. Moreover, this practice is known to such an extent that it can be analysed and taught to others. Descriptions always include topics about the afterlife and it is implied that the state gained in breath practice is the same as the state gained after death as it is in the ṚV (see Jurewicz 2010a).

There is a great consistency between stages of the practice, regardless if their exponent is a king (Ajātaśatru), or a Brahmin (Yājñavalkya) or a god (Indra), or an unknown exponent (as in the TU). The novelty of the Upaniṣadic teachers is not a belief in rebirth[244] but a practice which allowed its agents to overcome death during their life in the same way it had been possible thanks to Soma. And, moreover, thanks to this practice, one is not reborn again which was not the case in the ṚV.

Although abstract and general concepts are commonly used in the early Upaniṣads conceptual metaphors are still in use. The concept of eating, in terms of which subjective-objective cognition is conceived, appears even in abstract contexts. The concept of drinking sap is used to conceive liberating cognition. The composers use source domains such as those of a spider which

[243] Renou (1953) shows how the Upaniṣadic philosophical debates continue the earlier *brahmodyas* described in the Brāhmaṇas; very often their participants are the same. This also confirms the close conceptual relationship between these two layers of the texts.

[244] For this problem see also next chapter.

emits thread, the sparks of a fire and a dike which separates and unites two receptacles of water in order to conceive the relationship between the unmanifest and manifest aspect of reality. The concept of a king who rules his subjects is used to conceive the relationship between the innermost self of man and his breath. The metaphor of play is used in contexts to highlight the pleasure which is the motive and result of play and this is used to conceive the self-sufficiency of reality which is not forced by any external factor to create the world. The concept of sleep is also elaborated to present the manifestation of reality in man and the stages of liberating cognition. In order to recognise them, the tools of cognitive linguistics is indispensable. Its use allows us to see consistency and coherence in seemingly obscure fragments and shows the conscious elaboration of earlier tradition.

Chapter Five

Afterlife and the belief in rebirth

In this chapter, I will analyse two pre-Upaniṣadic accounts of belief in rebirth, namely, that of JB (1.17-18, 1.45-50) and of JUB (3.7-28). I will also discuss the account of the KU 1 which displays conceptual links not only with other Upaniṣadic theories presented earlier (BU 6.2.9-16 and CU 5.4-10, see chapter 4.3.1), but also with the JB and JUB.

Many scholars assume rebirth theory was introduced during the time of the early Upaniṣads and came from royal circles that adopted non-Brāhmaṇical concepts and taught the Brahmins about them[1]. According to some scholars, the reasons a number of exponents of the teachings are Kṣatriyas lay in the historical and socio-political conditions of the time (Keith (1989[1925]: 493ff. Olivelle (1998: 11–12), Black (2007: 101ff.). Yet, scholars like Tull (1989), Killingley (1997) have presented evidence for earlier accounts of the rebirth theory.

In Jurewicz (2008b, 2010), I have shown that the concept of rebirth is attested already in the ṚV. Cremation is conceived in terms of a sacrifice in which the deceased is a Somic oblation. As during sacrifices performed in his life he reaches the sun where, having drunk Soma from the solar source, he transforms himself into a perfect being called Aṅgiras. It is believed that on the sun he meets his fathers and Yama. The deeds he performed during his life, (*iṣṭāpūrtá*, hapax in the RV) influence him which is conceived in terms of their union with him (ṚV 10.10.14.8). Then he comes back in the form of rain to be reborn as a member of his own family[2]. In this way, he realises the

---

1 Garbe ([1897] 2004), Deussen ([1919] 2000), Frauwallner (1990: 93ff), Butzenberger (1996), partly refuted by Bodewitz (1999a: 116–117), Bronkhorst (2007).

2 See also Bergaigne 1963 [1878–83], I: 100, Macdonell (1897: 166), Oberlies 1998: 478–483.

sacrificial cycle realised during his life. On a more general level, he takes part in the transformation of reality which manifests itself in its fiery and Somic aspects in creation, in the world's functioning and in human ritual activity.

I have also shown that traces of the belief in rebirth are present in earlier thought (AVŚ 11.5.13-14, chapter 2.2.1, 15.7.2-5, chapter 2.2.2, ŚB 10.4.3.10-11, chapters 3.3). In the Upaniṣad, the conviction about rebirth is attested not only in the famous descriptions of two paths in the BU and the CU, and in the teaching of Yājñavalkya (chapters 4.3.1, 4.4.2.3), but also in AU 3.4, CU 5.17.9-10, TU 2.1.1 (see chapters 4.1.3, 4.3.2, 4.4.2.5). In most of these places, the concept of rebirth is evoked metonymically which may imply that it belonged to shared knowledge and, therefore, the composers of the texts did not feel it was necessary to express it in more detail. I have shown (see chapter 4.3.1) that the expositions of Pravāhaṇa Jailvali in the BU and the CU concerning the afterlife state are deeply immersed in earlier Vedic tradition and this will be confirmed again in this chapter[3]. We will also see that the context of the expositions of the JB and JUB attesting the rebirth theory is purely Brahminic. In the KU, the exponent is not clear. This is in accordance with Black (2007: 104) who writes:

> 'It is clear, however, that the ideas voiced by the Kṣatriya characters, despite what the character claim, are not particularly new to the Vedic tradition, and that therefore, the motive of Kṣatriya authorship is a literary fiction.' [4]

Even if one accepts that some aspects of the belief in rebirth had come from outside of Vedic circles, within Vedic tradition there is a place for accepting these aspects and their redefinition according to its assumptions. My aim in this chapter is the same as my aim for the whole book which is to show the development of concepts and their redefinition within the main Brahminic tradition of the early Veda.

The quotations of the JB are from Vira, Chandra (1986([1955]), the quotation of the JUB and of the KU are from the Titus Text Database[5]. Translations are by Bodewitz (1973), Oertel (1896, 1898) and Olivelle (1998).

---

3 As Black (2007: 101-102) writes: 'Pravāhaṇas's claims that this teaching is known only by Kṣatriyas is clearly not a factual representation of the origins of this discourse but rather part of the literary presentation of teachings in the Upaniṣads'.

4 In a similar way Lindquist (2013: 81) interprets the figure of Yājñavalkya as a literary figure and argues that this interpretation makes us 'move beyond subjective reader-response interpretation about the 'authenticity' of a figure and turns towards investigating the literal nature of this figure and the value placed in him by tradition'.

5 http://titus.uni-frankfurt.de/texte/etcs/ind/aind/ved/sv/jub/jub.htm; http://titus.uni-frankfurt.de/texte/etcs/ind/aind/ved/rv/upanisad/kausup/kausu.htm

5.1. Accounts of the *Jaiminīya Brāhmaṇa* (1.17-18, 1.45-50)

In this section, I will discuss two accounts of the afterlife state presented in JB 1.17-18 and in JB 1.45-50. In JB 1.17, the role of the Agnihotra in the creation of the ritual self of the sacrificer is described and the sacrificer is called 'one who has two selves' (*dvyātman*). The exposition of JB 1.45-50 is also placed within the context of Agnihotra and begins with the description of the functioning of reality in the model of the Five Fires followed by a description of the two kinds of afterlife path. I will concentrate on the latter account and I will refer to JB 1.18 when it is needed.

Bodewitz (1973) in his translation of the JB divided part 1.45-50 into two. He discusses separately the state of the deceased (1.45-46, 49-50) and the cremation rite (1.46-49). This misses the meaning of the description the aim of which is to show the role of the cremation rite and the role of those who perform it for the situation of the deceased. The text is difficult and I am not claiming that I am able to reconstruct its whole meaning. However, it is possible to understand the main intention of its composer.

I would propose the following construction of JB 1.45-50. Firstly, the author describes the functioning of the world conceived in terms of the model of the Five Fires (JB 1.45). Then he describes the afterlife of those who do not have the proper cremation rite and do not possess right knowledge about themselves. They come back to be reborn (JB 1.46). Then the composer describes the cremation rite in detail (JB 1.45-49) in order to show that, together with right knowledge, it influences the future life in that the deceased does not come back to the world (JB 1.50).

The conceptual network created in the description of the JB is as follows. The first input space is the concept of the deceased which includes his life. The image schema of CAUSE-EFFECT, which is the next input space, imparts to the blend the causal relationship between life and the afterlife state. This image schema also justifies the influence of relatives who remain on earth and perform cremation rite on the afterlife state; this concept is the next input space. The next input spaces are the concept of a journey to an abode and the image schemas of SOURCE-PATH-GOAL and VERTICALITY. The sixth input space is the cosmos. The generic space is the concept of transformation. In the blend, the deceased travels up across the spheres of the cosmos towards the abode in terms of which the aim of his journey is conceived[6].

6 For the ritual journey to heaven, see also Smith (1989: 14 ff.).

5.1.1. The model of the Five Fires in the *Jaiminīya Brāhmaṇa* and the first afterlife path

The fire in the model of the Five Fires presented in JB 1.45 is called Agni Vaiśvānara[7] and is identified with the sun (*ya eṣa tapati*), the thunder (*stanayitnu*), the earth (*pṛthivī*), man (*puruṣa*) and women (*strī*). The oblations are immortality and water (*amṛtam āpas*), king Soma (*somo rājā*), rain (*vṛṣṭi*), food (*anna*) and semen (*retas*).

The description ends with an explicit expression of rebirth: in the fifth oblation man is born from the gods and the heavenly waters speak with a man's voice[8]. The heavenly waters correspond to 'immortality' (*amṛta*) and 'waters' (*āpas*), i.e. the form of the deceased which was acquired at the cremation pyre (see below).

In the last sacrifice a man is placed on the cremation pyre and, thanks to his fiery essence, becomes fire and is transformed into oblation for the next fire which is death identified with the sun:

JB 1.46a

> *tasyā āhuter hutāyai puruṣo 'muṃ lokaṃ saṃbhavati | so 'sya lokaḥ punar utthāyai bhavati |*
>
> From this oblation when it has been offered man comes into existence (and goes) to yonder world. That it for him the world in which he resurges. (Bodewitz 1973)

As proposed above, in the early Veda the word *loka* can be interpreted as the space of experience realised in ritual activity. And this is stated in the JB: the yonder world is the world of the deceased which appears so that he could arise (*so 'sya lokaḥ punar utthāyai bhavati*). The form of this world depends on the ritual action performed by the deceased during his life and by those who perform the cremation rite. It also depends on his knowledge about himself.

One may presume that the following description refers to the state realised at the borderline sphere of the cosmos:

---

7 Like in ŚB 10.6.3, see chapter 4.4.2.1. Hayakawa (2014) sees this version as combination of 'two lines of thoughts, namely Agni's ascent in the cremation and his descent in the Third Soma-Pressing'. In my view, this version is the result of the efforts of the composers of JB to express explicitly the cosmologic and ritual model assumed already in the ṚV (see Jurewicz 2010a).

8 JB 1.45: *so 'tra pañcamyāṃ visṛṣṭyāṃ puruṣo devebhyo jāyate | pañcamyāṃ visṛṣṭyāṃ divyā āpaḥ puruṣavāco bhavanti |*.

JB 1.46b

tasya haitasya devasyāhorātre ardhamāsā māsā rtavas saṃvatsaro goptā ya eṣa tapati | ahorātre pracare | taṃ hartūnām eko yaḥ kūṭahasto raśminā pratyavetya pṛchati ko 'si puruṣeti | sa kiṃ vidvan pravṛñjyāt | tasya ha praharati |

Of that god who shines here night and day, the half-months, the months, the seasons and the year are the guards. Night and day are forerunners (who announce his coming). To him one of the seasons, who has hammer in his hand, comes down along a ray of light and asks him: 'Who at thou, man?' In case he has some (but not the perfect) knowledge he may withhold (his name from the interrogator). Then he strikes him (with his hammer).

The composer metonymically evokes the concept of time *via* concepts of its divisions: days and nights, half-months, months and seasons which are called the guardians of the sun. In ŚB 2.3.3.12, the situation of a person who performs Agnihotra is conceived in terms of a chariot driver who looks down at the revolving wheels of his chariot in terms of which the days and the nights are conceived; this image will be used in the KU 1.4 to describe the state of the liberated person (see section 5.3)[9]. Contrary to those who do not perform Agnihotra, he is free of the influence of time and is not killed by it as are those who are below time's wheels and are killed by them.

In the JB, the composer activates the metaphor THE SUN IS A KING; the composer of the KU presents this source domain in full detail (see section 5.3). Within the frame of this metaphor, the king has his guardians who are first to meet the visitor and also prevent those unwanted from seeing the king. One of the seasons is conceived in terms of a guardian with a hammer. The season asks the deceased person's name and if he possesses the right knowledge he may – as Bodewitz translates the verb *pra vṛj-* – withhold his name.

Houben, in his analysis of the meaning of the verb *pra vṛj-*, proposes to understand it in a positive sense as 'to inflect' 'set apart' or 'set aside' or in a negative sense as 'to exclude', 'to avoid' (esp. in the compound *pari vṛj-*)' (2007: 6). He argues that such an interpretation suits ritual contexts better than the meaning 'to place at the fire'. However, there are contexts in the ŚB where this latter meaning is the most probable. In ŚB 7.1.2.6, this verb is used to denote the placing of dead Prajāpati into the fire by the gods; thanks to its heating power Prajāpati will be transformed into the cosmos (ŚB 7.1.2.6: *táṃ devā́ agnaú prā́vṛñjan | tád yá enam právṛktam agnír ā́rohad*). The verb *prá vṛj-* is then used to express the heating of the fire pan (ŚB 7.1.2.10: *tā́m agnaú právṛṇakti yáthaivaìnam adó devā́ḥ prā́vṛñjaṃs tád yá enām právṛktām*

[9] ŚB 2.3.3.12, TB 3.11.7.5. In JB 1.11, the sun which carries the sacrificer beyond death is compared to an elephant.

agnír āróhati) and this activity is explained by the creative activity of the gods. The results are the same as in case of Prajāpati: the sacrificer's self will be composed under the heating power of fire.

The meaning 'to place at the fire' is also more suitable in other contexts. In ŚB 4.4.1.7, in the explanation of the meaning of the libation to Savitar in the evening pressing during the Agniṣṭoma ritual, the composer identifies Savitar with the mind (*mánas*) and breath (*prāṇá*) of the sacrificer (ŚB 4.4.1.1, 7). The proper performance of this libation ensures that mind and the breath will be not placed on the fire (*máno ha vā́ asya savitā́ nén máno 'gnaú pravṛṇájānī́ti prāṇo ha vā́ asya savitā́ nét prāṇám agnaú pravṛṇájānī́ti*). In a similar context the verb *prá vṛj-* is used in ŚB 11.5.9.11 in the description of the optional libation of Soma (*adābhyagraha*). Its proper performance ensures that speech is not placed on the fire (*tát sómam evàitat sómāya juhoti tátho vā́cam agnaú ná právṛṇakti*). In both cases the meaning 'to set apart' would be less convincing.

The interpretation 'to place at the fire' is also more convincing in ŚB 1.8.3.19. This section describes the after-offerings (*anuyāja*) in the Darśapūrṇamāsa ritual. In ŚB 1.8.3.16, the bundle of grass covering the altar (*prastará*) is identified with the sacrificer (*yájamāno vaí prastaráḥ*). Then it is said that if the Adhvaryu throws the whole *prastará* into the fire, the sacrificer would quickly die (*sá yát kṛtsnám prastarám anupraháret kṣipré ha yájamāno 'múṃ lokám iyāt*). Because of that the Adhvaryu takes only a single stalk of *prastará*. In ŚB 1.8.3.17-18, the proper and safe way of throwing the stalk into fire is described. Then the composer states:

ŚB 1.8.3.19

áthāgnī́d āhānupráharéti | tád yátrāsyétara ātmā́gaṃs tád evā̀syaitád gamayéty evàitád āha tū́ṣṇī́m evā̀nuprahṛ́tya cakṣuṣpā́ agne 'si cákṣur mepāhī́tyātmā́nam úpaspṛ́śati téno ápyātmā́naṃ nā̀nuprávṛṇakti |

The Āgnīdhra says (to the Adhvaryu), 'Throw the single stalk after (the prastara)!' – 'whither his (the sacrificer's) other self went, thither make it now go,' this is what he thereby says. (The Adhvaryu) having thrown it silently after, touches himself, with the text (Vāc S. II, 16 f): 'Guardian of the eye art thou, O Agni; guard mine eye!' In this way also he does not throw himself into the fire after (the *prastara* or sacrificer).

Taking into account the two similar contexts using the verb *pra vṛj-*, it is more possible that the noun *ātmán* refers to the self of the Adhvaryu (ŚB 1.9.2.17, 3.8.5.5)[10]. In this context the meaning 'to place at the fire' is more suitable.

[10] And in this way it is interpreted by Eggeling (1882).

Let us also look at the use of the verb *prá vr̥j-* in ŚB 14.3.2.22-30 in the explanation of the Pravargya sacrifice (the section about the expiatory ceremonies). Here various aspects of the cosmos are identified with the Pravargya ritual (*saṃvatsará, imé lokā́ḥ, imé devátāḥ*), then the sacrificer (*yájamāna*), then various sacrifices (*agnihotrá, darśapūrṇamāsá, cātúrmāsya, paśubandhá*) and finally *sóma* which metonymically evokes Soma sacrifices. Their elements or phases are identified with phases of the process which takes part during the sacrifice which are called *právr̥kta, rucitá* and *pinvitá* which Eggeling translates as: 'when it is placed on the fire', 'when it is burning-hot' and 'when it flows'. The latter two participles activate the R̥gvedic general model of reality according to which it firstly manifests its fiery aspect and then its liquid one. This model is realised in the sacrifice, so one should assume that the participle *právr̥kta* activates the meaning of heating which is done on fire. The concept of heating is most distinctly expressed in the identification of a year with Pravargya: spring is *právr̥kta*, summer is *rucitá* and autumn is *pinvitá*. It reflects the growth of heat during the seasons ending with the rains. In the case of the sacrifice, it is his self, *ātmán*, which is called *právr̥kta*, his offspring *rucitá* and his cattle *pinvitá*. Thus the ritual process realises successful transformation of man *via* his substitute which is placed in fire. This transformation is conceived and ritually realised in terms of a shining pot which is heated and of milk which brims.

These accounts show that the verb *prá vr̥j-* is also used to denote the act of heating one's *ātmán* at the sacrificial fire. In the case of Prajāpati, it is his own *ātmán*, in the case of the sacrificer, it is his *ātmán* which is burnt *via* its substitutes because, as it has been shown, during sacrifice the ritual *ātmán* of the sacrificer is composed and it should not be destroyed by fire (see chapter 3.1.1). So it is possible that the deceased, who knows something about the meaning of ritual, does the same as during his life: he tries to compose his *ātmán* and its substitutes as he did during his life but in a way which leads to its destruction.

In the R̥V, the verb *vr̥j-* is often used to denote killing[11] and it also denotes the activity of fire (R̥V 3.29.6, 4.7.10, 7.3.4). The recipient could also evoke this meaning: the deceased offers himself in fire in terms of which death is conceived. Then the following sentence (*tasya ha praharati*) express the destruction of the sacrificer's self which is the result of his fatal mistake; the destruction is conceived in terms of being struck by a hammer. Thus the deceased is not allowed to approach the sun.

[11] E.g. R̥V 1.54.5 (with *ní*), R̥V 1.129.3 (with *pári*), 1.53. 9 (with *ní, cakréṇa*), 5.29.10 (with *ní*, 2.17.6 *vájreṇa*), 1.101.2, 5.32.8 (with *ní*), 6.18.8, 7, 18.12 (with *ní*), , 6.26.3, 10.8.9 (with *párā*), 1.33.5 (with *párā*).

In JB 1.18 the deceased, having presented to the gods his good and bad deeds (*iyad asya sādhu kṛtam iyat pāpam*), rises with the smoke of the funeral fire and reaches the seasons who are the guardians of the sun. Then he should recite the stanza *vicakṣanād*... which will be analysed below and the seasons then let him go to the sun. It is the sun who asks him who he is. If he mentions his name or the name of his family name (*gotra*), the sun answers:

JB 1.18a

taṃ hāha yas te 'yaṃ mayy ātmābhud eṣa te saḥ iti |

That self of yours that has been in me, that is yours[12] (Bodewitz 1973)

The recipient may presume that the sun takes the *ātman* of the sacrifice being the same *ātman* which he tried to create during his life (see JB 1.17: *sa yaj juhoti yas sādhu karoty etasyām evaitat devayonāv ātmānam siñcati* | *yo 'syātmāmuṣminn āditye saṃbhavati*). According to the JUB (3.10.4), it is the sun which gives life to man when he is born and dies for the first time, i.e. when he appears in his mother's womb[13]. The sun which is the cosmic form of fire (ŚB 2.3.3.7) takes away the self of the sacrificer. I am tempted to suggest that the two syllables *hāha* (*ha āha*) may trigger the recipient to hear the sun cruelly laugh at the deceased as if saying: "Ha, ha, this is your self that has just been in me! Look at it! It is now mine!" Devoid of the self, the deceased is overtaken by time metonymically evoked by the concept of the seasons which drag him by his leg. Within the frame of this conceptualisation, *ātman* is conceived in terms of man which foreshadows its later conceptualisation in these terms in the Upaniṣads (e.g. BU 1.4.1, see chapter 4.1.1, AU, see chapter 4.1.3). The world he creates for himself is again the world influenced by time:

JB 1.18.6b

tasmin hātman pratipatta ṛtavas saṃpalāyya padgrhītena apakarṣanti | *tasya hāhoratre lokam āpnutaḥ* |

After that Self has been received back, the seasons from all sides run towards him, grasp him by his feet and drag him away. Night and day take possession of his world (Bodewitz 1973)

JB 1.46 describes this subjection to time in a more detailed way:

---

12 Bodewitz (1973) adds '(again)'.

13 Moreover, as we will see, in the JUB the parts of the sacrificer who wins immortality are given back by various elements of cosmos, see section 5.2.3.

JB 1.46c

tasya ha pratirāddhasya tredhā sādhukṛtyā vinaśyati | sa tṛtīyam ādatte | diśo 'nu tṛtīyaṃ vyeti | tṛtīyena sahemaṃ lokam abhyavaiti | sa yo hāsya dānajito loko bhavati tasmin niramate | tam u ha vai tato mṛtyur evāntata āpnoti | anavajito hāsya punarmṛtyur bhavati sa ya evaṃvit syāt |

Of him when he has stopped the good deeds disappear in three parts. He (i.e. the Ṛtu) takes one third. One third diffuses in the air. Together with one third he (i.e. the deceased) descends in the direction of this world. The world which is won by him on account of his gifts, in that he stops. Thereupon even him Death ultimately reaches. Repeated dying is not overcome by him who knows (only) thus. (Bodewitz 1973)

The good deeds of the deceased are divided into three: the first are taken by the season, the second are dispersed in the space and with the third he comes back to this world. Bodewitz (1973) translates it as 'descends in the direction of this world' and explains in the note that he translates the sentence in this way because 'reaching this earth seems to be excluded here', without giving any reasons for his assumption (1973: 119). And he then argues that the concept of *punarmṛtyu* 'obviously point to a life in yonder world', but he gives no argument for his claim. We can take into account the literal meaning of the verb *abhyave-*, that is 'to go down, descend' and understand that the deceased comes back to 'this world', i.e. the earth and is born according to that which he has given during his previous life. According to JUB 3.11.3 during the second birth and death, which is initiation (*dīkṣā*), man is born for a sacrificial fee (*dakṣinā*). One cannot exclude that *dakṣiṇā* is also meant here and that the future birth of the deceased depends on how much he offered to the Brahmins during his life. Since *dakṣiṇā* is the final act of sacrifice, this concept is metonymically evoked here on the basis of the metonymy THE LAST PHASE OF THE PROCESS FOR THE WHOLE PROCESS (Radden, Kövecses 1999: 49). This would mean that the final form of the deceased depends on his ritual activity, i.e. on his acts.

5.1.2. The second afterlife path

In JB 1.47, the description of cremation is presented which ends with the description of the second path followed by the deceased. As I have already said, the fact that the composer inserts this description here implies that properly performed cremation is important for the future lot of the deceased.

It is worth noting that there is a close connection between the first sacrifice performed by a man who has become a householder (Agnyādheya) and cremation; it is attested in JB 1.1-2. The composer describes the creation of the sacrificer's breaths (*anna*, *manas*, *cakṣus*, *śrotra*, *prāna* and *vāc*) during the ritual of installing the sacrificer's fires. Then he says that when the sacrificer dies his breaths come back to the cremation fire and from it he is born again. The stanza which expresses this relationship and the form of the deceased is the same as in JB 1.47[14] (see below). Since this description begins the exegesis of the Agnihotra, one can presume that it is implied that the sacrificer, having installed his fires, should perform the daily Agnihotra in order to become immortal after his death. This close connection is more explicitly expressed in the description of the Agnihotra in the ŚB immediately after the main cosmogony explaining this ritual:

ŚB 2.2.4.7-8

sá hutvā́ prajā́patiḥ | prá cā́jāyatātsyatáś cāgnér mṛtyór ātmā́nam atrāyata sá yó haiváṃ vidvā́n agnihotráṃ juhóty etā́ṃ haivá prájātim prájāyate yā́ṃ prajā́patiḥ prā́jāyataivám u haivā̀tsyatò 'gnér mṛtyór ātmā́naṃ trāyate | (7)
sa yátra mriyáte | yátrainam agnā́v abhyādádhati tád eṣò 'gnér ádhijāyaté 'thāsya śárīram evā̀gnír dahati tád yáthā pitúr vā mātúr vā jā́yetaivám eṣò 'gnér ádhijāyate śáśvaddha vā́ eṣá ná sámbhavati yò 'gnihotráṃ ná juhóti tásmād vā́ agnihotráṃ hotávyam | (8)

And Prajāpati, having performed offering, reproduced himself, and saved himself from Agni, Death, as he was about to devour him. And, verily, whosoever, knowing this, offers the Agnihotra, reproduces himself by offspring even as Prajāpati reproduced himself; and saves himself from Agni, Death, when he is about to devour him. (7)
And when he dies, and when they place him on the fire, then he is born (again) out of the fire, and the fire only consumes his body. Even as he is born from his father and mother, so is he born from the fire. But he who offers not the Agnihotra, verily, he does not come into life at all: therefore the Agnihotra should by all means be offered. (8)

Taking this into account, it is not surprising that the author of JB 1.45-50 decided to enrich the earlier description of the afterlife (JB 1.18) with a description of a cremation properly performed.

The body of the deceased is prepared for cremation: its impure elements (hair, beard, feces) are removed and thrown into a hole dug earlier and then covered by sand. Thus his *pāpman* is covered (*pāpmānam evāsya tat pracchādayanti*, JB 1.47). In the early Veda, *pāpman* is not only used in reference to sin (as Bodewitz translates this word, 1973: 140), but also in reference to death (ŚB 8.4.2.1-14, 8.4.3.1, 10.4.4.1, 14.4.1.11). In my view, it

[14] JB 1.2: *asmād vai tvam ajāyathā eṣa tvaj jāyatāṃ svāh.*

is in this way that the future immortality of the deceased is presented within the frame of the ritual. Then the deceased is placed between the fires, clarified butter is melted on the Gārhapatya fire and offered in the Āhavanīya fire with a stanza which expresses the relationship between fire and man:

JB 1.47a

> *ayaṃ vai tvad asmād asi tvam | etad ayaṃ te yonir asya yonis tvam |*
> *pitā putrāya lokakṛj jātavedo naya hy enaṃ sukṛtām yatra lokaḥ |*
> *asmād vai tvam ajāyathā eṣa tvaj jāyatām svāhā |*
>
> He has come into existence through thee, thou through him. He is thy womb, his womb thou art. As a father clearing the way for his son lead him, Jātavedas, to the world of the virtuous. From him thou wast born, he must be born from thee, svāhā!

In verses *c–d* the composer seems to elaborate ṚV 10.16.4cd (*yā́s te śivā́s tanúvo jātavedas tā́bhir vahainaṃ sukṛ́tām ulokám*). The concept 'favourable bodies' (*śivā́s tanúvo*) of Agni are evoked here *via* the concepts of a father and his son. Their relationship is based on love which is the basis for the favourable attitude of cremation fire towards the deceased.

Verses *e–f* of the stanza are the same as the verses quoted in the beginning of the JB (1.2, see above). In the ŚB, there is a cosmogony which discusses the relationship between man and fire and their mutual interdependence (2.3.3.1-6). As a man keeps fire in Agnihotra during his life, in the same way fire keeps man after his death. This concept is evoked here.

The composer of the JB then states:

JB 1.47b

> *so 'ta āhutimayo manomayaḥ prāṇamayaś cakṣurmayaś śrotramayo vaṅgmayo ṛṅgmayo yajurmayas sāmamayo brahmamayo hiraṇyamayo 'mṛtas saṃbhavati |*
>
> He arises immortal form from this (fire) in order of an oblation, consisting of mind, breath, sight, hearing, speech, Ṛc, Yajus, Sāman, Brahman and gold. (Bodewitz 1973)

As I have shown, according to the Ṛgvedic model the deceased placed on a funeral pyre becomes the Somic oblation (Jurewicz 2010a: 294). JB 1.2, in its description of what happens to an Āhitāgni when he dies, describes the deceased in the same way as is described here. In both cases, the deceased becomes a form composed of the oblations, of his breaths and the sounds of the Veda. The noun *brahman* in *brahmamaya* refers either to the Veda as a whole or to the Atharvaveda which was the Veda ascribed to the Brahman-priests. In the same way, the immortal self of the sacrificer built during the Agnicayana ritual is described in the ŚB (see chapter 3.4).

The compound *hiraṇyamaya* evokes the concept of the purification of gold. In the ṚV, this metaphor is mostly used to conceive the kindling of fire and the purification of Soma but also thinking (Jurewicz 2010a). In ŚB 6.1.3, creation is conceived in terms of transformations of Prajāpati's sweat the final product of which is gold (see chapter 3.5.1)[15]. As I have also shown, the verb *saṃ kṛ-*, which is used to denote the creation of *ātman* of Prajāpati during creation and the sacrificer during ritual (especially during Agnicayana), generally expresses transformations under the influence of heat and such is transformation of gold (see chapter 3.4).

The fact that the ritual transformation of the sacrificer was conceived in the Brāhmaṇas in terms of the purification of gold needs more research. For the moment I will refer to *Taittirīya Brāhmaṇa* 3.11.7.3 which says that the body of the Nāciketa fire altar is golden (*híraṇyaṃ vā́ agnér nāciketásya śárīram*) and that the sacrificer who knows that, goes to the heavenly world with his body (*sáśarīra evá svargáṃ lokám eti*)[16]. There he shines with radiance and fame (*téjasā yáśasā*) as a burning golden disc (3.11.7.3-4). Since the fire altar is the visible form of the *ātmán* of the sacrificer, which is built of the sounds of the Veda (*ṛk*, *yajus*, *sāman*, ŚB 4.3.4.5, 10.5.1.5, 11.2.6.13), I would argue that the author of the *Taittirīya Brāhmaṇa* implies that the sacrificer's body is also conceived in terms of being gold. Because of that, he can reach the sun without being burnt by it. Then the *Taittirīya Brāhmaṇa* presents a cosmogony which clearly evokes the process of gold purification: urged by his desire of creation Prajāpati creates gold and casts it into the fire three times, but he does not like this (*Taittirīya Brāhmaṇa* 3.11.8.6). So the fourth time he casts it into his heart which is Agni Vaiśvānara. Fire is the first manifest form of Prajāpati and Prajāpati's second manifestation is conceived in terms of gold. One could presume that on the first three occasions Prajāpati was not able confirm his identity with his manifest part. The fourth time he realises that what he creates is an integral part of himself and thus the identity of both his aspects is confirmed. This act is conceived in terms of burning gold in fire within Prajāpati himself: he realises that the fire he created in the beginning is the fire identical with himself. Then it is said that gold, which is the smallest of treasures, is most dear because it is born in the heart (*tásmād dhíraṇyaṃ kániṣṭhaṃ dhánānām | bhuñját priyátamam | hṛdayajám̐ hí*). It is implied

15 The composer of the JUB 3.17.3 in its description of the afterlife also evokes the process of cleansing metals under the influence of heat to present the way the way the Brahman-priest cures the mistakes which may occur during sacrificial performance.

16 See Smith (2016).

here that the ritual transformation of the sacrificer's *ātman* is conceived in terms of the purification of gold too. The conceptualisation of immortality in terms of gold is well attested in the ŚB (5.2.1.20 , 5.3.5.15, 5.4.1.14, 6.7.1.2, 10.4.1.6, 12.8.1.22). The *ātman* of the sacrificer, created in ritual, is conceived as a golden treasure in his heart.

At the same time, Agni's seed is conceived in terms of gold (ŚB 2.1.1.5, 3.3.1.34.5.1.15, 12.4.3.2). In ŚB 12.4.3.2, where the expiatory ceremonies of the Agnihotra are discussed, it is said that if fire goes out before the second libation is offered, the sacrificer may offer gold because it is Agni's seed and 'and the father is the same as the son, and the son is the same as the father'[17]. In this concise way, the recipient is triggered to evoke the general domain of Procreation and the scenario of insemination and development of man who is the same as the seed and conceived in terms of gold. The logic of this scenario, together with the whole ritual context, implies that the immortal self of the sacrificer is conceived in these terms.

The same is implied in the exegesis of the Agnicayana where the act of placing fire in the fire vessel (*ukhā́*) during initiation (*dīkṣā́*) is conceived in terms of insemination and is understood as the pouring of the *ātmán* of the sacrificer composed of metres (ŚB 10.4.1.2, 10.4.2.29). The conceptual network created here consists of five input spaces: the general domain of Procreation in its specific realisation of insemination and the development of man, the general domain of Cleansing By Heat in its specific realisation of the purification of gold, the actual ritual performance and the creation of the *ātmán* of the sacrificer. The generic space is the concept of transformation. In the blend, just as man evolves from seed and as gold is purified by fire, so in the same way the immortal self of the sacrificer is created while the altar is built; if correctly accomplished the end result will be an adult man and purified gold. This blend also implies conceptualisation of the sacrificer's self in terms of gold.

Let us come back to the description of JB 1.47b. The accounts just presented allow me to interpret the qualification of the deceased as *hiraṇyamaya* as activating the metaphor CREATION OF THE IMMORTAL SELF IS PURIFICATION OF GOLD. The fact that the body of the deceased will be burnt on the cremation pyre confirms my assumption. The body of the deceased will be transformed and purified under the influence of fire as gold, when heated, is transformed and purified.

Now the dead body is covered with sacrificial implements and with the parts of the body of the *anustaraṇī* cow in close correspondence: heart on

[17] ŚB 12.4.3.1: *agnér vā́ etád réto yád dhiraṇyaṃ yá u vaí putráḥ sá pitā́ yáḥ pitā́ sá putrás tásmā́d dhiraṇyam abhíjuhuyā́d etád evá tátrakárma* |

heart, fore-legs on arms etc.[18]; finally he is covered with its skin. Already in the ṚV a goat was offered as an oblation to the cremation pyre, so that it does not destroy the dead person (ṚV 10.16.4). For the same reason the body was covered with a cow's skin (ṚV 10.16.7). I would argue that the same is meant here: the part (*bhāga*) which will be taken by the death (conceived in terms of fire, JB 1.12) is not the deceased but a cow. The deceased is redeemed by that oblation just as he redeemed himself by all the oblations he gave to fire in his life. Moreover, the instrument to kill the cow is the same as the instrument which is used by the season to strike the dead who do not possess the right knowledge (*kūṭa*, JB 1.49). So every mortal part of the deceased is already killed in ritual: it is not him who is killed by the season, but the cow which is killed by priests instead of the deceased.

The explanation of the essence of the smoke of the cremation fire is based on this action, namely, making the deceased free from his mortal body:

JB 1.49a

tasyopādīptasya dhūma eva śarīraṃ dhunoti | sa yad dhunoti tasmād dhunaḥ | dhuno ha vai nāmaiṣa | taṃ dhūma iti parokṣam ācakṣate parokṣeṇaiva | parokṣapriyā iva hi devaḥ |

Of him when he has caught fire the smoke (*dhūma*) shakes off the body. Because it shakes off (*dhunoti*) therefore it is *dhuna*. In fact it is *dhuna* by name. The call it mystically *dhūma* in a mystic way of speaking. For the gods are fond of the mystic. (Bodewitz 1973)

The properly performed cremation allows the dead person to rise up through the night, the day, the half-month of the waning moon, the half-month of the waxing moon and finally to the month:

JB 1.49b

dhūmād va rātrim apyeti rātriyā ahar ahno 'pochantīpakṣam apochantīpakṣād āpūryamāṇapakṣam āpūryamāṇapakṣān māsam | te atra māse śarīraṃ cāsuś ca saṃgachāte |

From the smoke he goes to the night, from the night to the day, from the day to the half-month of the waning moon, from the half-month of the waning moon to the half-month of the waxing moon, from the half-month of the waxing moon to the month. There in the month both the body and the life-spirit come together. (Bodewitz 1973)

[18] For correspondence of parts of the deceased and the cow's body, see Oertel (1898).

The fact that the deceased is conceived as going through bright and dark divisions of time implies that he mentally embraces the whole manifest aspect; the same idea is implied by the JUB (see section 5.2.3). As we have seen, in the CU and the BU the bright and dark divisions of time are split into two: the fully liberated are united with the bright part while those who return to the earth unite with the dark part (see chapter 4.3.1). In the JB, when the deceased reaches the month, his breath and his body come together that would imply that he regains his *ātman* built during rituals performed in his life and after his death.

As in the previous case, the guardian of the sun comes and asks the same question, but now the correct answer is given:

JB 1.50a

taṃ hartūnām eko yaḥ kūṭahasto raśminā pratyavetya pṛchati ko 'si puruṣeti | *taṃ pratibrūyāt* |
vicakṣaṇād ṛtavo reta ābhṛtam | *ardhamasyaṃ prasutāt pitryāvataḥ iti* |
yad ado vicakṣaṇaṃ somaṃ rājānaṃ juhvati tat tat |

O, seasons, from the radiant one, which is pressed out every half month, from the one who is connected with the pitṛs the seed is produced'. That they offer there the radiant Soma, that (is meant by) this. (Bodewitz 1973)

In order to interpret the first two verses, I will refer to the Ṛgvedic general model of reality transformation. According to that model, fire in which Soma is poured becomes the sun. When it reaches zenith Soma, is finally purified in the sun and comes back to the earth in the form of rain. The deceased follows the same route: burnt on the sacrificial pyre, he becomes the Somic oblation, reaches the sun in zenith and then comes back to the earth in the form of rain (Jurewicz 2010a[19]). The first two verses in a concise way evoke this model. The composer in his commentary interprets *vicakṣaṇa* as Soma. This agrees with the Ṛgvedic use of this word which mostly refers to Soma (Gonda 1963: 32–33). For the present argument it is important to note that in several stanzas Soma, qualified as *vicakṣaṇá,* is presented in his solar aspect: it is presented as mounting a chariot of the sun, as standing in the sky and illuminating space and it is also called *pátir diváh* and *divó viṣṭambhá upamó vicakṣaṇáḥ* which implies its solar form (ṚV 9.74.1, 9.85.9, 9.86.11, 35). Moreover, in three stanzas *vicakṣaṇá* is the epithet of the sun (ṚV 1.50.8, 10.37.8, 4.53.2) and in one place (ṚV 3.3.10) it refers to Agni in its solar

[19] For the svargá lóka located in zenith in the Brāhmaṇas, see Klaus (2004: 166 ff.).

aspect[20]. The word *vicakṣaṇá* is also used in ṚV 1.164.12 to denote the visible form of the sun which is placed in the nearer half of the sky (see chapter 1.6).

In the ṚV, the adjective *pítryavant*, which appears in the next stanza, is used once in the context of pressing Soma:

ṚV 9.46.2

páriṣkṛtāsa índavo yóṣeva pítriyāvatī |
vāyúṃ sómā asṛkṣata ||

The drops, adorned like a maiden with her patrimony[21], the soma drinks have been released to Vayu.

Soma is compared to a maiden who is adorned for a wedding. In ṚV 4.58.9, streams of clarified butter which are identified with Soma are compared in a similar way with the verb *añj-*, 'to put a balm', used in that case. As I have argued, the concept of putting on balm activates the general domain of Cleansing By Heat the specific realisations of which were used to conceive, among others meanings, the purification of Soma (Jurewicz 2010a). The same domain is evoked here in order to express this process. The verb *páriṣ kṛ-* is also used in the context of the purification of Soma (ṚV 9.14.2, 9.39.2, 9.43.3, 9.46.2, 9.61.13, 9.86.24, 9.99.2, 9.105.2, 9.113.4). Although it means 'to adorn', it is possible that the concept of adorning also activated the concept of putting on balm as part of the general preparations before a wedding[22].

Since, according to the general model of reality transformation, Soma was purified not on earth but also in the sun, the last verse can be interpreted not only as an offering to Vāyu, but also its appearance in space in the form of rain. Qualification of the sun in the JB as *pítryavant* could evoke this way of thinking about the purification of Soma attested in ṚV 9.46.2.

In his interpretation of the verse *ardhamasyaṃ prasutāt pitryāvataḥ*, Bodewitz (1973: 59, note 22) treats the word *pitryavant-* as 'an old epithet of Soma, here identified with the moon which is pressed out'. Within the frames of my argument, this word refers to Soma identified with the sun. It is called *pitryavant*, 'connected with fathers', because it was believed that the deceased meet his fathers on the sun. The noun *ardhamāsya* may also evoke the

---

20 It is worth adding that the word *vicakṣaṇa* was used by the Dīkṣita (JB 2.64: *vicakṣaṇavatīm vācam vadati (...) prāṇo vai vicakṣaṇas | tasya vāg eva mithunam*), see Caland, Henry (1906: 21). According to Heesterman (1962: 13), the specific speech is one of similarities between the Dīkṣita and the Vrātya in terms of which reality is conceived in the *Vrātyakāṇḍa*.

21 In their translation, Brereton and Jamison call this simile 'a striking image of the soma drops adorned like a girl for the marriage' (2014: 1272).

22 This is the case in some usages of the verb *alaṃ kṛ-* (Gonda 1975b), see section 5.3.

concept of the moon which in post- Ṛgvedic thought became more and more important. The verse *ardhamasyaṃ prasutāt pitryāvataḥ* can be interpreted as creating a blend in which the Ṛgvedic concept of the sun (evoked by words *vicakṣaṇa* and *prasutāt pitryāvataḥ*) is fused with the later concept of the moon (evoked by *ardhamāsyam*). As will be shown, the ambivalent power of the sun is divided in JUB 3.12.4 (see section 5.2). Its favourable power is identified with the sun itself which allows the deceased to go further. Its dangerous power is identified with the moon from which the deceased comes back to the earth in the form of rain.

So I would interpret the first two verses of the stanza *vicakṣaṇād*... as follows. Soma offered on earth becomes the sun. The rain-making function of the sun is conceived in terms of the moon. Soma becomes conceived in terms of semen (RAIN IS SEMEN). This is exactly what is expressed in the model of the Five Fires presented in JB 1.45: immortality and water (*amṛtam āpas*) are poured into the sun, from which Soma appears which is then poured into the thunder. Thus rain appears (in this model the concept of the moon is not activated). Immortality is the part of the deceased which survives his death. It is his *ātmán* built in rituals performed during his life. This is the body (*śarīra*) which is gained by the deceased when he reaches the sun (JB 1.49).

The identification of the deceased with water can be justified on the basis of the ṚV where Soma is often identified with water[23]. This identification may be attested in JUB 3.10.9: *atho yad evainam etad asmāl lokāt pretaṃ cityām ādadhaty atho yā evaitā avokṣaṇīyā āpas tā eva sa tato 'nusambhavati prāṇam v eva prāṇo hy āpaḥ.* Oertel (1896) translated *tatas* as relating to waters and the whole sentence as '...now what waters for sprinkling are, after those he thence comes into existence and after breath also'. If we understand that *tatas* refers to the moment of placing the deceased in the funeral pyre, we could understand that after this moment he becomes waters and breath (*prāṇa*). Breath can be identified with 'the life-spirit', *asu*. Because of that the composer JB 1.49 says that the body and the life spirit of the deceased come together (*te atra māse śarīraṃ cāsuś ca saṃgachāte*).

In the model of the Five Fires presented in JB 1.4, the creation of rain from the sun is presented in two stages: firstly the deceased in the form of immortality and water is poured into the sun[24]. It is worth noting that according to CU (3.1.2, 3.2.1, 3.3.1, 3.4.1, 3.5.1), the parts of rays of the sun, identified with the ṚV, YV, SV, AV and *brahman*, are called 'immortal waters' (*amṛtā āpas*). If this identification was accepted by the composers of the JB, we could assume that the form of immortality and water also refers to

---

[23] E.g. ṚV 1.134.2, 3.35.8, 9.32.3, 9.74.3, 9.74.8, 9.103.2 passim. See Srinivasan (1979: 61 ff.).
[24] In the BU and CU he has the form of *śraddhā*, see chapter 4.3.1.

the immortal self of the sacrificer made from the sounds of sacred speech. In this process, Soma appears which is then poured into the thunder (*stanayitnu*). The thunder metonymically evokes the concept of storm and lightning which is the manifestation of fire in space. Bodewitz, in his notes to these verses, also notices this similarity: 'The Seasons offer King Soma just as the gods in the *pañcāgnividyā* (second sacrifice)' (1973: 122). It is also possible that the concept of thunder is meant to metonymically activate the concept of Indra whose weapon is a thunderbolt, *vájra*, and who is the prototypical Soma drinker. All this confirms my interpretation that the first two verses of the stanza *vicakṣaṇād...* evoke the first three stages of the world's functioning presented in the model of the Five Fires.

The following verses of the stanza present the next stages of the cosmological process that has been presented in JB 1.45:

JB 1.50b

taṃ ma puṃsi kartary erayadhvam iti |
puṃsi hy enam kartary erayante |

'As such you sent me in a man as[25] agent' – For they send him here in a man as their agent (Bodewitz 1973)

The deceased enters a man in the form of semen as expressed in the fourth sacrifice of the model presented in JB 1.45 according to which man eats food, which is the form the deceased and semen enter man. The next stage corresponds to the fifth stage when the deceased person in the form of semen is placed in the womb of his future mother and then is born:

JB 1.50c

puṃsaḥ kartur mātary āsiṣikta iti
mātari hy enam asiñcanti |
sa upajāyopajāyamānas trayodaśena dvādaśopamāsah iti |
eṣa trayodaśo ya eṣa tapati |

'From that man, your agent, you emitted me in a mother'. – For he (the father) emits him in a mother. 'Thus I am produced, being added by the thirteenfold one as the additional month of the twelve'. It is the thirteenfold one which burns here. (Bodewitz 1973)

Conceptualisation of the deceased who is born by the thirteen month implies that the symbolic interval of pregnancy was twelve months. Bergaigne (1963

25 Bodewitz (1973) adds 'your'.

[1878–83], II: 123 ff.) and Heesterman (1957: 34 ff.)[26] discuss the problem of the formation of numbers by adding an extra one which encompasses all the entities: 'the extra element summarises and encompasses the totality number to which it is added' (Heesterman 1957: 35). Further Heesterman argues that

> the summarising element represents the new birth, the recommencement of the totality's unfolding as it is strikingly shown by the speculations on the thirteenth month, which as an embryo enters seasons again (1957: 36)

In a note, he refers to ṚV 10.72.8-9 which presents Aditi who goes to heaven with seven sons and the eighth one is thrown away 'for procreation but also for death' (ṚV 10.72.9c: *prajā́yai mṛtyáve tuvat*, see chapter 1.5). Heesterman's interpretation concerns the Śunāsīrīyam rite which 'marks not only the close of the *cāturmāsya* year, but, like the Āgrayaṇa iṣṭi, also and in the first place the transition to the new year' (Heesterman 1957: 33). Taking this into account, the recipient may understand that the deceased is born to live again and die again.

The JB identifies 'the thirteenthfold one' (*trayodaśa*) with the sun (*ya eṣa tapati*). Since the concept of the sun metonymically evokes the concept of time, the recipient may understand that the power of time is meant which makes the entities grow and become mature. In the present case, time matures the embryo in his mother's womb. There is, however, more meaning in this sentence. Heesterman (1957: 33) argues that 'the thirteenth month is the embryonic year which (re-)enters the seasons'. He refers to ŚB 8.4.1.19: 'the year, as an embryo, in the shape of the thirteenth month, enters the seasons' (*saṃvatsaró ha trayodaśo mā́so gárbho bhūtvá 'rtū́n právíśati*). Then he argues that 'the rebirth of the year implies that man is also reborn' and refers to *Taittirīya Brāhmaṇa* 1.5.5.6[27].

The recipient may then understand that the deceased is identified with the sun which is reborn at the winter solstice. Thus, in his answer to season, the deceased not only reveals his knowledge about his origin but also about his identity with the sun. The deceased is the sun, because he comes from the sun having been poured into it as the first oblation in the model of the Five Fires and because the son is identical with his father. Within the frames of this conceptualisation, it may be argued that now the deceased wants to realise his identity with that part of the sun which is 'in the upper half of heaven' (*diva (...) páre árdhe*, ṚV 1.164.12ab) and which is, as I have argued, the

[26] See also Knipe (1975), Gonda (1976a), Srinivasan (1997: 71 ff.).

[27] *ékaṃ mā́sam údasṛjat | parameṣṭhī́ prajā́bhyaḥ | téna ābhyó máha ā́vahat | amṛ́taṃ mártyābhyaḥ | prajā́m ánu prájāyase | tád u té mártya amṛ́tam |*

sun cognised in supernatural cognition. As such it is changeless, contrary to its aspect called *vicakṣaṇa,* and is perceived in everyday cognition (described in ṚV 1.164.12cd).

JB 1.50d

taṃ vide prati tad vide 'ham |
taṃ martavo 'mṛtaṃ anayadhvam dvādaśatrayodaśena pitrā |
tayā mātrā tayā śraddhayā tenānnādyena tena satyena
ahar me pitā rātrir mātā | satyam asmi |
te martavo 'mṛtam ānayadhvam iti |

'This I know, of this I am sure. So lead me, O Seasons, to immortality, through the twelve- or thirteenfold father, through his mother, through his faith, through this food, through his truth. Day is my father, night my mother. I am truth. So lead me, O Seasons, to immortality' (Bodewitz 1973)

The deceased reveals who he is because he knows his origin. He has come into being in the cycle of rebirth which is already described in the RV: having reached the sun and spent some time in happiness and immortality with his fathers, he came back to earth in the form of rain. If we put this in terms of the BU and the CU descriptions, we could say that he knows that till now he has been walking the path of the fathers (*pitṛyāna*). Now, thanks to his knowledge, he can go further. The factors which will allow him to do so are faith (*śraddhā*), food-eating (*annādya*) and truth (*satya*). Both translators of the JB interpret the word *śraddhā* as the faith of the deceased though. If we take into account the description in the JUB 3.11.7, it is the faith of those who remain on earth which has the greatest impact on the afterlife (see section 5.2). The concept of 'food-eating' (*annādya*) introduces the concepts of cognition and power which were conceived in these terms in the Veda.

Then the metaphor THE SUN IS THE KING is again elaborated: the seasons, conceived in terms of the guardians, lead him to the abode of the king. Having reached the sun, the deceased becomes one of the gods:

JB 1.50e

tam hartava ānayante | yathā vidvān vidvāṃsaṃ yathā jānan jānantam evaṃ hainam ṛtava ānayante | taṃ hātyarjayante | sa haiṣa na manuṣyo ya evaṃ veda | devānāṃ ha vai sa eko ya evaṃvit |

Him the seasons take with them. As one who knows one who like-wise knows, as one who understands one who likewise understands so the seasons take him with them. They admit him (to heaven). He who knows thus is not a human being; he is one of the gods if he has this knowledge. (Bodewitz 1973)

Similarly to ṚV 10.14.8, the deceased meets his fathers, but the JB elaborates this topic in more detail:

JB 1.50f

taṃ ha vai manojavasaḥ pitaraś ca pitāmahāś ca pratyāgachanti tataḥ kiṃ na āhārṣīr iti | tān pratibrūyād yat kiṃ ca puṇyam akarma tad yuṣmākam iti | tasya putrā dāyam upayanti pitaraḥ sādhukṛtyām dviṣantah pāpakṛtyām |

The father and grandfather, swift as thought, approach him (saying): 'What, dear son, have you brought to us?'. He should answer them: 'Whatever good I have done, that is yours'. His sons enter upon his inheritance, his fathers upon (the effect of) his good deeds, his enemies upon (the effects of) his evil deeds. (Bodewitz 1973)

As in the case of the deceased who did not know themselves, the deeds of the deceased are divided into three. Everything he did to enlarge his wealth becomes the heritage of his sons, the good deeds go to his fathers and the wrong ones go to his enemies; the same idea is elaborated in KU 1.4 (see section 5.3). Since the deeds are done during life, the recipient understands that here it is their results that are meant and that they are beneficial for his ancestors and destructive for his enemies. This means that the composer of the JB accepts the belief that consequences of one's action last longer than the action itself and they can influence not only its agent, but also other people. This is a very common human belief and I would not differentiate it from so called 'karmic retribution' the principle of which is the same. The difference consists on who is to bear the consequences: the agent or other people. In the JB and KU (see sections 5.1.1, 5.3), it is not only the agent, but also other people whereas in the JUB (see section 5.2.2), BU and CU (see chapter 4.3.1) it is the agent. I would see this difference as a shift of accents rather than a radical change in thinking. Moreover, it seems that it is the deceased who decides what will happen to his deeds, as he can distribute them according to his will and is not just deprived of them. As we remember in the previous case (JB 1.46, see section 5.1.1), the deeds of the deceased were distributed without his will.

Then the deceased becomes one with the sun without the danger that the sun will burn him:

JB 1.50g

sa evam etat tredhā vibhajyaitasya salokatām apyeti ya eṣa tapati |

Having thus made this threefold division he goes to co-existence in one world with the one that burns here. (Bodewitz 1973)

From what has been said it follows that the JB presents two possibilities for the afterlife which the BU and CU will elaborate more precisely. The first possibility ends with a return to the state of life and death and the second in union with the sun. There are three factors on which the afterlife depends. The first is the deeds deceased performed during his life. The second is knowledge of one's origin. The third is somehow connected with a properly performed cremation. The insertion of a description of cremation between the two afterlife paths is not random and conveys a meaning which should be reconstructed. In the description of the first path, the cremation rite is mentioned only generally as a part of a model of the Five Fires. In the description of the second path, the cremation rite is described with more details and its author evokes a *mantra* addressed to fire which is supposed not to destroy the deceased, but to give him immortality. He also presents the ritual acts which redeem the deceased person from being killed by the season.

My analysis of the JB shows that it is strongly grounded in earlier thought. The path which leads to liberation is the path which is already present in the ṚV. The JB description is placed within the teaching of Agnihotra and it is not introduced by a Kṣatriya. Moreover, it is consistent with the context in which this passage appears. As I have shown elsewhere (Jurewicz 2004), the successive stages of functioning of the cosmos can be seen as the successive acts of offering milk into fire which repeats the first creative act of Prajāpati in which he offered milk to fire and thus redeemed himself from total annihilation (ŚB 2.2.4, see chapter 3.1.1). Viewed from this perspective, the model of the Five Fires presents the functioning of the cosmos in terms of Agnihotra which ensures the safe manifestation of Prajāpati within its frames. There is a close similarity between Prajāpati who creates fire from himself and the sacrificer who, in the Agnyādheya rite, kindles fires which are identified with his breaths, i.e. with his self (JB 1.1-2)[28]. In this fire-self the sacrificer has to perform the Agnihotra in order to obtain long life and immortality after death as Prajāpati did *in illo tempore* and does all the time in order to manifest himself as the cosmos. It is worth adding that in the model of the Five Fires the composer of JB 1.45 uses the word *visṛṣṭi* in reference to the cosmic sacrifices as if he wanted to emphasise the creative role of the processes described in the model.

Bronkhorst (2007) claims that the difference between the earlier Vedic thought and the culture of Magadha is the belief in transmigration which in the next incarnation depends on previous deeds. He claims that such a belief is not attested in the early Veda (2007: 115). Taking into account the evidence of the JB, the problem is more complex. According to this text, the future

[28] The detailed analysis of the Agnyādheya has been done by Krick (1982).

incarnation depends on deeds. Firstly, it depends on gifts the deceased gave during his life (in the first path). Secondly, it depends on deeds of those who are still alive and can perform the proper cremation rite (in the second path). This line of thinking is continued in the JUB (see section 5.2). It is worthwhile mentioning that even in the ṚV the concept of deeds (*iṣṭāpūrtá*, ṚV 10.14.8), which unite with the deceased in the sun, imply their influence on him.

Moreover, as I have already mentioned, contrary to other accounts analysed in this book, the JB does not place this exposition within the context of the debate. The two possible ways of the deceased are seen as the result of the proper performance of the Agnihotra and the cremation rite. This also weakens Bronkhorst's hypothesis about the non-Brāhmaṇical source of a belief in rebirth.

5.2. Account of the *Jaiminīyopaniṣad Brāhmaṇa* (3.7-28)

The JUB is the next early account of a belief in three kinds of afterlife. The text is difficult and is immersed in cultural knowledge about the role of the Udgātar and the interpretation of the Sāman-chant[29], but it is possible to reconstruct the main features as to what happens to man after death.

According to this account man, is born and dies three times: during birth, during initiation and when he dies (JUB 3.8.9-10, 3.9.1-8). I will concentrate on the description of what happens after death. The role of the Udgātar in this process is indispensable. I will not go into detail about correspondences between parts of the mantras sung by the Udgātar on the one side and activities and objects on the other, but, generally speaking, there is an ontological link between those two spheres and because of this the Udgātar can influence the afterlife lot of man[30].

In JUB 3.10.10, the composer presents the role of the Udgātar in the following way. When the Udgātar says *vāc*, he carries the deceased beyond the Agni, when he says *huṃ*, he carries the deceased beyond Vayu and when

[29] For the formation of the JUB, see Fuiji (1997).

[30] Malamoud describes the role of the Udgātar who helps the Sattrin, who died during performance of Sattra, to reach the world of the fathers: 'la mélodie (*sāman*) est caractéristique du dieu de la mort Yama, car le but est d'aider le mort à parvenir au royaume de Yama' (2002c: 97). He says that ṚV 10.189, which is an invocation to the Sun, is not clearly connected with the situation and looks for reasons for its recitation in its traditional attribution to the Queen of Serpents (2002c: 97–98). I would rather argue that the content of the hymn is in place here because it is the sun which should be reached by the dead sacrificer. For cognitive analysis of selected sections of JUB 3.10.10-3.13.10, see Jurewicz (2016e).

he says *bhā*, he carries the deceased beyond the moon[31]. In the Veda, Agni is an aspect of the earth and the wind is an aspect of space, so the recipient can metonymically activate these concepts (AGNI FOR EARTH, WIND FOR SPACE[32]). As far as the moon is concerned, its concept metonymically activates the sky (MOON FOR THE SKY) and the sphere of the cosmos from which men come back to the earth (MOON FOR THE YONDER WORLD)[33]. This is elaborated in later parts of the exposition (JUB 13.14.6 ff.). Together with the deceased the Udgātar carries himself up (JUB 3.10.11)[34].

In this passage, the composer creates a conceptual network which consists of four input spaces. The first input space is the Udgātar who sings the Sāman-chant in the ritual place. The second input space is the immortal part of the deceased. The third input space is the cosmos composed of three spheres: the earth, the space and the sky. The fourth is the concept of a journey. The generic space is the concept of transformation and the image schemas of VERTICALITY and SOURCE-PATH-GOAL.

In the blend, singing is the cause of the transformation of the deceased, conceived in terms of the upward journey across the spheres of the cosmos. We may presume that the Udgātar, when he sings in the ritual place, activates his ritual self with whose aid he follows the deceased. The role of recitation in this process is highlighted *via* the use of the word *prāṇa* which is mentioned as one of the factors of the process described in this passage (JUB 3.10.11). The input spaces of the Udgātar and the deceased are linked with a cause-effect relationship. In the blend, it is compressed into relations of identity. This

31 JUB 3.10.10: *taṃ ha vā evaṃvid udgātā yajamānam om ity etenākṣareṇādityam mṛtyum ativahati vāg ity agniṃ hum iti vāyum bhā iti candramasam* | In the first sentence the composer introduces the general topic of his exposition which is how the deceased safely passes the sun on which death threatens him and goes further. For analysis of this passage see Fuiji (1987b).

32 The nature of these metonymies depends on the way the relationship between fire and wind on the one hand and earth and space on the other was conceived. If fire and wind were conceived as inhabitants of the earth and space, then the metonymy can be modelled as INHABITANTS FOR PLACE (Radden, Kövecses 1999: 41). However, if it is conceived more generally in terms of a container (earth, space), then fire and wind are its content (CONTENT FOR CONTAINER, Radden, Kövecses 1999: 41). The issue of the nature of the Vedic metonymies needs a separate study.

33 The nature of this metonymy also depends of the nature of relationship between the moon and the yonder world. For example, it is possible to understand this relationship in terms of the relationship between the concrete and the visible (the moon) and the abstract and the invisible (the yonder world). As Radden, Kövecses (1999: 45) write: 'Our basic human experience relates to concrete objects, which have more salience for us than abstract objects' and this is reflected in conceptual metonymies, e.g. we say *to save one's skin* for 'to save one's life' (1999: 46).

34 JUB 3.10.11: *tān vā etān mṛtyūn sāmnodgātātmānaṃ ca yajamānaṃ cātivahaty om ity etenākṣareṇa prāṇenāmunādityena* |

compression strengthens the efficacy of the Udgātar's activity in the minds of the participants of the ritual. The activity of the Udgātar is a visible sign of the transformations of the deceased which take place when he sings. This is the basic blend which will be elaborated in the further description.

In JUB 3.11.4 the composer states when a man dies, 'he becomes faith' and is 'born to a world' (*sa śraddhām evābhisambhavati lokam abhijāyate*). If the recipient interprets the word *loka* as the space of experience realised in ritual activity, he will understand that the deceased is reborn to an experience. It will not only depend on his deeds and his knowledge, but first of all on the Udgātar's recitation. Now the Udgātar sings the Gāyatra Sāman three times. With the first turn, the earth is won by the deceased, with the second space and with the third the yonder world (JUB 3.11.5-7). Together with the world, one wins everything which there is in these spheres of the cosmos. There is a correspondence between the first two spheres won after death and the spheres won during the first and second birth (i.e. insemination and *dīkṣā*). These are space (*āśā*) and the sacrificial fee (*dakṣiṇā*, JUB 3.11.2-3). There is also correspondence between the forms of the deceased. The first is breath (*prāṇa*), the biological self of man which allows him to move in space. The second are metres (*chandāṃsi*), i. e. the immortal self of man created in the rituals which end with the offering of the sacrificial fee to the priests. It is thus implied that the deceased repeats his life while he is conducted by the Udgātar to the yonder world. The last form of the deceased with which he wins experience in the yonder world is faith, though it is implied by the composer of the JUB that it is not only the faith of the deceased (as I have argued before, Jurewicz 2004), but, first of all, the faith of those who remain on earth:

JUB 3.11.7

> *tad etayā cainaṃ śraddhayā samardhayati yayaivainam etac chraddhayāgnāv abhyādadhati sam ayam ito bhaviṣyatīti* |
>
> Thus he causes him to thrive with that faith with which faith they lay him into fire (saying): 'this one, from here, will come to life'. (Oertel 1896)

Then it is said that the Udgātar gives the deceased to this world or to this space of experience in which he will be born (*etaṃ cāsmai lokam prayacchati yam abhijāyate*, JUB 3.11.7).

It may be presumed that the composer is now describing the state of the deceased who has reached the borderline sphere of the cosmos conceived as his presence on the sun. He now states that the deceased, having reached the yonder world, is followed by death:

JUB 3.12.2

taṃ ha svarge loke santam mṛtyur anvety aśanayā |

After him, being in the heavenly world, death goes, hunger. (Oertel 1896)

This would mean that death of the body is not the death of the whole person. Although the body is destroyed, the immortal self composed in ritual performed during life remains and now this very self is in danger. I would argue that the word *punarmṛtyu*, so often mentioned in the Brāhmaṇas, refers to the concept of the death of this immortal self. Death is conceived in terms of hunger (see BU 1.2.1, chapter 4.1.1), and hunger is, in turn, conceived in terms of a living being who follows the deceased. The Udgātar repels death with the sound *hiṅ*:

JUB 3.12.3

śrīr vā eṣā prajāpatis sāmno yad dhiṅkāraḥ tam id udgātā śriyā prajāpatinā hiṅkāreṇa mṛtyum apasedhati |

The *hiṅkara* is the fortune (excellence), Prajāpati of the Sāman. That death the Udgātar drives away by means of fortune, of Prajāpati, of the *hiṅkara.* (Oertel 1896)

The composer explains that the sound *hiṅ* is *śrī*, excellence, and Prajāpati of the Sāman. Thus he enriches the conceptual network with further input spaces. The first of them is activated by the concept of *śrī* which activates the Ṛgvedic concept of fame understood as the supernatural immortal state realised in the sun thanks to the ritual (see chapter 1.7). As I have shown, in the ŚB the dangerous aspect of the sun is very much elaborated. The sun is often identified with death (e.g. ŚB 2.3.3.7) and conceived in terms of a hungry being which has to be fed in sacrifice so that it does not kill the sacrificer. This cultural knowledge about the sun is transferred into the blend and the recipient understands that the death, which threatens the deceased, is the dangerous power of the sun. The logic of the input space of the journey implies that the deceased has passed the sphere of the moon (which is described in JUB 3.10.10) and that the yonder world is located in the sun which is above the moon.

Qualification of the sound *hiṅ* as 'Prajāpati of the Sāman' (*prajāpatis sāmnaḥ*) activates the next input space of the complex blend created by the composer. It is the concept of Prajāpati in terms of which the creative power of reality is conceived in the Brāhmaṇas. In the blend, the deceased reaches the sun and is confronted with its dangerous power. However, the sound *hiṅ* incites the beneficial aspect of the sun and death is expelled. The efficient power of the sound *hiṅ* comes from its identification with Prajāpati who in *illo tempore* expelled death which had threatened him (see e.g. ŚB 2.2.4).

The composer of the JUB evokes yet another source domain to explain this efficacy. The Udgātar should additionally pronounce the syllables *huṃ mā* (JUB 3.12.4). It is explained that by saying *huṃ mā*, he drives away death a as a better person drives away a worse one who trembles before him (JUB 3.12.5). In this case, the influence of the Udgātar's speech is conceived in terms of a confrontation between two persons. The recipient may activate the cosmogonic fight of Prajāpati with death and conceive the influence of the Udgātar's speech in these terms.

Then the composer explains the meanings of the syllables *huṃ mā*. In this way, the Udgātar says to death 'Do not now go hither, where the sacrificer now is' (3.12.4)[35]. This explanation evokes a metonymy which gives access to the whole event *via* its initial phase (Radden, Kövecses 1999: 49). By saying *mā*, the Udgātar can expect that death, conceived in terms of a person, will unfold the whole sentence from its initial syllable *mā* and will run away. In the same metonymic way, the second meaning of the phrase *hum ma* is explained: *mā* is the first syllable of the word *māsa*, the moon[36]. By saying *mā*, the Udgātar shows the place where death is expected to run to: it is the moon. Thus he splits the ambivalent power of the sun and places its dangerous aspect into another heavenly luminary body.

According to the third explanation, *mā* means *bhā* (JUB 3.12.6)[37]. This explanation is called 'as if cryptic' (*parokṣeṇeva*). Such a qualification not only refers to the conventional definitions of words which are presented in the ritual exegesis[38]. It is also connected with the linguistic knowledge of the composer who recognises that sounds *mā* and *bhā* are produced in the same way as far as articulation is concerned and that both are labial. The composer concludes, however, that the Udgātar should say *mā-* because this syllable activates all three meanings just discussed unlike *bhā-* (JUB 3.12.6). In other words, it is more general.

In the first half of the next chapter (JUB 3.13), the composer enumerates three kinds of second syllable of the Sāman-chant added to *hiṅ*. Three desires are mentioned: the desire for lustre in the sacred lore (*brahmavarcas*), the desire for cattle (*paśu*) and the desire for fortune or glory (*śrī*). It is not

---

35 3.2.14: *mātra nu gā yatraitad yajamāna* |

36 3.12.6: *yan mety āha candramā vai mā māsaḥ eṣa ha vai mā māsaḥ* |

37 3.11.6: *bhā iti haitat parokṣeṇeva yasmād v eva mety āha yad v eva mety āhaitāni trīṇi tasmān mety brūyāt* |

38 Gonda (1955–1956).

clear whose desires are being described here, those of the Udgātar or of the deceased. If they refer to the deceased, this would imply that his return to the earth is taken into account. It could be argued that the three social states are metonymically evoked here: the Brahmin state is evoked by sacred lore, the Vaiśya state by cattle and the Kṣatriya state by *śrī* which is conceptually connected with the royal rule[39]. Such a future rebirth is presented in the JUB 3.28.4 (see section 5.2.3).

According to JUB 3.13.1, *huṃ bhā* is recited for the fulfilment of the desire for the splendour of sacred lore (*brahmavarcas*). The conceptual link between *bhā* and *brahmavarcas* is explained in the following way: the splendour of the sacred lore shines (*bhāti*). The metonymy THE INITIAL PHASE OF THE PROCESS FOR THE WHOLE PROCESS in its specific realisation of THE INITIAL SYLLABLE FOR THE WHOLE WORD/PHRASE/SENTENCE is activated here[40]. Listening to the phrase *huṃ bhā*, the recipient is expected to unfold it into the verbal form *bhāti* and activate the concept of its subject which is *brahmavarcas* and a person which filled with it. Both activations are based on the metonymy ACTION FOR AGENT[41]. In the first case, the agent is abstract (*brahmavarcas*) and in the second case, the agent is man.

The fulfilment of the desire for cattle is caused by the phrase *huṃ bo* because *bo* is the sound of cattle. The fulfilment of the desire for excellence is caused by the phrase *huṃ bag* because in this way excellence is extolled (JUB 3.13.2-3)[42]. These explanations are also based on metonymy. In the case of cattle, it is the metonymy SOUND OF THE AGENT FOR AGENT; *bo* is an onomatopoeic sound for bellowing[43]. The case of excellence is more difficult. It may be presumed that the recipient is expected to activate the whole situation, when someone is excellent and others admire him saying *bag*![44]

---

[39] Three social classes are metonymically evoked *via* the concepts of their salient activities which can be seen as the instantiation of more general metonymies: DEFINING PROPERTY FOR CATEGORY (Radden, Kövecses 1999: 35) and ACTION FOR AGENT Radden, Kövecses 1999: 37).

[40] Radden, Kövecses (1999: 49) argue that etymology of *creed* provides a historical illustration of this metonymy: '*creed* derives from the word of Apostles' Creed, *Credo in unum Deum*, 'I believe in one God'.

[41] Radden, Kövecses (1999: 37).

[42] JUB 3.13.1 *bhā iti brahmavarcasakāmasya bhātīva hi brahmavarcasam* |
hum bo iti paśukāmasya bo iti ha paśavo vāśyante |
hum bag iti śrīkāmasya bag iti ha śriyam paṇāyanti |

[43] This would be an example of metonymic abstraction (Paivio: 2007: 292), it is similar to the onomatopoeic *bow wow* which is the metonymic extension of the vocal property of dogs. This metonymy can be seen as a variation of metonymy INSTRUMENT FOR PRODUCT (as in: 'Did you hear *the whistle*?' for 'its sound', Radden, Kövecses 1999: 40).

[44] The next three sentences of the paragraph concerns specific next issues connected with the recitation of the Sāman which needs more research which goes beyond the aim of the present book.

I will leave other issues connected with the recitation of the Sāman. From the point of view of the afterlife of the deceased, it is important what happens when the Udgātar says the *nidhana* (conclusion) of the Sāman. The composer discusses the results of the recitation of the syllables *ovā* analysed later as *oṃ vā* (JUB 3.13.12, Fuiji 1987a, 2009/2010).

JUB 3.13.7

> *anto vai sāmno nidhanam antas svargo lokānām anto bradhnasya viṣṭapam* |
>
> Verily, the nidhana is the end of the *sāman*, heaven is the end of the worlds, the summit is the end of the ruddy one. (Oertel 1896)

Now the composer reverts to the basic conceptual network created in JUB 3.10.10. The input space of the Udgātar who sings Sāman-chant is elaborated and its final part called *nidhana* is highlighted. The input space of the world is enriched with the concept of its end. The input space of the journey is elaborated in that now its aim is specified and it is conceived in terms of a summit. Thus the composer metonymically introduces the concept of a mountain or a tree as the new input space of the conceptual network. In the blend, the cosmos is conceived in these terms. Such a conceptualisation of the cosmos is attested already in the ṚV (Jurewicz 2010a: 304–305, 315).

The next input space of the conceptual network is the concept of cognition. It is activated *via* the words *bradhnasya* and *viṣṭap*. Although they do not stand in apposition (*viṣṭap* stands in apposition to *anta*), in the ṚV the phrase *bradhnásya viṣṭáp* is used twice in very significant contexts. In ṚV 9.113.10, it is used to denote the sun which men reach in Somic exultation and where they gain immortality both in life and after death. In ṚV 8.69.7, it denotes the place where the poet went with Indra after they had both drunk Soma and became friends; in the hymn this place is called 'a house' (*gṛhá*). Somic exultation conceived in terms of friendship with the god Varuṇa is also presented in ṚV 1.25.17 (Jurewicz 2010a: 407) and 7.87-88 (Jurewicz 2010a: 415–416). In the latter hymns (7.87.6, 7.88.3), the poet creates the image of himself and Varuṇa swinging on a golden swing in terms of which the sun is conceived. If the recipient of the JUB activates those Ṛgvedic usages of *bradhnásya viṣṭáp*, he will understand the place to which the composer refers in the phrase *anto bradhnasya viṣṭapam* is the sun. It is worth noting that according to the ṚV, the place reached by people under the influence of Soma and after death is conceived in terms of the sun (Jurewicz 2010a: 294 ff.). Since the sun has already been reached by the deceased, the recipient may presume that he now goes further. This seems to be implied by the composer who states that the

Udgātar with the aid of the syllable *oṃ* places the deceased in the heavenly world (*svarga loka* in JUB 3.13.8).

The wording of the sentence *anto vai sāmno nidhanam antas svargo lokānām anto bradhnasya viṣṭapam* is such that it builds sets of correspondences between the input spaces of the Udgātar and of the world which are realised as identical in the blend: the *nidhana* is identical with heavenly word (*svarga*) and with the summit (*viṣṭap*), i.e. the sun. At the same time, the singing can be put in a spatial structure according to the image schema of VERTICALITY where *nidhana* is the highest point of the Sāman-chant.

The crucial role of the speech of the Udgātar in shaping the afterlife state of the deceased is expressed in the next sentences of the JUB:

JUB 3.13.9-10

ya u ha vā apakṣo vṛkṣāgraṃ gacchaty ava vai sa tataḥ padyate atha yad vai pakṣī vṛkṣāgre yad asidhārāyāṃ yat kṣuradhārāyām āste na vai sa tato 'vapadyate pakṣābhyāṃ hi saṃyata āste | (9)
tam etad udgātā yajamānam om ity etenākṣareṇa svarapakṣaṃ kṛtvānte svarge loke dadhāti sa yathā pakṣy abibhyad āsītaivam eva svarge loke 'bibhyad āste 'thācarati | (10)

Verily he who without wings goes up to the top of a tree, he falls down. But if one having wings sits on the top of a tree, or on the edge of a sword, or on the edge of the razor, verily he does not fall from it. For he sits supported by his wings. (9)
Thus the Udgātar, making him, the sacrificer, by means of that syllable *oṃ* posses sound as wings, puts him in the end in the heavenly world. As one with wings would sit without fear in the heavenly world, (and) likewise moves about. (10) (Oertel 1896)

The input space of a mountain and a tree is profiled and the image of man climbing it is introduced: man falls because he does not have wings. This scenario is transferred into the blend. Within its frames, the activity of the Udgātar is conceived in terms of endowing a man with wings.

The recipient also may imagine the Udgātar, who accompanies the deceased, in terms of a bird. Thus the image created by the composer is very close to that of ṚV 1.164.20-22 which presents two birds sitting on the same tree. Moreover, in these stanzas the supernatural knowledge leading to the recognition of reality is conceived in terms of climbing a tree (Jurewicz 2010a: 304–305). If the recipient activates this conceptualisation, he will again activates the concept of transformations under the influence of Soma. This activation is confirmed in that this state is conceived in terms of the acquisition of wings by man in the ṚV (ṚV 10.119.2-3,11-12, Jurewicz 2010a: 178). In this way, the internally contradictory state realised in Somic exultation is conceived as man who normally does not fly is now is able to fly (Jurewicz 2010a: 177 ff.).

In the blend, the immortal self of the deceased is conceived in terms of man who climbs a tree and reaches its top. Everyday knowledge informs the recipient that man is too heavy to remain there contrary to birds which can safely sit on the tops of trees and on thin, sharps edges such as swords and razors because they can keep balance thanks to their wings. The influence of the *nidhana* is conceived in these terms. The immortal self of the deceased is created during his journey along the spheres of cosmos thanks to the Udgātar's recitation. The recipient may activate the conceptualisation of *axis mundi* in terms of tree (attested already in the ṚV, Jurewicz 2010a: 304–305). He will then understand the afterlife transformations in terms of climbing along the *axis mundi* which the deceased climbs during his afterlife journey.

The final moment of this transformation is conceived in terms of the acquisition of wings. Now the composer activates the image schema of BALANCE to conceive the safe situation of the deceased. It is worth noting that keeping balance involves slight swinging. Thus the recipient may activate the concept of a swing in terms of which the sun is conceived in the ṚV 7.87.5, 7.88.3 discussed above. Since the sun is also conceived in terms of a bird, the recipient understands that the deceased becomes identical with the sun. The nature of this identity is elaborated in further description of the JUB 3.14.2-5 (see section 5.2.2).

The image of a bird sitting on a sharp edge of a razor or sword foreshadows the dreadful situation of the deceased who lacks proper knowledge about this identity. It is conceived in terms of a living being who is cut into two halves by the sharp edge of a razor or a sword.

5.2.1. The first afterlife path

The deceased is now asked who he is by the sun (JUB 3.14). The text is almost the same as in JB 1.18: if the deceased answers with his name or the name of his *gotra*, the sun will take his self away and the seasons will drag him away and occupy his world. Thus he is destroyed by time metonymically evoked by the seasons (3.14.2). This is the first path of the deceased. Probably this is the path of those who, according to BU 6.2.16 and CU 5.10.8, do not know the two paths and because of that they are reborn in the miserable form of beings the life of which is useless (see chapter 4.3.1). Here, however, it is implied that such people disappear forever (see also JUB 3.14.11, analysed below, section 5.2.2).

5.2.2. The second afterlife path

Having described the first path of the deceased, the composer of the JUB comes back to the issue of the Sāman and the correspondences of its syllables with parts of the world:

JUB 3.13.11-13

te ha vā ete akṣare devalokaś caiva manuṣyalokaś ca ādityaś ca ha vā ete akṣare candramāś ca | (11)
āditya eva devalokaś candramā manuṣyalokaḥ | *om ity ādityo vāg iti candramāḥ* | (12)
tam etad udgātā yajamānam om ity etenākṣareṇādityaṃ devalokaṃ gamayati | (13)

The same two syllables are the world of the gods and the world of man. (11) The sun these two syllables are, and the moon. The sun is the world of the gods, (and) the moon is the world of man. The sun is *oṃ*, the moon is *vāc*. (12) Thus the Udgātar causes him, the sacrificer, to go to the heavenly world by means of this syllable *oṃ*. (13) (Oertel 1896)

In JUB 3.13.7, it is said that the *nidhana* consists of two syllables: *o* and *va* (*atha vā ato nidhanam eva ovā iti dve akṣare*). As Fuiji (2009/2010: 29) writes, '[i]n many places of the JUB, the sound *o* of the repeated *o va* is regarded as the sacred syllable *oṃ*, and *va* as the divine entity *vāc*'. It may be assumed that when the Udgātar says *o*[*ṃ*], he leads the deceased to the sun which is the world of the gods and when he says *vā*[*c*], he leads the deceased to the moon.

Now the composer presents the right answer which should be given by the deceased; the text is the same as in JB 1.18 and the sun is similarly cruel in his laugh:

JUB 3.14.2-5

tasmā u haitena prabruvīta ko 'ham asmi suvas tvam sa tvāṃ svargyaṃ svar agām iti | (3)
ko ha vai prajāpatir atha haivaṃvid eva suvargaḥ sa hi suvar gacchati | (4)
taṃ hāha yas tvam asi so 'ham asmi yo 'ham asmi sa tvam asy ehīti | (5)

To him he should answer thus: 'Who (*ka*) am I, heaven (art) thou. As such I have gone to thee, the heavenly heaven.' (3)
Verily Prajāpati is who (*ka*), and he who knows thus is heaven going; for he goes to heaven. (4)
He says to him: 'Who thou art, that one am I; who I am, that art are thou; come!' (5) (Oertel 1896)

If the deceased knows his identity with the sun and Prajāpati, he will go further. His situation is described as follows:

JUB 13.14.6

sa etam eva sukṛtarasam praviśati | yad u ha vā asmiṁl loke manuṣyā yajante yat sādhu kurvanti tad eṣām ūrdhvam annādyam utsīdati | tad amuṃ candramasam manuṣyalokam praviśati |

He enters this sap of good deeds.
And what men in this world sacrifice, what good (deeds) they do, that of them rises upward (as) food-eating; it enters yonder moon, the world of men. (Oertel 1896)

In the first sentence, the deceased is presented as entering the sap of good deeds. The verb *pra viś-* (*praviśati*) activates conceptualisation of the change of the deceased in terms of entering a container; within the frames of this conceptualisation states are conceived in terms of containers. The word *rasa* in the compound *sukṛtarasa* activates conceptualisation of the change of the deceased in terms of drinking a juice. The first part of the compound, *sukṛta*, activates the concept of good deeds which the deceased performed in his life. The recipient may understand that the composer of the JUB presents the influence of deeds on the state of the deceased. Within the frames of this conceptualisation, the results of action are conceived in terms of juice which is available to people after their death[45]. As previously shown the composers of the ŚB and the Upaniṣads elaborate the concept of drinking sap, *rasa*, as the source domain for liberating cognition. This is motivated by the memory of the state realised in Somic exultation which is the ideal of the supernatural state. The account of JUB 3.14.6 shows an important change in the use of this source domain because here the influence of previous deeds is conceived in its terms and not in terms of a liberated state. We can see that the later conceptualisation of the afterlife state is grounded in earlier Vedic tradition.

In the next sentence, the composer of JUB 3.14.6 explains how this influence is possible. He says that the deeds performed by the deceased rise upwards and become 'the food-eating' (*annādya*) as Oertel (1896) translates but this word can also mean 'food'[46] and is located at the moon. The concept

[45] In the later thought, the influence of action is conceived in terms of eating the fruits of what has been sown during life. The basic conceptualisation is the same: the source domain is preparation of something edible and its eating. The change in source domains is caused by a change in cultural experience: Soma is lost and the agriculture becomes one of the main occupations of Indian society.

[46] This double meaning is motivated by metonymies AGENT FOR ACTION, ACTION FOR THE OBJECT OF ACTION.

of sap is metonymically compressed with the container in which it is located, i.e. the moon (metaphors: MOON IS CONTAINER, SAP IS CONTENT OF CONTAINER and the metonymy: CONTAINER FOR CONTENTS, CONTENTS FOR CONTAINER).

The conceptual network is elaborated in the following way. Its input spaces are concepts of the moon, of the deceased with his life, the concept of preparation and drinking sap and the image schemas of CONTAINER and of CAUSE-EFFECT. The generic space is the concept of transformation. In the blend, the deceased enters the moon and is able to be influenced (*annādya* as food-eating) by his previous deeds conceived in terms of sap (*annādya* as food). Within the frames of this conceptualisation, the recipient may understand *rasa* not as sap but as the life-giving part of food. The influence of previous actions is conceived in terms of drinking the sap.

It should be noticed that the composer mentions separately sacrificial deeds (*yad* (...) *yajante*) and good deeds (*yat sādhu kurvanti*) which would imply that not only performance of the ritual influences the afterlife state.

Taking into account what is said in JUB 3.13.13 that the Udgātar leads the deceased to the sun, I would assume that the deceased reaches the sun which is the world of the gods (JUB 3.13.12), but cannot go further and comes back to the moon (i.e. the world of men, JUB 3.13.12) where he is influenced by his good deeds. This will be confirmed at the end of the chapter.

The deceased who takes the path now described will be reborn again:

JUB 3.14.7

tasyedam mānuṣanikāśanam aṇḍam udare 'ntas sambhavati | tasyordhvam annādyam utsīdati stanāv abhi | sa yad ājāyate 'thāsmai mātā stanam annādyam prayacchati |

This human-like egg of him comes into being within the belly. Of it the food eating rises upward toward the two breasts. When he is born, then the mother offers her breast to him for food-eating. (Oertel 1896)

The composer now explains how rebirth is possible. The way good deeds influence man is conceived in the same way as the production of milk of a pregnant woman. The concept of pregnant woman is the next input space of the network. In the blend, man's previous deeds reaches the moon and influences him in the same way as in micro-scale food (*annādya*), which is milk, reaches the breasts of his mother and can be drunk. The input space of preparation and drinking sap gives coherence to both processes. On the moon, the deceased drinks *rasa* and in a similar way when he is reborn he drinks milk the quality of which depends on his previous deeds.

The role of sacrifice is then presented as the necessary factor for rebirth:

JUB 3.14.8-9

ajāto ha vai tāvat puruṣo yāvan na yajate | sa yajñenaiva jāyate |
sa yathāṇḍam prathamanirbhiṇṇam evam eva | (8)
tadā taṃ ha vā evaṃvid udgātā yajamānam om ity etenākṣareṇādityaṃ devalokaṃ gamayati | vāg ity asmā uttareṇākṣareṇa candramasam annādyam akṣitim prayacchati | (9)

Verily unborn is the man in so far as he does not sacrifice. It is through the sacrifice that he is born: just as an egg burst first.
Then the Udgātar knowing thus causes him, the sacrificer, through this syllable, viz. *oṃ*, to enter the sun, the world of the gods. By means of the next syllable, viz. *vāc*, he gives him moon, food-eating, imperishableness. (Oertel 1896)

The deceased, thanks to deeds performed in the previous life which shaped his afterlife state and his shape in his mother womb, is born again; the concept of birth is evoked by the simile of a burst egg. The concept of hatching a bird is the next input space of the network. As we have seen, it is well entrenched in the cosmogonies of the ŚB (see chapters 3.2.1, 3.2.2[47]). The difference lies in that now this concept is used to conceive the state of man and not creation. The concept of an egg which first bursts is difficult to reconstruct but, taking into account that further on (JUB 3.14.11) the composer evokes the concept of a broken egg, one can presume that now safe birth is presented. This is confirmed by the first two sentences in which the composer states that a man who does not offer sacrifices is unborn because one can be born only through sacrifice.

The next passage (JUB 3.14.9) seems to summarise what has been said till now[48]. It recalls the description of JB 3.13.12 where two syllables of the *nidhana* are analysed.

When the Udgātar says *o*[*ṃ*], he leads the deceased to the sun. Then he says *vā*[*c*] and thus he brings the deceased to the earth ensuring his safe rebirth ('food, imperishableness', *annādyam akṣitim*). But in order to do that, the Udgātar has to have correct knowledge about the meaning of the Sāman-chant. If he does not, the destiny of the deceased is miserable:

---

47 It is also possible that the concept of the 'dead egg' (*mārtāṇḍá*, ṚV 10.72.8-9, see chapter 1.5) is evoked here too.

48 JUB 3.14.9: *tadā taṃ ha vā evaṃvid udgātā yajamānam om ity etenākṣareṇādityaṃ devalokaṃ gamayati | vāg ity asmā uttareṇākṣareṇa candramasam annādyam akṣitim prayacchati |*

JUB 3.14.10-12

atha yasyaitad avidvān udgāyati na haivainaṃ devalokaṃ gamayati no enam annādyena samardhayati | (10)
sa yathāṇḍaṃ vidigdhaṃ śayītānnādyam alabʰamānam evam eva vidigdhaś śete 'nnādyam alabhamānaḥ | (11)
tasmād u haivaṃvidam evodgāpayeta|evaṃvid ihaivodgātar iti hūtaḥ pratiśṛṇuyāt | (12)

But whose Udgītha one not knowing thus sings, verily he does not cause him to enter the world of the gods, nor to thrive through food-eating (10).
As an egg would lie besmeared (?), not receiving food, so he lies besmeared (?), not receiving any food (11).
Therefore he should cause only one knowing thus to sing the Udgītha. Only one knowing thus here being addressed with 'O Udgātar' should answer. (12) (Oertel 1896)

The composer evokes the concept of a broken egg with white flowing from it; from the logic of the scenario the recipient understands that the nestling dies[49]. In these terms, the situation of those who are do not have an Udgātar with the right knowledge is conceived. Conceptualisation of his situation in terms of a broken egg implies that they follow the first path and are totally destroyed.

5.2.3. The third afterlife path

The third path is described in JUB 3.20-28 and is, as Fuiji (2011: 106) writes, 'most probably the earliest Upaniṣad' which 'includes a long passage on rebirth'. He summarises these chapters as follows:

> Here the journey of the deceased through the entities represents the gradual process of the recovery of his own body after death by getting back his vital functions and bodily elements which have been deposited in the corresponding cosmic entities. From this passage in the JUB, it can be reasonably inferred that the similar journey of the deceased in the theory of the devayāna and pitṛyāna must have the same purpose, that is, the recovery of the body after death by regaining vital functions and bodily elements from the cosmic entities. (Fuiji 2011: 107)

The description of the third path begins with an analysis of the relationship between speech and mind and, correspondingly, between the three priests who pronounce mantras during sacrifice (Hotar, Udgātar, Adhvaryu) and the silent

[49] A similar image, although more elaborated, is activated in ŚB 6.1.1.12, see chapter 3.2.2.

Brahman-priest[50]. Speech is connected with the descendants of Viśvamitra and mind with the descendants of Vasiṣṭha. The Brahman-priest is identified with the *evaṃvid*, 'the person who knows in this way' (JUB 3.15.3: *tad u vā āhur evaṃvid eva brahmā*).

In order to explain the role of the Veda, a version of the initial cosmogony of the JUB is repeated (3.15.4-9): Prajāpati wants to create beings, heat himself and creates three worlds. Then, in successive acts of heating, he creates the sap (*rasa*) of the three worlds which are Agni, Vāyu and Āditya. Their sap (*rasa*) are *Ṛgveda*, *Yajurveda*, *Sāmaveda* and their sap (*rasa*) are the sounds *bhūr*, *bhuvaḥ*, *svaḥ*. These sounds are called 'the brightness of the threefold knowledge' and it is stated that the world is as great as they are (JUB 3.15.9 *tad dha vai trayyai vidyāyai śukram etāvad idaṃ sarvam*). Thus the composer conceives creation in terms of the preparation of sap the last form of which is the most perfect. This may bring to the recipient's mind the Ṛgvedic experience of the preparation of Soma juice and activate the general domain of Cleansing By Heat.

The next paragraph explains the role of priests in the sacrifice. The composer identifies sacrifice with wind and conceives it in terms of a walking man or a chariot which leaves tracks. The relationship between the mind and speech is conceived in terms of tracks. The Hotar, Udgātar and Adhvaryu perform the sacrifice with speech, and Brahman with the mind and because of this he is silent. If he spoke, the sacrifice would have only one track and would be like a man with one leg or a chariot with one wheel. The sacrifice with a silent Brahman-priest is conceived in terms of a man with two legs and a chariot with two wheels.

In the next paragraph (JUB 3.17), the role of Brahman-priest is explained: if there is mistake from in the Ṛk-stanza, the Yajus-formula, or the Sāman-chant, the Brahman-priest corrects it. He cures them with the exclamations *bhūr*, *bhuvas*, *svar*, created by Prajāpati as the shining essence of the Veda (see above, JUB 3.15.4-9). The composer stresses that the Brahman-priest should get half of the sacrificial share while the remaining half is for the three other priests and that he should possess true knowledge because everything that exists is within him (JUB 3.17.5-10).

Having described the right recitation of the after-verses of the verses called *stomabhāga* (JUB 3.18), the composer explains the role of the speech and of *oṃ* in the sacrifice:

---

50 For the role of the Brahman-priests in Vedic ritual, see Bodewitz (1983).

JUB 3.19.1

athaiṣa vācā vajram udgṛhṇāti | yad āha somaḥ pavata iti vopāvartadhvam iti vā vācaiva tad vāco vajraṃ vigṛhyate vācas satyenātimucyate |

Now with speech he takes up a thunderbolt. In that he says either 'Soma cleanses itself' or 'Turn ye hither', thereby with speech that thunderbolt of speech is taken apart (?), by the truth of speech he is released. (Oertel 1896)

In the ṚV, the fight between Indra and Vṛtra was one of the important source domains in which sacrifice was conceived (Jurewicz 2010a). It is especially elaborated in the exegesis of the Darśapūrṇamāsa (e.g. ŚB 1[51]). The source domain of fight is also elaborated as the fight of the gods against demons (*daivāsura*, see ŚB 11.1.6.9, see chapter 3.5.2). Within the frames of this conceptualisation, a thunderbolt is the weapon with which Indra and the gods fight and the sacrificer re-enacts their activity at the sacrificial ground. In terms of a thunderbolt, the ambivalent power of speech is conceived with both aspects: dangerous and beneficial. The dangerous one should be directed against the enemies of the sacrificer and not against himself or the sacrifice. The recipient is expected to activate this conceptualisation here: the speech carries its own power conceived in terms of the thunderbolt[52]. A *mantra* properly pronounced (beginning with words *somaḥ pavate* or *upāvartadhvam*) separates this power (one could also argue this ensures it is aimed in the correct direction), then it is released, i.e. thrown in that direction with the aid of the truth of speech. One can presume that such a speech can only be created by 'him who knows in this way' (*evaṃvid*) because only he knows the true meaning of words which are ontologically the same as that they denote. It is then repeated that the after-verse should end with *oṃ*.

Now, in order to explain the importance of the syllable *oṃ*, another version of the initial cosmogony is presented. The gods went to the yonder world thanks to the threefold knowledge, but they do not want men to follow them. They press the knowledge, but are not able to press one syllable which is *oṃ*. The syllable is called 'full of sap' (*sarasa*) which implies that it conceived in terms of a closed container filled with liquid so completely that it is too hard to destroy. Such a conceptualisation of the syllable *oṃ* may direct the mind of the recipient towards ṚV 1.164.22 the composer of which conceives the content of the sacred knowledge in terms of a sweet fruit on the top of a tree (see chapter 1.6).

51 For the description of the Darśapūrṇamāsa, see Rustagi (1981).

52 For conceptualisation of speech in terms of thunderbolt (*vajra*), see Gonda (1993: 62).

This is confirmed as at the end of the paragraph as it is said that *oṃ* is the foundation for three Vedas and for priests and that by placing the sacrificer in this syllable the priests carry him to the heavenly world:

JUB 3.19.6-7

etad dha vā akṣaraṃ trayyai vidyāyai pratiṣṭhā om iti vai hotā pratiṣṭhita om ity adhvaryur om ity udgātā | (6)
etad dha vā akṣaraṃ vedānāṃ triviṣṭapam etasmin vā akṣara ṛtvijo yajamānam ādhāya svarge loke samudūhanti | *tasmād om ity evānumantrayeta* | (7)

Verily this same syllable is the firm stand of the threefold knowledge. (Saying) *oṃ* the Hotar stands firm, (saying) *oṃ* the Adhvaryu, (saying *oṃ*) the Udgātar. (6) Verily this same syllable is the triple heaven (?) of the Veda. The priests having placed the sacrificer in this syllable carry him up together into the heavenly world. Therefore he should recite the after-verse (saying) *oṃ* only. (7) (Oertel 1896)

The syllable *oṃ* is called the threefold summit of the Vedas (*vedānāṃ triviṣṭapam*). The word *triviṣṭap* is used in JUB 3.13.7 which explained the cosmic role of the *nidhana*; there the summit was defined as the end of the 'ruddy' (3.13.7: *anto vai sāmno nidhanam antas svargo lokānām anto bradhnasya viṣṭapam*). As I have argued, the concept of summit refers to the sun which is the heavenly world placed at the end of worlds and time. The number 'three' in *triviṣṭap* refers to three Vedas because *oṃ*, as the syllable which is the essence of the Vedas, comprises them. If the recipient activates the blend created in the previous passages, he will understand that the deceased and the Udgātar are now on the top of the cosmic tree and the syllable *oṃ*, conceived in terms of a sweet berry, becomes his foundation (*pratiṣṭhā*, see chapter 3.2.2) a starting point for the further journey within the range of the sun.

The following passages of the JUB are difficult to understood fully in the present stage of research, but their main line of thought can be reconstructed. The description of the path of the deceased can be divided into two parts: the first part describes his journey to the end of the world and time, in other words, to the borderline sphere of the cosmos. The second seems to refer to the states which are realised when this border is crossed. It is possible that the second part also refers to some meditative stages similarly to the TU (see chapter 4.4.2.5) and the KU (see section 5.3).

The description begins with the following stanza:

JUB 3.20.1

guhāsi devo 'sy upavāsy
upa taṃ vāyasva yo 'smān dveṣṭi
yaṃ ca vayaṃ dviṣmaḥ |

'Thou art in secret, thou art a god, thou art on-blowing; blow on him who hates us and whom we hate.' (Oertel 1896)

In Ṛgvedic descriptions of the vision of the poets, the first stanza describes its final aim (ṚV 4.1.10, 4.58.1, Jurewicz 2010a). The aim of this stanza is the same. The word *gúhā* is used in the ṚV in reference to various objects which are hidden and found (the precious ones such as cattle, e.g. ṚV 1.65.1 or fire, e.g. ṚV 5.11.6). As I have shown, the concept of looking for a hidden, precious object becomes the source domain for the conceptualisation of creation and cognition and this is attested in the use of the word *nidhí*, 'treasure, treasury', which is used in such contexts ṚV 1.130.3, 2.24.6 (Jurewicz 2010a). In a more abstract context, the word *gúhā* is used in 10.45.2d to qualify the secret name of Agni (*vidmā́ te nā́ma paramáṃ gúhā yád*) and in ṚV 1.164.45 to qualify the three hidden parts of speech (see chapter 1.6). As previously mentioned, the word *gúhā* is also used in AVŚ 2.1.1 in the abstract meaning of the object of knowledge of reality (see chapter 2.4)[53].

The sentence *guhāsi* expresses then the aim of the journey which the deceased is expected to follow. In the context of the JUB 3.20.1, this aim is Agni. Taking into account earlier background, the recipient may understand Agni in the aspect of the earth at the beginning the journey the aim of which is Agni in its solar form. This interpretation is confirmed by the following verses of the stanza.

Then the hidden aim is understood more generally as the god (*devo 'sy*) who blows (*upavāsy*) and is expected to blow on those who hate the poets and whom they hate (*upa taṃ vāyasva yo 'smān dveṣṭi yaṃ ca vayaṃ dviṣmaḥ*). Such a qualification inevitably triggers the recipient to think about the wind but the whole sentence is again motivated by earlier thinking. As mentioned, in the early Veda there was a close conceptual link between the concept of fire and the concept of wind. In the ṚV, fire is presented as blowing (with use of the verb *dham-*, ṚV 5.9.5) and the expelling of enemies is conceived in terms of blowing them away[54]. In most cases, it is Indra who expels the enemies in this way; one may presume that he does it when he is heated

[53] For the concept of hidden self in the Upaniṣads, see Ganeri (2011).
[54] e.g. ṚV 1.33.5, 9; 1.51.5, 5.31.9, 8.3.20, 8.89.2, 10.55.8, 10.145.2

with Soma which kindles his internal fire now released in a terrifying blast against enemies (see Jurewicz 2010a: 360 ff.).

The last phrase of the stanza (*yo 'smān dveṣṭi yaṃ ca vayaṃ dviṣmaḥ*) is used in AVŚ 2.11.3b and, in a slightly different way, in AVŚ 2.21, 2.22, 2.23: Agni, the sun, the moon and waters are asked to burn (*práti tap-*, *práti śuc-*, *práti arc-*) and to carry away (*práti hṛ-*) the enemies of the composer. They are also asked to deprive enemies of their brilliance (*téjas*). A similar phrase is used in AVŚ 3.27 where the poet wishes that his enemies are placed within the jaws of gods (*yò 'smā́n dvéṣṭi yáṃ vayáṃ dviṣmás táṃ vo jámbhe dadhmaḥ*)[55].

AVŚ 10.5.15-21 is also interesting from the point of view of the present analysis. Whitney (1905) gives the title of the hymn "Preparation and use of the water-thunderbolts". The hymn begins with the identification of waters with strength (*bála*), manly power (*vīryà*) and the manliness (*nṛmṇá*) of Indra (AVŚ 10.5.1-6). In this way, the androgynic character of waters is expressed: they are both male and female. The male aspect of waters is further elaborated and waters are identified with *bhāgá* (Whitney: 'portion') and *śukrá* (Whitney: 'sperm') of Agni, Indra, Soma, Mitra and Varuṇa, fathers and Savitar (10.5.7-14). If we take into account that the word *bhāgá* also activates the meaning of a woman's generating power in the AVŚ, then we would see that here the poet is describing the act of insemination of waters which can be performed thanks to their androgynous nature. The waters are yoked by the poet 'for conquering junction', as Whitney translated *jiṣṇáve yógāya*; in my opinion, *yóga* means here martial activity as in the ṚV (Oberlies 1998). They are sent into the world on the basis of Prajāpati's order (*prajā́pater vo dhā́mnāsmaí lokā́ya sādaye*). The poet wants to get a shining state (*várco asmā́su dhatta*) thanks to waters; only then will he be able to produce rain.

Then various elements of waters are thrown against the enemies of the composer which is expressed in the same way as in JUB 3.20.1 (*téna tám abhyátisṛjāmo yò3 'smā́n dvéṣṭi yáṃ vayáṃ dviṣmáḥ*). These elements are again *bhāgá*, then wave (ūrmí), calf (*vatsá*), bull (*vṛṣabhá*), golden germ (*hiraṇyagarbhá*), the heavenly dappled stone of waters (*apā́ṃ áśmā pṛ́śnir divyó*) and fires (*agnáyas*). The sequence in which the elements are evoked implies that the scenario of pregnancy and of the growth of a calf are blended with the cosmological scenario. The word *bhāgá* evokes the concept of woman's generating power while the concepts of wave and of the golden germ

[55] The form *dadhmaḥ* may phonetically evoke the verb *dham-*, used in the ṚV in the context of expelling enemies.

metonymically evoke the concept of a womb filled with amniotic fluid. The logic of the general domain of Procreation implies that the embryo evolves into a calf and a full-grown bull. The concept of the heavenly dappled stone refers to the sun (see chapter 2.4) conceived in terms of a bull. The final form of water are fires which can be understood as the rays of the sun and the shining drops of rain which destroy the enemies who hate the composer and whom the composer hates (see AVŚ 15.1.7-8, chapter 2.2.2).

Taking all this into account, I would argue that the concept of the aim of the journey expressed in the JUB 3.20.1-18, 3.28.1 is motivated by earlier concepts although here it is conceived in a more abstract way. The aim is Agni in its solar form which has power to destroy the enemies of the deceased.

JUB 3.20.2

mahināsi bahulāsi bṛhaty asi rohiṇy asy apannāsi |

'Thou art great, thou art abundant, thou art extended, thou art ruddy, thou art not fallen.' (Oertel 1896)

The epithets are in feminine gender and highlight the extension and permanence of the object which makes the recipient think about the earth. The epithet *rohiṇī* is used in reference to the earth in AVŚ 12.1.11c. Since according to the etymology of the word 'earth', broadness and extension are its essence (ŚB 6.1.1.15, see chapter 3.2.2), it may be inferred that the deceased knows the essence of the earth.

The next verse formulates the wish of the deceased to exist which is based on the identity of the cognising subject with the cognised object stated by the verse (it will be repeated several times more, see below):

JUB 3.20.3

sambhūr devo 'si sam aham bhūyāsam ābhūtir asy ābhūyāsam bhūtir asi bhūyāsam |

Thou art a god coming into existence; may I come into existence. Thou art existence; may I exist. Thou art becoming; may I become.' (Oertel 1896)

The next sentence (which also repeated later) is difficult to interpret:

JUB 2.30.4

yās te prajā upadiṣṭā nāhaṃ tava tāḥ paryemi upa te tā diśāmi |

'What offspring of thee is declared, that (offspring) of thee I do not comprehend. That (offspring) of thee I declare' (Oertel 1896)

I would guess (contrary to Oertel 1896) that the first phrase is spoken by the earth who in this way asks about the nature of its identity with the deceased conceived in terms of offspring. The offspring is the same as the father, he is conceived as his self, so there are rational grounds for conceptualisation of essence in these terms. The phrase *upa te tā diśāmi* is spoken by the deceased and is continued in the next sentence:

JUB 3.20.5

nāma me śarīram me pratiṣṭhā me tan me tvayi tan me mopahṛthā itīmām pṛthivīm avocat |

'My name, my body, my foundation: that of me is in thee. Do not take that of me into thee,' thus he said to this earth. (Oertel 1896)

Everything that is stable in a man comes from the earth. In the two afterlife paths described earlier, the *ātman* of the deceased was taken by the sun. Now, it seems that the deceased can rebuild himself from the parts of the world and in this way finally survive death.

Then the earth greets the deceased and the following dialogue is presented:

JUB 3.20.6-8

tam iyam āgatam pṛthivī pratinandaty ayaṃ te bhagavo lokaḥ saha nāv ayaṃ loka iti | (6)
yad vāva me tvayīty āha tad vāva me punar dehīti | (7)
kiṃ nu te mayīti nāma me śarīram me pratiṣṭhā me tan me tvayi tan me punar dehīti tad asmā iyam pṛthivī punar dadāti | (8)

Him having come to this earth joyfully receives (saying): 'Thine, O reverend sir, is this world. This world is ours in common'. (6)
'Verily that of me is in thee,' he says, 'give that back to me.' (7)
'What now of thee is there in me?' 'My name, my body, my foundation. That of me is in thee; give that back to me.' That this earth gives back to him. (8) (Oertel 1896)

The earth gives the deceased 'this world' (*ayaṃ loka*). If we interpret *loka* as space of experience, we can understand that the deceased can now experience everything that is connected with the earth. This space of experience will be enlarged each step of the journey. The deceased wants to get back the elements of his *ātman* which belong to the earth. These are: name (*nāman*), body (*śarīra*) and foundation (*pratiṣṭhā*). One may presume that name and body give the deceased back his identity. Conceptualisation of the earth as the foundation is well entrenched in the earlier thought (see e.g. ŚB 6.1.1.15, chapter 3.2.2, BU 1.2.2, chapter 4.1.1). In Vedic cosmogonies, the creative power of reality first builds the foundation which will allow it to continue creation. Now the deceased reaches the starting point for his further journey.

Then the deceased asks the earth to convey him to fire; this means that he knows the next step of his journey:

JUB 3.20.9

tām āha pra mā vāheti kim abhīti agnim iti tam agnim abhipravahati |

He says to her: 'Carry me forth' 'To what?' 'To Agni.' She carries him forth to Agni. (Oertel 1896)

Then the situation repeats. The deceased recites verses which define Agni's features and it is emphasised that those who know them becomes endowed with those features:

JUB 3.20.10

so 'gnim āhābhijid asy abhijayyāsam lokajid asi lokaṃ jayyāsam attir asy annam adyāsam annādo bhavati yas tvaivaṃ veda |

He says to Agni: 'Victorious art you, may I be victorious; world-conquering art thou, may I conquer the world, eating art thou, may I eat food; food-eating becomes he who knoweth thee thus.' (Oertel 1896)

Agni is conceived as a victorious entity already in the ṚV (Jurewicz 2010a) while its conceptualisation in terms of a food-eating entity is also deeply entrenched in Vedic thinking.

Then the composer repeats the same content as expressed earlier. In JUB 3.20.3-5 the deceased expresses his wish to exist based on the identity of himself and Agni, Agni asks about this identity and the deceased answers what elements of him are in Agni:

JUB 3.20.13

tapo me tejo me 'nnam me vāṅ me tan me tvayi tan me mopahṛthā ity agnim avocat |

My heat[56], my splendour, my food, my speech. Do not take that of me into thee,' thus he said to Agni. (Oertel 1896)

56 Oertel (1896): 'penance'.

Everything which is connected with heat in man (*tapas*, *tejas*) comes from fire. Fire, present in the stomach, is the giver of food. Finally, speech is conceived in terms of fire (see chapter 3.1.1).

Then Agni greets the deceased, gives him experience of his world and returns to the deceased his fiery elements. Since cognition is conceived in terms of heating, the recipient understands that now the deceased is endowed with the ability to cognise, speak and eat.

Agni carries the deceased to the wind (Vāyu). Again its essential features are enumerated:

JUB 3.21.2-4

sa vāyum āha yat purastād vāsīndro rājā bhūto vāsi yad dakṣiṇato vāsīśāno bhūto vāsi yat paścād vāsi varuṇo rājā bhūto vāsi yad uttarato vāsi somo rājā bhūto vāsi yad upariṣṭād avavāsi prajāpatir bhūto 'vavāsi | (2)
vrātyo 'sy ekavrātyo 'navasṛṣṭo devānām bilam apyadhāḥ | (3)
tava prajās tavauṣadhyas tavāpo vicalitam anuvicalanti | (4)

He says to Vayu: 'In that thou blowest from the front (the east), thou blowest as king Indra. In that thou blowest from the right (the south), thou blowest as the Lord. In that thou blowest from above (the west), thou blowest as king Varuṇa. In that thou blowest from above (the north), thou blowest down as Prajāpati. (2)
Thou art the Vrātya, the only Vrātya, not released of the gods (?). (3)
Thou hast closed the opening
The progeny, the herbs, the waters follow after thy departing' (4) (Oertel 1896)

Wind, according to the direction from which it blows, is identified with the main gods. The recipient may think about ṚV 2.1 where Agni is identified with the all Ṛgvedic gods accordingly to their behaviour.

However, a more clear reference is the *Vrātyakāṇḍa* where reality is conceived in terms of Vrātya. As has been shown, Vrātya incites Prajāpati who, at the end of creation, becomes *Vrātya* who alone encompasses the world (see chapter 2.2.2). The verb *ánu ví cal-* is also used in the *Vrātyakāṇḍa* to express the activity of reality and in JUB 3.21.4 it expresses the specific nature of wind which makes everything move.

Wind is qualified as *'navasṛṣṭo devānāṃ bilam apyadhāḥ*. The word *bila* literally means 'opening'. In AVŚ 18.4.30, it is used in a context which may shed some light on its interpretation in the JUB. This hymn belongs to the funeral hymns:

AVŚ 18.4.30

kóśaṃ duhanti kaláśaṃ cáturbilam íḍāṃ dhenúṃ mádhumatīṃ svastáye |
ū́rjaṃ mádantīm áditiṃ jáneṣv ágne mā́ hiṃsīḥ paramé vyòman ||

The milk a receptacle (*kośa*), a jar with four orfices, *iḍā* (as) milch-cow rich in honey, in order to well being; revelling refreshment, Aditi among the people, injure do not, O Agni, in the highest firmament (*vyoman*). (Whitney 1905)

Verse *a* presents the image of milking a receptacle, *kóśa*. In the ṚV, this concept is used as the source domain for the conceptualisation of the sun from which Soma flows (Jurewicz 2010a: 164 ff.). The concept of the sun is also meant here and the appearance of rain is conceived in terms of milking. The receptacle is presented as having four openings (*bíla*) and the concept of cow, introduced in verse *b*, may prompt to recipient to metonymically think about a cow's udder which has four teats and in terms of which the sun is also conceived in the ṚV[57]. From the point of view of my present analysis, verse *d* is important. The composer here asks Agni not to injure him in the highest heaven (*paramá vyòman*). As stated this concept is used in the ṚV to denote the borderline sphere of the cosmos conceived in terms of the sun which is reached by the sacrificer during life and after death. If the recipient of JUB 3.21.3 activates this concept of the sun, he will understand wind as the power which closes the openings of the sun and thus makes rain impossible if not loosened by the gods. But when the wind opens the opening and rain is loosened, it makes the rain appear with all its results: water flows, plants grow and progeny is possible. The last result is probably based on the belief that the deceased are reborn in plants which again supports the thesis that this belief was well entrenched in early Vedic times. The fact that the Atharvavedic stanza belongs to the funeral hymns makes activation of this stanza in the context of the JUB more probable.

Then the verses which state the identity of the deceased with Vāyu are again repeated. The deceased enumerates his features which come from the wind. These are exhalation (*prāṇa*), inhalation (*apāna*) and learning:

[57] On my view, conceptualisation of the sun in terms of udder with four teats is evoked in ṚV 1.62.6d: *mádhuarṇaso nadíyaś cátasraḥ*, 8.100.10c *cátasra ū́rjaṃ duduhe páyāṃsi*, 9.74.6c: *cátasro nā́bho níhitā avó divó*, and, metonymically, 9.89.5a: *cátasra īṃ ghṛtadúhaḥ sacante*. See also Jurewicz (2014a).

JUB 3.21.7

> *prāṇāpānau me śrutam me tan me tvayi tan me mopahṛthā iti vāyum avocat* |
>
> My exhalation and inhalation[58], my learning, that of thee is in me. That of me do not take into thyself,' he said to Vayu' (Oertel 1896)

The wind then greets the deceased, the experience of the deceased is again expanded and he recovers his features which come from the wind (JUB 3.21.8-10).

The reconstruction of the deceased looks as follows: he is endowed with name, body and foundation, with heat (*tapas* and *tejas*), food and speech, with breath and learning. While the earth's elements gives him identity and a starting point for further transformations, the fire's elements gives him the ability to function as living[59] and thinking[60] entity. The elements of wind give him the ability for practice which leads to supernatural cognition. In BU 2.3, a concentration on wind and breath is the starting point of this cognition (see chapter 4.4.2.2). It is possible that 'learning', *śruta*, refers to everything the deceased learnt in his life which forms the intellectual basis for liberating practice. In this stage, the deceased can repeat it and thus go further.

This would mean that, having reached the wind, he crosses an important barrier. This is also confirmed in that the next part of his journey is described more shortly. The subsequent spheres of the cosmos transfer him from one to another and the deceased does not recite the preliminary verses, but is immediately admitted by the spheres. When he knows which part of him belongs to a sphere, he receives it back and is carried to the next sphere. In each stage, the space of experience of the deceased is enlarged with the perspective of the consecutive spheres.

Wind carries the deceased to the sphere of space (*antarikṣaloka*) from which he gains back his space (*ākāśa*, JUB 3.21.11-14). It can refer to the spatial dimension of the afterlife form of the deceased. The world of space carries him to the quarters (*diśas*) from which he gains back his hearing (JUB 3.22.1-4). The quarters carry him to the sphere of day and night (*ahorātra*) from which he recovers his imperishableness (*akṣiti*, JUB 3.22.5-8). Since days and nights are the result of the sun's circular movement in the sky, it is implied that the deceased crosses the sphere subjected to time and because of

---

58 Oertel (1896): 'breath and exhalation'.

59 Metonymy FOOD FOR LIFE (instantiation of metonymy CAUSE FOR EFFECT, Radden, Kövecses 1999: 38).

60 Metonymy SPEECH FOR THINKING (EXTERNAL SYMPTOM FOR THE INTERNAL PROCESS; this metonymy is governed by the cognitive principle CONCRETE OVER ABSTRACT in its specific instantiation BODILY OVER MENTAL).

that he cannot perish. During the next three stages of his journey the deceased finally reconstructs his immortal body which is conceived in terms of a living organism. The days and nights lead him to the halves of a month which give him 'these petty joints' (*imāni kṣudrāṇi parvāṇi*, JUB 3.231.4). The halves of months lead him to the months (*māsa*) which give him back 'these gross joints' (*imāni sthūlāni parvāṇi*, JUB 3.23.5-8). The months carry him to the seasons who give him back 'these chief joints' (*imāni jyāyāṁsi parvāṇi*, JUB 3.24.1-4). The seasons lead him to the year which gives him back 'his self' (*ayam ma ātmā*, JUB 3.24.5-8). This word is used in the sense of the whole person which gives the deceased his identity.

The next two spheres are those which belong to the heavenly Gandharvas and the Apsarases from which he receives respectively: 'fragrance, joy and delight' (*gandha*, *moda*, *pramoda*) and 'laughter, play and sexual union' (*hāsa*, *krīḷā*, *mithuna*[61], JUB 3.25). This description presents the state of happiness gained by the deceased who, thanks to his immortal body, is able to experience various kinds of pleasure. In ṚV 9.113.11ab, the state gained thanks to Soma during life and after death is conceived in terms of a place where various kinds of happiness can be experienced (Jurewicz 2010a); the nouns that metonymically evoke this happiness are almost the same as those used in the JUB (*yátrānandā́ś ca módā́ś ca múdaḥ pramúda ā́sate*). In the Upaniṣads (e.g. BU 4.3.21, see chapter 4.4, 4.4.2.5), the images of sexual union and pleasure are used to conceive the state gained during liberation[62]. In its definition of the fourth state of *ātman*, CU 8.12.3 creates an image of a king, who laughs and plays, in order to present the image of ultimate happiness (see chapter 4.4.2.4). The concept of smelling is also used in the KU to conceive a very subtle cognitive stage realised by the deceased on his way to *brahman* (see section 5.3).

But this state of happiness is not the final stage of the deceased's journey. The Apsarases lead him further to the sky (*div*) which gives him back his satisfaction (*tṛpti*) because, it is explained, the sky is 'satisfied once for all, as it were' (*sakṛt tṛpteva hy eṣā*, JUB 3.26.1-4). The word *tṛpti* is also used in the Ṛgvedic description of immortal happiness gained thanks to Soma (ṚV 9.113.10c: *svadhā́ ca yátra tṛ́ptiś ca*). Its use implies that the deceased becomes fully satisfied having experienced the states conceived in terms of the worlds of the Gandharvas and the Apsarases. But the sky leads him further to the gods who give him back his immortality (*amṛta*, JUB 3.26.5-8).

61 Oertel (1896) translates *mithuna* as 'sexual pleasure'.

62 See also Olivelle (1997).

Now the description becomes the same as in the beginning which implies that the final stages of the afterlife journey are as difficult as the first (earth – fire – wind, see above). The gods lead the deceased to the sun (JUB 3.27.1). The deceased expresses his knowledge about the nature of the sun in the following verses:

JUB 3.27.2

> *sa ādityam āha vibhūḥ purastāt sampat paścāt samyaṅ tvam asi samīco manuṣyān aroṣī ruṣatas ta ṛṣiḥ pāpmānaṃ hanti apahatapāpmā bhavati yas tvaivaṃ veda* |
>
> Extensive art thou in the east, success (?) in the west. Thou art collective. Thou hast been angry with the collective men; of thee that art angry the sage (*ṛṣi*) kills the evil. (Oertel 1896)

The first sentence seems to evoke the scenario of the day: the sun when it rises extends its rays and its going down is conceived in terms of achieving the goal of the journey (SOURCE-PATH-GOAL image schema) which is metonymically evoked by the general noun *saṃpad.* Conceptualisation of the sun as a killing entity is characteristic for the thinking of the ŚB (see chapter 3.3). The adjective *saṃyañc* (translated by Oertel as 'collective') means not only 'going along with or together, turned together or in one direction', hence 'combined, united', but also 'entire, whole, complete' (which seems to be a further extension of the first meaning). Thus the feature of the sun expressed as *saṃyañc* denotes its fullness. Most difficult to understand is the sun's anger against people who also possess this feature. It is possible the fact that the seer (*ṛṣi*) mentioned in the passage can use the anger of the sun against evil-death is the consequence of the fact that the seer partakes in the nature of the sun. This is expressed by the last sentence which states that who knows the features of the sun is also able to kill the evil-death.

Then the verses expressing the deceased's wish to exist are repeated. They are based on the assumption of his identity with the sun (like in JB 1.18[63]). The deceased is asked about the aspects of his nature which are in the sun and which are conceived in terms of his offspring. These features are power (*ojas*), strength (*bala*) and sight (*cakṣus*, JUB 3.27.5). They are given back to the deceased by the sun (JUB 3.27.8) and the deceased asks the sun to carry him further to the moon (JUB 3.27.9). To it he says:

63 *ko 'ham asmi suvas tvam | sa tvāṃ svargyaṃ svar agām |*

JUB 3.27.10-11

satyasya panthā na tvā jahāti amṛtasya panthā na tvā jahāti | (10)
navo-navo bhavasi jāyamāno bharo nāma brāhmaṇa upāsse
tasmāt te satyā ubhaye devamanuṣyā annādyam bharanti annādo bhavati yas tvaivaṃ veda | (11)

'The path of truth forsakes thee not; the path of immortality forsakes thee not. (10) Anew and anew thou becomes, being born. Burden by name, a *Bráhman*, thou dost worship. Therefore the true, both gods and men, bring food for thee. Food-eating becometh he who knoweth thee thus.' (11)

The first sentence evokes the description of the moon which appears in ṚV 10.85.19 (with *bhavati* instead of *bhavasi*) and in AVŚ 7.81.2 (with *bhavasi*). The feature of the moon which is food-eating is implied already in the description of the second path in the JUB (see section 5.2.2)[64]. It is worth adding that the way of thinking about the moon seems to be motivated by the Ṛgvedic way of thinking about fire which is also described as constantly new (e.g. ṚV 3.11.5.c) and as the eater of food. It is again expressed that knowledge of the essence of the moon endows the knower with it.

Then the deceased again repeats his wish to exist and enumerates his features which are the basis of his identity with the moon: these are mind (*manas*), semen (*retas*) and offspring (*prajā́*, JUB 3.27.17). The conceptual connection between mind and moon is already stated in ṚV 10.90.13 while identification with semen and with offspring is built on the basis of the assumption that the place from which the deceased returns to the earth is conceived in terms of the moon (see above, JUB 3.14.6, see section 5.2.2). It is worth adding that when the deceased repeats his aspects which come from the moon he adds one more: it is *punaḥsambhūti*, 'the second birth'.

The state which is gained by the deceased in his afterlife journey, called 'the world of *brahman*' (*brahmaloka*), is conceived in terms of his free wandering between the sun and the moon:

JUB 3.27.18, 3.28.1-4

tam āha pra mā vaheti | (3.27.18)
kim abhīti brahmaṇo lokam iti tam ādityam abhipravahati | (3.28.1)
sa ādityam āha pra mā vaheti kim abhīti brahmaṇo lokam iti
taṃ candramasam abhipravahati sa evam ete devate anusaṃcarati | (2)

64 In the description of the *pitṛyāna* in the CU, BU, the moon is conceived in terms of food eaten by the gods, see chapter 4.3.1.

eṣo 'nto 'taḥ paraḥ pravāho nāsti
yān u kāṁś cātaḥ prāco lokān abhyavādiṣma te sarva āptā bhavanti te jitās teṣv asya sarveṣu kāmacāro bhavati ya evaṃ veda | (3)
sa yadi kāmayeta punar ihājāyeyeti yasmin kule 'bhidhyāyed yadi brāhmaṇakule yadi rājakule tasminn ājāyate sa etam eva lokam punaḥ prajānann abhyārohann eti | (4)

He says to it: 'Carry me forth.' (3.27.18)
'To what?' 'To the world of *brahman*.' It carries him forth to the sun. (3.28.1) He says to the sun: 'Carry me forth'. 'To what?' 'To the world of *brahman*.' It carries him forth to the moon. He thus wanders to and fro between these divinities. (2)
There is no carrying forth beyond this (limit). And all the worlds beyond (this limit) of which we have spoken, they are all obtained, they are conquered, in all there is unrestricted movement for him who knows thus. (3)
If he should wish: 'May I be born here again,' on whatever family he might fix his thoughts, be it a Brāhman-family, be it a royal family, into that he is born. He keeps on ascending to this world again-fore knowing. (4)[65]

The deceased is presented as moving freely between the sun and the moon. In the Ṛgvedic description of the immortal happiness realised under the influence of Soma, the same concept of unrestricted freedom conceived in terms of the possibility for free movement is presented (ṚV 9.113.9 *yátrānukāmáṃ cáraṇaṃ trināké tridivé diváḥ*). The compound *kāmacāra* is used in CU 8.1.6 (see chapter 4.4.2.4) in the description of final liberation. It is very probable that the composers of those Upaniṣads drew upon the JUB's description of the final situation of the dead.

Another similarity between the JUB and the Upaniṣadic descriptions is that the state of liberation can be reversed and if one so desires one can be reborn and begin again to cognise in a subjective-objective way (CU 8.12.4-5, see chapter 4.4.2.4). In this state, one may also choose the form of the future birth which is realised thanks to his cognitive activity (*yasmin kule 'bhidhyāyed* (...) *tasminn ājāyate*). Such a description of the deceased brings to mind the Upaniṣadic descriptions of the liberated person conceived as *satyasaṃkalpa* (CU 3.14.2, see chapter 4.4.2.1, CU 8.1.4, 8.7.1, see chapter 4.4.2.4). In this state, there is no division between subject and object and thinking is enough to transform being. We can see that this way of thinking is attested already in the JUB.

The last sentence shows that in the times of the JUB there were already people who did not want to be reborn:

---

[65] As Fuiji (2011: 108, note 19) writes: 'This is one of the early passages which explicitly refer to the deceased's rebirth on earth'.

JUB 3.28.5

tad u hovāca śāṭyāyanir bahuvyāhito vā ayam bahuśo lokaḥ
etasya vai kāmāya nu bruvate [vā] śrāmyanti vā ka etat prāsya punar iheyād atraiva syād iti |

And *Śāṭyāyani* said: 'Ofttimes, indeed, this world is very ill. Now for the sake of it they talk to each other or toil (saying): 'Who having thrown away would come here again? He would be only there.' (Oertel 1896)

This formulation most probably reflects the existence of ascetic communities which rejected the possibility of rebirth and looked for final liberation.

*

The possibility of rebirth was well known. The problem was how to escape from it. It seems that the crucial difference between the second and the third path described in the JUB lies in whether or not the Sāman has *oṃ* as its ending syllable. If it ends with *oṃ*, the deceased is finally liberated although he still has a possibility to come back to earth and to be reborn. Contrary to the ṚV, the deceased has a choice. Freedom, conceived in terms of wandering between the sun and the moon, is the most important feature of the liberated state.

If the Sāman is sung without *oṃ*, the deceased reaches the moon; then he is reborn. Moreover, in this case, the results of his deeds (the ritual deeds, *yad yajante*, and the good deeds, *yat sādhu kurvanti*, JUB 3.14.6) reach the moon where the deceased is influenced by them conceived in terms of drinking sap.

The proper singing of the Sāman and one's deeds in life are not the only factors affecting the afterlife. The next is correct knowledge about oneself. If the deceased lacks such knowledge, he is annihilated. As can be seen, the knowledge is vast and concerns ontic correspondences between one's body and cosmic entities.

The exposition just analysed is preceded by a story which presents four Veda students Sudakṣiṇa Kṣaimi, Prācīnaśāli and the two Jābāla brothers, Śukra and Gośru. Sudakṣiṇa Kṣaimi asks 'what of the sacrifice (can be) immediately (gained), what is obvious'[66]. They enter into discussion[67] and it is Sudakṣiṇa Kṣaimi who is the exponent of the theory outlined above. His angry colleagues call him 'Śūdra'(JUB 3.7.5) and 'Śūdraka' (JUB 3.9.9). As Black (2007) shows, Brahmins in their discussion were often aggressive

[66] *atha ha sma sudakṣiṇaḥ kṣaimir yad eva yajñasyāñjo yat suviditaṃ tad dha smaiva pṛcchati* | (3.7.4) (translation by Witzel 1987c).

[67] It is analyzed thoroughly by Witzel (1987c).

towards each other and to call a Brahmin 'a Śūdra' must have been very offensive. The Śūdras (contrary to the Kṣatriyas and Vaiśyas) could not learn the Veda and, moreover, Sudakṣiṇa Kṣaimi does not want a discussion without an audience like a Śūdra (JUB 3.7.6)[68]. Finally, he must have been close to his teacher if he knew that the teacher considered his colleagues so easy to defeat[69]. The construction of the exposition is common for Brāhmaṇic teaching. Firstly, Sudakṣiṇa Kṣaimi presents his view in a general way. He mentions the three deaths of man (during birth, during initiation and during cremation JUB 3.8.10-3.9.1.8) and the crucial role of the Udgātar who carries each man across death. Then Sudakṣiṇa Kṣaimi leaves the place where the discussion was held. The younger Jābāla brothers asks about the meaning of Sudakṣiṇa Kṣaimi's exposition and one is reminded of Prajāpati's teachings in the CU 8.7 (see chapter 4.4.2.4), where his first general teaching is not understood by Virocana and Indra. Then the elder Jābāla repeates what Sudakṣiṇa Kṣaimi has told them: it is the Udgātar who carries the deceased across death (JUB 3.9.9). And again the close relationship between the teacher and Sudakṣiṇa Kṣaimi is expressed because the elder brother adds:

JUB 3.10.1

taṃ vāva bhagavas te pitodgātāram amanyateti hovāca |

'Your father indeed has thought of him (S.K.) as an Udgātar'[70] (Witzel 1987b)

However, the relatives of Prācīnaśāli do not agree that Sudakṣiṇa Kṣaimi should be chosen as an Udgātar and they chose Kāṇḍviya as the Udgātar and Prācīnaśāli as the Brahman-priest. It is implied that the debate takes place again and is won by Sudakṣiṇa Kṣaimi who looks down on at his opponent and says:

JUB 3.10.3

taṃ hābhyavekṣyovācaivam eṣa brāhmaṇo moghāya vādāya nāglāyat sa nāṇu sāmno 'nvicchatīti ati haivainaṃ tac cakre |

'Thus has this Brahmin not been tired of useless talk. He does not seek the subtle of the Sāman'. – He did this beyond him (overcome him) (Witzel 1987c)

And then the detailed explanation analysed above is presented which is the teaching of Sudakṣiṇa Kṣaimi.

---

68 See also Witzel (1987c: 397).

69 JUB 3.8.4: *ma ācāryas suyamān amanyateti* |

70 This is not surprising then that the debate was so heated; probably Jābālas were very jealous of Sudakṣina Kṣaimi, especially if the teacher who preferred him was their father.

The whole context is purely Brāhmaṇical and, moreover, the main issue is not what happens to man after death but the role of the Udgātar and other priests in this process. There is a general agreement about the three deaths of man; the elder Jābāla explains to the younger that Sudakṣiṇa Kṣaimi was talking about the Udgātar who carries the deceased across the three deaths with aid of the Sāman. And this is indeed the main topic of the second teaching of Sudakṣiṇa Kṣaimi: he tries to establish in great detail the correspondences between each part of the Sāman and the afterlife journey of the deceased.

5.3. The afterlife paths according to the *Kauṣītaki Upaniṣad* 1

The composer of the KU puts his description about the afterlife state in the frame of teaching given by Citra Gārgyāyani (Frenz 1968/1969) to Uddālaka Āruṇi and his son Śvetaketu. The name of the teacher is interpreted by some scholars as Gaṅgyāyani and by others as the name of a king (Olivelle 1998). Bodewitz (2002) argues that the form Gārgyāyani is more probable because there is no mention in the Upaniṣads about a king Citra Gaṅgyāyani (although a king Citra is mentioned in the ṚV). On the other hand, 'the Gārgyas and their descendants were teachers and specialists of ritual' (2002: 9). This controversy again shows that the role of the Kṣatriya in introducing the concept of rebirth is not as certain as assumed by many scholars.

The composer of the KU concentrates on the states of liberation realised by the deceased in a very detailed way as it may be presumed they have mentally reached the unmanifest aspect of reality. This may be the reason for the variety of variants of this chapter (Olivelle 1998, Bodewitz 2002), because the topic is extremely subtle and new. At the same time, the composer includes and redefines many earlier Vedic concepts and there is no doubt that he knew it very well.

The general conceptual network elaborated by the composer consists of the following input spaces. The first input space is the afterlife state of man including his deeds and the second is reality. The next input space is the concept of a journey to an abode. The next input spaces are the image schemas of VERTICALITY, SOURCE-PATH-GOAL, and CAUSE-EFFECT. The conceptual network is enriched with the next input space, namely, the concept of cognition which leads to the realisation of the supernatural state seen as unity with *brahman*. Cognition is conceived in terms of eating (specific realisation of the general domain of Cooking) which is the next input space. In the blend, the input space of journey to an abode is specified as a journey across various places to reach a king's land. The causal influence of deeds is limited to those who will be reborn. The realisation of final liberation also depends on recitations performed by the deceased during his life. The generic space is the concept of transformation.

KU 1.2

sa hovāca | ye vai ke cāsmāl lokāt prayanti candramasam eva te sarve gacchanti | teṣāṃ prāṇaiḥ pūrvapakṣa āpyāyate | tān aparapakṣeṇa prajanayati | etad vai svargasya lokasya dvāraṃ yac candramāḥ | taṃ yaḥ pratyāha tam atisṛjate | atha ya enam na pratyāha tam iha vṛṣṭir bhūtvā varṣati | sa iha kīṭo vā pataṅgo vā matsyo vā śakunir vā siṃho vā varāho vā parasvān vā śārdūlo vā puruṣo vānyo vā teṣu teṣu sthāneṣu pratyājāyate yathākarma yathāvidyam |

When people depart from this world, it is to the moon that they all go. By means of their breaths[71] the moon swells up in the fortnight of waxing, and through the fortnight of waning it propels them to new birth. Now, the moon is the door to the heavenly world. It allows those who answer its question to pass. As to those who do not answer its question, after they have become rain, it rains them down here to the earth, where they are born in these various conditions – as a worm, an insect, a fish, a bird, a lion, a boar, a rhinoceros, a tiger, a man, or some other creature – each in accordance with his actions and with his knowledge. (Olivelle 1998)

The path of the deceased is described shortly. There is no reference either to Agnihotra (as in the JB, BU and CU) or to the role of the Udgātar (as in the JUB) or even to the cremation rite. This impliesthat the role of the ritual is not so important for the state realised by man after death.

The deceased reaches the moon. This testifies the characteristic change in the evaluation of the sun and the moon in Vedic thinking that was connected with a change of climate. The positive features of the sun ascribed to it by the Ṛgvedic poets disappear in the ŚB and, beginning with the Upaniṣads, they are included within the concept of the moon. At the same time, the moon is presented as growing with the breath of the dead[72], so its conceptualisation is the same as in the BU and the CU (see chapter 4.3.1). The moon is called the door to heaven (*svargasya lokasya dvāraṃ*) but, at the same time, it is conceived in terms of a door-keeper who asks questions as seasons did in the JB 1.46 (see section 5.1.1; in the JUB it is the sun who asks questions, see section 5.2.1). In the KU, the concepts of the door and the door-keeper are metonymically compressed (see section 5.3). Thus the moon becomes the source domain for conceptualisation of the borderline sphere between the two aspects of reality.

71 Olivelle (1998): 'lifebreaths'.

72 KU 4.2: *candramasy annam.*

Now, if the deceased correctly answers its questions, he will be allowed to go further. If he does not, he will become rain and will be reborn; the KU is quite explicit in this. The rain as the form of the dead is already attested in the ṚV (Jurewicz 2010a: 3010 ff.); as we have seen, later texts present the path of the dead to final happiness in a more elaborate way. The composer of the KU metonymically compresses it into its most important form which transfers the deceased from the moon to earthly life. The factors of future rebirth are deed (*karman*) and knowledge (*vidyā*) as in the JB (see section 5.1.1-2).

Now the question of the moon is presented:

KU 1.1-2

tam āgataṃ pṛcchati ko'sīti | *taṃ pratibrūyād* | (1)
vicakṣaṇād ṛtavo reta ābhṛtam pañcadaśāt prasūtāt pitryāvataḥ |
tan mā puṃsi kartary erayadhvaṃ puṃsā kartrā mātari māsiṣikta ||
sa upajāya upajāyamāno dvādaśena trayodaśopamāsaḥ |
pitrā saṃ tad vide 'haṃ prati tad vide 'haṃ
tan ma ṛtavo 'mṛtyava ābharadhvam||
tena satyena tena tapasa ṛtur asmy ārtavo 'smi ko 'smi tvam asmi | *iti tam atisṛjate* | (2)

When someone approaches it, the moon asks: 'Who are you?' And he should reply: 'The semen, O Seasons, is gathered from the radiant one, from the one with fifteen parts, from the one who is born, from the one linked to the fathers. Then you sent me into a man, the agent, and, through that man as the agent you poured me into a mother. Here I am born, given birth to as an addition, as the thirteenth, the added month, by a father of twelve parts. I recognise it. I understand it. Se lead me, O Seasons, to immortality, by that truth, by that austerity – I am the season! I am the offspring of the season! Who am I? I am you!' The moon lets him pass. (Olivelle 1998)

The correct answer is the stanza already presented in the JB 1.50 (see section 5.1.2). In the JB, the stanza fits the context because the deceased answers questions from one of the seasons. Here, the answer is to the moon which shows that the stanza is probably quoted here from the JB; it is also possible that the stanza was widely known as the correct answer for ensuring happiness after death. One can assume that the composer implies that, similarly to the JB, knowledge about the origin of the earth opens the way to immortality.

The composer of the KU changes the last verses of the stanza. In the JB, the factors which lead the deceased to immortality are śraddhā, *annādya* and *satya,* here it is *satya* and *tapas*. *Śraddhā* refers to the state of man after death which depends on the ritual activity of those who are on earth (see JUB

3.11.7, section 5.2). Since, as already stated, the KU does not refer to any ritual, the concept of *śraddhā* becomes unnecessary. The term *annāda* is still used in the KU as the ideal of man (KU 2.1.14, 2.2.14, 2.9.5,7,9,11,13), but the metaphor of eating is gradually vanishing in the Upaniṣads and probably losing its meaningful power. On the other hand, in the early Upaniṣads the word *tapas* begins to be used in reference to practice which led to supernatural consciousness. This is the same word that in the ṚV was used to denote the heat of the sun and fire and also the heat which overwhelmed man under the influence of Soma (Jurewicz 2010a: 193–194). The fact that this word is used in reference to a mental practice agrees with my hypothesis that the search for immortality was motivated by the memory of the state gained under the influence of Soma attested in the ṚV.

Then the deceased is presented as going along the path of gods (*devayāna*) and reaching the worlds of fire, wind, Varuṇa, Indra and Prajāpati (KU 1.3). It may be presumed that these worlds belong to the borderline sphere between the two aspects of reality. Interpretation of the word *loka* as the space of experience strengthens the meaning of transformation of the deceased in the blend. The deceased is conceived in terms of a traveller who visits various places and this experience changes him.

Finally, the deceased reaches the world of *brahman*. The recipient may assume that the unmanifest aspect of reality is conceived in these terms. The experience realised in this state is analysed in the KU in a remarkably extensive way, contrary to the brief descriptions of the BU and the CU. A similar specificity in the description of the stages of liberation can be seen in JUB 3.20-28 (see section 5.2.3), although the stages are conceived in a different way. There is one more difference between these two accounts. While the composer of the JUB describes the state realised at the borderline sphere of the cosmos, the composer of the KU refers to what happens when the deceased reaches the unmanifest aspect of reality.

The unmanifest aspect of reality is conceived in terms of a garden with a lake (*hrada*), a river (*nadī*) guarded by a watchman (*yastihā*), a tree (*vṛkṣa*), a courtyard (*saṃsthāna*), and a palace (*āyatana*) with two doorkeepers (*dvāragopa*) in which there is a hall (*pramita*) with a throne (*āsandī*) and a couch (*paryaṅka*, KU 1.3). In the blend, the transformations of the deceased are conceived in terms of the journey to a king's palace. As I have mentioned many times, the concept of conquest of land is used in the ṚV to conceive cognition under the influence of Soma. In the KU, this concept is profiled in a way which reflects social changes: in the new societal context, the use of images of palaces of rich kings to conceptualise mental states was meaningful.

KU 1.3a

sa āgacchaty āraṃ hradam | taṃ manasātyeti | tam ṛtvāsamprativido majjanti | sa āgacchati muhūrtān yaṣṭihān | te'smād apadravanti | sa āgacchati vijarāṃ nadīm | tāṃ manasaivātyeti | tat sukṛtaduṣkṛte dhunute | tasya priyā jñātayaḥ sukṛtam upayanti apriyā duṣkṛtam | tad yathā rathena dhāvayan rathacakre paryavekṣetaivam ahorātre paryavekṣata evaṃ sukṛtaduṣkṛte sarvāṇi ca dvandvāni | sa eṣa visukṛto viduṣkṛto brahma vidvān brahmaivābhipraiti |

He first arrives to the lake Āra. He crosses it with his mind, but those who go into it without a complete knowledge drown in it. Then he arrives near the watchmen Muhūrta, but they flee from him. Then he arrives at the river Vijarā which he crosses with just his mind. There he shakes off his good and bad deeds, which fall upon his relatives – the good deeds upon the one he likes and the bad deeds upon the ones he dislikes. It is like this – as a man driving on a chariot would look down and observe the two wheels of the chariot, the good and bad deeds, and all the pairs of opposites. Freed from his good and bad deeds, this man, who has knowledge of *brahman*, goes on to *brahman*. (Olivelle 1998)

That the transformation of the deceased are mental can be inferred from that he crosses the lake and the river with his mind (*manasā*). In this way, the next input space of the network is conceived which is the concept of cognition. It is said that those who do not have correct knowledge (but still were wise enough to reach this state) drown in the lake. The logic of the input space of the journey which is elaborated in the blend, allows the recipient to understand that the purification of all kinds of deeds, both good and bad, is conceived in terms of bathing in a river which the deceased crosses to get to the kingdom. In the ṚV, the afterlife purification of the deceased is performed by Soma in the sun: he is supposed to come back to the earth having left behind all imperfections (Jurewicz 2010a: 317). This again shows that the composer of the KU evoked earlier tradition to present his views.

This is also confirmed in that the verb *dhū-*, used to express the result of purification from deeds, brings the recipient's mind to the JB 1.49 the composer of which explains the essence of the smoke of the sacrificial fire as being the ability to remove (*dhū-*) the body from the deceased; this essence is expressed by its name *dhūma* (see section 5.1.2). The composer of KU 1.4 uses the same verb, although it does not refer to the cremation fire and its object the good and bad deeds of the deceased. Moreover, the deeds of the deceased are divided in a similar way as in the JB 1.50 (see section 5.1.2): the good deeds of the deceased become the share of relatives while the bad deeds are the share for his enemies.

Then the deceased is presented as the chariot driver who can see the revolving wheels of his chariot. This image is created in ŚB 2.3.3.12 in the description of the Agnihotra to conceive the sacrificer who, thanks to his daily performance of sacrifice, realises the ultimate state. He reaches the borderline sphere of the manifest aspect of reality and is not subjected to the influence of time. This again shows the motivating influence of the earlier thought because, as we have seen, the exposition of the afterlife in the JB constitutes a part of a larger discussion on the Agnihotra rite. Although one could presume that the deceased, having reached the world of *brahman*, is already freed from time, the composer introduces the concept of moments (*muhūrta*) conceived in terms of river watchmen. They are presented as flying away from the deceased. If the recipient evokes the concept of internal heat (*tapas*) which fills the deceased, he can imagine the watchmen who, having seen him, are so terrified of his fiery appearance that they fly away without fighting. In these terms, the final liberation from the influence of time is conceived. The image of a man riding on his chariot agrees with the logic of the blend as the deceased, having been freed from time, is conceived in terms of a victorious warrior who continues his ride towards his king's land. The recipient may presume that the river Vijarā is the border of the kingdom; it has been crossed by the deceased.

KU 1.4b

priyā ca mānasī | pratirūpā ca cākṣuṣī | puṣpāṇy ādāyānayato vai ca jagāti ambāścāmbālī caivānyāś cāpsaraso' mbikādāyaḥ | tam itthaṃvid āgacchati taṃ brahmāha abhidhāvata mama yaśasā vijarāṃ vā ayaṃ nadīṃ prāpan na vā ayaṃ jarayiṣyatīti | taṃ pañcaśatāny apsarasāṃ pratiyanti śataṃ mālyahastāḥ śatam āñjanahastāḥ śataṃ cūrṇahastāḥ śataṃ vāsohastāḥ śataṃ phalahastāḥ | taṃ brahmālaṅkāreṇālaṅkurvanti | sa brahmālaṅkāreṇālaṅkṛto vidvān brahmābhipraiti |

The beloved Mānasī and her twin Cakṣuṣī have picked flowers and bring them here – so also the two Jagāti, Ambā and Ambālī, and other celestial nymphs such as Ambikā. As the man who knows this is approaching, *Brahman* tells them: 'Run to him with my glory! He has already arrived at the river Vijarā! He will never grow old!' Five hundred celestial nymphs go out to meet him – one hundred carrying garlands, one hundred carrying lotions, one hundred carrying cosmetic powders, one hundred carrying cloths, and one hundred carrying fruits. And they adorn him with the ornaments of *brahman*. Then, decked with the ornaments of *brahman*, this man, who has the knowledge of *brahman*, goes on to *brahman*. (Olivelle 1998)

Brahman is conceived in terms of a king who sends his maiden servants with flowers and orders to adorn the guest in terms of which the deceased is conceived. They are told to serve him with *brahman's* glory (*yaśas*). *Yaśas* is one of the words used in the ṚV to denote the concept of fame realised in the sun under the influence of Soma (see chapter 1.7). This also strengthens the meaning of the cognitive nature of the transformation of the deceased.

The further transformation of the deceased is conceived in terms of adorning (*alaṃ kṛ-*) by five hundred young maidens. The image of young maidens serving a male activates the model of Child Of The Waters and the general domain of Cleansing By Heat. As I have shown, the specific source realisations of this general domain are processes which make their objects beautiful and shining under the influence of heat and they were used to conceive cognition (Jurewicz 2010a). One of the specific realisations of the general domain of Cleansing By Heat is applying balm. In ṚV 4.58, thoughts are presented as young women who put balm on themselves before a wedding (*kanyà iva vahatúm étavā́ u añjí añjānā́ abhí cākaśīmi*, ṚV 4.58.9ab). It is possible that the meaning of applying balm is still active in the KU. As Gonda (1975b: 265) shows, the verb *alaṃ kṛ-* is used in this meaning in some contexts of the *Kauśikasūtra* (1.31.7 II = 35.3 I) and the ŚB (13.8.4.7). Referring to the passage of the *Śāṅhkāyana Āraṇyaka* 3.4, he writes that 'here too these *alaṃkārās* are not merely things that are pleasing the eye'. Since the social circumstances have changed, the source domain is profiled in a different way.

The concept of Apsarases in the conceptualisation of the afterlife state of man is also evoked in JUB 3.25.5-6 to conceive the experience of ultimate happiness (see section 5.2.3). Although the concept of sexual pleasure is not explicitly evoked, it is implied by the whole scene created by the composer. In the blend, the deceased becomes more and more perfect thanks to the cognition he performs.

Then the deceased is presented as entering the king's garden and palace and he acquires more and more subtle forms. The composer enriches the conceptual network with the general domain of Cooking in its specific realisation of eating. The further cognitive transformation of the deceased will be conceived in these terms in the blend.

When the deceased arrives at the tree of Ilya, the fragrance of *brahman* permeates him. When he arrives at the courtyard of Sālajya, the flavour of *brahman* permeates him. When he arrives at the palace of Aparājita, the radiance of *brahman* permeates him. The scenario activated here is the scenario of approaching food: firstly the agent can smell it and then can taste it, when he eats. This is the next input space of the conceptual network created by the composer. In the blend, transformations of the deceased are conceived as cognitive. Since eating is the source domain for conceptualisation of subjective-objective cognition the recipient understands that duality in this state is not yet suspended. It is worth noting that this source domain is activated in the descriptions of the elaborate and subtle stages of the liberating processes (BU 2.3.2-5, see chapter 4.4.2.2, BU 4.2.3, see chapter 4.4.2.3) which shows consistency in their conceptualisation. In the ŚB, conceptualisation of cognition in terms of eating allows its composer to highlight the meaning of total identification of the object of cognition into the subject as the food becomes the same with its eater (see chapter 3.1.1). It is possible that the composer of the KU wants to highlight the same meaning.

Then the deceased is presented as reaching the palace as a result of which he is pervaded by *brahman*'s radiance. In this way, the composer elaborates the target domain of cognition conceived now in terms of light. The doorkeepers, Indra and Prajāpati, flee from him probably being afraid of his radiance (similarly to the *muhūrtas* in KU 1.4) and the entrance to the hall is open. Then it is said that the deceased is permeated with the glory (*yaśas*) of *brahman*. As we remember, glory was brought by the maiden servants (KU 1.4b) so the recipient will understand that now it finally fills the deceased. At the same time, the state realised under the influence of Soma is evoked (see chapter 1.7).

The further transformations of the deceased are conceived in terms of approaching the throne. It is composed of the Sāman-chants: the front legs are Bṛhat and Rathaṃtara, the back legs are Śyaita and Naudhasa and its supports are Vairūpa, Vairāja, Śākvara and Raivata[73]. The concept of a king sitting in a throne composed of the chants and elements of time is elaborated in the cosmogonic description in AVŚ 15.3 (see chapter 2.2.2). Such a conceptualisation of this state implies the importance of the sacred recitation accompanied by breath practice performed by the deceased during his life which allows him to create his immortal self (see chapter 3.4). It is also possible that the composer of the KU refers here to the description of the JUB where the immortal self of the deceased is presented as composed of the Sāman-chants performed by the priests on earth (see section 5.2).

The throne is called *prajñā*, insight[74]. This word is used (interchangeably with *prajñāna*) in the third chapter of the AU 3.3 to express the ontic role of cognition as the basis of the manifest aspect of reality identified with *brahman* (see chapter 4.1.3). *Prajñā* is the condition of liberation after death (AU 3.4). Seen against this context, the identification of the throne of *brahman* with insight is fully justified. The composer explains this identification in that one

---

73 In the similar way the throne of the sun is conceived in JB 2.25 and the king's throne in the Rājasūya ritual, see chapter 2.2.2. Bodewitz (2002: 18, note 45) points out that it is surprising that the role of Sāman chants is emphasised here because KU belongs to the Ṛgvedic school. However, careful analysis of Vedic texts shows that the division into schools, as far as the conceptual level is concerned, is not so strict and that there was a general common conceptual basis shared by the composers who freely recruited from it when they needed.

74 Olivelle (1998) translates *prajñā* as 'knowledge' (ad AU) and 'wisdom' (ad KU).

sees with the aid of wisdom (*prajñayā hi vipaśyati*). Such an explanation evokes the compound *prajñānetṛ* which is used in the AU to express the cognitive ability of the manifest aspect. The recipient now understands that in this stage the deceased can use his insight in order to finally liberate his self composed of the Sāman-chants.

The next step is conceived in terms of approaching a couch. It is identified with breath (*prāṇa*). Its four legs are composed of past (*bhūta*) and future (*bhavya*), splendour (*śrī*) and nourishment (*irā*), other parts are the Sāman-chants: Bṛhat, Rathaṃtara, Bhadra, Yajnayajñīya, the Ṛk-stanzas and the Sāman-chants generally, the Yajus formulas, Soma stalks (*somaṃśava*), the High Chant (*udgītha*) and splendor (*śrī*) again. The fact that the splendor (*śrī*) is mentioned twice (as one of the back legs and as the pillow) emphasises the importance of this concept which in the ṚV is used to denote the state of immortality achieved under the influence of Soma (see chapter 1.7). Here the whole Veda is presented, not only the Sāman-chants, which implies that the recitation of the whole of sacred knowledge is necessary to reach final liberation. Two kinds of seat, the throne and the couch, may refer to the JUB's concept of the final liberation conceived in terms of wandering between the sun and the moon (see section 5.2.3).

Identification of the couch with breath (*prāṇa*) metonymically evokes breath practice connected with recitation during which insight (*prajñā*) is realised and thanks to which final liberation can be achieved. Identification of the coverlet (*upastaraṇa*) with Soma stalks metonymically evokes the Ṛgvedic concepts of Somic exultation. The word *upastaraṇa* is used in the ṚV 9.69.5 in the description of Soma, purified in two vessels, and conceived in terms of a king who puts on a bright, clean garment; the back of the sky is his other garment and the coverlet is made of clouds[75]. Since this word appears in the ṚV only once, I would argue that the composer meant to evoke this stanza in order to show that the state he describes is the same state as that described by the Ṛgvedic poets.

Brahman sits on the coach and the deceased is presented as mounting with his foot on the couch (*tasmin brahmāste | tam itthaṃvit pādenaivāgra ārohati*, KU 1.5[76]). *Brahman* is conceived in terms of a king who asks the deceased questions about his identity which is, as one can presume, normal practice when someone enters someone else's home:

---

[75] ṚV 9.69.5: *ámṛktena rúśatā vā́sasā hárir | ámartiyo nirṇijānáḥ pári vyata | divás pṛṣṭhám barhánā nirṇíje kṛta upastáraṇaṃ camúvor nabhasmáyam* || See also ṚV 9.71.1.

[76] For the details of this source domain, see Bodewitz (2002: 19, notes 48, 49).

KU 1.5-6

taṃ brahmāha ko 'sīti | taṃ pratibrūyāt (5)
ṛtur asmi | ārtavo 'smi | ākāśād yoneḥ sambhūto bhāryāyai retaḥ saṃvatsarasya tejo bhūtasya bhūtasyātmā | bhūtasya bhūtasya tvam ātmāsi | yas tvam asi so 'ham asmīti | tam āha ko 'ham asmīti | satyam iti brūyāt | kiṃ tad yat satyam iti | yad anyad devebhyaś ca prāṇebhyaś ca tat sat | atha yad devāś ca prāṇāś ca tat tyaṃ | tad etayā vācābhivyāhriyate satyam iti | etāvad idaṃ sarvam idaṃ sarvam asītyevainaṃ tad āha | (6)

Brahman then asks him: 'Who are you?'. (5)
He should reply: 'I am the season! I am the offspring of the season. I was born from the womb of space as the semen for the wife, the radiance of the years, as the self (*ātman*) of everything. You are the self of every being. I am who you are'. *Brahman* then asks him: 'Who am I?'. And he should reply: 'The real.' 'What is the real?' '*Sat* is whatever is other than the gods and the breaths[77] (*prāṇa*), while *Tyam* consists of the gods and the breaths[78]. All of that is comprehended by this word 'real' (*satyam*). That is the full extent of this whole world. And you are this whole world' (6) (Olivelle 1998)

The correct answer is the same as that which should to be given to the moon in KU 1.1-2: the deceased calls himself the season and the child of the season. But the answer is elaborated in a more abstract way: the deceased is born from the womb of space and he is the semen of light. In BU 1.4.3, space is identified with woman (see chapter 4.1.2). The concept of light metonymically evokes the concept of the sun. Thus the recipient understands that the deceased is the offspring of the sun which is his father. Since the son is identical with his father the meaning of the correct answer is the same as in the JB and the JUB: the deceased knows his identity with the sun. But it seems that these concepts are not necessary to understand the meaning of the stanza which concludes that the dead person is *ātman* of every being in the same way as *brahman*.

The answer also evokes AU 3.1-3 where the question about *ātman* is asked (*ko 'yam ātmeti vayam upāsmahe*) and the answer is that *ātman* is *brahman*, Indra, Prajāpati, all the gods and everything that is manifest (AU 3.3). It is worth mentioning that the composer of the KU uses the names of Indra and Prajāpati to refer to the doorkeepers guarding the entrance to the hall (KU 1.5). The recipient may presume that they are the last obstacle which the deceased has to overcome. In ŚB 6.1.1.2, the concept of Indra denotes the main breath of reality which manifests in the beginning of creation and Prajāpati is the name of its creative power (see chapter 3.2.2). In AVŚ 11.5,

[77] Olivelle (1998): 'lifebreaths'.
[78] Olivelle (1998): 'lifebreaths'.

15.1.6, this power is conceived in terms of Indra (see chapters 2.2.1, 2.2.2) which, as I have argued, continues the Ṛgvedic conceptualisation of Agni who manifests as Indra in the cosmos (Jurewicz 2010a: 360–363). Taking into account that the stages of liberating cognition are realised in reverse order to the stages of creation, the concepts of Indra and Prajāpati can be seen as the source domains to conceive the state when the deceased realises his identity with the manifest aspects[79]. The fact that in AU 3.3 they are mentioned immediately after *brahman* implies the same (*eṣa brahmā eṣa indraḥ eṣa prajāpatiḥ ete sarve devāḥ*).

Then the composer plays with the word *satya* divided into two meaningful parts: the part *sat* and the part *tyam*[80]. *Sat* refers to what is beyond the gods and the breaths and *tyam* to the gods and the breaths. So the recipient may understand that *sat* refers to the unmanifest aspect of reality and *tyam* to the manifest. Similarly to BU 2.3.2-5 (see chapter 4.4.2.2), the second part of the word *satyam*, which is *tyam*, metonymically prompts man to search for its first part which is *sat*. In the same way, the manifest aspect of reality is the starting point for cognition of its manifest aspect. However, in the next sentence, the composer describes *sattyam* as *etāvad idaṃ sarvam* which in BU 1.4.6 is used to denote the range of what is manifest and what can be conceived in terms of Agni and Soma (see chapter 4.1.2). In this way, the composer can narrow the meaning of *satya* to the manifest aspect and imply that creative transformations are real. In the same way, the meaning of *satya* is narrowed in BU 2.3. At the same time, he again evokes, *via* the concepts of Agni and Soma, the earliest Ṛgvedic background.

Then a stanza is quoted:

KU 1.7a

yajūdaraḥ sāmaśirā asāv ṛṅmūrtir avyayaḥ |
sa brahmeti sa vijñeya ṛṣir brahmamayo mahān iti |

Yajus is the belly, Sāman, the head; the Ṛg is the body of this great seer. He is imperishable, he consists of *brahman*. 'He is *brahman*' – so should he be known. (Olivelle 1998)

Taking into account that in the preceding sentence the meaning of the word *satya* refers to the manifest aspect of reality, I would argue that the aim of this stanza is to elaborate this concept. The manifest aspect is conceived in terms

[79] See AVŚ 15.6, 15.14.21, see chapter 2.2.2. The final sequence Indra – Virāj – Prajāpati appears also in AVŚ 15.5-6.

[80] For the play with the word *satya*, see also chapter 4.1.5.

of the seer (*ṛṣi*), composed of sounds of the Veda. The concept of *ṛṣi* is used in ŚB 6.1.1.1 to conceive the manifest aspect of reality (see chapter 3.2.2). His belly is composed of the Yajus-formulas, his head of the Sāman-chants and the Ṛk-stanzas are his visible appearance (*mūrti*). Thus the recipient is prompted to unfold the logic of this source domain and to understand that the seer if filled with the sounds of the Veda thanks to his recitation.

The fact that the composer enumerates only these three elements of the body can be explained as being motivated by the earlier tradition, attested in the ŚB, where the first form of the world is conceived in terms of a hungry belly (see chapter 3.1.1). The concept of the head, in a very concise way, evokes the conceptualisation of creation in terms of human growth; the final creation of cosmos is conceived in terms of an adult man who stands up[81]. The cosmos is the visible form of reality and the word *mūrti* is used in AU 1.3.2 in the description of the creation of an object of cognition (see chapter 4.3.1). The fact that the manifest aspect is conceived as composed of the sounds of the Veda evokes the same conceptualisation presented in ŚB 10.4.2.22 where the first manifest form of the world is conceived as composed of Vedic sounds. Qualification of the seer as great may also activate the concept of greatness in terms of which the first form of the manifest aspect is conceived (see chapter 2.2.2). This form is identified with *brahman*.

The role of subjective-objective cognition is then discussed. The composer enumerates nine cognitive faculties which are mind, speech, sense of smell, sight, hearing, taste, hands, sexual organ and feet with which aspects of *brahman* can be cognised. It is worth mentioning that AU 1.4 enumerates the same seven cognitive faculties which appear in the creative process but excludes hands and feet; the concept of hand also involves the concept of touching. The last cognitive organ is insight *prajñā* with whose aid the thought (*dhī*) and the desires (*kāma*) of *brahman* can be known.

According to the cosmogony of the AU, reality, having manifested itself in the cosmos and man, realises that it can be cognised in subjective-objective cognition but does not know who is he (*atha ko 'ham*, AU 1.3.11, see chapter 4.1.3). Then it enters through the cranium of its cosmic and human manifestation and experiences its identity with all reality called *brahman*. The composer of the KU seems to refer to the same moment in human cognition. Subjective-objective cognition gives only partial knowledge of reality and full knowledge can only be gained with the aid of insight (*prajñā*). Partial cognition of reality is seen by BU 1.4.7 (see chapter 4.1.2) in the same way. Insight gives man access to the thoughts (*dhī*) and desires (*kāma*) of

81 These are specific realisations of the general domain of Procreation.

brahman. Bodewitz (2002) considers the enumeration presented in KU 1.7 as 'careless'[82], but it can be seen that it is very well motivated if we take into consideration the broader context.

In this concise way the final cognition of *brahman* is presented as man is able to experience *brahman*'s cognitive and emotional powers. The word *dhī* in the ṚV is used to denote the visionary thought which leads to supernatural cognition (ṚV 1.139.2)[83] and the use of this word again introduces the earlier conceptual background. The concept of desire (*kāma*) evokes the concept of liberation understood as a state in which it is possible to realise all desires and intentions (*satyakāma*, *satyasaṃkalpa*, see chapter 4.4.2.1, and 4.4.2.4). Thus understood, *prajñā* is the only cognitive faculty which enables liberation (see AU 3.1-3, chapter 4.1.3). At the end of his description the composer of the KU states that *brahman* gives its world to the deceased:

KU 1.7b

tam āha āpo vai khalu me lokam 'yaṃ te 'sāv iti |

Brahman then tells him: 'I see that you have truly attained my world. It is yours, so-and-so!' (Olivelle 1998)

From the source domain the recipient can imagine a king who shares his kingdom with his guest. In the target domain, if the recipient understands *loka* as the space of experience, he can infer that the deceased takes part in *brahman's* experience with all its thoughts and desires[84].

It is worth noting that the phrase *āpo vai khalu me lokam* can also be interpreted as 'truly, my world is water' (Syrkin 1992). This ambiguity is attested in earlier tradition. According to ŚB 6.1.1.9, Prajapati creates waters which are identified with speech thanks to which is he pervades everything that is manifest. This is the reason for the etymology of the word 'waters' (*ā́pas*) which comes from the verb 'to attain' (*āp-*). Water, identified with speech, is the first form of the manifest aspect of reality. A recipient of the KU well versed in tradition, can be expected to activate the ambiguity of the phrase *āpo vai khalu me lokam*. Thus he will understand that the liberating state encompasses the state described in the Brāhmaṇas and, at the same

82 Bodewitz (2002: 54): 'Here we have a careless enumeration of the *indriyāṇi* (the senses) and the *karmendriyāṇi* mixed with some prāṇas (vital powers) and supplemented with *prajñā* and *śarīra*.'

83 See Gonda (1963).

84 *sā yā brahmaṇo jitir yā vyaṣṭis tāṃ jitiṃ jayati tāṃ vyaṣṭiṃ vyaśnute ya evaṃ veda ya evaṃ veda* |

time, goes beyond that state to achieve unity with the whole of reality called *brahman*. The next chapters of the KU present life and practice with lead to liberation after death. However, this topic goes beyond the scope of the present study.

5.4. Conclusion

Fuiji (2011) traces back the concept of the afterlife presented in the JUB. He enumerates three conceptual strands which existed separately in earlier thought and which are now united in a coherent whole. These are:

1. The concept of the deceased's new body after death.
2. The correspondence between the vital functions and the cosmic entities.
3. The making of the self (*ātman*) in the rituals (Fuiji 2011: 108).

Thus he shows the early background for the concept of rebirth which is confirmed by my research.

As can be seen from the above analysis, the belief in rebirth is not only attested in the JB and JUB, but is also grounded in the earlier thought. The afterlife state depends on what the deceased has done during his life: on his ritual deeds and on his knowledge. It also depends on the activity of those who remain on earth, on how the cremation is done, on proper recitation by the priests and on the faith of the deceased's relatives. The composers of the JB and the JUB present this topic in detail. They do not present a new theory of the afterlife situation of man, just the opposite; their exposition draws on the earlier Brahminic context and cannot be fully understood without reference to it.

In the KU, the path which leads to rebirth is presented in a concise way, contrary to the other path which is identified with liberating cognition. The composer mentions only deeds committed in life as the causal factor influencing the form acquired in rebirth. On the other hand, he emphasises the role of breath practice connected with recitation as the main cause of the possibility to realise final liberation.

Let me briefly summarise the conceptualisation of the afterlife state presented in the texts analysed in this chapter and in the BU and the CU discussed in the previous chapter (4.4). The tools of cognitive linguistics allow me to compare on a general level. The composers of all accounts create similar conceptual networks. The image schematic input spaces are the same. These are VERTICALITY, SOURCE-PATH-GOAL, and CAUSE-EFFECT. The image schema of VERTICALITY imparts to the blend conceptualisation of the afterlife state in terms of moving upwards. The image schema of SOURCE-PATH-GOAL imparts to the blend the meaning of intentional action undertaken by a conscious agent. The image schema of CAUSE-EFFECT provides the ground for the conviction that a man's life influences his state after death. In the blend, the form of a living man is the same as his earlier deeds.

The composers of the JB, the JUB and the KU introduce the input space of the journey to the abode of a king. Thus they can present the afterlife state in terms of common experience. They variously elaborate this input space in the blend. While the composers of the JB and the JUB use this input space to conceive two possible afterlife states, the composer of the KU focus on elaborating it to conceive the liberating state. In my view, the composers of the BU and the CU do not activate this input space in their description, which makes it more abstract. Their composers metonymically activate the consecutive stages of the process conceived in general terms of SOURCE-PATH-GOAL schema *via* the words denoting parts of the cosmos and the divisions of time. This implies that they could assume their recipients would easily activate shared knowledge about the afterlife state. The path leading to rebirth is presented in the KU in the same way. This attests that it is not rebirth that is the new part of their expositions.

The composers of the BU, the CU and the KU introduce the concept of reality as the input space of their conceptual network. This agrees with my claim that the cognition of the unmanifest aspect of reality appeared only in the Upaniṣads. In the JB and the JUB, the deceased reaches the state of the borderline of the cosmos and their composers analyse this problem from the point of view of a particular man. The same individual perspective is elaborated in the KU but the aim of the afterlife journey is the unmanifest aspect. Its composer shows that liberating cognition is the realisation of the creative activity of reality in reverse order (the recipient needs to refer to the AU to activate this meaning). The composers of the BU and the CU create a general model which allows for an understanding of reality in terms of men who are reborn and men who are liberated.

The exposition of the KU is unique in its elaboration of the final stages during which unity with the unmanifest aspect is realised and in the identification of this process with liberating cognition. This is consistent with the general assumption of the Upaniṣadic philosophers about this cognition. This is the new content when compared with earlier tradition and this was the secret of the Brahminic teachers of that time. The accounts of the BU and the CU which are most abstract and general can be seen as just the last phase of the process of creation of a theory about rebirth and liberation.

General conclusion

The main aim of this book is to reconstruct the Vedic foundations of Indian philosophy. I have analysed selected fragments of the Śruti texts which I have treated as representative for the consecutive stages of development of thought to show its consistency in accepted axioms, in arguments and in conclusions. However, this thought is most often expressed in non-literal language the analysis of which needs a methodology which would render it possible to go beyond the words that express thought so as to understand their mutual relationship and their meaning. I have chosen models proposed by cognitive linguistics. Their use not only helped me to reconstruct basic aspects of the Vedic thought. It also allowed me to reconstruct the beginnings and formation of abstract concepts and the terms which express them. Since the mental operations that are modelled by cognitive linguistics are universal, the research done in this book contributes to the more general field of the beginnings of human philosophical thinking.

1. The way the abstract concepts are built

The models of conceptual metonymy, metaphor and blending make possible to reconstruct the ways the abstract concepts were built. It has been shown that the logic of the source domain is implanted in the target domain and this allows for an understanding of the latter. The experience evoked by the source domain is often violated in order to convey the abstract meaning of the target domain. The final creation of the abstract concept is due to the blending of the input spaces already transformed and to the new ones. This conscious effort to create abstract concepts is especially attested in the hymns of the late ṚV and of the AV. The role of the experience is crucial not only for the creation of the abstract concepts but also for their understanding. If it is culturally specific and its logic has not been incorporated into the target concept or blend in such a way that it could be understood without reference to it and if it cannot be reconstructed by the context, the abstract concept cannot be understood. This is the one of the reasons why many abstract concepts, coined in the late ṚV and in the AV, has been lost in later Indian tradition.

The tendency for abstraction and generalisation can also be seen in the development of the ritual exegesis. It has been shown in the insightful research of Patton (1996, 2005). In the conclusion of her book on the development of the Vedic Canon (Patton 1996), she writes that

> one can view the destiny of the Veda as the process of abstraction. In the Purāṇa, Vedic mantra is reduced into a smaller and smaller symbolic unit, its actual contents abstracted to such an extent that it becomes a single concept or an image as opposed to a series of full-length utterances. To be sure, on could describe this development of increasing ignorance as increasing ignorance of the contents of the Veda. However, one could also describe it as an attempt at commentarial totalisation through condensation. The Veda does not need to be 'explained'; it simply needs to be 'referred to' in order for its power to work. (1996: 444)

The reference is just at hand, or maybe we should say 'at mind' of the composers and those recipients of the Canon who knew the texts by heart. The human ability for metonymic and metaphoric activations of the contents encapsulated in the short *mantra* was the ground for their meaningfulness.

In her next book (Patton 1995), Patton shows how the explanations of the ritual usage of various *mantras* presented in the consecutive layers of the Vedic tradition are the proofs for generalisation. The specific context of the utterance of *mantras* becomes generalised in that a *mantra* can be used in various situations (e.g. 1995: 122, 124, 129, 130–131, 148, 186, 188). The price is that the concepts lose their semantic richness and ambiguity. Patton (2005: 136–137) analyses how the contradictory ritual and metaphysical context of the Pravargya ritual created in the early Vedic exegesis were lost in its interpretation by the Vidhāna exegesis. While in the early thinking 'an atmosphere of both possibility and impossibility, presence and absence is created' in the later 'all that is unseen is meant to be destroyed' (Patton 2005: 136 and 137). The ambivalence is lost and reality is to some extent simplified within the regime of two-valued logic. As I have argued elsewhere (Jurewicz 2010a), the same happened to many other concepts of the early Veda which, in course of the development of thought and the search for abstraction, lost its multivalent meaning.

The investigation by Patton confirms the tendency of ritual thought towards abstraction and generalisation. Her research confirms the role of conceptual metonymy in this process. As she shows the later general usage of the *mantras* is not random. It is motivated by the earlier thinking and is guided by its rational interpretation

2. The development of the early Vedic philosophy

Let me reconstruct the main lines of development of Vedic thought. An attempts are made in the late hymns of the ṚV to create an abstract and general apparatus that is both conceptual and verbal. This endeavour is continued in the hymns of the AV. Already in the late ṚV and the AVŚ, we can see the efforts made to create metaphysical theories based on the assumption of one reality which manifests itself during creation. These theories elaborate the general model of reality transformations which was created in the earlier strands of the ṚV (Jurewicz 2010a). According to this model, reality is Agni composed of its own aspect and of the opposing aspect conceived in terms of Soma. Reality alternatively manifests its aspects during creation, in the cosmos and in men who perform ritual. The composers of the ṚV and AVŚ also look for concepts other than Agni and Soma to express these metaphysical assumptions; however, their motivating influence can be seen. Moreover, the conviction of the composers that Agni is the ultimate principle of reality is preserved.

The new concepts in terms of which reality is conceived are those concepts connected with human being beginning with the concept of *puruṣa* and speech (*vā́c*) in the ṚV, then breath (*prā́ṇa*), the Brahmacārin (Brahmacārín) and the Vrātya (Vrā́tya). Other concepts are the Maker of Everything (*viśvákarman*, the ṚV) and the pillar (*skambhá*, the AV) which are also blends with man as one of their input spaces. The choice of concepts is, I would argue, connected with the growing role of recitation and breath practices which are necessary for proper recitation. At the same time, it logically follows the earlier Ṛgvedic assumption that Agni, under the influence of Soma, manifests in man in order to cognise itself through him as if through a lens and thus unity of reality is realised in microscale.

Another general concept elaborated by the composers of the ṚV and AVŚ is the concept of time. It is elaborated in ṚV 1.164 the composer of which see it as the cosmic manifestation of reality (see chapter 1.6). The experience of time is closely connected with the experience of recitation and breathing in that this experience enhances the awareness of the passage of time and of the possibility of its division into wholes which are particular sounds and consecutive in- and outbreaths. So the attempts to conceptualise time in a philosophical way can also be seen as rooted in the breath practices connected with recitation. In two hymns of the AV, time (*kālá*) is seen as the principle of reality. Its thirteenth book which is dedicated to The Ruddy One (*róhita*), can also be seen as expressing the fundamental role of time because the movement of the sun on the sky is a visible manifestation of its passage. However, as I have shown, the concept of *róhita* is also grounded in the Ṛgvedic belief that the sun is the solar form of Agni.

The composers of AVŚ are not only influenced by Ṛgvedic thought but they are also aware of this influence. Moreover, they consciously want to incorporate their thought within the frame of the Ṛgvedic background and show they are speaking about the same basic metaphysical models.

The composers of the ŚB, on the one hand, continue the earlier philosophical tradition and, on the other, introduce new elements. The main continuity is that reality is still conceived as Agni which manifests its opposing aspects in creation and in man. However, the role of ritual as the sphere in which man can realise his unity with reality is very much enlarged. In the ṚV and the AV, ritual is one of various experiences activated in the descriptions and is seen as the starting point of the processes explained by the general model of reality transformation. In the Brāhmaṇas, the ritual becomes the main focus of philosophical investigation. Yet, the focus of the Brāhmaṇic thinkers on ritual does not mean that they are uninterested in the cosmos and themselves. They elaborate the blend already created by the composers of the ṚV which consists of two main input spaces: the concept of ritual actually performed and the concept of the manifest aspect of reality. In the blend, the former input space gives topology and scenario to the latter. The sacrificial place is the whole world and ritual is the activity which creates and sustains it. This blend allows for conceptualisation of sacrifice as the model of the world which is identical with it. Contrary to modern scientific models (such as the large Hadron collider), in the sacrificial model of the Brāhmaṇas, whatever happens in the sacrifice happens in the world. As Wheelock (1989: 108) writes: 'the ritual setting is not is a symbolic simulacrum of the cosmos but a point of control over those (i.e. cosmic, JJ) forces'.

Within this ritual frame, the composers of the ŚB analyse the problem of creation of the world and its functioning (which, as in the ṚV, repeats creation) and the role of man. The central figure of the cosmogony is Prajāpati, conceived in terms of man (which also continues earlier conceptualisations of reality in these terms). The composers activate various experiential concepts and the tools of cognitive linguistics shows how coherently and consciously they used them to create complex metaphors and blends. Thanks to that we can see that the authors of the ŚB do not create a primitive vision of a hungry or sexually active god but rather a very abstract concept of the Absolute whose main attribute is freedom which allows it to deny all its attributes, existence included. The main schema of creation agrees with the general model of reality transformation which, on a more general level, assumes alternative transformation of the fiery and liquid aspects of reality. While in Ṛgvedic thought, the liquid is Soma, in the ŚB it is water, milk, sweat, and semen.

This alternative transformation is re-enacted in ritual. I will give here one example though much research has still to be done in this field (see below). In his analysis of the concept of Dakṣinā (the fee paid to the priests after ritual), Heesterman writes:

> In the broad outline the sacrifice may be described as a periodical quickening ritual by which the universe is recreated. In the sacrifice are summed up the two opposite poles of the cyclical rhythm of cosmos: birth and death, ascension and descent, concentration and dispersion. It epitomises the time cycle and follows the sun on its daily (or yearly) course round the world. (246)

He, then, investigates the speculations on the Dakṣinā which are attested in the passages of the Brāhmaṇas which deal with the Gārgya Trirātra, the three-day Soma sacrifice during which a thousand cows are to be given to the priests. I will not go into details of his deep analysis, but will limit myself to his general conclusions on the meaning of this ritual. The three days of Trirātra represent 'three successive stages of the cosmogony', namely, 'earth, heaven and rain; or sunrise, zenith, sunset. The underlying pattern seems to be a cyclical sun wise movement around the universe' (Heesterman 1959: 252). I will briefly look at the first set of cosmic counterparts of which rain is the last phase. It agrees with the general model of reality transformation. Heesterman himself writes that '[t]he descending phase, connected with death (...) and with sunset is less in evidence' (1959: 253). He adds that this link can be traced 'in Vādhūla's identification of the *dakṣinās* with rain' (1959: 253). The author also looks for this link in the correspondence between the cows given on the third day and their identification with speech (*vāc*) and the identification of speech with a stream of water and Sarasvati (1959: 253–254). These identifications allow him to interpret the Dakṣinā-giving as expressing the cosmology.

My research allows me to add a further interpretation. The distribution of cows took place in the midday of each day of the Trirātra. According to the general model of reality transformation, in this moment of the day, the final purification of Soma in the sun in zenith takes place which is conceptualised as the appearance of rain. The moment of giving a thousand cows to the priests could be seen as ritually re-enacting this cosmic process. Then the sacrificer receives back one cow. As Heesterman puts it:

> After the distribution of the thousand cows he (i.e. the sacrificer, JJ) is, therefore, like prototype Prajāpati, 'emptied out' and must be 'swelled again' (ŚB 4.5.8.6-9). In this respect particular importance is attached to the thousandth cow. (...) [t]his thousandth cow, by virtue of her being the last, encompasses the others, is as important as the other ones together; at the same time it (re)produces the thousand cows. (1959: 247)

Within the frames of the general model of reality transformation, when the sacrificer distributes the cows to the priests, the rise of the sun is metonymically re-enacted *via* the concept of the midday. Then, when the cow is returned, the appearance of rain is re-enacted. Taking into account the identification of cows with speech, the situation re-enacted in ritual is exactly the same as the situation of men described in ṚV 1.164 (see chapter 1.6). Speech, conceived in terms of a cow, goes away with the rising sun and returns when the sun reaches zenith. One can presume that mentally the sacrificer is in the sun, but experientially is on earth and the final result of his ritual activity is rain which comes from the sun. In terms of rain all kind of valuable goods are conceived.

The role of man is conceived in the ŚB similarly as in earlier Vedic texts. Man is expected to repeat in his cognitive activity the creative transformations of reality. It is done in ritual performed both during life and after death when those who remain on earth are responsible for its proper performance. The composers of the ŚB devote much of their composition to explain how the immortal self is built during sacrifices due to the fact that Soma was not in use and that a new and rational way of explaining this process was needed.

It has been shown that the composers of the late ŚB more clearly express the cognitive nature of the manifestation of reality. Such a conceptualisation is present already in the ṚV (Jurewicz 2010a) and the early ŚB expresses it with the use of metaphors. The composers of the Upaniṣads continue this way of thinking about reality and express it in explicit language. Their philosophers also look for abstract concepts which could grasp the real nature of the relationship between the unmanifest and manifest aspects of reality. The ambivalence of reality, conceived in the earlier thought in terms of the opposition of its fiery and liquid aspects, is now seen as the opposition of subject and object of cognition. The construction of this philosophical apparatus is grounded in the earlier tradition and is its logical implication. There are many parts of the Upaniṣad exposition which cannot be understood without reference to tradition. An amazing example of continuity of tradition is the concept of *śrī* which is used in the very specific context of super-natural cognition throughout all its usages. Authors of histories of Indian philosophy usually take out the explicit passages which are not so numerous in the pre-Buddhist Upaniṣads. Thus they distort their exposition. Moreover, they formulate on this basis a general statement about the beginnings of Indian philosophy as being attested only in the Upaniṣads which, as we have seen, is false.

Philosophical concepts are created in the Upaniṣads not only in the rational inquiry of the earlier tradition and its adjustment and elaboration according to the contemporary needs but also in breath practice connected with recitation. This is in accordance with the assumption of the primary nature of cognition in early Vedic philosophy. This assumption allows its composers to analyse reality within the frames of their own experience leading to supernatural cognition. This basic frame begins already in the ṚV where cognition under the influence of Soma gives the poets insight into the deepest layers of what is manifest, expressed in words and poems. The search for a method of gaining such an insight without Soma is attested already in the ŚB and has been finally perfected in the early Upaniṣads. This new cognitive method results in enhancement of the scope of what can be cognised. While the earlier philosophers can grasp the manifest aspect with its borderline sphere, the Upaniṣadic ones go beyond it and try to understand what is unmanifest. The latter problem becomes a more and more important focus for their investigation. The paradoxical nature of this super-natural cognition is preserved but now it is expressed in terms of going beyond the subjective-objective divisions.

The Upaniṣadic thinkers elaborate the role of human beings in the model of the Five Fires (*pañcāgnividyā*) which encompasses both aspects of reality. The manifest aspect is realised through mortal men who perform ritual, the unmanifest one is realised through those who are liberated. This model blends the concept of sacrifice and the concept of subjective-objective cognition to conceive the structure of the manifest aspect. The unmanifest aspect is not described in this model but it is elaborated in many other passages of the Upaniṣads together with the methods for its recognition. While according to the composers of the Brāhmaṇas, the sacrifice is the model of reality, the Upaniṣadic thinkers shift it into man who in his liberating cognition realises the unity of reality. Such a view of man as a model is elaborated in the later Tantra tradition (Wheelock 1989).

I do not intend to neglect the important differences between the consecutive layers of early Indian thought. Just the opposite, the cognitive tools provide the meta-language which facilitates comparison on the general level, diachronically and synchronically. This approach allows me to show how various concepts changed, how old concepts were reinterpreted within new conceptual frames, how some disappeared and new ones appeared. I also looked for reasons for these changes, but was more interested in the internal logic of the development of thought than in external historical and social conditions. Nevertheless, there is one external condition that seems to me crucial for understanding changes in early Indian philosophy which needs more attention and further research. This is the loss of Soma and the memory of its influence on the human mind, constantly refreshed during everyday recitation.

The relevance of this problem has become more and more visible to me during this research. The ways of looking how to get Somic experience without Soma are not presented in the texts explicitly, but as my research continued I was more and more convinced about the very important role of recitation and breathing in this process. I would now like to present just a few examples that are not analysed in this book to show that these processes are worth further consideration.

3. Early breath practice connected with recitation

As I have just mentioned, the problem of the reconstruction of the role of breath practice connected with recitation in the early Vedic texts will be now only very generally outlined. I will also outline the main possible fields for its investigation. Firstly, this study would need to analysis the use of the word *prāṇa* and other Sanskrit words denoting kinds of breath. These words appear already in the ṚV and AVŚ. According to Zysk (1993: 200), ṚV 10.189 is 'the earliest indication that breathing involves a twofold process of taking in and expelling air' (ṚV 10.189b: *asyá prāṇā́d apānatī́*[1]). He also argues that

[1] This hymn is devoted to the serpent queen (Sarparājñī). In their commentary Jamison, Brereton (2014: 1660) write: 'There are no signs of snakes, much more less their queen'. However, this meaning somehow must have been present because it is recited during the *prasarpaṇa* ceremony which takes place in the Agniṣṭoma ritual (Caland, Henry 1906: 171, Malamoud, 2005c: 121–122, Patton: 2005: 182–183). The priests form a procession, keeping their cloths. In this way, they are simulating the movement of a snake, move towards the place where they will sing the Bahiṣpavamāna laud. Fuiji (1986: 20) explain symbolism of the rite in the following way: 'In the symbolism of the Soma sacrifices, the heavenly world is represented by the *mahāvedi* and the boundary of the latter is regarded as that between the heavenly world and this world. It seems that this symbolic function of the *mahāvedi* comes into operation when the Bahiṣpavamāna laud has been chanted, for the act of creeping northwards (which also means 'Bahiṣpavamāna) to the Cātvāla pit shows that until the laud the heavenly world is still above and its entrance is the sun with which the Cātvāla pit is symbolically identified.'

the poet sees the resemblance between the appearance and disappearance of a celestial body in the cosmos and 'the regular process of a human inhalation and exhalation'. Zysk identifies the body with the moon, though I rather agree with Jamison, Brereton (2014: 1659–1660) who interpret the hymn as being set at the dawn sacrifice and playing 'with the various sources of light that compete at that time: the sun and the ritual fire, as well as Dawn'. Within the frame of the general model of reality transformation we can see that homology is set between fire which becomes the sun and human breathing.

The experience evoked in ṚV 10.189 to conceive these processes is the growth of a bull (*gaúḥ pṛ́śnir*, ṚV 10.189.1). Its growth is conceived in terms of stepping upon (*ā́ kram-*); the image-schema of VERTICALITY is also evoked by the concept of the sun (*svàr*, ṚV 10.189.1.c). The bull reaches its mother and father (ṚV 10.189.1ab) and then moves around, breathes and looks out (ṚV 10.189.2). The experience is violated, because while the subject of the first stanza is masculine (*ayám gaúḥ pṛ́śnir*), the subject of the second stanza is feminine (*apānatī́*). So the conceptual network created by the composer is as follows: the concept of a bull and cow, the concept of the sunrise and of a breathing man. In the blend, sunrise and breathing are the same processes and they are conceived in terms of transformations of an animal. Since the sun is filled with rain which emerges from it, the recipient may presume that the man also sweats (Jurewicz 2010a: 266–267, 381–383). The internally contradictory appearance of rain from the sun and of sweat from a heated man is conceived in terms of the transformation of a bull into a cow at zenith. Rain and sweat are conceived in terms of milk flowing from the cow's udder.

In ṚV 10.189.3c, the concept of speech (*vā́c*) appears which is 'established for a bird' (*vā́k pataṃgā́ya dhīyate*). Thus the input space of breathing is enlarged with concept of morning recitation[2]. The coherence of the blend is strengthened as the concept of a calf which follows its mother and during that time grows is used as the source domain to conceive not only the rising sun but also cognition expressed in speech by the poets (ṚV 1.164.5, 9, see chapter 1.6). It is further strengthened in that Agni which appears in its solar form in the morning is conceived in the same way. The identity between the cosmic (sunrise) and human (recitation with breathing) processes is also established by the identity of Agni which in the morning manifests

(See also Fuiji (1987b: 1004, Bodewitz (1990: 210, note 33). And this meaning of the sunrise and the possibility to reach zenith by man is the topic of ṚV 10.189. This ritual use of the ṚV is a good example that the concepts do not have to be explicitly expressed in words to be properly understood and that the later ritual exegesis understands them perfectly.

2 Jamison, Brereton (2014: 1660): 'The association of speech with the bird is also found in the Pataṃga hymn (10.177) and probably reflects the importance of ritual speech at the dawn sacrifice.'

in cosmos as the sun and in man as the final subject and object of cognition (see ṚV 1.164, see chapter 1.6, see Jurewicz 2010a).

This short analysis of ṚV 10.189 shows us that in the investigation of the beginnings of breath practice connected with recitation one should also analyse its metaphorical conceptualisations, especially those the source domain of which is concept of cow, bull and calf. The hymns of the AVŚ should be investigated along this line.

As has been shown, conceptualisation of recitation connected with breath in terms of a growing bull is attested in BU 2.2 (see chapter 4.4.2.2). I would like to quote here one more Upaniṣadic fragment which attests the connection between liberating cognition and breathing during recitation. In TU 1.6.1, reality manifest in the space within the heart and is conceived in terms of golden man which consists of mind (*sa ya eṣo 'ntarhṛdaya ākāśaḥ | tasminn ayaṃ puruṣo manomayaḥ | amṛto hiraṇmayaḥ*).

Then a place is mentioned, between the two palates like a nipple or a teat (*stana*) which Malamoud (1996c) interprets (with a quotation mark) as the uvula. It is called *indrayoni*. Olivelle (1998) translates it as 'Indra's passage' but I think that it should be interpreted literally as Indra's womb (Angot 2007, I). The main breath is conceived in terms of Indra in the early Veda (ŚB 6.1.1.2, see chapter 3.2.2) and, if the recipient activates this concept, he will understand that the beginnings of breathing are described here conceived in terms of an embryo. Reality passes through this place and 'arrives at the place where the hair-roots divide, forming a gap between the two cranial bones' (*yatrāsau keśānto vivartate | vyapohya śīrṣakapāle*, Malamoud 1996c: 71)[3]. This description of the TU refers to the experience of the emission of voice during which a breath raises the uvula and the sound reaches the head voice and registers when the tone resonates in the agent's head[4].

Then the composer of TU 1.6.1-2, describes the stages of liberating cognition during which man realises his identity with successive parts of the cosmos while he pronounces the calls. He realises his identity with the earth when he says *bhūr*, with the wind when he says *bhuvas*, with the sun when he says *svar*. Finally, saying *mahas*, he realises his identity with *brahman* (*bhūrityagnau pratitiṣṭhati | bhuva iti vāyau |* (1.6.1) *suvar ity āditye | maha iti brahmaṇi |*, 1.6.2). Then he becomes liberated which is conceived in terms of becoming a king (*āpnoti svārājyam*). He is also presented as the lord of cognitive faculties: of thinking, of sight, of hearing and of perception

[3] The experience described in AVŚ 10.2.26-28, 33 can be interpreted in the same way (chapter 2.5.1.1).

[4] I use the European terms to describe the emission of the voice, but the transformations of the body during the emission of voice based on diaphragm breathing are universal.

(*āpnoti manasaspatim* | *vākpatiś cakṣuṣpatiḥ* | *śrotrapatir vijñānapatiḥ*). The recipient understands that cognitive powers are conceived in terms of a king's subjects and that he masters their functioning. It is worth noting that faculties are connected with cognition (mind, sight[5], perception) and recitation (speech, hearing). The further description also activates experience of recitation connected with breathing. Man becomes *brahman* whose body is space (*ākāśaśarīraṃ brahma*) and whose pleasure is breath *prāṇārāmam*. I will come back to this description below. The recipient may understand this stage as the stage in which man masters his breath which produces the voice freely without any effort. The cognitive nature of this stage is confirmed by man's qualification as him whose self is truth (*satyātman*). It is also evoked in the qualification of man as someone whose delight is mind (*mana ānandam*). In the end of the description man is qualified as 'completely tranquil and immortal' (*śānti samṛddham amṛtam*).

It can be seen then that the composer presents liberating cognition as realised during breath practice and recitation. These processes are also conceived here in terms of the growth of a living being. This conceptualisation is evoked *via* the concept of *indrayoni*. At the macro scale, the image-schema of VERTICALITY is evoked *via* the concepts of consecutive spheres of the cosmos with which man identifies himself. These spheres in vertical order start from the earth and end in *brahman* which is above the sun. In micro scale, this image is evoked *via* the concept of breath which begins in the heart (the chest register) and goes up to the head (the head register). This process is conceived in terms of the growth of Indra[6].

The next important concept when looking for the traces of breathing practice connected with recitation is *brahman*. This concept has been analysed by several scholars (Renou 1948–1949, Gonda 1950, Thieme 1952[7]). I will begin will Thieme's interpretation who interprets its meaning in the ṚV as 'die (dichterische) Formulierung' and 'sprachliche Formung'. For my argument it is important that, in some usages of the word *brahman* in the ṚV, he sees an analogy between the creation of poetic speech and the formation of the embryo (Thieme 1952: 113–116). Putting this in the cognitive models, these usages betray conceptualisation of the creation of poetic speech in terms of the growth of an embryo which agrees with the conceptualisation presented by Thieme. I would argue that the experience of proper breathing during the

---

[5] COGNITION IS SEEING.

[6] For an analysis of cognition realised through *prāṇa* described in KU, see Bakker (1982). He, however, does not refer to the specific experience of breathing.

[7] For a comparative analysis of this concept within the frames of larger philosophical context, see Tate (1982).

emission of voice is also ground for this conceptualisation. The muscles in the lower part of the belly should be tensed to keep the diaphragm in an appropriate state for recitation. This may give an experience which could be interpreted as similar to the experience of a pregnant woman.

In his analysis of the concept of *brahman* and its meaning, Gonda (1950) argues in favour of the etymology of this word which is the verb *bṛh-*, 'to grow, swell, expand'. He shows that this verb is often used in contexts expressing the creation of a basis for something (1950: 29, 45–50). In ŚB 6.1.1.8, Prajāpati creates a basis (*pratiṣṭhā́*) which allows him to continue creation (see chapter 3.2.2). This basis is called *bráhman* and *trayī́ vidyā́*, and its meaning of knowledge gained in education is clear (*tásmād anū́cya prátitiṣṭhati pratiṣṭhā́ hy èṣā́ yad bráhma*). Such a conceptualisation of *bráhman*, i.e. knowledge realised in recitation and breathing, refers to the same experience during speaking as described above. Long recitation needs deep breathing which gives the agent the feeling of a centre that is located in the lower half of his torso below the diaphragm. It is felt physically as the growth of stability within one's belly which fills the body and gives support to it. The agent feels as if he is filled with air which becomes his internal support. This is probably the experiential root of the description of the liberated man as *brahman* which is *ākāśaśarīra* and *prāṇārāma* (TU 1.6.2). The body of the reciter becomes a space filled with breath and this feeing gives him pleasure.

In their interpretations of *brahman*, scholars treat this concept as an ontological one. I am not going to challenge their views here. I am just proposing the experiential ground known to trained singers which could ground its etymology. It is the physical experience of a base felt in the lower part of the body which grows while breathing and recitation goes on filling the body of the reciter. Taking this into account, the priest *brahman* is not only someone who remembers the Veda, but also someone who masters his breath to such an extent that he can recite it for a long time without effort. Thus he can externalise in words the content which grows in him and fills him completely.

The next important word for the investigation of the breath practice connected with recitation is *mantra* which, interestingly enough, appears mostly in the late maṇḍalas of the ṚV (Findly 1989). The contexts of its usages are such that it is difficult to reconstruct the experience which could motivate thinking about it. In ṚV 1.67.4b, 7.7.6b, the verb *takṣ-*, 'to carve, to chop' is used which betrays the conceptualisation of creation of hymns in these terms that is well entrenched in the ṚV. In ṚV 7.32.13a, it is qualified as *súdhita* and *supéśas* which implies its conceptualisation in terms of an object which is made perfectly and beautifully; the same conceptualisation of thinking is activated with the use of the general domain of Cleansing By Heat. The lack of a concrete context for the word *mantra* shows that already in the late ṚV it was an abstract word which was used to name a specific verbal expression pronounced by specific agents and in specific situations. Findly (1989: 27) defines it as 'the vehicle for reflection' and then writes:

> the power of the word as a performative utterance becomes crystallised in the notion of *mantra*. No other term for ritual speech in the *Ṛgveda* is seen to express as clearly the agentive quality of speech as much as mantra, where priest's growing sensitivity to the pure power of pronounced speech, as an instrument for the insight already deemed so central it is finally put into concrete form. (1989: 28).

This sensitivity to the power of pronounced speech is built during proper recitation supported by proper breathing. Findly also interprets the concept of *áṃhas* which is evoked in some hymns of the ṚV connected with recitation of *mantra*, as the concept which 'makes the development of mantra so important for, in the end, the reason speech must be performative which is to carry man beyond the boundaries of death' (1989: 41). It is not surprising that the experience of breathing during recitation of *mantra* could be seen as a remedium against the fear of death especially when Soma, which gave the experience of immortality (Jurewicz 2010a: 181–182), was no longer available.

It is also worth adding that the name of *mantras* used in Tantric practice, i.e. *bīja mantras*, literally 'seed/semen *mantras*' may reflect conceptualisation of breathing and recitation in terms of growing an animal or a plant. As Wheelock (1989: 103) writes 'these monosyllabic vocables, in theory are sonic manifestations of basic cosmic powers (*śaktis*); literally, seeds of the fundamental constituents of the universe'. And a bit later: 'the *bīja mantras* are not felt to be mere symbols of elements, they *are* the cosmic forms in essential form.' Within the frame of cognitive explanation the *bīja mantras* metonymically activate the corresponding elements of reality. The metaphoric conceptualisation reinforces the metonymic thinking. The *bīja mantras* encapsulate the parts of reality which grow when a *mantra* is uttered just as a plant grows from its seed. Their utterance leads to the realisation of man with reality.

So the reconstruction of the early Vedic breath practices connected with recitation should be conveyed on several levels. It should be based not only on the search of words (such as *prāṇa*, *brahman*, *mantra*) but also on the search for source domains in terms of which recitation and breathing are conceived. The implications of such investigations are important for understanding the development of Indian philosophy: the roots of classical yoga lie in the efforts of the Vedic thinkers who were so concerned with the proper expression of their tradition preserved in words. The loss of Soma is the next important factor amplifying these efforts.

4. Other topics for the further research

As far as general study of the development of abstract concepts in the early Veda is concerned, the Ṛgvedic hymns devoted to All Gods (Viśve Devas) are still waiting for their cognitive analysis. Their difficulty lies in that the composers of these hymns use terms they wanted to be abstract and which could be understood without activation of their experiential motivation. The same kind of investigation should be done on many hymns of the AVŚ in both its versions. The models proposed by cognitive linguistics will be very helpful in this investigation because they render it possible to construct maps of metonymic and metaphoric thinking which will constitute the basis for the further research.

A cognitive analysis should also be done on the specific concepts concerned which at first glance seem not to be philosophical, for example the concept of *rasa* or the concept of wind (*vāyu*). These concepts are not only abstract in the later Veda, but they are also important for the reconstruction of the early breath practice connected with recitation. Other concepts worth cognitive analysis are the concepts of gods in the Vedic ritual. Their use betrays the tendency towards abstraction because their rich meaning which is elaborated in the ṚV is later narrowed to bundles of prototypical features which become the basis for the conceptualisation of abstract concepts of agencies and states. The concept of Indra in terms of which the main breath is conceived is a good example of this tendency.

The next topic of investigation is how the Ṛgvedic philosophical models are re-enacted in ritual. I have already briefly analysed how the general model of reality transformation is re-enacted in the Trirātra rite. Let me shortly refer to the Rājasūya ritual to outline rather more how the philosophical models created in the ṚV are re-enacted in ritual. During the unction rite, the consecrated king who stands upright with his hands raised is the ritual embodiment of the *axis mundi* (Heesterman 1957: 120). Yet, he is also re-enacting the rise of the sun to zenith while the water with which he is anointed corresponds to rain which comes from the sun. Thus the most important moment of the ritual of the royal consecration is patterned according to the general model of reality transformation. There is another model which is evoked in this rite. The four priests who consecrate the kings can be seen as the ritual embodiment of waters in the model of Child of the Waters who feed Agni (Heesterman 1957: 86–87[8]). The composers of the Brāhmaṇa evoke this model in their exegesis of this rite, although the child is identified with Varuṇa and not with Agni (Heesterman 1957: 85 ff.). Thus the ritual becomes a visible form of the most abstract philosophical thinking as it is the physical expression of the model of reality.

Finally, research for traces of the belief in rebirth should not be limited to those texts which explicitly express it. As I have shown, it is possible that the belief in rebirth within the range of one's family or clan was so well entrenched in early Vedic thinking that the composers did not feel necessary to elaborate it more extensively. It is the same in European tradition where texts explicitly discussing the problem of rebirth after death are difficult to find. Yet, according to our European assumptions, rebirth is not the case whereas the Vedic assumption is that it is the case. In other words, the argument *ex absentia* is not very helpful in this context. As Obeyesekere (2000) shows the belief in rebirth has been quite widespread. It is also attested in the late ṚV (Jurewicz 2008b, 2010a). Taking into account the fact that the composers of the ṚV aimed at the creation of general metaphysical models, it can be assumed that later generations of thinkers took this belief for granted. It motivated their thinking about cosmological and metaphysical issues.

This topic is reconsidered again in the Upaniṣads when a new practice is found which leads to the possibility of *not being reborn.* Throughout the early Veda, the state reached after death was the state which was reached during supernatural cognition performed in one's life. According to the earlier tradition, attested in the Saṃhitās and the Brāhmaṇas, the range of the supernatural cognition was the borderline sphere between the two aspects of reality, so it was believed that everyone came back to the earth after death. The Upaniṣadic practice allowed the practitioners to reach the unmanifest aspect of reality. This resulted in the belief that those who perform cognition in the proper way, finally merge with this aspect and realise the state in which one could choose if he wanted to come back to manifest reality or not.

---

[8] In BU 1.4.11, the priestly power (*bráhman*) is conceived in terms of the womb of the royal power (*kṣatrá*). 'Therefore, even if a king should rise to the summit of power, it is to the priestly power that he returns in the end as to his own womb' (Olivelle 1998). Such a conceptualisation of the priestly power justifies interpretation of priests in terms of waters.

*

Human philosophical thought can rationally develop not only in the way European philosophy sees it. Mankind looks for answers for the most fundamental questions about themselves in the world and about the world itself in various ways. The early Indian thinkers tried to find the answer to these questions in rational thinking, although its form is different from that proposed by the ancient Greeks. The work of the composers of the early Veda shows that human rationality does not expresses itself only in the form of statements that are created in accordance with requirements of divalent logic and its implications. Lakoff and Johnson call metaphor 'imaginative rationality' (1980: 193):

> Reason, at the very last, involves categorisation, entailment, and inference. Imagination, in one of its many aspects, involves seeing one kind of thing in terms of another king of thing – what we have called metaphorical thought.

The art of blending can also be seen in this way. Abstract philosophical concepts can be seen as the result of cooperation of mind and imagination realised in a conscious way in the minds of philosophers. The way early Indian thinkers developed concepts and philosophical models did differ from the way they were developed by the ancient Greeks, but this does not mean that their activity was not conscious and rational.

In the conclusion to his analysis of the Ṛgvedic religion, Witzel (2004b: 626) writes that it is a system 'just like any other religion, though one *still digesting* recent influences from the Hindukush and the Greater Panjab'. He also shows the historical and cultural complexity of this system. In Jurewicz (2010a), I have shown how the Ṛgvedic composers created metaphysical models and abstract terms. Although my approach was not a socio-historical one, the efforts of the Ṛgvedic poets can be seen as part of the 'digestion' (as Witzel puts it) of their earlier tradition. This conceptual system became the heritage of the later generation of Vedic thinkers which was then further elaborated and developed. My approach which combines Indological and cognitive tools shows that the Vedic texts attest conscious efforts to create philosophical thought and appropriate language. They can be witnessed and reconstructed because it does not differ very much from any human creative thought. In other words, we are in unique position to witness the development of philosophy seen as a part of larger human intellectual endeavour.

Warszawa – Oxford – Puszcza Augustowska

Bibliography

1. Primary sources

AVŚ = *Atharva-Veda Saṃhitā. Śaunaka Recension.* http://titus.uni-frankfurt.de/texte/etcs/ind/aind/ved/av/avs/avs.htm

AU = *Aitareya-Upaniṣad.* http://titus.uni-frankfurt.de/texte/etcs/ind/aind/ved/rv/upanisad/aitup/aitup.htm

BU = *Bṛhad-Āraṇyaka-Upaniṣad. Mādhyandina-Recension / Kāṇva-Recension.* http://titus.uni-frankfurt.de/texte/etcs/ind/aind/ved/yvw/upanisad/bau/bau.htm

CU = *Chāndogya-Upaniṣad.* http://titus.uni-frankfurt.de/texte/etcs/ind/aind/ved/sv/upanisad/chup/chup.htm

JB = Vira R., Chandra L. 1986[1955]. (eds.) *Jaiminīya Brahmaṇa of the Sāmaveda.* Delhi, Varanasi, Patna, Madras: Motilal Banarsidass

JUB = *Jaiminīya-Upaniṣad-Brāhmaṇa.* http://titus.uni-frankfurt.de/texte/etcs/ind/aind/ved/sv/jub/jub.htm

KU = *Kauṣītaki-Upaniṣad.* http://titus.uni-frankfurt.de/texte/etcs/ind/aind/ved/rv/upanisad/kausup/kausu.htm

ṚV = Holland G.B., van Nooten B. 1994. *Rig Veda: A Metrically Restored Text With an Introduction and Notes.* Cambridge, Massachusetts: Department of Sanskrit and Indian Studies. (Thomson K., Slocum J.: http://www.utexas.edu/cola/centers/lrc/RV/RV00.html)

ŚB = *Śatapatha-Brāhmaṇa, Mādhyandina Recension.* http://titus.uni-frankfurt.de/texte/etcs/ind/aind/ved/yvw/sbm/sbm.htm

Taittirīya-Brāhmaṇa. http://titus.uni-frankfurt.de/texte/etcs/ind/aind/ved/yvs/tb/tb.htm

TU = *Taittirīya-Upaniṣad.* http://titus.uni-frankfurt.de/texte/etcs/ind/aind/ved/yvs/upanisad/taittup/taitt.htm

Weber A. (ed.). 1885. *The Śatapatha-Brāhmaṇa in the Mādhyandina-Śākhā. With extracts from the commentaries of Sāyaṇa, Harisvāmin and Dvivedānga.* London: Williams and Norgate.

2. Secondary sources

Alper H.P. (ed.) 1989. *Mantra.* Albany, NY: State University of New York Press.

Amin T., Smith C.L., Wiser M. 2014. 'Student Conceptions and Conceptual Change: Three Overlapping Phases of Research'. In: Lederman, Abell 2014: 57–81.

Angot M. 2007. *Taittirīya-Upaniṣad avec le commentaire de Śaṃkara. Introduction, texte et traduction.* 2 vols. Paris: College de France.

Arole M. 1987. 'Significance of the Tortoise in Sacrifices and its Archaeological Correlation'. *Indica* 24, 45–46: 15–17.

Auboyer J. 1968. *Le trône et son symbolisme dans l'Inde ancienne.* Paris: Presses Universitaires de France.

Bakker H.T. 1982. 'On the Origin of the Sāṃkhya Philosophy'. *Wiener Zeitschrift für die Kunde Südasiens*, 24: 117–148.

Bakker H.T. 2007. 'Human Sacrifice (Puruṣamedha), Construction of Sacrifice and the Origin of the Idea of the "Man of the Homestead" (Vāstupuruṣa)'. In: Bremmer 2007: 179–194.

Balbir N., Pinault G.J. (eds.) 1996. *Langue, style et structure dans le monde indien. Centenaire de Louis Renou.* Paris: Librairie Honoré Champion.

Balcerowicz P., Mejor M. (eds.) 2004. *Essays in Indian Philosophy, Religion & Literature.* Delhi: Motilal Banarsidass.

Bareja-Starzyńska A., Mejor M. (eds.) 2012. *Oriental Studies – Past and Present. Proceeding of the International Conference of Oriental Studies.* Warsaw 2010. Rocznik Orientalistyczny 65, 1.

Barsalou L.W. 1999. 'Perceptual Symbol Systems'. Behavioral and Brain Sciences, 22: 577–66.

Barsalou L.W. 2003. 'Abstraction in Perceptual Symbol Systems'. *Philosophical Transactions of the Royal Society B*, 358: 1177–1187.

Barsalou L.W. 2005a. 'Abstraction as Dynamic Interpretation in Perceptual Symbol Systems' In: Gershkoff-Stowe, Rakison 2005: 389–431.

Barsalou L.W., Wiener-Hastings K. 2005b. 'Situating Abstract Concepts'. In: Pecher, Zwaan 2005: 129–163.

Bechert H. (ed.) 1992. *The Dating of the Historical Buddha/Die Datierung des historischen Buddha.* Part 2. (Symposien zur Buddhismusforschung, IV, 2) Göttingen: Vandenhoeck & Ruprecht.

Begg I. 1972. 'Recall of Meaningful Phrases, *Journal of Verbal Learning and Verbal Behavior*, 11: 431–439.

Bender E. (ed.) 1962. *Indological Studies in Honor of W. Norman Brown.* American Oriental Series. Vol 47. New Haven: American Oriental Society.

Bergaigne A. 1963 [1878–83]. *La religion védique d'après les hymnes du Rig-Veda.* 3 vols. Paris: Librairie Honoré Champion.

Bhattacharya D. 1977. 'Cosmogony and Rituo-Philosophical History of the *Atharvaveda*'. *Vishveshvaranand Indological Journal* 15, 1: 1–12.

Bhattacharya C. 1978. 'The Doctrine of Four in the Early Upaniṣads and Some Connected Problems'. *Journal of Indian Philosophy* 6: 1–34.

Bhattacharya G. 1986. *Studies in Memory of Dr D. C. Sircar.* Delhi: Sri Satguru.

Biardeau M. 1981. *Études de mythologie hindoue. Tome I. Cosmogonies purāṇiques.* Paris: Publications de l'École Française d'extrême Orient.

Black B. 2007. *The character of the Self in Ancient India. Priests, Kings, and Women in the Early Upaniṣads.* Albany, NY: State University of New York Press.

Blair C.J. 1961. *Heat in the Rig Veda and Atharva Veda. A General Survey with Particular Attention to Some Aspects and Problems*. New Haven, Connecticut: American Oriental Society.

Blanchard L. 2012. 'Burning Yourself: *Paticca Samuppāda* as a Description of the Arising of A False Sense of Self Modeled on Vedic Rituals'. *Journal of the Oxford Centre for Buddhist Studies* 2: 36–83 (http://jocbs.org/index.php/jocbs/article/view/14).

Blezer H.W.A. 1992. 'Prāṇa. Aspects of Theory and Evidence for Practice in late-brāhmaṇical and early-Upaniṣadic thought'. In: Hoek, Kolff, Oort 1992: 20–49.

Bloomfield M. 1891. 'Contribution to the Interpretation of the Veda. Third Series'. *Journal of American Oriental Society* 15: 143–188.

Bloomfield M. 1897. *Hymns of the Atharva-Veda together with Extracts from the Ritual Books and Commentaries*. Sacred Books of the East. Vol. 42. Oxford: Clarendon Press.

Bloomfield M. 1899. *The Atharvaveda'*. Strassburg: Verlag Von Karl J. Trübner.

Bloomfield M. 1915. 'On Etymology and Meaning of the Sanskrit Root *varj*'. *Journal of American Oriental Society* 35: 273–288.

Bockarova M., Danesi M., Núñez R. (eds.) 2012. *Semiotics and Cognitive Science Articles on the Nature of Mathematics*. Munich: Lincom Europa.

Bodewitz H.W. 1973. *Jaiminīya Brāhmaṇa I, 1–65: Translation [from the Sanskrit] and Commentary with a Study of Agnihotra and Prāṇāgnihotra*. Leiden: E.J. Brill.

Bodewitz H.W. 1974. 'Vedic Dhāvayati "To Drive"'. *Indo-Iranian Journal* 16: 81–95.

Bodewitz H.W. 1982. 'The Waters in Vedic Cosmic Classifications'. *Indologica Taurinensia* 10: 45–54.

Bodewitz H.W. 1983. 'The Fourth Priest (the Brahmán) in Vedic Ritual'. In: Kloppenborg 1983: 33–68.

Bodewitz H.W. 1990. *The Jyotiṣṭoma Ritual. Jaiminīya Brāhmaṇa* I, 66–364. Leiden: E.J. Brill.

Bodewitz H.W. 1991. *Light, Soul and Visions in the Veda*. Poona: Bhandarkar Oriental Research Institute.

Bodewitz H.W. 1992. 'King Prāṇa'. In: Hoek, Kolff, Oort 1992, 60–64.

Bodewitz, H.W. 1996a. The *Pañcāgnividyā* and the *Pitryāna / Devayāna*. In: Goswami, Chutia 1996: 51–57.

Bodewitz H.W. 1996b. 'Redeath and its Relation to Rebirth and Release'. *Studien zur Indologie und Iranistik* 20: 27–46.

Bodewitz H.W. 1997a. *The Daily Evening and Morning Offering. Agnihotra According to the Brāhmaṇas*. Leiden: E.J. Brill.

Bodewitz H.W. 1997b. 'The Hindu Doctrine of Transmigration: Its Origin and Background'. *Indologica Taurinensia* 23–24: 583–605.

Bodewitz H.W. 1999a. 'Yonder World in the *Atharvaveda*'. *Indo-Iranian Journal* 42, 2: 107–120.

Bodewitz H.W. 1999b. 'Pits, Pitfalls and the Underworld in the Veda'. *Indo-Iranian Journal* 42, 3: 211–226.

Bodewitz H.W. 2000a. 'Classifications and Yonder World in the Veda'. *Wiener Zeitschrift für die Kunde Süd- und Ostasiens* 44: 19–59.

Bodewitz H.W. 2000b. 'Distance and Death in the Veda'. *Asiatische Studien / Études Asiatiques* 54, 1: 103–117.

Bodewitz H.W. 2001. 'Citra's Question in KauṣU. 1.1'. In: *Indo-Iranian Journal* 44: 265–268.

Bodewitz. H.W. 2002a. 'The Dark and Deep Underworld in the Veda'. *Journal of the American Oriental Society* 122, 2: 213–223.

Bodewitz. H.W. 2002b. *Kauṣītaki Upaniṣad. Translation and Commentary with an Appendix Śāṃkhāyana Āraṇyaka IX–XI.* Groningen: Egbert Forsten.

Boot I., Pecher D. 2011. 'Representation of Categories. Metaphorical Use of the Container Schema'. *Experimental Psychology* 58, 2: 162–170.

Borghi A.M., Capirci O., Gianfreda G., Volterra V. 2014. 'The Body and the Fading Away of Abstract Concepts and Words: A Sign Language Analysis.' *Frontiers in Psychology*, 5, 29: 811 (1–13), (http://www.ncbi.nlm.nih.gov/pubmed/25120515).

Borkent M., Dancygier B., Hinnell J. (eds.). Language and the Creative Mind. Stanford, CA: CSLI Publications.

Bosch L.P. van den. 1985. 'The Āprī Hymns of the *Ṛgveda* and their Interpretation'. *Indo-Iranian Journal* 28, 2: 95–122, 3: 169–191.

Bremmer J.N. (ed.) 2007. *The Strange World of Human Sacrifice.* Leuven, Paris, Duddley, MA: Peeters.

Brereton J.P. 1981. *The Ṛgvedic Ādityas.* New Haven, Connecticut: American Oriental Society.

Brereton J.P. 1982. The Particle *iva* in Vedic Prose'. *Journal of the American Oriental Society* 102: 443–450.

Brereton J.P. 1991. 'Cosmographic Images in the *Bṛhadāraṇyaka Upaniṣad*'. *Indo-Iranian Journal* 34, 1: 1–17.

Brereton J.P. 1996. 'Yājñavalkya 's curse.' *Studien zur Indologie and Iranistik* 20: 47–57.

Brockington J. 1990. *Święta nić hinduizmu. Hinduizm w jego ciągłości i różnorodności.* Warszawa: Instytut Wydawniczy PAX (translation of *The Sacred Thread. Hinduizm in its continuity and Diversity* 1985).

Bronkhorst J. 1982. 'Some observations on the *padapāṭha* of the *Ṛgveda*'. *Indo-Iranian Journal* 24: 181–189.

Bronkhorst J. 2007. *Greater Magadha. Studies in the Culture of Early India.* Leiden, Boston: E.J. Brill

Brown N.W. 1931. 'The Sources and Nature of the *púruṣa* in the *Puruṣasūkta* (Rigveda 10.90)'. *Journal of the American Oriental Studies* 51: 108–118.

Brown N.W. 1968a. 'Agni, Sun, Sacrifice, and Vāc. A Sacerdotal Ode by Dīrghatamas (Rig Veda 1.164). *Journal of the American Oriental Society* 88: 199–218.

Brown N.W. 1968b. 'The Creative Role of the Goddess Vāc in the Rig Veda'. In: Heesterman, Schokker, Subramoniam 1968: 393–398.

Brenzinger M., Kraska-Szlenk I. (eds.). 2014. *The Body in Language Comparative Studies of Linguistic Embodiment.* Leiden: E.J. Brill.

Buitenen J.A.B. van 1988a. 'The Large Ātman'. In: Rocher 1988: 209–222.

Buitenen J.A.B. van 1988b. 'The Speculations on the Name "Satyam" in the Upaniṣads'. In: Rocher 1988: 263–272.

Buitenen J.A.B. van 1988c. '*Vācārambhaṇam*'. In: Rocher 1988: 5–12.

Buitenen J.A.B. van 1988d. '*Vācārambhaṇam* Reconsidered'. In: Rocher 1988: 121–134.

Butzenberger K. 1996. 'Doctrine of Transmigration. I'. *Berliner Indologische Studien* 9/10: 55–118.

Butzenberger K. 1998. 'Ancient Indian Conceptions on Man's Destiny After Death. The Beginnings and the Early Development of the Doctrine of Transmigration. Doctrine of Transmigration. II'. *Berliner Indologische Studien* 11/12: 1–84.

Caballero R., Díaz Vera J. E. *Sensuous Cognition. Exploration into Human Experience: Imagination, (E)motion and Perception* . Berlin/Boston: Mouton de Gruyter.

Caillat C. (ed.) 1989. *Dialects dans les litteratures indo-āryennes.* Paris: de Boccard.

Caland W., Henry V. 1906. *L'Agniṣṭoma. Description complète de la forme normale du sacrifice de Soma dans le culte védique.* 2 vols. Paris: Ernest Leroux.

Candotti M.P., Pontillo T. 'Aims and Functions of Vrātyastoma Performances. A Historical Appraisal'. In: Pontillo, Bignami, Dore, Mucciarelli 2015: 154–215.

Cánovas C.P. 2010. 'Conceptual Blending Theory and the History of Emotions'. *Proceedings of the Workshop on Cognitive Social Science, Cogsci 2010.* (http://www.neuro humanitiestudies.eu/archivio/ConceptualBlendingandtheHistoryofEmotions.pdf).

Cánovas C.P. 2011. 'The Genesis of the Arrows of Love: Diachronic Conceptual Integration in Greek Mythology'. *American Journal of Philology* 132, 4: 553–579.

Cánovas C.P., Antović, M. (forthcoming a). 'Introduction: Oral poetics and cognitive science'. In: Cánovas, Antović (forthcoming).

Cánovas, C.P., Antović, M. (forthcoming b). 'Construction grammar and oral formulaic theory'. In: Cánovas, Antović (forthcoming).

Cánovas, C.P., Antović, M. (eds. forthcoming). *Oral Poetics and Cognitive Science.* Berlin: Mouton de Gruyter.

Cavallin C. 2011. *The Efficacy of Sacrifice. Correspondences in the Rigvedic Brāhmaṇas.* Saarbrücken: LAP LAMBERT Academic Publishing.

Cavallin C. 2013. *Ritualization and Human Interiority.* Copenhagen: Museum Tusculanum Press.

Chłopicki W., Pawelec A., Pokojska A. (eds.) 2007. *Cognition in Language: Volume in Honour of Professor Elżbieta Tabakowska. Review of Cognitive Linguistics.* Kraków: Tertium.

Choudhary R. 1964. *Vrātyas in Ancient India.* The Chowkhamba Sanskrit Series. Vol. 38. Varanasi: Chowkhamba Sanskrit Series Office.

Cienki A. 2007. 'Frames, Idealized Cognitive Models, and Domains'. In: Geeraerts, Cuyckens 170–188.

Cienki A., Müller C. 2008a. 'Metaphor, Gesture, and Thought'. In: Gibbs 2008: 483–501.

Cienki A. Müller C. 2008b. *Metaphor and Gesture.* Amsterdam, Philadelphia: John Benjamins Publishing Company.

Clark A. 2008. *Supersizing the Mind: Embodiment, Action, and Cognitive Extension.* Oxford, New York: Oxford University Press.

Clark A., Chalmers D. 1998. 'The Extended Mind'. *Analysis* 58: 10–23.

Clausner T.C., Croft W. 1999. 'Domains and Image Schemas'. *Cognitive Linguistics* 10–1, 1–31.

Coomaraswamy A.K. 1935. 'Angel and Titan: an Essay in Vedic Ontology'. *Journal of the American Oriental Society* 55: 373–419.

Coomaraswamy A.K. 1946. *áty atiṣṭhad daśāṅgulám. Journal of the American Oriental Society* 66, 2: 145–161.

Coulson, S., Van Petten, C. 2002. 'Conceptual Integration and Metaphor: An Event-related Potential Study. *Memory and Cognition* 30: 958–968.

Coulson, S., Matlock, T. 2001. 'Metaphor and the Space Structuring Model. *Metaphor and Symbol* 16: 295–316.

Croft W., Cruse D.A. 2004. *Cognitive Linguistics*. Cambridge: Cambridge University Press.

Crangle E.F. 1994. *The Origin and Development of Early Indian Contemplative Practices*. Wiesbaden: Harrasowitz Verlag.

Collins B. 2014. *The Head Beneath the Altar. Hindu Mythology and the Critique of Sacrifice*. East Lansing, Michigan: Michigan State University Press.

Connolly P., Hamilton S. (eds.). *Indian Insights: Buddhism, Brahmanism and Bhakti. Papers from the Spalding Symposium on Indian Religions*. London: Luzac Oriental.

Coulson S. 2000. Semantic Leaps: Frame-shifting and Conceptual Blending in Meaning-Construction. Cambridge: Cambridge University Press.

Coulson S., Oakley T. 2000. 'Blending Basic'. *Cognitive Linguistics* 11, 2, 4: 176–196.

Coulson S., Oakley T. 2005. 'Blending and Coded Meaning. Literal and Figurative Meaning in Cognitive Semantics'. *Journal of Pragmatics* 37, 1510–1536.

Grady J., Oakley T., Coulson S. 2007. 'Blending and Metaphor'. In: Evans, Berger, Zinken (eds.): 420–440.

Covill L. 2009. *A Metaphorical Study of Saundarananda*. Delhi: Motilal Banarsidass.

Croft W., Cruse D. A. 2004. *Cognitive Linguistics*. Cambridge: Cambridge University Press.

Dancygier B. 2006. 'What Can Blending Do For You?'. *Language and Literature* 15, 1: 5–15.

Dange S.A. 2000. *Images from Vedic Hymns and Rituals*. New Delhi: Aryan Books International.

Dasgupta S.D. 1951–1955. *A History of Indian Philosophy*. 5 vols. Cambridge: Cambridge University Press (first edition 1922, 1932, 1940, 1949, 1955).

Deussen P. 2000 [1919]. *A History of Indian Philosophy*. Vol. 1. Delhi: Motilal Banarsidass.

Dhavalikar M.K. 1975, 'The Beginning of Coinage in India'. *World Archaeology*, 6, 3: 330–338

Diez Velasco O.I. (2001/2002). 'Metaphor, Metonymy, and Image-schemas. An Analysis of Conceptual Interaction Patterns.' *Journal of English Studies*, 3: 47–63.

Doniger O'Flaherty W. 1981. *The Rigveda: An Anthology*. Harmondsworth, UK: Penguin Books.

Doniger O'Flaherty W. 1987. *Tales of Sex and Violence. Folklore, Sacrifice, and Danger in the Jaiminīya Brāhmaṇa*. Delhi: Motilal Banarsidass.

Dore M. 2015. 'The Ekavrātya, Indra and the Sun'. In: Pontillo, Bignami, Dore, Mucciarelli 2015, 33–54.

Dore M., Pontillo T. 2013. 'What Do Vrātyas Have To Do with Long-stalked Plants? *Darbha*, *kuśa*, *śara* and *iṣīkā* in Vedic and Classical Sources'. *Pandanus*, 150th Anniversary of the Birth of Moriz Winternitz Seminar 4: 35–61.

Dreyfus B.W, Gupta A., Redish E.F. 2014. 'Applying Conceptual Blending to Model Coordinated Use of Multiple Ontological Metaphors' (arXiv:1412.1693v2 [physics.ed-ph]).

Dumont P.E. 1927. *L'Aśvamedha, description du sacrifice solennel du cheval dans le culte védique d'après les textes du Yajurveda blanc (Vājasaneyisaṃhitā, Śatapatha-brāhmaṇa, Kātyāyanaśrautasūtra)*. Paris: P. Geuthner.

Dumont P.E. 1939. *L'Agnihotra. Description de l'agnihotra dans le ritual védique.* Baltimore: The John Hopkins Press.

Edgerton F. 1920. 'The Philosophic Material of the Atharva Veda'. In: *Studies in honor of Maurice Bloomfield.* New Haven: Yale University Press, 117–135.

Edgerton F. 1965. *The Beginnings in of Indian Philosophy.* London: George Allen & Unwin Ltd.

Eggeling J. 1882, 1885, 1894, 1897, 1900. *The Śatapatha Brāhmaṇa.* Sacred Books of the East. Vols. 12, 26, 41, 43, 44. Oxford: Clarendon Press.

Elizarenkova T. Ja. 1989. *Rigveda. Mandaly I–IV.* Moskva: Nauka.

Elizarenkova T. Ja. 1995. *Rigveda. Mandaly V–VIII.* Moskva: Nauka.

Elizarenkova T. Ja. 1999. *Rigveda. Mandaly IX–X.* Moskva: Nauka.

Erdosy G. (ed.) 1995. *The Indo-Aryans of Ancient South Asia. Language, Material Culture and Ethnicity.* Berlin, New York: Walter de Gruyter.

Evans V. 2004. *The Structure of Time. Language, Meaning and Temporal Cognition.* Amsterdam, Philadelphia: John Benjamins Publishing Company.

Evans V. 2006. 'Lexical Concepts, Cognitive Models and Meaning-construction'. *Cognitive Linguistics* 17, 4: 491–534.

Evans V., Green M. 2006. *Cognitive Linguistics. An Introduction.* Edinburgh: Edinburgh University Press.

Evans V., Bergen B., Zinken J. 2007 'The Cognitive linguistics Enterprise: An Overview'. In: Evans, Bergen B. and Zinken J. 2007: 2–36.

Evans, V., Bergen, B., Zinken J. (eds). 2007. *The Cognitive Linguistics Reader: Advances in Cognitive Linguistics.* Equinox Publishing Ltd, London.

Falk H. 1986. *Bruderschaft und Würfelspiel. Untersuchungen zur Entwicklungsgeschichte des vedischen Opfers.* Freiburg: Hedwig Falk.

Falk H. (ed.) 1987. *Hinduismus und Buddhismus. Festschrift für Ulrich Schneider.* Freiburg: Hedwig Falk.

Falk H. 1989. Soma I and II. *Bulletin of the School of Oriental and African Studies* 52, 1: 77–90.

Fauconnier G. 2005. Compression and Emergent Space. In: S. Huang: *Language and Linguistics.* 6.4: 523–538.

Fauconnier G., Turner M. 1988. 'Conceptual Integration Networks'. Cognitive Science 22, 2: 133–187.

Fauconnier G., Turner M. 2000. 'Compression and Global Insight'. *Cognitive Linguistics* 11, 3–4: 283–304.

Fauconnier G., Turner M. 2003. *The Way We Think. Conceptual Blending and the Mind's Hidden Complexities.* New York: Basic Books.

Feldman J.A. 2006. *From Molecule to Metaphor. A Neural Theory of Language.* Cambridge, MA: MIT Press.

Findly E.B. 1989. '*Mántra Kaviśastá*: Speech as Performative in the *Ṛgveda*'. In: Alper 1989: 15–47.

Forceville Ch. 2005. 'Visual Representations of the Idealized Cognitive Model of *Anger* in the Asterix Album *La Zizanie*'. *Journal of Pragmatics* 37: 69–88.

Forceville Ch. 2008. 'Metaphor in Pictures and Multimodal Representations'. In: Gibbs 2008: 462–482.

Forceville Ch., Urios-Aparisi E. (eds.) 2009. *Multimodal Metaphor*. The Hague: Mouton de Gruyter.

Frauwallner E. 1990 [1953] . *Historia filozofii indyjskiej*. 2 vols. Warszawa: Państwowe Wydawnictwo Naukowe (translation of *Geschichte der indischen Philosophie* 1953).

Freeman M. 2002. 'Cognitive Mapping in Literary Analysis'. *Style* 36, 3: 466–483.

Freeman M. 2007. 'Poetic Iconicity'. In: Chłopicki, Pawelec, Pokojska 2007: 472–501.

Freeman M. 2008. 'Reading Readers Reading a Poem: From Conceptual to Cognitive integration', *Cognitive Semiotics* 2: 102–128.

Freeman M. 2012 'Blending and Beyond: Form and Feeling in Poetic Iconicity'. In: Jaén, Simon 2012: 127–143.

Frenz A. 1968/69. 'Kauṣītaki Upaniṣad'. *Indo-Iranian Journal* 11: 79–129.

Fuiji M. 1986. 'The Bahiṣpavamāna Ritual of the Jaiminīyas. *Nachikaneyama Ronso (Philosophy)* 20: 3–25.

Fuiji M. 1987a. 'On the Unexpressed *Gāyatra-Sāman* in the Jaiminīya-Upaniṣad-Brāhmaṇa'. *Journal of Indian and Buddhist Studies* (*Indogaku Bukkyōgaku Kenkyū*) 32, 2: 1121–1123

Fuiji M. 1987b. 'The *Gāyatra* and Ascension to Heaven. (Jaiminīya-Upaniṣad-Brāhmaṇa 1, 1–7, 3, 11–14). *Journal of Indian and Buddhist Studies* (*Indogaku Bukkyōgaku Kenkyū*) 35, 2: 1002–1005.

Fuiji M. 1997. 'On the Formation and Transmission of the Jaiminīya-Upaniṣad-Brāhmaṇa. In: Witzel 1997: 89–102.

Fuiji M. 2009/2010. 'The *Gāyatra-Sāman*: Chanting Innovations in the Sāmavedic Brāhmaṇas and Upaniṣad. *ZINBUN* 42: 1–37.

Fuiji M. 2011. 'The Recovery of the Body After Death: A Prehistory of the Devayāna and Pitṛyāna'. In: Tikkanen, Butters: 103–120.

Gadamer H-G. 1993 [1975]. *Prawda i metoda. Zarys hermeneutyki filozoficznej.* Kraków: inter esse (translation of *Warheit und Methode. Grundzüge einer philosophischen Hermeneutik* 1975).

Ganeri J. 2007. *The Concealed Art of The Soul. Theories of Self and Practices of Truth in Indian Ethic and Epistemology.* New York: Oxford University Press.

Garbe R. 2004 [1897]. *The Philosophy of Ancient India.* Montana: Kessinger Publishing.

Garzilli E. 1996. (ed.) *Translating, Translations, Translators: From India to the West.* Harvard Oriental Series, Opera Minora 1. Cambridge Massachusetts: Harvard University Press.

Geeraerts D., Cuyckens H. (eds.) 2007. *The Oxford Handbook of Cognitive Linguistics*. New York: Oxford University Press.

Geertz C. 1973. *The Interpretation of Cultures*, New York: Basic Books.

Geertz C. 1973a. 'The Impact of the Concept of Culture on the Concept of Man'. In: Geertz 1973: 33–52.

Geertz C. 1973b. 'Religion As a Cultural System'. In: Geertz 1973: 87–125.

Geldner K. F. 1951, 1957. *Der Rigveda. Aus dem Sanskrit ins Deutsche übersetzt und mit einem laufenden Kommentar versehen.* 3 vols. Cambridge, Massachusetts: Department of Sanskrit and Indian Studies.

Gershkoff-Stowe L., Rakison D. (eds.), *Building Object Categories*. Carnegie Symposium Series. Majwah, NJ: Erlbaum.

Gibbs R.W. 2005a. 'Embodiment in Metaphorical Imagination'. In: Pecher, Zwaan 2005: 65–92.

Gibbs R.W. 2005b. *Embodiment and Cognitive Science.* New York: Cambridge University Press.

Gibbs, R.W.(ed.) 2008. *The Cambridge Handbook of Metaphor and Thought.* New York: Cambridge University Press.

Gibbs R.W. , Matlock T. 2008. 'Metaphor, Imagination, and Simulation. Psycholinguistic Evidence'. In: Gibbs 2008: 161–176.

Girard R. 1993[1972]. *Sacrum i przemoc.* Poznań: Brama (Translation of *La violence et le sacré* 1972).

Givón T. 1998. 'On the Co-evolution of Language, Mind and Brain. *Evolution of Communication* 2, 45–116.

Glucklich A. 1994. *The Sense of Adharma.* Oxford, New York, Toronto: Oxford University Press.

Gombrich R. 1992. 'Dating the Buddha: A Red Herring Revealed'. In: Bechert 1992: 237–259.

Gonda J. 1954. *Aspects of Early Viṣṇuism.* Utrecht: N.V.A. Oosthoek's Uitgevers Maatschappij.

Gonda J. 1959a. *Four Studies in the Language of the Veda.* The Hague: Mouton & Co.

Gonda J. 1959b. *Epithets in the Ṛgveda.* The Hague: Mouton & Co.

Gonda J. 1963. *The Vision of the Vedic Poets.* The Hague: Mouton & Co.

Gonda J. 1965. *The Savayajñas.* Amsterdam: Noord-Hollandsche Uitgevers Maatschappij.

Gonda J. 1966. *Loka. World and Heaven in the Veda.* Amsterdam: Noord-Hollandsche Uitgevers Maatschappij.

Gonda J. 1969. *Ancient Indian Kinship from the Religious Point of View.* Leiden: E.J. Brill.

Gonda J. 1975a. 'The Meaning of Sanskrit *mahas* and its Relatives'. In: *Selected Studies. Presented to the Author by the Staff of the Oriental Institute Utrecht University, on the Occasion of His 70th Birthday.* Volume II. *Sanskrit Word Studies.* Leiden: E.J. Brill, 450–485.

Gonda J. 1975b. 'The Meaning of the Word *Alaṃkāra*'. In: *Selected Studies. Presented to the Author by the Staff of the Oriental Institute Utrecht University, on the Occasion of His 70th Birthday.* Volume II. *Sanskrit Word Studies.* Leiden: E.J. Brill: 258–275.

Gonda J. 1975c. 'Āyatana'. In: *Selected Studies. Presented to the Author by the Staff of the Oriental Institute Utrecht University, on the Occasion of His 70th Birthday.* Volume II. *Sanskrit Word Studies.* Leiden: E.J. Brill: 179–257.

Gonda J. 1976a. *Triads in the Veda.* Amsterdam: North Holland Publishing Company.

Gonda J. 1976b. *Viṣṇuism and Śivaism. A Comparison.* New Delhi: Munshiram Manoharlal Publishers.

Gonda J. 1985. *Pūṣan and Sarasvati.* Amsterdam, Oxford, New York: North-Holland Publishing Company.

Gonda J. 1986. 'Mind and Moon'. In: Bhattacharya 1986: 147–160.

Goswami A.K., Chutia D. (eds). 1996. *Studies on Indology: Professor Mukund Madhava Sharma Felicitation Volume.* Delhi: Sri Satguru Publications.

Gotō T. 1987. *Die 'I. Präsensklasse' im Vedischen.* Wien: Verlag der Österreichischen Akademie der Wissenschaften.

Gotō T. 1996. 'Zur Lehre Śāṇḍilyas: zwischen Brāhmaṇa und Upaniṣad'. In: Balbir, Pinault 1996: 71–89.

Gotō T. 2005. 'Yājnavalkya's Characterisation of Ātman and the Four Kinds of Suffering in Early Buddhism'. *Electronic Journal of Vedic Studies* 12–2: 71–85.

Grady J. 1997. *Foundations of Meaning: Primary Metaphors and Primary Stress*. PhD. Dissertations, Department of Linguistics, Department of Linguistics, University of Berkeley (http://escholarship.org/uc/item/3g9427m2#page-4).

Grady J. 2005. 'Primary Metaphors as Inputs to Conceptual Integration'. *Journal of Pragmatics* 37: 1595–1614.

Grady J. 2007. 'Metaphor'. In: Geeraerts, Cuyckens 2007: 188–213.

Grady J., Oakley T., Coulson S. 2007. 'Blending and Metaphor'. In: Evans, Berger, Zinken 2007: 420–440.

Grassmann H. 1999 [1873–1875]. *Wörterbuch zum Ṛgveda*. Delhi: Motilal Banarsidass (first edition: Leipzig 1873–1875).

Gren-Eklund G. 1978. *A Study of Nominal Sentences in the Oldest Upaniṣads*. (Acta Universitatis Upsaliensis, Studia Indoeuropaea Upsaliensia, 3. Uppsala: Almquist & Wiksell.

Griffiths A., Houben J. E. M. (eds.) 2004. *The Vedas. Texts, Language and Ritual. Proceedings of the Third International Vedic Workshop, Leiden 2002*. Groningen: Egbert Forsten.

Griffiths A., Schmiedchen A. 2007. *The Atharvaveda and its Paippalādaśākhā: Historical and Philological Papers on a Vedic Tradition*. Aachen: Shaker Verlag.

Grimal F., Dejenne N. (eds.) 2010. *Forms and Uses of the Commentary in the Indian World*. Pondichery: Institute Français de Pondichery.

Grinshpon J. 2003. *Crisis and Knowledge. The Upanishadic Experience and Storytelling*. New Delhi: Oxford University Press.

Gupta B. 2012. *An Introduction to Indian Philosophy. Perspectives on Reality, Knowledge, and Freedom*. New York, Abingdon: Routledge.

Hacker P. 1963. 'Śraddhā'. *Wiener Zeitschrift für die Kunde Süd- und Ostasiens* 7: 151–189.

Hamilton S. 2000. *Early Buddhism: A New Approach. The I of the Beholder*. Richmond, Surrey: Curzon Press.

Hampe B. 2005. 'Image schemas in Cognitive Linguistics: Introduction'. In: Hampe, Grady 2005, 1–14.

Hampe B., Grady J.E. (eds.) 2005. *From Perception to Meaning. Image Schemas in Cognitive Linguistics*. Berlin, New York: Mouton de Gruyter.

Hara M. 1992. 'Śraddhā in the Sense of Desire'. *Asiatische Studien : Zeitschrift der Schweizerischen Asiengesellschaft / Études asiatiques : Revue de la Société Suisse – Asie* 46: 180–194.

Harakawa J., Nagai Y., Taura T. 'Study on Conceptual Synthesis in Design Creation. Role of Thematic Relation in Creativity'. International Design Congress IASDR 2005, 10 (kobe-u.ac.jp).

Hauer J.W. 1927. *Der Vrātya. Untersuchungen über die nichtbrahmanische Religion Altindiens*. Stuttgart: W. Kohlhammer.

Hayakawa A. 2014. *Circulation of Fire in the Veda*. Zürich, Berlin: LIT Verlag.

Havelock E.A. 1983. 'The Linguistic Task of the Presocratics'. In: Robb 1983, 7–82.

Havelock E.A. 2006[1986]. *Muza uczy się pisać. Rozważania o oralności i piśmiennictwie w kulturze Zachodu.* Warszawa: Wydawnictwa Uniwersytetu Warszawskiego (translation of *The Muse Learns to Write. Reflections on Orality and Literacy from Antiquity to the Present* 1986).

Heesterman J.C. 1957. *The Ancient Indian Royal Consecration. The Rājasūya Described According to the Yajus Texts and Annoted.* 'S-Gravenhage: Mouton & Co.

Heesterman J.C. 1957. 'Reflections on the Significance of the *Dáksinā*'. *Indo-Iranian Journal* 4: 241–258

Heesterman J.C. 1962. 'Vrātya and Sacrifice'. *Indo-Iranian Journal* 6, 1–37

Heesterman J.C. 1983. 'Other Folk's Fire'. In: Staal 1983: 76–94

Heesterman J.C. 1985a. 'Brahmin, Ritual, and Renouncer'. In: Heesterman 1985, 26–44

Heesterman J.C. 1985b. 'Vedic Sacrifice and Transcendence'. In: Heesterman 1985, 81–94

Heesterman J. C. 1985c. 'Kauṭilya and the Ancient Indian State'. In: Heesterman 1985, 128–140.

Heesterman J.C.1985d. 'The conundrum of the King's Authority'. In: Heesterman 1985, 108–127.

Heesterman J.C. 1985. *The Inner Conflict of Tradition. Essays in Indian Ritual, Kinship, and Society.* Chicago and London: The University of Chicago Press.

Heesterman J.C. 1987. 'Self-Sacrifice in Vedic Ritual'. In: Shaked, Shulman, Stroumsa 1987: 91–106.

Heesterman J.C. 1993. *The Broken World of Sacrifice. An Essay in Ancient Indian Ritual.* Chicago and London: The University of Chicago Press.

Heesterman J.C., Schokker . H., Subramoniam V. I. (eds.).1968. *Pratidanam. Indian, Iranian and Indo-European Studies Presented to Franciscus Bernardus Jacobus Kuiper on His Sixtieth Birthday.* The Hague, Paris: Mouton.

Heine B. 2002. 'On the Role of Context in Grammaticalisation'. In: Wischer, Diewald 2002: 83–101.

Hillebrandt A. 1990[1927–29]. *Vedic Mythology.* 2 vols. Delhi: Motilal Banarsidass (translation of *Vedische Mythologie* 1927–29).

Hock H.H. (ed.) 2016 (forthcoming). *Selected Papers from the Veda Session of the 16th World Sanskrit Conference.* New Delhi: DK Printworld, Bangkok: Silpakorn University.

Hoek A.W. van den, Kolff D.H.A., Oort M.S. (eds.) 1992. *Ritual, State and History in South Asia. Essays in Honour of J.C. Heesterman.* Leiden–New York–Köln: E.J. Brill .

Hoffmann K. 1975. *Aufsätze zur Indo-Iranistik. Hrsg. von J. Narten.* Wiesbaden: Marwick.

Houben J.E.M. *The Pravargya Brāhmaṇa of the Taittirīya Āraṇyaka: An Ancient Commentary on the Pravargya Ritual. Introduction, Translation, and Notes.* Delhi: Motilal Banarsidass.

Houben J.E.M. 2000a. 'The Ritual Pragmatics of a Vedic hymns: the "Riddle Hymn" and the Pravargya Ritual'. *Journal of the American Oriental Society* 120, 4: 499–536.

Houben J.E.M. 2000b. 'On the Earliest Attestable Forms of the Pravargya Ritual: Ṛg-vedic References to the Gharma-pravargya, especially in the Atri Family Book (Book 5)'. *Indo-Iranian Journal* 43: 1–25.

Houben J.E.M. 2003. 'The Soma-Haoma Problem: Introductory Overview and Observations on the Discussion'. *Electronic Journal of Vedic Studies* 9, 1a.

Houben J. 2007. '*pra-vargyà-, pari-*vargyà-, *vāsudeva-várgya-*'. *Electronic Journal of Vedic Studies* 14, 1.

Huizinga J. 1985[1939]. *Homo ludens. Zabawa jako źródło kultury*. Warszawa: Czytelnik (translation of *Homo ludens. Proeve eener bepaling van het spelelement de kultuur* 1939).

Hulin M. 1978. *A History of Indian Literature. Vol. 6. Scientific and Technical Literature. Part 3, Fasc. 3. Sāṃkhya literature*. Wiesbaden: Harrasowitz Verlag.

Jaén I., Simon J.J. (eds.). 2012. Cognitive Literary Studies: Current Themes and New Directions. Austin: Texas University Press.

Jamison S.W. 1991. *The Ravenous Hyenas and the Wounded Sun. Myth and Ritual in Ancient India.* Ithaca, London: Cornell University Press.

Jamison S.W. 2002. 'Poetry and Purpose in the *Ṛgveda*: structuring enigmas'. In: Griffiths, Houben 2002: 237–249.

Jamison S.W. 2007. *The Rig Veda Between Two Worlds. Le Ṛgveda entre deux mondes*. Paris: de Boccard.

Jamison S.W. 2015. 'Ślesa in the *Ṛgveda*? Poetic Effects in *Ṛg Veda* 10.29.1'. *International Journal of Hindu Studies* 19, 157–170.

Jamison S. W, Brereton J. P. 2014. *The Rigveda: The Earliest Religious Poetry of India*. 3 vols. Oxford and New York: South Asia Research.

Jamison S. W., Witzel M. 2003. 'Vedic Hinduism'. In: Sharma 2003: 65–113.

Jelec A. 2014. *Are Abstract Concepts Like Dinosaurs Feathers? Conceptual Metaphor Theory and Conceptualisation strategies in Gesture of Blind and Visually Impaired Children.* Poznań: Wydawnictwo Naukowe UAM.

Johnson W. 1976. 'On the Ṛg Vedic Riddle of the Two Birds in the Fig Tree (1.164.20-22) and the Discovery of the Vedic Speculative Symposium'. *Journal of the American Oriental Society* 96, 2: 248–258.

Johnson M. 1987. *The Body in the Mind. The Bodily Basis of Meaning, Imagination, and Reason*. Chicago, London: The University of Chicago Press.

Johnson M. 2008. 'Philosophy's Debt to Metaphor'. In: Gibbs 2008: 39–52.

Jurewicz J. 1994. *O imionach i kształtach Jednego. Monizm indyjskiej filozofii tradycji*. (*On Names and Forms of The One. Monism of Indian Smṛti Philosophy*). Warszawa: Państwowe Wydawnictwo Naukowe.

Jurewicz J. 1997. 'The Fiery Self. The Ṛgvedic Roots of the Upaniṣadic Concept of *Ātman*'. In: Stasik, Trynkowska 1997: 123–137.

Jurewicz J. 2004. 'Prajāpati, the Fire and the *Pañcāgnividyā*'. In: Balcerowicz, Mejor 2004: 45–60.

Jurewicz J. 2005[2000] „Playing with Fire: The *Pratītyasamutpāda* from the Perspective of Vedic Thought". In: Williams 2005: 169–187 (first edition: *The Journal of the Pali Text Society* XXVI, 2000, s. 77–105).

Jurewicz J. 2006. „Spring, Well and Bucket in the *Ṛgveda*". In: Stasik, Trynkowska 2006: 252–275.

Jurewicz J. 2008a. 'Anger and Cognition. Conceptual Metaphor in the *Ṛgveda*'. *Rocznik Orientalistyczny*. 61, 1: 7–19.

Jurewicz J. 2008b. 'Rebirth Eschatology in the *Ṛgveda*. In Search for Roots of Transmigration'. *Indologica Taurinensia*. 38: 183–210.

Jurewicz J. 2008c. Rygwedyjskie źródła pojęcia 'majestat' (*śrī*) w «Brahmanie stu dróg»". In: Sierakowska-Dyndo, Surdykowska 2008: 89–106.

Jurewicz J. 2010a. *Fire and Cognition in the Ṛgveda*. Warszawa: Dom Wydawniczy Elipsa.

Jurewicz J. 2010b. 'Fortess (*púr*, *pura*) in the Veda as a Metaphor for Self (*ātmán*)'. In: Stasik, Trynkowska 2010: 13–35.

Jurewicz J. 2010c. 'Kreacja świata a cztery stany Jestestwa w filozofii upaniszad" ('Creation of the World and Four States of *Ātman* in the Upaniṣadic Philosophy'). *Przegląd Orientalistyczny*: 1–2: 3–8.

Jurewicz J. 2012a. '*Tátaḥ ksarati akṣáram*. A History of a Philosophical Notion'. *Indologica Taurinensia* 38: 106–121.

Jurewicz 2012b. What Ancient Indian Cosmogonies Tell Us About Language?" In: Bareja-Starzyńska, Mejor 2012: 75–89.

Jurewicz J. 2013a. 'How the General and Abstract Concepts Were Construed in the *Ṛgveda* (Based on the Example of the Concept *ámhas*)'. In: Stasik, Trynkowska 2013: 215–232.

Jurewicz J. 2013b. 'Twarz i maska jako Inny i Ten Sam w staroindyjskich kosmogoniach' ('Face and Mask as the Other and the Same in the Old Indian Cosmogonies'). In: Konarska 2013: 81–94.

Jurewicz J. 2014a. 'The Cow's Body as the Source Domain of Philosophical Metaphors in the *Ṛgveda*. The Case of 'Udder' (*ū́dhar*). In: Brenzinger, Kraska-Szlenk 2014, 98–116.

Jurewicz J. 2014 b. 'Ancient Indian Ritual as a Multimodal Metaphor'. In: Świerzowska, Bąkowska-Czerner 2014: 75–106.

Jurewicz J. 2016a (forthcoming). 'The Concept of *ṛtá* in the *Ṛgveda*'. In: Seaford 2016: 28–39.

Jurewicz J. 2016b (forthcoming). 'The Continuity of the Vedic Tradition: *Atharvaveda* 2.1 and the *Ṛgveda*'. In: Hock 2016.

Jurewicz J. 2016c. (forthcoming). 'Etymologies in the Brāhmaṇas and the *Ṛgveda*: A Case Study of "Fire's Precedence"'. In: Parpola, Koskikallio 2016: 251–270.

Jurewicz J. 2016d (forthcoming). 'The Meaning of Ritual in the Brāhmaṇas'. In: Thompson, Payne 2016.

Jurewicz J. 2016e (forthcoming). The Power of Sacred Speech in the Ancient India (on the Example of the *Jaiminīyopaniṣad Brāhmaṇa*). In: Lisiecki, Milne, Yanchevskaya 2016.

Jurewicz J. 2016f (forthcoming). 'Prajāpati is Hungry. How Concept of Eating Can Be Used in Philosophy'. In: Pieruccini, Rossi 2016.

Kaelber W.O. 1975. 'Tapas, Birth, and Spiritual Rebirth in the Veda'. *History of Religions* 15, 2: 343–386.

Kaelber W. O. 1990. *Tapta Mārga. Ascetism and Initiation in Vedic India*. Delhi: Sri Satguru Publications.

Kane P.V. 1968–1975. *History of Dharmaśāstra*. 5 Vols. Poona: Bhandarkar Oriental Research Institute.

Keith A.B. 1989 [1925]. *The Religion and Philosophy of the Veda and Upanishads*. 2 vols. Delhi: Motilal Banarsidass.

Khare R.S. *Culture and Reality. Essays on Hindu System of Managing Foods.* Simla: Indian Institute of Advanced Study.

Killingley D., 1997. 'The Paths of the Dead and the Five Fires'. In: P. Connolly, S. Hamilton 1997: 1–20.

Klaus K. 2004. *Die altindische Kosmologie nach den Brāhmaṇas dargestellt.* Marburg: Indica et Tibetica Verlag.

Kloppenborg R. (ed.) 1983. *Selected Studies on Ritual in the Indian Religions. Eassys to D.J. Hoens.* Leiden: E.J. Brill.

Knipe D.M. 1972. 'One Fire, Three Fires, Five Fires'. *History of Religions* 12: 28–41.

Knipe D.M. 1975. *In the Image of Fire. Vedic Experiences of Heat.* Delhi, Varanasi, Patna: Motilal Banarsidass.

Köhler H.-W. 1973. *Śrad-dhā in der vedischen und altbuddhistischen Literatur.* Wiesbaden: Franz Steiner Verlag.

Kołakowski L. 1990. *Horror metaphysicus.* Warszawa: Res Publica.

Konarska K. (ed.) 2013. *Maski, twarze, pyski. Colloquia Anthropologica et Communicative.* Wrocław: Wydawnictwo Uniwersytetu Wrocławskiego.

Kousta, S.-T., Vigliocco, G., Vinson, D., Andrews, M., & Del Campo, E. 2011. 'The Representation of Abstract Words: Why Emotion Matters'. *Journal of Experimental Psychology: General* 140: 14–34.

Kövecses Z. 2008. 'Metaphor and Emotion'. In: Gibbs 2008, 380–396.

Kövecses Z. 2011[2006]. *Język, umysł, kultura. Praktyczne wprowadzenie.* Kraków: Universitas (translation of *Language, Mind and Culture. A Practical Introduction* 2006).

Kramrisch S. 'Pūṣan'. *Journal of the American Oriental Society* 81: 104–122.

Krech V., Steinicke M. (2012) Dynamiken der Religionsgeschichte zwischen Asien und Europa. Leiden: E.J. Brill.

Krick H. 1982. *Das Ritual der Feuergrundung (Agnyādheya).* Wien: Austrian Academy ofSciences Press.

Krzeszowski T. 1997. *Angels and Devils in Hell: Elements of Axiology in Semantics.* Warszawa: Energeia.

Kudelska M. 2009. *Dlaczego istnieje raczej „Ja" niż „to"?.* Kraków: Wydawnictwo Uniwersytetu Jagiellońskiego.

Kuiper F.B.J 1957. '*Vācārambhaṇam*'. *Indo-Iranian Journal* 1: 155–159.

Kuiper F.B.J. 1962. 'The Three Strides of Viṣṇu'. In: Bender 1962: 137–151.

Kuiper F.B.J. 1964. 'The Bliss of Aša'. *Indo-Iranian Journal* 7, 2: 96–129.

Kuiper F.B.J. 1992. 'Nabhrâj and the Purchase of Soma'. In: Hoek, Kolff, Oort 1992: 179–197.

Kuiper F.B.J. 1996. 'Gandharva and Soma'. *Studien zur Indologie und Iranistic.*20: 225–255.

Kulikov L.I., Rusanov M. (eds.) 2008. *Indologica: T. Ya. Elizarenkova Memorial Volume.* Vol. 1. Moskva: Russian State University for the Humanities.

Kulke H. 1992. 'The Rājasūya. A Paradigm of Early State Formation?'. In: Hoek, Kolff, Oort 1992, 188–198.

Kulke H.. Rothermund D. 2008 [1986]. *A History of India.* London, New York: Routledge Taylor & Francis Group (second Indian reprint).

Kumar F. 1991. *The Philosophies of India. A New Approach.* New York, Ontario: The Edwin Mellen Press.

Lakoff G. 1987. *Women, Fire, and Dangerous Things. What Categories Reveal about the Mind*. Chicago and London: University of Chicago Press.

Lakoff G. 1990. 'The Invariance Hypothesis: Is Abstract Reason Based on Image-schemas?'. *Cognitive Linguistics* 1, 1: 39–74.

Lakoff G., Johnson M. 1980. *Metaphors We Live By*. Chicago: The University of Chicago Press.

Lakoff G., Turner M. 1989. *More Than Cool Reason. A Field Guide To Poetic Metaphor*. Chicago: The University of Chicago Press.

Lakoff G., Johnson M. 1999. *Philosophy in the Flesh. The Embodied Mind and its Challenge to Western Thought*. New York: Basic Books.

Lakoff G., Núñez R. 2000. *Where Mathematics Comes from: How the Embodied Mind Brings Mathematics into Being*. New York: Basic Books.

Larson G.J. 1969. *Classical Sāṃkhya: An Interpretation of Its History and Meaning*. Delhi: Motilal Banarsidass.

Lederman N., Abell S. (eds.) 2014. *Handbook of Research in Science Education*. New York: Routledge.

Lelli D. 2015. 'The *Paippālada Saṃhitā* of the *Atharvaveda* and the Royal Rituals. Evidence from Kāṇḍa Fifteen'. In: Pontillo, Bignami, Dore, Mucciarelli 2015: 376–397.

Levi S. 1898. *La doctrine du sacrifice dans les Brāhmaṇas*. Paris: Ernest Leroux

Lewandowska-Tomaszczyk B., Kwiatkowska A. (eds.) 2004. *Imagery in Language. Festschrift in Honour of Professor Ronald W. Langacker*. Frankfurt/Main: Lang.

Lidova N. 1994. *Drama and Ritual of Early Hinduism*. Delhi: Motilal Banarsidass.

Lindquist S.E. 2013. 'One Yājñavalkya… Two? On the (Questionable) Historicity of a Literary Figure'. In Lindquist 2013: 69–82.

Lindquist S.E. 2013. *Religion and Identity in South Asia and Beyond. Essays in Honor of Patrick Olivelle*. London, New York, Delhi: Anthem Press.

Lisiecki M., Milne L., Yanchevskaya N. (eds.) 2016. (forthcoming). *Power and Speech: Mythology of the Social and the Sacred*. Toruń: Eikon.

Logan R.K. 2008. *The Extended Mind. The Emergence of Language, Human Mind, and Culture*. Toronto, Buffalo, London: University of Toronto Press.

Lubin T. 2010. 'Brāhmaṇa as Commentary'. In: Grimal, Dejenne 2010: 1–22.

Lubotsky Alexander. 1997. *A Ṛgvedic Word-Concordance*. 2 vols. New Haven, Connecticut: American Oriental Society.

Ludvik C. 2007. *Sarasvatī. Riverine Goddess of Knowledge: From the Manuscript-carrying Vīṇā-player to the Weapon-wielding Defender of the Dharma*. Leiden, Boston: E.J. Brill

Maaley Z.A., Yu N. 2011. *Embodiment via Body Parts. Studies from Various Languages and Cultures*. Amsterdam, Philadelphia: John Benjamins Publishing Company.

Macdonell A.A. 1897. *Vedic Mythology*. Strassburg: Verlag Von Karl J. Trübner.

Macdonnell A.A, Keith A.B. 1967. *Vedic Index of Names and Subjects*. 2 vols. Delhi: Motilal Banarsidass.

Magnone P. 2015. 'ΓΝΩΘΙ ΣΕΑΥΤΟΝ – आत्मैव विजिज्ञासितव्य: The Eye as Mirror of the Self in India and Greece'. A provisional version based on the Kolkata conference paper. *Consciousness, Value and Reality: East and West. Panel: Self and Consciousness: East and West*. University of Kolkata, 6–8.01.2015.

Maienborn C., Heusinger K. von, Portner P. (eds.) 2011. *Semantics: An International Handbook of Natural Language Meaning*. Vol. 1. Berlin, Boston: Walter de Gruyter.

Malamoud Ch. (ed.) 1968. *Mélanges d' indianisme à la mémoire de Louis Renou*. Paris: Éditions E. de Boccard.

Malamoud Ch. 1966. *Cooking the world. Ritual and Thought in Ancient India*. Delhi: Oxford University Press.

Malamoud Ch. 1996a. 'The Vedic God of Wrath'. In: Malamoud 1996: 144–155.

Malamoud Ch. 1996b: 'Cooking the World'. In: Malamoud 1996: 23–53.

Malamoud Ch. 1996c: 'The Pierced Brick'. In: Malamoud 1996: 54–73.

Malamoud Ch. 1997. *Svādhyāya: récitation personelle du Veda Taittirīya-Āranyaka. Livre II: texte; traduit et commenté par Charles Malamoud*. Paris: Institut de Civilisation Indienne.

Malamoud Ch. 2002a. 'A Body Made of Words and Poetic Meters'. In: Shulman, Stroumsa 2002, 19–28.

Malamoud Ch. 2002b. 'La dualité, la mort, la loi'. In: Malamoud 2002, 13–33.

Malamoud Ch. 2002c. 'Le sacrifice des os'. In: Malamoud 2002: 91–105.

Malamoud Ch. 2002. *Le jumeau solaire*. Paris: Éditions du Seuil.

Malamoud Ch. 2005a. 'Un corps fait de parole et de rhytmes poétiques'. In: Malamoud 2005, 15–32.

Malamoud Ch. 2005b. 'Cosmologie prescriptive'. In: Malamoud 2005, 83–104.

Malamoud Ch. 2005c. 'Rite, simulacre, theâtre. In: Malamoud 2005: 121–141.

Malamoud Ch. 2005. *La danse des pierres. Études sur la scène sacrificielle dans l'Inde ancienne*. Paris: Éditions du Seuil.

Malamoud Ch. 2005 (1). *Féminité de la parole. Études sur l'Inde ancienne*. Paris: Albin Michel.

Mandler, J.M. 1992. 'How to Build a Baby: II. Conceptual Primitives. *Psychological Review* 99, 587–604.

Mandler, J.M. 2000. 'Perceptual and Conceptual Processes in Infancy'. *Journal of Cognition and Development*, 1, 1: 3–36.

Mandler J.M. 2004. *The Foundation of Mind. Origins of Conceptual Thought*. New York: Oxford University Press.

Mandler J.M. 2008. 'On the Birth and Growth of Concepts'. *Philosophical Psychology* 21, 2: 207–230.

Mandler J.M. 2010a. 'The Spatial Foundations of the Conceptual System'. *Language and Cognition* 2, 1: 21–44.

Mandler, J.M. 2012a. 'On the Spatial Foundations of the Conceptual System and Its Enrichment'. *Cognitive Science* 36: 421–451.

Mandler, J.M. 2012b. 'The Spatial Foundations of the Conceptual System'. *Language and Cognition* 2, 1: 21–44.

Mandler J.M., McDonough L. 1996. 'Drinking and Driving Don't Mix: Inductive Generalization in Infancy'. *Cognition* 59, 307–335.

Mandler J.M., Cánovas C.P. 2014. 'On Defining Image Schemas'. *Language and Cognition*. (http://dx.doi.org/10.1017/langcog.2014.14).

Mayrhofer M. 1992, 1996. *Etymologisches Wörterbuch des Altindoarischen*. 2 Vols. Heidelberg: Carl Winter Universitätsverlag.

McNamara P. 2006. *Where God and Science Meet. How Brain and Evolutionary Studies Alter Our Understanding of Religion*. Westport, Connecticut, London: Praeger.

McNeill D. 1992. *Hand and Mind. What Gestures Reveal About Thought*. Chicago, London: The University of Chicago Press.

Michaels A. 2004. Hinduism: Past and Present. Princeton: Princeton University Press.

Minchin E. 2001. *Homer and the Resources of Memory. Some Applications of Cognitive Theory to the Iliad and the Odyssey*. Oxford: Oxford University Press.

Minchin E. 2008. 'Communication without Words: Body Language, 'Pictureability', and Memorability in the Iliad 17'. *Ordia Prima. Revista de Estudios Clásicos* 7, 17–38.

Minchin. E. 2011. 'Themes and Mental Moulds: Roger Schank, Malcolm Wilcox and the Creation of Character in Homer'. *Classical Quarterly* 61.2: 323–345.

Minkowski. Ch.Z. 1992 *Priesthood in Ancient India. A Study of the Maitrāvaruṇa Priest*. Vienna: Sammlung de Nobili.

Mitchiner J.E. 1982. *Traditions of Seven Ṛṣis*. Delhi, Varanasi, Patna: Motilal Banarsidass.

Mittelberg I. 2002. 'The Visual Memory of Grammar: Iconographical and Metaphorical Insights'. (http://www.metaphorik.de/de/journal/02/visual-memory-grammar-iconographical-and-metaphorical-insights.html).

Mittelberg I. 2003. 'Making Grammar Visible: The Use of Metaphoric Gestures to Represent.

Grammatical Categories and Structures'. In J. Streeck (Ed.), *Proceedings of the First Congress of the International Society for Gesture Studies: 'Gesture – The Living Medium, University of Texas at Austin*. (http://www.humtec.rwth-aachen.de/index.php?article_id=953&clang=1).

Moore J.D., Stenning K. (eds.). 2001. Proceedings of the Twenty-Third Annual Conference of the Cognitive Science Society. Mahvah, New Jersey: Lawrence Erlbaum Associates.

Mucciarelli E. 2015. 'Lost Speech: The Poetry of Sattrins'. In: Pontillo, Bignami, Dore, Mucciarelli 2015: 65–98.

Mus P. 1962 . 'De nouveau sur *Ṛgveda* 10.90? Sociologie d'une grammaire'. In: Bender 1962: 165–185.

Mus P. 1968. 'Oú finit Puruṣa?'. In Malamoud 1968: 539–563.

Mylius K. 1965. *Geographische Untersuchungen zur Entstehungsgegend des Śatapatha-Brahmana*. Wissenschaftliche Zeitschrift d. Universität Leipzig 14, 759–761.

Nagai Y., Taura T., Mukai F. 2009. 'Concept Blending and Dissimilarity: Factors for Creative Concept Generation Process'. *Design Studies* 30 648–675. (kobe-u.ac.jp).

Nagy G. 1974. *Comparative Studies in Greek and Indic meter*. Cambridge, Massachusetts: Harvard University Press.

Núñez N. 2008. 'Conceptual Metaphor, Human Cognition, and the Nature of Mathematics'. In: Gibbs 2008: 339–362.

Nyberg H. 1995. 'The Problem of the Āryans and the Soma: The Botanical Evidence'. In: Erdosy 1995: 382–406.

Oakley T. 2007. 'Image Schemas'. In Geeraerts, Cuyckens 2007: 214–235.

Oberlies T., 1998. *Die Religion des Ṛgveda. Erster Teil. Das religiöse System des Ṛgveda*. Wien: Institut für Indologie der Universität Wien.

Obeyesekere G., 2002. *Imagining Karma. Ethical Transformation in Amerindian, Buddhist, and Greek Rebirth.* Berkeley, Los Angeles, London: University of California Press.

Özçalişkan Ş., Stites L.J. 2013. 'Moving across metaphorical spaces over developmental time'. In: Caballero, Díaz-Vera 2013: 221–205.

Oertel H. 1896. 'The *Jaiminīya* or *Talavakāra Upaniṣad Brāhmaṇa*'. *Journal of the American Oriental Society* 16: 79–260.

Oertel H. 1898. 'Contributions from the *Jaiminīya Brāhmaṇa* to the History of the Brāhmaṇa Literature'. *Journal of the American Oriental Society* 19: 97–125.

Oldenberg H. 1993[1894]. *The Religion of the Veda.* Delhi: Motilal Banarsidass (translation of *Die Religion des Veda* 1894).

Oldenberg H. 2005[1888]. *Prolegomena on Metre and Textual History of the Ṛgveda.* Delhi: Motilal Banarsidass (translation of *Metrische und textgeschichtliche Prolegomena zu einer kritischen Rigveda-Ausgabe* 1888).

Olivelle P. 1993. The Āśrama System. The History and Hermeneutics of a Religious Institution. New York: Oxford University Press.

Olivelle P. 1997. 'Orgasmic Rapture and Divine Ecstasy: The Semantic History of Ānanda'. *Journal of Indian Philosophy* 25: 153–180.

Olivelle P. 1998. *The Early Upaniṣad. Annotated Text and Translation.* New York, Oxford: Oxford University Press.

Olivelle P. 2012. 'Kings, Ascetics, and Brahmins: The Socio-Political Context of Ancient Indian Religions.' In: Krech, Steinicke 2012: 117–135.

Ortony A. 1993[1979]. *Metaphor and Thought.* New York, Melbourne: Cambridge University Press.

Paivio A. 2006 'Dual Coding Theory and Education'. Draft chapter for the conference on "Pathways to Literacy Achievement for High Poverty Children". The University of Michigan School of Education, September 29–October 1, 2006, (http://www.csuchico.edu/~nschwartz/paivio.pdf).

Paivio A. 2007. *Mind and Its Evolution: A Dual Coding Theoretical Approach.* Mahwah, New Jersey: Lawrence Erlbaum Associates.

Paivio A., Walsh M. 1993[1979]. 'Psychological Processes in Metaphor Comprehension and Memory.' In: Ortony 1993(1979): 307–328.

Panther K.-U., Radden G. (eds.) 1999. *Metonymy in Language and Thought.* Amsterdam, Philadephia: John Benjamins Publishing Company.

Panther K-U, Thornburg L.L. 2004 'The Role of Conceptual Metonymy in Meaning Construction' (http://www.metaphorik.de/de/journal/06/role-conceptual-metonymy-meaning-construction.html).

Patton L. 1996. *Myth as Argument. The Bṛhaddevatā as Canonical Commentary.* Berlin, New York: Walter de Gruyter.

Patton L. 2005. *Bringing the Gods to Mind. Mantra and Ritual in Early Indian Sacrifice.* Berkeley, Los Angeles, London: University of California Press.

Parpola A. 1983. 'The Pre-Vedic Indian Background of the Śrauta Rituals'. In: Staal 1983: 41–75.

Parpola A. 1992. 'The Metamorphoses of Mahiṣa Asura and Prajāpati'. In: Hoek, Kolff, Oort 1992: 275–308.

Parpola A. 1995. 'The Problem of the Aryans and the Soma: Textual-linguistic and Archaeological Evidence'. In: Erdosy 1995: 353–381.

Parpola A. 2005. The Nāsatyas, the chariot and Proto-Aryan religion. *Journal of Indological Studies* 16–17 (2004–2005): 1–63. Kyoto: Association for the Study of Indian Thought.

Parpola A. 2007. 'Human Sacrifice in India in Vedic Times and Before'. In: Bremmer 2007: 157–194.

Parpola A. 2015. *The Roots of Hinduism. The Early Aryans and the Indus Civilization*. Oxford: Oxford University Press.

Parpola A., Koskikallio P. (eds.) 2016. *Vedic Investigations*. Delhi: Motilal Banarsidass

Patyal H.Ch. 1978–1979. 'Tortoise in the Vedic Mythology and Ritual'. *Bulletin of Deccan Research Institute* 38: 1-7-115.

Pecher D., Zwaan R. (eds.) 2005. *Grounding Cognition. The Role of Perception and Action in Memory, Language, and Thinking*. New York: Cambridge University Press.

Pecher D., Boot I., Van Dantzig S. 2011. 'Abstract Concepts: Sensory-Motor Grounding, Metaphors, and Beyond'. In: Ross 2011: 217–248.

Pieruccini C., Rossi P.M. (eds.) 2016 (forthcoming). *A World of Nourishment. Reflections on Food in Indian Culture*. Series *Consonanze*, Università degli Studi di Milano, Dipartimento di Studi letterari, filologici e linguistici.

Prinz J.J. 2005. 'Passionate Thoughts: The Emotional Embodiment of Moral Concepts'. In: Pecher, Zwaan 2005: 93–114.

Pollet G. (ed.) 1987. *India and the Ancient World. History, Trade and Culture before A.D. 650. P.H.L. Eggermont Jubilee Volume*, Orientalia Lovaniensia Analecta 25, Leuven: Departement Oriëntalistiek.

Pontillo T., Bignami C., Dore M., Mucciarelli E. (eds.) 2015. *The Volatile World of Sovereignty. The Vrātya Problem and Kinship in South Asia*. New Delhi: DK Printworld.

Porto Requejo M.D. 2007. 'The Role of Context in Word Meaning Construction: A Case Study'. *International Journal of English Studies* 7, 1: 169–173.

Potdar K.R. 1944–46, 1946–47. 'Āpri Hymns in the *Ṛgveda*. A Study and a Theory'. *Journal of the University of Bombay* 13–14: 26–43, 15–16: 28–57.

Potter K. et al. (eds.) 1981–2015. *Encyclopedia of Indian Philosophies*. 22 Vols (four in press). Delhi: Motilal Banarsidass, Princeton, N.J.: Princeton University Press.

Proferes T. 2007. *Vedic Ideals of Sovereignty and the Poetics of Power*. New Haven, Connecticut: American Oriental Society.

Radden G. 2004. 'The Metonymic Folk Model Of Language'. In: Lewandowska--Tomaszczyk, Kwiatkowska 2004: 543–565.

Radden G., Kövecses Z. 1999. 'Towards a Theory of Metonymy'. In: Panther, Radden 1999: 17–59.

Ramscar, M., Matlock, T., Boroditsky, L. 2010. 'Time, Motion and Meaning – The Experiential Basis of Abstract Thought'. In: Smith, Mix, Gasser 2010: 67–86.

Rau W. 1957. *Staat und Gesellschaft im alten Indien, nach den Brāhmaṇas dargestellt*. Wiesbaden: Otto Harassowitz.

Rau W. 1974. *Metalle und Metallgeräte im vedischen Indien*. Mainz: Verlag der Akademie der Wissenschaften und der Literatur.

Reat N.R. 1990. *The Origins of Indian Psychology*. Berkeley: Asian Humanities Press.

Renou L. 1947. *Les écoles vediques et la formation du Veda*. Paris: Imprimerie Nationale.

Renou L. 1948–1949. 'Sur la notion de *bráhman*'. *Journal Asiatique* 236–2377: 7–46.

Renou L. 1953. 'Le Passage des Brahmaṇa aux Upaniṣad'. *Journal of the American Oriental Society* 73, 3: 138–144.

Renou L. 1958. *Études sur le vocabulaire du Ṛgveda*. Pondichéry: Institut Français d'Indologie.

Renou L. 1960. Védique *púrīṣa*. *Indo-Iranian Journal* 4: 104–110.

Renou L. 1965. 'Sur quelques mots du *Ṛgveda*'. *Journal of the American Oriental Society* 85: 79–85.

Renou L. 1955–1969 (EVP). *Études védiques et Pāṇinéennes*. 17 vols. Publications de l'Institut de Civilisation Indiennes (fasc. 1, 2, 4, 6, 9–10, 12, 14, 16–18, 20, 22–23, 30). Paris: de Boccard.

Richardson M., Spivey M.J., Edelman Sh., Naples A.J. 2001. '"Language is Spatial": Experimental Evidence for Image Schemas of Concrete and Abstract Verbs'. In: Moore, Stenning 2001: 845–850.

Robb K. (ed.) 1983. *Language and Thought in Early Greek Philosophy.* LaSalle IL: Hegeler Institute.

Rocher L. (ed.) 1988. *Studies in Indian Literature and Philosophy. Collected Articles of J.A.B. van Buitenen.* Delhi, Varanasi, Patna: Motilal Banarsidass.

Rocher L. 1994. 'Orality and Textuality in the Indian Context'. *Sino-Platonic Papers* 49: 1–28.

Roebuck W. 2000. *The Upaniṣads.* London: Penguin Books.

Rohrer T. 2007. 'Embodiment and Experientialism', In: Geeraerts, Cuyckens 2007: 25–48.

Ross B. (ed.) 2011. *The Psychology of Learning and Motivation,* Vol. 54, Burlington: Academic Press.

Rustagi U. (1981). *Darśapūrṇamāsa (A Comparative Ritualistic Study)*. Delhi, Varanasi: Bharatiya Vidya Prakashan.

Salomon R. 1995. 'On the Origin of the Early Indian Scripts'. *Journal of the American Oriental Society* 115, 2: 271–279.

Salomon R. 1998. *Indian Epigraphy*. New Delhi: Munshiram Manoharlal Publishers.

Scharfe H. 2002. *Education in Ancient India.* Leiden, Boston, Köln: E.J. Brill.

Scheftelowitz I. 1906. *Die Apokryphen des Ṛgveda*. Breslau: M. & H. Marcus.

Schmithausen L. 1993/1994. 'Men, Animal and Plants in the Rebirth Passages of the Early Upaniṣads'. *Journal of the Royal Asiatic Society of Sri Lanka* 38: 141–162.

Schmithausen L. 1994. 'Zur Textgeschichte der *pañcāgnividyā*'. *Wiener Zeitschrift für die Kunde Südasiens* 38: 43–60.

Sharma A. (ed.) 2003. *The Study of Hinduism*. Columbia, South Carolina: University of South Carolina Press.

Schank R. C, Abelson R. P. 1977. *Script, Plans, Goals and Understanding. An Inquiry into Human Knowledge Structures.* Hillsdale, New Jersey: Lawrence Erlbaum Associates

Schank R.C., Abelson R.P. 1995. 'Knowledge and Memory: The Real Story'. In: Wyer 1995: 1–88.

Schayer S. 2012[1938] *Contributions to the Problem of Time in Indian Philosophy.* Warsaw Research Centre of Buddhist Studies, Faculty of Oriental Studies, University of Warsaw.

Schmidt H.-P. 1968. *Bṛhaspati und Indra. Untresuchungen zur Vedischen Mythologie und Kulturgeschichte*. Wiesbaden: Otto Harassowitz.

Schmidt H.-P. 1992. 'The Place of *Ṛgveda* 4.42 in the Ancient Indian Royal Ritual'. In: Hoek, Kolff, Oort 1992: 323–346.

Scholem G. 1969[1960]. *On the Kaballah and its Symbolism*. New York: Schocken Books (translation of *Zur Kabbala und ihrer Symbolik* 1960).

Seaford R. 2004. *Money and the Early Greek Mind. Homer, Philosophy, Tragedy*. Cambridge: Cambridge University Press.

Seaford R. 2016 (forthcoming). *Universe and Inner Self in Early Indian and Early Greek Thought*. Edinburgh: Edinburgh University Press.

Shaked S., Shulman D., Stroumsa G.G. (eds.) 1987. *Essays on Transformation, Revolution and Permanence in the History of Religions Dedicated to R.J. Zwi Werblowsky* (Studies in the History of Religions, Supplements to Numen, L), Leiden: E.J. Brill.

Shulman D., Stroumsa G.G. (eds.) 2002. *Self and Self-Transformation in the History of Religions*. Oxford: Oxford University Press.

Sierakowska-Dyndo J., Surdykowska S. (eds.). 2008. *Posłuchaj fletu trzcinowego...* Warszawa: Wydawnictwa Uniwersytetu Warszawskiego.

Slaje W. 2001a. 'Water and Salt (I): Yājñavalkya's *Saindhava Dṛṣṭānta* (BĀU II, 4.12)'. *Indo-Iranian Journal* 44, 1: 25–57.

Slaje W. 2001b. 'Water and Salt (II): 'Material' Causality and Hylozoic Thought in the Yājñavalkya-Maitreyī Dialogue?'. *Indo-Iranian Journal* 44, 4: 299–327.

Slaje W. 2002. 'Water and Salt (III): An Analysis and New Translation of the Yājñavalkya-Maitreyī Dialogue'. *Indo-Iranian Journal* 45: 205–220.

Slaje W. 2010. *'Néti néti'. On the Meaning of an Upaniṣadic Citation of Some Renown Hindu Texts and Western Minds*. Stuttgart: Franz Steiner Verlag.

Smith B.K. 1985. 'Sacrifice and Being. Prajāpati's Cosmic Emission and its Consequences'. *Numen* 32, 1: 71–87.

Smith B.K. 1989. *Reflections on Resemblance, Ritual and Religion*. New York: Oxford University Press.

Smith B.K. 1994. *Classifying Universe. The Ancient Varṇa System and the Origin of Caste*. New York, Oxford: Oxford University Press.

Smith B. K., Doniger W. 1989. 'Sacrifice and Substitution: Ritual Mystification and Mythical Demystification'. *Numen* 36, 2: 189–224.

Smith C. 2016 (forthcoming). 'The *Kaṭhopaniṣad* and the Deconstruction of the Fire Altar'. In: Wenthe, Byrd, DeLisi 2016.

Smith L., Mix K., Gasser M. (eds.) 2010. Spatial Foundations of Cognition and Language. Oxford: Oxford University Press.

Snyder B. 2000. *Music and Memory: An Introduction*. Cambridge, MA: MIT Press.

Sørensen J. 2007. *A Cognitive Theory of Magic*. Lanham, New York, Toronto, Plymouth UK: Altamira Press.

Sparreboom M. 1985. *Chariots in the Veda*. Leiden: E.J. Brill.

Srinivasan D. 1979. *Concept of Cow in the Ṛgveda*. Delhi: Motilal Banarsidass.

Srinivasan D. M. 1997. *Many Heads, Arms and Eyes. Origin, Meaning and Form of Multiplicity in Indian Art*. Leiden, New York, Köln: E.J. Brill.

Staal J.F. 1979. 'The Meaninglessness of Ritual'. *Numen* 26, 1: 2–22.

Staal J.F. 1983 (in collaboration with C.V. Somayajipad and M. Itti Ravi Nambudiri). *Agni: The Vedic Ritual of the Fire Altar*. 2 vols. Berkeley: Asian Humanities Press.

Staal J.F. 1986. *The Fidelity of Oral Tradition and The Origins Of Science*. Amsterdam: North-Holland Publishing Company.

Staal J.F. 2001. 'How a Psychoactive Substance Becomes a Ritual. The Case of Soma'. *Social Research. An International Quarterly of the Social Sciences* 68, 3: 745–778 (http://frtitsstaal.googlepages.com/soma2001).

Stasik B., Trynkowska A. (eds.) 1997. *Teaching on India in Central and Eastern Europe. Contributions to the 1st Central & Eastern European Indological Conference on Regional Cooperation* (Warsaw, 15–17 September 2005). Warszawa: Dom Wydawniczy Elipsa.

Stasik D., Trynkowska A. (eds.). 2006. *India in Warsaw. Indie w Warszawie. Tom upamiętniający 50-lecie powojennej historii indologii na Uniwersytecie Warszawskim (2003/2004)*. Warszawa: Dom Wydawniczy Elipsa.

Stasik D., Trynkowska (eds.). 2010. *The City and the Forest in Indian Literature and Art*. Warszawa: Dom Wydawniczy Elipsa.

Stasik D., Trynkowska A. (eds.) 2013. *CEENIS. Current Research Series*. Vol 1. Warszawa: Dom Wydawniczy Elipsa.

Stuhrmann R. 2006. 'Capturing Light in the *Ṛgveda*: Soma Seen Botanically, Pharmacologically, and in the Eyes of the Kavis'. *Electronic Journal of Vedic Studies* 13, 1: 1–93.

Sweetser E. 1990. *From Etymology to Pragmatics. Metaphorical and Cultural Aspects of Semantic Structure*. Cambridge: Cambridge University Press.

Sweetser E. 2000. 'Blended Spaces and Perfomativity'. *Cognitive Linguistics* 11, 3/4: 305–333.

Szelid V. 2010. 'Flowers of Love. Cognitive Linguistic Analysis of Moldavian Southern Csángó Folksongs'. *Acta Universitatis Sapientiae, Philologica*, 2, 2, 221–236.

Szwedek A. 2008. 'Objectification: A New Theory of Metaphor'. *Lund Studies in English* 112, 308–317.

Świerzowska A., Bąkowska-Czerner G. (eds.) 2014. *Magical Texts In Ancient Indian Civilisations. The Polish Journal of the Art and Culture* 9, 1.

Talbot R.F. 1995. *Sacred Sacrifice. Ritual Paradigms in Vedic Religion and Early Christianity*. New York: Peter Lang.

Talmy L. 1988. 'Force Dynamics in Language and Cognition'. *Cognitive Science* 12: 49–100.

Talmy L. 2000. *Toward a Cognitive Semantics. Typology and Process in Concept Structuring*. Cambridge MA. The MIT Press.

Tate P.D. 1982. 'Comparative Hermeneutics: Heidegger, the Pre-Socratics, and the 'Ṛgveda'. *Philosophy East and West* 32, 1: 47–59.

Taura T., Yukari N., Tanaka Sh. 'Design Space Blending – A Key for Creative Design'. *DS 35: Proceedings ICED 05, the 15th International Conference on Engineering Design*, Melbourne, Australia, 15.–18.08.2005. (http://designsociety.org/publication/23131/design_space_blending_-_a_key_for_creative_design).

Taura T, Nagai Y. 2013. *Concept Generation for Design Creativity. A Systematized Theory and Methodology*. London, Heidelberg, New York, Dordrecht: Springer.

Taylor J.R. 2002. *Cognitive Grammar*. Oxford, New York: Oxford University Press.
Taylor J.R. 2011. 'Prototype Theory'. In: Maienborn, Heusinger, Portner 2011: 643–663.
Thapar R. 1966. *History of Early India: From the Origins to Ad 1300: Volume 1*. London: Penguin Books.
Thieme P. 1952. 'Bráhman'. *Zeitschrift der Deutschen Morgenländischen Gesellschaft* 102: 91–129.
Thieme P. 1985. 'The First Verse of the *Triṣaptīyam* (AV, Ś 1.1 ~ AV, P 1.6) and the Beginnings of Sanskrit Linguistics'. *Journal of the American Oriental Society* 105, 3: 559–565.
Thieme P. 1987. 'Das Rätsel ṚV 1.164.15-16'. In: Falk 1987: 329–339.
Thite G.U. (1975). *Sacrifice in the Brahmana-Texts*. Poona: University of Poona.
Thompson G. 1997. 'The *Brahmodya* and Vedic Discourse'. *Journal of the American Oriental Society* 117.1: 13–37.
Thompson G., Payne R. K. (eds.) 2016 (forthcoming). *On Meaning and Mantras: Essays in Honor of Frits Staal*. Institute of Buddhist Studies and BDK America.
Tikkanen B., Butters A. M. (eds.) 2011. *Pūrvāparaprajñābhinandanam. East and West, Past and Present. Indological and Other Essays in Honour of Klaus Karttunen*. Helsinki: Finnish Oriental Society.
Toporov V.N. 'Sarasvati – reka, rec', krasnorecije'. In: Kulikov, Rusanov 2008: 39–62.
Tull H.W., 1989. *The Vedic Origins of Karma. Cosmos as Man in Ancient Indian Myth and Ritual*. New York: State University of New York Press.
Turner M. 1996. *The Literary Mind*. New York, Oxford: Oxford University Press.
Turner M. (ed.) 2006. *The Artful Mind Cognitive Science and the Riddle of Human Creativity*. Oxford: Oxford University Press.
Turner M. 2006. 'The Art of Compression'. In: Turner 2006: 93–114.
Turner M. 2007. 'Conceptual Integration'. In: Geeraerts, Cuyckens 2007: 377–393.
Turner M. 2012. 'Mental Packing and Unpacking in Mathematics'. In: Bockarova, Danesi, Núñez 201: 248–267.
Tyler, Andrea and Vyvyan Evans. (2001). 'Reconsidering Prepositional Polysemy Networks: The Case of Over'. *Language*, 77, 4: 724–65.
Tyler, A., Evans V. 2003. *The Semantics of English Prepositions: Spatial Scenes, Embodied Meaning and Cognition*. Cambridge: Cambridge University Press.
Wasson R. G. 1968. *Soma: Divine Mushroom of Immortality*. New York: Harcourt, Brace, Jovanovich.
Weber A. 1914[1852.] *The History of Indian Literature*. London: K. Paul, Trench, Trübner (translation of *Akademische Vorlesungen über indische Litteraturgeschichte* 1852).
Wenthe M., Byrd A., DeLisi J. (eds.) 2016 (forthcoming). *Tavet Tat Satyam*. Ann Arbour: Beech Stave Press.
Wheelock W.T. 1989. 'Mantra in Vedic and Tantric Ritual'. In: Alper 1989: 96–122.
Whitaker J.L. 2011. *Strong Arms and Drinking Strength. Masculinity, Violence, and the Body in Ancient India*. New York: Oxford University Press.
Whitney W.D. 1905. *Atharva-Veda Saṃhitā*. 2 vols. Cambridge Massachusetts: Harvard University Press.
Wilcox Ph. P. 2004. 'A Cognitive Key: Metonymic and Metaphorical Mappings in ASL'. *Cognitive Linguistics* 15, 2: 197–222.

Williams P. (ed.) 2005. *Buddhism. Critical Concepts of Religious Studies*. Abingdon, New York: Routledge.

Windisch, E. 1908. *Buddha's Geburt und die Lehre von der Seelenwanderung*. Leipzig: B.G. Trübner.

Winkelman M. 2006. 'Cross-Cultural Assessments of Shamanism as A Biogenetic Foundation for Religion. In: McNamara 2006: 139–159.

Winter B., Matlock T. 2013. 'Creativity and the Sensorimotor Grounding of Mathematics'. In: Borkent, Dancygier, Hinnell 2013, 37–48.

Wischer I., Diewald G. *New Reflections of Grammaticalisation*. Amsterdam, Philadephia: John Benjamins Publishing Company.

Witzel M. 1979. 'On Magical Thought in the Veda'. Leiden: Universitaire Pers Leiden; (http://crossasia-repository.ub.uni-heidelberg.de/90/).

Witzel M. 1984. 'Sur le chemin du ciel'. *Bulletin des Études Indiennes* 2: 213–279.

Witzel M. 1987a. 'On the Origin of the Literary Device of the "Frame Story' in Old Indian Literature'. In: Falk 1987: 380–414.

Witzel M. 1987b. 'On the Localisation of Vedic Texts and Schools (Materials on Vedic Śākhās' In: Pollet 1987, 173–213.

Witzel M. 1897c. 'The Case of the Shattered Head.' *Studien zur Indologie unde Iranistik*. 13/14: 363–415.

Witzel M. 1989. 'Tracing the Vedic Dialects'. In: Caillat: 1989: 97–264.

Witzel M. 1992. 'Meaningful Ritual. Vedic, Medieval, and Contemporary Concepts in the Nepalese Agnihotra Ritual'. In: Hoek, Kolff, Oort 1992: 774–828.

Witzel M. 1995a. 'Early Indian History: Linguistic and Textual Parametres'. In: Erdosy 1995: 85–125.

Witzel M. 1995b. 'Ṛgvedic History: Poets, Chieftains and Polities'. In: Erdosy 1995: 306–352.

Witzel M. 1995c. 'Early Sanskritisation. Origins and development of the Kuru State'. *Electronic Journal Of Vedic Studies* 1, 4: 1–2.

Witzel M. 1996. 'How to Enter the Vedic Mind? Strategies in Translating a Brāhmaṇa Text'. In: Garzilli 1996: 163–176.

Witzel M. (ed.) 1997. *Inside the Texts. Beyond the Texts. New Approaches to the Study Of The Vedas. Proceedings of the International Vedic Workshop. Harvard University, June 1989.* Cambridge, Massachusetts: Department of Sanskrit and Indian Studies.

Witzel M. 1997. 'The Development of the Vedic Canon and its Schools: the Social and Political Milieu'. In: Witzel 1997: 257–346.

Witzel M. 2010. *Das alte Indien*. München: Verlaf C.H. Beck.

Witzel M. 2004b. 'The Ṛgvedic Religious System and its Central Asian and Hindukush Antecedents'. In: Griffith, Houben 2004: 580–636.

Witzel M. 2012. *The Origins of the World's Mythologies*. Oxford, New York, Auckland: Oxford University Press.

Witzel M., Gotō T. 2007. *Rig-Veda. Das heilige Wissen. Erster und zweiter Liederkreis*. Frankfurt: Verlag der Weltreligionen.

Wyer R. S.(ed.)1995. *Knowledge and Memory. Advances in Social Cognition. Vol. 2*. Hillsdale, New Jersey, Hove, UK: Lawrence Erlbaum Associates.

Yu N. 2008. 'Metaphor from Body and Culture'. In: Gibbs 2008, 247–261.
Zelinsky-Wibbelt C. 2000. *Discourse and the Continuity of Reference. Representing Mental Categorization*. Berlin, New York: Mouton de Gruyter.
Zwaan R. 2014. 'Embodiment and Language Comprehension: Reframing the Discussion'. *Trends in Cognitive Science* 18, 5, 229–234 (http://dx.doi.org/10.1016/j.tics.2014.02.008).
Zysk K.G. 'The Science of Respiration and the Doctrine of the Bodily Winds in Ancient India'. *Journal of the American Oriental Society* 113, 2: 198–213.

Index (English, Latin, Greek)

C.

G.

H.

T.

Y.

Z.

Index (Sanskrit)

Index
(fragments discussed in the book)

Atharvaveda

Ṛgveda

Brāhmaṇas

Jaiminīya Brāhmaṇa

Jaiminīya Upaniṣad Brāhmaṇa

Śatapatha Brāhmaṇa

Upaniṣads

Aitareya Upaniṣad

Bṛhadāraṇyaka Upaniṣad

Chāndogya Upaniṣad

Kauṣītaki Upaniṣad

Taittirīya Upaniṣad